7

CORK

History & *Society*

Interdisciplinary Essays on the
History of an Irish County

Editors:
PATRICK O'FLANAGAN
CORNELIUS G. BUTTIMER

Editorial Advisor:
GERARD O'BRIEN

GEOGRAPHY PUBLICATIONS

Published in Ireland by
Geography Publications,
Kennington Road,
Templeogue, Dublin 6W

© The authors 1993

ISBN 0 906602 22 x

Design and typesetting by Phototype-Set, Lee Road, Dublin Industrial Estate
Printed by Colour Books
Bound by Museum Bookbinding

Contents

List of Figures

List of Plates

List of Tables

Contributors

T. C. Barnard
Fellow and Tutor, Hertford College, Oxford University

John Bradley
Lecturer, Department of Archaeology, University College, Dublin

Cornelius G. Buttimer
Lecturer, Department of Modern Irish, University College, Cork

Nicholas Canny
Professor, Department of History, University College, Galway

Maura Cronin
Lecturer, Department of History, Mary Immaculate College, Limerick

L. M. Cullen
Professor, Department of History, Trinity College, Dublin

Ian d'Alton
Department of Finance, Dublin

David Dickson
Lecturer, Department of Modern History, Trinity College, Dublin

Angela Fahy
Department of Geography, University College, Cork

Andrew Halpin
Dublin City Archaeologist, Dublin Corporation

Peter Hart
Research Fellow, The Institute of Social and Economic Research, Memorial University of Newfoundland

Patrick Hickey, C.C.
Drinagh, county Cork

Kevin Hourihan
Lecturer, Department of Geography, University College, Cork

John A. Murphy
Emeritus Professor, University College, Cork

Peter Murray
Curator, Crawford Municipal Art Gallery, Cork

Kenneth Nicholls
Lecturer, Department of Irish History, University College, Cork

A. F. O'Brien
Lecturer, Department of Medieval History, University College, Cork

John B. O'Brien
Lecturer, Department of Modern History, University College, Cork

Breandán Ó Buachalla
Professor, Department of Modern Irish, University College, Dublin

Diarmaid Ó Catháin
Solicitor, Court-house Chambers, Cork

Donnchadh Ó Corráin
Associate Professor, Department of Irish History, University College, Cork

Gearóid Ó Crualaoich
Lecturer, Department of Irish History/Centre for Folklore and Ethnology, University College, Cork

Patrick O'Flanagan
Associate Professor, Department of Geography, University College, Cork

Diarmuid Ó Murchadha
Crosshaven, county Cork

Pádraig Ó Riain
Professor, Department of Early and Medieval Irish, University College, Cork

William J. Smyth
Professor, Department of Geography, University College, Cork

Preface

Cork: history and society is the sixth volume in the present county history series to appear under the imprint of Geography Publications. The conventions established in the earlier titles are by and large followed here, with the exception that this work is confined solely to the documented historical period. Although Cork is the principal focus of attention, it will be apparent that many contributors have chosen to set their research in a context which includes Ireland generally, Atlantic and continental Europe and North America. The region may thus be seen in a broader comparative perspective while being primarily studied for its own sake.

The volume has benefitted from a previously-established tradition of writing on the Cork area, dating in earnest from the seventeenth century. It draws especially on the scholarship of the Cork Historical and Archaeological Society. By means of its field-work, lectures and *Journal,* the latter organisation has made a sustained contribution to our understanding of city and county for over one hundred years. Other local societies in county Cork have placed researchers under a similar obligation.

The index is intended to provide a selective guide to those places which recur most frequently. We trust that readers will find in the work as a whole a stimulating treatment of a complex and diverse county for the millenium and a half with which *Cork: history and society* is concerned.

Patrick O'Flanagan
Neil Buttimer

Cork – June, 1993

Acknowledgements

We wish to acknowledge the invaluable assistance received from various sources without which this project would not have come to fruition. We are grateful to the following institutions for their generous financial support in aid of publication: University College, Cork, and in particular its President, Dr Michael P. Mortell, Mr Michael Kelleher, Finance Officer and Secretary, Mr Cyril Deasy, Assistant Finance Officer and Secretary, and other members of the Finance Committee, together with Mr J. J. Kett, Development Officer. We thank Cork Corporation, particularly the office of the Town Clerk; the General Purposes Committee of Cork County Council and Mr Edward Marnane, County Secretary; the Senate of the National University of Ireland, and the University of Ulster.

We are indebted to all who participated in typing various drafts of the different contributions, particularly to Noreen McDowell, Ann Phelan, Ann Lynch, Ann Donovan and Colette Horgan of U.C.C.'s Department of Geography, Elmarie Uí Cheallacháin and Siobhán Ní Dhonghaile of the Departments of Early and Medieval and Modern Irish, Kay Doyle of the Department of Spanish, Helen Kinsley and her staff of the Secretarial Centre and the staff of Central Bureau Services, Cork.

Michael Murphy, Cartographer, Department of Geography, drafted and reproduced all of the figures in the volume with his customary care, precision and good humour. Dan Murphy of the same department courteously and whole-heartedly aided in many aspects of the work's preparation and conclusion. Our thanks goes to Peter Murray, Curator, Crawford Municipal Art Gallery, for his expert advice on the selection of illustrations for the volume generally, and particularly with regard to items in his own institution, kindly copied together with items from elsewhere by Niall Moore, Gallery Photographer. We are similarly obliged to Tomás Tyner of U.C.C.'s Audio-Visual Services unit for his painstaking reproduction of several of the book's other illustrations. Denis Power of the Archaeological Survey of County Cork, based at U.C.C., generously assisted in the selection of photographs from the Survey's collection.

For permission to reproduce illustrative materials in their care we record our indebtedness to the following persons and organisations: J. V. Bond, Principal, Ashton School, Cork, Stella Cherry, Curator, Cork Public Museum, Eugene Gillan and especially Michael Mulcahy, Curator, Kinsale Regional Museum and the museum authorities who retain copyright for plate 15.3, Patricia McCarthy, Archivist, Cork Archives Institute, Bernard Meehan and Stuart Ó Seanóir, Trinity College Library, Dublin, Richard Wood, Fota House, Cork; the Department of Irish Folklore, University College, Dublin, the trustees of the Keith St Joseph collection, Cambridge University, and the National Library of Ireland.

The staff of Boole Library, U.C.C, provided sterling support to the editors and many of the contributors. We especially thank Dilys Bateman, Pat Connolly, Peadar Cranitch, Helen Moloney-Davis and Eithne O'Halloran. The assistance of Kieran Burke of Cork City Library, Tim Cadogan of Cork County Library, and staff in the National Library of Ireland, the Royal Irish Academy and Trinity College, Dublin, is gratefully acknowledged. Various other forms of support were kindly extended by Traolach Ó Ríordáin, Virginia Teehan, Archivist, U.C.C., Feargal Ó Brolcháin and Deirdre Early, Geraldine Fagan and Noel Forde and Eileen and Terry Maddock, John A. Murphy, Kenneth Nicholls, Cormac Ó Gráda and anonymous referees. We also wish to thank the Arts Faculty Fund, U.C.C., for research support.

We heartily thank Michael Lynam of Phototype-set Limited, Dublin, for his courteous, patient and professional assistance at every stage of the work's preparation for publication. His colleagues Christy Nolan, who designed the cover jacket, and also Rory O'Neill and Noel Murphy who assisted with the production, have placed us under a similar obligation. Colour Books and Museum Bookbinding printed and bound the volume with their customary care. We express appreciation to Dr Gerard O'Brien of the Department of History, Magee College, Derry, for his editorial advice.

The title would neither have been contemplated nor concluded without the inspiration and sustained support of William Nolan, instigator and publisher of this series. We are indebted to him and to Teresa Nolan for their enthusiastic commitment to the undertaking. Their counsel and guidance particularly in the concluding phase of the work are acknowledged. Noreen Buttimer and Ríoghnach O'Flanagan and our respective families deserve our thanks for their forbearance and support throughout the entire project.

Finally, we express fulsome gratitude to our contributors for their dedication, patience and unstinting co-operation in the preparation of this volume.

List of Abbreviations

A. Clon.	D. Murphy (ed.), *The annals of Clonmacnoise* (Dublin, 1896)
Acts privy council	*Acts of the privy council of England, 1542-7* [etc.] (London, 1890 -)
A.F.M.	J. O'Donovan, *Annals of the kingdom of Ireland by the Four Masters* (Dublin, 1848-51)
A.L.C.	W. M. Hennessy (ed.), *Annals of Loch Cé* (London, 1871)
Anal. Hib.	*Analecta Hibernica*
Ann. Inisf./A.I.	S. Mac Airt (ed.), *The annals of Inisfallen* (Dublin, 1951)
Archiv. Hib.	*Archivium Hibernicum*
A. Tig.	W. Stokes (ed.), 'The annals of Tigernach' in *Revue Celtique*, xvi-xviii (1895-97)
A.U.²	S. Mac Airt and G. Mac Niocaill (ed.), *The annals of Ulster (to A.D. 1131)* (Dublin, 1983)
B.B.	R. Atkinson, *The Book of Ballymote,* photolithographic facsimile (Dublin, 1887)
Barnard, *Cromwellian Ire.*	T. C. Barnard, *Cromwellian Ireland: English government and reform in Ireland 1649-60* (Oxford, 1975)
Bennett, *Bandon*	G. Bennett, *History of Bandon* (Cork, 1869)
Best and Lawlor, *Mart. Tallaght*	R. I. Best and H. J. Lawlor, *The martyrology of Tallaght* (London, 1931)
Bielenberg, *Cork industry*	A. Bielenberg, *Cork's industrial revolution, 1780-1880: development or decline?* (Cork, 1991)
Bk Uí Maine	R. A. S. Macalister, *The Book of Uí Maine, otherwise called 'The Book of the O'Kellys',* facsimile (Dublin, 1942)
B.L.	British Library
B.M. cat. Ir. MSS	S. H. O'Grady, R. Flower and M. Dillon, *Catalogue of Irish manuscripts in the British Museum,* 3 vols (London, 1926-1953)
Bodl.	Bodleian Library, Oxford
Bolster, *Diocese of Cork,* i-iii	E. Bolster, A *history of the diocese of of Cork, from the earliest times to the Reformation* (Shannon, 1972) [i], ... *from the Reformation to the Penal era* (Cork, 1982) [ii], ... *from the Penal era to the Famine* (Cork, 1989) [iii]
Brady, *Clerical records*	W. Maziere Brady, *Clerical and parochial records of Cork, Cloyne, and Ross,* 3 vols (Dublin, 1863-4)

Brady and Gillespie, *Natives and newcomers*	C. Brady and R. Gillespie (ed.), *Natives and newcomers: essays on the making of Irish colonial society 1534-1641* (Dublin, 1986)
Burke, 'Cork'	T. Burke, 'Aspects of the population geography of county Cork', unpublished Ph.D. thesis, University of Birmingham (1967)
Burke, 'Eighteenth-century Cork	idem, 'County Cork in the eighteenth century' in *Geographical Review,* xli (1972), pp 61-81
Butel and Cullen, *Cities and merchants*	P. Butel and L. M. Cullen, *Cities and merchants: French and Irish perspectives on urban development, 1500-1900* (Dublin, 1986)
Butler, *Gleanings*	W. F. T. Butler, *Gleanings from Irish history* (London, 1925)
Butlin, *Town*	R. A. Butlin (ed.), *The development of the Irish town* (London, 1977)
Byrne, *Irish kings*	F. J. Byrne, *Irish kings and high-kings* (London, 1973)
C.A.I.	Cork Archives Institute
Cal. Carew MSS	*Calendar of Carew manuscripts preserved in the archiepiscopal library at Lambeth, 1515-74* [etc.], 6 vols (London, 1867-73)
Cal. close rolls	*Calendar of the close rolls, 1272-9* [etc.] (London, 1900 -)
Cal. doc. Ire.	*Calendar of documents relating to Ireland,* ed. H. S. Sweetman and G. F. Handcock, 5 vols (London, 1875-86)
Cal. justic. rolls Ire.	*Calendar of the justiciar rolls of Ireland,* ed. J. Mills *et al.,* 3 vols (Dublin, 1905-)
Cal. papal letters	*Calendar of entries in the papal registers relating to Great Britain and Ireland: papal letters, 1198-1304* [etc.] (London, 1893 -)
Cal. papal petitions	*Calendar of entries in the papal registers relating to Great Britain and Ireland: petitions to the Pope, 1342-1419* (London, 1896)
Cal. pat. rolls	*Calendar of patent rolls, 1232-47* [etc.] (London, 1906 -)
Cal pat. rolls Ire., Hen. VIII - Eliz.	*Calendar of patent and close rolls of chancery in Ireland, Henry VIII to 18th Elizabeth,* ed. J. Morrin (Dublin, 1861).
Cal. pat. rolls Ire., Jas I	*Irish patent rolls of James I: facsimile of the Irish record commissioners' calendar* (Dublin, 1966)
Cal. patent and close rolls	*Rotulorum patentium et clausorum cancellariae Hiberniae calendarium.,* ed. E.

	Tresham (Irish Record Commission, 1828)
Cal. S.P. dom.	*Calendar of state papers, domestic series, 1547-80* [etc.] (London, 1856 -)
Cal. S.P. Ire.,	*Calendar of the state papers relating to Ireland, 1509-1573* [etc.], 24 vols (London, 1860-1911)
Cal. treas. papers	*Calendar of treasury papers, 1557-1696* [etc.] 6 vols (London, 1868-89)
Caulfield, *Cork*	idem, *The council book of the corporation of Cork* (Guildford, 1876)
Caulfield, *Youghal*	idem, *The council book of the corporation of Youghal* (Guildford, 1878)
Caulfield, *Kinsale*	R. Caulfield (ed.), *The council book of the corporation of Kinsale* (Guildford, 1879)
C.C.	*Cork Constitution*
C.E.	*Cork Examiner*
Census Ire.,	*A census of Ireland circa 1659,* ed. S. Pender, I.M.C. (Dublin, 1939)
C.E.P.	*Cork Evening Post*
Chart. privil. immun.	*Chartae, privilegia et immunitates, being transcripts of charters and privileges to cities, towns, abbeys and other bodies corporate, ... 1171-1395* (Dublin, 1829-89)
Chartul. St Mary's, Dublin	*Chartularies of St Mary's Abbey, Dublin, and annals of Ireland, 1162-1370,* ed. J. T. Gilbert (1884-6)
Chron. Scot.	W. M. Hennessy, *Chronicum Scotorum* (London, 1866)
Civil Survey	*The Civil Survey, A.D. 1654-56,* 10 vols, ed. R. C. Simington (Dublin, 1931-61)
C.M.C.	*Cork Mercantile Chronicle*
Collect. Hib.	*Collectanea Hibernica: sources for Irish history* (Dublin, 1958-)
Common ground	K. Whelan and W. Smyth (ed.), *Common ground: essays on the historical geography of Ireland presented to T. Jones Hughes* (Cork, 1988)
Commons' jn. Ire.	*Journals of the house of commons of the kingdom of Ireland ...* (1613-1791), 28 vols (Dublin, 1753-91; reprinted and continued, 1613-1800, 19 vols (Dublin, 1796-1800)
Cork Hist. Soc. Jn.	*Journal of the Cork Historical and Archaeological Society*
Cox, 'Regnum'	R. Cox, 'Regnum Corcagiense; or a description of the kingdom of Cork', ed. R. Day in *Cork Hist. Soc. Jn.,* viii (1902), pp 65-83

Crotty, *Ir. agric. prod.*	R. D. Crotty, *Irish agricultural production: its volume and structure* (Cork, 1966)
C.S.	Civil Survey
C.S.O., R.P.	Chief Secretary's Office, Registered Papers
Cullen, *Emergence*	L. M. Cullen, *The emergence of modern Ireland 1600-1900* (London, 1981)
Cullen and Furet, *Ire. and France*	L. M. Cullen and F. Furet (ed.), *Ireland and France 17th-20th centuries: towards a comparative study of rural history* (Paris, 1980)
d'Alton, *Protestant society*	I. d'Alton, *Protestant society and politics in Cork 1812-1844* (Cork, 1980)
de Brún, *Cnuasach Thorna*	P. de Brún, *Clár lámhscríbhinní Gaeilge Choláiste Ollscoile Chorcaí: cnuasach Thorna*, 2 vols (Corcaigh, 1967)
Dickson, 'Cork region'	D. Dickson, 'An economic history of the Cork region in the eighteenth century', unpublished Ph.D. thesis, T.C.D. (1977)
Donnelly, *Land and people*	J. S. Donnelly, Jr, *The land and the people of nineteenth-century Cork* (London, 1975)
D.S.	Down Survey
Dublin	F. H. A. Aalen and K. Whelan, *Dublin city and county* (Dublin, 1992)
Ec. hist. rev.	*Economic history review*
ed.	edited by or edition
E.H.R.	*English Historical Review*
Extents Ir. mon. possessions	*Extents of Irish monastic possessions, 1540-1541, from manuscripts in the Public Records Office, London,* ed. N. B. White, I.M.C. (Dublin, 1943)
Fiants Ire., Hen. VIII [etc.]	'Calendar to fiants of the reign of Henry VIII ...' [etc.] in *P.R.I. rep. D.K. 7-22* (Dublin, 1875-90)
F.J.	*Freeman's Journal*
Folia Gadelica	P. de Brún, S. Ó Coileáin and P. Ó Riain (ed.), *Folia Gadelica: essays presented to R. A. Breatnach* (Cork, 1983)
Geneal. tracts	T. Ó Raithbheartaigh (ed.), *Genealogical tracts* (Dublin, 1932)
Gibson, *Cork*	Revd C. B. Gibson, *The history of the county and city of Cork,* 2 vols (Cork, 1861-64)
Gormanston reg.	J. Mills and M. J. McEnery (ed.), *Calendar of the Gormanston register* (Dublin, 1916)
Griffith, *Valuation*	*General valuation of rateable property in Ireland* [printed tenement valuation, 1851-52]
Harkness and	D. Harkness and M. O'Dowd (ed.), *The town*

O'Dowd, *Town*	*in Ireland,* Historical Studies XIII (Belfast, 1981)
Hayes, *Sources*	R. J. Hayes (ed.), *Manuscript sources for the history of Irish civilisation,* 11 vols (Boston, Mass., 1965)
Hib. Chron.	*Hibernian Chronicle*
H.C.	House of Commons
H.M.C.	Historical Manuscripts Commission
Hogan, *Onomasticon*	E. Hogan, *Onomasticon Goedelicum locorum et tribuum Hiberniae et Scotiae* (Dublin, 1910)
Hore and Graves, *Southern & eastern counties*	H. F. Hore and J. Graves (ed.), *The social state of the southern and eastern counties of Ireland in the sixteenth century* (Dublin, 1868-9)
I.F.C.	Irish Folklore Commission
I.H.S.	*Irish Historical Studies*
I.M.C.	Irish Manuscripts Commission
Ir. Econ. Soc. Hist. Jn.	*Journal of Irish Economic and Social History*
Ir. Geneal.	*The Irish Genealogist*
Ir. Geog.	*Irish Geography*
Ir. Jurist	*Irish Jurist*
I.T.	*Irish Times*
Jn. Hist. Geog.	*Journal of Historical Geography*
Kerry Hist. Soc. Jn.	*Journal of the Kerry Historical and Archaelogical Society*
Kilkenny	W. Nolan and K. Whelan (ed)., *Kilkenny: history and society* (Dublin, 1990)
Lewis, *Topog. dict. Ire.*	S. Lewis, *Topographical dictionary of Ireland,* 2 vols with atlas (London, 1837)
L.L.	R. Atkinson, *The Book of Leinster,* autotype facsimile (Dublin, 1880) / R. I. Best *et al.,* (ed.), *The Book of Leinster,* diplomatic ed., 6 vols (Dublin, 1954-83)
Lr Muin.	T. Ó Donnchadha (ed.), An *Leabhar Muimhneach* (Dublin, 1940)
Lydon, *Lordship*	J. F. Lydon, *The lordship of Ireland in the middle ages* (Dublin and London, 1972)
McCarthy-Morrogh, *Plantation*	M. McCarthy-Morrogh, *The Munster plantation: English migration to southern Ireland 1583- 1641* (Oxford, 1986)
MacLysaght, *Ir. families*	E. MacLysaght, *Irish families: their names, arms and origins* (Dublin, 1957)
Mac Niocaill, *Na buirgéisí*	G. Mac Niocaill, *Na buirgéisí xii-xv aois,* 2 vols (Baile Átha Cliath, 1964)
Má Nuad clár	P. Ó Fiannachta *et al., Lámhscríbhinní*

	Gaeilge Choláiste Phádraig Má Nuad: clár, 8 vols (Má Nuad, 1965-80)
Mason, *Survey*	W. Shaw Mason, *A statistical account or parochial survey of Ireland,* 3 vols (Dublin, 1814-19)
Misc. Ir. annals	S. Ó hInnse (ed.), *Miscellaneous Irish annals* (Dublin, 1947)
Moran, *Spicil. Ossor.*	P. F. Moran, *Spicilegium Ossoriense,* 3 vols, (Dublin, 1874-84)
MS(S)	Manuscript(s)
N.A.	National Archives
n.d.	no date
New hist. Ire.	*New history of Ireland,* especially vols II, A. Cosgrove (ed.), *Medieval Ireland (1169-1534)* (Oxford, 1987), III, T. W. Moody, F. X. Martin and F. J. Byrne (ed.), *Early modern Ireland 1534-1691* (Oxford, 1976), and IV, T. W. Moody and W. E. Vaughan (ed.), *Eighteenth-century Ireland 1691-1800* (Oxford, 1986)
Nicholls, *Gaelic Ire.*	K. W. Nicholls, *Gaelic and Gaelicized Ireland in the middle ages* (Dublin, 1972)
N.L.I.	National Library of Ireland
N.L.I. cat. Ir. MSS	N. Ní Sheaghdha *et al, Catalogue of Irish manuscripts in the National Library of Ireland* (Dublin, 1961 -)
O'Brien, *Corpus geneal. Hib.*	M. A. O'Brien, *Corpus genealogiarum Hiberniae,* i (Dublin, 1962)
Ó Conchúir, *Scríobh. Chorc.*	B. Ó Conchúir, *Scríobhaithe Chorcaí* (Baile Átha Cliath, 1982)
O'Connor, *Limerick*	P. J. O'Connor, *Exploring Limerick's past: an historical geography of urban development in county and city* (Limerick, 1985)
O'Donovan, *Misc. Celt. Soc.*	J. O'Donovan (ed.), *Miscellany of the Celtic Society* (Dublin, 1849 [1851])
Ó Fiannachta, *Mionchnuasaigh*	P. Ó Fiannachta, *Clár lámhscríbhinní Gaeilge: leabharlanna na cléire agus mionchnuasaigh,* 2 vols (Baile Átha Cliath, 1978-80)
O'Flanagan, *Bandon*	P. O'Flanagan, *Bandon,* R.I.A., Irish Historic Towns Atlas, No. 3 (Dublin, 1988)
Ormond deeds	E. Curtis (ed.), *Calendar of Ormond deeds, 1172-1350* [etc.], 6 vols (Dublin, 1932-43)
Orrery papers	E. MacLysaght (ed.), *Calendar of the Orrery papers* (Dublin, 1941)
O.S.	Ordnance Survey of Ireland

Ó Murchadha,
Family names

D. Ó Murchadha, *Family names of county Cork* (Dún Laoghaire, 1985)

Orpen,
Normans

G. H. Orpen, *Ireland under the Normans, 1169-1333,* 4 vols (Oxford, 1911-20)

O'Sullivan,
Econ. hist. Cork city

W. O'Sullivan, *The economic history of Cork city, from the earliest times to the act of union* (Cork, 1937)

O'Sullivan Beare,
Hist. cath. Ibern.

Philip O'Sullivan Beare, *Historiae catholicae Iberniae compendium,* ed. M. Kelly (1850)

Otway-Ruthven,
Medieval Ire.

A. J. Otway-Ruthven, A *history of medieval Ireland* (London, 1968)

Pacata Hibernia

[Thomas Stafford], *Pacata hibernia: Ireland appeased and reduced ...* (London, 1663; 2 vols, Dublin, 1810; ed. S. H. O'Grady, 2 vols, London, 1896)

Parl. gaz.

Parliamentary gazetteer of Ireland, 1844-45, 3 vols (Dublin, London and Edinburgh, 1846)

Pat. rolls Ire., Jas I

A repertory of the inrolments on the patent rolls of chancery in Ireland commencing with the reign of James I, ed. J. C. Erck (Dublin, 1846-52)

Peritia

Peritia: journal of the Medieval Academy of Ireland

pers. comm.

personal communication

Petty,
Hib. Del.

Sir W. Petty, *Hibernia Delineatio* (1685), 'Atlas of Ireland', ed. F. Graham (Newcastle upon Tyne, 1968)

Pipe roll Ire. 1211-12

O. Davies and D. B. Quinn (ed.), 'The Irish pipe roll of 14 John, 1211-1212' in *U.J.A.,* 3rd series, iv, supp. (July 1941)

Pocoke, *Tour*

Dr R. Pocoke, *A tour in Ireland in 1752,* ed. G. Stokes (Dublin, 1891)

Power, *Crichad*

P. Power (ed.), *Crichad an Chaoilli: being the topography of ancient Fermoy* (Cork, 1931)

P.R.I. rep. D.K. 1 [etc.]

First [etc.] *report of the deputy keeper of the public records [of England],* 2 vols (London, 1840 -)

P.R.O.

Public Record Office, London

Proc . king's council, Ire. 1392-3

A roll of the proceedings of the king's council in Ireland for a portion of the sixteenth year of the reign of Richard II, 1392-93, ed. J. Graves (London, 1877)

P.R.O.I.

Public Record Office, Ireland

P.R.O.N.I.

Public Record Office, Northern Ireland

Quart. Bul. Ir. Georg. Soc.

Quarterly bulletin of the Irish Georgian society

Quinn, 'Plantation'	D. B. Quinn, 'The Munster plantation: problems and opportunities' in *Cork Hist. Soc. Jn.*, lxxi (1966), pp 19-41
Red Bk Kildare	G. Mac Niocaill (ed.), *The Red Book of the earls of Kildare* (Dublin, 1964)
R.I.A.	Royal Irish Academy
R.I.A. cat. Ir. MSS	T. F. O'Rahilly *et al.*, *Catalogue of Irish manuscripts in the Royal Irish Academy* (Dublin, 1926-70)
R.I.A. Proc.	*Proceedings of the Royal Irish Academy*
R.I.A. Trans.	*Transactions of the Royal Irish Academy*
Reg. St Thomas, Dublin	*Register of the abbey of St Thomas the Martyr, Dublin,* ed. J. T. Gilbert (London, 1889)
Richardson and Sayles, *Ir. parl. in middle ages*	H. G. Richardson and G. O. Sayles, *The Irish parliament in the middle ages* (Philadelphia, 1952; reissue, 1964)
Richardson and Sayles, *Parl. & councils med. Ire.,* i	H. G. Richardson and G. O. Sayles, *Parliaments and councils of medieval Ireland,* i (Dublin, 1947)
Rot. chart.	*Rotuli chartarum in Turri Londinensi asservati, 1199-1216* (London, 1837)
Rot. pat. Hib.	*Rotulorum patentium et clausorum cancellariae Hiberniae calendarium* (Dublin, 1828)
R.S.A.I. Jn .	*Journal of the Royal Society of Antiquaries of Ireland*
R.T.É.	Radió Telefís Éireann
Rymer, *Foedera*	T. Rymer (ed.), *Foedera, conventiones, litterae et cujuscunque generis acta publica,* 12 vols (London, 1704-11)
Smith, *Cork*	C. Smith, *The antient and present state of the county and city of Cork,* 2 vols (Cork, 1750)
S.O.C.P.	State of the Country Papers
S.P. Hen. VIII	*State papers, Henry VIII,* 11 vols (London, 1830-52)
Spillar, *Bandon*	W. A. Spillar, *A short topographical and statistical account of the Bandon union* (Bandon, 1844)
S.P.O.	State Paper Office
S.R.	*Southern Reporter*
Stat. Ire.	*The statutes at large passed in the parliaments held in Ireland* ... (1310-1761, 8 vols, Dublin, 1765; 1310-1800, 20 vols, Dublin, 1786-1801)
Stat. Ire.,	*Statute rolls of* the *parliament of Ireland,*

Hen. VI	reign of King Henry VI, ed. F. H. Berry (Dublin, 1910)
Stat. Ire., 1-12 Edw. IV	Statute rolls of the parliament of Ireland, 1st to the 12th years of the reign of King Edward IV, ed. H. F. Berry (Dublin, 1914)
Stat. Ire., 12-22 Edw. IV	Statute rolls of the parliament of Ireland, 12th and 13th years of the reign of King Edward IV, ed. J. F. Morrissey (Dublin, 1939)
Stokes, Mart. Gorman	W. Stokes, The martyrology of Gorman (London, 1895)
Stokes, Mart. Oengus	W. Stokes, The martyrology of Oengus the Culdee (London, 1905)
Studia Hib.	Studia Hibernica
Taylor and Skinner, Maps	G. Taylor and A. Skinner, Maps of the roads of Ireland (London and Dublin, 1778)
T.C.D.	Trinity College, Dublin
T.C.D. cat. Ir. MSS	T. K. Abbott and E. J. Gwynn, Catalogue of Irish manuscripts in the library of Trinity College, Dublin (Dublin, 1921)
Theiner, Vetera mon.	A. Theiner, Vetera monumenta Hibernorum et Scotorum (Rome, 1864)
Tipperary	W. Nolan and T. McGrath (ed.), Tipperary: history and society (Dublin, 1985)
Todd and Reeves, Mart. Donegal	J. H. Todd and W. Reeves (ed.), The martyrology of Donegal (Dublin, 1864)
Townsend, Cork	Revd H. Townsend, Statistical survey of the county of Cork, with observations on the means of improvement (Dublin, 1810)
Tuckey, Cork remembrancer	F. H. Tuckey, The county and city of Cork remembrancer (Cork, 1837)
U.C.C.	University College, Cork
U.C.D.	University College, Dublin
U.J.A.	Ulster Journal of Archaeology
vol(s)	Volume(s)
Watson, Almanack	J. Watson (and others), The gentleman and citizen's almanack (Dublin, 1729-1844)
Webster, Cork	C. A. Webster, The diocese of Cork (Cork, 1920)
Windele, Cork	J. Windele, Historical and descriptive notices of the city of Cork and its vicinity (Cork, 1839)
Young, Tour	A. Young, Tour in Ireland (1780)

Chapter 1

CORK: ANATOMY AND ESSENCE

JOHN A. MURPHY

'The county', says Donnelly, 'has some claim to be regarded as a microcosm of the whole country'.[1] While historical geographers may demur at this as simplistic special pleading, enthusiastic Corkonians will complacently accept the description as a richly-deserved compliment, happily equating 'microcosm' with 'model' or 'exemplar'. More seriously, Donnelly is here pinpointing the salient feature of the county's physical geography, the contrast between a fertile east and a rugged west. The east in this sense comprises not only the rich tracts of farm, park and estate between Youghal and the lower Lee but the good land extending north into the middle Blackwater valley with its many demesnes and beyond that again into Golden Vale country. West Cork stretches beyond Macroom, into Nadd and the Boggeraghs in one direction, and in the other to the watershed of 'the county bounds', and away to the mountains and deep bays of Carbery and the far-flung Beara peninsula.

As well as being the largest Irish county, Cork was for long the most populous. Indeed, to those Elizabethan planners who finalised the boundaries of the medieval administrative divisions it seemed a good idea at one stage to have two compact counties, east and west of the city, instead of the unwieldy and rather incoherent unit which was eventually allowed to survive.[2] In Gaelic Ireland there was little in common between Carbery and Muskerry, still less between those areas and Imokilly. Yet, just as English rule created Irish nationalism, so too alien administration forged a county identity. Unlike less strong-featured counties, Cork was always much more than a mere geographical expression. Physically, the county may lack real cohesion or homogeneity, in contrast, say, to Wexford. East Cork shades imperceptibly across the Blackwater into Waterford, and mountainous south-west Cork is really Kerry country: indeed, Beara was part of Elizabethan Desmond and it still belongs to the diocese of Kerry. However, a certain countervailing pattern of unity is supplied by the parallel rivers of Blackwater, Lee and Bandon, flowing east and south into the Celtic Sea.

The ancient ecclesiastical dioceses of Cloyne, Cork and Ross correspond generally to the river parallels, forming three unequal, and uneven, east-west divisions. Cloyne reaches north to the Limerick boundary, while ceding the Cork part of the Sliabh Luachra area to the diocese of Kerry. Cork has its northern limit along the river Lee, but swoops north of the city to breach the Anglo-Norman cathedral division of Uí Chorb Liatháin. The three dioceses, long since combined in one Church of Ireland administration, retain distinct personae, difficult to define or describe. Cork is certainly more dominant in the public perception, partly because of a succession of strong individualistic bishops, partly because of the urban status of its see. Cloyne, with its modern cathedral seat at Cobh, has a more rural and reticent character appropriate to the tranquil backwater that was its original headquarters, although it is also distinguished by rich and strong town parishes, such as Mitchelstown and Mallow.

Of particular interest is the tiny coastal diocese of Ross, extending from Courtmacsherry Bay to Cape Clear, having its ancient see at Rosscarbery and its modern centre at Skibbereen, and corresponding in territorial extent to the old kingdom of Corcu Loígde. Ross has played its part in the story of Irish Catholicism, and the name of its Cromwellian martyr-bishop, Boetius MacEgan, is familiar to generations of schoolchildren. But it also has had a chequered history of mergers with its neighbours, mainly because of its smallness and consequent lack of viability. When the Bishop of Cork took over Ross in a controversial *anschluss* in 1958 the ensuing furore in the occupied diocese was considerable and prolonged. Resistance was as much locally patriotic as ecclesiastical. It was felt that 'the honour of the little diocese' was at stake and that a regional personality was being obliterated. The self-esteem of a historic area, already badly shaken by unemployment and emigration, was now being dealt a further and unwarranted blow, or so it was indignantly perceived. Ross had had no resident ordinary since Bishop Moynihan's translation to Kerry in 1953 and it greatly resented the implication that it could not maintain a bishop in the style to which he had been accustomed or to which he was entitled. Although the crusading enthusiasm to save Ross permeated all classes, not least the professions and the hard-headed businessmen, it was the clergy themselves who bridled most indignantly, if for the most part in silence, at such iniquitous ecclesiastical imperialism. Thus it was that in the 1980s a local priest-hero publicly rejected Cork jurisdiction as invalid and illegal, and carried his defiance to the extent of breaking the civil law. Like Luther he appealed from a pope ill-informed to a pope better-informed, and, in a well-established historical pattern of local loyalty his parishioners dramatically refused the ministrations of the pastor sent to replace the turbulent priest.

In all this Ross passion one large component was resentment of Cork metropolitan power. Even in the most harmonious of times there is some tension in the balance between the city and, in varying degrees, different areas of the county. On the whole the tension is a healthy one and there is none of that disproportionate and suffocating dominance which Dublin exercises over its small county and further afield. Yet the city of Cork is undeniably the commercial, cultural and services mecca not only of the county but of the province of Munster. And the county's orientation towards the city at its coastal centre is symbolically reflected in the fact that the county takes its name from the city, which is not invariably the case throughout Ireland.

Traditionally, the city has a mentality as incorrigibly urban as a large metropolis. Sir Fopling Flutter's deep distrust of the countryside – 'Beyond Hyde Park all is a desert' – would be heartily endorsed by the quintessential urban Corkonian. Civilisation crumbles at Carrigrohane, Macroom is *ultima thule* and dragons lurk at Mushera. County people are not admitted to the plenitude of Corkiness, so to speak, being merely 'Kerrymen with shoes', to quote a contemporary Cork comedian.[3] This tongue-in-cheek condescension is countered by a rural perception of the city's inhabitants as sly and arrogant. However, these town-country semi-serious tensions are subsumed in a general Cork personality, recognised as distinctive by natives and outsiders alike. Not all attributed Cork characteristics (in varying degrees common to city and county) are appealing or attractive. 'There is a bumptiousness in the Cork temperament', observed that shrewd revolutionary, Ernie O'Malley, himself a Mayo man. 'They resemble the Gascons: quick and volatile, but they seem too conscious of their qualities, as if they are surprised at possessing them'.[4] One might add that people tend to act up to the perceived image. An agreed list of characteristics might categorise Cork people as cute (in the Irish rather than the American usage) if not wily and cunning opinionated, self-satisfied and self-confident, sometimes to the point of *hubris*; pushing and ambitious, with a legendary penchant for taking over the top jobs nationally; able, witty and garrulous and ostensibly friendly and charming but clannish to a degree.

The renowned Cork accent has long been commented upon by observers and travellers, and badly imitated by envious outsiders. It was the proud name given to an O'Brienite newspaper early in the century,[5] after a notorious disruption of a political meeting, when one faction was recognised by its distinctive speech. A recent B.B.C. television series on the development of English dealt with Hiberno-English as spoken in Cork, and used sub-titles as an aid to understanding the conversation of workers in a northside brewery. Cork viewers were torn between resentment at the depiction of their standard English as a patois, and pride that interpretative help was essential for unravelling the mysteries of their highly distinctive speech. In an age of instant global communication through radio and television, in addition to the influence of the cinema, it is remarkable that local accents should have survived the universal levelling process. However, a rich local slang[6] is regrettably disappearing from Cork city, as are nuances of locality within the general 'accent', though class variations still range from fruity patrician tones to an adenoidal plebian whine.

The distinctive Cork personality is so marked that it must have been in the course of development long before county boundaries became a reality with the growth of local government in the nineteenth century. Many counties did not have such a pre-existing regional character. In Cork's case, as has been said, the regional personality transcends any urban-rural divisions, and loyalty to Cork spans the class spectrum.

The important role of the Gaelic Athletic Association in the social, cultural and political history of modern Ireland is amply documented. One aspect of its significance that is not adequately appreciated, perhaps, is its formative influence in shaping county identity and county loyalty. These were defined and sharpened in two ways: first, through club or parochial rivalry for primacy within the county area; secondly, and far more importantly, through phenomenal public interest in the inter-county games of the provincial and 'All-Ireland' championships. Just as various class and local interests are subsumed in a composite Cork personality and character, so too club, parochial and urban-rural rivalries are subordinated to a single loyalty at inter-county level. It is one of the many ironies of Irish nationalism that it is the Gaelic Athletic Association which finally nativised and successfully popularised a British-imposed administrative division. County loyalties go right up to the county line – and stop there. This sense of county identity is no less real for being somewhat artificially formalised at its boundaries.

A corollary of fanatical county loyalty is the creation of a certain demonology where the county's arch-rivals are concerned, Kerry in Gaelic football and Tipperary in hurling. Such hostilities are, of course, somewhat unreal (given, for example, the almost identical sub-culture and one-time political union of south-west Cork and south Kerry) but are passionately felt for all that – only in the sporting sphere, of course, and there only for the duration of the championship season. It should be noted that fierce county loyalty and fervour were particularly in evidence in the autumn of 1990 when Cork achieved a unique hurling-football double in the All-Ireland championships. The red and white county colours (corresponding to the limestone and old red sandstone facings of Shandon steeple, the most symbolic of Cork landmarks) fluttered proudly on business and public buildings alongside, or often instead of, the national tricolour. All this half-seriously suggests that, if the utopian European Community dreams of real regionalisation ever come true, Cork would be an authentic focus of the much-vaunted principle of subsidiarity of function. In the G.A.A. context, two final points (no pun intended) are worth making. First, though county and city are conjoined enthusiastically in victory, with some rural areas supplying outstanding individuals in hurling and football, the main strength now resides in urban clubs, reflecting the general Irish trend of rural depopulation, emigration and the superior attraction of city lights. Secondly, in attempting to distil the essence of a county, it would be difficult to exaggerate the importance of sport in general and of the G.A.A. games in particular as expressions of Cork pride, even *hubris*, and of the urge to excel. Though 1990 was a striking example of this in many codes, the most symbolic personification of Cork's sporting prowess is undoubtedly Jack Lynch, a 'dual' star of the 1940s in hurling and football and subsequently (and by no means co-incidentally) as Taoiseach, the most popular political leader since Daniel O'Connell, in the generous opinion of Lynch's main political opponent, Liam Cosgrave.[7] Jack Lynch is also, in all probability, the most popular Corkman of all time.

If the city centrally serves, rather than dominates, the county, there is an equally pleasing balance in the distribution of lesser urban settlements throughout the countryside, from the rich tillage and pasture of east Cork to the rugged terrain of the west – from Youghal through Kinsale to Castletownbere along the coast, and inland from Fermoy and Mallow to Bandon and Skibbereen. There are picturesque villages and market towns with a native feel, as well as settler or semi-planned towns. Whatever their individual flavour or relative state of prosperity, the county towns have been vastly improved by the modernisation process since mid-century, and energetically-organised festivals of great variety have brought light, colour and life to what were very dingy streets a hundred years ago.

As with other Irish counties, religion is a predominant aspect of the county Cork landscape. Pre-Christian antiquities, Christianised rituals, surviving cults of local saints, elegant Protestant churches and robust Catholic architecture of the resurgent 1800-1960 period, all attest to the central role of religion in the lives of Cork people since the dawn of history. The stone circles of west Cork and the numerous holy wells throughout the county merge insensibly into the immemorial 'rounds' in honour of St Gobnait at Ballyvourney, St Olan at Aghabullogue and St Finbarr at Gougane Barra, the latter cult being the subject of severe ecclesiastical censure in the early nineteenth century because of its riotous excesses.[8] In mid-county, about a mile east of Macroom, there is an ancient well in a characteristic arboreal setting (albeit much vulgarised by tasteless modernisation) which is associated with penitential Holy Week rounds and with the veneration of the seventh-century Saxon St Berrihert, who laboured in different parts of the county and the centre of whose still vigorous cult is in the village of Tullylease, in the north-west. Just across the road from the Macroom well is a successful semi-conductor plant, affording welcome local employment. This juxtaposition of ultra-modern technology and pre-Christian antiquity is a striking symbol of the continuity of human settlement.

From medieval times and later, there are rich memorials of former ecclesiastical splendours and of thriving pre-Reformation religious communities. One thinks of Buttevant and Timoleague but above all of the splendid Franciscan ruin at Kilcrea Abbey, standing serenely in the rich and tranquil pasture-land of the Bride valley, only a mile away from the busy Cork-Killarney N 22 route. There are also numerous reminders of Gaelic power in its twilight years. Kilcrea was sponsored by Cormac Láidir Mac Carthaigh, Lord of Muskerry, the munificent builder of Blarney and other mid-Cork castles, a contemporary Irish version of Lorenzo de Medici (It was an exiled Mac Carthy lady in Lous XIV's Paris who made the magnificently arrogant Cork response to a maid urging her to hasten to the window to observe *le roi soleil* returning after a famous victory. 'I have seen', she said, not bothering to lift her head from her embroidery, 'I have seen Mac Carthy entering Blarney and what can Paris offer to *equal* that?'[9]). Near Kanturk is a monumental never-quite-finished castle, built by the Mac Carthy lord of Duhallow in defiance of Gloriana's ban on such impudent pretensions. In the extreme east of the county, just on the Cork side of the Blackwater estuary, the coastal town of Youghal reflects a blend of ambiences[10] – an Anglicised nineteenth-century watering resort, the urban mecca of the native Irish from the Déise country a century or two ago (*maidin Domhnaigh's mé ag dul go hEochaill*), the Elizabethan base of courtier-explorer Raleigh and adventurer Boyle, and once a nucleus of a proposed collegiate seat of learning. Various buildings express these presences, and the clock-tower spanning the main street is like an eastern gateway to the county.

Youghal is in the barony of Imokilly and the sub-county divisions still have some importance today, mainly in G.A.A. competitions. The Cork baronies each have their own flavour, and are yet another aspect of the county's richness. Muskerry, Duhallow and Carbery evoke strongly distinct regional resonances and are celebrated, as they say, in song and story. As a native Macrompian, I once felt a surge of pride when, as a fledgling researcher studying the Confederate war, I read in the mid-seventeenth century *Commentarius Rinuccinianus* that Macroom was *emporium Muscriae!*[11]

To return to the religious landscape, we must not overlook a notable Protestant colouring. We would naturally expect to find in Cork city a significant residue of an erstwhile political and commercial ascendancy but a fairly large rural Protestant presence – despite depopulation, probably the most substantial in the State outside metropolitan Dublin – is at first sight somewhat surprising. Bandon,[12] in origin a plantation settlement, was for long distinguished from other county towns by its strongly, and at times aggressively, Protestant complexion. The political folklore tells of Bandon's Orange bucks sallying forth to challenge signs of Catholic resurgence in neighbouring towns. Generations of Catholic children in Cork became familiar with the gibe 'In Bandon even the pigs are Protestant', and they exulted in the alleged graffito-retort to the legendary warning at the town gates: 'Turk, Jew and atheist may enter here but never a papist'. The Catholic response was: 'Whoever wrote this wrote it well/The same is writ on the gates of hell'.

From Bandon south-west to the peninsular extremities of Carbery, there is still a perceptible Protestant vein, generally Anglican but including some later sects. An exceptional concentration in the Toormore/Altar area, between Schull and Goleen, recalls a dramatic evangelical episode of the Famine period, associated with the charismatic missionary personality of the Rev. William Allen Fisher.[13]

Protestant places of worship throughout the county, as in the country at large, greatly enhance the man-made landscape, being as aesthetically pleasing in location as in design. Equally enriching is the Protestant or Anglo-Irish voice in literature, varying across the spectrum of time and style from Somerville and Ross to Elizabeth Bowen. More controversial, socially and politically, is the role of the Protestant landed gentry, symbolised by the distribution of the remains of Big Houses across the county. Nationalists would claim that the suffering of West Cork Protestants during the turmoil of the early 1920s – by way of property destruction, personal intimidation, expulsion and murder – was a strategic necessity rather than an exercise in revenge, yet there were regrettable instances of ugly sectarianism.[14] Happily, harmony and tolerance now characterise contemporary Catholic-Protestant relations, in part an ironic consequence of the tragic polarisation in Northern Ireland and its impact on the South.

We move now to what would be generally, perhaps mistakenly,

regarded as a totally different cultural world from that of Cork
Protestants. County Cork has two residual Gaeltachtaí, Oileán Chléire
(Clear Island) and Cúil Aodha, the latter being the only inland Irish-
speaking pocket in the country, if we except the county Meath
colonies. The Cork Gaeltachtaí are not *primarily* Irish-speaking,
numbering a few hundred habitual native speakers over some square
miles,[15] but the areas give a very distinctive flavour to these parts of the
county. The *seanchas* tradition is strong in both Cork Gaeltachtaí, and
the people of Cúil Aodha have preserved and developed a popular
bardic and musical culture, to the great enrichment of their appreciative
fellow-Corkonians. Whatever the outlook for Irish as a living
community language in the county, it need hardly be said that a
knowledge of the Irish originals of place-names is an indispensable key
for unlocking the meaning of the landscape in Cork, as elsewhere.

The rural road network is denser in Cork than in any other county,
and this greatly facilitates walking or cycling, especially in the western
reaches of the county. But all roads, in a sense, lead to the city which
is the essential focus of the county and from which the county takes its
name. *Omnes viae urbem Corcagiam tendunt.* Corcach Mór Mumhan
(the great marsh of Munster) was the earlier name of the more modern
'Corcaigh'. The marsh (still used colloquially to describe the old heart
of the city) was where the river Lee became estuarial, threading itself
through various islands which were built over in the course of time.
Much of the modern city centre, including the principal (St Patrick)
street, arose over closed-in waters from the late eighteenth century.
This completed the lengthy process of consolidating a marshy delta
into one long island. Before that last stage, the medieval and post-
medieval fortified town comprised a compact area around the axis of
the main street running from North to South Gate Bridge. Old Cork
was bounded by the two main channels of the river, famously
described by Spenser who was married, so the tradition says, in
Christchurch:

> The spreading Lee that like an island fayre
> Encloseth Cork with his divided flood.

Sixteenth-century maps of the city give a clear picture which is borne
out by this description of 1586:

> It is of oval form, enclosed with walls, and encompassed
> with the channel of the River which also crosses it, and
> is not accessible except by bridges: lying along as it were
> in one direct street with a bridge over it.

Meanwhile over the last two centuries, the city spread itself up the steep hills to the north and the gentler incline to the south. After a classic European pattern, a 'north' and 'south'-side dichotomy emerged with various forms of rivalry developing between two areas of real or imagined dissimilarities.

St Finbarr, some of our scholars now assert, was not a real historical personage or, an even more shocking heresy, may not have been a Cork man at all![16] He has nonetheless an unshakeable place in the popular tradition as the eponymous Cork patron saint, and it is arguable that he has closer links with Cork than any other Irish town has with its patron. As well as linking Catholic and Protestant traditions, he transcends and unites city and county. Born in mid-county, so the tradition goes, he set up his monastic retreat in the 'green isle' of the scenic and mountainous valley named after him, Gougane Barra, and later moved down the Lee from source to mouth, or at least to estuarial head-water. In doing so, he made the river an essential symbol of city and county unity. The seventh-century monastic school of St Finbarr at Gillabbey, near the present University College, Cork site, was the seminal urban settlement from which developed the Viking town (of which, curiously, we know little, archaeologically speaking) and the medieval trading city and port.

Throughout the diocese, but particularly in the city, the saint's name is popular and ubiquitous, attesting to a remarkable pride in tradition and a strong local *pietas*. The ecclesiastical and academic legacies of St Finbarr still flourish. A College crest carries the legend, 'Ionad Bhairre, Scoil na Mumhan'. Another College motto runs, 'Where Finbarr taught, let Munster learn'. In various spelling combinations, he gives his name to the imposing neo-Gothic (Saint FinBarre's) Church of Ireland cathedral dominating the inner south-side of the city, to various other churches and schools, and to the diocesan seminary. He is further commemorated by hospitals, social and sporting clubs and a famed hurling team:

> The Rockies thought that they were stars/Till they met the St Finbarr's.

Finbarr, Barry or Barra is still a favourite Christian name in city and diocese. Thus Cork's earliest ecclesiastical tradition is also its most enduring one.

'A city of tattered grace' is one striking description of Cork city.[17] This really applies to the genteel grandeur of Montenotte and Sunday's Well rising sharply to the north over the river valley. Here were built the imposing mansions of the merchant princes who presided over the city's prosperous nineteenth-century economy, based on the butter market and the provisioning trade. The winding channels of the Lee, the numerous and beautiful bridges and the steep hills make for an endless variety of Italianate vistas, glimpsed from mid-stream bridges or through narrow alleyways. These views often feature Cork's most famous landmark, the clock tower of St Anne's, Shandon, with its nostalgic bells 'that sound so grand on the pleasant waters of the river Lee,' in Fr Prout's celebrated lines. 'Tattered', however, is an epithet no longer applicable to the bustling business centre. Enlightened municipal management policies have long since arrested and reversed inner city dereliction in Cork. Patrick Street is a joy for the promenader, the Grand Parade has been rescued from decay, and mean alleys have been transformed into delightful retreats of restaurants and boutiques. Cork as a whole has a satisfying human scale, and walking, except to the most far-flung suburbs, is a feasible and enjoyable proposition. Cultural life is also fulfilling in a city where there is thriving literary and artistic activity.

A benign adaptation of a Virgilian phrase,[18] *statio bene fida carinis*, 'a trustworthy anchorage for ships', is the motto on the city's crest. It is significant that Cork thus identifies itself primarily with the spacious harbour rather than with the city or the rich hinterland. Indeed, it is the harbour in all its dimensions that explains historically why Cork, rather than, say, Kinsale evolved as the principal urban settlement in the county. The harbour was of great strategic importance in the days of British naval supremacy, and the return of the naval bases in Cork harbour and elsewhere to Irish jurisdiction in 1938 completed the process of sovereignty-transfer begun in 1922. The growth of Queenstown, later Cobh, was a reflection of garrison power but the town was also the port of departure for the post-famine exodus across the Atlantic. The harbour channelled Cork's valuable provisioning trade and the regular commercial trade with Bristol and other British ports, as well as with Continental centres. Grain, coal, fruit and timber imports developed storage and warehouse facilities in the dock area. All this harbour activity, as well as the vital business of dredging, comes under the auspices of the Harbour Commissioners whose splendid office, interior and facade, is one of the city's most notable architectural features. Today, large cross-channel and continental ferries constitute another dimension of harbour business, as do the numerous industrial and chemical sites from Little Island to the lower harbour in the Ringaskiddy area. Beyond the harbour mouth is the rich fishing ground of the Celtic Sea and the flowing resource of natural gas.

'Where Finbarr taught let Munster learn'. If Cork is outstandingly a port and harbour city, it is no less a university town, though the citizens have tended to take this aspect for granted over the century and a half since the Queen's College was instituted. In terms of location and scale the handsome College buildings and riverside grounds are admirably situated on the western approaches within a mile of the city centre, and they lend a distinctive and elegant appearance to a large neighbourhood. In terms of the local economy, and considered as a bustling academic village, University College, Cork generates considerable spending power. For over half a century its pioneering adult education programmes have provided a far-flung and vital community service throughout the province of Munster. In the vicinity of Cork itself, the College has vigorously stimulated scholarship and the arts. In its primary function of supplying higher education and professional training it remains the premier third-level institution in the city and the province, despite the challenges presented by the arrival of new institutions. The pattern of student intake has been remarkably consistent over the decades. The largest proportion of students has always come from the city itself, and the rest are supplied by the county and the province, particularly south Munster. A student body with its family and social roots deep in the area has tended to be a conservative force in the community but it has also made for solidity and continuity in the Cork academic tradition.

Archaeologists and historians at the university are making a major contribution to the study of the county's past. However, it must be said that as far as history is concerned, up to quite recently when region and locality rather than nation became the acceptable, if not the necessary, models of research, the real enthusiasm for Cork's antiquities was shown by amateur local historians. Archaeology, on the other hand, has long since brought a high degree of professionalism to local investigations in city and county. The region is an extremely fruitful one for archaeological study since there is ample evidence of extensive human settlement from a very early period. The Ordnance Survey Six Inch maps show over ten thousand archaeological monuments in the county. Extensive and systematic study of every known archaeological and historical site is being carried out by the Cork Archaeological Survey, based in U.C.C. This work is a race against the ravages of time and of a radically changing agrarian economy. Deep ploughing, fence clearance, land reclamation, intensive cattle grazing, tree planting and sand and gravel quarrying are some of the ways in which our links with the past can be damaged and destroyed. Informing public opinion about the significance of ancient monuments is an important task for the archaeologist whenever time can be taken off from the investigation of megalithic tombs, stone circles, *fulachta fiadha*, ring-forts, ogham stones – and in a later period – castles, tower houses, abbeys and mills.

Urban archaeology, though calling for a different approach, is no less important. A number of successful excavations has taken place within the medieval city though none of these has had the dramatic significance of Wood Quay in Dublin or of work carried out in Waterford. There is one intriguing *negative* aspect about Cork urban excavation to date. Since the city, as a centre of trading and port activity, owes its initial development to Viking settlement, it is curious that however rewarding in other respects, urban excavations have so far produced no Viking or Ostman remains. Doubtless, further investigations on different sites will yield appropriate results in time.

The history of the county, or perhaps history *in* the county, is a vast and patchy fabric, destined never to be completed. If the dead Cork generations could be consulted, they would probably agree with the maxim that all history is local history. So-called national events and movements were reflected and expressed in local issues and through local personalities. The pulse of history beats strongly from early Christian cults and legends, through the interaction of Gael and Norman, the sixteenth and seventeenth-century upheavals in religion, land ownership and political power (with Kinsale fortuitously becoming the synonym for the final collapse of the Gaelic world), the social and economic changes of the early modern period and the nationalist resurgence which led to an independent Ireland, a period in which Cork played a disproportionately important part. As is the case with other counties, historical geographers are coming to make a major contribution to our understanding of urban settlement and of the patterns of social history in general. All students of the Cork past are now greatly facilitated by the increasing availability of properly-organised municipal and academic archives. An extremely welcome aspect of the work of investigating and recording the history of the county is the fruitful co-operation, despite intermittent tensions, of local historians and professional academics. The pre-eminent focus of their joint endeavours is the Cork Historical and Archaeological Society which celebrated its centenary in 1991 and whose *Journal* has been published annually over the century, with the understandable exception of the convulsive civil war year of 1923. The *Journal* is by far the largest repository of Cork archaeological and historical studies. Intent on preserving, investigating and recording what seemed to them to be the threatened antiquities of city and county, the founding members dedicated themselves to perpetuating and developing the labours of such antiquaries as Smith, Crofton Croker and Caulfield. After a century of achievement, the Society continues to unfold new pages of the Cork past and occasionally publishes exceptionally informative special volumes. As a constant and inspiring presence in the scholarly life of Cork, the Society may justly take some credit for the publication of several valuable monographs on the educational, genealogical, architectural and economic history of city and county.

In the corpus of humorous Cork stories, a significant anecdote concerns the American visitor who hired a taxi-driver to take him on a sight-seeing tour around the city. On parting with a substantial fare after completing an unexpectedly wide orbit, he ruefully observed, 'I never knew this place was so big'. Came the instant tongue-in-cheek answer, 'Big, is it, sir? No one knows the size of Cork'. Cork, city and county, has a complacent sense of its own largeness which in turn provokes gibes such as 'vainglorious Lilliput' (in Tom Flanagan's novel *The Tenants of time*).[19] It also likes to flaunt the soubriquet of 'rebel Cork', being blissfully unaware for the most part that the designation began as a derogatory one at the time when the city briefly supported the cause of the Yorkist pretender, Perkin Warbeck, in 1495. Ironically, in view of the English royalist origins of the term, 'rebel' has strong connotations of republican resistance to British rule earlier in this century, perhaps with particular reference to the revered figures of the martyred Lords Mayor, Tomás MacCurtain and Terence MacSwiney, and later to Cork's rearguard resistance to the infant Irish Free State. 'Rebel' is also used more widely as a synonym of a sturdily independent attitude of mind. That independent mentality is the essence, in the eyes of Cork people at least, of the most distinctive county personality in Ireland.

References

1. Donnelly, *Land and people*, p. 2.
2. C..Litton Falkiner, *Illustrations of Irish history and topography* (London 1904), p. 132, note 1, where Carte papers, lxi, p. 337 is cited.
3. Niall Tóibín.
4. E. O'Malley, *On another man's wound* (Dublin, 1979), p. 198.
5. *The Cork accent;* cf. W. O'Brien, *An olive branch in Ireland and its history* (London, 1910), p. 467.
6. S. Beecher, *A dictionary of Cork slang,* 2nd ed. (Cork, 1991).
7. *Irish Press,* 6 Dec. 1979.
8. Bolster, *Diocese of Cork,* ii, pp 237-40.
9. W. J. O'N. Daunt, *Personal recollections of the late Daniel O'Connell, MP* (London, 1848), i, p. 45.
10. A. Orme, 'Youghal, County Cork – growth, decay resurgence' in *Ir. Geog.,* vi (1966), pp 121-149.
11. B. O'Farrell and D. O'Connell, *Commentarius Rinuccinianus,* I.M.C. (Dublin, 1932), i, p. 488.
12. O'Flanagan, *Bandon.*
13. See D. Bowen, *The Protestant crusade in Ireland, 1800-70* (Dublin, 1978), pp 168-89; P. Hickey, 'A study of four peninsular parishes in west Cork, 1796-

1855', unpublished M.A. thesis, U.C.C. (1980), pp 107 ff., 502 ff.

14. M. Hopkinson, *Green against green: the Irish civil war* (Dublin, 1988), pp 195-7; K. Bowen, *Protestants in a Catholic state* (Dublin, 1983), pp 22-25; P. Buckland, *Irish Unionism,* i (Dublin, 1972), pp 213 ff.

15. R. Hindley, *The death of the Irish language* (London and New York, 1990), pp 117-124.

16. P. Ó Riain, 'Barra Naofa: tuairisc an Irisleabhair air' in *Cork Hist. Soc. Jn.*, xcvi (1991), pp 117-24.

17. 'A city of tattered grace, probably the most seductive and loquacious in Western Europe': see J. Matthews, *Voices: a life of Frank O'Connor* (Dublin, 1983), p. 5.

18. 'Statio *male* fida carinis', Virgil, *Aeneid,* ii, 23.

19. T. Flanagan, *The tenants of time* (London-New York, 1988). For another 'Lilliput' reference, see S. Ó Faoláin, *An Irish journey* (London, 1940), p. 85.

Chapter 2

THE TOPOGRAPHICAL DEVELOPMENT OF SCANDINAVIAN AND ANGLO-NORMAN CORK

JOHN BRADLEY AND ANDREW HALPIN

Cork is unique among Irish cities. It is the only one which has experienced all phases of Irish urban development. Some towns were founded by the Vikings, others by planters, others again by landlords and industrialists. Cork alone has experienced them all. It originated as a monastic centre, it was transformed into a Scandinavian port; it was expanded by the Anglo-Normans; it was enlarged by English colonists in the sixteenth and seventeenth centuries; it was remodelled in Georgian and Victorian times when spacious streets and elegant town houses were constructed; its docks, warehouses and rows of artisan dwellings attest the impact of the industrial revolution; and in our own time, it has experienced both the growth of substantial suburbs and the beginnings of inner-city renewal. For well over a thousand years Cork has attracted *Gael* and *Gall* alike and the modern city reflects the fusion of many diverse cultural traditions. This paper is concerned with the early stages of Cork's growth, with the first eight hundred years or so of its development, during which it altered from a monastery, whose inmates were devoted to the contemplation of spiritual things, into a formidably walled city, whose citizens devoted themselves to the pursuit of trade and industry and whose activities took them along most of the Atlantic seaboard of Europe. The physical growth stages in this development have not previously been identified systematically. The purpose of this paper is to chart these changes, beginning with a few remarks on prehistoric activity before we go on to examine the nature of the earliest settlements.

In prehistoric times the site of the future city was frequented by people on a number of occasions, but there is no evidence for actual settlement. Three flat axeheads and one halberd of Early Bronze Age date (*c.* 2000-*c.* 1400 B.C.), and three bronze swords, two socketed axeheads, one spearhead and two chapes of Later Bronze Age date (*c.* 1200-*c.* 700 B.C.) have been found within the immediate environs of the city.[1] These may have been casually lost or deposited as votive offerings. The best-known archaeological artefact from Cork, the set of three bronze objects known as the Cork Horns, was almost certainly a votive deposit.[2] It was found in 1909 in river mud near the South Jetties, where the main channel of the Lee meets the sea. The objects formed part of a cap probably made in the first century A.D.

The early monastic foundation

The earliest settlement at Cork was the monastery dedicated to St Finbarr or Bairre. Various dates in the sixth and early seventh centuries have been suggested for its foundation, but the actual date is unknown.[3] There is no reliable information on the early monastery in the Lives of Finbarr and, despite local tradition, little is known of the saint himself. Indeed it has been suggested that he is a replicate of Finnian of Moville, whose cult may have been adopted at Cork and given a local flavour by connecting the latter saint with places in the valley of the Lee.[4] According to this view the cult of Finbarr, alias Finnian, was originally a widespread phenomenon also found for instance in Moville, Clonard, Cornwall and Scotland. When, however, the monastery of Cork began to develop and acquire importance within Munster the local character of the saint became more significant. This may have led to conflict with other monasteries, particularly those affiliated to the cult of Finbarr, and it could possibly explain the battle of 807 between the monasteries of Cork and Clonfert which resulted in a 'countless slaughter of ecclesiastical men, and of the noblest of the *familia* of Corcach'.[5]

Whatever about Finbarr's identity, the monastery was evidently in existence by 682 when Suibne, abbot of Cork, died.[6] Abbots are subsequently recorded in the annals until the twelfth century, while bishops are noted from the late ninth century onwards. The annalistic references are largely confined to brief notices of burnings, but it is evident that by the eleventh century Cork was already one of the most important monasteries in Munster. It was plundered by the Vikings on many occasions, the first being in 821, but other raids occurred in 839 and 913.[7] The annals continue to record attacks on Cork after the foundation of the Scandinavian settlement but it is difficult to know whether these relate to the monastery or to the town. Such raids are recorded in 962, 978, 1013, 1089 and 1098.[8] In the attack of 1081 both houses and churches were destroyed.[9] This may be an allusion to structures within the monastic enclosure but it could also refer to the plundering of both the monastery and the town. In the early eleventh century the monastery came under the control of Brian Bóromha for a time. It was in the hands of the local Ua Selbaig family, however, for most of that century before reverting to Dál Cais domination *c.* 1085.[10]

In 1118 Diarmait Ua Briain, king of Munster, died at Cork and the large territory assigned to the diocese of Cork at the synod of Ráith Breasail in 1111 is probably a measure of the extent of Dál Cais influence at this time. After Diarmait's death this area was re-divided and the dioceses of Cloyne and Ross were formed. The monastery suffered during the twelfth century largely because it was caught up in power struggles between the Uí Briain of Thomond, the Meic Charthaig of Desmond and the Uí Chonchobair of Connacht. After the partition of Munster in 1118, Cork appears to have come under the control of the Mac Carthaig kings of Desmond. The church was burned in 1126 and in 1151 the monastery was pillaged by the Uí Briain.[11] Other burnings are recorded in 1116, on two occasions in 1143 and once in 1152, but it is unclear whether these references relate to the monastery or the town, or both.[12]

Practically nothing is known of the physical appearance of the early monastery but at least its position can be identified. It was located on a prominent ridge offering a commanding view of the marshy estuary of the river Lee. The placename St Finbar's Cave, later the site of the Augustinian foundation known as Gill Abbey, may have been an initial hermitage but, if so, the focus of the monastery subsequently moved eastwards to more open ground where there was room to build. The present cathedral occupies the site of its medieval predecessors. Romanesque fragments in the chapter house indicate that there was a prestigious pre-Norman church on the site,[13] while a description of 1644 records the presence of

> an old tower, ten to twelve feet in circumference and more than one hundred feet high; which they firmly hold to have been built by St Barre.[14]

This tower is shown on many early maps a short distance east of the cathedral and was almost certainly a round tower of tenth- to twelfth-century date.[15] The extent of the monastic enclosure is difficult to gauge but both the form of the present churchyard and the curve of Barrack Street are tell-tale signs of the former existence of major curving boundaries. An examination of Rocque's map of 1759 reveals its site. The street block bounded by Dean Street, Vicar Street and Barrack Street is divided longitudinally by a major plot boundary. This plot boundary is continued in the block immediately to the east towards the seventeenth-century Elizabeth Fort, where the curving alignment is preserved in Keyser's Hill. West of the cathedral, the former line is indicated by a long property boundary north of Gillabbey Street, while on the north the steep escarpment forms a natural boundary.

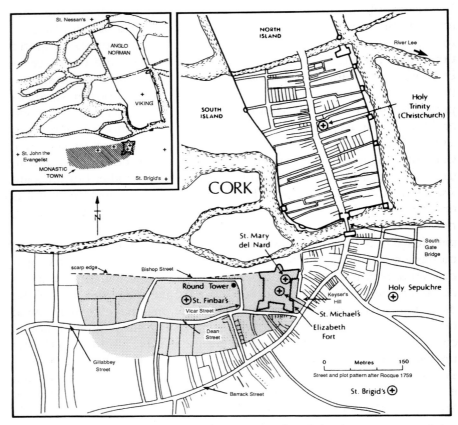

Figure 2.1   Plan of Cork showing the position of St Finbarr's monastery and the Scandinavian town. The plot pattern is based on Rocque's map of 1759 with the late medieval and Elizabethan defences interpolated.

Accordingly the monastery would seem to have been located within a D-shaped enclosure with its back formed by the cliff dropping to the river Lee below.

The Scandinavian town

The presence of a monastery may have attracted the initial Vikings to Cork but the estuarine situation provided them with an ideal haven. The foundation date of the Scandinavian settlement has not been recorded but, on analogy with Viking activities elsewhere at this time, a date of *c.* 845 is unlikely to be far wrong. The first reference to their presence at Cork is in 848 when Olchobar, king of Cashel, following up victories at Sciath Nechtain and Dún Maele Tuili, besieged the Viking *dún* of Cork.[16] The Viking settlement seems to have survived, however, because in 867 the death of Gnimhbeolu, 'chief of the foreigners of Cork', is recorded.[17]

The nature of this ninth-century settlement, whether fortress or trading town, is unknown. The entry in the *Fragmentary annals of Ireland* recounting the death of Gnimhbeolu (Gnim Cinnsiolaigh) describes Cork as a *purt* but this section of the annals was compiled in the mid-eleventh century and it may relate more to conditions at that time rather than two centuries before.[18] Nothing further is known of a Viking presence at Cork until the renewed phase of Scandinavian activity in the early tenth century, and it may be that 867 marked the end of the first Viking settlement at Cork. In 915 the Norse plundered the monastery of Cork and this may have been the prelude to a renewed occupation by them.[19] In the previous year a large Scandinavian expedition arrived at Waterford and two years later Dublin was refounded by them.[20] It is tempting to think, as the twelfth-century author of the *Cogadh Gaedhel re Gallaibh* would have us believe, that it was part of this fleet which plundered Cork and resettled there.[21] It would certainly provide a convenient explanation for the re-establishment of Cork and the colonisation of the barony of Kerrycurrihy, later known as the 'cantred of the Ostmen'.[22] The reference to the robbery of Cork by the fleet of the Ladgmanns in 962 is probably best interpreted as a battle between rival Viking groups.[23] In 1088 an attempted raid on Cork by a combination of the Norse of Dublin, Wexford and Waterford was repulsed with great slaughter by the local tribe, the Uí Echach Muman.[24] The relationship between the town and the monastery is unknown, but it is reasonable to infer from this battle that, like the monastery, the town was also under the control of native Irish dynasties. In 1134 Cormac Mac Carthaig assembled the *Gaill* of Cork, among others, when preparing to proceed into Connacht,[25] and Jefferies has suggested that Mac Carthaig established a fort at Shandon from where he could dominate the town immediately across the river to the south.[26] The last that is heard of Hiberno-Scandinavian Cork is the account by Giraldus Cambrensis of the sea battle between a fleet of thirty-two ships from Cork under Gilbert son of Turgerius and a Norman fleet under Adam de Hereford.[27] Although the Norse of Cork were defeated the incident is valuable in that it provides an insight into the size of the town's fleet [Fig. 2.1].

It is evident from the documentary sources that the monastery and the Scandinavian town co-existed. Physically, however, there would appear to have been two distinct settlements. The precise extent of the Scandinavian town cannot be determined from documentary sources but there is little doubt about its general area. Brooks, Jefferies and Candon have discussed a number of charters which contain important topographical information about the pre-Norman settlement.[28] These grants date to the initial years of Anglo-Norman activity (1177-82);

because they were issued soon after the takeover and prior to the period of intensive colonisation which occurred later it can be assumed that the structures and features referred to, like their former owners (who are occasionally named), belonged to pre-Norman times. From these charters it appears that the south island was the nucleus of the town, but it had a suburb linked by a bridge on the south bank in the Lower Barrack Street Area. The north island, then known as Dungarvan, may also have been a suburb, and there was probably some settlement in the vicinity of Shandon.

The south island was clearly regarded as the core of the city from the initial days of the Anglo-Norman occupation. In the early records it is denoted by the word *civitas,* whereas *villa* is used for the built-up area on the south bank.[29] This linguistic distinction would seem to indicate that the configuration of the south island was visibly (and perhaps administratively) distinct. This could be explained by the existence of a defensive wall; its possible presence should not surprise us in view of the excavated evidence from Dublin and Waterford and the documentary evidence for Limerick and Wexford.[30] The fact that Robert FitzStephen and Milo de Cogan *besieged* Cork in 1177 indicates that it possessed fortifications of some kind.[31] This is supported by the references in the earliest Anglo-Norman records to the gate (*porta*) of Cork and to the presence of burgages both within and without the walls.[32] Gilbert son of Turgerius, the last Ostman ruler of Cork, had a hall (*curia*) with an attached chapel and a number of burgages within the *civitas*.[33] The possible presence of burgesses and burgages within Hiberno-Scandinavian Cork should not be ruled out. Both Dublin and Killaloe appear to have had the status of boroughs in pre-Norman times, and evidence of a burgage plot pattern has been recovered in excavations at Dublin, Waterford and Wexford.[34] These plots, like their post-medieval successors, would have been arranged at right angles to the street, in this instance South Main Street, which ran the length of south island and was itself aligned north-south. Within the *civitas* was the parish church of Holy Trinity (Christchurch), a dedication also found in the Scandinavian towns of Dublin and Waterford where it is normally interpreted as an indication of contact with Canterbury. There is evidence also for contact further afield. The Romanesque voussoirs at St Fin Barre's Cathedral indicate influence from Poitou. It has been argued that Cork was one of the avenues by which sculptural and architectural motifs were channeled into Munster during the first half of the twelfth century.[35] Although it has been stated that no archaeological evidence for Viking-age Cork existed on the south island this is no longer true. A recent reassessment of the excavations on the site of Holy Trinity College has identified artefacts of pre-Norman date among the objects uncovered. While it is still too soon to know the full implications of this discovery, it supports the other evidence that the south island was the nucleus of Viking-age Cork.

In identifying the extent of settlement on the south bank of the Lee one document is particularly significant. This is a grant of land to St Nicholas' Priory, Exeter, which it specifies as bounded firstly by the curtilages of the burgesses of Cork, secondly by the 'cross of Cameleire upon the water', thirdly by a 'little harbour', and fourthly by 'the way which leads up to the church of St Sepulchre and the great water'.[36] Some of the locations mentioned in this grant can be identified. The church of St Sepulchre stood on the site of the modern church of St Nicholas' and the road leading towards it and onto the 'great water' (that is the river Lee) may be identified with the modern Douglas Street.[37] The 'little harbour' was located near Parliament Bridge, between Sullivan's Quay and Cove Street.[38] It appears then that the plot of land was located west of the harbour, north of Douglas Street and east of the burgesses' curtilages which were presumably located on the east side of Barrack Street. This grant indicates that part of the Scandinavian town occupied the area immediately south of South Gate Bridge. The extent of the settlement is unknown, however, but it is possible that it extended westwards to Keyser's Lane, because this is a street name which appears to be of Scandinavian origin.[39] This suburban settlement was evidently unwalled, as Candon has pointed out,[40] otherwise the grants would have specified the defences as a boundary rather than the burgesses' curtilages. If the settlement extended as far as Keyser's Lane then it indicates an area of overlap between the Scandinavian town and its ecclesiastical counterpart. This suburb was linked to the south island by a bridge, almost certainly to be identified with that referred to in 1163 as a *droichet*[41] on the site later occupied by South Gate Bridge.

The church of the Holy Sepulchre is described in these charters as lying outside the town and it seems that other churches may have catered for the occupants of this area also. The churches of St Michael, St Mary del Nard and St Brigid, first attested in 1199, were probably founded in pre-Norman times. The decretal letter of Innocent III in 1199 provides the sole evidence for the existence of a church dedicated to St Michael at Cork and it specifies that it was sited within the same churchyard as St Mary del Nard.[42] Dedications to Michael and Brigid are known from the Hiberno-Scandinavian towns of Dublin, Wexford and Waterford, but only in the case of Dublin can one be absolutely certain of their pre-Norman date. The Anglo-Normans had a strong devotion to St Mary, but the possibility of a pre-Norman origin, hinted at by the continued use into the later middle ages of the appelation 'del Nard' (Ir.

an t-ard, 'the height'), should be borne in mind. The cathedrals of Limerick and Tuam are dedicated to St Mary and indicate that her cult had powerful supporters in twelfth-century Ireland. St Michael's and St Mary's del Nard would seem to have been sited within the ecclesiastical enclosure of St Finbarr's, within which there is also evidence for a guest-house and an abbot's dwelling in the twelfth century.[43]

In the later middle ages the area adjacent to these churches was known as the 'Fayth', a name derived from *faithche,* which is first mentioned in the twelfth-century *Aislinge Meic Conglinne.*[44] Although usually translated as 'green' this was an area of peace in front of a dwelling, church or town.[45] At Dublin, for instance, the *faithche* lay outside the walls, to the west, and was the place where the *margad,* 'market', or *oenach,* 'assembly', was held; in Wexford it was also outside the walls and lay immediately south-east of the town beside the church of St Michael.[46] At Cork it functioned in the twelfth century as a place of punishment and execution and was evidently large because an area known as *Imaire in aingil,* 'the angel's ridge', lay within it.[47] At a later stage it is known that St Nicholas' Church (*alias* the church of the Holy Sepulchre) lay within the Fayth.[48] In the Anglo-Norman period the Fayth was the name applied to the feudal manor of the bishops of Cork, later known as the manor of St Finbarr's.[49] Associated with this manor was an independent borough first evidenced in 1282.[50] It has been suggested that this borough was established by the bishop to accommodate the Ostmen dispossessed by the Anglo-Normans, but it seems more likely that, like the Irishtown of Kilkenny, the bishop's borough developed out of a pre-Norman settlement over which the church already exercised considerable control.[51] On the west side of St Fin Barre's Cathedral the Augustinian priory of St John the Baptist (Gill Abbey) was established by Cormac Mac Carthaig, king of Desmond, prior to his death in 1138.[52]

The north island was known as Dungarvan, a name which suggests the presence of an enclosure, perhaps a secular ring-fort. Candon has argued that there may have been a small fort here which was later superseded by St Peter's Church.[53] It may be, however, that the *dún* was originally the fortress of Hiberno-Scandinavian Cork, equivalent to Dundory in Waterford.[54] St Peter's Church is itself probably of pre-Norman origin, in keeping with its counterparts at Waterford and Dublin.[55] On the north bank of the Lee was St Nessan's Church which had a water-mill associated with it. The church is first mentioned in a charter of 1180 and the mill is referred to in a grant which was issued before 1183.[56] Like their counterparts on the south bank the references occur too early in the Anglo-Norman takeover to reflect new buildings and seem to represent the parceling out of pre-existing structures. St

Nessan's stood on the site later occupied by St Catherine's parish church, while the mill-race and mill lay to the west.[57] The stream still flows under North Abbey Square but it is now culverted over. On the north bank also was an old castle, perhaps the remains of a fortification built by Cormac Mac Carthaig.[58] It was evidently of sufficient importance to give its name to this area, Shandon, *sean dún,* 'the old fort'.

Anglo-Norman Cork

The beginnings of Anglo-Norman Cork may be traced to the submission of Diarmait Mac Carthaig, king of Desmond, to Henry II at Waterford in 1171.[59] Giraldus Cambrensis states that Henry placed a royal governor and officials in charge of Cork at this time, but the period 1171-77 is an obscure one in the city's history. In 1173 the town's Viking fleet attacked the Normans at Youghal and this suggests that, despite the appointment of a governor, Cork was not under Anglo-Norman control. In 1176 Diarmait Mac Carthaig was overthrown and imprisoned by his son, Cormac Liathánach, and recalling his oath of fealty to Henry II, he sought help from Raymond le Gros who assisted him and marched on Cork.[60] In the following year, 1177, Henry II changed his policy towards Ireland. His ten-year-old son, John, was created Lord of Ireland and large tracts of Munster were granted to Anglo-Norman adventurers in order that his son would have the support of a series of loyal barons.[61] The kingdom of Cork (Desmond) was granted to Miles de Cogan and Robert FitzStephen, who were also to have custody of the city on behalf of the king.[62] In the same year de Cogan and FitzStephen took possession of the city. Giraldus states that they were 'honorably received by the citizens and a knight, Richard of London, who at that time was governor of the city',[63] but the Irish annals record that they were taken to Cork by Muirchertach Ua Briain, son of the king of Thomond, and together they beseiged the city and plundered it.[64] Almost immediately, the Anglo-Normans began to colonise and expand the city, and the important series of charters already noted, dating to between 1177 and 1185, chronicle these developments.[65]

Henry II's action in 1177 changed Cork into a royal city. It probably received a charter of incorporation, but the earliest surviving charter is that granted by John, as lord of Ireland, *c.* 1189.[66] This confirmed all the land of the city to the citizens of Cork, to be held according to the laws of Bristol. It did not enumerate the city's privileges, however, and throughout the middle ages it was Cork's second charter of 1242 which was regarded as the basic charter of liberties. This charter was confirmed and elaborated upon on many subsequent occasions.[67]

The government of the city was at first placed in the hands of custodians appointed directly by the crown. Miles de Cogan and Robert

FitzStephen were its first custodians and Giraldus Cambrensis states that Raymond le Gros succeeded them after relieving Cork from an Irish siege in 1182. Otherwise, however, nothing is known about the government of Cork during the first 30-40 years of the Anglo-Norman invasion. A reference to the sheriff in Cork in 1211 probably refers to Thomas Bluet, sheriff of Waterford and husband of Miles de Cogan's heiress, Margarita, who in 1211-12 accounted for monies spent on the walls of Cork.[68] Subsequent royal governors included Thomas FitzAnthony, appointed in 1215, Henry of London, archbishop of Dublin, in 1223, and Peter de Rivall in 1232.[69] De Rivall, dismissed in 1234, is the last recorded royal governor but the beginnings of municipal government are still unclear.[70] Henry III's charter of 1242 contains an apparent reference to the provost of the city but it is not certain if it indicates the existence of a municipal authority or not.[71] The earliest undoubted evidence is in 1281 when the payment of a fine by 'the mayor and commonalty' of Cork is recorded.[72]

Cork's wealth in the thirteenth and fourteenth centuries was based upon its position as the principal port of south-west Ireland.[73] The custom returns of Irish ports in the period 1276 to 1333 indicate that Cork was the third most important port of Ireland, after New Ross and Waterford, and that it accounted for 17 per cent of all Irish trade.[74] The principal exports were agricultural produce from the Cork hinterland: hides, skins, wool, grain and beef.[75] The principal imports were wine, cloth and spices. Trade was conducted primarily with England and Scotland, through the ports of Bristol and Carlisle, and also with France. O'Sullivan suggested that most of this trade was conducted by foreign merchants, such as the Frescobaldi and Riccardi of Lucca, rather than by the citizens of Cork themselves, but this view seems to exaggerate the role of the Italian merchant venturers.[76] The existence of a strong seafaring tradition among the citizens cannot be doubted. In 1241 and 1300, for instance, the citizens of Cork were commanded to send ships to aid the king in his military expeditions against Wales and Scotland.[77]

From about the middle of the fourteenth century this picture of commercial prosperity and wealth begins to decline. Cork appears increasingly as an exposed and embattled outpost in a hostile environment dominated by the resurgent Irish and Gaelicised Anglo-Normans. Trade becomes less a profitable commercial venture than a lifeline preserving the city's existence. Contemporary records frequently request remission of the fee farm and other dues because the city was no longer able to pay. The Black Death of 1349 may have been a major factor in Cork's decline because it is immediately afterwards that the first references to serious difficulties occur. The plague had a severe effect. In 1351 the jurors of an inquisition recorded that 'in the time of the said pestilence the greater part of the citizens of Cork and other faithful men of the king dwelling there went the way of all flesh'.[78] In the same year Edward III postponed the payment of the fee farm of the city because the citizens had pleaded inability to pay as a result of the pestilence and attacks by the native Irish.[79] In 1354 the king remitted all arrears of the fee farm and halved the amount to be paid for the succeeding five years. In addition to the effects of the 'late pestilence' and wars, Cork's impoverishment at this time was also attributed to the fact that one-fourth of the city had lately been burned by accident.[80] A further allowance on arrears was granted in 1355-6 because of the city's impoverishment through fires, disease and the cost of defending itself against the enemy, but also on account of Cork's service in the war of 1352 against Diarmait mac Diarmada Mac Carthaig, lord of Múscraige, when the city sent 172 men in the company of the justiciar, Sir Thomas de Rokeby.[81]

Further remissions of the fee farm were granted in 1376, 1380 and 1382.[82] In 1376, moreover, it was recorded that the suburbs of Cork had been burned 'by an assault of certain Irish enemies and English rebels' within the previous two years.[83] There are indications about this time that the city's food supply was becoming a matter of serious concern. In 1386 and 1387 Richard II granted licences to a number of merchants to buy grain and ship it to Cork because of the barrenness of the surrounding countryside.[84] In 1388 the mayor and bailiffs were empowered to command all those who held lands or goods in the city to live there and to defend them, and not to leave Cork without royal licence to do so.[85] In 1389, however, the king gave the citizens licence to leave the city in order to buy grain to support themselves.[86] In the same year legislation was passed to protect shipping bringing grain to Cork, and in 1390 the king granted the citizens of Cork licence to buy grain in any Irish port.[87] In 1393, John of Desmond, eldest son of the Earl of Desmond, was authorised to provide protection for the hawkers and carriers of victuals and corn from the county of Limerick to the city of Cork (along with Youghal and Limerick), where the inhabitants were unable to support themselves because of the destruction of the neighbouring countryside.[88] In 1400 the king pardoned the mayor and citizens of Cork of amercements amounting to £200 and four years' farm of the city, in order to encourage them to resist the king's enemies, for the safety of the city.[89] When a further remission of fee farm and amercements was granted in 1423, it was recorded that Cork had 'for some years past been almost continuously beset by Irish rebels, so that none could go in or out without paying tribute to the said rebels'.[90] In 1450 the Irish parliament passed an act to protect the merchants of Cork, Waterford and other places coming to Dublin, Drogheda and

Malahide to buy corn and once again it was noted that, because of attacks by 'Irish enemies and English rebels', the lands around these cities could not be tilled, resulting in food shortages.[91] In 1462, Edward IV noted that Cork had eleven parish churches attached to the city and suburbs stretching apparently for one mile on either side, north and south, but that these had been 'wasted and destroyed by the rebels for the past fifty years'.[92] This would appear to be an accurate summary of the difficulties experienced by Cork since the mid-fourteenth century.

The latest recorded legislation relating to the difficulties experienced by Cork at this period is a licence granted to the citizens in 1463 to buy and sell merchandise to and from Irishmen.[93] This had previously been prohibited but it was recognised that the citizens could not survive without such trade. There are no further records of the cancellation or remission of dues owed to the crown by the city, but, as O'Sullivan points out, this is much more likely to indicate that such dues were no longer being paid rather than that no difficulty in payment was being experienced.[94] Towards the end of the fifteenth century Cork became deeply involved in the cause of the Yorkist pretender, Perkin Warbeck, who landed at Cork on both of his Irish visits, in 1491 and 1497. There is a tradition that Cork was disenfranchised as a result of its support for Warbeck but there is no documentary evidence to support it.[95] A possible indication that the normal municipal functions of the city were interrupted at this time comes in the appointment by Henry VII in 1499 of Maurice Roche, William Tirry, Edward Collys and Edward FitzDave Tirry, citizens of Cork, as receivers and collectors of custom in the port, of the profits of the fee farm and land-gavel and all other dues of the king, and to supervise and govern the city.[96]

Layout, houses, market-places, bridges

The Anglo-Norman city was built on two islands in the marshy estuary of the river Lee. The street pattern of Anglo-Norman Cork was linear, based on the north-south axis of the main street with lanes running at right angles, giving access to individual properties and to the town wall. In the suburbs the street pattern seems to have followed the line of existing routeways, but it is difficult to be certain whether streets such as Douglas Street follow the medieval route precisely or not.

Within the walled city, the burgage plots were probably long narrow strips extending at right angles from the main street to the walls. No contemporary information on the size of these plots is known, but there are several fifteenth- and sixteenth-century references to messuages extending from the main street to the city walls.[97] Excavations at the College of the Holy Trinity, on South Main Street, found that the property units were long narrow strips of ground about

20 to 25 feet in width, extending from the main street to the town wall.[98] These plots were delimited by post and wattle fences which were later replaced by stone walls. The remains of a probable property boundary were also found in the excavations at Grand Parade.[99]

Little is known of the form of Cork's housing during the medieval period. Part of a landgable roll survives listing the presence of 162 houses in the mid-fifteenth century[100] but, unfortunately, it does not indicate their exact position. The roll is incomplete but nonetheless it shows that late medieval Cork was densely built up. The Civil Survey of 1653-4 enumerates over 350 properties, providing many details of their size and construction, and it is clear that the seventeenth-century town was also densely occupied.[101]

Stone houses were present from at least the fourteenth century but it is not known how common they were. Clear references to stone houses occur in 1306 when John de Wynchedon bequeathed to his sons two such houses near Holy Trinity church, and in 1314-15 when a stone house belonging to Nicholas de la Wythye was taken over by the crown to be used as a prison.[102] The 'great stone house', formerly belonging to Walter Reych, is referred to in 1442, and the buildings known as Skiddy's Castle and the 'Paradise Castle' were constructed around this time.[103] It is likely that many of these buildings were fortified stone houses similar to those which survive in Ardee, Carlingford and Kinsale. An account of 1620 described domestic housing in Cork as 'of stone, and built after the Irish forme, which is Castlewise, and with narrow windows, more for strength than for beauty, but they begin to beautify it in better forme'.[104]

The excavations at Holy Trinity College, South Main Street, uncovered the remains of timber-framed and post-and-wattle houses on the street frontage.[105] These had floors consisting of brushwood, wicker-work matting or spreads of gravel and were dated to the late twelfth and early thirteenth centuries. To the rear of these were a variety of lean-to and free-standing sheds, and behind these again was an open area which may have been partly cultivated, although the excavation results suggested that it was used primarily as a rubbish dump. From the early fourteenth century the timber houses were gradually replaced by stone-built houses with slate or stone-tiled roofs and stone flags, cobbles or timber flooring. At St Peter's Market excavations uncovered the remains of two houses constructed in the late thirteenth/early fourteenth century.[106] The earlier had a floor of limestone flags while the later was a simple structure with mud walls.

There are no direct references to a market-place within the medieval city but there can be little doubt that it was anywhere other than in Main Street. The *Pacata Hibernia* (*c.* 1600), Speed (*c.* 1610) and

Hardiman (c. 1601) maps all show a market cross at the southern end of North Main Street. North of the walled city, in Shandon, the street known as Old Market Place was named 'Old Market Place' on Phillips' map of 1685. It is probably to be identified with the 'Market Greene' referred to in 1663-4.[107] Henry III's charter of 1241-2 stipulated that the citizens of Cork should plead all cases at their Guildhall, but no further references are known to it until 1577.[108] The guildhall may well have been the same building as the tholsel first referred to in 1442.[109] This appears to have stood on the site later occupied by the Exchange built in 1708-10.[110]

The port of Cork is first mentioned in 1207.[111] No contemporary documents provide information on the precise location of the medieval port and quays, but it is clear that in the sixteenth and seventeenth centuries the port was the channel of the river flowing between the north and south islands, on the east of the central bridge. The present Castle Street, situated immediately north of this channel was originally the quayside serving this port. It is shown thus on the maps of *Pacata Hibernia* (c. 1600), Hardiman (c. 1601) and Speed (c. 1610). The *Pacata* map, indeed, shows two ships berthed in this channel. A number of late sixteenth- and early seventeenth-century documents refer to the 'key' of Cork, situated beside the castle, that is the 'king's old castle', supporting the cartographic evidence for the location of the quay.[112]

Information on industries and crafts in medieval Cork is almost totally lacking. The only significant evidence relates to mills, several of which are attested in medieval documents. Mills were attached to most of the religious foundations, including the Augustinian house at Gill Abbey,[113] the Dominican friary,[114] the Franciscan friary,[115] the Augustinian friary,[116] the Benedictine hospital priory[117] and the church of St Nessan.[118] Prince John held a mill, probably the king's mill referred to in a deed of 1177-82, which was apparently situated outside the city to the west.[119] One particular mill stands out because of the frequency with which it is mentioned and because its location within the town can be plotted. In or before 1348 the mayor and community of Cork granted to William FitzWalter Droup an area of land, 80 perches long and 2 perches wide, in Cork and Dungarvan, extending from the channel of the Lee to the middle bridge of the city, along with the watercourse flowing through that land, for the purpose of building a mill. In 1392 this grant was confirmed to Phillip Stone and his wife Joanna, grand-daughter and heiress of William Droup.[120] It stood on the north side of Mill Street (roughly corresponding to modern Liberty Street) beside the channel of the river which separated the north and south islands of the city, and is referred to as Droop's Mill throughout the seventeenth and eighteenth centuries.[121]

The bridge connecting the south island to the south bank is thought

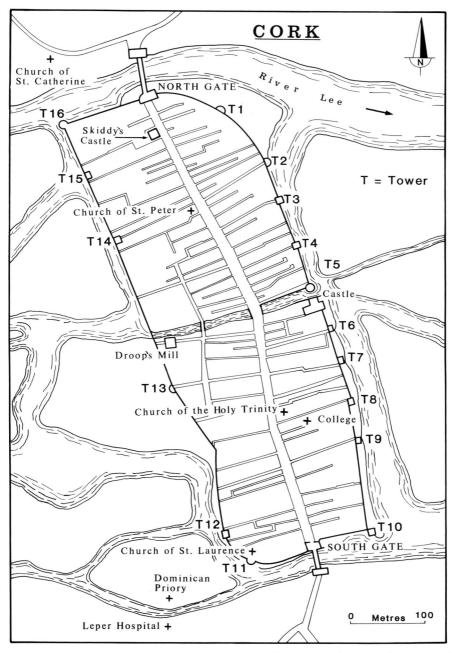

Figure 2.2   Outline sketch of Anglo-Norman Cork showing the main documented features within the walled city.

to have existed in pre-Norman times, but the presence of two other bridges can also be demonstrated before the end of the twelfth century. One connected the north and south islands while the other linked the north island to the north bank of the Lee. It is possible that they are of pre-Norman origin. A charter of Philip de Barry, dated to 1183 by Brooks, granted 'two carucates of land next to the bridge of Dungarvan' to St Thomas' Abbey, Dublin.[122] Between 1223 and 1230 Gerald de Prendergast granted land at Enniscorthy to St Thomas' Abbey in exchange for these same two carucates, which were then stated to be 'in the vill of Shandon beside the bridge of Cork'.[123] Thus it would seem that the 'bridge of Dungarvan' in 1183 and the 'bridge of Cork' in 1223-30 were one and the same. This connected the north island of the city (Dungarvan) to the north bank of the river Lee (Shandon), and was almost certainly on the site of the modern Griffith Bridge. A grant of John, as lord of Ireland, dating to between 1191 and 1199, granted the Benedictine cell of St John the Evangelist 'two burgages in Dungarvan at the head of the bridge opposite [? the city]'.[124] This probably refers to a bridge between the north and south islands. A bridge 'between the city [south island] and Dungarvan [north island] is specifically mentioned in a charter of Richard de Careu, who died in 1199.[125] This bridge would have been located roughly at the junction of South Main Street and Castle Street [Fig. 2.2].

References to the bridges of Cork prior to the seventeenth century are rare although the murage grant of 1284 made provision for repairs to the bridges which were described as ruinous[126] The *Pacata Hibernia* (*c.* 1600), Hardiman (*c.* 1601) and Speed (*c.* 1610) maps give an indication of the appearance of the bridges in the late sixteenth and early seventeenth centuries. The north and south bridges are represented as balustraded timber structures, each defended at both ends by two-storied gatehouses. Further defensive outworks are apparently indicated on the north and south banks of the river. This may explain a reference in 1631 to 'the old wall or *baricado* without the North gate, being the defence of the said gate'.[127] The bridge linking the two islands, however, is clearly represented as being stone-built. A deed of 1392, for instance, records that in or before 1348, William son of Walter Droup had been granted land extending 'from the channel of the Lee to the furthest part of the stone column of the middle bridge of the city'.[128] In the survey and valuation of Cork *c.* 1663-4, Christopher Rye was noted as holding a three-storied slated house in Mill Street (modern Liberty Street) 'over the stone bridge', which presumably refers to this central bridge.[129]

The castle and town defences
Caulfield read John's charter to Cork as confirming to the citizens 'all

enclosure of land of the city of Cork, except a place in the same city, which he [John] keeps to make a fortress'.[130] Other translations have been offered for this clause, however, and the first definite evidence for the existence of a castle is in 1206 when the *Annals of Inisfallen* note that the castle of Cork was built by the foreigners. In 1230 the same annals record the destruction of *cloch Corcaigi* which Mac Airt has translated as 'the stone castle of Corcach', indicating that the castle of 1206 was probably a stone structure.[131] In 1232 Peter de Rivall was given custody of the castle, implying that it was rebuilt soon after the burning.[132] Its subsequent history is obscure although incidental references indicate that it continued to function until the late fifteenth century. The latest reference to a constable of the castle occurs in 1467-8 when Thomas Copner is so described.[133] In 1537 it was granted to the citizens by Henry VIII[134] and in January 1610 the corporation ordered that the 'old walls and vaults' of the old King's Castle be pulled down to make way for the building of the new court-house.[135] The earliest contemporary evidence for the location of the castle is a grant of 1608 which positions the 'Kinges castle, on the s[outh] side of the key neere and uppon the walle of the Cittie of Corcke'.[136] This indicates that it was in the angle between Castle Street and Grand Parade, on the site subsequently occupied by the court-house built between 1610 and 1612. The strategic importance of this location was twofold. Firstly, it controlled the port of the medieval city and, secondly, assuming that the south island was fully enclosed in the early thirteenth century, the castle would have occupied the north-east angle of the city's defences, a pattern whlch is known from other Anglo-Norman towns in Ireland.[137]

The medieval gaol in Cork appears to have been situated within the castle and in the fifteenth century, at least, the constable of the castle was also custodian of the gaol.[138] In 1269-70 Prince Edward (later Edward I) ordered the rebuilding of the gaol and in 1279-80 over £83 was spent on construction work.[139] The royal accounts for 1296-99 include an allowance for repairs to the gaol and further rebuilding was apparently in progress in 1326.[140]

As indicated above it is probable that the Hiberno-Scandinavian town of Cork was fortified before the Anglo-Norman conquest. The Anglo-Normans, however, expanded and enhanced the circuit. Work was clearly in progress in 1211-12 when £55 5s. 6d. was spent on the walls, and in 1218 when Thomas FitzAnthony, the king's bailiff of Cork, was assigned three years' farm of the city in order to fortify it.[141] From the fourteenth century onwards Cork became an increasingly isolated frontier town; upkeep of the walls was a constant concern to the citizens. Murage grants and records of repairs are numerous up to the late seventeenth century. Repairs were necessary as much as a result of threats from the Irish and Anglo-Irish as of erosion caused by the city's position in the tidal estuary of the Lee.[142]

Contemporary maps and documents yield much information on the appearance of Cork's walls in the late sixteenth and early seventeenth centuries, although little can be said with certainty for earlier periods. The most important of these maps are the *Pacata Hibernia* map of *c.* 1585-1600, Hardiman's (*c.* 1601) and Speed's (*c.* 1610). These show a number of gates and mural towers in the circuit of the walls, but unfortunately the maps do not correspond exactly; consequently the location and number of these structures cannot be reconstructed with certainty. There appear to have been sixteen mural towers, however, and at least two gates.[143] The walls enclosed a sub-rectangular area measuring roughly 645m north-south and 225m east-west, an area of roughly 14.5 hectares. Archaeological excavations have uncovered sections of the town wall at St Peter's Market, Christchurch Lane and Grand Parade.[144] Where well preserved, the masonry consists of limestone ashlar, the outer face tends to be battered above a stepped plinth and it is about 4m thick at the base but narrows to 2.35m as it rises.

Churches and religious houses

Early attempts to install Anglo-Norman bishops appear to have proved unsuccessful and the see of Cork remained largely in Irish hands until the fourteenth century.[145] Little is known about the fabric of the cathedral at this time but it is likely that it was rebuilt in Gothic style. The surviving chapter house door, built into the south-east corner of the graveyard wall, is of thirteenth-century date, but there is a strong tradition that it was moved here from the Dominican friary.[146] The cathedral was modified in the seventeenth century but it was seriously damaged in the siege of 1690 and was replaced in 1735.[147] The eighteenth-century structure was itself replaced by the present building constructed between 1867 and 1870 [Fig. 2.3].

The parish church of Holy Trinity was in existence before 1185 and it has already been suggested that it is of pre-Norman origin.[148] The advowson was in the hands of the crown and appointments were made by the king.[149] Little is known of its medieval appearance but there were at least two side-chapels. The mid-fifteenth century landgable roll of Cork refers to a Lady Chapel and there was also a chapel dedicated to St James.[150] The Hardiman map (*c.* 1601) depicts the building as a large church consisting of a nave with north and south aisles and a square tower at the west end. The present church dates from the 1720s, but parts of the crypt, which houses a fine collection of burial monuments, may be of medieval date.[151] In 1482

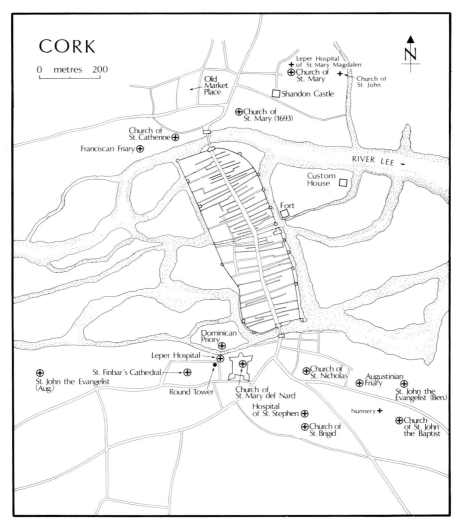

CORK

0   metres   200

Leper Hospital
+ of St. Mary Magdalen
⊕ Church of   +
St. Mary   Church of
St. John

Old
Market
Place   □ Shandon Castle

⊕ Church of
St. Mary (1693)

Church of
St. Catherine ⊕

Franciscan Friary ⊕

RIVER LEE →

Custom
House □

Fort
□

Dominican
Priory
⊕

Leper Hospital
⊕

⊕   St. Finbar's Cathedral   ⊕
St. John the Evangelist
(Aug.)
Round Tower   Church of
St. Mary del Nard

⊕ Church of
St. Nicholas   Augustinian
⊕ Friary
St. John the
Evangelist (Ben.)

Hospital
of St. Stephen ⊕   Nunnery +

⊕ Church of
St. Brigid

⊕ Church
of St. John
the Baptist

Figure 2.3   Outline sketch of Anglo-Norman Cork showing the main documented
features outside the walled city.

Philip Goold founded a chantry college for eight priests and built a
stone college nearby.[152] Excavations in 1975 located the fragmentary
remains of the college along the south side of Christ Church Lane,
south of the present church. It was a rectangular stone building
measuring 20m by 8m.

St Catherine's parish church is first mentioned in a charter of Gerald
de Prendergast dated 1223-30, but it has been suggested that it
replaced an earlier dedication to St Nessan.[153] It was located in Shandon
and was annexed to St Mary's, Shandon, in 1617.[154] St Mary's itself was

valued at six marks in the ecclesiastical taxation of 1302-6.[155] In the fourteenth century the patronage of the church belonged to the de Rochford family who had inherited the borough of Shandon from the de Prendergasts.[156] The church was demolished during the siege of 1690 and in 1693 a new site was granted at the foot of Shandon Street.[157] The site of the church was cleared in 1930 and is now used as a children's playground.[158]

A number of churches are known only from incidental references. The decretal letter of Innocent III in 1199[159] mentions the church of St John *in civitate*. This suggests that it was within the walls since St Peter's church is similarly described. The Civil Survey of Cork (1653-4) lists a St John's Lane in the south-east quarter, somewhere between Holy Trinity Church and the Castle, and tombs have been found in this area.[160] The presence of a church in Shandon also dedicated to St John is indicated by the will of John de Wynchedon made in 1306.[161] This may account for the presence of a St John's Street east of Shandon today. A mill called 'John's Mill' situated near Shandon Church (and presumably on the Kiln river) is referred to in 1663-4 and, while it is impossible to be certain, it may have taken its name from the church.[162]

A church dedicated to St Laurence is known from sixteenth-century references.[163] It was located on the site later occupied by Beamish and Crawford's Brewery, on the west side of South Main Street, where St Laurence's Lane is referred to in 1666.[164] The sole evidence for the existence of St Philip's Church is the will of John de Wynchedon, 1306.[165] It has been suggested that it was located in the same general area as St Brigid's and St Stephen's on the south side of the walled city.[166]

The Anglo-Normans founded at least five new religious houses and three hospitals in the course of the late twelfth and thirteenth centuries. The Benedictine priory of St John the Evangelist was founded *c*. 1191 and was endowed by John as earl of Morton between 1191 and 1199.[167] A deed of 1323 indicates that the priory stood to the north of St John the Baptist's (Knights Hospitaller) and east of the Augustinian friary.[168] From this it appears that it stood on the north side of Douglas Street to the east of the Augustinian friary. The earliest reference to the Augustinian friary ('Red Abbey') occurs in the will of John de Wynchedon, dated to 1306.[169] A late thirteenth-century date for the foundation seems likely. The Dominican friary was established in 1229 by Philip de Barry, nephew of Robert FitzStephen.[170] It stood on an island immediately west of the city, towards its southern end, and because of this it was generally called 'St Mary's of the Isle'. There is some uncertainty over the foundation date of the Franciscan friary. It was in Shandon, where the de Prendergasts were lords in the thirteenth century, and accordingly they are likely candidates as founders. A date of *c.* 1240 has been proposed and, in this context, it might be suggested that when Gerald de Prendergast repossessed two carucates in Shandon from St Thomas' Abbey, Dublin, it was with the purpose of endowing the Franciscan friary.[171] The friary was dedicated to the Blessed Virgin and is frequently referred to as St Mary's of Shandon. Its position can be fixed quite accurately from seventeenth-century maps. It stood on the north bank of the river, west of the North Bridge, near the bend in the Lee where St Vincent's Bridge now stands.

The Knights Hospitallers' house of St John the Baptist was an early foundation. It is referred to in a deed of 1177-82 and may even be of pre-Norman date.[172] The church was situated in the old St John's graveyard on the south side of Douglas Street, east of Nicholas Street.[173] The nunnery of St John the Baptist was founded shortly after 1279 but was still not built by 1301.[174] Nothing more is known of this convent which seems to have had only a brief existence. It was located in St John's Street (the modern Douglas Street).

St Stephen's leper hospital was founded before 1277.[175] It was located on the site of the Blue-Coat School in the south suburbs.[176] The hospital of St Mary Magdalen in Shandon is known only from the will of John de Wynchedon who bequeathed 40*d.* in 1306 'to the lepers of the church of St. Mary Magdalene, Shandon'.[177] It may have been attached to the church of St Mary at Shandon. John de Wynchedon also bequeathed 2*s.* to the 'lepers residing beside the bridge near the priory of the Friars Preachers'.[178] The house would appear to have been situated just north of St Fin Barre's Cathedral, beside a bridge leading to the Dominican priory, but nothing further is known about it after 1306.

Suburbs

Suburban developments occurred on both the north and south banks of the river Lee. Shandon was developed as a separate borough, presumably by the lords of Shandon. The grant of 1183 indicates that Philip de Barry was the first Anglo-Norman lord of Shandon but the de Prendergasts obtained rights to the area shortly afterwards. In 1290 John de Cogan and Maurice de Rochford were lords of Shandon, a position which they clearly inherited as heirs of Gerald de Prendergast.[179] The earliest evidence for the existence of a borough occurs in a deed of 1223-30 which mentions a burgage in Shandon.[180] The burgesses of Cork resented the existence of a rival market in Shandon and took steps to prevent it.[181] This must have had an adverse effect on Shandon's development; it suffered even further with the Gaelic resurgence and economic decline of the later fourteenth century. In 1374-6, the suburbs of Cork were burned by 'certain Irish enemies and English rebels',[182] while in 1462 the suburbs of Cork 'within the space of a mile' were described as wasted and destroyed for the previous fifty years.[183] Although Shandon is not mentioned by name, it presumably shared the fate of these suburbs.

After 1183 the next reference to a castle at Shandon occurs in 1531 when it seems to refer to a different structure.[184] The 1183 grant makes it clear that the 'old castle' was situated near the stream flowing from the mill of St Nessan which was located west of Griffith Bridge, in the vicinity of North Abbey Square.[185] It occupied a different site to the sixteenth- and seventeenth-century castle which, according to contemporary maps, was located some distance to the east.

On the south side of the city was another suburban borough, known variously as 'Faythe', 'le Fairgh', or 'Fayd', which is derived from the *faithche,* or 'green' of Cork, mentioned in the twelfth-century *Aislinge Meic Conglinne.* In the Anglo-Norman period this name was applied to the feudal manor of the bishop of Cork, later known as the manor of St Finbarr's.[186] Associated with the manor was a borough, first referred to in 1282 in the royal escheator's accounts for revenues from the bishopric, which makes it clear that the bishop was the patron of the borough.[187] In 1376, when Edward III pardoned the city of Cork for its rents of that year, the sum of 86 marks was said to include payment for 'a hamlet without the walls thereof, called, "La Fathe"'.[188] This suggests that the citizens of Cork held the borough of Fayth to farm as they did the borough of Shandon. Like Shandon also, Fayth is presumably included in the references to the destruction of the suburbs of Cork in the late fourteenth and fifteenth centuries. The complete absence of references to the borough in the later medieval period suggests that it collapsed under the weight of these attacks. The corporation of Cork were apparently making payments of the fee farm of the 'Fahie' or 'Fahe' as late as 1609-11.[189] In 1690 and in 1722 the corporation made enquiries into what rights they held in the manor when it seems they were even uncertain of its precise location.[190] The precise extent of the borough is uncertain but it probably lay close to the cathedral and bishop's court, as Bolster has suggested.[191] Both the priory of St John the Evangelist and the church of St Nicholas are described as situated in 'le Fairgh'.[192] It may be that the early fourteenth-century extra-mural settlement in St John's Street also formed part of the Fayth. In particular the reference of 1320-3 to Thomas Cogan, provost, and Nicholas Wrench, bailiff of the street of St John near Cork, indicates that it was a borough settlement.[193] St John's Street may simply have been an alternative name for the Fayth.

Conclusions

The topographical development of medieval Cork can be divided into three stages. The first consists of the foundation of St Finbarr's monastery on the high ground of the river Lee's south bank. Nothing is known of the spatial arrangements of this early monastery; what information we have derives from the twelfth century when there was at least one prestigious church and a number of subsidiary ones set, apparently, within a large D-shaped enclosure. The second stage is represented by the development of a Scandinavian (and later Hiberno-Scandinavian) town. Its nucleus was on the south island where it was established probably in the tenth century. Its location in the marshy ground below the monastic site suggests that a *modus vivendi* was worked out between the church and the townspeople from the beginning, otherwise the newcomers would simply have sequestered the monastery itself. Indeed, the interaction between the monastic site and the Scandinavian town was of central importance for the development of medieval Cork. It led to a concentration of settlement on the south bank and it probably explains why the cathedral of Cork remained outside the city defences throughout the middle ages. The monastery appears to have had a secular settlement associated with it but, morphologically, it seems fair to say that the Scandinavian settlement functioned as the monastic town of Cork.

On the eve of the Anglo-Norman invasion settlement would seem to have been concentrated in two locations, along the south bank and, linked with it by a bridge, on the south island which was probably walled. Running north, however, across the marshy estuary was the routeway, linking the north bank with south island, which was to become North Main Street. On north island itself there may have been settlements in the vicinity of St Peter's Church and the fort of Dungarvan while, further north, there was the church of St Nessan and its associated water-mill.

The third stage of development commenced with the arrival of the Anglo-Normans in 1177. By the end of the twelfth century they had introduced new colonists and expanded the built-up area to include the north island. In the course of the thirteenth century they established a complex settlement infra-structure which governed the physical development of Cork until the seventeenth century. They founded a series of large religious houses, they built the defences which delimited the city and they created new suburbs on the north and south banks. Despite this powerful impact, however, it appears that the Anglo-Normans did not change the existing layout in any dramatic way. Rather they seem to have continued the topograpical patterns of development already in place by the time of their arrival.

Acknowledgments

Our interest in Cork City was sparked off by our work for the Urban Archaeology Survey which was commissioned by the Office of Public Works. We wish to thank the Commissioners and their staff for their help in the course of that survey. We are also grateful to Heather King, Anthony Candon, Maurice Hurley, Aodh Ó Tuama and Denis Power for their expert knowledge and assistance.

References

1. P. Harbison, *The axes of the Early Bronze Age in Ireland* (Munich, 1969), p. 26: no. 552; National Museum of Ireland, Irish Antiquities Collection 1939:50; J. M. Allen, D. Britton and H. H. Coghlan, *Metallurgical reports on British and Irish Bronze Age implements and weapons in the Pitt Rivers Museum* (Oxford, 1970), pp 66-7: no. 11; P. Harbison, *The daggers and halberds of the Early Bronze Age in Ireland* (Munich, 1969), p. 40: no. 159; *Catalogue of the important collection of Irish stone and bronze implements, personaal ornaments, etc formed by Robert Day* (London, 1913), p. 44: lot 316; S. M. Nicholson, *Catalogue of the prehistoric metalwork in Merseyside County Museums* (Liverpool, 1980), p. 42: nos. 42-3; J. Evans, *The ancient bronze implements of Great Britain and Ireland* (London, 1881), p. 140; G. Eogan, *Catalogue of Irish bronze swords* (Dublin, 1965), pp 49-50.

2. M. J. O Kelly, 'The Cork Horns, the Petrie Crown and the Bann Disc' in *Cork Hist. Soc. Jn.,* lxvi (1961), pp 1-12; B. Raftery, *La Tène in Ireland: problems of origins and chronology* (Marburg, 1984), p. 312.

3. C. J. F. MacCarthy, 'The Celtic monastery of Cork' in *Cork Hist. Soc. Jn.,* xlviii (1943), p. 4; A. Gwynn and R. N. Hadcock, *Medieval religious houses: Ireland* (London, 1970), p. 66.

4. P. Ó Riain, 'St Finnbar: a study in a cult' in *Cork Hist. Soc. Jn.,* lxxxii (1977), pp 69-72; idem, 'Another Cork charter: the life of Saint Finbarr' in *Cork Hist. Soc. Jn.,* xc (1985), p. 4.

5. *A.U.²*: 807.

6. *A.F.M.:* 682; *A.U.²*: 681; *A. Tig.*: 681.

7. *A.F.M.:* 820; *A.U.²*: 838; *A. Clon.*: 910.

8. *A.F.M.:* 960, 1012, 1089, 1098; *Ann. Inisf.*: 978, 1012; *Chron. Scot.*: 1011.

9. *A.F.M., Ann. Inisf., A.L.C.*

10. Gwynn and Hadcock, *Med. relig. houses,* p. 66; Bolster, *Diocese of Cork,* i, pp 54-5.

11. *A.F.M., A.L.C.*: 1126; *Misc. Ir. Annals,* p. 33.

12. *A.F.M.:* 1116, 1143; *Misc. Ir. Annals,* p. 35.

13. J. Bradley and H. A. King, 'Romanesque voussoirs from St Fin Barre's Cathedral, Cork' in *R.S.A.I. Jn.,* cxv (1985), pp 146-51.

14. P. F. Moran (ed.), *Monasticon hibernicum by Mervyn Archdall* [hereafter *Monasticon hib.*], i (Dublin 1873), p. 114.

15. G. L. Barrow, *The round towers of Ireland* (Dublin, 1979), p. 71.

16. *A.F.M.:* 846, *Chron. Scot.*: 848.

17. *A.F.M.:* 865.

18. J. N. Radner (ed.), *Fragmentary annals of Ireland* (Dublin, 1978), p. 125.

19. *A.F.M.:* 913; *Chron. Scot.*: 914.

20. J. Bradley, 'The topographical development of Scandinavian Dublin' in *Dublin,* pp 44-5; J. Bradley and A. Halpin, 'The topographical development of Scandinavian and Anglo-Norman Waterford' in *Waterford,* p. 105.

21. J. H. Todd (ed.), *Cogadh Gaedhel re Gallaibh: the war of the Gaedhil with the Gaill* (London, 1867), p. 31.

22. H. A. Jefferies, 'The history and topography of Viking Cork' in *Cork Hist. Soc. Jn.,* xc (1985), p. 16; J. Bradley, 'The interpretation of Scandinavian settlement in Ireland' in idem (ed.), *Settlement and society in medieval Ireland: studies presented to F. X. Martin, O.S.A.* (Kilkenny, 1988), p. 65.

23. *A.F.M.:* 960.

24. *A.F.M.*

25. *Misc. Ir. Annals,* p. 23.

26. H. A. Jefferies, 'Desmond: the early years and the career of Cormac MacCarthy' in *Cork Hist. Soc. Jn.,* lxxxviii (1983), p. 87. It is possible, of course, that the place-name Shandon may derive from the fort built by Olchobar in 848, see *Chron. Scot.:* 848.

27. A. B. Scott and F. X. Martin (ed.), *Expugnatio Hibernica: the Conquest of Ireland by Giraldus Cambrensis* (Dublin, 1978) [hereafter *Expug. Hib.*], p. 137.

28. E. St John Brooks, 'Unpublished charters relating to Ireland, 1177-82, from the archives of the city of Exeter' in *R.I.A. Proc.* xliii, C (1936), nos. 5-7, 13-17, 23 and 26; Jefferies, 'Viking Cork', pp 17-21; A. Candon, 'The Cork suburb of Dungarvan' in *Cork Hist. Soc. Jn.,* xc (1985), pp 93-5.

29. This distinction was pointed out by H. A. Jefferies, 'The founding of Anglo-Norman Cork 1177-1185' in *Cork Hist. Soc. Jn.,* xci (1986), p. 33. He believed that the *civitas* was a newly-founded Anglo-Norman town and that the *villa* was the site of the Scandinavian town. The time-scale of the charters, however, and the recently reassessed archaeological evidence do not support this view.

30. *Murus* is the word used by Giraldus Cambrensis to describe the town wall at Wexford (*Expug. Hib.,* p. 32, line 32, also defended by a fosse, ibid., line 34), Waterford (ibid., p. 64, line 16), Dublin (ibid., p. 66, line 14), and Limerick (ibid., p. 150, line 30). The twelfth-century pre-Norman defences of Dublin and Waterford were built of stone, see P. F. Wallace, 'Dublin's waterfront at Wood Quay: 900-1317', in G. Milne and B. Hobley (ed.), *Waterfront archaeology in Britain and Northern Europe* (London, 1981), pp 109-18, and M. F. Hurley, 'Late Viking age settlement in Waterford' in *Waterford,* pp 52-4.

31. *Ann. Inisf., Misc. Ir. Annals.*

32. *Reg. St Thomas, Dublin,* p. 215; *Ir. mon. deeds 1200-1600,* p. 227.

33. *Reg. St Thomas, Dublin,* no. ccxlviii.

34. M. Rule (ed.), *Eadmeri historia novorum in Anglia* (London, 1884), p. 297; J. Bradley, 'Killaloe: a pre-Norman borough?' in *Peritia* (in press).

35. Bradley and King, 'Romanesque voussoirs'; J. Bradley, 'The sarcophagus at Cormac's Chapel, Cashel' in *North Munster Antiquarian Journal,* xxvi (1984), p. 32.

36. Brooks, 'Unpublished charters from Exeter', pp 336-8.

37. Brooks, 'Unpublished charters from Exeter', p. 337; Jefferies, 'Viking Cork', p. 19, suggests that it is Cove Street.

38. Brooks, 'Unpublished charters from Exeter', p. 337; Jefferies, 'Viking Cork', pp 19-20.

39. Jefferies, 'Viking Cork', p. 20 and note 61.

40. Candon, 'The Cork suburb of Dungarvan', p. 93.

41. *A.F.M., Ann. Tig.*

42. M. P. Sheehy (ed.), *Pontificia hibernica: medieval papal chancery documents relating to Ireland 640-1261* [hereafter *Pontificia hib.*], i (Dublin 1962), p. 106.

43. K. Meyer (ed.), *Aislinge Meic Conglinne: the Vision of MacConglinne, a Middle-Irish wonder tale* (London, 1892), p. 11, line 9; p. 31 line 6.

44. Ibid., p. 13, line 25; p. 29 line 10.
45. C. Doherty, 'Exchange and trade in early medieval Ireland' in *R.S.A.I. Jn.,* cx (1980), p. 83.
46. Ibid.; B. Colfer, 'Medieval Wexford' in *Old Wexford Society Journal,* xiii (1990-91), pp 22-3.
47. *Aislinge,* p. 21, line 9; ibid., p. 31, line 16.
48. P.R.O.I., MS RC 7/12, p. 254.
49. Webster, *Cork,* p. 178; Bolster, *Diocese of Cork,* i, p. 159.
50. *P.R.I. rep. D.K.* 36, p. 60.
51. Nicholls quoted in Jefferies, 'Anglo-Norman Cork', p. 32; J. Bradley, 'The early development of the medieval town of Kilkenny' in *Kilkenny,* p. 66.
52. Gwynn and Hadcock, *Med. relig. houses,* p. 150.
53. Candon, 'The Cork suburb of Dungarvan', p. 96.
54. Bradley and Halpin, 'Scandinavian and Anglo-Norman Waterford', p. 108.
55. Bradley, 'Scandinavian Dublin', p. 51; Bradley and Halpin, 'Scandinavian and Anglo-Norman Waterford', p. 111.
56. *Reg. St Thomas, Dublin,* pp 205, 220; Brooks, 'Unpublished charters from Exeter', p. 341.
57. Compare *Reg. St Thomas, Dublin,* pp 186, 205.
58. *Reg. St Thomas, Dublin,* p. 205; Jefferies, 'The career of Cormac Mac Carthy', p. 87.
59. *Expug. Hib.,* p. 93.
60. Ibid., p. 165.
61. F. X. Martin, 'The first Normans in Munster' in *Cork Hist. Soc. Jn.,* lxxvi (1971), p. 69.
62. Orpen, *Normans,* ii, p. 32.
63. *Expug. Hib.,* p. 185.
64. *Ann. Inisf.; Misc. Ir. Annals,* p. 63.
65. *Reg. St Thomas, Dublin,* pp 202, 215; Brooks, 'Unpublished charters from Exeter', pp 322-5, 335-8.
66. See *Cal. doc. Ire. 1171-1251,* no. 572; Otway-Ruthven, *Medieval Ire.,* p. 123. Mac Niocaill, *Na buirgéisí,* i, p. 158; A. F. O Brien, 'The development of the privileges, liberties and immunities of medieval Cork and the growth of an urban autonomy *c.* 1189 to 1500' in *Cork Hist. Soc. Jn.,* xc (1985), p. 49.
67. O'Brien, 'Medieval Cork', pp 50-61.
68. *Ann. Inisf.; Misc. Ir. Annals,* p. 89; O. Davies and D. B. Quinn (ed.), 'The Irish pipe roll of 14 John 1211-1212' in *Ulster Journal of Archaeoloqy,* 3rd series, iv (1941), supplement, p. 49.
69. *Cal. doc. Ire., 1171-1251,* nos. 576, 1060, 1972, 1976; Orpen, *Normans,* iii, pp 178-9.
70. Orpen, *Normans,* iii, p. 182.
71. Translated as 'mayor' by O'Sullivan, *Econ. hist. Cork city,* p. 284.
72. *Cal. doc. Ire., 1252-1284,* p. 382.
73. B. Graham, 'The towns of medieval Ireland' in Butlin, *Town,* p. 41.
74. Ibid., pp 39-41.
75. O'Sullivan, *Econ. hist. Cork city,* pp 38-9.
76. Ibid., p. 40.
77. *Cal. doc. Ire., 1171-1251,* no. 2532; *Cal. doc. Ire., 1293-1301,* no. 777.
78. Otway-Ruthven, *Medieval Ire.,* p. 268.
79. *Cal. pat. rolls, 1350-1354,* pp 117-8.
80. *Cal. pat. rolls, 1354-1358,* p. 87.

81. *Rot. pat. Hib.,* p. 63, no. 129.
82. *Cal. pat. rolls, 1374-1377;* p. 309; *Rot. pat. Hib.,* p. 109, no. 78; ibid., p. 116, no. 24.
83. *Cal. pat. rolls, 1374-1377,* p. 207.
84. *Rot. pat. Hib.,* p. 136, nos 185, 186, 188, 197.
85. *Cal. close rolls,* 1385-1389, pp 521-22.
86. *Rot. pat. Hib.,* p. 142, no. 244.
87. *Chart. privil. immun.,* p. 87; *Rot. pat. Hib.,* p. 146, no. 217.
88. J. Graves (ed.), *A roll of the proceedings of king's council in Ireland 16 Ric. II* (London, 1877), pp 120-22.
89. *Cal. pat. rolls, 1399-1401,* p. 400.
90. *Cal. pat. rolls, 1422-1429,* pp 105-6.
91. *Stat. Ire. Hen. VI,* pp 171, 237-9.
92. *Cal. pat. rolls, 1461-1467,* p. 214.
93. *Stat. Ire. 1-12 Edw IV,* pp 139-41.
94. O'Sullivan, *Econ. hist. Cork city,* p. 51.
95. Ibid., p. 59.
96. *Rot. pat. Hib.,* p. 272, no. 13.
97. For instance R. Caulfield, 'Chartae Tyrryanae relating to Cork and its vicinity' in *The topographer and genealogist,* iii (1858), pp 111-13, 116-18, 120.
98. D. Twohig, 'Cork city' in *Excavations 1974,* pp 11-12; idem, 'Cork city: South Main Street' in *Excavations 1975-76,* pp 26-7; idem, 'Cork city excavations 1974-77' in *Bulletin of the Irish historic settlement group,* v (1978), pp 19-22; idem, 'Archaeological heritage' in *C.E.,* 'History of Cork' series, article no. 13, 27 Mar., 1985.
99. M. Hurley and D. Power, 'The medieval town wall of Cork' in *Cork Hist. Soc. Jn.,* lxxxvi (1981), pp 1-20.
100. Mac Niocaill, *Na buirgéisí,* ii, pp 589-95.
101. *Civil Survey,* vi, pp 397-497.
102. D. O'Sullivan, 'The testament of John de Wynchedon of Cork, anno 1306' in *Cork Hist. Soc. Jn.,* lxi (1956), p. 79; *P.R.I. rep. D.K. 39,* pp 51, 71; *Rot. pat. Hib.,* p. 22, no. 70.
103. Caulfield, 'Chartae Tyrryanae', p. 113 and note 2; T. A. Lunham, 'Skiddy's Castle' in *Cork Hist. Soc. Jn.,* xiv (1908), p. 81; Mac Niocaill, *Na buirgéisí,* ii, p. 594 and Candon, 'The Cork suburb of Dungarvan', p. 98.
104. J. Buckley, 'The siege of Cork, 1642' in *Cork Hist. Soc. Jn.,* xxii (1916), p. 12.
105. Twohig, 'Cork city excavations', pp 19-22.
106. M. F. Hurley, 'Excavations in medieval Cork: St Peter's Market' in *Cork Hist. Soc. Jn.,* xci (1986), pp 11-15.
107. *Civil Survey,* vi, p 453.
108. *Cal. doc. Ire., 1171-1251,* no. 2552; *Cal. Carew MSS., 1575-1588,* p. 482.
109. Caulfield, 'Chartae Tyrryanae', p. 113.
110. C. J. F. MacCarthy, 'An antiquary's notebook 1' in *Cork Hist. Soc. Jn.,* lxxxvi (1981), pp 63-5.
111. *Cal. doc. Ire., 1171-1251,* no. 348.
112. *P.R.I. rep. D.K. 16,* p. 274, no. 5950; *Pat. rolls Ire., Jas I,* ed. Erck, ii, pp 474, 585.
113. *Extents Ir. mon. possessions,* p. 142.
114. Ibid., p. 139; it is shown on both the *Pacata Hibernia* and Hardiman maps.
115. *P.R.I. rep. D.K. 11,* p. 125: no. 184.
116. *Extents Ir. mon. possessions,* p. 140.

117. Bolster, *Diocese of Cork*, i, pp 151-2; *Cal. doc. Ire. 1171-1251*, no. 1437.
118. *Reg. St Thomas, Dublin*, p. 205.
119. Bolster, *Diocese of Cork*, i, pp 151-2; *Reg. St Thomas, Dublin*, p. 215.
120. *Rot. pat. Hib.*, p. 182, no. 68.
121. Caulfield, *Cork*, pp 32, 115-6; *Civil Survey*, vi, p. 410; R.I.A., MS Southwell papers, 753-6.
122. Brooks, 'Unpublished charters from Exeter', p. 334; *Reg. St Thomas, Dublin*, p. 205.
123. *Reg. St Thomas, Dublin*, p. 186.
124. Bolster, *Diocese of Cork*, i, pp 151-2.
125. *Reg. St Thomas, Dublin*, pp 213-4; *Ann. Inisf.:* 1199.
126. *Cal. doc. Ire., 1252-1284*, no. 2247.
127. Caulfield, *Cork*, p. 157.
128. *Rot. pat. Hib.*, p. 182, no. 68.
129. *Civil Survey*, vi, p. 432.
130. Caulfield, *Cork*, p. x.
131. *Ann. Inisf.*, p. 347.
132. *Cal. doc. Ire., 1171-1251*, nos. 1972, 1976.
133. *Stat. Ire., 1-12 Edw IV*, p. 559.
134. J. Gairdner (ed.), *Letters and papers of Henry VIII*, xi, pt. i (London, 1890), p. 351; O'Sullivan, *Econ. hist. Cork city*, p. 293.
135. Caulfield, *Cork*, p. 15, where it is incorrectly dated it to 1609.
136. *Pat. rolls Jas I*, ed. Erck, ii, p. 474.
137. See J. Bradley, 'Planned Anglo-Norman towns in Ireland' in H. B. Clarke and A. Simms (ed.), *The comparative history of urban origins in non-Roman Europe* (Oxford, 1985), p. 444.
138. Compare *Rot. pat. Hib.*, p. 165, no. 209, p. 206, no. 100. See *Pat. rolls Jas I*, ed. Erck, ii, pp 622-9.
139. *P.R.I. rep. D.K.* 35, p. 49; *P.R.I. rep. D.K.* 36, pp 44, 51.
140. *P.R.I. rep. D.K.* 37, p. 30; *Stat. Ire. John-Hen V*, p. 219; *Rot. pat. Hib.*, p. 35, no. 54.
141. *Pipe roll Ire. 1211-12*, p. 49; *Cal. doc. Ire. 1171-1251*, no. 842.
142. The murage grants are cited in A. Thomas, *The walled towns of Ireland*, ii (Dublin, 1992), pp 63-4. The 1303 grant was collected until 1317, see *Rot. pat. Hib.*, p. 6, no. 80; *Chart. privil. immun.*, p. 48; *P.R.I. rep. D.K.* 39, p. 71.
143. Descriptions of the wall are to be found in Thomas, *Walled towns*, ii, pp 60-7 and J. Bradley, A. Halpin and H. A. King, *Cork city* (Urban Archaeology Survey xiv, 2), pp 46-52. The latter was a report commissioned by the Office of Public Works in 1985.
144. Hurley, 'St Peter's Market', pp 15-19; D. Twohig, 'Cork city excavations 1974-77', p. 21; M. F. Hurley and D. Power, 'The medieval town wall of Cork' in *Cork Hist. Soc. Jn.*, lxxxvi (1981), pp 1-20; M. F. Hurley, 'Excavations of part of the medieval city wall at Grand Parade, Cork' in *Cork Hist. Soc. Jn.*, xc (1985), pp 65-90.
145. Gwynn and Hadcock, *Med. relig. houses*, p. 66.
146. Smith, *Cork* (1893 ed.), i, p. 423; M. A. O Leary, 'Monumenta vetera Coragiensia being a survey of all antiquarian remains in and around the city of Cork', unpublished M.A. thesis, U.C.C. (1931), p. 339; D. M. Waterman, 'Somersetshire and other foreign building stone in medieval Ireland c. l175-1400' in *Ulster Journal of Archaeology*, xxxiii (1970), p. 66.
147. Webster, *Cork*, p. 127.
148. *Reg. St Thomas, Dublin*, p. 214.

149. *Rot. pat. Hib.,* p. 118, no. 119; ibid., p. 205, no. 60; see *Stat. Ire., Hen VI,* pp 541-5; *Cal. papal letters, 1471-84,* p. 144.

150. Mac Niocaill, *Na buirgéisí,* ii, pp 592-3; Brady, *Clerical records,* i, p. 109; Webster, *Cork,* p. 134 notes 25-7.

151. According to Windele, *Cork,* p. 46, the church was demolished in 1717 and the present church built in 1720. Webster, *Cork,* p. 135, and J. J. O Shea, 'The churches of the Church of Ireland in Cork city' in *Cork Hist. Soc. Jn.,* xlviii (1943), p. 31, substitute dates of 1716 and 1720-6 for its demolition and reconstruction. The medieval and seventeenth-century memorials are deseribed in Bradley et al. *Cork city,* pp 59-65.

152. Gwynn and Hadcock, *Med. relig. houses,* p. 359.

153. Candon, 'The Cork suburb of Dungarvan', p. 94.

154. Brady, *Clerical records,* i, pp 281-2; Caulfield, *Cork,* p. 144; O'Sullivan, 'The testament of John de Wynchedon', p. 85.

155. *Cal. doc. Ire., 1302-1307,* p. 308; see O'Sullivan, 'The testament of John de Wynchedon', p. 78, for the first clear reference to the dedication.

156. E. St John Brooks, *Knights fees in counties Wexford, Carlow and Kilkenny: 13th-15th century* (Dublin, 1950), p. 140.

157. Smith, *Cork* (1893 ed.), p. 408.

158. O'Leary, 'Monumenta vetera Corcagiensia', p. 49. A referee has suggested to us that the site of the church may be a little north-west of that shown on figs. 2-3; see *Gentleman's Magazine,* April 1865, p. 270, and *Civil Survey,* vi, p. 450.

159. *Pontificia hib.,* i, p. 106.

160. *Civil Survey,* vi, p. 418; Smith, *Cork* (1815 ed.), i, p. 383; Windele, *Cork,* p. 64.

161. O'Sullivan, 'The testament of John de Wynchedon', p. 78.

162. *Civil Survey,* vi, p. 464.

163. *Monasticon hib.,* i, p. 126; Webster, *Cork,* p. 137, note 40.

164. Windele, *Cork,* p. 53; Webster, *Cork,* p. 138, notes 41 and 46; see T. A. Lunham, 'Historical notices of old Cork' in *Cork Hist. Soc. Jn.,* xiii (1907), p. 65.

165. O'Sullivan, 'The testament of John de Wynchedon', p. 78.

166. Ibid., p. 85.

167. Gwynn and Hadcock, *Med. relig. houses,* pp 104-5; Bolster, *Diocese of Cork,* i, pp 151-2; see *Cal. doc. Ire., 1171-1251,* no. 1437.

168. N.L.I., MS D.25886.

169. O'Sullivan, 'The testament of John de Wynchedon', pp 76-7.

170. *Monasticon hib.,* i, pp 121-5; D. O'Sullivan, 'The monastic establishments of medieval Cork' in *Cork Hist. Soc. Jn.,* xlviii (1943), p. 14; Gwynn and Hadcock, *Med. relig. houses,* p. 224.

171. Gwynn and Hadcock, *Med. relig. houses,* p. 246; *Reg. St Thomas, Dublin,* pp 186, 205.

172. Brooks, 'Unpublished charters from Exeter', p. 336; several Cork deeds of the same date are witnessed by members of the order, ibid., pp 323, 339, 358.

173. C. G. Doran, 'The old church of the Knights of St John of Jerusalem, Cork' in *Cork Hist. Soc. Jn.,* ii (1893), pp 188-90; Brooks, 'Unpublished charters from Exeter', p. 337; Both Bolster, *Diocese of Cork,* i, p. 133, and O'Sullivan, 'Monastic establishments', p. 11, however, place it further north near George's Quay, in the vicinity of St Finbarr's presbytery.

174. *Cal. justic rolls Ire., 1295-1303,* p. 154; *Cal. doc. Ire., 1293-1301,* no. 801; *Cal. doc. Ire., 1302-1307,* no. 98.

175. Gwynn and Hadcock, *Med. relig. houses,* p. 348.

176. T. A. Lunham, 'Bishop Dive Downes' visitation of his diocese, 1699-1702' in *Cork*

Hist. Soc. Jn., xv (1909), pp 88, 179.
177. O'Sullivan, 'The testament of John de Wynchedon', p. 78.
178. Ibid., p. 79.
179. Brooks, *Knights fees,* p. 140; *Cal. doc. Ire., 1285-1292,* p. 307.
180. *Reg. St Thomas, Dublin,* p. 186.
181. *Cal. doc. Ire., 1285-1292,* p. 307; *Cal. justic. rolls Ire., 1295-1303,* pp 313, 334-5.
182. *Cal. pat. rolls, 1374-1377,* p. 207.
183. *Cal. pat. rolls, 1461-1467,* p. 214.
184. J. Coleman, 'The old castles around Cork harbour' in *Cork Hist. Soc. Jn.,* xx (1914), p. 163, note 1.
185. *Reg. St Thomas, Dublin,* p. 205.
186. Webster, *Cork,* p. 178; Bolster, *Diocese of Cork,* i, p. 159.
187. *P.R.I. rep. D.K.* 36, p. 60.
188. *Cal. pat. rolls, 1374-1377,* p. 309.
189. Caulfield, *Cork,* pp 12, 14, 16, 25.
190. Ibid., pp 213, 426.
191. Bolster, *Diocese of Cork,* i, p. 164.
192. *Rot. pat. Hib.,* p. 111, no. 58; P.R.O.I., MS RC. 7/12, p. 254.
193. *P.R.I. rep. D.K. 42,* p. 49; see ibid. 43, pp 29, 52 and *Cal. justic. rolls Ire.,* 1295-1303, p. 313.

Chapter 3

'TO BE NAMED IS TO EXIST': THE INSTRUCTIVE CASE OF ACHADH BOLG (*AGHABULLOGE*)

PÁDRAIG Ó RIAIN

'No undertaking is so difficult as that of getting a great name'.[1] Comprising even now no more than a cluster of buildings – a church, public house, shop and some residences – Aghabulloge (in Irish: *Achadh Bolg*), the site of an early Christian foundation, can never have aspired to more than a very modest version of the 'great name' contemplated by La Bruyère.[2] In fact, to be noticed at all in writing by the correct form of its name presented Aghabulloge with almost intractable difficulty from the start. For eight hundred years or so of its history, from about 830 to the early 1600s, despite many available opportunities, the name failed to be properly recorded. The purpose of this article is to chronicle the circumstances that hindered this minor medieval church achieving what was no more than its due, a proper place in the written record. Aghabulloge's case history presents problems which are fairly typical of the relatively richly-documented early topography of the Cork area. The methodology used here, therefore, may well be found useful in other similar situations.

The Múscraige tribal background

Aghabulloge's story cannot be separated from the history of the area in which fate has located it. Known at the beginning of the period under review, between about 800 and 1200, as Múscraige Mitine, this was the most southerly of the several Múscraige kingdoms, which extended in a narrow and almost unbroken line from the river Lee northwards to the river Brosna near Birr.[3] Historically confined to Munster, where they were a so-called subject people, the Múscraige traced their remote origins elsewhere, to the district around Tara.[4] This fiction, which is already set forth in an origin-legend dating to about 800, had a quite transparent aim.[5] It enabled the Múscraige to bask in the reflected glory of association with a place which had come to be regarded as the symbolic seat of Irish high-kingship states.[6]

Honour by association was similarly achieved in relation to Munster.

Here, according to the Múscraige origin-legend, land for settlement was first sought from the 'sons of Ailill' – another name for the dominant Munster dynasty, the Eoganachta – at a place called Bregon.[7] This was the district just west of Cashel which gave its name to one of the several historical Múscraige kingdoms, Múscraige Bregoin, later Múscraige Uí Chuirc.[8] The purpose of the legend is again quite clear. Cashel was to Munster as Tara was to Ireland, the symbolic seat of sovereignty.[9] To have had a part in its history, therefore, was to share in the sovereignty it symbolized. Indeed, a separate origin-legend written about the same time for the Eoganachta acknowledges this by conceding to the Múscraige prior possession of the actual Rock of Cashel.[10]

The historical reality reflected by the legend was the 'most favoured nation status' accorded by the Eoganachta to the Múscraige.[11] This was exemplified in a number of ways. The first hostage ever taken by the king of Cashel, for instance, the initial token, as it were, of his power, reputedly belonged to the Múscraige.[12] Similarly, in certain circumstances, the king of the Múscraige Bregoin was seated beside the king of Cashel, which was an important privilege.[13] And when ninth-century Armagh propagandists brought Saint Patrick to Munster, they too showed their appreciation of the local 'pecking order' by having him visit churches in Múscraige Bregoin straight after Cashel.[14]

However, the Múscraige Mitine can have had little access to the privileges which accrued to their more northerly brethren. Not only were they geographically the most southerly representatives of the Múscraige, they were also vassals of one of the least important segments of the Eoganachta, the Uí Echach of Raithliu, now Garranes in the parish of Templemartin, barony of Kinalmeaky.[15] These latter, who held the rich lands of the baronies of Kinalea and Kinalmeaky, had no share in the kingship of Munster before about the middle of the tenth century. Only then, with all the other Eoganachta segments in decline following the rise of the Dál Cais, did they succeed in providing one or two largely ineffectual kings of Cashel.[16]

The relative unimportance of the Múscraige Mitine is borne out by the fact that they are mentioned only once in the annals of the period before 1000.[17] Despite this, however, they have one claim to fame denied to all other branches of the Múscraige. They are still remembered in two modern administrative denominations, a deanery and a barony.[18] Characteristically, only the lesser of the two administrative divisions, the deanery of Muscrylin, really owes its name to the Múscraige Mitine.

Now comprising fifteen parishes north of the river Lee, the rural deanery of Muscrylin (in modern Irish Múscraighe Uí Fhloinn) in the

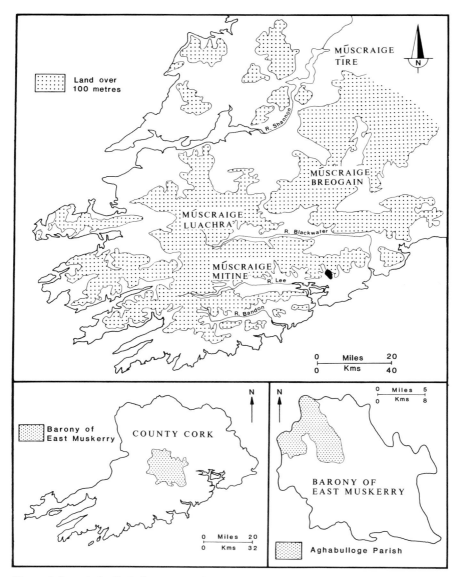

Figure 3.1   Achadh Bolg: territorial and tribal context.

Church of Ireland divisions of the diocese of Cloyne takes its name
from Ó Floinn, the head of the O Flynns or Uí Fhloinn, who held the
former kingdom in the twelfth century. The origins of the Uí Fhloinn
have been the subject of disagreement. In an article on the formation
of the kingdom of Desmond published in 1983, Henry Alan Jefferies
described the O Flynns as 'a branch of the Eoganacht Locha Léin

recently [that is, about 1100] excluded from the kingship' of the area around Killarney.[19] These O Flynns had lost out to the O Donoghues of Ceinél Láegaire in Uí Echach who, in turn, had been forced to move westwards under pressure from their cousins, the O Mahonys.[20] Jefferies produced no evidence, however, to sustain his claim that the O Flynns of Loch Léin then moved eastwards into Múscraige Mitine.

An alternative explanation was provided by Diarmuid Ó Murchadha in 1985. Discussing the Uí Fhloinn of Muskerry, he drew attention to the pedigrees of the Múscraige Mitine where, he stated, 'the next in line for the kingship was Flann, son of Blathmac'.[21] This Flann, according to Ó Murchadha, may have been the ancestor of the Uí Fhloinn. In fact, the Uí Fhloinn traced their descent to Flann's brother, Airmedach son of Blathmac.[22] First bearing the tribal name Uí Blathmaic after the founder of the dynasty, the family later took the surname Uí Fhloinn from Flann mac Flannchada. Like many other originators of surnames, this Flann may be dated approximately to the period 950 to 1000.[23] Two early twelfth-century annals entries, for 1110 and 1115, in fact add Flannchad's name to that of Flann in recording obits of heads of the family.[24]

At least up to the end of the twelfth century, the area designated by the name Muscrylin (Múscraighe Uí Fhloinn) continued to be known as Múscraige Mitine. An annals entry for 1201 describes how Muirchertach Ua Briain, accompanied by Norman adventurers, sent 'plundering parties' into Múscraige Mitine before proceeding southwards to Cenn Eich, now Kinneigh in the barony of East Carbery.[25] The forces of Domnall Mór Mac Carthaig, the last 'king of Cork', were no doubt the object of this raid.[26] The track followed by it was a well-trodden one. Exactly fifty years earlier, in 1151, the O Briens had similarly traversed Múscraige before going on to Cenn Eich in pursuit of Domnall's father, Diarmait Mac Carthaig.[27]

Still later, albeit in reference to pre-Norman Ireland, Giolla na Naomh Ó hUidhrín, the historian and poet who died in 1420, referred to Múscraige Mitine, adding that it was controlled by Ó Floinn.[28] While nowhere attested in its Irish form before the eighteenth century, Múscraighe Uí Fhloinn must have gained some currency by the thirteenth.[29] Certainly, in the papal taxation of the diocese of Cloyne for 1291, the term used is 'Muscrilyn'.[30] Ironically, by then also the O Flynns appear already to have lost effective control of the territory to new rulers, first the Norman family de Cogan, then the Meic Carthaig or Mac Carthys of Muskerry.

In 1207, when it was granted by King John to Richard de Cogan, Múscraige Mitine became the Norman cantred of 'Muscry Omittone'.[31] The Cogans retained nominal control of the area until 1439 when they released their rights to the Earl of Desmond.[32] In the meantime, however, the Mac Carthys had come into possession, their first 'lord of Muskerry' being Diarmait Mór Mac Cormaic who was slain in 1367.[33]

Already under the Cogans, 'Old Muskerry', a name used for the original territory of Múscraige Mitine, or Múscraige Uí Fhloinn, had increased in size. By 1600, however, Muskerry had come to denote an even larger territory. Continuous expansion on the part of the Mac Carthys of Muskerry, mostly at the expense of their neighbours south of the river Lee, led to the emergence of a huge lordship.[34] Its extent is now reflected in the 37 parishes and more than 311,000 acres of the barony of Muskerry.[35] By having it as the name of their lordship, therefore, the Mac Carthys, a family of Eoganachta descent, were instrumental in securing a place for the name Muskerry on the modern map of south Munster. If left entirely in the hands of its indigenous rulers, the name would no doubt still have become attached to a modern deanery. But that would almost certainly have been the sum of the topographical legacy of the Múscraige Mitine. And, as we shall now see, what applies to the impact on the record of the Múscraige in general is equally valid for the church of Aghabulloge in particular.

Some early misunderstandings

Now the head of a union or district in the Roman Catholic divisions of the diocese of Cloyne, Aghabulloge was very probably the chief church of the eastern section of Múscraige Mitine.[36] Macroom, formerly Achad Dorbchon, may have had the same status in the western part of the kingdom. Be this as it may, the chances of the church being noticed in writing were no doubt in direct proportion to the prominence attained by Múscraige itself. It is hardly a coincidence, therefore, that Aghabulloge's first 'near mention' occurred at a time when Múscraige Mitine had succeeded in attracting attention to itself.

What was happening in Múscraige Mitine in the early ninth century is unclear. Whatever it may have been, however, it culminated in a series of bloody battles in 828 which, according to the Annals of Inisfallen, left at least 370 dead.[37] Included among the dead was Éladach, king of the Uí Echach, nominally the overlord of the Múscraige, who, in alliance with the Corcu Loígde and Ciarraige Cuirche, had invaded Mitine only to be defeated and slain.[38] Éladach's involvement in the affair is attributed by the annalist to the designs of the monastic community of Cork. This may mean that some ecclesiastical matter, perhaps connected with the progress of the anchoritic movement, was the bone of contention which led to the battles. Eoganacht and Múscraige churches were otherwise very much involved in this reform. It should also be pointed out, however, that the Múscraige Mitine pedigrees embedded in the text of the Múscraige origin-legend are datable to about this time.[39] It may be, therefore, that the Múscraige Mitine were then beginning to adopt a more independent political stance.

The anchoritic movement of the early ninth century, which was centred on the ecclesiastical foundations of Finglas and Tallaght, enabled many churches to enter the written record for the first, and sometimes the only, time.[40] This was because it led to a revision of the liturgy which, in turn, produced the necessity for a new, more national, martyrology of saints.[41] The text which ensued, now known as the Martyrology of Tallaght, was compiled sometime after 826 and before 833.[42] The author was very probably a cleric named Óengus, who, almost simultaneously, composed a metrical martyrology of saints out of the Martyrology of Tallaght.[43] In any case, the author clearly depended on lists supplied to him by churches throughout the country.[44] Since the anchoritic reform was particularly strong in Munster, it may be assumed that many lists of southern saints and clerics reached the Tallaght cleric. Furthermore, almost certainly included in at least one of these lists was the name and church of the principal saint of the Múscraige Mitine. What then transpired may be gleaned from a study of the saints commemorated, according to the Martyrology of Tallaght, on 5 September.

As now preserved in the twelfth-century Book of Leinster, the earliest surviving manuscript to contain a copy of the Martyrology of Tallaght, the list of Irish saints for 5 September reads as follows:[45]

> Elacho (uel Eolang) Achaid Bó
> Eolog anchorita
> Et Duib Scuili
> Faithlenn dechoin.
> '[The feasts of] Eolach (or Eolang) of Achad Bó, of Eolach the anchorite, of Dub Scuile and of Faithliu the deacon'.

Even though the first two entries bore exactly the same name, the martyrologist had clearly decided that he was dealing with distinct saints. It may be that he had allowed himself to be persuaded by differing descriptions in what were presumably separate sources. Experience shows, however, that where a doublet of this kind occurs, whether it be in Irish or other martyrologies, the saints concerned were originally identical.[46] In other words, Eolach, patron of the church named Achad Bó, and Eolach the anchorite, alleged holder of a then very highly-regarded office, were almost certainly one and the same.

The martyrologist thus began his list for 5 September by creating two saints out of one. His successors were more perceptive. On the available evidence all subsequent martyrologists discovered and corrected his error.[47] Even the Franciscan friar, Mícheál Ó Cléirigh, who, when compiling the Martyrology of Donegal in 1630, otherwise reproduced almost mechanically the names contained in his sources, ignored the second saint named at 5 September.[48] Neither Ó Cléirigh nor any other martyrologist appears, however, to have noticed a much more serious second error contained in the Tallaght text for 5 September, the failure to assign to Eolach, alias Eolang, the proper name of his church.

By the early ninth century, Achad Bó (in English Aghaboe), the chief church of the powerful kingdom of Osraige, later Ossory, had already figured prominently in the written record.[49] Obits of its abbots are on record for the years 619, 695, 789, 813 and 822.[50] Together with its patron, Cainnech, Aghaboe was among the churches mentioned by Adamnán in the Life he composed for Columba of Iona shortly before 700.[51] Nowhere else, however, in what was a substantial dossier by any standards, is there mention of a saint named Eolach (or Eolang) in connexion with the church.[52] That the martyrologist nonetheless chose to assign this saint to Aghaboe in his list for 5 September remains, therefore, to be explained.

On the face of it, the explanation is a very simple one. The saint variously named Eolach or Eolang was in fact patron of Aghabulloge. Wittingly or unwittingly, therefore, the Tallaght cleric had gone against what must have been the reading of his source, namely *Achaid Bolg.[53] If made unwittingly, and I can see no reason why it should have been otherwise, then the mistake was greatly facilitated by the close similarity of the two names. Understandable as the mistake may be in these circumstances, however, it deprived Aghabulloge effectively of a place in the Irish martyrological tradition.

Once written down, a mistake of this kind is almost ineradicable. Within a very short time, in fact before 833, Óengus of Tallaght, who may have committed the error in the first place, set the seal on it by glorifying in song 'holy Eolang of Achad Bó'.[54] Eolang may well have deserved Óengus's description of him as 'a beauteous pillar, a triumph of piety'. He did not, however, merit attachment to Aghaboe. Yet so enduring did this mistake become that the last of the native martyrologists, Mícheál Ó Cléirigh, went on to compound it. Assigning Eolang to Aghaboe, he added the claim that the saint belonged to the race of Conaire, in other words to the Múscraige.[55] So he did, according to the genealogical tradition, but, as Ó Cléirigh must have known, only as patron of Aghabulloge.[56]

Once only in the eight hundred years or so of the Irish martyrological tradition was an attempt made to put right the error committed at Tallaght between 826 and 833. This was at an uncertain date, probably in the later twelfth century, when a martyrology was being composed for a church somewhere in Meath, possibly at Duleek.[57] The martyrologist, who appears to have worked mainly from an annotated copy of the Martyrology of Óengus, first wrote *Eoluing Aichid Bó*, '[feast] of Eolang of Aghaboe', at 5 September. Then, presumably on reflection, he qualified this statement by adding *nó Aigthi Bolg*.[58] Clearly, the intention was to restore Eolang to Aghabulloge. As if fated to be misrepresented, however, the name of the Muskerry church was written down in a totally unacceptable form. The correct genitive of *Achad* or *Aiched*, which the martyrologist had just written down in connnexion with Aghaboe, was *Achaid* or *Aichid*.[59] Could it be that he was misguided by a separate written source into supplying the name with an unacceptable genitive *aigthi*? Or was it the case that, knowing the name only from oral sources, he wrongly assumed that *aigthi* was a fair representation of its sound? Whatever its origins, the scribal error in this case meant that Aghabulloge was now nowhere properly recorded within the Irish martyrological tradition.

Outside the martyrological tradition, Aghabulloge's record was likewise plagued by scribal slips or oversights. As in the martyrologies, however, the cue elsewhere for mention of the church was invariably provided by its saint. Thus in a prose and verse account of the nine principal saints of the Múscraige, which must have been composed before about 1150, Eolang was included among *trí senóire,* 'three elders'.[60] Omitted in the verse, the name of the church attached to Eolang in the prose text is *Athbi Bolg* (dative case) in Múscraige Mitine. As in the Meath martyrology, the clear intention was to assign Eolang to the church of Aghabulloge. Again, however, the first element of the name is presented in a totally unacceptable form. *Athbi*, more properly *aithbe,* is attested only in the sense of 'ebb' or related metaphorical meanings.[61]

Lying neither near the sea nor a tidal waterway, the Irish form of the name Aghabullogue could not be composed of the element *aithbe* in the sense of 'ebb'. Moreover, none of the metaphorical meanings of the word, which include such concepts as 'decline', suit the location of the church.[62] In any case, the word is very rarely attested in place-names. As in the example from the Meath martyrology, therefore, we must again assume that in this instance, the scribe or his source wrote *athbi (aithbe)* in mistake for **achaid/aichid*. And even if *aithbi* must seem an unlikely realisation of achaid *(aichid),* here, as in the previous case, the scribe may simply have been swayed by phonetic considerations.[63]

Towards correction

Already the subject, then, of numerous errors of judgement,

Aghabulloge might have expected better treatment from the next writer to have given it his attention. This was the author of the Life of Saint Finbarr who, unlike all previous commentators, had strong local connections.[64] Without exception, the texts under consideration up to now had emanated from churches far removed from Aghabulloge. Finbarr's Life, on the other hand, was composed a mere ten miles or so away in Cork. Furthermore, as the plot of the Life makes plain, the internal affairs of Múscraige Mitine, including those of the church of Aghabulloge, appear to have been of considerable interest to the saint's biographer.

Composed on internal evidence sometime between 1196 and 1201, Finbarr's Life set out a case for Cork's right to jurisdiction over large parts or even the whole of the neighbouring dioceses of Ross and Cloyne.[65] In other words, the concern of its author was to document the entitlement of Cork to lands lost to it at the Synod of Kells-Mellifont in 1152, which had previously been granted to it at the synod of Ráith Bresail in 1111. At the earlier synod, the river Blackwater and the sea had been respectively named as the northern and southern boundaries of the diocese of Cork.[66] Prior to 1152, therefore, when they came to form part of the diocese of Cloyne, the lands of Múscraige Mitine, which lay between the Blackwater and the Lee, had in fact belonged to the diocese of Cork.

In making his case, Finbarr's biographer skilfully deployed the traditional means of his genre. Thus, tradition being of paramount consideration in such compositions, he deliberately set out to document certain crucial associations of his subject, the benefits of which, so it was believed, devolved in turn on each successor of the saint. Associations established for the saint in this way constituted precedents which implicitly dated back to the very beginning of local Christianity. It goes without saying that the incumbent bishop of Cork, when Finbarr's Life was composed, was included in this succession.

To establish title in this way, it was necessary only to take representative churches into account. In dealing, therefore, with Múscraige Mitine, Finbarr's biographer concentrated on two main foundations. One of these, Achad Dorbchon or Macroom, may have been the chief church of the western segment of the kingdom.[67] The other, Aghabulloge, appears to have occupied the same position in relation to the eastern segment of Múscraige.[68] The more western church, Achad Dorbchon, was given early prominence in the Life as the location of Finbarr's parental home.[69] The author's apparent purpose was to give to Múscraige Mitine the distinction of having 'hosted' Finbarr in his earliest years, which represented one of the first chapters in the history of local Christianity. Later in the Life, the saint's biographer identified Achad

Dorbchon as the first local church to have been founded by Finbarr.[70] Again, the message would not have been lost on his audience. The founder rights enjoyed by Finbarr in connexion with the putative chief church of the western segment of Múscraige devolved as a matter of course on the saint's successor, the head of the church and diocese of Cork.

No other saint is named in association with Achad Dorbchon.[71] It may be, therefore, that there was no rival cult to contend with. It was altogether different in Aghabulloge. There, Eolang's cult was long established. Consequently, if Aghabulloge was to be introduced into Finbarr's Life, Eolang had also to be accommodated. The opportunity to do this came towards the end of the Life where Finbarr is described as having given his mentor, Bishop Mac Cuirb, the honour of being the first occupant of the newly consecrated cemetery at Cork.[72] With a view to replacing Bishop Mac Cuirb as a confessor, Finbarr is then brought to Eolang's church. The show of deference implicit in this journey was a pretext only. It enabled Eolang to demonstrate even greater deference by obliging Finbarr to return to Cork where, and where only, he would agree to see him. Subsequently, on meeting Finbarr, Eolang

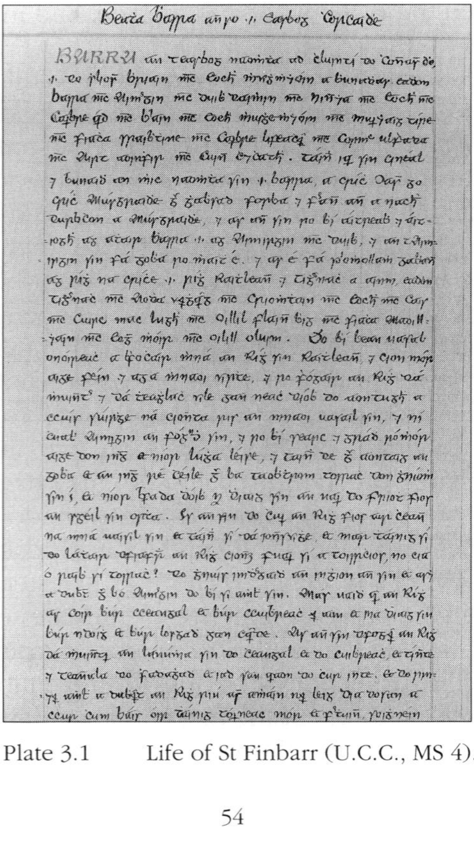

Plate 3.1   Life of St Finbarr (U.C.C., MS 4).

is described as having offered the Cork saint his church, as well as his body and soul, *in eternum,* 'in perpetuity'.

The implications of this set piece are again self-evident. Eolang, founder saint of Aghabulloge, is presented as having conceded to Finbarr jurisdiction over his church. It follows from this primordial action that he had bound his successor at Aghabulloge to recognise the same authority in the person of Finbarr's successor, the bishop of Cork. Taken together, the parts played by Achad Dorbchon and Eolang of Aghabulloge in Finbarr's Life present a totally fictitious but, on the face of it, otherwise unanswerable case in favour of Cork's title to juris-diction over Múscraige Mitine. From our point of view, however, the irony of all this is that, despite the very real prominence accorded to it by Finbarr's biographer, and despite the specification of its *familia,* 'community', and *mansorius,* 'hospitaller', nowhere in the Life is Eolang's church actually named![73] Moreover, it took some four hundred years and many subsequent revisions of Finbarr's Life before this omission was finally rectified.

Following its composition between 1196 and 1201, Finbarr's Life went through a series of new redactions.[74] After about twenty years it was adapted from Latin into the vernacular. Sometime later it was twice revised in Latin and also given a synoptic breviary form. Finally, in the early seventeenth century, the vernacular Life underwent a thorough revision.[75] In part the intention of the reviser was to make the Life more easily understood by an audience unfamiliar with the intricacies of early thirteenth-century Irish. Also, very plainly, however, he was concerned with giving Eolang's church an even more prominent place in the Life.

In the early thirteenth-century vernacular version a list had been added of saints who attended Finbarr's school on Loch Irce, now Gougane Barra.[76] First in the list was Saint Eolang, who is described as the saint's *oite,* 'tutor'.[77] In the revised version of the list Eolang is no longer described as Finbarr's tutor. Rather is he the saint 'who founded Aghabulloge' *(do bheannaigh a nAchadh Bholg).*[78] Thus, finally, in the early seventeenth century, at the tail-end, as it were, of Eolang's recorded tradition, which had begun in Tallaght between 826 and 833, the name of his church was correctly written down. Why did it take so long?

As already pointed out, the various distortions undergone by the name, *Achaid Bó* (genitive) in the Martyrology of Tallaght, *Aigthi Bolg* (genitive) in the Meath Martyrology, and *Athbi Bolg* (dative) in the Book of Leinster poem on the nine principal saints of the Múscraige, had been placed on record by scribes far removed from Aghabulloge. Their main interest was in the saint, but none of them is likely to have been sufficiently *au fait* with him or with his sphere of influence to have had a good idea of the correct name of his church. Belonging to the community of the church of Cork, the author of the original Life of Saint Finbarr was no doubt thoroughly familiar both with the saint, in whom he had a vital interest, and with his church. Neither he, however, nor any subsequent redactor of his work, save one, appears to have considered it necessary actually to name the church. The exception, who, as already stated, lived sometime in the early seventeenth century, must have had good reason, therefore, to rectify the omission. Could it be that he belonged to the church of Aghabulloge?

Whoever it was that revised Finbarr's vernacular Life plainly had a special interest in Aghabulloge. Thus, not only did he avail of the first opportunity to name the church founded by Eolang, he made precisely the same comment when next the saint was mentioned.[79] Also, in describing how the Lord agreed to act as Finbarr's confessor, he built upon his source by locating *ulaidh Eolaing*, 'the stone marking Eolang's tomb', which allegedly stood at the scene of the miracle, in Aghabulloge.[80] In doing so, he defied the firm intention of the author of his source which was to locate the miracle in Cork.[81] That he nonetheless chose to do so, however, clearly implies that the reviser of Finbarr's Life resented Cork's claim to Eolang's tomb.

There is, then, strong internal evidence to support the view that the reviser of the Life had a very special interest in the church of Aghabulloge. It is hardly a coincidence, therefore, that several manuscript witnesses to his work explicitly acknowledge 'O Cremin of Aghabulloge's Book' as their ultimate source.[82] A hereditary ecclesiastical family, the Uí Chruimín or O Cremins were already settled at Aghabulloge in the fifteenth century when they are mentioned in *annates*.[83] They were still there in 1600 when, not unexpectedly, perhaps, in view of the history of the name of their church, in a list of the four hereditary church families still surviving in Muskerry, they were mistakenly called the O Cronins.[84] They may not have survived much longer at Aghabulloge. Certainly by 1654, when the Civil Survey, which ignores them, was made, they appear to have lost their hereditary lands.[85] By then, however, one of their number, apparently the head of the family, the Ó Cruimín, had either compiled or arranged to have compiled the book containing the revised modern version of Finbarr's vernacular Life.

How long the now lost book survived is uncertain. About 1700, however, it was at the disposal of Eoghan Ó Caoimh (1656-1726), a very well-known scribe, who transcribed from it a copy of Finbarr's Life.[86] Ó Caoimh's transcript is also lost but it later served as the direct or ultimate source of five other copies of the Life.[87] After 1700 Ó Cruimín's book appears to have continued in circulation. Thus, about 1750 it was again at the disposal of a Cork scribe, Seán Ó Murchú na Ráithíneach (1700-62), who used it without acknowledgement.[88] From his transcript, which still survives, were drawn no fewer than fifteen modern manuscript copies of Finbarr's Life. This includes the latest copy known to me which was made about 1871 by the Protestant clergyman, James Goodman (1828-96) of Skibbereen.[89] Between the time of its composition, therefore, in the early seventeenth century and the late nineteenth century, the Aghabulloge redaction effectively represented the received version of Finbarr's Life. If compensation were needed for the exclusion of the name of the church from all previous versions of the Life, it could hardly have been attained in a more striking fashion. So in order to have its name properly recorded, the little church of Achadh Bolg, in the parish of Aghabulloge and barony of Muskerry, finally had to call on its own resources.

References

1. La Bruyère is quoted, without reference to a source, in H. Percy Jones, *Dictionary of foreign phrases and classical quotations* (Edinburgh, 1913), p. 246.
2. Aghabulloge is now the name of a parish in the barony of East Muskerry. While not used of a townland as such, the name is also attached to the local village. The name may originally have been attached to a large bivallate ring-fort adjoining the village on the edge of the townland of Dromatimore. The remains of the early Christian foundation are a short distance away in the townland of Coolineagh.
3. For the traditional extent of the Múscraige lands see L. Gwynn, 'De Shíl Chonairi Móir' in *Ériu*, vi (1912), pp 130-43, especially p. 141. The second element in the tribal name, for which I adopt the form Mitine, is variously attested as *Mit(t)ine, Mitine, Mit(t)aine, Mithain* etc. It seems to contain the same suffix as *Mairtine*, a tribal/territorial name in mid-Munster. In deference to previous scholarship I write the suffix with a short *i*.
4. Ibid., pp 138-40.
5. The language of the text is compatible with a date in the Old-Irish period, that is 700-900 A.D. Moreover, embedded in the text are some pedigrees of the Múscraige Mitine which relate to the period about 800 A.D.
6. For the emergence of the notion of 'high-kingship' see Byrne, *Irish kings*, pp 52-4.
7. Gwynn, 'De Shíl Chonairi Móir', p. 141.
8. This kingdom presumably corresponds to the area comprised by the later deanery of Muskerry in the diocese of Cashel.
9. For a discussion of Cashel see Byrne, *Irish kings*, pp 184-99.
10. M. Dillon, 'The story of the Finding of Cashel' in *Ériu*, xvi (1952), pp 61-73, especially p. 68, § 1. Allegedly, Cashel was first 'found' by the swineherds of the kings of Éile and Múscraige, whose territories marched in the area. For another version, which mentions only the swineherd of the king of Múscraige see Byrne, *Irish kings*, p. 186.
11. Byrne, *Irish kings*, p. 45.
12. Dillon, 'The story of the Finding of Cashel', p. 71, §§ 4-5.

13. Ibid., p. 71, § 5, where the mythological precedent for this privilege is also set out. This relates how the king of the Múscraige was the first to arrive at the inaugural Feast of Cashel.

14. W. Stokes, *The tripartite Life of Patrick*, i (London, 1887), p. 197.

15. For an account of the circumstances surrounding the identification of Raithliu with Garranes see P. Ó Riain, 'Barra Naofa: tuairisc an irisleabhair air' in *Cork Hist. Soc. Jn.*, xcvi (1991), pp 117-24.

16. For a recent discussion of the Uí Echach see M. Herbert and P. Ó Riain (ed.), *Betha Adamnáin: the Irish Life of Adamnán*, Irish Texts Society, liv (London, 1988), pp 22-4.

17. The relevant entry is contained only in the Munster Annals of Inisfallen, s.a. 828. See below at note 37.

18. Two other Múscraige kingdoms, Múscraige Tíre in north Tipperary and Múscraige Bregoin in south Tipperary, were likewise remembered in names of deaneries in the dioceses of Killaloe and Cashel respectively. Neither of them, however, is remembered in the name of a secular administrative division.

19. H. A. Jefferies, 'Desmond: the early years, and the career of Cormac Mac Carthy' in *Cork Hist. Soc. Jn.*, lxxxviii (1983), pp 81-99, especially p. 83. See note 29 for another mistaken descent proposed for the O Flynns of Muskerry.

20. Jefferies' account of the O Donoghues in 'Desmond before the Norman invasion: a political study' in *Cork Hist. Soc. Jn.*, lxxxix (1984), pp 12-32, especially p. 24, does not take sufficient account of the O Mahonys.

21. Ó Murchadha, *Family names*, p. 153.

22. For the Uí Blathmaic see S. Pender, 'A guide to Irish genealogical collections' in *Anal. Hib.*, vii (1934), p. 125; to Pender's single reference add T.C.D., MS H.2.7, f. 115 a 30, *B.B.*, f. 145 e 50, Bodl., MS Rawl. B 486, f. 45v (23v).

23. For a recent discussion of the evolution of surnames see B. Ó Cuív, 'Aspects of Irish personal names' in *Celtica*, xviii (1986), pp 151-84, especially pp 179-84.

24. *Ann. Inisf.*, p. 268 (s.a. 1110), p. 272 (s.a. 1115).

25. Ibid., p. 328 (s.a. 1201).

26. According to ibid., p. 322 (s.a. 1196), Domnall had been 'put in control of his own town' of Cork. In a decretal letter sent by Pope Innocent III to the archbishops of Armagh and Cashel and the bishop of Killaloe in 1198, reference is made to *rex Corcaie*, who was, presumably, Domnall; see M. P. Sheehy (ed.), *Pontificia Hibernica,* i (Dublin, 1962), p. 94.

27. S. Ó hInnse (ed.), *Miscellaneous Irish annals* (Dublin, 1947), p. 32 (s.a. 1151).

28. J. Carney (ed.), *Topographical poems* (Dublin, 1943), p. 50. Ó hUidhrín also refers to an Ó Maoil Fhábhaill overlord in connection with the kingdom. This is one of the indications of its having been divided into two segments.

29. The earliest examples of the name in Irish known to me are in J. O'Brien, *Focalóir Gaoidhilge-Sax-Bhéarla or an Irish-English dictionary* (Paris, 1768), pp 247, pp 358. O'Brien also named the eastern and western boundaries of the kingdom as the Dripsey river and Ballyvourney. Furthermore, he stated, wrongly, that the O Flynns were a branch of the O Donoghues.

30. *Cal. doc. Ire., 1302-07,* pp 302-307, 315.

31. See D. Ó Murchadha, 'Where was Insovenach?' in *Cork Hist. Soc. Jn.*, lxiv (1959), pp 57-62.

32. See E. Donnelly, 'The lords of Fermoy' in *Cork Hist. Soc. Jn.,* xl (1935), pp 37-42, especially p. 41.

33. For a grant of lands around Macroom to the Mac Carthys in 1353 see Otway-Ruthven, *Medieval Ire.*, p. 279. See also Ó Murchadha, *Family names*, p. 58.

34. Butler, *Gleanings*, p. 107 note.
35. For the exact acreage see *General alphabetical index to the townlands and towns, parishes and baronies of Ireland* (Dublin, 1861), p. 966. The barony is now divided into two sections, East and West.
36. As pointed out above (note 28), mention of two ruling families in Ó hUidhrín's poem suggests that the kingdom was divided into two main segments. This may also be inferred from the emphasis placed in the Life of Saint Finbarr on two churches in the area, Macroom and Aghabulloge. See below at note 67.
37. *Ann. Inisf.*, p. 126 (s.a. 828).
38. On the face of it, the site of the battle is not named. On the assumption that part of the entry has been lost, Diarmuid Ó Murchadha has suggested, very perceptively, that the first word, the otherwise unattested *Baccrad,* may be what remains of a reference to the 'Boggeragh Mountains' in Muskerry, which, significantly perhaps, formed the northern boundary of the civil parish of Aghabulloge; see D. Ó Murchadha, 'The Ciarraighe Cuirche' in *Cork Hist. Soc. Jn.,* lxxiii (1968), pp 60-70, especially p. 66 note.
39. For the main pedigree of the Múscraige Mitine see O'Brien, *Corpus geneal.,* pp 371-2. The scribe of the Book of Leinster, who is followed by O'Brien, extrapolated this pedigree from the original legend. Its final entries can be dated, by generation count, to the period 750-800.
40. For a general account of the anchoritic movement see P. O'Dwyer, *Céli Dé: spiritual reform in Ireland* (Dublin, 1981).
41. No Irish martyrology survives from before this period. It may be, however, that individual churches preserved lists of names to be commemorated. In describing his sources, for instance, Óengus of Tallaght, who wrote before 833, referred to 'Ireland's host of books'; Stokes, *Mart. Oengus*, p. 270.
42. Best and Jackson Lawlor, *Mart. Tallaght.* See also P. Ó Riain, 'The Tallaght martyrologies, redated' in *Cambridge medieval Celtic studies,* xx (Winter 1990), pp 21-38.
43. See note 41.
44. A systematic examination of the sources underlying the text has yet to be undertaken. As I hope to show elsewhere however, it does seem possible to identify lists supplied by particular churches.
45. Best and Lawlor, *Mart. Tallaght*, 68 (*L.L.,* f. 362c). Some morphological notes are in order. *Elacho*, which is elsewhere found as *Eologo* (P. Ó Riain, *Corpus genealogiarum sanctorum Hiberniae* (Dublin, 1985), p. 143 (= § 707.256)), is the genitive of *Eolach (Eolog)* from **Eo-Lug*, literally 'Yew-Lug'. The variant *Eolang* was declined differently, with genitive *Eolaing.*
46. P. Ó Riain, 'The composition of the Irish section of the Calendar of Saints' in *Dinnseanchas*, vi (1975), pp 77-92, especially p. 80.
47. In one text (Stokes, *Mart. Gorman*), it is not possible to say for certain whether the martyrologist took *Eolach* as a name or, as Stokes thought, an adjective meaning 'erudite'.
48. Todd and Reeves, *Mart. Donegal*, p. 236.
49. From the sixth or seventh century, when the Corcu Loígde, who favoured Seirkieran, lost control of Osraige, Aghaboe was the chief church of the kingdom. It retained this position until after the arrival of the Normans when the see was moved to Kilkenny.
50. All dates are from *A.U.*[2]
51. A. O. Anderson and M. O. Anderson (ed.), *Adomnan's Life of Columba* (London, 1961), p. 352. For a discussion of Cainnech's role see P. Ó Riain, 'Cainnech alias

Colum Cille, patron of Ossory' in *Folia Gadelica*, pp 20-35.

52. The Eolach assigned to Cainnech's 'home' church of Drumachose in the barony of Keenaght, county Derry, in P. Walsh (ed.), *Genealogiae regum et sanctorum Hiberniae* (Maynooth, 1918), p. 123, §10, is nowhere else attested.

53. The genitive form is necessary after the name of the saint.

54. Stokes, *Mart. Oengus*, p. 192.

55. Todd and Reeves, *Mart. Donegal*, p. 236.

56. In Walsh, *Genealogiae*, pp 78-9, which was compiled in the same year as the Martyrology of Donegal, Ó Cléirigh and his companions used a tract on the nine saints of the Múscraige which specifically assigns Eolang to Aghabulloge. Curiously, however, it was left to J. Colgan to fill in Eolang's name and church in this section of the *Genealogiae!*

57. This recently-discovered martyrology has been edited in A. V. Brovarone and F. Granucci, 'Il Calendario Irlandese del codice D iv 18 della Bibliotheca Nazionale di Torino' in *Archivo glottologico Italano*, lxvi (1981), pp 133-88. W. O'Sullivan, 'Additional medieval Meath manuscripts' in *Ríocht na Midhe*, viii (1987), pp 68-9, mentions Duleek as a likely place of origin of this manuscript.

58. Brovarone and Granucci, 'Il Calendario Irlandese', p. 64.

59. Misled by the form in the manuscript, Granucci (ibid., p. 70) wrongly assigned it to *agad*, 'face'.

60. Ó Riain, *Corpus*, pp 109-10 (§ 665).

61. In a note added to Walsh, *Genealogiae*, p. 78, Colgan, no doubt mystified by the *athbi* form of his source, 'rationalised' the name as *Ath Biobholcc*.

62. E. G. Quin (general ed.), *Dictionary of the Irish language*, compact edition (Dublin, 1983), p. 32.

63. I know of no example of a name in *achad* followed by a word beginning with *b* being anglicised as *af(f)-*.

64. The standard editions of Finbarr's Life are in C. Plummer (ed.), *Vitae sanctorum Hiberniae*, i (Oxford, 1910), pp 65-74, and idem, *Bethada naem nÉrenn: Lives of Irish saints*, i (Oxford, 1922), pp 11-22. I am preparing a new edition of the vernacular Life.

65. P. Ó Riain, 'Another Cork charter: the Life of Saint Finbarr' in *Cork Hist. Soc. Jn.*, xc (1985), pp 1-13. I have since revised the date on the basis of further internal evidence.

66. J. MacErlean, 'Synod of Ráith Breasail' in *Archiv. Hib.*, iii (1914), pp 1-33, especially p. 15.

67. For the identity of Achad Dorbchon with Macroom see L. Ó Buachalla, 'The homeplace of St. Finbarr' in *Cork Hist. Soc. Jn.*, lxviii (1963), pp 104-6.

68. See note 36.

69. Plummer, *Vitae*, i, p. 66, §2; idem., *Bethada*, i, p. 11, § I.

70. Plummer, *Vitae*, i, p. 70, § 12; idem., *Bethada*, i, p. 16, §25.

71. A list added in the vernacular Life (Plummer, *Bethada*, i, p. 15, § 22) mentions a Saint Lasar in connexion with Achad Dorbchon. It seems that an otherwise unknown sister of Finbarr was intended.

72. Plummer, *Vitae*, i, p. 71, §13; idem., *Bethada*, i, p. 18, § 35.

73. Plummer, *Vitae*, i, p. 72, §14; cf. idem., *Bethada*, i, p. 18, § 36; p. 37.

74. For a discussion of the various redactions of the Life see Ó Riain, 'Another Cork charter'. A much more thorough investigation will form part of my edition (in preparation) of the Life.

75. This is the redaction known to Plummer, who quotes from it extensively in *Bethada*, i, as the 'later Irish Life' (= Ir.2.).

76. Plummer, *Bethada*, i, p. 15, § 21.

77. I know of no other reference to Eolang as 'tutor' of Finbarr.

78. Plummer, *Bethada*, i, p. 15, §21 (variant reading from Ir.2.).

79. Ibid., p. 17, § 32. In this case, Plummer failed to note the variant reading.

80. Ibid., p. 19, § 39. In this case also, Plummer failed to note the variant reading.

81. In the Ó Murchú version of the seventeenth-century redaction (see below note 88), the reference to Aghabulloge is omitted at this point. I take it that Ó Murchú here corrected his source.

82. Plummer, *Bethada*, i, p. 22, § 51 (variant reading Ir.2.).

83. D. Buckley (ed.), 'Obligationes pro annatis diocesis Cloynensis' in *Archiv. Hib.*, xxiv (1961), p. 13, § 41, p. 20, § 62, p. 22, § 71. The dates are 1492 and 1493. The family name is variously spelt 'Ocrunyn', 'Ocrwnun', and 'Ocromin'. The name of the church is variously spelt 'Acchobolog', 'Achabolug' and 'Achaboloch'.

84. Butler, *Gleanings*, pp 117, 253. Aghabulloge is not named but the assumption is that these were the O Cremins. I wish to thank Diarmuid Ó Murchadha for this reference.

85. *Civil Survey*, vi, pp 364-68. On the other hand, the lack of any reference to them may have been due to the fact that, presumably, their property was 'bishop's land'. The receipt of crown rents in Munster for 1625 (B.L., MS 4772) mentions 'Conogher O Cromyne' as tenant of lands named 'Tuoghballoge' (Aghabulloge) and 'Montercomen' (Muintir Chruimín?) under the Earl of Cork and Thomas Roper.

86. For Eoghan Ó Caoimh see Ó Conchúir, *Scríobh. Chorc.*, pp 33-36. About 1700 Ó Caoimh was in the employ of Bishop Mac Sleighne (*ob.* 1712) of Cork, for whom he may have made his copy of Finbarr's Life.

87. My edition in preparation of the Life of Finbarr will contain a detailed discussion of these five manuscripts.

88. Ó Murchú's version survives in two copies. One, an acephalous copy in R.I.A., MS 23 M 50, pp 129-36, was transcribed between 1740 and 1758. The other, in Saint Colman's College, Fermoy, MS 24, pp 354-72, was made for Father Domhnall Ó Cearbhaill in 1761. The second copy represents the ultimate source of the fifteen later copies of the text.

89. U.C.C., MS 4, pp 76-88; see B. Ó Conchúir, *Clár lámhscríbhinní Gaeilge Choláiste Ollscoile Chorcaí: cnuasach Uí Mhurchú* (Baile Átha Cliath, 1991), pp 9-14, especially pp 10-11.

Plate 3.2   Mizen Head (Cambridge University Collection of air photographs).

Chapter 4

CORCU LOÍGDE: LAND AND FAMILIES

DONNCHADH Ó CORRÁIN

The Corcu Loígde (earlier known as Dáirine) were an important and far-flung group of dynasties in Munster in the very early middle ages.[1] However, they did not manage to maintain their position and with the expansion of the Eoganacht in the seventh and eighth centuries they declined greatly.[2] By the twelfth century they had been pushed into the south-west of the present county of Cork. Their territory is often equated with that of the diocese of Ross[3] but this is not quite accurate. There are fairly extensive and early genealogies of the Corcu Loígde but they are difficult to interpret for several reasons: they are fragmentary, they are a compilation of materials drawn from different historical strata and we lack enough annalistic entries to assess the data properly.[4]

One of the most interesting texts contained in the genealogies is a list of landholders that survives in five of the eight manuscript copies of the genealogies consulted for this chapter. It gives a geographical description of a portion of an Irish kingdom in the twelfth century, lists the lords and landholding gentry families of seven local lordships and gives some idea of the social structure of the aristocracy. It is variously known as *Duc(h)usaich Corco Laidi so,* 'The hereditary proprietors of Corcu Loígde' *(Lec.); Crichairecht Corco Laige ann so .... Fondaigect an .xxx. meadhonaig and so .i. Duthaig I Cobthaig,*[5] 'The boundaries of Corcu Loígde .... the mearing of the middle cantred, i.e. O'Coffey's country' *(B.B.); Da thuathaib Corco Laidi ⁊ da duchasacaib a tuath and seo,* 'Concerning the territories of Corcu Loígde and the hereditary proprietors of their territories' (U, and with minor differences, F); and simply 'Corca Laige' in H due, very likely, to the imperfect state of the text. F is a copy of U and is of no independent value: I do not, therefore, print it in the Appendix below with the texts of *B.B.,* H and U.[6] There are, in fact, two recensions of the tract. Recension I, the older, is best preserved in *Lec.;* it occurs in H where the last paragraph is missing and in *B.B.,* where however it has come under the influence of the second recension to a very limited degree. Recension II occurs in U (and, of course, in F) and must reflect a later period when Uí Chobthaig had come to power. Here the entire order of the tract (west to east) is reversed; Tuath Uí Duib dá leithe is placed at the head; the territories are listed east-west; and Ó Cobthaig replaces Ó Duib dá leithe as ruler of his territory.[7]

Only three technical terms worth noting occur in the tract which, for the most part, is interesting as a twelfth-century list of family names. The first is *tuath*. This term has been much discussed and there is a good deal of confusion about it. Binchy thought it was the tribe over which his imagined archaic Irish king ruled[8] and others have asserted on very doubtful evidence that there were between 80 and 150 of these in the country at any given time.[9] Whatever about the archaic period, where we have little more evidence than the uninformed guesses of linguists, the term, when used historically of Irish kingdoms and regions, can quite properly be translated 'territory, local lordship, local community'. It is more like a small group of parishes than a kingdom.

The ruler of the *tuath* in the earlier period is called *rí*, 'king', and Binchy has made much of etymologies that would tie this term to the archaic, sacral and Indo-European. He asserted that the *rí tuaithe*, 'king of a *tuath*', was the true king and that any higher king, even the king of a province, was merely a glorified king of a *tuath*. The evidence for this remarkable assertion is thin, the argument tendentious. In the contemporary annals of the eighth century kings who must have been kings of *tuatha* or of even larger units are referred to as *duces*, and in the ninth century this title is extended to even more significant overkings. It is rendered in Irish as *toísech, tigerna* – the normal term for the ruler of a *tuath* in the present tract.[10] An excellent example for the twelfth century occurs in a charter originally written into the Book of Kells and dated to c. 1129 x 1146. Here Cellach Ua Cellaig, *rí Breg*, 'king of Brega', appears as a guarantor with Ua Dondgaile, *toísech tuaithi Cnogba*, 'lord of the *tuath* of Knowth'.[11] *Toísech* is the normal name for the lord of a *tuath* in the twelfth-century tract 'Crichad an Chaoilli' that lists the land-owners of the territory of Fermoy in north Cork.[12] In our text, the term *toísech dúthchusa* means 'hereditary lord', the term *dúthchas* being understood as 'patrimony, inheritance'.

The third term is *óclach dúthchusa* or *óclach dúthaid* of whom there are seventy mentioned by name in the present compilation (I shall argue soon that there may have been many more). The term is rendered 'servitor, vassal' and will very likely correspond to a degree in its semantic range to Latin *iuvenis;* this range of meanings, stretching from servitor to vassal, is well attested in Irish usage from the twelfth to the fifteenth centuries.[13]

Mac Niocaill finds the number of *óclaig* significant: namely, that their number is excessive.[14] However, a careful reading of the *Lec.* and *B.B.* texts will tend to indicate that they may have been even more

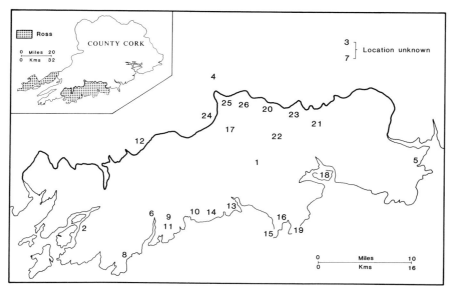

Figure 4.1   Corcu Loígde territorial divisions
             Source: Duchusaich Corco Laidi so

Numbers denote places mentioned in commentary, viz.

1	*Benn Fhinn*	2	*Tráig Omna*
3	*Féith na hImgona*	4	*Béal Átha Buidi*
5	*Tráig Claen acon Carruig*	6	*Cend Mara*
7	*Bél Átha Semand*	8	*Bend Sídáin*
9	*An Garrga*	10	*Loch an Bricin*
11	*Midros*	12	*Bél an Átha Solais*
13	*Fersad Ruis*	14	*Tráig Long*
15	*Góilín na Gaethnemtha*	16	*Dún Déide*
17	*Bél Átha na Leice*	18	*Ailén Indse Duine*
19	*Dún Eogain*	20	*Glaise Draigneach*
21	*Béal Átha na hUidri*	22	*Achad Aible*
23	*Grellach na Gruime*	24	*Cluain da Mael*
25	*Gort na Daibche*	26	*Loch an Tairb*

numerous. In *Lec.*, in giving the form of family names the scribe fluctuates between the usual abbreviation (*.h.*, which may be singular or plural and which I have expanded in my edition below as *Uí*) and the singular form of the surname prefix (*Ó*). This occurs in 23 out of 70 cases in *Lec.* Of these 16 are ambiguous: the abbreviation could be singular or plural. The remaining seven (.h. Chiabain, .h. Chertaig, .h. Aingle, .h. Adaim, .h. Chaingni, .h. Odradain, .h. Aeda) are quite clearly grammatically plural. It is certain, then, in the case of these seven, and likely in the case of the other 16, that these were families in which there were two or more persons bearing the title *óclach dúthaid*. This interpretation is strengthened by two other considerations. First, the scribe distinguishes between singular and plural in these cases: of the 47 examples where the singular form of the surname is used, it is certain in the case of seven (O hOcain, O hUrmoltaich, O hUainidi, O hIairisnich, O hIarnan, O hAinbith) that the use of the singular is deliberate. Second, one can observe the disappearance of this distinction in the manuscripts: in *B.B.* there are only four examples of *.h.* (or an equivalent plural form), in H only one (I Mothla), in U and F all have become singulars. I would argue that *Lec.* preserves an earlier stage of the text and with it significant historical information on the possible numbers of the *óclaig:* each surname in the plural will repre-sent two or more *óclaig.* Given that much land was held by the church in this area and that much else of it is mountainous, bogland or otherwise unprofitable, the *óglaig* of this portion of Corcu Loígde must have been landowners of very modest means.

Let us take an admittedly speculative example: *Tuath Uí Chonneid.* As I shall argue below, this *tuath* consists of the parish of Myross and a portion of the parish of Kilfaughtnabeg together with a very uncertain amount of the upland parish of Kilmacabea. Let us make the relatively generous assumption that all Myross lay within the territory, half of Kilfaughtnabeg and one-third of Kilmacabea, and that the *óclaig* could be holders of church land as much as secular land. This gives a total of 10,267 acres. The names of three *óclaig* are mentioned in the singular. Those of two others (Uí Chaingni and Uí Dubchonna) are in the plural, and let us assume the minimum, namely, that they represent between them four *óclaig.* This gives a total of seven *óclaig* for this *tuath.* Let us make the further assumption that Ó Conneid, the lord of the *tuath,* owned twice as much land as an *óclach.* This would make Ó Conneid the owner of 2,282 acres and the average *óclach* the holder of 1,141 acres of land, profitable and unprofitable. The *óclach,* it would appear, was a gentleman-farmer, better bred than appointed.[15]

Nonetheless, despite their narrow resources and long history of expropriation by natives and foreigners, the hereditary proprietors of this portion of Corcu Loígde maintained themselves with great tenacity, if we may judge from the large proportion of their surnames that survives to this day.

The Lecan text

Lec., f. 113 r° b 41: Duc*hus* aich Corco Laidi so

§1. Duthaich hI Gilla Michil o F*h*eith na hImgona co Cend Mara 7 o Beind S*h*idain co Bel Atha Semand 7 as iad so a oclaich duthaich .i.

O Duib Arda ⁊ O Dunlaing ⁊ O hOcain ⁊ O Dubacain ⁊ *Uí* Meic Eidich ⁊ *Uí* Chiabain ⁊ *Uí* Chertaig ⁊ *Uí* Buadaig ⁊ *Uí* Mongain ⁊ *Uí* Doirc ⁊ *Uí* Meic Con ⁊ *Uí* Aingle ⁊ *Uí* Mothla ⁊ *Uí* Mail Edair ⁊ *Uí* Adaim ⁊ *Uí* Bairr ⁊ *Uí* Rosna.

§2. Tuath *Uí* Conneid .i. an Garrga, o Chind Mara co Loch an Bricin ⁊ o Midros co Bel in Atha Solais. O Conneid a taisech. Is iad so a oclaich duc*chusa* .i. O Muimnich ⁊ O Drochruaimnig ⁊ O Fuailchin ⁊ *Uí* Chaingni ⁊ *Uí* Duib Chonna.

§3. Tuath Ruis .i. Tuath in Dolaich, o Loch in Bricin co Fiad Ruis ⁊ o Thraig Long co Sid na Fear (i) Find. O Laegaire a taiseach duch*usa*. Is iad so a oclaid duc*husa* .i. O Ruaidri ⁊ O Lonan ⁊ O Laidid ⁊ O Torpa ⁊ O hUrmoltaich ⁊ O Mirin ⁊ O Meic Dairic ⁊ O Tuaraide ⁊ O Trena ⁊ O hUainidi ⁊ O Cerdin.

§4. Tuath O nAengusa o Fersaid Ruis co Goilin na Gaethnemtha ⁊ o Dun Deidi co Bel Atha na Leici. O hAengusa a taiseach duch*usa*. Is iad so a oclaid duthaid .i. *Uí* Corrbuidi ⁊ *Uí* Dubaill ⁊ O Dunndin ⁊ O Mudain ⁊ O hAidne ⁊ O Mainchin ⁊ O Cuis ⁊ O Cuili ⁊ O Dercain ⁊ O hIairisnich ⁊ *Uí* Odradain ⁊ O Greisi [⁊] O Cuilin ⁊ O Sindaich.

§5. Tuath O Fit(h)chellaich o Goilin na Gait(h)nema co hAilen Indsi Duin[e] ⁊ o Dun Eogain co Glaisi Draignech. O Fithchellaig a taiseach *dúthchusa*. Is iad so a oclaich *dúthaid:* O Cormaic ⁊ O Dondaman ⁊ O Dubchon ⁊ O hIarnan ⁊ O Nuallan ⁊ O Croinin ⁊ O Sifi ⁊ O hAinbith.

§6. Tuath O nDungalaich o Ailen Indsi Duine co Bel Atha na hUidri ⁊ o Grellaich na Gruimi co hAc(h)ad Aib(le). O Dungaile a taiseach *dúthchusa*. Is iad so a oclaich *dúthaid* .i. *Uí* Mail Cumad ⁊ *Uí* Aeda o Cluain da Mael ⁊ O Loingsich ⁊ O Mael Temin ⁊ O Cellaich ⁊ O Maelguirm ⁊ O Selbaich ⁊ O Gabadan.
§7. Tuath hI Duib da Leithi: o Bel Atha na hUigri co Bel Atha Buidi ⁊ o Gurt na Daibchi co Loch an Tairb. O Dub da Leithi a taiseach. Is iad so a oclaith *dúthaid:* *Uí* Mail Chellaich ⁊ *Uí* Duibleanda ⁊ *Uí* Mail Chorma ⁊ O Cuileandain ⁊ O Bruadair ⁊ O Dunadaich ⁊ O Lathim.

Commentary on the tuatha and place-names

B.B. (p. 201 b 9-15) and H (col. 758.32) introduce the tract with the titles *Crichairecht Corco Laige ann so* and *Corca Laige* respectively and the following two quatrains:

O Beind Fhinn (go Traig) co Traig Omna
siar co Feith na hImgona
o Bel Atha Buidi buaid
co Traig Clain acon Carruig

.uii. n-easgaib .xx. co han
do gab Ross na fod findban
o re Fachtna mbind bladhaig
co re nosmur nDungalaigh.[16]

'From Benn Fhinn to Tráig Omna, westwards to Féith na hImgona, from pre-eminent Bél Átha Buidi to Tráig Claen at the Carraig.'

'Twenty-seven bishops famously ruled Ross of the fair lands from the time of melodious and famous Fachtna to the renowned time of Dúngalach.'

Benn Fhinn (1).[17] Its identity is uncertain, but could be equivalent of *Cnoc Finn,* Knockfeen, a hill over 600 feet which overlooks the present church of Castleventry. This is a townland name. J. T. Collins, however, has suggested that it is identical with Mounteen hill, east of Ballinascarty. A tumulus on the top is marked Mullaghseefin in the Ordnance Survey maps.[18] *Tráig Omna* (2) is Tragomna, on the coast to the south of Skibbereen. *Féith na hImgona* (3) is unidentified.[19] *Béal Átha Buidi* (4) is Bealaboy Bridge: it joined the townlands of Moreagh, parish of Fanlobbus, barony of Carbery West and Nedinagh West, parish of Fanlobbus, barony of Carbery West. It was the site of a fair. *Tráig Claen acon Carruig* (5) is Broadstrand, outside Courtmacsherry and the Horse Rock. This looks very like an extent of the diocese of Ross less its detached western portion which makes up the deanery of Beare (the parishes of Killaconenagh, Kilnamanagh, Kilcatherine and Kilcaskan). At the synod of Ráith Bresail (A.D. 1111) this latter area was assigned to the diocese of Ráith Maige Deiscirt (Kerry) whilst the remainder of Ross was made part of Cork.[20] With the setting up of the twelfth-century diocese of Ross at the synod of Kells-Mellifont in 1152, this portion was taken from the diocese of Ráith Maige Deiscirt and became a detached part of Ross. We do not know what political competition led to these results, but it is reasonable to believe that these quatrains formed part of the ecclesiastical dossier of the clergy of Ross in the period between 1111 and 1152. In part, the quatrain delimits the area with which the distribution tract is concerned and, given this and their association together, it is likely that they are contemporary.

§1. *Dúthaig Uí Gilla Michíl. Féith na hImgona* (3), though unidentified, must lie to the west of Tragomna and is likely, as we have seen, to be at the western extremity of the main portion of the diocese of Ross. It is very likely then to extend to a point that will include the parish of Kilcoe at the head of Roaringwater Bay. *Cend Mara* (6) may be the inmost part of the harbour of Castlehaven.[21] *Bél Átha Semand* (7) is unidentified but it may be a ford on the Saivnose, a tributary of the Ilen.[22] *Bend Sídáin* (8) is Beenteeane, a hill in the townland of Farranconnor, parish of Castlehaven, barony of West Carbery. Quarry states: 'The highest cliff on the southern coast of Castlehaven, as still known by this name'.[23] This *tuath* occupied the basin of the Ilen (from its junction with the Saivenose, or thereabouts) to the sea and included the parishes of Abbeystrowry, Castlehaven, Creagh, Tullagh, Clear and very probably Aghadown and Kilcoe to the west. This would correspond to the western portion of the deanery of Collimore et Collibeg.[24]

§2. *Tuath Uí Conneid. An Garrga* (9), 'the Garden', is the name of a fertile district in the parish of Myross.[25] *Loch an Bricin* (10) is the present designation of a lake a little east of Glandore Harbour.[26] *Midross* (11), a townland and parish to the west of Glandore Harbour. *Bél an Átha Solais* (12), said to be *Áth Solais*, Aughsollis, a ford on the river Ilen about a mile west of Skibbereen, but it must be on the Saivenose. This *tuath* runs from the harbour of Castlehaven to the east of Glandore Harbour and from Myross northwards to a point on the Saivnose river (?). It includes the entire coastline from Castlehaven around to and including Glandore Harbour. It is equal to the parish of Myross and a portion of Kilfaughtnabeg and Kilmacabea.

§3. *Tuath Ruis (Tuath in Dolaich). Fersad Ruis* (13): O'Donovan accepted the faulty manuscript reading of *Lec., Fiad Ruis.* It is evidently the sand-bar in Rosscarbery Bay.[27] *Tráig Long* (14) is Tralong Bay. *Síd na Fear i Find* is 'now Shee Hill',[28] but I do not know its location. *Tuath Ruis,* that is *Tuath in Dolaich:* from a little to the east of Glandore Harbour to the sand-bar on Rosscarbery Bay and from Tralong Bay inland to a point unknown called Shee Hill.

§4. *Tuath Ó nAengusa. Góilín na Gaethnemtha* (15) is 'the townland of Ganniv, parish of Rathbarry, barony of Ibane and Barryroe . . . the Góilín is probably Dirk Bay'.[29] *Dún Déide* (16) is the 'modern townland of Dundeady, parish of Rathbarry, barony of Ibane and Barryroe'.[30] *Béal Átha na Leice* (17) is at or near the stream issuing from Curraghlicky Lake.[31] This *tuath* is made up of the coastal strip from Rosscarbery Bay to Dirk Bay and a narrow strip of mountain and river valleys stretching north-west to Curraghlicky Lake.

Plate 4.1   North-west from Rosscarbery (Cambridge University Collection of air
photographs).

§5. *Tuath Ó bFithchellaig. Ailén Indse Duine* (18) is Inchydoney, parish of Island, barony of Carbery East.[32] The island is a prebend of the diocese of Ross.[33] *Dún Eogain* (19) is 'Dunowen, parish of Ardfield, barony of Ibane and Barryroe'.[34] *Glaise Draignech* (20) is probably the Glashagloragh river and including the townlands of Inchattin, Sarue, Clashatarriff, Maulvirane, Derrybaun, Castleventry, Foxhall, Killeigh, Coonagay, Knockfeen, Coolcraheen. Ó Niatháin argues[35] that *Achad Aible* mentioned as a boundary of *Tuath Ó nDúngalaig* is Aghagilla townland, parish of Castleventry, barony of Ibane and Barryroe. It is a western limit of the *tuath* in question and therefore an eastern limit of *Tuath Ó bhFithchellaig. Béal Átha na hUidri* (see below) was also probably on the eastern boundary of *Tuath Ó bhFithchellaig. Tuath Ó bhFithchellaig* occurs as Twohmweallhah in the Down Survey map of the parish of Castleventry. The form Toughveala is still applied popularly to the eastern part of the townland of Coolnagay. The final element of the name is also found in the name of the parish of Ard*field*.[36] *Tuath Ó Fithchellaig* is equivalent to the coastline from Dirk Bay to Inchidoney and a strip of land stretching inland in a north-west direction as far as the upper reaches of the Glasgloragh and Argideen rivers.

§6. *Tuath Ó nDúngalaig. Béal Átha na hUidri* (21) 'is on the Argideen river between the townlands of Bealad West parish of Kilkerranmore, barony of Ibane and Barryroe and Knocks, parish of Kilkerranmore, barony of Ibane and Barryroe'.[37] *Achad Aible* (22): Ó Niatháin argues[38] that *Achad Aible* mentioned as a boundary of *Tuath Ó nDúngalaig* is Aghagilla townland, parish of Castleventry, barony of Ibane and Barryroe. All manuscripts except *Lec.* read *Achad Aible* and *Lec.*'s *co hAcadaib* should be emended to *co hAchad Aible. Grellach na Gruime/Cruimhe* (23) 'now Grillagh in the parish of Kilnagross [O.S. 122]'.[39] *Cluain da Mael* (24) is now obsolete.[40] *Tuath Ó nDúngalaig*: the good coastal lowlands about Clonakilty and further north the fertile basin of the Argideen and its foothills – the parishes of Kilgarriff, Island, Templebryan, Kilnagross, or parts of them.

§7. *Tuath Uí Duib dá leithe.*[41] *Béal Átha Buide* (4) 'joined the townlands of Moreagh, p. Fanlobbus, b. Carbery W and Nedinagh West, p. Fanlobbus, b. Carbery W . . . . Its exact position coincided with that of the present Bealaboy Bridge – site of a fair'.[42] *Gort na Daibche* (25) 'is the townland of Gortnadihy, in the parish of Kilmeen'.[43] *Loch an Tairb* (26) 'is a lake shown on S.O. [that is O.S. 121] as Lough Atariff, lying partly in the parish of Drinagh and partly in the parish of Kilmeen'.[44] *Tuath Uí Duib dá leithe:* the uplands stretching south of the Bandon river – most of the parish of Kilmeen and a small portion of Kilkerranmore, and, in its northern extremity, a small portion of Ballymoney and Fanlobbus in the diocese of Cork.

The eastern portion of the diocese of Ross, namely the parishes of Kilmaloda, Timoleague, Abbeymahon, Donaghmore, Lislee, Kilsillagh, Templequinlan and Templeomalus, that is the greater part of the deanery of Timoleague, is not touched upon in this survey. It seems that the deanery of Timoleague corresponds to Uí Badamna,[45] an important part of the territory of Corcu Loígde excluded from the present survey. In the west, as we have seen, the detached deanery of Beare – the parishes of Kilaconeanagh, Kilnamanagh, Kilcatherine and Kilcaskin – is also excluded though there were Uí Etersceoil in Bérre. In fact, the distribution tract covers only the deaneries of Ross and of Colliemore et Collibeg (namely Corcu Loígde Mór and Corcu Loígde Becc). The intervening parishes of the diocese of Cork (know as Fonn Iartharach) – Caheragh, Schull, Kilmoe, Durrus, Kilcrohane and Kilmocomoge – will very probably have been under O'Driscoll over-lordship at least for some of the twelfth century and were occupied in part at least by Uí Báire Árann and Uí Chonchobair of Corcu Loígde Cúile.[46]

Alphabetical list of surnames in the tract[47]

Ó Bairr 'now Barr', O'D. Not Ó Báire. West Cork attestation? It could have been partly absorbed by Barry.

Ó Bruadair 'now Broderick and Broder', O'D. Broderick very well attested in Cork. It has tended to replace Broder as a more fashionable form.

Ó Buadaig 'now Buaig, the g pronounced. They consider themselves Sullivans'.[48] This form seems now to have been replaced by Boohig, which is well attested in west Cork. Bogue (< Ó Buadhaigh) is another form also attested in Cork.

Ó Caingni 'now obsolete', O'D. Now (O) Cagney, well attested in Cork.

Ó Cellaig (O) Kelly. Well attested in west Cork.

Ó Cerdín. 'Kerdin. Curdin', O'D. Unknown? Could be absorbed by Cairns, Kearns, Kerins.

Ó Certaig 'obsolete' O'D. Not so! Now Carthy, Carty, both attested in west Cork. The name Carthy, Carty would inevitably have been absorbed in part by McCarthy.

Ó Ciabáin 'now Keevan', O'D. ML.: (O) Keevan, Kevane; Kevane in west Cork at Bandon.

Ó Conneid Eochaid Cind Reithi o tait *Uí* C(h)onaill Cathrach Durlais 7 *Uí* C(h)onneid'.[49] Probably survives as Kenn(e)y.

Ó Cormaic 'now Cormick', O'D. Now Cormac, and Cormack.

O Corrbuide 'now Corby', O'D. ? Corboy, Corry. I do not find.

Ó Cróinín. In Munster, only Corcu Loígde. An erenagh family.[50]

Ó Cúile 'now Cooley', O'D. ? Cowley, Cull(e)y – both attested in Cork.

Ó Cuileandáin 'now Cullenan', O'D. (O) Cullinan(e). O Collenane, O Cullenane, O Collynane in the Fiants for Cork.

Ó Cuilín 'now Cullen'. Cullen is well attested in Cork. Probably partly absorbed by Collins.[51]

O Cuis 'now Cas and Hussey', O'D. Now Quish and Cush, both attested in Cork.

Ó Dercáin 'now Derkan', O'D. Now Dorgan and possibly Durkin.

Ó Doirc 'now Durk and Dark', O'D. Unknown?

Ó Dondamáin now (O) Donovan and completely confused with Uí Dondubáin of Uí Chairpre Aebda (according to O'D.).

Ó Drochruaimnig ruaimnech 'hairy'; seems to be a variant of *ruainnech,* which could give *Drooney, *Drewny. ML. has (O) Dro(o)ney which he tends to locate in Clare 'rarely found elsewhere'. Is this attested in west Cork?

Ó Dubagáin 'now Doogan and Duggan', O'D. Common.[52]

Ó Dubáin 'now Duane, Dwan and Downes', O'D. Duane, Dwane, Downes, Kidney are well attested in Cork.

Ó Dubchon 'obsolete', O'D. Doohan (still found in Clonakilty), Doughan. O Dwghune, O Dughune in the Fiants for south Kerry.

Ó Duib Arda 'now Doorty, a name still extant and numerous in . . . Cork', O'D. If so, not in ML. Doherty, Dougherty, Dehorty are possible variants; probably has become Doherty in county Cork; I Doherty, O Doghertie in the Fiants show that the surname Ó Dochartaigh existed in Cork and in west Cork.

Ó Duib Chonna. Now Doheny. Well attested.

Ó Duib dá Leithe 'now Dowdall'; P. Woulfe, *Sloinnte Gaedheal is Gall* (Dublin, 1927), p. 51, equates it with Dudley; Ó Niatháin, *Dinnseanchas,* i, pt. 3 (1965), p. 68, suggests Dullea, Delea as an anglicisation. Dudley and Dowdall are attested for Cork; Dullea is very well attested in west Cork; Del(l)ea is also well attested. K. W. Nicholls (pers. comm.) suggests that Dulea is Anglo-Norman.

Ó Duibleanda 'obsolete', O'D. Possibly absorbed by Dillon.

Ó Dunadaig 'now Downey and Denny', O'D. Downey and Downing are well attested in Cork; Denny much less so.

Ó Dúngalaig, Ó Dúngaile 'now Donnelly', O'D. Well attested in Cork.

Ó Dúnlaing 'now Dowling or Doolin', O'D. Dooling, Doolan, Dowling are all found in Cork. O Dowlinge, O Dowlin in the Fiants.

Ó Dunndín 'now Dinneen and latterly Downing', O'D. Din(n)een and Downing extremely well attested in west Cork.[53]

Ó Fithchellaig 'now anglicized Feehily, Feely, and even Field', O'D. Feehily, Feehely, Fehil(l)y, Feely, Field are all attested for Cork. Of that family were Maurice (de Portu) *Flos mundi,* archbishop of Tuam (1506-13) and Domnall Ua Fithchellaig (Donald O Fihely), Oxford graduate and annalist. They held Ballymacrown down to the seventeenth century (K. W. Nicholls).

Ó Fuailchin vv.ll. Ualchin, H; Tuaillchin, F. Very uncertain. It could be realised as Folan; with epenthesis, as Hoolahan, Hoolihan. The latter is very well attested in west Cork. *Foulihan would be absorbed by the former.

Ó Gabadáin 'now Gavan, locally "muintir-Ghabhain"', O'D. (O) Gavan, Gavin and, probably, Gowan, Gowen.

Ó Gilla Michíl not now known, perhaps Michael(s).

Ó Greisi 'obsolete', O'D.

Ó hÁdaim 'now obsolete', O'D. One would expect this to be anglicised Adam(s) and, in fact, this name is well attested in west Cork. One would expect some confusion with MacAdam(s) < Mac Ádhaimh, which is attested for the same area.

Ó hAeda ó Cluain dá Mael 'now O'Hea and Hayes', O'D. O'Hea had a small castle one mile south-west of Clonakilty at Ahamilly. Well known clergy in the diocese of Ross.[54] The identity of Cluain dá Mael is uncertain. O'Hea is well attested in west Cork.[55]

Ó hAengusa (O) Hennesssy, well attested in Cork.[56]

Ó hAidne 'now Hyney', O'D.? Hynie, Hiney. Hiney attested in Cork. Partly absorbed by Hynes, which is well attested in Cork.

Ó hAinbítha 'now Hanvey and Hanafey', O'D. Now Hanvey.

Ó hAingle Well attested in Beara (including Beare Island and Bantry) in the form Hanley.

Ó hlairisnich. 'obsolete', O'D. Unknown?

Ó hlarnáin 'now Mac Iarran', O'D. Hernon, Hernan, both attested in Cork.

Ó hócáin (O) Hogan.

Ó hUainide 'now Hooney or Green', O'D. Well attested.

Ó hUrmoltaich 'now anglicized Tromulty and Hamilton', O'D. Hamilton very well attested. I do not find Tromulty.

Ó Laegaire O'Leary. O'D. thinks that the family was driven into the parish of Inchegeelagh or Iveleary to which it gave its name.[57]

Ó Laidid 'now Liddy or Laddy', O'D. Liddy attested Cork.

Ó Lathim 'Lahiff, Lahy and Leahy', O'D. O Laithimh, *B.B.,* U, F. Probably originally Ó Flaithim.

Ó Loingsich 'now Lynch, Lynchy or Lingshy', O'D. Now Lynch.[58]

Ó Lonain 'now Lannin and Lennane', O'D. Lannin, Lenane, Lennon (and its frequent fancy anglicisation Leonard) attested in Cork.

Ó Mael Chellaich 'now obsolete', O'D. I do not find. Probably absorbed by Kelly.

Ó Mael Chorma 'obsolete', O'D.

Ó Mael Cumad 'now obsolete', O'D.

Ó Mael Étair U/F have Mael Petair, wrongly. This name possibly gives Leader, of which ML. (p. 191) says it was established in county Cork in the mid-seventeenth century; by the mid-nineteenth it had become very numerous, though it is now much less so. Of Mulpeters ML. (p. 228) states: 'Ó Maolpheadair (devotee of St Peter). Originally of Co. Cork, later Leix and Offaly'. A guess based on the footnote in O'Donovan, *Misc. Celt. Soc.*?

Ó Mael Temin 'obsolete', O'D. I do not find.

Ó Maelguirm 'obsolete', O'D.

Ó Maic Dairic 'now obsolete', O'D. I do not find.

Ó Mainchin 'now Mannin', O'D. The Fiants for south Kerry have Manahan, O Manihan, Y Vanihine. Manning, Mannion are extremely well attested in Cork and west Cork; Mannix well attested in Cork; Manahan also attested in Cork.

Ó Meic Con 'now Macken', O'D. Macken attested in Cork.

Ó Meic Étig has become Mac Ceidigh, Mac Eidigh, now (Mac) Keady. M' Keaddie in the Fiants for Carbery. According to Thomas Swanton[59] still extant near Bantry in mid-nineteenth century.

Ó Mirín 'Mirreen', O'D. I do not find.

Ó Mongáin 'Mongan and Mangan. Still extant near Dromaleague', O'D. Mangan well attested in west Cork, Mongan less so.

Ó Mothla 'now O'Mothola, Mohilly; extant near Dromaleague', according to Thomas Swanton.[60] '(O) Mohilly, Moakley . . . A Co. Cork name', ML. These are probably separate names since they have a different distribution. The common form now is Mohally, which is well attested in Cork.

Ó Mudáin 'now Modan. The parish of Ballymodan took its name from this family', O'D. I do not find.

Ó Muimnich 'now Moyny', O'D. Very probably the well attested Cork and west Cork Mean(e)y family. The Fiants for Carbery have O Moynig, O Moynie.

Ó Nualláin 'now Nowlan or Nolan', O'D. Nolan well attested in Cork.

Ó Odradáin 'now Horan', O'D. Horan.

Ó Rosna 'now obsolete', O'D. '(O) Rosney. O Rosna. A rare Corca Laoidhe name which is extant in Co. Kerry', ML. (p. 261). It is now also extant in Cork city.

Ó Ruaidri 'Rory, Rodgers', O'D. Ro(d)gers well attested in Cork.

Ó Selbaig 'now Shallow and Shelly', O'D. (O) Shally, Shalvey, Shalloo, Shallow, Shell(e)y, Shalloe. Well attested in Cork. The Uí Shelbaig, hereditary abbots of Cork down to the twelfth century, belong to a different family, but now both will be mixed up.

Ó Sifi 'unknown', O'D. O Sithbi, *B.B.*; O Sifigh, U; O Sife, H; O Sifigh, F. The basic form is probably Ó Síthbe; probably absorbed by Sheehy, which is quite common in west Cork.

Ó Sindaich 'now Shinny or Fox; extant near Dromaleague', O'D. (O) Shinnick, characteristically Cork; may have also been translated Fox.

Ó Torpa 'now Torpy', O'D. Now (O) Torpey. Attested in Cork.

Ó Trena 'obsolete', O'D. I do not find.

Ó Tuaraide 'now obsolete', O'D. O hUarraide, *B.B.*, O Uaraig, U; O Tuairigh, F; O Uaraig, H.? (O) Furey, attested in Cork.

Appendix

The other manuscript recensions

B.B., p. 201 b.16

Duthaig I Gilla Michil o Feith na hImgona co Cend Mara 7 o Beind Sidhain co Bel Atha Semann. As iad seo a oglaigh duthaig .i. O Duib Arda 7 O Dunlaing 7 O hOgain 7 O Dubagain, O Meic Eidig 7 O Ciabain 7 O Cerdaig, O Buadaigh, O Mongan, O Doirc, O Meic Con, *Ui* Aingle, *Ui* Mothla, *Ui* Mael Edair, O hAdaim, O Bairr, O Rosna.

Tuath *Ui* Conneid .i. an Garrda, o Cind Mara co Loch an Bricin 7 o Midhros co Bel an Atha Solais. O Conneid a taiseach. As iad a hoglaich duthaig .i. O Muimnig, O Fuailcin, O Caingni, O Duib Conna.
Tuath Ruis .i. Tuath in Dolaig, o Loch an Bricin co Fersaid Ruis 7 o Traig Long co Sidh na Fer Find. O Laegaire a taisech. As iad a oglaich .i. O Ruadri, O Lonan, O Laidi, O Torpa, O hUrmoltaig, O Mirin, O Meic Dairig, O hUarraide, O Trena, O hUainigi, O Cerdin.

Tuat[h O n]Aengusa (c)o Fersaid Ruis co Goilin na Gaithnemtha 7 o Dhun Deidi co Bel Atha na Leicci. O hAengusa a thaisech. As iad a oclaigh .i. O Corrbuidhi, O Dubain, O Duindin, O Mudain, O hAidhne, O Manchin, O Cuis, O Cuile, O Dergain, O hIaraisnigh, O hOdragan, O Gresin, O Cuilein, O Sindaig.

Tuath O Fichill*aig* o Goilin na Gaithneama co hAilen Indsi Duine 7 o Dhun Eogain co Glaissi Draigneac. O Ficheallaigh a taisech. As iad a oglaich .i. O Cormaic, O Dondamhan, O Dubchon, O hIarnan, O Nuallan, O Croinin, O Sithbi, O hAinbith.

Tuath hUa nDunlaing uel Ua Dungalaig .i. o Oilen Indsi Duine co Bel Atha na hUidri 7 o Greallaig na Gruime co hAchad Aible. O Dungalaig a taisech. As iad a oglaich .i. O Mael Cumad, O hAeda o Cluain da Mael, O Loingsig, O Mael Teimin, O Cellaig, O(m) Maelguirm, O Muireadhaig, O Sealbaig, O Gabadan.

Tuath I Duib da Leithi o Bel Atha na hUidhri co Bel Atha Buidhi, o Ghort na Daibchi co Loch an Tairb. As iad a oglaich .i. *Ui* Mail Cellaig, O Duibleanda, O Mail Corma, O Cuilennain, O Bruadair, O Dunadaig, O Laithimh.

H 3. 17, col. 758.38

Dutaig a Cill Mithil [759] o Feth na hImgolla co Ceand Mara [7] o Beand Sigain co Bel Atha Senain. As iat so a oglai duthaig: O Duib Ara 7 O Dunlaing 7 O hOgain 7 O Dubacain 7 O Mail Edig 7 O Ciabain, O Ceartaig, O Buagaid, O Mongain, O Doirc, O Coniacla, I Mothla, O Mail Petair, O hAdaim, O Bairr, O Rosna.

Tuath O Conned annso .i. in Carrda, o Cind Mara co Loch an Bricin 7 o Midros co Bel Atha Solais. O Conead a taiseach. O Muimnig fos. O Drochruamnig fois. O Ualcin, O Cainginid, O Dun Conna.

Tuath Rois .i. Tuath Annola ho Loch an Briccin co Fersait Ruis o Traig na Long co Sigh Fer Find taire. O Laegaire a taiseach. O Ruadri(r), O Longain, O Laige, O Torpa, O Urmaltaig, O Mirin, O Meic Dearc, O Uaraig, O Cerdin.
Tuath O nAengusa o Fersait co Golin na Gaithnama, o Tun Dede co Bel Atha na Lice. O hAengusa a taiseach. O Corrbaide, O Dubain, O Duindin, O Muadain, O Adna, O Mancin, O Cuis, O Caile, O Deragain, O Ciarasnaid, O hOgragain, O Gresin, O Cuilen, O Sindaig.

Tuath O Fithceallaig o Golin na Gaethnena co hAilig ind Innsi Duine 7 o Dun Eogain co Glaise Draignech. O Fithceallaig a taiseach. O Cormaic, O Donnamain, O Duibcon, O Ciarain, O Mallain, O Cronin, O Sife, O hAnbith.

Tuath I Dungalaid o Golin Inse Duine co Bel Atha na hUigri, o Greallaig na Gruime co Achad Aible. O Dungalaig a taiseach. O Mail Comad, O Aega o Cluain da Meall, O Lonnsig, O Mail Temen, O

Cairellaig, O *Maillgruirm*, O(m) Muiredaig, O Sealbaig, O Gabadain.

U f. 34 v° b 33

DA THUATHAIB CORCO LAIDI 7 DA DUCHASACAIB A TUATH
AND SEO

Duthaigh hI Cobthaigh .i.Tuath .H. nDuibh da Leithi o Bel Atha na
Buidri [*modified to* hUidri] co Bel Atha Buidh(e) 7 o Gort na Dabcha
co Loch in Tairb. A oglaith duthaigh .i. O Mael Ceallaig 7 O Duib
Lenda 7 O Mael Corma 7 O Cuilindain 7 O Bruadair 7 O Dulladaigh
7 O Laithim.

Tuath I Dungalaigh o Oilen Indsi Duini co Bel Atha na hUidhri 7 o
Greallaig na Cruimhi co hAchadh Aibli. A oglaid duthaig .i. O Mail
Comadh 7 O hAedha o Chluain da Mhael 7 O Loingsigh 7 O Mael
Teimhin 7 O hAilealla 7 O Mail Guirm 7 O Muireadaigh 7 O
Sealbaigh 7 O Cadhan.

Tuath O Ficheallaigh .i. o Gaiblin in Gaithneamha co hOilen Indsi
Duini o Dhun Eoghain co Glaisi Draighnecha. A oglaigh duthaigh sein
.i. O Comraig 7 O Dondubhan 7 O Dubchon 7 O hIarnain 7 O
Nuallain 7 O Croinin 7 O Sifigh 7 O hAinbith.

Tuath O nAengusa o Fersaid Ros co Gaibhlin in Gaithneamha 7 o
Dhun Deide co Bel Atha na Leice. A oglaigh duthaigh hI Aengusa .i. O
Corrbuighi 7 O Dubain 7 O Duindin 7 O Mudain 7 O hAidhni 7 O
Mainchin 7 O Coisi 7 O Dreaan 7 O hAirisnigh 7 O Thograin 7 O
Greisin 7 O Cuilin 7 O Sindaigh.

Tuath I Laedhairi .i. Tuath an Dolaidh o Fearsad Ruis co Loch in
Bhricin 7 o Thraig Long co Sith na Fer Fhinn. Oglaidh duthaigh na
tuaithi sin .i. O Ruairi 7 O Lonan 7 O Laidhidh 7 O Torpa 7 O
Thuaraigh 7 O Treana 7 O hUainighi 7 O Ceirdin.

Tuath O Ceindeidid .i. an Garrdha o Loch in Bricin co Ceann Mara 7 O
Mhidhros co Bel in Atha Solais. O Coindeid 7 O Muimnigh a taisigh.
Oglaig dutaigh doib O Drochruimnigh 7 O Thuaillchin 7 O Caingni 7
O Dubconda.

Tuath I Ghilla Mhichil o Feith na hImgona co Ceand Mara 7 o Beind
Sidhain co Bel Atha na Seamand as iad so a hoglaigh duthaig .i. O
Duibh Ardar 7 O Dunlaing 7 O Thogan 7 O Muireidid 7 O Dubagan

O Ciaban 7O Ceartaigh 7O Buadaig 7O Mongain 7O Doirc 7O Meic Con 7O hAingli 7O Mothla 7O Mael Peadair 7O hAdhaim 7O Rosna 7O Bairr. Is don tuaith sin da bhi in fer ina inmhi fein is fhearr eineach 7 eagna tainig dan tuaith sin riam co fis duindi .i. fer inaid Bearchan .i. in Bicairi Mor O Gilla Micil risa raiti Sparan Oslaicthi.[61]

References

1. For manuscript sigla cited in the present introduction not already given in this volume's List of Abbreviations see below, note 4.

2. G. Mac Niocaill, *Ireland before the Vikings* (Dublin, 1972), pp 33-34; Byrne, *Irish kings*, pp 180-82; W. Carrigan, *The history and antiquities of the diocese of Ossory*, i (Dublin, 1905; repr. 1981), pp 27-34; L. Ó Buachalla, 'Contributions towards the political history of Munster 450-800 AD' in *Cork Hist. Soc. Jn.*, lxix (1954), pp 111-26 (Carrigan's and Ó Buachalla's works must be read with caution because they accept as historical material which is legendary).

3. O'Donovan, *Misc. Celt. Soc.*, p. 141; Hogan, *Onomasticon*, s.v. Corcu Laigde; D. A. Binchy, *Scéla Cano meic Gartnáin*, Mediaeval and Modern Irish Series, xviii (Dublin, 1963), p. xxiv.

4. The early genealogies are found in the following manuscripts and editions: Bodl., MS Rawlinson B 502, f. 155 a 3-b 26, ed. in O'Brien, *Corpus geneal. Hib.*, pp 256-63; *L.L.*, vi, pp 1410-14; T.C.D., MS H 2. 7, cols. 85 a 9-89 b 17 (unedited); *Lec.*, ff 110 v° a 1-113 r° c 51, ed. with translation, notes and some variants from *B.B.* and Mac Firbhisigh (for which see below) in O'Donovan, *Misc. Celt. Soc.*, pp 2-58; *B.B.*, pp 196 e 1-202.23; R. A. S. Macalister (ed.), *The book of Uí Maine* [hereafter U] (Dublin, 1942), ff 34 r° a 62-v° d 36; T.C.D., MS H 3. 17, cols. 757.1-760.23 (unedited); U.C.D., MS Add. Ir. 14 [= Mac Firbhisigh, Book of Genealogies, hereafter F], pp 673-78 (unedited).

5. *.i. Duthaig I Chobthaig* is probably a misplaced gloss.

6. I am much indebted to the generosity of Dr Nollaig Ó Muraíle who kindly supplied me with a copy of F. The text will appear in the edition which he is preparing of Mac Firbhisigh's Book of Genealogies.

7. D. Ó Corrain, 'Uí Chobthaigh and their pedigree' in *Ériu*, xxx (1979), pp 168-73.

8. D. A. Binchy, 'Secular institutions' in M. Dillon (ed.), *Early Irish society* (Dublin, 1954), pp 52-65; idem, 'The passing of the old order' in B. Ó Cuív (ed.), *Proceedings of the international congress of Celtic studies held in Dublin, 6-10 July, 1959* (Dublin, 1962), pp 119-24; idem, *Celtic and Anglo-Saxon kingship* (Oxford, 1970), pp 3-30; F. J. Byrne, 'Tribes and tribalism in early Ireland' in *Ériu*, xx (1971), pp 128-66.

9. E. MacNeill, *Early Irish laws and institutions* (Dublin, 1935), p. 96; Byrne, 'Tribes and tribalism', p. 160; Byrne, *Irish kings*, p. 7.

10. *A.U.*,² *dux*, s.a. 732, 756, 771, 790, 796, 867, 869, 870, 872, 877, 879, 883, 884, 912, 917, 932, 933, 934, 935; *toísech*, s.a. 869, 914 (tris), 916, 1007, 1026, 1055, 1073, 1075, 1082 (bis); *tigern(a)*, s.a. 719, 740.

11. G. Mac Niocaill, *Notitiae as Leabhar Cheanannais 1033-1161* (Dublin, 1961), p. 26.

12. J. G. O'Keeffe, 'The ancient territory of Fermoy' in *Ériu*, x (1926-28), pp 170-89 (pp 173-76); Power, *Crichad*.

13. *D.I.L.*, s. v. óclach; G. Mac Niocaill, 'A propos du vocabulaire social irlandais du bas moyen âge' in *Études Celtiques*, xii (1970-71), pp 512-46, especially pp 524-36.

14. Mac Niocaill, *Ireland before the Vikings*, p. 534.

15. Note that in the title of the tract in *Lec.* the term *dúthchasach,* 'hereditary proprietor', refers to both the *toísech (dúthchusa)* and the *óclach dúthchusa.*

16. In printing the *B.B.* text of the first quatrain O'Donovan, *Misc. Celt. Soc.*, p. 48, took it to be prose. H's copy of the quatrains is defective. The second quatrain is found in the same position in *Lec.* with the introductory remark: *do gobadar .uii. n-easpaig fiched do Cland Lugdach Ros o Fachtna mac Maenaich co Dungalach mac Folachtaich amail adbert* ...: 'Twenty-seven bishops of the race of Lugaid ruled Ross from Fachtna son of Maenach to Dungalach son of Folachtach as (the poet) said' (O'Donovan, *Misc. Celt. Soc.*, p. 46 = *Lec.*, f. 113 r° b 31)

17. These numbers refer to the numbered locations on the accompanying figure.

18. J. T. Collins, 'The O'Heas of south-west Cork' in *Cork Hist. Soc. Jn.* li (1946), pp 97-107, especially p. 98 note.

19. Compare *Lec.*, f. 112 v° b 4 = O'Donovan, *Misc. Celt. Soc.*, p. 38.20: 'Da mac Threna mc Duach .i. Mac Eirc Oengus. Tri meic Coinchindi ingine Cathhad .i. Mac Erc Oengus. Conall Claen in tres mac. Is e sin Cenel Coinchindi o Fheith na hImgona co Droiched Lacha hImchada'.

20. O.S., *Map of monastic Ireland*, 2nd ed. (Dublin, 1979) for medieval diocesan boundaries; J. MacErlean, 'Synod of Ráith Breasail: boundaries of the diocese or Ireland' in *Archiv. Hib.,* iii (1914), pp 1-33, especially p. 9.

21. O'Donovan, *Misc. Celt. Soc.*, p. 88.

22. Ibid.

23. Ibid.

24. M. A. Murphy, 'The royal visitation of Cork, Cloyne, Ross and the College of Youghal' in *Archiv. Hib.*, ii (1913), pp 173-215, especially pp 206-10.

25. Cf. *Lec.*, f. 111 r° a 13-15: 'Clann Chathra meic Eidirsceoil .i. Cland Fhind in Garrga'. O'Donovan, *Misc. Celt. Soc.*, p. 10.10, adds from *B.B.*: 'Mac Raith mac Cathna mic Edersceoil as lais do ronadh teampull mor Fachtna i Ros Ailithir'.

26. O'Donovan, *Misc. Celt. Soc.*, p. 89.

27. P. Ó Niathain, 'Tuath Ó bhFithcheallaigh' in *Dinnseanchas*, i, pt. I (1964), pp 12-14, especially p. 12.

28. Ibid., p. 52.

29. Ibid.

30. Ibid.

31. O'Donovan, *Misc. Celt. Soc.*, p. 90.

32. Ó Niathain, 'Tuath Ó bhFithcheallaigh', p. 12.

33. O'Donovan, *Misc. Celt. Soc.,* p. 90.

34. Ó Niatháin, 'Tuath Ó bhFithcheallaigh', p. 12.

35. Ibid., p. 14.

36. Ibid.

37. Ibid., and also marked on Ó Niatháin's map. See J. Coombes, 'Obligationes pro annatis diocesis Rossensis' in *Archiv. Hib.*, xxxix (1970), p. 36, note 11, for further references to these places which were prebends in the fourteenth century.

38. Ó Niatháin, 'Tuath Ó bhFithcheallaigh', p. 14.

39. O'Donovan, *Misc. Celt. Soc.*, p. 54.

40. Ibid., p. 55.

41. Compare P. Ó Niatháin, 'Tuath Uí Dhuibhdáleithe' in *Dinnseanchas*, i, pt. 3 (1965), pp 67-68 plus map.

42. Ibid.

43. Ibid., p. 67.

44. Ibid.

45. Abbeymahon (Fons Vivus) was founded by Diarmait Mac Carthaig in 1172, referred to as 'seanmainistir O Madamhna', *Ann. Inisf.*, s.a. 1231.3; the 'manistir nuó darighneadh i Gregan i ní[b] Badhamhna', ibid., s.a. 1278.2, refers to Abbeymahon which was moved from the original site to Creggan (I owe this information to the kindness of my colleague, Mr K. W. Nicholls). See further the references to the half-cantred of Obaddamnia, Obathebme (= Uí Badamna) in K. W. Nicholls, 'Some unpublished Barry charters' in *Anal. Hib.*, xxvii (1972), pp 113-19.

46. O'Donovan, *Misc. Celt. Soc.*, pp 42-44 = *Lec.*, f. 112 v° d 11, f. 112 v° d 23.

47. The following abbreviations are used in the commentary in this list: O'D. = O'Donovan's notes on family names in *Misc. Celt. Soc.*; ML. = Edward MacLysaght, *The surnames of Ireland* (Dublin 1973). The certain identification of surnames with given families is full of difficulties, since the same surnames recur in different families and the records are very fragmentary. Of the families here listed, we can posit that 52 or more survive to the present day. Further research may show that even more survive. On the other hand, Mr K. W. Nicholls (pers. comm.) is very doubtful that so many surnames could have survived and feels that such a rate of survival implies a very static society.

48. T. Swanton in O'Donovan, *Misc. Celt. Soc.*, p. 50 note.

49. O'Donovan, *Misc. Celt. Soc.* p. 46.1.

50. Ó Murchadha, *Family names*, pp 104-06.

51. Ibid., p. 83.

52. Ibid., pp 133-36.

53. Ibid., pp 137-39.

54. Coombes, 'Obligationes', pp 33-48.

55. Collins, 'The O'Heas of south-west Cork', pp 97-107; Ó Murchadha, *Family names*, pp 156-61.

56. Ó Murchadha, *Family names*, pp 162-65.

57. Ibid., pp 206-14; see also Chapter Seven in this volume.

58. Ó Murchadha, *Family names*, pp 221-23.

59. In O'Donovan, *Misc. Celt. Soc.* p. 50 note.

60. Ibid.

61. I am grateful to the President and Council of the R.I.A. and to the Provost and Fellows of T.C.D. for permission to print this text from manuscripts under their care.

Plate 4.2   Rosscarbery (Cork Archaeological Survey).

Chapter 5

POLITICS, ECONOMY AND SOCIETY: THE DEVELOPMENT OF CORK AND THE IRISH SOUTH-COAST REGION *c.* 1170 TO *c.* 1583

A. F. O'BRIEN

This chapter sets out to evaluate the salient elements of the organisation, development and evolution of the region comprising essentially the present county Cork in the period from the Anglo-Norman (or Anglo-French) conquest and settlement of much of the region in the late twelfth and early thirteenth centuries until the sixteenth century. The paper consists of a synthesis of my own publications in the area, original research which I present here for the first time and, finally, an overview of the growing body of scholarship concerned with later medieval Ireland. This is the first presentation of such a synthesis to my knowledge for the Cork region or, indeed, for any other Irish area in the period. The guiding principle is to bring clarity to a political, economic and social situation of considerable complexity and apparent confusion. The article is written in the belief that the circumstances of later medieval Ireland are critically important for our understanding of the totality of the development of Irish civilisation.

Anglo-Norman invasion: context and significance

In a recent seminal study,[1] Canon C. A. Empey has described the context of the Anglo-Norman invasion of Ireland. Because of the significance of his paper, Empey's conclusions are sketched here at the outset. Later sections discuss the general concerns raised in this introduction and develop them in detail for the Cork region in the period under review.

Canon Empey has argued that the Anglo-Norman conquest of much of Ireland in the late twelfth and early thirteenth centuries, 'was haphazard, incomplete, and unevenly sustained'. Thus 'the kingdoms of Ireland fell piecemeal over an extended period into the hands of adventurers acting for the most part independently of each other when they were not actually in conflict. The desire to create a strong monarchy was remote from the minds of men who sought only to establish themselves firmly within the borders of their lordships.' In this respect the conquest of Ireland differed fundamentally from that of England a century earlier. There were other differences also between the Irish and English situations, notably the fact that 'in England, the conquest was predominantly aristocratic in character: it was not followed by a significant influx of non-military classes from France.' Accordingly, few settlers were attracted from overseas to the new colonial towns in England and fewer still to the existing Anglo-Danish towns, whereas 'in Ireland, and to a lesser degree in Wales, the picture was very different: here the Anglo-Norman towns recruited their populations almost entirely from England and north-western Europe. Nowhere is the difference between the conquests more evident: though less complete in its military and political consequences, the invasion of Ireland resulted in a significant inflow of non-military classes – particularly in the south and east – of a kind scarcely visible in England a century earlier'.[2]

Furthermore, 'equally significant is the wider economic context in which the conquest of Ireland occurred. In the twelfth century, European society experienced an unprecedented prosperity that reached its climax only in the succeeding century. This was manifested in a steady increase in population, a rapid expansion of agriculture, and, most obviously, in the formation of innumerable villages and towns'.[3] Empey points out that 'while these conditions were experienced in the older, settled regions of Europe, they were all the more visible along the Slavonic and Celtic fringes and that most of these developments gained momentum only in the twelfth century, which suggests that the conquest of England occurred too prematurely to benefit from such conditions'.[4] From this he concludes that it seems that 'the heyday of colonial enterprise in these islands was confined to a fairly clearly defined band of time, say from 1100 to 1275'. Accordingly, 'had Ireland been conquered by William in 1066, or by Edward I in 1282, the character of the ensuing settlement would surely have been fundamentally different from that which actually occurred in 1169. In the long term Ireland might have emerged as firmly Gaelic as England was to become securely English'.[5]

The fact that the conquest was never complete affected the subsequent history, not least the political history, of medieval Ireland. Because of the Gaelic revival and colonial decline, later medieval Ireland was politically fragmented and culturally mixed. Nonetheless, as Empey has pointed out,[6] 'in spite of everything – the Gaelic recovery, economic decline, the virtual collapse of royal authority – the fact remains that Ireland would never again be Gaelic in the sense that it

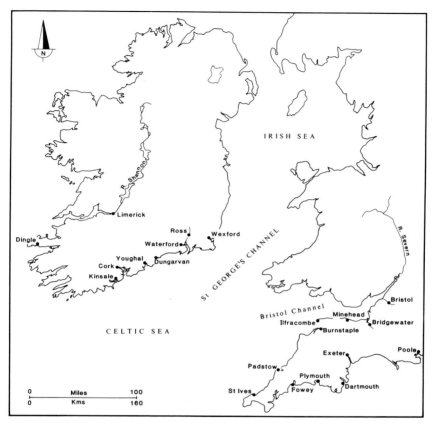

Figure 5.1   Medieval ports in southern Ireland and south-west England.

had been before 1169'. On the other hand, because the conquest –
partial though it may have been – occurred in economic and
demographic circumstances which were profoundly favourable for
colonisation and settlement, it had a more profound impact on the Irish
economy and polity than the Norman conquest ever had on England.
The crucial difference between the two was the scale and intensity of
colonisation. The most important consequence of the Anglo-Norman
invasion of Ireland, certainly as far as settlement is concerned, was the
introduction of manorial economy and organisation. The introduction
of the manorial economy, based as it was on intensive arable
agriculture, profoundly altered much of the landscape. There was a
significant shift from pastoral husbandry to arable farming in many
areas. In the Cork region this was particularly the case in the north,
east and south-east of the present county Cork. There was also in these

locations a consequential feudalisation of society. The classical kindred organisation of Irish society was particularly suitable for pastoral husbandry, but arable farming worked better with either servile or wage labour. These changes transcended in importance the introduction of new political masters into the conquered areas.

Empey's argument that the new colonial settlements in Ireland attracted significant immigration on the part of non-military tenants is an important one, but one which has not gone unchallenged. Inevitably, given the nature of the evidence, there is room for dis-agreement here. However, his thesis appears to be supported by some of the family names of settlers which have survived. In the Cork region, the names of burgesses of the town of Youghal, drawn up in 1351, constitute a case in point.[7] While some of this nomenclature is English, Welsh place-names are strongly represented also. Although it is possible that some Irish people, adapting themselves to the culture of the new rulers, abandoned their Irish names and substituted for them English ones, particularly names derived from crafts or trades, it is less likely that they would have adopted names derived from Welsh topography. These names, therefore, are much more likely to have been those of immigrant settlers or their descendants. Moreover, the surviving records of the Dublin guild merchant and the freemen rolls of the thirteenth century provide ample evidence of an influx of persons not only from England, Wales and Scotland but also from parts of continental Europe.[8] These people added significantly to the mercantile life of medieval Dublin and other towns and, together with native Irish and (in the port towns of Viking origin) the surviving Ostmen, formed the merchant class of the principal Irish towns whose economic fortunes were greatly boosted by the vast and rapid economic growth and expansion of the thirteenth century.

THE THIRTEENTH CENTURY: THE HEYDAY OF EXPANSION, SETTLEMENT AND ECONOMIC GROWTH

Foundation

Western Europe as a whole, between the late twelfth and the early fourteenth centuries, witnessed extensive and rapid economic growth. Thus the introduction of the manorial system and intensive arable agriculture into Ireland, the crucial first phase of the Anglo-Norman settlement, occurred against a background of favourable economic and demographic conditions not only in Ireland but in Europe as a whole. 'There is no doubt ... that Norman lords of every degree were determined to develop intensive demesne farming as an important element in their programme of settlement, and that this was related directly to the buoyant conditions of an expanding European economy.'[9] The impact of the new agricultural organisation and methods can be seen most strikingly in the vast quantities of cereals shipped from Ireland, either by way of trade or as supplies or render, in the course of the thirteenth century.[10]

The growth of towns

The Cork region contributed significantly to this enhanced agricultural production. The surplus production of agriculture was the bedrock of a new, reinvigorated trade, both internal and external, and that trade, in turn, was an essential pre-condition for the growth of towns. In practice the growth of towns and the growth of trade were two interconnected phenomena. The growth of towns and an urban mercantile class greatly facilitated and promoted the growth of both internal and external trade. Economic advantages accrued from the foundation of towns in this period and towns became an important element in the new pattern of settlement. As Empey points out, 'that Norman lords tried to exploit the economic potential of their lordships to the maximum can be most clearly demonstrated by the lavish scale of their urban foundations'.[11] However, the lord's concern was not primarily economic; it was military and strategic. Thus, 'the economic development of the Anglo-Norman lordships in Ireland was ... an integral part of the original seignorial design: it was not simply a response to favourable trading conditions. Towns were founded chiefly with the intention of channelling the trade of a particular lordship through a market controlled by the lord. While he may well have pondered the full range of their economic potential, his primary motive was to exclude others from reaping the direct profits of trading with his tenants'.[12]

The spate of borough foundation and renewal in Ireland in the thirteenth century testifies strongly to the scale of colonisation by the new feudal lords and the importance of the borough to them in mobilising the resources of their lands. In this connection the question of burgage tenure (essentially the term burgage was applied first to land when a borough was created by charter where no town existed before, as was the case with many boroughs in Ireland)[13] was particularly important. Therefore:

> as in the case of the demesne land, and the major tenements in general, the amount of land held by burgage tenure almost certainly represents the investment of the founding lord. Thus it is the measure of the importance he attached to town-building in the context of his overall design for his lordship. Since the town

was the manor in its trading capacity, it is not surprising that the largest urban foundations are identified with the capital manors of the great lords.[14]

Empey's analysis of six of Theobald Walter's capital boroughs in Tipperary and Kilkenny suggests that solid inducements were offered in order to attract settlers. 'The fact that Walter was prepared to make such a considerable territorial investment in his towns is a reflection of the significance he attached to the development of trade in his lordship, not only for the sake of profit, but because he needed the skills that the burgesses could provide'.[15] This pattern was replicated in the Cork region, for example, in the case of Youghal, Kinsale and Dungarvan. These boroughs (Youghal and Dungarvan have been studied in some detail)[16] belong to the category which Empey describes as that to which 'the greater part of the boroughs founded by Anglo-Norman lords undoubtedly belonged', namely 'the type of borough commonly found in the single manor attached either to the demesne of some lordship or held as a fief by a knight'.[17]

Political and economic factors combined in Ireland to promote urban growth, particularly in the thirteenth century. Many of the newly-established boroughs were, of course, quite small and amounted to little more than a present-day Irish village. Some of them, indeed, were doomed to failure; these were either stillborn or they failed to survive the economic contraction of the later fourteenth century, compounded by visitations of bubonic plague (the Black Death) and the developing political instability promoted, particularly, by increasing attacks by Irish enemies and English rebels.[18]

The following are examples of important urban development in the region. 'The real founder of Youghal as a medieval town appears to have been Maurice fitz Gerald II, the second baron of Offaly, who had obtained seisin of the lands of his father, including Imokilly, in 1215. He colonised Youghal with citizens of Bristol "who gave to it the trading characteristics it long retained".'[19] Almost certainly, 'the borough acquired a charter of basic liberties at an early stage, probably in the early thirteenth century'.[20] Accordingly, 'by the later thirteenth century . . . Youghal was the major component of the extensive and important manor of Inchiquin . . . and had already become a major Irish seaport trading town with an extensive overseas trade. Its importance to the lords of Inchiquin in the late thirteenth century is shown by the fact that in 1288 the revenue it yielded represented almost 61 per cent of the total extent of the manor. The total burgages of the town amounted to 18 ploughlands or 2,160 customary acres which, in turn, represented as much as 4,560 (if not even more) statute acres lying both in the town itself and in the common fields adjacent to it which were held by the burgesses'.[21]

The nearby borough of Dungarvan had been founded 'some time about 1205 at latest'[22] by the English crown which 'seems to have made determined attempts to promote the fortunes of its new borough. This included, notably, the grant, made by King John on 3 July 1215 to his burgesses of Dungarvan, of all the liberties and free customs of Breteuil, the small Norman town whose liberties and customs became the model for so many of the smaller boroughs in England (particularly those in the west country) and in Ireland in the thirteenth century.'[23] Other grants by the crown followed, including a grant of pontage in 1308.[24] Thirteenth-century Dungarvan was a small but important borough and its revenues were far from insignificant. 'In the period October 1234 to October 1235 and Easter 1262 to Easter 1263, rent amounting, respectively, to £10.17s. and £13.14s. . . . accrued to the crown from the town of Dungarvan alone' while in 1282 an inquisition found that 'the burgesses of Dungarvan paid £13.17s.4d. yearly for their burgages'.[25] While other revenues accruing from the manor of Dungarvan seem to have declined in the second half of the thirteenth century, burgage rents appear to have maintained their value. Thus in 1298 an inquisition found that the burgesses of Dungarvan held '12 carcates in their burgages for which they paid a rent of £13.13s.4d. yearly'.[26] Dungarvan appears to have been 'a small borough with very many of its considerable burgages, if not the majority, lying outside the town in the common fields. As such it was similar to many Irish boroughs such as Sligo, Rindown and Roscommon.'[27] Although Dungarvan managed to survive in the difficult political and economic circumstances which obtained in the later middle ages (in that period its fortunes were strongly promoted by successive earls of Desmond into whose hands it had passed)[28] it 'never became really important as a port, although in the thirteenth century it appeared possible that it might and in the later fifteenth century attempts were made to develop its trade.'[29] Indeed, in common with other port towns in the region, the late fifteenth century saw renewed economic activity and overseas trade in Dungarvan and its port[30] and in the late sixteenth century, in the course of the English conquest of Ireland, Dungarvan became a centre of considerable strategic importance.

The origins of Kinsale are more obscure but the growth and development of the town seems to have occurred in the course of the thirteenth century following the settlement of the area by the de Courcys. That settlement appears to have been begun by the early thirteenth century.[31] The port of Kinsale is likely to have developed by the early fourteenth century. A glimpse of the embryonic port is given by an escheator's account for the period 1301-06 which refers to the taking of a prisage of fish by the widow of Miles de Courcy at Ringrone and Kinsale in 1300. By the end of the century it was significant and enjoyed an active overseas trade.[32]

As part of the process of conquest and settlement in the late twelfth and thirteenth centuries many existing towns or proto-towns were revitalised and many new boroughs were established. In the Cork region the city of Cork was pre-eminent. It and the town of Youghal are examples of proto-towns which developed rapidly in new political and economic conditions, while Dungarvan is a striking example of a newly-founded borough. The development of the city of Cork is as follows:

> The potential of the seaport trading towns, founded by the Vikings about the late ninth or early tenth centuries, was recognized by the English monarchy from the outset of the conquest and settlement of much of Ireland. Thus, Dublin, Waterford, Cork and Limerick were reserved to the crown and, accordingly, became royal boroughs. In granting the kingdom of Cork and the whole demesne of Desmond to Robert fitz Stephen and Miles de Cogan in 1177, Henry II retained to the English crown in perpetuity the city of Cork and the lands of the Ostmen adjacent to it ... At the time of the Anglo-French invasion ... Cork consisted of a mixed settlement of Irish and Hiberno-Vikings ... The Hiberno-Vikings were traders and their overseas commerce brought about the development of the port of Cork which 'before the twelfth century ... was very small, and not very important.' With the coming of the Anglo-French invaders in the late twelfth century a whole new process of development was set in train. The Mac Carthy kings were displaced in the Cork area and fitz Stephen and de Cogan embarked on the sub-infeudation of their newly-acquired lands and the introduction of the manorial economy. The Hiberno-Viking settlement at Cork appears not to have been disturbed by the change of regime but certainly became subject to the ultimate authority of the English crown. In turn, the crown promoted the fortunes of the city of Cork and its port. This development was further facilitated by both the strategic importance of Cork for the political settlement imposed by the invader and the rapid economic growth, reflected in agriculture and commerce, which the twelfth and thirteenth centuries witnessed in Europe as a whole.[33]

Development

The development of the Irish boroughs in this period, therefore, must be seen as part of a wider European phenomenon. Building on the foundations well laid in the twelfth century, the thirteenth century witnessed a rapid and impressive growth in borough status, economy and privilege. In this process several distinct but interconnected elements can be discerned. All of these, from the late twelfth and early thirteenth century onwards, shaped the history of the boroughs in the feudalised area of the Cork region.[34]

First, there was an increasing emancipation of the borough and its inhabitants from control by, or interference on the part of, local landowners (that is feudal or other territorial lords) and, in the case of royal boroughs such as Cork, even by the crown itself. Second, as a consequence of that emancipation, the inhabitants of the boroughs, the burgesses, increasingly acquired the right freely to dispose of the lands which they held in the boroughs, that is to say the lands they held by burgage tenure; in other words they were emancipated also from the constraints and rigidity of feudal land tenure. Third, as their economic importance increased with the expansion and growth of trade (a striking feature of the thirteenth-century economy in Europe as a whole), the political power of the boroughs grew accordingly. In this way the boroughs were further emancipated from seigneurial, even royal, control and, as important centres of settlement, by extending even further their urban privileges, liberties and immunities in the later middle ages they developed to a greater degree their autonomy and legal personality.

In summary, we can say that if any borough was to prosper in the period, in addition to generating significant economic activity without which there could be no prosperity, it needed certain basic liberties and privileges. These can be described broadly as legal and jurisdictional, on the one hand, and social and economic, on the other, but they were, of course, completely interconnected. They were merely different facets of urban autonomy. It was essential that the borough, great or small, should be empowered to administer its own affairs in accordance with powers delegated to it. In the case of a major borough such as Cork that entailed self-government under the crown whereby the borough would be free of the direct jurisdiction of the various royal officials (most especially the sheriff) appointed by the crown to administer local government.

In the matter of law and jurisdiction, it was also essential that the burgesses should have their own borough court (the hundred court as it was called in England and Ireland) which would have competence in regard to such matters as suits concerning debts and pledges of all kinds – a most important matter in the context of trade and commerce – as well as suits concerning borough tenements. With regard to the latter, it should be said that liberty to dispose of borough lands and tenements at will and to convey them to others differentiated these burgage tenements from those land holdings subject to the provisions of feudal land tenure prescribed both by law and custom. Freedom in the matter of conveyance of real (or fixed) property was, of course, a liberty at law, but it was also an economic freedom. By the thirteenth century it was axiomatic that burgesses should have full control over their property, both real and personal, and this notion formed part of the developing mercantile or bourgeois ethos. Equally, the right of the burgesses to establish in their boroughs merchant guilds to control and regulate trade and to enjoy a virtual monopoly of trade therein was accepted and increasingly established.[35] Thus, legal and jurisdictional rights were closely bound up with social and economic privileges and they were increasingly strengthened by and reflected in borough charters.

Towns such as these, especially the major port towns, were utterly dependent for their survival on the surplus production of agriculture, both pastoral and arable. First, they needed to obtain foodstuffs from their agricultural hinterland and, second, much of their trade, including their overseas trade, consisted of the products of agriculture. For example, in the thirteenth and early fourteenth centuries, the principal Irish exports (apart from fish which seems to have been a constant export throughout the later middle ages) were wool, wool-fells and hides and cereals such as wheat and oats. Equally, in the same period, Ireland's staple imports included wine (especially from Gascony) and woollen cloth (especially from England). Both of these commodities, of course, were, either immediately or ultimately, the product of agriculture or husbandry. The sale of these commodities stimulated the trade of the Irish boroughs, but most especially the trade of the major seaport towns through which they were imported or exported. In the case of the smaller boroughs the trade was essentially local in scale, but many of these boroughs were particularly important as centres for collecting local produce for sale to the merchants of the major seaport trading towns who, in turn, exported it or, equally, as centres through which the same merchants could distribute and sell goods and merchandise which they imported through the seaports or which they bought from foreign traders there.

Markets and fairs

Not infrequently, lords, who established boroughs on their lands, sought from the crown licence to establish in them a weekly market or, in the case of the more important boroughs, a yearly fair. This was done in order to promote the economic fortunes of the borough and, thereby, enhance the lord's revenues. These smaller markets and market towns, which sprang up in the course of the thirteenth century particularly, constituted an extensive network of commercial traffic and an important part of the infrastructure of the growing agrarian and mercantile economy. Some examples can be cited to illustrate this important development in the Cork region [Fig. 6.2].

In 1234 Maurice fitz Gerald was granted royal licence to hold a weekly market every Saturday at his town of Youghal and a yearly fair there from 28 September to 12 October.[36] On 25 September of the same year David de Barry obtained licences to establish a weekly market, to be held every Saturday, and a yearly fair, to be held from 17 to 24 October, at his town of Buttevant and a weekly market, to be held on Tuesday, at Carrigtohill.[37]

Many similar markets and fairs were established throughout county Cork, and indeed much of Ireland (the grant of the right to hold a yearly fair for eight days from 31 July to 7 August made by Henry III to Dungarvan in 1242 is a case in point)[38] in the course of the thirteenth century, although, not infrequently, evidence of the date of their foundation has not survived. Often we have only indirect evidence of their existence as, for example, when disputes arose concerning them. The market and fair at Philip de Barry's borough of Innishannon, county Cork, appears to be such a case. Both the market and fair certainly existed by 1256 since in that year the burgesses of the city of Cork were in dispute with Philip in the king's court regarding that market and fair.[39] Disputes of this kind were far from unusual because tensions, usually generated by trading competition, between rival boroughs were commonplace and often militated against joint action in pursuance of common interests. Thus in the thirteenth century there appears to have been constant competition between Cork and Youghal. Likewise in 1290 the burgesses of Shandon, which belonged to John de Cogan and Maurice de Rochford, complained to Edward I that the citizens of Cork were preventing them from trading as they were wont to trade.[40] Plainly, Shandon, because it lay in very close proximity to Cork, was overshadowed and dominated by the latter.

While the most important markets and all the fairs were associated with the major boroughs, some smaller markets not associated with boroughs also existed. An example of such a market was that which, at the end of the thirteenth century or the beginning of the fourteenth, apparently existed at Kyl or Kyleocofthy near Clonakilty.[41] That the growth of market towns in the Cork region in the thirteenth century was extensive can be noted from a list of them drawn up by the sheriff of Cork in June 1299.[42] These ports and market towns included the city of Cork and the towns of Timoleague, Carrigtohill, Buttevant, Ballyhay (near Charleville), Midleton, Castlemartyr, Cloyne, Mogeely, Tallow, Corkbeg (on Cork Harbour, south-east of Cobh), Glanworth, Castlelyons, Shandon, Mallow, Bridgetown (south of Castletownroche on the river Blackwater), Ballynamona (south of Mallow, near Mourneabbey), Carrig (between Mallow and Killavullen), Kilworth, Mitchelstown, Ballynoe (south-east of Fermoy), Carrigrohane (on the river Lee, west of Cork city), Ballinacurra (at the mouth of the river Owencurra, south of Midleton), Doneraile, Dunbulloge (north of Cork city), Innishannon (on the river Bandon, north-east of Bandon), Grenagh (near Rathduff), Ballyhooly (east of Mallow), Kinsale, Ringrone (south-east of Kinsale), Ringcurran (beside Kinsale), Athnowen (or St Mary, Owen or Ovens), Castlemore, Ballinaboy (south-west of Cork city), Carrigaline, Douglas and 'del Fayth' (namely the bishop's town in the present Barrack St./Dean St. area of Cork city). In addition, in the course of *quo warranto* inquiries,[43] markets were said to function at Dunnamark near Bantry (this is one of the few markets known to have existed in west Cork) and at Uí Fhearghusa (north-west of Youghal on the present Waterford-Cork border). In the same inquiries fairs were said to exist at Buttevant, Carrigtohill, Castlelyons, Timoleague, Innishannon and Ballynamona. A striking feature of this distribution of market towns is the concentration of them in mid and east Cork. This is not surprising since these areas were the most manorialised (and as such the areas of most intensive arable agriculture) in the Cork region and the territory of county Cork in which the conquest and settlement had taken deepest root [Fig. 6.2].

The cluster of market towns, diffused principally throughout north and east county Cork, were all strategically placed and together these boroughs and markets constituted an extensive network of commercial traffic. Not infrequently they were situated on or at important inland routes, the fordable points of rivers (Carrigrohane is a case in point) or at locations on the coast where they afforded access to the sea for towns or like settlements further inland (Kinsale, Ringrone, Ringcurran, Ballynacorra, and Corkbeg are examples of this kind of settlement). As already indicated, before too long Kinsale was to become in its own right an important seaport in county Cork and, as such, ranked with Youghal and the port of Cork, all three of which became important regional centres of maritime trade. Moreover, the ports of Kinsale, Cork, and Youghal were at the mouths of three major Munster river networks (respectively, the Bandon, the Lee, and the Blackwater). This gave these centres an important geographical advantage in that heavy and bulky cargo, such as timber, which could not be conveyed overland, could be transported by water to them and shipped overseas. 'Internal trading routes, radiating outwards from the seaport towns in county

Cork linked those ports with the market towns of the county and even with towns further afield. (The established trading route between the port of Cork and the town of Kilmallock, county Limerick, is a case in point.) Together these boroughs and markets constituted an extensive network of commercial traffic.'[44]

Some of these market towns, such as Shandon and 'del Fayth', which now are part of Cork city, at the end of the thirteenth century were separate boroughs whose interests could also conflict with those of the city of Cork and its burgesses. The conflict, in matters of trade, between Cork city and Shandon has already been noted. Others which were situated quite close to Cork city (Douglas and Carrigaline are instances of this) show how localised some kinds of trading activity could be. Timoleague, the port and market furthest to the west in the list drawn up in 1299 (although, as already indicated, apparently not the only market in west county Cork at that time), evidently was an important local market and, in all probability, an active local port.

Together these market towns (and it must be noted that there were boroughs which did not attract markets) show how far manorial organisation had proceeded, particularly in north and east county Cork, as part of the general pattern of settlement in the century or so following the Anglo-French invasion. This was a complex process in which, not infrequently, newly-established centres could rest on and overlay existing structures. It has been pointed out that 'the indissoluble link between the landholding system and the foundation of urban settlements in Ireland is central to an understanding of the historical settlement geography of the period and the influence of the pre-existing framework must always be borne in mind when discussing the distribution and location of the medieval towns of the island'.[45]

Trade and the underlying economy

New and extensive settlement, agricultural and urban, helped to promote the considerable economic growth which thirteenth-century Ireland witnessed; economic development in this period was boosted also by the inflow of settlers and increased population to which reference has already been made. With agricultural innovation and increased profitability, which encouraged the growth of demesne farming, a vast surplus of corn was available for export from much of Ireland in the thirteenth and early fourteenth centuries. Other factors also promoted overseas trade. Thus:

> political developments in the period also had important economic
> consequences. With the creation of the English lordship of Ireland
> by Henry II, Ireland became part of the dominions of the crown of

England. This intensified existing trading and cultural links with England, especially Chester, Bristol and (later) other developing ports in the English west country such as Bridgwater, and with Gascony (for long a source of wine supply for Ireland) and Normandy, which likewise had an established pattern of trade with Ireland. The political connection with England had economic effects in other ways also. Irish commerce was further promoted, particularly in the later thirteenth and early fourteenth centuries, by an influx of Italian merchant bankers who acted as tax collectors for the English crown. In this capacity, they collected in Ireland, as in England, the Great or Ancient Custom, which was imposed by Edward I on the export of wool, woolfells and hides in 1275. Quite quickly they extended their activities beyond tax gathering and engaged in large scale, not least speculative, trading ventures.

Irish overseas trade extended beyond the dominions of the English crown and, in the course of the thirteenth century particularly, an extensive trading network linking Ireland with important commercial centres in continental Europe was developed. The basic trading area on the European mainland extended from the Low Countries to south-west France, although activity appears to have been more concentrated on the latter region.[46]

Trade, therefore, played a particularly important part in the development of the Irish towns, particularly the seaport towns. Cork, Youghal and Kinsale owed much, as seaport towns, to their feudal overlords (in the case of Cork, the English crown), on the one hand, and to the economic revolution of the thirteenth century, on the other. While the growth of urban autonomy was not absolutely necessary for the development of trade, certainly the intensification of trade was essential for urban development. In practice, the two phenomena were closely interlinked. Trade and commerce, on the scale which the thirteenth century produced, required the coming into being of professional merchants operating within a new framework totally freed from the constraints of feudalism. The town was an essential component of that framework and increasingly came to be dominated by an urban patriciate comprised of the greater merchants.[47]

The various commodities set out in the murage grant made to Cork in 1284[48] 'may reasonably be taken to contain all the most important [goods traded in the city], many of which can be corroborated from other sources.'[49] The commodities exported from the port of Cork (and similar commodities were exported from Youghal, at that time, and from Kinsale, slightly later), as set out in that grant, may be categorised as follows: wool, wool-fells and hides and skins of wild animals; manufactured goods such as Irish cloth and Irish frieze mantles (for which there was a constant demand overseas). They also included beef (although this does not appear to have been a significant export in the later middle ages, cattle being valued more for their hides than their flesh) and fish (particularly herring, salmon, conger, ling, hake and milwell or cod). Animals such as oxen, cows, horses, hogs, pigs, sheep and goats were exported; also cereals (particularly wheat) and oatmeal, timber and boards (especially shipboards and staves for the manufacture of barrels).

Commonly imported products consisted of the following: wine; English and French cloth; canvas; manufactured goods, such as utensils and mercury; spices (such as pepper) and dyestuffs (such as alum and woad). In addition, certain kinds of merchandise (such as wax and honey) which could be either imported or exported are listed.

In summary, the principal Irish exports in the thirteenth and early fourteenth centuries, apart from fish, were wool, wool-fells and hides. Substantial quantities of these were exported through the major ports. An example will illustrate this traffic in the Cork region. In 1335, Vincent Percival, Nicholas Hemmyng, Sinolda la Mercer and Adam Recche, burgesses and merchants of Cork, freighted in Cork a ship, called le Rudecog of Howth, with wool, wool-fells and hides to be transported to Normandy.[50]

From 1275 onwards these exports were taxed. We have considerable, though by no means complete, information regarding receipts from the Great Custom.[51] Some figures will illustrate the scale of this trade in the period 1275 to 1345. It should be emphasised that these figures are likely to understate the total volume of exports, since they are incomplete, and, in any event, the receipts do not include merchandise successfully smuggled abroad.[52]

In the period 1275 to 1340, £5369. 4s. 6d. accrued to the Irish exchequer from the equivalent of some 4,425,810 fleeces exported from the port of Cork, while in the same period, £870. 18s. 5d. accrued from the export of the equivalent of some 805,737 fleeces from the neighbouring port of Youghal. However, the accounts for the period September 1278 to October 1279 conflate the returns from both Cork and Youghal. Thus, receipts of £442. 16s. 2¾d., which would represent some 398,531 fleeces, were paid into the exchequer. In the light of the general pattern of payments, it is reasonable to surmise that most of the money accrued in the port of Cork. The port of Dingle exported the equivalent of at least 72,105 fleeces, yielding a customs revenue of £81. 4s. 6½d., in the period 1277 to 1302. Dingle is important in this context. Although not, of course, part of the Cork region, it was one of the cluster of ports in the south and south-west of Ireland (the others were Cork, Kinsale, Youghal, and Dungarvan, now familiar to us from the preceding account) which, in the course of the fourteenth and fifteenth centuries, came under the control of the earls of Desmond.[53]

The total value of receipts from the Great Custom from all twelve Irish ports, for which we have information, in the above period was £27,335. 10s. 9d. which would represent approximately 24,713,395 fleeces. Of the total amount received, about 6,320 accrued in the ports of Cork, Youghal and Dingle. This sum would represent some 5,702,183 fleeces exported. Accordingly, customs receipts and exports from Cork, Youghal and Dingle represented 23 per cent of the total from all twelve Irish ports. Dingle's contribution, however, was quite small and does not affect the picture greatly. If Dingle is excluded, then the ports of Cork and Youghal together generated a customs revenue of about £6,240, the equivalent of about 5,231,547 fleeces or 21 per cent of the total exported from all twelve ports. It is, nonetheless, clear from the figures that the port of Cork was preeminent in this region (certainly as far as these exports are concerned in the period); its exports of wool, wool-fells and hides constituted about 18 per cent of the total known to have been exported from all twelve ports. Indeed, of the leading five ports of the twelve, Cork ranked third, closely following New Ross and Waterford (the south-east together with the river valleys of the Suir, Nore and Barrow was another Irish region profoundly affected by the revolution in pastoral husbandry and arable agriculture in the thirteenth century) but considerably ahead of Drogheda and Dublin, while Youghal ranked appreciably lower. It ranked sixth, but the value of its exports represented only 28 per cent or so of the value of those of Dublin which ranked fifth in order of magnitude. Finally, Dingle, with only 0.3 per cent of the total, was very much lower down the scale, being followed only by Wexford with about 0.25 per cent.

However, for the reasons already stated together with the fact that they relate only to the export of wool, wool-fells and hides, the only commodities which attracted the Great Custom, these figures must be treated with caution. The picture they present should not be regarded as absolute. Above all, they must not be viewed as an indicator of the relative ranking of Irish ports over the later medieval period as a whole. For example, both Youghal and Wexford, which it would seem barely feature as wool, wool-fell and hide exporters in the thirteenth century, were major Irish trading ports in the later fifteenth and earlier sixteenth centuries.[54]

Thus the total receipt from Cork exports is very impressive (and Cork was only one of the exporting ports) and testifies strongly to the advance of the manorial, agricultural economy in Ireland, not least in the south and south-east, in the thirteenth century. Clearly, there was substantial clearance of woodland with a consequential development of pastoral husbandry as well as arable agriculture. Woodland clearance would also account for the considerable quantities of timber and shipboards available for export, notably in the thirteenth century but also in the later fifteenth and sixteenth centuries, a point developed below. However, Irish wool was inferior to English wool. In Flanders, for example, English, Scottish and Irish wool were ranked in that order as regards quality. Irish wool, therefore, was often mixed with the better quality English. In England, demand for Irish wool was not very great. It was at its strongest when there was a shortage in English supplies due to, for example, the outbreak of disease such as murrain in sheep.[55] About 1350, for example, John de Wynchedon, John Mably, Robert Droup, John Lombard, John Codde and Andrew Kynald, all merchants of Cork, shipped wool to England for sale. However, the wool remained unsold because of its poor quality and it was, therefore, re-exported to Flanders.[56]

By contrast with wool, there was a strong demand for Irish hides, not only in continental Europe but in England also. Since Ireland, most especially Gaelic Ireland, was rich in cattle, there was a constant source of supply throughout the middle ages. Thus 'there was ... a flourishing trade with Italy, especially in the hides which went to supply the leather industry there. Enormous numbers of hides were exported annually, reflecting the huge herds of cattle which were such a dominant feature of the Irish country scene.'[57] Indeed, the Cork region continued to be a major supplier of cattle produce into modern times.[58] Therefore, despite the impressive export of wool and wool-fells, particularly in the late thirteenth and early fourteenth centuries, hides (especially cattle hides) probably featured more strongly in Irish exports over the later medieval period as a whole, although we have not sufficient statistical material with which to attempt to quantify hide exports. The equally strong development of arable agriculture in the thirteenth century is indicated by, for example, the substantial quantities of cereals produced. Some of this production was used to feed the growing urban population especially, but considerable quantities were available also for export. Thus agricultural and urban development were closely interlinked.

By the late thirteenth and early fourteenth centuries, Ireland was a major producer of cereals, especially oats, wheat and barley. 'It appears ... that in the thirteenth century large areas of arable land were held in demesne and cultivated by tenants-in-chief, and it is clear that at the same time a considerable amount of land was brought under the plough

Plate 5.1   Youghal (Cork Archaeological Survey).

and improved agricultural methods were introduced with a consequent expansion in the production of cereals, so that by the middle of the century a large surplus was available for export'.[59] The enhanced prospect of profit was a major stimulus to production: 'there can be no doubt that the demesne lands on the manors were worked for profit. Much of the grain produced and many of the animals raised were intended for market. Naturally the home market consumed much of the available surplus, but a surprisingly large amount was exported. Many religious houses in Britain, and even France, procured considerable quantities of wheat and oats in Ireland, often from manors which belonged to them or to their Irish daughter houses. Merchants bought Irish grain for export. There was a particularly lively trade with Gascony, and especially with Bordeaux, where wine provided a profitable return cargo'.[60] This vast expansion in cereal production is clear also from the amount purveyed in Ireland to the king's use, principally to supply the royal armies in their campaigns in Wales, Scotland, and Gascony. As J. F. Lydon has pointed out, 'Ireland proved herself one of the king's great storehouses of grain, if not the main one'.[61]

The royal purveyors were active in many regions of the east and south of Ireland and considerable quantities of provisions were sent to the king's armies through Irish ports including Cork and Youghal. Some examples illustrate the character of this traffic. In 1295 the Irish administration was instructed to obtain as quickly as possible ten or twelve or more shiploads of good wheat and oats from merchants in the areas around Cork and Youghal and to send them to the royal army in Gascony.[62] In the same year 'a great quantity of wheat, wine and other victuals were shipped to Wales from Dublin, Cork and Youghal.'[63] In the same year also, in connection with the Welsh war, 'a merchant of Youghal, Peter de Parys (or Paris) ... was appointed [by Edward I] to supervise all the shipping arrangements [in Ireland], to seize the necessary vessels [to transport supplies] and to persuade or impress criminals and "malefactors" to serve as mariners. Two weeks after his appointment de Parys was ordered to seize thirty or forty ships to carry these supplies which gives us some idea of the volume of provisions which Edward expected to be shipped from Ireland.'[64] In 1296-7 the same Peter de Paris was engaged in arranging the shipping of a large amount of wheat and oats from the Irish ports to Gascony.[65] In that period, supplies of corn were sent to Gascony from, among other ports, Cork and Youghal. Thus in March 1297 the *Grace Dieu* of Cork and the *Snake* brought, respectively, 340 quarters and 250 crannocks[66] of wheat from Cork to Gascony, while, in the same month, 14 quarters of wheat and 259 quarters of oats and 410 quarters of wheat were shipped to Gascony from Youghal on, respectively, the *God's Ship* and

La Cogge Sancti Spiritus of Youghal. In the following year and in 1299 wheat, oats, wines, meat, fish and other victuals were purveyed at Cork, Youghal and Waterford and elsewhere in Munster for the king's expedition to Scotland,[67] while 'between January and March 1302 wine to the value of £237.4.5. was shipped from Cork'.[68]

In addition to supplies of victuals (principally grain such as wheat and oats, legumes such as peas and beans, fish, especially dried fish, and wine) purveyed to the king's use in mounting these military campaigns, shipping was also provided by the Irish seaport towns (the activities of Peter de Paris in this regard have already been noted). In 1301, for example, the following towns were instructed to provide for the war in Scotland the following numbers of ships: Cork (2), Waterford (1), Dublin (1), Youghal (3), New Ross (2) and Drogheda (1).[69]

The royal purveyors in individual ports were usually drawn from the ranks of the urban patriciate which consisted of the prominent merchants of the town. In the period 1299 to 1300 John de Wynchedon, whose background will be examined presently, and Walter Reych or Reyht, mayor of Cork, were royal purveyors in that city of victuals which were to be sent to the royal army in Scotland, while in the same period John de Pembroke and John Brun acted in a similar capacity in Youghal.[70] With William Pollard, John de Wynchedon was again assigned to act in Cork in the period 1300 to 1301.[71]

Although purveyance was not trade, strictly speaking, the vast quantities of cereals and other foodstuffs involved point to the production in Ireland, not least in the Cork area, of a considerable surplus which could be available for trade, while the availability of large quantities of imported commodities, such as wine, likewise purveyed to the king's use, testifies to a greatly increased supply of these products as a result of a vast expansion in overseas trade. As Lydon has pointed out:

> it is important for us to realise that the economy of Ireland in the thirteenth century was sufficiently advanced to enable the Anglo-Norman colony there to participate in the military enterprises of the king. Internal commerce and overseas trade, particularly the wine trade with the continent, were necessary pre-requisites for such participation. Towns and ports, merchant companies and traders, agriculture of a high order were equally important; without them the king's commissariat could never have been organized. A flourishing commercial and agricultural society meant also that the prosperity of the country was such that the royal income was not insufficient to meet the government's needs,

and even provided a surplus of money which could be utilised by the king outside Ireland. Finally, the degree of order which prevailed throughout the colony was sufficiently high to allow the resources of the country to be applied to external affairs.[72]

The merchant classes

John de Wynchedon was a member of one of the leading merchant families in Cork in the later middle ages. Some biographical details demonstrate the continuing importance of this patrician and mercantile family and, by extension, the class to which he belonged. One of John de Wynchedon's sons, Richard, flourished in the middle years of the fourteenth century.[73] Richard's son, another John, apparently was even more prominent in commerce, law and public life.[74] As already indicated, he was a member of a consortium which exported wool to England and Flanders about 1350. In 1346 he had been appointed one of the supervisors of the keepers of the peace in county Cork, and in December 1358 he was appointed one of the keepers of the peace in that county. Earlier that year he had been commissioned to hear and arbitrate a dispute between Miles de Courcy and his tenants, on the one hand, and Richard Óg Barrett, on the other. In the period 1355-7 he had been directed to have an inquisition made in county Cork and in 1355 he acted as an attorney. In 1356 he was involved in litigation involving the assize of novel disseisin, while his commercial and financial activities are further indicated by the fact that, in 1358, he was engaged in a suit for the recovery of a debt of 109s. 3d. His son, also Richard,[75] was one of the justices of gaol delivery in Cork in 1372 and apparently again in 1381-82. In 1382 he was also one of those appointed to sell 1,000 cows which had been paid as a fine to the king by Richard Óg Barrett who was strongly established in Muskerry. Richard de Wynchedon's son, John, who was given letters of protection in 1386, was accused of various (unspecified) felonies in 1392 and was pardoned of them about 1406. Nonetheless, his public service activities were significant. In 1401 and 1410 he was engaged in the taking of the assize of novel disseisin. In 1404, with two other prominent Cork merchants and burgesses John Galwey and William Gowlys, he was commissioned to enquire into the conduct of the king's officials in counties Cork and Limerick. In September 1408, with Thomas son of John earl of Desmond, he was appointed a justice in counties Cork, Limerick and Kerry. Finally, towards the end of the reign of Henry IV (1399-1413), he was one of the collectors of the king's customs in the port of Cork. Little further is known about the de Wynchedon family until, it would seem, the late fifteenth century when we catch additional glimpses of them. In 1480, for example, a William de

Wynchedon was active in Cork's trade with Bristol.[76] Indeed, a landgable roll for Cork, which seems to date from the fifteenth century, contains a Thomas, a William and a John de Wynchedon.[77]

The John de Wynchedon of the late thirteenth and early fourteenth centuries was prominent in the ranks of the urban patriciate of Cork. That situation is clearly reflected in the terms of his will,[78] dated at Cork 6 July 1306, not only in regard to the amount and value of property which he devised, but also in relation to his social standing generally to which his role as a major urban benefactor testifies. Thus in addition to bequests made to his children, to various friends and business associates (these latter throw much light on the close personal and commercial bonds linking the great town merchants, a factor which contributed to the maintenance of their urban hegemony) and to his servants and retainers, different sums of money were left to the principal Cork churches and to other ecclesiastical bodies and institutions. These latter may be summarised as follows.

In addition to various amounts given for the maintenance of individual priests, the sum of £10. 1s. was provided for the fabric-fund or other capital costs of the following churches in Cork city and Shandon: the parish church of St Finbar,[79] the church of the Holy Trinity,[80] the priory church of the Augustinian friars,[81] the church of St Peter,[82] the church of St Katharine of Shandon,[83] the church of St Mary of Shandon,[84] the church of St John (the Baptist),[85] the church and leper house of St Mary Magdalen, Shandon,[86] the church of St Philip,[87] the church of St Brigid,[88] the church of St Stephen and the lazar house and friary of St Stephen.[89]

John de Wynchedon, apparently, was survived by seven sons and three daughters. One son, Richard, whose career has already been briefly reviewed, was one of the executors of the will (the other two being William de Hardepie (or Hardepirie) and William of Youghal, whose wife was a beneficiary) and, therefore, may have been the eldest. To him de Wynchedon bequeathed 'the holding of Robert Coffyn' (Coffyn likewise was one of the beneficiaries) and £22 'out of the revenues from the administration of my estates and those properties held [by us] in common' and 'the proportion of all animals [that is livestock] belonging to me which are in the hands of William Martin and John Gwgyn' together with one-third 'of the house of which William Sage held possession'. Another son, William, was given a stone house near the church of the Holy Trinity, Cork, while another stone house, adjacent to the above, went to a further son, Nicholas.

Reference to stone houses reflects the trend towards more construction in stone which seems to have begun about the late thirteenth or early fourteenth centuries. 'The earliest houses built within the medieval town [of Cork] ... were constructed of timber and roofed with either thatch or timber shingles. Floors consisted of brushwood, wickerwork matting or spreads of gravel trampled into the underlying peat .... Beginning in about 1300 and continuing on into the next century many of the timber houses of the main street frontage began to be rebuilt in stone with slate or stone tiles replacing the thatch or timber shingles as roofing materials. Floors of brushwood, wickerwork matting and gravel were replaced by stone flags, cobbles or timber flooring. The main street and some of the lanes may have been surface dressed with stone chippings or gravel on a regular basis. Stone built drains and sewers were put in to remove more efficiently and hygienically rainwater, waste and sewage and these drains were eventually extended out to and probably through the town wall to empty into the open water channel beyond'.[90]

Two other sons, Walter and Thomas, were given possession of, respectively, a 'holding in Dungarvan[91] which I bought from Helena de Stackpol' and 'my holding which I purchased in the street of St John the Evangelist, Cork.' In addition, two sons, Adam and John, who were, respectively, Franciscan and Dominican friars (both of these religious orders together with the Augustinians were particularly favoured in the will and received various charitable bequests) were given £5 each. Indeed, a striking feature of the will is the way it reflects the importance in the religious and civic life of Cork which the orders of friars had attained by the end of the thirteenth century. A comparison with contemporary developments in France is particularly useful here. In France, these mendicant orders were especially attracted to the towns and they both reflected the growth of the town in the thirteenth century and further shaped its development.[92]

Finally, one daughter, Alice, was given three marks, while £10 went to the remaining two daughters, Isabel and Ellen. None of the daughters received a bequest of fixed property. In devising his fixed property, de Wynchedon followed the principle of the entail which in later medieval England and Ireland increasingly was used to secure greater control over the descent of real property and, particularly, to ensure that it would not permanently be alienated from the main body of the estate.[93] Thus his will stipulated the following: 'I likewise will and do ordain that my children, to whom I have bequeathed houses or holdings under the terms of this instrument, retain them for themselves during their own and their offsprings' lives, with the proviso that if they die without issue, the said houses and tenements shall revert to my heirs.'

The principal secular beneficiaries of de Wynchedon's will, apart from his children and servants, were Clarice and Alice, daughters of William Curcle, John Malros, William Granger, Roger Hemd and his wife, Adam le Smal, Audeon le Barbour, Philip Millar, Robert Coffyn, William Demet, Warin Vallens (that is Wallens or Walshe), John son of Walter Reich (or Reyht), 'whom I sponsored at the baptismal font', Alice Vaceryn, John de Baddeby and the wife of William of Youghal. The witnesses were Martin Moryn, Nicholas le Mercer and Stephen Cole, all citizens of Cork. At least some of these people were prominent in Cork's mercantile and civic life. For example, John de Baddeby paid the fee farm of the city to the Irish exchequer in 1292,[94] while William of Youghal made similar payments in 1309 and 1310.[95] William de Hardepirie, Nicholas le Mercer and Stephen Cole were among the controllers of the new custom in the port of Cork in 1302-04,[96] a position which testifies strongly to their mercantile status.

An inventory of de Wynchedon's assets and their value reveals that he was possessed of considerable stock in trade and other goods, particularly cereals and livestock, having a total value of £169. 19s. 8d. The following are the details of these goods: 87 acres of wheat worth £13. 1s.; 100 acres of oats worth £15; 10 acres of barley and peas worth £1. 10s.; 519 wethers worth £17. 6s.; 320 sheep worth £8; 38 oxen worth £76; 12 cows worth £34; nine horses worth £1. 16s.; two foals worth £2; nine sets of harness worth £1. 6s. 8d. In addition, debts due to him, by pledge or other written agreement, amounted to £377.

John de Wynchedon's will illustrates vividly the demographic, economic and physical growth which had taken place in Cork and the Cork region in the course of the thirteenth century. Both agricultural and urban settlement had greatly expanded. The development of agriculture and commerce had been facilitated by the growth of a commercial infrastructure of towns and markets. The major boroughs, such as Cork, had seen the emergence of a wealthy merchant class and an urban patriciate. Likewise, these boroughs had experienced a marked expansion in their autonomy and had acquired a defined legal personality which freed them from the constraints of feudal law and custom and, in particular, provided a legal framework for the solution of problems which particularly affected the urban merchant class, such as the securing and settlement of debts and the free disposition of real property. The will also testifies to the physical development of boroughs like Cork in the course of the century. A striking feature is the number of churches, both parish churches (in the fifteenth century Cork was reported to have eleven parishes)[97] and those belonging to the new mendicant orders of friars, which, it would seem, by Irish standards, were richly endowed and maintained. Likewise, the trend towards greater construction in stone, in both public works and domestic dwellings, is also reflected in the will. Together these are yardsticks of change, development and growing prosperity.

CRISIS OF THE ENGLISH LORDSHIP OF IRELAND: DECLINE, CONTRACTION AND INSTABILITY IN THE CORK REGION IN THE LATER MIDDLE AGES *c.* 1300-*c.* 1440

By the early fourteenth century, however, the English lordship of Ireland was already showing signs of crisis which deepened as the century progressed and continued until the early fifteenth century. The new conditions which now set in profoundly affected the politics, economy and society of the Cork region and placed its development on a different course. The causes of the crisis were both political and economic, but the two interacted on each other, producing a malaise far greater than either alone could have generated. The nature and scale of the fourteenth-century upheaval and its consequences are investigated in what follows.

Turbulence, crime and civil disobedience

The conquest of Ireland had never been complete and this made possible the later medieval Gaelic Irish resurgence and recovery. Henry II's disposition of the Mac Carthy kingdom of Cork had not been followed by either the total subjugation or the assimilation of the Gaelic Irish. Nevertheless, much of Munster had come under the control of the invader. 'It was in this way that Desmond was rapidly invaded ... with the Geraldines very much to the fore.' So successful were the invaders that 'on the whole this proved to be one of the most peacefully settled areas in feudal Ireland' and 'relations with the Mac Carthys remained good.' However, following the death of Cormac Finn Mac Carthaig trouble began as 'the settlers became enmeshed in a succession quarrel.' In the warfare which followed 'Desmond became a land of war' and much of the settlement was overthrown. Following the destruction of the royal army at Callan near Kenmare in 1261, Fingen Mac Carthaig destroyed 'the settlement on all sides' and, although he was killed in an attack on Kinsale, these events represent 'a great turning point in the history of Desmond' and 'there was no way in which the settlement could be restored'. Thus, 'when Thomas fitz Maurice came of age in 1282 an inquisition revealed that, while his lands in Kerry and Limerick were still valuable, those listed in Desmond were worth either 'nothing, for they all lie in the power of the Irish' or were worth a fraction of their former value 'as nearly the whole has been destroyed by the war of the Irish'. Gaelic Desmond was thereby made secure to the end of the middle ages and a massive contraction of the land of peace had taken place in the south-west of Ireland.[98]

In Thomond also, in the later thirteenth century, relations between the O'Brien rulers and the Anglo-Norman colony became increasingly inflamed as 'new grants further eroded their [the O'Briens'] position and feudal settlements were made across the Shannon.'⁹⁹ This unstable situation was compounded by the development of a 'great split among the O'Briens'. The internecine warfare which followed not only involved Gaelic Thomond but the colony also as 'Anglo-Irish as well were ranged on opposite sides.' The turning-point in Thomond was the killing of Richard de Clare by Muirchertach O'Brien at Dysert O'Dea in 1318. 'It was the virtual end of feudal Thomond, for though Quin was held for a brief period and Bunratty was kept up by the government, they were both taken by the O'Briens within a few years. To the end of the middle ages the O'Briens remained in control of Thomond.'¹⁰⁰

Thus 'there is no doubt that in the second half of the thirteenth century the land of peace ... began slowly to contract as a Gaelic resurgence enlarged the land of war .... Marchlands appeared in areas that formerly had been deep in the land of peace.'¹⁰¹ The revival of the Irish kingships was 'part of the new pattern that had emerged from the breakup of the old feudal structure which the settlers had imposed. The Dublin government, the English king, and the Gaill and Gaedhil alike now had to find a way of living within the new structure that was shaping Ireland.'¹⁰² The Gaelic revival in both Desmond and Thomond affected adversely the fortunes of the Anglo-Irish port towns of county Cork and the inland settlements, urban and agrarian, which had been so closely connected with them in the thirteenth century.

In Desmond the Mac Carthys continued to be a force to be reckoned with throughout the later middle ages, although from time to time they could be, and were, successfully resisted. For example, in 1298 and again in 1302 Domnall Óg Mac Carthy was forced to pay fines for his offences.¹⁰³ However, not infrequently, resistance entailed the launching of a full-scale military campaign. In December 1317 Dermot Mac Carthy, described as 'prince of the Irish of Desmond', was pardoned for his involvement in the Bruce invasion.¹⁰⁴ Among those pardoned with him, however, were certain Anglo-Irish, including Philip de Cogan. This latter development is one of the greatest importance for it marks the emergence of the 'rebel English' in later medieval Irish society. The 'rebel English', who appear in increasing numbers from the early fourteenth century on, not only aggravated the government's problem of enforcing the law but confused relations with Gaelic Ireland as well .... in the south Maurice fitz Thomas, later first earl of Desmond, was allied with O Briain and Mac Carthaig .... in Munster Barrys, Cogans, and Roches were only some of the great names listed as rebels'.¹⁰⁵

This development was greatly promoted by 'the disturbed state of the country' which 'resulted in a collapse of the rule of law in some localities. The courts became less active. The Dublin bench adjourned cases in 1316 because it was impossible for parties to get to the city without peril to their lives on account of the dangerous conditions on the roads to the city and the continuous presence of enemies'.[106] An increase in crime, lawlessness and general turbulence was a notable feature of the Irish lordship in the second decade of the fourteenth century, especially in the period 1315 to 1318, a period for which we have considerable information from which we can draw some useful (not least statistical) conclusions.

A recent study[107] has shown that 198 cases of homicide are recorded in the justiciary rolls for the period 1295 to 1318 and that the highest incidence of this felony (36 cases in all) occurred in 1318, a year which also saw the highest recorded incidence of larceny. Homicide 'accounts for 16.2 per cent of all felonies of which we have records in the period 1295-1314 and 18.3 per cent in the period 1314-18, a period which saw considerable turbulence and lawlessness.' This pattern is indicated clearly by the incidence of indictments: 'the percentage of larceny indictments rises in the early fourteenth century and accounts for 46.9 per cent of the total over the period 1295-1314 and for 51.7 per cent over the period 1314-1318'. In 1311, 74 of all the 139 indictments (or 53 per cent of the total) were concerned with larceny, while 1317 saw a similar pattern, namely 73 of the total 136 or 53 per cent.

A striking feature of this latter statistic, however, is that 45 of the total of 136 occurred in county Cork. Indeed, all statistics of serious crime in this period show a higher than average incidence in the Cork region. The incidence of arson in 1317 was highest in Cork which saw some 12 indictments in all. Cork was to the fore also in regard to an increasingly common crime in this period, namely the phenomenon 'of groups of men coming together with standards and banners displayed to flout the king's authority'. For example, in county Cork in 1312 certain men are recorded as having 'openly set themselves at war against the standard of the king with standards displayed' .... The participants involved in all of these cases appear to have made a point of being conspicuous and to [have] set themselves [openly] against the king's authority.' This whole pattern of increased and aggravated crime, especially in 1316 and 1317, produced 'a marked increase in the number of remittances and pardons granted to criminals indicted of crimes generally, but particularly in regard to larceny, burglary, homicide and receiving.' The Cork region was particularly important in relation to this development. 'A total of 1224 remittances are recorded for the period 1295-1318' of which 236 (or 19 per cent) were granted in 1316 and 863 (or 71 per cent) in 1317, 'the majority of the large scale remittances being found in Cork in 1316 and, especially, 1317'.

No doubt this factor reflected, as much as anything else, the degree to which the whole system of government and royal authority was coming under strain, not least in the southern region of the lordship, in the early fourteenth century. In these circumstances, not alone was the administration of law and justice rendered exceedingly difficult but also, when apprehended (not infrequently a difficult operation in itself), persons indicted of serious infractions of the law, including open rebellion, could be granted remittances. One suspects that the authorities simply could not cope with a breakdown of public order and government on this scale. For example, in 1317 'in one case involving 363 persons in Cork . . . a fine of £2,000 was imposed with the addition of the penalty of military service to be done in the future.' Furthermore, the system of remittances appears to have expanded in the second decade of the fourteenth century. Thus 'the number of remittances from 1310-1318 outnumbered the total number of indictments in the period 1295-1318. [The system of remittances] was a short-term solution to a political and legal problem of control that seemed insurmountable to the Irish authorities'. From all of this evidence, then, it can be concluded that 'crime in early fourteenth century Ireland was rising as a response to the political and socio-economic climate . . . of the time. The fact that the number of remittances and pardons [was] also experiencing an upward trend demonstrates the number of crimes which were not being called to justice due to administrative problems being experienced by the authorities'.

The malaise which now developed was greater than any which could have been caused simply by a soaring increase in crime and popular disturbance, important as they were. The emergence of the 'rebel English' as a significant force 'highlights the loosening of the feudal bond which was evident all over the lordship. Even in the thirteenth century something like a clan system was emerging in feudal Ireland. But it was the confusion of unending raids and wars and the lack of adequate governance that made the family bond important again. With it went 'bastard feudalism', which produced a new family based, not on the ties of blood, but on service and fees'.[108] These 'rebels were motivated in many different ways, though personal gain was always the main driving force. Mainly they seem to have been people who had little or no hope of fortune, being younger brothers or from cadet branches of lineages'.[109] These people were at the disposal of any magnate who was willing and able to muster them. One such magnate was Maurice fitz Thomas, an important figure in the politics of the Cork region and in Munster generally in the first half of the fourteenth century. He was created earl of Desmond in 1329 and 'his notorious career of crime and rebellion spanned the years from 1319 to 1346 ... His forays into east Cork and Waterford were more than simple raids, they were more in the nature of military campaigns: we read of his army moving forward with standards raised and flags flying. They brought him into violent conflict with Barrys, Cogans, and Roches, and ultimately with the Powers. Maurice had allies from those parts, too, and doubtless they were using him to work off old scores against local rivals.'[110]

The activities of the 'rebel English' added considerably to the general lawlessness and disorder of the fourteenth century. Moreover, this situation was compounded by the activities of the Gaelic Irish who could muster sufficient strength to threaten the colony and cause it grievous damage, not least economic, but who were never sufficiently strong a force to undermine it completely. Segmental rivalries among the Gaelic Irish prevented the emergence of a strong Gaelic power. Indeed, a recent seminal study of Anglo-Irish relations in the period from the late twelfth to the end of the fourteenth century[111] has pointed to 'the progressive crumbling that afflicted the provincial [Irish] kingships themselves in the course of the thirteenth century. As baronial power expanded, their wealth declined and their dynastic instability was exploited and intensified; this instability was to ensure that no O'Connor or O'Brien would be in a position to deliver the backing of Gaelic Connacht or Thomond to Edward Bruce during the Scottish invasion in the years 1315-18'. Accordingly, by the fourteenth century, 'there was ... no question of [the English chancery] conceding royal titles to the Irish as there might still have been in the 1240s; they are referred to as *duces, principales,* or merely by family name in the manner of clan chiefs.' Moreover, the level of population of the Gaelic Irish was inadequate to permit their overthrowing completely the colony, which at its core was (relative to the Gaelic Irish) quite strongly established, even had they wished to do so. The relationship between the Gaelic Irish and the colonists, neither of whom constituted monolithic groupings or represented monolithic interests, was complex. It ranged from serious political and economic contacts, which evidently were often quite amicable, to outright banditry and despoliation but, in regard to the latter, it must be emphasized that the activities of the Gaelic Irish did not differ in kind from those of the 'rebel English'.

As the influence of the English crown and its administration in Dublin declined, what the Cork region, like so much of Ireland, lacked in the fourteenth century was government by some established political authority. The absence of such an authority was a striking feature of political and economic life in the region in the fourteenth century. In the early fourteenth century 'constant disorders [were] associated with the de Cantetons and Roches in Wexford and Cork'.[112] The Cantetons (or Cauntons or de Cauntetons) were one of the great southern and

Munster lineages,[113] some members of which, notably Maurice, had become notorious felons even before the end of the thirteenth century.[114] Furthermore, 'through the 1320s Maurice fitz Thomas had used [his rout] to ravage the counties of Limerick, Cork and Waterford, allying himself with the Cantetons, and with Brian O'Brien of Thomond and Dermot Mac Carthy of Desmond.'[115] Again, in 1344-5, fitz Thomas, now earl of Desmond, was supported in Munster by 'members of his own kindred, headed by Thomas fitz John "the nephew", and followers with several Munster lineages such as Cauntons, St Aubyns, Cogans, and de Valles'[116] and was alleged to have 'formed a sworn confederacy with, among others, various de Mandevilles, Barrys, Cantetons and Mac Carthys to form a single "covin" against the king of England.'[117]

The role of the Mac Carthys in these events is particularly significant. Dermot MacCarthy, known as 'Mac Dermot' and a cousin of the reigning king of Desmond, and who became lord of Muskerry and Duhallow, was associated with Maurice fitz Thomas throughout his rebellious career.[118] In 1336 the justiciar, John Darcy, led an expedition against Dermot Mac Carthy, Domnall Mac Carthy and other 'felons' in county Cork.[119] Dermot Mac Carthy survived the military expedition against the first earl of Desmond in 1345-6 which resulted in Desmond's submission. However, Mac Carthy's fortunes began to wane following the appointment of Sir Thomas Rokeby as justiciar in 1349. Rokeby embarked on a campaign against Mac Carthy in September 1352.[120] 'Rokeby's own force was about 1,000 men at its largest, including a number of Irish in the later stages of the campaign, and he seems to have been joined by Cormac Mac Carthy of Desmond, acting independently .... The campaign was over by the end of January 1353 and had clearly been a complete success; the colonists were re-established in the valley of the Lee, and "Mac Dermot" was driven out of Muskerry. On 1 February Cormac Mac Carthy was granted extensive lands in Muskerry "among the woods", and though Mac Dermot's descendants continued to hold Duhallow the later lords of Muskerry were the descendants of Cormac's second son .... it is not surprising that after he [Rokeby] had been superseded in 1355 the mayor and citizens of Cork wrote to the king praising "the evident usefulness of his good works" and urging his reappointment.'[121] Rokeby had some success in Thomond also where he forced Mac Namara to submit (1352) and rebuilt the castle of Bunratty, but success in this region was very limited and the castle 'seems to have been lost again by 1355.'[122]

Expeditions of the kind mounted by Rokeby were not only expensive but also they were limited both in scope and duration, not least because increasingly the royal government lacked the resources of men, money and materials necessary to consolidate the gains of war even when campaigns were militarily successful. Accordingly, by 1358-9, only a few years after Rokeby's impressive military campaign in the Cork region, collectors had been appointed to ensure payment of the subsidy of 2s., to be levied on every carucate of cultivated land, granted to the king by the community of county Cork to fight the Irish enemies.[123] This renewed outbreak seems to have been due, at least in part, to the temporary eclipse in the power of the earldom of Desmond following the first earl's death in 1356 and that of his son, Maurice, in 1359 when it was reported that 'a great commotion and warlike disturbance [had been] raised by the Irish enemies and English rebels in Munster'.[124] If so, this development testifies strongly to one basic political fact which the circumstances and conditions obtaining in the region following the military defeat of the first earl of Desmond by the government in 1346 had made abundantly clear. Even after his defeat, Desmond continued to dispose of 'continuing power and influence' and both he and his successors were essential for the stability of their region.[125]

One may cite the following as examples of continued instability. In 1359 it was alleged that William son of John de Barry and Miles son of Miles de Courcy 'on account of certain supposed grievances, had invaded in a warlike manner the lands of Richard Og Barrett and others, and burned their houses'. Barry and de Courcy were ordered to desist from such activities and, rather, 'to seek for justice from the law, to which they had promised to submit.'[126] At the same time John de Wynchedon, Cormac Mac Carthy and others were assigned to investigate the dispute between the two parties, while the sheriff of Cork and the keepers of the peace there were directed to arrest the offenders. In 1365 Barrett was granted lands in Muskerry by the lieutenant, Lionel of Clarence, in the course of his campaign in the Cork region[127] but, in 1377, we hear of an expedition against the Barretts, described as 'rebels in the county of Cork'.[128] Again, in 1381-2, the mayor and bailiffs of Cork were directed 'to provide sufficient horses to take Richard Og Barrett and other hostages of lez Barretes, being in their custody' to Waterford.[129] John Bryt and Richard Wynchedon were ordered to receive from William son of Sir William de Barry the 1,000 cattle, surrendered to Philip by Richard Óg Barrett and his son, William, and others 'by way of a fine for divers treasons', and to dispose of them to the king's advantage.[130]

The quest for stability entailed a major transfer of power from the royal government in Ireland to, in the province of Munster, the rising earldoms of Ormond and Desmond. As far as the erosion of the colony was concerned matters were even worse in Thomond, which was now dominated by the unchallenged power of the O'Briens. However, in the late fourteenth century it continued to be an area of prolonged warfare in the course of which the city of Limerick was burnt and, apparently, destroyed to a considerable extent.[131] Moreover, not only was county Limerick disturbed as the royal government campaigned against the O'Briens, but county Cork also was threatened. In 1373, for example, the earl of Desmond and others were ordered to defend their lands in county Limerick while the men of county Cork were arrayed for its defence. As the government attempted to contain this deteriorating situation, Cork and Youghal, together with Limerick and Kilmallock, became important centres from which the authorities directed operations, a striking example of the importance of the towns in the defence of the colony. However, prolonged warfare on this scale resulted in the destruction of large tracts of the Irish lordship which included the overthrowing of settlements and the killing of tenants.

A notable feature of these disturbed political conditions was the growing importance of the earls of Ormond and Desmond in Irish, and especially Munster, politics. In 1386, for example, together with the sheriff of Cork, Desmond was given senior command in regard to the defence of Munster. Furthermore, the history of these campaigns against O'Brien graphically illustrates the basic political realities confronting the later medieval English lordship of Ireland. With adequate finance, campaigns could be and indeed were mounted with varying degrees of success. Political successes against the Irish enemies could be gained by playing on rivalries between different elements or segments of the Gaelic Irish or by buying allies. But without overwhelming resources such objectives were difficult to achieve and the resulting gains were even more difficult to keep.

The decline of English government

The history of the English lordship of Ireland in the fourteenth century was one of increasing fragmentation, both political and economic. This, however, was accompanied by major changes in the structure of the Anglo-Irish nobility and landholding as lesser lords (in Munster these were primarily the earls of Ormond and Desmond) made determined efforts 'to expand their territories and to promote themselves to the first rank'.[132] This process whereby power more and more passed from royal to seigneurial hands, already evident by the end of the fourteenth century, is demonstrated graphically by a petition presented to the Irish council, on the occasion of the meeting of the Hilary parliament of 1393. The petitioner, John fitz Gerald, was son and heir of the third earl of Desmond who succeeded his father in 1398. In his petition he declared that:

the king's cities of Cork and Limerick and the town of Youghal are situated in the marches, and the country round the said cities and town are so destroyed and ruined by the enemies of our Lord the King and by the English rebels, that the people in the same cannot support themselves for lack of victuals without the aid of the people of the country of Limerick, and the hawkers and carriers of victuals, corn and other merchandizes to the said parts do not dare and should not be able to go and repair to comfort and victual the said cities and town without safe conduct.

Accordingly, he sought and obtained from the council authority:

to convey the said carriers and hawkers in going and returning from these cities and towns, he receiving therefor the customary fees, giving it in command to all the faithful lieges of our Lord the King, that they be obedient and attending to the said John in making the convoy aforesaid and this in aid of the lieges of our Lord the King in these parts.[133]

John fitz Gerald's petition, in focusing on the physical fragmentation of the colony and the consequential further isolation of whole segments of it, did not misrepresent the situation. 'The ... political turbulence and lawlessness – the basic feature of life in the Irish march – contributed greatly to economic dislocation also. Internal trading routes linking particularly the seaport towns ... with the network of market towns and markets in the interior (the development of which had been such a striking feature of the growth of the economy and polity of Ireland in the thirteenth century), became more difficult and hazardous to traverse, at least for so long as the hinterland lacked government by some firm authority.'[134] This determining situation was already apparent quite early in the century and coincided with the impact of the Bruce invasion on the colony and the serious outbreak of crime, lawlessness and turbulence to which attention has already been drawn.

Clearly the charter granted to Cork city in 1318[135] 'strikingly illustrates the degree of disruption and upheaval which the colony was already experiencing by the early fourteenth century'. It provided that normally 'on election, the mayor of Cork was to be permitted to take his oath of office before his predecessor rather than in the exchequer in Dublin'. The king, 'in making this concession, indicated that he was doing so because of the fact that Dublin and Cork were far apart and, therefore, no safe passage between them could be guaranteed in the event of war or rebellion on the part of the Gaelic Irish and that, accordingly, it was necessary to provide for the security of the citizens of Cork.' Significantly, in January 1331 a similar concession was made by the crown to the citizens of Waterford who, in seeking it, had pleaded inability to travel to Dublin 'on account of the distance and perils of the way' and had recited the concession in this regard which Cork already enjoyed.[136] By mid-century the hazards of communication with the royal administration in Dublin and travel within the king's Irish lordship had, if anything, evidently worsened. In March 1361 the sheriff of county Cork, John Lombard, was empowered by the king to render his account at the Irish exchequer by means of an attorney. This was done in response to petition by Lombard who argued that his county was 100 leagues distant from Dublin and that 'many of the towns and places through which the road from the county to Dublin passes have been conquered and are held by the king's Irish enemies so that none of his subjects can pass without very great peril unless with a very great company and force of armed men'.[137]

The developing role of the Anglo-Irish magnates and their earldoms as centres of government and political stability is also shown by the petition made to the council in 1392 by Thomas, son of the second earl of Ormond, for recompense of £20 on foot of the costs incurred by him in upholding and defending the king's lieges in the counties of Cork, Tipperary, and Kilkenny in the preceding four or five years.[138] Again in 1393 Thomas petitioned[139] the council for a grant to him and Nicholas White, king's sergeant, of 'a commission of enquiry in the counties of Cork and Limerick, and the cross of the county of Tipperary concerning all manner [of] treasons, trespasses, felonies, conspiracies, champerties, extortions, oppressions, contempts, deceits, falsities, and all other matters done there contrary to the peace, and them to hear and determine, as well at the suit of the King as of the party and to deliver gaols there of those persons indicted, and to hold assizes of novel disseisin, mort dancestor, juries, certificates and attaints by writs of our Lord the King, and also to hold all other pleas of trespass, debt, account, covenant, detainer, and all other contracts there without the King's writ, and them to hear and determine according to the law and custom of Ireland, and power to make and deliver King's writs touching the matter aforesaid, for the profit of our said Lord the King and of the lieges there, since by default of law there, the lieges who are not able to sue elsewhere out of their own country may be disinherited and foreclosed of their rights.' The council acceded to Thomas's petition.

These grants to Butler and John of Desmond are particularly important. Their consequences were to be of far-reaching significance for they represented the conferring on members of the ruling houses of the rising Munster earldoms of licence to exercise in their regions 'what was in reality regalian power.'[140] The royal administration, however, lacked any alternative. Bereft of adequate resources, not least financial, the choice confronting the government was either between rule by these territorial lords, which offered some prospect of stability, or continuing anarchy. The government bowed to realities. The fact that it did so marked an important point of departure in the history of the medieval Irish lordship and that of the rising Anglo-Irish earldoms. This political role of the great Anglo-Irish magnates represents a significant stage in the growth of seigneurial power and competence. As such, the activities of these magnates in the later fourteenth century (and even more so in the fifteenth) contrasts sharply with that, apparently, to be discerned at an earlier date. Thus 'when the Kilkenny parliament of 1310 heard the report of a special commission appointed to investigate the recent steep rise in prices, it laid the blame squarely on "those of great lineage" who regularly robbed merchants of their goods as they travelled through the country or held them to ransom, and who also were in the habit of taking "bread, wine, beer, flesh, and other victuals and things saleable, wherever they may be, without making reasonable payment".'[141]

It would, therefore, appear that, as the fourteenth century progressed, 'the political vacuum created by the retreat of royal authority in Ireland was filled for the most part by the great territorial magnates whose role increasingly changed from one of destabilising the polity of the Irish lordship to that of constituting in their own regions new centres of power and stability. These magnates, consequently, increasingly "represented forces which ... were seen to be more dynamic and immediate than were either the authority of the royal administration in Dublin or the still more remote authority of the king".'[142] Of course this new political structure took some time to evolve, but, certainly by the mid-fifteenth century, the earldom of Desmond was a major power in Munster. That reality was reflected in the appointment, in 1443, of James, sixth earl of Desmond, to govern and keep the counties of Cork, Waterford, Limerick, and Kerry.[143] Prior to the consolidation of these new forces, however, the region continued to be troubled by political turbulence and instability and by a general lawlessness, all of which undermined further the authority of the royal administration.

In the fourteenth century, although military campaigns by the government against both the Gaelic Irish and 'rebel English' were not unknown (those mounted by John Darcy in 1335 and Rokeby in 1352-3 have already been noted, while 'between 1361 and 1376 there were five military expeditions to Ireland ... led by English chief governors ... and all were heavily financed from England'),[144] financial constraints alone precluded their being employed as the normal instrument for dealing with the military threat to the colony. This was not least because any military solution necessarily entailed expenditure greatly in excess of that spent on the campaign itself. It was necessary to follow up successful warfare with significant settlement buttressed by some measure of military occupation and, for both financial and demographic reasons, that simply was not possible in the bleak conditions of the fourteenth century. Therefore, in the light of the totality of conditions obtaining in both Ireland and England in that century, the two expeditions mounted by Richard II in 1394 and 1399 were exceptional. Not alone were they ultimately unsuccessful, but they entailed major expenditure. Since finance on this scale no longer was available to the king from revenue accruing to him in his Irish lordship, it then represented a significant drain on the English exchequer.

Some figures can be adduced to demonstrate the decline in royal revenues in Ireland in the fourteenth and fifteenth centuries. It has been calculated that 'the average annual revenue in the period 1278-99 was £6,300. For the period 1368-84 it had fallen to £2,512. The sums are pitifully small in themselves; there had been a serious decline and the downward trend was to continue .... the burden on the English treasury for Ireland became increasingly serious in the later fourteenth century until in the fifteenth "the incapacity of the English government to find ready money reduced any subvention from this source to vanishing point". This had dire consequences for the defence of the colony'.[145] Thus 'figures for the last years of the reign of Edward I show a fall from £6,112 in 1301-2 to as little as £3,641 in 1305-6. There was a brief recovery to £5,893 in 1306-7 and £5,237 in 1307-8. But thereafter the decline continued year by year: £3,477, £2,586, £3,003, £2,865.'[146] Again, in 1324-5 total receipts accruing to the Irish exchequer appear to have amounted to £2,488,[147] while in 1328-29, 1329-30, 1330-31 and 1331-32 receipts amounted to, respectively, £1,329, £1,420, £1,363 and £1,268, a total of £5,380 for that four-year period.[148] Thereafter the pattern of decline continued. In 1332-3 the revenue recovered somewhat, but only momentarily, when it yielded £2,994. However, it quickly decreased again to £1,526 in 1337-8, £1,336 in 1338-9 and £1,243 in 1339-40.[149] In 1361 'payment could not be made because the treasury was empty'[150] while the Irish pipe rolls for the last seven years of the reign of Edward III (the period c. June 1370 to June 1377) are said to have indicated that 'the revenue and profits of Ireland did not amount unto £1,000 per annum'.[151]

A further memorandum,[152] apparently of decisions made by Richard II for the governance of Ireland (the precise date is not given but from internal evidence it would seem to have been dated sometime after 1394), noted that 'the revenues [of Ireland] are so small, because great taxes and talliages (sometimes 20s. on the ploughland) have been levied by the armed men of every country, who were made accountable, not to the Exchequer, but to various persons ... ; also because the former great subsidies on merchandises (cloth, grain, iron, salt, hides, wool, wine, salmon, etc.) have not been granted to the King since his departure from Ireland.' The decline of customs revenue was particularly important. Beginning in the fourteenth century, 'it is apparent that royal revenue [from the fee-farm rents of the royal boroughs and the customs revenues accruing in the port towns of the Irish lordship] was very seriously diminished' principally as a result of large-scale remissions which 'began, apparently, as an ad hoc response to the declining fortunes of the Irish lordship in general and the boroughs in particular, brought about by both political and economic factors in the course of the fourteenth century'.[153]

The same memorandum noted many other causes of the malaise affecting the king's Irish lordship. Of particular importance in regard to the subject of this study – indicating as it does the continuing fragmentation of the lordship as both a territorial unit and one subject to governance by common institutions of government exercising authority in the name of the English crown – was the assertion that 'the English rebels, as the Butlers, Tobines, Powers, Burkes, Geraudines, Barets, and many other sects by sufferance of their chieftaines, make such riot that the liege people is destroyed' and that 'the mayors of Dublin and Cork and other cities will not suffer searches to be made by the Treasurer within their bailiwicks.'[154] This latter charge presumably refers to the growing financial autonomy, at least as far as the crown was concerned, of the royal boroughs and the port towns to which reference has already been made.[155]

Thus the financial pressures which the royal administration in Ireland experienced in the later fourteenth and fifteenth centuries – it has been said that in 1433 'the revenue of Ireland fell short of the expense of keeping it by four thousand marks'[156] – compounded the impact of other difficulties and rendered the government increasingly powerless to cope with the range of problems and crises which confronted it. Sometime in the reign of Edward III – again the precise date is not given, but it may well have been in the 1370s, a decade which saw heavy and extensive military campaigning – we are told[157] that the expenses of the war against the Irish amounted to £1,037, that is to say, in the light of the figures set out above, an expenditure equivalent to almost one year's yield of revenue. Again, 'in 1360 the earl of Ormond, who was then justiciar, had to finance a campaign in Leinster out of his own resources'.[158]

Colonial reaction

As the lordship visibly declined, the consciousness of the colonists that

Plate 5.2   Kinsale (Cambridge University Collection of air photographs).

they were a distinct ethnic group intensified. By the early fourteenth century 'the "English in Ireland" ... were recognisably a distinct breed, preserving and developing an identity of their own'.[159] This 'Anglo-Irish political identity emerged out of the peculiar strains experienced by a colonial ruling elite harassed by insecurity, and feeling itself neglected, misunderstood or undervalued by a ruler whose mind was of necessity elsewhere.'[160] Accordingly, 'during the later fourteenth and fifteenth centuries the community of the lordship established a habit of bringing itself to the attention of the king through formal messages, usually drawn up in parliaments and great councils, and transmitted to England through publicly-chosen envoys. Typical examples of the *genre* contain complaints about governmental abuses, criticisms of absentee land-holders, and descriptions of the perilous state of the lordship and requests for assistance from Westminster.'[161] In 1441, for example, the colony requested the king to 'ordayne a mightie lord of ... your realme of England for to be your lieutenant of the said land [of Ireland]'. [162]

In the event, Richard, duke of York, was appointed lieutenant in December 1447. Initially York enjoyed significant military success in Ulster, the midlands and in south Leinster. By 1449 some of York's entourage were euphoric but 'an antidote to such euphoria was soon provided by a report to York from the citizens of Cork, Kinsale, and Youghal, who requested that the lieutenant and council should come to Cork to quell the disorder inside that county. In particular they complained of the dissensions among the lords of English descent which had become so widespread that much of the county had passed into the hands of the Gaelic Irish. Unless measures were taken to end these destructive quarrels, they claimed, "we are all cast away, and then farewell Munster for ever". If York and the council refused to act, then they would complain directly to the king'.[163] This petition almost certainly exaggerated the situation. By the mid-fifteenth century the Cork region was much more stable than it had been a century earlier, not least because of the entrenchment of Geraldine power there and at least the beginnings of economic recovery. In any event, like all self-interested petitions to the crown, that of the three boroughs in 1449 contained more than an element of propaganda. As Frame has pointed out, 'more than we perhaps realize, our image of late medieval Ireland has been formed by this propaganda'.[164]

Because of these prevailing political conditions, the fourteenth century, in particular, saw continuing destabilisation of the colony. Although, as we have seen, important and powerful military expeditions were mounted by the king – 'at certain moments Ireland impinged more sharply on the consciousness of the English government than has usually been allowed'[165] – in an attempt to remedy the situation, increasingly the colony had to depend on its own declining resources in order to maintain its defences. Some examples of this latter development can be cited. 'In May 1372 . . . the mayor of Cork and the sovereign of Youghal were directed to attend with six of their "better, worthy and shrewd burgesses" a council to be convened at Ballyhack, Co. Wexford, in June to discuss the defence of the king's lieges in Ireland.'[166] Attention has already been directed to instances of successful, though rather localised, military resistance to Gaelic Irish encroachment. However, as the century progressed, 'numerous licences were issued to those living on the border of the colony, permitting them to negotiate with the neighbouring Gaelic Irish and also, on occasion, to trade with them'[167] and negotiations of this kind, rather than military campaigns, became the norm.

Already in February 1345 John de Wynchedon, to whom reference has earlier been made, together with William son of John de Barry and Miles de Courcy, was commissioned to treat with Dermot Mac Carthy, otherwise known as 'Mac Dermot' who, as previously indicated, had been a threat to the colony since at least the 1330s and who had survived the defeat of the rebellious first earl of Desmond with whom he had been associated. In September 1382, the mayor and citizens of Cork were empowered 'to treat for peace and truces with the Irish rebels'.[168] Again, in October 1384 Robert Thame and John Lombard, citizen of Cork,[169] were appointed 'to hold parleys with the Irish enemies and English rebels and to treat with them',[170] while in May 1387 John Bryt, one of the justices of gaol delivery in county Cork, was licensed 'to treat with Irish enemies and English rebels in this county although they should have been indicted for seditions, felonies etc. and to bring them to peace as well as he could.'[171] Although this approach was no substitute for a policy of conquest and settlement, a policy which for both financial and demographic reasons simply could not be pursued, at least it did something to arrest or minimise the onslaughts on the colony and, thereby, ensure its survival. Moreover, in appropriate circumstances, additional advantage could be gained from contacts of this kind. Certainly by the fifteenth century contacts with the Gaelic Irish produced significant gain for the colonists by opening up opportunities for substantial trading between the colony and Gaelic Ireland to the mutual advantage of both. An important consequence of the initiation of this approach or policy of negotiating settlements was that it introduced an element of ambiguity into the relations between the colonists and their Gaelic neighbours. Henceforward, that relationship ceased to be overwhelmingly negative and acquired some positive qualities also. Indeed, it has been pointed out that 'in cultural complexion and style of life Gaelic lords probably differed no more from their Anglo-Irish neighbours than some Anglo-Irish (or indeed some Gaelic) lords differed from others. Marriage and other bonds of alliance had long crossed and blurred national boundaries and loyalties were largely local and personal in a society marked by violent competition and feud.'[172] Again, the complexity of the relationship between the two races is indicated by the fact that:

> it is necessary to recall that the forces opposing the 'Irish enemies' contained large numbers of Irish troops, some of them led by Gaelic lords indistinguishable from those against whom expeditions were aimed, and others by men of English status who were heavily influenced by Irish culture and social habits .... Later medieval Ireland, like other frontier societies, had its share of ambiguities. The working of practical relationships ... often seems at ... odds with the attitudes of the Lordship's ruling groups as they appear in legislation or in formal messages to the king and Council in England .... 'the frontier' is to be understood as a process of interaction.[173]

This essentially symbiotic relationship did much to shape both the polity and the economy of late medieval and, indeed, of early modern Ireland.

Demographic and economic deterioration

The decline of the colony in the fourteenth and early fifteenth centuries was manifested not only by the course of political development described above but also by profound economic crisis. That malaise was due both to internal conditions, of which growing political dis-location constituted an important element, and external circumstances, notably the impact of natural catastrophes such as plague, famine, and demographic contraction of the kind which Europe as a whole witnessed in this period. Disasters wrought by the hand of man, especially prolonged and intensive warfare, also took their toll. Again, in common with Europe as a whole, the economic crisis which now set in was reflected most especially in agriculture. The new economic and social conditions were the complete antithesis of those which had obtained in the heyday of the colony in the thirteenth century, which was a period of growth and expansion on all fronts.

The onset of the Black Death – the visitations of bubonic plague – in the mid-fourteenth century was particularly devastating in its effects.[174] Moreover, subsequently in the fourteenth, fifteenth and early sixteenth centuries there were other outbreaks of various other plagues and pestilences in the region. We learn that there were occurrences, either in Munster in general or the city of Cork in particular in 1361, 1370, 1383, 1447, 1504, 1522 and 1535, but we know nothing about the nature of these plagues or their economic and social consequences.[175] By 1348 'Irish urban life and trade was declining. The plague aggravated existing tendencies and wrought untold damage to the cities'.[176] For example, 'in listing 91 burgesses [in Youghal in 1351] we are told that no fewer than 39 are represented by their heirs, which suggests a recent heavy mortality. The desertion of [the neighbouring borough of] Kinsalebeg where all the burgages were described as waste, a phenomenon which appears to have been quite recent, can almost certainly be attributed to the plague'.[177] The substantial waste in Youghal was probably also due, in some degree, to the assault on the town by the first earl of Desmond in July 1344. Therefore political turbulence and natural catastrophe 'interacted on each other producing a malaise greater than either alone could have brought about, and this continued to be a constant element in the history of later medieval Ireland, especially in the second half of the fourteenth century and the early decades of the fifteenth'.[178]

While the plague had an immediate impact on the towns, ultimately it affected agrarian settlement also, leading to a massive decline in the area under cultivation. 'By the later fourteenth century ... political conditions compounded the effects of economic contraction conse-quent on the decline in population and the widespread abandonment of settlement, particularly that of thirteenth-century origin'.[179] The full effects of this in Ireland will only be seen when many more regional and local studies than we have at our disposal at present have been made. For present purposes one such study of a manor in the Cork region can be cited. The manor of Inchiquin in east county Cork[180] had contained three boroughs, Inchiquin itself, Youghal and Kinsalebeg, the latter adjacent to Youghal but lying in county Waterford. By the later fourteenth century, as already noted, Kinsalebeg had been deserted, while Inchiquin[181] had at least been largely eclipsed; like Youghal and Kinsalebeg, it had suffered serious waste and destruction of burgage tenements.[182] Other known deserted rural-boroughs in county Cork are Kilmaclenine,[183] three miles south-west of Buttevant, Ringrone[184] near Kinsale and Donoughmore.

By the middle of the fourteenth century the decline of the colony was marked by a growing demographic crisis. A notable feature of the new situation was, on the one hand, the increase of absenteeism on the part of many of the great landowners and, on the other, a developing trend towards emigration, a flight from the colony, by agricultural labourers and artisans. The latter, particularly, added to the growing economic contraction consequent on the abandoning of whole areas of settlement, and altered profoundly the balance between the Gaelic Irish and the settlers. Thus 'licences to receive Gaelic Irish tenants on their estates underline the difficulty experienced by many Anglo-Irish landholders in finding men of English descent to undertake tenancies, particularly in the border areas .... There were problems, too, in maintaining a sufficient work force on estates'.[185]

The government tried to arrest both developments. Absentee landowners were obliged by statute to return to Ireland to defend their lands,[186] while it also became normal to legislate against unlicensed emigration. In 1344 the mayor and bailiffs of Cork 'were required to cause proclamation to be made ... that no [person], with the exception of merchants and their servants, should be permitted to pass out of Ireland, without the king's special licence; and to arrest all persons offending and to seize their ships, masters and mariners'.[187] A similar proclamation appears to have been made at Cork on 18 May 1359,[188] while in March 1360 'writs were directed to the sovereign and bailiffs of Youghal, and the mayor and bailiffs of Cork ordering them to prevent persons from going to foreign parts'.[189] In July 1388 a royal writ to the mayor and bailiffs of Cork, responding to information received regarding the weakened condition of the city,[190] directed them to summon before them 'all citizens, merchants and others ... who have lands or goods within the city and on the king's behalf to command them to reside there ... for its defence'.[191] It is evident that legislation prohibiting migration was frequently breached. In September 1381, for example, Henry Greff, a mariner from Pembroke, was pardoned for transporting 'certain men from the port of the city of Cork overseas without licence'.[192] Nonetheless, with whatever success, attempts were made to enforce the statute. In October 1384, John Wayt, one of the bailiffs of Cork, was licensed to go overseas on business.[193] 'The parliament of 1410 claimed that so many labourers and servants had gone abroad that "the husbandry and tillage of the same land is on the point of being altogether destroyed and wasted"; and it laid down that in future any mariner who was discovered conveying a labourer or servant abroad, without licence from the administration, should forfeit his ship. Officers were appointed to enforce this statute, but not, it would seem, with a great deal of success'.[194]

Three of those appointed in 1413 were John de Wynchedon, referred to above, John Galwey of Kinsale, a member of a prominent merchant family in both Cork and Kinsale, and John Meagh, likewise a member of an important Cork mercantile family.[195] Indeed, their appointment probably was due, at least in part, to the fact that their mercantile activities singularly fitted them for a task which entailed some familiarity with ports, shipping and shipping movements. These measures, however, proved equally ineffective since 'those who were determined to cross to England must have found it comparatively easy to do so. By 1421 the colonists were complaining that 'tenants, artificers, and labourers ... daily depart in great numbers ... to the kingdom of England and remain there', and they asked the king to provide some remedy for this drain on the colony's resources. But in 1429 many labourers and servants were reported to be emigrating without licence, and parliament passed a further statute attempting to restrain them'.[196]

This picture of decline, political, economic and social, is vividly illustrated by a petition[197] to the king sent by John Lombard, citizen of Cork and later sheriff of the county, in May 1359. It was dispatched about the time when it was reported that 'a great commotion and warlike disturbance [had been] raised by the Irish enemies and English rebels in Munster[198] and when a subsidy of 2s. from each cultivated plough-land had been granted by the community of county Cork to muster forces to attack those Irish enemies.[199] In his petition Lombard recalled that the king had given him custody of the castle of Gynes [Cloghroe], county Cork, together with thirty plough-lands, to be held forever. But he complained that 'he could scarcely cause any part of the land to be inhabited on account of the frequent invasions of the Irish as well as English malefactors and rebels, and that any, whom he could get, would render him little or nothing for the same, and designed to go away, being impoverished from hostile incursions, robberies, and depredations; and thus he could not obtain as much as he had expended in the custody of the castle.' In response to this petition the king directed the Irish treasurer that 'if the rents and annual profits received were insufficient for the custody, then to cause him [Lombard] to be exonerated from the arrears due to the treasury'.

Thus the effects of decline and contraction, not least of agriculture, were felt particularly in south and south-east Munster. Consequently, the region ceased to be a producer of surplus cereals. It will be recalled that several Irish regions including Munster had been major exporters of grain in the heyday of agricultural growth and expansion in the thirteenth century. The region became, rather, an importer. Accordingly, ports such as Cork, Youghal and Kinsale became centres through which essential supplies of wheat, oats, barley and legumes were imported. Not infrequently, the three ports were grouped together for this purpose.

From about the mid-fourteenth century onwards Cork and the other towns of its region were in fact dependent for their economic survival on imports of this kind. In 1376, for example, the burgesses of Youghal who, we are told, 'had been devastated by the Roches and

Clangibbons', were permitted 'to carry three ship loads of corn from any harbour in the county of Dublin or in those of Meath or Louth for their relief'.[200] Already in October 1375 authorisation had been given to Richard Reve to transport 100 crannocks of wheat to Youghal and Cork.[201] In 1389 the burgesses of Cork petitioned the king for licence to import cereals.[202] In their petition they maintained that 'their city and the parts adjacent thereto were so destroyed that they would be obliged to leave that desolate place altogether unless they were supplied with fruits.' In response to their petition the king, in January 1390, informed the admiral and other officers of the crown in Ireland that 'he had granted the citizens and commons of Cork liberty to buy corn in any of the ports in Ireland as it was impossible to reside there without a great supply of food'.[203]

The necessity to import corn and other foodstuffs into Cork, Youghal, and Kinsale emerged quite early in the fourteenth century and, no doubt, was a consequence of the turbulent and disastrous opening decades of that century. Thereafter the need intensified and continued throughout the fifteenth and early sixteenth centuries at least, notwithstanding the marked economic recovery which Cork and the south-coast region, in common with other regions of Ireland, witnessed certainly from the later fifteenth century onwards.[204] The provenance of these supplies is a matter of some interest. For the most part they came from other regions of Ireland, notably the northern part of the Pale, from England, especially the West Country, and, to a lesser extent, from France, particularly from the late fifteenth century onwards as trade revived with that country following the ending of the Hundred Years War.

Some examples, ranging in date from the early fourteenth century (when the crown still permitted the export of grain from Ireland)[205] to the mid-fifteenth, illustrate the evolution of the situation. In May 1330 Richard Bele, Robert Fraunceys and Augustine Geyner, merchants of Cork, shipped corn for Ireland, presumably to Cork, in the port of Bristol.[206] Again in February 1331 Henry Neuland and Thomas Rycol, likewise merchants of Cork, bought corn in Somerset and Gloucestershire for shipment to Wales or Ireland, while in May 1333 Neuland and another Cork merchant, Stephen Travers, were licensed to ship 600 quarters of corn to Ireland through the port of Bristol. A similar licence, of even date, issued to two other Cork merchants, Walter de Kerdyf or Cardiff and Henry Skidy.[207] Not all the merchants engaged in this trade were Irish. English merchants and mariners, particularly from the West Country, were active in the Irish trade. Thus we learn that in February 1371 two Somerset merchants, William Holeweye of Wellington and Richard atte Mille of Bridgwater, were authorized to load 500 quarters of barley and 500 quarters of beans in the port of Bridgwater for shipment to Cork, Waterford, Cardiff and Carmarthen.[208] While most supplies from England originated in and were shipped from the West Country, there were other sources of supply. In May 1364, for example, two Cork merchants, David Roche and John Pomfret, were licensed to ship 100 quarters of wheat and 60 quarters of beans in the port of Shorham, in Sussex, and to bring them to Ireland.[209]

By the late fourteenth century, as the crisis deepened, the need to supply the southern ports had become very pressing; more and more corn was shipped from Leinster, most especially from counties Dublin, Meath and Louth, the northern tier of the emerging Pale. Some of these cargoes, like those sent from the west of England in the late fifteenth and early sixteenth centuries, were quite small, but in the aggregate they were substantial enough, becoming quite significant as the frequency of shipments increased. The following are some examples of this traffic. In 1375 Walter Gaude was licensed to bring two weys of corn to Cork, Youghal or Kinsale.[210] Again, in October 1386 William Sygyn, Thomas Mernagh and John Wayt, of Cork, were empowered to buy six weys of wheat, barley and oats in Wexford and to bring them to Cork or Kinsale. In December following, the same William Sygyn (who with John Galwey was appointed admiral 'in certain ports in Co Cork' in 1381)[211] was licensed to buy six weys of corn, barley and oats in counties Dublin and Meath. Gregory Hore was similarly authorized 'to buy and carry to the city of Cork or the town of Kinsale eight weys of corn and oats'.[212] In the following January, William Horsley and John Lovell were given licence to buy, respectively, two weys of corn, a half wey of barley, one wey of oats and one wey of beans in county Dublin for shipment to Cork, Youghal or Kinsale and four weys of corn in any port of counties Dublin and Meath and to transport them to Cork by ship.[213] In the fifteenth century matters were no better. Thus in February 1410 (in which year, we are told, there was a dearth of corn in Ireland)[214] John Conyll, a Cork merchant, received licence to buy four weys of corn in Ireland and to transport them to Cork,[215] while in 1422 Robert Taylor, a merchant of Swords, was permitted to supply corn to Kinsale.[216] A general permit for merchants of Cork, Kinsale, Youghal, Waterford, Kilkenny and Wexford to transport corn from the ports of Dublin and Drogheda was granted by the Irish parliament in 1449 and, in 1450, parliament again ordained that merchants might ship corn to Cork.[217]

The above are but some of the instances of cereal importation which the surviving records permit us to glimpse. Buffeted by fissiparous forces of all kinds, the colony declined rapidly in the course of the fourteenth and early fifteenth centuries. It experienced a major agricultural collapse, clearly indicated by the fact that, in contrast with the thirteenth-century situation when substantial quantities of grain were exported, the Cork region became utterly dependent on imported supplies of corn and legumes. In this period of demographic and economic contraction agriculture was, for the most part, replaced by pastoral husbandry. Economic activity was very badly affected also by the prevailing internal and external conditions which disrupted both domestic and overseas trade. Growing lawlessness, political turbulence and instability played a major part in undermining the network of established internal trading routes which had been developed in the thirteenth century. Equally, the Hundred Years War, with growing hostilities at sea and the development of piracy, disrupted maritime trading routes and led to the destruction of shipping.[218] Political disintegration and economic malaise interacted on each other and seriously undermined the colony. In all the circumstances it was only with difficulty that the colony managed to survive. Yet it managed to do so for, despite all the bleakness of the colony's circumstances in the later middle ages, there were some positive developments also. One of these has already been identified, namely the changing role of the earldoms of Ormond and Desmond, to the point that, far from destabilising the polity and economy as they had done in the earlier fourteenth century, by the end of that century they had become, or at least were in process of becoming, cohesive forces in society, constituting centres of political power, government and stability in the Munster region. In this way their consolidation removed much of the turbulence and anarchy which, at an earlier stage, had promoted their growth and development. The final part of the present chapter develops this point and examines broadly the other positive elements in the otherwise inauspicious circumstances of the colony in the late middle ages.

REVIVAL AND RENEWAL: POLITICAL STABILITY AND ECONOMIC EXPANSION c. 1440 TO c. 1500

Survival of the towns

Gaelic Ireland, because of its own weaknesses and rivalries, was never able completely to overrun the colony even when the latter was at its weakest and subject to greatest threat. The position of the colony was further strengthened by the fact that it continued to dispose of certain resources and to enjoy certain advantages. The development of urban life had been one of the great achievements of the colony in the epoch of its foundation in the thirteenth century. However damaged the towns were by the catastrophic events of the fourteenth century, much of the life they had generated survived. This is particularly true of the major port towns of the region, Cork, Youghal and Kinsale. By surviving they were particularly well placed to form bridges between Gaelic and English Ireland, not least by way of trade, and, as the economy in Ireland and in western Europe generally recovered in the later fifteenth century, these towns, as the major maritime trading centres of the region, grew increasingly wealthy and their urban partricates stronger. In this way both the port towns themselves and their ruling élites became even more entrenched.

Of course the towns suffered grievously, but it would seem that the fortunes of the inland centres were more adversely affected than were those of the port towns. After all, even in the worst of circumstances, the latter could maintain communications by sea. Indeed, from a parliamentary record of 1447 we know that the Irish administration was very much intent on securing and maintaining sea communications between, on the one hand, Dublin, Drogheda, Malahide and Dalkey and, on the other, Wexford, Waterford and Cork,[219] while the importance of coastal shipping traffic in the matter of supplying the port towns of the south with essential foodstuffs has already been noted. Reference has previously been made to the disruption of the network of market towns which had flowered in the thirteenth century. In 1318 John son of David de Barry's town of Buttevant was given a murage grant of £105 from the issues of the town due to the exchequer and, in the following March, the burgesses of Henry de Cogan's town of Ballynamona (or the 'Newtown of Monemore') received a murage grant of £67. 6s. 8d. from the issues which they owed to the crown.[220] While it is true that murage grants were much more complex 'than a simple matter of raising money to build walls to defend the town',[221] the dating of these grants is significant since we know that widespread turbulence and lawlessness existed in county Cork in that decade in general and in the period 1316-18 in particular.

It can be suggested, therefore, that the purpose of such murage grants was primarily defensive. Moreover, because of the fact that they were situated in north Cork and thus close to zones of military activity in Thomond, these two towns were particularly vulnerable and their situation parlous. Certainly, military activity appears to have been endemic in this region. According to Francis Tuckey, about 1409 the king forgave Sir John Barry, sheriff of Cork, all his debts 'in consequence of his having, for some years, supported at his own expense the burdens of the wars in the county by reason of his office', while about 1415 fines imposed on him for non-attendance at the king's courts were remitted 'in consequence of his having stated that he was unable to attend as his men and horses had been killed in the war with the Irish'.[222] The scale of military activity in this period is further illustrated by the fact that on 10 December 1429 James, earl of Desmond, was granted £100 'because he has daily kept horsemen and footmen at his own costs to deter the enemy in Munster and Connacht in relief of the faithful lieges'.[223] Notwithstanding the impact of warfare, it is, however, possible to exaggerate the degree of decay and destruction which the towns experienced. For example, the will of David Lombard, 'Captain of his nation', dated 1479, refers to property 'in eadem villa [Buttevant] infra muros eiusdem ville situatis'.[224] Again, 'in 1517 the episcopal see of Rosscarbery, in a purely Gaelic area, was a walled town with two gates and nearly two hundred houses'.[225]

The port towns of the region, with their backs to the sea, were more fortunate in their situation than were the inland towns, although some of the latter undoubtedly fared better than others. Philip de Barry's town of Innishannon with its ferry on the Bandon is a case in point.[226] Nevertheless, in the period of decline and contraction even the port towns suffered many privations, although it should be emphasised that, in seeking concessions or support from government, they tended to exaggerate their plight.[227]

In January 1381 the mayor and bailiffs of Cork[228] made represent-ations to the crown about their situation. They claimed that the city and its inhabitants were so impoverished by robberies and the like that 'some of the more substantial of the citizens designed to go away' and that 'the city from its situation, was liable to be conquered by enemies unless it were defended by a force of armed men'.[229] In December 1384 a chimney tax was imposed in the city in order to pay watchmen 'who were posted on the borders of the enemy',[230] while in 1406 we are told that the city of Cork 'was so encumbered with evil neighbours, the Irish outlaws, that ... the inhabitants were forced to watch their gates continually, to keep them shut ... from sun set to sun arising, nor suffer any stranger to enter them with his weapon... They walked out at seasons for recreation "with strength of men furnished, they matched in wedlock among themselves, so that well nigh the whole city was allied together" '.[231] Intermarriage, one suspects, had less to do with the besieged nature of life in the city than with a policy espoused by the urban patriciate to maintain its oligarchical status, privileges and advantages by means of marriage settlements.

In January 1382 it was reported that Kinsale had been attacked by Spanish enemies[232] and in 1389-90 the citizens were granted exemption from attending parliaments on the grounds that 'the town lay in the midst of rebels'.[233] Further action in aid of the town's maintenance and defence followed. In March 1400 the citizens were given a murage grant for 15 years and this grant was subsequently renewed.[234] Again, on 16 January 1409 'because of its poverty', the town was accorded a privilege by the crown whereby 'no foreign merchant nor anyone henceforward [might] retail or brew ale or sell by retail merchandise or any victuals within the town without licence of the ... provost and commonalty'.[235] As already noted, Youghal was similarly threatened. In April 1376 its neighbourhood was reported to have been wasted by the Roches, Clangibbons and other marauders,[236] that is to say by rebel English of the kind who, together with Gaelic Irish, had earlier been mustered by the first earl of Desmond to serve in his 'rout'.

From this consideration of the subject it is clear that the towns of the colony were being subjected to intolerable pressure by political and economic circumstances. Yet it is equally clear that the English crown was making significant attempts to aid them. This was particularly so in the case of the seaport towns and the royal boroughs which could be assisted financially by a number of measures. Indeed, the latter are a striking feature of royal policy in the fourteenth and fifteenth centuries.[237] 'This policy marks a new departure, the emergence of a defensive strategy for such important elements of the Irish lordship as the seaport towns [many of which were royal boroughs] and it reflects government recognition, no doubt prompted by important local interests, of Irish realities. This strategy [which clearly emerged in the course of the fourteenth century] was further elaborated and extended ... in the fifteenth century. Accordingly, we can discern in royal policy towards the towns in later medieval Ireland the harbinger of that pursued, even more forcefully and cogently, by government in sixteenth-century Ireland'.[238]

That policy was essentially twofold. Increasingly, the crown permitted the royal boroughs to retain to their own use the fee-farm rents due to the crown yearly while, at much the same time, the port towns (many of which were royal boroughs) were permitted to keep the receipts accruing from the royal customs in their ports. 'The purpose of these grants to the port towns [and royal boroughs] of royal revenue, accruing principally from the customs and fee-farm rents is quite clear. They were designed to bolster the fortunes of the towns which were governed by English law and which were loyal, or at least presumed to be loyal, to the crown and its administration in Ireland as bastions against a Gaelic Irish resurgence, the ambitions of rebel English or, indeed, those of self-interested Anglo-Irish territorial magnates'.[239] In the Cork region, the towns principally affected by this policy were Cork, Youghal and Kinsale. Of these, Cork alone was a royal borough and, therefore, it alone was granted remission, in whole or in part, of fee-farm rent due to the crown. Grants of remission of fee-farm, or grants remitting fines due for non-payment, are known to have been made in 1316, 1342, 1351, 1354, 1375, 1388, 1389, 1392, 1400, 1423, 1462, 1482 and 1500. The grant of 1423 included a further endowment of 20 marks a year for three years out of 'the great custom called the 'coket', while that of 1462 also included the revenues accruing from the cocket custom'.[240] Similar concessions regarding the customs levies were made to Youghal and Kinsale in the course of the fourteenth and fifteenth centuries.[241] In making these concessions 'the government simply made a virtue of necessity'.[242]

The towns and Gaelic Ireland

Thus even in the exceedingly difficult circumstances of the later fourteenth and early fifteenth centuries, many of the towns managed to survive and, with the revival of trade in the later fifteenth and early sixteenth centuries, some of them, particularly the port towns, managed to generate a modest prosperity. That situation has been described as follows:

> The collapse of the Anglo-Irish colony and the retreat of English administration and control which took place during the course of the fourteenth century left the port towns of the southern and western coasts, including Cork, isolated among territories ruled by Gaelic and Gaelicised lords.
>
> Although in the early portion of the fifteenth century their position would seem to have been one of considerable stress and their relations with their neighbours generally hostile, by the second half of the century a *modus vivendi* appears to have been reached which, coinciding with an upturn in foreign trade, led to an improvement in the position of the towns which by 1500, although small, were prosperous and, by Irish standards, rich.[243]

These developments, therefore, accord with the observation made above, namely that, certainly by the later fourteenth century, relations between the colonists and the Gaelic Irish were not entirely negative. The political interests of both could be accommodated as circumstances warranted and trading relations of all kinds entered into to the mutual advantage of both ethnic communities. Thus 'in times of constant war, the towns were hardly able to promote their trade, and, accordingly, they used to be given permission from time to time to conclude truces with the enemy outside and to trade with him. Waterford was granted such permission in 1345, Cork in 1382, Limerick in 1391 and Kinsale in 1400. New Ross was permitted in 1402 to arrange truces with the Irish and to sell food to them. In 1463, parliament granted a general permission to Cork, Limerick, Waterford and Youghal to sell every kind of merchandise, with the exception of arms, to the Irish and to buy from them'.[244] The reasons for this permission are clearly recited in the statute. 'Whereas the profit of every market, city and town in this land, depends principally on the resort of Irish people bringing their merchandise to the said cities and towns, and the inhabitants in the said cities and towns durst not buy and sell with the said Irish people, by reason of certain acts and statutes made against them in this land, which is a very great injury to the said inhabitants in the said cities and towns, especially to those who adjoin the marches. Whereupon ... [it] is ordained ... that the inhabitants in the cities of Cork and Limerick, Waterford and Youghal, may lawfully buy and sell all manner of merchandise from and to Irishmen, without any hurt or hindrance ...'.[245] By the late fifteenth century parliamentary licences of this kind were normal and, we may suspect, they merely gave formal, legal expression to what had for long been done in practice. Nowhere was the symbiotic relationship between Gaelic Ireland and the English lordship more succinctly expressed than in the terms of that parliamentary statute of 1463.

While advantageous to Gaelic Ireland, trade between it and the lordship was essential for the prosperity of many of the merchants of the towns of the colony. Some of the latter, it should be emphasised, were Gaelic Irish in origin who, by means of grants of denization, enjoyed the benefits of English law which permitted them to engage in trade in the king's dominions and to secure their interests in English law.[246] Some examples illustrate this development for the Cork region. 'An important case in point ... is the O'Ronayne or Ronan family which acquired considerable property in Cork, Kinsale and Youghal and ranked among the urban patriciate there from the later fifteenth century onwards'.[247] Thus 'in 1487 Maurice Ronayne was simultaneously a freeman of Cork, of Youghal and of Kinsale, seemingly a not unusual situation'.[248] 'On 12 September 1467, the king, probably at the instance of the earl of Desmond, granted to Philip O'Ronane, "being of the Irish nation", that he and his descendants "be of free state and condition and from all manner of Irish servitude free and quit and that they may use the English law ... and that they answer and be answered in any of our courts whatsoever ... and that they be able to acquire all manner of lands, tenements, rents, services, offices and other possessions and hold, occupy and enjoy them, their heirs and assigns for ever'.[249] In February 1425 a similar grant of denization was granted to Robert Holohan (*Holbane*) and Margaret Barry, his wife, on the grounds that 'he and his ancestors were, from the time of the conquest of Ireland, themselves faithful liege men of the king, and had also associated with faithful liege men of the king'.[250]

Evidently in response to changing conditions and new needs, as the fifteenth century progressed, such grants of denization became more common.[251] Consequently, the racial composition of the towns of the lordship became even more mixed and, we can assume, ties with Gaelic Ireland were strengthened. The situation had thus radically changed from that which had obtained in the thirteenth and fourteenth centuries when attempts had been made to prevent Irishmen from being appointed to ecclesiastical benefices or to public or civil office in the towns. For example, in 1279-80 concern had been expressed following an allegation that an Irishman had been appointed customer in Cork, while in November 1360 the mayor and bailiffs of Cork were directed by the king not to permit Irishmen to be appointed to civic office or to ecclesiastical benefices.[252] As already indicated, by the later fifteenth century relations, not least commercial relations, between the lordship and Gaelic Ireland had become much more complex.

Political and economic regeneration

Strong trading contacts between the two nations were reflected in the pattern and structure of Irish overseas trade which, moreover, became increasingly buoyant in the late fifteenth and early sixteenth centuries.[253] The tempo of trade in that period quickened since Cork, Youghal and Kinsale, by royal prescription, were permitted to retain to their own use the customs revenues accruing in their ports. The increased volume of trade added considerably to municipal wealth; Cork, of course, was further aided by being relieved of the obligation to pay its fee farm. These factors together with the augmentation in the late fifteenth century of Cork's area of jurisdiction to encompass much more of Cork harbour[254] show that the city of Cork was in the process of recovering a position it had seemed to be in danger of losing a century or so earlier. In the later fifteenth century Cork's development as a major Irish seaport town, a process begun in the late twelfth or early thirteenth centuries, was being renewed. That development was due both to political and economic factors, the salient features of which were the evolution and enlargement of Cork's borough status, financial and other concessions made to it by the crown, the growth of its overseas trade in the later middle ages as a whole, and the recovery, both economic and political, which the later middle ages witnessed. Accordingly, this chapter should properly conclude with some further observations regarding growing political stability in the Cork region from the later fifteenth century onwards.

It has already been contended in the present study that the fourteenth century was a period of transition in which power in significant areas of the lordship passed more and more from royal to seigneurial hands. In the Munster area the rising earldoms of Ormond and Desmond arrogated more political authority to themselves. In struggling to establish their own political power bases and in contending with each other and with others they contributed in no small degree to the growing disorder and instability which the fourteenth century in particular witnessed. These were the conditions which gave rise to the celebrated and bizarre occurrence in 1380 when Edmund 'Mortimer and other leading members of the administration were present [in the chapel of Dublin Castle for a requiem mass for Mortimer's wife] to hear the celebrant, Richard Wye, bishop of Cloyne, introduce into the mass a new preface, which he sang with a loud voice: "there are two in Munster who destroy us and our goods, namely the earl of Ormond and the earl of Desmond with their followers, whom in the end the Lord will destroy, through Jesus Christ, our Lord, Amen."' Yet at much the same time as the bishop vented his feelings and frustrations at the activities of Ormond and Desmond, the latter was active in the field in defence of the colony against the Gaelic Irish. In this respect, the government was becoming increasingly dependent on him and his likes to defend the king's subjects in Ireland.

Indeed, a decade or so later the crown's growing dependence on these rising earldoms to maintain any semblance of royal authority in whole regions of the lordship reached a further stage of development with, as indicated above, the granting to them of a significant measure of regalian power. Thus, the rising earldoms of the lordship were permitted to assume more of the responsibility of governing themselves and thereby establish a defensive bulwark against the Gaelic Irish and rebel English. In effect, this policy operated in parallel with that of buttressing the towns as bastions of English power in Ireland to which attention has already been directed. The former entailed conciliating, principally, the rising power of Ormond and Desmond. In reality, of course, the crown really had no alternative. Those who could govern were to be permitted to do so and, as far as possible, they were to be associated with the interests of the crown and those of the royal administration in Dublin. These two interests, it should be said, did not necessarily exactly coincide. This policy, therefore, was arrived at *faute de mieux* and merely recognised the fact that new centres of power, the great earldoms, had come into being.[255] Indeed, the earldom of Desmond became the greatest power in Munster. By the fifteenth century, therefore, primarily for reasons of self-interest, Desmond, as already noted, had become a mainstay of the colony in that region.

In 1420, for example, the burgesses of Cork paid a subsidy of 17*s.* 5*d.* and the commonalty of the county of Cork a subsidy of £14. 6*s.* 8*d.* to the earl of Ormond, the king's lieutenant in Ireland. These payments represented a total of £15. 4s. 1d. out of a grand total of 300 marks paid by way of this subsidy. The city of Cork's payment is remarkably small and can be compared with the 36s. 8d. paid by Kinsale. Limerick paid 148s., Dublin 233s. 4d., Drogheda 133s. 3½d., Wexford 284s., and Kilkenny 532s. Cork's small payment may be due to tension between the earls of Ormond and Desmond, since the latter dominated Cork. Indeed, of the towns only New Ross paid a smaller amount than Cork, 5s. 7d., but that port was evidently in some decline by the fifteenth century. A further 42s. were paid by the clergy of county Cork.[256]

The emergence of this political structure in late medieval Ireland had serious implications for the towns, especially the port towns. 'Waterford was dominated by the earls of Ormond whose earldom and power, certainly by the late fifteenth century, was able to provide security and stability for the town. Dungarvan, Youghal, Cork, and Kinsale were likewise dominated by the earls of Desmond who played a similar role in their affairs'.[257] Thus 'as royal authority was eroded, the vacuum was filled by the rising power of the feudal earldoms. These feudal lords, in pursuance of their own interests, permitted the towns a measure of autonomy, in the same way as the crown had, and even obtained from the king grants extending urban autonomy in important respects.'[258] While the feudal lords did much to support the towns which they had come to control and in general provided a political stability which promoted their economic fortunes, it must be remembered that for this they exacted a price, not only financial but also political. This is strikingly demonstrated by the history of the Simnel and Warbeck affairs in the last decade or so of the fifteenth century.[259]

Both these pretenders to the English crown received considerable support in Ireland, especially in Munster, from both Gaelic and Anglo-Irish lords alike. The notable exception, however, was Waterford, the *urbs intacta,* which was dominated by the earl of Ormond. In 1488, during the Simnel affair, Sir Richard Edgecombe landed at Kinsale and forced the lords Barry and Courcy and the town authorities to take oaths of fealty. Warbeck landed at Cork in 1491 and was supported by Desmond and the mayor of the city, John Walters (or Water). Again, Waterford strenuously resisted. Although Warbeck attracted support from many quarters including Gaelic Ireland, much of it appears to have been merely opportunistic and 'genuine commitment to Warbeck's cause was probably confined to parts of Munster'.[260] Like Simnel's, Warbeck's cause was unsuccessful, but for at least some of those associated with him the consequences of his failure were much more serious. 'By march [1496] Desmond had agreed to a ... pledge for his future good behaviour: he would deliver his son and heir to the city of Cork for a year .... Three days later, in return for the promise of a pardon he swore an oath of allegiance with detailed clauses about his future conduct, but evaded giving better security. Desmond, Youghal town, and most Old English magnates in Cos. Cork, Kerry and Waterford were pardoned in August 1496, but Lord Barry and John Water, mayor of Cork, were specifically excluded: Water was later arrested by Kildare and executed in London with Warbeck in 1499. Cork and Kinsale remained for some time in a kind of legal limbo: Kildare received their oaths in 1498 and Cork finally received a new charter [the previous one having been forfeited by the rebellion of its citizens] only in 1500'.[261] Thus, among those pardoned in the aftermath of the Warbeck affair were Maurice earl of Desmond, Thomas, John and Gerald of Desmond, John fitz Gerald of Desmond and Gerald and Thomas fitz Garret of Desmond as well as the archbishop of Cashel and the bishops of Waterford and Lismore and Cork and Cloyne, Maurice Lord Roche, James Lord Courcy, James Lord Barret, Lord Maurice the White Knight, Lord Maurice the Knight of Kerry, Edmund fitz Maurice, baron of Glanmores (that is to say Clanmaurice, namely Kerry), Lord Barry and the mayors and bailiffs of Cork and Youghal.[262]

The mainstay of this party or faction was, of course, the earl of Desmond. It was his political and territorial position which either influenced or determined the attitude of other Anglo-Irish lords in the region as well as that of the borough authorities in Cork, Kinsale and Youghal. Their 'Yorkist' sentiment was in conflict with Ormond's 'Lancastrian' position. The latter determined the attitude of the borough authorities in Waterford, the *urbs intacta*, who steadfastly resisted both Simnel and Warbeck. Accordingly, at the heart of Yorkist-Lancastrian factionalism in Munster was the long-standing conflict between the two great Munster earldoms, Desmond and Ormond. More than the strength of Yorkist sentiment in the south-Munster region, the political interventions of Simnel and Warbeck show the strength of the earl of Desmond's power there. That power was based on his affinity, the number of his retainers and the strength of his retinue and his associates. But, above all, it rested on his extensive territories in the region and, in drawing the study to a close, attention should now be directed to these.[263]

Regarding 'the power structure in the regions immediately surrounding Cork' in the fifteenth century, K. W. Nicholls has emphasised 'the importance of the Desmonds in the neighbourhood.' He has pointed out that 'Robert Cogan, lord of Kerrycurrihy, was still listed among the magnates of County Cork in 1421, but in 1439 he sold his lands (including Carrigrohan) to James, sixth earl of Desmond' and that 'east of [Cork] harbour, the barony of Imokilly[264] – whose feudal centre was Inchiquin near Youghal – was finally, after a century of dispute, brought firmly under Desmond control in this same period and a branch of the Geraldines installed as its hereditary Seneschals.' In this connection he argues that 'it is hard not to believe that the union of the two sides of Cork harbour under the direct control of the great ruling family of Munster, once it had been firmly consolidated, did not dramatically improve the security situation for shipping coming up to Cork itself and so lead to a revival of its trade at the expense of Kinsale.' He points out that 'besides Kerrycurrihy and Imokilly, the Desmonds held scattered lands in Kinelea – such as Noughaval – and elsewhere in the county, and although their outlying castles and manors in West Cork would seem to have been abandoned to the Mac Carthys in the fourteenth century, the earls claimed tributes out of the territories ruled by the two great houses of Mac Carthy Mor and Mac Carthy Reagh (of Carbery) and seem to have collected them with some regularity'.[265] It is evident, therefore, that Cork, Youghal, Kinsale and Dungarvan were either part of Desmond's lands or greatly overshadowed by them. After the collapse of the Desmond rebellion in 1583 and the forfeiture of the earl's lands, it was found that while the earl 'possessed relatively little land in Cork' (those lands which he possessed, however, were very strategically situated, giving the earl control over much of the south coast and dominance over a cluster of important port towns there), 'certain rents and services swelled the total value of his estate to over £1,500'.[266]

Though not unchallenged in the south Munster area (there was, for example, constant conflict between Desmond and the Mac Carthy lords despite intermarriage),[267] by the late middle ages the earldom of Desmond was the major power in Munster, if we exclude the earldom of Ormond, and certainly Desmond power was preponderant in the region extending from Cork city to Dungarvan. The defeat of the earl in his rebellion against the English crown in 1583 and the consequential forfeiture of the Desmond lands removed an essential mainstay of the political system in Munster which had come into being in the course of the fourteenth and early fifteenth centuries. It left Munster and Ireland in general open to the full English conquest which the later sixteenth and early seventeenth centuries witnessed. That conquest was effected largely by means of a policy of plantation, which a surplus population in England at that time permitted, combined with colonisation financed by venture capital. With these developments the political structure of late medieval Munster passed into history and the modern era began.

Conclusion

The Anglo-Norman conquest and settlement of much of the Munster

Plate 5.3   Liscarroll Castle (Cork Archaeological Survey).

region in the late twelfth and thirteenth centuries was followed by unparalleled economic growth and development which changed the very physical configuration of large tracts of the region. This was due not only to the general economic expansion which Europe as a whole witnessed in that period, but also to the introduction of the manorial economy into Ireland and a significant wave of immigration. By the fourteenth century, however, the colony in Ireland was in decline in both its political and economic dimensions. Nonetheless, the colony once established was never completely overturned. On the contrary, it managed to survive in very difficult circumstances. In this regard, the role of successive earls of Desmond in the late middle ages was particularly significant as the earldom came to constitute a new centre of political stability and order, in effect substituting in many ways for that provided by the English crown at an earlier stage.

From the outset the towns, and especially the seaport towns, had constituted an important element of the colony. They were particularly adversely affected by the troubled conditions of the later fourteenth and early fifteenth centuries. However, with varying degrees of success they managed to survive, although towns such as Buttevant by the fifteenth century were decayed. Indeed, the seaport towns especially, enjoyed a modest prosperity arising, not least, from their position as trading centres. In this, even in the darkest days of political and economic troubles, they were buttressed by the political protection and support given to them by the earls of Desmond, by considerable financial concessions made to them by the English crown and by the fact that, in an era of general population decline in the colony and migration from it, there was some movement into the port towns although, of course, there was significant emigration from them also. Thus 'many of the most prominent families of the patriciate [of the port towns] were large landowners from the countryside who had moved into the city to escape the exactions of the Gaelicised lords. Such were the Tirrys and the Sarsfields from Barrymore, the Miaghs from Kerrycurrihy, the Roches of Dunderrow near Kinsale and the Whytes of Killaminoge near Innishannon. These retained their rural lands until with the reimposition of English rule in Elizabethan times they were able once again to enjoy them unmolested, but they did not then give up their urban position'.[268]

This urban patriciate would appear to have supported the English crown during the Desmond rebellion and wars, to have welcomed Desmond's defeat in 1583 and the reimposition of English rule which, no doubt, offered the prospect of stability and commercial prosperity. This was accomplished by a second English conquest and settlement, underpinned, as was the first, by the availability in England of a surplus population which could be transferred to Ireland for re-settlement. This was the essence of the new policy of plantation which emerged long before the Desmond rebellion. It has been pointed out that after 1534 English policy regarding Ireland began to envisage the necessity for a thorough conquest of Ireland to be secured by 'colonisation by new English settlers either on a local or a national basis. At its most extreme it called for the clearing of the Irish out of Ireland and their replacement by Englishmen'.[269] Thereby 'Tudor conciliation in Ireland – the policy that marked the closing years of the reign of Henry VIII – gave way to Tudor conquest'.[270]

The policy of the military suppression of Gaelic Ireland to be followed by the colonisation of extensive tracts of Gaelic Irish territory increasingly came to the fore in the period between 1543 (when the policy of conciliating the Gaelic Irish rulers by bringing them into a feudal relationship with the English crown was abandoned) and 1565 when Sir Henry Sidney, a prominent exponent of colonisation, was appointed lord deputy of Ireland. It would appear that between these two dates a shift in social thinking had taken place in England. It has been argued that English thinking had evolved to the point that, inspired by the model of imperial Spain and its treatment of the native Indian population of the Spanish colonies, there now existed in England a mature ideology of colonisation.[271] In Munster its implementation was facilitated by the Desmond collapse and was promoted by the English government as a joint enterprise between the crown and private interests. In the course of these profound changes, the merchant class of Youghal and Kinsale was augmented by newcomers from England, although Cork appears to have resisted this development.[272] Its medieval patriciate was, however, displaced in 1652 when the 'ancient natives and inhabitants of the citty of Cork' were expelled from the city by the New English.[273] The new and greatly extended merchant class of the port towns contributed significantly to the process of colonisation, including the exploitation of resources, most notably the clearing of woodland, and to the urban growth and economic expansion which seventeenth-century Munster witnessed.

Accordingly, by the early seventeenth century, as a consequence of English military victory and subsequent colonisation, Ireland had become a colony dominated politically and commercially by its sister kingdom, England. Even Irish commercial interests had been made subservient to the interests of the developing English mercantilist state[274] and its ruling class. In Ireland 'a ruling class had been created, riddled with cultural, religious and economic differences, but united against Catholicism and Gaelic tradition'.[275] This development marked in Munster, as indeed in Ireland as a whole, the passing not only of the mixed polity which was so striking a feature of later medieval Ireland but even of the Gaelic order itself.

Acknowledgement

This paper was prepared with the assistance of a grant from U.C.C.'s Arts Faculty Fund, which is gratefully acknowledged.

References

1. C. A. Empey, 'Conquest and settlement: patterns of Anglo-Norman settlement in north Munster and south Leinster' in *Ir. Econ. Soc. Hist. Jn.*, xiii (1986), pp 5-31.
2. Ibid., p. 7.
3. Ibid.
4. Ibid., pp 7-8. The argument regarding contemporary German expansion into central and eastern Europe is an important one and Empey is right to emphasize the parallel between this and the Anglo-Norman colonisation of Ireland. For a further discussion of this question see H. B. Clarke and A. Simms (ed.), *The comparative history of urban origins in non-Roman Europe: Ireland, Wales, Denmark, Germany, Poland and Russia from the ninth to the thirteenth century,* British Archaeological Reports International Series 255 (Oxford, 1985).
5. Empey, 'Conquest and settlement', p. 7.
6. Ibid., p. 5.
7. A. F. O'Brien, 'Medieval Youghal: the development of an Irish seaport trading town, c. 1200 to c. 1500' in *Peritia,* v (1986), pp 346-378, especially pp 353-5.
8. Dublin Corporation Archives, MSS D/Corp 1/1, 1/2, 1/3. Extracts from these rolls are printed in J. T. Gilbert, *Historic and municipal documents of Ireland 1172-1320* (London, 1870), but this work has been superseded by a full edition of the rolls recently published. See P. Connolly and G. Martin (ed.), *The Dublin guild merchant roll, c. 1190-1265* (Dublin, 1992).
9. Empey, 'Conquest and settlement', p. 20.
10. For an examination of Irish agricultural growth in general in the thirteenth century see M. C. Lyons, 'Manorial administration and the manorial economy in Ireland, *c.* 1200 – *c.* 1377', unpublished Ph.D. thesis, T.C.D. (1984) and K. Down, 'Colonial society and economy in the high middle ages' in *New hist. Ire.,* ii, pp 439-490.
11. Empey, 'Conquest and settlement', p. 21.
12. Ibid., pp 9-10.
13. M. de Wolf Hemmeon, *Burgage tenure in medieval England* (Cambridge, Mass., 1914), pp 92-3. In Ireland, as in Wales, the burgage rent was fixed at one shilling per burgage; see Empey, 'Conquest and settlement', p. 21; O'Brien, 'Medieval Youghal', pp 349-50.
14. Empey, 'Conquest and settlement', pp 21-2.
15. Ibid., pp 22-3.
16. O'Brien, 'Medieval Youghal' and idem, 'The development and evolution of the medieval borough and port of Dungarvan county Waterford *c.* 1200 to *c.* 1530' in *Cork Hist. Soc. Jn.,* xcii (1987), pp 85-94.
17. Empey, 'Conquest and settlement', p. 24. For the sub-infeudation of much of east county Cork and the question of borough foundation and burgage tenure in that area in the thirteenth and fourteenth centuries see R. Caulfield, *Rotulus pipae Clonensis* (Cork, 1859).

18. This point is developed below in regard to the three boroughs of the manor of Inchiquin, county Cork (Youghal, Inchiquin, and Kinsalebeg), of which only Youghal survived.
19. O'Brien, 'Medieval Youghal', p. 347.
20. Ibid., pp 371-2, 377.
21. Ibid., p. 355.
22. O'Brien, 'Medieval Dungarvan', p. 85.
23. Ibid., pp 85-6.
24. Ibid., p. 88.
25. Ibid.
26. Ibid.
27. Ibid., p. 89.
28. Ibid.
29. Ibid.
30. This point is developed below.
31. *Cal. doc. Ire., 1293-1301,* no. 75; ibid., *1302-7,* no. 85; *Cal. justic. rolls Ire., 1295-1303,* p. 451; Orpen, *Normans,* iii, pp 123-4. On the death of Miles de Courcy without male heir in 1353 his manor of Ringrone with the rents of the town of Kinsale and the profits of the hundred court there passed to his four sisters, Margaret, Joan, Catherine and Anastasia; see Tuckey, *Cork remembrancer,* p. 22.
32. *Cal. close rolls, 1392-6,* pp 219-20; A. F. O'Brien, 'The royal boroughs, the seaport towns and royal revenue in medieval Ireland' in *R.S.A.I. Jn.,* cxviii (1988), pp 13-26 (hereinafter cited as O'Brien, 'Royal revenue'); *Cal. Carew MSS (Bk. Howth),* pp 370-71.
33. For what follows and for a more detailed discussion of the development of the medieval city of Cork see A. F. O'Brien, 'The development of the privileges, liberties and immunities of medieval Cork and the growth of an urban autonomy *c.* 1189 to 1500' in *Cork Hist. Soc. Jn.,* xc (1985), pp 46-64. See also *Cal. Carew MSS (Bk. Howth),* pp 95, 232, 346, 454. Cork is a striking example of a proto-town whose character was altered by 'the Anglo-Norman colonists who changed the balance decisively in favour of trade in those parts of Ireland that were intensively settled by them.' For a discussion of towns and proto-towns see H. B. Clarke and A. Simms, 'Towards a comparative history of urban origins' in Clarke and Simms, *Urban origins,* pp 669-714, and the same authors' 'Analogy versus theory: a rejoinder' in *Jn. Hist. Geog.,* xiii (1987), pp 57-63.
34. For what follows particularly in the matter of urban privileges, liberties and immunities see O'Brien, 'Medieval Youghal', 'Medieval Dungarvan', 'Medieval Cork'.
35. For merchant guilds see C. Gross, *The gild merchant* (Oxford, 1890).
36. *Cal. doc. Ire., 1171-1251,* no. 2182; *Cal. close rolls, 1231-4,* pp 523-4; *Cal. Carew MSS (Bk. Howth),* p. 397.
37. *Cal. doc. Ire., 1171-1251,* nos. 2170, 2183; *Cal. close rolls, 1231-4,* p. 524; *Cal. Carew MSS (Bk. Howth),* p. 370.
38. *Cal. pat. rolls, 1232-47,* p. 318; *Cal. doc. Ire., 1171-1241,* no. 2569; T. Carte (ed.), *Catalogue des rolles Gascons, Normans et François, conservés dans les archives de la tour de Londres* (London, 1743), i, p. 2.
39. *Cal. doc. Ire., 1252-84,* no. 497; *Cal. close rolls, 1254-6,* p. 411; *Cal. Carew MSS (Bk. Howth),* p. 396.
40. *Cal. doc. Ire., 1285-92,* no. 622.
41. I am indebted to Mr K. W. Nicholls for this information.
42. For what follows regarding markets and fairs in county Cork in the thirteenth

century see P.R.O.I., Plea Rolls (29 Edw. I), R.C. 7/9, pp 205-214 and *Cal. justic. rolls Ire., 1295-1303*, p. 265.

43. These enquiries were begun by Edward I at the outset of his reign and were conducted in the period 1274 to 1294. They were aimed at those who claimed the right to exercise jurisdiction delegated to them by the crown. Such persons were obliged to justify the privileges they claimed. For a discussion of the enquiries see T. F. T. Plunkett, *Legislation of Edward I* (Oxford, 1949), pp 148-9 and D. W. Sutherland, *Quo warranto proceedings in the reign of Edward I, 1278-1294* (Oxford, 1963).

44. P.R.O.I., Plea Rolls (29 Edw. I), R.C. 7/9, pp 205-214 and *Cal. justic. rolls Ire., 1295-1303*, p. 265. Established trading routes, however, by bringing different towns into close association with each other could generate their own trading tensions. For example, in 1287 the mayor and bailiffs of Cork proceeded in the king's court against John Silvestre and other burgesses of Kilmallock on the grounds that the latter had impeded the burgesses of Cork 'in freely buying and selling by wholesale or retail their merchandise in the said town of Kilmallock as they had been wont to do from the foundation of their city' (*Cal. doc. Ire., 1285-92*, no. 310). Similar tensions, also generated by trading competition, existed between Cork, on the one hand, and Youghal and Kinsale, on the other (T.C.D., MS 2013, no. 269A).

45. B. J. Graham, 'The towns of medieval Ireland' in Butlin, *Town*, p. 33.

46. See A. F. O'Brien, 'Europe centre and periphery: the significance of development and change in the medieval Irish economy' forthcoming in K. Fritze (ed.), *Trade and culture in the northern seas* (hereinafter cited as O'Brien, 'Medieval Irish economy'). The whole question of the medieval Irish economy and Irish overseas trade will be considered in detail in my study *The foundations of the medieval Irish economy c. 1000 to c. 1550*, forthcoming.

47. For the urban patriciate in one Irish town see O'Brien, 'Medieval Youghal', pp 366-7. For a discussion of the Cork patriciate see below. A discussion of the role of the urban patriciate in Ireland will be found in Mac Niocaill, *Na buirgéisí*.

48. For Cork's murage grant see O'Brien, 'Medieval Cork'. For the use of revenue accruing from murage grants see O'Brien, 'Royal revenue'.

49. O'Sullivan, *Econ. hist. Cork city*, p. 36. However, it is important to emphasize that not all of these commodities were of equal importance in overseas trade. Some, if they featured at all, were only of marginal significance.

50. *Cal. pat. rolls, 1334-38*, pp 147-8.

51. Revenues accruing from customs receipts in the ports of Dublin, Cork, Dingle, Drogheda, Youghal, Galway, Wexford, Limerick, Waterford, New Ross and 'the Ulster ports' (Coleraine and Carrickfergus), set out in the receipt rolls of the Irish exchequer, have been tabulated by Mac Niocaill, *Na buirgéisí*, ii, pp 523-28. The calculations on pp 15-16 are based on those tables.

52. The operation of the customs system in later medieval Ireland is considered in O'Brien, 'Royal revenue'.

53. A. F. O'Brien, 'The territorial ambitions of Maurice fitz Thomas, first earl of Desmond, with particular reference to the barony and manor of Inchiquin, co. Cork' in *R.I.A. Proc.*, C, lxxxii (1982), pp 59-88; O'Brien, 'Royal revenue'.

54. This point is developed below, pp 45-57.

55. Lydon, *Lordship*, p. 90.

56. *Cal. pat. rolls, 1354-58*, pp 405-6.

57. Lydon, *Lordship*, p. 99.

58. As O'Sullivan has pointed out, in the late seventeenth century 'there is ample

evidence to show that Cork was ... becoming a recognised port of call for all transatlantic shipping, and was establishing an organised victualling trade where a ready market could be found for all manner of cattle produce including hides'; see *Econ. hist. Cork city*, p. 128.

59. Down, 'Manorial administration'.
60. Lydon, *Lordship*, p. 89.
61. Ibid., p. 90; J. F. Lydon, 'Ireland's participation in the military activities of English kings in the thirteenth and early fourteenth century', unpublished Ph.D. thesis, University of London (1955), pp 195-96.
62. Lydon, 'Ireland's participation', p. 192.
63. Ibid., pp 174-75.
64. Ibid., p. 173.
65. Ibid., p. 193.
66. The crannock was the equivalent of the English quarter; see Lydon, *Lordship*, p. 89.
67. Lydon, 'Ireland's participation', Appendix vii, pp xvi-xxi.
68. Ibid., p. 237.
69. Ibid., pp 241-42; *Cal. doc. Ire., 1299-1301*, no. 777.
70. *Cal. doc. Ire., 1299-1301*, nos. 333, 634; *P.R.I. rep. D.K. 38*, p. 50.
71. *Cal. doc. Ire., 1302-7*, no. 58; *P.R.I. rep. D.K.* 38, p. 56; P.R.O., Exchequer Accounts Various, E101/233/16.
72. Lydon, 'Ireland's participation', pp 64-5. For the implications of the royal policy of drawing on Irish resources in support of its activities overseas in the matter of minting and supply of coinage and its movement abroad, the counterpart of purveyance, see M. Dolley, *Medieval Anglo-Irish coins* (London, 1972), pp 6-14.
73. *Rot. pat. Hib.*, pp 32, 33.
74. Ibid., pp 52, 58, 62, 65, 66, 70, 72, 103, 110, 111, 113, 114; Tuckey, *Cork remembrancer*, p. 22; P.R.O.I., Ferguson MSS: Collections from Memoranda Rolls (47-48 Edw. III), R.C. 8/30, pp 345-8, 439.
75. P.R.O.I., Ferguson MSS: Collections from Memoranda Rolls (2 Hen. V), R.C. 8/34, p. 473; *Rot. pat. Hib.*, pp 127, 149, 165, 178, 184, 186, 194.
76. E. M. Carus-Wilson, *The overseas trade of Bristol* (Bristol, 1937), pp 238, 257, 264.
77. Mac Niocaill, *Na buirgéisí*, ii, pp 589-95.
78. For the following details of de Wynchedon's will see D. O'Sullivan, 'The testament of John de Wynchedon of Cork anno 1306' in *Cork Hist. Soc. Jn.*, lx (1956), pp 75-88.
79. This was 'the early fourteenth century parish church of St Finbar, the site of which is now occupied by the Church of Ireland Cathedral of St Finbar.'
80. 'This church stood on the eastern side of the present South Main Street and was within the walls of the mediaeval city of Cork. The site is now occupied by the present-day Christ Church (Church of Ireland).'
81. 'This priory was situated outside the walls of the mediaeval city of Cork on the south shore of the river Lee and appears to have been founded during the reign of Edward I (1272-1307)'.
82. The church of St Peter was 'an early thirteenth century church' which was one of the 'two parish churches within the walls of the mediaeval city', the other being the church of the Holy Trinity, and stood 'on the western side of North Main Street'.
83. According to O'Sullivan 'this church was in the ancient parish of St Mary, Shandon but the exact site of it has been forgotten'. However, Mr K. W. Nicholls informs me that St Katherine's church, Shandon, stood on the south side of

Blarney St. at the west corner of the steps leading down to the North Mall and that the church was destroyed by the seventeenth century.

84. 'The thirteenth century church of St Mary stood on the site now occupied by the church of St Anne (C. of Ireland) on Shandon Hill.'

85. 'This was the church attached to the nunnery of St John the Baptist which was founded in the thirteenth century to the east of the Shandon area .... Its site was near the Kiln River which flows into the north channel of the Lee at Pope's Quay in the neighbourhood of St John's Street.'

86. 'It was situated on Shandon Hill to the west, perhaps, of the mediaeval St Mary's church in the same district.'

87. The site of this church is not clear, but O'Sullivan suggests that it may have been 'on the south side of the River Lee further to the south-east of the walled city in that area wherein stood the churches of St Brigid, St Stephen and St John the Evangelist.'

88. 'The church of St Brigid stood on the summit of Tower Street within an ancient ring-fort.'

89. 'Outside the walls of mediaeval Cork, in the southern suburbs and situated in the present constitutional parish of St Nicholas was an interesting thirteenth century establishment, namely St Stephen's Priory and Lazar Hospital. It derived its name from a small church dedicated to St Stephen which exercised parochial juris-diction over a small area, in part of which stood the hospital and priory buildings, long before the union of the parish of St Stephen with the parish of St Nicholas. St Stephen's Church stood in Stephen Street ....'

90. D. C. Twohig, 'Archaeological heritage' in *History of Cork* in *C.E.*, 27 Mar. 1985 (all further references to *C.E.* are to articles in the newspaper's *History of Cork* series). We are told that in October 1303 the city of Cork was given permission to pay, from tolls levied on foot of its murage grant, 'the expense of a conduit for supplying the city with water' (Tuckey, *Cork remembrancer*, p. 16) while, certainly by 1381 if not even earlier, the middle bridge of the city was said to be made of stone (ibid., p. 33). Another example of a stone house in Cork in this period was that belonging to Nicholas de la Wythye, likewise a prominent burgess and merchant of Cork, in 1318 (ibid., p. 18; *Rot. pat. Hib.*, pp 22, 27).

91. Dungarvan appears to have been a suburb of Cork. It is described by O'Sullivan as 'consisting of a principal street lying north and east having walls to the east and west and is always stated to be in the suburbs and in Shandon parish.'

92. J. Le Goff, 'Croissance et prise de conscience urbaine', in G. Duby (ed.), *Histoire de la France urbaine: la ville médiévale* (Paris, 1980), ii, pp 189-240 (pp 234-39). In Ireland 'the introduction and spread of the friars was ... predominantly an Anglo-Irish phenomenon. But it was by no means exclusively so. All four orders were patronized by native Irish rulers and though houses of friars were for the most part situated in the towns of the colony, each had a significant native Irish element both in the form of houses established in predominantly Irish areas and ... in the form of Irishmen in houses in the predominantly English area'; see J. A. Watt, *The church and the two nations in medieval Ireland* (Cambridge, 1970), pp 176-7. For the role of the friars in the thirteenth century Irish episcopate see also A. F. O'Brien, 'Episcopal elections in Ireland c. 1254-72' in *R.I.A. Proc.*, C, lxxiii (1973), pp 129-76.

93. See J. M. W. Bean, *The decline of English feudalism 1215-1540* (Manchester, 1968). For the question of the rights of burgesses in devising or otherwise disposing of real property, in accordance with privileges conferred on them by charter, see O'Brien, 'Medieval Cork'.

94. R.I.A., MS 12 D 10, p. 85; *P.R.I. rep. D.K.* 39, p. 47. For the fee farm of Cork and payment of it see O'Brien, 'Medieval Cork' and 'Royal revenue'.

95. P.R.O., Exchequer Accounts Various, E101/235/18; 235/22; *P.R.I. rep. D.K.* 39, p. 32; P.R.O.I., Transcript of Memoranda Rolls, 3 Edw. II, R.C.8/4, p. 418.

96. P.R.O.I., Transcript of Memoranda Rolls, 31-32 Edw. I, R.C.8/1, p. 275. For the customs system and its operation see N. S. B. Gras, *The early English customs system* (Cambridge, Mass., 1915).

97. R.I.A., MS 12 I 4.

98. For what follows see J. Lydon, 'A land of war' in *New hist. Ire.,* ii, pp 240-274, especially pp 251-2. The magnitude of the campaign launched by the government against Finín Mac Carthy can be seen from the fact that in 1261-2 the sum of £27. 11s. 8d. was expended 'in buying fish and wheat, and expenses of sending [these supplies] to Cork to the army which [the justiciar] William de Dene led into Desmond against Fynyn Mac Karthy and his accomplices, enemies of the lord Edward' (*P.R.I. rep. D.K. 35,* p. 49).

99. Lydon, 'A land of war', pp 251, 253. For the consequences of this in regard to the de Clare lands in east county Cork see O'Brien, 'Territorial ambitions'.

100. Ibid., p. 256.

101. Ibid., p. 241.

102. J. Lydon, 'The impact of the Bruce invasion, 1315-27' in *New hist. Ire.,* ii, pp 275-302, especially p. 302.

103. P.R.O., Exchequer Accounts Various, E101/233/7; 233/16. Cf. also the case of Dermot MacCarthy discussed below. We are told that, in 1301, Domnall Mac Carthy Reagh and the Irish of Carbery killed John de Courcy, baron of Kinsale and Ringrone, and his brother Patrick in a battle at Inchydoney and that John de Courcy's grandson, Miles de Courcy, likewise baron of Kinsale, defeated Finín MacCarthy Mór 'with a great army of his followers in a battle near Ringrone and drove them into the Bandon river where many of them were drowned'; see Tuckey, *Cork remembrancer,* p. 16.

104. *Rot. pat. Hib.,* p. 25; Tuckey, *Cork remembrancer,* p. 17; Lydon, 'Bruce invasion', pp 284-5.

105. Lydon, 'Bruce invasion', p. 279.

106. Ibid., p. 296.

107. J. de Foubert, 'Crime, punishment and popular disturbance in later medieval Ireland', unpublished M.A. thesis, U.C.C. (1990).

108. Lydon, 'Bruce invasion', p. 297.

109. Ibid., p. 279.

110. Ibid., pp 297-9.

111. R. Frame, 'England and Ireland, 1171-1399' in M. Jones and M. Vale (ed.), *England and her neighbours 1066-1453: essays in honour of Pierre Chaplais* (London, 1989), pp 139-155, especially p. 149.

112. Otway-Ruthven, *Medieval Ire.,* p. 272.

113. R. Frame, *English lordship in Ireland 1318-1361* (Oxford, 1982), pp 18, 168. In 1329 Hugh Canteton, with many others of his family and kin, was killed in a conflict involving the Roches and Barrys (*Cal. Carew MSS (Bk. Howth),* p. 328) while in 1336 Guy Canteton, described as 'a felon and rebel', was captured near Cork by Robert Canteton; see Tuckey, *Cork remembrancer,* p. 21. Sometime before 1359 Gerald son of Peter Canteton gave a pledge of security to the crown in respect of the good conduct of his kin and, in turn, he was empowered to punish such of them as might offend. Accordingly, in July 1359 he and the sheriff of Cork were directed by the king 'to chastise those who had lately invaded his

faithful people of the county Cork in a hostile manner and had collected great spoil and to restore their goods to those from whom they had been seized'; see Tuckey, *Cork remembrancer*, p. 24.

114. Lydon, 'A land of war', p. 263; P.R.O., Exchequer Accounts Various, E101/231/6; 233/16; 236/14.

115. Otway-Ruthven, *Medieval Ire.*, p. 249.

116. Frame, *English lordship*, p. 274. Ironically, in 1340 fitz Thomas and David de Canteton were among those appointed to report the names of those in county Cork who had been 'adherents of divers Irish in rebellion against the king, forming unlawful assemblies there and in parts adjacent, [and] breaking the king's peace' (*Cal. pat. rolls, 1340-43*, p. 93).

117. Otway-Ruthven, *Medieval Ire.*, p. 262. For the career of Maurice fitz Thomas see G. O. Sayles, 'The rebellious first earl of Desmond' in J. A. Watt, J. B. Morrall and F. X. Martin (ed.), *Medieval studies presented to Aubrey Gwynn S.J.* (Dublin, 1961), pp 203-29.

118. Sayles, 'The rebellions first earl of Desmond', pp 205, 216, 220.

119. Tuckey, *Cork remembrancer*, p. 21. See also the action in that year against Guy Canteton discussed above (note 113).

120. Otway-Ruthven, *Medieval Ire.*, pp. 279-80.

121. Ibid.; Tuckey, *Cork remembrancer*, pp 20, 22; *Rot. pat. Hib.*, p. 58; P.R.O., *List of Ancient Correspondence*, xxxviii, no. 26. Evidently the government continued to exert pressure on Dermot Mac Carthy for, in 1366, he was obliged to pay a fine of 500 cows valued at £20. 13s. 4d., in order to have the king's peace; see P.R.O., Exchequer Accounts Various, E101/244/9.

122. Otway-Ruthven, *Medieval Ire.*, p. 280.

123. *Rot. pat. Hib.*, p. 72; Tuckey, *Cork remembrancer*, p. 24. As Frame has pointed out 'the intimate relation between the habit of local taxation and the prevalence of regionalized warfare seems clear' (R. Frame, 'Military service in the lordship of Ireland 1290-1360: institutions and society on the Anglo-Gaelic frontier' in R. Bartlett and A. Mac Kay (ed.), *Medieval frontier societies* (Oxford, 1989), pp 101-126 (p. 113)).

124. Tuckey, *Cork remembrancer*, p. 24.

125. O'Brien, 'Territorial ambitions', pp 76-7, 85.

126. Tuckey, *Cork remembrancer* p. 23; *Rot. pat. Hib.*, p. 72.

127. Otway-Ruthven, *Medieval Ire.*, p. 294.

128. Tuckey, *Cork remembrancer*, p. 27.

129. *Rot. pat. Hib.*, p. 118; Tuckey, *Cork remembrancer*, p. 29.

130. *Rot. pat. Hib.*, pp 114, 118; Tuckey, *Cork remembrancer*, p. 29.

131. For what follows see Otway-Ruthven, *Medieval Ire.*, pp 298, 300, 301, 303, 304, 305, 306, 309-38. See also Tuckey, *Cork remembrancer*, pp 25, 30, 31, 32; *Rot. pat. Hib.*, p. 101.

132. O'Brien, 'Territorial ambitions', p. 60.

133. *Proc. king's council, Ire., 1392-3*, pp 120-23; Richardson and Sayles, *Ir. parl. in middle ages*, pp 89-90.

134. O'Brien, 'Medieval Youghal', p. 359.

135. O'Brien, 'Medieval Cork', pp 56-7.

136. *Cal. pat. rolls, 1330-34*, p. 43.

137. Ibid., 1358-61, p. 573.

138. *Proc. king's council, Ire., 1392-3*, pp 19-21. Thomas Butler, son of the second earl of Ormond, was killed by John fitz Thomas, son of Sir Thomas 'the nephew' in 1396, for whose death the earl of Desmond, on behalf of his 'nation', agreed

to pay the earl of Ormond the sum of 800 marks of silver; see K. W. Nicholls, 'Late medieval Irish annals: two fragments' in *Peritia,* ii (1983), pp 87-102 (p. 90).

139. Ibid., pp 108-110.
140. O'Brien, 'Medieval Youghal', p. 363.
141. Lydon, 'Bruce invasion', p. 278.
142. O'Brien, 'Medieval Youghal', p. 362.
143. Tuckey, *Cork remembrancer,* p. 37; *Cal Carew MSS (Bk. Howth),* p. 370.
144. P. Connolly, 'The financing of English expeditions to Ireland, 1361-1376' in J. Lydon (ed.), *England and Ireland in the later middle ages* (Dublin, 1981), pp 104-21, especially p. 104.
145. J. A. Watt, 'The Anglo-Irish colony under strain, 1327-99' in *New hist. Ire., ii,* pp 366-7, 376.
146. Lydon, 'Bruce invasion', pp 275-6.
147. P.R.O., Exchequer Accounts Various, E101/540/12.
148. *Cal. Carew MSS,* vi, p. 484.
149. R. Frame, 'English policies and Anglo-Irish attitudes in the crisis of 1341-1342' in J. Lydon (ed.), *England and Ireland in the later middle ages* (Dublin, 1981), pp 86-103, especially p. 88.
150. Connolly, 'The financing of English expeditions', p. 105.
151. *Cal. Carew MSS,* vi, pp 454-5. Because the original rolls have been destroyed it is not possible to confirm this figure. However, Frame has argued that the yield of £1,243 for the period 1339-40 represents the 'nadir [of the revenue] under Edward III'; see Frame, 'English policies', p. 88. What is important to note, however, is the general pattern of decline rather than the apparent yield in any one year.
152. *Cal. Carew MSS (Bk. Howth),* pp 384-5.
153. O'Brien, 'Royal revenue', p. 25.
154. *Cal. Carew MSS (Bk. Howth),* p. 385.
155. This matter is developed further on pp 45-51.
156. Tuckey, *Cork remembrancer,* p. 37.
157. *Cal. Carew MSS (Bk. Howth),* p. 484. We are told that in July 1376 'a parliamentary subsidy was assessed upon Munster, Kilkenny and Wexford, of which the county of Cork was to pay 45 marks, the city of Cork £10, and the cities of Waterford and Limerick £10'; see Tuckey, *Cork remembrancer,* p. 27.
158. Connolly, 'The financing of English expeditions', p. 105.
159. Watt, 'Anglo-Irish colony', p. 352.
160. Frame, 'English policies', p. 100.
161. Ibid.; Watt, 'Anglo-Irish colony', p. 367.
162. A. Cosgrove, 'Anglo-Ireland and the Yorkist cause, 1447-60' in *New hist. Ire., ii,* pp 557-568, especially pp 557-60.
163. Ibid. See also O'Brien, 'Medieval Youghal'.
164. Frame, 'English policies', p. 100. By their very nature petitions to the crown seeking assistance or redress of grievances tended to exaggerate the plight of the petitioners. For instances of such petitions from the major Irish port towns and the royal boroughs see O'Brien, 'Royal revenue' and 'Medieval Youghal'.
165. Frame, *English lordship,* p. 331.
166. O'Brien, 'Medieval Youghal', p. 357.
167. A. Cosgrove, 'The emergence of the Pale, 1399-1447' in *New hist. Ire.,* ii, pp 533-556, especially pp. 551-2.
168. *Cal. pat. rolls, 1381-5,* p. 166; *Rot. pat. Hib.,* p. 49.
169. Tuckey, *Cork remembrancer,* p. 23.

170. Ibid., p. 30.
171. Ibid., p. 31; *Rot. pat. Hib.,* p. 136.
172. Frame, 'Frontier institutions and society', p. 120.
173. Ibid., pp 124-5.
174. O'Brien, 'Medieval Youghal', pp 356-7. For a study of the impact of the Black Death on Ireland see M. Kelly, 'The Black Death in Ireland', unpublished M.A. thesis, U.C.C. (1972).
175. Tuckey, *Cork remembrancer,* pp 22, 25, 30, 37, 45, 46.
176. Kelly, 'The Black Death', p. 77.
177. This information is given by Professor Otway-Ruthven in her as yet unpublished paper 'The medieval Irish town'. For a discussion of burgesses and burgages in Youghal see my 'Medieval Youghal'.
178. O'Brien, 'Medieval Youghal', p. 357.
179. Ibid., p. 360.
180. For the evolution and development of this important manor see my 'The settlement of Imokilly and the formation and descent of the manor of Inchiquin, Co. Cork' in *Cork Hist. Soc. Jn.,* lxxxvi (1982), pp 21-26.
181. O'Brien, 'Medieval Youghal', p. 356 note 36.
182. Ibid., p. 352.
183. R. E. Glasscock, 'The study of deserted medieval settlements in Ireland' and 'Gazetteer of deserted towns, rural-boroughs, and nucleated settlements in Ireland', both articles in M. Beresford and J. G. Hurst (ed.), *Deserted medieval villages* (Guildford and London, 1971), pp 279-301. Glasscock lists only this borough for county Cork. His list, however, is only a preliminary one.
184. 'By 1473 the burgesses would seem to have disappeared from Ringrone, Co. Cork, for in that year James Curci, son of Nicholas Curci, lord of Rinron and Kinsale, granted to Rory son of Melmory Mc Beha, *medicus,* half a ploughland of arable land in the burgagery of Rinron'; see Otway-Ruthven, 'The medieval Irish town'.
185. Cosgrove, 'The emergence of the Pale', pp 552-3.
186. Otway-Ruthven, *Medieval Ire.,* p. 296.
187. Tuckey, *Cork remembrancer,* p. 21.
188. Ibid., p. 23.
189. Ibid., p. 25.
190. For this point see also p. 47.
191. *Cal. close rolls, 1385-9,* pp 521-2.
192. *Rot. pat. Hib.,* p. 110; Tuckey, *Cork remembrancer,* p. 30.
193. *Rot. pat. Hib.,* p. 131; Tuckey, *Cork remembrancer,* p. 31.
194. Cosgrove, 'The emergence of the Pale', pp 552-3.
195. *Rot. pat. Hib.,* p. 201; Tuckey, *Cork remembrancer,* p. 35.
196. Cosgrove, 'The Emergence of the Pale', p. 553.
197. Tuckey, *Cork remembrancer,* p. 23.
198. Ibid., p. 24.
199. Ibid.
200. R.I.A., MS 12 I 4.
201. *Rot. pat. Hib.,* p. 95. In Ireland the crannock of wheat varied in quantity but could be as much as eight bushels; see R. E. Zupko, *A dictionary of weights and measures for the British Isles: the middle ages to the twentieth century* (Philadelphia, 1983), p. 100.
202. Tuckey, *Cork remembrancer,* p. 32.
203. Ibid.; *Rot. pat. Hib.,* pp 142, 146.

204. This point is discussed further on pp 45-57.
205. See, for example, the Nottingham ordinance, dated about 1343 or 1344, concerning the export of corn and other commodities; see *Cal. Carew MSS (Bk. Howth)*, p. 458.
206. *Cal. close rolls, 1330-33*, p. 140.
207. *Cal. pat. rolls, 1330-34*, pp 75, 431.
208. Ibid., 1370-74, p. 52.
209. Ibid., 1361-4, p. 499.
210. *Rot. pat. Hib.*, p. 96. The size of the wey varied with the product, but in the case of barley, corn and malt it was the equivalent of 40 bushels; see Zupko, *A dictionary of weights and measures*, p. 434.
211. Tuckey, *Cork remembrancer*, p. 29.
212. Ibid., p. 31; *Rot. pat. Hib.*, p. 136.
213. *Rot. pat. Hib.*, p. 136.
214. Tuckey, *Cork remembrancer*, p. 35.
215. *Rot. pat. Hib.*, p. 196.
216. Tuckey, *Cork remembrancer*, p. 36. This is a striking illustration of the role of merchants from, or using, the small but active ports in county Dublin in this and other maritime trade.
217. *Stat. Ire., Hen. VI*, pp 171, 237-9.
218. For a further discussion of this see my 'Royal revenue'. T. O'Neill, *Merchants and mariners in medieval Ireland* (Dublin, 1987), although apparently inaccurate in important respects, has a useful, but anecdotal, discussion of piracy.
219. *Stat. Ire., Hen. VI*, p. 71.
220. *Rot. pat. Hib.*, p. 25.
221. O'Brien, 'Medieval Cork', p. 59 and 'Royal revenue'.
222. Tuckey, *Cork remembrancer*, p. 35.
223. College of Arms, William Lynch's Calendar of Irish Memoranda Rolls (Henry VI) p. 25. (I am indebted to Mr K. W. Nicholls for this reference).
224. I am indebted to Mr K. W. Nicholls for letting me consult his transcript of J. F. Ainsworth's transcript of the will which is in the Lombard Collection in N.L.I.
225. K. Nicholls, 'Gaelic society and economy in the high middle ages' in *New hist. Ire., ii*, pp 397-438, especially p. 399. Mr Nicholls draws my attention also to the position of Ardfert, county Kerry, which, he points out, in the fifteenth century had a municipal government and in which, even in Elizabethan times, there seems still to have been an urban presence. Clearly, towns and urban life existed outside English Ireland, while it is easy to exaggerate the degree of destruction and decay which both experienced in frontier or contested regions.
226. Tuckey, *Cork remembrancer*, p. 35. Innishannon, moreover, was an important element in the river traffic of the Bandon, not least in the transportation of timber, linking Innishannon with the port town of Kinsale certainly in the late fifteenth and early sixteenth centuries.
227. For a full discussion of this point see O'Brien, 'Royal revenue'.
228. William Sygyn, merchant, to whom reference has already been made in the matter of the importation of cereals and who in 1386 was licensed to export 30 pipes of salmon (*Rot. pat. Hib.*, p. 127) was mayor while William Any and David Candewyk were bailiffs.
229. Tuckey, *Cork remembrancer*, pp 28-9; *Rot. pat. Hib.*, p. 114.
230. Tuckey, *Cork remembrancer*, p. 31.
231. Ibid., pp 34-5. Undoubtedly this picture of Cork's distress is greatly exaggerated at least in some respects. Tuckey's description of the situation regarding inter-

marriage appears to have been inspired by Fynes Moryson's observation that Cork 'is so compassed with rebellious neighbours, as they of old not daring to marry their daughters to them, the custom grew, and continues to this day that by mutual marriages one with another all the citizens are of kin in some degree of affinity'; see F. Moryson, *An history of Ireland from the year 1599 to 1603 with a short narration of the state of the kingdom from the year 1169 to which is added a description of Ireland* (Dublin, 1735), ii, p. 360.

232. *Rot. pat. Hib.,* p. 114; Tuckey, *Cork remembrancer,* p. 29.
233. *Rot. pat. Hib.,* p. 142; Tuckey, *Cork remembrancer,* p. 32.
234. *Rot. pat. Hib.,* p. 190.
235. Ibid.; Tuckey, *Cork remembrancer,* p. 35.
236. Tuckey, *Cork remembrancer,* p. 26; S. Hayman, *The annals of Youghal* (Youghal, 1848), p. 14.
237. For what follows see O'Brien, 'Medieval Youghal' and 'Royal revenue'.
238. O'Brien, 'Medieval Youghal', p. 359.
239. Ibid., pp 365-6.
240. O'Brien, 'Royal revenue', pp 16-18.
241. Ibid., pp 16 ff.
242. Ibid., pp 25-6.
243. K. W. Nicholls, 'Merchant families prosper' in *C.E.,* 6 Mar. 1985.
244. Mac Niocaill, *Na buirgéisí,* ii, pp 394-5. 'The burgesses of Youghal were the recipients of a charter in the year 1404 which conferred upon them a licence to treat with rebels. Ten years later they received a similar charter extending the period of treating with rebels'; see J. J. Webb, *Municipal government in Ireland* (Dublin, 1918), pp 80-81.
245. *Stat. Ire., 1-12 Edw. IV,* pp 138-40.
246. For a discussion of the role of English law in the towns of the colony, particularly in regard to the mercantile activities of the Gaelic Irish inhabitants of these towns, see O'Brien, 'Medieval Youghal', pp 366-7.
247. Ibid.
248. K. W. Nicholls, 'Two islands, one street' in *C.E.,* 13 Mar. 1985.
249. O'Brien, 'Medieval Youghal', pp 366-7.
250. Tuckey, *Cork remembrancer,* p. 36.
251. For grants of denization see G. J. Hand, 'The status of the native Irish in the lordship of Ireland 1272-1331' in *Ir. Jurist* (1966), pp 93-115 and B. Murphy, 'The status of the native Irish after 1331' in *Ir. Jurist* (1967), pp 116-28.
252. Mac Niocaill, *Na buirgéisí,* ii, pp 351, 351 note 77, 398; *Cal. pat. rolls, 1358-61,* pp 492-3, 501.
253. The structure of the medieval Irish economy and the pattern of Irish internal and external trade will be examined in my forthcoming study, *The foundations of the medieval Irish economy c. 1000 to c. 1550.*
254. See my 'Medieval Cork'.
255. O'Brien, 'Medieval Youghal'; A. Cosgrove, 'Ireland beyond the Pale, 1399-1460' in *New hist. Ire.,* ii, pp 569-590.
256. *Cal. Carew MSS (Bk. Howth),* pp 337-9.
257. O'Brien, 'Royal revenue', p. 24.
258. Ibid. In this connection the matter of developing urban autonomy is particularly important. A striking instance of this is to be seen in the royal grant of 1463 to Dungarvan; see O'Brien, 'Medieval Dungarvan', pp 87, 91-2.
259. For Simnel and Warbeck in Ireland see Otway-Ruthven, *Medieval Ire.,* pp 403-8; Tuckey, *Cork remembrancer,* pp 41-2, 42-3, 44-5; S. G. Ellis, *Tudor Ireland:*

crown, community and the conflict of cultures 1470-1603 (London, 1985), pp 76-7; D. B. Quinn, 'Aristocratic autonomy, 1460-94' in *New hist. Ire.,* ii, pp 591-618. The names of those who submitted to Edgecombe at Kinsale will be found in Caulfield, *Kinsale,* p. xiv.

260. Ibid., p. 77.

261. Ibid.; Tuckey, *Cork remembrancer,* pp 42-3, 44, 45; N.L.I., MS 23310, ff 63-4.

262. P.R.O.I., Ferguson MSS (Collections from Memoranda Rolls), 1A49 135, p. 347; R.I.A., MS 12 I 4, pp 339-40.

263. They need be described here only in broad outline as they are discussed in some detail by Mr K. W. Nicholls elsewhere in the present volume. For what follows see Nicholls, 'Merchant families'.

264. The territory of Imokilly included Inchiquin, Clonpriest, Killeagh and Kilcredan. It came into the possession of the earl of Desmond sometime between 1429 and 1462. Its descent is discussed in my 'Imokilly'.

265. Ibid.

266. Mac Carthy-Morrogh, *Plantation,* p. 14.

267. Nicholls, 'Merchant families'.

268. Nicholls, 'Two islands'.

269. D. B. Quinn, 'Ireland and sixteenth-century European expansion' in T. D. Williams (ed.), *Historical studies,* i (London, 1958), pp 22-32.

270. B. Bradshaw, 'Native reaction to the westward enterprise: a case-study in Gaelic ideology' in K. R. Andrews, N. P. Canny and P. E. H. Hair (ed.), *The westward enterprise: English activities in Ireland, the Atlantic, and America 1480-1650* (Liverpool, 1978), pp 66-80, especially p. 67.

271. N. P. Canny, 'The ideology of English colonization: from Ireland to America' in *William and Mary Quarterly,* 3rd series, xxx (1973), pp 575-98, especially pp 593-5.

272. MacCarthy-Morrogh, *Plantation.*

273. Nicholls, 'Two islands'. The list of those expelled contains 253 names including '36 Goolds, 28 Roches, 19 Tirrys, 18 Gallweys, 18 Coppingers and 18 Meades or Miaghs (two forms of the same name). The Sarsfields, Morroghs and Mortells each numbered ten'.

274. K. S. Bottigheimer, 'Kingdom and colony: Ireland in the westward enterprise, 1536-1660' in Andrews, Canny and Hair (ed.), *The westward enterprise,* pp 45-64, especially p. 63.

275. Ibid.

Plate 5.4   Motte at Kilmaclenine (Cambridge Collection of air photographs).

Plate 5.5   Old Head of Kinsale (Cambridge Collection of air photographs).

Chapter 6

THE DEVELOPMENT OF LORDSHIP IN COUNTY CORK, 1300-1600

KENNETH NICHOLLS

Sixteenth-century Ireland, as is well known, was divided politically into a multitude of small but more or less autonomous lordships, known in Irish as *pobal* or *oireacht*[1] and ruled by lords of Gaelic or Anglo-Norman origin, the main distinction being that in the latter succession normally – though not invariably[2] – went by primogeniture to the eldest son or nearest male heir, while in those of Gaelic origin it theoretically devolved to the 'eldest and worthiest', a phrase to be understood in the materialistic sense as 'richest' or 'most powerful',[3] and in practice was frequently fought over between rival claimants. While the rule of primogeniture, where it was followed, must have afforded the Munster lords of Anglo-French origin, less vulnerable to the claims of their kinsmen, a greater degree of authority over the latter, in practice the Gaelic lordships of the region seem also to have been remarkably stable and this is probably not merely an impression conveyed by the lack of detailed annalistic evidence. (An exception is Duhallow, where the MacDonogh lordship was fought over throughout the sixteenth century by the rival lines descended from two brothers[4]). In terms of land law, also, there would seem by the sixteenth century to have been little difference in practical terms between the former colonial regions where younger sons and brothers were entitled to receive a portion of the land[5] and the adjacent Gaelic ones where (in contrast to the practice in most other parts of Ireland, where equal division was the rule) the chief could make the division himself and so assign the largest portion to himself and his immediate kinsmen or even in some cases exclude altogether those whom he disfavoured.[6]

In county Cork the two major lords of Anglo-French stock whose interests lay entirely within the county were Lords Barry, or *Barrach Mor,* 'the great Barry, as he was called to distinguish him from the two lesser Barry lords, Barry Oge (*Barrach Og,* 'the young lord Barry') in Kinelea and Barry Roe (*Barrach Ruadh,* 'the Red Lord Barry' in Ibane) and Roche of Fermoy. Neither of these admitted the superiority of the Geraldine earls of Desmond, who ruled directly over a considerable part of the county, notably Imokilly, Kerrycurrihy and Kinnatalloon, with various scattered lands elsewhere, and received tribute from the small lordships of the Barrets and Courcys, as well as from Beare and from MacCarthy Reagh's great territory of Carbery. The city of Cork seems to have looked to them as protectors against the local lords.[7] The Condons, the FitzGibbon lords of Kilmore, and the much greater FitzGibbon house of the White Knights (*an Ridire Fionn*), most of whose territory, however, lay across the border in Tipperary and Limerick), completed the list of ruling lords of Anglo-French origin. In the west of the county, the three great MacCarthy lords – MacDonayh (*Mac Donnchadha*) of Duhallow, MacCarthy of Muskerry, and MacCarthy Reagh (*Mac Carthaigh Riabhach*) of Carbery, represented branches of the former royal line of Desmond, whose head (who by this time had abandoned the title of king of Desmond to be known as MacCarthy *Mór*), although his power base lay further west in the present County Kerry, exercised a direct overlordship over O Sullivan Beare and the autonomous MacCarthy septs in Beare and Bantry and a lesser degree of superiority in Duhallow, while collecting tribute from the Barret lordship and claiming a virtually ineffective overlordship in Muskerry.[8] The powerful and grasping MacCarthys of Muskerry seem to have exercised a degree of control within their territory rare for Gaelic rulers, but both MacDonogh and MacCarthy Reagh were overlords to a number of powerful local lords who enjoyed considerable autonomy of their own and constituted political forces to be reckoned with. Such were O Keefe, O Callaghan and MacAuliffe in Duhallow and the two O Mahonys, the two O Donovans, the two O Driscolls, with O Crowley and some local MacCarthy chiefs, in Carbery. In 1579 the remote overlord, MacCarthy *Mór,* had 'made' an O Callaghan chief, apparently without reference to the then MacDonogh.[9] Each of these lords, even those in a defined relationship of subordination, sought to maximise his degree of autonomy and to exercise what was in fact a sovereign, or in contemporary parlance 'imperial', authority,[10] and even such a minor sub-chief as MacMaug Condon, head of a branch of that lineage which even in the fourteenth century had acted independently of its lineage heads, seems to have claimed what was in effect an independent authority in his lands.[11] Each lord levied taxation almost at will and appointed judges and officials within his territory.[12] On him depended the maintenance of such law and order as existed, and their positions in this regard was confirmed by Henry VIII's Munster ordinances of 1541[13] which sought, in a policy subsequently to be totally abandoned, to extend English authority on the basis of a modified version of native Irish law.

By contrast, if we turn back to the year 1300 we find that, while the western third of the present county was left to the rule of various

MacCarthy princes and their clients, the remainder was under the control of an efficient county administration, conforming to the normal practice of England itself and responsible to the administration in Dublin and in the last resort to the king of England himself, even if the social and political realities, not only the incessant frontier pressure from the increasingly aggressive Gaelic Irish, but, more seriously, the multiplication of the lordly lineages and the social instability to which this gave rise, were increasingly transforming it into an empty shell. And this administration was a royal one, depending on the king's officials and not on local lords. While the latter enjoyed massive resources in land and retainers, and in the ever-multiplying members of their lineages, their political and judicial authority was, in strict legal theory, minimal if not non-existent. By European standards, the centralisation of authority and of justice, which to those historians reared in the English tradition seems the normal system, was quite exceptional. In France, in Scotland, in most of feudalised Europe the decentralisation of administration and of justice in the hands of the local lords was the accepted norm: in England, the activities of kings from Henry II onwards, culminating in the massive efforts of Edward I, had rendered it almost obsolete, and its survival in the March of Wales was seen as requiring a special – and bogus – historical justification.[14] In Ireland, although the first two (and greatest) grants made by Henry II, those of Leinster to Richard 'Strongbow', earl of Pembroke, and of Meath to Hugh de Lacy, had carried extensive jurisdictional powers, and the now lost grant of Ulster must have done the same,[15] none of the later grants made by Henry or his son John followed these precedents. Henry's grant to Miles de Cogan and Robert fitz Stephen of the 'kingdom of Cork' (i.e. the MacCarthy kingdom whose capital – if such a term is warranted was probably at Shandon beside Cork[16]) con-ferred no such powers, and although those enfeoffed by knightly tenure in Munster, as elsewhere in Ireland, seem to have assumed that they enjoyed the usual powers of baronial jurisdiction, to hang thieves and conduct the ordeals and judicial duels by which proof was obtained in such cases, yet when King John confirmed to Gerald fitz Maurice the grants which he held in Leinster and Munster, the latter (which included Oglassin, the later barony of Inchiquin) by grant from Robert fitz Stephen, he stated precisely that he added these powers of his own gift.[17] The same king's grant of Kerrycurrihy to Philip de Prendergast conveyed only the vaguest jurisdictional rights.[18] Never-theless, at the *quo warranto* proceedings of 1301 in county Cork John de Barry claimed the basic baronial jurisdiction of gallows, infangethef (the right to hang thieves caught in the act), *vetita namia* (improper distraint) and fines for shedding blood (where 'Englishmen' were involved) in his manors of Buttevant, Castlelyons, Rathbarry and Lislee. Philip de Barry of Kinelea claimed the same rights and, in addition, outfangethef (the right to try in one's court and hang a stranger who commits theft upon one's lands) in all his lands, John de Cogan claimed only *vetita namia* and bloodshed at Shandon, Carrgrohan and Dundrinan, as (apparently) did Maurice de Carew in his demesne manors of Dunnamark, Dounemakothemound and CastleCory (Ballinacurra).[19] We do not know the outcome of these proceedings, but it is unlikely to have been favourable; the royal justices were unfriendly to such rights unless backed by a specifically worded royal grant, and in England, where they had once been common, they had by this date become obsolescent if not obsolete under the twin-pronged attack of direct royal challenge and an increasingly efficient and all-pervasive system of royal justice.[20] The impression that one gains from the printed Justiciary Rolls – all that remains to us of criminal records from medieval Ireland – and the criminal cases from the Munster counties recorded in them is that baronial justice had ceased to be of much significance in this regard. Only three references to it from South Munster, all from 1295. Thomas de Saresfeld of Glanmire – a vassal of the Crown at fifth remove![21] – claimed to have the right of gallows over all native Gaelic thieves, and William de Ridelesford (a vassal of the bishop of Cork at Ballymolmichill, the modern Rochfordstown, a corruption of Ridesfordstown) successfully claimed that a native Irishwoman, accused of receiving a thief – itself a capital offence – should be returned to him for trial. The third instance was in County Kerry.[22] The success of Ridelesford's claim may have been affected by the fact that he was a vassal of the bishop, and that the Irish bishops had waged a long – though admittedly often unsuccessful – struggle to get their jurisdictional rights acknowledged by the Crown. Saresfeld was convicted of exceeding his jurisdictional powers – he had the right to try theft but not the offence of permitting the escape of a thief – but it may be noted that the charter by which he held his lands did not contain any clauses conferring jurisdiction.[23] What is more significant is that the right claimed was only to try Gaelic Irish offenders – perhaps Ridelesford claimed no more either – and that in 1301 it was only when the claim to collect bloodshed fines applied to 'Englishmen' that the lords found it necessary to enter it; such rights over their Gaelic tenants were taken for granted. The question of a connection between the replacement of baronial justice in Ireland by royal and the formalisation of the 'exception of Irishry', the exclusion of the Gaelic Irish from legal rights, is an interesting one which has not received attention, but the opposition of the Irish baronage to the wholesale enfranchisement of the Gaelic Irish is easy to explain if it would have meant losing the

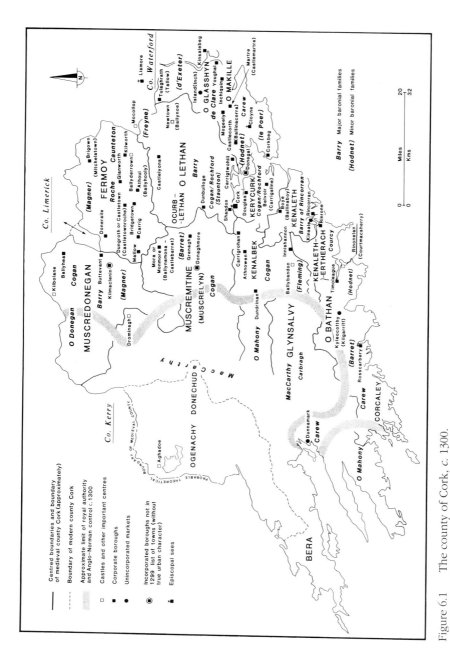

Figure 6.1   The county of Cork, c. 1300.

Source: The primary authority for the cantreds of county Cork is: L. Ó Buachalla, 'An early eighteenth-century placename-list for Anglo-Norman Cork' in *Dinnseanchas*, ii (1966-67), pp 1-12, 39-50, 61-7.

jurisdiction which they had retained over them while losing it over their English tenants.

The decline of royal authority

Nevertheless, whatever such claims, the impression one gets from the Justiciary Rolls is of a royal justice as ubiquitously efficient in prosecuting offenders as it was in contemporary England, even if few of those so prosecuted were in the end convicted. Due to the destruction of the records, we do not know for how long into the fourteenth century the King's justices continued to try criminal please on a regular basis in county Cork, but civil pleas concerning land, after dwindling off for some time, seem to have appeared for the last time in the rolls of 1390-91.[24] Commissions to royal justices for the Munster counties continued to be issued during the first half of the fifteenth century.[25] We do not know the extent of their activity; it seems likely that it did not extend beyond the port towns and their immediate vicinity. In 1475 two citizens of Cork doubled as justices of assize in County Cork and as judges to Lord Barry when they heard a case involving land in Shandon, a suburb of Cork but in the Barry lordship.[26] During the same period intermittent links continued between the county and the Dublin Parliament and administration, though sometimes perhaps more apparent than real. In 1420-21 the county of Cork, with the city, the town of Kinsale, and the clergy of Cork and Cloyne (but not, significantly, Ross) joined in voting a grant to the lord lieutenant, and some magnates and others of the county were appointed to assess its imposition,[27] but on the one hand the lord lieutenant in question was the earl of Ormond, still lord of Youghal and the barony of Inchiquin, and on the other the county representatives who consented to it are given as John Mythe (Miagh or Meade), who had also been elected as a burgess to represent the city, and Thomas Halle, a County Dublin man with no apparent Cork connections.[28] It would look as if the county had in fact sent no representatives to the Parliament, and that two were hastily nominated in Dublin for the purpose of giving consent. A similar event occurred when the earl of Desmond, as Lord Deputy, summoned a Parliament in 1463. Although Desmond was a major magnate in county Cork, his brother Gerald, as its sheriff, nominated two Kildare men, Sir Roger Penkeston and Robert Rocheford, to serve as its representatives; because no members had been sent 'for a long time', an Act of Parliament was necessary to enable him to levy their salary from the county.[29] Could Desmond not raise two reliable anglophones in county Cork? Nonetheless, there were some more genuine contacts by the magnates of the county. In 1450 an Act was passed to grant livery of their lands to Lords Barry, Roche and Courcy (the fact that this was done shows both that the lords in question were concerned about their legal title and that the normal administrative processes were not operative in the region),[30] and in 1477 Maurice Lord Roche obtained an act for the legitimation of his eldest son David, born before the arrival of the dispensation for his parents' marriage and so legitimate in Canon but not in English law.[31] We know that Lord Barry attended Parliament in 1520.[32] of the county administrative system, the office of sheriff continued to be filled by local lords in the early fifteenth century, David, Lord Roche and William, Lord Barry each occupying it,[33] while in 1463 it was held, as we have seen, by Sir Gerald of Desmond. There-after there appears to be no record until after 1500, when Sir Gerald's son, Sir John fitz Gerrot, lord of the Decies, is found in continuous occupation, although his possessions only barely touched the border of the county.[34] It is clear that the sheriffdom of Cork, as almost invariably in Ireland, while ceasing to be an effective arm of royal administration never afforded a useful power base to its holders, and that the example of Waterford, where the sheriffdom was converted by Richard Power and his son Piers into a local lordship independent of royal control, was in Irish terms unique. Even more significant in terms of the atrophy and death of the former institutions of royal government in the changing political and social climate of the fifteenth century was the failure of the earls of Desmond to maintain in existence the hereditary sergeantship of Cork, which they held in common with those of Kerry and Waterford.[35] In the colonial period it was an office of considerable profit and authority, and as late as 1376 we find Sir Maurice fitz Richard, as the earl's deputy in the sergeantship of the county, leasing for 6 years to Patrick fitz Robert de Courcy the office of sergeant in the three of East and West Kenaleath and Kenalbeg, for a down payment of £2 and a yearly render of £4.[36] By the sixteenth century the office would appear to have disappeared without trace. Yet one must not assume that with the passing of royal control and the institutions of royal government all trace of the feudal colonial world likewise disappeared. In 1520 'Royal Service', the scutage due from knights' fees, appears incongruously among the otherwise Gaelic names of exactions imposed by Lord Barry;[37] one need not suppose that it was only collected when scutage was proclaimed in Dublin, or even retained a link with the latter event. In 1592 a later Lord Barry was still holding manorial courts,[38] and it is probable that their tradition had been uninterrupted, although again we might question what kind of law was being administered in them in the sixteenth century.

The growth of Gaelic power
In 1300 about a third of the present county was – if we may judge from

the absence of references in the records of administration – outside the control of the royal government and left to the rule of the MacCarthys and their subordinate Irish lords. Nevertheless some degree of control by Anglo-French lords may have extended further into this region than we can confirm. The fact that Castletownbere and the surrounding lands were in the following centuries an enclave of MacCarthy land surrounded by, but quite independent of, the O Sullivan lordship suggests that we have here the survival of an Anglo-French manorial demesne, as we know to have been the case at Dunnamark in Bantry. Here the former Carew manorial centre and what were presumably its demesne lands belonged to a branch of the MacCarthy Mor house, again independent of the same O Sullivan lords of the surrounding lands.[39] From Dunnamark, where a market was still being held in 1300,[40] a strip of Anglo-French territory extended southeastwards through the Ilen valley to the coast, and extended eastward, so far as we can ascertain, to meet the solid colonial settlement in Ibane (Obathun), bypassing both the inland regions and the southwestern peninsulas. Between 1289 and 1300 we find Maurice de Carew engaged in suing various O Mahonys, MacCarthys, O Dalys and others for lands which he describes as in Caheragh[41] but which must in fact have lain largely in these peninsulas, the latter O Mahony and O Daly territories. A similar situation may have existed in the Blackwater valley, if the manor of Dromayn or Dromany which David de Barry successfully recovered in 1300 from Cormac MacCarthy[42] is to be identified, as seems likely, with Drominagh in Dromtarriff Parish. David alleged that Cormac's recently deceased father Feidhlimidh had dispossessed his own father, the elder David, but it is possible that Feidhlimidh's occupancy had been a tenancy at will rather than a forcible seizure, and all along the frontier, as elsewhere in Ireland, there must have been lands left in the occupation of the Irish in return for some token of rent. Unfortunately the information recorded above which we owe to the obsessive litigiousness of Maurice de Carew is atypical, and in general we know little or nothing of the internal arrangements in the Gaelic regions. Their earlier political geography had been totally transformed not only by Anglo-French invasion and the establishment within them of MacCarthy princes, but also by the arrival of Gaelic ruling lineages driven out of the regions taken over by the colonists, such as the O Sullivans or the O Donovans who were already present by 1201[43] in the O Mahony territory, to which they were to transfer the name of their former territory in county Limerick, Uí Cairbre or Carbery. In the early thirteenth century the western part of this region was in the hands of a Diarmaid MacCarthy, feudal tenant of the cantred of Glanshalewy (Clann Sealbhaigh) but it appears lord not only of the rural deanery of that name but also of the more western district known as Fonnieragh (*Fonn Iartharach*).[44] By 1232 Domhnall Got MacCarthy, ancestor of the later MacCarthys Reagh, was moving into the area,[45] where the O Mahony lordship was eventually split into eastern and western sections, separated not only by the territories of Domhnall Ruadh's descendants but by those of the O Donovans and of the new lineage of Ó Cruadhlaoich (O Crowley), whose claim to Connacht origin suggests that in 1283, when they first appear,[46] they were also recent immigrants to the region. One of the rare references to territorial changes to be found in the Irish annals was when in 1280 Domhnall Ruadh MacCarthy, nominal king of Desmond, divided up the territories under his rule, giving the northern districts to Feidhlimidh MacCarthy and those south of the Lee to Domhnall Got's youngest son and eventual successor, Domhnall Og Maol.[47] Through the fourteenth and fifteenth centuries the latter's descendants gradually destroyed the Anglo-French presence in West Cork. It is to be noted that the territories of the septs descended from Domhnall Og Maol's elder brothers lay in the far west of Carbery, while those of the septs of fifteenth-century origin were in the more recent conquests in the east.

But if information on the formation of the clan lordships within Carbery is scanty, that on the emergence of those in Duhallow, other than that of the overlord MacDonoghs, is almost non-existent. The O Keefes (*Ó Caoimh*) had been rulers of Fermoy at the time of the conquest, and Corc O Caoimh (died 1259) is styled of Fermoy in a royal letter summoning him to serve in person in Henry III's Scottish campaign of 1244.[48] The summons shows that he was one of the Gaelic lords whose territorial status was recognised by the English administration in Ireland, but Fermoy had had Anglo-French lords since the 1180s and was one of the most heavily settled and enfeoffed areas. Although there may still have been a minor O Keefe presence there in 1300,[49] it is almost certain that by that date they had already moved into their later homeland on the upper Blackwater, a hypothesis supported by their feud with the Barrets, who had territorial claims in that area, and who slew the O Keefe chief, Thomas mac Mailduin, in 1283.[50] We have no information whatever regarding the beginnings of the O Callaghan or MacAuliffe lordships. An annalistic reference to the O Callaghans in 1283 even suggests that they were then in Carbery,[51] but this may be misleading. Both O Callaghans and O Keefes, including the probable chiefs of both lineages, are named among the leaders of the force which Diarmaid mac Diarmada MacCarthy and Domhnall MacCarthy of Carbery led into Duhallow to slay Sir Robert de Barry, custodian of the Barry lands, in 1345.[52] But the fact that the townlands named as harried by them in that campaign lay in the later O Callaghan lordship tells us no more than that the latter, if already formed, did not stretch so far as to include them.

Two of the major baronial lordships of the colonial period, those of the Carews and the Cogans, failed to survive as such into the sixteenth century. The collapse of the Carew lordship is perhaps unsurprising, given its lack of a solid territorial base outside the vulnerable frontier territory in West Cork. Maurice de Carew had tried to make the most of his rights, as heir of Robert fitz Stephen, to the overlordship of half the 'kingdom of Cork' (which included County Kerry and part of Limerick as well as Cork), but his son Thomas was to be the last of his line. No doubt realising that he could no longer maintain his position, at some date before 1326 he conveyed his remaining rights as overlord, along with Dunnamark and the other lands in West Cork, to Maurice fitz Thomas, first earl of Desmond. It is significant that the Desmonds, as will be seen, were equally unable to keep control of these lands. Thomas had previously granted his feudal overlordship of the Barry lands to David de Barry, who thus became a direct tenant of the Crown.[53] After him the remaining Carews quickly declined into minor landlords in Imokilly, while the old Carew *caput* of Castlecorth (Ballinacurra) was taken over by the Barrys.[54] The collapse of the Cogan lordship, on the other hand, would appear surprising, given both its territorial extent and the numerical strength of the lineage. In 1300 the Cogans controlled perhaps the largest accumulation of landed power in the county, stretching from the Limerick border to Cork Harbour. The nucleus of this was the cantredal lordship of Muscrymittine, which occupied the territory between the Blackwater and the Lee, with its baronial centre at the place known in Latin as *Mora* and otherwise varyingly called the Newtown of Monemore, Moretown or Ballynamona, or, later, Castlemore or Castle-Barret. South of the Lee, and in the cantred of Kenelbek, the main line of the Cogans held the manor of Dundrinan (Castlemore near Crookstown) in the upper Bride valley under the lords of the cantred, the Barrys of Rincorran. The lower Bride valley was held, partly from the bishops of Cork, and partly perhaps as a sub-fee of Dundrinan, by the junior branch of the lineage, the Cogans of Hycheston (Garryhesty). Further east, Carrigrohane (-more) was held by the main line from the bishops.[55] The acquisition (through the first marriage of John (I) de Cogan) of half the Prendergast inheritance brought the Cogans the manor of Balaghath (Ballyhea) in the north (where they already held Rathcogan, the modern Charleville, as a sub-fee) and a half share in the manors of Beaver (Carrigaline) and Shandon, corresponding respectively to the cantred of Kerycurk and the district of Ocurblethan. Both Balaghath and Shandon were held under the Barrys, and the northern lands were separated from the rest of the Cogan lands, which formed a continuum, by a belt of Barry territory. In addition, there were lands in the south-west of which we know little, and very extensive territories in Connacht. The fact that the other half of the Prendergast inheritance had passed to the knightly family of Rocheford, who never developed into a lineage, made the Cogans the dominant force in Kerycurk and Ocurblethan, where their territories enclosed the city of Cork (where they claimed the hereditary custody of the south gate) on almost all sides.[56] John (I) de Cogan, however, had before his death in 1279 alienated much of the inheritance, including *Mora* and Kilshannig and the Connacht lands, in favour of the sons of his second marriage. In the event the surviving son, Master Henry (who abandoned a clerical career in favour of a secular one) obtained from his nephew John (III) the manor of Balaghath and a life interest in Beaver and other lands (parts of the Prendergast inheritance) in exchange for those his father had given him.[57] Since Henry survived until 1336 and his surviving son, Master William, also a cleric, and a client of the first earl of Desmond, until 1367 at least this represented a serious diminution of the Cogan inheritance, although it still remained a great one. John (III) had been succeeded in 1311 by a minor son Milo, who was killed, soon after coming of age, at the battle of Athlahan (Ballylahan and Strade, county Mayo) in 1316, leaving his brother Piers, also a minor, as heir.[58] During the minorities of Milo and Piers the headship of the lineage was exercised by David de Cogan, perhaps an elder and illegitimate half-brother, and it was he who led the Cogans when their lands were ravaged 'from Cloch Muchoba (Cloghmacow) to Barnahely' by the Barrys and Roches in the course of the furious lineage war which ravaged County Cork. On February 29 1317 those Barrys and Roches who, on account of the 'robberies, arsons, homicides and very many other misdeeds on the lands of those of the surname of the Cogans' which they had committed, had been reluctant to appear at Cork before the Justiciar, Edmond le Botiller, arrived on safe conducts and were admitted to the King's peace for a fine of £2,000, two-thirds of which was immediately remitted to them on condition of their serving in the Justiciar's forces against the Scots, for this was in the middle of the Bruce invasion. On 18 December following the various lineage leaders of County Cork, among them David de Cogan, appeared before the Justiciar and agreed to make peace between themselves, to give hostages, and not to quarter their horses or their kernes and other 'idlemen' except on their own unfree tenants (betaghs). Only David (IV) de Barry, heir to that lordship, refused to submit with his kinsmen and remained in rebellion until he finally submitted in 1320.[59] In the same year Henry de Cogan and his overlord John de Barry, who had been co-operating in the defence of Muscrydonegan against the MacCarthys, fell out when Barry made peace without consulting Henry.[60] David was still acting as lineage head in 1320[61]; Piers was of age in 1326 but dead by 1330, again leaving a minor heir.[62] In these circumstances the Cogan lordship, perhaps already gravely weakened by the events of 1317, was in no condition to withstand the Gaelic attack which was to fall upon it.

It is possible that the Macroom region had been under effective MacCarthy control since the 1260s, and that the colonial frontier between the Blackwater and the Lee, and in the Bride valley to the south, remained largely static through the following half-century. The fact that the natural frontier at the hill of Cloghmacow just west of the present Crookstown, where the Bride emerges from the hills to enter its wide lower valley, is mentioned as the western limit of the Cogan lands in 1317 suggests that an equilibrium had been reached in the area, with the lands west of the line being occupied by the Gaelic Irish. In the second quarter of the fourteenth century the reoccupation of territory by the MacCarthys acquired a new momentum. This movement, however, was not the work of the nominal kings of Desmond but of their cousin and enemy, Diarmaid mac Diarmada MacCarthy, known to the English as MacDermot, a close and ambitious ally of the ambitious Maurice fitz Thomas, first earl of Desmond.[63] The targets of this expansionary movement were the Barry and Cogan lordships, temporarily linked through the marriage of David (IV) de Barry to Margaret Wogan, widow of Piers de Cogan and mother of the young heir Henry.[64] In December 1331 David was granted custody of the heir and his lands, but although he manfully warred with Diarmaid mac Diarmada, against whom he refortified the castle of Dundrinan, he was ousted for a time by the influential prior of the Hospitallers, Roger Outlawe, and did not regain control until 1337, this time, however, without having to account for the rents.[65] David was alive in May, 1344 but died soon after, leaving a ten-year old heir; on August 11 of the following year his kinsman Sir Robert de Barry, who had been granted custody of his lands, was slain in battle in Duhallow with many others by 'MacDermot' and Domhnall Cairbreach MacCarthy, allegedly at the instigation of Desmond. In 1347 custody of Liscarroll, the frontier fortress of the Barry power in North Cork, was granted to David's widow and her ten-year-old son and heir, and it was not until January 1349 that Sir Robert's son John was confirmed in his father's custody of the Barry lands.[66] The young Cogan heir, having come of age, had formal livery in august 1347, but was dead within a year, when his brother Walter succeeded and had livery in turn.[67] In these circumstances defence of the frontier against the Gaelic expansion, probably in any case hopeless, became impossible. When Sir Thomas de Rokeby, justiciar of Ireland, conducted his successful career against MacDermot in the autumn and winter of 1352-3 it was too late, at least for Walter de Cogan and his vassals. The justiciar proclaimed that the former landowners should return and reoccupy their lands, under pain of forfeiting them, but we are told that it was not until after the death of MacDermot, slain with his eldest son Donnchadh by the O Sullivans in 1356 or 1357,[68] that some of them dared to do so. In any case, Rokeby appeared at first to ignore the Cogan claims, immediately after the campaign granting – or rather, confirming – Macroom and many other lands to Cormac MacCarthy.[69] Cormac, the nominal king of Desmond, had joined in the campaign against MacDermot; his relations with the English administration seem to have continued, as in 1358 he was one of those commissioned to hear and determine the feud between the Barrets on the one hand and the Courcys and Barrys Og on the other. He died in 1359.[70] At the same time as the grant to Cormac Rokeby granted to John Lombard, a Cork citizen and royal official of Italian banking stock, the lands which had belonged to Ralph de Gynes, a Cogan vassal who had died without heirs and whose castle at Cloghroe had been in Gaelic hands.[71] Then, turning to his own advantage, he induced or compelled the hapless Walter de Cogan, first to grant to him a life-tenancy of the manor of Moreton (that is to say, the cantred of Muscrimittine), and then to release it in fee to de Rokeby and his heirs.[72]

After the death of MacDermot peace, we are told, was established on the frontier, and some of the previous landowners, notably Geoffrey de Cogan of Hycheston and his vassals, moved to reoccupy their lands, in some cases installing members of the MacCarthy clan as tenants. Trouble, however, soon broke out again, interrupting the attempt of Piers de Cogan, who had succeeded his brother Walter, to overthrow the latter's conveyance to Rokeby.[73] When the new Lord Lieutenant, the king's son, Lionel, Duke of Clarence, came south in 1365 and 1366 he seems, as Rokeby had done, to have regarded the Cogan lands in Muscrimittine as *terra nullius* and at his free disposal. The main beneficiaries of Lionel's grants were the rising lineage of the Barrets.

The rise of the Barrets

The Barrets, another Cambro-Norman lineage,[74] had been important in both Desmond and Connacht since the early thirteenth century. Sir William Barrett, probably the third William, had been killed in a private battle in northern Connacht in 1281. His main interests in County Cork had been in the far south-west, where he held Castlegeyth (Castleventry) and Clardor (Glandore), as well as lands from the see of

Ross, but he also held Grenagh in the later Barrets Barony as a fief of the Cogans.[75] The 'sons of William Barret', who slew O Keefe in 1283, were presumably his brothers; William's heir and namesake was a child who did not come of age until 1299; he died between 1311 and 1313, leaving only daughters.[76] Thereafter the representation of the lineage in Connacht and in Desmond diverged, while the lands in west Cork soon fell out of family possession. The custody of Grenagh was entrusted (by September 1313) by the Crown – in whose custody the Cogan lordship then lay – to Robert Barret, perhaps the dead man's uncle or perhaps a son and namesake of the latter, in which case he would be 'the son of Robert Barret' who slew and was slain by Fionnghuine O Keefe in 1317, as he was dead in the latter year when the custody was confirmed to his son William in reward for Robert's staunch defence of the marches against the Irish.[77] Grenagh, however, was not the only Barret holding in this area: Thomas Barret fitz John was litigating for the advowson of Garrycloyne in 1327.[78] The John fitz John Barret who held Garrycloyne in 1353 must have been a descendant of his. Garrycloyne belonged to a line of Barrets down to the seventeenth century.[79] However, another Thomas Barret 'of Dessemond', this time the son of a Richard, was one of the Anglo-Irish magnates whom Edward III summoned to accompany him in his invasion of Scotland in May 1335.[80] It was perhaps this Thomas's son who turns up, along with three other sons of a Richard Barret William, John and another Richard – in MacDermot's army in 1345.[81] By 1355 William Barret, presumably the man of 1345, was chief of the lineage.[82] By 1358 he had been replaced in this position by Richard Óg Barret, presumably his brother, who was to be the main beneficiary of Clarence's grants. By that year also Richard Óg and his kinsmen were engaged in a furious feud with the southern lords, Miles de Courcy and William de Barry Óg (to give him the later title of his line).[83] The probable area of contention was the cantred of Kinalmeaky, of which Barry was lord, where Courcy held lands and into which the Barrets were probably already moving.

Although on his way to Munster in 1366 Clarence had made on July 16 a grant of lands (now lost) to a Philip Ballagh Barret,[84] perhaps the Philip who was hostage for his father William in 1355, the grant made by him to Richard Óg on September 20 was in its terms a spectacular one. It conveyed to him and his heirs all the lands from the Lee to the Awynmor (Blackwater) in the cantred of Muscrymytyn, and all those from the Lee southwards to the Bride, from Inniscarra in the east to Inchiall (in Knocknagoul) and Moraghcolagh (perhaps Mallagh) in the west, along with all the lands of Dundrinan and Bruyn.[85] All these lands were said to have been reconquered by Clarence after having been wasted by the Irish, so short had been the effect of Rokeby's campaigns. Under colour of this grant, Richard Og and his kinsmen, including the sons of John Boy and of William Cnap Barret – probably his brothers of 1345 – proceeded not only to oust Geoffrey de Cogan and those of the other former landowners who had returned to their lands but also to expel John Lombard who had already by 1356 been at law with a Barret over Ardamadane, on the ill-defined northern limits of his grant[86] – from some of his lands, including Oldcastle which he had purchased from its former owner.[87] The ousted landowners obtained legal judgements against Richard Óg and his kinsmen: it is extremely unlikely that these had any effect, and from then on the Barrets were to replace the Cogans in the latter's mid-Cork territories.

Piers de Cogan the younger had eventually inherited what was left of the northern lands on the death of Master William, but died childless, like his brothers, in July 1371: his legal heirs in the female line were John de la Roche, lord of Fermoy, and another Roche, the outlawed Sir William, but his heir of entail was his distant kinsman Geoffrey of Hycheston. After his death it was recorded that no rents were received from *Mora* 'on account of destruction by the Barrets', and very little from the northern lands, on account of 'destruction by the Geraldines', the FitzGibbon clan who were to be the later lords of that area.[88] A deal would seem to have been eventually struck between the legal heirs by which John de la Roche secured possession of Ballyhea and its dependencies, subject to a yearly rent of £4 to Geoffrey and his heirs, and in 1405 John's son Maurice Roche quitclaimed all the lands south of the Awnmor to Geoffrey's sons Robert and Miles, an arrangement which did not prevent the greater part of the parish of Whitechurch (in the old Muscrymittine) becoming and remaining a detached portion of the Roche lordship of Fermoy.[89] In 1439 Robert Cogan conveyed away all his lands, including his claim to Dundrinan and the Newtown of Monmor with Muscrymittine to James, Earl of Desmond, whose grandson in 1494 confirmed the Barret possession of at least the Muscrymittine lands by releasing to Sir James Bared, captain of his nation, all the earl's right and claim in the district (*rus*) of Ballynemona.[90]

Clarence's generous grant to the Barrets had not imbued them with a spirit of loyalty to the English administration in Ireland; eleven years later than were in open rebellion, a state which continued until Richard Óg, his son William and others of the family decided, or were compelled, to buy peace by surrendering hostages and paying a fine of a thousand cows in January 1383.[91] In 1387, however, John Barret was a keeper of the peace in that strange list which included the MacCarthy lords of Muskerry and Duhallow.[92] Although the Barret lordship in mid-Cork was gradually eaten away by the eastern expansion of the

Muskerry MacCarthys – the process will be considered later leaving the geographically broken and fragmented territory which survived as the Barony of Barretts until the boundary reforms of 1837 – it also continued to expand in the old cantred of Kinalmeaky south of the Lee. Ballincollig was acquired from the last of the eponym family, the Coles, in 1468, while Carrigrohan (another former Cogan possession) was for a time in Barret hands.[93] The Barrets paid tribute both to MacCarthy Mor and perhaps a result of the treaty by which they submitted to him in 1426, not long after they had been temporarily expelled from their territory by the MacCarthys – to the earl of Desmond, while they themselves were overlords of the MacCarthy sept called the Clan McDonnell, whose lands lay on both banks of the Lee above Inniscarra.[94] In the late sixteenth century several disputed successions led to intra-lineage violence among the Barrets. In the end, although the male heir, Edmond Barret, retained the chieftaincy and the castle of Ballincollig, as did his son William after him, most of the lands passed by English law to his cousin Catherine, or rather to her husband Andrew Barret, a Cork merchant's son who had been educated at the Inns of Court in London.[95]

The rise of Muskerry

We do not know if a now lost grant of lands by Lionel, Duke of Clarence to Domhnall MacCarthy, Cormac's eldest son and 'captain of the Irish of Desmond'[96] on 11 May 1365 had reference to lands in the present County Cork, but in any case the beneficiaries of Rokeby's grant to Cormac were to be the descendants of Domhnall's younger brothers, Diarmaid (known to later generations as Diarmaid Mor Muscraighe) and Eoghan. Diarmaid mac Diarmada, as we have seen, had been killed with his eldest son Donnchadh (the eponym of the later MacDonoghs of Duhallow) in 1356 or 1357: another son, Diarmaid *mac Láimhe,* may have taken over his father's position in Duhallow until his own violent death in 1363.[97] The next of that line on whom we have concrete information is Donnchadh's son Cormac, who died in 1403.[98] Diarmaid Mor, who was killed in treachery by the O Mahonys in 1381 (suggesting that, like his namesake, he was attempting to extend his possessions into their territory south of the Lee), married Catherine de la Roche of Fermoy, a granddaughter through her mother of the first earl of Desmond.[99] In 1387 his eldest son Tadhg was one of two MacCarthy lords included, remarkably, in a royal commission of the peace for county Cork; the other, even more remarkably, was MacDermot's grandson, Cormac mac Donnchadha of Duhallow.[100] After the death, some time after 1411, of the third of Diarmaid's sons to rule Muskerry, Feidhlimidh, it seems likely that the territory fell under the control of their cousins Cormac and Domhnall, the sons of Eoghan. That this was the case is strongly suggested by the fact that in 1421 these two brothers seized possession of the Barret territory, which they occupied for a year, defeating at Carrigrohane a combined MacCarthy Reagh-Roche expedition against them.[101] It is hard to see how this could have been effected without control of at least part of Muskerry, and there would seem to be also a lacuna in the succession of Diarmaid Mor's descendants at this time. It would also appear from the title of *adhbhar tigherna* of Desmond given to a grandson of Diarmaid Mor in 1411[102] that the descendants of Cormac were not yet segregated into territorially distinct lines. Domhnall mac Eoghain was killed in 1435 by Diarmaid's grandson Tadhg mac Cormaic, who in 1461 was succeeded as lord of Muskerry by his eldest surviving son, the famous Cormac mac Taidhg, founder of Kilcrea Friary and builder of Blarney.[103] We do not know when and how the MacCarthys of Muskerry took possession (granted in 1365, as we have seen, to the Barrets) and imposed a heavy overlordship on the O Mahony septs who surrounded it. The O Mahonys of Kinalmeaky, only slightly to the south, were subject to MacCarthy Reagh, and it is possible that the fierce campaign in 1449 between the lord of Muskerry, assisted by MacCarthy Mor's sons, and MacCarthy Reagh[104] was connected with the formation of the later frontier in this region, cutting through the old cantred of Kinelmeaky. If the traditional date of 1465 for the foundation by Cormac mac Taidhg of the Observant Franciscan Friary of Kilcrea[105] is correct and if it followed the usual fifteenth-century pattern of being established close to a lord's residence, then the erection of the nearly MacCarthy castle must have antedated it by at least some years. Had the MacCarthys actually secured possession of Castlemore when they erected Kilcrea Castle a few miles away? Mathghamhain O Mahony, chief of the Clann Finghin sept whose territory surrounded Castlemore was of sufficient importance to merit an obit in the MacFirbisigh annals in 1466[106] was Castlemore for a time in O Mahony hands? In the area south of the Lee and Bride, Muskerry expansion pushed southward from Kilcrea to occupy the northern upland fringe of Kinelea, leaving the level country in the hands of its lords, the Barrys Óg.

On the east, the expansion of Muskerry at the expense of the Barrets and others was a haphazard process which left an extremely frag-mented border, as the various lands which fell onto MacCarthy hands were added to Muskerry. The building of the castle of Blarney has been traditionally dated at 1440, but the will of David Lombard in 1479 suggests – although it does not conclusively establish – that 'Blarnach' and 'Clocroga' (Cloghroe) were still in his hands[107] and a date in the 1480s seems more likely. In Elizabethan times the continuing Lombard claim to Blarney was exploited in the struggle for its possession by the rival MacCarthy cousins, Cormac mac Diarmada and the sons of his uncle Sir Cormac mac Taidhg.[108] The earlier Cormac's brother, Eoghan, who was to slay his brother in 1495 and rule as lord for three years until himself slain by his nephew Cormac Óg in alliance with Sir Thomas of Desmond. Along with Eoghan was slain Edmond mac Dubhdara MacSweeney, a galloglass leader invited from Tir Conaill by Cormac mac Taidhg, and whose three sons and their descendants were to become a very important force in Muskerry.[109] Eoghan had in 1488 acquired Cloghphilip from its owner, John Barret;[110] we do not know how voluntary the conveyance was, or how he acquired, as he did, the remainder of 'Twogh-Cloghroe' which, as has been noticed, was Lombard land. Cormac mac Taidhg's occupation (with the consent of the young earl of Desmond whom he was supporting) of the castle of Carrigrohane during the struggle for control of the Desmond earldom in 1469-70,[111] does not seem to have endured, but he achieved a further expansionary step when, shortly before his death, he secured the preceptorship of the Knights Hospitallers' commandery of Mourne (until then usually held by one of the Roches) for his twelve-year-old son Donnchadh.[112] This gave not only lands on the border of Barret and Roche territory but also control of the rectorial tithes of almost all the old Cogan lordship. Donnchadh was subsequently *tánaiste* to his brother Cormac Óg, while the preceptory was afterwards held by the latter's son Diarmaid, finally ending up in the hands of Sir Cormac mac Taidhg and his descendants.[113]

The eastward growth of Muskerry went on, gradually encircling the city of Cork. In 1597 Nicholas Browne declared that the MacCarthys had forcibly compelled the Barrets to yield up CastleInch and a branch of the Roches Carrignavar.[114] Neither, however, was gained without a struggle. Castle-Inch was included in the livery of her lands granted to the Barret heiress, Catherine, in 1588, and was in the custody of her servants in 1593, when it was besieged (and taken ?) by Cormac mac Diarmada.[115] Thereafter it seems to have remained with the MacCarthys. Carrignavar was an even more hard-won acquisition, since there was a rival claim from the Desmonds, perhaps as part of the Cogan lordship of Ocurblethan, in which it lay. Sir John of Desmond was in possession in the 1570s, mortgaging it in 1578 for £50 to Justice John Meagh or Meade, who maintained possession against both the Crown (who wanted it for the Plantation) and the MacCarthys.[116] Cormac mac Diarmada, after some difficulty, succeeded in having it included in his regrant of 9 May 1589.[117] This was the furthest extension of MacCarthy territory; ironically it was the last piece of property to remain with their descendants, who held Carrignavar down to modern times. Also north of the Lee, the MacCarthys took over the entire parish of Currykippane,[118] just outside the city of Cork, as well as various scattered lands in Barrets' Country. Those which they retained endured as detached fragments of the barony of Muskerry down to 1837,[119] while others, such as the lands in Grenagh Parish known as MacWilliam's Lands and those in Carrigrohanbeg Parish, eventually returned to the Barrets, in spite of figuring in Cormac mac Diarmada's surrender and regrant of 1589.[120] Can we hypothesise a deal involving the trading off of the claims to these lands and to Castle-Inch? It is to be remarked, however, that the lands of East Pluckanes, which Sir Cormac mac Taidhg and his wife acquired (under the name of Ballyknock) from its Barret owners in 1575, and which subsequently belonged to his descendants,[121] remained in the barony of Barrets. South of the Lee the lords of Muskerry acquired the lands of Garrandarragh, Ballincranig and Gortagoulane, and Kilmurriheen.[122] A final acquisition was the concession by the leper hospital of St. Stephen's outside Cork, in return for a free supply of firewood from the woods of Blarney, of free entertainment for the lords of Muskerry, their servants and horses, whenever they came to Cork.[123]

Eoghan MacCarthy, the lord from 1495 to 1498, had, as has been mentioned, acquired Cloghphilip and the rest of 'TwoghCloghroe', and his descendants continued for a time to expand their land-acquisitions before finally collapsing. In 1566 three grandsons of Eoghan's, the brothers Eoghan, Carrthach and Donnchadh, sons of Tadhg, acquired Ballygarvan in Kerrycurrihy from Patrick Meade of Kinsale,[124] and perhaps the neighbouring Ballea, which also seems to have been Meade or Meagh land, was acquired by them about this time. The two MacCarthy brothers who conveyed their right to Ballyhemiken near Carrigaline to Richard Boyle in 1616[125] probably also belonged to this sept. But at some time in the 1570s the entire lands of the sept, not only Cloghroe but also Ballygarvan and (if it did belong to them) Ballea had come to the hands of the then lord of Muskerry, Sir Cormac mac Taidhg, who was to bequeath them to his sons with the recommendation that they should 'reasonably agree for some rent or other allowance' during their lives to the three then representatives of the sept, 'for any their challenge to any part of Cloghroe'.[126]

But the most spectacular expansion of Muskerry power to the east was one that was not destined to last. This was when in 1535 Cormac Óg persuaded the wretched English-educated heir to the earldom of Desmond, James (who was contracted to marry his daughter) to grant to him the entire manor of Carrigaline, corresponding to the cantred of Kerrycurrihy. Cormac Óg in consequence ruled Kerrycurrihy for the short period before his death in 1536, as did his son Tadhg, until he was expelled and Kerrycurrihy recovered by the new earl James and his brother Maurice.[127]

The Barrys

The fate of the Barry lordship was very different from that of the Cogans, losses of territory to the MacCarthys of Duhallow in the north-west and to the Desmonds in the east being compensated for by acquisitions elsewhere. The hiving off the West Cork possessions to a junior branch, later known as the Barrys Roe (*an Barrach Ruadh,* 'the Red Lord Barry') and founded by Sir William *Maol* (died 1373) would have strengthened the Barry interest rather than weakening it, by giving that area a resident lord and allowing the main line, who became known as Barrymore (*an Barrach Mór*), to concentrate their attention on their other territories. David (IV) de Barry had had, shortly before his death, to contend with the claims of a distant kinsman, Adam fitz William de Barry of Rathcormack, who sued him in Dublin for the entire Barry inheritance, and subsequently with his own immediate kinsmen, waged open war against him.[128] The occupation of much of the Barry lordship in Muscridonegan by the descendants of 'MacDermot', the MacDonogh MacCarthys, and the O Callaghans was under way in the time of 'MacDermot' himself, but may have been a fairly long drawn out process. It left the Barry lordship in the north restricted to the compact area known as Orrery, centred on the castle and borough of Buttevant and the castle of Liscarroll, with an outlying enclave in the Magner holding around Castlemagner. In the sixteenth century the Barrys formally styled themselves 'lord of Olyehayn and Orryry', though they were commonly called *an Barrach Mór.*[129] Buttevant had several small town 'castles' as well as Lord Barry's castle, and the Lombard family maintained a strong presence there.[130] Moyge, the earlier Moyglauragh, was disputed between the Barrys and the FitzGibbons of Kilmore in Elizabethan times as it had been in 1404.[131] By the time that David (V) de Barry came of age in 1356[132] the eastern manors of Knockmourne and Ballynoe (the Newtown of Olethan), which had belonged to the de Freyne family, had come into the hands of the first earl of Desmond,[133] and in the following period this area was to be subtracted from the Barry lordship, developing into the later barony of Kinnatalloon.[134]

But the gains by the Barrys in the late medieval period were at least equal to their losses. Great Island had been part of the cantred of Imokilly, its eastern portion belonging to the Carews and the western to the Hodnets: in the course of the fourteenth century it was annexed by the Barrys (profiting by the establishment there already of some of their clansmen) and became 'Lord Barry's Great Island'. East of this, various fragments of the Carew lordship in Imokilly were absorbed into Barrymore: the parish of Mogeesha, largely belonging to the Hodnets: Castlecorth (Ballinacurra) itself, acquired by Sir William *Maol,* but which may have reverted, like his lands at Rathcobane, to the main line, and Titeskin, another piece of Carew land.[135] Garranekinnefeake, the home in the fifteenth and sixteenth centuries of a junior branch of the Barrymores, was probably the Kenlegestoun [*sic*] which David (IV) de Barry was holding in 1344.[136] Finally, in 1364 David (V) was mesne lord of Aghada between the bishops of Cloyne and its owners, the Magners:[137] this ensured that it, and some tiny scattered fragments of Magner land, were reckoned as parts of Barrymore.[138] Finally, at some date unknown to us, but probably in the early fifteenth century, the Lords Barry took over the manor and castle of Shandon and its dependent territory of Ocurblethan, which had belonged in equal halves to the Cogans and to the Rochfords and their successors in title, the earls of Kildare.[139] Presumably there was some conveyance, or one would have thought that the Desmonds, to whom the Cogan lands (including Shandon) had been granted in 1439, or the Kildares would have asserted some claim, but only Carrignavar escaped the Barry lordship. In the late fifteenth century the Barry interests in this area were strengthened by the more or less forcible acquisition of Rahanisky and its dependent lands. David Lombard in his will (1479) declared bitterly that he had never sold or given Rahanisky to the late Lord William Barry and had only yielded it to the present Lord Barry [John] during his own lifetime, through fear of death and of the plundering of his other lands and goods, and in return for an annuity which was never paid.[140] Rahanisky, nevertheless, remained with the Barrys.

David (V) de Barry, in whose time the connection with the ancestral Welsh home, Manorbier, was finally ended when he granted it to the Windsor family,[141] died in 1393 and was succeeded by his son John, already married to a daughter of Earl Gerald of Desmond;[142] by this time all the ruling lords of County Cork were closely linked by marriage with that great Geraldine house. Thereafter the line of lords continued until the death in 1557 of James fitz John, the last of three sonless brothers, when the lordship and lands passed under an entail executed by his brother and predecessor Edmond, to his remote kinsman and namesake, James fitz Richard, already Barry Roe. The nearest male agnate, Edmond Barry of Rathcobane, released his claim to James fitz Richard three years later, as did later James fitz John's daughter.[143] James fitz Richard appears to have been the first Lord Barry to assume the totally spurious 'Viscountcy' of Buttevant.

A feature of Olethan or Barrymore in the sixteenth century is the number of new landed families of Gaelic origin which established themselves in the territory. These included O Briens from north Munster at Coyllnacorra (Kilcor) at Ballyhamsherry, Ballynella and Pellick, O Cahills at Rathcobane and elsewhere, and especially O Keefes, whose main houses were at Glennafreghane (Glenville) and Dunbolloge, while a third line held Knocknahorgan and Conyengally (the modern Coneybeg and Trantstown).[144] It is possible that the arrival of these newcomers was closely connected with the emergence of the system by which Lord Barry, like other lords, would take over lands whose owners proved unable to cultivate them or to pay his tribute, and dispose of them as his own, allowing the hereditary owners a quarter of the rent he received.[145] In a further development of this system, by 1576 it had become usual for Lord Barry (like Lord Roche in Fermoy) to simply take over, in lieu of his exactions, three quarters of every free-holder's land and set it to whatever tenant he willed.[146] Given Irish conditions of the day, it is probable that there were some septs or individuals too powerful or dangerous to be treated in this way: never-theless the system was general in Munster. It must be as a consequence of this system that we find the Lords Barry mortgaging lands which we know to have been the inheritance of others: the Tirry lands in Gortroe Parish (to their hereditary owner!) and Belvelly (Hodnet land) in 1521, and Ballinacurra before 1580.[147] The process might involve a great deal of violence: in 1548 Edmond Tirry, one of the bailiffs of Cork, was brutally murdered by the Barrys while returning from Lord Barry's 'Parliament in his own country, holden on a hill' in the Irish fashion, where he had sought to obtain restitution of his own lands which were detained by Lord Barry, and in 1578 Lord Deputy Sidney was petitioned by an unfortunate landowner under Lord Roche whom the latter had kept in irons until he had surrendered seven and a half out of the eight ploughlands of his inheritance, on the understanding that he would have the remaining half ploughland free of exactions, an agreement which Lord Roche did not bother to honour.[148] It was perhaps as a result of this kind of annexation that Edmond, Lord Barry was in possession of Glennafreghane when he granted it to Domhnall O Keefe in or around 1550; the Barrys of Rathcormack, known as MacAdams from their prominent fourteenth-century ancestor, subsequently claimed it as their inheritance.[149] Nevertheless, some of the newcomers would seem to have acquired a more legitimate claim to their holdings: the O Briens of Kilcor were themselves for over sixty years victims of the system, being ousted from their lands by successive Lords Barry and the tenants they installed.[150] The most successful of these immigrant lineages was that of the O Keefes, one of whom, Luige (*Lughaidh*) mac Airt (a brother of the Domhnall who acquired Glennafreghane), occurs as a large-scale farmer of lands, holding in this way the lands of the Barrys of Kildinan and the MacAdams of Rathcormack, each of which amounted to several thousand acres, and many other members of the lineage are found at this period established through Barrymore, no doubt first as tenants and mortgagees, though many graduated to becoming proprietors.[151] The O Cahills were less numerous, but made a spectacular rise to major landed proprietors between 1560 and 1641.[152]

The founder of the house of Barry roe was Sir William fitz David de Barry, known (at least to later generations) as Sir William *Maol* ('the Bald'), who died in his eighties in 1373.[153] During most of his career he is styled of Rathgobban (Rathcobane) in Olethan:[154] at some time before 1356, but apparently after 1345, he acquired the western Barry territory, Ibane and the adjacent lands, from his nephew David (V), perhaps as part of a deal which involved the surrender after his death of Rathcobane and Castlecorth.[155] By 1356 he was also in possession of the former Barret fee of Castellnegeyth (Castleventry), although Richard Barret was claiming it.[156] The latter pedigrees (which are confused about his place in the Barry line) state that his son and successor, and the ancestor of the later Barrys Roe, was a Laurence, but in fact Sir William *Maol's* son and heir was another William, who survived until at least 1392.[157] If this William was the William *Rothe (*Ruadb*) de Barry who was custodian of the temporalities of the see of Ross in 1379-80,[158] then we have the origin of the title Barry Roe, and go on to suspect that the later pedigrees have fused father and son into a single individual and that Laurence may have been the son of the younger William, which would indeed fit in better with the chronology of his descendants. On 8 May 1390 William fitz William de Barry had royal letters of protection in consideration of the fact that most of his tenants in Obathoun and Drommanagh had been destroyed by the Irish.[159] Drommanagh is surely the Dromany which David de Barry had claimed against Cormac MacCarthy in 1301, and to be identified with Drominagh in Dromtarriff Parish in Duhallow: in 1527 the then Barryroe, styling himself ' lord of Ybawna and Tryuchamenach' (the 'Middle Cantred', the western part of the Barry possessions in this area, lying outside the original district of *Ui Badhamhna*),[160] was possessed of a rent 'in the country of Captain O Coya*m*',[161] a name which can only be explained as *Ó Caoimh,* O Keefe, to whom Drominagh then belonged. Hardly anything is known of the history of the Barrys Roe during the fifteenth century. At some time in the century the lordship was cut almost in half by the loss of the castle of Clonakilty (which under the English form of the name, Coyltescastell, had been in the hands of Sir William Maol at his death)[162] and the surrounding district, known as Tuoghnakilly, which were absorbed into the MacCarthy Reagh territory. The fact that this area subsequently belonged to the descendants of Cormac mac Donnchadha MacCarthy, contender for the lordship of Carbery until his capture by his cousins in 1477 and subsequent castration, suggests that it was he who seized them from the Barrys.[163] A further loss of territory to MacCarthy Reagh became enshrined, unusually, in the ecclesiastical arrangements when Amhlaoibh Ó Cruadhlaoich (Crowley), lord of Coill tSealbhaigh, on account of the 'deadly enmities' which existed between the inhabitants of his lands in the parish of Cruary and those of the rest of the parish (the later Templeomalus, and a lay advowson of the Anglo-French Arundel lineage), erected a church at Kilnagross and persuaded the bishop of Ross (probably Aodh O Driscoll, 147294) to erect it into a separate parish, an arrangement confirmed by the pope in 1493.[164] The area subsequently became a detached portion of the O Crowley sub-lordship of Kiltallow (*Coill tSealbhaigh*), the original territory of which lay north of the River Bandon, although the fact that, unlike the original territory, it paid no tribute to MacCarthy Reagh suggests that it may still in the sixteenth century have been regarded as in some sense part of Ibane. Further MacCarthy Reagh expansion led to the detachment from Ibane at some later date of Killavarrig in Timoleague Parish, although the Barrys continued to claim tribute from it[165] and to the acquisition (probably by Domhnall MacCarthy Reagh, died 1528) of Dunowen at the southern tip of the western peninsula, although Lord Barry was disputing its ownership in 1592.[166] In addition, the MacCarthys Reagh claimed a tribute out of the remaining territory of Ibane, and in 1542 Lord Barry Roe, like his neighbour Lord Courcy, was 'always of the retinue and company of [MacCarthy Reagh] to all journeys and hostings at his call'.[167] Within Ibane itself the changing political circumstances had led to a reversal of the former relationship between the Barry Roe and the Hodnets. Whereas in the thirteenth centuries the Barry manor of Lislee had been held as a feudal fief from the Hodnet manor of Rynnanylan, the later Courtmacsherry, by the sixteenth century the Hodnets were said to hold Courtmacsherry of the Barry manor of Timoleague, paying a heavy rent and providing free quarters for horses, as did the Arundels and other landowners of Ibane.[168]

In the mid-sixteenth century the Barry Roe lordship was racked by a succession dispute in which James fitz Richard Barry, whose father had been bastardised by an annulment, slew or exiled his cousins and made himself lord. As has been mentioned, on the death of James, Lord Barry Mor in December 1557 he, James fitz Richard, succeeded him in that lordship also under an entail made by the dead lord's brother and predecessor. He found it necessary, however, to buy off the claims to the Barry Roe lordship of his surviving cousin, David Og, with a massive grant of former Barry Mor lands,[169] thus removing him from Ibane. James fitz Richard, however, did not intend that the two lordships should remain united: on 14 June 1568 he granted the Barry Roe lordship to his third son William, who accordingly held it until his death late in 1584. On that event, however, his elder brother David Barry *Mór,* Viscount Buttevant, seized it also on the pretext of the illegitimacy of William's sons, the eldest of whom, James, only succeeded in retaining the manor of Lislee.[170]

The decline of the Courcys

The Courcys of Kinsale and Rinrone had been, like the Carews, one of the overlord lineages of the 'Kingdom of Cork', but the territory under their direct control consisted in effect of the cantred of West Kinelea (Kenelethertherach) and a few ad~acent lands, including the manor and borough of Kinsale on the opposite side of the Bandon or Glashlin River. The position of the Courcys on the south-western frontier placed them in the front line of opposition to the rising MacCarthys of Carbery, with whom and their client sub-chiefs their relations would seem to have been much worse than were those of the Carews. Miles de Courcy had defeated and killed the otherwise triumphant Finghln MacCarthy when the latter attacked Rinrone in 1261; Miles's son and successor John was killed by Finghln's brother Domhnall *Og (Maol)* in 1294; and in 1339 two grandsons of this John, sons of the ruling lord Miles (II), and another Councy, were killed by the Carberymen.[171] Miles (II) acquired many lands in the cantred of Kenelbek, which was held of him by William de Barry of Rincorran, and thus became a sub-vassal of his own vassal, a situation which led to litigation over their respective claims in 1335.[172] Miles's surviving son and successor, being apparently childless and having only sisters, executed in 1358 a rather curious entail to secure the integrity of the lordship and its continuance in the name of Courcy.[173] The first designated in remainder, however, was not a close male agnate but a very distant clansman, Sir Nicholas de Courcy of Ballycrenan, who however was the husband of Miles's youngest sister Anastasia. Failing male heirs from Nicholas and Anastasia, the remainders were to a long list of Courcys and their male heirs. We do not know if Sir Nicholas, who died in 1366,[174] survived Miles: the inquisition *post mortem* on the latter was taken in 1372,[175] and it was very unusual at that period to delay the taking of an inquisition so long after the death. There are some indications that Sir Nicholas did in fact succeed, in which case Miles must have died before 1366, but this seems unlikely.[176] Sir Nicholas and Anastasia left only a daughter, Margaret, who married Sir Maurice fitz Thomas and was ancestress of the Knights of Kerry, who held Killowny and other lands in Courcy's country until they disposed of them in the sixteenth century.[177] The next Lord Courcy whom we know of was the third in remainder of 1358, John fitz Miles, who died at some time before 1393.[178]

In the fifteenth and sixteenth centuries the Courcys were known under the title of MacPatrick (*Mac Padraigín*), derived either from the first of their ancestors to occupy the lordship, Patrick de Courcy who inherited from his mother Margaret de Cogan, or from an early fifteenth-century lord, the grandfather of James fitz Nicholas, 'lord of Rinrone and of the town of Kinsale' who by a charter of 11 April 1475 granted to Rory son of Melmory McBeha, *medicus,* and his heirs half a carucate of land in the burgagery of Rinrone, along with medicinal dignity and liberty throughout his lordship, with the profits arising from it, thus in effect creating an *ollamb*ship in medicine for the grantee, who was probably an immigrant from Scotland and the ancestor of the Bayes family.[179] After James's death in 1499 the lordship was usurped by his younger brother David, archdeacon of Cork,[180] although accounts differ in describing the circumstances. Sir George Carew, in his Courcy genealogy, says that David deposed his idiot nephew Edmond, although he himself had an elder brother Nicholas living, whose grandson John was 'an old man living in 1601 who ought to have been the Lord Courcy, as Gerald the late lord confessed'.[181] Another account, however, says that Nicholas succeeded the idiot nephew and was then dispossessed by his brother.[182] David's son and successor, John was perhaps the Shon de Cowrse to whom the earl of Kildare presented a horse in 1515, though the form of the name is unusual; ten years later, as lord of Kynsale, he ceded a mark (13s 4d) yearly as protection money to the earl during his lifetime.[183] The sixteenth-century Lords Courcy interfered in the municipal government of the town of Kinsale, granting, for example, exemptions from municipal office, and receiving a payment called 'book money'.[184]

Between the fourteenth and sixteenth centuries the Courcy lordship gradually shrank in the face of continued encroachment by the MacCarthys of Carbery. In any case, by the late fifteenth century the Courcy's territory had become restricted to the area enshrined in the pre-1837 barony of that name, and in 1542 'MacPatrick Courcy', like his neighbour Lord Barry Roe, was 'always of the retinue and company' of MacCarthy Reagh whenever summoned by the latter to join him on an expedition.[185] Perhaps to secure protection against this too-powerful neighbour, by the late sixteenth century Lord Courcy was paying an annual tribute of 5 marks and a penny (£3 6s. 9d.) 'halface money' to the earl of Desmond.[186] But MacCarthy penetration continued, and in 1588 it could be said that the then lord of Carbery, Sir Owen MacCarthy, had enlarged his possessions by getting the Lord Courcy's country and other lands.[187] This was a result of the actions of Gerald who succeeded his father John as Lord Courcy some time after 1538, in first mortgaging and then disposing outright of all his lands. Much of this was to Kinsale merchants and lesser local men, but in 1558 he mortgaged Rinrone itself to Donnchadh MacCarthy for £50 and 40 milch cows. A series of other mortgages to Donnchadh (who became MacCarthy Reagh in 1566) followed, and finally on 9 March 1583 Gerald released all the mortgaged lands to Sir Donnchadh's son, the famous Florence MacCarthy. In December 1584 he mortgaged his other manor, Downmacpatrick or Old Head (the earlier Oldernes) to Sir Donnchadh's brother and successor, Sir Eoghan, reserving a life tenancy for himself and his wife; in August 1594 he conveyed the fee simple of these lands also to Florence.

In May 1581 Gerald had entailed his lands on his cousin, Edmond Óg Courcy of Kilnacloona, and on Gerald's death in 1599 Edmond's son John succeeded to the title of Lord Courcy and what little, if any, was left of the inheritance.[188] It was probably because the Courcys (as former tenants-in-chief) had been recognised, like the Barrys and Roches, as peers of Parliament when the latter dignity had become defined in the fifteenth century and that therefore the king and the Dublin administration were not prepared to allow the heir to fall into destitution, that the new Lord Courcy was successful in recovering much or most of the lands alienated by his predecessor, in spite of the opposition of Florence MacCarthy – indeed the deep disfavour with which the latter, a prisoner in the Tower of London, was regarded by the Government may also have played a part in the outcome.[189] Whatever the reasons, the Courcys, having sunk almost to extinction, regained their position, and their landed estate descended intact until the late nineteenth century.

Barry Óg

The lordship of the Barrys Óg of Rincorran had originally extended to the two cantreds of Keneleth (Kinelea) and Kenelbek, the inheritance of their ancestress Hilarie de Cogan, although the strength of the Cogan presence in Kenelbek must have prevented them from exercising much power or influence there.[190] In the fifteenth century the lordship suffered erosion at the hands both of the MacCarthys Reagh and the lords of Muskerry, while in the Elizabethan period, like that of the Courcys, it suffered a total collapse. The fourteenth century heads of this line, Sir William fitz John de Barry and his son Philip fitz William had played an important role in the politics of the county, the latter seeming to be particularly relied upon by the royal administration.[191] Philip's son Odo (Irish *Eada,* the latter Anglo-Irish *Eddy*) was lord of

Kinelea in 1421,[192] but thereafter we have no information on the lineage until the then lord, Thomas, submitted to Sir Richard Edgecumbe when the latter touched in at Kinsale in the aftermath of the Simnel affair in 1487.[193] At some time in the fifteenth century they lost the western part of Innishannon parish to the MacCarthys Reagh, who built there the castle of Dundaniel (Doundaniyer) at some unknown date, but in any case before 1515: in 1475 a rival MacCarthy, Cormac mac Donnchadha, unsuccessfully petitioned the pope that his lands in the west of Innishannon parish should be erected into a separate parish on account of the obstruction by fortifications of the road between them and the parish church.[194] As in the case of Kilnagross, already cited, the fact that the right of presentation to Innishannon church belonged to the Barrys may also have been an important consideration.[195] During this period, too, the acquisition by the earls of Desmond of extensive lands in Kinelea may have subtracted from the authority of its lords.[196] Nevertheless, the lordship seem to have continued a prosperous existence, and on 20 October 1553 Philip Barry Óg, 'captain of his nation and lord of Kinnalega',[197] obtained from Queen Mary I Letters Patent confirming him in possession of all the lands which had belonged to his father William, Lord Barry, or any other of his predecessors, and which should descend to Philip by hereditary right in 'Kinaghlee', along with the customs of the port of Oysterhaven.[198] Philip, however, was childless and on his death in 1566 was succeeded by his brother Sir Thomas, under whom the lordship fell into complete disarray. In 1566 Richard Roche of Britfieldstown obtained a decree from the Queen's Commissioners freeing his lands from the 'coin and livery, cuddy and all other Irish exactions and impositions' which Barry Óg had imposed on him,[199] a foretaste of the disintegration of the latter's authority. By 1580 Sir Thomas could be referred to as 'a poor beggarly capten of a countrie called Kynaley, whose simplicity is such, that he maketh of a proper soil of a countrie nothing to be accounted on'.[200] An inquisition in 1584 declared that 'Barry Oge is but chief of his nation, and is not lord of the country',[201] a statement quite at variance with both the historical facts and the situation of eighteen years earlier. Sir Thomas died in April 1590, like his brother, without legitimate issue, and after having mortgaged or sold most of his lands as well as allowing his power to be dissipated. The vultures – in this case, the English administrators in Munster – were already closing in, hoping to declare his heir Henry Barry illegitimate and seize what was left of the possessions.[202] In the event, like Florence MacCarthy in the Courcy's country, they were unsuccessful, and Henry Barry succeeded to Rincorran. An inquisition held in 1618 set about securing his title by the quite false findings that Sir Thomas was the son of the Philip who had secured Queen Mary's patent, and that Henry's father John Barry was another son of this Philip, instead of his uncle![203]

Roche and Condon

The Roche lordship of Fermoy in north-eastern Cork, by contrast with most of the others we have discussed, changed little in extent between the fourteenth and sixteenth centuries. The acquisition of the Cogan lands in the north after 1372 extended it beyond the bounds of the old cantred of Fermoy on the west, but all in fact that came to the Roches were the demesne lands of the manor of Ballyhay, with a small adjacent area and a number of chief rents.[204] The remainder of the old Cogan lordship in this area became an independent lordship under that branch of the FitzGibbon Geraldines known as the lords of the Great Wood, or of Kilmore.[205] The enclave of the Roche lordship in Whitechurch Parish probably owed its origin less to the Cogan inheritance than with the ownership of land within it by Roches.[206] In the east, the Roche lordship was entangled in an intricate mesh with that of the Condons (originally de Caunteton), also carved out of the old cantred of Fermoy, and a continuing feud subsisted between the two lineages, going back to the acquisition by marriage of the Caunteton manor of Glanworth by a thirteenth-century lord of Fermoy. As part of Glanworth manor, the Roches claimed chief rents out of many Condon lands. Whereas the Roche succession passed in an unbroken descent from father to son or grandson from the thirteenth to the seventeenth century,[207] the succession of the Condons had been broken in the fourteenth. The then head of the lineage, Sir Maurice, had been killed by the Roches while in open rebellion in Leinster (where he also held lands) in 1308, and his kinsman Sir David captured and hanged in Dublin. Furious wars followed between the Roches and the Condons, who in 1311 captured David de la Roche, Lord of Fermoy, but released him (we are told) in return for pardon and the restitution of their lands.[208] Maurice's son Sir William, thus restored, was the leader of the lineage during their furious war with the Roches in 1316-17, when Fermoy was devastated by their mutual plunderings and burnings. Sir William died in 1321, allegedly leaving a five-year old heir, but – perhaps on the pretext of the heir's illegitimacy – his brother Sir David succeeded to the lands.[209] On 1 October 1340, while serving as sheriff of county Cork, he was slain at Kilworth by his nephews, the sons of Sir William, the leader of whom, David (was he the alleged heir of 1321?) seized possession of the chief Caunton (as the surname was already shortened) manor of Ballyderown. One of the charges against the first earl of Desmond was that four years later he had received the slayers into his peace, but David at least was afterwards captured and hanged.[210] The nearest agnates would seem to have been Sir David's brother, Edmond[211] and after him his son William fitz Edmond, but the effective headship had passed to more distant cousins, the sons of Piers de Caunton of Clondulane. In 1346 Gerald fitz Piers de Caunton was one of the keepers of the peace in the cantred of Fermoy: in 1355 he was one of those who elected a sheriff of the county, and in 1356 one of the assessors and collectors of the subsidy voted by the community of county Cork to maintain an armed force for their defence. Another and different side to Gerald's activities is shown when it was recorded in July 1358 that whereas he had been granted authority over all those of his surname, except William fitz Robert de Caunton and his son (the ancestors of the later house of MacMaug Condon), he was commanded to chastise those of them who had attacked and robbed the lieges of county Cork, and to restore the goods taken.[212] Two months earlier Sir David's daughter Elizabeth and her husband Maurice fitz Nicholas of Kerry had judgement for possession of Ballyderown against Gerald and his brother Raymond. On Elizabeth's death and that of her child ten years later William fitz Edmond was her legal heir and seems to have secured possession of Ballyderown; he served soon after as sheriff of Cork, but may then have returned to England, where he held lands.[213] By 1377 Gerald (who is described in 1373 as having been outlawed) had been succeeded as lineage-head by his brother Raymond, who in that year captured Sir David de Barry of O Lethan and Miles de Staunton, 'magnates of the county' whom he kept prisoner until they were exchanged for his own son and nephew, prisoners in Cork gaol.[214] It was surely the same Raymond, now an old man, and his son William who were appointed keepers of the peace in that strange list for county Cork in 1387.[215] As usual, the history of the lineage then becomes obscure, and the pedigree taken down by Sir George Carew cannot be relied upon before the middle of the fifteenth century, when Raymond son of Raymond kyech (*Caoich*) Conduyn was chieftain and interfered to support by force a candidate for the abbacy of Fermoy.[216]

In the thirteenth century David de la Roche had added the great manor of Glanworth to his existing lordship by his marriage with a Caunteton heiress, Amice, a transfer which led to continual litigation and eventually feud between the lineages.[217] But during the course of the fourteenth century many other Caunteton holdings came into Roche hands, probably on the extinction of the lines which held them: Carrickdoonan, Cregg, Ballyhendon and the great manor of Athoull (Ballyhooley), the inheritance of a very prominent Caunteton branch.[218] The result was the emergence of the highly complex boundary which was enshrined in the later baronies as they remained until 1837. The corner of Condon's Country which is in Castlelyons and Knockmourne parishes must have originally belonged to the Barry Lordship of Olethan. On the northern frontier of the Condon lordship an extremely complex situation existed in the sixteenth century, a situation which gave rise to the double barony name, Condons and Clangibbon. The territory known as Clangibbon, ruled by the Geraldine house of the White Knights,[219] lay largely in Counties Limerick and Tipperary: it extended across the Cork frontier in a number of places to include Ardskeagh, Oldcastletown and the surrounding lands, and in the east, Mitchelstown or Brigown, where the lands of the White Knights were intermingled with surviving Condon landholdings. Their ancestor Sir Maurice fitz Thomas held Brigown in 1366, having replaced its former holders, the St Mitchels (eponyms of Mitchelstown) at some date after 1340.[220] Mitchelstown and Oldcastletown were the usual residences of the sixteenth-century White Knights. Between them the district known as Kiltymabins, covering the northern part of Marshallstown Parish, was for the purposes of both rent and lordship authority to have been under the condominium of the White Knight and the autonomous but declining Condon subchief known as MacMaug, whose castle of Carriganoura stood a little to the south. The details of the arrangement are extremely interesting.[221] The White Knights seem also to have made a claim to the overlordship of Farrahy and the other lands of the Cushing family until they released it to Lord Roche in 1530.[222]

David Condon, chief of the name in 1551 and 1552, was succeeded as 'captain and chief of his name' by his brother Richard, who occupied that position in 1564,[223] doubtless during the minority of David's son and eventual successor, the redoubtable rebel Patrick Condon. The latter at first lost his lands to the Munster plantation, but succeeded in obtaining the reversal of his forfeiture on the grounds that his attainder had not been for his part in the Desmond rising but for having previously burned, allegedly in the pursuit of robbers, the Roche castle of Ballyhendon.[224] After his death during the second Desmond rising which he had joined but soon left, his son David succeeded in holding on to the Condon lands for a period, and received a regrant by letters patent in 1610.[225]

The growth of Desmond power

Maurice fitz Thomas, the first Geraldine earl of Desmond, had commenced his career with a very slender territorial base in the present county Cork, consisting of the manor of Mallow (which his father had obtained from one of the Roches by an advantageous exchange for lands in Connacht that were soon to be lost to the Irish!), of half a cantred in Corcaley (*Corca Laoighdhe*) in the far south-west, and of a minor holding in Duhallow.[226] In addition, as has been noted, he held the hereditary sergeancy of south Munster, including Cork, still a valuable asset. His first major acquisition was when he obtained from the last Carew lord, Thomas, the manor of Dunnamark (along with, presumably, Dun mic Odhmainn and the other Carew lands in the south-west) and his residual overlordships over half the 'kingdom of Cork'. Desmond's claims in this respect were promptly challenged by the Crown, concerned at this accession of authority to the earl, although their exercise by the Carews had never been disputed.[227] Maurice's overlordship was one of his weapons in his attempt to secure control of the great barony of Inchiquin, which included the town of Youghal and most of the present barony of Imokilly, and which had descended to absentee English coheirs, but his attempt failed, and Inchiquin came under the control of the earls of Ormond. In 1402-04 the third earl of Ormond, as 'lord of half the barony of Inchiquin and farmer of the other half' was the acknowledged ruler of Imokilly, and as such granted to the bishop of Cloyne, his city, clergy and tenants, exemption from the maintenance of kerne and other unlawful exactions which might be imposed in his, the earl's, name. Ormond granted the half of Inchiquin which belonged to him to his niece and unofficial spouse, Katherine of Desmond, and it is possible that she subsequently granted her interest to her brother, Earl James of Desmond, but in 1420 the fourth (White) earl of Ormond acquired the other half of the barony from its absentee owners. Two years later he granted the office of keeper and governor of Inchiquin, Imokilly and Youghal to the earl of Desmond for life, and in 1429 he granted the barony as a dowry for his daughter who was to marry Desmond's son and heir. The couple were children and Desmond was to have custody of the lands in the meantime, but if the marriage ever took place it was quickly terminated by the bride's death without children.[228] Nevertheless Inchiquin thereafter remained with the Desmonds. The office of seneschal of the courts of the barony, granted to Desmond in 1422, must be that which Desmond granted to the Geraldine Richard fitz Maurice, whose descendants were to be the hereditary seneschals of Imokilly, with their seat at Castlemartyr. It is just possible, however, that their office had absorbed some residual authority of the sergeancy of the county, which had been held by Richard's father Sir Maurice fitz Richard. In 1403 (?) an elder son of the latter, David, had entered into an agreement with the bishop of Cloyne, the text of which is unfortunately incomplete, but from which it is clear that he had been a thorn in the bishop's side who now promised to mend his ways and to protect the bishop's interests. If any of David's own men, or those of his brothers, should rob from the bishop or his tenants, David would restore the stolen goods within eight days, under the penalty of paying double their value.[229] In return for this it appears that the bishop recognized a claim to lands, and in the following two centuries the descendants of Sir Maurice, in their many branches, became the dominant landed clan in Imokilly, besides producing two bishops of Cloyne and innumerable other clerics. The most successful of all was the famous John fitz Edmond, Dean of Cloyne in succession to his father and grandfather, who acquired an immense landed estate during the course of his career, besides being a stock-owner on an enormous scale.[230]

The Carew lands in West Cork proved an even worse bargain for the first earl of Desmond and, like his existing hereditary estate in that area, were soon to be lost to the MacCarthys of Carbery. An expedition by Maurice in 1326 (probably immediately after acquiring the lands) in alliance with a local MacCarthy pretender, Donnchadh, succeeded in rebuilding the Carew castle of Dún Mac Odhmainn but ended in disaster when it was defeated with heavy loss by Domhnall (*Cam*) MacCarthy. Only the intervention of Cormac MacCarthy of Desmond allowed the future earl to escape.[231] Desmond's subsequent disgrace, when for a time the manor of Dunnamark was actually committed by the administration to the custody of Domhnall *Cam's* son,[232] cannot have helped the situation, and thereafter the claim to the West Cork lands became more and more nominal. It left the earls with a group of rectorial advowsons in the area which Earl Thomas was to use as part of the endowment of his collegiate church of Youghal in 1464,[233] but we cannot say whether the annual rent of 67¾ beeves which the earls of Desmond received out of Carbery in the sixteenth century was a direct outcome of these claims.[234] A more substantial acquisition by Desmond was that of the manors of Knockmourne and Ballynoe, mentioned above, creating the solid block of Desmond lands which became the barony of Kinnatalloon. This estate was to receive a further accretion in 1460, when William, Lord Barry, granted Conna and other lands to his son-in-law Earl Thomas of Desmond and his countess Alice Barry.[235] But Maurice fitz Thomas's power in the county was never simply a matter of acquiring landed possessions or feudal authority. One can see from the names on the lists of his supporters how he drew into his clientage so many of the Munster gentry, not only his own Geraldine kinsmen, the discontented like Adam de Barry or the lineage-heads without feudal status, like the Barrets and the sons of Piers de Caunton, but the heads of many established knightly families as well.[236] To enter into Desmond's clientage was safer than to remain outside it. Yet in the end Desmond's power, which had promised to become totally dominant in south and west Munster and perhaps even to establish an autonomous principality there, broke when confronted with decisive action by the representatives of royal government in Ireland, notably Ralph de Ufford,[237] and it was not until his grandson's time that the Desmond power was once more set on an expansionist course.

That grandson, James, had secured possession of the earldom after defeating his nephew Thomas.[238] I have already referred to his acquisition of Inchiquin, which made him and his successors lords of the important seaport town of Youghal. In 1430 he acquired Kilcolman and other lands from William, Lord Barry, and in 1439, from Robert Cogan, last of his house, the lordship of Kerrycurrihy and claims to the rest of the Cogan inheritance.[239] In 1442 came the manor of Garth or Ballingarry in Kinelea.[240] In 1445 he set himself right with the Crown by obtaining, from London, a royal license entitling him to absent himself from the Irish and to acquire lands without further specific royal license.[241] The acquisition of Kerrycurrihy brought the Desmonds into close relations with the city of Cork, and in 1470 it was the mayor, who after the victory of the forces supporting the young James against his uncle Gerald of the Decies, proclaimed him earl at Cork.[242] In 1548, not long after a period when Kerrycurrihy had been in the hands of the MacCarthys, the citizens declared that they always looked to Desmond for protection against the other local lords.[243] There are some indications, however, that in the early sixteenth century Kerrycurrihy may have become an appanage for Sir Thomas of Desmond, younger brother of the then earl and himself earl in succession to his nephew from 1529. In 1505 his wife, Gilis ny Cormyk, a sister of Cormac Óg of Muskerry, had a five-years lease of the Kildare lands of Currabinny, last fragment of the Rochford inheritance.[244] In the second half of the sixteenth century many of the Desmond lands were hived off to provide appanages for younger sons: Kerrycurrihy on an irregular basis for Maurice, brother of Earl James fitz John; Conna, Knockmourn, Aghern and Ballynoe, comprising between them most of Kinnatalloon, by deed of 1554 for the disinherited son of Earl James's first annulled marriage, Sir Thomas; Mallow, Carrignavar, Kilcolman, the newly acquired Mogeely in Kinnatalloon, and other lands, for James's younger son, Sir John of Desmond.[245]

A grant made in the aftermath of the Warbeck rebellion to Maurice earl of Desmond (who had been the main mover therein) of the customs, cocket (custom of hides) and prise wines (a cask out of every ship) in Kinsale, Youghal and Baltimore to hold during pleasure was interpreted by later earls as a permanent grant, becoming a further cause of hostility with the Ormond Butlers, who reasserted their hereditary right to the prise wines (outside the city of Cork, which had an unquestioned right to them in the city).[246] It is to be noted that the

1497 grant, made at Dublin, totally ignored, insofar as Baltimore was concerned, the grant made at London to Finghln MacCarthy Reagh ten years previously. Baltimore is not however mentioned in the later Ormond-Desmond disputes over the prise wines.

The MacCarthy Reaghs

The last great lordship of county Cork which has not so far been touched on, except incidentally, was that of the MacCarthys Reagh of Carbery. The exact details of the formation of their enormous lordship, and of the various sub-lordships within it, must remain with rare exceptions hidden from us. The problem is well illustrated by the case of the O Driscolls (*Ó hEidirsceoil*) where we have a few annalistic obits from the early thirteenth century and thereafter no information until they emerge as the most powerful of maritime lords in the fifteenth, and no evidence at all as to how they reasserted themselves in an area at least superficially occupied by Anglo-French landowners, though in 1300 significantly outside the scope of royal criminal justice.[247] During the late thirteenth and early fourteenth centuries the headship of the Carbery MacCarthys was exercised successively by three Domhnalls, all known to their contemporaries as Domhnall Cairbreach (Carbragh, etc) and not by the epithets attached to their names by the genealogists, *maol, cam* and *glas* respectively. The last of these was succeeded after 1356 by his brother Cormac Donn, 'lord of Ui Eachach (the O Mahony territories) and Ui Cairbre', who was slain in 1366 by his nephew Domhnall. Two years later Cormac's son Diarmaid, presumably contesting the lordship, was captured by the same Domhnall and handed over to the English, who put him to death.[248] From another son of Cormac Donn descended the important house of the MacCarthys of Gleanacroim, whose dissensions in Elizabethan times are well documented.[249]

We do not know if the Domhnall of 1366 and 1368 is the Domhnall *Riabhach* from whom the later title of MacCarthy Reagh is derived, and who died as lord of Carbery in 1414, as the latter had also an older brother Domhnall *Óg*,[250] but a long period of rule *Riabhach* would help to explain why the title of MacCarthy Reagh replaced that of MacCarthy Carbragh. However, Domhnall *Riabhach's* rule was not undisputed: Domhnall MacCarthy Cluasach ('Big Ears') who died in 1409, a grandson of Desmond's ally Donnchadh and chief of the sept known as Clan Dermot in West Carbery, is styled MacCarthy *Cairbreach* by one source in 1398, and his son Diarmaid was rldhamhna (eligible successor) of Uí Cairbre at his death in 1418.[251] There is no evidence of a later attempt by the Clan Dermot to seize the lordship of Carbery, although they remained of importance. Three sons of Domhnall

Riabhach succeeded as lords in turn, but after the death of the second, Donnchadh, in 1453, the rule of his brother Diarmaid *an Duna* came to be disputed by Donnchadh's son Cormac. In the struggle for the earldom of Desmond between Sir Gerald and his nephew James in 1469-70, Cormac, then *tanaiste* to his uncle, was a close ally of Gerrot and succeeded with his help in deposing his uncle Diarmaid, taking prisoner two of his sons and capturing the castles of Coolmain, Kilgobban and Monteen.[252] In 1473 Cormac is described as ruling Carbery, while Diarmaid was nominally MacCarthy Cairbreach.[253] In 1477, however, Cormac was defeated and captured at Knocknalurgan near Carrigaline by Diarmaid's sons and their maternal uncle, Cormac mac Taidhg of Muskerry with the aid of their imported MacSweeney galloglass, and was castrated and blinded before being released as no longer a danger.[254] Diarmaid was evidently already dead: his eldest son Finghln was now installed as lord.

The descendants of Cormac mac Donnchadha remained in posses-sion of extensive lands in Carbery. To them belonged the districts of 'Tuogh Iniskyen, Twoghe Ballynydeihie and Twoghenykillihie', centred respectively on Inniskeane, Ballinadee and Clonakilty, and known collectively by the name Tanaistah (*tánaisteacht*, the tanist's country' (members of the sept are sometimes referred to as 'tanist of Carbery').[255] The heads of the lineage bore the curious titles, which are almost synonymous, of 'Cawnnigonturdye' (*Ceann i gcontabhairte*, 'the chieftain in controversy' or 'Cawne ganawris' (*Ceann go n-amhras*, 'the doubtful chieftain').[256] They were entitled to, or at least claimed, a third part of all the customs of ships and boats received by MacCarthy Reagh in Baltimore and the other harbours of Carbery, until Finghin mac Eoghain 'Mac Ingan Auras' (*mac cinn go n-amhras*), the last chief of the house, was dispossessed of much of his possessions by Sir Donnchadh MacCarthy Reagh. He was eventually slain in 1600 and his remaining possessions confiscated.[257]

Finghin MacCarthy Reagh ruled until 1505. After the Simnel affair and Sir Richard Edgecumbe's consequent expedition to Cork he and Cormac mac Taidhg of Muskerry made advances to King Henry VII, and were rewarded with grants of English liberty and, in the case of Finghin ('Florence'), a grant to him and his heirs for ever of the customs, cockets and prises of wines on his lands west of the Old Head of Kinsale.[258] It was doubtless on account of this grant that the ports of Baltimore and Crookhaven claimed in 1610 to be exempt from customs,[259] but otherwise the MacCarthys Reagh seem to have made remarkably little use of it. The treaty made by Finghin with the earl of Kildare, newly returned to Ireland as Lord Deputy, on 20 November 1496, can be taken as a genuine event, even though the first portion of the text preserved to us seems a spurious accretion.²⁶⁰ Finghin had married a daughter of the earl of Desmond, who was remembered as the builder of the castle of Benduff;²⁶¹ their son Domhnall, who had been given as a hostage to Kildare in 1497, succeeded after the brief reign of an uncle.²⁶² Domhnall married Kildare's daughter Eleanor, and on 28 September, 1513, as 'prince of the Carberymen' (*Carbriniencium princeps*) he entered into a remarkable indenture with his wife. By this he granted to her for her life the manor of Doundaniyer (Dundaniel) and half of all the lordship (*dominium*) which he might obtain in any way, swearing on the Gospels to keep the bargain. It is clear that *dominium* here means not political authority but land ownership, 'landlordship'. He further agreed to appoint and remove those of his officers and officials whom he might lawfully remove (i.e. who did not have a hereditary right?) at the will and counsel of Eleanor whenever it seemed fit to her. Finally, he agreed that if those 'Scots' whom he now had, namely *gallogle chlenesuene* (*galloglaigh Chloinne Suibhne*) were not conformable to Eleanor's will he would expel them and bring in others in their place at her will and counsel. The agreement was witnessed by, among others, her sister Margaret, wife of Piers Butler with whom Domhnall had entered into a treaty of mutual assistance in the previous January.²⁶³ In the event the MacSweenys remained. Two of their leaders, Brian and Donnchadh, had been invited from Tir Conaill by Finghin to serve him as galloglass. After Donnchadh's death his son Maolmuire, a child, had returned to the north, but on reaching manhood had come back to Munster, this time to serve MacCarthy Mor. Some of his sons were to move into Carbery, where the other sept, descended from Brian through his son, another Maolmuire (*Bacach*) were already established. Between the two septs there subsisted 'mortal malice, so much as whensoever any of them did meet they did assuredly fight, and many great slaughters have been committed on each other. The cause of their malice is that either sept do think themselves of better descent than the other'. The MacSweenys were for this time on to be a major political factor in the MacCarthy territories, as the MacSheehy galloglass were to be in the Desmond ones, but, except for those in Muskerry and Duhallow at the very end of the period, they never acquired landed property, although 'of such credit and force they would make the greatest lords of the province both in fear of them and glad of their friendship'.²⁶⁴ The bonaght (*buannacht*), the tax imposed on the country for their maintenance' was probably the heaviest of all Irish impositions.

Four sons of Domhnall and Eleanor, Cormac (*na h-áine*), Finghin, Donnchadh and Eoghan, all knighted in their time, were to rule over Carbery between 1531 and 1593. Cormac had to contend with his namesake, 'cousin and adversary', Cormac 'Caunnigonturdye', and when MacCarthy Reagh was at war with the city of Cork in 1538 (acting as part of the so-called 'Geraldine League' against King Henry VIII, of which his mother Eleanor, now married to Maghnus O Donnell of Tir Conaill, was a principal organiser) the citizens provided boats to ferry the rival Cormac and his men to an attack upon Carbery and Ibane.[265] As has been remarked, the last two of his brothers, Sir Donnchadh (died 1576) and Sir Eoghan, almost succeeded in annexing to Carbery what remained of the Courcy lordship. The last ruling MacCarthy Reagh was his nephew, Domhnall (*na piopaI*) son of Cormac, who outlived the end of the old order, surviving until 1612.

In the three centuries between 1303 and 1603 the political wheel in county Cork, as elsewhere in the south and east of Ireland, turned full circle, from being part of a centralized unitary state back to the same situation. In 1303 the lords and the dominant lineages were increasingly becoming autonomous political forces; after 1603 the lords for a period still retained power and influence, but as magnates within the unitary state, with their position increasingly eroded both by the growth of the English settler community – one of whose members, Richard Boyle, first earl of Cork, quickly achieved magnate status – and in most cases by religious alienation from the ruling state. But in between there was a period when the lords conducted themselves, as has been said, as independent sovereign powers, enforcing their own wishes and interests as laws upon their subjects and making war and peace for themselves. Not all the great lineages of the colonial period shared in this development to independent authority, whose roots (as I hope has been made clear) were in the Gaelic rather than the English legacy. When Steven Ellis, in rejecting the concept of 'Gaelicization', speaks of 'the practices ... which develop naturally where power is decentralized',[266] he is, I think, begging the question. The decentralization of power, even in a limited administrative sense, was a concept profoundly alien to the English polity as it developed under the monarchs from John onwards, and one normally absent from their Irish policies. (The interesting exception is the period of the Mortimer ascendancy from 1326 to 1330, when power rested not with the king but with a private member of the baronage, and which saw the erection of the new liberties of Kerry and Tipperary.) The re-assertion of personal rule by Edward III saw a reversion to the former policy, and the successful crushing, in two distinct but similar interventions, of the autonomist ambitions of the first earl of Desmond, even though this policy was becoming daily more out of touch with Irish realities. In practice, the fourteenth-century English administration in Ireland, like that of the Elizabethan period, was capable of effective and decisive

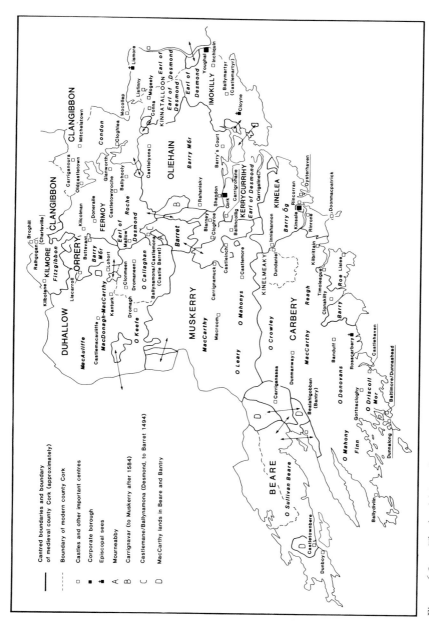

Figure 6.2   The lordships of county Cork, c. 1570.

military intervention but incapable of establishing or maintaining peace and order. The refusal of the English governmental system – in marked contrast to the Scottish – to permit the decentralization of power to local lords meant that the latter, when compelled by the exigencies of their situation to assume authority, assumed it in a Gaelic guise, as the model readily and obviously available to them. In the list of Lord Barry's exactions in 1519-20 the feudal 'Royal service' appears incongruously among a series of Gaelic terms (largely referring to food-renders): *coinnmheadh, aithne (?), soirthean, srath, ceithearn tigh, cion dubh*,[267] perhaps a reflection of the comparative contributions of the two systems to that prevailing in the sixteenth century.

Under Henry VIII, his Dublin administration, largely dominated by Palesmen, in seeking to reassert royal authority, was content at first to accept the existing decentralized power structures, a policy exemplified, as I noted, in the Munster ordinances of 1541[268] and in the generous terms accorded in the early surrenders and regrants, a concession to lordly authority which was soon discontinued.[269] By Elizabethan times, while traces of this policy continued to persist, it had in general been abandoned for one of coercion and the forced imposition of English norms. This new policy, of 'coercion and colonization', seems to have found its first throughgoing exposition in the Munster of the 1560s. The development of religious division between rulers and ruled – the Irish were offered, and accepted, the Counter-Reformation before being offered the Reformation in any meaningful way – was a powerful factor operating to promote a harder policy, and Munster, the most open to influences from the Iberian Peninsula and the Mediterranean of all the Irish regions, again led the way in this. And finally the sheer intractability of so many of the Irish lords and of the *mic rígh* – the swarming members of the ruling lineages who were the real curse of the Gaelic polity – must have discouraged even those pragmatist officials who sought to work through the existing system. Irish lords and their kinsmen must often have reacted to eulogies of law and order and exhortations to cherish the real producers of wealth in much the same way as present-day Irish politicians confronted with environmental arguments. The attitude of Sir Niall *Garbh* O Donnell cannot have been unique.[270] Between all these factors, the coercionist policy, attuned as it was to the centralized nature of the English system and the exclusivist nature of English law, was perhaps bound to triumph. In any case, the centralization of power and authority – if not always in so extreme a degree – was perhaps the major distinctive element in the 'modern' Europe which emerged in the course of the seventeenth century. It was surely in recognition of this fact that the insurgent Irish of the 1640s called, not for the anachronistic recreation of autonomous local lordships, but for the constitutional rights of English subjects.

References

1. For a discussion of the nature of the Irish 'lordship' of this period see my forthcoming *Late medieval Ireland: law and institutions*. The term 'Cane *poble*' *(ceann pobail)*, 'head of a pobal') was the standard title used of lesser lords; see Hore and Graves, *Southern and eastern counties*, p. 277.

2. K. W. Nicholls, 'Gaelic society and economy' in *New Hist. Ire.*, ii , p. 424. A notable example is the usurpation of the Courcy lordship by David Courcy *c.* 1500 (see below). The matter is however complicated both by the question of illegitimacies, technical or otherwise, which might either be ignored in practice (as in the case of Lord Roche in 1477, referred to below, or, possibly the children of David Courcy, an archdeacon although almost certainly not in major orders) or used as a pretext to facilitate usurpation, as when Sir Gerald of Desmond tried to bastardise his nephews in 1469 (*Cal. papal letters*, xii, p. 67). For the dispensation for their parents' marriage, 1455, (ibid., xi, p. 232), and by that of the temporary exercise of rule by a kinsman during the minority of the heir, as in the case of Richard Condon in 1564 (below) and possibly that of Edmond Roche in 1450 (below, n. 207).

3. *Geneal. Tracts,* pp. 30-1. I will discuss this question in my *Late medieval Ireland: law and institutions.*

4. Late genealogies can be an extremely misleading guide; nevertheless 'closed' successions, passing within comparatively narrow groups of kinsmen, seem to have characterised the Gaelic lordships of this region. See Nicholls, 'Gaelic society and economy', pp 424-5. For the MacDonoghs, see Lambeth MS 626 ff 9ᵛ-10ᵛ.

5. K. W. Nicholls, 'Some documents on Irish law and custom in the sixteenth century' in *Anal. Hib.*, xxvi, pp 115-7. The case of the Barrys of Ballinacurra is a good example of partible inheritance, see N.A., Salved Chancery Pleadings (henceforth C.P.), I., 89; AA, 204.

6. The case of the O'Callaghans is an extreme example. In 1594 the three brothers of the then chief held 14 ploughlands between them, their first cousin 1½, and a second cousin one ploughland. No other member of the chiefly sept held land, although others were certainly living (N.L.I., MS 15, p. 478). Butler's account of the O'Callaghans (*Gleanings,* pp. 91-2) is extremely unsatisfactory, due largely to his reliance on the appallingly inaccurate Gilman. In the case of the O'Mullanes, landowners under the O'Callaghans, we are told that the 'eldest and worthiest' of the sept was entitled to hold the lands of Brittas and Glantane see N.A., Ferguson MS vii, f. 390.

7. Caulfield, *Cork,* pp siv-xv.

8. There is a reasonably good if occasionally inaccurate account of the MacCarthy lordships and their sub-lords in Butler, *Gleanings.*

9. Inquisition of 20 April 1609, Cork Inquisitions in O.S. MSS, R.I.A. (henceforth C.I.), i, pp 137-48.

10. See the famous tract in *S.P. Hen. VIII,* iii, 1, pp 1-30, usually dated in 1515, although the name of Cormac mac Taidhg (died 1494) as lord of Muskerry suggests perhaps a date in the mid-1490s.

11. C.I., i, pp 103-6. Inquisition of 29 April 1605. For the semi-autonomous position

of the MacMaug ancestors in the thirteenth century see below.

12. Nicholls, 'Gaelic society and economy', pp 427-30. There is little information on lord's officers in this region. See Caulfield, *Kinsale*, p. 369, however, the grant of an official and exclusive right of medical practice (in fact, an *ollamhnacht*) by James, Lord Courcy (below). In 1531 John Wenth was judge of Kinelea.

13. Printed in Moran, *Spicil. Ossor.*, iii, pp 13-8, from S.P. 63/20/78. There is another text in S.P. 60/10/21-2.

14. R. R. Davies, 'Kings, lords and liberties in the March of Wales, 1066-1272' in *Transactions of Royal Historical Society*, 5th ser., xxix (1979), pp 41-61.

15. Otway-Ruthven, *Medieval Ire.*, pp 181-3.

16. H. A. Jefferies, 'The history and topography of Viking Cork' in *Cork Hist. Soc. Jn.*, xc, p. 17.

17. *Red Bk. Kildare*, no. 1.

18. *Rotuli Chartarum, 1199-1216*, 171b. 'Soc and sac, toll and team, infangenethef'. For the meaninglessness of these terms (except perhaps infangethef) even by the late twelfth century see N. G. Hurnard, 'The Anglo-Norman Franchises' in *E.H.R.*, lxvii (1949), pp 289-323, 433-60. John's charter of Muscrymitine to Richard de Cogan (*Rotuli Chartarum, 1199-1216*, 173) contains no jurisdictional clauses.

19. N.A., R.C. 7/9, pp 205-18. As with all of the Record Commission's transcripts, one cannot assume that the abridged version accurately reflects the original.

20. Davies, 'Kings and lords': Hurnard, Anglo Norman franchises; M. T. Clanchy, 'The franchise of return of writs' in *Transactions of the Royal Historical Society*, 5th ser., xvii (1967), pp 59-79. For the process in Ireland, K. W. Nicholls, 'Anglo-French Ireland and after' in *Peritia*, i (1982), pp 376-7.

21. The Sarsfields held of the Stauntons, who held of the Prendergast coheirs of Ocurblethan, who held of the Barrys of Olethan, who held of the Carews, heirs of Robert fitz Stephen.

22. *Cal. Justic. Rolls Ire., 1295-1303*, pp 35, 45, 95.

23. N.L.I., MS D.25, 225.

24. Genealogical Office, Dublin (henceforth G.O.), MS 192, passim. But see. Caulfield, *Kinsale*, p. 436.

25. *Rot. Pat. Hib.*, passim.

26. C.A.I., deed of 20 June, 1475, Coppinger MSS.

27. Richardson and Sayles, *Parl. and councils Med. Ire.*, i, pp 142-3, 146, 160, 165-6.

28. *Rot. Pat. Hib.*, pp 217b, 227 et passim. He seems to have been a professional administrator.

29. *Stat. Ire., 1-12 Edw. iv*, 262-3. The comments of Richardson and Sayles in *Ir. Parl. in middle Ages*, p. 180, are misconceived.

30. *Stat. Ire., Henry vi*, pp 176-7. See Bodl., MS Laud. Misc. 613, pp 288-9.

31. *Stat. Ire., 12-22 Edw. iv*, pp 468-9.

32. R. Caulfield (ed.), 'Chartae Tyrryanae' in *Topographer and Genealogist*, iii (1858), p. 117.

33. *Rot. Pat. Hib.*, pp 219b, 264b. William Barry is returned as sheriff in 1466 (N.A., R.C. 8/41, pp 23-4, 28-31). He may have been reappointed in place of the rebel Sir Gerald. He was certainly dead however by 1468, and the name may simply have been mechanically repeated from an earlier date, ignoring Sir Gerald's appointment.

34. N.A., R.C. 8/43, pp 155, 205, 261. His return as sheriff of Waterford in 1494 (ibid., p. 97) may simply be due to haplography by the nineteenth-century transcriber.

35. A. J. Otway-Ruthven, 'Anglo-Irish shire government in the thirteenth century' in

I.H.S., v/17, pp 22-3; *Ormond Deeds*, iii, p. 34.

36. B.L., Add. MS 4790, f. 113.
37. 'Chartae Tyrryanae', pp 117, 118.
38. N.A., C.P., G.22.
39. Butler, *Gleanings*, pp 60-62. The eponym of Clan Donnell Roe was the son of Eoghan, brother of the kings Diarmaid (died 1325) and Cormac (died 1359). Diarmaid Bearrtha, the ancestor of Clan Dermot in Bere, was the son of Cormac's son Domhnall Og, died 1391 or 1392 (*Lr. Muin*, p. 151; T.C.D., MS H.1.12 (1286) (B), ff lb-c, 2a).
40. N.A., R.C. 7/9, p. 212.
41. N.A., R.C. 7/2, pp 322-3; 7/5, p. 410; 7/8, p. 409; 7/9, p. 119. Most of the O Mahonys named can be identified in the genealogies. See K. Nicholls, 'A new source for O Mahony genealogy' in *O'Mahony Journal*, vi (1976), pp 11-15. The other names which appear are O Coghlans and O Fynekils.
42. N.A., R.C. 7/8, p. 409; 7/9, p. 119. Cormac was the son of Feidhlimidh (see n. 47 below).
43. *A.I.*, 1201.12; *Misc. Ir. Annals*, 1201.2.
44. N.A., R.C. 7/1, pp 246-7, 263; Nicholls, 'Anglo-French Ireland and after', p. 383 (where the footnote reference is misprinted). In 1297 and 1300 Maurice de Carew alleged that the lands claimed by him in this area had been taken from his grandfather by Diarmaid MacCarthy (above, n. 41). The identity of this Diarmaid must remain obscure; Diarmaid son of Cormac Og Liathanach died in 1234, in his father's lifetime (A.I., 1234.2, 1244.1) and Cormac Og Liathanach's espousal of the monastic life seems to have taken place only shortly before his death (*Cal. Doc. Ire., 1171-1251*, no. 276). Perhaps Cormac had two sons called Diarmaid, as he had two named Domhnall. There is no reference to a cantred of Fonieragh in any source, although there was a rural deanery of that name: it may have been included in the cantred of Glinshalwy, although this seems unlikely.
45. *A.I.*, 1232.2.
46. *A.I.*, 1283.5.
47. *A.I.*, 1280.5. This Feidhlimidh who died 1300 ('from whom Clann Feidhlimidh in Uí Conaill') was the son of Finghin (died 1249) son of Diarmaid of Dun Droighnein (*Bk Uí Maine*, 28r c).
48. *Cal. Doc. Ire.*, 1171-1251, no. 2716.
49. If 'le Wyth Okyf' of the list of vills is, as seems likely, to be read as Lewyth (*Lughaidh*) OKyf see L. O Buachalla (ed.), 'An early fourteenth-century place-name list for Anglo-Norman Cork' in *Dinnseanchas*, ii/2 (1966), p. 39.
50. *A.I.*, 1283.2; cf. 1316.2. William Barret held Alle of Piers le Botiller at his death in 1281 (*Cal. Justic. Rolls Ire. 1295-1303*, p. 278); these le Botillers are described variously as holding Allith and Drissan (Drishane in Muskerry Barony?) of Thomas de Multon (N.A., R.C. 7/13 (iv, p. 43) or of John de Barry (R.C. 7/11, p. 385 = N.A., M.2550, f. 210). Alle or Allith was probably the upper Blackwater valley, the parish of Cullen, adjoining Drishane, was known as Cullin Alla See D. Buckley (ed.), 'Obligationes pro Annatis Diocesis Cloyensis' in *Arch. Hib.*, xxiv (1961), p. 9. For the relationship between the Multons, the le Botillers and the Barrys see K.W. Nicholls, 'The Butlers of Aherlow and Owles' in *Journal of the Butler Society*, i/2 (1969), pp 123-8.
51. *A.I.*, 1283.4.
52. G. O. Sayles (ed.), 'The legal proceedings against the first earl of Desmond' in *Anal. Hib.*, xxiii, pp 39, 40. Mac Raith Ó Ceallachain and Diarmaid Ó Caoimh,

there mentioned, end the respective genealogies in *Bk Ui Maine,* f. 28r a; Mac Raith was ancestor of the Later O Callaghan chiefs. Of the places mentioned, Curraghbower south of the Blackwater and Drumrastill and Gortbofinna north of it can be identified.

53. A. F. O'Brien, 'The territorial ambitions of Maurice fitz Thomas, first earl of Desmond, with particular reference to the barony and manor of Inchiquin, Co. Cork' in *R.I.A. Proc.* 82 C (1982), pp 61-4; *Rot. Pat. Hib.,* 68, 70; P. Mac Cotter, 'The Carews of Cork' in *Cork Hist. Soc. Jn.* (forthcoming). I am grateful to Mr MacCotter for discussion of problems and information regarding his article.

54. MacCotter, 'Carews', R. Caulfield (ed.), *Rotulus Pipae Clonensis* (Cork, 1859), pp 4, 42-3.

55. N.A., R.C. 8/20, Dundrinan, pp 192-4; Carrigrohane, the fragmentary rent-roll of the bishopric of Cork, probably *c.* 1362-5 (Bolster, *Diocese of Cork,* i, pp 169-70, wildly misdated at 1456! The names of Piers and Geoffrey de Cogan establish the date).

56. N.A., R.C. 7/3, p. 416.

57. N.A., R.C. 7/5, pp 395 (where for *pater* read *frater*), p. 419; *Cal. Justic. Rolls, 6 Edw. ii,* p. 160; R.C. 8/21, pp 453, 475 (where for *Nicholas* read *John*), pp 542 ff.; *Cal. Close Rolls, 1333-37,* p. 61; *Cal. Pat. Rolls 1334-38,* p. 303; G.O., MS 191, p. 229; MS 192, p. 222. For William, R. Frame, *English lordship in Ireland, 1318-1361,* p. 290; *Rotulus Pipae Clonensis,* pp 13, 25-6.

58. *A.I.,* 1316.4; *A. Conn.,* 1316-4; *Rot. Pat. Hib.,* 24b.

59. *A.I.,* 1317.2 (the initial *c* of *Cloch muchoba* is lost through damage to the text); N.A., Cal. Justic. Roll, 5-11 Edw. II, pp 53-9; R. Frame, 'The Bruces in Ireland' in *I.H.S.,* xix/73 (1974), pp 34-5; G.O., MS 190, p. 135 = R.C. 7/12, pp 148-51.

60. R. Frame, 'War and peace in the medieval lordship of Ireland' in J. Lydon (ed.), *The English in medieval Ireland,* pp 139-40.

61. G.O., MS 190, pp 181-2.

62. *Cal. Fine Rolls,* 1327-37, p. 291; *Rot. Pat. Hib.,* 33; N.A., R.C. 8/17, pp 72, 351.

63. For his genealogy, and a list of his sons, see T.C.D., MS H.1.12 (1286) B, p. 1c.

64. G.O., MS 191, p. 73. Margaret Wogan (G.O., MS 192, p. 96) must have been a daughter of the Justiciar Sir John Wogan, to whom Piers de Cogan's custody had been granted in 1317 *(Rot. Pat. Hib.,* 24). After David de Barry's death she married Sir William fitz Gerald (P.R.O. E.101/241). Her fourth husband was Sir Nicholas de Courcy (N.A., Ferguson, MS xiv, p. 27).

65. *Cal. Fine Rolls, 1327-37,* p. 291; ibid., *1337-47,* pp 8-9; *Cal. Pat. Rolls,* p. 518.

66. *Anal. Hib.,* xxiii, pp 32-3, 37, 39, 40, 41 (Giving the correct date for Sir Robert's death, 11 Aug. 1345). The date of 15 Sept. given in two inquisitions made some years later (ibid., pp 25, 31) may be due to confusion between the feast of the Nativity of the B.V.M. and that of the Assumption; Clyn, *Annals,* p. 31; B.L., Add. MS 4790, f. 35; N.L.I., MS 761, p. 151.

67. N.L.I., MS 761, pp 148, 150.

68. *A.U.,* ii, p. 502; *A.F.M.,* iii, p. 610. *A. Conn.,* 1356.6 is unclear, and has been misunderstood by the translator. The Annals of Lecan placed the deaths in 1357 (*A.F.M.,* 3rd ed. (Dublin, 1990), Introduction, App.).

69. A. J. Otway-Ruthven, 'Ireland in the 1350s: Sir Thomas de Rokeby and his successors' in *R.S.A.I. Jn.,* xcvii (1967), pp 49-51. The reference to the monthly suit which Cormac's ancestors had been accustomed to make to the Cork county court seems to imply that they had long occupied the lands. The rent reserved was 20*s.,* a faling (Irish mantle) and a lance yearly; by 1368 it was 18 years in arrears! (N.L.I., MS 761, pp 210-11). For Rokeby's proclamation, and the land-

owners' delayed response, see N.A., R.C. 8/29, pp 705-4

70. *Rot. Pat. Hib.,* 70; *A.U.,* ii, p. 508.
71. Nicholls, 'Anglo-French Ireland and after', pp 396-7, note 5.
72. N.A., R.C. 8/29, pp 686-96.
73. Ibid., notes 85, 87 below.
74. See H. F. Hore, 'On Irish families of Welsh extraction' in *Archaeologia Cambrensis,* n.s. 3 (1852), p. 148; H. Owen, *Old Pembroke families* (London, 1902), pp 117-8. The Irish genealogists made them Cymric, but this seems to be incorrect.
75. *A. Conn.,* 1281-4; *Cal. Justic. Rolls Ire., 1295-1303,* pp 277-8, 336-7. Fresketh, another fee of Sir William's, is Ardskeagh *(Fert Sceith);* for the location of his fee of Alle, see above, note 50. The modern name Castleventry is a *hapax legomenon* for *castrum venti,* a translation of *Caisleán na gaoithe.*
76. *Rot. Pat. Hib.,* 25, 33. He was living in 1311 (N.A., R.C. 8/5, p. 83) but died before the termination of the escheatorship of Walter de Islip in Sept. 1313.
77. *A.I.,* 1316.2; *Rot. Pat. Hib.,* 25. For Robert the uncle, *Cal. Justic. Rolls Ire., 1295-1303,* p. 312; for Robert fitz Robert, ibid., *1308-1313,* p. 200.
78. N.A., R.C., 8/15, p. 138.
79. His lands are given as one of the northern boundaries of Lombard's grant (above, note 71). For the Barrets of Garrycloyne see *Acts Privy Council,* xv *(1587-88),* p. 185, xvi (1588), pp 101-2.
80. Rymer, *Foedera,* xxiii, pp 643-4.
81. *Anal. Hib.,* xxiii, pp 39, 40.
82. *Rot. Pat. Hib.,* 59.
83. Ibid., 71, 72.
84. B.L., Add. MS 19868, f. 30. Could this have been Cloghphilip, although the latter appears to lie in the middle of Lombard's grant? On the other hand, if this was the Philip who was hostage in 1362 *(Rot. Pat. Hib.,* 59), Rathduff and the adjacent lands in the east of Grenagh parish were known in the late sixteenth century by the name of 'MacWilliam's Lands' (N.A., C.P., G.384); could this have been the location of Philip's grant? More probably the eponym was the William fitz Robert of 1317.
85. N.A., R.C. 8/29, pp 705-7. The name of Bruyn was preserved in that of the River Broen, see *C.S.,* vi, pp 304-5.
86. *Rot. Pat. Hib.,* 65. The northern limits of Lombard's grant were the lands of Lawellyn son of Houyth (Hwfa?) and of John fitz John Barret. Presumably Blarney in Garrycloyne Parish, had been Gynes land, and so fell within Lombard's grant.
87. N.A., R.C. 8/29, pp 716-29. The lands lost by Lombard besides Oldcastle were Mamokyth, either the present Kilnamucky, or across the stream to its east: see the Cloghphilip charter of 1488, Cnoknemarw (Knocknamarriff), Faigh next Mayoly (Faha next Magooly) and Glascartan (unidentified).
88. *Rot. Pat. Hib.,* 100b. The custody of Piers's lands was committed to Philip fitz William de Barry of Rincorran. For the heirs of entail, G.O., MS 192, p. 222, referring to the entail, allegedly executed by John (III) de Cogan *(Ormond Deeds,* iii, no. 346 = N.L.I., D. 1962.) The date as given cannot be correct: John (III) died in 1311, while Richard de Cogan of Huntspill (Somerset), a remainderman, did not succeed his father Thomas until 1315. It is possible, indeed likely, that the deed is a forgery of the reign of Edward III.
89. *Cal. Carew MSS, Bk. of Howth, Misc.,* p. 363. Balecath and Coganrath in

Muscryedonegan had been included in an entail made by John de la Roche in 1386 (Lambeth, MS 635, f. 32). For the southern Roche enclave see note 206 below.

90. *Cal. Carew MSS, Bk. of Howth, Misc.*, pp 362-3; *Bodl. Laud. Misc.*, MS 611, f. 87ᵛ. James fitz Thomas, the 'Súgán' earl of Desmond, however, made some claims to this Castlemore, see *Cal. Pat. Rolls Ire. Jas. I*, 162b. Robert Cogan left a daughter Ellen, who married William Tyrry of Cork; her great-grandson Patrick Tyrry appears to have claimed lands in her name in 1596 (N.A., Betham gen. abstracts, Misc. Ser. 23, p. 66).

91. *Rot. Pat. Hib.*, 100b, 114b, 118: Otway-Ruthven, *Medieval Ire.*, p. 315.

92. N.L.I., MS 4, f. 30. It is possible that John is an error for William; John Roth Barry in the same list, would appear to be William Roth.

93. *Cal. Carew MSS, 1603-1624*, pp 260-1; ibid., *Bk. of Howth, Misc.*, p. 398.

94. Ibid., p. 397; Butler, *Gleanings*, pp 131-3: C.I. ii, p. 260; N.A., C.P., M.10.

95. Butler, *Gleanings*, pp 133-6; N.L.I., Lombard MSS (unsorted collection), bond of John Bareth fitz Robert of Cork, merchant, to James Mathew of do., [30] May, 25 Eliz.

96. Bodl. Rawl, MS B 502, f. 91ᵛ.

97. *A.F.M.*, iii, p. 626 note If the dating at 1364 of the holding of Kilcorcran in Duhallow by a Dermot MacCarthy, *Rotulus Pipae Clonensis*, p. 15, is correct, this could be MacDermot's youngest son, Diarmaid *an phréacháin*.

98. *A.F.M.*, iv, p. 778.

99. *A.U.*, iii, p. 6; Theiner, *Vetera mon.*, p. 279; *Rot. Pat. Hib.*, 98 (*Anna* and *Amia* are interchangeable: the latter became Áine in Irish).

100. N.L.I., MS 4, f. 30.

101. *Misc. Ir. Annals*, p. 111: for the true year see *A.U.*, iii, p. 90.

102. *A.F.M.*, iv, p. 806, corrected from *A. Conn.* 1411.19. It appears from Lambeth, MS 635, f. 25 that individual's real name was Diarmaid.

103. *A.U.*, iii, p. 134, 204; *A. Conn.* 1455.10.

104. J. O'Donovan (ed.), 'Annals of Ireland, from the year 1443 to 1468' in *Miscellany of the Irish Archaeological Society*, pp 223-4.

105. 'Brevis synopsis provinciae Hyberniae fratrum minorum' in *Anal. Hib.*, vi, p. 159.

106. O'Donovan, 'Annals', p. 261. For his genealogy see Nicholls, 'A new source for O'Mahony genealogy', p. 14.

107. Will of David Lumbard, 'captain of his nation', formerly in Lombard MSS. The original would appear to have been lost or destroyed before the collection reached the N.L.I. There remain [i] a transcript by the late J. Ainsworth, see N.L.I., Reports on private collections, no. 46, [ii] A damaged examplification made in 1627 (N.L.I., Lombard MSS).

108. U.C.C., Library, MS U.83/5, passim; N.A., C.P., G. 21.

109. *A.U.*, iii, pp 384, 428; *A.F.M.*, iv, pp 1212, 1246.

110. U.C.C., Library, MS U.83/5, f. 11.

111. B. Ó Cuív (ed), 'A fragment of Irish annals' in *Celtica*, xiv (1981), p. 94. I strongly disagree with Professor Ó Cuív regarding the probable provenance of these annals; it must seriously be considered whether this is not an extract from the otherwise lost annals compiled by Donald Ó Fihely (S. Ó hInnse, *Misc. Ir. Annals*, ix-x). Ware gives extracts from O Fihely for the years 1279 and 1466 (B.L., Add. MS 4821 ff. 102ᵛ, 109.

112. *Cal. Papal Letters*, xvi, no. 347; A. Bolster (ed.), 'Obligationes pro annatis diocesis Coragiensis' in *Arch. Hib.*, xxix, p. 26. The Donat MacCarthy, precentor of Cork,

previously provided in 1492, see *Cal. Papal Letters*, xv, no. 891, xvi, nos 90, 146, 225; *Arch. Hib.*, xxix, p. 21, is surely the same person, although his age is stated as 13 in 1493. There is no mention of him in the later bull of provision .

113. *Fiants, Ire. Henry VIII*, no. 461; see *Extents of Irish monastic possessions*, p. 104.

114. J. Buckley (ed.), 'Munster in 1597' in *Cork Hist. Soc. Jn.*, n.s. xii (1906), p. 66.

115. *Fiants, Ire., Elizabeth*, no. 5183; *H.M.C., Egmont*, i, p. 25.

116. Butler, *Gleanings*, p. 237; *Cal. S.P. Ire., 1586-88*, p. 941; College of Arms, London, *Cal. Ir. Memoranda Roll*, vol. 'Philip and Mary to James I', p. 340 (28 Elizabeth); *Cal. Carew MSS, 1515-74*, p. 417; Lambeth, MS 627, ff 106, 127; N.A., C.P., I.192.

117. *Fiants, Ire., Eliz.*, no. 5333; *Cal. Pat. Rolls Ire. Eliz.*, pp 153, 170. It is not in his surrender (Fiants, 5330).

118. Currykippane had belonged in the fourteenth century to the ancestors of the Cogans (later Gogans) of Barnahely, see G.O., MS 192, p. 142.

119. *C.S.*, vi, pp xxxcv, 376-9. The D.S. map of Barrets Barony shows the townlands of Ballymorisheen and Ballyvaloon, in Grenagh Parish, as part of Muskerry; I can find no other reference to this, nor to there being a MacCarthy interest.

120. These lands were Grenagh, Glencam and Rathduff, in Grenagh Parish; Carrigrohanbeg and Coolatanvally, in Carrigrohanbeg Parish. N.A., C.P. 0.88, is a claim of Cormac MacCarthy against Andrew Barret and others for 16 ploughlands whose names are illegible. Sir Cormac mac Taidhg left his part of 'MacWilliam's lands' in his will, see *Cork Hist. Soc. Jn.*, 1st ser. i (1982), pp 196-8; these were the lands in Grenagh Parish mentioned above (C.P., G. 384).

121. U.C.C., Library, MS U.83/5, f. 14. The boundaries given for Ballyknock in the deed correspond to those of the D.S. denomination of East Pluckanes, held by Charles Oge Carthy.

122. *C.S.*, vi, p. 382; *Fiants, Ire., Elizabeth*, 5330, 5333; *Cal. Pat. Rolls Ire. Jas.* I, pp 488-9; N.A., C.P. K249. Kilmurriheen had passed with Carrignamuck to Ceallachan mac Taidhg and his son Cormac.

123. *Cal. Pat. Rolls Ire., Jas.* I, p. 489b.

124. U.C.C., Library, MS U.83/5, ff 17-8, with an interesting remainder in tail to the heirs of their ancestor Thadeus son of Cormac [died 1461] and Joan daughter of the White Knight. The second of these three brothers, Carthach (*Carucus,* Korragh) mcTeig mcOwen of Cloghroo, made his will in 1579, see R. Caulfield (ed.), 'Wills and inventories, Cork, *temp.* Mary and Elizabeth' in *Gentleman's Magazine*, (Jan. 1862), pp 30-1.

125. R. Grosart (ed.), *Lismore Papers*, 1st ser., i, p. 187. These brothers, Phelim and Dermot mcDonogh, were possibly sons of the Donogh mcPhelim (mcFynin mcOwen, *Fiants, Ire., Eliz.*, no. 3551) mentioned in Sir Cormac mac Taidhg's will.

126. See n. 120, above.

127. P.R.O., S.P. 63/1/168/10, i, f. 22ᵛ; Caulfield, *Kinsale*, pp 423-5 = N.L.I., D. 23, 909.

128. *Anal. Hib.*, xxiii, pp 32-3: *Rot. Pat. Hib.*, 68 (better in N.A., Lodge MSS, Records of the Rolls, i, p. 24).

129. 'Chartae Tyrryanae', pp 116, 118. In 1553 the then Lord Barry signs himself simply 'Edmond Barry Mor', see B.L. Add. MS 19868, f. 10.

130. Will of David Lombard (note 107 above).

131. *Rot. Pat. Hib.*, 165b; P.R.O., S.P. 63/1/168/10, i, f. 000.

132. *Cal. Inquisitions post mortem,* x, no. 299. Note that this inquisition appears, as calendared, to insert an extra David into the descent. This, however, is unsustainable.

133. *Rot. Pat. Hib.,* 58, 60b; *Ormond Deeds,* iii, pp 34-5. The Freynes had inherited these lands from their ancestor Sir Odo de Barry (N.A., R.C. 7/12, pp 387, 398).

134. In 1460 William Lord Barry granted Conna, Cooladurragh and Ballytrasna, along with Mocollop in County Waterford and various rents, to his son-in-law Earl Thomas and the latter's wife *(Lismore Papers,* 1st ser., i, p. 132). The name Kinnatalloon had formerly a much wider significance: the parish of Gortroe was in the 'lordship of Kynealtalwn', see 'Chartae Tyrranae', p. 116.

135. For all these see Mac Cotter, 'Carews'.

136. *Rot. Pat. Hib.,* 46b.

137. *Rotulus Pipae Clonensis,* p. 4.

138. For these see *Census of Ireland, 1841, Report,* County tables, pp 190-1. There were, however, further important changes between 1841 and the issuing of the 1st edition of the six-inch O.S. maps.

139. Piers de Cogan still held half at his death in 1372 (Rot. *Pat. Hib.,* l00b). For the Kildare half see *Red Bk. Kildare,* nos 149, 151; K. W. Nicholls, 'Some place-names from the Red Book of the earls of Kildare' in *Dinnseanchas,* iii (1968-9), pp 33-4; P.R.O.N.I., D.3078/2/1/1; G. MacNiocaill (ed.), *Crown surveys of lands 1540-41, with the Kildare rental begun in 1518,* (Dublin, I.M.C., 1992), p. 310, merely repeating the information from the *Red Bk.,* suggesting the Kildares had no real holdings there. The fact that they retained the advowson of Shandon vicarage (ibid., p. 278: Brady, *Clerical records,* i, pp 281-2, 284) as the Barrymores did of the rectory suggests also that the Kildares had never formally disposed of their half, but that the Barrys had legitimately acquired the Cogan half. Did they acquire it from the Desmonds by exchange, perhaps for Conna etc. in 1460? The manor and castle certainly belonged to Lord Barry in 1533, see R. Caulfield (ed.), 'Early charters relating to the city and county of Cork' in *Gentleman's Magazine,* (April, 1865), p. 450.

140. See note 107 above.

141. *Cal. Pat. Rolls, Henry IV, 1399-1401,* p. 233; see *Cal. Fine Rolls, 1383-91,* pp 66, 87; *Cal. Inquis p.m.; Richard II,* iii, p. 69.

142. N.L.I., MS 4, f. 80. This John appears as Philip by an editorial misreading in *Rotulus Pipae Clonensis,* pp 54, 55; cf. *Johannis* elsewhere in the same document. Nicholas fitz John Barry of Castellethan, who occurs among local lords as an assessor in county Cork in 1421, see Richardson and Sayles, *Parl. and councils med. Ire.,* i, p. 165, might *possibly* be an elder son of John who briefly succeeded his father, but this seems unlikely.

143. Rev. Edmond Barry, 'Barrymore' in *Cork Hist. Soc. Jn.,* n.s., v (1899), pp 219-20, vi (1900), pp 81-86. For the obits of Edmond and James, Lords Barry (showing the unreliability of inquisition dates), see S. H. O'Grady, *B.M. cat. Ir. MSS,* i, p. 201.

144. C.I., vi, pp 59-60, 72; vii p. 243. For O Keefe of Knocknahorgan, *Cal. Pat. Rolls Ire. Jas.* I, p. 141. Conyengally is the *Cannaidhe* of *Lr. Muim,* p. 200.

145. K. W. Nicholls, *Land, law and society in sixteenth-century Ireland,* N.U.I. O'Donnell Lecture (Dublin, 1976), pp 145, 24, notes 48, 49.

146. Hore and Graves, *Southern and eastern counties,* p. 272 (where 'third parte' should read 'three partes'); *Cal. Pat. Rolls Ire., Henry VIII-Elizabeth,* p. 532; P.R.O., S.P. 63/168/10, i, f. 22ᵛ.

147. 'Chartae Tyrryanae', pp 116-9; Caulfield, 'Wills and inventories', p. 256.

148. Caulfield, *Cork,* pp xiv-xv; *Cal. Carew MSS, 1574-1588,* p. 147.

149. N.A., C.P., AA. 44.

150. Barry, 'Barrymore', pp 197-202.

151. Nicholls, *Land, law and society*, pp 11, 23, note 30; *Fiants, Ire., Elizabeth*, e.g. nos 1075, 2247, 2253, 2274, 3079, 3974, 6845, 6566; N.A., C.P., B. 260; Book of Survey and Distribution, Barrymore Barony. For the genealogy of the main line, *Lr. Muim.*, pp 198-200 (where the children given to the first Domhnall on p. 199 in fact belong to his grandfather and namesake).

152. Barry, 'Barrymore', *Cork Hist. Soc. Jn.*, n.s. viii (1902), pp 7-9; C.I., iii, pp 63-5, 120-3, 134-5.

153. Barry, 'Barrymore', *Cork Hist. Soc. Jn.*, n.s. vi (1900), p. 69. The same source gives the obit within the month of his wife, Margaret de Courcy, but this cannot be correct: she survived to claim dower in 1378. For his longevity and vigour, *Rotulus Pipae Clonensis*, p. 35.

154. Rathcobane seems to have been part of the lands of Dromor Odyryn which he detained from successive bishops of Cloyne, see *Rotulus Pipae Clonensis*, pp 33-5. The Walter de Barry to whom he gave lands there (ibid., p. 34; *Rot. Pat. Hib.*, f. 59) was probably an illegitimate son, born early in his career.

155. Obathne still belonged to the minor David (V) in 1345 (B.L., Add. MS 4790, f. 35); the lands there had been taken into the King's hands by 1359 as alienated without licence to Sir William, see *Rot. Pat. Hib.*, 59.

156. *Rot. Pat. Hib.*, 65a.

157. G.O., MS 192, pp 198, 221; Richardson and Sayles, *Parl. and Councils med. Ire.*, i, p. 61.

158. *Rot. Pat. Hib.*, 106, 'Roche' for Rothe. Is the 'John Roch' de Barry, a keeper of the peace in County Cork in 1387, see N.L.I. MS 4, f. 30, an error for William Roth? An Adam son of William Rothe de Barry occurs along with William son of Sir William in 1387 (G.O., MS 192, p. 207).

159. *Rot. Pat. Hib.*, 142b.

160. K.W. Nicholls, 'Some unpublished Barry charters' in *Anal. Hib.*, xxvii, pp 113-4.

161. Marsh's Library, Dublin, MS C.1.20.

162. G.O., MS 192, pp 198, 221.

163. *Cal. Pat. Rolls Ire., Jas* I, p. 289, and see below, note 254.

164. *Cal. Papal Letters*, xvi, no. 110. The names have been badly mangled by the curial clerk, the editor, or both. For the Arundel's advowson of Templeomalus, Brady, *Clerical records*, ii, p. 550.

165. *Cal. Pat. Rolls Ire. Jas* I, p. 79.

166. [P. L.] Laine, *Genealogie de la maison de Mac-Carthy* (Paris, 1839), p. 93; N.A., C.P. E.84.

167. *Ormond Deeds*, iv, no. 280.

168. Nicholls, 'Some unpublished Barry charters', p. 114: C.I., iii, pp 185-9.

169. Barry, 'Barrymore', *Cork Hist. Soc. Jn.*, n.s. vii (1901), pp 65-77.

170. Ibid., vi (1990), pp 134-37; Lambeth, MS 627 f. 71^v. James's eldest son, Richard, was born deaf and dumb but survived to a great age.

171. *Cal. Justic. Rolls Ire. 1295-1303*, pp 101, 143 (for Domhnall Baiscneach MacCarthy, named as one of the slayers, *Bk. Ui Maine*, f. 28r b); D. F. Gleeson (ed.), 'Annals of Nenagh' in *Anal. Hib.*, xii, p. 159. One of these sons was perhaps the Eustace who was his father's hostage in 1320 (G.O., MS 190, p. 181).

172. N.A., R.C., 8/20, pp 192-4.

173. B.L., Cotton MS Titus B xi (2), f. 00. This copy has annotations in the hand of Sir George Carew.

174. This date, given by Carew (Lambeth, MS 62, f. 102^v) from 'Cork Cathedral' is

confirmed by N.A., R.C. 8, p. 432, mentioning his widow Margaret (for whom see above, note 64).

175. Lambeth, MS 635, f. 4 (from which N.A., M. 2550, f. 127 is copied); an abridged version in Bodl., MS. Laud. Misc. 613, pp 286-7. See also *Rot. Pat. Hib.*, 83b.

176. Nicholas de Courcy is named as tenant of Kinsale in the Cork episcopal rental, which I date *c*. 1362-72 (above, note 55).

177. Inquisition post mortem on Gerald, Lord Courcy, 7 Dec. 1604, reciting earlier inquisition post mortem of 16 Aug. 1601 (Bodl., MS Talbot B.16.21). For Margaret see N.A. M.2550, f. 79^v = T.C.D., MS F.4.18, f. 200^v = G.O., MS 192, p. 229; R.C. 8/31, p. 501. Her sister Katherine was not by Anastacia Courcy (*Rot. Pat. Hib.*, 83b) and was presumably the child of Margaret Wogan: was she 'the Knight Courcy's daughter' from whom the MacCarthy sept called *Sliocht Inghine an Ridire* took its descent (*Lr. Muim.*, p. 151) and so second wife of Domhnall Og MacCarthy, king of Desmond (died 1393)?

178. An inquisition post mortem on this John, dated 16 Richard II, survived in the P.R.O., Dublin, until 1922, see *P.R.I. rep D.K.* 28 app., p. 40. See G.O., MS 192, p. 268.

179. Bodl., Laud Misc., MS 613, pp 280 = B.L., Cotton MS Titus B. xi (2), f. 179. The boundaries given would fit Ringfinnan, which later belonged to the Bayes family, and the name Morianus, found in the latter, could be an anglicisation of Maolmuire. For the lineage see J. Bannerman, *The Beatons: a medical kindred in the classical Gaelic tradition* (Edinburgh, 1986), pp 34-5.

180. There seems little doubt that the David who usurped the lordship was the David whose ecclesiastical career can be traced through the papal registers. John, son of an archdeacon, provided as rector of Kilgobban in 1493 (*Cal. Papal Letters*, xvi, no. 220) would then be the John who was subsequently lord, and Nicholas, son of the Archdeacon Coursy, slain in 1513 (Lambeth, MS 626, f. 102^v) would also agree with one of David's sons (Lambeth, MS 635, f. 139). David Lecurcy [*sic*], of baronial race, was provided as rector of Kilgobban in 1468 and soon after, having delated the incumbent, David Myagh, as archdeacon of Cork (*Cal. Papal Letters*, x, pp xxi, 289, 713). He became rector of Rinrone in 1486 (ibid., xiv, pp 32, 125) and drops out of the records after 1490 (ibid., xv, nos 235, 564).

181. Lambeth, MS 635, f. 139. The date given for James's death (Laud Misc., MS 613, p. 289) may not be reliable: his son Richard is said to have prececeased him by three years (ibid.). In 1591 John fitzJohn fitz Nicholas Courcy joined Lord Courcy in a conveyance of Coolbane and Garrylucas (inquis. cited, note 177).

182. S.P. 63/214/36; U.C.C., Library, MS, 'Kinsale manorial papers'.

183. *Crown surveys of lands, 1540-41*, pp 263, 364. This John was living in 1538 (inquisit. cited, note 177).

184. Caulfield, *Kinsale*, pp xvii, 370; inquis. cited n. 177.

185. *Ormond Deeds*, iv, no. 280.

186. Lambeth, MS 627, f. 104^v. For 'halface' money, worth a third more than sterling, see M. Dolley and G. Mac Niocaill, 'Some coin-names in *Ceart Uí Neill*' in *Studia Celtica*, ii (1967), pp 119-24.

187. *Cal. S.P. Ire., 1586-8*, p. 585.

188. Inquis. cited, note 177, *Fiants, Ire., Elizabeth*, no. 5029; D. MacCarthy, *The life and letters of Florence MacCarthy Mor* (London, 1867; repr. Cork, 1975), pp 41, 124, 135, 139. Gerald Lord Courcy sometimes associated kinsmen with him in his conveyances, suggesting that these were their recognized portions (*cion*

fineachais or *cuid fineachais*) of the lands: John fitz John fitz Nicholas in that of Coolbane and Garrylucas, and the sons of his uncle James (a priest and rector of Rinrone and Templetrine: Lambeth, MS 635, f. 139; 'Obligationes pro annatis diocesis Corcagiensis', pp 31-2 in that of Dromdough.

189. *Cal. S.P. Ire., 1611-14,* pp 172-3, 507-8; MacCarthy, *Life and letters,* pp 381-4, 395-6; *Cal. Pat. Rolls Ire., Jas. I,* pp 473, 497.

190. The cantred of Kenelbek (*Cineal mBeice:* Kinelmeaky) extended right up to the outskirts of Cork, the stream called Glassynysheanaghe (the Glasheen river) marking the boundary in the suburbs between it and Kerrycurrihy (B.L., Add. MS 19868, f. 9).

191. Inquisition post mortem on Miles de Courcy (note 175 above); N.A., R.C. 8/17, pp 58-9; 8/20, pp 192-4; *Rot. Pat. Hib.,* 65, 69b, l00b, 114b, 148, 150; N.L.I., MS 4, f. 30.

192. Richardson and Sayles, *Parl. and councils med. Ire.,* i, p. 167; *Rot. Pat. Hib.,* 206; *Cal. Pat. Rolls Ire. Henry VIII-Elizabeth,* p. 532.

193. Caulfield, *Kinsale,* p. xiv. It is this Thomas, and not the Sir Thomas of Elizabethan times, who ends the genealogy in *Lr. Muim.,* p. 284. He appears to have died childless and been succeeded by his brother Philip, lord of Kinalea in 1516 (Caulfield, *Kinsale,* p. 367). Thomas is omitted (no doubt as having died childless) from the genealogy in Lambeth, MS 635, f. 133, where Philip and their father William are given.

194. N.L.I., D.1999 (ii); *Cal. Papal Letters,* xii, p. 428.

195. It was alienated by Philip Barry Og to Patrick Myaghe in 1541, see Caulfield, *Kinsale,* p. 368.

196. Caulfield, *Kinsale,* p. xiii; below, note 240.

197. Caulfield, *Kinsale,* p. 368.

198. *Cal. Pat. Rolls, Philip and Mary,* i, *1553-4,* p. 65.

199. *Cal. Pat. Rolls Ire. Henry VIII-Elizabeth,* p. 533. The Lady Katherine referred to was Philip Barry Og's widow, the daughter of Earl Thomas of Desmond; cf. further the inquisitions referred to in note 203.

200. P.R.O., S.P. 63/71/8.

201. Lambeth, MS 627, f. 175.

202. *Cal. S.P. Ire., 1586-88,* p. 320; *1588-92,* pp 497, 515; *1592-96,* p. 11 ('Sir Robert' is a mistake for Sir Thomas); *Acts Privy Council 1591-92,* pp 471-2.

203. Inquisition of 26 Aug. 16 Jas., C.I. ii, pp 28-40; cf. another of 15 Aug. 1620 (ibid., pp 113-9). Sir Thomas mortgaged his tributes from various lands to the landowners. For the true relationship of Henry, Sir Thomas and their pre-decessors see Lambeth, MS 635, f. 133: *Acts Privy Council, 1591,* p. 313.

204. *Cal. Pat. Rolls Ire., Jas.* I, p. 209. See, S.P. 63/1/168/10, i, f. 25ᵛ-26ᵛ.

205. Henry McGibbon, who was disputing the possession of Moylawryth (Moyge) in 1401 (*Rot. Pat. Hib.,* 165b) must have been the ancestor of this line for whom Lambeth, MS 626, f. 94 declares to have been of a different, though Geraldine, origin to the White Knights. There is remarkably little information on them.

206. Part of it, the townlands of Coolowen and Farranastig, properly Farranrostig, 'Roche's land, see *C.S.,* vi, p. 493, was transferred to the newly erected county of the city (later the barony of Cork) in 1608; the remainder was in Fermoy until 1837 (note 138 above). See also *C.S.,* vi, p. 383.

207. In 1450, however, an Edmond Roche (who cannot be placed in the genealogy) seems to have been a chieftain in this area (*Cal. Papal Letters,* x, p. 454. The Roches, however, were alleged to have a tradition of conflict with their eldest sons: *Cal. S.P. Ire. 1586-88,* p. 3.

208. *A.I.* 1309.1, 1311.2; *Cal. Justic. Rolls Ire., 1308-1314,* pp 159-61; *Chartul. St. Mary's Dublin,* ii, pp 281, 338.

209. *N.A., Cal. Justic. Rolls, 9-11 Edw. ii,* pp 60ff.; *Cal. Justic. Rolls, 11 Edw. ii* (iv; Plea Roll no. 119), pp 3952, 65-7; Clyn, *Annals,* p. 19; 'Exsul', 'The Clinton family' in *Ancestor,* x (1904), pp 36-41.

210. *Cal. Inquis. post mortem,* x, no. 176; 'The Clinton Family' in *Anal. Hib.,* xli, xxiii, p. 34; B.L., Add. MS 4790, f. 108ᵛ; *Rot. Pat. Hib.,* 59b.

211. This Edmond had briefly possession of Ballyderown in 1335 (N.A., R.C. 8/15, pp 273, 386); in 1340 he was holding Glyndowyn, county Limerick, formerly part of Sir Maurice's lands *(Gormanston reg.,* p. 115).

212. *Rot. Pat. Hib.,* 52, 56b, 65b, 69. He and his brother Raymond had been among Desmond's followers (see *Anal. Hib.,* xxiii, p. 33). 'Gerald fitz *William* de Caunton of Clondolan' (ibid., p. 38) must be a *hapax legomenon.*

213. *Rot. Pat. Hib.,* 65, 70b; *Cal. inquis. post mortem,* xii, no. 113; B.L., Add. MS 4790, f. 108ᵛ; N.A., R.C. 8/29, p. 15. The William fitz *Reimund* de Caunton who (or his heirs) was to be distrained (Nov. 1376) for the relief of the manor of Ballyderown, which he held in chief (R.C. 8/31, p. 368) must surely be an error for William fitz *Emund.*

214. B.L., Add. MS 4780, f. 108ᵛ; *Rot. Pat. Hib.,* 102b. Raymond was in fact probably chief by 1367 (G.O., MS 192, p. 158).

215. N.L.I., MS 4, f. 30. Raymond's father, Piers de Caunton of Clondulane, was dead by 1322, when his widow claimed her dower against his son Gerald (R.C. 8/13, p. 510).

216. According to Carew (Lambeth, MS 635, f. 163) the Raymond or Redmond who married Ellen or Evelin Roche (a marriage confirmed by dispensation March 1440) (*Cal. Papal Letters,* ix, pp 70, 114) was the son of another Raymond and grandson of Raymond fitz Piers. This might seem too short: nevertheless it seems as though Raymond fitz Piers was known as Raymond Keogh (K...gh, *Rot. Pat. Hib.,* 65) in which case the Raymond of 1450 would be his son, born in his old age, and the husband of Evelin Roche his grandson, thus confirming Carew. According to the latter William Carragh, son of Raymond fitz Piers, was illegitimate. He may have been the grandfather of the Thomas fitz Raymond fitz William Condon who acquired Marshalstown in 1445 (C.I., i, p. 106).

217. See esp. N.A., R.C. 7/1, p. 252; *Cal. Justic. Rolls Ire., 1295-1303,* pp 383-5.

218. The last of the Cauntetons of Athoull would seem to have been Gregory fitz Robert de Caunteton, living in 1344 (B.L., Add. Chart. 13, 599; *Anal. Hib.,* xxiii, p. 38), son of Sir Robert fitz Gregory.

219. The traditional (and published) pedigrees of the early White Knights bear no resemblance to anything to be found in contemporary records. The following succession would seem to be firmly established: Sir Thomas fitz Gilbert, Sir Maurice fitz Thomas, Maurice fitz Maurice, the last-named being presumably the Sir Maurice Whyteknight of 1401 (*Cal. Pat. Rolls, 1399-1401,* p. 451) and the White Knight *(an Ridire Fionn)* who died in 1419 (*A.F.M.,* iv, p. 840).

220. *Rotulus Pipae Clonensis,* p. 12; N.A., R.C. 7/12, p. 478; G.O. MS 191, p. 269.

221. C.I., i, pp 103-6. The surname MacMaug must be derived either from Mathew fitz William de Caunteton in the late thirteenth century or his greatgrandson Mathew fitz William of 1366.

222. *R.S.A.I. Jn.,* xv (1879-82), pp 650-55.

223. *Fiants, Ire., Edward* vi, nos 862 ('of Horston', 'Hoar stone' that is *Cloch liath*), 1096 ('of Cloghle'); P.R.O., S.P. 63/14/52.

224. A. Sheehan. 'Official reactions to native land claims in the Plantation of Munster' in *I.H.S.*, xxiii/92 (1983), pp 307-8.

225. See J. F. Casey, 'Land ownership in North Cork 1584-1641', unpublished Ph.D. thesis, N.U.I. (1988).

226. *Cal. Inquis. post mortem,* ii, no. 437, very inaccurately calendared also in *Cal. doc. Ire., 1252-12~4,* no. 1912. Clonlathtyn and Dromynargyl (Dromanarrigle, Kilmeen parish) were held of Sir William Rokele, husband of the Fitz Elias heiress, see K. W. Nicholls, 'The early Keatings' in *Ir. Geneal.,* V/3 (1976), pp 287-8. The half cantred in Corkeleye was presumably that which had belonged to his ancestor Thomas fitz Anthony; see K. W. Nicholls, 'Some place-names from *Pontificia Hibernica*' in *Dinnseanchas,* iii (1969), p. 96.

227. Orpen, *Normans,* iv, pp 236-7; A. F. O'Brien, 'The political ambitions of Maurice fitz Thomas, first earl of Desmond', pp 61-63.

228. Ibid., pp 61, 84; *Rotulus Pipae Clonensis,* pp 57-60. Katherine of Desmond also acquired the manor of Rincrew, immediately east of Youghal: she granted it in 1443 to her nephew Gerald fitz James, afterwards lord of the Decies, see R.I.A., MS 3 B 40.

229. Lambeth, MS 635, f. 183; *Rotulus Pipae Clonensis,* pp 60-61. Maurice fitz Richard's father, Sir Richard fitz Maurice, had been involved in the administration of Inchiquin in the 1340s (O'Brien, 'Maurice Fitz Thomas', p. 75).

230. Mr P. Mac Cotter promises a definitive study of John fitz Edmond and his land-holdings. For his stock, see P.R.O., S.P. 3/83/29.

231. *A.I.,* '1321' (1326), 4; *A.F.M.,* iii, p. 534. Donnchadh MacCarthy must be Donnchadh son of Diarmaid Reamhar, ancestor of the Clan Dermot. I cannot accept the identification of Dún Mic Odhmainn with Myross, proposed by Diarmuid Ó Murchadha. See Mac Cotter, 'Carews'.

232. N.A., R.C. 8/15, pp 273, 496. 'Dovenaldus filius Douenaldi Carberagh', MacCarthy must be Domhnall *glas.*

233. *Cal. Papal Letters,* xii, p. 624.

234. Lambeth, MS 627, f. 107 (in case of default of delivery, the amount was to be doubled); *Cal. Pat. Rolls Ire., Jas. I,* p. 284.

235. Above, note 134.

236. See the lists of his supporters in Sayles (ed.), 'Legal proceedings' in *Anal. Hib.,* xxiii, pp 5-46.

237. On Desmond the standard writings are those of R. Frame, 'The justiciarship of Ralph Ufford: warfare and politics in fourteenth-century Ireland' in *Stud. Hib.,* xiii (1973), pp 7-47; idem, 'Power and society in the lordship of Ireland, 1272-1377' in *Past and Present,* 76 (1977), pp 3-33; idem, *English lordship in Ireland, 1318-1361.* See also, O'Brien, 'Territorial ambitions'.

238. K. W. Nicholls, 'Fragments of Irish annals' in *Peritia,* ii (1982), pp 88-9.

239. Guildford Record Office, Midleton MSS, box 95; *Cal. Carew MSS, Bk. of Howth,* pp 362-3.

240. Ibid., p. 397, where 'Gale' is an error for Garthe, Ballingarry, an old possession of the Brit family; cf. Lambeth, MS 627, f. 103.

241. *Cal. Pat. Rolls Henry VI* 1441-46, p. 358.

242. Ó Cuív, 'A fragment of Irish annals', pp 95, 99.

243. Caulfield, *Cork,* pp xiv-xv.

244. *Cal. Carew MSS, Bk. of Howth,* p. 397; *Crown Surveys of lands,* 1540-41, p. 245; K. W. Nicholls, 'Some place-names from *The Red Book of the earls of Kildare*' in *Dinnseanchas,* iii (1968), p. 33.

245. *Cal. S.P. Ire.* 1509-74, p. 273; *Cal. S.P. Ire. 1574-85,* p. 19; Bodl., MS Laud. Misc. 611, f. 87; above, note 116; P.R.O., S.P. 63/1/168/10, i, f. 25ᵛ (cf. *Bk. of Howth,* p. 398, line 28, where 'Edw. IV' should read 'Edw. VI').

246. *Ormond Deeds,* iii, pp 254-5; iv, pp 153-4, 197; v., pp 110-11, 174; *Acts Privy Council, Ire.,* pp 57, 237; Lambeth, MS 627, f. 107ᵛ. Desmond could only claim 'through long continuance of possession in himself and his ancestors', without documentary title.

247. No O Driscolls appear in the published *Justiciary Rolls.* For the O Driscolls, see O'Donovan, *Misc. Celt. Soc.* (Dublin, 1849), p. 327-403.

248. *Rot. Pat. Hib.,* 58b; *A. Conn.,* 1366.4; 1368.7. The fourteen sons of Cormac Donn are listed in T.C.D., MS H.1.12 (1286), B. p. 2a.

249. D. MacCarthy (Glas), *A historical pedigree of the Sliochd Feidhlimidh: the MacCarthys of Gleannacroim* (Exeter, n.d.).

250. *A.F.M.,* iv, pp 816-7; T.C.D., MS H.1.12 (1286) B. p. 2a. It would appear that Kilbrittain was Domhnall's residence at his death.

251. *A.F.M.,* 3rd ed. (1990), Introduction, app., s.a. 1398; *A.F.M.,* iii, p. 800; *A. Conn.,* 1418.10.

252. *A.U.,* iii, p. 178; Ó Cuív, 'A fragment of Irish annals', pp 93-99. Note that the Cormac mentioned in the later part of 1468.4 is Cormac mac Taidhg of Muskerry.

253. *Z.C.P.,* ii (1899), p. 4; P. Walsh (ed.), *Leabhar Chlainne Suibhne* (Dublin, 1920), pp 56-7; *A.U.,* iii, p. 264; *A.F.M.,* iv, p. 110. Cormac survived, in spite of this treatment, until 1503 (*A.F.M.,* v, p. 1270).

254. *Cal. Pat. Rolls Ire., Jas. I,* pp 51, 79, 310 (where Kilgarriff (in Twoghenykillihie) and Killaneety and Ballybolane (in Twoghe Ballynydeihie) are both described as in Tanaisteh); cf. Butler, *Gleanings,* p. 175. For the title of 'tanist' applied to members of this sept, Lambeth, MS 599, f. 39 (Finghin mac Eoghain); MS 635, f. 170ᵛ (Domhnall *Rabach* mac Cormaic). Two sons of this Domhnall *Rabach* were landowners in Tuogh Montine (*Fiants, Ire., Elizabeth,* nos 6515, 6770).

255. I am grateful to Professor Donnchadh Ó Corráin for his assistance in solving the mystery of these titles, often presented in corrupt form, which seem so obvious when interpreted.

256. *Ormond Deeds,* iv, no. 280.

257. *Cal. Pat. Rolls Ire., Jas. I,* pp 51, 79. For his rebellion, *Cal. S.P. Ire., 1598-99,* p. 499. There were two *inquisitions post mortem* (19 Dec. 1603; 16 July 1607) on this Finghin in the Exchequer series: I am grateful to Mr P. Mac Cotter and Mrs J. A. C. Richardson for copies of the abstracts of them made by W. Lynch (London, College of Arms, Cal. of Exchequer Inquisitions, Ire.), which give a great deal of information on the sept. There is also an inquisition (29 Apr. 1615) on his father Eoghan, *alias* Cawne mcGanawris, allegedly slain in 1559 (C.I., vii, pp 4-6); also in Exchequer series. For 'Mac Ingan Auras', Butler, *Gleanings,* p. 174 (misidentified).

258. *Cal. Pat. Rolls Henry VII,* p. 226; cf. *Ormond Deeds,* iii, no. 273.

259. V. Treadwell, 'The establishment of the farm of the Irish customs, 1603-1613' in *E.H.R.,* xciii (1978), p. 588.

260. Laine, *Genealogie de Mac-Carthy,* pp 85-87.

261. *A.F.M.,* v, p. 1288. *Dun na mBend,* mentioned along with *Bend dubh,* is certainly not Dunmanway, as O'Donovan hazarded. I suspect the linking ⁊ is really an *i,* and that the names are alternatives.

262. Laine, *Genealogie de Mac-Carthy,* p. 89.

263. N.L.I., D. 1999 (i, 11). The marriage treaty is briefly and incorrectly handled in *Ormond Deeds,* iv, no. 16.

264. Walsh, *Leabhar Chlainne Suibhne,* pp 56-7; Lambeth, MS 635, ff. 13^v-14, 189^v-90; *U.J.A.*, 1st ser., v (1860), pp 318-9.
265. *Ormond Deeds,* iv, no. 1280 = N.L.I., D.2375-6.
266. S. G. Ellis, *Tudor Ireland* (London, 1985), p. 48.
267. 'Chartae Tyrryanae', pp 117-8.
268. See note 13 above.
269. Ellis, *Tudor Ireland*, p. 251.
270. *Cal. S.P. Ire. 1600-01*, pp 289-90.

Plate 6.1   Timoleague Abbey (Cambridge University Collection of air photographs).

Chapter 7

GAELIC LAND TENURE IN COUNTY CORK: UÍBH LAOGHAIRE IN THE SEVENTEENTH CENTURY

DIARMUID Ó MURCHADHA

Throughout the sixteenth century a number of minor Gaelic lordships flourished in county Cork, dependent to a greater or lesser extent upon one or other of the three major branches of the Mac Carthys who were effectively overlords of the entire western half of the county. Because the Mac Carthys regained control of Muskerry at a comparatively late stage – probably during the fourteenth century – those who had previously established themselves there maintained a degree of independence which lasted into the seventeenth century. 'Freeholders' is the term used in a Carew document, c. 1600,[1] to describe the O Learys and three clans of O Mahonys – Clann Fhínghin, Clann Chonchobhair and the clan of Uí Fhlainn Lua. Following these were 'Countries in Muskrye' with ecclesiastical associations – O Healys of Donaghmore, O Herlihys of Ballyvourney, O Longs of Cannaway and O Cremins of Aghabullogue. All had their traditional systems of land usage and division, a pattern in which the Mac Carthys liked to be represented.

Uíbh Laoghaire (Inchigeelagh parish) was perhaps the area least affected by the Mac Carthy hegemony. It was an insignificant lordship in an upland district, one not considered worthy of mention either in official English documents or in Irish annals or bardic poetry prior to the late sixteenth century.[2] This remoteness from extraneous influences brought about a legal system, particularly in respect of land division, which developed unhindered from Brehon law, adapted to local requirements, right up to 1638 when the last division took place.

Because the results of this final allotment have been, so to speak, fossilised for us in the Civil Survey of Muskerry barony (a survey which did not differentiate between feudal and Gaelic-type landholding), we are provided with a valuable illustration of the manner in which the lands of a sept were shared out among its leading members prior to the upheavals of the seventeenth century. The study of the working of this system is the chief purpose of this article. It also examines the effects of the intrusion of the English legal system on the old, following confiscations and royal grants, and in particular the influence of Richard Boyle, the chief beneficiary of such dealings.

Extent of the territory

The Uí Laoghaire territory embraced the valley of the infant river Lee, from its origins in the mountains encircling Gougane Barra, through Lough Allua to its junction with the Toon, the river which marks the northern boundary of the parish for most of its length. Southwards, the Shehy mountains separate Uíbh Laoghaire from Bantry and East Carbery. It was more or less coterminous with the civil and ecclesiastical parish of Inchigeelagh, county Cork's third most extensive parish – but with the following differences: (1) The north-west corner of the parish, comprising fifteen modern townlands, was in 1641 owned and occupied by a branch of the Mac Carthys, Clann Charthaigh Eachruis. (2) In 1493 the townlands of Deshure, Cooldorragha, Shanacashel, Cusduff, Clonmoyle and two others were detached from the eastern side of Inchigeelagh parish and joined to some townlands from Macloneigh to form the new parish of Kilmichael.[3] It is likely that this adjustment of boundaries was based on an existing territorial division. Uí Fhlainn Lua was O Mahony territory (the new vicar was to be Mathew O Mahony) and the papal mandate makes special reference to the enmities between the people of the Kilmichael area and those in Inchigeelagh and Macloneigh. (3) At some time subsequent to the surveys of the seventeenth century, an additional 11 townlands (5,576 acres) were added to the civil (and ecclesiastical) parish of Inchigeelagh on its southern boundary. These townlands, centred around Coolmountain, were formerly in the parish of Fanlobbus. They lie south of the Shehy mountain barrier, and geographically (as well as topographically) form part of Carbery [Fig. 7.1].

Accordingly, none of the three above-mentioned areas will be taken into consideration here. The remainder, totalling in modern terms 34,442 statute acres, constitutes the Uí Laoghaire lands in respect of which various statistics will be provided.

The Mac Carthys

Two Uí Laoghaire families in south Munster are recorded in early sources, one at Castletownroche[4] and the other among the Corca Laoighdhe.[5] The latter is the one associated with the sixteenth/ seventeenth-century Uí Laoghaire by the genealogists of that era (see Appendix A). In the absence of an alternative derivation, I am assuming that the tradition of a migration from Corca Laoighdhe is historically genuine.

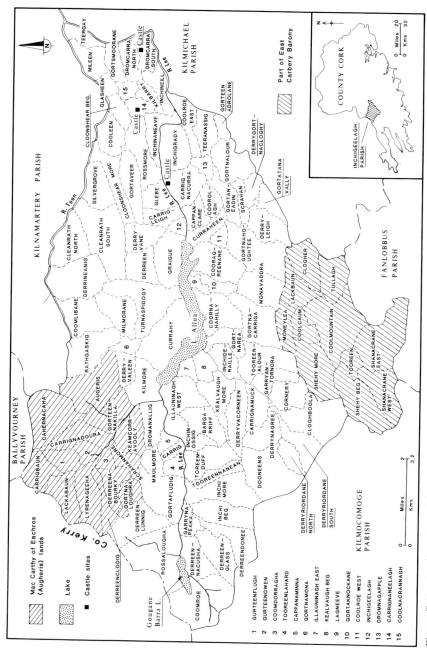

Figure 7.1 Inchigeela parish.

215

As one of the leading families of Corca Laoighdhe the Uí Laoghaire occupied a reasonably fertile strip of coastal territory on the peninsula between Rosscarbery and Glandore. They were known as Uí Laoghaire Ruis Ó gCairbre and their territory as Tuath Ruis, also Tuath in Dolaich.[6] In the early thirteenth century, following the division of Mac Carthy's kingdom of Cork, the half-cantred of Rosyletir (*Ros Ailithir*) consisting of three territories, one of which was named Doleht Ilecheri (*Dolach Uí Laoghaire*), was occupied by one of the Butler family. Prior to 1229 Henry Le Botiller bestowed it on his son-in-law, David de Barry, head of the powerful Barry family.[7]

It is most likely then that in the first quarter of the thirteenth century the Uí Laoghaire were forced out of their original homeland around Rosscarbery. They may not, however, have immediately forsaken the west-Cork coastline. They could have at first moved further west, into Schull parish where there are townlands named Derryleary and Scrahanyleary (*Doire/Screathan Uí Laoghaire*).[8] But it is generally assumed that they settled in Inchigeelagh parish at an early stage.[9]

On the basis of the vague and somewhat biased remarks of Nicholas Browne[10] and Sir William Herbert[11] it has frequently been stated that the O Learys occupied Inchigeelagh as an independent clan until forced by the Mac Carthys to pay rents and services. It is more likely that they settled there under the aegis of the Mac Carthys. Despite its remoteness, Inchigeelagh was hardly a 'no man's land' before their arrival. The abundance of such archaeological sites as wedge-tombs, standing stones, stone alignments, as well as many ring-forts, two cashels and a crannóg[12] indicates a continuity of occupation for many centuries before the coming of the Normans. As part of the kingdom of Desmond it may also have provided a secure refuge for Mac Carthy leaders pursued by Norman antagonists.

The decline of the Cambro-Norman settlement in the fourteenth century led to a re-establishment of Mac Carthy dominance in Muskerry. In 1352 the Justiciar, Sir Thomas Rokeby, drove the rebellious Diarmaid mac Diarmada (Mac Carthy) out of Muskerry.[13] Rokeby was aided by Diarmaid's rival, Cormac Mac Carthy, who in 1353 was rewarded with a grant of lands in and around Macroom and Macloneigh, as well as some in county Kerry.[14] Cormac made his second son, Diarmaid, 'lord of Muskerry', and eventually the Mac Carthys asserted that lordship, extending their sway beyond 'old Muskerry' (north of the Lee) into the O Mahony territories to the south, so that the modern baronies of East and West Muskerry embrace both sides of the Lee valley.

Interestingly, one area granted to Cormac in 1353, and not then connected with either Muskerry or Múscraighe Luachra but isolated *inter silvas*, was named 'Islagagh'. This probably represents the earliest reference we have to Inchigeelagh, by then no doubt occupied by the Uí Laoghaire, although we have no account of their activities until Elizabethan times.

'Among the woods' it certainly was, and among the mountains as well, its inaccessible position segregating its inhabitants to a large extent from their Gaelic neighbours, and almost totally from English government influences. This isolation seems to have extended even to church organisation. No church is recorded there in 1199[15] nor in the early fourteenth-century taxation lists.[16] Inchigeelagh first appears in the Papal records in 1479[17] and again in 1493 when a disputed clerical appointment was followed by the erection of a new parish at Kilmichael.[18]

By 1510 a Mac Carthy cleric was vicar of Inchigeelagh[19] and in 1540 the rectory of Inchigeelagh was divided between Gill Abbey and Mourne Abbey,[20] both in the sphere of influence of the Mac Carthys of Muskerry. In the lay domain, the rights of the Mac Carthys over the whole of Muskerry were officially recognised through a royal regrant in 1578 to Cormac mac Taidhg of lands surrendered by him in the previous year. The grant included the territory of Iveleary and the lands of its two strongholds, Carrignaneelagh and Carrignacurra.[21] A similar surrender by and regrant to Cormac mac Diarmada took place in 1589.[22] It was about that year that a raid by Thomas Butler, Earl of Ormond, on Uíbh Laoghaire was referred to in an Irish praise-poem as an injury to the Mac Carthys.[23]

Early seventeenth-century inquisitions make it clear that an annual rent was payable to the lord of Muskerry by the O Learys. A surrender by and regrant to Cormac Mac Carthy (son of Cormac mac Diarmada) in 1620 specifies a rent of 24 beeves and £7 2s. 3d. English money out of Iveleary, though it names only townlands north of the Lee.[24] That this was the rent payable for the whole territory, however, is confirmed by a similar regrant in 1639[25] and by the Civil Survey.[26] Carew's account informs us that in 1600 the *tánaiste* of Muskerry (Cormac mac Taidhg) claimed the right to two days' and nights' refection in Uíbh Laoghaire every quarter, or two marks sterling in place of each refection. Furthermore, he was entitled to a payment of £4 9s. every time a new chief of the Uí Laoghaire was elected.[27]

Apart from these reasonably tolerable exactions, the Uí Laoghaire did not suffer from the encroachments of their Mac Carthy overlords, to whom they paid a lump sum communally, rather than individual head-rents as was usual elsewhere in Muskerry. This integral independence was obviously due in part to the inhospitable terrain and the rampart of encircling hills. But there may have been an early agreement, pre-dating the lordship of Muskerry, perhaps as far back as the original Uí Laoghaire settlement in Inchigeelagh.

As already mentioned, the entire north-west corner of the parish around Augeris (*Eachros*), totalling 5,397 statute acres or 13.5 per cent of the old parish, was allotted to a segment of the Mac Carthys. The only source[28] to give their ancestry derives them from an otherwise unnoticed fifth son of Cormac Fionn (*ob.* 1247) named Donnchadh na Dromann, so that it appears they were not a sub-sept of the Muskerry Mac Carthys. They paid a separate annual rent of £8 to the lord of Muskerry.[29] They also had their own chapel-of-ease (the ruin of which is known as Teampaillín Eachruis) and in 1540 Eachros was regarded as a rectory separate from Inchigeelagh.[30]

Local names

The very place-names of Uíbh Laoghaire reflect its imperviousness to outside influences. In the Normanised or semi-Normanised parts of Ireland the use of *baile* (or *-ton*) to denote a farmstead/holding spread like wildfire across the landscape. Out of a total of 428 townlands in the barony of Imokilly in east Cork, for example, 132 (30.8 per cent) begin with 'Bally-/Ballin-' or end in '-town'. Not one of the 118 townlands in present-day Inchigeelagh parish does so,[31] and fewer than 10 per cent embody personal or family names.

In Uíbh Laoghaire the most frequent initial place-name elements are *Daire* or *Doire/Doirín*, an 'oakwood' or 'grove', and *Gort/Goirtín*, a 'plot of land'. Other natural features such as *Inse*, 'river-meadow', *Carraig*, 'rock', *Cúm*, 'coomb', *Cuar*, 'concavity', *Drom*, 'ridge' are also in evidence. The purely descriptive – almost poetic – style of such names as *Cúm Dorcha*, 'the dark recess', or *Tuairín na nÉan*, 'little lea of the birds', contrasts sharply with the more prosaic Ballyrobert or Ballinvarrig so frequently found in the east of the county, a product of the totally practical Norman-style approach to naming, based on owner-occupation.

In regard to personal names too, the influx of biblical and Germanic names introduced by the Normans and frequently taken up by Gaelic septs (for example Geoffrey by the O Donoghues, Philip by the O Sullivans, John by the O Mahonys) seems to have left the O Learys practically untouched. True, Tomás Mór and Tomás Óg occur in the Ó Laoghaire genealogy (see Appendix A), but as late as 1641, out of the thirty-three occupiers of the ancestral lands, most of whom had their fathers' names appended to theirs, Donogh mac Shane is the only instance of a personal name showing Norman influence.[32]

It may then be safely assumed that the customs, the laws and in particular the system of land division in use among the Uí Laoghaire owe little to common law or to Norman feudal practice. The allotment of land to clan members must be studied in the light of what we know of Gaelic tradition in this matter. It was, for example, customary in most Gaelic lordships to elect a lord or chief from among the *deirbhfhine*, the group consisting of men whose father, grandfather or great-grandfather had been chief.[33] Clans subject to overlords had their chiefs elected by an assembly of the gentlemen of the lordship, presided over by the overlord.[34] There is an account of such an assembly in Uíbh Laoghaire in 1592 when the reigning chief, Art Ó Laoghaire, retired (or was deposed) to be replaced by a younger brother, Amhlaoibh. The latter was elected by the chief men of Muskerry and had the white rod of office delivered to him by Cormac mac Dermod Mac Carthy.[35]

After such an election – normally caused by the death of a reigning chief – a redistribution of clan lands took place, with the lion's share usually falling to the chief himself and to those most closely related to him. Those at the fringes of the *deirbhfhine* generally found themselves pushed into less fertile and ever-decreasing landholdings.

Chiefs or lords

DIARMAID (fl. *c.* 1540)
Diarmaid (5)[36] who lived in the early sixteenth century is the first of the Uí Laoghaire to be definitely named as lord.[37] He probably succeeded his cousin, Tadhg (4).

CONCHOBHAR (*ob. c.* 1576)
The earliest chief in respect of whom we get detailed information is Conchobhar (10) who died about 1576.[38] He was a son of Diarmaid (5), and described as of Manyn (also spelt Mannen and Manninge). This was a well-known and well-populated place *c.* 1600[39] but the name disappeared soon afterwards. The residence was undoubtedly part of the settlement which later became the village of Inchigeelagh, about 400 metres to the west of the old church, and in the townland of Carrigleigh.[40] It was not one of the three tower-houses (Carrignaneelagh, Carrignacurra, Dromcarra) in which Conchobhar's successors lived,[41] but an older-type residence in a strategic position commanding the river-crossing.[42]

In contrast to the mountainous area around Gougane Barra, the eastern portion of the parish contains the most level and most fertile agricultural land, so it was there that the chief members of the clan built their residences and claimed their birthright.

The 1626 inquisition into Conchobhar's lands found that he had been in possession of the following townlands: Glassinbolloge (Glasheen), East Clonserrye (Cloonshear Beg), Gortdirraclye (between Milleen and Teergay), Mullinvarodig (Milleen), Turnaspidogy, Inchinaneave, Derryvane. Each townland, irrespective of fertility or size

(Turnaspidogy was almost six times Gortdirraclye), was rated as a half-carucate, worth 2s. per annum, so that his total estate was 3.5 carucates, worth 14s. per annum. The river Lee appears to have played an important role in land division; it is noticeable that all Conchobhar's estate lay to the north of the river.

ART (c. 1572–1592)

Before Conchobhar died in 1576 he may have already seen his son, Art (20), succeed him. 'Arthur O Leary of Carignygyelagh, gentleman' is included in a pardon to the leading men of Muskerry in May 1573.[43] His father is probably the 'Conogher mc Dermodie O Leary of Inshygyelaghe' further down the list.

Carraig na nGeimhleach ('rock of the captives', a name obviously to be associated with Inse Geimhleach) was not at that time a townland name. Its use as Art's address in 1573 indicates that by then his tower-house had been established there, the first of its kind in the territory.[44] The nearby chapel-of-ease of Kilbarry was probably built around the same time.[45]

A possible rival claimant to the lordship was Art's uncle, Diarmaid Óg (11). Although described as 'Dermod Oig of Carrignegyellagh' in a pardon dated 6 September 1577,[46] he had probably left there after Conchobhar's death in 1576, moving south of the Lee to occupy (perhaps to build) what seems to have been regarded as the tánaiste's tower-house at Carrignacurra.[47] In Cormac mac Taidhg's surrender and regrant (dated 8 September 1577 and 20 July 1578 respectively) the lands of both Carrignaneelagh and Carrignacurra are listed.[48]

Art, as chief representative of the sept, did not – openly at any rate – support the Earl of Desmond's rebellion. The pardons given on 3 June 1584[49] to 'Arthur O Lery alias O Lery of Carrignagilagh' and to his brothers, Amhlaoibh Ruadh and Conchobhar, seem to have been in the nature of indemnities. But Diarmaid Óg was in a different category. A separate pardon for 'Dermot Oge and his men' was issued on 9 July 1584.[50] He was described as 'of Karrignekorie, gent'. The pardon extended to two sons (Tadhg and Domhnall), a daughter, Ellen, and fourteen other followers. Apparently Diarmaid Óg, unencumbered by cares of office, had been active in the rebellion and his pardon was provisional on appearing before commissioners and giving security to keep the peace. This he must have failed to do, for although he was not among those attainted by Act of Parliament in 1586,[51] an inquisition held in Shandon Castle, Cork, on 9 September 1588[52] named him as having been concerned in the Earl's rebellion.

Diarmaid Óg's attainder could have had disastrous consequences, such as the confiscation and plantation which Kinalmeaky endured following the killing of Conchobhar O Mahony – one who had never been considered its chief. But the remoteness of the Uí Laoghaire lands put confiscation in abeyance. Carrignacurra and Carrignaneelagh were confirmed as part of Cormac mac Dermot Mac Carthy's domain in the following year.[53]

On 18 September 1592 Art O Leary joined with Cormac, his overlord, in signing an agreement with the Commissioners appointed to make an annual 'composition' (an amalgamation of all cesses and feudal dues), amounting to £35 for the whole barony of Muskerry.[54] Whether putting his 'X' to the agreement aroused the ire of his independent-minded clan, or for some other reason, before the year was out Art had been replaced by his younger brother, Amhlaoibh (21), duly elected by the chief men of Muskerry, as mentioned above (p. 219).

But Amhlaoibh did not displace Art from Carrignaneelagh Castle, nor Diarmaid Óg's family from Carrignacurra. Tower-houses, as well as being prestigious, were expensive to construct, and once built, they tended to remain with the family of the founder. Dromcarra Castle, of later construction, was similarly inherited.

Furthermore, while Art lived no redistribution of clan lands seems to have taken place. When he died in 1597 his castle of Carrignaneelagh had a manorial-type three carucates attached to it, lands mainly contiguous to the castle, east and west (Coolnacranagh, Rossmore (including Gortaveer) and Carrigleigh, with West Currahy further to the west) – 1,160 Down Survey acres (approximately 2,200 statute acres). Art also held another three carucates to the north of the river Lee – Dromcarra N/S, Inchineill, Kilbarry, Gortincronogie (Inchigeelagh townland), Cleanrath and Derriveaghe (part of Rossalougha) – a total of approximately 3,000 statute acres. As well as that he had rents out of lands both north and south of the Lee. The northern townlands were Teergay, Gortiderryclea, Glasheen and Cloonshear Beg, which provided an annual rent of 5s. 9d. each (6s. 9d. out of Teergay). South of the river the rent-paying townlands were paired, each pair paying 11s. 6d. – Coornahahilly/Monvaddra; Farrenmorroe (part of Cappanclare)/Coolroe; Cooragreenane/Rathtahiffe (part of Gortnahoughtee); Gortnalour/Gortaneadin. His total annual rents came to £3 10s.[55] Calculating on the Down Survey acreages, the percentage of the Uí Laoghaire septlands controlled by Art at the time of his death amounted to 30.9 per cent and most of his portion, it must be borne in mind, lay in the more fertile eastern section.

AMHLAOIBH (1592–1600)

Art's brother and successor, Amhlaoibh (21), endeavoured to fulfil expectations of a more fiery leadership. In 1598 (according to an inquisition held in 1604)[56] when Hugh O Neill's rebellion had spread to Munster, he joined the forces of William Burke, then conducting a successful campaign against Thomas Norreys, President of Munster. By the autumn of 1600 Carew had succeeded in crushing the rebellion and 'pacifying' Munster. It was just at this latter period that Amhlaoibh took the field again, not against the Queen's supporters but to attack the rebel Donnchadh Maol, one of the Carbery Mac Carthys whose men had intruded on Muskerry in search of stolen cattle. About 100 of the O Learys followed the Carbery men back into the O Crowley country where a sharp engagement took place, resulting in the loss to the O Learys of their chief and ten others of the principal members of the family along with some more of lesser note.[57]

In a second inquisition into Amhlaoibh's lands taken in 1627[58] the date of his death is given as 23 December 1600 and the place as 'apud Mannen'. This may indicate that Amhlaoibh was borne from the battle-field to die of his wounds at home. But it could also be an attempt to conceal the circumstances of his death, reflecting the same political shrewdness which denied his possession of the lion's share of the lands such as Art had enjoyed. While the 1604 inquisition merely stated that Amhlaoibh's (unnamed) lands of Mannen amounted to four carucates, the second one named only three pairs of townlands, each pair estimated at half a carucate with an annual value of 5s. As it happens, each half-carucate consisted of a townland in the sought-after north-east corner, joined to one south of the river: Gortdiracly/Inchi Beg; Milleen/Inchi More; Cloonshear More/Garryantornora. His declared total share of 6.5 per cent of the lands still looks suspiciously small when compared to Art's massive 30.9 per cent. Was this perhaps an endeavour to circumvent confiscation?

Of the ten other leading members of the sept who, according to Carew, lost their lives in 1600, one was Tadhg (40), son and heir of Art of Carrignaneelagh. Three others named as 'slain in rebellion' were Conogher, Teige and Donell.[59] Conchobhar (22) was brother to Art and Amhlaoibh; Tadhg (13) may have been their youngest uncle.[60] Domhnall (51) was probably 'Donell M'Dermott O Learye of Carrickleevan, attainted',[61] a brother of Tadhg Meirgeach (50). A third brother, Art (52), was also noted as slain, in Carew's pedigree.

DONNCHADH (1601–38)

Following the disaster of December 1600 and the slaying of Amhlaoibh and Conchobhar, a fourth brother, Donnchadh (23), was elected chief forthwith.[62] Since the tower-houses were occupied by the families of their founders, Donnchadh continued to reside in the old homestead at Mannen, though he seems to have moved to Carrignaneelagh for a time – according to a jurors list of 1606[63] – leaving Amhlaoibh's son, Tadhg, at Mannen. He was married to Eibhlís, daughter of one of the Carbery O Crowleys (the slayers of his brothers, according to Carew).

The losses incurred by the O Learys did not curb their rebelliousness. Following the fall of Dunboy in 1602, O Sullivan Bear led a force of 1,000 men into Muskerry. He laid siege to and captured the castles of Carrignacurra (*Chorirupes*) and Dundareirke (*Munimentum jucundi prospectus*), forcing the inhabitants who surrendered to join his rebellion.[64] Cormac Mac Carthy, lord of Muskerry, was imprisoned in Cork but escaped and joined O Sullivan in capturing Carrigaphooka Castle. Later in the year Mac Carthy submitted and was pardoned, one of the conditions being 'that you have brought in the O Learies and other loose and suspected people, inhabitants of Muscry, and put in an assurance for their subjection to Her Majesty'.[65]

DOMHNALL (1638 – c. 1650)
The last old-style chief of the Uí Laoghaire was Domhnall (42) son of Art (20). He succeeded his uncle, Donnchadh, in 1638. His landholdings will be dealt with further on.

Confiscations
What D. B. Quinn calls 'the second plantation of Munster'[66] (*post* 1603) has never been studied as closely as the first, though its effects proved sometimes more enduring. In the case of the Uí Laoghaire, Diarmaid Óg's attainder for his part in the Desmond rebellion was not followed up until Amhlaoibh joined William Burke's forces in 1598 and was killed in 1600. The inquisition (see note 58) which found that Amhlaoibh had died without having been pardoned for his rebellious activities was held on 14 August 1604. On 6 December of the same year Thomas Hibbotts and John King were, for a fine of £10, granted a 21-year lease of various confiscated lands, including 'the towne and landes of Mannen in Muskerie, cont. 4 quars, with all chiefries, rentes, services and dueties sometymes belonging to Awliffe O Learie, chief of his name, attainted; and now extended at the yerelie rente of 20s. irishe'.[67]

Hibbotts and King were two careerist office-holders. The former began as an agent to the Treasurer of Ireland in 1600; he was responsible for transporting the Queen's treasure to England. He became Clerk of the Casualties in 1606 and Chancellor of the Exchequer in 1617, following which he was knighted. He finished his days in Carrickfergus.[68]

King started as secretary to Sir Richard Bingham in 1585. Following Bingham's fall from grace he transferred his allegiance to Carew who recommended him as 'honnest, sufficient and discreet'. In 1601 he became Collector of the First Fruits and Deputy-Treasurer of Ireland. He later settled in Ballinasloe, was knighted and became M.P. for county Roscommon. He held the office of Clerk of Crown and Hanaper before he died.[69]

A survey of leased Crown lands taken in 1606-07 confirms the grant of 'Maymen, in Muskerry, late in possession of Awliffe O'Flerry, chief of his sept, attainted' to King and Hibbotts.[70] The same survey found Edward Becher[71] to be the lessee of Carrignaneelagh, Carrickleevan and Carrignacurra, late possessions of Teige M'Arte (40), Donell M'Dermott (51) and Teige Merrigoogh (50) O Learie, respectively. All three were described as 'attainted', though whether because they were involved in the conflict with the Carbery men or for previous rebellion is not clear.

But Becher does not seem to have had any patent for those lands and on 31 January 1609 a new royal patent was issued, this time to Francis Gofton, 'one of the auditors of the imprest'. This outright grant of extensive lands spread over thirteen counties included the whole of Iveleary – '6½ qrs. in the towns and fields of Maninge, Caricknecory and Carrickenegealagh; parcel of the estate of Dermot Oge O Learie, attainted; and of Awliffe, Conogher, Teige, Donell and Teige M'Arte O Learie slain in rebellion'.[72] The annual rent was 20s. However, King and Hibbotts still held a 21-year lease of Mannen dating from 1604, and Donnogh O Leary, occupying Mannen as the assign of John King, was liable for the annual rent of 20s. up to 1625.[73]

The King/Hibbotts lease and the Gofton grant must have borne in upon the O Learys a realisation that in the post-Kinsale era even the remote fastnesses of Uíbh Laoghaire were no longer immune to the ordinances of English law. Litigation was discovered as a weapon that could be used to contest the customary share-out of septlands.

In a Chancery pleading[74] of c. 1611, Donough (23) O Leary, the then chief, answered the plea of his nephew, a son of the former chief, Art (20). The plaintiff, whose name is missing, was probably Connoghor (41);[75] he was dissatisfied with his share, in particular with the loss of Currahy, Kilbarry, Graigue and certain yearly rents out of other lands. Donnogh's defence was that when the lordship was held by his elder brother, Awliffe (21), Connogher's elder brother, Teig (40) mac Airt, never contested the division 'by the said costome'. Awliffe, he said, was succeeded by his next brother, Connoghor (22),[76] and then by himself (Donnogh) who held the lordship peaceably for ten years or so. His brother, Dermod Roo (24), and his half-brother, Lysagh (27), who were cited as co-defendants, pleaded likewise:

And for the other lands comprized in the byll the deffs. says that there be divers other of the sept of O Leary which enioy the same

as theire portions by division by costom of the country tyme out
of mynde used in yvileary paying certain rents and duetyes to O
Leary for the tyme being which the pl. ought to impleade and not
this Donnogh O Leary.

The defence plea of immemorial custom, made before Francis Aungier,
Master of the Rolls, and Robert Leycester, an attorney in the Chancery,
appears to have been successful, since no change in the status quo can
be detected. But further legal transactions took place.

Gofton's title to lands in county Cork, remote though they were,
attracted the immediate attention of the acquisitive Richard Boyle, then
in the process of empire-building. Within six months Boyle had
purchased Gofton's rights in Uíbh Laoghaire, but that was only the
beginning of a convoluted legal process. Realising that the Gofton grant
was complicated by the King lease (Hibbotts appears to have bowed
out) and even more so by the impermanent pattern of land tenure
practised by the O Learys, Boyle with his customary shrewdness
concentrated on obtaining a mortgage payment by making use of the
men in possession. The method by which this was achieved was later
revealed in a series of seven inquisitions into O Leary lands, obviously
instigated by Boyle himself, and held in the years 1625-6-7.[77] (The
escheator, William Wiseman, who presided at all seven, happened to
be Boyle's agent in Bandon where he occupied a newly-built
mansion).[78]

Two inquisitions – Teige (50) of Carrignacurra (*ob.* 1616) and Art
(20) of Carrignaneelagh (*ob.* 1597) – had already been held when
Boyle must have realised that the jurors were ending with the bland
statement that they did not know what the rents and services were or
to whom they were payable. Those two inquisitions were later
duplicated, but with addenda full of extra legal details. Two further
inquisitions, Connor (10) of Mannen (*ob. c.* 1576) and Dermod mac
Teige mac Fynin (*ob.* 1596), representative of a marginalised branch
pushed into the mountainous southerly regions of Coornahahilly, were
each supplied with the same addendum. The seventh inquisition –
Awliffe (21) of Mannen – found that various rents and debts were
payable out of his lands to Richard, Earl of Cork.

According to the legal addenda, the lands of Iveleary, granted by
patent to Francis Gofton[79] on 31 January 1609, were on 10 July 1609
sold by Gofton to Richard Boyle who took possession. On 28 March
1612 Boyle enfeoffed Donnchadh O Leary (23) (the then chief) and
Conchobhar (41), eldest surving son of Art, for the sum of £421,[80] on
condition that the two would join with Boyle in giving separate title-
deeds for their lands to other O Leary landholders then in possession,

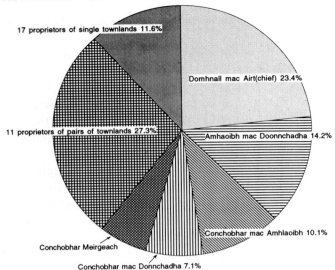

Figure 7.2   a   Land tenure, *c.* 1650
Source: Civil Survey.

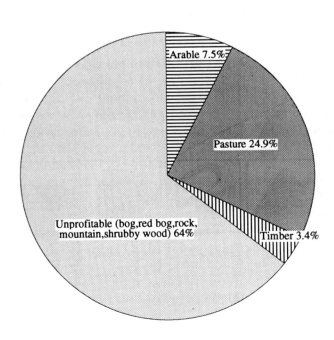

Figure 7.2   b   Land type, *c.* 1650
Source: Civil Survey.

for a consideration of £25 per carucate. Accordingly, Donnchadh and Conchobhar took possession and then mortgaged the property to Boyle for £421. (So far, no money had changed hands; Boyle had merely exchanged his title for a mortgage).[81]

On 13 January 1621 (spurred on perhaps by Cormac Óg Mac Carthy's surrender and regrant of the previous month)[82] Boyle, together with three O Learys, Donnchadh, Amhlaoibh (46), his son and heir, and Domhnall (42), third son and now heir[83] of Art, for a sum of £421 mortgaged the lands to Andrew Comyn and George Creagh for the use of Geoffrey Galwey for his life. Boyle recorded in his diary the receipt from Galwey of £249 7s. 5d. on 31 January 1620 (1621 new style) and a further £50 on 17 March.[84] Galwey (Sir Geoffrey, Bart. from 1624) was the mayor of Limerick who crossed swords with Sir George Carew in 1600. He was a lawyer,[85] a prominent Catholic figure, and generally a thorn in the side of the establishment. He died in 1636 and was buried in the Galwey chapel of St Multose, Kinsale.[86]

A further complication was introduced in the following year on 20 March 1622 when Boyle apparently surrendered his rights to the Crown so that new letters patent could be issued, this time to Sir James Craig, a Scottish undertaker based in county Cavan,[87] as part of a grant worth 200 marks per annum.[88] The grant was worded like Gofton's – 'Iveleary, 6½ quarters in the town and lands of Maninge, Carrignecorry and Carrigkengealagh', with a yearly rent of 20s. out of same. Furthermore, he had permission to create the lands of Iveleary into a manor, with the usual powers, and a licence to hold a Saturday market and a fair on 15 June on the lands of Dromcarra. The inquisitions too recorded this patent and a further transaction on the following day when Craig once more enfeoffed Andrew Comyn with those premises for the use of Geoffrey Galwey. Whether money changed hands at this point is not clear.[89]

One result was the emergence of Dromcarra as a centre of note and the building of a tower-house there. We know that Donnchadh Ó Laoghaire, the chief, who appears to have been at Mannen up to 1625, spent his declining years at Dromcarra Castle, living as a country gentleman in the privacy of his walled garden and orchard. His son and heir, Amhlaoibh, registered Donnchadh's death in Ulster's office,[90] giving his date of demise as 4 January 1637 (1638) and tracing his pedigree back to Mac Con. (The arms supplied featured a hound, gules, impaled with the azure boar of the O Crowleys).[91]

Sir Geoffrey Galwey died earlier, on 2 April 1636, and according to the inquisition[92] into his lands he remained the mortagee of all Iveleary with the exception of Coornahahilly, Monvaddra, Coolroe, Farrenmurrine, Gortdiracly, Inchi Beg, Inchi More, Milleen, Cloonshear

More and Garryantornora. His grandson and heir is mentioned only twice in the Civil Survey of Inchigeelagh parish: as the mortgagee of Teergay (Arthur O Leary) and the lessor of Ratheahiff.[93]

Boyle's rights were limited to 'the timber wood and Ayeries of great Hawks' – not very productive as he notes ruefully in his diary, 9 July 1625: 'And I had out of my eyry in O Learies country a tercell of a goshawk onely'.[94] His very comprehensive rental book of 1637 makes no reference to any rents from Muskerry.[95]

Accordingly, it would seem that despite all the legal dealings of the first four decades of the seventeenth century, the overall impact on the life-style of the Uí Laoghaire was negligible. After the death of Donnchadh in 1638 the title of Ó Laoghaire went, not to his son and heir, but presumably by election to Domhnall (42), eldest surviving son of Art (20). At this juncture the septlands would have had their final apportioning – probably one of the last of its kind in the country. The details of ownership in accordance with the hereditary system of land division were accepted and fully recorded for posterity in the Civil Survey.

The surveys

Most of the Catholic landowners in Munster were either involved in or sympathetic to the rebellion which broke out on 23 October 1641. Many of them attended the General Assembly of the Irish Confederation of Kilkenny in 1644. Among them was Donnel O Leary.[96] By then a total of 537 county Cork landowners had been declared outlaws. Sixteen of the O Learys were among these.[97] Although the name of Domhnall and those of about half the other O Leary landowners were omitted, none escaped the net once the war finally ended in 1652. Commissioners were then appointed to carry out, mainly during the years 1654-5, what has become known as the Civil Survey – an inventory of all forfeited lands, giving the exact boundaries of parishes and townlands, proprietors in 1641, and the quality and valuation of the lands.[98] This was followed in 1655-6 by Sir William Petty's 'Down Survey' which utilised the findings of the Civil Survey but was accompanied by detailed maps (valuations were omitted). The main difference between the surveys is that the Civil Survey used the old measurements – plowlands, gneeves and 'Irish' acres (which varied enormously) – in order to provide a rough estimate, while the Down Survey used a standardised 'plantation' acre of 7,840 square yards,[99] or 1.6 times the statute acre – though in the case of Inchigeelagh parish Petty's acres are roughly twice the statute ones.[100]

The work of the Down Survey map-makers has frequently, and deservedly, been praised for its accuracy and completeness, but the same recognition has not been accorded the Civil Survey, without whose exhaustive delineations of boundaries and details of ownership the work of the Down Survey could not have been so quickly or effectively completed. One reason for this efficiency was the appointment, by the county Commissioners, of panels of local jurors for each barony. For Muskerry a jury of 15 included six Mac Carthys, an O Donovan, an O Daly, a Murphy, a Mac Sweeney and Aulife O Leary, perhaps Donnchadh's son and heir who had been passed over for the chieftaincy. Between them they had completed the correction of the errors of the survey by 17 September 1655.[101]

The only major divergence between the Civil Survey and the Down Survey is in regard to the number of O Leary landowners declared to be deceased. The Civil Survey has the unusually high number of 23; the Down Survey has only 5, but includes Domhnall (the chief) which the Civil Survey does not (*The Book of Survey and Distribution* [hereafter B.S.D.], compiled at a later date and closely linked to the Down Survey, has 6). Both surveys are in agreement as to the identity of the thirty-three O Learys who shared the septlands in 1641.[102] The following section attempts to relate the status of each of these land-holders to his actual holding.

Since, generally, the Civil Survey is the more accurate and more detailed in regard to situation and boundaries,[103] unless otherwise stated it can be taken that all details derive from it, except in the case of area measurements where the Down Survey is more exact. Petty's plantation acres are used throughout the section.

Principal landholders

I.   Domhnall (42) succeeded his uncle, Donnchadh (23), as chief in 1638. He occupied Carrignaneelagh Castle (valued at £150, with a mill valued at £2) and 13 townlands totalling 2,923 plantation acres. Although this works out as 16 per cent of the total acreage of Uíbh Laoghaire, his valuation (£30 9s.) accounted for 20.2 per cent, since he owned 23.4 per cent of the arable land. The largest and most fertile portion consisted of seven contiguous townlands, both east and west of the castle, from Inchigeelagh (village) to Gortsmoorane on the eastern boundary. A second portion, in the mid-west, consisted of Derryvaleen, Gortnamona, Kilmore, West Currahy and Illauninagh West. The last-named townland is south of the river; Domhnall's only other southern one was Carrignamuck. He held another isolated townland, Derrenlunnig,[104] in the mountainous area near Gougane Barra.

II.   The second-largest share fell to Amhlaoibh (46), elder son and heir of Donnchadh, the previous chief. His acreage (15 per cent) was

Plate 7.1   Carrignacurra Castle.

almost as large as Domhnall's but his share of arable (14.2 per cent) and his valuation of £19 14s. (13.1 per cent) were smaller. His 'demolished'[105] castle of Dromcarra with its small ruined garden and orchard was valued at £110. His demesne of Dromcarra (N/S) and Inchineill comprised the south-east angle of the territory. The other townlands were Cleanrath, East Currahy, Dromanallig, Coomlibane, Milmorane and Rossalougha, all lying north of the river Lee.

III.   Next in extent was Conchobhar (44), son of Amhlaoibh (21), the chief killed in 1600. For some reason Conchobhar resided in the Mac Carthy enclave at Gortinacolly, near Augeris. But he held Milleenavarodig/Gortdiracloy (now Milleen), Cloonshear (now Cooleen) and Diryargid (Silvergrove) north of the Lee as well as Inchi Beg, Inchi More and Maughinmugh (between Garryantornora and Tooreenalour) to the south. He owned 10.1 per cent of the arable land and 11.1 per cent of the total valuation.

IV.   Next came Conchobhar (47), the second son of Donnchadh. He resided in East Graigue and also held Gortcronogy (now Inchigeelagh townland) and Dirineknockroe (Derreen). South of the river he had Culeask and East Illauninagh, the two Kealvaughs, West Cooragreenane and Derrygortnacloghy – 7.1 per cent of the arable land, 7.7 per cent of the valuation.

V.   For Conchobhar Meirgeach (60) of Carrignacurra, see below, pp 222, 233-4. (These constituted the big five in the 1638 share-out, the first four being sons of previous chiefs. Between them they had occupied the three tower-houses, together with 52.9 per cent of the total clan lands (56.5 per cent of the pasture, 56.6 per cent of the timber and 58.9 per cent of the arable). Their percentage of the total valuation amounted to 65.9 per cent).

VI.   For Conchobhar (62), son of Art, see below, p. 219.

VII.   Laoiseach (27) belonged to an earlier generation; he was the only surviving son of Conchobhar (10) who died in 1576. But because he was a son by a second marriage (to one of the Mac Sweeneys of Desmond) he was treated as a grandson rather than as a son, which meant that he got one townland in the more fertile east plus a second in the west or south – in his case Inchinaneave (£3) and Gortafludig (£2). The latter held about 150 acres of timber.

Similarly treated were some of Conchobhar's grandsons, those whose fathers (Conchobhar (22) and Diarmaid Ruadh (24)) had never been chiefs.

VIII. Art (45) son of Conchobhar was allotted Teergay (£4) and Cornery (c. 13s.).

IX. Tadhg (48) son of Diarmaid Ruadh was allotted Bargarriff (£2) and Dooneens (16s.). Both are south of the river, but Tadgh resided in Glasheen.

X. Glasheen (£2 1s.) was the property of Tadhg son of Domhnall[106] who lived in (and owned) Turnaspidogy (£4), both being north of the Lee.

Five others had pairs of townlands, almost all south of the river and decreasing in valuation. Because the Uí Laoghaire used such a limited range of personal names, it is difficult to trace their relationship to the main stem; some of them will be referred to below. Following them (in status) we find seventeen proprietors of single townlands. It would be simplistic to assume that all of these were great-grandchildren of former chiefs, pushed to the outer perimeter of the *deirbhfhine* system. Perhaps some were. But in a closely-knit community such as Uí Laoghaire strict adherence to a legal sytem could give rise to bitter animosity on the part of once-powerful segments whose entitlements had declined. One way to avoid this without compromising the rights of the *deirbhfhine* was the granting of leases by the chief.

Art (20) of Carrignaneelagh (*ob.* 1597) derived annual rent amounting to £3 10s. from 12 townlands which included Coornahahilly and Monvaddra, Farranmurrine and Coolroe,[107] occupied by Dermod mac Teige mac Fynin who died in 1596. Dermod's lineage is not traceable. In his inquisition *post mortem*[108] no rent is specified other than a head-rent to Mac Carthy. If Dermod had held a lease, his heir (Tadeus) could not easily be displaced. In fact, in 1641 Teige (Dermod's son) was still in possession of Coornahahilly while Donogh (another son) had Monvaddra, or at least half of it. The other half was occupied by Finine mac Teige, perhaps Teige's son, who, jointly with his brother, Daniel, also held Ratheahiffe (now part of Gortnahoughtee). Dermod's two pairs of townlands were among those not mortgaged to Sir Geoffrey Galwey in 1636,[109] but Galwey's grandson appears to have been the lessor of Ratheahiff in 1641.[110] Finine survived the Cromwellian wars and in his will (1670) bequeathed his lands to his grandson and namesake.[111] Perhaps a brother to Finine was Dermod mac Teige, the 'inheritor as is alleged' of Milleen and Inchi More, both of which Cnogher (44) mac Auliff held in 1641 by virtue of a letter of attorney from Dermod.[112]

But apart from such new developments as leases and mortgages,[113] it was also necessary to allow for the attachment of a particular family to the old homestead.[114] Not only tower-houses were affected; it would seem that every Inchigeelaghman's home was his castle.

To take one example: Cooragreenane (*Cuar a' Ghrianáin*, a 'sunny concavity') is a remote and mountainous spot on the south shore of Lough Allua, 572 statute acres of which only 15 per cent was arable and pasture in 1641. Conoghor mac Awly O'Leary was a husbandman or farmer there in 1577. In 1601 his sons, Dermod and Donell mac Conoghor mac Awliff, occupied it, along with his brother Mahown mac Awliff.[115] In 1641 it was still mainly occupied by Dermod's son (Cnogher mac Dermott mac Cnogher) who could hardly have qualified for it under the *deirbhfhine* system. The only diminution was that about one-sixth of the townland had been given to Connor (47) mac Donough and renamed West Cooragreenane.

A possible reason then for the large number of divided townlands in the early seventeenth century is the reluctance to evict a family from an ancestral homestead – obviously resistance to eviction had roots that went deeper than Land League times[116] – giving rise to the alternative solution of allowing the family to keep half the townland while the other half went into the melting-pot.

Nine townlands in Uíbh Laoghaire, mainly in the poorer western area, were divided into either East/West or North/South: Dromcarra, Illauninagh, Kealvaugh, Derryriordane, Coolroe, Currahy, Cooragreenane, Gortnalour, Monvaddra (the last four are no longer so divided). Cloonshear was divided into three parts, two of which went to the 'big five', while Cloonshear Beg (that is, east) was the property of smallholder Donough mac Auliff *alias* Gearh. But his home was in the middle part, Cloonshear (now Cooleen), owned by Cnogher (44) mac Auliffe who in turn resided at Gorteenakilla. Donough may have been an illegitimate brother.

With regard to the 17 single-townland holdings, though they appear extensive on paper, they lay mostly on the western side and their mountainous nature greatly lessened their value. The average amount of arable land was 8.5 acres, and of pasture 38.6 acres, while the average valuation was £1 1s. At the bottom of the ladder we find Finnin and Conor mac Dermot. The former held 538 acres in Derreenacusha but 532 (99 per cent) of these were bog and rocks, and his valuation was 13s. Conor of Inshircoongwogane (near Gougane Barra) had about 160 acres of which 97.5 per cent comprised bogland; his valuation was 4s. 6d.

Rules were by no means inflexible. Technically, Conchobhar Meirgeach (60) of Carrignacurra was entitled only to a great-grandson's share, since his grandfather, Diarmaid Óg (11), had never been elected chief. But politically Diarmaid Óg had been a powerful figure during the Desmond rebellion, and his removal south of the river to erect Carrignacurra Castle has the appearance of forming a new dynastic segment. It would have been difficult if not divisive to attempt to lessen the Carrignacurra portion, so Conchobhar was left with Cloghbarra, Cloughboola, Tooreenalour, Carrignacurra, Inchigrady and Cappaclare, all in the more rugged southern division and containing but 6.3 per cent of the arable land. (His valuation of £20 17s. was inflated by the inclusion of the valuation of the (demolished) castle and mill). Apart from Carrignacurra and Inchigrady, these were different townlands to those held by his father, Tadhg (50), but the acreage was much the same. Tadhg, however, had held about as much land again in mortgage in the northern half.[117]

Another member of that segment was his cousin, Conchobhar (62), son of Art (52), who held some small townlands south of the Lee – Dirineveluesty (now part of Dooneens), Derryleigh, Gorteenadrolane, Gortatanavally, with a total valuation of £3 5s. 6d. Obviously dissatisfied with his lot, at an inquisition into his cousin, Tadhg's (ob. 1616) lands taken in April 1637, Conchobhar put in his claim to be the rightful heir to Carrignacurra castle and lands.[118] Also south of the river was Diarmaid Óg (72) who held Teeranassig (£2 2s.) and Derryvacorneen (£1 12s.) – not much arable land but 29 acres of timber in the former were valued at £5.[119] If, as seems likely, he was son of Dermod (61) mac Donel O Leary of Teeranassig who acted as attorney for Mac Carthy of Augeris in 1619,[120] and Dermod's father was the Domhnall (51) killed in 1600, then Diarmuid Óg was a second cousin of Conchobhar Meirgeach's sons.

Non-landowners

Logically, the next generation to succeed the single-townland proprietors would become landless. Although this did not always happen, there must have been quite a number of tradesmen, labourers and others. Migration to alternative areas was of course an option.[121] One such migrant was Donnchadh an Chuasáin (34), elder son of Tadhg (13). He was resident in Macroom in 1601.[122] Of the large number of O Learys in Uíbh Laoghaire who are mentioned in the Elizabethan fiants between 1573 and 1601,[123] not more than sixteen have their occupations listed. Four were 'gentlemen' (family heads living in tower-houses), two were 'yeomen' (other landholders), four were 'husbandmen' (farmers), four were 'kern' (soldiers), one a ' farmer' and one a 'labourer'. The sample is small, but it indicates that not all were landholders.

Hardly mentioned at all in the records are the inhabitants who were not O Learys. But the fiants show that they were there, again mainly as husbandmen and kerns (with one piper). Six bore the surname O Cronyne (the Cronins were mainly at Carrignacurra); there were two O Sullivans and one each of O Moynaghan, O Moroghow, O Ring, O Rien, O Croly, O Hallaghane, O Hanglen, O Downe, O Martnant, McSwyny.

Post-Cromwellian era

The Civil Survey depicts Uíbh Laoghaire as utterly devastated by the Cromwellian campaign. Two of its tower-houses lay in ruins while the third, Carrignaneelagh, was garrisoned by soldiers. Only the bare walls of the parish church remained standing. 'No other buildings, not as much as an Irish Cabbin'.[124] A massive disruption of the old order had come about, and since under English law the land no longer belonged to the Uí Laoghaire, no further redistributions took place. Presumably some of the former proprietors or their families remained in occupation while awaiting the inevitable displacement. In the interim period there is no record of lands in Inchigeelagh parish being allotted to soldiers or adventurers, although nearby Macroom Castle, with over 3,000 acres in Muskerry, was granted by Cromwell to Admiral William Penn in 1655.[125] Penn was later compensated for handing over his Muskerry lands[126] to the new Earl of Clancarty (formerly Lord Muskerry) who had his outlawry reversed following the restoration, and all his estates in Muskerry restored by Charles II.[127]

In this way the O Learys lost their previous status as semi-independent landowners and became mere tenants of Clancarty. The Earl promised the former freeholders that he would buy the estates from them in trust and so they desisted from any claims. But Cormac died in 1665 and his son (Callaghan) was not disposed to give any special consideration to his former freeholders, so that they, led by Conchobhar O Leary of Carrignacurra, took legal action against him, but to no effect.[128] The grant to Callaghan's son, Donnogh, in 1677, includes practically all the townlands in Inchigeelagh parish.[129]

Clancarty did try to make amends by granting extensive leases to some of the O Learys, but to many of that independent-minded sept this was not acceptable. Some removed to county Clare,[130] others joined the Wild Geese,[131] while many became outlaws in the mountains.[132] The main (Carrignaneelagh) branch eventually moved to Drishane and Millstreet.[133]

Other branches, however, helped to maintain the sense of continuity. Diarmaid Óg Buidhe of Inchideraille and Derreenglass (1641) was probably grandfather of Dermod Lery *alias* Buy of the same places whose will was proved in 1700.[134] (He, in turn, was probably ancestor of the O Learys Buidhe of Tooreenanean of whom the best-known was the poet, Máire Bhuidhe).[135] Dermod's widow, Helen, became tenant of not only his ten townlands but of eleven others as well, totalling 2,707 acres, all later included in the Hollow Blades Company's purchase following Clancarty's forfeiture.[136]

The O Learys Meirgeach of Carrignacurra fared better. Conchobhar (80) who died in 1699[137] was head of this branch in the late seventeenth century, but his more ambitious relative, Céadach,[138] assembled leases from other O Learys[139] and joined to these the Carrignacurra lands when Conchobhar appointed him guardian of his two young sons.[140] Although the fee simple of Céadach's 5,212 acres was purchased by the Hollow Blades Company, his lease of 99 years dating from 1677[141] was recognised. As Captain Keadagh Leary of Carrignacurra he had been successful in his claim for restoration in 1699.[142] A settlement was later agreed between Céadach and the sons of Conchobhar, and although the Masters family acquired the castle site shortly afterwards, Conchobhar junior (91) in his will (1753) was described as 'of Carrignacurra', which he left to his son Timothy (101).[143]

Clancarty's fortunes rose and fell with James II. On 11 June 1691 he was attainted for high treason and an inquisition on 15 August 1694 declared all his lands to be forfeited.[144] Many of his followers took to the hills. A list of 'friends, relations and harbourers of Tories' in 1694 listed fourteen O Learys (and just one Mac Sweeney) in Gougane Barra and Iveleary.[145]

Later Uíbh Laoghaire personalities

Yet by 1700, just before the sale of the Clancarty estates and despite the ravages of wars and confiscations, there were approximately 130 'cabins' on the lands of Uíbh Laoghaire, not counting six 'good farmhouses', one with a grist mill and another (Céadach's in Teergay) 'a good stone house, slated, 2 stories high with barn and stable'.[146] The speed and tenacity with which the local population re-established itself is surely a testimony to that sturdy independence which had permeated the way of life in Uíbh Laoghaire for many generations. It is hardly a coincidence that from this one remote upland parish emanated some of the most notable of what might be termed anti-establishment personages and events throughout succeeding centuries, incidents which in Gaelic folk-memory have always had a symbolic impact far above and beyond their actual historical significance.

Munster's most widely-known (and best-lamented) folk-hero of the eighteenth century, Art Ó Laoghaire (*ob.* 1773), was proudly declared to be of the best blood in Uíbh Laoghaire.[147] The early nineteenth century witnessed a Whiteboy action at Keimaniagh, where an English soldier was killed by Conchobhar Buidhe Ó Laoghaire, an affray stirringly celebrated by his sister, Máire Bhuidhe, one of the best-known of Irish woman poets.[148]

Even in this century, in the early days of the Gaelic League, the influence and prolific writings of an tAthair Peadar Ó Laoghaire (1839-1920) who claimed descent from the owners of Carrignacurra Castle,[149] allied to the local traditional life-style, led to the founding in Ballingeary of the first and most famous of the 'Coláistí Gaeilge', a symbol of the burgeoning desire to re-establish a separate national identity.

References

1. Lambeth Palace, Carew MS 635, f. 180. See *Cal. Carew MSS, 1589-1600,* p. 513. A fuller treatment of the document may be found in Butler, *Gleanings,* p. 117.
2. There is not a single reference to the name in Hogan, *Onomasticon,* though one may be found in a Butler poem of *c.* 1589 (see note 23). Little has been written in modern times on the Uí Laoghaire, apart from the introduction and appendices to D. Ó Donnchú, *Filíocht Mháire Bhuidhe Ní Laoghaire* (Baile Átha Cliath, 1931), and a chapter in my own *Family names,* pp 206-214.
3. Text of Papal mandate printed in Bolster, *Diocese of Cork,* i, pp 277-280.
4. Power, *Crichad,* p. 49.
5. See account of that dynasty by Donnchadh Ó Corráin in this volume.
6. 'Geinealach Chorca Laidhe', in O'Donovan, *Misc. Celt. Soc.,* pp 50-52.
7. Details of these transactions are to be found in K. W. Nicholls (ed.), 'Some unpublished Barry charters' in *Anal. Hib.,* xxvii (1972), pp 113-17.
8. That not all the Uí Laoghaire left the area is shown by the occurrence of the name among the clergy of Ross. Thomas Olegeri, of the diocese of Ross, was granted a vicarage in the diocese of Lincoln in England prior to 1343 (*Cal. papal petitions,* p. 73). John Olaegere was chancellor of Ross in 1448 as was Matheus Ylegary in 1494 (*Cal. papal letters 1447-1455,* p. 380 and *1492-1498,* p. 636). There were 67 of the name in Carbery in 1659 (*Census Ire., 1659,* pp 215, 221, 228).
9. O'Donovan, *Misc. Celt. Soc.,* p. 52 note, put it 'about the period of the English invasion'.
10. B.L., MS Titus B 13, f. 508, ed. in *Cork Hist. Soc. Jn.,* xii (1906), p. 67.
11. *Cal. S.P. Ire., 1586-1588,* p. 545.
12. Cork Archaeological Survey, *Sites and monuments record, county Cork* (Cork, 1989).
13. J. Otway-Ruthven, 'Ireland in the 1350s' in *R.S.A.I. Jn.,* xcvii (1967), pp 47-59.
14. The grant is referred to in a treasurer's account of 1371 (copy in N.L.I., MS 761, pp 210-11) which notes that Cormac already owed 18 years' rent.
15. See decretal letter reproduced in Bolster, *Diocese of Cork,* i, p. 98.
16. *Cal. doc. Ire., 1302-1307,* pp 310, 321.
17. *Annata ... ecclesie de Insygeyleach;* see M. A. Bolster (ed.), 'Obligationes pro annatis Diocesis Corcagiensis' in *Archiv. Hib.,* xxix (1970), p. 10. Inse Geimhleach, 'Inch of the hostages', is a secular place-name with no ecclesiastical connotations. The second element reappears in the name Carraig na

nGeimhleach (Carrignaneelagh), the site of the principal O Leary tower-house in Elizabethan times.

18. *Cal. papal letters, 1492-98*, pp 63, 93. Inchigeelagh is included in a list of churches dated 1437 in Webster, *Cork*, p. 402 (from a document in P.R.O.I. subsequently destroyed). But the inclusion of Kilmichael (see p. 2) makes this dating suspect.

19. *Annatae* in Bolster, 'Obligationes', p. 31.

20. *Extents Ir. mon. possessions,* pp 105, 143.

21. Fiant Eliz., 3373 (Fiants of Queen Elizabeth quoted are taken from *P.R.I. rep. D.K.,* nos. 11-13, 15-18, where they are printed in numerical order. See also *Cal. pat. rolls, Ire., Eliz.,* p. 170.

22. Fiants Eliz., 5330, 5333.

23. J. Carney (ed.), *Poems on the Butlers* (Dublin, 1945), p. 76.

24. *Cal. pat. rolls, Ire., Jas. I,* p. 489. See also Cork Inq., no. 47, p. 89. (Since frequent reference will be made to these Chancery inquisitions, it may be noted that the original copies perished in the Four Courts in 1922. However, transcripts made for the Record Commissioners in the 1820s survive. There are five volumes of Cork inquisitions in the N.A., Chancery Cal. Inq., vols. 2-6. These in turn were copied for the Ordnance Survey in the 1830s and those copies are in the R.I.A. Library (six vols. including an index of places). The numbering is the same in both sets which match very closely. I have used the pagination of the R.I.A. set which is the more easily consulted since it has been microfilmed).

25. N.A., Lodge MSS: Records of the Rolls, vol. 6, p. 318. '24 in-calf cows' takes the place of '24 beeves'.

26. *Civil Survey,* vi, p. 337. '2 white groats' in place of '2s 3d'. (Vol. vi deals mainly with county Waterford but the addenda include the barony of Muskerry, the only part of county Cork for which the survey is available).

27. *Cal. Carew MSS., 1589-1600,* p. 511.

28. T.C.D., MS H.1.7, f. 137b, in T. ÓDonnchadha, *An Leabhar Muimhneach,* p. 430.

29. *Civil Survey,* vi, pp 336-7.

30. *Extents Ir. mon. possessions,* p. 105. At one stage it was even claimed as part of Cloyne diocese; see Brady, *Clerical records,* i, p. 120; ii, p. 73.

31. *Baile* does appear at the end of Gortatanavally *(Gort an tseanbhaile).*

32. Names such as Laurence and Ferdinand which appear in *Civil Survey* are obvious 'translations' of Laoiseach and Fearganainm.

33. D. Ó Corráin, *Ireland before the Normans* (Dublin, 1972), p. 37.

34. Nicholls, *Gaelic Ire.,* p. 28.

35. Cork Inq., no. 4, p. 92.

36. The numbers in brackets correspond with those used in the pedigrees in Appendices B and C. Numbers are not wholly consecutive but are intended to reflect generation depth. 10-13 are the sons of Diarmaid (5), 20-35 his grandchildren, 38-48 his great-grandchildren. In Appendix C the 50s correspond to Appendix B's 20-35.

37. By Carew in his pedigree (see Appendix B).

38. Cork Inq., no. 54.

39. See, e.g., Fiants Eliz., 6467, 6539, 6571, 6701.

40. The present townland arrangement is confusing. The original Inchigeelagh (churchyard) is in the townland of Glebe; most of the village, as far as the bridge, is in Carrigleigh; west of that is a small townland now called Inchigeelagh (Gortcronogy in *Civil Survey*). It seems likely that because Mannen was so close to the church site of Inchigeelagh that it adopted its name. (I would no longer

equate Mannen with the obsolete townland of Magninenagh/Maughinmugh, as I did in my *Family names*, p. 208).

41. That none of these was built before the 1570s is apparent from the documentary sources, also from Lythe's fairly detailed map of Munster *c.* 1570 (published in *S.P. Hen. VIII*, ii, pt. iii) which shows no names or sites whatever in Iveleary.

42. 'On the premises (Carrigleigh) is the decay'd bridge of Inshygeelagh', *Civil Survey*, vi, p. 326. The military barrack built there later and described by Smith, *Cork* (1893 ed.), i, p. 165, as 'built in a stone fort of four bastions, erected on the north end of a bridge over the Lee', was probably on the site of 'Mannen'.

43. Fiant Eliz., 2264.

44. A stone with the initials 'A. L.', said to have come from a razed castle of the O Learys, was recorded by Canon J. Lyons in *Cork Hist. Soc. Jn.*, iiA (1893), p. 77.

45. See Brady, *Clerical records*, i, p. 120. Kilbarry is shown on the *Pacata Hibernia* map of *c.* 1600.

46. Fiant Eliz., 3083.

47. The shell of Carrignacurrra castle still stands on its rock overlooking the Lee which is wide and shallow at that point. *Carraig na Cora* means 'rock of the weir'; at the time of the Civil Survey the nearby eel-weir was demolished and decayed (*Civil Survey*, vi, p. 290).

48. Fiant Eliz., 3373.

49. Fiant Eliz., 4416.

50. Fiant Eliz., 4485.

51. *Stat. Ire.*, i, pp 418 ff.

52. Smith, *Cork* (1893 ed.), i, p. 29.

53. Fiant Eliz., 5330, 5333.

54. *Cal. Carew MSS, 1589-1600*, p. 69.

55. Cork. Inq., nos. 33, 53.

56. Cork Inq., no. 4. (The name 'Owen de O Leary' in this inq. is probably a copyist's error for 'nomen de O Leary').

57. This is Carew's account, as given in *Pacata Hibernia*, i, p. 133. The battle took place in the O Crowley country of Coill tSealbhaigh (parish of Fanlobbus) according to Smith, *Cork* (1893 ed.), i, p. 17. Carew in his pedigree (see Appendices B/C) says that they were slain by the O Crowleys.

58. Cork Inq., no. 84, pp 167-8.

59. *Cal. pat. rolls Ire., Jas. I,* p. 128.

60. Not Tadhg Meirgeach as shown in Carew's pedigree (see notes to Appendix C).

61. *Cal. S.P. Ire., 1606-1608*, p. 66. 'Carrickleevan' may be today's Gortnacarriga (Courygrohan in D.S.).

62. He is described as 'Donough O Lerie alias O Leyerie, of Manen' in Fiant Eliz., 6467, a pardon dated 16 Feb. 1601.

63. Inquisition published by R. Caulfield in *Gentleman's Magazine* (Sept. 1862), p. 301.

64. O'Sullivan Beare, *Hist. cath. ibern.*, p. 239.

65. B.L., MS Harl. 697 ('Council Book of Munster') published in Caulfield, *Kinsale*, p. 302.

66. D. B. Quinn, 'The Munster plantation: problems and opportunities' in *Cork Hist. Soc. Jn.*, lxxi (1966), p. 35.

67. J. C. Erck, *A repertory of the inrolments on the patent rolls of Chancery in Ireland* (Dublin, 1846), p. 84. See also *Cal. Pat. Rolls, Ire., Jas. I,* p. 39.

68. *Cal. S.P. Ire., 1600*, p. 410; *1601-03*, p. 36; *1603-06*, p. 429; *1615-25*, p. 148; *1633-47*, p. 63.

69. *Cal. S.P. Ire., 1574-85*, p. 571; *1596-97*, p. 128; *1600-01*, p. 280; *1601-03*, p. 121; *1611-14*, pp 162, 362; *1625-32*, p. 632.

70. *Cal. S.P. Ire., 1606-08*, p. 66. Through faulty transcription or punctuation 'Maymen' is allotted to Robert Morgan rather than to King and Hibbotts, who follow directly on the list.

71. Son of undertaker Phane Becher, he was appointed Escheator of Munster and became a burgess of Bandon at its incorporation in 1612 *(Cal. S.P. Ire., 1611-14*, pp 198, 293).

72. *Cal. pat. rolls, Ire., Jas. I*, p. 128. (The next entry (no. 76) is misleading; Gofton did not alieniate all his lands etc. to Colley Phillips, but merely a rectory in King's county, as shown by a fuller transcript in Erck, *Repertory*, p. 467). Gofton, the auditor, first came to Ireland with Mountjoy early in 1600. Ten years later he was granted the abbey of Assaroe which he passed on to Sir H. Folliott *(Cal. S.P. Ire., 1599-1600*, p. 382; *1608-10*, p. 573).

73. B.L., MS 4772, Receipts of Crown Rents in Munster, 1625 (from a copy made by R. Caulfield in 1873, U.C.C. Library, MS U 83, box 3).

74. N.A., Salved Chancery Pleadings, F. 38 (somewhat damaged by fire). I wish to thank Mr K. W. Nicholls of U.C.C. for drawing my attention to that document – and also for his useful suggestions in relation to other parts of this article.

75. According to the inquisitions referred to in note 77, Boyle's dealings in 1612 were with Donogh and *Conogher;* by 1620 this had altered to Donogh, *Donell* and Awliff (the last-named being Donogh's son). Conogher must have died between 1612 and 1620. Donell got livery (for a fine of £10) on 3 Mar. 1628 (1629); see N.A. Lodge MSS., Wardships, etc., i, p. 84.

76. Actually, Conoghor and Awliffe were slain at the same time, according to Carew's pedigree, but it may not have been considered politic to refer to this.

77. Cork Inq., nos. 23, 33, 53, 54, 55, 57, 84.

78. See M. MacCarthy Morrogh, 'The foundation of Bandon, Co. Cork' in *Cork Hist. Soc. Jn.*, xci (1986), p. 60, and O'Flanagan, *Bandon*, p. 3.

79. Gofton is misspelt 'Goston' throughout the inquisition transcripts. Likewise, A. B. Grosart in his edition of the *Lismore papers* (1st ser. [1886], i, p. 271) has 'Sir ffrances gastons original deed').

80. *In consideracione summe quadragint' et vigint' et unius librorum* should obviously read *quadringent' et*. Boyle in his diary mentions a sum of £400 *(Lismore Papers*, 1st ser., ii, p. 5).

81. He charged O Leary a sum of £19 half-yearly ('Easter Rent'), that is £1 per ploughland; see *Lismore papers*, 1st ser., i, p. 72 (11 May 1615).

82. See note 24 above.

83. Although Boyle wrote 'Cnogher' in his diary on 30 Jan. 1620 (1621). 'Jno Leary' of the same entry should probably read 'Ive Leary'.

84. *Lismore papers*, 1st ser., ii, pp 5, 10.

85. He was admitted to Gray's Inn on 13 Aug. 1590; see *Ir. Jurist*, v (1970), p. 107.

86. See H. Blackall, 'The Galweys of Munster' in *Cork Hist. Soc. Jn.*, lxxi (1966), p. 150; lxxii (1967), pp 125-6. Andrew Comyn was probably brother-in-law of Geoffrey, whose wife was Anne Comyn, daughter of the mayor of Limerick in 1583.

87. *Cal. S.P. Ire., 1611-14*, pp 202, 317; *1615-25*, p. 222.

88. *Cal. pat, rolls, Ire., Jas. I*, pp 531-2.

89. Craig was still liable for the rent of Dromcarra fair and lands in 1625 (see note 73).

90. Genealogical Office, Funeral Entries, vol. vii, p. 267.

91. A different coat of arms is shown in MacLysaght, *Irish families,* 3rd ed., plate xix, along with the absurd motto, 'Laidir is e Lear Righ'.

92. Cork Inq., no. 445.

93. *Civil Survey,* vi, pp 323, 336.

94. *Civil Survey,* vi, p. 323. *Lismore papers,* 1st ser., ii, p. 161.

95. N.L.I., MS 6239.

96. J. T. Gilbert (ed.), *History of the Irish Confederation* (Dublin, 1885), iii, p. 216.

97. *Anal. Hib.,* xxiii (1966), p. 334.

98. J. P. Prendergast, *The Cromwellian settlement of Ireland,* 3rd ed., (Dublin, 1922), pp 201-204.

99. T. A. Larcom, *History of the Cromwellian survey of Ireland A.D. 1655-6* (Dublin 1851), p. 36.

100. S. Ó Domhnaill, 'The maps of the Down Survey' in *I.H.S.,* iii (1943), p. 383, maintains that Petty's area measurements are 10 per cent to 15 per cent too small.

101. *Civil Survey,* vi, p. 380.

102. Not including Cnogher O Connell whose appearance as proprietor of Garryantornora is singular. Perhaps he came of a family of turners after one of whom the townland was called *Gaorthadh an tornóra.*

103. Where the terrain proved difficult of access, Petty's surveyors tended to lump several townlands together in a confusing manner. (Around Gougane Barra there are ten in one measurement). This confusion extends to the I.M.C.'s printed version of *Civil Survey,* where figures from D.S. are put under the C.S. acreage, though often the two figures related to areas with different boundaries. Inchigeelagh parish was admeasured in 1656 by W. Crawley, using a scale of 160 Irish perches per square inch; see W. H. Hardinge, 'Surveys in Ireland, 1640 to 1688' in *R.I.A. Trans.,* xxiv (1867), p. 82.

104. Written 'Dirivicanlongy' in C.S. and 'Derrivecanlongy' in D.S., the original form appears to have been *Doire Mhic an Longaidh.*

105. A sketch of the inside of Dromcarra Castle by John Windele in 1832 shows enormous breaches in the north, south and east walls, obviously a deliberate slighting (R.I.A., Windele MS 12 19, p. 337). The ruined walls stood until 1968 when they were levelled because of their dangerous condition.

106. Teige McDonl in C.S. is probably correct, though he appears as Teige McDermod in D.S./B.S.D., and in Christopher Gough's list; see J. O'Hart, *Irish landed gentry* (Dublin, 1887), pp 274-5 – apparently through being confused with Teige McDermod Roe.

107. Cork Inq., no. 33.

108. Cork Inq., no. 57.

109. Cork Inq., no. 445.

110. *Civil Survey,* vi, p. 336. Ratheahiff is no longer a townland, but the rath from which it was named is still extant, in the townland of Gortnahoughtee.

111. Ó Donnchú, *Filíocht Mháire Bhuidhe,* p. 82.

112. *Civil Survey,* vi, pp 324, 332.

113. Tadhg Meirgeach held five townlands in mortgage from Cnogher mac Teige mac Arte (Cork Inq., no. 257).

114. For an example of a division dispute arising from just such an attachment see K. W. Nicholls, 'Gaelic Landownership in Tipperary' in *Tipperary,* p. 101.

115. Fiants Eliz., 3083, 6539.

116. See P. W. Joyce, *A social history of ancient Ireland* (London, 1903), i, p. 204.

117. Cork Inq., nos. 23, 55, 257.

118. Cork Inq., no. 417.
119. *Civil Survey*, vi, p. 334.
120. U.C.C. Library, Caulfield MSS quoted in S. Ó Coindealbháin, *The story of Iveleary* (Dundalk, [n.d.]), p. 18.
121. The 1659 poll-tax *(Census Ire. 1659)* accounted for 42 O Learys in East Carbery, 11 in West Carbery, 14 in Kilbrittain, 8 in Ibane and Barryroe, 21 in Kinalmeaky and 24 in Cork city and liberties (Muskerry is not recorded). By 1890 (O) Leary was one of the ten most numerous surnames in county Cork, and in 62nd place in the whole of Ireland; see R. E. Matheson, *Special report on surnames in Ireland* (Dublin, 1909), pp 7, 33.
122. Fiant Eliz., 6701.
123. Fiants Eliz., 4485, 4764, 5506, 5688, 6486, 6539, 6571, 6764.
124. *Civil Survey*, vi, p. 323.
125. N.A., Lodge MSS: Records of the Rolls, vol. vi, p. 415.
126. *Cal. S.P. Ire., 1660-62*, p. 449 (28 Oct. 1661).
127. H.M.C., *The MSS of the House of Lords 1697-99,* new ser., (London, 1905), iii, p. 48; *Stat. Ire.*, ii, p. 256.
128. *Cal. treas. bks, 1669-72*, pp 1068-1070, 1086.
129. Appendix to *Fifteenth annual report from the Commissioners on the public records of Ireland* (1824-5), p. 240.
130. Daniell O Leary, gent., his son, Dermott, and Teige Leary, gent., were *tituladoes* there in 1659 *(Census Ire. 1659,* pp 182,184).
131. Many of the name were officers in the Spanish army in the early eighteenth century; see, for example, M. Walsh (ed.), *Spanish knights of Irish origin,* i (Dublin, 1960), pp 63, 90.
132. Rewards were offered in 1694 for the capture of six of the name who had fled to the mountains – including Dermot Leary of Iveleary *(Cal. S.P. dom., 1694-5,* p. 353).
133. Daniel O Leary, *alias* O Leary, claimed that he had a 99-year lease (given by Clancarty, 1 May, 1677) of Gortsmoorane, Kilbarry and other lands but his claim was disallowed at Chichester House in 1700 (*A list of the claims* ... (Dublin, 1701), p. 145, no. 1347). Arthur Mc Daniell Leary of Drishane, gent., was outlawed (for overseas treason) in 1690 *(Anal. Hib.,* xxii (1960), p. 68). The tomb of the last in the male line, (Denis) O Leary of Millstreet, *ob.* 1783, is in the old Drishane graveyard.
134. See will in Ó Donnchú, *Filíocht Mháire Bhuidhe*, p. 84.
135. Ibid., p. 12.
136. N.L.I., *Book of postings*, p. 85.
137. Index to wills in *Cork Hist. Soc. Jn.*, iii (1897), p. 119.
138. 'Céadach Meirgeach' died in 1723 and was lamented by Domhnall na Tuile Mac Carthaigh (U.C.C., Torna MSS, T.8, pp 5-12: see de Brún, *Cnuasach Thorna,* i, p. 221).
139. See various deeds referred to in supplement to the *Eighth report of the commissioners of the public records of Ireland* (1819), p. 616. One of the leases (1677) was to Lissigh O Leary. He could have been the father of Céadach and so great-grandfather of the famous Art Ó Laoghaire (*A Airt Uí Laoghaire Mhic Conchubhair, Mhic Céadaigh Mhic Laoisigh Uí Laoghaire, Aniar ón nGaortha; ... A ghaoil Thaidhg Mheirgigh na scabal,* quoted in the work cited below, note 147).
140. Ó Donnchú, *Filíocht Mháire Bhuidhe*, p. 11.
141. N.L.I., *Book of postings*, pp 82-85.
142. *Anal. Hib.*, xxii (1960), p. 114.

143. Will published in Ó Donnchú, *Filíocht Mháire Bhuidhe,* p. 85.

144. N.A., Exchequer Cal. Inq., vol. 2 (Clare and Cork), p. 44. This is an abbreviated schedule; only some of the Iveleary townlands are listed. A fuller survey of Clancarty's forfeited lands in Muskerry (B.L., MS 17,508, copied by Richard Caulfield in 1881 and published in *Cork Hist. Soc. Jn.,* vi (1900), pp 253-6) lists practically all the townlands of Inchigeelagh parish. The acreage does not derive from D.S., but the total for the parish (19,578 acres) approximates to that of D.S. (20,965). This survey provided the sale figures shown in N.L.I., *Book of postings.*

145. *P.R.I. rep. D.K.* no. 57, p. 488.

146. N.L.I., *Book of postings,* pp 82-85.

147. S. Ó Tuama (ed.), *Caoineadh Airt Uí Laoghaire* (Baile Átha Cliath, 1961). See also note 139.

148. D. Ó Donnchú, *Filíocht Mháire Bhuidhe.*

149. P. Ó Laoghaire, *Mo scéal féin* (Baile Átha Cliath, 1915).

Appendix A
Uí Laoghaire genealogies

Two genealogies of the Uí Laoghaire are available in printed form. The older one comes from the O Clery Book of Genealogies [hereafter O Clery] ed. by S. Pender in *Anal. Hib.*, xviii, p. 163:

> Tadhg m Lughdha a ch m Airt m Dunluing m Amhlaoibh m Con mumhan m Tómáis óig m Tomais Mhóir m Maoil seachlainn m Taidg m Donnchada m Con mumhan m Diarmada m Donnchada na tuinne m Taidhg m Concobair cliodhna m Eirc m Aonghusa m Maine m Rossa m Dunluing m Fiachach m Laóghaire (o atát úi Laoghaire) m Rossa m Eirc m Treana m Dúach m Mic Con mic Maicníadh.

Maicniadh was an *alias* for Lughaidh Laoighdhe, ancestor of the Corca Laoighdhe, according to 'Geinealach Chorca Laidhe' in O'Donovan *Misc. Celt. Soc.*, p. 8.

The second genealogy is taken from U.C.C. Library, MS Murphy 62, p. 385, transcribed by Eoghan Ó Caoimh in 1703 (published in Ó Donnchadha, *An Leabhar Muimhneach* [hereafter *L.M.*], p. 282).

> Dómhnall: mac Airt, mic Conchubhair, mic Diarmada, mic Taidhg, mic Airt, mic Dúnlaing, mic Amhlaoibh, mic Conmhumhan, mic Amhlaoibh, mic Tomáis Óig, mic Tomáis Mhóir, mic Maoilseachloinn, mic Taidhg, mic Maoilseachloinn, mic Taidhg, mic Donnchadha, mic Conmhumhan, mic Diarmuda, mic Diarmuda, mic Donnchadha na Tuinne, mic Taidhg, mic Conchubhair Chliodhna, mic Eirc, mic Aonghusa, mic Maine, mic Rosa, mic Dúnlaing, mic Fiacha, mic Laoghaire (ó n-abarthar Aoibh Laoghaire), mic Eirc mic Tréana, mic Donnchadha, mic Fátha Canann, mic Meic Con, *ut supra.*

Some divergences in this second genealogy are also to be found in that sent in to Ulster's office by the son of Donnchadh Ó Laoghaire in 1638 (Geneal. Office, Funeral Entries [hereafter Fun. entry], vii, p. 267). This in turn was used by W. Betham to 'correct' the O Clery genealogy in his copy of Roger O Ferrall's *Linea Antiqua* (now in N.L.I.), ii, p. 453.

A third (unpublished) genealogy is to be found in Bodl., University College MS 103, f. 27 [hereafter U.C.], compiled for Carew in the early seventeenth century. It is practically indentical with O Clery except that it begins with Art mac Conchubhair (indicating that it originated in the period *c.* 1572-1592) and has 'm. Dunchadha' (as against 'm. Duach') near the end. But it also contains valuable details of collateral branches not available elsewhere, so providing the basis for Carew's own pedigree (see Appendices B/C).

APPENDIX B

Ó Laoghaire pedigree, c. 1500-1650

Based mainly on Carew's MSS: Lambeth, MS 635, f. 156 and U.C., f. 27.

Art (1)

Lughaidh (2) Tadhg (3)

Tadhg (4) Diarmaid (5)

Conchobhar (10) = (a) Mac Carthy = (b) Mac Sweeney Diarmaid Óg (11) Domhnall (12) Tadhg (13)
(see Appendix C)

Art (20) Amhlaoibh Ruadh (21) (*ob.* 1597) Conchobhar (22) (*ob.* 1600) Donnchadh an Ghaorthaidh (23) (*ob.* 1638) Diarmaid Ruadh (24) Dau. (25) Dau. (26) Laoiseach (27) Conchobhar na Cairge (30) Diarmaid (31) Donnchadh (32) Domhnall (33) Donnchadh an Chuasáin (34) Art (35)

Tadhg (40) (*ob.* 1600) Conchobhar (41) Domhnall (42) (b. 1575) Tadhg (43) Conchobhar (44) Art (45) Amhlaoibh (46) Conchobhar (47) Tadhg (48) George (38) Dau. (39)

245

Appendix B
Notes

(1)	Art m. Dúnlaing m. Amhlaoibh (as in Appendix A).
(2)-(5)	See Appendix A (O Clery, *L.M.*, U.C.).
	Diarmaid (5) married Ellen, daughter of Cormocke McDermod (Mac Carthy) of Drishane (Car.).
(10)	*L.M.*; U.C.; Cork Inq., no. 54. Conchobhar's first wife was a Mac Carthy of Tuath na Dromann and his second a daughter of Maolmhuire Mac Sweeney of Desmond (Car.).
(11)	U.C.; Car.; founder of the Carrignacurra branch (see Appendix C).
(12)-(13)	U.C.
(20)	*L.M.* Married to one of the O Moroghies (Car.).
(21)	U.C. Married to one of the O Keeffes (Car.).
(22)	U.C. Married to one of the O Moroghies (Car.).
(23)	U.C. Married Ellice, daughter of Dermod mac Teige O Crowley (*alias* O Crowley) of Toome in Carbery (Fun. entry, 1638).
(24)	U.C. Married daughter of Moroghe mac Dermod O Regan in Carbery (Car.); 'Shilie ny Murroghoe' (Fiant Eliz., 6467).
(25)	Married one of the 'Mc Shees' of Imokilly (Car.).
(26)	Married (i) O Donovan, (ii) Raghnall oge duffe (Car.).
(27)	U.C. Married to one of the O Mahonys of Muskerry (Car.).
(30)-(35)	U.C.
(38)	Married Giles, daughter of Donell Mac Carthy of Bealamoyre (Funeral certificate of Donell Mac Carthy, 1637; copy in U.C.C. Library, Caulfield MSS, U 83, box 7).
(39)	Ellin, married Teig Mac Carthy of Bealamoyre (ibid.).
(40)	Car.; *Cal. S.P. Ire. 1606-08,* p. 66.
(41)	Lived at Carrignaneelagh (Car.).
(42)	*L.M.* Chief in 1641 (*Civil Survey,* p. 325).
(43)	Car. Born in 1574 (Cork Inq. 84).
(44)	*Civil Survey,* p. 324.
(45)	B.S.D., county Cork, p. 32.
(46)	Married (i) Ellen, daughter of Awliffe O Leyne of Jordanstown; (ii) Shily, daughter of Geoffrey O Donoghue, *alias* O Donoghue of the Glen (Fun. entry, 1638).
(47)	Married Onora, daughter of Art O Leary of Gortatanavally (ibid.).
(48)	*Civil Survey,* p. 333.

Appendix C
Ó Laoghaire of Carrignacurra, c. 1580-1750

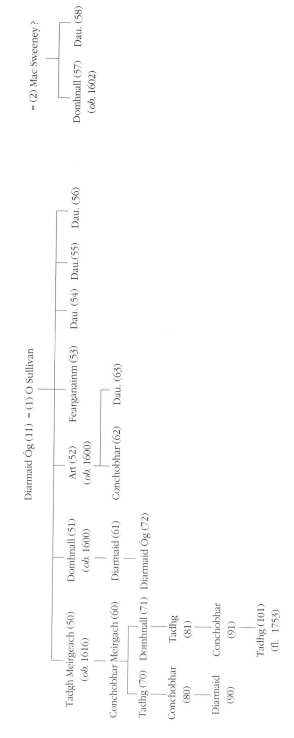

247

Appendix C
Notes

(11)   See Appendix B. There is some ambivalence here in Car. Diarmaid Óg married a daughter of Mac Flynn of Desmond, but an entry on the right makes it appear he also married a daughter of Moylemurry mac Donoghowe Swyne. The numbers 1, 2 ... over sons Teige, etc. were changed to 2, 3, etc., but U.C. names Tadhg as the eldest son.

(50)   U.C. Married daughter of Donell mac Teig Mange in Desmond (Car.). Carew says he was slain in 1600, but three Cork Inqs. (23, 55, 417) give 1 Mar. 1615 (1616) as date of death. No. 417 also tells us that his widow (Sheely) married secondly Dermott Mc Murtagh (Ó Muircheartaigh) *alias* Dermot O'Dingle of Ballynacourty (Boyle's agent in county Kerry). This remarriage appears to have taken place during Teig's lifetime, as it is also noted in Car.

Sheely was partoned for her remarriage without licence on 4 Mar. 1639 (1640), see N.A., Lodge MSS, Wardships etc., i, p. 119.

(51)   U.C. Married daughter of Brian mac Owen Mac Sweeney (Car.).

(52)   U.C. Married daughter of Brian Óg dubh Mac Sweeney (Car.).

(53)   U.C.; Car.; Fiants Eliz., 6467, 6764.

(54)   Married (i) Rory mac Donogh Mac Sweeney of Desmond, (ii) Moriertagh mac Rory Mac Shee (Car.).

(55)   Married (i) – Mac Sweeney, (ii) Thomas Óg of the island in Kerry (Car.); 'Ellen nyne Dermod O Leary, wife (of) Tho. oge Gerrald' (Fiant Eliz., 6524).

(56)   Married Cormac Mac Flynn mac Cormac of Gleann an Chroim (Car.).

(57)   'Donell ne Lane O Lerie slayne by Moronighe (?) McBrian McDonn¹ Swynie in anno 1602' (Car.).

(58)   Married Teig mac Donel Og mac Carthy of Tuath na Dromann (Car.).

(60)   *Civil Survey,* p. 333; Cork Inq., no. 417.

(61), (72)   See p. 19.

(62)   *Civil Survey,* p. 333; Cork Inq., no. 417.

(63)   Married Rory mac Donell mac Sweeney of Desmond (Car.).

(70), (71)   Mentioned in will of 1663 (Ó Donnchú, *Filíocht Mháire Bhuidhe,* p. 81).

(80)   Will in 1699 (*Cork Hist. Soc. Jn.,* iii (1897), p. 119).

(81)   *P.R.I. rep. D.K.,* no. 57, p. 488.

(90), (91), (101) Wills 1699 and 1753 (Ó Donnchú, *Filíocht Mháire Bhuidhe,* pp 11, 85).

Chapter 8

THE 1641 DEPOSITIONS AS A SOURCE FOR THE WRITING OF SOCIAL HISTORY: COUNTY CORK AS A CASE STUDY

NICHOLAS CANNY

Introduction: the sources

This essay is addressed to those interested in local history and more especially the history of county Cork, to encourage them to make use of the collection of material known as the 1641 depositions for the purpose of better understanding social conditions within their country and its various regions during the first half of the seventeenth century.

That such encouragement is necessary is explained by the fact that this material has not received the attention it deserves for the purpose of writing social history, either because people have little idea of what is contained within the collection or because they are discouraged by the absence of any systematic ordering of the documents in the collection. Perhaps also they have been convinced by a long tradition of historical writing that the evidence in the depositions is so biased in nature as to be useless to any historian who might wish to present an objective appraisal of the events associated with the 1641 rising in Ireland[1]. It is not my purpose to reject the suggestion of bias or to conceal the fact that the depositions were collected for the specific purpose of assisting the efforts of Protestant officials in Ireland to identify and take revenge upon those Catholics who were involved with the onslaught which they had launched against the Protestant community in Ireland during the winter and spring of 1641-2.

This factor of bias should not deter us, because all sources are biased in one way or the other, and it is the responsibility of historians to extract whatever information they can from all surviving fragments of the past, always taking account of the purpose which lay behind the compilation of the evidence in the first instance. Nor, it must be said, is it unusual for historians to make use of hostile or unsympathetic evidence to further their enquiries into their chosen subject. Most of what we know of the Peasants' Revolt in Germany comes from accounts compiled by those who suppressed it, and almost everything that is known of the Counter-Revolution in France has been gleaned from the testimony of ardent revolutionaries who lacked sympathy with the cause of the insurgents. Similarly with Irish history, those who have reconstructed the events leading up to the insurrection of 1798 and its aftermath have relied principally on information compiled by the government from its network of informers, and the records of Dublin Castle have also proved a most fruitful source for historians who have studied the Irish nationalist struggle for independence in the twentieth century.[2]

Such parallels suggest that the depositions might even be employed for reconstructing the course of events during the early stages of disturbances that followed upon the uprising of 1641, and they have been used for this purpose by Michael Perceval-Maxwell.[3] They are more evidently useful for the purpose of understanding the extent, location and character of the English settler presence in Ireland at the point when the insurrection occurred, because the question of bias does not affect the extraction of such raw data from what is a complex source. As will be suggested in this paper, the reports made by these settlers in their depositions also shed much light on their economic activities in Ireland and on their social interaction with the broader community in the decades before 1641. This information, in turn, reveals something of the social and economic circumstances of the indigenous population, and a close examination of the testimony of the deponents makes it possible to identify the principal leaders of the insurrection in each county of Ireland as well as many of the participants who were accused of having been involved in the uprising within each locality.

Before embarking on an analysis of the depositions for county Cork, which may serve as a model for the examination of similar evidence relating to other counties, it is appropriate to say something of the origin and character of the manuscripts which will give some indication of the strengths as well as the limitations of the depositions as a source for social history.[4] The most important consideration for the researcher to bear in mind is that there are two distinct elements within this single archival source. The first and more extensive element derives from sworn statements collected by officials of the Dublin government during the closing months of 1641 and through the spring and summer months of 1642 from Protestant settlers in Ireland (and some Irish Protestants also) who had endured the rising of the previous months.

This exercise was conducted at a time when the government was confident that its authority would soon be restored, and the purpose behind the compilation of depositions from all parts of the country seems principally to have been to establish what had been lost to the Protestant interest during the course of the disturbances, so that due compensation could be exacted from those responsible. To this end, deponents were required to identify themselves by name, by exact place of residence in Ireland (including townland, parish, barony and county), and by social position or occupation. Then, according to the rigid formula that was followed, each deponent listed all property, goods and chattels that had been lost, as well as all sources of income that had been disrupted as a consequence of the insurrection.

These inventories included debts owing to the deponents and rents due to them from property, but no account was taken of debts owed by the deponents to others or of rents paid by them to the owners of any property which they leased from their landlords. Those deponents who were artisans usually estimated the annual income which they derived from the pursuit of their crafts, but again nothing was said of any outlays involved. A price was also placed on any investment which deponents had made in their property, through building or improvement, and account was also taken of entry fines paid by them upon taking up occupancy of any property, and of the number of unexpired years on any leases which they held. These valuations were thus statements of income rather than estimations of wealth, because little was said of the expenditures associated with their endeavours in Ireland. Then, because compensation was the principal objective in view when these statements were collected, the deponents identified those who had attacked them or had deprived them of goods and property. In the course of doing so, they usually made specific mention of any atrocities they had witnessed or heard reported, as well as of any physical or verbal abuse suffered by themselves, and again they identified those who had been responsible.

In several instances this accusatory aspect of the deposition became the primary element and extended to several pages of closely-written script, and in several instances also (usually in the case of wealthy landowners or entrepreneurs) the inventory of lost possessions extended into several folios. These were highly exceptional depositions however and the more typical document was terse and no more than two pages in length.

The objective of acquiring quick compensation and recovery of property, which lay behind the compilation of depositions, was defeated once it became clear that the government's authority would not be quickly restored. Protestant disappointment and uncertainty about the future are explained by the fact that the English government, which might have been expected to come to the immediate assistance of the settler community in Ireland, was preoccupied with a challenge to its own domestic authority. In these circumstances, some leaders of the Protestant community in Ireland employed the evidence assembled in the depositions for a purpose for which it had never been intended: the drafting of hundreds of pamphlets designed to alert the competing factions in England to the plight of the Protestant community in Ireland. The general thrust of these pamphlets was to the effect that the 1641 rising was but a dimension of a general Catholic conspiracy to massacre the entire Protestant community in Ireland. In their effort to lend authority to this thesis, the pamphleteers drew heavily upon the accusatory passages in the depositions which were cited out of context.[5] This selective use of the depositions tended to convey the impression that the entire body of testimony collected was directly related to murder and atrocity.

This legacy, which still endures even among well-regarded historians, was strengthened by the further use to which the depositions were put in the decade after their compilation. At this point it had become clear that the struggle being fought out in Ireland was not merely to determine what compensation would be made to dispossessed Protestants, but that it was a fight to the finish which would result either in the total supremacy or the total overthrow of the Protestant interest in Ireland. As the years progressed and as Protestant victory seemed ever more likely with the accession to power of Oliver Cromwell in England, officials in Dublin began to make preparations for the moment when they could effect the destruction of those who had initiated the disturbances in 1641 and 1642. Resort was again made to the depositions, this time to isolate those individuals in the Irish Catholic community who had been identified by the deponents as having been involved in the disturbances. Then, when Cromwellian authority was established everywhere in Ireland, these named individuals, or those of them who were still alive in the aftermath of the war, were summoned before the courts and obliged to account for their movements at the time when the alleged attacks and atrocities had occurred.

At this point the original depositions were being used as evidence for the prosecution, but where they wished to do so the accused were given the opportunity to make sworn statements professing their innocence and explaining where they had been when the alleged offences occurred. Whenever the accused took advantage of this opportunity, they saw the need to bring forward witnesses who would bear out their testimony, and these corroborating statements were frequently countered by yet other witnesses for the state. This entire process of charge and counter-charge generated an enormous body of material which is related to, but distinct from, the original depositions of 1641-2. The differences, apart from date, are that this second series of sworn statements is of a different format and relates specifically to incidents that had occurred more than eleven years previously. This second series of depositions provides little information of social and economic conditions in Ireland previous to 1641, and in so far as it contributes to our store of knowledge it is because the deponents on this occasion always stated their ages.

Because they were so closely associated and inter-connected during the court proceedings of the 1650s, these two very different documentary elements came to be filed together and have been identified as a single source, known generally as the 1641 depositions. This identification was strengthened because, at some point in the nineteenth century, the entire body of material was reorganised along county lines and bound in thirty-one volumes which are deposited in the library of Trinity College, Dublin.

While the material is arranged according to county, there is not an even spread of the material among the counties. The distribution is explained as much by the ferocity of the attack that beset the settler community in 1641 as it is by the relative density of settlement in the first instance. Thus there are almost as few sworn statements for such counties as Donegal and Armagh where British settlement was dense as there are for the counties in Connacht where Protestant settlers were thin on the ground. The county for which most evidence survives is Cork, and this is as much a reflection of its size and the density of settlement as it is of the fact that the settler community there withstood the assault of 1641-2 better than their counterparts elsewhere in Ireland. It is appropriate, therefore, that this case study of the uses to which the depositions might be put by the social historian should be based on the material from county Cork.

County Cork's depositions

There are four volumes of depositions for county Cork and these are identified as Trinity College, Dublin, manuscript numbers 822, 823, 824 and 825. Attention for the purposes of this paper, was confined to the first category of depositions, those made by Protestants in 1641 and 1642, and these are included in each of the four volumes and interspersed with the material which derives from the court proceedings of the 1650s. There are 911 depositions of this first category contained within the four volumes, but seven of the 911 have been identified as belonging to other counties. This leaves us with a total of 904 sworn statements filed by Protestant residents of county Cork in the aftermath of the 1641 rising.

The ordering of the depositions within the four volumes does not follow any apparent logic, and an effort has been made, in the Appendix to this paper, to list the deponents under their parish of residence, showing in each case the volume number and folio number of the deposition as well as the name, townland address and social position or occupation of each deponent from each parish listed. The spelling of parish and townland names has, in every instance, been compared with the standard form provided in the Census of 1851, and question marks indicate where doubt exists over the identification of place-names. Some margin of error is bound to have entered into this exercise with the result that a small number of deponents may now be listed under an incorrect parish address, and I have been unable to identify sixteen of the place-names either because of the poor condition of the manuscript or because the deponent did not provide a full address. More frequently deponents did not supply details on social position or occupation and such deficiencies are noted by the letters n.s.g., which signify 'no status given'. The parishes have been listed in alphabetical order in the Appendix, and an effort has been made to preserve the manuscript spelling of parishes and townlands in square brackets where this differs significantly from the 1851 standard.

This arrangement of the Cork depositions under civil parish headings is designed as an aid to the local historian who may wish to consult the depositions for a single parish or cluster of parishes without having to wade through the entire four volumes. This arrangement has also facilitated the making of a map (devised by Patrick O'Flanagan) which reveals how the deponents were distributed throughout the county. The distribution of this segment of the settler population provides some impression of how the total settler population was dispersed at the moment when the insurrection occurred (Fig. 8.1).

Distribution of settlers

The fact that the 904 deponents from county Cork were distributed throughout 134 parishes makes it clear that there must have been English settlers in every part of the county. The further fact that 309 of these deponents were clustered in but ten parishes, and that a few of these were contiguous parishes, reveals that the distribution of the deponents was far from even throughout the county. This point is further borne out by the fact that 66 of the 134 parishes had three deponents or fewer. The general impression about the distribution of Protestant settlement in county Cork conveyed by the depositions is that there was some English presence almost everywhere in the county but that the settlement was very thick indeed in particular regions. These regions of dense settlement were determined as much by the existence of natural resources as they were by the ownership of land. For example it appears from the map that there was a continuous line of relatively dense settlement in the valleys of the Blackwater, the Lee and

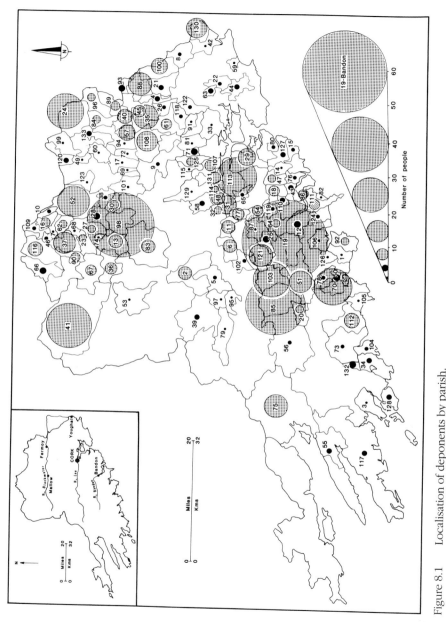

Figure 8.1   Localisation of deponents by parish.
Source: 1641 depositions.

the Bandon rivers, and this phenomenon would emerge even more clearly if settlement in west county Waterford was included. A significant settler presence along the coastline of west Cork, where fishing attracted settlement, is also suggested by the distribution of deponents, but the most striking feature of all is the suggestion of sizeable urban settlement in county Cork.

The largest cluster of deponents, sixty-two in all, came from the parishes of Ballymodan and Kilbrogan which together included the town of Bandon, and there is a further cluster of eighteen deponents from the nearby parish of Kinneigh which included the village of Castletown. The twenty-six deponents who came forward from the parish of Kilgarriff almost all belonged to the town of Clonakilty which suggests a sizeable English settlement there, and the twenty-five deponents from the parish of Brigown are explained by the presence of Mitchelstown in that parish. Similarly, the thirty-one deponents from the parish of Clonfert belonged principally to the towns, Newmarket and Kanturk, in that parish, and almost all of the forty-eight deponents from the parish of Mallow were residents of the town of the same name. The overwhelming majority of these urban deponents were artisans who rented property in the towns, but most of them also leased farms of land in the surrounding countryside. The multi-faceted activity of the deponents as artisans, farmers, traders, money-lenders and middlemen provides clear evidence that these towns were important centres of proto-industry, and it is possible that some of these Cork urban settlements surpassed the plantation towns in Ulster both in terms of the size of their settler communities and of their economic importance. It is also possible, or even probable, that some regions of county Cork, and most notably the Bandon river valley, were more densely settled with migrants from Britain than any area of comparable size in the province of Ulster.[6]

The list of deponents that has been arranged along parish lines permits us to dwell only in the realm of possibilities and probabilities, because a mere fraction of the settler community, and these usually heads of households who had losses to report, came forward to make depositions in the aftermath of the 1641 rising. That the list is only the tip of a much larger iceberg is clear from the depositions themselves, because almost all deponents identified several other relatives or settlers who had lived in their immediate vicinity previous to the out-break of hostilities. These could be settlers who had been killed, injured or humiliated during the course of the early hostilities; or settlers who had defected to the enemy at the moment of onslaught and saved themselves by going to mass; or settlers who had been indebted to the deponents but who could no longer meet their obligations because they had been ruined by the insurrection. Even the simplest of depositions enables the investigator to add to the store of names of settlers, while a detailed deposition by a merchant or gentleman can contribute up to a score of extra settler names. Peter Scus, a yeoman from Glanbarahan (823, f. 18), was unable to provide any list of those who were indebted to him because 'his papers and writings' were in England. However, he partly compensated for this deficiency in his deposition by his further testimony that 'Thomas[ine] Ford alias Tippery of Castlehaven of the said county, spinster; Richard Carpenter of the same, fisherman; Gabriel Perkins of the same, fisherman; Ralph Tomkin of the same, yeoman; Arthur Bohena of the same, weaver; Thomas Powell of the same, yeoman; and Nathaniel Blight of the same, fisherman; and a son of John Gregory of the same, yeoman; and a servant of Thomas Hancocke of the same' had all been murdered at the end of May 1642.

This example made by a person of modest circumstances reveals that a systematic analysis of the depositions would enable a researcher to increase the list of identified settlers in county Cork, or any region of that county, at least sixfold. This exercise would produce a list of possibly 5,500 named individuals who had settled in county Cork before 1641. Most of these individuals would have been members of a family, which means that the 5,500 named individuals would account for approximately 9,125 settlers who belonged to their families. And this figure would still represent only a fraction of the total settler presence in the county.[7]

The compilation of such an extensive list, derived from a close scrutiny of the depositions, should be of immense interest to genealogists since it would point to the precise location and first occurrence in Cork of a completely new stock of family names which was now being added to the surnames which derive from earlier waves of settlement in the county. What could be done in this matter for county Cork could obviously be replicated for other counties, but it is unlikely if the depositions for any other county in Ireland would produce a list of say 5,500 names that could be compiled from the depositions for county Cork. A full list which would include the names of those settlers mentioned in the depositions, as well as the deponents themselves, would still be far from being a comprehensive list of all Protestants from abroad who had settled in the county in the decades before 1641. Nevertheless such a list, or even the preliminary list of the 904 deponents that has been attached as an Appendix to this paper, should make it possible to test some assumptions about British migration into Cork, and into Munster generally, that have been made by previous historians of the subject.

Newcomer origins

David B. Quinn was the first historian who attempted to consider the question of English plantation and settlement in Munster in a broader context.[8] In the course of sketching out a subject which he believed to be in urgent need of investigation, he suggested that English migration into Munster during the sixteenth and into the seventeenth century had come mostly from the south-west of England. This suggestion was taken up by the present author in several publications, and in some of these an analogy was drawn between the province of Munster which attracted a sizeable number of migrants (estimated at 15,000) from the south-west of England, and the province of Ulster which drew settlers principally from lowland Scotland and the north-west of England. This same point was taken up independently by Dr Michael MacCarthy-Morrogh, again drawing upon the suggestion of Quinn, but he carried it further to suggest that 'the special relationship of Munster to the south-west of England' resulted in the settled areas of the province becoming anglicised to the point where it was 'akin to a slightly raffish county on the English borders'. This, as MacCarthy-Morrogh was at pains to point out, was as much a consequence of almost half a century of peace and prosperity as it was of English settlement in the province. However this anglicised appearance of the province is advanced by him to support his further theory that Munster was not colonised by England as much as it was developed as a natural extension of the English south-west, with people passing to and fro by water between Munster and the south-west of England as easily as they did by road between Devon and London. This ease of passage explains for MacCarthy-Morrogh how his estimated settler population of 22,000 people came to arrive in Munster, and he assumes that the overwhelming majority of these had their origin in the English south-west as well as making their crossing to Ireland from there. And this supposition in turn lends authority to MacCarthy-Morrogh's general conclusion that 'in economic terms south Munster and south-west England were fast becoming one unit'.

This concern of Dr MacCarthy-Morrogh to establish his case that Munster was becoming a social and economic extension of England, and not a colony of that country, seems to derive as much from his misunderstanding of social conditions in Britain's trans-Atlantic colonies in the seventeenth century as it does from his desire to strike out with an argument of his own rather than to provide supporting evidence for the suggestions of others. In so far as his argument rests on the character of the migration from England to Ireland, it relies almost altogether on supposition.[9] Apart from a few documented instances, such as that of Sir William Hull whose origins can be traced to Devon,[10] we are left to take it on trust that the vast majority of his suggested 22,000 migrants to Munster were natives of the south-west of England. No fault should be attributed to Dr MacCarthy-Morrogh for not citing evidence because proof is not readily available. The surviving sources do provide details of the regular commercial contacts that were established between ports such as Youghal and Kinsale on the south coast of Cork and Bristol and Minehead on the Severn basin; occasional references are to be found to cattle being shipped from Cork ports to the south of England and even of their being grazed on common land after their arrival in England; and there is one fascinating glimpse of fawns accompanied by goats on which they suckled, being shipped by the earl of Cork from the south of England for the stocking of his deer park at Lismore Castle.[11] On the movement of people, however, the sources are silent; it is only very occasionally that one encounters a passing reference in the sources to the place of origin of a settler in Munster, or of an Irish person in the south-west of England.

The depositions do not provide any immediate solution to this problem of origin because the Protestant deponents from county Cork revealed nothing of their place of origin other than the description 'British Protestant' or 'Irish Protestant', and in the case of a solitary deponent, Valentine Gordon of Bantry (823, f. 169), the description, 'spinster and Scottish Protestant'. Even these claims to national origin are not always reliable, because some deponents whose names would suggest that they were of continental birth, for example Agmondesham Muschamp of Carrigaline (823, f. 187) still went by the description, British Protestant. However the fact that we have a list of 904 deponents for county Cork, and that this can be expanded upwards to about 5,500 names, should make it possible to establish whether a migration pattern from the English south-west to the province of Munster did in fact exist. This could be done most readily by referring the list to social historians of the various counties of the English West Country and of Wales. These have studied their regions with a microscopic precision and they would immediately recognise any occurrence in Ireland of name patterns with which they are acquainted from the study of their own seventeenth-century communities. Should no such recurrence happen, then we must suppose that many of the English settlers in county Cork originally came from a much wider area than the English West Country.

It is now my own belief that this test will prove negative and that we will be left to conclude that the settlers came from a very wide area of England and not from a single region. This impression has been formed because of the clustering of settlers with particular skills in particular areas of county Cork. This clustering suggests that these artisans or skilled farm workers were recruited by entrepreneurs or landowners rather than that they happened to settle together after a casual migration. That skilled personnel would have had to be recruited is suggested by the experience of the towns of Springfield and Marblehead in seventeenth-century Massachusetts. Each of these communities of English migrants was established around commercial endeavours which required skilled personnel who were engaged only after a process of recruitment which extended over an extensive area of the dominions of the British crown.[12]

If we are to accept the logic of this argument then we must suppose that the presence of four tanners, three butchers, a weaver, a feltmaker, a blacksmith, a wheeler, a shoemaker, a sawyer and a malster among the forty-two deponents from the parish of Kinneagh did not happen by chance. It is more likely that they were invited to settle there by William Richardson of Castletown, who described himself as a clothier (823 f. 80) or by Richard Samell the chandler (824, f. 200), or by an entrepreneur in nearby Bandon such as Henry Turner (824, ff 118-9), or by a landlord or gentleman in the vicinity. And if artisans with this range of skills were deliberately drawn to settle in the parish, it is more unlikely that they came from a single locality or region in England.

Should this hold true for the artisan communities of county Cork it would hold true also for the farmers among the deponents. Skilled agriculturalists with the capital necessary to pay entry fines or develop their farms were extremely hard to come by in England, it is unlikely that the very large number of skilled yeomen and husbandmen who appear among the deponents for county Cork could have been drawn from a single sector of England. It is far more likely that landowners who had an interest in attracting such tenants to their estates would have trawled over an extensive area of England and would have made contact with landowners in all parts of that country in their search for suitable tenants. That such searches were conducted is also suggested by the close coincidence between the agricultural specialisms followed by gentlemen on their home farms and those pursued by the yeomen and husbandmen who rented land from them.

We learn of such specialisms from a close reading of the depositions themselves. The presence of John Slade, a shepherd, in the parish of Kilbrin (822, f. 116) seems without significance until we consider the deposition of Jonas Smith (822, f. 161), the only gentleman deponent from the same parish. In his inventory of goods, Smith reveals that he was engaged in mixed farming on his home farm, but with sheep-raising as the most important constituent element, since he valued his loss in sheep at £495 out of his total estimated loss of £1,498. This evidence would suggest that Slade had been invited by Smith to serve as his shepherd, a suggestion that is all the more plausible since Slade did not detail any personal losses in his deposition. This John Slade was a man of mature years because he had a daughter, Mary, who corroborated his testimony, and it may have been he, whose skill as a shepherd would have been required by Jonas Smith, who was the first of his family to make his way to Kilbrin. If so he was soon followed by relatives, because another John Slade, this time a yeoman, also entered a deposition from the parish of Kilbrin (822, f. 137) and a second deposition (825, f. 283) on behalf of his father, Thomas Slade, who had an extensive farm in the parish of Clare Abbey in county Clare.

This latter shred of information opens the possibility that the Slades came to Kilbrin not directly from England but from county Clare, where the first of their number could have been settled by the earl of Thomond.[13]

Patterns of settlement

The existence of kinship clusters among the settlers as well as the existence of common economic interests would suggest that Cork had a sequence of settler communities established in particular localities rather than a broad-spectrum settler society covering the expanse of the entire county. This impression is sustained by an investigation of the economic information that is contained within the depositions for the county. Attention has already been drawn to the deposition of Peter Scus which alludes to several Protestants associated with fishing in the vicinity of Glanbarahan. Other deponents from the same area such as Richard Christmas, a clothmaker from the parish of Kilmacabea (823, ff 74-5), provided evidence of the same phenomenon. Christmas, listed those Protestants who, to his knowledge, had been killed; these included George Griffin of Castlehaven, fishermen, Peter Wren of Leap, fisherman, and Gabriel Perkins and Nathaniel Blight of Castlehaven, also fishermen. Deponents from that same locality, who had no direct involvement with fishing, revealed through their listing of those who were indebted to them that their network of commercial contact was linked closely and almost exclusively with the series of settler communities that were situated along the west coast of county Cork.

Thus, Thomas Doggin of Castlehaven (823, f. 1), although a yeoman farmer, identified his English Protestant debtors as Thomas Numan of Baltimore; Henry Evers of Clonakilty; John Racklife of Castlehaven; Richard Heard of Castlehaven; and, the two exceptions, Daniel Pool of Ballymodan and Thomas Caple of Inishannon. Even allowing for the two exceptions, the contacts of Doggin were very localised and this local dimension to the world of settlers-of-modest-means is borne out by their frequent reference to kinsfolk who lived in close proximity to them. Communities of settlers with special skills such as the fishing communities at Castlehaven, Glanbarahan and further west would presumably have made contact with the wider world through such entrepreneurs as Sir William Hull of the 'island' of Schull, or Otto Redish and his associates in the town of Youghal, or Tristram Whitcombe of Kinsale. Hull has left us in his deposition (824, ff 253-9) with one of the most detailed inventories that exist for anywhere in Europe during the early-modern centuries of the equipment required for the furnishing of a fishing palace. Otto Redish and his associates Frances Gibbons and Elizabeth Lewis, both widows of Youghal, had been 'partners in the trade of fishing'. They valued at £267 their loss of 'implements necessary to trade of fishing' (822, f. 194), and Whitcombe of Kinsale (822, ff 26-7) placed a value of £140 on his 'fishing palace' at Ballymalloe which has been 'demolished' during the disturbances.

What information we have on the fishermen and their families who established themselves in the settler communities along the coastline of county Cork comes to us from third parties, because we have no depositions from any of those fishermen. Some, as we saw, were killed and the majority are likely to have slipped back to England in their boats at the first outbreak of disturbances in the county. Artisans were much less mobile, which explains why we have hundreds of depositions from artisan settlers on the basis of which we can advance much more confident conclusions about the niches that they had carved out for themselves in seventeenth-century county Cork.

Artisans

Most artisans, regardless of craft, claimed losses for their initial investment in establishing themselves in their trade, but this was seldom a significant sum. Richard Christmas of Kilmacabea (823, f. 745) placed a value of £5 on the implements of his trade, a further £5 on 'English wool and stockcards', and a value of £40 on the lease, with eight years to run, on one tucking mill, eight acres of land and a dwelling house. Similarly with Henry Tatardall, a tanner who had settled in the parish of Myross (823, f. 141); he placed a value of £2 on his implements of trade and £10 on a lease of a portion of land with nineteen years unexpired on which he had built a tanyard. Of much greater loss to Tatardall were his leather and tanned hides which he valued at £42 10s. Both of these revealed in their depositions that they were also involved with farming but on a minor scale, and that money from within their immediate vicinity was owed to them when the insurrection broke out.

Other artisans such as John Holland, a blacksmith from the town of Enniskeen (822, f. 30), revealed a greater involvement with agriculture.

Holland, who was sick and had his wife Diana depose on his behalf, claimed that he had enjoyed an annual income of £10 'from the benefit of his trade', and an annual profit of £5 'above the landlord's rent' from the lease that he farmed. On this he raised cows, horses, one mare, corn and hay, and he also possessed houses in Enniskeen valued at £10. Gosse, the miller, seems to have been even more securely established in farming, with one lease for three lives which he valued at £4 per annum above the landlord's rent, and a second lease with twenty-one years unexpired which had reaped a profit of £2 above the landlord's rent. Gosse, like Holland, was engaged in mixed agriculture but with the balance in favour of tillage farming, since he placed a value of £67 on his hay and corn in the haggard and £20 on the cows and heifers which he had lost.

The greater wealth of Holland and Gosse over Christmas and Tatardall would suggest either that they were longer settled in the county, and had invested the profits of their trade in the acquisition of farms, or else that an artisanal hierarchy existed, and that those, like millers and blacksmiths, who provided an essential service to the farming population, could demand leases of land before they agreed to settle in any given community. Whichever the case, it does appear that the way upwards on the social scale for an artisan was through the acquisition of farming land, sometimes supplemented by urban property.

This is suggested by the depositions of several who assumed the designation 'yeoman' or 'gentleman' but who revealed in their inventories that they were skilled artisans. One example is Thomas Lowe from the townland of Derrycoole in the parish of Kilbrogan (825, f. 130). This yeoman, for so he described himself, enjoyed an annual income of £10 from the twenty-four year lease which he held in that townland, and a further income of £7 per annum from a lease for one life. But if he was a yeoman in 1642, he had once been a tanner, because he valued at £4 5s. a 180-year lease of a 'parcel of land and a tanyard' at Newcestown, and he placed a value of £40 on his invest-ment in the tanyard itself. Similarly with the case of Robert Horne, gentleman (823, f. 114) from the parish of Kinneigh. Yeoman might have been a more appropriate social category than gentleman, because the farm, which he held on a forty-one year lease, rendered him but a modest profit. However, he was also a malster, and presumably had originally been such because he valued at £2 10s. the 'necessaries for malting', including 'hareclot and two great cisterns, one screen and other things', and he also had 'newly built a fair malt house which with other houses and tenements was worth twenty pounds per annum'. And he seems to have had every intention of making a further investment in building because he claimed a loss amounting to £10 10s. for 'wood, lime and boards'. Another who had made the transition from malster to gentleman was Humfry Hunt of Clonakilty (823, f. 49), but a few who described themselves as artisans appear to have reinvested in business and achieved spectacular success while also making some profit from farming and investment in urban property. One of the most conspicuous in this respect was Henry Turner of Bandonbridge who claimed to have lost £774 through the rebellion but who still described himself as 'free-burgess and clothier'.

Turner is the Cork settler whose deposition (824, ff 118-9) is most frequently cited because of his claim that he was involved in the export of broad cloths to Mr John Quarles of Amsterdam, 'a Dutch merchant but an English man', and he placed a value of £400 per annum on this trade. This, as well as his description of himself, suggests that he saw himself primarily as a businessman and manufacturer. However he also claimed to have lost tenements and farms, to the value of £150, which he held on a forty-eight year lease, and the 'land of Gaggan' which he valued at £10. The stock on this land, oxen, cows, heifers, a bull, a gelding and some nags, were valued at £130, and he also claimed to have lost £20 when his houses and garden plots in Sugar Lane near the North Gate of Bandon were deliberately destroyed lest the enemy should shelter in them. Turner listed a further loss of £30 because his seven houses in Bandon had been burnt by the rebels. Thus it appears that even Henry Turner had diversified his interests and invested heavily in land and property, even if his principal interest was in manufacturing and trade.

Most artisans, including those who laid claims to gentility, provided a list of those who were indebted to them at the outset of the insurrection. The total sums owed to artisans was usually not great, which means that the individual amounts due to them were small. These amounts were generally not stated but the names of the debtors were usually provided, sometimes accompanied by status or occupation, and place of residence of the debtors. Such details, which reveal that those indebted to artisans were usually from within the same locality as themselves, suggest that the normal working lives of the artisan deponents were lived within these localities.

The fact that the artisans usually distinguished between Protestant and Catholic debtors indicated that all who lived within these narrow circuits were bound together in the shared world of work. Moreover, these worlds would appear to have been even more circumscribed because artisans frequently mentioned that the debts were due to them by individuals engaged upon the same crafts as themselves; for example clothworkers being owed money by weavers, or tanners being owed money by shoemakers or broguemakers. In such instances it was probably not money that was owed to the deponents but rather raw materials which they would have advanced to subordinate artisans under a putting-out system of employment.

If we return once more to the deposition of Richard Christmas of Kilmacabea (823, ff 74-5), we find that he claimed a total loss in debts of 'nine score and six pounds.' Those indebted to him were eight, named 'impoverished Protestants' who included 'James Cleland clerk' and two who were deceased. Then he named fifteen Irish debtors of whom twelve, starting with Fyneen Mc Cormac Carty of Bantry, were described as 'gent'; one, Donogh McFyneen Carty of Kilmacabea, a 'masspriest'; and two, Thomas Condon of 'the Lepp' and Teig Leah of 'the Ard' as weavers. Humfry Hunt of Clonakilty (823, f. 49) claimed to have had twenty-one British Protestant debtors and his list included the name of Richard Christmas as well as 'Mr. Cleveland, clerk'. His Irish debtors were nine in number and read as follows: 'Donnell McCormack of the same, husbandman; Donogh Morrgath of Kilgariff parish, husbandman; John O Rierdane of the Leppe in the said county, gent; John O'Daly of the same, tailor; John O'Molowna of the same, weaver; John O'Hea of the same, gent; Daniell McOwen of Kilgarriff aforesaid, husbandman; John McDaniell of Rosse in the said county, brogue-maker, all in actual rebellion'. Such instances, which could be mul-tiplied a hundredfold, bear testimony to the narrow world in which those artisans lived, and reveal also how a painstaking study of all the depositions for any given locality would make it possible to learn much more than we know of the lives of the natives as well as the new-comers who lived and worked and died within these localities.

Another feature which emerges from the depositions is that the wealthier the deponent, the wider his or her geographical horizons. We already noted the case of Henry Turner whose contacts extended to Amsterdam, but his list of debtors suggests that his ambit of influence within county Cork while not local was still regional. This list which extends to something like one hundred people was made up almost entirely of the names of Irishmen with addresses which extended from Cork city westwards to Bantry, and of a smaller number of English and Old English merchants from such towns as Cork, Baltimore, Bantry, Templetrine and Ballydehob. The list, interestingly, included 'Old Lady Muskery and her son Owen Chartie', and also a great number of Irish people from the town of Bandon, which puts paid to the idea that this was entirely an English settlement. The fact that many of those who owed debts to Turner were described as gentlemen would suggest either that he was involved in the local sale of his broadcloth or that he was involved in money lending. If the latter, his business was on a small scale because his total outstanding debts amounted only to £322. A further snippet of evidence that suggests that Henry Turner was tied to the local world of commerce and manufacturing while participating also in international commerce comes to us from the deposition of John Langton, a gentleman of Bandonbridge (823, f. 51). In this, Langton revealed that he was jointly responsible with Henry Turner for the maintenance of a farm, held on a thirty-one year lease from 'the consistory of the diocese of Cork', for and on the behalf of 'Edmund, John, Margaret and Henry Rufin the children and orphans of Matthew Rufin, deceased'.

Such a moving proof of Turner's loyalty to his neighbours should not conceal the important role which he and other large-scale manufacturers played in drawing the series of artisan-based settler communities in west county Cork into a single regional economy through their trading activity. The function of drawing the several economic regions within the county and within the southern half of Ireland into a single unit was left to the great trading merchants of Kinsale and Youghal and to the lesser merchants and chapmen of these port towns and such inland towns as Mallow and Mitchelstown. Those whose depositions provide the most detailed information on this function were Thomas Turner of Youghal, merchant (824, f. 93), Tristram Whitcombe of Kinsale, merchant (822, ff 26-7), Jonas Clone of Youghal, merchant (824, f. 251), and Stephen Clove of Youghal, merchant (823, f. 58). Each of these drew a distinction between the 'disabled English Protestants' and the 'Irish rebels' who had been indebted to them. In the case of the former, the deponents merely listed their names, thus implying that those English people listed were close neighbours or residents of the same region as themselves. This list in the case of Thomas Turner, whose total debts were estimated by him at £693, extended to one hundred and fifty names.

Tristram Whitcombe, who estimated his debts as having been worth £3,986 17s. 10d., divided his English Protestant debtors into three categories: those who were 'debtors by speciality', 'debtors upon account' and 'debtors for certain goods'. He listed twenty-seven names under the first category, seventeen under the second, and he provided no names for the third, they being 'divers other poor people'. After this enumeration, he listed five names of 'impoverished papists and Irish' from Kinsale who were also 'debtors of account', and then a long list of Irish rebel debtors with addresses which extended throughout counties Cork, Limerick and Waterford. Whitcombe, as was noted previously, owned a fishing palace; he revealed in his deposition that he was the occupier of extensive farming lands with leases valued at £680; and he was also involved in the timber trade with losses of 'tuns of timber, cords of wood, and pipe staves' valued at £152 10*s*. His greatest business, however, must have been in money-lending, because only this would explain the huge sum that he claimed was owing to him at the outset of the insurrection.

The other merchant deponents we have identified appear to have been directly involved in trading, and the credit extended by them to retailers was probably in the form of consumer goods for which they would have been paid by these middlemen after sale. If such was the case, these merchant depositions would make it possible to trace a map suggesting the orbit of commercial influence of each Cork town for which depositions exist, and these depositions also identify many Irish people who were involved with trade in the towns of the southern half of Ireland. Jonas Clone, for instance, was owed money by 'Edmund Bryen of Clohine, County Tipperary, mercer; Hugh McCahir of Iland Co. Kerry, gent; Edmund Hackett of Waterford, merchant; Dennis O'Dwyer of Birr, King's County, mercer; John Cleer, city of Kilkenny, merchant; Nicholas Arthur of Cullen, County Limerick, merchant; Philip O'Breda of Mitchelstown, mercer; Richard Comerford and Richard Bourke of Callen, Co. Kilkenny, mercers; William Banfield and William Smith of Birr, merchants; Henry Hendley and Thomas Hendley of Downe, Co. Cork, gents; Hugh Rigley of Cloghbegg, Co. Longford, mercer; Henry Neale of the city of Waterford, merchant; Edward Comyn of Fethard, Co. Tipperary, chapman'. A second list by Clone (822, f. 310), which included all the above names, was more extensive and included further names of traders in Birr and Ballinvale, county Longford, as well as several in county Roscommon. The list devised by Thomas Turner of rebel traders who were in debt to him was concentrated on counties Cork, Limerick, Waterford and Tipperary and included the names of three 'English papists now notorious rebels', John and Anthony Rushell of Aglis, county Waterford and George Carter of Thurles, county Tipperary, who apparently had established themselves as traders in Ireland. Stephen Clove, the chapman from Youghal, was unable to provide a comprehensive list of his Irish rebel debtors because his 'bills and bonds' were kept in England, but those whose names he could recall were all in Birr, King's County. More helpfully Clove detailed the commodities in which he had been trading, these being 'six hundred weight of tobacco, linen yarn, linen cloth, wool and one pack of feathers'.

Other deponents, such as Jonas Clone, revealed how they maintained contact with the outside world, while still others explain how they developed an inland trade in Ireland. Jonas Clone mentioned that he and his partners had lost four hundred weight of tobacco and ninety- four barrels of salt as well as 'a quarter part' of the barque, the

William of Youghal, when that vessel was taken by pirates at Wexford. How the imported tobacco was marketed in Ireland is explained by the deposition of Symon Lightfoot (823, f. 24), who described himself as a blacksmith of Kinsale, but who was obviously a man of many parts because he claimed a loss of £12 for 'a horse laden with tobacco and one pair of scales and weights'. The development by Youghal of its remarkable network of influence is explained by the deposition of Richard Newman, carrier (822, f. 155), where he claimed the loss of 'ten pack horses with furnishings'; these, together with the packhorses of other carriers who did not make depositions, would have been used to convey imported goods, such as tobacco and salt, as far afield as Birr, Longford and Roscommon, in exchange for linen, wool and such other commodities of the countryside as would have attracted a market abroad.

Yeomen and husbandmen

The vast majority of the deponents from county Cork were associated strictly with the rural economy and the overwhelming majority of these described themselves as yeoman or husbandman. Most of these were involved in mixed agriculture with a balance in favour of either stock raising or tillage farming; the balance being determined presumably by the nature of the soil, the preference of the landlord, the previous experience of the farmers and the availability of markets. Ellias Cotterell, yeoman (825, f. 41), held a farm at Buttevant on an eighteen year lease from Thomas Betworth, Esq., and he had two other leases of farms in the same parish. Since Betworth was the only landlord mentioned by him, we can take it that it was Betworth who first established Cotterell in the locality. On these three farms Cotterell suffered a loss of £20 in cows and dry cattle; a loss in sheep to the value of £40; a horse valued at £3; and a loss in corn 'threshed and in stack' to the value of £20. Cotterell was therefore primarily a raiser of livestock, and the fact that he had expanded his activity to secondary farms meant that he lived well above subsistence level. Other yeomen, like Ralph Oliver of Whiddy Island (825, f. 28), were also involved in stock raising but were closer to the margins of subsistence because they held a lease of only one farm. Thomas Paddeson, a husbandman in the parish of Kilgarriff (822, f. 38), also had but one farm, but it must have been a large farm because he declared a loss of £46 10s. in corn in the haggard and house; a further loss of corn in the ground to the value of £18 and a loss in livestock to the value of £45 14s. Paddeson revealed something of his industry when he claimed a loss of £30 'expended upon near forty acres of land provided for next summer's tillage'. Peter Warner, a yeoman from the parish of Ballymartle, suffered a heavy loss, which he valued at £50, for the charges involved in 'building, ditching and improving'. He was primarily a livestock farmer but, in a passing reference to a loss of 'three horses laden with apples', Warner revealed that he was seeking to supplement his income from alternative agriculture. Sara Butler, a widow from the parish of Kilbrogan (825, f. 75), revealed that she was principally involved in stock raising, with a loss valued at £30 in livestock, and a loss of £14 for 'corn in the ground'. Then, almost as an afterthought, she added a claim of 11s. for losses in 'poultry and milk tubs', thus drawing attention to a supplementary income that may have fallen within the female domain and that would have been overlooked by most male deponents.

When the farmer deponents presented lists of people who were indebted to them, as for example Ellias Cotterell of Buttevant (825, f. 41), these came from the same locality as themselves and included 'Irish rebels' as well as 'British Protestant' debtors. Also when farmers bore testimony to murders or atrocities, as in the case of Peter Scus of Glanbarahan (823, f. 18), these usually related to incidents that had occurred close to their parish of residence. Most of these assaults and atrocities were attributed to Irish people resident within the same parish or from close by. There is also much evidence in the depositions that kinship networks had been established both as a consequence of natural increase among the settlers and because of intermarriage between settlers of roughly equal rank who resided within the same locality. Thomas Paddeson, a husbandman from the parish of Kilgarriff (822, f. 38), mentioned that 'his brothers and sisters, John Paddison, William Paddison, Robert Paddison and Eleanor Paddison, were stripped naked' by Teig O'Hea, a 'householder' of Kilgarriff and other rebels from parishes nearby. Then in the deposition of John Thomas, a tailor from the parish of Britway (822, f. 126), we learn that he owned a herd of cattle jointly with 'his uncle William Hussey, yeoman'.

Such references point to the confined world of the yeomen and husbandmen who, with their families, had settled in county Cork during the first half of the seventeenth century. The evidence also makes it clear, as in the case of the artisan communities, that we must think of Cork being settled by a series of settler farming communities that stretched across the full width of the county. There was, as we saw, considerable social interaction, including marriage, between farming and artisan families among the settlers; the farmers appear also to have established neighbourly relations with Irish people of similar social position who lived within the same locality. The extent of such interactions was, we might suppose, reliant on the density of settlement in any given area, with settler farmers who lived in relative isolation from other settlers being forced to establish closer contacts with Catholic neighbours. Not all Irish were Catholic, however, even at this rank, as we learn from the deposition of Thomas Butler of Tullyglass in the parish of Kilbrogan who described himself as husbandman and Irish Protestant (825, f. 10). Nor, for that matter, did one have to be English to be an improving tenant, as is again clear from the deposition of Thomas Butler, where mention was made of his investment 'in manuring, building and enclosing'.

Improving at this level was probably dictated by the landlord, and contact with the world outside the particular community was also probably made through the landlord. This is certainly suggested by those of the settlers who assumed the description 'gentleman' when making their depositions. Most who adopted the title gentleman, as also that of esquire, were middlemen who leased property from head landlords and who rented out part of what they held to yeomen and husbandmen. These, like Anthony Mansell of Ballyhustie in the barony of Duhallow (825, f. 133), were usually exemplary farmers with well-stocked and well-furnished home farms. Mansell was primarily involved in tillage farming, so he had working oxen as well as cows and young cattle, and had 'mares, horses, geldings, stone horses and colts' to the value of £70. His principal loss, valued at £190, was in grain both 'standing in rick' and 'corn on ground'; and he had also suffered a loss of 'waynes, harrows, yokes and chains'. As well as being skilled agriculturalists and informed improvers, the gentlemen among the settlers also held several parcels of land in several localities and sometimes by different tenures.

Tenurial practices

The sheer variety and complexity of the tenurial arrangements that could obtain can be witnessed in the deposition of Randall Warner of Kilcolman in the parish of Desertserges (825, f. 155). Warner held freehold land in Kilcolman where he had his residence and also in the townland of Cashilbeg in the neighbouring barony of Carbery. To this were added two leases in the townland of Deregragh which were good for fifteen and ten years respectively; two leases in the parish of Kinneigh for twelve years and one year; a lease in the parish of Murragh with one year unexpired and several other leases there valued at £180; a lease of several tenements in Enniskeen, parish of Kinneigh, and a twenty-five year lease of a quarter ploughland in Clonreage. To these properties, which were not far distant from Warner's residence, was added a lease of Lisekrimey in the barony of Ibawne 'having a tenure of the life of Lady Viscount Buttevant' at £28 profit per annum and after her decease a tenure of 100 years at £40 profit per annum.

The complexity and geographic extent of these tenurial provisions is one indicator of the widespread influence of these gentlemen deponents. Their influence was further underlined by the money which they had given on loan to a wide range of people, frequently, as in the case of Charles James of Britfield's town (825, f. 38), secured by 'mortgages, bills and bonds'. The influence of those who assumed the more elevated status of esquire was correspondingly greater, as in the case of William Groves of Caherduggan (825, f. 170), who held a parcel of land in county Kerry as well as his prime holding in north county Cork. These gentlemen also had contact with the wider world through military service. Giles Cooke, for example, (824, f. 115) was an exemplary tenant of the earl of Cork on 'his manor of Fermoy' and had been given a thirty-one year lease dated from 25 January 1635. He had also come into the possession of a lease of Ballymacpatrick in the barony of Condons and Clangibbon in return for a 'bond of £200' which he had given to Richard FitzDavid Condon. At the same time, however, he served as ensign to Captain James Finch and, in that capacity, would presumably have had responsibilities which would have brought him well beyond the bounds of county Cork.

Middle-ranking clergy would have enjoyed the same status as gentlemen and esquires and their sphere of influence would also have been regional or even provincial. Henry Rugg (824, f. 238), who enjoyed a prebendary in the diocese of Cloyne, itemised a list of leases in several baronies of county Cork which matched those of any gentleman and he also appears to have been heavily involved with sheep farming, having had a flock of 1,568 sheep and 500 lambs. Rugg also listed a wide range of people who were indebted to him, as did also Thomas Fryth, Archdeacon of Ross and justice of the peace for Cork and Kerry (825, f. 142). Fryth was a brother of the deceased John Fryth, gentleman of Cork, whose property he had inherited, and he claimed the loss of extensive properties and church livings throughout western county Cork and into county Kerry.

Above all these on the social scale were the head landowners whose political influence extended throughout the kingdom, and in a few instances to the kingdom of England. The principal of these was the earl of Cork but no deposition was returned for any of his several properties, although we do have returns from several of his tenants who seemed to take pride in mentioning that they held their leases from him. We also have depositions for two of the principal head landlords in the county, Sir Philip Perceval (824, f. 166) and Sir Warham St Leger, president of Munster (824, f. 112). Perceval, a senior official in the Dublin administration, was stated to have been absent in England by John Hodder from Churchtown, who deposed on his behalf. We can take it that Hodder was Perceval's agent, because Perceval was an absentee proprietor, and Hodder merely stated Perceval's loss in rental income as £2,587 a year, and his losses in livestock, cows, horses, mares and sheep worth £2,866. These figures correspond reasonably well with what we know of the Perceval property from the estate records,[14] and the size of Perceval's rental income is a clear indication of the level of his influence. The St Leger return was also made by agents, who declared him to have had an annual income of £1,786 from manors in the baronies of Orrery and Duhallow in county Cork, in the barony of Middle Third in county Tipperary and two manors in Queen's county. This extent of property, together with the level of income and office which he enjoyed, all point to the political stature that Sir William St Leger enjoyed both within the province and within the kingdom.

This account suggests that a clear hierarchy of landownership existed, and that those at the upper reaches of the pyramid provided unity and leadership to what was a diverse and dispersed rural settler community, in the same way that the principal merchants and manu-facturers drew together the artisans among the settlers. There is much evidence to suggest that the principal Protestant landowners and clergy in the county believed that they had a responsibility to do just that. Of the merchants, Tristram Whitcombe published two pamphlets in the years after 1642 to spur the Protestants in the county to greater effort to recover their position. The shrill and persistent exhortations to unity made by successive generations of social leaders from among the Protestant population in county Cork suggests that they feared that they would not succeed in their attempt to shape the settlers scattered over this broad county into a single community, guided by a common purpose and bonded by a shared religion.[15]

Irish landowners

The wide-ranging economic and social interest of what was a diverse settler population is one reason why bonding of the type favoured by the élite Protestants was so difficult to achieve. Another reason which emerges also from a close study of the depositions is that a great number of the Protestant settlers in the county, gentlemen as well as farmers and artisans, rented property from Irish rather than settler landowners and looked to these rather than to the settler élite as their natural leaders and protectors.

This development was not surprising on the property of such Irish landowners as the earl of Barrymore who had been raised in a Protestant environment from an early age by the earl of Cork and then married to one of Cork's daughters. We can take it that Barrymore was principally responsible for establishing a sizeable settler community at his seat at Castlelyons, of whom seventeen came forward to make depositions. Other Irish landowners who were committed to the Protestant interest, such as Tobias Welsh of Doneraile (825, f. 106), would presumably have been active recruiters of English settlers on their properties. Irish Catholic proprietors, for a variety of reasons, seem also to have settled foreign Protestants on their properties. Some apparently had no choice but to do so because they had run into financial difficulty and sought to resolve their problems by settling property on their creditors. Giles Cooke of Fermoy (824, f. 115), who was primarily a tenant of the earl of Cork, also held property from Richard FitzDavid Condon of Ballymacpatrick who, in exchange for a loan of £200, had given him a bond 'for the enjoying of a lease ... in the abovesaid barony of Condons'. A similar example was Walter Baldwin of Templemartin (823, ff 165-8) who held some freehold land and a variety of parcels leased from different landowners, including Dermot Mac Donnell Mc Fynen. This latter, as Baldwin stated it, was as security on a 'loan of £80' which Baldwin had extended to the Irishman.

Arrangements of this kind which derived from the financial need of Irish proprietors are not likely to have fostered any devotion among tenants for their landlords. Neither would those arrangements where foreign Protestants held leases of property from several Irish land-owners. John Strange of Doneraile, esq. (825, f. 253), had one lease for eight years from Teige McCurtain which reaped him £15 profit per annum; a second lease for eight years 'part of Cnogher Curten's land' which produced an annual profit of £10; and a third farm 'at Castleton', probably from Lord Roche who had his residence there, which produced an annual profit of £40. Strange, who was also sergeant-at-arms for the province of Munster, would presumably have had ready cash for the payment of entry fines, and it is likely this which made him an attractive tenant for the Irish landowners because only Cnogher Curten is mentioned as having been in debt to him. The lease which John Horsey, clerk, of Mitchelstown (824, f. 62) held from James Condon seems to have been independent of any outstanding debts, but it is likely to have been supplementary to the church lands which he would have enjoyed by virtue of his office. Agmondesham Muschamp of Carrigaline, esq. (823, f. 187), also enjoyed several leases including one for twelve years on 'part of Barry Oge's land', and another, also for twelve years, of a 'farm on the Lord of Muskerry's land'. However the combined annual profit of £76 from these two leases was but a fraction of the £254 annual income which came to him from land and is unlikely to have influenced his political outlook.

The situation was different for those Protestant gentlemen who held their primary lease from an Irish Catholic lord. One such was Isacke Filpott of the parish of Lislee (825, f. 307). He held an eight-year lease in the townland of Agha where he maintained livestock to the value of £482 10s. Filpott had proved himself an improving tenant and had built 'a good dwelling house' together with 'other out houses, paying but a grain of pepper yearly' for the same. His land, and the buildings which he had constructed on it, was apparently held from William Barry of Lislerin because Filpott left a substantial portion of his cattle in Barry's custody when the insurrection broke out. This resort to an Irish Catholic lord for protection at the moment of danger was not unusual for a settler in county Cork. Walter Baldwin of Templemartin (823, ff 165-8) who, as we saw, was wealthy in his own right and was renting property from several head landlords, sought protection from the Lord of Muskerry at the outset of the rebellion 'because of his former acquaintance with him'. Nor was this a sheer act of desperation because, as Baldwin testified, Lord Muskerry 'in this deponent's hearing seemed to be very zealous for the English party in his country and threatened to hang and prosecute those who disturbed them'. This zeal of Lord Muskerry's is, of course, not surprising because the rental income which British tenants paid to enterprising Irish Catholic landowners such as he would have been necessary to sustain his position. Besides that, British tenants filled vital functions for some Irish landowners. Benjamin Baxter, a husbandman from Kilbolane (822, f. 98) was, for instance, a gate porter in the castle of Sir William Power, and Anthony Hussie of Blarney (823, f. 66) was a 'park-keeper' to Lord Muskerry. The position of miller seems also to have been of critical importance to a Catholic landowner, as is suggested by the narration of Matthew Boultar (825, f. 27) who rented property from James Condon. That landlord approached Boultar as a candid friend at the outset of the rebellion and advised him as follows: 'Matthew turn back again to your home and farm and I will undertake your safety for that the Irish will be too strong for you'.

In the event, those Catholic landowners in county Cork who wished to provide protection for their British tenants were unable to do so, and some who initially remained loyal to the crown later became deeply involved in the insurrection. The circumstances that brought about this change of heart are a subject that requires special attention, but one aspect of that subject that comes to light from a close reading of the depositions for county Cork is the extent to which the British tenants of Irish Catholic landowners were the agents of their own destruction. It is already apparent from the evidence of Matthew Boultar that he drew the wrath of his landlord upon himself by seeking to abandon his position, thus depriving James Condon of his services as a miller and of his rent as a tenant. Looked at from Condon's point of view this was a breach of contract, and he seems to have striven to salvage something from the wreckage of his estate by distraining the goods of those British tenants who were deserting him in this fashion. We have evidence from the deposition of John Horsey, clerk (824, f. 62), who also held land from Condon, that he acted in this way and 'possessed himself of his said lease'. We then learn from the deposition of Andrew Lacy (824, f. 56) how this action of Condon's, which was designed to protect his own interest, involved him in open conflict with the representatives of the crown. This occurred when Lord Barrymore, in an effort to forestall Condon's actions, dispatched a troop of eleven musketeers and a sergeant 'to the town of Coole to thresh corn of Richard Peard of Coole and bring it to Castlelyons to prevent the Condon rebels from having it'. On the third day of the threshing the Condons intervened to prevent this incursion on their sphere of influence and the two groups came to blows. This resulted in the death of the ten troopers. In this action, we are told by Lacy, 'Richard Condon always struck upon them the first blow with his sword and then the rebels would fall upon them with their skeins and pikes till they were murdered'.

By thus piecing together the witness of several deponents we learn how one Irish landowner, in this case James Condon, moved from being a defender of his British tenants to being an upholder of his own interest, and finally to becoming a murderer and rebel, at least in the eyes of the crown authorities. This process was set in motion by his British tenants; we find evidence of a similar process from several other deponents but from none more graphically than Nicholas Blight, yeoman, of the parish of Rathway (822, f. 123). Blight had been a tenant of 'Teige O'Brien of Kilmecurry' and had lived in peace until 1 March 1642 when he learned that 'the rebel forces' were not far off from his farm. Then, 'fearing they should in their accustomed manner seize upon the deponents goods and persons', he moved with 'part of his said cattle for refuge towards Youghal', only to be overtaken by four or five armed men sent after him by his landlord. These 'in the king's highway towards Youghal violently and with force and arms did then and there take away this deponent's said cattle and carried them back again'. This action, which Blight interpreted as rebellious, would have been considered necessary by O'Brien to preserve his interest in a tenant who had entered into a contract with him.

These examples show that a careful use of the depositions would reveal as much of how the British settlement in county Cork was challenged and disturbed by the uprising of 1641-2 as it would of the constitution of that settlement before the onslaught of that year. A close study of the evidence would also reveal that the insurrection in Cork, as in other counties, assumed a different form in the several different regions of the county, and that these configurations were determined both by the character of the settlement that had taken place in the decades before 1641 as well as by external factors.[16] The external factor that exerted the most potent influence was the arrival in the northern sector of the county of an Irish Catholic army determined on the overthrow of the defensible positions that still remained under Protestant control. When this threatened, many Protestant settlers fled from the path of the oncoming army and took refuge in the fortified towns. Then ensued the sieges of such towns as Mallow, Mitchelstown and Newmarket, with the associated loss of life and destruction to property both within the towns and in the surrounding countryside. Detailed lists were provided by the deponents of those Protestants who were killed in these actions, but these 'murders' were attributed rather impersonally to Lord Mountgarret's army or to 'the forces of Donagh Mac Carty' (824, ff 48-9). Lists of the officers of these forces were sometimes provided, as they were by John Horsey, clerk of Mitchelstown (824, f. 62), but even then the deponents seem to have seen themselves as the luckless victims of a war which did not have its origin within their own community. Personal rancour seldom entered into these narrations other than when local Catholic notables were seen to have taken the part of the invading army. Such instances were carefully documented, as when Richard Gethings, a gentleman from Doneraile (822, f. 66), noted the presence in Mountgarret's army of John Roche of Ballenemonagh, gent, who 'took away the deponent's debt-boards and carried them to his said castle of Ballenemonagh'.

The second general configuration that the insurrection in county Cork assumed was when Irish Catholic gentlemen followed the example of the invading forces and raised private bands of their own, which engaged in raiding parties directed against the Protestant settlers over a wide area. Some of these gentlemen came from within the county, but more often they appear to have belonged to neighbouring baronies in counties Limerick, Kerry and Tipperary. Thus, for example, John Hodder (824, f. 166) was able to identify Edmund Fitzgerald, Gerald McEnery and Eddy Lacy, all of county Limerick, as those who took possession of the property of Sir Philip Perceval. Such statements could be used, as indeed they were by the courts of the 1650s, to construct lists of those Catholic gentlemen who took up arms during the early stages of the insurrection in county Cork.[17]

The third general pattern that can be identified in the insurrection, and that which evoked greatest bitterness from the deponents, was when they and their acquaintances were attacked by people from their own localities with whom they previously had cordial dealings. Some of these incidents, as we saw, were provoked by the precipitate action of the settlers; others occurred when settlers were attacked by neighbours who had fostered some grievance against them; and yet other incidents happened because greedy adventurers took advantage of the breakdown in authority to enrich themselves at the expense of everybody who was vulnerable.

Instances of the first kind of action have already been cited; examples of the other two kinds of assault can be found in the depositions for almost any given locality, and deponents also detailed the atrocities and indignities endured by them at the hands of their assailants. When combined, these various elements suggest a general onslaught of the Catholic population in the county upon the recent settlers. This may be the impression that the deponents wished to convey and it is generallly borne out by the evidence. However, there are occasional references which point to some degree of complexity in this popular insurgency. John Rowe, a yeoman from the parish of Mogeely (823, f. 84), complained that his cattle had been stolen by 'Anthony Scriviner an English Protestant living in the said parish', and Walter Baldwin (823, ff 165-8) complained bitterly of 'John Simons the Frenchman formerly living in Bandonbridge and formerly a professed Protestant and since this rebellion turned papist and brags oftentimes ... of killing and slaughtering the English and Protestants'. Then to further complicate matters, there are several references to the counsel offered by Irish Catholics to their Protestant neighbours on how they could save themselves from attack. Henry Tatardall, tanner (823, f. 141), for example, cited how Richard Welsh, broguemaker, was 'very earnest with this deponent and others to go to Mass, he said you would do well to do so for the king is here with us and is gone to Mass'.

Further questions

The true character of the revolt, like the true character of British settlement in the county, will be better understood when the depositions for each locality and region are studied and correlated. Such a microscopic analysis of the source would also shed some light on how the two populations in the county – natives and newcomers – interacted with each other during the decades of peace preceding the insurrection.

There are frequent references to clusters of Irish people who had conformed to the established Protestant church during the years of peace, only to revert to their original Catholicism when they were confronted by the insurrection; there are occasional references to individual Irishmen, such as John Gardiner of Ardfert (825, f. 142), who had taken up the Protestant ministry for material reward until the outbreak of the revolt and who would then have 'turned friar but the papists refuse to admit him because he is of so notorious evil and scandalous conversation'; and there are more frequent references in the depositions to Irish men and women who had become so steadfast in their Protestant beliefs that they suffered the persecution and death of a martyr rather than renounce them. Only a close study of the particular situations of these several people would explain their different responses to the reformation message, and such a study would also help explain why many of the settlers turned to Catholicism at the first onset of the revolt, while the majority were seemingly prepared to endure any privation rather than take such a step.

A close analysis of the source may also reveal something of the language which the two populations used to communicate with each other. Every mention of direct speech cited in this paper implies that natives and newcomers, whether they were gentlemen, artisans or husbandmen, spoke to each other in the English language, and several other passages of direct speech, dealing with such abstruse subjects as theology and political philosophy, seem also to have been enunciated in English by the insurgents. The consistency of this reportage suggests that the native population in county Cork were more proficient in the use of the English language then were their counterparts elsewhere in the country. This is not surprising when we take account of an ever-increasing government involvement in the county since the 1560s, and the intensive settlement that had been established there by the 1640s. What is surprising however, is the suggestion that the leaders of the insurrection in Cork spoke English even among themselves. This impression is conveyed by the several deponents who report conversations they had overheard while prisoners among the insurgents. Edward Harris of the parish of Kilshannig (825, f. 22) reported that 'he heard the said Callaghans discussing together about these troublesome times, he ... heard them severally say that they had his Majesty's commission for what they did or words to that effect'. This reference could be taken to mean that Harris knew Irish and was synopsising a conversation that he heard spoken in that language, but this interpretation seems hardly permissable in the absence of any specific references to the settlers in county Cork being able to comprehend or speak the Irish language, because we do have such references relating to settlers in other counties. There is however one reference that I have encountered, but among the deposition material from the 1650s, which makes it clear that some of the Irish population could communicate in English and Irish. The evidence in question came from George Gould of Kinsale (824, f. 9) who, at the time of presenting his testimony in the

1650s, declared himself to be aged thirty. He must have been about twenty therefore in 1642 when he travelled from his 'first winter quarters' in Kerry to Blarney 'to buy tobacco'. There he held conversation with the rebels who, he states, 'answered in Irish'. Gould would have been Old English rather than settler but his testimony implies that he spoke in English to the rebels while understanding their Irish responses, and that they spoke in Irish but comprehended his questions in English. What held true of an Old English resident of Kinsale may also have been true of a settler in the same town, which implies that the famous tobacco trading encounter described in *Pairlement Chloinne Tomáis* may have been closer to every-day experience in seventeenth-century Munster than has been allowed for.[18]

The fact that such critical questions can be raised about cultural encounters between natives and newcomers in county Cork is a measure of the importance of the depositions for the investigation of the social history of the county during the seventeenth century. The questions that have been addressed in the course of writing this paper are but some of those than can be partially resolved, and another historian working through the same material might raise a significantly different set of questions.

The answers supplied have been deliberately tentative because they are based on a superficial inspection of all the evidence for the county rather than on a close scrutiny of the depositions for any particular region. The chapter is thus intended to be an invitation to further research rather than a final statement; and the most important element is the Appendix (ss p. 281) which will make it possible for those who accept this invitation to proceed with their work of investigation with less effort than I had to expend on the task.

References

1. The tradition goes back at least to Irish Catholic historians of the eighteenth century but has been given a recent imprimatur in R. F. Foster, *Modern Ireland, 1600-1972* (London, 1988), pp 85-7 and in the review by K. Theodore Hoppen of that book in *I.H.S.*, xxvi (1989), pp 304-6. There is no evidence that either of these present-day historians has studied any of the depositions in the original.

2. W. Scribner, *Popular culture and popular movements in Reformation Germany* (London, 1988); R. Dupuy, *De la revolution à la chouannerie* (Paris, 1988); T. Bartlett (ed.), 'Defenders and defenderism in 1795' in *I.H.S.*, xxiv (1985), pp 373-394; F. X. Martin (ed.), *The Irish volunteers, 1913-1915* (Dublin, 1963).

3. M. Perceval Maxwell, 'The Ulster rising of 1641 and the depositions' in *I.H.S.*, xxi (1978), pp 144-167. See also W. Love, 'Civil war in Ireland' in *Emory University quarterly*, xxii (1966), pp 57-72.

4. A. Clarke, 'The 1641 depositions' in P. Fox (ed.), *Treasures of the library of Trinity College, Dublin* (Dublin, 1986), pp 111-122.

5.   P. Loupes, 'Le jardin Irlandais des supplices: la grande rébellion de 1641 vue à travers les pamphlets anglais' in L. Bergeron and L. Cullen (ed.), *Culture et pratiques politiques en France et en Irlande, XVIè-XVIIIè siècles* (Paris, 1991), pp 41-61.

6.   This general line of argument was originally put forward in N. Canny, 'Migration and opportunity: Britain, Ireland and the new world' in *Ir. Econ. Soc. Hist. Jn.,* xii (1985), pp 7-32. The contention that Munster attracted a higher calibre of settler than Ulster became the subject of a debate between Canny and R. Gillespie in *Ir. Econ. Soc. Hist. Jn.,* xiii (1986), pp 90-99 and a slightly modified version of the original statement has been published in N. Canny, *Kingdom and colony: Ireland in the Atlantic world, 1560-1800* (Baltimore, Md., 1988), pp 69-102. M. Perceval-Maxwell has also come to the support of the Gillespie position in *Ir. Econ. Soc. Hist.,* xiv (1987), pp 59-61. Neither Gillespie nor Perceval-Maxwell has confronted the evidence from Munster and this presentation of the material for one county of that province justifies a restatement of the original proposition, now sustained by copious reference to the evidence from county Cork.

7.   If 5,500 names of Protestant settlers can be extrapolated from the statements of the 904 documents (and 5,500 is a conservative estimate), this suggests a total number within the families of those 5,500 individuals of 9,125 people. This figure is arrived at by dividing the 5,500, mostly adult male, names by 3.14 to get an idea of the number of settler families present, and multiplying the product by 5.21 to convert the estimated number of families into an estimated number of people. This is the conversion procedure employed by R. Gillespie, *Colonial Ulster: the settlement of east Ulster, 1600-1641* (Cork, 1985), p. 55. This, it should be said, is a very conservative procedure, since most names among the 5,500 seem to have been heads of households.

8.   D. B. Quinn, 'The Munster plantation: problem and opportunities' in *Cork Hist. Soc. Jn.,* lxxi (1966), pp 19-40; D. B. Quinn, *Raleigh and the British empire* (London, 1973), pp 103-124; N. Canny, 'The Irish background to Penn's experiment' in R. S. Dunn and M. M. Dunn (ed.), *The world of William Penn* (Philadelphia, 1986), pp 139-156; Canny, 'Migration and opportunity'; Canny, *Kingdom and colony*, pp 69-102; N. Canny, 'The marginal kingdom: Ireland as a problem in the first British empire" in B. Bailyn and P. D. Morgan (ed.), *Strangers within the realm: cultural margins of the first British empire* (Chapel Hill, N.C., 1991), pp 35-66; McCarthy-Morrogh, *Plantation*; M. Mac Carthy-Morrogh, 'The English presence in early seventeenth century Munster' in Brady and Gillespie, *Natives and newcomers,* pp 171-190; M. Mac Carthy-Morrogh, 'Credit and remittance: monetary problems in early seventeenth-century Munster' in *Ir. Econ. Soc. Hist. Jn.,* xiv (1987), pp 6-19.

9.   Little fault attaches to Dr MacCarthy-Morrogh for his misunderstanding because historians of England and Scotland, as also historians of Ireland, devote scant attention to the rich and rewarding literature on the developing British Atlantic world of the seventeenth century. An especially good recent example which draws attention to the 'English' character of one area of settlement in America is L. Green Carr, P. D. Morgan and J. B. Russö (ed.), *Colonial Chesapeake society* (Chapel Hill, N.C., 1988).

10. MacCarthy-Morrogh, *Plantation,* p. 219.

11. MacCarthy-Morrogh, 'The English presence in ... Munster'; D. Woodward, 'The Anglo-Irish livestock trade of the seventeenth century' in *I.H.S.,* xviii (1973), pp 489-523; B.L., MS Royal 17 A, xxxvii, f. 11v, where reference is made to cattle 'even from Ireland' being grazed on Sedgmoor, Somerset, during the early

seventeenth century. I owe this latter reference to Dr Joan Thirsk. The reference to the conveyance of deer is among the Lismore papers at Chatsworth.

12. The method of tracing places of origin by surname sampling has been used for Scottish migration to Ulster in Gillespie, *Colonial Ulster*. This method is much less reliable for tracing English migration patterns. On Springfield and Marblehead see S. Innes, *Labor in a new land: economy and society in seventeenth-century Springfield* (Princeton, N.J., 1983); C. Heyrman, *Commerce and culture, the maritime communities of colonial Massachusetts, 1690-1750* (New York, 1984), especially pp 207-230. My misgivings on this issue have been upheld by Dr Joan Thirsk and Dr Todd Gray who have kindly read and commented on this paper. Dr Thirsk confirms my opinion that the Cork settlers come from many different parts of England, and Dr Gray feels certain that hardly any came from Cornwall.

13. The establishment of English and Dutch settlements in county Clare has been detailed in C. D. Ó Murchadha, 'Land and society in seventeenth-century Clare', unpublished Ph.D. thesis, University College, Galway (1982).

14. B.L., Add. MS 47,036 ff.

15. T. Whitcombe, *The truest intelligence from the province of Munster* (London, 1642); idem, *A sad relation of the miseries of the province of Munster* (London, 1645). On the exhortations of Protestant clergy in Munster during the early seventeenth century see A. Ford, *The Protestant reformation in Ireland 1590-1641* (Frankfurt am Main, 1985), pp 98-122, 193-242; for secular Protestant exhortations at the same time see N. Canny 'Identity formation in Ireland: the emergence of the Anglo-Irish' in N. Canny and A. Padgen (ed.), *Colonial identity in the Atlantic world, 1500-1800* (Princeton, 1987), pp 159-212, especially pp 164-180. For the later seventeenth century with a decided emphasis on Munster, see T. C. Barnard, 'Crisis of identity among Irish Protestants, 1641-1685' in *Past & Present*, cxxvi (May 1990), pp 39-83.

16. For a more general portrayal of the pattern of revolt based on a close reading of the depositions from other counties see N. Canny, 'In defence of the constitution: the nature of Irish revolt in the seventeenth century' in *Culture et pratiques politiques*, pp 23-40, Canny, 'The marginal kingdom'.

17. For a list compiled in the seventeenth century see K. Whelan, 'A list of those from county Wexford implicated in the 1641 rebellion' in *The Past*, xvii (1990), pp 24-53. This list, as Dr Whelan makes clear, was compiled for court use in 1642 but it is likely to have been drawn from depositions testimony. It is not accurate to describe such lists as a '"Who's Who" of Catholic Ireland' in the mid-seventeenth century because not all Catholics proprietors took up arms.

18. N. J. A. Williams (ed.), *Pairlement Chloinne Tomáis* (Dublin, 1981), pp 39-41.

Appendix

Roll of deponents

Parish numbers refer to figure 8.1. Localisation of deponents by parish. Here individual parishes are indicated by a number and the total number of deponents by a proportionate circle.

1. *Parish Abbeymahon, Barony Ibane*
   824.209   John Arthur, brother-in-law to Harry Sampson of Abbeymahon, yeoman.

2. *Parish Aghabulloge, Barony Muskerry*
823.205   Thomas Hurr of Dromtymon [Dromatimore], n.s.g.
823.218   John Oldis of Drumtymore [Dromatimore], n.s.g.
824.42   John Radcliffe of Caherow [Caherbaroul], gent.
824.212   Richard Boyle of Corrune [?], clerk.
825.55   Ellin Godson of Carkoo [?], wife.
825.115   Anthony Pullbanke of the Lecconeene [Lackaneen], n.s.g.
825.180   Robert Olders of Druntymore [Dromatimore], on behalf of Mary Gill, widow.
825.185   Robert Olders of Carhooe [Caherbaroul], yeoman.
825.269   Giles Denham of Lackanurie [Lacknahaghny], n.s.g.

3. *Parish Aghadown, Barony West Carbery*
825.15-16   Richard White of Inishbegneclery [Inishbeg], gent.

4. *Parish Aghern, Barony Kinnataloon*
822.58   Captain James Finch of Bally McKeoman [Ballymacsimon], parish Iragherne [Aghern], esq.
825.58   Robert Flower, town and parish of Ahan [Aghern], n.s.g.
825.311   Thomas More, town and parish of Agharren [Aghern], gent.

5. *Parish Aghinagh, Barony East Muskerry*
822.269   George Bostock of Carga Drowhett [Carrigadrohid], gent., ensign.
823.176   Thomas Burton of Gurtine Carrune [?], parish Agheny [Aghinagh], n.s.g.

6. *Parish Aglish, Barony East Muskerry*
822.36   Grace Jakman, Aglis [Aglish], widow.
822.73   Henry Mills of Fargus [Fergus], n.s.g.
822.77   Philip Tancocks of Curnady [Cronody], barony Barretts [?], n.s.g.
823.86   John Hathway, town and parish of Agly [Aglish], yeoman.
823.202   George Winsmore of Curnady [Cronody], n.s.g.
824.213   Thomas Nealde of Cornedie [Cronody], timberman.
825.56   Anthony Godson of Aglis, n.s.g.
825.83   Thomas Godson, n.s.g.
825.286   Morgan Mundyn of Kilnadoney [?], parish Aglis, Barony Barretts [?], minister.

7. *Parish Aglishdrinagh, Barony Orrery and Kilmore*
824.86   Nicholas Muncton of Ballindredin [Ballynadridren], gent.

8. *Parish Ardagh, Barony Imokilly*
823.119   Henry Bennit of Ballilega [Ballyneague], parish Ardagh, n.s.g.
823.133   William Lewellin of Courneveigh [Cornaveigh], gent.

9. *Parish Ardnageehy, Barony Barrymore*
822.61   Christopher Steevenson of Glanfrehan [?], parish Ardnagee [Ardnageehy], yeoman.
825.225   John Strort of Kilmartin [?], parish Ardnegreth [Ardnageehy], gent.

10. *Parish Ardskeagh, Barony Fermoy*
822.226   Robert Austen, yeoman.

822.227   Robert Austen, yeoman, on behalf of Edward Austen the younger, n.s.g.

11. *Parish Athnowen, Barony East Muskerry*
     (This incorporates the parish of Ovens)
     822.71   George Barkley of Knocknamore [Knockanemore], parish Ovens, n.s.g. (probably gent.)
     822.182   John Barkley of Maghernes [?], parish Ovens, barony Barretts [?], n.s.g.
     822.255   Robert Burden the younger of Grange, parish Ovens, n.s.g.
     823.48   William Dowe of Barnegore [Barnagore], parish Ovens, n.s.g.
     823.182   Elizabeth Shore and Ellen Burder of Sarsfield's Grange [?], [Grange], parish Ovens, n.s.g.
     823.199   Stephen Gaynes of Maghery [?], parish Ovens, yeoman.
     824.159   John Newton of Athnowen, clerk.
     825.98   William Barkley of Mullaghroe, parish Ovens, n.s.g.
     825.147   Robert Burdon, Sarsfield's Grange [?], [Grange], parish Ovens, n.s.g.

12. *Parish Ballinadee, Barony East Carbery*
     823.120-1 Edward Rashly of Cloncomise [Cloncouse], gent.
     823.144   Hilkiagh Hussey, clerk.
     824.71   John Fleming of Kilmacsymon [Kilmacsimon], gent.
     824.172   John Martin of Corrowry [?], yeoman.

13. *Parish Ballyclogh, Baronies Duhallow and Orrery*
     822.154   William Ind of Gortbofinnigh [Gortbofinna], yeoman.
     823.35   John Sampson of Gornegrasse [Gortnagross], yeoman.
     823.45   Edward Mitchel, town and parish of Ballyclogh, husbandman.
     823.125   William Morley of Dromcostell [Dromrastill], tanner.
     824.152   Edmund Cock, miller.
     824.261-4 Nicholas Philpot, esq.
     825.3   Roger Lorymer, Dramdoney, gent.
     825.65   Robert Treegose of Gortnegrosse [Gortnagross], yeoman.
     825.161   Edward Michell, Ballylogh [Ballyclogh], husbandman.

14. *Parish Ballyfeard, Barony Kinalea*
     825.196   Henry Cooke of Ballingarry, gent.

15. *Parish Ballyfoyle, Barony Kinalea*
     825.11   Edward Beecher, Ballefoyle [Ballyfoyle], gent.
     825.38   Charles James of Britfieldstown, gent.

16. *Parish Ballyhay, Barony Fermoy*
     822.2   William Gowers, yeoman.
     823.41-2   Robert Meade of Broghill, esq.
     823.209   Digorye Trix of Ballyhay, mercer.
     824.233
     and 241   Thomas Parsons of Kilcolman [?], husbandman.
     825.28   James Baldwins of Ballyhay, clothier.
     825.277   William Bird of Ballyhay, gent.

17. *Parish Ballyhooly, Barony Fermoy*
    823.184   Percival Gibson of Ballyhowly [Ballyhooly], gent.

18. *Parish Ballymartle, Barony Kinalea*
    822.200   William Dangell of Carbecarron [?], yeoman.
    823.97   Peter Warner of Ballymaholas [?], [Ballynalouhy], parish Ballymac-daniel [?], [Ballymartle], yeoman.
    823.123   Edward Reney, town and parish of Ballymartle, yeoman.
    824.216   William Mead of Balintubridg [Ballintober], esq.
    825.74   Thomas Hichions, town and parish of Ballymartle, husbandman.
    825.149   Elizabeth Cleyes, wife to Richard Cleyes of Donnemus [?], [Dooneen], parish Ballymacdaniel [?], [Ballymartle], hewer.
    825.197   George Jolly of Ballynicholas parish [?], Ballymitchell [Ballymartle], yeoman.

19. *Parishes Ballymodan and Kilbrogan, Barony Kinalmeaky*
    822.8   John Woodroffe, provost of Bandon.
    822.45   William James of Kilbrogan, yeoman.
    822.46   John Abbott of Knock [?], yeoman.
    822.62   Amy Taylor, town and parish Ballymodan, widow.
    822.80   Robert Bathurst of Bandon, hatter.
    822.86   Richard Abbott, Tullyglass, parish Kilbrogan, yeoman.
    822.162   George Fenton of Bandon, merchant.
    822.172   Andrew Woodly of Bandonbridge, gent.
    822.198   Thomas Franklin of Bandon, butcher.
    822.206   George Wright of Derrygarriff [Derrycoole], parish Kilbrogan, gent.
    822.211   William Cary of Conckeyarran [Knocknagarrane], parish Ballymodan, yeoman.
    822.219   Richard Webb of Killybeg [Kilbeg], parish Kilbrogan, yeoman.
    822.258   Susanna Forde of Gaggan, Ballymodan, spinster, on behalf of Mary Forde, widow.
    822.263   James Elwell of Bandonbridge, yeoman.
    822.265   John Newman, on behalf of Elizabeth Newman Gagin [Gaggan], parish Ballymodan, widow.
    822.267   Amy Maskline of Callethram [Callatrim], parish Kilbrogan, widow.
    822.287   William Dun, parish Ballymodan, yeoman.
    823.51   John Langton of Bandon, parish Kilbrogan, gent.
    823.111   Samuel Poole of Knocknameela [Knockaveale] parish Ballymodan, leather tanner.
    823.129   William Sellach of Gagin [Gaggan], parish, Ballymodan, tanner.
    824.33   Thomas Fuller of Ballemoodan [Ballymodan], yeoman.
    824.38   Samuel Sanders of Derrycool [Derrycoole], yeoman.
    824.48-9   Henry Boswell *alias* Bosville of Cooltra [Callatrim], gent.
    824.50   Ann Gates *alias* Barber of the bog, widow.
    824.54   Emmet Draper of Ballymodan, widow of yeoman.
    824.85   John Snary of Bandonbridge, clerk, rector of Kilbrogan.
    824.118/9   Henry Turner of Bandonbridge, clothier.
    824.168   Francis Bernard of Mussells [Mishells], yeoman.
    824.170   Anne Hasell, widow and Joyce Deane, servant town of Bandon.
    824.194   Christopher Trenaman of the Shennagh [Shinagh], n.s.g.
    824.201   Anne Williams of Larragh [Laragh], wife to Robert Williams, butcher.

824.210	Frances Gillett of Kilgobban [?], parish Ballymodan, husbandman.
824.242	John Landen of Bandon, merchant.
825.10	Thomas Butler of Tullaghglass [Tullyglass], parish Kilbrogan, husbandman, Irish Protestant.
825.36	James Maye of Bandonbridge, n.s.g.
825.62	Anthony Shipward or Sheepheard of Bandon, clothier.
825.66	John and Francis Bemish, town of Bandon, yeomen.
825.75	Sara Butler of Malligatto [Mallowgatton], parish Kilbrogan, widow.
825.81	Ralph Fuller of Derrygariffe, parish Kilbrogan, yeoman.
825.82	Charles Nicholet, town of Bandon, clerk.
825.90	Benedict Ford of Bandon, husbandman.
825.96	Arthur Burchell of Knockmeda [Knockaveale], parish Ballymodan, yeoman.
825.108	Marie Congdon, wife of Robert Congdon, yeoman.
825.128	William Bull of Kilbrogan, hellier [haulier].
825.130	Thomas Lowe of Derrycoole parish Kilbrogan, yeoman.
825.144	William Heynes or Haindes of Bandon, shoemaker.
825.150	Daniel Howard of Bandonbridge, gent.
825.151	Mary Berry, relict of Richard Berry of Gaggan, parish Ballymodan, widow.
825.176	John Collins of Clancoole Begg [Clancool Beg], parish Ballymodan, yeoman.
825.181	Thomas French the younger of Collytran [Collatrim], parish Kilbrogan, yeoman.
825.201	Thomas Standon of Colfada [?], [Colfada], parish Kilbrogan, yeoman.
825.203	Richard Bemish of West Gullath [Gully], parish Ballymodan, yeoman.
825.204	George Dugney of Ballemodan [Ballymodan], carrier.
825.210	Mathew Johnson of Kilbrogan, husbandman.
825.223	Anne Cox of Messels [Mishells], parish Kilbrogan, widow.
825.231	Thomas Rogin of Hurtin [?], parish Kilbrogan, wheeler.
825.239	Francis Sunester, Curren [Carhoon], parish Kilbrogan, yeoman.
825.250	Richard Hulin of Gortine [Gurteen], parish Kilbrogan, yeoman.
825.281	Samuel Burchell of Ballemodan [Ballymodan], yeoman.
825.290	John Lissen of Messels [Mishells], parish Kilbrogan, yeoman.
825.291	John Harrott of Shonagh [Shinagh], parish Kilbrogan, yeoman.
825.302	Mabel Waterman, wife to Jacob Waterman of Currie Cloth [Corravreeda], n.s.g.

20. *Parish Ballymoney, Barony East Carbery*

823.107	Robert Coate of Shanoways [Shanaway], yeoman.
823.145	Katherine Cotes of Shanoways [Shanaway], widow of Robert, yeoman.
823.197	John Fripps of Shanoway [Shanaway], husbandman.
824.31	William Warren, yeoman.
825.189	Margaret Brothers of West Derrigeagh [West Derrigra], widow.

21. *Parish Ballynoe, Barony Kinnatalloon*

822.72	John Pardner, yeoman.
823.54	Thomas Vezy of Clanreagh [Glenreagh], husbandman.
824.95	William Vesey, Gleanreagh [Glenreagh], husbandman.

22. *Parish Ballyoughtera, Barony Imokilly*
    822.74   Robert Blake of Dromaddamore, yeoman.
    824.90   Lieutenant William Cade of Kilmurry [?], [Killurrigal], parish Balliethor
               [Ballyoughtera]; his mother Izabella Cade, of Glannageare
               [Glennageare], widow.

23. *Parish Bregoge, Barony Orrery and Kilmore*
    822.74   Giles Bustead of Tullagh [Tullig], n.s.g. (probably gent.).
    822.88   John Runnig, yeoman.
    822.92   John Runnig for and on behalf of William Damier, gent.
    824.147   John Henton of Bregoge, shepherd.
    825.295   John Rany of Bregoge, yeoman.

24. *Parish Brigown, Barony Condons and Clangibbon (includes Mitchelstown)*
    822.13   Ann Blissett, widow.
    822.128   Thomas Mansell, gent.
    822.191   William Adams and John Grute on behalf of Jacob Blackwell, gent.
    823.36   Hugh Bunckar of Briggowne [Brigown], parish Mitchelstown,
               husbandman.
    823.71   Robert Hogbin, town and parish Mitchelstown, shoemaker.
    823.83   Ann Ormon, spinster.
    823.149   Henry Halbord, shoemaker.
    823.180   William Field, gardener.
    824.25   William Harding, gent.
    824.62   John Horsey of Cooleregan [Coolyregan], clerk.
    824.108   John Horsey of Coolregan [Coolyregan].
    824.149   William Damer, tailor.
    824.153   Alexander Cashell, yeoman.
    825.5   Elizabeth Bastar, n.s.g.
    825.27   Matthew Boultar of Curragheruman [Curraghmere], parish Bregan
               [Brigown], miller.
    825.45-6   Stephen Towse, merchant.
    825.68   William Adams of Cargane [Carrigane], husbandman.
    825.135   John Stichson, husbandman.
    825.136   John Gulliams, miller.
    825.137   Thomas Coollman the elder, carpenter.
    825.138   John Pope of Mitchelstown, tailor.
    825.139   Julian Blissett, widow, Irish Protestant.
    825.140   Ann Perry widow of Edward Pierry, clerk.
    825.285   William Raymond, malster.
    825.287   John Grutes of Garrane [?], parish Mitchelstown, husbandman.

25. *Parish Brinny, Barony Kinalmeaky*
    822.247   Mary Lee of Finagh [Finnis], widow.
    825.255   Tristram Hake of Kilpatrick, parish Breny [Brinny], yeoman.
    825.258   Robert Christman of Kilpatrick, yeoman.
    825.280   Philip White, town and parish Breny [Brinny], fuller.

26. *Parish Britway, Barony Barrymore*
    822.123   Nicholas Blight of Coolekaedane [Coolkinedane], yeoman.
    822.126   John Thomas of Coolnedane [Coolkinedane], tailor.

27. *Parish Buttevant, Barony Orrery and Kilmore*
   822.207   Owen McSwiney, Irish Protestant, n.s.g.
   822.220   Phillip Farneham, Ballyvolane [?], yeoman.
   825.41   Ellias Cotterell, yeoman.
   825.51   William Kingsmill of Ballybegg [Ballybeg], squire.
   825.141   Robert Robinson of Roaclogh [Rathclare], yeoman.

28. *Parish Caherduggan, Barony Fermoy*
   822.275   John Brice, tailor.
   825.170   William Groves of Cardowgan [Caherduggan], esq.
   825.208   Roger Kennedy, yeoman, Irish Protestant.
   825.289   Richard Lane of Croighykery [Curraghakerry], parish Kilfada [?], barony Fermoy, yeoman.

29. *Parish Carrigaline, Barony Cork*
   822.51   Richard Hayes of Kinyglery [Kilnaglery] on behalf of his brother-in-law William Best, n.s.g.
   822.76   William Hoade of Aghmartin [?], Barony Kinalmeaky [?], n.s.g. (probably gent.).
   822.186   John Richard of Killowen [?], parish Carigolane, Barony Muskerry [?], n.s.g.
   822.237   Nathaniel Peade, parish Cargylion [Carrigaline], n.s.g.
   822.252   William Daunt, gent.
   823.65   William Daunt, n.s.g.
   823.187   Agmondesham Muschamp of Ballinre [Ballinrea], esq.
   824.43   Robert Beckett, clerk.
   824.199   Edward Jefford of Ballinbuisigg [Ballinvarosig], n.s.g.
   825.59   Richard Heyes of Cargylion [Carrigaline], n.s.g.
   825.103   Ellen Bigg of Cargylion [Carrigaline], widow.
   825.232   William Green of Ballinemela [Ballinimlagh], parish Cargyline [Carrigaline], n.s.g.

30. *Parish Carrigleamleary, Barony Fermoy*
   822.31   John Polard, Cargamalira [?], [Carrigleamleary], n.s.g.
   823.31   Roger Gill of Kilconaway [Kilcanway], gent.
   823.44   Edward Gill, town and parish of Carrigleamleary, n.s.g.
   823.126   Ann Atway, widow.
   825.153   Charles Hargill of Cargymalery [Carrigleamleary], esq.
   825.257   Elis Cullinan, gent.

31. *Parish Carrigrohane, Baronies Cork and East Muskerry*
   822.236   Thomas Hak of Cooleroogh, parish Coregrohane [Carrigrohane], county of the city of Cork, n.s.g.
   822.284   Hugh Burrowes, parish of Carrigrohane in the county of the city of Cork, n.s.g.
   823.159   John McEdmond of Carrigleamleary, Irish Protestant, servant to Mr. John Love.
   823.159   Abraham Ashton, n.s.g.
   823.160   Henry Bargery, n.s.g.
   823.183   Abrame Ashton, yeoman.
   823.191   John Love, n.s.g.

824.141   Richard Hoop, n.s.g.

825.85   Edward Rubie, yeoman.

825.86   James Martin, yeoman.

825.91   Henry Gilman, n.s.g.

825.118   Henry Rooby, tanner.

825.272   Richard Knowles of Killegroghan [?], [Carrigrohane], Cork city, n.s.g.

32.   *Parish Carrigrohanebeg, Barony East Muskerry*

822.175   William Howard of Lackintoine [Lackenshoneen], parish Killigroghan-Beg [Carrigrohane Beg], n.s.g.

822.245   John Oldis, gent.

823.57   Christopher Hewdon, parish Killogrohan Begg [Carrigrohanebleg], barony Barretts [?], n.s.g.

825.237   Thomas Somersett of Dromsmore, [Dromasmole], parish Killgrohan Begg [Carrigrohanebeg], Barony Muskerry, n.s.g.

825.265   Donogh Fenan of Inishtony [?], yeoman, Irish Protestant.

33.   *Parish Carrigtohill, Barony Barrymore*

822.67   Augustine Kingsmill of Barryscourt, clerk.

34.   *Parish Castlehaven, Barony West Carbery*

823.1   Thomas Doggin, yeoman.

824.100   John Stukly, clerk.

825.184   Daniel Poole of Smoorane [Smorane], yeoman.

35.   *Parish Castlelyons, Baronies Barrymore and Condons and Clangibbon*

822.202   Hugh Ellott of Ballyoran [Ballyarra], parish Cassillion [Castlelyons], glover.

822.222   Richard Vowell of Glanorooferm [Glenarousky], yeoman.

822.225   Joan O Colleman, wife to Teige O Colleman, Irish Protestant, yeoman.

822.232   Richard Seller of Kilmecurry [Kilcor], yeoman.

822.233   Sara Tucker, wife to William Tucker, yeoman.

822.240   Michael Rowe of Kilmecurry [Kilcor], yeoman.

823.12   Eliner Wright of Ballyora [Ballyarra], widow.

823.17   Mary Smith, town and parish of Castlelyons, widow.

823.39   Mary Payne of Kilbarry, widow.

824.40   John Petters of Ballinatty [?], miller.

824.56   Andrew Lacy, town and parish Castlelyons.

824.59   Frances Osborne, wife to Henry Osborne of Carbertrey [Currabeha].

824.117   William Numan of Glanderoust [Glennrousk], yeoman.

824.244   Elizabeth Ennington for husband William Ennington, n.s.g.

825.54   Henry Kennet of Ballynorea [Ballyarra], yeoman.

825.271   Thomas Witherdon of Ballyoran [?], [Ballyarra], yeoman.

825.308   John Mark of Corbeth [Currabeha], yeoman.

36.   *Parish Castlemagner, Barony Duhallow*

822.150   Robert Hayle of Ballytobber [Ballintobber], husbandman.

822.151   Christina Wiseman, on behalf of sick husband, n.s.g.

822.254   Swithin Noble, yeoman.

823.124   Richard Gould, town of Castlemacnoe [Castlemagner], carpenter.

825.1   Richard Sollace of Kilbritt [?], gent.

825.8	Patrick Cryne, clerk.
825.95	Thomas Righton of Ballygibbin [Ballygiblin], n.s.g.
825.274	Jane Weekes of Ballintobber, widow.

37. *Parish Churchtown, Barony Orrery and Kilmore (cited parish Bruheny)*

822.87	William Young of Carrigene [Carrigeen], yeoman.
822.101	Francis Percivall of Moggan [?], gent.
822.215	Edmund Stripps of Cregin Court [Cregganacourty], yeoman.
822.246	James Button of Ballymachugh [?], parish Brookeny [?], yeoman.
823.28	William Holyday, clerk.
823.64	Anthony Wiseman of Ballinvalligh [Ballybahallagh], yeoman.
824.41	John Hodder of Ballymaccowe [?], esq., on behalf of Barth Atterton, esq.
824.166	John Hodder, esq., on behalf of Sir Philip Percival.
824.191	Richard Bowley of Kilgrogan [?], yeoman.
825.71	Edmond Martin of Welchestown [Walshestown], husbandman.
825.72	William Holyday, clerk.
825.74	Edward Holland of Greggan Courty [Cregganacourty], cooper.
825.116	John Gingell of Mogane [?], parish Brooheny, yeoman.
825.125	Thomas Murroe of Ballyvallis [Ballybahallagh], parish Ballytemple [?], carpenter.
825.168	Henry Wiseman of Mogan [?], parish Brewheny, yeoman.

38. *Parish Clenor, Barony Fermoy.*

822.4	John Latchford of Killuragh, parish Clanur [Clenor], yeoman.
823.113	Walter Gill of Ballinard [?], parish Cleanore [Clenor], gent.

39. *Parish Clondrohid, Barony Muskerry*

825.109	Elizabeth Allen, wife to William Allen, clerk, of Gratrixtown [?].
825.127	Richard Croker of Clondrohatt [Clondrohid], gent.
825.270	Richard Barnes of Carrigfooky [Carrigaphooca], n.s.g.

40. *Parish Clondulane, Barony Condons and Clangibbon*

822.33	Robert Gosse of Cargibrick [Carrigbrick], miller.
822.102	George Pooke of Ballinreess [?], husbandman.
822.147	Grace Strevett of Garrymore [Garrynoe].
823.8	Haniball Horsey of Cargybrick [Carrigabrick], gent.
823.85	John Prattat of Shanecloghir [Shanacloon], husbandman.
824.160	Henry Arnold, parish Clandelane [Clondulane], n.s.g.
824.184	John Sims of Cargybuck [Carrigabrick], carpenter.
825.158	Edward Hitchins Cargybrick [Carrigabrick], weaver.
825.226	Richard Phillips of Carybrick [Carrigabrick], yeoman.
825.249	William Merets, gent.

41. *Parish Clonfert, Barony Duhallow (includes towns of Kanturk and Newmarket)*

822.1	Thomas Percivall of Ballylaghan [?], parish Newmarket, husbandman.
822.7	William Coker, Newmarket town, carpenter.
822.9	Mary Meades, of Rossecon [Rossacon], parish Newmarket, widow.
822.17	William Ullin of Newmarket, yeoman.
822.22	Ralph Steers of Newmarket, blacksmith.
822.41	John Richman the elder, Newmarket, husbandman.

822.48	William Hoder of Glanturk [Kanturk], tanner.
822.52	James Ford of Glanturk [Kanturk], n.s.g.
822.99	Robert Keirby, town of Newmarket, husbandman.
822.117	Thomas Haynes of Duragill [Duarrigle], carpenter.
822.259	Kathleen Wall, Newmarket, parish Clonfarta [Clonfert], widow.
823.25	Richard Gafley of Chane Parky [Park], parish Newmarket, tanner.
823.73	Mary Parker of Newmarket, widow.
823.155	John Warren of Newmarket, parish Clonfadda [Clonfert], tanner.
824.67	Thomas Grant of Newmarket, shoemaker.
824.68	George Tanner of Newmarket, baker.
824.177	Alice Bretrish of Newmarket, widow.
824.179	John Ellis of Newmarket.
824.217	Katherine Stackbird of Glananock [Glennamucklagh], widow.
824.218	Joan Inyver, town of Newmarket, widow.
825.20-21	Thomas Raymond, town of Newmarket, gent.
825.40	Robert Owgane of Newmarket, gent.
825.48-9	Juan Lee of Newmarket, widow.
825.77	John Powell of Newmarket, clerk, on behalf of Thomas Fisher, clerk, of Mallow and Winifred Foard of Newmarket, spinster.
825.88	Richard Richman of Clonferto [Clonfert], husbandman.
825.105	John Woodmason on behalf of his brother Joseph and his sister Margaret, spinster.
825.119	Katherin Hall of Newmarket, widow.
825.121	John Woodmason of Clanturke [Kanturk], parish Newmarket, cooper.
825.244	Thomas Owgan of Ballymacceral [?], parish Newmarket, n.s.g.
825.259	Robert Howes of Newmarket, innkeeper.
825.298	Gilbert Barthlet of Newmarket, slater.

42. *Parish Clonpriest, Barony Imokilly*

822.261	Robert Rookes, Ballykelly [Ballykilty], gent.

43. *Parish Clontead, Barony Kinsale*

822.21	John Pulham, Castlevallename [Coolvallanbeg], clerk.
824.192	Nicholas Ham of Ballyrustick [?], [Ballinrichard], gent.
825.198	Elizabeth Smale, wife of Henry Smale of Bulleston [Butlerstown], yeoman.

44. *Parish Cloyne, Barony Imokilly*

822.203	Phellim Fitzsimons, clerk, Irish Protestant.
823.101	John Binnes, Cloyne, clerk.
823.131	Rice Wight, Cloyne, clerk.
824.238	Henry Rugg, clerk.

45. *Parish Coole, Baronies Condons and Clangibbon, Barrymore and Kinnatalloon*

823.138	William Rowe, yeoman.
822.169	Helen Baynard, widow.
822.231	James Bruce of Coole, clerk.
823.45	George Streat, town and parish Coole, barony Kinnatalloon, yeoman.
824.58	John Whetcome, gent.
824.84	Richard Cooper, yeoman.
824.111	Richard Pearl, husbandman.

824.202   John Barretts, yeoman.

46. *Parish Cooliney, Barony Orrery and Kilmore*
    822.164   William Holcorne, of Cooline parish [Cooliney], gent.
    824.32   George Hakes, yeoman.

47. *Parish Cullen, Barony Kinalea*
    822.176   Elizabeth Woolson, widow.
    823.127   Katherin Spencer, of Cargy [Carrigeen], parish Cullane, widow.
    823.229   Millisent Owen of Garrigine [Carrigeen], parish Cullane, widow.
    824.109   William Doare of Coolin [probably Cullen], n.s.g.
    824.154   Robert Gill of Carrigine [Carrigeen], husbandman.

48. *Parish Currykippane, Barony of Cork*
    822.37   John Looby of Clochine [Clogheen], yeoman.
    822.66   Anthony Hussie of Blarney, park-keeper.
    824.20   John Jennings, Corromrowhoe [Coolymurraghue], n.s.g.
    824.89   William Atwell of Blarney, husbandman.
    824.197   Thomas Woolcock of Carraborrahoe [Coolymurraghue].
    824.227   Als Holyday, n.s.g.
    825.32   Baptist Lawrence of Cloghimes [Clogheen], n.s.g.
    825.211   John Spred, Cork city, n.s.g.
    825.241   William Jennings of Coorvurlin [?], n.s.g. (probably miller).

49. *Parish Derryvillane, Barony Condons and Clangibbon*
    824.144   Richard Mansell, son to Captain Thomas Mansell.

50. *Parish Desert, Barony Ibane and Barryroe*
    822.165   Robert Bramble of Desert, Barony Duhallow [?], mariner.
    823.63   Robert Rickett of Ballybroman [?], parish Disert [Desert], n.s.g. (probably a tanner).
    824.203   Sasana Charles of Ballybronian [?], widow.
    825.175   Bridgett Iagnes of Cahirgall [Cahergall], widow.

51. *Parish Desertserges, Barony East Carbery and Kinalmeaky*
    822.12   Robert Salmon, on behalf of Ann Salmon of Arkyth [Ardkitt].
    822.188   Nicholas Harte of Briglany [Breaghna], husbandman.
    822.212   Michael Chatterton of Kilcolman, carpenter.
    822.264   Thomas Townsend of Arkett [Ardkitt], husbandman.
    824.15   Ann Fottrell, wife to Richard, n.s.g.
    824.23-4   Perergrine Banister of Farnisery [Farrannasheshery], esq.,
    824.35   Elizabeth Stower, parish of Kilcolman [?], weaver.
    825.61   Thomas Harris of Ardkitt West, gent.
    825.76   William Glen of Arkett West [Ardkitt], mason.
    825.104   William Recraste, town and parish of Desert, yeoman.
    825.111   William Wright of Farronsesty [Farrannasheshery], yeoman.
    825.126   Mary Horne of Capreknockane [?], widow.
    825.155   Randall Warner of Kilcolman, gent.
    825.245   Thomas Harrison of Knocknegillagh [?], [Knocknacullen], yeoman.
    825.248   Thomas Haynds of Kilcolman, yeoman.

52. *Parish Doneraile, Barony Fermoy*

822.24	Henry Pepp, gent.
822.29	Richard Basted of Rossacke [Rossagh], yeoman.
822.37	John Owgan, n.s.g.
822.56-7	Denis Pepper of Kylblocks, [?] [Kilbrack], parish Dumeragh [?], on behalf of D. Pepper, Snr., n.s.g.
822.66	Richard Gethings of Ballinaderne [Ballyandrew], gent.
822.95	William Holmes of Doneraile, gent.
822.108	Thomas Martin of Doneraile, gent., on behalf of daughters Anne Fowle and Dorothy Martin.
822.122	Robert Saunders, town and parish of Doneraile, gent.
822.196	Richard Groves of Carrigine [Carrigeen], gent.
822.213	William Acocks of Doneraile, n.s.g.
822.224	David Thomas of Doneraile, n.s.g.
823.153	Simon Brudges of Doneraile, n.s.g.
823.192	Garret Hadrington of Doneraile, n.s.g.
824.46	William Cook of Carkar [Carker], yeoman.
824.112	Three deponents on behalf of Sir William St Leger (*viz.* Richard Gettings, gent.; Thomas Rice, gent.; George Dent, all Doneraile).
825.2	Joan Lane of Doneraile, widow.
825.35	William Burnham of Croagh [Croaghnacree], gent.
825.106	Tobias Welsh of Doneraile, gent.
825.205	Edward White of Doneraile, joiner.
825.230	Thomas Martin of Doneraile, gent.
825.253	John Strange of Doneraile, esq.
825.278	Lewis Michell of Doneraile, n.s.g.

53. *Parish Dromtarriff, Barony Duhallow*

823.215	Robert Brimble, of Disert [?], parish Drumagh, Barony Duhallow [possibly townland of Dromagh, parish Dromtarriff]. Deposition by John Hodder, parish Churchtown, esq.

54. *Parish Dunderrow, Barony Kinalea*

822.185	Josias Farlow of Ballimallisant [?], esq.
823.22	John Shippward, gent.
823.100	William Aleshine, town and parish Downerowe [Dunderrow], yeoman.
823.142	Ann, late wife of Thomas Slater, now wife of Edmund Nicholson of Kinsale, merchant.
823.194	William Phillips, butcher.
825.193	Francis Skinner husbandman.
825.253	Henry Smale, yeoman.

55. *Parish Durrus, Barony Bere and Bantry (see also Kilmocomoge parish)*

823.76	Martha May and brother Nathaniel May of Bantry, he is described as a yeoman.
824.211	Nicholas Harvy, late Blackrock [?], yeoman.
825.23	Ralph Oliver of Whiddy Island, yeoman.
	[Note Bantry and Whiddy Island are included in the 1851 census in the parish of Kilmocomoge.]

56. *Parish Fanlobbus, Barony East Carbery*
   824.142 Alis Robinson of Knockeduff [Knockaghaduff], widow.
   825.84   Nathanid Richards of Westmarch [Manch West], yeoman.

57. *Parishes Fermoy and Kilcrumper, Baronies Condons and Clangibbon and Fermoy*
   822.34   Agnes Pope, parish Fermoy, widow.
   822.170 Sir Arthur Hyde of Carrignedy [?], parish Carrigneedy [?].
   823.60   Samuel Hutchings of Mullinepook [?], parish Kilcrump [Kilcrumper], yeoman.
   823.89   Thomas Bulman of the Coole in Fermoy, parish Kilcrumper, yeoman.
   823.95   Faith Anger of Farmoy [Fermoy], parish Kilcrumper, spinster, on behalf of her husband Anthony Anger, absent in England.
   824.96   John Wyett, town of Fermoy, gent.
   824.97   Richard Dashwood of Fermoy, parish Kilcrumper, yeoman.
   824.99   Ann Hope of Fermoy, parish Kilcrumper, wife to Alexander Hope, blacksmith enlisted in army.
   824.102 Julian Wyett, town of Fermoy, n.s.g.
   824.115 Giles Cooke of Fermoy, parish Kilcrumper, gent.
   824.225 John Parr of Fermoy, parish Kilcrumper, merchant.

   [Note that in the census of 1851 Fermoy constituted a single parish in the Barony of Condons and Clangibbon and Kilcrumper was a distinct parish divided between the baronies of Condons and Clangibbon and that of Fermoy. This distinction does not appear to have prevailed in 1641.]

58. *Parish Garrycloyne, Barony East Muskerry*
   823.93   Adam Newman of Blarney, n.s.g.
   824.228 John Welsh of Freefelscastle [?], county and city of Cork, n.s.g.
   825.178 William Hudsen of Blarney, n.s.g.

59. *Parish Garryvoe, Barony Imokilly*
   825.235 Thomas Hole, town and parish of Ballyhennick [Ballyhimikin], gent.

60. *Parish Glanworth, Barony Condons and Clangibbon*
   824.158 Robert Nixon of Manning, yeoman.

61. *Parish Gortroe, Barony Barrymore*
   822.241 Henry Turgare of Pursuvantstown [?], yeoman.
   824.190 George Saier of Ballinterig [Ballinterry], husbandman.
   825.14   Richard White of Scartynarrow [?], parish Gort [?], [Gortroe], husbandman.
   825.64   Margery Howell of Claquill [Clykeel], widow.
   825.164 Robert Rodger of Gurtane, [Gortroe] [?], yeoman.
   825.190 John Durdane, n.s.g.
   825.310 Clement Trock of Crophebode [Curraghphilibbode], yeoman.

62. *Parish Imphrick, Barony Fermoy*
   822.91   John Toller, yeoman.
   822.171 William Conway of Ballyhowry [Ballyhoura], *alias* Kilwallicke, gent.

822.210 Robert Shinkwin of Ballyhaury [Ballyhoura], shoemaker.
823.16
and 224 John Dore of Ballyhosgrane [?], parish Emortick [Imphrick], gent.
825.162 Robert Rice of Lisballihag [Lisballyhay], parish Embrick [Imphrick], yeoman.

63. *Parish Inchinabacky, Barony Barrymore*
823.112 Evan Gevan of Inishinbarry [Inchinabacky], n.s.g.
823.117 William Ward of Insanaboke [Inchinabacky], husbandman.
824.207 Thomas Badnidge, esq.

64. *Parish Inishannon, Baronies Kinalea and East Carbery*
822.183 Jane Bayly, parish Eneshannig [Inishannon], widow.
823.128 William Burlingham of Sheemanish [Shevanish], yeoman.
824.229 Symon Smith of Corrint [?], [Corranure], yeoman.
824.230 Dermot and Teig O'Coughlan, late of Drummkeen [Dromkeen], malsters.
825.227 Elizabeth Nelins, widow.

65. *Parish Inishkenny, Barony Cork*
824.198 William Lone, parish Inskenry [Inishkenny], Cork city, n.s.g.
825.172 Cyprian Hawkins of Ardrostick [Ardarostig], Barony Kerrycurrihy [?], n.s.g.

66. *Parish Kilbolane, Barony Orrery and Kilmore*
822.98 Benjamin Baxter of Kilbolane, husbandman.
823.88 John Hopkins of Kilbolane, embroiderer.
823.135 Henry Fudge of Kilbolane, husbandman.
824.60 Benjamin Baxter, husbandman

67. *Parish Kilbrin, Barony Duhallow*
822.116 John Slade of Ballycriston [Ballyhest], shepherd.
822.161 Jonas Smith of Ballymacpierce [Ballymacpierce], gent.
822.187 John Slade of Ballyrihine [Ballyrusheen], yeoman.
824.176 Thomas Johnson, town of Ballintobber [?], miller.
825.42 Jane Ellis of Dromonargall [Drominagure], widow.
825.283 John Slade of Ballyriskin [Ballyrusheen], yeoman (on behalf of his father in county Clare).
825.316 John Morris of Garrans [Garranmacgarrett], yeoman.

68. *Parish Kilbroney, Barony Orrery and Kilmore*
825.229 Thomas Hill of Ballinbooly [Ballinguile], yeoman.

Parish of Kilcumper: see under Fermoy

69. *Parish Kilcrummer, Barony Fermoy*
823.15 Ann Dowdall of Reny [Renny], Barony Fermoy, widow.

70. *Parish Kilgarriff, Barony West Carbery*
822.10 Rebecca Barnham, widow, Clonakilty.
822.38 Thomas Paddeson, Lisburnett [?], husbandman.

822.82   Joan Vincent of Clonakilty, wife.

822.89   James Martin of Clonakilty, yeoman.

822.96   Thomas Holland of Curraugh [Carhoo], gent.

822.103   Ann Baker of Clonakilty, widow.

822.106   George Stukly of Clonakilty, gent.

822.137   William Bodell of Clankelly, [Clonakilty] [?], yeoman.

822.141   Kathern Fisher of Clonakilty, widow.

822.166   John Austine, burough of Clonakilty, tanner.

822.242   William Strangway, Clonakilty, gent.

822.288   James Dyer of Skartagh [Scartagh], borough Cloghlikelly [?], clerk.

823.49   Humfry Hunt of Clonakilty, gent.

823.53   Thomas Worrall of Clonakilty, innkeeper.

823.204   Charles Hitchins of Clonakilty, husbandman.

824.27   Walter Bird of Clonakilty, esq.

824.145   Thomas Jude of Clonakilty, feltmonger.

824.175   William Sleman of Clonakilty, yeoman.

824.220   Lewis Harris of Clonakilty, cooper.

824.222   Nicholas Coker of Clonakilty, yeoman.

825.113   Jane Savell, wife of Robert Savell, yeoman.

825.148   Rebecca Bennett, wife to Nicholas Bennett, tanner.

825.194   Thomas Sermon, Clonakilty, yeoman.

825.247   Thomas Kingson of Clonakilty, yeoman.

825.263   Joan Hamilton wife to George Hamilton, yeoman of Kilty [?]

825.267   James Pace of Clonakilty, shoemaker.

71.   *Parish Killaspugmullane, Barony Barrymore*

822.47   Henry Harris of Conygallike [?], [Coolnacaha] [?], n.s.g.

822.178   Agnis Tuker of Crosane [?], [Kilrussane], parish Kilmalane [?], [Killaspugmullane], widow.

822.234   Henry Barnes of Coshan [?], parish Kilnemollan [?], [Killaspugmullane], yeoman.

824.178   Robert Hawkins of Connegally [?], [Coolnacha], n.s.g.

72.   *Parish Killathy, Barony Fermoy*

824.18   Leonard Tily of Ballymacphilip, husbandman.

Parish Kilowen: see under Murragh

73.   *Parish Kilmacabea, Baronies East and West Carbery*

823.74-5   Richard Christmas of Cappaonabagh [Cappanabohy], parish Kilmacgibby [Kilmacabea], clothmaker.

825.222   John Minor of the Leap, parish Kilmackubby [Kilmacabea], merchant.

74.   *Parish Kilmaclenine, Barony Orrery and Kilmore*

825.148   Henry Lashfoord of Kilmackerin [?], [Kilmaclenine], husbandman.

75.   *Parish Kilmocomoge, Barony Bantry (see also parish Durrus)*

822.142   Thomas Moorecocke of Dromanare [Dromdoneen], wheelwright.

822.249   Thomas Heyford of Bantry, gent.

822.273   Thomas Henry of Whiddy, yeoman.

823.23   John Browne of Whiddy, yeoman.

823.55	William Wood of Carir Inshikeene [?], [Inchinarihen] [?]., joiner.
823.87	John Winter of Bantry, parish K., husbandman.
823.100	John Lak of Whiddy Island, husbandman.
823.122	Thomas Moorcock, Dromanara [?], [Dromdoneen], parish K., yeoman.
823.143	Edmund McCarty of Bantry, yeoman.
823.169	Valentine Gordon of Bantry, spinster, Scottish Protestant.
823.190	Anthony Blunt of Bantry, yeoman.
824.149	Agnis Tucker, of Whiddy Island, widow.
824.223	Katherin Heyford, wife of Owen Heyford of Bantry, n.s.g.
825.7	Christopher Speringe of Bantry, timberman.
825.264	William French of Kilmacom [Kilmocomoge], tanner.
825.318	Robert Collins of Whiddy, yeoman.

76. *Parish Kilmonoge, Barony Kinalea*
822.25	Giles Massrey, Belgooley [Belgooly], miller.
824.29	John Mosley, Belgooly, n.s.g. (probably gent.).

77. *Parish Kilnaglory, Baronies Cork and East Muskerry*
822.260	Edward Bennett of Ballynora, n.s.g.
822.276	Katherin Vestment of Ballinagally [Ballingilly], widow.
823.33	Katherin Allard of Coolebane [?], widow.
823.164	John Skinner of Minchullick [?], n.s.g. (probably gent.).
824.44	William Burdon, n.s.g.
824.248	Robert Milton of Ballynora, husbandman.
825.50	John Whiteing, n.s.g.
825.200	Robert Milton of Ballynora, n.s.g.

78. *Parish Kilnagross, Barony East Carbery*
822.40	Henry Bennett of Gallens [Gallanes], yeoman.
823.196	Joan Barguff of Gullam [?], [Gallanes], widow.

79. *Parish Kilnamartery, Barony West Muskerry*
823.222	Joan Hupp, wife of John Hoop, town Clogheny [?] [Clogheena], n.s.g.

80. *Parish Kilpatrick, Barony Kinalea*
823.137	Thomas Dant of Gortigenane [Gortigrenane], esq. (deposition made by Wiliam Da[u]nt of Carrigaline).
825.214	Lawrence Spenser of Kilpatrick, yeoman.

81. *Parish Kilquane, Barony Barrymore*
824.151	Gregory Aldworth, gent.

82. *Parish Kilroan, Barony Courceys*
825.199	Phebe How on behalf of John How, gent., her husband of Ballinbooly [?], parish Coortupptin [probably townland of Courtaparteen, parish Kilroan], barony Courceys.

83. *Parish Kilshannig, Barony Duhallow*
822.23	Samuel Willies of Rathcoman [?], barony Orrery [?], mason.
822.30	William Jul of Carriglan [Carrigleena], yeoman.
822.55	John Busted of Gortmolery [Gortmolire], yeoman.

823.217	Thomas Gilborne of Sharrough [Sharragh], n.s.g.
824.22	William Busted of Gortevelaire [Gortmolire], yeoman.
825.22	Edward Harris of Rathcoman [?], husbandman.
825.60	Emanuell Faire of Kilvalide [?], [Kilvealaton] [?], clerk.
825.217	Mary Sumers of Carrigalane [Carrigeleena], spinster, Irish Protestant.
825.275	Robert Faier of Killvallidie [Kilvealaton], n.s.g.

84. *Parish Kilworth, Barony Condons and Clangibbon*

822.97	Samuel Andrews of Kilworth, yeoman.
822.217	James Olifer, town and parish of Kilworth, yeoman.
824.17	William Mitchell of Glanseskin, parish Kilworth, yeoman.
824.21	John Leynard of Glanseskin, parish Kilworth, yeoman.
824.161	George Blackburne, town of Kilworth, yeoman.

85. *Parish Kinneigh, Barony East Carbery*

822.20	John Sampson of Castleton [Castletown], tanner.
822.49	Ralph Woodley of East Tedes [Teadies], n.s.g. (probably gent.).
822.54	Diana Holland, wife to John H. of Enniskeen, blacksmith.
822.64	Richard Fripps, Hurtline [?], husbandman.
822.65	John Newelocke of Drummedeclaugh [Dromidiclogh], yeoman.
822.114	John Browne of Inishkyan [Enniskeen], yeoman.
822.134	George Baskam of Arleak [Anaharlick], husbandman.
822.136	Richard Baskains of Aherlick [Anaharlick], husbandman.
822.251	Nicholas Suite of Castletown, husbandman.
822.257	Philip Jagoe of Iniskeen [Enniskeen], yeoman.
822.268	Cheney Polden of Castletown, ensign to Captain Banister.
822.274	William Redwood of Castletown, butcher.
823.79	Judith Radcliff, wife to Richard Radcliff and widow of William Cobbe of Inishkien, n.s.g.
823.80	William Richardson of Castletown, clothier.
823.82	John Stannine of Inishkyen [Enniskeen], husbandman.
823.91	Als Bayle of Ardcostick [?], parish Inishken [Enniskeen], n.s.g.
823.114	Robert Horne, town Inishkene [Enniskeen], gent.
823.118	John White of Corknostowick [?], weaver.
823.140	John Fullbrooke, of Inishkyen, yeoman.
823.148	Hugh Wellington of Eniskeane, feltmaker.
823.177	William Ward of Castletown, tanner.
823.185	John Steevens of Eniskeane, butcher.
823.220	Richard Sampson, n.s.g.
824.36	William Roe, town of Iniskeane [Enniskeen], tanner.
824.196	Thomas Kinsey, clerk.
824.200	Richard Samell, chandler.
824.214	Nicholas Heard of Trumfeelty [?], n.s.g.
825.13	Richard White of Castletown, clerk.
825.34	Robert Shut of Castletown, gent.
825.37	Thomas Moorecock of Bekrof [Buckree], wheeler.
825.80	George Johns of Castleton, yeoman.
825.97	Edmund Michell of Chaine O Moricke [?], shoemaker.
825.124	Richard Bickam of Skyethen [?], yeoman.
825.146	Edward Arthur, sawyer.
825.165	John Polden of Castleton, gent.

825.182   George Ellett of Castletown, n.s.g.
825.183   Richard White, clerk for his son Gabriel White, n.s.g.
825.220   Hugh Williams of Inishkyrth [?], butcher.
825.252   Richard Shute of Castletown, n.s.g. (probably gent.).
825.282   Richard Sargeant of Castletown, malster.
825.301   John Smith of Gurtirow [Gurteenroe], husbandman.
825.314   Thomas Lassells of Dromtyclugh [Dromidiclogh], tanner.

86. *Parish Kinsale, Barony Kinsale*
822.26-7   Tristram Whitcombe, merchant.
822.152   William Vincents, servant to William Thomas, esq.
823.24   Symon Lightfoot, blacksmith.
823.189   Edward Lassells, gent.
823.213   John Buckingham, gent.
825.212   Robert Southwell, gent. (really malster).
825.228   John Rowe, merchant.

87. *Parish Knockavilly, Barony Kinnalea*
823.29   Randall Holland of Garryhankane [Garryhankard], clerk.

88. *Parish Knockmourne, Barony Kinatalloon*
822.16   Richard Winchester, clothier.
822.146   Hugh Mansell, yeoman.
822.139   Richard Seward of Ballinbrody [Ballybride] and Charles Seward, n.s.g.
823.78   Thomas Abram, yeoman.
823.221   Thomas Fudge of Ballybred [Ballybride], yeoman.
823.225   Richard Seward of Ballybrody [Ballybride], n.s.g.
824.92   William Clay of Ulconer [Kilcoran], yeoman.
824.104   Richard Clay of Ulconor [Kilcoran], yeoman.
824.143   Edward Jerman of Cooldoragh [Cooladurragh], yeoman.
824.182   John Cloud of Coneky [Conna], husbandman.
824.183   Robert Danborne of Cargeen [Carrigeen], yeoman.
824.187   Edward Rogers of Balydas [Ballydaw], butcher.
824.193   Philip Bleight, clothier.
824.205   Elizabeth Pope, wife of William Pope of Coolebane [Coolbaun], n.s.g.
824.260   William Whittyer of Ballibridge [Ballybride], yeoman.
825.319   Joan Markes, wife of Thomas Markes of Corbert [?], n.s.g.

89. *Parish Leitrim, Barony Condons and Clangibbon*
822.70   John Sprange of Arglen [?], parish [?], Litrum [Leitrim], millwright.
822.79   Edward Collins of Ardlinbridge [?], soapmaker, for and on behalf of Anabelle Emry of Ardlinbridge [?], parish Lehin [?], [Leitrim], widow.
824.73   Robert Lake of Kilmurry, timberman.
824.83   July Mitchell, wife to Richard Mitchell of Arglinbridge [?], parish Letrium [Leitrim], n.s.g.
824.103   Augustine Ludgate of Arlinbridge, parish Leitrium [Leitrim], yeoman.
824.180   Thomas Powell of Kilmory [Kilmurry], parish Leitrim, yeoman.

90. *Parish Liscarroll, Barony Orrery and Kilmore*
822.119   Sagn [?] Smart, wife of Robert Smart, widow.

822.277	Elizabeth Twait, Irish Protestant, widow.
822.285	Thomas Williams of Moegg [Moyge], parish L., n.s.g.
825.70	John Fisher of Kilbridg [?], gent., on behalf of Mary Goddard, spinster.
825.132	John Fisher of Kilbride [?], gent.
825.297	Samuel Savedg of Liscarroll, parish Bruhenye [?], yeoman.

91. *Parish Lisgoold, Barony Barrymore*
   824.188   Philip Huddy of Ballygarrt [?], yeoman.

92. *Parish Lislee, Barony Ibane and Barryroe*
   822.105   Daniel Maxfield, carpenter.
   822.184   John Arthur, son to Joan Laborne *alias* Arthurtown and parish Lisby [Lislee]; Joan a widow.
   823.94   Florence Bryan on behalf of grandson Thomas Jomeck, n.s.g., of Colen Coshery [?], [Cullenagh], parish Lesly [Lislee], n.s.g.
   825.12   Richard White of Cargine [Carrigeen], yeoman.
   825.293   John Arthur, town, yeoman (also hewer).
   825.307   Isacke Filpott of Agha, gent.

93. *Parish Lismore and Mocollop, Barony Condons and Clangibbon (county Cork only)*
   822.84   Edward Ingrey of Lynone [?], parish Castle Mocollop, gent.
   823.3   Francis Cook of Ballymacklase [?], skinner.
   824.76   Thomas Carter, gent.
   824.107   Richard Helliard of Ballamaglas [?], yeoman.

94. *Parish Litter, Barony Condons and Clangibbon*
   823.61   Thomas Smith, clerk.

95. *Parish Macloneigh, Barony West Muskerry*
   822.163   Henry Cooke of Ballyglassan, parish Macdonagh [Macloneigh], Barony of Muskerry, yeoman.

96. *Parish Macroney, Barony Condons and Clangibbon*
   822.197   Richard West, yeoman.
   823.32   William Howell of Curmon [?], parish Morrony [?], [Macroney], Barony Fermoy, glover.
   823.34   Walker Williams of Macroney, n.s.g. (either shoemaker or tanner).
   824.236   Thomas Stout of Kilclogh, yeoman.
   825.304   Alexander Crease, n.s.g.

97. *Parish Macroom, Barony West Muskerry*
   822.60   William Taylor, town and parish Macrom [?], [Macroom], n.s.g.
   823.70   Humphrey Warren, n.s.g.
   825.268   James Bruner of Macroum [Macroom], n.s.g.

98. *Parish Mallow, Baronies Fermoy and Duhallow*
   822.3   Philip Vaghane, Jnr., of Mallow, gent.
   822.14   George Chimery the younger on behalf of G.C. the elder, merchant.
   822.28   Katharine Hudson, widow.
   822.32   Elizabeth Maguire, widow, British Protestant.

822.42	Amy Standish, town of Mallow, widow.
822.83	Donell Shigham, late of Mallow, Irish Protestant, yeoman.
822.90	Francis Bidell for Randall Clayton, gent.
822.94	Edy Forest, wife of John F. of Mallow, carpenter.
822.143	Arthur Kingsmill of Mallow, clerk.
822.158	Thomas Haynes of Mallow, merchant.
822.199	Thomas Fisher, town and parish of Mallow, clerk.
822.223	Thomas Morris, Mallow, n.s.g.
822.230	Philip Vaughan of Mallow, yeoman.
822.238	Ann Cockinge, widow.
822.239	William Holmes of Mallow, n.s.g.
822.282	Stephen Chymery of Mallow, yeoman.
823.2	Edmund Stiles, n.s.g.
823.4-5	Arthur Bettesworth, gent.
823.11	Richard Aldworthy, yeoman.
823.19	Thomas Bettsworth of Mallow, esq.
823.96	Robert Darling, tailor.
823.116	Timothy Lee of Mallow, yeoman.
823.198	Frances Badell of Mallow, gent.
824.88	Henry Kniverton of Mallow, n.s.g. (gent. or malster).
824.150	John Rice of Mallow, weaver.
824.173	Thomas Blake of Mallow, n.s.g.
824.206	Robert Stanton of Mallow, yeoman.
824.215	John Wiseman of Mallow, cooper.
824.221	Christopher Wright of Mallow, yeoman.
825.18	Richard Williamson, gent.
825.67	Thomas Fisher, clerk.
825.73	Philip Vaughan, the elder, yeoman.
825.159	John Collins of Mallow, yeoman.
825.160	Thomas Wright of Mallow, dyer.
825.166	William Rowse of Mallow, yeoman.
825.167	Francis Bertridge of Mallow, n.s.g.
825.215	John Bastry of Mallow, yeoman.
825.216	John Hagan of Mallow, shoemaker.
825.218	John Godsell, the younger of Ballydahill [Ballydahin], skinner.
825.221	Steven Chinery, town and parish of Mallow, maltmaker.
825.238	Robert Walker of Ballindalin [Ballydahin], parish Mallow, n.s.g.
825.246	John Collins of Mallow, yeoman.
825.261	Thomas Bettsworth, town and parish of Mallow, esq.
825.300	William Wakelet of Mallow, weaver.
825.309	Gregory Newman of Mallow, gent.
825.313	Alice Timberlake, wife to John Timberlake, smith.
825.315	George Keitely of Mallow, gent.
825.320	John Marnes of Mallow, miller.

99. *Parish Marshalstown, Barony Condons and Clangibbon*
825.63	Elizabeth Mitchell, relict of Robert Mitchell, husbandman.

100. *Parish Mogeely, Barony Kinnatalloon*
822.156	James Andrews of Curreglass [?], yeoman.
823.6	Walter Croker of Curriglass [?], gent.

823.7	Barnard Guppy of Shanekill, yeoman.
823.9	John Russell of Glanballiconlane [?], husbandman.
823.77	John Williams of Balleren [?], n.s.g.
823.84	John Rowe of Templevally [?], yeoman.
823.136	Edward Markam of Leckbeake [?], shearman.
824.80	Samuel Blancher of Garret James [Garranejames], yeoman.
824.155	John Rowe of Templevally [?], husbandman.
825.114	Theodore Cumby of Templevalley [?], husbandman.
825.288	Simon Randall of Gortnawherne [?], husbandman.

101. *Parish Monaniny, Barony Fermoy*
822.100   John Marton of Ballygriffin, shepherd.

102. *Parish Moviddy, Barony Muskerry*
822.278   Dorothy Burt of Garran and Buddagh *alias* the Knock Lough [Garranehamuddagh], late wife to Jo Burte, yeoman, now wife to Hugh Winter of Kinsale, ropemaker.
823.163   William Beard, clerk.

103. *Parish Murragh, Barony Kinalmeaky (note that Murragh included the parish of Killowen in 1851 census)*

822.11	Thomasin Dun of Killowen, widow.
822.133	Hirah Gilslan of Morragh [Murragh], clerk.
822.205	John Pressley of Killowen, yeoman.
822.266	Alice Warrs, widow.
822.272	Eleanor Johnson of New Liston [?], [Newcestown], widow.
823.13	Thomas Arthur of Marragh [Murragh], sawyer.
823.14	Thomas Rubie, Ballylemett [?], n.s.g.
823.193	John James of Callaghglasse [Tullyglass], yeoman.
823.201	Joseph Scott of Killineere [Killaneer], chandler.
824.19	Stephen Shorting of Marragh [Murragh], yeoman.
824.30	John Greenfield of Tullaghglasse [Tullyglass], yeoman.
824.167	Edward Clerk, gent.
824.171	John Ware of Newseton [Newcestown], yeoman.
825.44	Daniel Perkins of Bengor [Bengour], tanner.
825.78	Elizabeth Clerk, widow, deposition by her son-in-law John Bond.
825.79	Alre Paul of Malbegg [Maw-beg], deposition by John Bond.
825.99	John Baker of Killowen [?], husbandman.
825.112	Richard Bell, town and parish of Morra [Murragh], yeoman.
825.123	Thomas Hill of Killoyen [Killowen], husbandman.
825.177	Robert Heale and Mary Long of Killowen, yeoman.
825.187	Henry Young, town and parish of Morrath [Murragh], yeoman.
825.202	Richard Lucas of Newcoston [Newcestown], yeoman.
825.219	Robert Warr of Farrenkanlogh [?], [Farranthomas], yeoman.
825.251	Edward Oldis of Mabeg [Maw-beg], husbandman.
825.292	Humphrey Woad of Kilmeere [Killaneer], yeoman.

104. *Parish Myross, Barony West Carbery*
823.141   Henry Tatardall of Brade, tanner.
823.210   Henry Pomeroy of Ballincolly [Ballincolla], yeoman.

105. *Parish Rathbarry, Barony Ibane and Barryroe*
    824.105   William Jobson of Dowenore [Donoure], gent.

106. *Parish Rathclarin, Barony East Carbery*
    823.146   Iseak Philpott the younger of Cloncalla [Clooncalla], gent.

107. *Parish Rathcooney, Barony of Cork*
    822.104   Robert Piersy of Ballincrokegg [?], [Ballincrokig], searcher of port.
    822.235   George Kelly of Cork, parson of rectory of Rathcooney and prebend of St Michael's, clerk.
    823.92   Henry Ware, n.s.g.
    823.219   Roger Beer, town and parish of Rathcooney, tanner.
    825.69   Gregory French of Garranbuy [Garraneboy], yeoman.
    825.242   Charles Gay of Knockargen [Knocknahorgan], on behalf of John Tucker of same, his father-in-law, n.s.g.
    825.284   Thomas Sheane of Knockorgen [Knocknahorgan], Cork city, n.s.g.

108. *Parish Rathcormack, Barony Barrymore*
    822.189   Philip Upham of Kilbruen [Kilbrien], yeoman.
    822.250   Elizabeth Buck, on behalf of children of Joan Lanard, widow, deceased sister to deponent.
    822.279   Elizabeth Buck of Lisneguard [Lisnagar demesne], on behalf of ailing husband, George Buck, n.s.g.
    823.40   Joane Crews of Mawlane [Maulane], yeoman.
    823.59   Henry Normon, town and parish of Rathcormack, yeoman.
    823.67   Edward Liffe, miller.
    823.72   Nicholas Parker, yeoman.
    824.39   William Foster, yeoman.
    824.55   Joan Lunn, widow of shoemaker.
    824.146   Thomas Herrington, husbandman.
    825.33   William Murryfield of Craghtymore [Curraghteemore], yeoman.
    825.93   Adrian Morefield of Craftymore [Curraghteemore], yeoman.
    825.134   Philip Upham, son of Robert Upham of Kilbrien, yeoman.
    825.306   Pillip Brock of Rathcormack, yeoman.

109. *Parish Rathgoggan, Barony Orrery and Kilmore*
    823.38   Phillip Cross, town and parish of Rathgoggan, yeoman.
    823.48   Daniel Whittle of Rathgogan [Rathgoggan], n.s.g.

110. *Parish Ringcurran, Barony Kinalea*
    823.98   Robert Milner of Sillpoint [Scilly], near Kinsale, clerk.
    824.157   Henry Saunderburg of Cappuch [Cappagh], yeoman.
    824.186   Thomas Martin of Kippa [Cappagh], yeoman.

111. *Parish Ringrone, Baronies Courceys and Kinsale*
    822.18-9   Eperetus Bellew of Ballymacredmond, gent.
    822.124   John Bellew, son of Nicholas Bellew of Evagh [?], gent.
    824.51   John Marsh of Oldcourt, gent.
    824.174   Thomas Tieepes of Corrwhoe [Currahoo], yeoman.
    824.189   Elizabeth Sutton, relict of Thomas Sutton of Ballifidina [?], widow.

824.219	John Marsh, Oldcourt, gent., on behalf of Mary Nicholson, widow absent in England.
825.209	John Temple of Castle Park [Castlepark], gent.

112. *Parish Ross, Barony East Carbery*

822.167	Roger Waters of Dunedo [?], [Downeen], parish Ross Carbery, husband-man.
822.177	Ann Sellers of Bohowna [Bohonagh], parish New Carbry [Ross Carbery], widow.
823.50	Richard Channing of Rosebarry [?], [Ross], husbandman.
823.138-9	Osmond Crode of Carrigronmore [Carrigagrenane], husbandman.
823.152	Edmund Gillingham, town and parish of Rosscarbery, yeoman.
824.45	Ann Horsey, widow and Helen Horsey, spinster.
825.6	Christian Bolton of Rosscarberry [Ross], widow.
825.24	John Yew of Cahiron [?], [Cahermore], yeoman.
825.30	Thomas Boyle of Ross, clerk.
825.142	Thomas Fryth, Archdeacon of Ross and J.P. for Cork and Kerry, clerk.

113. *Parish St Finbarr's, Barony of Cork*

822.35	Thomas Nevell, parish St F., esq.
822.168	John Chappell of Kilcomine [Killumney], parish St Barries [St Finbarr's], gent.
822.179	Thomas Nevell of Ballinicurrig [Ballincurrig], esq.
822.193	Eleanore Acalley, wife to Robert Acalley of Killhumeny [Killumney], n.s.g.
822.229	John Freeman, n.s.g.
822.244	Thomas Spencer of Gortaglane [Gortagoulane], n.s.g.
822.281	Mary Smith of Gill Abbey [Gillabbey], parish St Barry's [St Finbarr's], widow.
823.103	Abraham Battin of Gurtagolane [Gortagoulane], n.s.g.
823.105	Anthony Watts, n.s.g.
823.109	Thomas Bennett; Edward Johns; Robert Bayly; Richard Bennell, all clerks of St Finbarr's.
823.110	Dorcas Hall, widow.
823.115	William Browne, n.s.g.
823.181	Henry Whetcroft of Cork, yeoman.
824.34	Thomas Pinchon of Ballinspeckbey [Ballinaspig-beg], n.s.g.
824.140	Henry Smart, yeoman.
824.164	Richard French, ironmonger.
824.224	John Hall, clerk.
824.231	Henry Bryan of Inshegaggen [Inchegaggin], n.s.g.
824.249	Thomas Roberts, clerk.
825.53	Francis Butterfieid, husbandman.
825.120	Robert Kellye, parish St Barry's, husbandman.
825.186	Hugh Burrowes the elder of Magellin [?], parish St. Barries, n.s.g.
825.188	Christopher Band of St. Barries, n.s.g.
825.234	John Gilman the younger, n.s.g.
825.240	Gartwright Wilson of Killadywood [?], on behalf of her husband Robert Wilson, n.s.g.
825.243	James Deacon of Gurtagolane [Gortagoulane], n.s.g.
825.276	William Wheeler, n.s.g.

825.294   Israel Taylor, clerk.

114.   *Parish of St Mary's Shandon, Barony of Cork*
822.253   William Knight, n.s.g.
824.234   Robert Fennell of the North Abbey [?], county of the city of Cork, merchant.
825.94   Thomas Martin of St Mary Shandon, Cork city, n.s.g.
825.154   Justance Hall of Half Mile House [?], n.s.g.
825.179   Thomas Morley of St Mary's Shandon, n.s.g.
825.233   Thomas Martin and Thomas Morley of St Mary's Shandon, n.s.g.

115.   *Parish St Michael's, Barony Barrymore*
824.185   Mary Ward, the quarter, parish of St Michael, county Cork, n.s.g.

116.   *Parish Shandrum, Barony Orrery and Kilmore*
822.6   Thomas Williams of Loske, parish Ballinekelly [Ballynakilla], gent.
822.43-4   John Damian of Curryglass, wheeler.
822.120   John Hardon of Killmore [Kilmagoura], husbandman.
822.214   John Fisher of Kilrahan [Killabraher], yeoman.
822.243   John Hunt of Curragh Clonbou [Curraghcloonabro], husbandman.
824.53   Elias Fitch of Kilmagower [Kilmagoura], yeoman.
824.81   Thomas Meade of Old Orchard [?], gent.
824.204   William Greene of Newtowne [Newtown], n.s.g.
825.145   James Mitchell of Curriglasse [Curryglass], husbandman.
825.299   William Williamson, town and parish of Balynykilly [Ballynakilla], gent.

117.   *Parish Skull, Barony West Carbery*
822.135   Thomas Way, clerk.
823.212   John Northeran of Lencom [Leamcon], yeoman.
824.253-9   Sir William Hull, knight.

118.   *Parish Templeboden, Barony Barrymore*
823.47   Edward Way of Templebodan, n.s.g.
824.114   John Meiger, Ballyvodin [?], [Templebodan], Barony Barrymore, shepherd.

119.   *Parish Templemichael, Barony Kinalea*
823.206   Francis Oster of Clothniedownan [Clogheenduane], n.s.g.
825.29   William Robinson of Temple Michelliagh [Templemichael], clerk.

120.   *Parish Templemolaga, Barony Condons and Clangibbon*
822.109-10   Jasper Horsey of Ballyshurdane, gent.
823.227-8   Edward Horsey of Athcroff [?], gent.
824.74   Jasper Horsey of Ballyshordane [Ballyshurdane], gent.

121.   *Parish Templemartin, Barony Kinalmeaky*
822.190   John Quarry of Granahoonick [?], [Graigue], yeoman.
822.216   Robert Lane, late of Derrybeth [?], parish Temple [?], yeoman.
822.218   John Launcelate of Cottyvarth [?], parish Temple [?], yeoman.
822.256   Steven Barrett of Farmavan [Farranhavane], yeoman.

822.262	Stephen Cregan of Skirtinmuch [Scartnamuck], n.s.g.
823.10	Thomas Sherowe of Deryverth [?], parish Templetan [?], [Templemartin], yeoman.
823.165-8	Walter Baldwin of Granahoonick [?], [Graigue], yeoman.
823.186	David Arthure of Fynagh [?], yeoman.
824.47	Augustine Hicks of Shanloghane [Shanacloyne], yeoman.
824.163	Giles Dangar of Granaheny [?], [Graigue], tanner.
824.181	Richard Wilsheene of Agreenagh [?], Barony Barretts [?], n.s.g.
825.43	William Sarsfield of Garran [Garranes], clerk.
825.47	Richard Keele of Currovardy [Curravordy], clothier.
825.92	Henry Vizard of Coravordye [Curravordy], yeoman.
825.163	Robert Cripps of Aghineenagh [?], parish Templemortagh [?], [Templemartin], barony Barretts [?], n.s.g.
825.266	Walter Baldinge, brother to James Baldinge of Lisnegatt [Lisnagat], gent.

122. *Parish Templenacarriga, Barony Barrymore*

822.221	Nicholas Whetham of Ballyelyney [Ballymacsliney], yeoman.
823.102	John Soolevan of Cargysmall [?], [Carrigogna], parish Templenecarrig [Templenacarriga], Barony Agnacorroe [?].

123. *Parish Templeroan, Barony Fermoy*

824.87	William Smith of Ballymundra [Ballyhourode], gent.

124. *Parish Templetrine, Barony East Carbery*

822.201	Samuel Pawyly of Garretstown [Garrettstown], n.s.g.
825.256	John Sweate of Ballydownis, gent.

125. *Parish Templeusque, Barony Barrymore*

822.159	Samuel Croft of Connygally [Coneybeg], husbandman.
822.271	Alexander Durdane of Killologha [Killalough], husbandman.
823.30	Philipp Dardane of Cashery [Crushyriree], widow.
823.203	Samuel Croft of Conygally [Coneybeg], n.s.g.
825.195	Michell Dundann of Killclogh [Killalogh], n.s.g.

126. *Parish Timoleague, Barony Ibane and Barryroe*

823.223	George Davis of Timoleague, husbandman.

127. *Parish Tracton, Barony Kinalea*

822.146	James Daunt of Tracton Abbey, esq.
824.195	John Brien of Farrenbrien [Farranbrien], British Protestant [?], n.s.g.
825.191	William Allen of Farrenderacly [?], yeoman.

128. *Parish Tullagh, Barony West Carbery*

824.162	Elizabeth Rogers, town and parish of Tullagh, widow.
825.173	Jonathan Bennett of Bandon, on behalf of himself and his two brothers Thomas and Amos, all sons of Roger Bennett, a merchant of Baltimore Castle.
825.273	Thomas Mokes of Baltymore [Baltimore], n.s.g.

129. *Parish Whitechurch, Barony Barretts*

    824.78   William Stewart of the quarter [?], barony Decies [?], county Cork. (This belongs to county Waterford where there is a parish of White-church, barony of Decies-without-Drum with a townland Bridge-water)

130. *Parish Youghal, Barony Imokilly*

    822.111   John Clone, Youghal, merchant.
    822.113   Thomas Hincks for Margery Hazard, widow.
    822.155   Richard Newman of Youghal, carrier.
    822.194   John Redish and Thomas Beard, Youghal, gents.
    822.208   Richard Myers, town and parish of Youghal, gent.
    823.58   Stephen Clove of Youghal, chapman.
    823.132   Thomas Hinckes, merchant and Mary his wife.
    823.170-5   Therlagh Kelly, Youghal, gent., Irish Protestant.
    823.216   Francis Kerrine of Youghal, widow of merchant.
    824.93   Thomas Turner of Youghal, merchant.
    824.98   David Blayney, clerk.
    823.131 and
    824.251   Jonas Clone, town and parish of Youghal, merchant.
    824.246   Nicholas Stout, gent.
    825.101   Thomas Beard of Youghal, gent.

131. *Cork city (deponents who identified themselves with the city of Cork and who could not be assigned to an identifiable parish. Other city deponents appear under parishes of Carrigrohane, Currykippane, Garrycloyne, Inishkenny, Rathcooney, St Finbarr's, St Mary's, Shandon.*

    822.69   Henry Hawkes of Powllymore in the parish of Gallygrahane, the county of the city of Cork, n.s.g.
    822.248   Mary Cudmore, Christchurch parish within the city of Cork, widow.
    823.27   Edward Osborne of Glannekittane, county of the city of Cork, gent.
    823.106   Thomas Banks, minister of Christchurch, city of Cork, clerk.
    823.108   James Piercy of Cork in the county of the city of Cork, gent. and controller of the port of Cork.
    825.122   William Kinge of Cork city (no parish cited), gent.
    825.206   John Gilman, the elder, of Currisure, barony Barretts, within the county of the city of Cork, n.s.g.
    825.303   William Smarte of Synane, in the city of Cork, yeoman.

132. *Parish Glanbarahan, Barony Carbery* (note that no such parish has been located in the 1851 census, with the result that the name of the parish itself and the names of the townlands cannot be checked against that standard. It appears from internal evidence that the parish was close to Castlehaven and may, by 1851, have been absorbed into the parish of Castlehaven)

    823.18   Peter Scuse of Driffane [possibly Drishane, parish Castlehaven], parish Glanbrahan, Barony Carbery, yeoman.
    823.211   John Woods of Gortreagh, parish Glanbrahan, Barony Carbery, husbandman.
    823.214   Richard Scusse of Driffane [possibly Drishane], parish Glanabaroha, yeoman.
    825.169   Ann Ratcliffe of Derrylieth [possibly Derryleigh, parish Castlehaven], parish Glanbarraghan, widow.

133. *Parish Killurd, Barony Fermoy and Condons and Clangibbon* (note that no such parish has been identified in the 1851 census. It appears from internal evidence that this parish lay close to the parish of Kilworth, barony Condons and Clangibbon)

   822.78   John Lachford, town and parish of Killurd, husbandman.
   822.180   Mary Smith, wife to Thomas Smith, town and parish of Killurd, innholder.
   824.232   John Wright, parish Killurd, mercer.

134. *County Cork deponents from unidentified parishes*

   822.107   John Andrews of Ballyoniste and parish of [?] Elldades, no barony cited, husbandman.
   822.130   John Savadge of Ballycomin, parish of Knovall, barony Kymelbore [?], [Kilmore[, county Cork, yeoman.
   822.145   Richard Parsons of Ballyvard, parish Glanura [?], no barony cited, county Cork, shepherd.
   822.160   John Heger of Clanrogge, parish Cary [?], barony Carbery, yeoman.
   822.192   Nicholas Waite of Carrigalome, parish Lenagh [?], Barony East Carbery, husbandman.
   822-204   John Farneham of Caseyknocke in the county of Cork, gent.
   823.21   Cathrin Roberts, relict of George Roberts, parish Unnderkett [?], barony Duhallow, widow.
   823.56   Thomas Price of Tonnyglossy, parish Clenckler [?], barony Barry-more, shipwright.
   823.160ᵛ   Ann Sarjeant, wife of Symen Sarjeant, townland of Ballinasbugg, n.s.g.
   823.195   John Martin for his son Leonard Martin of Cole, parish Glantunda [?], barony Kinalea, yeoman.
   824.37   John Robinson of Gurtine, parish Mohey [?], barony Muskerry, n.s.g.
   825.39   Mary Cumbes of Downedonnell, parish Bre [?], barony Kinalmeaky, widow.
   825.110   An Ryan of Shartnanore, parish [illegible], barony Imokilly, widow.
   825.133   Anthony Mansell of Ballyhustie, barony Duhallow, gent.
   825.224   George Childs of Castlemor, barony Barretts, husbandman.
   825.305   Thomas Scuse of Dennycow, parish Ardes [?], barony Carbery, yeoman.

135. *Cork depositions incorrectly assigned by county*

   823.52   Robert Hunt, properly belongs with county Limerick.
   823.157-8 William Eames, properly belongs with county Limerick.
   823.161   Anthony Sherwin, properly belongs with county Limerick.
   824.3-4   William Bushop, more relevant to counties Monaghan and Meath.
   824.78   William Stewart, may properly belongs with county Waterford.
   825.25   Sir Robert Tirrell, properly belongs with county Limerick.
   825.283   John Slade, on behalf of his father, property belongs to county Clare.

Parish Ovens: see under Athnowen
(No parish of Ovens appears in the 1851 census but the area previously covered by that has been absorbed into the parish of Athnowen, Barony East Muskerry).

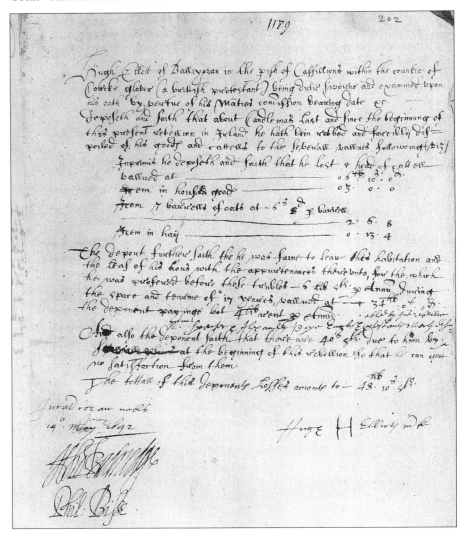

Plate 8.1   Cork deposition: Hugh Ellott of Ballyoran (T.C.D., MS 822 f. 202).

Chapter 9

THE POLITICAL, MATERIAL AND MENTAL CULTURE OF THE CORK SETTLERS, *c.* 1650-1700

T. C. BARNARD

County Cork has been lucky in its early and its recent historians. Without their researches this essay, avowedly impressionistic and anecdotal, could not have been attempted. As it is I diffidently squeeze between the titans a study of a little explored and formative period which may at least identify problems for further pursuit.[1]

Introduction

Richard Cox, the first Cork Protestant to stand back and reflect on his home county in the 1680s, emphasised three visible features. He shared the zest of his kind for 'improvement'. The past interested him enough to record ecclesiastical ruins, but here he may simply have cribbed the format of Sir James Ware and English antiquaries. Cox also catalogued nearly two dozen mansions, and in doing so prefigured those later annalists of the new English order who equated the county with its owners and saw their residences as oases of gentility and taste.

An interest in big houses may tell us something of Cox the lawyer's aspirations, for he was thrusting himself into the enchanted circle of big house owners. Yet it was a fascination shared by county Cork's next historian (and the first to be published), Dr Charles Smith. In the 1740s Smith itemised about 200 seats. This apparently dramatic increase may alert us to underlying changes: most obviously, spreading prosperity. Smith, however, had an incentive to thoroughness unknown by Cox, namely the need to list new houses comprehensively in order to entice their owners into subscribing to his publication.[2]

Neither Cox nor Smith was indulging a snobbish whimsy in recording gentlemen's seats. Rather each acknowledged the symbolic as well as utilitarian importance of the houses. These mansions, the hubs of estates now owned by Protestants, indicated a network of manors enmeshing the county in which a new world was in the making, and implied other settler achievements: remodelled and enlarged villages endowed with freshly built schools, market houses, almshouses and (sometimes) churches. Architecture made manifest the aims of the Protestant settlers: to enrich themselves and their neighbours and thereby to accomplish what the government had willed when it had placed them on their acres, a stable Protestant society. Thus the houses inventoried by Cox and Smith consciously displayed the different and allegedly better values of the newcomers. Cox indeed asserted that the inferior condition of the native Irish was most tellingly illustrated by their failure to build in brick and stone, an axiom widely accepted by other English commentators. Even the pre-Reformation structures which he admired he took to be the work of the earlier invaders, such as the Vikings and the Anglo-Normans. Culture and religion, Cox argued, had depressed the Catholic Irish, habituating them to dwell in 'cabins which are worse than hogstyes'. Through enforced changes in building, he hoped, the Irish would become 'neat and clean about your persons, and in your houses ... to which in truth you are naturally inclined'.[3] It is true that throughout Europe the supporters of the revived classicism behaved as if engaged on a crusade in which more than style was at stake.[4] In the Irish context, however, a developing enthusiasm for classical symmetry complicated an approach to architecture already rich in qualitative judgements, seeing it as a vital – because so visible – assertion of English superiority.

England in the early eighteenth century has been called 'a federation of country houses'.[5] Thus, if we follow Cox and Smith in seeing county Cork in a similar light, we may be led towards important insights. Later writers have detected the essence of Protestant Ireland in its landed élites and in their members' distressingly transient homes. Some panegyrists occasionally seem keen to relive, at least vicariously, the landowners' aimless indolence. In understandable reaction the parasitic and enfeebling effects of 'landlordism' have been emphasised. Much of what the owners spent their money on has been adjudged archaic and anachronistic because not self-evidently productive. Passing their lives in a 'sealed-in, autonomous world of privilege', preoccupied with the 'fastidious display of arrogance', the landed classes' demise can be treated at once as inevitable, owing to their failure to adjust to new political, social and economic imperatives, and deserved. Their houses and parks, important works of art, by being degraded into 'zones of superfluity' can be left to vanish unlamented.[6]

This essay will not attempt to rehabilitate 'landlordism'. Instead it will dissolve that abstraction which turns individuals into a homogeneous and undifferentiated class, which is then all too easily censured. It will seek to penetrate and evoke the distinct worlds of the largest but often absent and unashamedly Anglo-Irish magnates, of the more modest proprietors and of the merchants, lawyers and office-holders whose roles in settler society are more often mentioned than analysed. If nothing else, something of this newly hidden Ireland will be conveyed: the varieties of behaviour and outlook, of wealth and ways of life.

A county community?

The focus of my study raises questions about using the county as the point of entry into later seventeenth-century Ireland. What starts as a convenience can turn into a major interpretative tool. The county, some of its English chroniclers claim, was more than an administrative unit. As its functions proliferated, and as local virtuosi and cartographers isolated its distinctive characteristics, so it became the principal arena for its leading inhabitants. The passionate attachment of the latter to the county, it has been argued, conflicted with and sometimes overrode obligations to national government.[7] In turn sceptics have stressed competing and frequently stronger loyalties, either political, cultural and ideological or (for the majority) more parochial and personal.[8] This controversy has yet to echo through Irish historiography. Certainly historians of nineteenth-century Ireland have based their enquiries on the county: two fine studies of Cork lead the field here.[9] But writers on early modern Ireland have preferred to deal either in provinces or in economic and geographical regions, without in detail discussing the methodological misgivings which may have caused them to eschew the county and favour the larger district.

Thus, in voluntarily confining myself to one county, albeit the largest and perhaps the richest in Ireland,[10] I shall seek to avoid the silent jump from a descriptive to an evaluative use of the county. Rather than assuming without demonstrating the existence of a cohesive county community, I shall discuss what sense of their county the settlers in Cork possessed. A second problem is that the shire, imported from England and by the seventeenth century reproducing in Ireland most of its features, encourages the belief that Cork society in essentials resembles what we might meet in the larger English and Welsh counties remote from London. Again this is a presumption worth discussing rather than silently accepting or rejecting, and such a discussion may help us decide whether Irish Protestant communities were colonial, provincial or a special Hibernian hybrid.

The very fact that counties were designed to ease Ireland's subjection to England may have weakened affection for and involvement in them among their residents. Attachment to a locality, *pace* MacDonagh,[11] strong among many in Ireland, was usually inspired by something more specific and obtrusive than the unwieldy and contrived construct of county Cork. Dickson has isolated thirteen different farming regions in South Munster, eight of them in county Cork itself, and each varying in its social and economic features.[12] The size of the county, the diversity of soils and terrain, the unevenness of settlement and the awkwardnesses of travel all retarded any well-developed county community. Furthermore the county, ragged at its edges, merged imperceptibly into west Waterford, south Limerick and south Kerry. The baronies along the Blackwater corridor, for example, belonged functionally to the economy and society of county Cork. Settlers from those parts of county Waterford were elected to represent Cork in parliament, to serve as clerk of the peace for county Cork and, in the case of the greatest, took his title from Cork.[13] The difficulties of holding together this large and disparate county were further suggested when it was proposed to split it administratively into ridings, when its quarter sessions were divided between a northern and southern circuit, and when ecclesiastical oversight was again shared between two Protestant bishops, of Cork and Ross and of Cloyne.[14]

Among the newcomers the wealthiest owned estates which ignored county boundaries and indeed the Irish Sea. The worlds of these magnificoes, with the growing popularity of the Grand Tour, reached beyond the British Isles. For the majority of settlers, of more modest means, the county was an irrelevance. If an administrative district impinged on them it was most likely to be the barony, the borough, the village, the townland or the parish. Yet clearly the county was something more than an abstraction in the minds of Dublin and London officials. The Cromwellians and their successors used it as the basis for redistributing lands. By the 1680s a fortunate few could buy Petty's maps published in *Hibernia Delineatio*, and see for themselves the extent and shape of their shire.[15] For Cox it offered a precise framework for systematising his local curiosity and pride.

Also by the 1680s the well-established cycle of quarter sessions and twice-yearly assizes was a social as well as business event. In April 1686 the assizes lasted seventeen days. Landowners from as far afield as Carbery and Bantry were drawn by them to Cork city. Leading settlers serving as high sheriff, magistrates or grand jurors, either formally through addresses and presentments or informally through talk, voiced their worries. In addition the need to choose members of parliament, frequent between 1654 and 1661 and again after 1692, required gatherings and might stimulate county-wide planning. On these occasions it could be convenient to parade county solidarity, even if we question its spontaneity and suspect it of being adventitious and partisan.[16]

In 1658 a Cork settler prefaced a complaint with the words 'since this county became a county'; over twenty years later the chaplain of Cork's pre-eminent politician eulogised his master as 'the cement of the country gentry where he lived'. In each case the writer, rather tenuously linked with county Cork, may have slipped for rhetorical effect into the categories borrowed from and appropriate to English experience. Similarly when the heir of Kanturk and Lohort returned to his estates in 1682, his uncle recommended that he study the foibles of the county's gentry. But once more the adviser, for long absent from Ireland, assumed too readily that a gentleman's life in Cork would conform to that of his English counterparts. More telling as an indicator of some sense of identity with the county was the praise by Cork's political boss of a parliamentary speaker in 1693: 'he is of our county'.[17]

Such sparse and often ambiguous evidence for settlers' identification with county Cork has to be balanced against examples of the hold of other, equally powerful allegiances. Elections, while they might oblige cooperation between gentry throughout the shire, were times when urgent national and international questions could divide rather than unite. The eagerness with which the denominations of Whig and Tory were taken up by the Cork gentry owed much to long-standing rivalries over policies and between personalities which stretched back to the early seventeenth century; the affiliations also offered new means of expressing the inchoate tensions between the eastern and western baronies of the county.[18]

The administrative net in which all who inhabited county Cork were to be caught trawled less than comprehensively. Boroughs, including Cork, Youghal, Kinsale and Clonakilty, held their own sessions, and brusquely repelled the county courts' encroachments. Towns struggled less successfully against being rated for county levies; failure to gain exemption bequeathed bitterness, and the county came to stand principally for taxes. A patron could popularly serve a borough by freeing its inhabitants from jury service in distant parts of the county, and by procuring a local meeting of the sessions or, better still, of the assizes, which attracted extra custom. Within most landowners' grasp was a grant of manorial courts through which useful services were dispensed to the immediate locality. If tenants benefitted thereby, county-wide activity was lessened.[19] In seventeenth-century England most counties which approached Cork in size were internally divided for administrative and judicial purposes, and even then the courts tended to attract as jurors, litigants and even as active magistrates those who lived closest.[20] It is likely that a similar situation prevailed in later seventeenth-century Cork and, if it did, reduced the gravitational field over which county administration was effective.

To the pull of parochial forces must be added those which operated on the men most likely to staff county government. By definition the richest, they were most encumbered with interests which ignored county borders. Their actions, rooted in family or self, might reflect impulses of loyalty to the Irish and English king, to the Protestant interest and religion (variously perceived), or ideas of honour, honesty and virtue. The province of Munster, although extinguished as an administrative reality in 1672, continued to mean something, and not just to its aggrieved and humiliated lord president. It, rather than the county, better coincided with the extent of the plantation which had first brought the ancestors of many Protestants to the region. It took more notice of the interdependence which agriculture, trade and shared marriages, culture and religion created. Political management, undertaken by Orrery in 1659 and 1663 and by Midleton and Shannon in the early eighteenth century, reached beyond county Cork's to south Munster's M.P.s.[21] The act to bridge the Blackwater at Cappoquin, procured in 1666 by Lord Cork, was intended to assist the several counties required to contribute to its cost.[22] Defence of land through the law, the commonest of the settlers' public activities, meant exploring a maze of courts: those of the province (until 1672), of the county, of the Tipperary palatinate at Clonmel and the four in Dublin. In addition settlers and their agents from other counties, most conspicuously from Kerry, visited Cork for the assizes, so robbing them of any exclusivity to the county.[23]

These preliminaries can be closed by returning to Richard Cox. His feelings of local attachment and pride had been encouraged by an invitation to contribute to a planned Irish atlas, the format of which itself hinted at the stronger sense of locality (though not always for county) among Ireland's settlers. But Cox's interest in Cork existed alongside, and was often subordinated to, a fierce zeal for the endangered Protestant interest in Ireland. In advising how England could regain Ireland in 1689, Cox proposed to tap localism. His understanding of the anxieties of his fellow Protestants, whether forced into exile or embattled in Cork, informed his scheme. Cox saw too how the experience of adversity and deracination, which he himself had shared, created a precocious Irish Protestant identity.[24] In English counties there seems to have been some correlation between the length of time during which families had been settled and the strength of their devotion to the county.[25] By that token, the Protestants of Cork, few of whom could trace back their ancestors more than two or three generations, would be unlikely to exhibit this sentiment. However, continuous threats, with estates overrun in the 1640s and again in 1689-90, stimulated a rapid growth of local engagement. The widespread reluctance to flee in 1689 arose, in some cases, from affection for the locality. Dublin, when compared to Cork, was 'this dog of a town'.

Once in England even well-connected refugees like Henry Boyle and his wife (Lord Inchiquin's daughter) longed only to return to county Cork. She in particular railed against Bristol, her temporary home, as the 'rudest place in the world'.[26] Nevertheless we must suppose, and this is clearest in the case of Cox, that sense of place embraced love of a particular estate and *locale*, a region or province, and the loose and shifting idea of Protestant or English Ireland.

Notables

Dickson has delineated the structure of the Cork settler community. In 1641 Catholics still owned two-thirds of the land; by the 1660s their share was halved; after the Williamite Wars of the 1690s it had dwindled to a meagre 8 per cent. Among the new owners Dickson detected an élite in south Munster of about twenty families who owned perhaps 20 per cent of the profitable acreage. Below these grandees he found a larger group, numbering approximately one hundred, who filled public office, in Dublin as M.P. or in the county as high sheriff, justice of the peace or grand juror. A yet larger group, of perhaps three hundred, holding 1,000 statute acres or more, had the wherewithal to play something other than a parochial role.[27] As in England, so in county Cork, income and its source determined entry into society and politics. £100 annually, derived from land, has been suggested as the minimum stake in Ireland to join the commission of the peace.[28] More difficult to gauge is the proportion these three hundred formed in Cork's total Protestant population. The best estimate for the settler population before 1641 is 22,000. In the later seventeenth century contemporary figures are guesses. Recovery and growth after the disruptions of the Confederate Wars were slow, and a total of 30,000 might be hazarded.[29]

Whatever the figure, the danger of generalising about this society from its leaders is evident. Yet we must begin with those nabobs, and not simply because their activities have left the clearest traces. Far from living exclusively in 'sealed-in' worlds, the landowners, through their demands, standards and preoccupations, touched numerous dependants, neighbours and poorer Protestants, and helped to refashion the society in which all lived. Also they ensured that Ireland was closely integrated into the British Isles and western Europe, and was assuredly neither an offshore colony nor a nearer America.

Economic as well as social pre-eminence belonged to the peers, for ennoblement customarily went still to those who could sustain the honour from an appropriate income. In 1700 ten peers owned land in the county, but six of them were absentees. A similar situation had prevailed in the previous forty years, and even those who normally resided might be disabled from playing their expected parts, leaving openings for men of more modest rank. Some who had gained land in Cork thanks to the upheavals of the civil wars had done so almost by chance, as for example Lord Anglesey who took no interest in county, as distinct from Irish, affairs.[30] Others, notably the second earl of Cork, loosened their ties with the region, as his transformation from Lord Cork to Lord Burlington aptly symbolised. Cork, although from time to time a visitor and a powerful champion of Irish concerns in the English House of Lords and at court, contributed more to settler society by his absence than his presence. In return he expected Irish remittances to fund his English building ventures.[31]

Judged by what we know of rentals, Lord Cork and Burlington overtopped all rivals, including his younger brothers. The empire of his father, the first earl, had been dismembered to provide for his numerous offspring. After 1650 four sons survived, each with a substantial holding in the county: the continuously absent Robert Boyle; the often resident Lord Shannon, with his 'mongrel' estate, partly in England and partly in Cork around Ballinrea; Lords Orrery and Cork. The last enjoyed the lion's portion: Lismore, Lisfinny, Tallow, Dungarvan, Youghal, Inchiquin, Bandon and Carbery. Moreover he added to his patrimony. In 1666 he spent £8,000 on confiscated property in Youghal, and in 1691, following his brother Robert's death, some of his father's lands reverted to him. Thus supplemented, his Irish rentals yielded over £20,000 and now, in contrast to his father, he also owned extensive English lands.[32]

Below Cork the hierarchies of wealth and status did not always coincide. Some peers, including Cork's brother Shannon, his nephew Barrymore and Inchiquin hovered near genteel penury.[33] The wealthy owners of Mitchelstown and Liscarrol for the moment remained commoners. The estates of Orrery, the Percevals and the Fentons (after 1670 amalgamated with those of the Kings from Roscommon) probably each yielded about £4,000 p.a.[34] Yet each owner, through the unpredictable impact of deaths, minorities, jointures, rent charges, extravagance and mounting debts, enjoyed in practice a considerably smaller income and often was incapable of leading settler society. The Percevals, for example had to escape the consequences of too close support of Ormonde and the king in the 1640s. Later a rapid sequence of premature deaths hit them. Only between 1652 and 1665 and again from 1680 to 1686 did the Percevals dictate local taste while disdaining the rough and tumble of politics.[35] The Kings of Boyle Abbey had inherited the Fenton estates through an heiress. The last Fenton widow remarried, and her new husband, Sir William Petty, gleefully added defence of her jointure rights to his other causes. The contentions

Plate 9.1   Boyle monument, St Mary's Collegiate Church, Youghal.

between the Pettys and the Kings were soon eclipsed by vicious fights within the King tribe itself. Estates elsewhere, the third Lord Kingston's marriage to a Catholic dairymaid, his own conversion and Jacobitism, trickery by his uncle and enforced sojourns abroad, rendered the owners of Mitchelstown nullities in Cork life.[36]

The Inchiquin O'Briens showed how indigenous families might survive by religious and political conformity to the new English order. Survival but hardly prosperity rewarded them in the later seventeenth century. In the labyrinth of the 1640s the first earl had taken several wrong turnings. In the 1650s he returned to his old faith and, accepting Spanish pay, governed a second province recently troubled by rebellion, Catalonia. After 1660 Inchiquin's past services brought him Rostellan. He now obliterated old quarrels with his neighbour and erstwhile adversary Orrery and cemented the unexpected friendship by a double marriage. Inchiquin's heir married one of Orrery's daughters, and a daughter married Orrery's younger son: conjunctions reminiscent of those contrived by Orrery's father and given added allure by the fact that Rostellan marched with Orrery's Imokilly estate. Trading on this link, the dying Inchiquin in 1673 entrusted his children to Orrery's care, a duty which the latter punctiliously performed. Family fortunes, estimated in 1689 at £2,530 p.a., remained precarious. Military commissions with the attendant pay and the delusive quest for heiresses were the strategies to keep afloat. Orrery had done what he could to assist his son-in-law, lodging him and his bride in his own mansion at Charleville, and delegating to him some of the presidential powers and allowances while away in England.

In 1686, now a widower, hard-up and politically suspect, the second earl of Inchiquin stalked an heiress in Dublin and, while staying in Herefordshire, bagged another. His bride, Lady Herbert of Cherbury, was the widow of a Kerry settler. However her main attractions, as Inchiquin disarmingly admitted, were a jointure of £1,000 p.a., £5,000 in jewels and a further £2,000 in cash. Acquaintances shook their heads and predicted that the countess 'will not find much joy'. But she proved equal to her husband and insisted on high-life in London. However Inchiquin had a second scheme to escape from his financial straits, another match with an heiress, this time for his son. The daughter-in-law, whose father was a wealthy London merchant, would bring a dowry of £8,000. Yet in the end, it seems, the girl's father, dissatisfied with the inadequate provision made by Inchiquin, backed out of the contract.[37] In 1689 Inchiquin and his Boyle brother-in-law led the Protestants who resisted the Catholic onslaught. Fighting was the only trade that either knew or could follow without derogation from his aristocratic standing. Earlier it had taken Inchiquin to Tangier, and it led each to his death: Henry Boyle of Castlemartyr in the Low Countries in 1693 and Inchiquin in Jamaica in 1692. The Inchiquins bowed out of Cork affairs until 1708 when the third earl returned to Rostellan and there launched a costly building campaign.[38]

Most remarkable among the titled owners was Orrery, self-appointed captain of the Cork Protestants. To compartmentalise Orrery's multifarious activities and to discuss his life at Charleville and Castlemartyr without reference to his other concerns – in Limerick, as governor and property-owner; throughout Munster as lord president; in Dublin, briefly as lord justice, then as privy councillor and peer; in London, first as a lobbyist and expert on all matters Irish, then as M.P. for Arundel and an active politician; and indeed as a voluminous writer and controversialist – would be unjust to a man whom few liked. He was the man who so impressed Cromwell and who governed Scotland for him; he steered M.P.s into offering Cromwell the crown, but then smoothed the way for Charles II's restoration in Ireland.[39] For a short space he ruled Ireland on the king's behalf and even when demoted from that job to which his talents fitted him so admirably (in his own estimation), he was constantly at Ormonde's elbow, chiding and chivvying, steadied his band of dependants, the 'Orreronians', in the Irish Commons. No doubt he exaggerated his achievements, although the evidence for his diplomatic and managerial skills is strong.[40] His consolation prize, of lord president of Munster, provided a wonderful pretext to deluge the governments in London and Dublin with admonitions.

Yet Orrery never sank into provincial inanition. He kept his seat in the English parliament and his entrée to the court. Through his own and his wife's relations he had access to the smart intellectual world of London and the English country house circuit. He retained his Somerset estate. Crippled and reduced to semi-invalidism, peremptorily dismissed as lord president in 1672, he morosely reviewed past and present, and warned of the new threats from France and Catholicism. He relived fading glories as he compiled his treatise on warfare and fanned the cooling embers of old passions as he prepared a history of the Confederate Wars. This then was the man who lorded it over Cork society until 1679.[41]

For the role which he aspired to fill, Orrery suffered several disadvantages. Some might suppose that the chief was his temperament, combative and irascible: tendencies perhaps worsened by the constant pain which he latterly endured. No more easily than any other Cromwellian collaborator could he shed the reputation for suppleness which, to the unfriendly (and there were plenty), smacked of treachery. Furthermore Orrery's eagerness to ingratiate himself with the returned Charles II stopped well short of masking his strongest convictions. His attacks on Catholicism as a political as well as religious system were unlikely to please a monarch whom he also berated for siphoning off the Irish revenue. Connected with his difficult opinions was his uncertain hold on royal and government favour. His numerous enemies, including those in county Cork, seized upon and magnified rumours of his impending ruin, particularly in 1669 when he faced impeachment in the English parliament, and, when he was dismissed as lord president, openly gloated. In fact he was too valuable a royal servant to be gratuitously antagonised by the complete withdrawal of favour.[42] His loss of office in 1672 was quickly compensated, most appositely by a generous pension and then with a new commission to oversee the military security of Munster. His state and status had hardly been impaired.[43]

The pension which the king had settled on Orrery highlighted another of his difficulties. His magnificence had to be supported from an income frankly inadequate to the task. Like so many others in Restoration Ireland Orrery had large expectations, and he constantly badgered friends and officials to assist him to the enjoyment of funds earmarked for him. Until these promises were honoured – in the most important case not until 1699 – he lived on an income which seldom exceeded £4,000 p.a.: small beer by the standards of the English peerage or, indeed, of his elder brother.[44] From this he must pay not only the normal expenses of a peer, educating and providing for his two sons and finding portions for his four daughters (at a cost of about £20,000), but also finance the grandiose rebuilding of Charleville (calculated at £20,000), and the more modest works at Castlemartyr, said to have cost £2,900. Four lengthy stays in London cost a further £20,000. The lawyer Cox, called in to unknot the family's tangles in the 1680s, remarked that Orrery's 'soul was much larger than his fortune, tho' he had great offices and a plentiful estate'. Contrary to the impression that Orrery sought to convey, the debts had not all been contracted by his extravagant heir; he himself had regularly been over-spending for decades.[45]

The detailed financing of Orrery's public career, and especially of the splendour with which he surrounded himself at Charleville, remain puzzling. His own analyses reveal the main sources of his income. If rents constituted about 60 per cent of the expected receipts in 1678, it was the lands in Imokilly and Limerick which he had gained through his own industry rather than those around Charleville inherited from his father which lifted him from the middling plateau to the pinnacle of local landed society. But rents alone did not guarantee his pre-eminence in Cork. The steady and certain income from provincial and military offices added another £1,500, or almost 40 per cent of the expected total.[46] Orrery's figures tell us of the dangers which menaced and which were already lapping his estates. On his death his salaries would cease, the two Cork holdings would be separated, his own patrimony descending to his heir, while Castlemartyr, subject to a life interest for his wife, would pass to the younger son. The Limerick properties, intended to endow his as yet unmarried daughter, had already been depleted to satisfy more pressing needs.

His eldest son's annual income of £1,050 was already eaten into by the £450 needed to service his debts and a further £500 payable to his estranged wife. In his case and in that of his younger brother, Henry, inheritor of Castlemartyr, worth £600 p.a. but liable to rent charges of over £300, only their pay as captains of horse gave them much disposable income. The worsening situation seems to have caused Orrery to scale down the size of a younger daughter's dowry and to borrow. Family fortunes deteriorated further in 1683 when the second earl's death obliged the estates to keep two dowagers, one of whom survived until 1710. These two widows, usually but not invariably resident in England, took at least 70 per cent of the estates' income. Only the long minority of the third earl, boarded in cheap continental *pensions* with cut-price servants, and the firing of the costly incubus of Charleville, enabled the Orrerys to survive.[47]

The first earl of Orrery had risen above the expectations of a younger son, and avoided the lot of another brother, Viscount Shannon, who on £1,000 p.a. contented himself with 'a neat house and a curious small park' and the crumbs of public employment left once Orrery had taken his pick, scrounged hospitality from his bachelor brother in England and unctuously commiserated with affluent eldest brothers.[48] Orrery by dextrous opportunism had raised his income to £4,000, but it was not of itself enough to live as he did. His spending on Charleville far surpassed his brother Cork's on Burlington House in London and that of most aristocratic builders in England.[49] Charleville, in its scale, its decoration and furnishings, was designed to rival the state which Ormonde kept at Kilkenny and Dublin Castle.[50] But in pitting himself against Ormonde, Orrery foolishly ignored the disparities which extended beyond rank, lineage and royal favour to their wealth. Ormonde's annual income approached £24,000. Orrery, in comparison, borrowed to pay for his finery. Of course his accounts hide the 'free gifts' and sweeteners which came his way as lord president. He was also accused, and was almost certainly guilty, of sharp practice when at the Restoration Cromwellian officers had conveyed their lands to him in trust, only to discover that he had then sold them and pocketed the proceeds. But even with these bonuses, we can assume that receipts fell short of his expenditure.[51]

We may speculate on, though we should not reflexively condemn, the monstrous vanity which made Orrery so spendthrift, to the detriment of his heirs. Here we seem to glimpse an early example of that insouciance which bedevilled numerous Protestant dynasties in Ireland. (It was also alleged to afflict English aristocrats). However such fecklessness, if attributed to Orrery, hardly fits with a picture of a man in all other respects shrewd and calculating. The heavy outlay on show was connected intimately with his local and national ambitions. Closer investigation of his houses and their contents will show his and other landowners' relationship to the wider world of objects, ideas and men which radiated from the 'armed' chairs in which they sat at the physical and symbolic centre of their possessions.[52] The lines of connection spread from their houses throughout Protestant Ireland into England and on into Europe and the expanding continents of Asia, Africa and America.

Buildings and possessions
Rolf Loeber first made us take seriously what the settlers built in later seventeenth-century Ireland.[53] But the lost civilisation of the settlers still awaits resuscitation, and in hunting their values and ideas, the details of that physical world, rarely now surviving but retrievable through inventories, bills, accounts or correspondence, can assist. The artifacts with which they were surrounded were laden with meanings, some literal, others symbolic, which need to be decoded.

From all descriptions, Charleville and Castlemartyr set the standard of modish splendour in Munster, as Orrery had intended. So we shall start there, moving on to the other mansion which in comfort and elegance may well have surpassed them – the Percevals' Burton House.[54] Charleville impressed initially by its size. As Orrery's heir less appreciatively commented, 'the only fault 'tis too big by one half'. But to Cox it was quite simply 'magnificent'. Its other novelty, implicit rather then explicit in contemporary accounts, was its style: its regular façades deliberately distinguished it from the asymmetrical mansions and towers which dotted south Munster, such as Orrery's father's castle at Lismore, and which had recently reached an apogee at Coppinger's Court.[55]

With more regard for effect than literal truth Orrery dated the laying of the foundation stone at Charleville to 29 May 1661, the first anniversary of Charles II's re-entry into London. Although habitable by 1663, work there fell into at least two distinct phases. Orrery hoped to have '2 or 3 rooms to entertain my friends, then every week I shall enlarge my quarters'. In 1664 the house was taxed on only twelve hearths; by 1667 the number had risen to fifty-six; and in 1680 to sixty-five. Like so many other landowners, both in England and Ireland,

Orrery demonstrated his virtuosity by apparently designing his houses himself. His own hope that he could turn his property in Limerick into 'the Covent Garden of that city' suggested both his yardstick and his grasp of the significance of the new classicism derived especially through Inigo Jones from Italy.[56] Although the final palatial scale of Charleville is well attested, its architectural details are more mysterious. Defensive features which in England had atrophied through long years of disuse (notwithstanding their brief resurrection during the civil wars) were more often, though not invariably, retained by house-builders in Restoration Ireland. Orrery was alive to these differences when he wrote of 'the little old fashioned flankers such as most noble men and gentlemen's houses have to this day in Ireland'. Indeed the retention of such flanking walls and gun emplacements may indicate not only what had survived earlier bombardments but also how lawless the owner conceived his locality still to be. In this respect, if Charleville did include these consciously martial airs, it contrasted with Orrery's more southerly seat at Castlemartyr. The latter, begun only in the late 1660s, intended originally as a modest seat for a younger son but expanded to forty hearths, lacked defences. Denser English settlement in Imokilly and greater Protestant confidence may have tempted Orrery to relax his habitual anxieties about Irish Catholic intentions.[57]

The grandeur of Charleville is better understood when we remember that it was here that Orrery literally held court. He claimed that he had doubled spending on it, to £20,000, in order to fit it for himself, the king's governor.[58] The presidential duties also explained the choice of this location rather than a site near Ballymaloe. From Charleville he could more easily oversee the province, reach his own properties at Askeaton and Limerick, and communicate with Dublin.[59] (Previous lords president had chosen nearby locations for their court, at Mallow and Doneraile). In turn litigants, witnesses, jurors and messengers could more readily reach headquarters. Once dismissed as lord president, Orrery promptly abandoned the house, transferring, ostensibly for reasons of health, to Castlemartyr.

With no plans, it is fruitless to conjecture whether Charleville followed the English vogue for the double-pile format or French-inspired sequences of rooms *en enfilade* and sets of lodgings for the principal inmate. Orrery, thanks to his travels and aspirations, could be expected to know the various settings deemed suitable for a peer and a representative of the monarch; so much comes across strongly when we see how he used and furnished his residences. The surviving lists of contents at Charleville and Castlemartyr at first seem to consist of meaningless lists of fabrics: 'sad coloured serge curtains and counterpane', 'curtains and valance with gilt leather fringe', 'grey serge bed with hangings', Indian coverlets, turkey-work carpets, fustian and calico window curtains, 'one white quilt with great yellow tassels', arras hangings, Indian taffeta, sarsnet and buckram, stools and chairs covered with red baize.[60] But this sense of profusion, a kaleidoscope of colours, patterns and textures, is precisely the point. Much of the house's capacity to impress came not so much from its wooden and caned furniture, which by later standards was sparse, but from the fabrics which hung at the windows and beds as curtains, on the walls as tapestries, draped over tables and beds as carpets, quilts and counterpanes, and on chairs and stools as embroidery and upholstery.[61] The foremost historian of these matters has observed 'in the decoration of interiors it was obviously the upholstered types of furniture which made the greatest impact', and the elaborately contrived beds usually constituted the most important pieces of furniture.[62] Judged by these standards, Orrery's houses and indeed the Percevals' Burton were well abreast of contemporary fashion, set in France and soon copied in England.

In other possessions Orrery displayed not only wealth and position but his awareness of continental currents and court standards. In the principal rooms pewter vessels, brass fire implements, sconces and candlesticks glittered; great looking-glasses refracted the light; clocks chimed; and a few prized bottle-shaped vases and lidded jars of oriental porcelain gaudily hinted at distant cultures. When guests came to dine, as they frequently did, they would be seated on chairs upholstered in 'Turkey' work, could admire the gilt leather hangings, the painted images of family and royalty, the green curtains at the three windows, the burnished wall sconces and fire dogs and the three turkey-work carpets removed from the tables only when the food was served. Meals too offered further chances to impress: through the quantity, variety and rarity of the foods and wines, by the silver dishes freshly engraved with Orrery's armorials in which they were served, by the dazzling glass and the fine linen napery.

What, we may ask, did the visitor make of all this? At Charleville, the litigants and tenants who thronged the town on market and court days would see only the bulk of the new house, its thriving plantations of recently planted oak and ash, the roofs and chimneys of the offices, stables and pigeon-house or the elaborate wrought iron gates which sharply demarcated the entry into the demesne. But the bustle of these houses in their heyday drew far more than the regular army of indoor and outdoor servants into their ambit. Neighbours, relations and clients constantly arrived on business or for entertainment.[63] In a few cases we can do more than guess at what feelings they carried back to their inevitably more modest homes. Many, no doubt, were indifferent to the carefully contrived physical setting, affected more by the plenty of food and drink or the sport offered in the billiard room or by the pedigree horses, hounds and hawks kept by Orrery.[64] Disdain was another reaction, at a show which verging on the vulgar invited censure.[65] Frank curiosity might result, for the ingenious and unusual contrivance appealed strongly to seventeenth-century minds.[66] Envy, when it arose, might fuel resentment against nobles with wealth to squander, and invite critical gossip about how Orrery had come by these riches. A further response was emulation when the visitor, captivated by a new fad, glimpsed what he (or she) might also do. Competition and imitation could be complex affairs, and did not automatically lead to the diffusion outwards and socially downwards of a habit. Nevertheless they should not be ignored as forces for change in later seventeenth-century Ireland.[67]

Let us trace more exactly the impact of the physical worlds which Orrery had so laboriously created. Through the houses, as well as from them, he simultaneously advanced his political career, controlled his lands and led his family. Orrery, alert to the significance of the latest buildings of his peers, saw what would best cater to his own sense of self-importance. In translating his dreams into actuality a wider set of influences came into play. His family and friends in Ireland (like Lord Conway) linked him with most of the foremost architects of the day.[68] His frequent travels kept him *au fait* with the latest developments. Then too there were the women of his family, notably his wife and daughter-in-law, both formidable. Ormonde confessed to Orrery that it had been his wife's and his architect's importunities which had persuaded him to add expensively to Kilkenny Castle. Orrery's sister-in-law, Lady Cork, oversaw the completion of Burlington House. The first Lady Orrery, a Howard reared in the now rather threadbare and old-fashioned splendour of Audley End and Charlton Park, and the head-strong Lady Broghill, a Sackville used to the fashionable luxury of Knole, can hardly have been silent as Orrery planned. Certainly Lady Orrery and one of her daughters jumped to fashion's stern commands.[69]

We cannot be precise about the influences which determined the appearance, inside and out, of the mansions of county Cork, other than to insist that they met the standards derived directly from England and the continent, but we can suggest some ways in which these buildings affected more than their immediate environs. £20,000 was the figure put on the final cost of Charleville: high even by English levels. When we remember the spate of similar though less grandiose and therefore less costly undertakings in the county, and the public edifices erected or improved in Cork city and other towns, we might suppose that they reflected and further fuelled a booming economy.[70] But because many materials and much of the labour could be supplied from the estate itself these works have usually been credited with only limited economic consequences.[71] Yet we should not underestimate what buildings on the scale of Charleville required, or imagine that estates were in this respect self-sufficient. Trees had to be felled, hauled from the woods, seasoned, squared and prepared; deal was imported; suitable stone had to be located, quarried and then transported to the site; brick and lime kilns were constructed, fuelled and manned. Draught oxen must be hired, roads and causeways repaired or made. The county and beyond were scoured for the craftsmen proficient in the specialised skills; experts were in short supply, not least because other landlords like Lord Cork and Perceval had snapped up the best; they were constantly at risk of being poached.[72] So it went on, for months, often for years, the incessant heaving and hauling, levelling, digging, chiselling, sawing and hammering. Even when the shell was finished, roofs needed to be tiled or slated, courts cobbled and paved, terraces gravelled, walls limed, rooms wainscoted, floored and ceiled, saplings planted, furniture turned and joined. Orrery, brutally frank that the indigenous Irish should serve as hewers of wood and drawers of water, might aim to employ only Protestants, but such specialists were few and the sheer volume of work obliged him to relax his embargo.[73] The tasks attracted the skilled, sometimes from England, but also schooled locals in crafts as masons, carpenters, glaziers, painters and gardeners, as well as offering much casual and unskilled employment.

The quest for suitable materials and workmen obliged landowners to look further than their own estates, and so strengthened the ties of dependence between neighbours and with more distant acquaintances. The hermetic and introverted world had, perforce, to admit these outside influences. But still it might be argued that whatever could not be supplied from the estate would simply be imported lock, stock and barrel from England, leaving these essentially English houses shallowly rooted in Irish soil. Undoubtedly many of the most sumptuous items in Cork houses had been shipped from England or the continent. Few of the array of textiles could be woven locally, and indeed spoke of the growing imports into Europe from the east. The statue, perhaps of marble, which caused such a commotion when Orrery had it sent via Youghal, was merely the most spectacular among a list of imports which included beds, silver, porcelain, inlaid cabinets and paintings.[74] Yet it seems unduly negative to assume that merchants and craftsmen in the province did not rise to (or profit from) the wealth and diversified tastes of the local landowners. Let us then look a little longer at a few of the articles conspicuous in establishments like Orrery's: silver, fabrics, ceramics, paintings and horses.

Silver had a special appeal, for above all commodities its intrinsic worth proclaimed wealth unequivocally. Much of the silver which crowded the tables first at Charleville and then at Castlemartyr – the cistern, the sixty-six plates (many of them emblazoned with Orrery's arms), the boxes for sugar, pepper and mustard, the tankards and syllabub cups, the pierced mazarin for straining fish and meat – was inherited by Orrery's widow. It weighed over 3,700 ounces. The dowager countess felt neither sentimental affection nor aesthetic delight in it. She regarded it simply as a resource which, since she no longer needed to maintain an establishment of her own, let alone keep up the port of her husband, she wished to sell to the highest bidder.[75] Like other owners of unwanted silver in county Cork she assumed that the best price would be given in London: a telling comment on how far the settlers were thought to lag behind the English nobility and gentry in civility and spending power. Yet Lady Orrery was wrong. Her silver was eventually bought by the pre-eminent Dublin goldsmith, Sir Abel Ram.[76] Was its fate to be melted down and fashioned into new wares, now bearing the heraldic devices of a different family clambering to the prominence which the Orrerys, at least temporarily, had lost? The interposition of the Williamite wars may well have condemned it to an ignoble but more obviously utilitarian fate.

The ubiquity of silver utensils among the Irish Protestant gentry is strongly suggested by the guilds of goldsmiths and other workers in precious metals which existed in Dublin and, since 1656, in Cork.[77] Such articles were wanted increasingly, not only for domestic use, but for ceremony and religion. The corporation of Youghal, for example, presented Orrery in 1661 with 'a pair of fair silver candlesticks, a tankard and a dozen plates'. Soon too freedom boxes were required in Cork, while landowners donated communion plate to their parish churches.[78] These requirements, and the need to repair or remodel older items, could be satisfied locally. Because so little identifiable provincial Irish silver of this period survives, we may be in danger of neglecting this result of the settlers' presence. In 1666 Orrery sent off a heavy consignment of silver, including two London hall-marked flagons, two more with Dublin marks and a spoon assayed at Cork. These unfashionable articles (how acquired, who can tell?) were melted down and made into plates, then engraved with Orrery's crest, a powder box for his wife and two communion chalices. This work, together with repairs to a cistern, candlesticks and a fruit dish, had been entrusted to John Bucknor. No gold or silver-smith of that name is recorded in England or Ireland. But in fact Bucknor was Orrery's tenant in Limerick city and was there designated as a 'goldsmith'. Orrery's ostentatious life at Charleville had created extra work for one inhabitant

Plate 9.2   Sugar casters in silver by R. Goble, Cork *c.* 1690 (National Museum of Ireland).

of Limerick, already specialising in the services covered by the term goldsmith; another of Orrery's Limerick tenants followed the same trade.[79]

Silver, I have argued, was a commodity in a category of its own. The varied textiles to be found in the Orrery and Perceval houses were unlikely to have been made locally. Although the textile industry, especially around Bandon, thrived, it principally supplied clothing materials. Local notables were keen to patronise it. In 1666 Orrery's heir reported how Ormonde, the lord lieutenant, had announced 'he will wear nothing but what is made in Ireland, so that we are all going to follow his example and are going to make us frieze clothes, a suit whereof will not cost 20s'.[80] That craze was short-lived. The linen – the sheets, tablecloths and napkins – which formed a large and valuable element in the possessions of many households could also be locally manufactured. Orrery boasted how he had lured Dutch weavers to settle in Charleville and Limerick; flax was planted on his lands and a weaver was employed in the house to supply its needs.[81] However the finest linens had still to be imported from the Low Countries. We know that on their trips to London the Orrerys patronised suppliers there. Yet, just as in the case of linen, so with the decorative furnishing fabrics, the clear signs of increased demand in Restoration Ireland stimulated efforts to meet it. Turkey-work with its vivid patterns and colours, in its authentic form expensively procured from the Levant, was soon more cheaply made in East Anglia.[82] Even before 1660 the enterprising had attempted to manufacture it in Ireland; after 1660 these efforts were redoubled, precisely because of increased demand. One entrepreneur in Dublin promised to make 'Turkey work carpets and covers for chairs as good and cheap as England can afford'. This may not have been an entirely empty boast, since Ormonde, the patron of this venture, owned at Kilkenny an Irish turkey-work carpet, while the projector himself, as a descendant remembered, dined in a large room 'hung with the best sort of tapestry'.[83]

Settlers who bought Irish fabrics would restrict their choice and fall behind the latest fashions. Those without the money or the chances to buy the new imports drew apart from their trend-setting neighbours, the truly Anglo-Irish. Yet quickly these distinctions were blurred. A merchant of Youghal, enriched through supplying imports to the local notables, aped some of their style. His Youghal house boasted a dozen turkey-work chairs and four matching cushions. In the same town one of Lord Cork's factotums, urged on by his wife, would use only the best plate and insisted on the latest and most colourful clothes.[84] Away from the busy ports where the newest commodities first appeared, they were less easily procured. Yet there were ways.

Another widow, this time Lady Perceval from Burton House, had in 1686 inherited, besides the contents of her chamber, her jewels, clothes, coach and horses, a third part of the plate and furniture of the recently built mansion. Lady Perceval, eager quickly to shake the dust of county Cork from her heels, decided to sell most of the goods. Curiously, feathers from mattresses were to be barrelled up and sent over to England. Less surprising was her view that a portrait of Lord Strafford and a chamber organ would find a readier market in London. Her crimson velvet bed 'lined with white silk embroidered' and with its set of paragon curtains, had been dismantled and sent to Cork. That too was to be shipped to England rather than being offered for sale in

Dublin, but now Mrs Pigott was to be allowed a sight of it, 'if by chance she have a fancy for it, tho' it is not likely that she will go to the price that it is appraised at'. Mrs Pigott did not splash out.

However the other goods which Lady Perceval ordered to be sold locally found a ready vent, the purchasers an interesting cross-section of Munster society. The biggest spender was 'Mr. Broderick', either Thomas landlord of Midleton or Alan the rising lawyer: he secured for £63 what had been expertly valued at £69. His wife picked up a Persian quilt. Others who bought included St Leger from Doneraile, Lady Aldworth from Newmarket, Mrs Mary Clayton from Mallow, Sir Thomas Southwell from Rathkeale in Limerick, and members of the Hodder, Badham and Evans families. Finally the troublesomely drunken clergyman from Charleville purchased a bell and close stool with its pan. Sales of this sort, whether voluntary or enforced, kept goods circulating. With this brisk market for the second-hand we may expect that these exotic luxuries, worn and scuffed, gradually descended into humbler homes. Novelties became familiar, spurring the quest for fresh rarities.[85]

The evidence from Burton House reveals another effect of the growing consumerism in the county. The Percevals' possessions had been evaluated by a professional. He sniffed at the old, knew that turkey-work 'was now too common to be smart, but could spot 'printed Kidderminster stuff'. This expert was 'Mr Virgin the upholsterer' from Cork. Upholsterers at this time not only sold much of what was needed to furnish a house, they could also double as interior decorators. Dublin by the 1680s contained several, one of whom was patronised by Lord Cork; now it seemed that Cork city had work for at least one. Virgin already knew the house and its contents, for he had valued them when its last owner died in 1680 and had since supplied some of the grander effects for the 'green room'.[86]

The ceramics to be found in these mansions pose more problems, but again show the diffusion of European tastes. What was recorded was mostly described as 'white earthenware', tin-glazed pottery often later lumped under the generic name of delft. Some of this, especially the white tiles commonly mentioned, had been imported from Holland, usually as ballast. Much more, the great earthen jugs, the cups, dishes, porringers and basins, and the newer 'blue stoneware', had probably been shipped over, again from Holland or the Rhineland and Britain.[87] Yet we cannot entirely discount the possiblity of local manufacture. Potters are recorded in the towns, and Lord Shannon wrote of one who could make plant pots. When Cork houses had quickly to be opened up and equipped earthenware plates and cups were to be had immediately in the locality.[88] Ceramic wares gradually displaced the more customary wood, pewter or silver; even slower to appear was porcelain, at this date manufactured only in the Orient. The Orrerys owned china, and its value and rarity are indicated by the care with which it had to be packed. The larger cargoes of oriental porcelain arriving in Europe coincided in time, and soon became closely associated with other imports, of chocolate, tea and coffee. The taste for these outlandish beverages, percolating through the wealthy, changed possessions and social habits.[89]

Tea as an import into Ireland is recorded only in the second decade of the eighteenth century. However silver teapots started to be made by Irish craftsmen a little earlier, and we may guess that tea-drinking as a ritual was known among the élite by the end of the seventeenth century.[90] The rare references to coffee and chocolate show that they were used in Dublin by the 1670s. Indeed one of Lord Cork's properties there, in or near Cork House, was used as a coffee house by 1667. Usually, though, friends from England procured parcels of coffee or chocolate as a special favour or gift.[91] The Orrerys, true to their roles as the pacesetters in county Cork, bought tea, a teapot and china cups or bowls from which to drink it. Alas, the date of their purchases is unknown, but it cannot be before the mid-1660s. Moreover they were bought while the Orrerys were staying at Powerscourt. This then would seem to be a fashion first introduced through Dublin. But other evidence, from a fashionable household near Dublin, reveals that in 1674 the prized tea which was being drunk there had been imported via Kinsale, so it may be that county Cork was unusually well-placed to pioneer this new taste.[92]

Paintings hung in the houses of Orrery, the Percevals and the latter's Kinsale relations, the Southwells; portraits were the favourites. The Castlemartyr dining-room and Lady Orrery's own chamber contained images of the king and queen, proclaiming a loyalty from which her husband had notoriously wavered. The Percevals, as we have seen, owned a painting of Charles I's controversial viceroy Strafford, and also portraits of the king's brother, the duke of York, and of Lady Orrery. Although descriptions are usually exiguous, other subjects included classical mythology, landscapes and a genre scene of a woman making sausages.[93] Many of these had first come from the continent. Thus the payments recorded in the accounts of those living in Ireland for pictures, for example the regular disbursements of Sir William Petty in Dublin from the 1650s, were to dealers who supplied the chosen images. But by the late 1670s, if not earlier, portraitists painted in Dublin; Petty and the Percevals had their likenesses done there. Insofar as later seventeenth-century Ireland possessed an artistic capital it was obviously Dublin. A telling indicator of this was the grant to a

Dutchman of a monopoly in auctioning pictures – presumably imports and perhaps the rejects of families like the Percevals and Boyles.[94]

These hints of a stirring interest in art occur at much the same time as they did in England. If Ireland is compared with the more distant parts of England and Wales, rather than with London, little divergence appears.[95] Nor should we too readily reject the notion of journeymen painters active in Munster. Their skills were in demand, often for humdrum tasks such as the marbling and graining of woodwork or the painting of hatchments and other heraldic achievements so conspicuous at the funerals which regularly punctuated settler society. After Sir John Perceval's burial in 1686 £10 was owed to Jeremy Stratton 'the painter', some of it clearly for work on the decor for the obsequies. More difficult to explain satisfactorily is the payment on Orrery's behalf to 'Huton' for the picture to adorn his son Henry's chamber. We do not know if Huton was Orrery's supplier, his upholsterer or the painter himself. Framed paintings, like porcelain, when found in Restoration Cork, were very much the perquisite of the Anglo-Irish élite. None was listed among the effects of the wealthy Youghal trader in 1673; he preferred the more useful, indeed (given his calling) essential, map of the world.[96]

The attitude of the settlers to these artifacts was startlingly prosaic. Only the hazards of survival, the consequent rarity and the workmanship have in time transformed these objects into works of art. Although building mania early infected some, conscious collecting, other than of books, probably did not begin until the eighteenth century. Here the added popularity of the Grand Tour, together with its changing itineraries, seem to have been vital factors. George Berkeley's glum predictions of how neighbours would react to an early eighteenth-century Perceval's booty should warn us against elevating ownership into connoisseurship: 'to feed their eyes with the sight of rusty medals and antique statues would (if I mistake not) seem to them something odd and insipid. The finest collection is not worth a groat where there is no one to admire and set a value on it, and our country seems to be the place in the world which is least furnished with virtuosi'.[97] Grandees with Cork estates, discouraged by the prevalent philistinism, used their rentals to finance their buying and building sprees elsewhere. County Cork's contribution to Burlingtonian Palladianism would be crucial, but indirect.[98] In default of aristocratic leadership, a succession of munificent bishops assumed the role. The contributions of Berkeley at Cloyne and Robert Clayton in Cork are well known. Significantly Smith stressed how Bishop Berkeley's example was 'so happy, that it had diffused itself'.[99] Less widely praised, but perhaps even more influential, had been the activities of Charles Crow, a predecessor of Berkeley at Cloyne. His library contained the English version of Vignola's *The regular architect* and a more recent architectural text-book translated by John Evelyn. In accordance with these published designs Crow rebuilt his episcopal palace and embellished the cathedral; he was also a generous patron of Irish silversmiths.[100] It would be dangerous to infer from this early eighteenth-century evidence that such cultivated enthusiasm already existed at the end of the seventeenth century. More usual then was indiscriminate endorsement of the new and what passed for the smart. Even so the social and perhaps cultural leadership provided by the bishop of Cork is suggested in 1678 when it was with him that the viceroy stayed while visiting the city.[101]

The vogue for building and adornment tightened Cork's dependence on England and Europe, whence ideas, materials and practitioners frequently came. But these new fashions elicited local responses. A surprising range of settlers turned their hands to designing; not only the self-confident Orrery, but former army officers whose experience had previously been limited to siege trains and fortifications, and surveyors trained to map and measure fields. Specialist skills were scarce, making versatility a necessity, though again this was not peculiar to Restoration Ireland; the same was true in provincial England.[102] Site inspections, the reading of plans and the supervision of craftsmen had to be added to the many duties of agents. As we have seen Orrery planned to employ only Protestant and English workers, but it is unlikely that such a self-denying ordinance could be observed. It is true that the most ambitious furnishings were imported, but some could be produced locally. At Burton, for example, Thomas Sweeny, a carpenter, constructed beds; the Irish harp was presumably made nearby. A local joiner fashioned the imposing wooden seats for Orrery and his wife in the church at Charleville and made an oval table for the earl, for 19*s*.[103]

Recreation

This showy and sometimes sophisticated world of classical harmonies, books, paintings and ideas was less typical of settler society than the stables and kennels. One Cork peer derided 'the coarse home-spun country gentlemen, [who] if you do not talk of dogs and horses to them, they will not ... talk of anything else to you'. In general, though, love of sport and animals bridged rather than widened the social and economic gap between the grandees and the squireens. Lord Cork, an *aficionado* of the chase, the card table, the billiard room and the bowling green, best exemplified this predominant trait.[104] The dual interests of leading settlers are also well captured in the rather pathetic lists of effects left by Sir Philip Perceval in 1680. Inventoried are his silver watch, his personal silver-gilt cutlery in its cases, family miniatures, rings, small volumes in French, Italian and Spanish, the bundles of leases and memoranda on which he was working as he took his inheritance in hand, and also fowling and birding guns and an alarming tangle of nets for entrapping quail, plovers and other birds. His stables housed more than fifty horses. Beagles had also been bought, and work begun on new kennels.[105]

Lady Broghill's objections to her husband, Orrery's heir, numerous enough, centred on being eaten 'out of house and home, for my lord's horses, dogs and strange company do devour most unconscionable'. Broghill's aptitudes were confined to horsemanship and animals. After his wife had bolted, he passed much of his time hunting over his absent uncle's lands around Lismore. Earlier, in trying to endear himself to his grandfather-in-law, Broghill had offered to procure in Ireland motley creatures suitable for sport or as pets: falcons, hawks, martens, wolf dogs, red deer, even a tame wolf cub.[106] Orrery, like most land-owners, built stables for the horses vital for work, travel and pleasure. The pack of hounds which he kept and the park which he created and stocked with deer diverted his frequent visitors. But, as in all else, his wish to excel was apparent. His mares he sent to his brother's distin-guished stud between Youghal and Lismore, there to be covered. Orrery prided himself particularly on an Arabian horse, but a neighbour coolly commented 'though he hath very good horses, he hath hardly one colt that is tolerably handsome'.[107]

Interest in and accomplishment with horses united many, and not only men or Protestant settlers. For Orrery it provided a bond with his old foe and new ally Inchiquin. Lord Cork presented horses of his own breeding to the king and duke of York and to a group of kinsmen and neighbours in Munster. However the £100 owed by Lord Antrim for a horse rankled. In Cork city a hard-working merchant confessed his weakness for the chase.[108] The quest for good animals, either for use or for breeding, obliged enquiries and travel to the remoter parts of Ireland. Perceval sent a messenger into Clare to discover whether Lord Thomond had a fine beast to sell; Jephson from Mallow Castle made a similar request of Inchiquin, only to be deterred by the outrageous asking price of £200. Concern to improve strains led to the import of animals. But, naturally, it was a two-way traffic. Again Lord Cork illustrated this. His horses constantly crossed the Irish Sea; stallions sent to improve the breed; mares and colts, together with spaniels and setting dogs, dispatched to Minehead, thence to amble to his stables in East Yorkshire. Irish hobbies of equable temperament were highly esteemed in England for short journeys; other unfortunate mares and foals were shipped to the West Indies. Something of the scale of this traffic is conveyed by Petty's assertion that in 1685 1,054 horses had been exported from Ireland to England: these the ones noticed by the customs men.[109]

Horses were vital to the life of the settlers. Less evidently utilitarian were horse-races. They had certainly taken place before 1641, and during the 1650s had offered a painless way for Lord Cork to impress Cromwellian notables at Youghal. In the 1680s when races were regularly run at the Curragh, Dublin emptied and the work of governing Ireland ceased. Landowners in Ulster as well as in Munster sponsored meetings with plates and purses for prizes.[110] These two horse-races, in which gentleman rode against gentleman, offered fresh occasions 'to compete and excel. Yet we should not think of this pastime as exclusive to the settler élite. In 1684 three Cork gentlemen, including Henry Boyle and Thomas Broderick, agreed with Youghal's richest merchant who was to build them stables on the South Green of the town as part of a project to popularise the already well-established races along the strand. The gentlemen had organised a subscription of £400 among their friends; they now expected Youghal corporation to add £200. From the invested proceeds two annual prizes of thirty guineas would be awarded. The merchant, not to be outdone, proposed himself to donate two extra prizes of £20 a piece. The scheme closely resembled many in England. Whether or not it succeeded, the races continued, and in the eighteenth century attracted modest municipal backing. A confluence of punters into the town could only benefit business and enable Youghal to withstand the competition from Cork city and other, newer settlements.[111]

The breeding, training and care of horses, and other animals, fostered wider contacts; wider in both the geographical and social senses. Smiths and farriers attended to equine needs. The Irish had long been valued for their skills with horses, readily finding work in England as grooms. The tradition persisted, as Lord Cork's groom 'Irish Will' indicated.[112] In Cork itself we can only guess the degree to which racial or religious tensions were forgotten in shared enthusiasm for a spirited mount. Horses could, but did not invariably, reduce friction. The quality of a horse easily advertised its owner's status and wealth. The gulf between those able to keep a horse of their own and those without was enormous: it determined, for example, whether or not one could travel readily and widely. Horse ownership differentiated settler from settler; also it marked off the bulk of the newcomers from the mass of the poorer Irish, so many of whose animals had been commandeered or killed during the Confederate Wars. As with other livestock, native horses differed from the improved strains introduced by the settlers, and once more taught the monotonous lesson of alleged English superiority. Even the treatment and feeding of horses could be read as an index of the cultural differences between natives and newcomers, and of the supposed barbarism of the Irish.[113]

This world of possessions, tentatively evoked, profited producers and suppliers. But merchants dared not depend entirely on the orders from fickle grandees, frequently absent and sometimes doubtfully solvent. One in Cork, keen to cash in on the greater range of goods which he could import, bewailed the conservatism of his customers. New lines, like Caudebec hats from Normandy, simply did not go. Traditionalism affected diet. He warned a correspondent that a consignment of wine, probably Portuguese, 'being not white nor rosy as smaller wines', would not sell, and that Bordeaux 'is à la mode' in Cork. Also demand was seasonal. Wine and dried fruits had to catch the Christmas market. Lent in turn greatly increased consumption of dried fish and pickled herrings, imported from Minehead, for Protestants as well as Catholics abstained during these weeks.[114] The fairs and markets, proliferating through landlord pressure, survived thanks to the greater volume of trade, and in themselves speeded the circulation of goods, new, second-hand and occasionally stolen, throughout provincial society.[115] The Irish flocked to these fairs, but (it has been implied) as sellers of what the prospering Protestants consumed. Some have suggested that cultural values as well as poverty inhibited the Irish from spending on the fripperies which, for the settlers, were turning from luxuries into necessities. Petty opined that Irish labourers needed only salt and tobacco to be self-sufficient, so simple were their tastes and so light their purses. However an eighteenth-century propagandist contrasted the frugality of Protestant tenants with the profligacy of Catholics who 'squander their substance at fairs and patterns'. It is not clear whether growing consumerism accentuated or blurred differences between natives and newcomers.[116]

With new goods, as has long been clear, came ideas. Recently it has been argued that the exchange of goods in itself constituted an exchange of ideas. As the familiar staples of the local economy were supplemented by strange imports, horizons widened and other worlds and values were glimpsed.[117] What we know of this linked traffic in commodities and ideas in later seventeenth-century Cork reminds us forcibly that it was an economic and cultural province. Dependence on, but not necessarily subservience to England and Europe, were the hallmarks of this society, at least in its upper and acquisitive reaches.

Dependants
Beguiled by their wealth, misled by the copious remains and too willing to accept them at their own valuation, have I let the Anglo-Irish bulk too large in this account?

If I have done so, I have followed the assessment of contemporaries who, oblivious to the hidden shifts in the structures of economy and society, explained growth, recession and dearth in terms of the impact of powerful individuals (or God). Modern historians may know better, and be able to show, for example, that the bans on exporting live cattle and woollens to England encouraged profitable diversification, or that the older habits of settlement and cultivation outlasted the newcomers' insistence on improvement. Even so it is accepted that landowners possessed in the lease a potent instrument with which to alter their district.[118] In the later seventeenth century Lord Cork, having unavailingly fought the Cattle Bill and entered his dissent in the Lords' journal, apocalyptically noted after its passage 'this is the second time an unhappy day for Ireland, on which day the rebellion broke out anno 1641'. In Cork city the merchant William Hovell anxiously watched the movements of the nobility, knowing from experience how the arrival of Ormonde and his entourage or the need for Cork, Shannon and Inchiquin to remit rents into England, affected the rate of exchange and his own business. Already, too, observers were worrying about the adverse effects of absenteeism, and specifically Cork's lengthening absences from Lismore.[119]

The demands of the leading landowners influenced the lower levels of Cork's society, and not simply like giant sponges sopping up wealth in rents. Small towns created or expanded by magnates, like Orrery's Charleville, felt the chill when their patrons shut up their mansions, and decayed unless they could develop other services.[120] In 1679 a census found sixty-six inmates at Castlemartyr. This establishment, while large, was smaller than those at Charleville or Lismore in their heydays. In addition to members of the immediate and extended family, it contained a variety of functionaries ranging from the chaplain and housekeeper to a trumpeter, housemaids and a hen-woman. A household of this size, as its menus and guest lists show, consumed royally. But although it employed its own baker and brewer and could eat what the garden and estate grew, it neither was, nor was intended to be, self-sufficient. Meat had to be bought at market; the many sorts of fish testified not only to the abundance but the regularity of landings from Ballycotton Bay.[121] Sugar, anchovies and capers, hogsheads of claret and pipes of canary were supplied by Cork and Youghal merchants.[122] The house, its stables and kennels, the gardens and park, even when empty of all but a skeleton staff on board wages, required upkeep. When we remember the thick scatter of these mansions, we can sense, even if we cannot quantify, the extra work. Employment had been created for masons and labourers, and spectacularly for domestic servants, perhaps the most common occupation of all.[123]

The more prestigious jobs tempted migrants from Britain, and, more importantly, sustained cadets of other settler families, enabling them to stay and often quietly to flourish.[124] The benefits conferred by high-spending landlords on lesser men can be illustrated if we consider four groups: squireens, agents, lawyers and merchants.

Orrey's first loyalty, like that of his father and many other dynasts, was to his family. An accomplished nepotist, he shared what he could, including his houses, with his close kinsmen and sons-in-law. Next he gratified his clients, using posts in the presidency, in the boroughs, in Limerick city and in the provincial militia. The Brodricks, the Foulkes, Sir Richard Kyrle and the Southwells may serve as examples of Cork gentry who orbited in Orrery's universe or escaped to a more congenial solar system.

Sir St John Brodrick had served as Orrery's provost-marshal in the 1650s. Staying on after 1660, he retained the post and had earned payment in Irish lands, set out around Ballyanen, adjacent to Orrery's Imokilly estate. Brodrick happily combined oversight of Orrery's lands and the construction of Charleville with the development of his own holdings. Keen to supplant Inchiquin as 'lord paramount' in Imokilly, he had his new settlement at Midleton incorporated as a parliamentary borough, with himself as its first sovereign, in 1671. In the 1670s, however, he took up residence at Wandsworth, but maintained his close ties with Orrery, now attending to the latter's Somerset estate.[125] Also in Wandsworth lived Brodrick's brother, Sir Allen: a very different career as a royalist conspirator and as Ormonde's henchman brought him too into Ireland. As surveyor-general, a commissioner in the court of claims and as farmer of the great apanage in Ireland bestowed on the duke of York he amassed wealth which, after his death in 1680, underwrote the Irish careers of his nephews, the sons of Sir St John. The future belonged to this second generation of Brodricks. By 1695 they had replaced the Boyles as the managers of south Munster's M.P.s, so that the Dublin parliament of that year was known as the 'Brodricks' Parliament'.[126]

Kyrle too had come to Ireland to fight and had stayed on. As he exploited his lands, south of Mallow, especially through ironworks, he soon fell into disrepute as a trickster and bad payer, and was hotly pursued by neighbours in the law courts. This unsavoury reputation did not, surprisingly, prevent his being considered as a suitable tenant for Charleville when, following the second earl's death, it was imperative to have it aired if it were not to fall completely derelict. Kyrle, however, opted for a fresh life. In 1684 he was chosen to govern Carolina and, having quickly antagonised settlers there, died within a year. Kyrle, originally from Herefordshire, had alighted for a while in county Cork like a migratory mosquito but left no more lasting traces than a few smarting settlers.[127]

More enduring were the Foulkes. Of a family probably settled in Munster before 1641, Sir Francis, like Brodrick and Kyrle, advanced through the profession of arms. In the 1650s Lord Cork leased him Camphire, good land at the junction of the rivers Blackwater and Bride, on which Foulke later claimed he had spent more than £2,000 in draining the bog and other improvements. With baroque courtesy he deferred to Lady Orrery, sending her presents of eggs and pigeons, and stoutly defended the local interests and reputation of her husband. But Foulke, perhaps like other veterans of the wars, adjusted imperfectly to the peace. By the 1670s, seriously in debt and threatened by Lord Cork with re-possession of Camphire, he was found a posting more to his inclinations when Orrery appointed him to govern Limerick city. This better approximated to the life of the camp after which Foulke hankered. In 1674 when there was talk of the Dutch recruiting regiments among the Protestants of Ireland, he was eager to volunteer, expecting after a couple of years to be able to sell his command and use the money to provide for his old age. But above all the prospect of fighting the French 'would make me young again'. He would, no doubt, have been pleased by the epitome of his character after his death in 1678: 'an honest gentleman and a good officer'. His widow kept Camphire, and pestered Orrery to let one of his best farms to her son. Another son, having served as a cornet in Orrery's own troop at Charleville in the 1660s, married into the local gentry and later helped to run Cork's affairs from Youghal and Lismore.[128]

Different because not satellites of the Boyles were the Southwells of Kinsale. A cadet of settlers in Limerick, Robert Southwell, using the post of customer of Kinsale as his springboard, was the first to emerge into wealth. In 1641 he valued the annual profits of the position at £100, and made £50 p.a. from the malt trade. Southwell had realised and assiduously exploited Kinsale's potential as a victualling centre. In 1649 his thirst for enrichment converged with his politics when he provisioned Prince Rupert's marauding royalist flotilla. Although he cooperated with, and again profited from, the Cromwellian usurpers, his principles could be unabashedly advertised after 1660, and underpinned a close relationship with Ormonde who used the Southwells as a counterweight to the pervasive Boyles. The Southwells' court connections were publicised when Prince Rupert stood as god-father to a Southwell grandson.[129]

In 1664 Robert Southwell totted up his income. In 1641 he had been lucky to clear £150 p.a.; now he enjoyed £1,014. This put him on a par with prominent gentlemen like Jephson of Mallow and indeed with the shabbier peers like Lord Shannon. Southwell had kept his brewing and malting business, which had quadrupled in value since 1641; otherwise his income came entirely from property in or near Kinsale. Because Southwell, apparently, owned no lands in England and seldom travelled beyond the county, we can regard him as an Irish Protestant rather than one of the Anglo-Irish. However, Southwell was hardly introverted, and his family's English links grew. No less than Orrery, Southwell subscribed to the cult of improvement. He invested in the local fisheries, to no permanent profit, and backed the bid to have Kinsale declared a free port. That campaign failed, but the expanding victualling trade benefitted Southwell: his tenants prospered and, after his death, his heir, normally living in England, negotiated to lease the family home as a navy office and their warehouses and cellars to the victuallers.[130]

In comparison with a magnate like Cork or Orrery, Robert Southwell's needs were modest. He expected to spend £943, well within his annual income. This sensible moderation seems to have been transmitted to his only surviving son. At the end of the 1650s, rather than plunge onto the dangerous switchback of public life, the younger Robert Southwell, fresh from Oxford, toured Europe. On his return, he assessed how best to make a name for himself. Ireland, he concluded, offered no posts which would stretch or adequately reward him. Thus it was, assisted by his father and probably by his English wife's marriage portion, he bought his way into government service. His principal investment, of £2,000, was in one of the clerkships of the English privy council, which carried a formal salary of £450. He was launched on a career which would take him as ambassador to several European courts, win him the presidency of the Royal Society (the only son of Kinsale to hold the office?) and eventually, in the 1690s, return him to Ireland as secretary of state. From his earnings he bought a Gloucestershire estate. He had not entirely severed his Irish links. Through his numerous well-placed contacts he promoted Kinsale's and his family's interests, now inseparable in his mind; Ormonde regularly confided his views on Ireland to him; in 1679 he inherited his father's Kinsale portfolio; and, after 1686, oversaw his brother-in-law, Perceval's, much more valuable north Cork estate. Most of his methodical and efficient control of the two Cork inheritances was exercised from a distance. In a generation the Southwells had changed from Kinsale Protestants to English landed gentlemen who happened to enjoy a useful Irish rental.[131]

These contrasted lives show how factors of chance, temperament, wit and patronage make it impossible to foretell which families would advance in status and wealth, which would stagnate and which would disappear or decline. The unequal distribution and use of opportunities are again shown in the achievements of agents. This was an attractive route which cadets of settler families could tread in order to maintain themselves in the province. Lionel Beecher, a sprig from that prolific Munster tree, had, so he alleged, traded in a substantial way at Youghal before the war. Early in the 1640s he had skipped back to North Devon, only to see the twelve ships in which he had a share sunk during the naval warfare of the 1650s. Back in Youghal after 1660 he demanded compensation for his losses and pleaded with Cork and Orrery for employment. Orrery entrusted him with rent collection and estate management. In this modest way Beecher turned into an effective pluralist. He acted as seneschal of Orrery's Askeaton manor (delegating the work to an English deputy); in addition he sought the seneschalship of Charleville. At home in Youghal he held the posts of land-waiter, deputy-surveyor and storekeeper of the customs. In 1669 he entreated Orrery to assist him to the post of surveyor of the customs in the port (in Cork's gift as Lord Treasurer of Ireland) – duties which might reasonably be expected to ease the import of the expensive requirements of Orrery's households. Beecher's comfortable life ended abruptly with Orrery's. Thereafter he was constantly bombarded with imperious demands from the dowager and with searching enquiries from her efficient Dublin agent. New disaster struck when at Christmas 1686 his house was burnt. Beecher smelt arson, his ties with the Boyles supposedly making him a target. It gave him a wonderful excuse for the disorder which had enveloped his care of the Boyles' affairs. What became of Beecher and his six children, and whether his duties had contributed to the rise of another settler dynasty, cannot be said.[132] After 1691 his work was being done by a member of a second family later to become prominent in the locality, the Longfields.[133]

Agencies generally benefited men already settled in the area. The concerns of large landowners, especially when their estates were scattered or they themselves were absent, created chances which the alert grabbed. Yet estates offered wider opportunities, as the case of Dr Jeremy Hall shows. Hall, from Yorkshire, arrived in Dublin about 1639 thanks to the patronage of another Yorkshireman, soon to be earl of Strafford, the viceroy of Ireland. A promising lad, Hall was put into Trinity, only to have whatever future he had mapped disrupted by the civil wars. He returned to England, collected a doctorate and a large library in London. However it was his pre-war Irish connections which decided his career after the Restoration. Hall, a fussing, valetudinarian bachelor, was soon in demand among the Anglo-Irish as a suitable governor for their sons when they toured Europe. Lords Roscommon (Cork's son-in-law) and Donegall used him thus, then Orrery. So struck with his talents was Orrery that he inveigled him into remaining in his employ. Hall returned to Dublin and there, by his meticulous oversight of the business and legal affairs, made himself indispensable to the family. Although devoted to the Boyles, he kept up his other connections. The second Lord Strafford, usually absent from Ireland, needed a reliable man on the spot to watch over his interests in county Wicklow, and Hall fitted the bill perfectly. So it was that he bustled about Dublin, instructing lawyers and attorneys, consulting government functionaries, cultivating the powerful and listening for gossip and rumour. Off he jogged into the countryside, to Powerscourt, to Blessington, and on his employers' affairs into Wicklow, Limerick and sometimes to Cork. His salary, £100 p.a., was often in arrear; frequently he threatened to resign or retire. But he did not desert the Boyles, and indeed lent the first earl money and by way of return acquired some of Orrery's Limerick houses. It was he who hastened to Charleville to attend the lonely deathbed of the second earl and to arrange his makeshift funeral; it was he who poked about in the church at Youghal and, tut-tutting at the rain falling through the window onto Orrery's new monuments, ordered repairs. He criss-crossed England and, when no suitable governor could be found, took the third earl to the continent. Hall had impinged only intermittently and temporarily on county Cork. Nevertheless, his presence in Ireland after the Restoration can be traced directly to the needs of Orrery and his Cork-based clan.[134]

The patterns of employment provided by the settlers, and their tendency to spill over into a world larger than county Cork, are repeated when we look at the lawyers. The clearest profiteers from the landowners' needs, the lawyers were the most unpopular. As Lord Shannon railed: 'lawyers ... are now in a manner entailed as a rent-charge on most large estates and families, and are become such a customary and necessary charge ... as rich men cannot live at ease on their estates without a lawyer's advice ...'.[135] Four will show how lawyers battened on Cork society.

William Worth, a Trinity graduate, was son and heir of county Cork's leading ecclesiastical politician in the 1650s. Many in the county could echo one planter's comment: 'I knew his father well. It will concern me to know him also'. Worth, bequeathed property in Cork city, began his practice there and by 1678 was its recorder. After he had been appointed as a baron of the exchequer in Dublin many Cork settlers turned to him to assist them through that legal maze. Worth, like other judges with his background, was dismissed in James II's reign, and temporarily forsook Ireland for England.[136]

Sir Standish Hartstonge hailed from Norfolk. His mother, the Standish heiress from Bruff in county Limerick, first made him think of Ireland.

The running and improvement of Bruff were easily combined with the duties of recorder of Limerick. Equally handy for Bruff was Charleville, and soon Hartstonge, having attracted Orrery's favour, was second justice of the presidency court. But while building this valuable provincial base, he also made a name in Dublin. His ascent resembled Worth's: office in the Tipperary palatinate court and then in the exchequer, and was also halted in the 1680s. He too, following his dismissal, returned to England where through his family and a succession of wives he owned much land. The law had enabled him to strengthen his position as a landowner and to work, almost at will, in England, Wales or Ireland; thanks to its estates the family continued as a power in eighteenth-century Limerick.[137]

More deeply rooted in county Cork was Richard Cox. Of settler stock, as an orphan he had first been cared for by his grandfather, Oxford graduate, music-lover, recorder and thrice-sovereign of Clonakilty. Next he was looked after by an uncle who happened to be seneschal of Lord Cork's Bandon estate. If we can believe Cox's disingenuous account, his own drive, a small legacy and the help of Lord Cork lifted him from a small-town attorney working in the local courts around Bandon into a London-trained lawyer. After a spell of somnolent contentment with his new wife at Clonakilty, he suddenly roused himself, resumed practice in Cork and landed the recordership of Kinsale. He claimed to have earned £500 in his first year, which he invested in land, 'kept my coach and lived well'. With remarkable prescience, Cox removed to England in 1687, offering his health as an excuse. There he fluently championed the Irish Protestant cause, developed an exile's affection for his homeland, and soon returned triumphantly to Ireland in the train of the conquering William III. Henceforward his pre-eminence was assured, subject only to the fierce interplay of party.[138]

Briefs and retainers had come the way of Worth, Hartstonge and Cox from their Munster neighbours and acquaintances, and, especially in their earlier years, helped them to succeed at the bar. Alan Brodrick most clearly shows the importance of the local base. A younger son of the creator of Midleton, Brodrick, another Oxford graduate, having been called at the Middle Temple in 1678, decided to ply for hire in Ireland. In the early 1680s he complained of the 'lamentable dull trade ... with us young men at the bar'. He affected more interest in the latest songs from London, especially if bawdy 'to comply with the female fancies', and in improving his rig with lace cravats, cuffs and a new peruke. He set about exploiting his family contacts in Cork and soon won the invaluable backing of Baron Worth, in whose house he lodged. With Worth's influence, he hoped to become recorder of Cork.

But others, including Cox, harboured the same ambition. As well as fawning on Worth, Brodrick built up an interest with the mayor and sheriffs, whom he served as counsel. He correctly calculated that if he could survive the first lean years then he would be rewarded. Survival was mightily helped when, again on Worth's recommendation, he was retained by several leading and litigious Cork landowners, including Inchiquin, Kingston, Clancarty and Lady Orrery. In his first year Brodrick estimated that he had earned £120; now, with the guaranteed retainers, he hoped to make £200. Even so his outgoings were heavy. The annual rent on his chambers amounted to £41; he kept two clerks, one of his own choosing, the other foisted on him by Worth and a Cork alderman as the price of their support; in addition he employed a man servant and a groom.[139]

Steadily Brodrick pushed forward. Fearful of the political uncertainty he contemplated buying land in England. Whether or not he did, by 1689 he was said to enjoy £300 p.a. from Irish land. Any indecision about whether to persist with an Irish career was banished by William III's victories. The power base which he had industriously constructed in Cork served him well. He was now appointed recorder and as king's sergeant commissioned to practise in the county. By 1697 he contentedly grumbled about the hectic round which took him from the House of Commons to Dublin Castle, the Council board, the King's Inns, the Customs House and to Munster. The hopeful young man had matured into a pompous heavy-weight who delighted in puncturing the pretensions of 'pert and saucy' young barristers. Much in demand at the bar, he could earn £10 daily – little when set against the £40 which successful English barristers could command – but enough to bring him £1,000 p.a. He admitted that the sum was 'very fair', but added smugly 'I have worked hard for it'.

As early as 1692 Brodrick, Cork city's M.P., was reckoned a politician of national standing. In Parliament he argued for its sole right to initiate money bills, resisted the executive's interference and managed other members. But local causes were not forgotten. In particular an issue which for some years had angered Cork merchants, and which Brodrick had been instructed to press, inspired his attacks on an oppressive and corrupt government. Since the 1680s Cork customs officers had collected tolls of quayage and cranage, brushing aside objections about their size and legality. Brodrick used these irksome exactions to document his general case against the administration.[140]

These successful lawyers sprang from the same soil as the land-owners, and as the former thrived they drew nourishment from their landed hosts. Judges and barristers, along with army officers, first felt the force of the Catholic revanche after 1685, when Catholics were again permitted officially to practise and replaced the Protestant judges. The Protestant lawyers, copying the adroit Catholic barristers earlier in the century, driven by self-interest and equipped with their training, led the attack on the Stuarts' Irish polices. This willingness to speak for the wider Irish Protestant cause may have rehabilitated the lawyers with the settlers whom they had entangled and fleeced.[141] Although obviously an important component in settler society, many unanswered questions remain about the role of the Irish legal profession. As among landowners, so among lawyers, a chasm yawned between the Anglo-Irish, like Cox and Brodrick, and the small-town attorney, content with the recordership of Clonakilty or Charleville and to ride the Munster circuit.

Similar differences separate the one or two merchants whose lives can be reconstructed in useful detail from the anonymous remainder. Trade in the rapidly growing Cork city, free from the stranglehold of a single local landowner, differed even from a merchant's life in the smaller ports. Inland, away from the shipping lanes with their constant arrivals, news and novelties, trade obeyed distinct rhythms. Youghal, still very much in the ambit of Lord Cork, had its handful of civic notables. There, in Raleigh's House lived the one man known to own and understand the recent acts of settlement and explanation: little wonder that he was the town's recorder.[142]

A tantalising glimpse into this world is offered by the inventory compiled in 1673 on the death of Samuel Hayman, one of Youghal's leading traders. Hayman's bequests totalled £2,590; his assets were valued at nearly £2,800. Modest prosperity, based in part on the financial services that he performed for Lord Cork, enabled him to live in solid comfort. In his house were some of the furnishings now taken for granted in the county's mansions: table carpets, an 'arras carpet', two looking glasses, linen, pewter, silver, books other than his 'Great Bible'. But much of Hayman's wealth lay in coin – he had kept £200 in silver and £40 in gold in his desk – and in merchandise, ranging from deal boards, rape seed, salt, glass bottles, canvas, broad cloth, dowlas, pitch and barrelled beef. He owned livestock, held leases on Youghal properties and on a substantial house in Minehead where his family had originated and where his brother and partner still lived. He also had shares in five ships and was owed money both locally and by others in Clonmel, Dublin, Ilfracombe, London, La Rochelle and Barbadoes. His fortune was to be shared equitably among his six children: the eldest son received £400; the others, regardless of sex, were each bequeathed £300. Hayman, as we would expect of a trader, belonged to a world united by the sea. Wherein, we may ask, lay the difference between his brother's life in Minehead and his in Youghal?[143]

Plate 9.3   Walter Raleigh's house, Youghal (Crawford Municipal Art Gallery/Cork V.E.C.).

Hayman's effects provide no clues about his perceptions of the world. Yet another merchant, William Hovell, originally from Kinsale but by the early 1680s established in Cork city, offers a refreshing perspective on the affairs of the county. Hard-working and cautious, Hovell rarely let slip a concern with something other than the rate of exchange or the price and quality of pilchards, butter and cloth. A business ethic is evident; for Hovell credit amounted to more than accumulated funds and hinged on reputation and honest dealing. Those who fell short, whether his own kin and apprentices or the egregious Sir Matthew Deane of Dromore, were roundly censured. Through his correspondents Hovell's world reached to the West Indies and the Mediterranean; his wife's people lived near Mallow; close relations remained in England. A man of some education – he could read but not write French – Hovell hardly typified the small-town huckster.[144] He, no less than Hayman, the lawyers and the landowners whom I have described, was Anglo-Irish rather than exclusively Irish in his orientation. If we can trust the estimate of his wealth in 1689, Hovell enjoyed an income from land of £320, which put him on a par with the middling gentry of the county, but above all else, what Hovell's letters reveal is the foreboding which turned to panic as Tyrconnel's plans unfolded.

From our vantage point the Protestants' ascent after 1649 looks steady and inevitable, so much so that expressions of alarm or doubt among seventeenth-century Protestants like Orrery tend either to be discounted or treated as fabrications. But unless we take seriously that sense of uncertainty about what their ultimate fate was to be we omit an essential ingredient in Protestant mentalities, and also fail to explain the sense of dangers escaped which expressed itself in vengeful triumphalism after 1691. The crises of James II's reign and the Williamite Wars were the experiences which most decisively shaped Protestant identities. Hovell in Cork expressed an almost craven Protestant loyalism in 1685 and hoped by appeasing James II to temper the king's catholicising intentions. Eagerly he recorded the news that the king had attended Protestant worship, and was thankful that Monmouth's rebellion had been suppressed without its spreading, as it had seemed that it might, from Somerset into Munster. But Hovell was tormented by lack of solid information, and begged his chief Dublin contact 'to advise anything of news, without any observations or animadversions thereon, but only bare and public matters of fact ... for we have here nothing certain'. One 'stupendous letter' from Dublin dissuaded Hovell from building in Cork. Reasons for alarm quickly multiplied, as Protestant judges and officers were replaced, as 'idolatrous mass is here celebrated openly in the midst of the city'; and as Catholics boasted of what further changes were in the offing. A palpable apprehension entered Hovell's comments by the summer of 1686. His habitual caution increased, limiting his remarks on public affairs to Latin saws and religious platitudes (heartfelt for all their conventionality). He reassured his Dublin friend that he immediately obliterated any opinions on politics in his letters lest they fall into the wrong hands and be misconstrued.

A cynic might conclude that Hovell bewailed the uncertainties because they depressed trade. Certainly recession accompanied the political instability, as did rising lawlessness. Thoughts of local investment were abandoned as merchants and landowners jostled to convey to England as much of their substance as possible.[145] In this atmosphere there were few material inducements to stay. Yet Hovell's attitudes should not be reduced to simple calculations of profit and loss. The flimsy structure of Protestant domination was creaking and collapsing, but, in complete contrast to 1641, the settlers had time to see what was happening and escape. Hovell planned to send his wife and children to England as early as 1686, but himself confessed 'I am loath to leave Ireland, but I fear we soon must'. Leave he did, but probably not until 1688. He saw this crisis not exclusively in personal or mercenary terms. For him, as for many of his coreligionists, it could be traced back to the 'massacres' which had begun on 23 October 1641 and which the Catholics now threatened to repeat. The plight of the Huguenots, so often paralleling that of the Irish Protestants, also dismayed him and reminded him of the seemingly inevitable antagonism between Catholics and Protestants. Hovell, rich and with English relations, fled; other Cork merchants stayed. One who did testified to the mood in December 1689. While at church in Cork, news arrived from Dublin 'of a massacre designed on us all on that day ... You cannot imagine what a fright and confusion it put all into, all running out with their swords in their hands and breaking the church windows to get out. Ever since every house is upon their guard and all keep watch. The Irish laugh at it and threaten for the disorder. But the burnt child dreads the fire, and all have not forgot.'[146]

Hovell revealed another aspect of the Cork Protestants' experience after 1685 which added to their nervousness: the absence of leadership. Orrery's death in 1679, convenient to Ormonde in his bid to damp down panic in Ireland over the ramifications of the Popish plot, had left a vacuum at the centre of Munster's affairs. Hovell believed that so long as Ormonde lived, no harm would befall the Protestant community: the duke's death in 1688 was accordingly a heavy blow. By then most local notables had removed themselves to the safety of England, although, as we have seen, Henry Boyle and Inchiquin attempted to rally the Protestant resistance. In default of effective lay leaders, it was the bishop of Cork, Edward Wetenhall, who stayed and did what he could to sustain Protestant morale during the dark days of 1690.[147] Only with the peace did the Coxes, Brodricks, Bernards and Boyles re-appear to head the local settlers.

Wider worlds

In discussing Hovell, I have introduced obliquely the matter so far glaringly missing from this account: Protestant relations with the bulk of the population. They may seem too uncomplicated to need much discussion; composed of loathing on the Irish side, and contempt on the part of the newcomers. But to suppose that Protestant attitudes were uniform, or that public utterances mirrored private behaviour, is to rest too heavily on the repellent writings of Orrery, Brodrick and Cox.[148] There was a tradition, at once more relaxed and more generous, which, while severely shaken by the scares of 1689-91, did not evaporate.[149] Personal experience mattered. The veterans of the confederate wars constantly guarded against any resurgence of the Catholic menace. For younger generations, sceptical of the dire warnings of their elders, James II's reign provided a rapid education. A new and uncompromising mood marked the later 1690s. The more that contemporaries in England treated the Irish Catholics as a joke rather than a threat, the more the Protestants of Ireland did what they could to prove the contrary and to protect themselves. Through by-laws the Cork boroughs imposed oaths and so excluded Catholics from their running. In Kinsale, for example, the more aggressively Protestant ethos was signalled by the decision in 1695 to celebrate the 29 September 1690 'as a day of public rejoicing by making bonfires, illuminations and other marks and demonstrations of joy', in thanks that 'the Protestants of this corporation were delivered out of the hands and power of their implacable enemies of Roman Catholic persuasion ...'[150]

The octogenarian Lord Cork and Burlington, who had fought the Irish in the 1640s and who had seen his own, his father's and brother's schemes for assimilating the Irish to English ways run like water into the sand, was especially bullish. He insisted that the now antiquated and generally obsolete requirement of military service be included in tenancies. He ordered his agents to destroy the cabins which had mushroomed in Lismore, 'so as this crew of vermin may be put out of that place'. Yet fearsome as the rhetoric is, what really lay behind it? Lord Cork's venom against the Irish was no worse than the abuse which he hurled at his family's long-standing enemies among the settlers, like the Pynes of Mogeley, one of whose sons was seeking to encroach on Cork's precious deer-park. All Cork asked of the poor

Irish was that they rebuild their cabins on the other side of the Blackwater; Catholics were still given tenancies. Similarly Orrery's worries about Catholics on his lands differed little from his fury when cottagers illicitly colonised the woods of his Somerset manor.[151] In Munster the poor and rootless, 'the rascal multitude', who obstructed the landowners' grandiose plans, happened, usually, to be Catholic and Irish, characteristics which easily explained why they impeded 'improvement'. Social equals among the Catholics, such as Clancarty (Ormonde's brother-in-law and the greatest Catholic landowner in Cork after 1660) or Sir James Cotter, had to be treated with grudging respect. Furthermore, at this higher level, assimilation still occurred, as the examples of Barrymore and both the Thomond and Inchiquin O'Briens showed.[152] Relations between the newcomers and natives are too complex to be dealt with in the compass of this essay: but let us remember that they were complex.

In conclusion one other distortion needs correcting. The worlds which I have tried to penetrate have been peopled overwhelmingly with men. But seventeenth-century Munster was a woman's world. Redoubtable wives and widows, headed by the two Lady Orrerys and Lady Petty, took their turns in directing estates. Lady Maynard of Curraglass had a profitable side-line as a money-lender. Robert Southwell's wife went from Kinsale into the hinterland of Mallow in a hired wooden calash to defend the family's interests. Lady Foulke like a tigress protected her sons. At Youghal after Edward Lawndy was drowned his widow took over the running of his extensive business; while Mrs. French traded in iron.[153] These examples are few and, no doubt, exceptional. However, one theme of this account has been the growing traffic between Cork and England. The excitement over and appetite for goods, the zest for rebuilding and redecoration, were feelings shared by women. It was Hovell's wife, for example, who insisted that their linen should be the best from the Low Countries.[154]

The commodities shipped across the Irish Sea united England and Ireland. Conspicuous among them were women. Yet endogamy distinguished the Irish Protestants from the Anglo-Irish. The former selected their wives from the neighbours' daughters, as the Tynte girls from Ballycrenan (the beauties of Restoration Cork) or later the children of Arthur Bernard of Bandon remind us. The Anglo-Irish, like Cork and Orrery, looked further afield, to other Irish provinces or to England.[155] Marriage alliances which traversed the Irish Sea further deepened Ireland's participation in the economic, social and cultural life of England. These arranged matches were sometimes attended by strains (though probably no more often than in England). The sense of dislocation felt by a bride from England was sensitively suggested by

Lord Broghill. He admitted that living 'at such a rambling rate as I have done for five or six years ... disabled me from being so kind to my wife as my inclinations do promote me to be'. He had done what he could, but the headstrong Lady Mary Sackville was dissatisfied. For those used to London, as she was, Broghill acknowledged that 'this country at first cannot but a little discompose any body that hath lived amongst the best company of England'. Some brides settled happily into the provincial ways, just as they might in Northumberland, Shropshire, Cornwall or Scotland; others, notoriously Lady Broghill, Mrs Freke of Rathbarry and Anne Jephson, did not.[156] As well as this important difference among the settlers as to where they sought spouses, there existed, or so Cox contended, a difference between Irish and English: the former lorded it over their wives, while the latter behaved more considerately.

We come back in the end to the difficulty of seeing beneath the thin but dazzling crust of Anglo-Irish to the Protestants whose lives were bounded by county Cork. We can conclude that the latter had less money, usually found brides within their own community, were more likely to be educated locally and at Trinity rather than in England and on the continent, and were less tied to English patrons. Whether these distinctive traits narrowed or softened attitudes, we can only conjecture. Those who crowded the favourite locations, around the basin of Cork harbour, along the banks of the Blackwater and Bandon rivers or in the environs of Mallow, Youghal and Kinsale, comfortable in the society of numerous like-minded neighbours, regularly and easily in touch with Dublin and England, probably lived more sophisticated existences than their few coreligionists who tried life beyond Macroom or around Skibbereen and Bantry. But even if the bucaneering Hulls of Leamcon, Richard Hutchins at Bantry and Richard Hedges isolated at Macroom lived more roughly than the Boyles and Percevals, they were not frontiersmen.[157] Such social and geographical contrasts are, moreover, commonplace: they can be instanced in most English and Welsh counties. Distance made county Cork lag behind metropolitan habits; so too did spending power, for in size and average wealth, while increasing, the settler élite hardly matched its equivalents in London or lowland England. Yet county Cork was not uniformly backward. By 1700 Cork city, Kinsale and Youghal were recognisably English towns. Those who travelled through the accessible and better populated baronies sensed familiarity, not strangeness.[158] Nor did remoteness and under-development make county Cork a colonial society. In some aspects it conformed better to the smartest metropolitan standards than Northumberland, Glamorgan and Yorkshire.[159] Cork, we must admit, was special among Irish counties; and though the populations of county Dublin, Antrim or Down may have resembled it in religion, structure and wealth, we can hardly treat it as a paradigm for, say, Mayo, Roscommon or Clare.

Cork was unlike any English county in that its landowners floated above a population different not only in wealth and culture, but also in race and religion. This feature has deluded some into supposing that the Protestant grandees are most appropriately likened to the colonists of north, or the *conquistadores* of Latin America. Instead it ought to recall the similarities between the Irish situation and that in most other seventeenth-century monarchies, from Scotland to Bohemia, from Russia to Spain, where ethnic and religious differences further complicated economic and social disparities.

References

1. My principal debts, as will become obvious, are to: D. Dickson, 'Cork region', unpublished Ph.D. thesis, T.C.D. 1977; MacCarthy-Morrogh, *Plantation*; M. MacCarthy-Morrogh, 'The English presence in early seventeenth century Munster' in Brady and Gillespie *Natives and newcomers*, pp 171-190; T. O. Ranger, 'The career of the first earl of Cork', unpublished D. Phil. Oxford, 1958; T. O. Ranger, 'Richard Boyle and the making of an Irish fortune' in *I.H.S.*, x (1957), pp 257-297.

2. S. P. Johnson (ed.), 'On a manuscript description of the city and county of Cork, *cir.* 1685, written by Sir Richard Cox' in *R.S.A.I. Jn.*, xxxii (1902), esp. p. 363; R. Day (ed.), R. Cox, 'Regnum Corcagiense; or a description of the kingdom of Cork', in *Cork Hist. Soc. Jn.*, 2nd ser., viii (1902) pp 89-97; D. Dickson, 'A description of county Cork, *c.*1741' in *Cork Hist. Soc. Jn.*, lxxvi (1971), pp 152-5; Smith, *Cork* (Dublin, 1750), i, sig. A[l]-[A4]; Cf. T. P. Connor, 'The making of *Vitruvius Britannicus* in *Architectural History*, xx (1977), pp 14-25.

3. K.[ent]A.[rchive].O[ffice]., hereafter K.A.O., Maidstone, Sackville MSS U. 269, C. 18/1; [R. Cox], *An essay for the conversion of the Irish, shewing that 'tis their duty and their interest to become Protestants* (Dublin, 1698), pp 10, 13; R. Cox, *Hibernia Anglicana* (London, 1689) i, sig. h1; W. Petty, *The political anatomy of Ireland* (London, 1691), pp 25, 27; W. Petty, *The present state of Ireland* (London, 1673), pp 101-4; J. Ware, *De Hibernia & antiquitatibus eius, disquisitiones* (London, 1654), ch. xxii, pp 94-6.

4. P. Borsay (ed.), *The English urban renaissance* (Oxford, 1989), pp 260-1; J. Evelyn, *An account of architects and architecture* (London, 1706), pp 7-10, 40; R. North, *Of Building,* in H. Colvin and J. Newman (ed.) (Oxford, 1981), pp 8, 10-13; R. Wittkower, *Architectural principles in the age of humanism* (London, 1967), pp 14-16.

5. H. J. Habbakuk, 'England' in A. Goodwin (ed.), *The European nobility in the eighteenth century* (London, 1967), p. 4; L. and J.C.F. Stone, *An open élite? England 1540-1880* (Oxford, 1984), pp 295-398; J. Summerson, 'The classical country in house in eighteenth century England' in *Royal Society of Arts Journal*, cvii (1959), p. 9.

6. Cullen, *Emergence*, pp 98-9; Cullen, 'Man, landscape and roads', in W. Nolan (ed.), *The shaping of Ireland: the geographical perspective* (Cork, 1986), pp 127-8; Knight of Glin [D. Fitzgerald], *et al., Vanishing country houses of Ireland* (Antrim, 1988), pp 26-32; T. Jones Hughes, 'Historical geography in Ireland from *circa*

1700' in G. L. Herries Davies (ed.), *Irish geography: the geographical society of Ireland golden jubilee 1934-1984* (Dublin, 1984), pp 156-60; O'Connor, *Limerick*, pp 81, 82.

7. A. Everitt, *The community of Kent and the Great Rebellion* (Leicester, 1966); idem., 'County and town: patterns of regional evolution in England' in *Transactions of the Royal Historical Society*, 5th series, xxix (1979), pp 79-107; V. Morgan, 'The cartographic image of 'the county' in early modern England' in ibid., pp 129-54; J. Morrill, *The revolt of the provinces* (London, 1976).

8. A. Coleby, *Central government and the localities: Hampshire 1649-1689* (Cambridge, 1987), pp 1-3; A. Fletcher, 'National and local awareness in the county communities' in H. Tomlinson (ed.), *Before the English Civil War* (London, 1983); C. Holmes, 'The county community in Stuart historiography' in *Journal of British Studies*, xix (1980), pp 54-73; A. Hughes, 'Warwickshire on the eve of the Civil War: a county community?' in *Midland History*, vii (1982), pp 42-72.

9. d'Alton, *Protestant society*; Donnelly, *Land and people*.

10. *R.S.A.I. Jn.*, xxxii (1902) p. 354; Cox, *Hibernia Anglicana*, ii, p. 95; J. Walton, 'The subsidy roll of county Waterford, 1662' in *Anal. Hib.*, xxx (1982), pp 51-2.

11. O. MacDonagh, *States of mind: a study of Anglo-Irish conflict* (London, 1983), pp 16-17; W.J. Smyth, *Explorations of place* in J. Lee (ed.), *Ireland: towards a sense of place* (Cork, 1985), pp 4-15.

12. Dickson, 'Cork region', p. 320 (map 2), ch. 5.

13. Chatsworth House, Derbyshire, Lismore MS 32/4 and 5; T. C. Barnard, 'Lord Broghill, Vincent Gookin and the Cork elections of 1659' in *E.H.R.*, lxxxviii (1973), p. 356; Anon, *A brief account of Mr. Valentine Greatraks* (London, 1666), p. 19.

14. D. Hayton, 'Tories and Whigs in county Cork, 1714' in *Cork Hist. Soc. Jn.*, lxxx (1975), p. 88; Caulfield, *Youghal*, p. 394.

15. W. Nolan, 'Some civil and ecclesiastical territorial divisions and their geographical significance', in W. Nolan (ed.), The shaping of Ireland, pp 73-4.

16. Farmar MSS Dublin Hovell to Frederick, 19 Feb. and 21 March 1683[4]; same to same, 15 Aug. 1684; same to Putland, 16 July 1686 (I am grateful to Dr. David Dickson for first alerting me to the value of this source); Guildford Muniment Room, Midleton MSS f. 195, MS 1248/1; B.L., Add. MSS 46937, f. 155; Petworth, Sussex, Orrery MSS G[eneral] S[eries] 30, letter of H. Boyle, 13 April 1686; Barnard, 'Lord Broghill', pp 352-65; Brady, *Clerical records*, i, pp xlviii-lvi; R. Buckley, *The proposal for sending back the nobility and gentry of Ireland* (London, 1690), p. 18.

17. Guildford, MS 1248/1, f. 259^v; B.L., Add. MS 46937, f. 73; *Egmont MSS* ii, p. 114; T. Morris, *A sermon preached at the funeral of the honourable Roger, earl of Orrery* (London, 1681), p. 39.

18. T. C. Barnard, 'Crises of identity among Irish Protestants, 1641-85' in *Past and Present*, cxxix (1990); K. Bottigheimer, *English money and Irish land* (Oxford 1971), pp 76-114; Hayton, 'Tories and Whigs', p. 89; MacCarthy-Morrogh, *Plantation*, pp 273-4, 283; J. A. Murphy, 'The politics of the Munster Protestants 1641-49' in *Cork Hist. Soc. Jn.*, lxxvi (1971), pp 1-20; Ranger, 'The first earl of Cork', ch. 10.

19. N.L.I., MS 7861, f. 156; K.A.O., U 269, C18/22; Bodl., Clarendon State Papers, 84, f. 168^v; Brady, *Clerical records*, i, pp l-lii; R. Day (ed.), 'Cooke's memoirs of Youghal, 1749' in *Cork Hist. Soc. Jn.*, 2nd series, ix (1903), p. 56; Dickson, 'Cork region', pp 236-40; MacCarthy-Morrogh, *Plantation*, pp 272; [J. F. Ainsworth]

'Manuscripts of the old corporation of Kinsale' in *Anal. Hib.*, xv (1944), pp 193, 203; D. Townshend (ed.), 'Notes on the Council Book of Clonakilty' in *Cork Hist. Soc. Jn.*, 2nd series, i (1895), p. 454.

20. A. Fletcher, *Reform in the provinces* (New Haven and London, 1986), pp 100-3, 122-30; G. C. F. Forster, 'The north riding justices and their sessions 1603-25' in *Northern History*, x (1975), pp 110-11; C. Herrup, *The common peace: participation and the criminal law in seventeenth-century England* (Cambridge, 1987), pp 57-8, 125.

21. Chatsworth, Lismore MS 32/3, 4 and 5; Bodl., Clarendon State Papers, 79, ff 100, 107^v, 184; Dickson, 'Cork region', pp 61-2, 127-8; D. Hayton, 'The beginnings of the undertaker system' in T. Bartlett and D. Hayton (ed.), *Penal era and golden age* (Belfast, 1979), pp 32-54; D. Hayton, 'Ireland and the English ministers, 1707-16', unpublished D. Phil. thesis, Oxford, 1975, pp 113-14.

22. Chatsworth, Lismore MS 33/63, 64, 67 and 70; Lord Cork's diary, 2 June 1665, 2 Dec. 1665, 15 June 1666, 17 Sep. 1666; *Stat. at large Ireland,* iii, p. 175.

23. Bowood House, Wiltshire, Petty MSS 14, p. 4, 17, items 53 and 75; McGill University Lib., Montreal, Osler MS 7612, letter of 21 June 1670.

24. T.C.D., MS 1180, ff 67-73 'Mr. Cox his paper on the reduction of Ireland sent to the Ld. Pres., 2 Dec. 1689'; R. Cox, *Aphorisms relating to the kingdom of Ireland* (London, 1689); *Hibernia Anglicana*, i, sig. bl^v-b2, d[2]-[d2^v]

25. B. G . Blackwood, 'The Lancashire gentry and the Great Rebellion', in *Chetham Soc.*, 3rd series, xxv (1978), pp 23-5; Everitt, *The community of Kent*, pp 36-7; Hughes, 'Warickshire', p. 46; J.S. Morrill, *Cheshire 1630~1660* (Oxford, 1974), pp 3-4.

26. Chatsworth, Lismore MS 33/69; Petworth, Orrery MSS G.S.27 (8 Jan. 1688/9, 19 Feb. 1688/9, 3 Aug. 1689).

27. Dickson, 'Cork region', pp 14-15, 17, 67; idem., 'Property and social structure in eighteenth-century south Munster', in Cullen and Furet *Ire. and France,* pp 129-30.

28. Dickson, 'Cork region', p. 65; Hayton, 'Ireland and the English ministers', pp 5-6.

29. 1641: MacCarthy-Morrogh, *Plantation,* p. 260; later figures: T.C.D., MS 1180, f. 69^v; Bodl., Clarendon State Papers, 84, ff l68^v-9; *Camden's Britannia 1695* (facsimile, Newton Abbott, 1971), p. 979, note k.; Dickson, 'Cork region', p. 420; *Seasonable advice to Protestants containing some means of reviving and strengthening the Protestant interest,* 2nd ed. (Cork, 1745) p. 9.

30. P.R.O.I., Books of Survey and Distribution, Cork.

31. T. C. Barnard, 'Land and the limits of loyalty: the second earl of Cork and first earl of Burlington (1612-1698)' in T. C. Barnard (ed.), *Lord Burlington: the man and his politics* (London, 1993).

32. Chatsworth, Lismore MSS, rentals of 1677, 1683, 1693, 1700; Viscount Shannon [F. Boyle], *Moral essays and discourses upon several subjects* (London, 1690), p. 60; R.E.W. Maddison, *The life of the honourable Robert Boyle, F.R.S.* (London, 1969), pp 258-9; Ranger, 'The first earl of Cork', pp. 135-66; D. Townshend, *The life and letters of the great earl of Cork* (London, 1904), pp 470-505.

33. For Barrymore: Chatsworth, Lismore MSS Cork's diary, 15 Sep. 1663, 12 June 1665, 8 Aug. 1671; N. Canny, *The upstart earl* (Cambridge, 1982), pp 47-8; G. E. C., *Complete peerage*, i, pp 443-4; MacCarthy-Morrogh, *Plantation*, p. 276.

34. T.C.D., MS 847. The figures in this list, probably compiled to assist the London committee which relieved refugees from Ireland in 1689, are supported in regard to landed wealth from other sources. Other types of income seem to have been recorded more haphazardly. At the very least it indicates the ranking of incomes:

R. Caulfield (ed.), *Journal of the Very Rev. Rowland Davies*, Camden Society (1857), p. 9.

35. U.C.C. Library, MS U. 55, Kinsale manorial papers (11 May, 1686); D. Hayton (ed.), 'An Irish parlimentary diary from the reign of Queen Anne' in *Anal. Hib.*, xxx (1982), pp 100-1; H.M.C., *Egmont MSS* i and ii, *passim*, and esp. ii, p. 113; [A. Meredith], *Ormond's curtain drawn* (London, 1646).

36. Bowood, Petty MSS 6, p. 148; 16, pp 84-5; 18, item 18; 19, items 247, 261; McGill University Library, Osler MS 7612, 16 April 1668, 28 July 1668, 17 Oct. 1668; G.E.C., *Complete peerage*, vii, pp 297-8; R. D. King-Harman, *The Kings, earls of Kingston* (Cambridge, 1959), pp 6-21.

37. Chatsworth, Lismore MSS Cork's diary, 12 Feb. 1668[9]; U.C.C. Library, MS U 55 (6 Nov. 1688); T.C.D., MS 847; Petworth, Orrery MSS G. S. 28 (12 Sep. 1673); E. MacLysaght (ed.), *Calendar of the Orrery papers*, I.M.C. (Dublin, 1941), pp 293, 297, 298, 301, 302, 311, 318, 320; J. A. Murphy, 'Inchiquin's change of religion' in *Cork Hist. Soc. Jn.*, lxxii (1967), pp 59-67; J. W. Walker (ed.), 'Hackness manuscripts and accounts', *Yorkshire Archaelogical Society,* record series, xcv (1938 for 1937), p. 12.

38. Chatsworth, Lismore MS 34/8; Petworth, Orrery MSS G.S. 30 (14 Jan 1688[9]); J. Ainsworth (ed.), *The Inchiquin manuscripts* I.M.C. (Dublin, 1961) p. 517; *The declaration of the nobility and gentry of the province of Munster* (London, 1689); Dickson, 'Cork region', pp 121-2; G.E.C., *Complete peerage*, vii, pp 52-3; K. M. Lynch, *Roger Boyle, first earl of Orrery* (Knoxville, 1965), p. 246.

39. Most thorough remains: Lynch, *Orrery,* supplemented for the years after 1660 by D.B. Henning (ed.), *The history of Parliament: the House of Commons 1660-1690* (London, 1983), i, pp 701-3. Before 1660: T. C. Barnard, 'Planters and policies in Cromwellian Ireland' in *Past and present,* cxi (1973), pp 57-9; F. Dow, *Cromwellian Scotland* (Edinburgh, 1979), pp 162-210; H. R. Trevor-Roper, *Religion, the Reformation and social change* (London, 1967), pp 433-7; for his Irish activities after 1660, a quartet of articles by L. Irwin, 'The suppression of the Irish presidency system' in *I.H.S.,* xxi (1980), pp 21-32; idem, 'The earl of Orrery and the military problems of restoration Munster' in *Irish Sword,* xxii (1977), pp 10-19; idem, 'The Irish Presidency courts, 1569-1672' in *Irish Jurst.,* xii (1977); idem, 'The rôle of the presidency in the economic development of Munster' in *Cork Hist. Soc. Jn.,* lxxxii (1977), pp 102-104; Dislike is clear in Bodl., MS Eng. Hist. C. 266, ff 9-10; H.M.C., *Ormonde MSS*, new series, iv, p. 301; Henning, *Commons 1660-1690*, pp 701-3; and (more recently) J.N. Healy, *The castles of county Cork* (Cork and Dublin, 1988), pp 118-19.

40. Chatsworth, Lismore MSS, Cork's diary, 1 and 2 July 1668; Bodl., Clarendon State Papers, 79, ff 100, 107[v]-8.

41. M. MacGarvie, *The book of Marston Bigot* (Buckingham, 1987); Petworth, Orrery MSS G.S. 30 (14 Feb [1680?]).

42. B.L., Add. MS 21484, f. 42[v]; Victoria and Albert Museum, Forster collection, Orrery MSS, i, f. 34; Bodl., Carte MS. 50, ff. 62[v], 68[v]; MS. Eng. Hist. C. 266, ff 15-16; Petworth, Orrery MSS G.S., 28 (14 and 30 Dec. 1669 12 Feb. 1669[70]); 29 (2 Oct. 1677); MacLysaght, *Orrery papers*, p. 183.

43. B.L., Add. MS 28085, ff 3, 5; Stowe MS 200, f. 125; Bodl., Carte MS 50, ff 154, 155.

44. Petworth, Orrery MSS G.S., 13 and 17; *Cal. S.P. Ire., 1666-9*, p. 282. For the income of English peers: J. V. Beckett, *The aristocracy in England 1660-1914* (Oxford, 1986), pp 288-9; G. S. Holmes, 'Gregory King and the social structure of pre-industrial England' in *Transactions of the Royal Historical Society,* 5th series,

xxvii (1977), pp 54, 66-7; L. Stone, *The crisis of the aristocracy* (Oxford, 1965), p. 762.

45. Information about expenditure is scattered throughout the Orrery papers at Petworth, but see especially G.S. 13 and 17, 27, 29 (letter of 30 April 1677) 30 (letter of 20 Oct. 1683). Also: B.L., Stowe MS 200, f. 255; MacLysaght, *Orrery papers,* pp 142-3, 163; Cox, 'Regnum Corcagiense', p. 177.

46. Petworth, Orrery MSS G.S. 17.

47. T.C.D., MS 847; K.A.O., U. 269, C. 18/26-8, C. 19/7-9; Petworth, Orrery MSS G.S. 29 (letter of 11 Sep. 1676); MacLysaght, *Orrery papers,* pp 156-7, 198, 242.

48. T.C.D., MS 847; B.L., Stowe MS 200, f. 148; Petworth, Orrery MSS G.S. 17 (inventory of Charleville, 18 March 1672[3]); Cox, 'Regnum Corcagiense', p. 162; G.E.C. *Complete peerage,* xi, p. 655; Maddison, *Robert Boyle,* p. 259; Shannon, *Moral essays,* pp 18-19, 41-69.

49. Burlington House, bought as a carcase by Orrery's brother, cost in all £5,000. While completely new palaces like Castle Howard or Burley-on-the-Hill, required £35,000 and £30,000 respectively, more modest,though nevertheless grand, additions and improvements could be done for £4,000 or £9,000. Chatsworth, Lismore MSS Cork's diary, 2 Feb. 1666[7], 27 March 1667, 4 Nov. 1667, 30 Jan. 1667[8]; 1 and 4 Feb. 1667[8]; 24 Nov. 1671, 5 May 1673; H. Colvin et al. (ed.), *Architectural drawings from Lowther Castle, Westmorland,* Society of Architectural Historians of Great Britain (1980), pp 9-10; H. Colvin, *Calke Abbey, Derbyshire* (London, 1985), p. 101; idem, 'Letters and papers relating to the rebuilding of Combe Abbey, Warwickshire' in *Walpole Society,* l (1984), p. 255; K. Downes, *English Baroque architecture* (London, 1966), p. 12; H. J. Habbakuk, 'Daniel Finch, 2nd earl of Nottingham, his house and estate' in J. H. Plumb (ed.), *Studies in social history* (London, 1955), pp 152-3; F. H. W. Sheppard (ed.), *Survey of London, xxxii, The parish of St James, Westminster,* part ii (London, 1963), p. 391.

50. H.M.C., *Egmont MSS* ii, p. 112; H.M.C., *Ormonde MSS* new series, vii, pp 498-513.

51. Surrey Record Office, Kingston-upon-Thames, MS 84/49/1-4; Petworth, Orrery MSS G.S. 28 (letters of 14 Nov. 1671 and 18 May 1672); MacLysaght, *Orrery papers,* pp 59-61, 77, 84-5, 146.

52. P. Thornton and M. Tomlin, 'The furniture and decoration of Ham House' in *Furniture history,* xxii (1980), pp 23, 44-5.

53. R. Loeber, A *biographical dictionary of architects in Ireland 1600-1720* (London, 1981); idem, 'Early classicism in Ireland', in *Arch. Hist.,* xxii (1979); idem, with J. O'Connell 'Eyrecourt Castle, Co. Galway' in *The GPA Irish Arts Review Yearbook* (1988), pp 40-8; idem, 'Irish country houses and castles of the late Caroline period' in *Quart. Bull. of the Ir. Georgian Soc.,* xvi (1973), pp 1-70.

54. The ground-plan of Burton, in B.L., Add. MSS 46948, ff 16-17, is reproduced by Loeber in *Quart. Bull. Ir. Georg. Soc.,* xvi (1973), frontispiece and in B. de Breffny and R. ffolliot, *The houses of Ireland* (London, 1975), p. 69. A conjectural reconstruction is illustrated in Loeber, 'Early classicism', plate 8.

55. K.A.O., U. 269, C. 18/22; Breffny and Folliott, *The houses of Ireland,* p. 67; R. Cox, 'Regnum Corcagiense', p. 177; M. Craig, *The architecture of Ireland from the earliest times to 1880* (London and Dublin, 1982), p. 117; Loeber, *Biographical dictionary,* pp 25-7; M. MacCarthy-Morrogh, The English presence in early seventeenth century Munster' in Brady and Gillespie, *Natives and newcomers,* pp 181-4; T. Milward (ed.), A *collection of the state letters of ... the first earl of Orrery* (London, 1752), i, pp 31-2; D. M. Waterman, 'Some Irish seventeenth-century houses and their architectural ancestry' in E.M. Jope (ed.), *Studies in building history* (London, 1961), pp 258-60.

56. Chatsworth, Lismore MS 33/14 and 16; B.L., Stowe MS 744, ff 123ᵛ; Petworth, Orrery MSS G.S. 17 (account of W. Cooper, 1664-71, pp 2,11); 29 (3 Feb. 1679[80]); Loeber, *Biographical dictionary*, pp 1, 25-9; *Milward, Orrery state letters*, i, p. 74.

57. Orrery's perception was right: Castlemartyr survived, not Charleville. B.L., Stowe MS 200, ff 214, 216, 255; Loeber, 'Irish country houses', pp 30-1; Lynch, *Orrery*, p. 201.

58. B.L., Stowe MS 200, ff. 26ᵛ; K.A.O., MS U. 269, C. 18/22; North, *Of building*, pp 29, 62, 93-94.

59. Orrery boasted that Kilkenny could be reached in a day and Dublin in two: B.L., Stowe MS 744, ff 158.

60. M. Girouard, *Life in the English country house* (London, 1978), pp 120-62. For two important survivals from the period: J. Cornforth, 'Powis Castle' in *Country Life*, 9 July, 1987; G. Jackson-Stops, 'Badminton' in *Country Life*, 9 and 16 April, 1987.

61. Petworth, Orrery MSS inventories in G.S. 14-17; MacLysaght, *Orrery papers*, pp 168-79.

62. P. Thornton, *Authentic decor: the domestic interior 1620-1920* (London, 1984), p. 58; Idem, *Seventeenth-century interior decoration in England, France and Holland* (New Haven and London, 1978), pp 97-216; K. M. Walton, 'An inventory of 1710 from Dyrham House' in *Furniture history*, xxii (1986), pp 27-75.

63. Guest lists are to be found in N.L.I., MS 34, ff 345 (partly printed in MacLysaght, *Orrery papers*, pp 215-17); Petworth, Orrery MSS G.S., 14.

64. Ibid., G.S., 17, glazier's bill, 1 Jan. 1678[9]; 28 April 1679. Billiard tables were now commonplace in aristocratic dwellings, billiard rooms less so. P. Jenkins, *The making of a ruling class: the Glamorgan gentry 1640-1790* (Cambridge, 1983), p. 253; D. Neave, *Londesborough* (Londesborough, 1977), p. 31; C. J. Phillips, *History of the Sackville family* (London, 1930), p. 356; Stone, *An open élite?*, p. 315; Thornton, *Seventeenth-century interior decoration*, p. 231; plates 224, 225; Thornton and Tomlin, '*Ham house*', p. 39.

65. Shannon, *Moral essays*, pp 5, 59-69; E. Wetenhall, *A sermon preached Octob. 23. 1692 before His Excellency the Lord Lieutenant ... in Christ Church, Dublin* (Dublin, 1692), pp 16, 18.

66. C. Morris (ed.), *The journeys of Celia Fiennes* (London, 1947), pp 97-8; M. Howard, *The early Tudor country house: architecture and politics 1490-1550* (London, 1987), pp 21-2.

67. P. Earle, *The making of the English middle class: business, society and family life in London 1660-1730* (London, 1989), pp 294-5; L. Weatherill, *Consumer behaviour and material culture in Britain 1660-1740* (London, 1988), pp 20-1, 79-84, 89-90, 194-6.

68. His brother Cork and Burlington's activities: Neave, *Londesborough*, p. 13; Sheppard, *Survey of London*, xxxii, pt. ii, p. 391; Lord Conway's, Chatsworth, Lismore MSS, Cork's diary, 13 Oct. 1663; H. M. Colvin, *A biographical dictionary of British Architects* (London, 1978), pp 431, 440; P. Leach, 'Ragley Hall' in *Archaeological Journal*, cxxviii (1971), pp 230-3; Loeber, 'Irish country houses', pp 16, 27, 33, 35.

69. Chatsworth, Lismore MSS Lady Burlington's memorandum book, 21 Dec., 1674; Petworth, Orrery MSS G.S. 16 (Tempest's bill); 27 (Letter of Lady Powerscourt, 13 Aug. [168?]); 29 (letter of 14 Aug. 1678); Phillips, *History of the Sackville family*, pp 573-70; Sheppard, *Survey of London*, xxxii, pt. ii, p. 391; Stone, *Crisis of the aristocracy*, pp 552-4.

70. With typical hyperbole Orrery alleged that £60,000 had been spent on new public buildings in Cork city; Cox suggests much more modest sums: B.L., Stowe MS 207, ff 34ᵛ; Cox, 'Regnum Corcagiense', p. 162.

71. Generally on methods of financing such work: Dickson, 'Cork region', pp 123-5; Loeber, Irish country houses, p. 37. For the needs of Orrery's operations: Petworth, Orrery MSS G.S. 10; Phillips, *History of the Sackville family*, p. 431.

72. Chatsworth, Lismore MS 32/111; Petworth, Orrery MSS G.S. 28 (letters of Brodrick, 24 June 1662, 7 July 1662 and undated [?1662]); MacLysaght, *Orrery papers*, pp 22-3, 38. For this tendency among other skilled craftsmen see, T. C. Barnard, 'An Anglo-Irish industrial venture' in *R.I.A. Proc.*, 85, C (1985), p. 118.

73. Orrery, *An answer to a scandalous letter lately printed and subscribed by Peter Walsh* (London, 1662), p. 65. The sentiment was later repeated by Swift.

74. Petworth, Orrery MSS G.S. 16 (Book of accounts 1667); 17 (W. Cooper's account); 28 (letter of 25 May 1669); 29 (20 Jan. 1679[80]).

75. Petworth, Orrery MSS G.S. 15; 29 (letters of 30 March and 29 April 1680); MacLysaght, *Orrery papers*, pp 13, 139, 234; B.L., Add. MS 47038, ff 7, 32; *Egmont MSS* ii, pp 87, 98.

76. H.M.C., Petworth, Orrery MSS G.S. 15 (list of plate sold); 30 (letter of 18 Jan. 1686[7]). For Ram: Bodl., Clarendon State Papers, 88, ff 260 D. Bennett, *Collecting Irish silver* (London, 1984), p. 152; *Irish silver 1630-1820,* exhibition catalogue (Dublin, 1971), p. 8; T.C.D., MS 847.

77. D. Bennett, *Irish Georgian silver* (London, 1972); E. M. Fahy, 'The Cork Goldsmiths' Company, 1657' in *Cork Hist. Soc. Jn.*, lviii (1953), pp 33-38.

78. Chatsworth, Lismore MS 31/111; B.L., Add. MS 47037, ff 44, 62; Caulfield, *Cork*, pp 209, 210; Day, 'Cooke's memoirs of Youghal, 1749', p. 42; Anon [A. Frekel], 'Mrs. Elizabeth Freke, her diary, 1671-1714' in *Cork Hist. Soc. Jn.*, 2nd series, xvii (1911), p. 9; *Irish silver 1630-1820*, p. 19; C. A. Webster, *The church plate of the diocese of Cork, Cloyne and Ross* (Cork, 1909), pp 11-13, 60, 62, 73-4, 115, 121.

79. Petworth, Orrery MSS G.S. 15 (Bucknor's account, 15 Dec. 1666); 16 (Limerick city rentals).

80. K.A.O., U. 269, C. 18/6; Dickson, 'Cork region', ii, pp 547-8.

81. N.L.I., MS D. 13351-13422, item 30 (This is item 52 in National Register of Archives report on MSS of Mrs. Hooper, Briars Cross, Limpsfield, Surrey), henceforward cited as D.13381 (inventory of Samuel Hayman, Youghal, 8 July 1673); B.L., Add. MS 47037, ff 24, 35, 45ᵛ, 46, 47ᵛ, 48ᵛ; Petworth, Orrery MSS G.S. 10, 14, 16; *Cal. S.P. Ire., 1666-9*, p. 367; L. Irwin, 'Politics, religion and economy: Cork in the seventeenth century' in *Cork Hist. Soc. Jn.*, lxxxv (1980), p. 12; MacLysaght, *Orrery papers*, pp 44, 271.

82. Earle, *The making of the English middle class*, pp 293-4, 386; R. Loeber, 'English and Irish sources for the history of Dutch economic activity' in *Ir. Ec. Soc. Hist.*, viii (1981), p. 71; Thornton, *Seventeenth-century interior decoration*, pp 110-11.

83. Chatsworth, Lismore MS 28/4; Bodl., Carte MSS 36, ff 521ᵛ; 66, f. 303; *A memoir of mistress Ann Fowkes* (Dublin, 1892), p. 27; H.M.C., *Ormonde MSS* new series, vii, p. 500.

84. Chatsworth, Lismore MS 34/46, 51, 64, 65; N.L.I., MS D.13381.

85. U.C.C. Library, MS U.55, letter of 19 June 1685; B.L., Add. MS 47038, ff 7, 26ᵛ-27, 32, 37.

86. Chatsworth, Lismore MS 32/46, 55 and 65; Cork's diary, 5 Jan. 1662[3]; 30 Sep. 1668; Bolton Abbey, MS 279, pp 15, 25, 30; Bolton Abbey MS 282, *s.v.* 28 Feb. 1661[2]; B.L., Add. MS 47037, ff 34, 46ᵛ; 47038, ff 22, 26. Petworth, Orrery MSS

G.S. 15 (Astley's bill); 16 (1667 accounts); Loeber, 'Irish country houses', p. 42; Townshend, *The great earl of Cork*, p. 477.

87. Bodl., Carte MS 36, ff 497[v]; B.L., Add. MS 47037, f. 23; Petworth, Orrery MSS G.S. 17 (receipt of 29 Nov. 1670 and inventories).

88. B.L., Add. MS 47037, ff 34, 46[v]; G. Boate, *Ireland's naturall history* (London, 1652), p. 159; Caulfield, *Youghal*, p. 295; M. Dunlevy, *Ceramics in Ireland* (Dublin, 1988), pp 14-16; *Egmont MSS* ii, pp 128-9; A. Lynch, 'Excavations of the late medieval town defences of Charlotte's Quay, Limerick, *R.I.A. Proc.*, 84, C (1984), p. 312; D. P. Sweetman, 'Some late seventeenth to eighteenth-century finds from Kilkenny Castle' in ibid., 81, C (1981), pp 251-3; Smith, *Cork*, i, pp 127-8.

89. Petworth, Orrery MSS G.S. 17 (inventory of 18 March 1672[3] and 6 Sep. 1676); MacLysaght, *Orrery papers*, p. 175; K. N. Chaudhuri, *The trading world of Asia and the English East India Company 1660-1760* (Cambridge, 1978), pp 277-81; pp 406-10; Earle, *The making of the English middle class*, pp 272, 281, 295, 299, 336, 387; T. Volker, *The Japanese porcelain trade and the Dutch East India Company after 1683* (Leiden, 1959); idem, *Porcelain and the Dutch East India Company 1602-1682* (Leiden, 1954); Weatherill, *Consumer behaviour*, pp 28, 32, 39, 41, 49, 61, 110-11, 158-9.

90. L.M. Cullen, *Anglo-Irish trade 1660-1800* (Manchester, 1968), pp 51-2; Bennett, *Irish Georgian silver*, p. 67.

91. Bowood, Petty MSS 6, item 53; 8, item 23; Chatsworth, Lismore MSS rental for 1677, p. 91; Guildford, MS 1248/1, f. 195; B.L., Stowe MS 744, ff 78[v]; Inner Temple; London, Misc. MSS 61, letter book of Essex, 1677, pp 90, 93, 96; Damer House, Roscrea, De Vesci MSS J/2, J/3, J/8.

92. Petworth, Orrery MSS G.S. 15.

93. B.L., Add. MS 47037, ff 23; 47038, ff 24[v], 32-32[v]; K.A.O., MS U. 269, C. 18/22; Petworth, Orrery MSS, G.S. 16 (1667 accounts); 17 (inventories of 18 March 1672[3], 6 Sep. 1676, 21 May 1677, 29 Oct. 1679); H.M.C., *Egmont MSS* ii, pp 16, 69, 98; MacLysaght, *Orrery papers*, p. 174.

94. Bowood, Petty MSS 19, p. 341; T.C.D., MS 2947, pp 20, 42, 54; B.L., Add. MS 47038, ff 32-32[v]; McGill, Osler MS 7612, 16 Feb. 1677[8]; A. Crookshank and Knight of Glin, [D. Fitzgerald], *Irish portraits 1660~1860* (Dublin, 1969), pp 12-13, 27-9; Jane Fenlon, 'The painter stainers companies of Dublin and London ...', in J. Fenlon, *et al., New perspectives: studies in art history in honour of Anne Crookshank* (Dublin, 1987), pp 101-6; H.M.C., *Egmont diary*, ii, 16; iii, pp 365-6; Loeber, *Biographical dictionary*, p. 109.

95. Borsay, *English urban renaissance*, p. 35; Earle, *Making of the English middle class*, pp 74, 295; Weatherill, *Consumer behaviour*, pp 10, 37, 40, 41, 49, 50, 54, 56, 63, 77, 79, 88, 169, 172, 177.

96. N.L.I., MS D. 13385; B.L., Add. MS 47038, f. 28[v]; Petworth, Orrery MSS G.S., 16 (account book of 1667); [J. Ainsworth], 'Doneraile papers' in *Anal. Hib.*, xv (1944), pp 350-1; H.M.C., *Egmont MSS* ii, p. 15; I. Pears, *The discovery of painting: the growth of interest in the arts in England 1680-1768* (New Haven and London, 1988), pp 112-19.

97. B. Rand, *Berkeley and Perceval* (Cambridge, 1914), p. 57. Petty hinted at a taste for collecting, which he did not share: McGill University Library, Osler MS 7612, 30 Dec. 1671.

98. Dickson, 'Cork region', pp 73-9.

99. E. Boyle, countess of Cork and Orrery, *The Orrery papers* (London, 1903), i, p. 206; Smith, *Cork*, i, p. 147.

100. R. Freart, *Parallel of the ancient architecture with the modern*, transl. J. Evelyn (London, 1706); G. Barozzi [Vignola], *The regular architect* (London, 1669). These books were given to St Finbarre's cathedral library and are now in U.C.C. Library, pressmarks S.11.13 and T.1.6. See too, *The petition of the Lord Bishop of Cloyn to the Honourable House of Commons* (n.p., n.d.), in Bodl, Tanner MS 33, f. 20; Webster, *Church plate*, pp 79, 83, 100, 101, 107, 111, 123-4 and the memorial tablet in Cloyne cathedral.

101. B.L., Add. MS 21484, ff 39^v. Wetenhall proved an intellectual as well as spiritual leader: Bowood, Petty MSS 6, series ii, 92; B.L., Add. MS 5853, ff 14, 16, 22-22^v; H.M.C., *Egmont MSS* ii, p. 76; K.T. Hoppen, *The Dublin Philosphical Society* (London, 1970), pp 45-6; Webster, *Cork*, pp 281-93.

102. Colvin, *British archit.ects*, p. 29; Loeber, *Biographical dictionary*, pp 4-7, 17-18, 25-9, 67, 101-3.

103. Chatsworth, Lismore MS 31/95; 32/84, 86, 182; B.L., Add. MS 47037, ff 22^v, 31, 48^v; Petworth, Orrery MSS G.S. 29 (letters of 23 and 30 April 1677). For the first earl of Cork and the Irish harp, Canny, *The upstart earl*, pp 128, 195.

104. Chatsworth, Lismore MSS 32/91, 188; Cork's diary, 28 Aug. 1660, 23, 26 and 30 July 1661, 9, 12, 16 and 22 Aug. 1661, 31 Aug 1663, 30 May 1665; Bolton Abbey and MS 279, account of 'play money' to 5 March 1662[3]; J. Fairfax-Blakeborough, *Northern turf history*, ii ([London] 1950), p. 143; Neave, *Londesborough* pp 13, 74; Shannon, *Moral essays*, p. 61. Jenkins, *Making of a ruling class*, pp 156, 165, 263-8.

105. B.L., Add. MS 47037, ff 20^v-21, 23, 24^v, 42^v, 43, 43^v, 45, 45^v; 47038, f. 31.

106. N.L.I., MS 7177, 20 July 1672, 25 July and 5 Sep. 1677; K.A.O., U. 269, C. 18/1, 12-23; MacLysaght, *Orrery papers*, p. 157; Phillips, *History of the Sackville family*, p. 432.

107. Orrery expected to spend £2,130 on his household, out of which £200 was assigned to the stables and liveries. Petworth, Orrery MSS G.S. 17; also G.S. 16 (13 Sep. 1669); 22 (23 Sep. 1665); 26 (14 June 1659); Chatsworth, Cork's diary, 30 June 1666 and 4 Sep. 1666; K.A.O., U. 269, C. 18/25; M. D. Jephson, *An Anglo-Irish miscellany: some records of the Jephsons of Mallow* (Dublin, 1964), p. 55; MacLysaght, *Orrery papers*, pp 38, 40, 284.

108. Chatsworth, Cork's diary, 6 Jan. 1661[2], 24 May 1662, 13 Nov. 1662, 26 Feb. 1662[3], 31 Aug. 1663, 30 Oct. 1663, 15 May 1665, 18 July 1666, 9 June 1669, 8 and 11 Nov. 1670; Farmar MSS, Dublin, 4 Sep. 1685.

109. Chatsworth, Lismore MS 31/95, 111; Cork's diary, 9 and 23 March 1659[60], 14 Sep. 1660, 13 March 1661[2], 7 June 1662, 17 May 1666, 30 April 1669, 13 June 1670, 18 Aug. 1671; N.L.I., MS 7177, 18 May 1672, 24 Sep. 1672, 18 June 1673, 2 Dec. 1673, 2 Oct. 1675, 6 Oct. 1675, 22 Dec. 1677, 1 June 1678; Farmar MSS 7 March 1683[4], 12 Sep. 1684; B.L., Add. MS 47037, ff 42^v, 45^v; Petworth, Orrery MSS G.S., 29 (15 Sep. 1681); 30 (8 Oct. 1687); Buckley, *The proposal for sending back the nobility and gentry*, p. 15; N. Canny, 'The Irish background to Penn's experiment' in R. S. and M. M. Dunn (ed.), *The world of William Penn* (Philadelphia, 1986), pp 146, 155; Caulfield, *Journal of Rowland Davies*, p. x; [A. Freke], 'Mrs Elizabeth Freke's diary', p. 11; Jephson, *An Anglo Irish miscellany*, p. 55; E. MacLysaght, *Irish life in the seventeenth century*, 3rd ed. (Shannon, 1969), pp 43-5; MacCarthy-Morrogh, *Plantation*, pp 129-30; C. H. Hull (ed.), *Economic writings of Sir William Petty* (Cambridge, 1899), ii, pp 593-4; Joan Thirsk, *Horses in early modern England* (Reading, 1978), pp 24, 26.

110. Bowood, Petty MSS 8, item 22; 9, item 39; Chatsworth, Cork's diary, 10 March

1654[5]; 3 Aug. 1658; B.L., Add. MS 28876, ff 17^v; Stowe MS 744, ff 74; MacLysaght, *Irish life*, p. 145.

111. Borsay, *English urban renaissance*, pp 180-96, 214-15, 355-67; Caulfield, *Youghal*, pp 365-6, 369-70, 436, 507; Thirsk, *Horses*, p. 22.

112. Chatsworth, Lismore MS 32/101; Cork's diary, 15 Nov. 1661; D. B. Quinn, *The Elizabethans and the Irish* (Ithaca, 1966), p. 151.

113. Farmar MSS, 30 Oct. 1685; K.A.O., U. 269, C. 18/5; Borsay, *The English urban renaissance*, pp 302-3; Petty, *Political anatomy*, p. 56; K. V. Thomas, *Man and the natural world* (London, 1983), pp 59-60.

114. Farmar MSS 30 Nov. 1683, 7 March 1683[4], 27 July 1684, 19 Sep. 1684, 12 Dec. 1684, 26 May 1685, 28 July 1685, 8 Sep. 1685, 24 Aug. 1686, 23 Sep. 1686.

115. For the fairs and markets: B.L., Add. MS 47038, ff 36^v; Petworth, Orrery MSS G.S. 17 (account of Dr Hall, 2 Nov. 1676); Caulfield, *Kinsale*, pp 348-53; J. Russel, *A new almanack for the year of our Lord 1690* (Dublin, 1690); R. Shepherd, *An almanack for the year of our Lord 1678* (Dublin, 1678); W. J. Smith (ed.), *Herbert correspondence* (Dublin and Cardiff, 1963), p. 282; A. White, *An almanack and prognostication for the year of our Lord 1665* (Dublin, 1665). For their significance: Dickson 'Cork region', pp 25, 520-1; P. O'Flanagan, 'Settlement, development and trading in Ireland, 1600-1800' in T. Devine and D. Dickson (ed.), *Ireland and Scotland* (Edinburgh, 1983), pp 146-150.

116. Cullen, *Emergence*, pp 107-8; idem, 'Incomes, social classes and economic growth in Ireland and Scotland 1600-1900' in Devine and Dickson (ed.), *Ireland and Scotland*, pp 252-6, 258; Hull, *Economic writings of Petty,* ii, pp 563-578; *Seasonable Advice to Protestants*, pp 19-20.

117. T. H. Breen, 'An empire of goods: the anglicization of colonial America' in *Journal of British Studies,* 25 (1986), pp 468-99.

118. Dickson, 'Cork region', pp 145, 154-69.

119. Chatsworth, Lismore MS Cork's diary, 23 Oct. 1666; Farmar MSS 4 Jan. 1683[4], 3 June 1684, 17 Oct. 1684, 5 June 1685, 24 Aug. 1686; Cox, 'Regnum Corcagiense', pp 70-1; R. Lawrence, *The interest of Ireland in its trade and wealth stated,* i, (Dublin, 1682), pp 84-9; MacLysaght, *Orrery papers*, p. 340; Petty, *Political anatomy* , p. 119.

120. K.A.O., U. 269, C. 18/26; Petworth, Orrery MSS G.S. 17 (account of Cooper) 29 (petition of 15 Sep. 1686; letters of 19 Nov. 1680, 27 Jan 1681[2], 22 April 1682); 30 (letters of 10 and 14 May 1686, 13 Dec. 1687, 21 Jan 1687[8]); MacLysaght, *Orrery papers*, pp 236, 245, 251, 284; Smith *Herbert correspondence*, p. 244.

121. N.L.I., MS 34, ff 345 (partly calendared in MacLysaght, *Orrery papers*, pp 313-17); Petworth, Orrery MSS G.S. 14. For Lord Cork's estate see, Chatsworth, Bolton Abbey MS 283, 'House book in Dublin, 1662'; *U.C.C. Library*, MS U. 55, letter of 18 Nov. 1662; for Ormonde's: H.M.C., *Ormonde MSS* new series, vii, pp 497-8.

122. Petworth, Orrery MSS G.S. 12 (6 Nov. 1669); 16 (1667 accounts); 29 (22 April 1679); M. Allen, *The Ballymaloe cookbook* (London, 1977), p. 44; Loeber, 'Irish country houses' p. 48; Petty, *Political anatomy*, p. 111.

123. Chatsworth, Lismore MS 32/64; 33/66; B.L., Add. MS 47037, ff 43, 47, 48; Petworth, Orrery MSS G.S. 15 (account of R. Newenham); 17 (accounts of Cooper and Lawndy); Dickson, 'Cork region', p. 139; C. Shammas, 'How self-sufficient was early America?' in *Journal of Interdisciplinary History,* xiii (1982), pp 249-68.

124. B.L., Add. MS 47038, ff 30^v; Petworth, Orrery MSS G.S. 13 (Memo); 2-8 (17 Nov. 1674); 29 (30 April 1677 and 5 and 22 April 1682); MacLysaght, *Orrery papers*, pp 240, 299, 314, 325; P. Nunn, 'Aristocratic estates and employment in South

Yorkshire, 1700-1800' in S. Pollard and C. Holmes (ed.), *Essays in the economic and social history of South Yorkshire* (Sheffield, 1976), pp 28-40.

125. Cambridge University Library, MS ff 2.2., ff 1-1ᵛ; *U.C.C. Library* , MS U. 45, Southwell shrievalty papers; Houghton Library, Harvard University MS 218 22F (Orrery MSS), 6 May 1664; Bodl., Carte MSS 36, f. 308; 54, f. 504; 59, f. 458; Petworth, Orrery MSS, G.S. 28, passim, but esp. 14 and 30 Dec. 1669; 29 (19 Oct. 1680); [Ainsworth], Kinsale, p. 165; *Animadversions on the proposal for sending back the nobility and gentry of Ireland* (London, 1690), pp 34-5; *Sr. St. John Broderick's vindication of himself* (London, 1690), pp 5, 17-19; Caulfield, *Kinsale*, p. 420; MacLysaght, *Orrery papers*, pp 240, 299, 314, 325; C. M. Tenison, 'Cork M.Ps', p. 177.

126. Guildford, MS 1248/1, ff 111-11ᵛ, 124, 279; Bodl., Clarendon State Papers 84, ff 400-2; M. F. Bond (ed.), *The diaries and papers of Sir Edward Dering* (London, 1976), p. 9; Henning, *Commons 1660~90*, i, pp 721-4; N. Salmon, *A short view of the families of the present Irish nobility* (London, 1759), p. 146; P. Seaward, *The cavalier Parliament and the reconstruction of the old regime* (Cambridge, 1989), pp 56, 84, 91-2, 222, 254, 310.

127. Bowood, Petty MSS 14, pp 50-1; 19, pp 37, 125, 126, 223, 274, 312, 323, 341. McGill, Osler MS 7612, 23 July 1670; Petworth, Orrery MSS G.S., 16 (Kyrle's account with Orrery, 11 April 1660); 29 (23 April 1677, 5 and 22 April 1662, 30 Oct. 1682); N.A., Books of Survey and Distribution, Cork; T. C. Barnard, 'Sir William Petty as Kerry ironmaster' in *R.I.A. Proc.*, 82, C (1982), pp 12, 22-3; Jephson, *Anglo-Irish miscellany*, p. 52; MacLysaght, *Orrery papers*, pp 70, 103, 132, 258, 269, 277, 337, 354; J. M. Sosin, *English America and the restoration monarchy of Charles II* (Lincoln, Nebraska 1980), p. 212; Tenison, 'Cork M.P.s', p. 523.

128. Chatsworth, Lismore MSS 32/55, 79 and 82; 33-178; 34-142, 55, 92, 104, 118, 135, 137; Lord Cork's diary, 2 June 1654, 16 Dec. 1654, 13 April 1658, 19 Oct. 1659, 14 Oct. 1662, 11 Nov. 1662, 9 Aug. 1665, 4 Sep. 1665, 22 July 1669, 20 June 1670, 3 Oct 1670, 23 July 1672; 1677 rental, p. 31; 1700 rental p. 25; N.L.I., MSS 7177, 1 May 1672, 5 June 1672, 13 Nov. 1672, 28 Dec. 1672, 5 and 12 May 1675, 9 June 1677, 26 Jan 1677[8]; 13249 (2); B. L. Stowe MS 200, ff 346, 361; Petworth, Orrery MSS G.S. 12 (1668 deposition of Digby Ffoulke); 28 (12 Feb. 1669[70], 16 Jan 1671[2], 27 Feb. 1673[4], 3 March 1673[4], 5 May 1674); 29 (26 March 1678). Bodl., Carte MS 54, ff 504-4ᵛ; Barnard, *E.H.R.*, lxxxviii, p. 356 and n. 2; H. F. Berry, 'J.P.s for the county of Cork' in *Cork Hist. Soc. Jn.*, 2nd series, iii (1897), p. 60; MacLysaght, *Orrery papers*, pp 318, 322, 331, 352; Tenison, 'Cork M.P.s', p. 378.

129. *U.C.C.* Library, MS U. 55, Kinsale manorial papers, 1626-61, esp. letter of 15 July 1654; T.C.D., MS 825, f. 212; B.L., Add. MS 46937, ff 98-9, 102; Henning, *Commons 1660-90*, iii, p. 459; MacCarthy-Morrogh, *Plantation*, pp 200, 245.

130. N.L.I., MS 14910, pp 2, 13-14; *T.C.D.*, MS 825, f. 212; *U.C.C.* Library, MS U. 55, Kinsale manorial papers, 1665-1675 passim; K.A.O., U. 1713 (Dering Southwell MSS) C. 3/23, 25, 32; C. 4/2-4; [Ainsworth], 'Kinsale', pp 216-24; T. C. Barnard, 'Fishing in seventeenth-century Kerry: the experience of Sir William Petty' in *Kerry Hist. Soc. Jn.*, xiv (1981), pp 15-16; Dickson, 'Cork region', pp 51-2, 163-4, 422-4, 488.

131. N.L.I., MS 14910, p. 13; U.C.C. Library, MS, U. 55, Southwell shrievalty papers; K.A.O., U. 1713, C. 1/1; T. C. Barnard, 'Sir William Petty, Irish landowner' in H. Lloyd-Jones *et al* (ed.), *History and imagination* (London, 1981), pp 216-17; Caulfield, *Kinsale*, pp 393-4; Henning, *Commons 1660~90*, iii, p. 459.

132. Chatsworth, Lismore MS 32/32; 1677 rental, p. 58; Petworth, Orrery MSS G.S., 28

(25 May 1669); 30 (4 March 1683[4], 24 March 1684[5], 25 May 1685, 27 Dec. 1686, 15 July 1687); Caulfield, *Youghal*, pp 230-1, 302, 314; MacLysaght, *Orrery papers*, pp 224, 247, 266-7, 271, 299, 314-15, 316, 322, 325, 341, 366; Townshend, *Great earl of Cork*, p. 501.

133. Houghton Library, Harvard University, MS 218 22F, leases made in 1692-4; Dickson, 'Cork region', p. 16.

134. Bowood, Petty MSS 19, item 1; Chatsworth, Lismore MS 32/68; Petworth, Orrery MSS G.S. 28-30, passim; P.R.O.N.I., D. 562/15; G.D. Burtchaell and T.U. Sadleir, *Alumni Dublinenses* (Dublin, 1935), p. 357; Lynch, *Orrery*, pp 113, 120, 122, 214; MacLysaght, *Orrery papers*, pp 223, 287, 295, 318, 325-6, 327. The monument in Youghal church survives.

135. Farmar MSS, letters of 27 June 1684 and 25 Aug, 1685; Shannon, *Moral essays*, p. 121.

136. Bowood, Petty MSS 9, item 110; 17, item 93; Petworth, Orrery MSS G.S., 29 (26 July 1681); F.E. Ball, *The judges of Ireland, 1221-1921* (New York, 1926), i, pp 358-9; T. C. Barnard, *Cromwellian Ireland* (Oxford, 1975) pp 118-22, 126-30, 151-2; MacLysaght, Orrery papers, pp 223, 283, 287, 294, 358.

137. Chatsworth, Lismore MSS Cork's diary, 1 Sep. 1666; Guildford, MS 1248/1, ff 256, 278[V]; Houghton Library, Harvard University, MS 218 22F (14 Dec. 1669, 14 Nov. 1671); B.L., Add. MS 28876, f. 269; Petworth, Orrery MSS G.S. 17 (Limerick rentals 1675); 28 (3 Jan 1671[2], 20 Feb. 1671[2], 30 April 1677, 19 Nov, 1680, 29 April 1680, 26 Oct, 1686); Ball, *Judges*, i, p. 357; [A. Freke], 'Mrs. Freke's diary', p. 15; R. Gillespie (ed.), *Settlement and survival on an Ulster estate* (Belfast, 1988), p. xxxviii, n. 79; Lawrence, *The interest of Ireland*, ii, p. 189; MacLysaght, *Orrery papers*, pp 31, 161, 164-5, 223, 277, 283, 292, 298; O'Connor, *Limerick*, pp 31, 43, 87; R.C.B. Oliver, 'The Hartstonges and Radnorshire', *Radnorshire Society Transactions*, xliii-xlv (1973-5); E. P. Shirley (ed.), 'Extracts from the journal of Thomas Dinely, esq ...', *Kilkenny and S.E. of Ire. Soc. Jn.*, new series, v (1864-6), p. 435; Tenison, 'Cork M.P.s', p. 424.

138. T.C.D. MS, 824, ff 27; Petworth, Orrery MSS G.S. 30 (21 Jan 1684[5], 23 July 1688); Ball, *Judges*, ii, p. 53; Caulfield, *Kinsale*, p. 434; R. Caulfield (ed.), *Autobiography of the Rt. Hon. Sir Richard Cox, Bart* (London, 1860); MacLysaght, *Orrery papers*, pp 324, 333, 361, 365. W. Harris (ed.), J. Ware, *The history and antiquities of Ireland* (Dublin, 1764), ii, pp 207-51.

139. T.C.D. MS 847; Guildford, MS 1248/1, ff 190, 195, 197, 198, 202; Ball, *Judges*, ii, pp 69-70.

140. Farmar MSS 22 Dec. 1685; Guildford, MS 1248/1, ff 204, 220, 255-6, 259-60, 261-2, 266, 268, 274, 276, 278, 282, 296; K.A.O., U. 1475 De L'Isle and Dudley MSS O. 126; Caulfield, *Cork*, pp 209, 214; Caulfield, Journal of Rowland Davies, pp 21, 60. For English barristers and their fees see: All Souls College, Oxford, MS 305 (life of Sir John King); G. Holmes, *Augustan England: professions, state and society* (London, 1982), pp 115-65; W.R. Prest, 'The English bar, 1550-1700' in Prest (ed.), *Lawyers in early modern Europe and America* (London, 1981), pp 65-85.

141. Holmes, *Augustan England*, pp 116-18.

142. Chatsworth, Lismore MS, rental of 1677, p. 58; Petworth, Orrery MSS G.S. 28 (20 and 24 March 1671[2]); Day, 'Cooke's memoirs of Youghal, 1749' in p. 57; Shirley 'Dineley's journal' p. 337; Tenison 'Cork M.P.s', p. 276.

143. N.L.I., D. 13381. See too, Chatsworth, Lismore MSS Cork's diary, 17 May 1665, 9 June 1671, 12 March 1671[2].

144. Farmar MSS 26 Dec. 1683, 4 Jan. 1683[4], 21 March 1683[4], 28 March 1684, 14

April 1684, 29 July 1684, 19 and 29 Aug. 1684, 12 Sep. 1684, 4 and 8 Nov. 1684, 16 and 24 Dec. 1684, 6 Jan 1684[5], 3 April 1685, 26 May 1685, 5 June 1685, 4 Aug. 1685, 18 May 1686. For other hints of a business ethic: D. Dickson and R. English, 'The La Touche dynasty' in D. Dickson (ed.), *The gorgeous mask: Dublin 1700-1850* (Dublin, 1987), pp 17-18.

145. Farmar MSS 17 and 24 Feb 1684[5], 22 May 1685, 23 and 30 June 1685, 3, 10, 14, 17 and 28 July 1685, 9 Oct. 1685, 1 Dec. 1685, 12 Jan. 1685[6], 19 March 1685[6], 30 March 1686, 6 and 27 April 1686, 25 May 1686, 4 June 1686, 23 July 1686. Also, U.C.C. Library, MS U. 55, 28 Sep. 1685, 19 June 1686; T.C.D., MS 847; Caulfield, *Cork*, p. 207; Caulfield, *Journal of Rowland Davies*, p. 4.

146. Guildford, MS 1248/1, f. 227.

147. T.C.D., MS 1181, ff 25-7; Farmar MSS 2 April 1685, 22 and 29 Sep. 1685, 25 May 1686; B.L., Add. MS 5853, ff 14-14^v.

148. *Sr. St. John Brodrick's vindication of himself*, p. 9; Cox, *Aphorisms relating to the kingdom of Ireland;* idem, *An essay for the conversion of the Irish*; idem, *Hibernia Anglicana*, Orrery, *An answer to a scandalous letter*; idem, *The Irish colours displayed* (London, 1662).

149. That tradition is discussed in T. C. Barnard, 'Crises of identity', pp 39-83.

150. Caulfield, *Cork*, p. 240; D. Hayton, 'From barbarian to burlesque: English images of the Irish, *c.* 1660-1750' in *Ir. Econ. and Soc. Hist.*, xv (1988), pp 5-31; M. Mulcahy (ed.), *Calendar of Kinsale documents*, i (Kinsale, 1988), pp 90, 93, 106.

151. Chatsworth, Lismore MS 34/51, 57, 91, 100, 101, 116, 121; N.L.I., MS 13226 (8 Oct. 1691, 24 March 1691[2]); Petworth, Orrery MSS G.S.27 (9 April [ ]); T. C. Barnard, 'Crisis of identity'.

152. Bodl., Clarendon State Papers, 84, f. 286^v; Petworth, Orrery MSS G.S. 28 (22 Jan. 1666[7]); 30 (13 April 1686); Ainsworth, ed., *Inchiquin MSS* p. 512; M. Bence-Jones, *Burke's guide to country houses, i, Ireland* (London, 1978), p. 6; G.E.C., *Complete peerage*, iii, pp 214-16; Johnson, 'Cox', p. 361; Tenison, 'Cork M.P.s', p. 276; P. Walsh, *The Irish colours folded* (London, 1662), p. 3.

153. Chatsworth, Lismore MS 33/78; Petworth, Orrery MSS G.S. 30 (10 May 1686, 10 and 14 March 1686, 10 and 14 March 1686 [7], 13 June 1688); H.M.C., *Egmont MSS* ii, p. 69; M. MacCarthy-Morrogh, 'Credit and remittance: monetary problems in early seventeenth-century Munster' in *Ir. Econ and Soc. Hist.*, xiv (1987), p. 6.

154. Farmar MSS 9 July 1684; J. Weatherill, 'A possession of one's own: women and consumer behaviour in England, 1660-1740' in *Journal of British Studies*, xxv (1986), pp 131-56.

155. Dickson, 'Cork region', p. 109; H. T. Fleming, 'Some notes on the Tynte family', *Cork Hist. Soc. Jn.*, 2nd series, ix (1903), pp 156-7; H.M.C., *Egmont MSS* ii, p. 33; A. P. W. Malcomson, *In pursuit of an heiress* (Antrim, 1982).

156. B.L., Add. MS 21127, f. 58; K.A.O., U. 269, C. 18/22 and 27; Petworth, Orrery MSS G.S. 29 (28 March, 1683); 30 (13 August 1685, 23 April 1686); [A Freke], 'Mrs. Freke's diary', pp 159-60; xvii (1912), pp 5, 9-12, 47-8, 95, 145; Jephson, *An Anglo-Irish miscellany,* pp 65-6.

157. B.L., Stowe MS 206, f. 335; 207, ff 247-7^v; Bodl., MS Top.Ireland c. 2, f. 27.

158. A. Crookshank and Knight of Glin [D. Fitzgerald], *The painters of Ireland* (London, 1978), p. 66, colour plate 12; Dickson, 'A description of Cork in 1741' p. 154; Shirley, 'Dineley's tour', pp 320-1; P. Harbison, 'P. Burke's painting of Youghal', *Cork Hist. Soc. Jn.* in lxxviii (1973), pp 66-79; J. Loveday, *Diary of a tour in 1732* (Edinburgh, 1890), pp 37-9.

159. Comparative material includes: A. Bagot and J. Munby (ed.), *'All things is well*

here': letters from Hugh James of Levens to James Grahme, 1692-95, Cumberland and Westmorland Antiquarian and Archaeological Society, x (1988); Blackwood, *The Lancashire gentry*; Earle, *The making of the English middle class*; Everitt, *The community of Kent*, pp 33-6, 42; A. Hughes, *Politics, society and civil war in Warwickshire 1620-60* (Cambridge, 1987), chs. 1 and 2; W. Hunt, *The puritan moment: the coming of revolution in an English county* (Cambridge, Mass., 1983), pp 14-18; Jenkins, *The making of a ruling class*; P. Roebuck, *Yorkshire baronets 1640-1760* (Oxford, 1980); Stone, *An open élite?*; D. Underdown, *Revel, riot and rebellion* (Oxford, 1985).

Plate 9.4   River Bride (Cambridge University Collection of air photographs).

Chapter 10

BUTTER COMES TO MARKET: THE ORIGINS OF COMMERCIAL DAIRYING IN COUNTY CORK

DAVID DICKSON

Butter, milk and cheese formed a central part in the nutrition of the inhabitants of the Cork region from at least Iron Age times. In a grass-abundant environment and in a society where cattle were the primary criterion of wealth, this is hardly surprising. There were, however, local differences in the intensity of dairy consumption according to habitat, and from the thirteenth century there was probably also a cultural dimension to dietary variations, with fuller dependence on 'white meats' in the more Gaelic parts of the county and a somewhat greater role for winter-sown cereals and pulses in the more Normanised areas in the east.[1] But the composition of rural diet and its evolution is notoriously difficult to reconstruct, even for the seventeenth century; only by the accumulation of archaeological evidence from medieval and post-medieval sites can we hope to clarify the picture.

A series of revolutionary changes in diet did however occur, or at least begin to occur, in seventeenth-century county Cork as in many other parts of the south (although probably earlier in certain districts of Cork than nearly anywhere else). There seem to have been five distinct elements in these dietary changes: a decline in the cultivation and consumption of various strains of pea and bean; an increased cultivation and consumption of wheat; an increased consumption of mutton, offal and other low-grade beef products, notably around Cork city; the diffusion of the potato as a 'garden' crop and a winter food, possibly linked to the spread of other garden crops such as the cabbage; and a decline in the relative importance of dairy products, in particular the eclipse of large-scale butter consumption. Butter had been strategically important in winter-time when milk was not available, and one must assume that there was a correlation, whatever the causal relationship, between the spread of the potato and the decline of butter.[2]

The few contemporary observations on diet by persons who knew south Munster, Vincent Gookin in the 1650s, Sir William Petty in the 1670s and John Stevens in 1689, highlighted only the visible and distinctly non-English aspects of the local diet. Gookin (not speaking specifically of Cork) mentioned how 'the Irish ... live themselves on the roots and fruits of their gardens, and on the milk of their cows, goats and sheep, and by selling their corn to the English'; Petty, also generalising one presumes from Munster observations, spoke of a diet of 'milk, sweet and sour, thick and thin, which is also their drink in summertime ... their food is bread in cakes, ... potatoes from August till May, mussels, cockles and oysters, near the sea, eggs and butter made very rancid by keeping in bogs'. Stevens in his well-known comments on a wartime journey from Bantry to Cork described the poor villagers west of Bandon who lived exclusively upon their potatoes and sour milk.[3]

The contrasts between coast and upland, between winter and summer diet, between the food of large land-holding families and of the small-holders, herdsmen and artisans, were never elaborated in such seventeenth-century comments. However, it is significant that in the next century travellers were less eloquent on the subject of butter and fresh milk consumption. Only the truly intrepid visitors like Bishop Pococke found traces of the older diet; writing from Bearhaven in August 1758 he noted that booleying herdsmen in the Beara hills 'live on new churned butter and milk'.[4] It is not until the early nineteenth century that we have any systematic information that allows firm conclusions on Cork diets and regional comparisons. But by then even skim milk was disappearing from the daily diet of the majority.[5] The old butter-centred diet was quite forgotten.

The earlier dietary changes, not least the decline in the home consumption of dairy products, were of course linked to the collapse of the old social order, but the immediate causes seem to have been the growth of population and the greater commercialisation of agricultural production, as a competitive market-in-farm tenancy replaced older less profit-sensitive arrangements. Butter in other words went to market, and on such a scale that Cork became the most important centre for commercial butter production in the Atlantic world.

The commerce in butter

In the early post-Cromwellian period live cattle and wool were the two most valuable exports from the county, but with a prohibition on the former trade to England after 1667 there was a decade of difficulty for all involved in the rural economy. An export trade in butter, heavily salted and packed into hardwood barrels, grew from insignificant levels in the 1660s to become a major feature in the maritime trade of the Cork and Kerry ports by the 1680s; an average of about 2,350 tons per annum was being shipped out from them in the years 1683-86 according to the customs records, and this constituted more than a third of total national exports of butter. The centre of the new trade in the 1680s was the port of Youghal, the main markets northern France and Flanders. The product was at that stage often designated 'English' butter, indicating the manner of its processing, not the type of farmer (or cow) which had produced it.[6]

Butter exports from the ports of counties Cork and Kerry grew in less spectacular fashion and somewhat erratically over the next hundred years; there was a trebling in volume during the century, with roughly 7,500 tons per annum being exported in the mid-1780s, after which time there was little long-term growth until the 1850s; in the century after the 1680s there had been approximately a doubling in the value of export butter.[7] It is on the first century of growth that this chapter will focus.

In the early stages of the external butter trade the leading merchants of Youghal and Cork obtained much of their supplies by contracting with a few large cow-owners to take their whole annual output at a fixed price; but by 1700, with growing butter exports from Cork city at highly volatile prices, intermediaries appeared to whom export merchants could direct their bulk orders and to whom cow-owners could entrust their produce as they brought it to the city, to sell it as and when prices were favourable. These intermediaries were also buyers in their own right, and although this was probably a development from their original role as factors, it had become their more normal manner of dealing by the second quarter of the eighteenth century. However, the city butter buyers had no monopoly of handling butter en route for export, as general merchants still dealt directly with country producers and also employed local dealers or innkeepers as agents to buy on commission at country towns, a practice that survived at least until the 1760s.[8]

The emergence of a pricing system agreed to and accepted by both butter buyers and export merchants was an indication of the formal role butter buyers were coming to play. A standard price was fixed in the city towards the beginning of each summer, once the scale of foreign orders became apparent. It might be adjusted by mutual agreement but was observed between the main butter buyers and the export merchants (if not by all butter buyers themselves). By the 1730s it was 'the custom of the city', applying at least to all corporation freemen, not 'to exceed the prefixed price' or 'price current' (later known as the cant price).[9] By this period the butter buyers were becoming more than mere factors and buyers: some butter merchants distributed to the smaller country producers at the beginning of each season the firkins in which the butter had to be salted and brought to market; to a lesser extent larger casks suitable for tropical markets were similarly given out (on the understanding that better salted butter would be brought back in them), and small adjustments in the scale of prices current were made for such butter.[10] These practices may have reflected a desire to improve the quality of butter reaching market or were perhaps only a result of the relative concentration of the coopering trade in Cork city, for even by 1700 most of the stoves used in the firkins were imported from the Baltic or New England.

Associated with this commercial development was the butter buyers' practice of making seasonal cash or credit advances to producers; this had been done in the Belfast region in the 1670s,[11] but seems unlikely to have emerged in Cork before the 1710s or 1720s. Until the second half of the eighteenth century advances can only have been given to a minority of actual producers. But by the nineteenth century it was one of the cornerstones of the city's control over Munster butter production.

From 1721 the corporation of Cork, like other city governments, was under a statutory obligation to maintain a public weigh-house and to employ officials whose primary function was to weigh all butter offered for sale in the city, and to brand casks according to weight. A highly publicised dispute erupted in the following year over the nomination and control of the weigh-masters which was in essence political,[12] but the storm around the issue suggests the economic importance attached to the weigh-house scheme from its inception. The amending legislation that followed the dispute introduced a further task for weigh-masters (or their deputies): the quality of the product was to be tested to check that it was 'merchantable'.[13] In such controls lay the origins of the Cork butter market and its distinctive features of quality control. However the (two) weigh-houses of the 1720s were not intended to be actual markets. At this time butter was only brought to the weigh-house after sales had been negotiated or confirmed between farmer and butter buyer, although as the main weighing cranes were sited in that part of the north suburbs – Mallow Lane – already associated with butter dealing before the legislation, the neighbourhood of the cranes was seen even in the 1730s as the focus of the trade: 'To establish a pair of machines in the margin of a city, to gather and retain a side of a country into a daily market, upon a single spot, is a custom ... unknown to any place but this'.[14] Only with further legislation in 1747 (specifically related to Cork) did it become obligatory for vendors to bring all their butter on entering the city directly to the weigh-house, to be 'tried, weighed and branded' *before* sale.[15] The negotiation of butter sales thereafter took place almost exclusively around the weighing yards, and the Mallow Lane one was to be the site of the Cork butter market throughout its history.

The origin of the Cork butter buyers was not, as has often been presumed, because of a need for intermediaries to handle the diverse types of butter brought to the city, each suitable for a different overseas market.[16] This function only emerged in the 1760s with the widening of the markets for Cork butters. The Caribbean market had dominated overseas markets since the 1690s and for that very heavily salted butter was required; Dutch and then British domestic demand began to rival the orders from the sugar-and-slave islands, and this involved the production of far more lightly-salted butter. Until the British market became important there had been no great need to classify the consistency and salt level of firkin butter coming to town, for the important distinction theretofore had lain between butter exported in the condition it reached Cork, going mainly to Europe and usually in quarter-bound firkins, and butter to which pickle was added, often after repacking in full-bound firkins or casks, which was destined for tropical markets; the latter was normally prepared under the supervision of export merchants and was known as 'rose' or 'harp and crown' butter – after the symbols branded on the barrel.[17]

This sophisticated and regulated market structure reinforced the power of Cork to draw dairy-owners and dairymen to the city, at the expense of country markets or smaller ports in the region. Cork had overtaken Youghal by 1700; by the third quarter of the eighteenth century the town at the Blackwater's mouth was handling less than 3 per cent of Cork city's total throughput.[18] In the western part of the county and in south Kerry the pattern was more complex; until the mid-century construction of the Cork-Kerry turnpike direct producer contact with Cork was rare; yet the combined shipments from the ports of Kinsale, Baltimore and Dingle were less than 2 per cent of Cork's in the first third of the century.[19] Part of the explanation for their poor showing was the delayed development of commercial dairying in the area, which only intensified in the second half of the eighteenth century; furthermore, some of the local butter was bought up by Cork merchants and exported directly to the continent with such goods as pilchards and hides. Some was clandestinely exported by local shippers who were predominantly engaged in smuggling high-duty goods from France, such as the O'Connells of Iveragh at mid-century.

Licit exports of butter from the western ports grew in the later eighteenth century, but by that stage Cork was receiving a very substantial proportion of its butter supply piecemeal from the west. Some of it was shipped on small coasters and hookers but the preponderance came by land; even at Nedeen (Kenmare), Arthur Young found in 1776 that the butter produced there 'was all carried to Cork on horses' backs'.[20] Much of it passed through Millstreet and along the

Kerry turnpike across the Boggeraghs. Until carts were introduced it took one man and a horse about a week to deliver two firkins (a hundredweight) to market and return home, an investment of time that outsiders queried: 'The people, ignorant, suspicious and perfectly idle, prefer this labour to letting their property out of their sight, though by sea carriage four-fifths of the expense is saved'.[21] Seasonal advances from Cork butter buyers were arranged with producers in these areas when the city buyers came out to country towns in the spring.

How far did Cork's unassailable control of butter marketing weaken the power of producers to determine prices and conditions of sale? Organisational developments in the trade were often treated with suspicion by producers. The fixed price system was attacked by one rural writer in 1734: '... not one buyer will exceed the other, so we are obliged to let them have our goods at their own prices having no other market to go to, thus are we managed and governed by them ...'.[22] Similarly the legislation in 1747 to channel all incoming butter through the city weigh-yards was seen as discriminating against the interests of rural producers. It is impossible to determine how far there really was a degree of urban exploitation; it undoubtedly existed, but there were certain countervailing forces: competition between city buyers for supplies existed in the good years, and this helped to preserve open market conditions. Furthermore, the big export merchants saw themselves as guardians of the butter trade and were always anxious to curb the butter buyers' 'excesses'. And even among the shippers themselves there seems to have been an abnormal degree of personal rivalry, a result of the commission trade where personal reputation was all-important.

The reorganisation of the Cork butter market and the creation of a new controlling body, the Committee of Merchants, illustrate these internal divisions. In March 1769 a group of twenty-three export merchants formed a voluntary association which sought, among other things, to become the 'public' body regulating the butter trade, specifically to assist the weigh-masters and augment them in their function of monitoring the quality of incoming butter by employing inspectors (at exporting merchants' expense) to grade the product on the basis of its consistency, its salt content and its freshness. The committee also determined to introduce a formal three-tier price system, based on three qualities of butter. Their initiative was ostensibly because of 'the visible decay of our butter trade, added to the severe losses which attended the adventurers in it'.[23] Yet exports in the previous years had been at a high level, and there is no evidence of any major price fall. It was also claimed that the 'honest maker of butter' had received less than the current price for all sorts, however good the quality, whereas butter buyers charged a premium on sales of 'prime' sorts to the export merchant.[24]

In fact the catalyst for this major institutional innovation was external: after the legislative changes of 1759 butter could be openly exported to England for the first time in eighty years. With the threat of greater competition from other producers in the markets that Cork had long dominated, an English market for butter was a welcome prospect, but it was one which Cork was not able to take full advantage of because of the high salt level in local butter. In 1768-69 Cork was handling over 35 per cent of total Irish butter exports, but only 18.5 per cent of the Irish butter going to Britain. By giving in effect a premium on lightly-salted butter in their new pricing structure, the Committee of Merchants hoped to rectify this. The project seems to have been welcomed by the country, as indeed dairy-owners had nothing to lose. However, there was active opposition from those merchants primarily involved in the Atlantic trade and from some butter buyers.[25] Richard Hare, then the largest export merchant in the city, was an opponent of the Committee; two years after its formation he acknowledged that butter at market was noticeably 'better' and fresher as a consequence of the scheme, but that it had hurt the West Indies trade. Thus he pointed out to one complaining client that 'what I shipped for you was exceeding good but for want of salt must have turned out bad in a warm climate'.[26] The scheme was indeed successful in that record butter prices were reached and exports to England rose sharply.

By 1774-75 Cork handled about 34 per cent of Irish butter exports to Britain, which was to remain its share of a growing market for the rest of the century. By 1777-78 Britain took up over half of Cork's exports, and over the last quarter of the century the average was 51 per cent.[27] Butter exports to the 'East Country' (primarily Germany) fell away earliest; Dutch and French markets were later abandoned. The American and Portuguese trades survived, and the second quality, saltier butter was the standard for tropical markets. Later, price flexibility developed between the different qualities according to relative demand, and it was not unknown for 'firsts' and 'seconds' to sell at the same price.

The complete control of the Committee of Merchants by an annually rotating panel of exporters was a source of early tension between city merchants and the Mallow Lane butter buyers. This escalated into a public dispute in 1785-86, but it was resolved on the basis of various compromises (most significant was the allocation of a substantial minority of the seats on the Committee to butter buyers),[28] and this actually strengthened the Committee's influence. The potential for a conflict of interest between butter buyers and exporters, and between

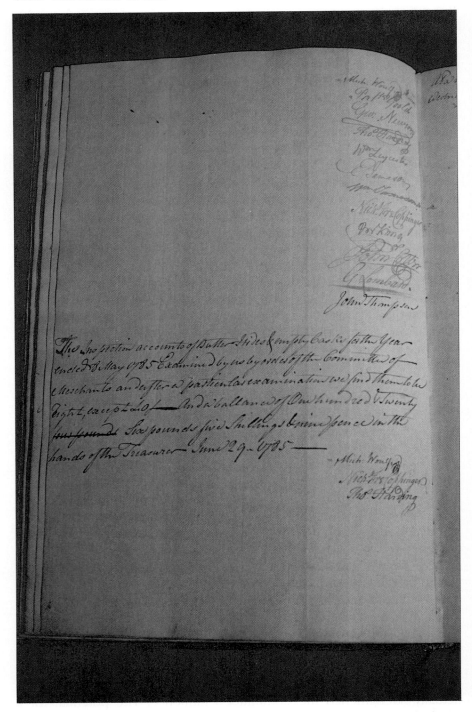

Plate 10.1   Page from Committee of Merchants' Minute Book (Cork Public Museum).

those dealing primarily with the English market and those with tropical ones, forced the Committee to develop a system of checks and balances in the manner of appointments, appeals and market regulation by which it achieved almost unintentionally a degree of impartiality and administrative effectiveness that was rare by the public standards of the eighteenth century. In spite of an increasing reliance on the small independent dairy farmers for supplies, butter quality was progressively improved in the 1780s;[29] that it was done at a period of sharply rising butter prices makes it the more remarkable.

If any group suffered from the hegemony of the Cork butter market during the eighteenth century, it was those with a stake in the country towns. The merchants in one or two centres did attempt to provide some of the services of Cork butter buyers, such as the giving out of firkins, but it was only with the decline in the demand for seasonal advances in the early nineteenth century, the extension of Anglo-Irish trade and shipping facilities in the wake of the expansion of the corn export trade, and the enactment of legislation facilitating the establishment of new country butter markets in 1822, that towns such as Youghal and Tralee once again began to challenge Cork city's monopoly.[30]

The organisation of production

The early history of commercial dairy farming in the Cork region, as distinct from the business history of butter, is fairly difficult to reconstruct from the historical sources. Who owned the dairy stock, who herded and milked them, and what effects on farming did the spread of dairying have? How far were higher-yielding milch cattle selectively bred, and what happened to calves and the surplus milk? The abundant parliamentary enquiries, newspapers and estate records of the nineteenth century are available for studying the background to the modern cooperative movement and to life before the creamery. But for earlier phases in the rise of Munster dairying the evidence is incomplete.

Management records of some of Cork's larger landed estates provide a few clues: agricultural land between the mid-seventeenth and the mid-eighteenth centuries was leased out for the most part in townland units, and most townland tenants – whether of Irish or new English background – were in no position directly to farm *all* the land they took on lease. For a variety of reasons large tenants were preferred by the gentry at that period, and these leaseholders in many districts earned their rent by building up massive stocks either of sheep, dry-stock or milch cows, the husbanding of which was contracted out to families who were usually rewarded in kind, in the form of subsistence agricultural holdings of a few acres or less. Dairy herds under the letting system were generally set with an agreed number of mature cows and in-calf heifers that had been bulled the previous summer. The dairyman's responsibilities were to mind the cattle, to milk them and to churn the butter. In the first half of the eighteenth century the prevailing practice was for dairymen to hand over in instalments a hundredweight of butter per cow to the dairy-owner, or to deliver such an amount to Cork and return him the receipts; there was the additional rent for 'privileges' called 'horn money', charged on each cow and usually paid off in labour. Whether this element originally related to a dairyman's right to keep the calves, or to a charge for the house, garden and grass that went with the cattle, is not clear.

The cow-owner had of course certain responsibilities. Firstly there was the job of actually acquiring cattle: a regular trade in two-year-old heifers grew up, based on the autumn and early spring fairs, supplied from within county Cork, from county Kerry and from county Limerick (if not further afield), and from these fairs cow-owners could make up their herds, often buying with the proviso that the heifer was a genuine 'springer' and would calve. Not surprisingly some cow-owners sought to avoid having to depend on fairs and instead maintained their dairies by rearing calves on their own account; this involved renting mountain farms nearby on which they placed their yearlings, or through setting them to upland herdsmen in other districts for two years. Once the full complement of cows based on the estimated grazing capacity of a farm was made up, the dairy-master could still have problems; cattle might not calve, might be injured or sicken, might go dry. Some dairy contracts placed the onus on the dairyman to replace all losses, to take his chance in effect, but the more common procedure was for the cow-owner to agree that if any cow could not produce an agreed output of milk during the season, the rent would be adjusted or the cow replaced.[31] It is less clear what happened in cases where the cattle were stolen, suffered injury or disease – eventualities which could be blamed on a dairyman's negligence; the frequency of complaints about defaulting dairymen suggests that normal practice was to put the blame on the dairyman.

If all went well, cows usually had a three- to five-year lactation span, yet one dairy-master, weighing up the various contingencies, claimed that '... dairies must [be] replenished every year with a third part, sometimes half of new milch cows, and the strippers sold for about half the money they cost ... the year before, – there are also vast casualties that cows ... are subject to, as deaths by various distempers as well as by poverty and many lost in bogs, clefts and mountains ...'.[32] Another cow-owner's estimate of hidden costs reckoned that every year one-fifth of his cows were strippers, at least three out of fifty died, and that a sixth of all obligations owed by dairymen would never be paid, although the last calculation was regarded by an estate agent reviewing these estimates as a gross exaggeration.[33] When old cows were phased out they could be quickly fattened by the cow-owner for sale in Cork, to be made up as poor-quality 'French' beef. The frequent appearance of old cows at country fairs as 'stores' suggests that many dairy-masters did not have fattening ground available. At times when 'French' beef prices were depressed, as in the early years of the American war, old cows were held back for an extra year or two.

The dairy contract was for a full year, so the responsibility for feeding cattle through the winter fell on the dairyman. The grass season was of course long, but for several months fodder was necessary, and this usually took the form of hay. Generally dairies were let with meadow ground, but in some cases dairymen were instructed to harvest hay from meadows in the hands of the dairy-master. Meadow ground was generally that part of a farm where grass was lushest; it would be fenced off about May Day, and the one crop of hay scythed in July and August. The stock of fodder was generally sufficient to bring cattle through most winters without actually impairing their health, but the weakness of cattle in the early spring months was proverbial. An active trade in hay developed at an early stage. Riverside farms and those with calcareous soils were more likely to have a surplus, while upland farms seem to have had a constant hay deficit: in severe winters cattle mortality was always greatest there. Substitutes were developed: furze, as well as being the standard hedge plant, was the source of cattle fodder (although used more widely for horses) along the meadow-scarce coast, while in the Kerry hills natural 'fenane' grass was harvested. Barley straw was also used, although not before the custom of burning the high stubble – still common in the 1740s – had died out. The new green crops began to be of importance in a few districts towards the end of the eighteenth century.

Cow-owners in many cases provided houses for their dairymen, and such 'dairy houses' had a room where the milk was kept; presumably with houses went some of the necessary butter-making utensils. Butter was most commonly made by the 'bonnyclabber' method: the milk was laid in shallow bowls (pecks) for several days 'till the cream comes off, but taking hold of it between the fingers, like a skin of leather, and some till it is mouldy ...'. The cream was churned, the resulting butter salted and kept in 'keelers' till barrelled in firkins for market.[34] The residual sour, thick butter-milk, the *bainne clabair* or 'bonnyclabber', remained a key part of the summer and autumn diet for the majority of the population.[35] Where there was an urban demand for *fresh* milk, unsour skim was produced by churning. The hand-operated dash churn was normally used, although manual and water-powered barrel churns were not unknown late in the century. One dairyman near Dripsey who was selling both butter and skim milk in the 1790s was supplied by his dairy-master with the appropriate equipment: a milk cart, three hand churns, and assorted keelers and milk cans.[36]

The origins of the actual dairy contract are unclear: it may have inherited certain features from West Country practice and come in with the Munster Plantation, or have evolved out of local herding conventions; the contracting out of dry cattle for a season to herdsmen, in return for a few acres of grazing with corn or potato ground or the right to the third or fourth sheaf of the harvest of other undertenants, was already well established in the late seventeenth century.[37] The usual dairy contract was for one year, running from Ladyday, but there were major variations, notably the extension of the dairy contract as a kind of lease. In 1722, for example, William Freeman – a large tenant on the Egmont estate – was changing the status of his dairymen at Kilbarry because of his own ill-health; he explained to his landlord that he had set some of the less improved parts of the farm to 'honest laborious dairymen who have lived under me on the lands for ten years past and rented my cows from year to year from me', and added, 'I have now agreed with them to hold part of my cattle with the land set to them for a term of years ...'.[38] Such an agreement could specify the mode of settlement as either butter or cash. An early cows-and-land contract, the lessor being a head landlord, Sir John Meade, relates to land in the Liberties of Kinsale: the farm with twenty cows was leased in 1692 for three years at a cash rent.[39]

The leasing of cows-and-land for cash was an alternative to the classic butter-payment system and indeed, after the 1760s, became increasingly the norm in many parts of county Cork, although the butter/horn-money mode dominated in west Cork for generations, and survived even in north Cork into the nineteenth century.[40] It was presumably more convenient for the dairy-*owner* to have a completely cash rent, for it can hardly have been in the dairy*man's* interest, given the annual nature of dairy agreements and the fluctuations from year to year in butter prices. Under the cash system, the rent per cow let was roughly fifty per cent above the average price of a hundredweight of butter at Cork in the previous year. The price per cow let was much higher within a few miles of Cork city and in the neighbourhood of towns (chiefly because of the market for milk and the supply of grain waste).[41] Given that most cattle (outside Kerry) were producing about a hundredweight of butter per annum, the fifty per cent loading, equivalent to horn money under the full dairy system, covered the dairyman's 'privileges': the house and a garden of an acre or two for potatoes and cabbage, which might initially be manured by the dairy-master, plus a grass allowance for one or two private cattle for every ten cows in the dairy, and usually the right to rear some or all of the calves.[42]

Dairymen and *gneevers*

The economic status of the dairyman, even when on no more than an annual contract, was considered superior to that of the tied labourer. Housing was distinct for a start, with the 'dairy house' a separate category from labourer's cottage or cabin on the more incisive estate surveys. Yet a dairyman had little prospect of entering the market on his own account to sell butter; all or nearly all being surrendered to the cow-owner. His family had at least the option of consuming the skim, but the only means of earning cash was by diverting some of the milk to the rearing of pigs or calves. In some cases the cow-owner took possession of all the calves in the autumn; in others the dairyman could keep the calves as long as they were cleared from the land before winter; a possible variation on this was where the dairyman was allowed to rear his calves, giving the cow-owner a proportion of the yearlings.[43]

By whatever means, these smallholding dairymen could thrive: among the bidders for lands on the well-documented Egmont estate were occasionally to be found ex-dairymen, such as three Sheehan brothers in 1747 who sought a farm of 130 Irish acres, and who offered to build a stone house and plant two acres of orchard; they were reckoned by the estate agent 'honest and industrious ... together deemed to be able to put sufficient stock on that farm', but added the agent, 'I don't think it likely that they ... will improve any land'.[44] Dairymen were often, it seems, required to give some guarantee for the cattle which they rented, but in spite of this, dairy-owners were constantly talking of the 'villainies' of defaulting dairymen, and in the words of one large cow-owner from the Decies side of the Blackwater, '... the rent of dairy cows ... is uncertain, attended with great loss. I know that I never one year with another could make twenty shillings ster. of the milk and grass of each dairy cow round; the difference 'twixt the prices I am to allow the dairymen for the butter and what I am promised by the merchants who but sometimes pays [*sic*] it, and the arrears of the dairyman which they [*sic*] never pay runs away with upwards of a third part of the sum they undertake to pay, and if they are changed every year it commonly turns to the same account ...'.[45] There was special pleading here, perhaps, but nonetheless the high incidence of defaulting can only have made the rate at which cows were set close to a true rack-rent. The 'horn money' which dairymen rendered over and above the butter could amount to over a dozen days' labour per cow, which with an average let of fifteen or twenty cows left dairymen with little opportunity for other agricultural activity, and the task of herding, milking and butter preparation in many cases became the responsibility of the women and teenagers.[46]

The distinction between the economically independent undertenant, sometimes called a *gneever* in local Hiberno-English, the man who owned his own cattle and also engaged in some tillage farming, and the dairyman, hiring his cattle and often occupying rather more land than a gneever, was not always clear. A dairyman's rent could be expressed in terms either of butter or money: a gneever's rent was normally fixed in money terms, but before the middle of the eighteenth century was often partly paid for in butter or worked off by labour. On the Egmont estate, undertenants had had agreements in the 1670s which fixed a money rent, determined by the number of cattle grazed, and a sheaf or 'corn' rent for tillage land,[47] but by the early eighteenth century sheaf payment seems to have disappeared from Cork practice; only butter and labour survived as alternatives to cash in the relations between tenants and undertenants. Gneever tenants, leasing perhaps 20 to 30 acres statute, would have been unable to pay their rent simply by labour, given current rent and wage levels (unless there were two adult males in the family), and access to cash must also have been limited for such families in the early eighteenth century. So even for the petty cow-owning undertenants a major part of their rent payments must have been in the form of butter from their own cattle. This was one land agent's belief in 1729: 'Upon the rise of lands lately which put the farmers under a necessity of altering their management of them, it is pretty universally practised in this country to set great part of their ground to Irish tenants for so much butter and so much money per acre, the money is commonly taken out in work ... it is much easier to pay that way than find money ...'.[48] A whole cohort of 1690s 31-year leases were expiring in the 1720s; the assumption that the new and markedly higher rents of that decade caused an alteration in management away from direct farming by large, townland tenants is highly plausible. Higher rents were forcing this type of lease-holder into the sub-contraction of production, either letting out land for butter and labour, or letting land and cows for rather more of the same.

The size of dairy herds, whether owned or hired, generally ranged from twenty to forty milch cows, the latter being about the upper limit that would be conveniently milked by one family. This did not alter noticeably in the course of the century where a farm was wholly given over to dairy, but much smaller herds were let out where dairymen were also engaging in other forms of farming. In the immediate vicinity of Cork city herds were sometimes larger; dairies of sixty and ninety were being offered for letting there in the 1760s, and cow-houses also seem to have been more prevalent, presumably because the opportunities for limited winter dairying made indoor feeding more important.[49] In some districts it was evidently the custom to drive the cattle at evening milking time to enclosed 'bawns' or yards, where they stayed the night 'for the sake of the grass' and the convenience of milkers. The construction of cow byres, by ordinary producers anyway, was quite exceptional.[50]

Herd size was in part determined by the family structure of labour. Herding sometimes, and milking invariably, were done by women, and in the great majority of cases labour was not drawn from outside the family for these tasks. It is indeed ironic that the hirers of cows were almost always men and presumably married men, whereas the main burden of dairying both in the field and at home fell on women.

A further influence against larger dairies was evidently the desire of cow-owners to spread the risks of default by individual dairymen. Where some form of security was sought from dairymen for the cattle put in their care, their normally meagre circumstances would have made it difficult for them to get guarantors to cover a very large number of cattle.

The normal size of dairies inside the letting system is fairly clear; the pattern of cattle ownership is more obscure. The owners of most of the 'commercial' cows in the region c. 1700 were the big townland tenants; the ownership of milch cows by labourers and dairymen themselves is impossible to estimate, but was probably relatively less than before the Williamite wars. Big cow-owners – dairy-masters – could be found leasing several townlands in the early eighteenth century, therefore controlling enough grass for many hundreds of cows. The proverbial rich man in the contemporary Munster Gaelic poetry was the *fear míle bó*,[51] and 1,200 dairy cows seems to have been the ceiling which the Egmont stewart in 1745 estimated 'some of our people have' in the Orrery/Duhallow area.[52] Dairy-masters in this league were probably strongest in the heady days of expansion between the 1710s and the 1730s, but a generation later they were only common in outlying parts of the county. As the average size of tenancies leased out by the gentry began to get smaller, so the huge dairy-owners became rarer, and even if there were 'depopulators' in parts of south Munster with herds of up to 800 cows still active in the 1770s, they were the exception in Cork.

The distribution of cow ownership was changing as small independent producers became more common after the 1740s. Many dairymen, where they could rear calves, went on to have some mature stock of their own. And many of the small gneever tenants, even in the early eighteenth century, had managed to keep a few dairy stock where there was suitable land. But the growth of owner-managed dairy farms of medium size was a process as long-drawn-out as the related decline of the large multi-townland tenant, and more than spanned the second half of the eighteenth century in county Cork.

This fundamental shift from the old dairy system of cow-owners and dependent dairymen cannot be precisely documented.[53] It was implicit in many developments, notably in the growth of seasonal credit from Cork butter merchants to producers; the demand for such loans was always more likely to come from those with bi-annual rent obligations, that is cattle-owning farmers who leased land, rather than dairymen who hired stock. The complete eclipse of the dairy system seems first to have occurred in the areas influenced earliest by the recovery in cereal prices, such as Imokilly, in the 1760s, and to have spread to other grassland areas as they reverted to mixed farming, only reaching the dairying parts of Kerry after 1800.

However, throughout south Munster medium-sized cattle-owning farmers were becoming continuously more numerous from the 1740s. The growing commitment by landlords against 'middlemen' who favoured smaller lettings, evident from the third quarter of the century, aided the process – and was also in part a response to it. Yet the transition was in no way complete even by 1800, and dairy-masters, albeit of more modest proportions, were to survive as a phenomenon in upland and remoter parts of west Cork and south Kerry until the late nineteenth century.[54]

Trends in the regional cattle trade bear out these changes. The sale of calves and yearlings out of the dairying areas, and of heifers into them, altered considerably between the late seventeenth century and 1800. Much of county Kerry had played a strategic role in the rearing of Cork calves (male and female), but this was before dairying spread into that county.[55] By the end of the eighteenth century Kerry had become a major dairying area and county Cork more mixed in its farming, so the east-west calf trade was far less important. The growth of smaller producers within Cork brought with it a greater tendency for the local rearing of a high proportion of calves;[56] in the Castletownroche area Arthur Young found that one calf was being reared for every two cows, with presumably the male calves being quickly disposed of.[57] In Kerry O'Brien estimated in 1800 that one calf was reared for every three cows, and that two calves in seventeen were sold out of the county as yearlings, the others being held till they were springers; nearly all of these must have been absorbed into local Kerry dairies if stocking levels were to be maintained.[58] Even after 1800 the stock of many of the dairy farmers, particularly in the south of the region, was noticeably lighter and closer to the old Irish breeds than in north Munster, which implies that the inflow of heifers from other regions was not important.[59]

The size of the independent dairy herd varied not least because it emerged in a mixed farming context. In the intensely farmed parishes in the western part of Cork Liberties the average number of cows per farm in 1798 was about five: no farmer had above twenty cows, but 26 per cent, thirty-five out of 135, held two-thirds of the total number, that is an average of about 14.5 cows each. Of the thirty-five larger cow-holders, hardly any can have been old-style dairymen, for with two exceptions there were also horses and significant tillage crops on every farm.[60] A few years later the top eleven 'common farmers' around Carrigaline were found to have had an average of twenty-four cows (which were seemingly their own).[61] A retrospective comment on farming towards the end of the eighteenth century in the Macroom area suggested that *every* farmer thereabouts was possessed of fourteen to twenty milch cows.[62] But just as the snug farming class with its own stock was consolidating itself, the declining earning power and falling incomes of the great army of agricultural labourers meant that access to milk, even sheep's milk, was shrinking: the loss of all milk from the labouring family's diet in the 1790s was in some districts a new step downwards in their degradation, in what was becoming a far more stratified rural society.[63]

A universal concomitant of dairying by the end of the eighteenth century was pig-keeping; indeed it was one of the ways by which a dairyman could hope to profit by his farm. Pigs were by no means restricted to cow-keepers, but whereas labourers and smaller farmers in tillage districts reared one to two pigs, considerably larger numbers were kept by dairy farmers, and it was they who held the breeding sows.[64] The pig and the dairy were complementary because sour milk, specifically the lower layer of bonnyclabber, was found to be an excellent feeding stuff.[65] It had not always been the case: pork exports from Cork were fairly modest before the late 1750s. However, from the time of the Seven Years War the trade became much larger and expanded gradually thereafter. On the farms of Castlemagner surveyed in 1744 there had been 1.2 pigs per house and approximately one pig for every five cows. Apart from the case of one dairyman who held with his twenty cows ten pigs, it would seem that most swine were kept for subsistence purposes.[66] Three decades later Young found a different position in Imokilly and north Cork: around Castlemartyr he was told that dairymen reared eight to ten pigs (that is approximately one pig per three cows), while around Castletownroche he reported that dairymen were rearing a pig for every cow on the farm, and at neighbouring Mitchelstown he was struck by the general profusion of swine.[67] In fact a one-to-one relationship was probably something of an exaggeration, because even in the western Liberties of Cork in 1798, where very high pig numbers might be expected, there were two pigs for every three cows, 3.7 pigs per farm.[68]

If sour milk was the dominant swine feed, it was not the only one; potatoes and cabbage were found to be economic too, and thus in tillage areas and among labourers who lacked cattle one or two pigs could be reared. In some cases final fattening was done by dairymen, but this was not general. By 1800 it was the marginal districts where dairying continued strong, and where potato culture was dominant, that attracted particular attention as pig-producing areas.

Milk yield

The organisation and geography of dairying therefore underwent a whole series of changes between the 1680s and 1800. Yet very little changed in the technology of production. The final question must be whether there was any productivity change, any fundamental improvement in milk yields. At first sight it would seem there was not: throughout the period where dairymen were paying in kind, the amount agreed to was generally one hundredweight of butter per cow. Such implied stability is surprising in the wider context of livestock production; there was a history of the importation of English breeds of cattle going back to the early days of the Munster plantation. It is of course possible that pre-eighteenth-century cattle imports had had proportionately greater impact than the more publicised new breeds introduced in the later part of the eighteenth century: whether native breeds would have been capable of producing the standard hundredweight remains doubtful. Late eighteenth-century descriptions of old and new breeds seldom rated them in terms of their annual butter production; weight, or daily milk output, were the usual measures, and in dairy contracts where guarantees were given of a cow's performance over a season they related only to milk yield.[69] From such evidence it seems likely that there was some rise in milk output towards the end of the period, but as no account was usually taken of butterfat content or lactation period, this does not necessarily indicate a rise in butter yields. Similarly there seems to have been a growth in the average weight of milch cows, but this need not have caused a proportional growth in milk or butter output.[70]

Heavier milch cattle were a by-product of more dramatic changes in beef production. As the export trade in salted beef expanded, the native Irish middle- and long-horn cattle were crossed with larger English breeds. The centres of this selective breeding were north

Munster and east Connacht. The results were evident in Cork market: five-year-old fat bullocks in the early eighteenth century had on average been somewhat under five hundredweight, whereas by 1810 they seem to have weighed (at the same age) around seven.[71] This improvement was achieved on the initiative of graziers and landowners *outside* the dairying districts, but the inter-regional flow of calves and heifers was sufficient by the late eighteenth century to affect cow size in much of the Cork region. A number of the new crosses such as that from the Staffordshire long-horn were distinctly less efficient milk producers than the cattle they replaced, while others had proportionate milk yields but shorter lactation periods; the Devon had lower yields but a high butterfat content. Of many it was observed that they were less adaptable to winter conditions than native stock, and less resistant to disease.[72]

The dairy stock that the new imports were modifying had consisted in the main of lowland, chiefly middle-horn cattle, of no precise colour and of indeterminate origin, which before fattening cannot have been more than three hundredweight. These were distinct on several counts from the smaller, black Kerry breed but, like it, they were popular because of their proportionately high milk yields and their tolerance of winter malnutrition.[73] The Kerry survived longer in near pure form, but the traits of both dominated the cattle stock of upland Kerry and Cork south of the Lee well beyond the eighteenth century.[74] In contrast, other parts of south Munster were more heavily influenced by the new breeds, and cattle size and shape in north and east Cork and lowland Kerry were undoubtedly changing. Some of the new long-horn crosses, notably the Leicester, Holderness and 'Dutch', do appear to have had beneficial effects on butter yields; Dutch or half-Dutch cattle, introduced in the 1750s and 1760s, may have been exceptional in that they were imported (by landowners and cow-owners) more for their milking than their beefing qualities. From such cattle 1.5 or 1.75 hundredweight of butter per annum was by the turn of the century fairly normal.[75] The absence of dairy contracts specifying payments of more than one hundredweight of butter is probably deceptive, for the areas in the county where these improved breeds were first introduced were also the districts where the classic dairy system disappeared earliest, and where wholly cash-based dairy contracts and then independent owner-producers predominated: parts of Imokilly and lowland north Cork, which since at least plantation times had been in the vanguard of agricultural change.

References

1. For a general analysis of Irish dietary evolution, see L. M. Cullen, 'Population growth and diet, 1600-1850' in J. M. Goldstrom and L. A. Clarkson (ed.), *Irish population, economy, and society: essays in honour of the late K. H. Connell* (Oxford , 1981), pp 97-103; Cullen, *Emergence,* pp 140-71. Also D. B. Quinn, *The Elizabethans and the Irish* (Ithaca, 1966), pp 62-7; J. O. Bartley, *Teague, Shenkin and Sawney* (Cork, 1954), pp 32-3, 121, 194.

2. Dickson, 'Cork region', pp 369-79.

3. V. Gookin, *The great case of transplantation in Ireland discussed* (London, 1655), p. 15; W. Petty, 'The political anatomy of Ireland' in *Tracts; chiefly relating to Ireland* ... (Dublin 1769), p. 355; Rev. R. H. Murray (ed.), *The journal of John Stevens* ... (Oxford, 1912), pp 46-7. See also the comments of the Italian Dean Massari, travelling from Kenmare to Kilkenny in 1645: 'butter is used abundantly with all kinds of food ...' in *I.T.,* 29 Aug. 1979.

4. P. Ó Maidín, 'Pococke's tour of south and south-west Ireland in 1758' in *Cork Hist. Soc. Jn.,* lxiii (1958), p. 90.

5. Dickson, 'Cork region', p. 405.

6. B.L., Add. MS 4,759; Dickson, 'Cork region', pp 44-6.

7. Eighteenth-century annual export totals by destination per port are extant in P.R.O., CUST/15. These long-term regional trends are derived from the data in Dickson, 'Cork region', Appendix tables *V* and *X.* For the nineteenth-century trade, see J. S. Donnelly, Jnr., 'Cork market: its role in the nineteenth-century butter trade' in *Studia Hib.,* xi (1971), pp 130-63; P. M. Solar, 'The Irish butter trade in the nineteenth century: new estimates and their implications' in *Studia Hib.,* xxv (1989-90), pp 134-58.

8. For direct dealing with export merchants, see P.R.O.N.I., D2707/A, Shannon MSS, 'A discourse between two countrymen', Nov. 1732. For country commission buyers see B.L., Add MS 46, 993*, Egmont MSS, pp 90-91 [N.L.I., Mic. p. 4677]. William Taylor, Ballymacow to Baron Perceval, 21 June 1728. Note where citations of the Egmont MSS in the B.L. are followed by an asterisk, this refers to the old classification system, which was changed subsequent to their microfilming by the N.L.I.; N.A., M7051, O'Donovan MSS, Daniel O'Donovan to Dr O'Donovan, 1 July 1768; P. Dineen, *Filidhe na Máighe* (Dublin, 1906), p. xxxvi.

9. See 'Discourse between two countrymen', 1732.

10. For example B.L., Add. MS 47,001B, ff 86, 112, Egmont MSS, Richard Purcell, Kanturk to Lord Perceval, 16 Oct. 1744, 31 May 1745, .

11. R. G. Gillespie (ed.), *Settlement and survival on an Ulster estate: the Brownlow leasebook 1667-1711* (Belfast, 1988), pp xxvi-vii.

12. It centred on the attempt by government to remove from the corporation the right to appoint and dismiss the weigh-masters, ostensibly because of complaints against the corporation that they had 'made use of the power vested in them to the prejudice of the country'; the government's aim was to appoint the two sitting Cork M.P.s, Hoare and Knapp, as weigh-masters; they were among the largest export merchants of the city and allegedly had the best reputations abroad. The dispute was in fact more a political quarrel between the Brodericks and their allies on the corporation and W. Conolly and his Cork supporters: P.R.O., S.P./63/382, ff 58, 64-6, William Conolly, Dublin to [-], 12 Dec. 1723; Duke of Grafton, Dublin to [Lord Cartaret] with memorandum, 14 Dec. 1723.

13. O'Sullivan, *Econ. hist. Cork city,* p. 156.

14. 'Alexander the Coppersmith', *Remarks upon the religion, trade, government,*

police, customs, manners and maladys of the city of Cork (Cork, 1737), 2nd ed. (Cork, 1974), pp 78-9 (pagination from 2nd ed.).

15. 21 Geo. II, c. 7. Cf. O'Sullivan, *Econ. hist. Cork city,* p. 157.

16. *Report from the select committee on the butter trade* ..., H.C. 1826 (406), v, p. 226; O'Sullivan, *Econ. hist. Cork city,* p. 266.

17. For example, Archives Departmentales de la Gironde, Pelet MSS 7.B. 1779 [N.L.I. Mic. p. 4,013], invoice with letter, Richard Bradshaw, Cork to Jean Pelet, Bordeaux, 20 Nov. 1743; also Calwell, Lawton and Carleton, Cork to Pelet, 30 July 1737; C.A.I., Hare letterbook [Richard Hare], Cork to John and David Brown, 12 May 1772.

18. P.R.O., CUST/15 at large.

19. Ibid.

20. Young, *Tour,* ii, p. 86; M. G. Moyles and P. de Brún (ed.), 'Charles O'Brien's agricultural survey of Kerry, 1800' in *Kerry Hist. Soc. Jn.,* i (1968), p. 116. The O'Connells were using both land and sea in their dealings with Cork city: U.C.D. School of Archives, P13/2/A/149, 151, 159, 170A, O'Connell MSS, Jerry McCrohan, Cork to Maurice O'Connell, 31 July, 6 Oct. 1788; Charles Casey, Cork to O'Connell, 27 Dec. 1793; Francis Segerson, Cork to O'Connell, 25 July 1805.

21. T.C.D., MS 4029-30, Daniel Beaufort's journals of Irish travels, 1788, i, p. 87; Representative Church Body Library, Dublin, MS 0/9, Beaufort's journals, 1806-7, i (2), p. 75; Townsend, *Cork,* pp 666-7; see S. Ní Chinnéide, 'A new view of eighteenth-century life in Kerry' in *Kerry Hist. Soc. Jn.,* vi (1973), p. 95.

22. 'Discourse between two countrymen', 1732.

23. Letter from 'Honestus' in *F.J.,* 3 June 1769.

24. Ibid.

25. C.A.I., Hare letterbook, copy, [Richard Hare], Cork to William Kirkpatrick, 4 Oct. 1771, p. 103; *F.J.,* 3 June 1769; *C.E.P.,* 15 June, 30 Oct., 27 Nov. 1769; *Hib. Chron.,* 7 May 1770.

26. C.A.I., Hare letterbook, [Hare] to Kirkpatrick; see [Hare] to Robert Barnevelt, 28 Mar. 1772, pp 281-2.

27. P.R.O., CUST/15 at large.

28. Cork Public Museum, Minutes of the Cork Committee of Merchants, 11 June 1785, 9 Feb. 1788, 21 May 1799.

29. Compare statements made at the meeting of country gentry and Cork merchants *re* the conduct of the butter trade in *C.E.P.,* 1 May 1786.

30. H.C., *Report . . . butter trade,* pp 223, 259.

31. N.L.I., Ainsworth Report 153, Agreement of memorandum, O'Donovan papers; Daniel O'Donovan and John Donoghue *et al.,* part of Kilgleny, 1762; Young, *Tour,* ii, pp 26-7, 122.

32. Ballynaparka House, Villierstown, county Waterford, Villiers Stuart MSS C/8, John Keily to Earl Grandison, 20 Oct. 1738. A stripper was a cow (as opposed to a heifer) that had not calved successfully and was therefore usually dry.

33. B.L., Add. MS 47,003*, Egmont MSS, Thomas Harris, 'Ballinliney' to Richard Daniel, 8 Nov. 1738; Daniel to the Earl of Egmont, [c. 14] Nov. 1738, pp 200-1, 204-6 [N.L.I. mic. p. 4,678].

34. Young, *Tour,* ii, p. 122; Rev. J. Radcliff, *A report on the agriculture and livestock of the county of Kerry* (Dublin, 1814), pp 121-2.

35. See advertisement for 'Mount Mary' in *Hib. Chron.,* 9 May 1782.

36. N.L.I., MS 7403, Earberry account books, A/c with John Linehan, 1791, Earberry account-book 1788-1809, p. 12.

37. See for example C.A.I., the account-book of Garret Fitzgerald 1652-74 (photocopy of MS).

38. The only direct evidence on how the herd system operated at this time comes from north Munster: N.L.I., MS 14,101, transcript of Lucas diary 1739/40-1, entry for 1 May 1741.

39. U.C.C. Library, Caulfield MSS 81, Memorandum of agreement, Sir John Meade and John Meade, Mellifontstown, 17 Jan. 1692[/3?], pp 5-6.

40. For example, C.A.I., Ryan-Purcell MSS account-book of John Purcell 1793-1806, the note of dairy setting made to John Creen, March 1806; Radcliff, *Agriculture of Kerry*, pp 118-9; Donnelly, *Land and people*, pp 142-5.

41. Burke, 'Eighteenth century Cork', where the rates for dairy lettings cited in Young are related in the first place to a distance factor; Burke argues that transport costs alone do not explain the decline in rates away from Cork city, but suggests that the extra advantage in proximity to Cork lay in the greater contact between producers and itinerant butter-buyers who were prepared to make cash advances. It seems far more likely that the factors cited here explain the higher near-urban rates; even between the immediate city zone and the outer liberties there seems to have been a considerable variation in rates, see N.A., Rebellion papers 620/36/14, Notice *re* dairy rates, *c.* 12 Mar. 1798.

42. For example, N.L.I., MS 7,043, Earberry account-book 1788-1809, account with John Linehan, 1791, p. 12.

43. The evidence for these arrangements is drawn from the 1770s (Young, *Tour*, ii, pp 11, 122, 133, 137) but it is assumed that they existed at an earlier date.

44. Copy, B.L., Add. MS 47,012*. Egmont MSS Purcell to Lord Perceval, 26 Jan. 1746/7 [N.L.I., Mic. p. 4,680].

45. Villiers Stuart MSS C/8, John Keily to Earl Grandison, 20 Oct, 1738.

46. Horn-money calculations are based on information given in B.L., Add. MS 47,088*, p. 29 [N.L.I. Mic p. 4,679], Egmont MSS, Purcell, Kanturk, to Lord Perceval, 22 July 1743; it is assumed here that the average daily wage was 4½d. For the role of women and teenagers see L. M. Cullen, *The hidden Ireland: reassessment of a concept* (Dublin, 1988), p. 25; N. Cullen, 'Women and the preparation of food in eighteenth-century Ireland' in M. MacCurtain and M. O'Dowd (ed.), *Women in early modern Ireland* (Edinburgh, 1991), p. 267; A. T. Lucas, *Cattle in ancient Ireland* (Kilkenny, 1989), p. 42.

47. R.I.A. MS 23.L. 49, Survey of the Perceval estates, 1677 pp 47, 51, 55.

48. B.L., Add. MS 46,994*, Egmont MSS p 125-6 [N.L.I. Mic. p. 4,677], William Taylor, Ballymacow to Viscount Perceval, 6 June 1729.

49. Taking a sample of actual settings and local estimates during the century of dairy lets (outside the city liberties), the average is about twenty-nine cows: U.C.C. Library, Caulfield MSS 81, pp 5-6 memorandum *re* Mellifont's town, Sir John Meade and John Meade, 17 Jan. 1692; N.L.I., Lismore Mss, MS 6,528, pp 40-1, note of dairy agreement with John Hallaghane, account-book 1724; B.L., Add. MS 47,001B, f. 55, Egmont MSS, Egmont survey, 1744; ref. to Ballybane dairies in Richard Purcell, Kanturk to Lord Perceval, 9 March 1743/4, B.L. Add., MS 47,008B, ff 68-9; Egmont MSS, note on Spittle farm, *c.*1746; N.L.I., Ainsworth report on papers in private keeping no. 153, O'Donovan papers; memorandum of agreement, Daniel O'Donovan and John Donohue *et al.*, part of Kilgleny, 1762; N.L.I., MS 7,043, Earberry account book, 1788-1809, p. 12, account with John Linehan, 1791; *Cork Journal*, 10 Feb. 1755, advertisement for dairy in Muskerry, and *Cork Chronicle*, 3 Feb. 1766, for two Castlelyons dairy farms; Young, *Tour*, ii, pp 11, 26, 60, 86, 119, 122; *Cork Journal*, 27 Dec. 1759, for a Lower Glanmire dairy being let with sixty cows, and *Cork Journal*, 26 Jan. 1765, a North Liberties dairy being let with ninety cows.

50. B.L., Add. MS 47,004B, f. 74, Egmont MSS, William Cooley to Lord Perceval, 15 June 1744; Lucas, *Cattle*, pp 25-31.

51. Cullen, *Hidden Ireland*, p. 19, quoting Seán na Ráithíneach.

52. B.L., Add MS 47,005A, f. 6, Egmont MSS,.Cooley to Perceval, 14 June 1745.

53. For the most explicit evidence for the shift, see Beaufort, 'Journal' in 1806-7, i (2), p. 65; Young, *Tour*, ii, p. 274; Townsend, *Cork*, pp 578-9; E. Wakefield, *An account of Ireland, statistical and political,* i (London, 1812), p. 323; Radcliff, *Agriculture of Kerry*, pp 119-20; J. Hall, *Tour through Ireland* (London, 1813), pp 211-2.

54. Townsend, *Cork*, p. 578; Donnelly, *Land and people*, pp 142-5.

55. W. J. Smith, *Herbert correspondence.* (Cardiff and Dublin, 1963), p. 337, John Jervis to Humphrey Owen, 4 June 1688.

56. Townsend, *Cork*, p. 581 (yet even in the district Townsend reported this, there was also some buying in from Limerick; ibid, p. 582).

57. Young, *Tour*, ii, p. 12, 274; Townsend, *Cork*, p. 546; Hall, *Tour*, p. 212. The only recorded veal production was in east Imokilly; Townsend, *Cork*, p. 614.

58. Moyles and de Brún, P. O'Brien's survey' 98; O'Brien's reference to 10,000 cows being sold annually at fairs, presumably meant old cows to be fattened.

59. Townsend, *Cork*, p. 607; Wakefield, *Account of Ireland*, i, pp 336, 340.

60. T.C.D., MS 1,182/1/31-7, Survey of farms in Carrigrohane, Currykippane and Kilnaglory, in Commissary-General letterbook, Cork 1798-9. If all holdings with ten or more cows are taken, this would cover 25.7 per cent of all the farmers in the sample (175) and they were in possession of approximately 66 per cent of all cows enumerated. The stock returns are obviously somewhat rounded.

61. T. Newenham, *A statistical and historical inquiry into the progress and magnitude of the population of Ireland* (London, 1805), pp 348-9.

62. J. O'Callaghan, *Usury or interest proved to be repugnant* (London, 1825), p. 135. Townsend suggested an average of forty cows per farmer in Imokilly (Townsend, *Cork*, p. 614), although it is not explicit whether this referred to independent dairies. In 1786 J. B. Bennett depicted *siológ* farmers as typically having ten to twelve milch cattle; see 'Fifth letter to the people by a Dublin shopkeeper' in *Hib. Chron.*, 23 Jan. 1786.

63. Dickson, 'Cork region', p. 405.

64. Wakefield, *Account of Ireland*, i, p. 353.

65. Radcliff, *Agriculture of Kerry*, p. 122.

66. B.L., Add. MS 47,011A, ff 51-2 Egmont, MSS. Survey of part of the Egmont estate, 1744.

67. Young, *Tour*, ii, pp. 13, 60, 275.

68. T.C.D., MS 1,182/1/31-7. Survey of Carrigrohane, etc. 1798 (See Note 60).

69. N.L.I., Ainsworth Rep. 153, Memorandum of agreement, Daniel O'Donovan and John Donoghue *et al.,* part of Kilgleny, 1762; Young, *Tour*, ii, pp 26-7; Townsend, *Cork*, pp 311, 547, 579.

70. Townsend, *Cork*, pp 311, 579; Radcliff, *Agriculture of Kerry*, pp 5-6, 118; H. Townsend, 'The parish and union of Kilgariff' in Mason, *Survey*, ii, p. 314; O'Donovan, *of livestock*, pp 111-2.

71. Young, *Tour*, ii, pp 260-1; *Munster Farmers' Magazine*, ii (1812-3), p. 158; C.A.I., Hare letterbook 1771-2, copy, [Richard Hare] to Roger Scully, 27 Sept. 1771; Young, *Tour*, ii, pp 260-1; Wakefield, *Account of Ireland*, i, pp 390, 750-1; O'Donovan, *Livestock in Ireland*, p. 111. Petty had assumed that a fattened oxen of six years weighed up to 7 cwt. in 1672, but like his other livestock data, this seems rather high; see Petty, *Political anatomy*, pp 336-7.

72. Townsend, *Cork*, p. 580; Wakefield,i, *Account of Ireland*, pp 334, 336, 340; O'Donovan, *Livestock in Ireland*, pp 170-2; Moyles and de Brún, 'O'Brien survey', p. 92.

73. Kerry cattle were only reckoned to give ½ cwt. p.a. by O'Brien, Moyles and de Brún, 'O'Brien survey', p. 97, but their stocking ratios – insofar as the coarse upland and rich lowland can be compared – were higher.

74. The oft-repeated assertion of the demise of the pure Kerry breed see 'O'Brien's survey', pp 92-3; Radcliff, *Agriculture of Kerry*, p. 145, missed the point that an 'impure' Kerry survived in spite of limited cross-breeding. See also Lewis, *Topog. Dict. Ire.*, i, p. 404.

75. For references to Dutch cattle, see *Munster Journal,* 4 Feb. 1750/1; cattle sale advertisement for Charleville herd; *Cork Journal,* 17 May 1756 at Mallow and at Cork itself (*C.E.P.*, 1 Oct. 1767), and the comment *c*.1816 in *Journal of the Royal Agricultural Society of England*, viii, p. 6, quoted in O'Donovan, *Livestock in Ireland*, p. 180. For references to the Holderness cross, see Young, *Tour,* ii, p. 27; Townsend, *Cork*, p. 579, and O'Donovan, *Livestock in Ireland*, p. 180. The origins of the Limerick (or Leicester) cross is less clear, but it seems to have been a popular dairy animal, see Townsend, *Cork*, p. 447; O'Donovan, *Livestock in Ireland*, pp 176, 179; Radcliff, *Agriculture of Kerry*, pp 118, 123, 192; Townsend, *Cork*, pp 579-80. Townsend states that Holderness crosses gave the equivalent of five to six gallons of milk; if it is taken that such might be the average over ninety days, and that three gallons of milk made a pound of butter, this would have produced about 1.5 cwt. p.a..

Chapter 11

THREE HUNDRED YEARS OF URBAN LIFE: VILLAGES AND TOWNS IN COUNTY CORK *c.* 1600 TO 1901

PATRICK O'FLANAGAN

County Cork has tempted many scholars as an arena in which to test issues of island-wide significance, because it has sometimes been perceived as a kind of best-fit microcosm or model of the island, encompassing now, as in the past, a bewildering range of societies and humanised landscapes.[1] The transcendant dimensions of the county draw inspiration in part from the qualities and eccentricities of some of the people who have become inextricably associated with it through their writings: suffice the instances of Richard Boyle, Richard Cox, Horatio Townsend and John Windele. Such an assertion must be qualified in several respects. The county never boasted of a national capital, but unlike the west of the country, county Cork has nurtured, for a millenium or more, a regional capital whose influence extends and has extended considerably beyond its boundaries. It has also sustained rich and varied suites of urban settlements whose ultimate roots are mainly medieval. In more recent times the impress of two formative phases of urban development is starkly visible in this extensive county and it is with these phases, their immediate aftermaths and their long term legacies that this chapter is essentially concerned. An attempt is made to identify and analyse the forces which both promoted and arrested urban development from the early years of the seventeenth-century – a period of immigration and early conflict – to the end of the nineteenth century. Particular attention is paid to the demographic aspects of urban existence, the early cartographic testaments and the detailed census material of 1901 in so far as it concerns living conditions and society.

The last two decades have seen much attention focused upon the analysis of urban centres after years of silence. Butlin's timely and very welcome piece, rescued urban studies from near oblivion. Fortunately there is now a plethora of material available which provides a useful yardstick for comparative purposes. Most recent efforts have been riveted on the larger towns and cities and apart from the Historical

Towns Atlas series of the Royal Irish Academy and O'Connor's excellent and purposeful work on county Limerick,[2] few have responded to Connell's earlier clarion call to examine our rich heritage of smaller urban places.[3]

One issue which has dogged urban studies in Ireland has been the quest to formulate and sustain some form of acceptable categorisation of Ireland's settlement structure. Some research appears as if emasculated by detailed typologies; others have avoided the thorny issue entirely. A classification system which attempts to span three centuries is clearly unworkable because the nature of these kinds of settlements has changed radically and substantially. However, in spite of these difficulties some degree of numerical rigour is essential when detailed data are available. Mere numbers by themselves are insufficient to determine urban status. Over the past four centuries at least, our towns and villages managed to nurture and sustain discrete occupational groups and particular class structures which were not replicated in the same proportions in contiguous rural areas. Institutions by themselves were not the touchstone of urban life or character; many never even lived up to the tasks expected of them by their instigators. Distinctive lifestyles defined the fundamental ethos of the lived experiences in our urban settlements and our sources are sometimes elastic enough to confirm or refute their existence.

Settlements of the seventeenth century

In the years immediately before the rebellion of 1641, county Cork could claim to have, by the standards of the time, a very respectable covering of urban settlements which had made a solid contribution to the county's economic performance throughout the early part of the century. Our knowledge of urban conditions in the county at the end of the previous century remains woefully inadequate and, ironically, Cox's impressionistic catalogue of urban settlements at the latter end of the seventeenth century provides no numerical perspectives.[4] What is beyond any doubt is that there had occurred a veritable urban revolution in the county between c. 1610 and c. 1641, exemplified by the foundation of many new, or expansions of existing, settlements.[5] Favourable economic circumstances, especially the intensification of long distance and overseas trade, and the arrival of many immigrants resuscitated and consolidated an earlier phase of the plantation; artesanal activity, garrison building and the commercialisation of the surplus, had conspired to provide auspicious circumstances for these innovations to transpire.[6]

It is not an easy task to distinguish the differences within and between urban settlements in seventeenth-century county Cork. This kind of confusion is exacerbated by contemporary designations which were applied to urban centres. Sources of the time with a countrywide remit, such as the Civil Survey, Petty's works and the 1659 'census' employ the term 'town' or 'village' interchangeably. Estate documents such as the voluminous Lismore papers tend to be more discriminating, but once again, there is often ambiguity between the terms town and townland.[7] Petty, for instance, refers simultaneously to Inishannon and Rosscarbery as villages and as towns. With only two short and narrow streets, less than six substantial houses, many cabins and a corn mill, Rosscarbery's claim to town status was more an aspiration than a reality. It probably harked back to its medieval heyday when it reportedly had at least two hundred houses. Even very modest settlements such as Baltimore (then known as Dunasead), Castlehaven and Glandore were called towns. Still only one settlement in the entire county, Coolniry, Shandrum parish in the barony of Duhallow was classified as a village in the 1659 'census'. Some authors have claimed that functional diversity is the sharpest measure of distinction between village and town.[8] Also the presence of certain kinds of institutions has been invoked as an index of rank. But many institutions such as courts were only activated very episodically and corporate status was not always tantamount to greater municipal independence as often centres were rigorously superintended by their owners or agents as was the case with the settlements on the Cork-Lismore estates. Many non-corporate centres grew rapidly to become larger than adjacent corporate ones. Some very active market centres developed well beyond the expectations of their founders while some corporate centres such as Doneraile struggled to maintain an urban identity.

Combinations of attributes facilitate to segregate settlements into different categories. Population totals, the proportion of new English, the physical extent of the built-up area, market and fair throughput, nodality in terms of accessibility to a developed hinterland, resident merchants, the distribution and sale of imported and luxury goods, complex occupational structures, a permanent garrison, significant religious functions, mills or other industrial activities, resident administrators and the involvement and patronage of a magnate were some of the salient features of urbanisation in early seventeenth-century county Cork. Before the middle of the century no one centre in the county could boast of having all these attributes. The incidence of combinations of these features at different settlements allows a crude ranking to be established as well as providing a yardstick to distinguish between villages and towns.

In the middle of the seventeenth century county Cork urban settlements had emerged along three distinctive axes (Fig. 11.1): they were the coast, especially east of Clonakilty, the valley of the river Bandon and the eastern section of the Blackwater/Bride system. This spread of settlements reflected several legacies and contemporary realities. The most ancient centres were on the coast and most of them can trace their initial roots to Viking/Norman times.[9] While some of the centres along the river valleys had undoubtedly venerable origins it was the plantation and the settlements of intrusive colonists from 1586 that engineered their growth or resusitation. Even at mid-century it is difficult to comprehensively portray the urban characteristics of the county as even the so-called 1659 'census' is by no means spatially complete. There are no data for Cloyne and other settlements in the barony of Imokilly. Information for such places as Kanturk, Midleton and Millstreet is also absent though data for some of these as well as other settlements are available from other near contemporaneous sources, such as maps, charts and correspondence, as well as rentals, tenures and valuations for some of the great properties such as the Lismore-Cork estate. Depositions, plantation commissioners' reports and muster-rolls furnish information for earlier decades and individually these sources give valuable insights about wealth, social status and especially occupations of intrusive elements.

Figure 11.1 depicts the distribution of urban centres, their ethnic composition and the incidence of garrisons and/or forts or other defensive structures. The 1659 'census' has been employed to supply population data while the Civil Survey and Petty's parish maps and their terriers furnished information about garrisons and forts. The inter-pretation of the 1659 'census' presents a range of complex problems, which fortunately, have been succinctly addressed. A multiplier of 2.5 has been suggested and this appears to be the best national estimate.[10] Here, however, a multiplier of 3.0 has been employed for the following reasons, even though it could be reasonably argued that it might overestimate conditions in many instances. Some settlements straddle one or even several different townlands: Bandon and Clonakilty are instances. In such cases a small increase is necessary to compensate for underestimation. It is quite possible that the numbers of Irish are generally underestimated especially in terms of entire household units – children, dependents and even relations. This appears to be the case if 1659 'census' totals are tallied against extant estate urban rental lists for native residents on the Lismore-Cork estate. Against the use of a multiplier of this magnitude is the fact that in areal denominations where the population exceeds one hundred people – the bottom threshold – not all the residents can be presumed to have lived in the chief centre. Such a presumption can, however, be mitigated by the fact that villages and towns appear to have been much more spatially

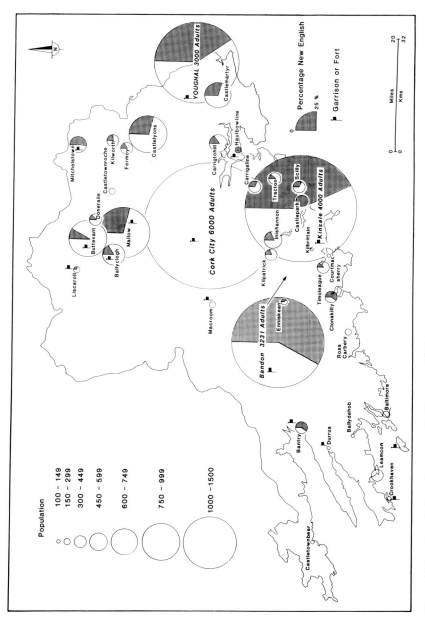

Figure 11.1   Population of towns and villages, c. 1659.
Source: *Census Ire., 1659.*

scattered than we are accustomed to today. The early seventeenth-century survey of Baltimore illustrates a settlement which straggled along the coast and perhaps even extended across to Sherkin Island.[11] In this way the distinctions between rural and urban were more blurred than they are today with craftspeople residing on the outer limits of the settlements and farmers often residing at the centres of the settlements.

Distribution

All of the settlements registering a population of one thousand plus (Fig. 11.1) can respectfully claim to be categorised as towns. Castlelyons (population 891) and Buttevant (population 836) form an intermediate rung between the towns and smaller villages. By contrast, Ballyclough and Mitchelstown had their respective population swelled by the presence of relatively sizable, presumably male-only, garrisons and accordingly cannot be regarded as higher order settlements. Small villages were the most frequently recorded element of the settlement hierarchy. Here villages are defined as a concentration of one hundred people or more (using the multiplier), and one or more of the criteria which embody urban living.[12] Nearly forty such centres can be identified in county Cork in *c.* 1659. The average recorded village population size at this time was 210 people. The vast majority of these settlements attained village status in the early decades of the seventeenth century. Most owe their rank at that time to intrusive settlement and development took place as a consequence of deliberate encouragement especially the foundation of fairs and markets and the attraction of skilled craftsmen-tenants from England. Originally, some sites were old medieval civil parish sites, while others were formerly opulent Anglo-Norman monastic centres, such as Midleton and Tracton. Few of them could claim to have been urban centres before the seventeenth century and those which managed to attain this status rarely sustained it due to the negative consequences of the Reformation and the political turbulence of late sixteenth-century Ireland.

Placed within a wider perspective, in county Cork, county Limerick, south-eastern county Clare and parts of east Leinster, towns and villages were a basic ingredient of country life. While spatially the division between town and countryside might have been blurred, no such ambiguity masked the differences in economic activities and occupation profiles, unlike in parts of Ulster, as indicated by Robinson, where village communities were complex and did not simply consist of small groups of farmers and their labourers.

Received wisdom implies that most villages grew between the early 1600's and the rebellion of 1641, and that thereafter many declined. Rental evidence confirms that a necklace of villages developed in the

Bandon valley as far west as Enniskeen before 1641, in an area where new English intrusion was most intense.[13] Centres such as Castletown-Kinneigh, Dundurrow, Kilpatrick and Newcestown can be cited as examples.[14] By 1659 Dundurrow had withered away and all of the other settlements returned population totals considerably lower than those suggested by rental evidence for the 1630's. Similar processes were at work around the Cork-Waterford borderland. The village of Kilmacow, which had been an active iron-working centre until the early 1640's had disappeared as a separate entity by 1659. Some settlements along the coast and possibly others inland had lost people before 1640. Crookhaven in the extreme south-west of the county, for example, is recorded as having 200 houses in the 1630's, while later reports for 1640 hint of a much smaller population. Well-documented vagaries in the presence of shoals of herring and particularly sprat may explain these kinds of population fluctuations. Centres such as Bandon and Macroom grew rapidly as a direct consequence of civil unrest. In 1643 Bandon is said to have had a population of '7000 souls'.[15] The claimant deliberately omitted to add that more than half of this total were refugees from the surrounding area. It is doubtful that Bandon maintained such a swollen population for very long; many residents and refugees are recorded as leaving for good and most seem to have returned to England. In contrast, the population of Macroom expanded as a consequence of the influx of many well-to-do Roman Catholic families who were evicted or burnt out of Cork city and many of these people who were encouraged to come here were to play a constructive rôle which greatly contributed to its prosperity.

Hierarchy

By 1659 the county's urban hierarchy had an unmistakably modern hue. Bandon and Mallow[16] were now added to the string of Anglo-Norman port centres of the coast. The only major subsequent additions to the larger towns were Fermoy, Midleton and Mitchelstown in the early years of the nineteenth century. The spatial disposition of villages is also striking. Most of them developed constellation-like around the larger and most dynamic members of the hierarchy; the Bandon valley from Enniskeen to Inishannon stands out clearly, as does the middle Blackwater valley pivoted on Mallow and as also the Fermoy-Tallow area to the east. Youghal, because of its location and physical constraints to more settlements in its immediate vicinity, stood alone. Easier sea communications elsewhere permitted settlements to scatter along the coast. Apart from Kanturk, Macroom and Newmarket, there were few notable settlements distant from the valleys of the Bandon and the Blackwater.

On the basis of supremacy of functions a number of different settlement types can be recognised in mid-seventeenth-century county Cork. Along the coast there was a necklace of minute fishing centres and both large and small ports: some of the larger ports also were important fishing centres as well as being involved in the export of fish throughout Atlantic Europe and even as far afield as colonial North America. Most of the smaller fishing centres were located west of Kinsale. Many of these were established by the Earl of Cork in some of his outlying westerly settlements such as Clonakilty, Bantry and Ballydehob.[17] Others crystalised around a series of *fish palaces* which had been developed by Hull, Boyle's tenant and sovereign of Clonakilty whose activities have been well documented by Went.[18] The *fish palaces* were essentially proto-industrial units where particularly pilchards, as well as, sprat and herring were cured or smoked and then barrelled for export. Consequently, these *fish palaces* were located at safe and sheltered landing places contiguous to the fishing grounds. The well known impressionistic sketch of Baltimore shows the boats and even the fishing gear employed by these early seventeenth-century fishermen.[19] In addition, Hull's famous deposition elucidates much about the entire range of technologies used both at sea and on land in this labour-intensive activity, as well as the commercial and financial dimensions of this enterprise. Because curing required a high labour input *fish palaces* often spawned small settlements. Hence such places as Baltimore, Bantry, Castletown, Castlehaven, Crookhaven, Courtmacsherry, Leamcon and Scilly, to name but some were all deeply involved in fishing. Then, as now, fish-shoals had the practice of appearing in abundance for a few short years and then vanishing inexplicably for longer periods.[20] It is more likely that the disappearance of these stocks rather than civil unrest was responsible for the withering of especially isolated settlements such as Kilmocamogue. The late 1620's and early 1630's seem to have been the period of the most vigorous expansion of these kinds of settlements. From then on a combination of stock depletion and/or disappearance as well as depressed economic conditions conspired to weaken these settlements and few ever managed to recover their vitality.

It is no coincidence that three of the largest settlements in the region were ports, all of which were engaged in long-distance commerce and trade and each of which could boast of complex and diverse social and ethnic structures. They also discharged administrative functions. Due to the region's strategic Atlantic location all of the ports became enmeshed in early seventeenth-century colonial trade, but because of its enormous harbour and immensely rich hinterland, Cork city, by the middle of the same century came singularly to dominate long-distance trade across the Atlantic. Kinsale and Youghal even more became involved with the Bristol Channel ports, and the ports of western France, northern Spain and with Portugal.[21] New English involvement at these centres even pre-dated the 1580s and several merhant ship-owners and fishermen settled in them. Intrusive settlement was initially most marked at Youghal being initially encouraged by Raleigh and much more so, later on, by Boyle. Cork city and Kinsale witnessed a flood of new English settlement during the Cromwellian period and in Kinsale especially, these Cromwellian families such as the Southwells played an influential rôle in the life of the town as major property owners and patrons.[22] Boyle remained forever unhappy with his meagre influence in Cork city and he devised a plan to erect a new port town at Beaver near Carrigaline to channel trade away from the city and direct commerce to it even from as far away as Bandon. Fortunately for the city these plans never materialised.

Military considerations spurred the emergence of another category of centre – though it is correct to note that few settlements entirely lacked a defensive capacity. Judging by the spatial disposition of garrisons and the absence of documents which indicate any general strategic plan their incidence relates seemingly to local considerations and perhaps occasionally to the military arrangements of some of the larger landed properties such as those of Boyle. Nearly all of the settlements in the west of the county had garrisons such as Crookhaven, Bantry (with 57 soldiers) and Four-Mile-Water which was located near present-day Durrus. All of these centres were isolated settlements and had been developed to protect fishing activities, prevent smuggling, and serve as a watch against potential coastal invasion. Another group of fortified centres had been built in the north-west of the county; these include Ballyclough, Buttevant, Liscarrol and Mallow (117 soldiers), and there was one sited at Mitchelstown (50 soldiers). Strangely, the villages of the Bandon valley were not fortified and few of them ever recovered from the onslaught of 1641. Bandon was designed as a major military redoubt. The ambitious 1621 plan of the town, which was only partially realised, indicates that even its streets were designed to repulse attackers who might breach its curiously inadequate walls. Cork city and some of its harbour centres, such as Haulbowline, as well as Youghal were well provisioned with all kinds of modern and effective defenses. Even Cape Clear Island had a fort which was occupied seasonally. Of them all, Bandon was the most militarised settlement in terms of its layout and its defensive capacity embodied in its design. It's qualities as a redoubt were symbolised by its enormous gatehouses and gates – even the river was fortified where it entered and exited from the town – its churches and its fort in which one of the churches

Christ Church was itself fortified). Cork city, Bandon, Kinsale and Youghal were the principal military settlements. Impressive fortifications in the form of large and extensive castles made Liscarroll, Macroom and Mallow members of a secondary league of military settlements. Garrisons and fort settlements or forts by themselves marked the military rear or vanguard of new English settlement depending on their locations.

Finally, there were many small villages which had developed as minor commercial and artesanal centres. In effect most of them were market centres which also held fairs episodically. Few sites which were entitled only to hold fairs emerged as urban centres. The Earl of Cork was the foremost instigator of market centre growth. He acquired patents for a string of settlements scattered throughout the county on his very extensive properties. Ballydehob, Ballymodan and Coolfadda at Bandon, Castlemore, Carrigaline, Castletown-Kinneigh, Clonakilty, Enniskeen, Fermoy, Kilpatrick, Newcestown and Tracton were the chief centres for which he sought and obtained patents.[23] Rentals show that in some instances he leased out the market and fair privileges, in others he leased only the market tolls and elsewhere he purchased market patents from the original grantees.

No other individual made such a singular contribution to urban development in early seventeenth-century Ireland. While Cork's work in this regard was by no means altruistic, his contribution was immeasurable as it facilitated and intensified commercialisation, not only on his own estates but also in a considerable orbit around them. His estate records and later depositions show that besides some farmers many artisans lived in these relatively small settlements. Other major land owners encouraged similar developments such as, Crooke (Baltimore), St Leger (Doneraile), Condon (Kilworth), MacCarthy (Macroom), Jephson (Mallow), Fenton (Mitchelstown) and Buttevant (its total swelled by the presence of a garrison). Castletownroche and Inishannon were of earlier origin.

Acting as conduits in every sense these small centres played a vital rôle which supported new English settlements and the initial objectives of the engineers of plantation policies. It is noteworthy that few of the early seignory centres emerged in full blown urban colours. Chronically unstable proprietorial conditions due to Gaelic rejection of the late sixteenth-century colonial settlement did not help, but it does not fully explain such a lack of growth although at Mallow a vibrant centre emerged to dominate the middle section of the Blackwater valley. By contrast, Macroom on the Lee valley seems to have been the only settlement of note that developed under the long term Gaelic tutelage. As its patrons, the MacCarthys seem to have been uniquely innovative as they enticed people from diverse backgrounds, including Cromwellian English recussants and dispossessed Cork city Catholics to settle there especially after the 1640s.[24] Plantation and intrusive settlement were not, however, always the engine of growth. Centres such as Cloyne, Timoleague and Tracton appear to have developed slowly. Undoubtedly, the aftermath of reformation and confiscation stunted their vitality. Nevertheless, Timoleague recorded a population total in excess of 400 people in 1659. Castlelyons remains an enigma. It could almost claim town status given its high returned population. Detached from the main centres of intrusive settlement its location in the bounteous Bride valley might explain its apparently above average size. It is also possible that we have here an instance of survival and growth from earlier times.

In summary it is evident that there was an urban revolution in the county in the early years of the seventeenth century which managed to strike deep roots, despite all the difficulties of the post 1641 period. In this way it was a formative phase of settlement emergence telescoped essentially into a mere twenty year period.[25] Most of these settlements attained urban status for the first time and the essential ingredients of the county's urban hierarchy were firmly put in place. What was also novel about this phase was the extraordinary number of brand new urban centres as well as the dramatic enlargement and expansion of some existing ones especially the leading port-towns.

Commercialisation

Market and fair foundation was the principal means through which commercialisation could be achieved.[26] Colonial control ensured that rigorous constraints were placed on the process as a means of ensuring equity between appellants and more basically as a device to regulate numbers as a plethora of centres competing in any area for trade could arrest rather than stimulate development. In the first half of the seventeenth century more than 90 per cent of the patents confirmed in county Cork were allocated to new English claimants. Ten per cent of the centres had their trading franchises granted to Gaelic owners such as Power (Shandrum), MacCarthy (Macroom), O'Donovan (Drumdaleague) and O'Callaghan at Dromina. The period between c. 1610 and c. 1630 was one of frenetic market and fair foundation. Over these years the rate of confirmation of patents of these institutions was more intense in county Cork, than elsewhere in Ireland. In all, close on eighty centres had patents allocated, or in the cases of older sites such as Castlelyons or Kinsale, they were reconfirmed. It was by no means axiomatic that market development led to urban development.

More than thirty sites can be identified where patents were confirmed but where durable settlements failed to appear. What kinds of places were they? Who held patents for them? Why did villages fail to materialise at these sites? They were a mixed bag of places and some could possibly have attained village status for some short period when no precise figures of their population were recorded. Others were seignorial centres, such as Carrigleamleary and Castlehyde; some were ancient civil parish centres and these kinds of sites did count small population nucleations with a castle, a church and several cabins. Others were older Anglo-Norman village sites such as the famous Cahirmee beside the ruins of Ballybeg abbey on the outskirts of Buttevant. The immediate proximity of more dynamic settelements, Buttevant and Mitchelstown in this context, precluded the potential for growth. Other centres were places where growth was expected but did not materialise because of the extreme isolation from prosperous rural areas; Apsley's port at Rincorlesky on Roaring-Water Bay is a good example of these specific difficulties.

Ethnicity and society

With few exceptions the dictum holds true that the larger the settlement the greater the proportion of new English residents in mid-seventeenth-century county Cork. Clonakilty seems to have been the only exception. Yet even the Clonakilty figure may be inflated as the total number of Irish is uncertain. Matters are made difficult here as the town extends over four townlands, none of which bears its specific name. There is no simple explanation for the disproportionate presence of the new English in county Cork's different size categories of urban settlements (Fig. 11.1). The nature, distribution and timing of several waves of new English intrusion is obviously relevant here.[27] Cork city, and to a lesser extent, Kinsale, were not subject to intense new English intrusion until after the 1640s. As MacCarthy Morrogh has indicated the confiscated lands of the late sixteenth century only included a proportion of the county's total area and one might correctly assume that urban centres on the plantation lands would have had higher proportions of new English.[28] The large number of new English settlers in some of the villages of south western county Cork shows that perceived economic opportunity was also a magnet of settler attraction outside the plantation lands. In the smaller villages new English rarely summed to more than a fifth of the total. In the larger villages their numbers seldom topped more than a quarter and in the larger towns proportions totalled from 40 per cent as at Kinsale and Youghal, to a maximum of more than 60 per cent at Bandon. Some other smaller settlements recorded many new English; Bantry and Mitchelstown are examples. Their totals are deceptive as they were inflated by the presence of a garrison of fifty soldiers apiece, who summed to almost 50 per cent of the settlements' residential total. Where garrisons have been identified they have not been subject to the multiplier and their raw complements have been added on to the rest as no compelling evidence attests to the presence of wives and children. What a contrast were circumstances here, by comparison to most of Ulster where the vast majority of urban residents at the same time were of colonial extraction.

Rapid urbanisation was not only a function of intrusive settlement as many people principally of Gaelic origin flocked to the new and pre-existing centres.[29] Such immigrants were initially tenants-at-will. Many lived in spatially confined pockets often referred to as an 'Irishtown' on the edges of the centres. Poverty may have been as potent a segregating agent as ethnicity. In such circumstances few would have had the capital to build new houses or pay high rents. In addition the degree of segregation was often diluted by the fact that new English settlers often moved to, and built houses on, the outskirts of the towns in order to evade the higher rents or obligations of residence within municipal boundaries. This was the case at Bandon and some other new settlements. But Bandon, with 60 per cent new English, was highly segregated. Could it be, then, that the greater the population of new English the more intense the degree of segregation? No documentary evidence suggests the same level of intensity of segregation in smaller settlements, where the numbers of intrusive people often totalled less than a quarter of all residents.

Intricate social structures were also characteristic of the towns of the county in the first half of the seventeenth century. Essentially three major social groups have been recognised. On top of the social plinth were major trading elements, the clothiers in particular, who were often involved in artesanal manufacturing, as at Bandon, Kinsale and Youghal. Members of this élite group were also land owners and rentier farmers. Wealthy rentiers seem to have more generally been a feature of the towns of ultimate Anglo-Norman origin. Contemporary evidence strongly indicates that craftsmen, mainly of new-English origin were the back-bone of the larger settlements and they were usually referred to as *mechanics*. Bennetts' impressive catalogue of tradesmen at Bandon may appear fanciful but evidence from parish registers, deeds, wills and depositions essentially confirms his assertions.[30] At the bottom of the social ladder were the Gaelic residents and a mixed bag of servants and menial workers of intrusive origin. Numerically, this was the largest group. Servants lived in the houses of their employers throughout the towns. In the new settlements these people were invariably new English. The poorer Gaelic residents lived outside the town centres often in small ghetto type sectors and rental evidence for these kinds of zones indicates that they were extremely volatile in the sense that there was a high through-put of people: few families remained in their residences over extended time periods and these facts are confirmed by contemporary rent rolls.

The presence and number of so-called *tituladoes* has been cited as a yardstick of urban rank. If this assertion has merit it means that most of the settlements in county Cork below a threshold of 500 people were in the lowest pecking order as few register the residence of such individuals. They were, in effect, only a feature of the larger centres and as a rule there was only a handful in each place. In the absence of any study of *tituladoe's* origins and the few pointers that exist seem to suggest that many were significant landowners, rentiers, farmers or combinations of these, the size of the resident merchant community in any town would appear to be a far more discriminating index of urban rank and urban vitality.

Settlement morphologies, housing and buildings.

Apart from Bandon, there is no evidence of sophisticated urban planning. It is difficult not to agree with the view that settlements were 'haphazard affairs ... with little evidence of planning'.[31] In terms of their sites and locations most settlements developed within the constraints of pre-existing social-territorial frameworks, modified by the carving out of larger plantation seignories. With few exceptions such as Bandon, Bantry and Clonakilty, most settlements expanded or emerged at pre-existing ecclesiastical or secular centres which were often of medieval origin, at focal points of the county's communication net or at strategic coastal locations. The casual appearance of many settlements was really a function of their size.

Excepting the larger ports, all impressionistically depicted on the Pacata maps, such as Cork, Kinsale and Youghal as well as Bandon, all of the other settlements were small consisting only of one or two streets. Macroom and Mallow had two streets while most of the rest such as Crookhaven had only one. Few of the streets were straight and even South Main Street at Bandon would be hard pressed to pass a test of straightness as the houses there do not appear to have been erected in line.

Petty's parish maps regrettably only furnish images of the outlines of the towns and some of the larger villages, which are too generalised to permit detailed reconstruction. The only available map, apart from Paccata, is one for Baltimore which indicates the centre as a loosely organised complex, with no obvious focus.[32] Then called Dunasead, the plan shows that the anatomy of Baltimore had developed in a difficult coastal site. The plan which pre-dates the famous so-called 'Algerine' raid shows that in the early to late 1620s there were two sectors of residential growth, one of which stretched around a cove in which boats are shown actively fishing pilchards. Here there were only cabins and chimney houses; nearby was a larger cluster of residences beside a 'castle' or small tower house. Here were some forty-six houses, ten of which were sited within the outer walls of the 'castle'. The other houses were organised in short rows which may have fronted streets. Five other 'castles' occupied pivotal positions on nearby islands and across the channel on the mainland opposite Baltimore. Beside the castles there was a church, the ruins of an abbey, quays, warehouses and probably pilchard presses which stress its maritime function. Most of the domestic residences were no more than modest and there were no slate houses. The plan gives a general impression of a scattered basic fishing settlement which, in spite of its dispersion, appears to have been functionally integrated.

Evidence from other contemporary sources confirms that Baltimore was typical of many other smaller settlements in that there were few public buildings except for a church, and castles or tower houses were the most frequent large secular buildings. Market houses and fair greens do not seem to have developed in these kinds of centres and thus apart from castle or church few appear to have had a clear focus. By contrast all of these elements were characteristic of the towns.

In the larger towns there was a much greater variety of housing styles. It is evident that the new English brought with them radically innovative architectural concepts and styles of domestic housing designs.[33] These were grafted on to an amalgam of Norman and Gaelic traditions. We know very little as yet about the results of the collision of these styles and tastes. Can we assume that imported styles were a feature of the new settlements and that mixture was the order of the day in the older port towns? It is clear that Boyle pursued a policy which attempted to rigorously introduce new English architectural practice. His stringent leasing conditions are a testament to his efforts in this regard but we do not know to what extent they were adhered to.[34]

Then as now housing types and the nature of the housing stock and its mix are a sure index of social structure and settlement vitality. Urban tower houses, extensive and elaborate gatehouses such as the North Gate at Bandon and mansion houses were occupied by the leading urban élite. By any standards Bandon, apart from Cork city, had the most varied ensemble of sumptuous and modern residences.[35] Occasionally large mansion houses were erected in some of the smaller settlements such as that built by Boyle for one of his sons at

Carrigaline, the St Leger mansion at Doneraile and the impressive 'castle' outside at Kanturk. In Bandon slate-roofed houses built of stone seem to have become the most popular house type within the walled area. These were the residences of the artesans and they replaced houses which employed timber in their fabrication because of the frequency of disastrous fires in the villages. Cabins were everywhere; 'there were many cabins but only six good houses at Rosscarbery'. At Castlehaven there were only two good 'English houses' and many cabins. At Macroom chimney-less cabins were dominant. Even at Bandon there were at least two extensive cabin suburbs outside the walls. The larger one was sited outside the East-Gate at Irishtown, and there was another beside the North Gate which was removed before the 1641 turmoil, as it hindered the gunners line of fire from the gatehouse. Cabins were not even contemplated by Boyle as an element of his housing portfolio. The speed with which they materialised and disappeared is a measure of the difficulties faced by their occupants. Many of them were of rounded proportions and usually very small. Often chimneyless and windowless they must have contrived to breed every conceivable kind of disease. All were single storied and most of their residents were tenants-at-will whom the agents note only occasionally in contemporary rentals and valuations.

Apart from Cork city, Macroom is the only other large settlement for which Civil Survey material has survived (Bandon's, and to a less satisfactory degree, Clonakilty's housing profiles are available in the Lismore papers). In Macroom, cabins were the least valuable dwelling, thatched houses and chimney houses were more desirable and some of them were up to thirty times more valuable than cabins. The chimney-houses came to Ireland towards the end of the sixteenth century and fifty years on they had become so popular that they were found in town and countryside alike and their owners came from all ethnic backgrounds. Slate houses were the most prized and valuable domestic residences, and on average they were five times more expensive than a chimney house. Macroom had only one; Bandon counted one hundred or more. As such they were the houses of the well-off urbanites and were seldom found outside towns. Mansion houses, gatehouses, and 'castles' were the abodes of the exclusive and the very rich who were very few in number.

Towns in county Cork could claim to have a varied suite of public buildings by the mid-seventeenth-century. Excluding buildings associated with defence and residence, there were churches (now all reformed), the market house (there were two at Bandon) symbolising its commercial life: there were sometimes court-houses, prisons or houses of correction, marshalseas and often a provosts' or sovereigns' house. Mills epitomised the processing dimensions of these towns, and Bandon's elaborate trundle-mills are surely the county's best known seventeenth-century mills. Completed in 1621 milling continued at the same site until it was destroyed in 1968. Warehouses, pilchard presses, *fish-palaces* and boat yards were elements of many of the coastal settlements. Brewhouses, inns, taverns, shops and tanyards were also recurrent features of the larger towns.

The diversity of economic activities was always reflected in the varied occupational structures of the larger towns: in them no one occupation was supreme; there was always a mix. Few extensive or wealthy farmers were residents of the larger towns, though many merchants and rentiers such as Richard Croft of Bandon did invest the proceeds of his lucrative trade in clothing, in land and in urban property. Maritime occupations were characteristic of the well established ports; in Kinsale and Youghal – carpenters, chandlers, merchants, boat-owners, seamen, rope and sail-makers and fishermen were popular occupations. Textile production absorbed many people and among them probably many women in Bandon, Clonakilty, Kinsale and Youghal; woolcombers, weavers, spinners, dyers and a host of other workers were evident in these settlements. Unlike other pursuits, most of their work was accomplished in their residences or back-yards and hence the most lucrative, labour-absorbent and skilled activity left no mark on the local urban fabric or morphology. Only in the fishing settlements in the south-west of the county did highly specialised occupational profiles emerge and these settlements proved to be much more vulnerable to the winds of change than other small centres with a more mixed occupational structure. Detailed analysis of depositions, wills and deeds must be awaited before we have a more comprehensive picture of the occupation mix of the villages and towns.[36] It is evident that they were not simply adjuncts to a prosperous farming sector, but that they also made a distinctive contribution to growing commercialisation. They were centres of crafts, processing and trade and the towns discharged crucial administrative and defensive functions. Mitchelstown, for instance, had apart from its garrison, many people working with leather, metal and wood. 'Gentlemen' were a rarity. By contrast, somnolent Doneraile with its pretentious airs and undeserved Parliamentary status was very much a gentlemen's village lorded over by the powerful St Legers. Mallow, a particularly populous and active inland centre was characterised by a distinctive mix of occupations. Depositions from 1643 show that it counted cobblers, dyers, coopers, maltmakers, tailors, tanners and weavers, all of whom claimed material loss.

Up to 1641 and extending to much later on in the century, if we can accept Cox's glowing account, a merchant élite was a fundamental element of the county's larger settlements. Mainly new English in origin this group became further consolidated after the 1650s when its members flooded into Cork city and Kinsale. In nearly all the towns and villages the so-called mechanics or crafts people were the productive kernel of society. Unlike in Ulster where it has been asserted that most of the urban centres acted as basic service nodes for the local gentry, in Munster and county Cork in particular export driven production underpinned the economies of the urban centres for part of the seventeenth-century and in turn supported a group of merchants and rentiers.[37] Landlord involvement in the superintendance of urban centres varied. Intense initial activity was often replaced by the more mundane concerns of lease allocation and rent collection. Having acted as early facilitators, most were, it seems, content to let the clothiers and crafts people get on with their work.

Given the export driven economy that served as a context for intrusive settlement to develop and flourish a colonial administration was installed which sought to stimulate the regional economy through the confirmation of trading franchises. The region's settlements were regarded as key elements to encourage commercialisation and in order to protect them a string of fortifications including walled towns, forts and garrisons was erected. Troops were frequently billeted in the settlements. Boyle's lease-books stress the military preparedness of many of his leading tenants. In may be that the military side of this chapter of settlement development in county Cork has been under-emphasised.

Stagnation c. 1660-1760

Between 1659 and 1798 no countrywide data base allows a detailed analysis of urban demographic behaviour. One however is left with a strong impression that after or even before the Williamite turbulence urban vitality at least froze, if it did not seriously decline in the first half of the eighteenth century. There were examples of spectacular per-formances and some striking new additions to the urban ensemble but they were unable to tilt the overall balance towards growth. Indeed up to the last quarter of the century the observations of noted locals such as Smith and many intrepid travellers were invariably negative when they mentioned the county's towns or villages. Cox's florid recital of the county's urban centres embodies the eulogistic echoes of the first Earl of Cork's earlier adulatory verbal cameo of his Bandonbridge (Fig. 11.2).[38] It is reminiscent of conditions in the 1630s. Still Cox's account is significant. He classifies the urban centres in three groups; first of all there were villages or pretty villages, then towns and finally

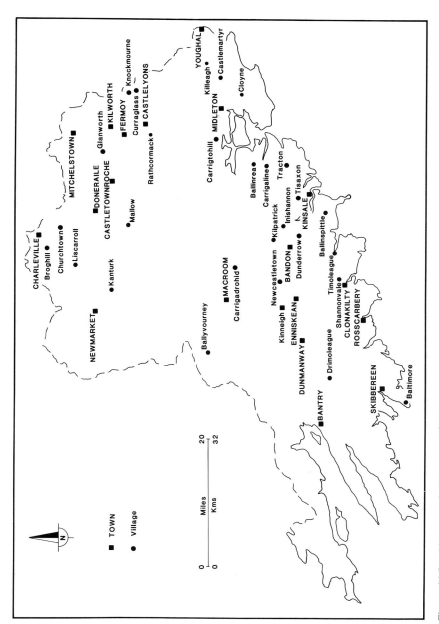

Figure 11.2   Towns and villages, c. 1680.
Source: Cox, *Regnum.*

he notes the presence of a handful of decayed or ruined villages. Some centres obtain particular commendation: Mallow is '... the best village in Ireland.' Dunmanway his home town, not surprisingly was a '... a fine English plantation'. He also emphasises the contribution of resident landlords and is particularly positive in relation to those who were embellishing the urban surrounds with parks which are mentioned at Midleton, Doneraile, Charleville and Castlemartyr. With 20,000 habitants, Cork city won pride of place. Egmont and Orrery activities nurtured the appearance of what were to emerge as important towns, namely Kanturk and Charleville which were the only major additions/expansions to the existing suite of centres. Ballyvourney was another locationally significant though small centre and its appearance was a consequence of the extension of the road net to Kenmare. New bridges accelerated growth at such centres as Fermoy and Mallow in 1666. The former bridge helped to radically transform the lower sector of the Blackwater valley by strengthening its connections with Cork city and simultaneously weakening its links with a less accessible Youghal. The building of many new seats was not the only testament to economic revival but so also was village creation at Ballinrea, Churchown or Burton Hall, Castlemartyr, Macroom, Kilbrittain and Midleton. Enniskeane according to Cox was 'flourishing' and Clonakilty was 'recovering' from the impact of the 1641 rebellion. Three centres are mentioned as ruined or decayed, namely Clonmeen, Glannor and Knockmourne beside Tallow. Despite its ambiguities and its optimism Cox's catalogue illustrates the tenacity of urban lifestyles in the county in the face of all the fall out from rebellion and economic and social dislocation. His rosy estimation stands in complete contrast to all the evidence which refers to urban conditions in the county over the subsequent seventy years.

Another cursory recital of the county urban institution character regrettably does not indicate anything about general conditions. Pratt in 1708 divides the county's urban centres into *boroughs* such as Baltimore, Bandon, Castlemartyr, Charleville, Clonakilty, Doneraile, Kinsale, Midleton, Rathcormach and Youghal. The other category recognised was *market towns* and Bantry, Buttevant, Castlelyons, Cloyne, Crookstown, Dunmanway, Enniskean, Fermoy, Kilworth, Mitchelstown, Newmarket, Rosscarbery, and Skibbereen were in this group.[39]

Village topographies of the eighteenth century
For a county the size of Cork with such a varied suite of urban centres, large estates and port towns of regional significance it is remarkable that so few urban plans and maps are available. The larger centres such

as Cork, Kinsale and Youghal were often surveyed but in the case of Bandon and some other towns several early eighteenth century maps have been mislaid. Fortunately surveys have survived for Doneraile (1728),[40] Enniskeane (1777)[41] Baltimore (1788),[42] Kanturk (1704+)[43] and Rosscarbery (1788).[44] This group of centres while by no means a cross section of types offers through their surveys a tantalising glimpse of its weak economic foundations especially if compared with periods in previous or subsequent centuries.

It is difficult to determine whether the 1728 representation of Doneraile was an aspiration plan like the 1621 plans of Bandon or if it was an accurate survey of the St Leger centre. Whatever the case something very like it came to fruition if it is compared to the early Ordnance Survey sheets. It anticipates the grand designs of Fermoy and Mitchelstown by nearly a century and in this respect it may be a unique blueprint for a very early planned estate centre. Geometrically conceived, even the river is blended in as part of its layout. Consisting of three district blocks, it was focused on a long linear street which was bisected by several lanes. Detached by a bridge from the remainder of the settlement was the castle and farm centre of the St Leger estate. Laid out beside it on a grand scale were the yards, stables, walled and formally laid out gardens, ponds, extensive enclosed orchards and not least large groves of trees which screened off the entire zone from the rest of Doneraile. Opposite the castle quarter was a small enclosed church, an open fair green and a mill on a small mill-race, all of which were connected to the outside world by a turnpike road. This sector was connected to the principal residential area of Doneraile by a bridge. Here were located the largest residences which comprised rows of substantial two and three storied houses facing the main street. Rows of small, perhaps single storied dwellings fronted the lanes on either side of these formally designed blocks. Behind these magnificent houses were lengthy but narrow enclosed gardens and small orchards very much in the style of Bernard Scalé's Bandon of 1777. The only public building was an impressive school-house. The south western sector of the town was more mixed in residential terms: as one moves from the centre some considerable three-storied houses are gradually replaced towards the edges by smaller houses and finally by what appears to be cabins. No public buildings were sited here and the gardens and plots although formally organised were by no means as classic or embellished as those elsewhere. In fact this sector has the air of being recently finished. Given the impressionistic and small scale proportions of the plan, housing numbers cannot be safely estimated nor can population totals be exptrapolated. By any standards, however, Doneraile was, or was intended to be, an extensive, daringly formally planned settlement which would qualify for the status of town in any league. In addition, it was the most ambitious and surely the most expensive addition to the county's urban ensemble during the eighteenth-century.

The remaining settlements of eighteenth-century county Cork for which cartographic records are available (that is, excepting the largest towns), are by no means as impressive as Doneraile; they were minute, apparently lacklustre and had no significant manufacturing or processing capacity. But at least the maps which have survived may indicate more about the typical than the exceptional. Enniskeane in the Bandon valley surveyed by Scalé in 1777 is a case in point. It was a very modest village with an estimated population of *c*. 210 people residing in thirty-four houses and a much larger number of cabins. Here there were few signs of affluent living or even comfort. It was essentially a rural agricultural settlement whose *raison d'être* was perhaps sustained by its weekly market. The only traces of well-being were two minute orchards and eighteen gardens which probably provided for domestic needs. Surrounded by many formally shaped fields devoted to arable and pastoral activities there was not even one public building sited at its core. Besides its population total its only claim to urban status was a mill, a possible tanyard and a tiny malt-house cum residence. Enniskeane emerged originally as a small plantation village at a critical crossing point of the river on the Earl of Cork's estate. It was essentially a small cabin settlement inhabited by a mixture of farmers, sellers and tradespeople. It presented a bedraggled appearance consisting of rows of houses, single houses and cabins placed at every conceivable angle to the main Bandon to Bantry road.

Kanturk and Rosscarbery were also fortunately surveyed and both settlements tell the tale of more direct landlord intervention by respectively the Percivals and the Freke's. Kanturk is unique to date in that three separate surveys are available for the eighteenth century; they are respectively for 1704 by Thomas Moland, for 1723 by John Smith and lastly for 1791 by John Purcell. It is the only centre for which we can obtain a cumulative pictorial assessment of change. Infant Kanturk like many other settlements in Ireland seems to have been dealt a devastating blow by the Jacobite-Williamite confrontation. Even by 1731 the young Percival heir described Kanturk as '... a wretched place and if left to itself would probably fall to ruin ...' This state of affairs was a far cry from his fathers' aspiration to develop it into an attractive plantation settlement in the 1670s. Cabins were the dominant type of domestic residence and there were also six 'workhouses' (for woolcombing) a wash-house, a salthouse and a small tobacco workhouse as well as the ruins of a 'old inn'. Ragged and disjointed would be kind descriptions of the settlement's layout. Yet the county's foremost historian, Smith, asserted that in the 1750s Kanturk was thriving. Landlord involvement in refashioning the settlement was weak and very episodic as the Percivals were rarely resident. Even though the centre had substantially expanded by the 1790s it still boasted of many untidy lanes and poor access roads. Freke's Rosscarbery is an example of an old, long declining and very tattered episcopal seat being furnished with an atmosphere of modernity by the arrangement of residences and shops around an attractive square beside its small cathedral. There was a barracks, a forge, a malthouse and a small tanyard. Aspirations of prosperity rested in its recently built market house, a market place, its fair green and a minute pond. Despite all that was new, cabins were everywhere even on the main street and the overall cabin to house ratio was three cabins to one house.

Blarney and Dunmanway and perhaps also Douglas were in the same league as Rosscarbery as planned centres; but these centres were developed or expanded as consciously founded industrial centres. Blarney was formally laid out during the last quarter of the eighteenth-century as a small manufacturing centre. Most of its houses were strung around a very modest square and a church, a handsome inn, a market house and four new bridges were put in place. An unsigned plan of the very early years of the subsequent century stressed that little expansion had taken place: there were then some thirty-eight houses, a tiny increase on the 1777 total of twenty-five houses. It would appear that most of those working in its mills lived outside the centre. Thomas Sherrard also surveyed Baltimore for Captain Freke. It was a miserable collection of huts which had no grounds whatever on which to claim urban status although it still maintained its borough status.

Manufacturing

Basic textile production was a well established feature of county Cork's larger urban centres especially in the early part of the seventeenth-century. Woollen based, most of its products were sent abroad for finishing. This tradition lingered on in such centres as Bandon, Kinsale and Youghal and it seems to have revived and strengthened in the subsequent century. The processing and manufacturing of agricultural products remained weakly developed and organized in all but a few settlements and, in most, it was an ephemeral activity. Kanturk's experience may be typical of many more places. It remained a minor woollen centre throughout the eighteenth century. It was provided with only a most rudimentary production capacity with its workhouses, washouses and storehouses. Still this activity was the most important employer with 104 part-time workers and at least 600 full-time workers most of whom lived outside the town in the countryside. Townsend confirms the continuity of this tradition into the nineteenth-century. Similar arrangements are reported in the vicinities of many other settlements. These kinds of activities bonded rural-urban inter-dependence and it may curiously help to explain why many of these settlements did not precipitate local waves of immigration of farming families. Even the families of labourers could combine textile working with their other responsibilities. A handful of villages such as Blarney, Douglas and Dunmanway developed in response to the foundation of a processing capacity. Bandon and later Midleton also rapidly expanded to become complexes of production. Few towns or large villages lacked a processing capacity by the early years of the nineteenth-century.

It is instructive to examine specific instances in order to understand the painful diffusion of these new functions throughout the county. Douglas and Dunmanway were among the first settlements to change and they share important characteristics.[45] Local entrepreneurship, the stimulus of the ideology on improvement and the support of a national facilitating institution, such as the Linen Board, helped to initiate or expand these activities. Undoubtedly Douglas was, besides being the earliest, the most ambitious project. Its strategic location on Cork Harbour enabled it to capture a city and an outside market. The story of Douglas is well known. Its earliest 'manufactury' goes back to 1726 and it initially relied on linen but later diversified into sailmaking and cotton production which underwrote village life for more than a century. A combination of individual dedication, Huguenot entre-preneurship and Cork city merchant capital served as midwife to the centre and supported its subsequent expansion. In 1750 over 500 people worked there, by 1810 there were more than 1,000 workers, but there is no evidence to suggest that there was a continuous growth in the labour force; it is more likely that a series of peaks and troughs occurred. It declined rapidly after the 1820s due, in large part, to its failure to maintain its hold on the North American market. No plan of Douglas is available but visitors confirm that it was not a very large centre and most of its operatives, as at Kanturk, lived in its immediate vicinity. Dunmanway founded by Bandonian Richard Cox was conceived as a model Protestant settlement to be sustained by linen production.[46] Founded in the 1740s it was a more modest enterprise than Douglas. Linen production was consolidated by the erection of a yarn market, a spinning school and premises were made available to attract skilled spinners from the north of Ireland.[47] Because of its isolation, its small scale and growing competition from other centres of production its heyday was telescoped into a few short years between *c.* 1747 to *c.* 1760. Young and subsequent writers fail to mention Dunmanway as a noteworthy textile centre. The historian of the Irish linen industry argued that either unrealistic ambitions and/or excessively large productive capacities explain the failure of many southern linen centres.[48] All that remained at Dunmanway in 1783 was a charter school and a fine seat.[49]

There were many other landlord sponsored linen production initiatives. Shannon involvement was responsible for the emergence of Clonakilty as an important centre with a market of regional signi-ficance. It had a 'factory' in 1769.[50] Bandon too was also part of this complex as was Inishannon which had its own small 'factory' and a bleachyard which 'formed a town'. After 1775 it was reported to be in long-term decline. Macroom may perhaps be also considered to be part of this net as one of Bandon's Bernard family moved there in 1702, bought lands on the outskirts of the town and had invested, by 1724, almost £2000, in linen production. Milling too was developed by the Bernards but it is impossible to build up a picture of its diffusion in the eighteenth century.[51]

North county Cork was also the centre for a series of small woollen driven settlements which combined this work with linen production. Here, not only processing linked town and village to the countryside in terms of the distribution of operatives but also in flows of raw materials and finished commodities. It generated regional and national connections besides linking these in turn to external markets. One observer noted that

'In the little town of Doneraile, in Mitchelstown, Mallow Kilworth, Kanturk and Newmarket are clothiers who buy up wool, employ combers in their houses ... they have a day fixed for the poor, to come in and take it on order to spin it into worsted ...
The clothiers export this worsted from Cork to Bristol and Norwich ...'[52]

The same writer noted that a proportion of the worsted was forwarded to Dublin whence it was then taken to the north and subsequently smuggled to England. Weavers were scattered throughout the countryside and they worked at their friezes and serges in their minute cabins. Clothiers organized the transport of finished goods to the towns and villages in small 'cars' and a contemporary noted seeing 500 of them in a line. So great was the demand for wool that often clothiers were obliged to attend markets at Ballinasloe and Mullingar and to transport wool back to county Cork.[53]

Apart from the unknown quantum of milling, textile production was the only manufacturing activity that was relatively widespread in eighteenth-century county Cork. Its impact would appear to have been most pervasive from *c.* 1725 to the 1770s when other kinds of production became more popular. Tanning and other related activities were also important but these seem to have been concentrated in the principal towns such as Bandon and Mallow. There were then two textile production zones that were neither utterly discrete and they both made a contribution to generating urban growth in the county. Although difficult to quantify in this respect these kinds of activities allowed a symbiosis to emerge between town and village and the countryside. These settlements were market and distribution centres for both raw materials and finished products. They also acted as the loci for the clothiers, merchants and both the skilled and many unskilled craftspeople. As centres of exchange they clearly facilitated the spread of a money economy which at least endowed many settlements with a sounder economic footing and aided their general growth. Physically these activities also helped to beget the building of market houses, schools of various kinds and probably led to improvements in domestic housing.

The development of Blarney in the 1760s represented a new initiative in manufacture driven urban growth which was to become common-place in the county in the early decades of the nineteenth-century. Initially probably not conceived as a major industrial complex it developed later on to be one of the county's most industrially diverse but surprisingly integrated centres. It was an early example of an industrial village with extremely modest beginings. Author Young notes that building began in 1765 and slowly grew to total ninety houses in 1777.[54] The initial phase was anchored around a bleach mill, and a 'linen manufactury'. Soon afterwards there were important additions which included a linen printing mill and two extensive bleach greens. By 1777 at least 300 people were employed, the vast majority of whom lived outside Blarney. Jefferys, the proprietor, soon afterwards erected a stocking mill, a woollen factory, a tucking mill for broadclothes, a gigg mill and a knapping mill. More facilities were shortly to be put on stream; these consisted of a leather mill, a bolting mill, a plating mill, a blade mill for implements and a paper mill. In sum almost a score of mills were erected within two decades. Most of them were driven by water power and in this way Blarney's development was a prelude for the kind of industrial evolution which transpired at Blackpool, Glanmire and to a lesser extent at Bandon and Midleton in the nineteenth-century.

Besides its size, variety of activities and technological innovation Blarney was distinctive in other respects. It may have been the county's first factory centred settlement and its originator also leased out many of the facilities which he built. Many aspects of the undertaking were generously subvented by the Dublin Society and public subscription. It also appears to have been the first instance in the county of the extensive harnessing of water power for productive purposes. In twenty five of Blarney's houses, Young counted four looms in each one and in each house there was a married couple and three apprentices besides children. The fact that Blarney managed to acquire such a range of units may help to explain why it struggled through leaner times in the 1820s and managed to revive again as a key manufacturing centre. In 1824, Croker reported that most of Blarney's houses were roofless and a fine crop of barley was ripening in the village square,[55] whilst Douglas with its more specialised facilities failed to weather its problems and only emerged as a dormitory centre when it was connected to the city by railway.

Landed involvement in the promotion of manufacturing seems, for whatever reason, to have been more often directed at linen centres especially in west county Cork. The Earl of Shannon for example, established a linen factory and a bleach green at Clonakilty in 1769 and there were ninety looms at work there. Another similar unit was built at Castlemartyr in 1774 which is reported to have given work to fifty people. Outliers of linen production, all small scale, were evident also at Macroom and Skibbereen over the same period.

Ethnicity

In the larger towns in the county there was a considerable but highly variable Protestant presence. Denominational segregation is reported from many of these kinds of centres and it appears to have been at its most extreme where Protestant totals were highest. Travellers comments, parish records and rent-rolls also confirm these patterns of exclusivity. Centres such as Mallow and Macroom were also sharply divided by religious lines even though Protestants represented less than a quarter of the total populations of these towns. Protestantism was by no means tantamount to monlithic Anglicanism. Anglicans usually counted to more than 50 percent of the total reformed church member-ship but another characteristic of nearly all of the county's larger towns was the presence of many different groups such as Methodists, Presbyterians of various hues, Episcopalians and Congregationalists. At its most extreme at Bandon, and particularly a feature of the garrison towns, this kind of confessional diversity was particularly evident at Clonakilty, Dunmanway, Mallow and Skibbereen especially towards the end of the eighteenth century. It seems that Protestant proportions radically increased in some few centres in the early years of the eighteenth century as a result of late forfeitures. Macroom is a good example of this. With the probable exception of Dunmanway (and this only in the period c. 1740 to 1760) the Protestant presence in the smaller towns and villages was infinitismal. In many, there were no reformed churches and if the case of Kanturk is typical (the first Anglican church was completed there in 1789) they often materialised as emblems of identity for a minority very conscious of its precarious position. It may well be that the mass-house was the badge of the village as mass-houses seem to have predated churches as in the case of Kanturk where one was erected in 1723 on the town common and here it also functioned as a school-house.[56]

Housing and public buildings

The few available estate maps, surveys and visitors impressions furnish some general insights into both the kinds of houses in the countys towns and villages as well as giving some clues regarding housing conditions. In every respect there were massive variations between all the settlements. The villages had few elaborate houses and many cabins. In spite of the presence of some fine residences, cabins were the most frequent type of dwelling in the county often by a factor of four cabins to one more elegant residence. Doneraile may be relevant here if we can accept the plan as representing reality. If this was the case, outside some of the larger towns such as Bandon or Youghal, Doneraile certainly could claim to have not only some of the most sumptuous town houses but also some of the most pleasing street-scapes in the county. A crude computation of its population in 1723 based on the number of houses would yield a total of c. 1000 people, most of whom lived in newly erected blocks of attractive gable-hearthed two-storied semi-detached residences. There are also some very impressive three storied residences with appealingly designed slate roofs. The most suspicious element of the plan is the paucity of cabins but it might represent a view of the settlement very shortly after the development work was completed.

In all the other settlements cabins were everywhere except in the very core areas of the larger settlements such as South Main Street at Bandon or The Square at Macroom. Rosscarbery's square was also cabin free.[57] If Enniskeane is more typical of smaller villages, there cabins outnumbered houses by a ratio of five to one.[58] The survey evidence stresses that it is oversimplistic to draw a distinction between houses and cabins. The excellent surveys of Kanturk and Bandon show that the housing stock was quite diverse. In 1731 at Kanturk, half of the entire stock consisted of single storied, thatched, mud-walled cabins measuring on average some thirty feet in length and some six feet in height. A further 45 per cent of the residences were stone walled thatched houses. There was only one two storied slated house and this was the newly erected agents residence.[59] The housing ensemble of Rosscarbery in 1788 was remarkably similar to that of Kanturk in terms of the house types. Sherrard, the surveyor, distinguished between cabins, houses and slate houses. Here, Frekes' programme of renewal endowed it with proportionately far more larger houses than in Kanturk.[60]

Apart from churches and mass-houses or chapels the absolute paucity of public buildings was a recurrent characteristic of the villages. Some boasted of market houses but they were rare and very unimpressive. Up to almost the end of the century Kanturks market house was a minute thatched single storied building measuring forty feet by sixteen and a half feet by ten feet. Even Rosscarbery's market house was a tiny affair. Indeed very few settlements could boast of a purpose built market place; here Rosscarbery was exceptional. Even formal Doneraile had to make do with a space between the castle and the church. Fair greens were more frequent but most however were very casual features. What was a ubiquitous element of the smaller settlements was the general absence of public buildings; there was indeed the odd school or elaborate residence, but the county's smaller settlements had to wait for the next century and the state to begin a rapid programme of service provision physically expressed in schools, dispensaries, post offices and police barracks.

Recognisable suburbs were a feature of the larger towns. Suburb as a term may not quite capture the lifestyles of these areas as they supported a high degree of functional independence. They had their own services and trades people and some had developed around clusters of leather workers, mills or breweries as at Bandon and Midleton. These suburbs were in origen of three distinct types. Some were descendants of seventeenth-century Irish towns as at Bandon, then more genteely known as Shannon Street and this phenomenon was also apparent at Youghal. Spontaneous industrial suburbs emerged as at Watergate Street in Bandon built around a collection of tanneries and Chapel Road focused around a gaggle of breweries and mills. Ballydaheen at Mallow evolved as a cabin settlement south of the river Blackwater and by mid-century at least a third of the towns population resided there chiefly in cabins.[61] Finally Macroom provides an example of a settlement with three active magnates two of whom added planned developments at the edges of the urban core and Masseytown is perhaps the county's best known example of a planned suburb.

Occupations
The Registry of Deeds offers one of the most promising locations to

investigate occupational structures in our towns and villages. We are sadly in the dark in relation to the identification and understanding of urban social structures. The problem with this source is that as a rule only local élites are noted. Even less is known about leasing policies and land-holding realities in our urban centres. We do not know whether most centres had witnessed the emergence of a rentier class which was such a prominent feature of the nineteenth-century. The municipal documents which have survived for the larger towns illustrate the diversity of occupation and social groups. A recent study of Macroom has employed O'Connor's succinct framework for the analysis of socio-spatial arrangements in the nineteenth-century.[62] Landlord involvement in the management of urban affairs was a crucial factor and the Hedges-Eyers, the Bernards and the Masseys' made important contributions. Indeed the Bernards encouraged skilled immigration of cloth workers to Macroom from Bandon. They were not alone in this respect as Cox at Dunmanway and the Earl of Shannon at Clonakilty and Thomas Adderly at Inishannon were involved in similar ventures. At the apex of the local urban pyramid were the professionals, the clergy, the law, medicine, the agents. merchants, clothiers and shipowners in the ports.[63] In the earlier half of the century the vast majority of those in this tier of society belonged to the reformed churches. The textile trade also sifted its own hierarchy; there were the clothier/factors at the top, then the skilled operatives, the combers, dyers and spinners and below these were the makers who lived in town and countryside. Milling reproduced itself in a similar fashion and it was closely associated with brewing and distilling which also extended to include brewhouses, malthouses and inns and Roman Catholics figured more prominently in this sector. Likewise, all aspects of leather-working employed hordes of people from button-makers to cobblers and interestingly cobbling was the largest employer of Protestant families at Macroom.

Service functions and occupations

Larger towns such as Bandon, Kinsale and Youghal had significant numbers of people engaged in what could be termed service activities deriving from the presence of tanning, milling and textile production. In the ports maritime activities also promoted occupations associated with processing and warehousing goods which were exported or imported as well as pursuits associated with boat building and fishing. Even in the larger centres, rentals and terriers seldom indicate the presence of shops. Villages in eighteenth-century county Cork only appear to have counted the most rudimentary services; even churches and chapels were a rarity. Some settlements seem to have relied particularly on services; in this respect Mallow is a case in point. Unlike Bandon, Macroom or Youghal it does not seem to have had a strong artesanal presence. In 1750 there was only a small textile mill and three grist mills in the town. But like the suite of settlements of plantation origins it had a sizable barrack population and maybe because of this there was also considerable denomination diversity. Within a range of ten miles it boasted of an incredible concentration of over fifty elaborate country seats plus country residences. It acted as the focus for the lavish and ostentatious lifestyles of this gentry set besides catering for the mundane needs of this wealthy group. This kind of rôle was solidified by Mallow's emergence as a fashionable spa centre in 1738. Decline set in after the 1760s which for most observers was the towns heyday as a resort and centre of society. In 1777 a visitor's diagnosis of the town's condition and immediate prospects was decidedly bleak, 'Without manufacture it subsists by the precarious trade of letting lodgings ... of late years it has been deserted'.[64]

Communications

Since the early seventeenth century and probably for long before this, Cork city was both a county and regional hub for overland roads. Until about the middle of the following century significant gaps in road coverage were evident especially in the north west and south-west of the county and along the border between counties Cork and Kerry. By the third quarter of the eighteenth-century most of the roads as we now know them were in place (Fig. 11.3). Scalé's Atlas of Ireland, and Taylor and Skinner's excellent road maps confirm these changes.[65] Scalé's maps also distinguish between major and secondary county roads and more critically Taylor and Skinner indicate the sites of turnpikes which were particularly a feature of the butter roads into Cork city from the north (Fig. 11.3). Road building undoubtedly helped some centres to expand; it facilitated the emergence of new settlements especially in the nineteenth-century and strengthened the regional role of Cork city with all its implications. Besides having obvious economic relevance many of these roads acquired military importance and several centres on them became the sites for important military barracks which both helped to spawn new settlements as at Inchageelagh or expand existing centres such as Millstreet, Mallow and Rosscarbery. The disposition of the major roads not only specified the salient trade routes, but it also contributed to shape the urban hierarchy in the nineteenth-century. Among these was the road leading to west Cork which extended to Bantry passing a necklace of coastal centres. Northwards, Mallow, Doneraile and Charleville linked Cork city to Limerick. The butter trade's requirements had led to important inter-

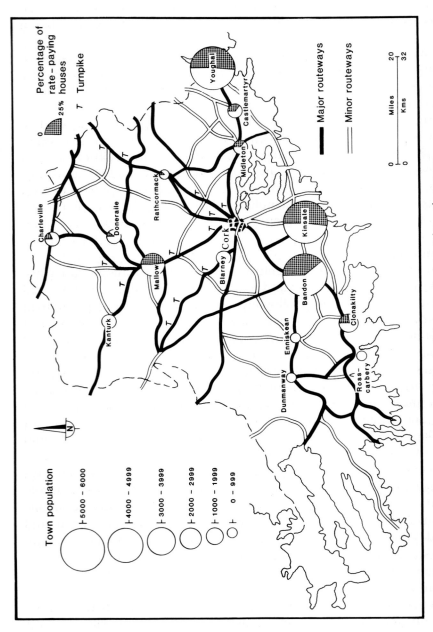

Figure 11.3   Settlement, communications and urban well-being in the late eighteenth century.
Sources: 1 Communications:- Scalé, *Hibernian atlas* (reference 65) and Taylor and Skinner, *Maps*; 2 Urban
well-being; *Commons jn. Ire*, xix (1800), pt. 2, Appendix, p. dcclxi, Hearth money returns).

county improvements between Cork and Kerry. Youghal remained in a cul-de-sac as the main Dublin road ran to Rathcormack, Fermoy and on to Kilworth where it struck north east and on to Cahir via Ballyporeen. Grand Jury and other municipal and private road building initiatives remain to be explored in detail. Without any countryside strategic plan, duplication resulted as in the case of the great butter road from Cork to Millstreet and on to Kerry.

Trade

With the exception of Cork city, Doneraile, Dunmanway and Mallow little evidence exists to indicate significant, or any urban growth in the first half of the eighteenth-century. For different reasons in each of these exceptional cases growth proved to be very ephemeral. The conditions of the smaller settlements such as Enniskeane, Kanturk and even Rosscarbery were no better. It may well have been that the only function which saved these settlements from extinction was their markets and fairs. The weak rate of trading franchise confirmation also indicates the poor economic condition of the county until the 1770s.[66] The market and fair 'surface' at least pinpoints the more economically active zones in the county (Fig. 11.4).

It illustrates that the Blackwater and Bride valleys were paramount in this respect. Besides these areas the fringes of Cork harbour extending as far as Youghal and an arc shaped corridor between Bantry and Skibbereen also stand out. The surface was nevertheless a ragged and discontinuous affair with many sharp edges. Almanack evidence for 1780 reveals an altogether different county trading topography (Fig. 11.5). A whole host of new locations was added on but what is crucial here is that the general spatial incidence of trading centres had not radically altered. What had transpired was a dramatic intensification of centres in areas already beside or near pre-existing trading places. Their names such as Annsgrove, Rockhill, Gooseberry Hill and Coolymurchoo illustrate that many medium sized landowners and petty gentry were involved in their creation. In addition as many as twenty per cent of the foundations were unlicensed indicating perhaps a very local response to improved trading conditions and a wider involvement of people from different backgrounds in marketing.

Hierarchy

By the close of the eighteenth century the essential configuration of the urban hierarchy had remained much as it was *c.* 1659. The one and only exception was the unprecedented growth of Cork city. If the estimates for the larger towns *c.* 1659 are correct these kinds of centres appear to have remained stagnant. Over such a lengthy period such a

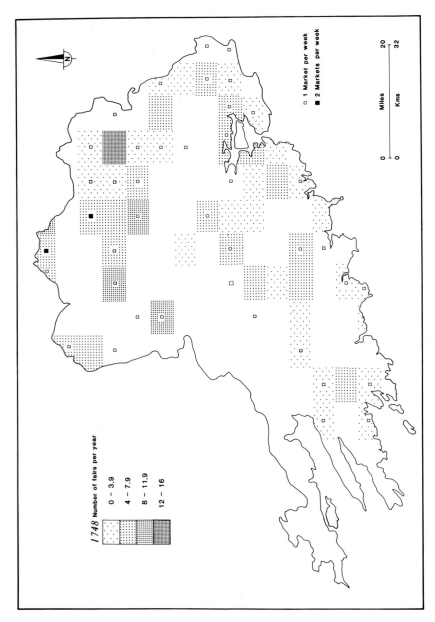

Figure 11.4   Market and fair incidence, 1748.
Source: Watson, *Almanac.*

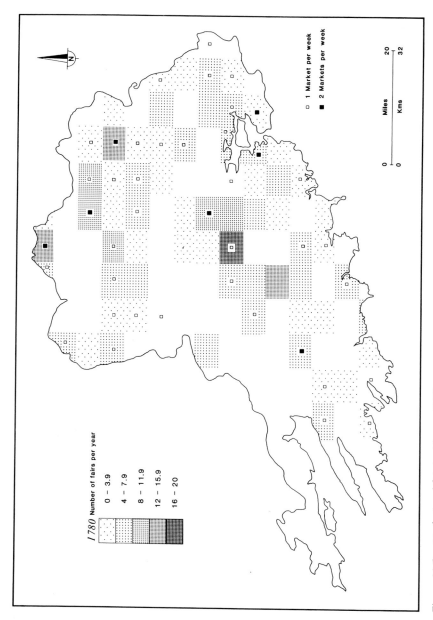

Figure 11.5   Market and fair incidence, 1780.
Source: Watson, *Almanac.*

paralysis is both difficult to either conceive or explain. From the few figures proffered by contemporary historians and observers the more likely explanation was one of decline followed by more noticeable growth in the last quarter of the century. The exceptional centres which did show growth in the 1740s and the 1750s all shed population in the 1760s. Mallow is an instance here; it's population can be estimated to be c. 2,560 in 1766; by 1775 it was only slightly more than 2,000. By all accounts during and after the 1790s all the towns and villages entered a period of intense growth the like of which was never recorded before or since.

Another interesting dimension of the settlements in the 1790s was each towns proportion of rate-paying houses which may be taken as a crude measure of vitality as expressed in housing conditions and valuations (Fig. 11.3).[67] Significant variations are evident in relation to towns and villages and between individual instances. In the towns on average at least 50 percent of the houses contributed but Bandons rate was lower at 43 percent. In the villages the proportion contributing was much more variable but always it was at a very weak level. At Castlemartyr, Charleville and Midleton it ranged from between 30 and 44 percent; elsewhere it was lower than 20 percent and in the case of Baltimore there was not one house involved. These data confirm the picture of the various surveys from different times over the century which demonstrate that economic conditions were extremely weak in the villages as few of them were able to support a wealthy tier of society.

It is very difficult to give credence to Smith's estimates of the county's urban population during the 1750s. If his figures are tallied with the more reliable urban hearth tax returns for 1798 the magnitude of the problem becomes clear. Smith cites, for instance, figures of 11,000 for Kinsale and 9,000 for Youghal. If a generous multiplier of five for the 1798 hearth-tax returns is employed the figures yielded for these towns are 5,115 and 5,875 respectively for 1788; Smith's estimate for Mallow in the same decade appears equally inflated and it is double the figure which can be extrapolated from a Mockler's 1775 house count of 400 units.[68] If Smith's estimate of 5,000 is matched with the total number of houses it would yield an average of ten residents per house which is impossible.

For these reasons, Burke's estimates of urban population totals which have been derived chiefly from Smith for the middle of the eighteenth century cannot be sustained.[69] Moreover there is no compelling evidence available to suggest that urban growth was more intense in south county Cork than elsewhere. Towns which did show definite growth only managed to sustain their increases for hardly more than two decades as was the case for Dunmanway and Mallow. The essential point seems to be that the southern coastal zone managed to sustain its large urban centres during the extended period of general population stagnation. Here in this area were already established the county's largest centres which had the most varied functional attributes. The legacies of earlier plantation settlement, better farming structures and crucially, advantages in terms of access to internal and external markets endowed the coastal zone with comparative strength which was to be dramatically realized in the early years of the following century.

Summary
Given that we have so little information about town and village life in the eighteenth-century it follows that it is exceedingly difficult to identify and measure the impact of those processes which either promoted or arrested urban growth in the county. Local factors seem to have been more potent agents in the early period when hinterlands were especially restricted given the generally poor means and methods of transport. The general amelioration in the condition and density of roads as the century wore on was certainly a growth promoter. The radial nature of so many centres is a measure of their rôle. Urban conditions in the post 1690s were characterised it seems by decline or at least stagnation; there was the absence of any fundamental economic rationale for their existence, apart from marketing. The paucity of public buildings and the absence of embellishments were common features especially of the smaller settlements. Relatively few new settlements were added to the existing stock; exceptions to this were Blarney, Doneraile, Douglas and probably Dunmanway, Charleville and Kanturk. It is also evident that the aftermath of the Williamite campaigns was very negative for towns and villages. Apart from Douglas, eighteenth-century manufacturing activity led only ephemeral bursts of growth as at Dunmanway. It appears that some of the larger towns experienced more sustained growth; none were to do this on the scale of Cork city which was the island's most dramatic case of expansion. Macroom, Mallow and Bandon are examples of towns which experienced moderate growth up to the 1770s and intense expansion thereafter. In all of these cases suburbs appeared beyond the town walls spreading outwards along the main axial routes. Like Bandon, Macroom had crystallised into three distinctive zones by the 1770s. Radically improved by its patron the core did not expand. Another local landed family, the Massey's built a suburb bearing their family name to the north-west of the core zone. Finally a poor cabin quarter latched itself around a Catholic mass-house on one of the

town's principal lanes. Other centres indubitably declined; Buttevant for instance was described by a visitor as 'a collection of the vilest cribs'. Burke cites the intensification of commercial grazing as an agent severely inhibiting urban expansion in north and north-west county Cork. But it was probably more complex than Burke asserts: textile production along cottage lines welded a symbiosis, rather than a dependance, between town and country. It may well be that factory based activity broke this down and prompted a massive exodus to the towns.

Growth, catastrophe and stagnation

Even as we approach the contemporary period little agreement is evident in the literature in relation to how best to define a town or a village. Villages have attracted the widest variations of definition and many are quite ambiguous and exceedingly imprecise. Nor is it likely that any generally acceptable definitions of these terms will win easy recognition in the context of nineteenth-century Ireland.

It may be worthwhile in this respect to re-examine the kinds of definitions employed by the census authorities and the criteria selected by the commissioners established to expedite the census. The 1841 Commission regarded 2,000 people as the critical threshold to categorise a town.[71] For them numbers of people was simply the salient element. The instructions given to Griffiths' teams of 'valuators and surveyors' also sheds light on the issue.[72] They were especially concerned with the knock-on value of prosperous settlements to immediately contiguous lands and for this reason they formulated a crude hierarchical set of settlement definitions:

Types of centres	Settlement status population
Villages	250 - 500
Small market towns	500 - 1,000
	1,000 - 2,000
Large market towns	2,000 - 4,000
	4,000 - 8,000
	8,000 - 15,000
	15,000 - 19,000
Cities	19,000 - 75,000
	75,000 +

They derived their categorizations from the following assumptions:

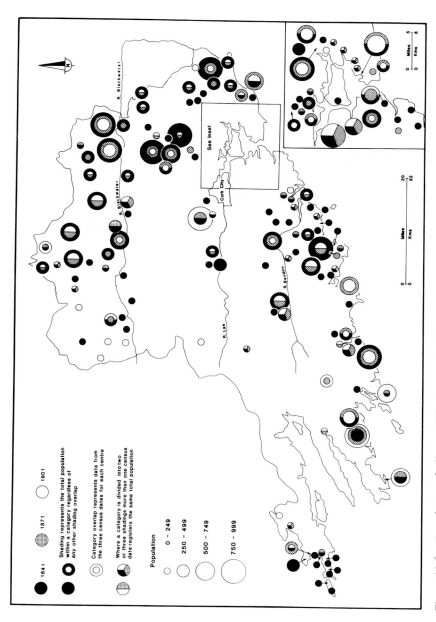

Figure 11.6   Population of villages, 1841, 1871 and 1901.
Source: Census.

villages, they reckoned did not increase the value of land, beyond the gardens or fields immediately behind the houses. Larger villages and small towns boosted values in an area within a three mile radius, whereas larger towns, up to a population of 15,000, influenced an area up to seven miles: while nine and a half miles marked the reach of cities. Within each area there was an outwardly decreasing zonation of value.

Exceptionally, several authors have advanced quantative categorizations of settlements. Currie, for instance has proposed a lower limit of 100 buildings or 500 residents for towns but he does not furnish a lower limit for village size.[73] Burke has advanced similar categories for county Cork but his population thresholds for some of them vary inexplicably.[74] To avoid randomness the census categories have been employed here. In the order of 190 settlements can be recognised as either towns or villages in nineteenth-century Cork but only a handful summed to more than 2,000 people. The preponderant majority were villages and the vast bulk of these counted less than 500 residents. The lower limit census threshold was twenty contiguous houses which would yield a population of some one hundred residents. What always counted for the census was the number of houses so in the aftermath of the Great Famine many places returned populations of below 100 people but with twenty occupied contiguous houses. The upper limit set for a village was 999 people. All the other settlements above this limit were designated as towns with the obvious exception of Cork city (Appendix 11.A).

With so many towns and villages it is tempting to suggest that an analysis of these kinds of settlements has more than countywide significance. If we employ the census definition we can only and confidently rely on the 1841 census as the censuses for the two preceding decades were not detailed or accurate enough for our purposes. It is possible to identify only twenty settlements above the 100 plus threshold in 1798 (Fig. 11.3). In 1841 there were 190 centres above this threshold which represents a staggering 900 percent increase in the number of centres. Also all of the existing settlements grew equally dramatically if we compare the 1798 estimates with the figures for 1841 (Figs. 11.6, 11.7). These kinds of generalizations need to be qualified in several respects: growth was not always a continuous process between 1798 and 1841. Some of the towns as we shall discover peaked between 1821 and 1830 and Bandon may have already been in early decline before 1820. Despite these qualifications it is abundantly clear that the population increase over these decades was far more intense in urban centres than in rural areas and natural increase combined with massive immigration was responsible for this dramatic and sustained growth. What brought about such changed

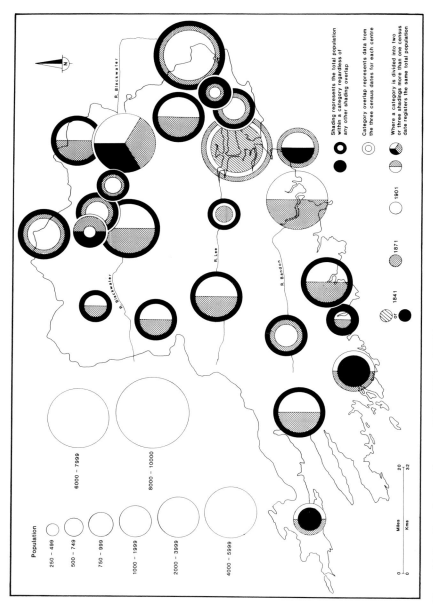

Figure 11.7   Population of towns, 1841, 1871 and 1901.
Source: Census.

431

circumstances? To what degree was urban growth premeditated and planned? What is starkly evident is that landlords played a very subsidiary role in urban genesis; nevertheless many made fundamental and decisive contributions towards modifying existing settlements and they attempted to cope as generously as they were able with the tremendous pressures for housing and services. Indeed there were elaborate and grandiose settlements founded such as Fermoy and Mitchelstown but they were very much the exception in a sea of spontaneous urbanization.[75] External, national and regional forces conspired and combined to unleash a short and very ephemeral burst of urban growth the like of which has never been experienced before or since in the county and in the country.

In order to identify and explain the interplay of these processes the settlements of the county have been divided into a number of distinctive categories each of which self-evidently indicates the primary processes which have promoted its emergence, survival or decline. The leading criteria employed relate to their functions as they were recorded in 1841. Few of the settlements founded earlier had sustained their early functions for one or more centuries such as the textile centres in south and west county Cork, the major ports being, of course, the leading exceptions. The functional mix of many places ebbed, intensified and was often replaced or substituted during the nineteenth-century. Many of the smaller villages owed their birth and continuity often to one single activity such as milling; these were the most volatile and ephemeral centres. Towns, that is centres of more than 1,000 residents, were different in that they maintained a mix of activities and frequently these functions ebbed and flowed and the numbers of people which they employed both directly and indirectly varied a lot. Some of the larger towns witnessed the emergence of veritable industrial complexes which prospered and they in turn fostered the growth of a range of services which towards the end of the century were to assume a paramount rôle in determining the fortunes of these towns.

Five major categories of settlements have been recognised in county Cork in 1841.[76] They were as follows: centres of primary production which included mining centres as well as ports and, or, fishing centres and clusters; manufacturing centres, market centres and communication centres complete the range of village types. There were also larger towns, satellite centres beside some towns and a handful of planned towns and villages (Fig. 11.8).

Centres of primary production

Four separate types of settlement can be recognised: there were centres associated with fishing, small ports, clusters and mining centres. The

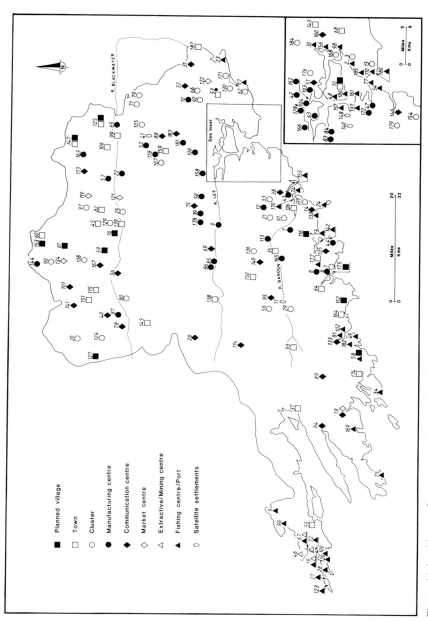

Figure 11.8   Types of settlements (for identification see Chapter 11, Appendix, pp 461-462).

distinction between fishing centres and small ports is clear because most of the fishing centres discharged this activity almost exclusively though some of them located on the extreme western peninsulas also combined mining with fishing. Smaller ports such as Crosshaven, Courtmacsherry and Farsid on Cork Harbour serviced small ships and sand-lighters and most of them also maintained a small fishing fleet. There were also several mining centres and a very numerous group of clusters.

Of all of the settlement types in this group the mining centres were the most discrete and ephemeral. By 1851 most of them had shrivelled up or were deserted. This was particularly the case with those centres on the western extremities of the Beara peninsula focused around Allihies. The complex of settlements developed around a private copper mining enterprise which involved the attraction of a number of skilled miners from Cornwall. Castletownbere's early growth stems from this time when it was linked by road to Allihies and through it the ore was exported abroad for smelting. All that remains of this brutal phase of extraction are the shafts, the Cornish miners 'village' and the gaunt remains of the entrepreneur Puxley's mansion, on the western outskirts of Castletownbere. Without the most elementary services, living conditions in these settlements were appalling and at Ballydonegan nearly 360 residents were recorded as living in 1841 in the most atrocious deprivation. Dromagh near Kanturk developed as a small centre focused on the extraction of low-grade coal deposits which were quickly worked out.

The entire coastline of the county was bedecked with a continuous necklace of generally small fishing centres. None of these was exclusively devoted to fishing as many of the families combined agriculture with fishing. Three types of centres dedicated to fishing may be recognised on the basis of their degree of specialization, the sophistication of their fishing activities and the size and continuity of the actual centres. To start there was a remote group of centres located on the western peninsulas and islands, notably Dursey Island, where some agriculture was combined with very basic fishing. Focused on Castletownbere and Bantry, the life-span of these settlements as villages rarely summed to more than a score of years. It was essentially an inshore unsophisticated and highly subsistent fishery. The many inlets and coves extending between Mizen Head and Youghal were the context for the emergence of the county's most specialized fishing communities and their villages. The first edition Ordnance Survey maps show that in these contexts such as at Carrigilihy or Laherne near Garrettstown the fieldscape adjacent to the centres was puckered out into an interminable maze of minute gardens and fields of irregular shapes. No doubt the erection of quays, breakwaters and small slips encouraged the emergence of settlements at these kinds of locations. Valuations from these locations stress that the residents held little land and in this way most residents were almost exclusively dependant upon the harvest of the sea. The steady improvement of the coastal infrastructure throughout the century included the provision of landing facilities and better roads in both these more isolated locations and in existing harbours such as Courtmacsherry where the Earl of Shannon's philanthropic zeal led to real improvements which helped to intensify a long-standing tradition in the area. It also encouraged the harvesting of wrack and seaweed, kelp production and the drawing of sea-sand and its transport inland to improve the land. Huge numbers of people were engaged in the harvesting, transport and spreading of these raw materials and it is no wonder that they acted to intensify village emergence and expansion in an area which recorded the highest rural population densities in pre-famine county Cork in the period immediately before the Great Famine.[77] Ring, Clonakilty's port, Timoleague, Courtmacsherry and Rosscarbery had fleets of small sand-lighters and shallow draught flat-bottomed seaweed harvesting craft besides longliners and inshore fishing boats. Ring alone counted 120 seaweed boats and more than a score of sand-lighters.[78] The lower harbour of Cork also possessed a number of small villages with similar dedications such as Aghada, Crosshaven, Farsid and Whitegate. In these centres basket-making and straw plaiting as well as net-making provided part-time employment for many women.

Finally all of the established ports and large villages from Bantry to Youghal supported substantial fishing fleets. World's End in Kinsale was an example of the emergence of a special fishing suburb on the edge of the town and Scilly became effectively another suburb on the opposite side of Kinsale Harbour. Ballycotton stands out as a remarkable example of a largely fish sustained village which managed, quite exceptionally to maintain a relatively stable demographic profile throughout the nineteenth-century. Castletownbere also owes its later growth to similar processes. Initially it was the supply and despatch centre for Allihies copper and it subsequently switched to fishing later on in the century, aided here no doubt by the laying out of good overland communications with Bantry. Its demographic behaviour is unique among the fishing centres and among most of the towns in the county (Fig. 11.9).

Compared with other sectors of Atlantic Europe, fishing in county Cork or indeed elsewhere in Ireland never served as a long-term promoter of urban growth, unlike southern Norway, eastern Scotland, Brittany and southern Galicia where it sponsored rapid nineteenth-century urbanization largely as a response to the growth of the pro-

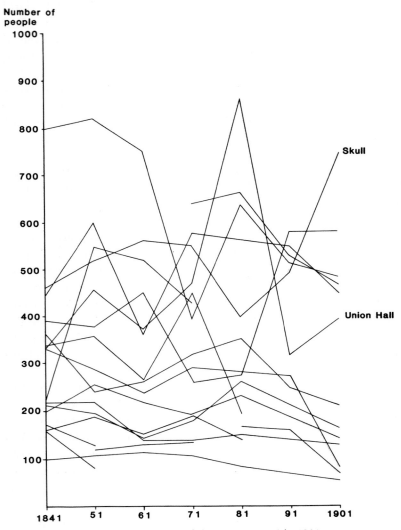

Figure 11.9   Population change in fishing centres, 1841-1901.
Source: Census.

cessing industry and technological sophistication at sea despite the
distance of these far-flung and isolated regions from their markets.
County Cork's fishing industry by comparison remained utterly under-
developed. Several short bursts of buoyancy were always marked by
the arrival of foreign boats which transported the fish abroad for
processing. But that is another story.

A glance at the demographic profiles of the fishing centres in general and especially the smaller ones confirms that most of them were ephemeral: associated with the demographic spring tide of the early decades of the century. The majority of them were swept away before the 1860s. The small fishing villages in Cork's lower harbour were more resilient because they maintained a greater mix of functions and some were to experience the knock-on effects of maritime industrialization in the upper harbour at least until the 1860s. But after that most of them nose-dived except for centres such as Crosshaven which subsequently acquired a reputation as a seaside resort. In the midst of inexorable decline some degree of hierarchialization was evident and it was revealed in the growth of a handful of centres such as Ballycotton and Union Hall. The variable demographic behaviour of the majority of fishing centres is a reflection of a range of unstable elements varying from fish supply to market demand. Small boats, meagre investment, scarcely any on-shore processing capacity, basic technology and poor organization were amongst the leading factors which arrested the progress of this sector and hence its capacity to drive urban growth.

The lifestyles and living conditions at the smaller centres were spartan as illustrated by Spillar's comments on Meelmore '... it stands (near Courtmacsherry) on nine acres of ground and consists of fifty-five houses of inferior description, mostly inhabited by fishermen and sailors. There are no shops in the town, which is of an irregular straggling and uninteresting appearance'.[79] Education and literacy were likewise at low levels there; only two men could read and write and 126 males and 107 females in the early 1830's could neither read nor write.

Some of these centres experienced some degree of terterization: this was the case at Crosshaven, Courtmacsherry and Glandore. The Earl of Shannon erected a pier at Courtmacsherry which engineered growth, stimulating fishing, coastal trading, sand and seaweed gathering and bathing.

> The healthy and sheltered situation of the town
> the salubrity of the atmosphere, the finished improvements
> and those constructing, the abundant supply of fish
> and all other kinds of provision have rendered it
> one of the most agreeable and fashionable bathing
> places on the south coast of Ireland.[80]

In the 1830s Courtmacsherry boasted of a small trading fleet, five of which were one hundred tons plus and two of which were ninety tons. Each of them made about eight trips a year to England importing an average of 8,000 tons of coal annually. Timber, salt and iron were also imported. Ten yawls were permanently involved in fishing and some sixty-six oared yawls were built there each year.

All of the larger towns along the coast discharged a broader range of port functions. Imports included iron, wood, salt and coal and each centre was characterised by the presence of many warehouses, mills and stores on their waterfronts. Towns which were located upstream of tidal limits such as Clonakilty and Midleton witnessed the growth of small ports to service their external trade. Ring and Ballinacurra acted respectively for these two centres and these saw the development of a range of processing and storage facilities which in the case of Ballinacurra was quite extensive and impressive. Many of these ports plummeted demographically in the immediate aftermath of the Great Famine; a few recovered somewhat in the 1870s only to decline again in the next decade (Fig. 11). Other small centres such as Timoleague managed to maintain for decades a coastal trade besides fishing and sand-collecting and ships exceptionally sailed from there as far afield as Portugal. The demographic haemorrhage experienced in these kinds of centres was not as severe as that felt in the fishing and manufacturing centres which were essentially overspecialised. In some few port centres landlord involvement was confined to investment in marine related infrastructure but in some instances such as Clonakilty, Courtmacsherry and Timoleague considerable changes resulted ranging from new housing and street layout to the emplacement of many tasteful embel-lishments. Schools, and some public buildings appeared but far more significant were infrastructural improvements such as the dredging of slobs, the building of piers, slips and wharfs and the clearance of silted harbours and their approaches as well as the enhancement of accessibility by the improvement of local roads.

Agricultural centres/clusters
These were by far the most numerous but by no means the most ubiquitous type of nucleated settlement. Unlike the fishing village however they had more varied origins but they shared many charac-teristics with them: they were very transitory phenomena counting few, if any, basic functions, and were often inhabited by kin groups. Housing and sanitation were usually appalling. The lifestyle which was an invariable characteristic is horrendously apparent in William Cobbett's description of a cluster beside Midleton which can most likely be identified as Walshtown:[81]

'I came here to see things with my own eyes; and, I have, *to-day,* been to see this BRODERICK's estate, which begins at about sixteen miles from this City of Cork; and the land of this sixteen miles, taking in two miles on each side of the road, the finest that you can possibly imagine. Ah! but, how did I find the *working people* upon this land of this Broderick? That is the question for you to ask, and for me to answer.

I went to a sort of hamlet near to the town of Midleton. It contained about 40 or 50 hovels. I went into several of them, and took down the names of the occupiers. They all consisted of mud-walls, with a covering of rafters and straw. None of them so good as the place where you keep your little horse. I took a particular account of the first that I went into. It was 21 feet long and 9 feet wide. The floor, the bare ground. No fire-place, no chimney, the fire (made of Potato-haulm) made on one side against the wall, and the smoke going out of a hole in the roof. No table, no chair: I sat to write upon a block of wood. Some stones for seats. No goods but *a pot*, and a shallow tub, for the pig and the family both to eat out of. There was one window, 9 inches by 5. and the glass broken half out. There was a mud-wall about 4 feet high to separate off the end of the shed for the family to sleep, lest the hog should kill and eat the little children when the father and mother were both out, and when the hog was shut in. No bed: no mattress; some large flat stones laid on other stones, to keep the bodies from the damp ground; some dirty straw and a bundle of rags were all the bedding. The man's names was Owen Gumbleton. *Five small children*; the mother, about thirty, naturally handsome, but worn into half-ugliness by hunger and filth; she had no shoes or stockings, no shift, a mere rag over her body and down to her knees. The man BUILT THIS PLACE HIMSELF, and yet he has to pay a *pound a year* for it with perhaps a rod of ground! Others, 25s. a year. *All built their own hovels,* and yet have to pay this rent. All the hogs were in the hovels today, it being coldish and squally; and then, you know hogs like cover. Gumbleton's hog was lying in the room; and in another hovel there was a fine large hog that had taken his bed close by the fire. There is a nasty dunghill (no privy) to each hovel. The dung that the hog makes *in the hovel* is carefully put into a heap by itself, as being the most precious. This dung and the pig are the main things to raise the rent and get fuel with. The poor creatures sometimes keep the dung in the hovel, when their hard-hearted tyrants will not suffer them to let it be at the door! So there they are, in a far worse state, Marshall, than any hog that you ever had in your life'.

Without detailed figures or a sound cartographic record it is very difficult to date their emergence and chart their growth. By 1850 most could no longer claim village status as they had fallen substantially below our threshold. By the time the large scale ordnance maps were revised later on in the century few of their sites even boasted of a handful of farm-houses, so the claim of this category of settlement to the status of village must remain ambiguous. Few maintained service functions and most of the houses belonged to farmers and landless elements, the majority of them being sustained by the most elementary primary production. Poverty was a salient feature also expressed in low literacy levels which were especially intense amongst the female residents and most were swept away by the effects of the Great Famine as these flotsam and jetsam communities were amongst the elements of society most vulnerable to any major natural disaster. Likewise it is not feasible to argue for village continuity since plantation times at centres such as Kilpatrick, Newcestown and Tracton. The reverse seems most likely and we seem to be dealing with the re-emergence of village life at favourable locations.

If we attempt to examine the origins and explain the distribution of these clusters we may be some way along the road towards identifing the processes which made and unmade them.[82] These kinds of settlements were especially a feature of a number of discrete zones which included the peninsulas and islands of south west county Cork, the bogs and moors of the north west of the county and certain very confined pockets along the Blackwater and Bride valleys. Finally, there was a small scattered group in the barony of Imokilly in the east of the county as well in the intensely Normanised and manorialised baronies of Courceys, Ibane and Barryroe, Kinsale, Kinalea and Kerrycurrihy. Of all these the most basic seem to have been the clusters in the west on the Beara peninsula and on Dursey and Bere islands such as Firkeel, Killough and Kilkiniken. In the Normanized sectors of the county, these kinds of centres were more durable and substantial in many respects. Houses were more impressive, farms were larger, enclosures were more permanent and where data are available, they suggest that literacy levels were higher. Instances of these kinds of clusters include Butlerstown and Lislevane in Ibane and Barryroe, Ballinspittal in Courceys, Nohoval in Kinalea and Ballinroostig, Churchtown, Ladysbridge and Shanagarry in Imokilly. In this latter barony clusters were quite numerous especially south of a line between Ballinacorra and Youghal, effectively following the course of todays main arterial road. The clusters were more resilient demographically; many of them managed to attract and to absorb a range of basic retail and state services. Craftspeople were a feature of their social content. Many also were recipients of earlier market and fair patents. West of Kinsale complex and ancient tenurial arrangements, fossilised open fields and the presence of extended families were recurrent features of these kinds of settlements. Griffiths Valuation indicates that intricate land-holding arrangements were in vogue and what appears to be partner-ship farming was occasionally a characteristic of these centres. In the absence of information which might shed more light on occupational structures in these kinds of centres our knowledge of lifestyles is meagre. For these reasons their claim to have village status is qualified and at most they could aspire to belong to the lowest rung of the settlement hierarchy.

Spillar's brief picture of Butlerstown is instructive in this respect. Here, there was an 'irregular street', with thirty houses some of which were 'tolerably built and good looking', there was also a chapel, two public houses, one good huxters shop a forge and a national school. Two masons and one cartmaker seem to have been the only skilled male trades people. Twenty-six males and sixteen females could read and write; whereas thirty-five males and thirty-seven females could neither read nor write. Despite Butlerstown's mediocre attainments in services and literacy they were a cut above those of the neighbouring fishing village of Meelmore.[83]

Along the Blackwater and Bride valleys, especially between Mallow and Fermoy a small number of clusters was also evident; Ballymagooley and Dromahana serve as instances of these kinds of centres. This was Munsters most conspicuously landlord embellished zone which continued eastwards to Lismore, Youghal and also on to Dungarvan. By the 1860s most of them had disappeared. It is probable that some resulted from landlord clearances which were a feature of parts of these zones and particularly an element of riverside and other highly esteemed locations. Many of these kinds of settlements had roadside locations and were hidden from the view of contiguous big houses by stands of trees.[84]

Finally another group of clusters can be recognised and their incidence was most noticeable in the barony of Duhallow in hilly, poorly drained upland country. Virtually all the nucleated settlements in this area were of very recent origin and were associated with the reclamation of heaths and moors and the laying out of new through all-weather roads across most unpromising countryside during a period of intense demographic expansion. Ballyhoolahan, Dernagree, Ballyhooleen and Gneeves are examples of these kinds of settlements which were surrounded by fieldscapes of very regular proportions recently gouged out by hand implements only to rapidly revert, for the most part, to rough grazing. Some few villages such as Dromina managed to survive but its future was underpinned by a major through route. Ballydesmond stands out as a rare example in this area of state intervention through land reclamation and internal colonization. Formerly known as Kingwilliamstown, it was a modest undertaking whose survival once again was assured by road development.

Communication centres

Road building was intensive in the early years of the nineteenth century and it was sponsored by a welter of institutions and individuals ranging from the state to particular landlords or, at their behest, grand juries. Buoyant economic conditions, population expansion and philantropy tinged with real needs prompted these enhancements. In this way roads and to a very minor extent railways acted as settlement catalysts especially at local nodes such as at bridges, important cross roads and in areas which had remained relatively isolated. Belgooly, Minane Bridge and Watergrasshill are telling examples of the results of these kinds of processes. Carrigtohill is an instance of an ancient centre which was revived by road development. Halfway House village and Sallys Cross Roads speak for themselves. In the far west of the county where few nucleations were evident roads helped to support settlements serving scattered and sparse communities and Ballymakeera, Freemount and Inchigeela are testaments to this. Banteer is the only example of a railway sponsored village.

Market centres

There were about a score of centres dispersed throughout the county which counted considerably larger populations that those which have been previously discussed. Instances of these villages include Ballydehob, Kildorrey, Killeigh, and Liscarroll.[85] Few of these centres managed to attract any manufacturing facilities but they shared a range of features. They were all market centres of more than local importance and most of them had seventeenth-century origins and had acquired market franchises early in their careers. With a rudimentary range of state services and retail outlets they were galvanised by the changes that brought many other smaller villages to their knees. This process of hierarchicalization is revealled by the dimuniation of market and fair centres (Fig. 11).

Manufacturing centres

After clusters, small manufacturing centres can be reckoned to have been the most numerous class of settlement. (Fig. 11.11). All of these had some basic manufacturing, processing or industrial function,[86] many of which derived their energy from water power. Some of the

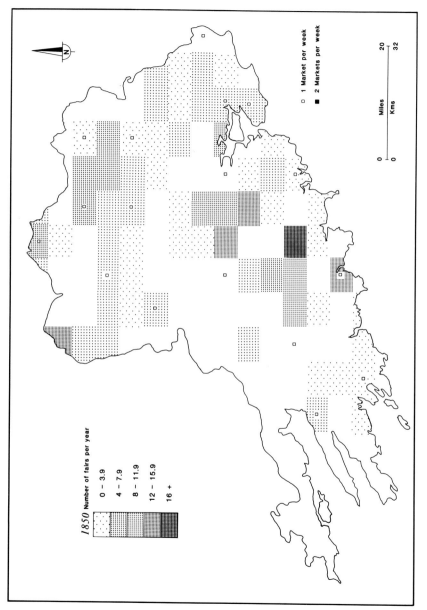

Figure 11.10   Market and fair incidence, 1850.
Source: *Fairs and markets rep.*

larger towns such as Bandon combined all of these functions and had emerged into industrial complexes where vertical integration was by no means unknown. (Fig. 11.11). The incidence of these kinds of centres was by no means an even one; there were several notable concentrations. Highly discrete factors exercised varying influences on their locations: among these can be counted the availability of water-power, propinquity to markets and ports, the presence of reserves of both skilled and unskilled labour, availability of raw materials and a local processing heritage. It is possible to recognise a group of very rudimentary settlements which emerged around milling and malting facilities. As one would expect they were located in areas of intensive arable farming and accessible water-power. They were very much a feature of the south of the county in the Bandon and Owenabui valleys; there were others also in the middle and eastern parts of the Lee, the Blackwater and Bride valleys and their tributaries. Ballinadee, Ballinascarthy and Enniskeane/Ballineen were examples in the Bandon valley. Rockmills and Castletownroche were outstanding instances of these kinds of villages in the north of the county. Another group of very simple mill villages can be recognised along the coastal zone especially between Cork Harbour and Rosscarbery and it included villages such as Arundelmills, Brownsmills and Newmills. In terms of their social content, transistory nature and lack of services these centres were similar in some respects to some clusters and fishing villages. Apart from their *raison d'être*, the mill, and perhaps the residence of the mill owner or millwright, housing conditions were generally appalling. Even the names of many of these settlements remind one of their very recent emergence. Most were of early nineteenth-century origin but many at least managed to maintain threshold populations for longer than the clusters and fishing villages. The failure of a mill was devastating: few ever continued to remain vibrant afterwards. Mills did not invariably seed settlements. Many small isolated mills were scattered through the grain growing sectors of the county and many were water-powered boulting, grist and tuck mills which were only active seasonally (Fig. 11.11).

Three major nodes of manufacturing-inspired villages can be recognised in the county. These were around or in the immediate vicinities of the large towns of Midleton, Bandon and finally Cork city. The group around Midleton was driven by the concentration of brewing and distilling industries and it extended to include Midleton's port, Ballinacorra and Clashavodig, Park North and Rathcoursey.[87]

The Butlerstown, Glanmire and Clashaboy river valleys acted as the locus for the growth of the most varied and sometimes quite vibrant group of compact industrial villages located a few miles to the north

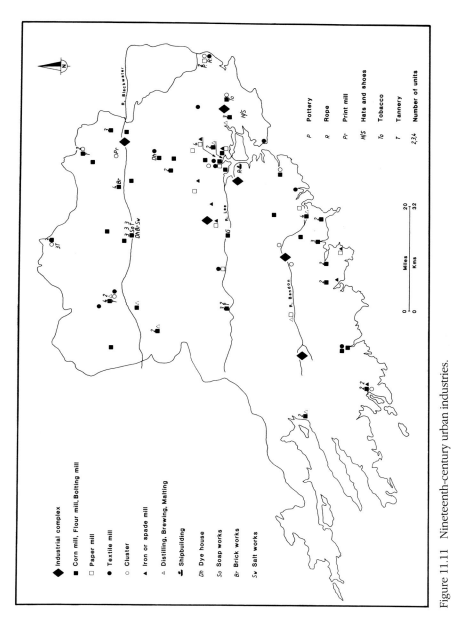

Figure 11.11   Nineteenth-century urban industries.
Sources: Directories; Lewis, *Topog. dict. Ire.*; *Pal gaz.*; Mason, *Survey*; Townsend, *Cork*, Bielenberg, *Cork industry*; Burke, 'Cork'; Dickson, 'Cork region'; O'Flanagan, *Bandon*; Spillar, *Bandon*.

east of Cork city. It included the villages of Brooklodge, Knockraha, New and (old) Glanmire, Poulacurry, Riverstown and Sallybrook and this zone of settlements extended northwards as far as Trantstown. Here were located nearly a dozen paper mills, bleach and cloth mills, corn mills, distilleries, woollen mills, slitting mills and iron-foundries producing agricultural tools. Apart from the greater Blackpool suburb of the city no other area in the county could rival this area in the range and number of units. Curiously this complex was also intensely specialised. Most of the villages were small, few of them ever attracting service functions and the average life-span of the centres totalled to no more than four decades. Often, as one industry failed another appeared almost in a leap-frog-like manner and there are many instances of buildings being refitted to accommodate new functions. By the end of the nineteenth-century the entire industrial complex had floundered; only the odd corn mill struggled on. Mass produced tools and textiles and large scale paper processing all emanating from external sources made the products of these small units uneconomic and gradually the villages shrivelled up apart from settlements such as Glanmire which was resusitated when a new arterial road to Dublin was laid out through it.

Bandon was also the focus of a mainly textile centred industrial complex; in addition milling, brewing and distilling were very significant.[88] With a population of c. 11,000 people in the 1820s and a claim of 14,000 in the decade before that, it was then the eighth largest town in Ireland. Linked to it within a radius of ten miles were a series of textile and grain mill settlements. Old Chapel, also known as Roundhill, was a major textile village located some few miles to the west. It was the residential focus of the magnificent and enormous Overton cotton mill located nearby. By all accounts Bandon had attained its maximum population in the 1820s and even possibly before that. The closure of Overton in 1827 marked the beginning of an extended and painfully long drawn-out period of decline. As at Midleton and in some other centres in the county this phase of industrial growth and urbanization was sponsored by local entre-preneurs whose personal investments and skills were crucial elements underpinning the success of the ventures. Some of Bandons' industrialists sought locations outside the cluttered confines of the town for the modern plants and this movement helped to spawn the mill villages of Derrygarriffe, Lisnegat and Mossgrove. The entire geography of the towns perimeter was refashioned at this time by these processes as was the morphology of its old core.

Finally two other well-known centres deserve special attention namely, Blarney and Douglas. The trajectories of both of these centres share some common threads: both had textiles to the forefront, both depended upon large scale labour intensive production processes and they were located very close to the capital of the region. Huguenot entrepreneurship was responsible for the startling growth of Douglas. Sail-making was replaced by four impressive woollen mills in the early decades of the nineteenth-century and it soon counted a similar tally of some 500 operatives as it had before. Nearby Donnybrook had also become incorporated into the complex in the 1820s. Later on its surroundings were to become a fashionable location for sumptuous suburbanization and the coming of a railway transformed it to become a suburb of the city after the textiles had failed (Fig. 11.12).

Blarney was a far more volatile centre in every respect as a consequence of fluctuations, substitutions and failures of some of its enterprises.[89] Among the county manufacturing centres its demography is unique in the nineteenth-century, when in decline like many other centres from the 1840s to the 1860s, it revived again and managed to sustain several increases in population.

Towns, planned towns and planned villages

By 1841 there were some thirty centres including Cork city recording resident populations of 1,000 plus. Two categories of towns can be recognised; there were those with populations of between 1,000 and 2,000 people in 1841, though few of these centres managed to sustain a population above the threshold of a thousand for more than a few decades. There was also a group of larger centres with populations exceeding 2,000 which formed the upper tier of the urban hierarchy. The evaluation of the populations of the larger centres can be complicated by one or more municipal boundary changes which reduce or inflate decennial population change.

One characteristic shared by all of the smaller towns, that is those with less than 2,000 residents, was their rapid, continuous and sometimes calamitous loss of people after 1840 (Fig. 11.13). Only two centres, namely Ballincollig and Castletownbeare break this form. Fishing stimulated the growth of Castletownbeare and the conglomerate of an East and a West village was fused toghter by the presence of a major munitions facility and military depôt. Most of these settlements failed to attract any significant manufacturing or processing rôles apart from some mills, grain stores and tanneries though some settlements such as Rosscarbery were minor textile centres at the end of the eighteenth-century. In essence they were large market centres whose trading roles had propelled their growth. Better communications and more organized marketing helped to slim significantly the numbers of these centres in the early decades of the nineteenth-century and only

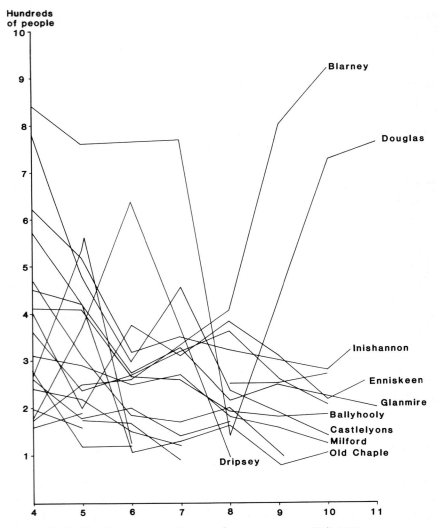

Figure 11.12   Population change in manufacturing centres, 1841-1901.
            Source: Census.

a dozen large towns still retained their weekly market function. In the general hierarchialization of retailing these smaller centres could never compete successfully with the larger towns.

The larger towns were an extremely mixed group in relation to their origins, functions and their social composition in the middle of the nineteenth-century. They ranged from grandiose and spectacularly con-

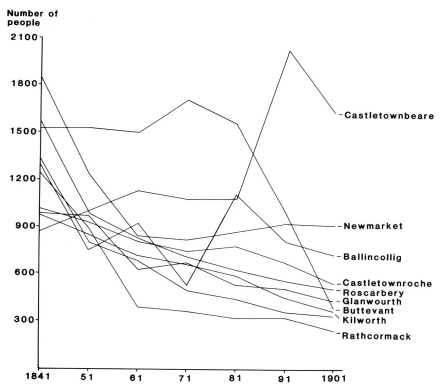

Number of people

Figure 11.13 Small town population change, 1841-1901.
Source: Census.

ceived and executed planned towns such as Fermoy and Mitchelstown to the demographically exceptional settlement of Queenstown later to be called Cobh. Begun in the early decades of the nineteenth-century as three separate developments with the landlord patronage of the Barrymores and the Midleton Brodericks and local entrepreneurial involvement at Rushbrooke its strategic maritime location facilitated its emergence as a transatlantic port of call. Many of the other large towns were considerably modified and/or embellished by their owners or patrons as transpired at Bantry, Clonakilty, Macroom and Mallow. Landlord participation was confined largely to the opening decades of the century before the calamaties and turmoil of subsequent years. Kanturk benefited greatly from the resourceful attentions of its local agent, Tierney,[90] while Skibbereen, with no patron developed along more *laissez faire* lines as exemplified by its circuitous street lines. It was a retailing centre *par execllence*. All of these large towns attracted a varying ensemble of manufacturing, processing, retailing, administrative and service functions. Local entrepreneurship, capital and technical adaptation were responsible for the emergence of industrial complexes at Bandon and Midleton. Anderson, Fermoy's developer also helped to procure milling and other processing facilities to secure the future of his efforts. Apart from acquiring some naval facilities at Kinsale this centre and Youghal were remarkable in as much as they singularly failed to attract the kinds or the range of activities that came to characterise Cork city, Bandon and Midleton. Both developed as classic retail-rentier societies where capital was invested in the apparent security of buildings rather than in higher risk manufacturing ventures. Retailing remained the backbone of urban life and contemporary directories confirm the presence of many professionals in law and medicine in these highly stratified towns.

Buoyant economic conditions and a dense population, could as in the case of Skibberreen without any patron, drive urban growth. Mallow, like Kinsale and Youghal failed to capitalise on the opportunities of its pivotal location for complex and little understood reasons:

> The appearance of the town is ancient and irregular,
> there are some good modern houses in the upper part,
> but the lower consists of mean looking shops; the first
> floor is let as a lodging ...[91]

So wrote Croker in the early 1820s. It was not until the following decade that the town began to be improved, when a new street was built to the north of the main street, the water supply was enhanced, the streets were flagged and footpaths were laid out. Still, in the 1830s, 60 per cent of its thousand odd houses were small thatched residences. Unlike the Bandon valley, Cork city and the Cork Harbour zone, the Blackwater valley experienced more modest urban growth in the years before the great Famine and most of the growth was dissipated amongst a large number of small settlements. Besides milling, industry developed a tenuous foothold in this zone and in this way urban vitality was even more dependant on the fortunes of farming.

The smaller, more modest and less pretentious estate village was a rarity: scarcely more than a half a dozen were built in the county. Each of them was the eccentric creation of a local magnate and amongst the best examples were Cecilstown and Ballyclough both of which were located near Mallow in a zone of elaborate seats and fine country houses. Castletownshend in the west of the county emerged in a similar context, namely a concentration of small but comfortable landed families in what became part of Sommerville and Ross country. Viewed in its perspective of a county which was already well supplied with villages and towns there was little scope for adding more and even less an economic rationale.

Housing in towns and villages

An over-emphasis upon demographic behaviour alone furnishes a false picture in that it suggests a scenario of inexorable and irreversible decline in all aspects of life and lifestyle. In spite of protracted demographic attrition and prolonged bouts of economic decline and stagnation, urban housing gradually improved in the latter half of the nineteenth-century. Both of the above processes facilitated these changes. All of this happened over a period when at least 50 per cent of the county's villages 'disappeared' failing as they did to be recorded as separate enumeration units. Hence the information arrayed on table 11.1 only refers to villages which maintained 100 plus residents or counted more than twenty occupied contiguous houses between 1840 and 1901.

The most telling indicator of poverty was the inflated incidence of class iv houses. The average figure for this class in 1841 for all towns and villages, was 26 percent; by 1861 this figure had fallen a massive 23 percent to only 6 percent and in the ensuing forty years, that is from 1861, it only fell by a further 3 percent. It is indeed tempting to argue that the 'improvement' in housing conditions essentially stemmed from the disappearance of the most marginal elements of urban society, namely the unskilled and propertyless. But as yet we know very little about the origins and the demographies of these people who lived in such miserable conditions. Were they a refugee-like element who moved in to town and village from even more grinding conditions in the surrounding countryside? Or did they constitute a more permanent if highly unstable group in the villages? Recent evidence from some of the larger urban centres in the region confirms that the bulk of these people were immigrants who flooded into these towns shortly after the early 1800's and precipitated explosive urban growth. Natural increase within the settlements alone could not explain such unprecedented growth.

The virtual elimination from the housing stock of class iv houses by 1901 witnessed subtle changes especially in the proportions of class ii and class iii houses. By comparison with 1840, housing conditions in the county's urban centres ranged from poor to quite comfortable in 1901. Still, in 1901 only 10 percent of housing belonged to class i which represents only a 5 per cent rise in this class in over sixty years.

Thousands
of people

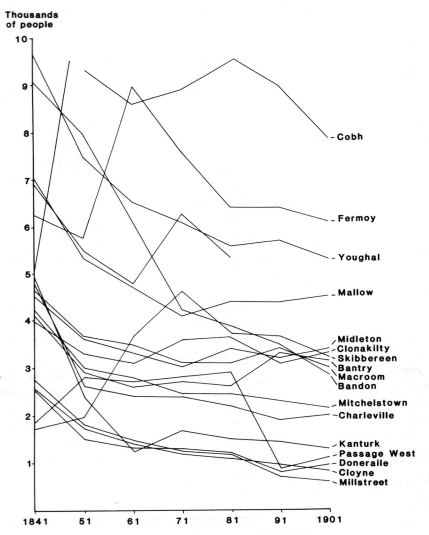

Figure 11.14   Population change in large towns, 1841-1901.
Source: Census.

Few villages had any class i houses and their most valuable buildings belonged to one of the churches or to the state. These kinds of general trends, however, mask important distinctions which characterise the different settlement types. At all times, towns with a population of 1,000 or more indicated profiles which exceed the average in favour of the better types of houses. Between 1841 and 1901, in towns whose population ranged between 1,000 and 2,000, there was almost a 200 per cent increase in the proportions of class i and class ii houses which must have represented the consolidation of affluent trading and professional classes. By 1901, more than two thirds of all residences in these places fell into these better classes.

In the earlier decades of the century, in the smaller settlements it was a very different story. Then, no doubt, reflecting the presence of a greater range of occupational and social groups, there was a more even distribution of housing classes though poorer quality houses tended to be more numerous. Matters even at that time were not as we might have expected them to be. For example, in some clusters in the east of the county such as Ballyhay, Dungourney and Ladysbridge there were up to 40 percent of houses belonging to class ii, reflecting the presence, according to Griffith and local parish records of some strong farmers and wealthy shopkeepers. Is it more than a coincidence that these kinds of clusters owe their ultimate origins to the Anglo-Normans and that they appear to have acted as local manorial and market centres for extended periods and in this way retained their nodal qualities?

Clusters which developed contiguous to larger settlements in the earlier part of the century exhibited some of the most appalling housing conditions: Ballymagooley beside Mallow, for instance, recorded sixty per cent of its dwellings as class iv. Similar deprivation was apparent in those kinds of clusters which had emerged on the edges of marginal land and this was the case in much of the barony of Duhallow: Dromina, Gneeves and Ladyscross are instances of settlements where class iv were so preponderant that this class of housing alone exceeded the combined totals of all the other classes by a factor of two. With few exceptions, Dromina being one, these settlements had very ephemeral lifespans. As a rule, settlements connected with fishing and manufacturing invariably were characterised by very poor housing. The fishing and mining centres of Beara peninsula were notorious in this respect; some of them, such as Caherkeen, Firkeel and Killough had only class iv houses. Moving along the coast in an easterly direction the minute kin-group fishing villages of Carrigilihy, Laherne and Trabolgan shared similar conditions. With good harbours, quays, a port function and overland connections some small ports witnessed the enlargement and enhancement of their housing stock through the growth of recreational activities. In this group of centres were Baltimore, Clonakilty, Rosscarbery, Schull, Timoleague and Crosshaven on Cork Harbour. In many of these settlements the housing profiles radically improved and by 1901 some of them could boast of more than 80 per cent of their houses cate-

Table 11.1
Housing classes, 1841, 1861 and 1901 (per cent)

Settlement types	1841				1861				1901			
	Class				Class				Class			
	i	ii	iii	iv	i	ii	iii	iv	i	iii	iii	iv
Town 1,000+ population	10	45	32	13	13	59	25	3	na	na	na	na
Towns 1,000-2,000 population	5	28	41	26	8	49	41	1	16	60	23	1
Fishing centres	3	21	36	40	6	52	36	6	9	72	18	1
Manufacturing centres												
Clusters	1	15	34	50	0	32	59	9	3	50	43	4
Estate villages	3	54	21	22	5	47	38	10	13	67	18	2
Market centres	3	34	43	20	6	47	38	9	6	59	21	4
Communication centres	1	26	37	36	5	48	41	6	7	61	32	0
Average (per cent)	4	33	37	26	6	46	42	6	9	60	20	3

Source: Censuses, 1841, 1861 and 1900.

gorised as class ii houses or even better; this was 20 per cent higher than the figure for either clusters or for manufacturing centres. Throughout the sixty odd years housing conditions remained comfortable in the planned villages. Most of them began their lives with more than half their total residences in the high quality bracket. Startling improvements in the housing stocks of road generated settlements and market towns were especially noticable. In this way housing profiles indicate a continuous, if modest, improvement in housing conditions in the county's villages and towns, for most of those people who were able to remain residents.

Occupations and society

What made villages different to towns and what made all urban centres different to the countryside? Functions and size were important differentiating criteria and so also was their social composition and their occupational structures. In order to conduct a preliminary investigation of these dimensions of urban life an arbitrary number of settlements was selected. These settlements have been allocated into the classes which have been already devised on the basis of their leading functional activities. Employing this kind of procedure for 1901 data has several drawbacks not least the fact that by 1901 some of these centres at least had lost their earlier functions or at best they had been diminished, by the substitution of other functions. A sequential analysis of trade directories might at first sight, be regarded as a fruitful and copious source to initiate such an analysis, but a preliminary examination yields conflicting results which strongly indicate that their enumerative procedures were unstandardised and in some cases *laissez faire*. Another major difficulty is that most treat only of the larger centres. Women and the unskilled are rarely mentioned and consequently it is not feasible to deal with the entire fabric of society. A brief examination of several directories between 1821 and 1896 indicates that in the early decades of the century tradespeople, especially those involved in leather working were particulary numerous. By the end of the century their numbers had declined substantially and the most numerous group comprised publicans, grocers and shopkeepers. Also, the numbers involved in specialised trades such as bakers and those working in metals had fallen off considerably. By comparison the 1901 manuscript census forms are an excellent source of social detail. They too, unfortunately have ambiguities and difficulties. It is often not possible, for example, to ascertain whether many craftspeople operated retail outlets or even to know how they traded their products. 'Farmer' is also a transparent definition as no evidence is available to indicate the size of their holdings or other crucial details.

Armstrong's classification system for occupational categories may well suit conditions in a much more urbanized and industrialized society, such as England in the last century. To be applied to small Irish urban settlements at the same time, significant modification is called for. Particular problems are evident with his classes iii, iv and v and as in England there is the quandary of farmers which is further accentuated here because no indication is evident on the manuscript census to show either size of farm or holding. Class iii becomes excessively bloated if certain occupations are allocated to it. Dress-makers, factory workers, fishermen, sailors, seamen and shop assistants have been categorised as class iv. All servants and labourers have been included in class v. No distinction has been made between agricultural labourers and other kinds of labourers.

Most of the manufacturing baggage of the county's settlements had long been swept away by 1901.[92] The odd grain mill struggled on but retail, wholesale and marketing activities were the lynchpins of the economies of the urban fabric. Another ubiquitous feature of these centres was that resident farmers were a rarity and this was also true of the few remaining clusters. Apart from the towns, professionals were few and where class ii numbers were more bloated this was usually the consequence of the presence of a convent or a large school. Everywhere, domestic servants and unskilled labourers were the preponderant elements of the active population. Craftspeople were more a feature of the larger settlements but there were clusters of them in some of the smaller centres. In the villages, the grocer-shopkeeper-publican, was the foremost element in class iii.

Variability in occupational structures was a recurrent feature of the county's urban fabric, both between settlements of the same class and settlements of different classes located contiguous to each other; compare for example – Ballinacorra, Carrigtohill, Farsid and Gyleen on the eastern shores of Cork Harbour (Table 11.2). The varying proportions in class v (which included the most unskilled) may in fact indicate critical differences between the settlements. Class v ranged from 13 percent at the small centre of Cullen to 64 percent at Knockraha-Knocknahorgan which was formerly an important member of the Glanmire manufacturing complex on the north eastern outskirts of Cork city. As a general rule the smaller the settlement was, the less differentiated was the occupational structure and the smaller the proportion of the class v category. Settlement types with an above average class v group included small planned villages, road generated centres and the remaining manufacturing centres. The most variable occupational structures were a feature of the clusters and a test of a larger sample of clusters sustained this result. In the market towns and villages more evenly distributed occupation structures were evident. Their general economic buoyancy over an extended period may help to explain this. For different reasons economic decline was a fact of life in the manufacturing centres and the planned villages which in many cases had lost their *raison d'être* by 1901: this may help to explain the low proportions of domestic servants and female employment in general and the inflated incidence of labourers. Glanmire was exceptional here, but it still retained some manufacturing facilities and enjoyed a boom as a consequence of becoming a route centre. Nodally located centres generally recorded high proportions of craftspeople who were allocated to the class iii category. The unstable nature of fishing and the extended process of port hierarchialization may help to explain the high incidence of the unskilled in these kinds of centres. In total contrast were the larger towns where the unskilled were proportionately less frequent. These conditions are not easy to account for as these kinds of centres potentially offered great scope for both employment and welfare for the weaker sections of society. Some of the larger settlements recorded lower proportions of professional people than was the case earlier in the century if we can trust the trade directories. It is clear from this initial examination of occupational

Table 11.2
Occupation structures in 1901 (per cent)

	Class i	Class ii	Class iii	Class iv	Class v
Planned centres					
Ballyclough	2	8	29	10	51
Castletownshend	1	7	21	25	46
Newtownshandrum	0	44	46	3	47
Communications centres					
Carrigtwohill	0	5	31	18	46
Churchtown	2	7	40	11	40
Freemount	0	5	42	12	41
Meelin	0	7	49	7	37
Ports					
Ballinacorra	0	3	23	25	49
Ballycotton	0	4	25	54*	17
Farsid	0	9	31	12	48
Gyleen	0	7	14	20	57
Clusters					
Cullen	0	9	47	31	13
Dromina	0	20	20	4	56
Scartlea	0	5	55	11	29
Manufacturing centres					
Glanmire	4	3	30	33	30
Knockraha	0	0	22	14	64
Milford	0	11	36	7	46
Poulacurry	0	7	43	13	37
Market centres					
Kildorrery	0	4	33	25	38
Liscarroll	0	8	25	23	44
Towns					
Castletownbere	1	6	43	11	39
Castlemartyr	2	2	61	6	29
Cloyne	3	10	38	23	26
Roscarberry	0	12	46	9	34

Source: 1901 MSS Census.

structures that highly localised circumstances exerted formative influences on their chararacter, vitality and potential for development as reflected in the variable occupational profiles.

Between the last quarter of the eighteenth-century and the end of the nineteenth-century town and village life in county Cork and elsewhere in Ireland had been transformed several times (Fig. 11.15). The period began with a phase of unfettered growth never experienced before or since. The subsequent demographic trajectories encapsulate the devastating and painful difficulties which had to be adapted to. Only the larger centres experienced significant morphological additions at the end of the nineteenth-century. Physically the cores of these settlements experienced little modification. The spacious squares and market houses and landlord enhanced main streets still acted as commercial, residential and trading hubs. Industrial dereliction was a feature of some centres that attracted industry later in their careers, while the movement of traditional industry at an early stage from the cores of some settlements such as Bandon saved them from this kind of blight. Entire sectors on the edges of many of the larger centres emerged to service the spiritual and worldly needs of the urban communities. Barrack building was a major growth industry earlier in the century and Fermoy's development is a local testament to its importance. Marketing and retail activity played a fundamental role in the economic transformation of the settlements in the latter half of the nineteenth-century. Bandon boasted of eleven different commodity markets ranging from fish to potatoes. Valuations, tithe surveys, rentals, election registers and trade directories confirm the proliferation of small shops and even of small multiple stores in the larger towns such as Bandon, Kinsale and Youghal. The railway also helped to refashion and extend the build-up of some centres, through the erection of a suite of physical paraphenalia ranging from stations to sidings and goods yards. The railway was a double edged innovation as it improved accessibility but also aided to consolidate and extend the marked penetration of Cork city which was to ultimately subvert the labour intensive but technologically unsophisticated local brewing, distilling and tanning concerns in such centres as Bandon, Clonakilty and Skibbereen.

Demographic decline was the watermark of all of the county's settlements during the latter half of the nineteenth-century, but this process masked considerable improvements in all aspects of living for those who managed to remain. This kind of progress was epitomised in the obliteration of the poorest elements of society and their houses. Public housing schemes, albeit modest, made their appearance at the end of the century in some of the larger towns such as Bandon, Kinsale

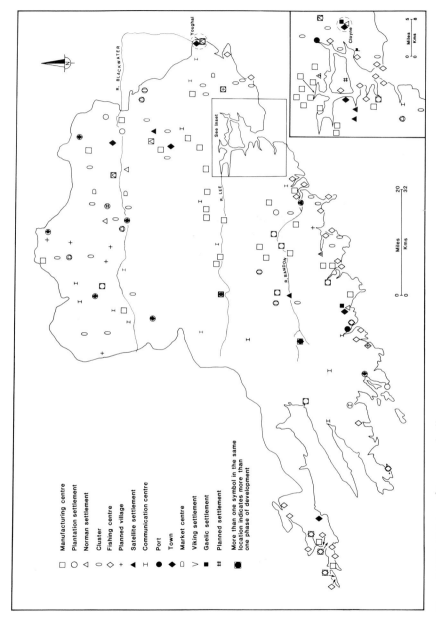

Figure 11.15   Origins of towns and villages.

and Mallow. It was the ultimate of a string of innovations which stretched back into the century and which included better sanitation, mains-water provision, public lighting, metalled streets and in some cases, public parks.

These developments were small compensations for the difficulties experienced by most urban centres. The failure of industry was indiscriminate in its consequences; even the presence of an important Atlantic port could not cushion the multitude of manufacturing centres around and within Cork city. More painful, but not less significant, was the loss of many small scale artesanal and craft activities such as coopering, tanning, leather work and textile production. By the end of the century the preponderant element in county Cork's towns and especially its villages were the unskilled. The gradual disintegration of the estate nexus in the county with its attendant social segmentation and ethnic segregation had also profound consequences especially for the larger settlements. Already in the early years of the nineteenth-century less than half of the county's largest towns – nineteen in all – could claim the involvement of an active land magnate in urban affairs. Even their ability to manipulate electoral affairs was eroded early, but their successors were often so deeply divided as to render constructive implementation of improvements virtually impossible.

The demise of manufacturing activities and the general decline of colonial institutions coupled with the consolidation of a new Catholic, and mainly later on, nationalist trader and professional class had other important repercussions. Some centres with large numbers of Protestant artisans such as Bandon reported their steady migration, which undoubtedly eased what had been sharply defined ethnic boundaries on a street by street basis.

While it is not difficult to isolate the general and particular processes which effectively weakened and undid many of the county's settlements in the latter end of the century, it is not as easy to pinpoint the mix of constructive processes which combined to unleash the county's most distinctive and dramatic phase of urban growth and expansion. We can pinpoint as being crucial in this respect the unrestrained demographic growth, the rôle of individual entrepreneurs as at Fermoy, or landlords as at Mitchelstown. Local entrepreneurship in the main, unleashed a powerful phase of industrial growth. The contribution of roads was often positive too.

It is very difficult to measure accurately the contribution of the Church of Ireland and the Roman Catholic Church to village emergence. The state played a crucial role through the erection and maintenance of many new services, such as schools, police barracks, and health facilities all over the island. The era of church building and the emplacement of these services coincided with substantial growth, rapid urbanization and to a lesser degree buoyant economic conditions. In most cases however, these institutions were grafted onto the existing settlement framework and thereby consolidated it. In some areas, especially in western Ireland, notably in parts of the baronies of Carbery and Muskerry in county Cork, these new institutions scattered almost randomly across the countryside where there were few settlements and where the density of population was low. Most of the sixty odd settlements recently cited as being chapel villages were already active market and fair centres since the late eighteenth-century, long before they had attracted either churches or other institutions.[93] Hence, only a mere handful of centres can be definitely ascribed institutional origins. Churches and state services more often than not did manage to gather around them more than a handful of houses and sometimes a retail outlet or two, but often counted less than a dozen residences. In such circumstances it was unlikely that such minute settlements ever supported village lifestyles. During the nineteenth-century the urban hierarchy at the upper level remained intact but transcendental changes were evident within it.' Cork city was still paramount and being the only centre where a significant concentration of industry remained, its position was further strengthened. Many of the remaining towns and villages continued in a spiral of decline that was not arrested until the 1970's.

Appendix A
Towns and villages in county Cork in 1840

Numbers indicate settlement locations depicted in figure 11.8

1.	Abbeystrand	17.	Ballycotton	31.	Ballynaleague
2.	Aghada Lower	18.	Ballydehob	32.	Ballynoe
3.	Aghada Upper	19.	Ballydonegan	33.	Ballytrooleen
4.	Allihies	20.	Ballyhoolahan	34.	Baltimore
5.	Ardgroom	21.	Ballyhooleen	35.	Bandon
6.	Arundelmills	22.	Ballyhooley	36.	Banteer
7.	Ballinadee	23.	Ballymackeen	37.	Bantry
8.	Ballinascarthy	24.	Ballymacoda	38.	Belgooley
9.	Ballincollig	25.	Ballymagooly	39.	Blarney
10.	Ballincurrig	26.	Ballymakera	40.	Boherboy
11.	Ballineen	27.	Ballynacallagh	41.	Bridesbridge
12.	Ballinhassig	28.	Ballynacarriga	42.	Brooklodge
13.	Ballinroostig		(Kilnamanagh)	43.	Brownsmills
14.	Ballinspittle	29.	Ballynacarriga	44.	Butlerstown
15.	Ballinvarry		(Ballymoney)	45.	Buttevant
16.	Ballyclough	30.	Ballynacorra	46.	Caherheen

47. Carrigaline
48. Carrigaloe
49. Carrigilihy
50. Carrignavar
51. Carrigtwohill
52. Castlelyons
53. Castlemartyr
54. Castlepoint
55. Castletown-Bearhaven
56. Castletownkinneigh
57. Castletownroche
58. Castletownsend
59. Cecilstown
60. Charleville
61. Churchtown
62. Churchtown
63. Clashavodig
64. Clonakilty
65. Clondullane/Ballynafauna
66. Clonmult
67. Cloonmines
68. Cloyne
69. Coachford
70. Cobh
71. Conna
72. Coulagh
73. Courtmacsherry
74. Cove
75. Crookhaven
76. Crookstown
77. Crosshaven
78. Cullen
79. Curraglass
80. Dernagree
81. Dock
82. Doneraile
83. Donnybrook
84. Douglas
85. Dripsey (Lower)
86. Dripsey (Upper)
87. Dromagh
88. Dromahana
89. Dromdaleague
90. Dromina
91. Dunderrow
92. Dungourney
93. Dunmanway
94. Durrus
95. Enniskeen
96. Eyries
97. Farahy
98. Farsid
99. Fermoy
100. Firkeen
101. Freemount
103. Glanmire (New Town)
104. Glanmire
105. Glantane
106. Glanworth
107. Glenville
108. Gneeves
109. Gogginstown
110. Gyleen
111. Halfway House
112. Inchageelagh
113. Inishshannon
114. Island Crossroads
115. Kanturk
116. Kilbrittain
117. Kilcoleman
118. Kildinan
119. Kildorrery
120. Kilkinniken
121. Kilavullen (Killawillan)
122. Killeagh
123. Kilmichael
124. Kiskeam
125. Kilworth
126. Kinsale
127. Knocknagree
128. Knockraha
129. Lachanalocha
130. Ladysbridge
131. Ladyscross
132. Laherne
133. Leap
134. Liscarroll
135. Lisvelane
136. Lisnagat
137. Loughanebeg
138. Macroom
139. Mallow
140. Maulbaun
141. Meelin
142. Meelmore
143. Midleton
144. Milford
145. Millstreet
146. Minane
147. Mitchelstown
148. Monkstown
149. Mossgrove
150. Newcestown
151. Newmarket
152. Newmills
153. Newtown Shandrum
154. Nohoval
155. Oysterhaven
156. Park North
157. Passage West
158. Poulacury
159. Rathcormack
160. Rathcoursey
161. Ringaskiddy
162. Riverstown
163. Rockmills
164. Rosscarbery
165. Roundhill-(Old Chapel)
166. Sallybrook
167. Sallyscross Roads
168. Scartlea
169. Schull
170. Scilly
171. Shanagarry
172. Shanbally
173. Shanballymore
174. Skibereen
175. South Ring
176. Springhill
177. Timoleague
178. Tower
179. Trabolgan
180. Tracton
181. Trantstown
182. Union Hall
183. Walshtown
184. Watergrasshill
185. Whitegate
186. Whitepoint
187. Youghal

References

1. Donnelly, *Land and people.*
2. Butlin, *Town*; O'Connor, *Limerick*; idem,'The maturation of town and village life in county Limerick in *Common ground*, pp 149-172.
3. P. Connell, *Changing forces shaping a nineteenth-century Irish town: a case study of Navan* (Maynooth, 1978); see also P. Flatrès, *Hamlet and village* (Rennes,1966); T. W. Freemon, 'The Irish county town' in *Ir. Geog.,* iii, pt. 1 i (1954), pp 12-13; T. Jones Hughes, 'Village and town in nineteenth-century Ireland' in *Ir. Geog.*, xiv (1981), pp 99-106; R. J. Hunter, 'Ulster plantation towns' in Harkness and O'Dowd, *Town*, pp 55-80; R. Gillespie, 'The small towns of Ulster, 1600-1700' in *Ulster Folklife*, xxxvi (1990), pp 23-31; for a wider perspective see J. Langton and G. Hoppe, *Town and county in the development of early modern Europe,* Historical Geography Research series, xi (London, 1983); B. Roberts, *The making of the English village* (London, 1987).
4. A. Sheehan, 'Irish towns in a period of change' in Brady and Gillespie, *Natives and Newcomers*, pp 93-120; R. Day (ed.), R. Cox, '*Regnum Corcagiense;* or a description of the Kingdom of Cork' ed. R. Day in *Cork Hist. Soc. Jn.*,viii (1902), pp 169-180; S. P. Johnston, (ed.), 'On a manuscript description of the city and county of Cork, *cir.* 1685 written by Sir Richard Cox' in *R.S.A.I. Jn.,* xxiii (1902), pp 351-377.
5. MacCarthy-Morrogh, *Plantation.*
6. K. R. Andrews, N. P. Canny and P. D. Hair (ed.), *The westward enterprise: English activities in Ireland, the Atlantic and the Americas, 1480-1650.* (Liverpool, 1976); D. P. Quinn, 'The Munster plantation: problems and opportunities' in *Cork Hist. Soc. Jn.* lxxi (1966), pp 19-40.
7. Chatsworth House MSS, *Calender of the Lismore manuscripts with an index of matters, A.D. 1396-1774, c.* 1900. Chatsworth House, Derbyshire.
8. P. Robinson, *The plantation of Ulster: British settlement in an Irish landscape, 1600-1670* (Dublin, 1984), p. 151; O'Connor, *Limerick.*
9. Caulfield, *Cork, Kinsale* and *Youghal;* A. F. O'Brien, 'Medieval Youghal: the development of an Irish seaport trading town, *c.* 1200 to *c.* 1500' in *Peritia,* v (1986), pp 346-378; idem, Politics, economy and society: the development of Cork and this Irish south coast region *c.* 1170 to *c.* 1583' in this volume; T. O'Neill, *Merchants and mariners in medieval Ireland* (Dublin, 1987).
10. W. J. Smyth, 'The nature and limitations of the 1659 census', typescript, 1987.
11. E.J. Priestley, 'An early seventeenth-century map of Baltimore' in *Cork Hist. Soc. Jn.,* lxxxix (1984), pp 55-58.
12. O'Connor, *Limerick;* W. J. Smyth, 'Society and settlement in seventeenth-century Ireland: the evidence of the 1659 census' in *Common ground,* pp 55-83; A. Simms and P. Fagan, 'Villages in county Dublin: their origins and inheritance' in *Dublin,* pp 79-119.
13. N.L.I., Lismore papers, MS 6139.
14. MacCarthy Morrogh, *Plantation,* pp 156-57.
15. A. B. Grossart, *The Lismore papers (second series), viz, selections from the private and public (or state) correspondence of Sir Richard Boyle, first and 'great' earl of Cork,* v, (London, 1888), p. 102; O'Flanagan, *Bandon,* p. 4.
16. H.F. Berry, 'The English settlement at Mallow under the Jephsons' in *Cork Hist. Soc. Jn.*, v (1906), pp 1-26.
17. K. Hourihan, 'Town growth in west Cork: Bantry 1600-1960' in *Cork Hist.Soc.Jn.,* lxxxii (1977), pp 83-97.
18. A. Went, 'Sir William Hull's losses in 1641' in *Cork Hist. Soc. Jn.,* ii (1947),

pp 55-68; for later seventeenth century activity see D.W. Ressinger (ed.), *Memoirs of the Reverend Jaques Fontaine, 1658-1728,* Huguenot Society, N.S., ii, (London, 1992). I would like to thank Mr C. J. Murphy of Castletownbere for providing this reference.

19.   Priestley, 'Map of Baltimore', pp 55-58.

20.   A. Went, 'Pilchards in the south of Ireland' in *Cork Hist. Soc. Jn.,* i (1946), pp 137-156.

21.   O'Sullivan, *Econ. hist. Cork city,* pp 83-131.

22.   Caulfield, *Kinsale.*

23.   *Report of the commissioners appointed to inquire into the state of the fairs and markets in Ireland,* xli (1852-53) 1647; P. O'Flanagan, 'Markets and fairs in Ireland 1600-1800: index of economic development and regional growth' in *Journal of Historical Geography,* ii, pt. 4 (1985) pp 364-378; Waterford County Library, Lismore, county Waterford, Lismore deed register.

24.   D. P. Ring, 'The historical geography of Macroom *c.* 1600-1900', unpublished M.A., thesis, U.C.C. (1991).

25.   R. J. Hunter, 'The settler population of an Ulster plantation county' in *Donegal Annual,* x (1971-73), pp 124-54; idem, 'Towns in the Ulster plantation' in *Stud. Hib.,* xi (1971), pp 40-79, Robinson, 'Ulster plantation', pp 172-192; R. Hunter, 'Ulster plantation towns' in Harkness and O'Dowd, *Town,* pp 55-80, and R. Gillespie, 'The origins and development of an Ulster urban network' in *I.H.S.,* xxiv (1984), pp 15-29.

26.   Cullen, *Emergence,* p. 25; O'Flanagan, 'Markets and fairs', pp 367-71, 373-77.

27.   A. R. Orme, 'Segregation as a feature of urban development in medieval and plantation Ireland' in *Geographical Viewpoint,* ii, pt. 3 (1971), pp 193-206; P. O'Flanagan, 'Urban minorities and majorities: Catholics and Protestants in Munster towns *c.* 1659-1850' in *Common Ground,* pp 129-148; M. MacCarthy Morrogh, 'The English presence in early seventeenth century Munster' in Brady and Gillespie, *Natives and newcomers,* pp 171-191.

28.   MacCarthy Morrogh, 'The Munster plantation; 1583-1641', unpublished Ph.D. thesis, University of London (1983), pp 419-420.

29.   MacCarthy Morrogh, 'The English presence', p. 183.

30.   G. Bennett, *The history of Bandon and the principle towns in the West Riding of Co. Cork* (Cork,1869), p. 100; N.L.I. Lismore papers, MS 6142.

31.   MacCarthy Morrogh, *Plantation,* p. 256.

32.   *Pacata Hibernia*, Priestley, 'Map of Baltimore'.

33.   C. Ó Danachair, 'Representations of houses on some Irish maps of 1600' in G. Jenkins (ed.), *Studies in folklife* (London, 1969), pp 91-103; P. Robinson, 'Vernacular housing in Ulster in the seventeenth-century' in *Ulster Folklife,* xxv (1969), pp 91-103; R. Hunter, 'Towns in the Ulster plantation' in *Stud. Hib.,* xi (1971), pp 40-79.

34.   R. Hunter, 'The Ulster plantation in the counties of Armagh and Cavan, 1608-41', unpublished M.Litt., T.C.D. (1969); N.L.I., MS 6139 Lismore papers, which give details of building conventions to be executed by different tenants; Robinson, *The plantation of Ulster.*

35.   O'Flanagan, *Bandon,* pp 3,15.

36.   N. Canny, 'The 1641 depositions as a source for the writing of social history' in this volume.

37.   Gillespie, 'Origins of towns', p. 24; R. Gillespie, 'The small towns of Ulster 1600-1700' in *Ulster folklife,* xxxvi (1990), pp 23-31.

38. Day, *'Regnum Corcagiense'*, pp 169-180; B.L., Add. MS 19832, f. 31, letter from Richard Boyle to Lord Coke, 13 April 1632.

39. H. Pratt, a map of the kingdom of Ireland newly corrected and improved by actual observations (Dublin, 1708). It includes four sheets of maps and two sheets of plans.

40. R. Hausler, 'An upright prospect of Doneraile town drawn for the Right Honourable Lord Visct. Doneraile', copy reproduced in J. Grove White, (ed.), *Historical and topographical notes etc. on Buttevant, Castletownroche, Doneraile, Mallow and places in their vicinity,* ii (Cork, 1905), p. 20.

41. C.A.I., Bernard Scalé, 'A survey of Bandon and the western districts ... in the estate of His Grace the Duke of Devonshire' (1775), microfilm copy.

42. Thomas Sherrard, 'A survey of the estate of Sir John Freke Baronet, in the county of Cork' (Dublin, 1788), a copy of which is in the rectory at Rosscarbery, see folios for Baltimore and Rosscarbery. I would like to thank Rev. G. Townley for his permission to examine the survey.

43. P. S. O'Sullivan, 'Land surveys and the mapping of eighteenth-century Kanturk,' in *Cork Hist. Soc. Jn.*, xcv, 254 (1990), pp 88-106; B.L., Add MS 47,043, Thomas Mollarn, 'A book of maps of the estate of Sir John Percival with reference ... showing the number of acres and the quality of each denomination ... and notes on improvements (1704); B.L., Add. MS 47009 C, John Smith, 'Map of the ploughland of Kanturk' (1723); C.A.I., John Purcell, MS 'A rent-roll and notes on land-use within the manor of Kanturk' (1791).

44. Scalé, 'A survey of Bandon'.

45. Book of leases, Douglas, county Cork 1710-1790, *Anal. Hib*, xv, pp 374-75.

46. D. G. Lockhart, 'Planned village development in Scotland and Ireland, 1700-1850' in T.M. Devine and D. Dickson (ed.), *Ireland and Scotland 1600-1850: parallels and contrasts in economic and social development* (Edinburgh, 1983), pp 132-145 and idem, 'Select documents xxxiii: Dunmanway Co. Cork, 1746-9' in *I.H.S.*, xx (1976), pp 215-218.

47. *I.C.J.*, vii, App. cvii. 1749, Letter from Sir Richard Cox to Thomas Prior.

48. C. Gill, *The rise of the Irish linen industry* (Oxford, 1925), p. 89

49. Taylor and Skinner, *Maps,* pp 167-185.

50. Young, *Tour,* i, p. 142.

51. Ring, 'Historical geography of Macroom', p. 76.

52. Young, *Tour,* i p. 390.

53. J. Percival Maxwell, *County and town under the Georges* (London, 1940), p. 237.

54. Young, *Tour,* i, p. 393

55. T. Crofton Croker, *Researches in the south of Ireland,* (Dublin, 1824), p. 291-92.

56. O'Sullivan, 'Survey of Kanturk', p. 93.

57. P. O'Flanagan, 'Bandon in the eighteenth-century: the view from a terrier and a survey', in *Bandon Hhistorical journal,* v (1989), pp 48-59

58. Scalé, 'Survey of Bandon'.

59. O'Sullivan, 'Survey of Kanturk'.

60. Sherrard, 'Sir Thomas Freke'.

61. E. Bolster, *A history of Mallow,* Cork Historical Guides (Cork, 1971), p. 27.

62. Ring, 'Historical geography of Macroom', p. 92.

63. D. Townshend, 'Notes on the council book of Clonakilty' in *Cork Hist. Soc. Jn.*, iii (1895), p. 47; R. ffolliot, 'Provincial town life in Munster' in *Irish Ancestor,* v (1973), p. 12; L. Clarkson, 'Armagh 1770: portrait of an urban community' in Harkness and O'Dowd, *Town,* pp 81-102.

64. T.Campbell, *A philosophical survey of the South of Ireland* (Dublin, 1977), p. 164

65. B. Scalé, 'Hibernian atlas or general description of the kingdom of Ireland, divided into provinces with its full sub-divisions of counties, baronies, etc. showing their boundaries, extent, soil, produce, content, measure, members of Parliament and number of colonists, also the cities, boroughs, villages, mountains, bogs, lakes, rivers and natural curiosities, together with the great and bye post roads. The whole taken from actual surveys and calculations'.(London, 1798), pp 33-34; Taylor and Skinner, *Maps,* pp 167-185.

66. 'Markets and fairs report..'

67. *I.C.J.,* 'A return of the return of hearth-money paid by the several cities, towns and boroughs, returning members to Parliament', xix (1800), pt.ii, App. p.dccclxi.

68. H. C. Brookfield, 'A microcosm of pre-famine Ireland – the Mallow district' in *Cork Hist. Soc. Jn.,* lvii no. 185 (1952.), pp 7-10.

69. Burke, 'Cork'.

70. Burke, 'Eighteenth-century Cork', p. 209.

71. Census, 1841, p. v-lv.

72. *H.M.S.O.,* Instruction to valuators and surveyors appointed under the 15th and 16th *Vict. Cap.* 63 for the uniform valuations of land and tenements in Ireland, (Dublin, 1853), pp 41-44, esp. p.42.

73. E. A. Currie, 'Settlement changes and their measurement: a case study from county Londonderry, 1833-1906' in Thomas (ed.), *Rural landscapes and communities* (Dublin, 1986), pp 93-119.

74. Burke, 'Cork'.

75. T. Jones Hughes, 'The origin and growth of towns in Ireland' in *University Review,* ii, (1960-1963), pp 8-15; N. Brunicardi, 'Fermoy 1841 to 1890: a local history', (Fermoy, 1978); D.N. Brunicardi,'Fermoy 1791-1840: A local history', (Fermoy, 1976); N.Brunicardi, 'Fermoy 1891-1940', (Fermoy, 1989); D.Vida Henning, 'Mitchelstown and its demesne in the year 1841' in *Ir.Geog.* ii, 3 (1951), pp 106-110 and School of Architecture, *U.C.D.,* Housing Research Unit, Mitchelstown: Heritage Park, (Cork, n.d.); L.M.Cullen *Irish towns and villages,* Dublin 1979.

76. J. Burtchell, County Waterford: society settlement and culture in the nineteenth century, unpublished B.A. dissertation, U.C.D., (n.d.); Simms and Fagan, 'Villages in county Dublin'; R.A. Williams, *The Berehaven copper mines,* British mining, viii, a monograph of the British mining society (Sheffield, 1991). In it there are excellent contemporary descriptions of mining villages and their social context.

77. Burke, 'Cork', p. 124 and J. Deady, 'Population growth in county Cork, 1815-1845, unpublished M.A. thesis, U.C.C., (1974).

78. W.A. Spillar, *Bandon,* pp 72-75.

79. Spillar, *Bandon,* p. 73; Mason, 'Statistical survey', pp 89-93.

80. Spillar, *Bandon,* p. 124.

81. G.D.H. and M. Cole, (ed.) *Rural rides by Wm.Cobbett,* iii, (London,1930), pp 898-899.

82. P. Flatrès, *Geographie rural de quatre countries Celtiques: Ireland, Galles, Cornwall et Man,* (Rennes,1957).

83. P. O'Flanagan, 'Rural change south of the river Bride in counties Cork and Waterford: the surveyors evidence' in *Ir.Geog.* xv (1982) pp 51-79; W. Nolan, 'Patterns of living in county Tipperary, 1750-1850' in Nolan, *Tipperary,* pp 288-324; T.Jones Hughes,'Land holding and settlement in county Tipperary in the nineteenth century' in Nolan, *Tipperary,* pp 339-366 and Simms and Fagan, 'Villages in Dublin county'.

84. Spillar, *Bandon.*

85. O'Flanagan, *Markets and fairs.*

86. Burke, 'Cork', p. 1; Andy Bielenberg, *Cork's industrial revolution 1780-1880: development or decline,* (Cork, 1991) and data from Young, *Tour;* Dickson, Cork region; Donnelly, *Land and people;* Lewis, *Topog. dict. Ire.;* Mason, *survey; Parl. Gaz;* Smith, *Cork;* Spillar, Bandon; Townsend, *Cork.*

87. H. O'Riordan, 'The economic and social development of nineteenth-century Midleton,' unpublished B.A. dissertation, U.C.C., (1982); Cork County Library, P. Ahern, A map of that part of the town of Cove and adjoining lands of the estate of the Rt. Hon. Lord Viscount Middleton (surveyed in 1811).

88. O'Flanagan, *Bandon.*

89. M. Meehan, 'The evolution of Blarney town: a geographical analysis', unpublished M.A. thesis, U.C.C, 1979; anon. Map of Blarney town (1803).

90. O'Sullivan, *Kanturk.*

91. Croker, 'Researches in south', pp 139-141.

92. W.A. Armstrong, The use of information about occupation, in E.A. Wrigley (ed.), *Nineteenth century society: essays in the use of quantative methods for the study of social data,* (Cambridge, 1972), pp 191-310 and P. Ryan, 'A consideration of the social classification of occupations for historical data sources' in *Chimera* (U.C.C.), iv (1989), pp 12-23.

93. P. O'Flanagan, 'Markets and fairs', p. 367; K. Whelan, 'A geography of society and culture in Ireland since 1800', unpublished Ph.D., thesis U.C.D., D. Gillmor, 'An investigation of villages in the republic of Ireland' in *Ir. Geog.,* xxi (1988), pp 57-68.

Plate 11.1   Doneraile village and court (Cork Archaeological Survey).

Chapter 12

THE MAKING OF A CORK JACOBITE

BREANDÁN Ó BUACHALLA

The intersection of literature and politics has been a major focus of public and academic discourse in Ireland in recent years. The canonical text is, of course, Yeats' oft-quoted 'Did words of mine send out/certain men the English shot?' and the responses both to that rhetorical question and the issues raised by it are as various as they are numerous.[1] Though conscious of the debate, I do not intend this essay[2] as a contribution to it, but rather as a more modest exercise: to attempt to correlate a specific literary text to the career of a specific political activist (for whom the text was written) and to delineate the intellectual and socio-cultural milieux which produced both text and activist. It is, in essence, an exercise in what Martines calls 'concatenation' – of relating the 'word' to its 'world'.[3]

The text and its background

The work in question is *Párliament na mBan,* 'The Parliament of Women',[4] which was written in 1697 by Fr Dónall Ó Colmáin as a didactic text for his pupil James Cotter (Séamas Óg Mac Coitir), the eldest son of Sir James Cotter of Ballinsperrig, Carrigtwohill, county Cork.[5] When edited by Professor Brian Ó Cuív in 1952, it was generally thought to be an original work, but scholars have since shown that it is in fact an adaptation from Latin sources. Parts of it were culled from preachers' handbooks, sermons, common-place books and manuals, while the first two sections are, in the main, a translation of one of Erasmus's *Colloquia familiaria.*[6] Erasmus wrote the work as a textbook for the sons of the rich whom he was tutoring – obviously in the tradition of the *speculum principis* – and it continued to be used in schools and by tutors for centuries after. It is not insignificant that it is as a tutor's manual that it also originally functioned in Ireland, the last text of Renaissance origin to be provided in Irish.

A short introduction by the author places the work in a local context and explains its genesis. There were, he writes, 'in the year 1697, in the Kingdom of Ireland thirty two noble, honourable, wise, sensible, prudent, exemplary, well-intentioned ladies' who were wont to communicate with each other and congregate together, particularly when matters 'appertaining to religion, conscience or anything which would promote the common good were being discussed'.[7] Having met in Cork, they decided to summon a parliament and erect an appropriate building in Glanmire on the outskirts of the city. Accordingly the parliament assembled on 10 June 1697 and it was attended by five hundred of the most understanding, wise, fluent, sensible women from all the counties of Ireland. Although the *Párliament* purports to describe the proceedings of this assembly, ostensibly dealing with the position of women in Ireland, it essentially consists of a series of didactic lectures or sermons which are utilised as a means of inculcating certain moral lessons. The dress and fashion of the day are severely criticised as are drunkenness, dancing, thieving, lust, backbiting, anger; prayer and the cardinal virtues are praised and promoted.

Some idea of the tone and contents of the subject-matter is provided by the following chapter headings:

> Lady Elenor's Oration on Prayer ... Elin O Flaherty's Oration on the Seven Capital or Mortal Sins ... Johanna of the Mountain's Oration on Covetousness, Temperate Maria's on Gluttony, Chaste Rose on Lust, Abaigil's on Sloth, Mild Ally's Oration on Anger, Charitable Bridget on Envy ....[8]

Each sermon is brought to a close with a pithy quatrain in *ambrán* ('song') metre which sums up and presents in mnemonic form the lesson of the sermon:

> Is é an raingce do ghríosann cuisleanna an chuirp,
> san ringce so smaointear turrainn gach uilc,
> san ringce so cítear buile 7 bruid,
> 's lé ringce théid mílte go hifrionn dubh.

> In dancing the pulses of the body beat,
> In dancing many an evil thought doth heat,
> in dancing madness we see here and woe,
> And by dancing thousands down to hell do go![9]

The text was obviously a popular one, particularly with Munster scribes, and there is some evidence to suggest that the material was used independently as religious and didactic matter during the eighteenth century; it was also translated into English.[10] Its significance however resides primarily in its original function – as a *speculum principis*[11] – and in the specific socio-cultural context that produced it: the local priest acting as tutor to the son of the local lord.[12]

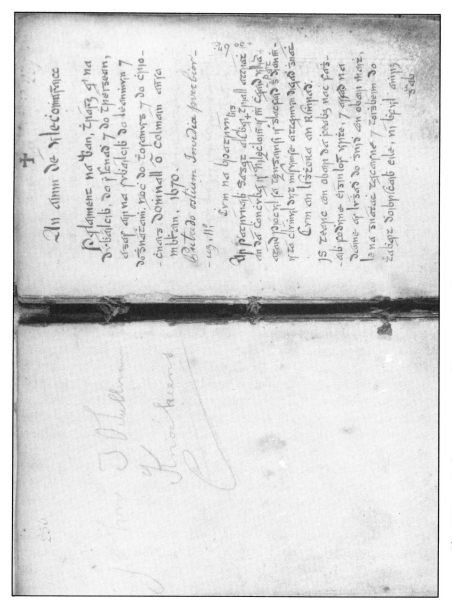

Plate 12.1   *Párliament na mBan* (U.C.C., MS Torna)

Sir James Cotter was one of Ireland's most prominent Royalists who had served the Stuarts diligently and consistently throughout his career and who had been well-rewarded for his services, particularly for his involvement in the killing of the regicide John Lyle.[13] Though he took a prominent part in the 'War of the Two Kings' (1689-91) and was in command of the Jacobite forces in Cork and its environs, he fortunately came within the articles of the Treaty of Limerick and, accordingly, remained in possession of his ancestral lands – a fairly typical repre-sentative of the remnants of the landed indigenous Catholic aristocracy. The Blackwater valley was however unusual in that several other families of the Catholic gentry (Hennessys, Nagles) in the area[14] had also retained their lands, thus rendering it atypical of the general Irish situation: it was, in several respects, an island of Catholic hegemony in a sea of Protestant ascendancy. The cohesion and collective prominence of these Catholic Cork gentry rendered its members both confident and conspicious and subsequently amenable to official attention, particularly since the same area – east Cork – was also the political base of the Whig faction in county Cork. The leading family of that faction were the Cotters' neighbours, the Brodericks of Midleton.[15]

The self-assurance of that Catholic gentry is well reflected in *Párliament na mBan* as are its rich polyglottic culture and its cultivated life-style, albeit one being lived out in the shadow and fear of persecution and dispossession. The fact that the approbations – in prose and verse – accompanying the text were written in Irish and Latin by both priest and layman testifies to the cultural context in which the piece was written;[16] the social context is revealed in the fact that James Cotter Junior was baptized by Dr Creagh, bishop of Cork, and that he had as godparents the same bishop and his maternal grandfather, Lord Louth.[17] *Párliament na mBan* not only reveals the Cotters' links with the clergy, literati and gentry of their time but the circumstances of its composition, cultivation and transmission afford a revealing insight into the socio-cultural nexus of priest/poet/patron which assiduously maintained an intellectual life among the indigenous gentry and which cultivated its aristocratic ethic. The social, cultural and religious lineaments of that ethic are both reflected and promoted in the work; there is also, I believe, a political dimension. This is neither explicit nor overt but is conveyed obliquely, not in the main text but in its encoding framework, particularly in the author's opening address to his pupil and in his closing admonition. In fact the textual evidence suggests that this framework was added later by the author and appended to a text which originally consisted of a collection of sermons.[18]

Ó Colmáin's foreword is addressed specifically to 'the noble youth, my loving pupil, Séamus Óg Mac Coitir' and he opens his address by asking 'if the proverb which we read in French'[19] be true: that it is impossible for any person in the world to make a suitable recompence to Almighty God, to his parents or to his teachers. It would be particularly difficult, he adds, 'for you, my beloved pupil' to give sufficient thanks to God for the innumerable noble qualities He had bestowed on him; to give thanks to his parents, not only for the lands and lordships they had 'in reserve' for him but also because they had joined him 'in consanguinity and affinity' to the nobility of Munster, Ulster, Connacht and Leinster.[20] As for his teachers, it were possible that in time he would realise 'with what assiduity and zeal I have endeavoured that stores of learning, irresistable darts of knowledge and the blaze of morality might be deeply poured into your mind'.[21] He continues:

We see that it is usual with eminent authors and tutors to write the life of some king, knight or noble personage, for regulating, modelling, and directing the conduct of their pupils. I therefore consider it incumbent on me to fix upon a rule for you also. Judicious men are of opinion that no exemplar other than that of your own father is necessary for you, as a mirror and guiding star; that you may imitate his good qualities and heroic achievements and appreciate the estimation in which he was held both at home and abroad by those who knew him. And in order that you may do this with the greater facility, I shall write for your instruction a sketch of his life, both from my own observation and hearsay.

First, if having a graceful person assists us in the discharge of worldly affairs, your father had a chest-strong waist, a bone-strong body, a valiant heart, a strong constitution, a martial countenance, and military perseverance. Moreover, if the good qualities of the soul be a noble gift of God, he had quick discernment, an acute and durable apprehension, sound senses, action to put a projected device in execution, resolution in peril, intrepidity in danger, magnanimity in trouble, ingenuity in defence, and foresight in devising plans. Moreover as everyman is known by his acts, and a tree by its fruit, it is unnecessary to observe that it was not by any sinister means that he acquired the large estates he possessed between the Blackwater and the sea. If it be praiseworthy in the estimation of the world, to merit and obtain the love and esteem of kings and princes, observe what confidence King Charles reposed in his strength, valour and performance when he gave him orders and authority to proceed with a small military force in quest of the traitor Lisle, and to cut him off, an action which Sir James executed with success, as a compensation for and to avenge the death of King Charles. And therefore it is not proper for any man to say or think that it was assassination or wilful murder he committed, in killing a proscribed traitor by the King's special command, but that it is rather to be considered so distinguished an action, that it seems to me and to other learned men, to deserve to be written in chronicles, in characters of gold, as a warning to the regicides of other ages. The King of England was so well pleased with this service, and the performance of it, that he made him a captain of his own lifeguard, and settled a considerable annual pension upon him besides; and afterwards appointed him Governor of the Islands[22] and when Sir James thought proper to return to his native country, the King made him Chief collector of his Rents and Revenues in this part of Munster. It is usual with those who are fortunate in the morning, to be so in the evening. Let us see what love King James had for him, after being with him in seven naval engagements and after being with him in the battle with the Duke of Monmouth, where Sir James behaved himself so gallantly that the King himself invested him with the order of Knighthood, for which also he made him Governor of the City of Cork, and afterwards Brigadier and Commander of all the garrisons in the vicinity thereof, and Sir James was well worthy of all those titles and trusts. For neither the voice of the cuckoo, nor the harmonious music of the harp sounded sweeter in his ears, than the sound of the trumpet, the whistling of harsh-sounding bullets, or the bellowing of the wide-mouthed cannon. The days of Glanworth and Kanturk can bear testimony to this, in which princes, field-officers and many hundred of horse and foot fell by the valour and magnanimity of Sir James.

Notwithstanding these exploits in war, he was not less useful in peace, but as the storms fall and descend heavily on high hills, so it fared with Sir James for no sooner was the whole nation reduced by King William (so that him whom they could not conquer by force of arms, they would compel to surrender by the intricacies of Law) than they at once entered eighteen lawsuits against him,[23] because certain they were if they could either defeat or take him out of the way, that all the other Gentlemen throughout Ireland would fall an easy prey to them. Yet as God is good, and provident in every strait, he endowed Sir James with such an undaunted spirit of wisdom and fortitude, as to oppose them effectually and force them to relinquish their base designs, to their shame and confusion, after much cost and contrariety! For, according to scripture, God humbles the proud and arrogant, and exhalts the humble and kind-hearted.

The service he rendered to the Catholic faith in Ireland[24] was not less conspicuous, for after the death of the Archbishop Brennan, there was no Roman Catholic Bishop in all Ireland, until the arrival of the Rt. Rev. John McSleiyne from beyond the seas. But then the times were so troublesome, the enemy so inveterate and implacable, the Irish themselves so weak and dispirited, that they were afraid of entertaining any Bishop lest some plot or treason might be formed against them. But Sir James was not at all daunted at this, for he hospitably received and entertained this eminent head of the Church more than three years privately and not only the clergy of Munster, but many from the other Provinces of Ireland daily called on and enquired for the Bishop, and held conferences and general councils in the Court of Ballynsperig. If it were not for this protection and asylum afforded by Sir James, it was impossible for this single eminent Prelate to remain in the Kingdom.

I did not here mention the great service he did the Irish Language in bestowing gold and silver to the learned, to performers on stringed and other musical instruments and to eminent poets.[25] The miscellaneous manuscript which can be produced, bears testimony to this, and which was composed for, and to perpetuate the exploits of the forementioned Knight.[26] There is scarcely a page in this book that is not the composition of some eminent scholar or poet, because the Knight was inclined to hand down to posterity the manners and customs of the truly hospitable Irish gentry. Nor is it to be wondered at that he loved learning and the lettered so much, because the more learned a man is, the more he loves the learned. Sir James understood and spoke fluently five or six languages, and that was of great utility to himself in his travels for many years throughout the different nations of Europe. But as St Paul said 'if a man spoke the languages of men and angels, and wanted charity it would avail him nothing'. Let us take a view of his charity and liberality to his friends and acquaintances, to both clergy and laity, but especially to poor Gentlemen who were reduced to want through the expulsion of their friends .....[27] And as this is so, who would not say that Sir James is the best son of his family, the defendor of the clergy, the protector of science, the terror of rebels, the hero of his relatives, the friend of the poor, the guardian of orphans, the honour of his country, and the champion of Princes.

There is for you, son of my heart, a pattern and sample, by which you may draw the lines of your conduct. There is for you the points of your compass by which you may steer your course

through this turbulent sea of the world so directly that you may
practice the virtues and avoid the vices of which this book treats,
that so you may land in safety in the haven of eternal glory which
is the heart and soul's desire and prayer of your ever faithful
servant, Daniel Coleman.

Neither the tone nor contents of that address could be deemed either
overtly political or offensive, yet when one considers that it was written
in the last decade of the seventeenth century for the eldest son of a
prominent Catholic Jacobite, one cannot but sense a subtle sub-text
highlighting certain facts and directing the pupil's attention in a certain
direction. Undoubtedly, parts of the address read like a traditional
bardic eulogy, albeit in prose, but other aspects, when read in the
specific circumstances of time, personages and place, assume a
contemporaneous relevance, however mutely expressed: the 'heroic
achievements' of Sir James Cotter, his 'foresight in devising plans', the
affirmation that it was 'not by any sinister means' that *he* had acquired
his large estates (the obvious implication being that the same could not
be said of others); the confidence 'King Charles reposed in his
strength'; his killing of the regicide John Lisle, which was not only 'to
be considered so distinguished an action', but deserved to be
remembered 'as a warning to the regicides of other ages'; what 'love
King James had for him'; his heroic actions the 'days of Glanworth and
Kanturk'; his 'wisdom and fortitude' in defeating the attempts to dis-
possess him at a time when 'the whole nation' had been 'reduced by
King William'; his inclination 'to hand down to posterity the manners
and customs of the truly hospitable Irish gentry'; and finally the
accolades applied to him: 'the defendor of the clergy ... the terror of
rebels ... the champion of Princes'.

The body of the text – the *Párliament* proper – does not take up or
reinforce any of those cryptic allusions; the moralistic and didactic tone
is maintained throughout as one sermon follows another without any
explicit reference to contemporaneous political concerns, but towards
the end of the work matter not entirely apolitical is again introduced.
Thus in the twenty-ninth sermon,

The truehearted Maria stept forth and said that Justice was the 2nd
cardinal virtue that follows wisdom ... it is justice that keeps the
people together and binds them peaceably in communion and
love with one another. Justice is the peace of the Commonwealth,
the defence of the country, the bond of society, the calm and
stillness of the sea and the fruitfullness of the ground. Justice may
be compared to the river Euphrates because this river when it

overflows its banks, it fertilizes the country round and causes a plentifull harvest. Also the Kingdom that is governed with justice possesses every good both publick and private ....[28]

Let justice be thy chief and constant care
Nor ever think against it to declare
But in your hearts let godly fear abide
And you'll not sin, while you on earth reside.[29]

The word corresponding to 'justice' in the original text – *ceart* – had a much wider semantic range than the translation denotes. It also signified 'rightful (rule)', 'righteous (kingship)' and had connotations of 'legal title', 'just claim' and the like.[30] Inherent in the concept of *ceart* when applied to rule or kingship was the belief that the beneficience of the country and its people depended ultimately on the rightfulness of the ruler which brought about, in Ó Colmáin's words 'the peace of the Commonwealth, the defense of the country, the bond of society, the calm and stillness of the sea and the fruitfullness of the ground'.[31] *Ceart* was a pivotal lexical item and concept in Irish Jacobite rhetoric and it was invoked constantly by the literati, but never as effectively as the potent use made of it by Ó Colmáin's contemporary and fellow Corkman, the poet Donnchadh Caoch Ó Mathúna, in the line *Ós ceart a cheart ina cheart go dtaga go luath.*[32]

There is no formal closure to the session of the parliament. The last speaker merely advises the members to abandon and avoid the vices discussed in the text and to contemplate and follow virtue and good deeds. They are urged to have respect, honour, reverence for the clergy, for the bishops and for the priests and they are especially urged to pray night and day that God may grant 'health of soul and body' to the bishop of Cork and Cloyne, Dr Sleyne.[33] Furthermore they are encouraged to pray 'for the nobles and the lowly across the sea that they might return safely and that none of them might fall into despair'. They should also pray for those of them who are still in this country and especially pray to God to grant 'prosperity, good fortune, grace, blessing, mercy and long life to the protector of the clergy, the most noble prince Sir James (son of Edmond) Cotter:

my affection, my love, my darling, my dear beloved/the prosperous rider of noble ever-spirited steeds/the hero who was not feeble in engaging in dangerous conflicts/and the guardian of the state who was never disloyal to his king ....[34]

The last line *(dá rígh nár chlaon)* could equally be translated 'who never yielded to his king'.[35] One presumes the ambiguity was conscious as either interpretation had obvious political connotations. Being loyal to one's king or submitting to him were no longer mere traditional virtues; for many they had become matters of life and death. It depended, of course, on which king one was loyal to since there was now – throughout the three kingdoms – a dynastic choice. As the English Jacobite Richard Savage expressed it:

> Two kings we have, the one is true
>   The other a pretender;
> To him, so called, is that name due
>   or him we call defender? ...
>
> No longer let us then mistake
>   The king for a pretender,
> Nor the pretender a king make
>   But right to right surrender.[36]

No one could be under any illusions as to the extent and object of Sir James Cotter's loyalty, nor, indeed, to which king his son's allegiance was being carefully nurtured and directed. It was hardly coincidental, one feels, that the auspicious date chosen by the author for the parliament to meet was 10 June – the Pretender's birthday. But even accepting the presence of a sub-text, a political framework encoding a didactic moralistic text, it is impossible now to retrieve its impact or quantify its influence on an impressionable youth. Nor have we any means of ascertaining Ó Colmáin's 'assiduity and zeal' as a teacher, nor his pupil's diligence or receptivity. Nevertheless, we do know that Sir Séamus Óg Mac Coitir, like his father, remained loyal to the Catholic church and patronised Irish learning[37] and that he also took up, on his father's death, the cause of their king – with tragic consequences.

Séamus Óg Mac Coitir

James Cotter was hanged on 7 May 1720 in Cork city. The official indictment was one of abducting and ravishing a member of the local Quaker community (Elizabeth Squibb), but popular opinion at the time and most scholars since have held that his death was, in essence, a political execution:

> It is said that government wrote to Mr. Dixon, collector of Cork about him and got such an account of his great disloyalty etc. that they determined to get rid of him ... It is very commonly said in the County that his political principles were in reality the cause of

this unhappy business having been so warmly taken up by the Government, who were glad to have such a means for humbling and getting rid of him ... He was executed through a conspiracy against him by the Government party, he being a very influential Jacobite, and a Roman Catholic and a most powerful Supporter of the Stuart Family against the House of Brunswick ....[38]

The circumstances connected with this affair and with the young Cotter's trial are very strange, and it is highly likely that the real reason for his execution was political ....[39]

He was executed on what was obviously a trumped up charge on 7 May 1720; his real crime was his Jacobite leanings – indeed he was the most active supporter of the Stuart cause in the south at that time.[40]

In the hope of getting a fair trial, Cotter surrendered himself in July 1719 to the sheriff of county Cork. His case was initially sent to the King's Bench in Dublin but he succeeded in having it transferred back to Cork where the trial took place the following March. The fact that he had been imprisoned throughout that period although bail had been granted, that the trial was postponed for over six months by rather dubious means, and that it was believed that witnesses were being bribed to give false testimony merely fuelled the grounds for suspicion concerning the affair.[41] The local political significance of the trial was highlighted by the fact that the presiding judge was none other than Sir St John Broderick,[42] Cotter's neighbour. That not only exacerbated the sectarian animosity but it also provided a human dimension to the tragedy which was not lost on the purveyors of popular lore:

That Mr. Broderick of Ballyanan was very much against Mr. Cotter, being jealous of him and from his wife having told him when going to the assises to take care to bring Mr. Cotter free ... He often heard it said that Mr. Cotter was in the habit of whipping Broderick at night, on the road between Middleton and Ballyanan and that Broderick having been told by his wife, when he was going to the Cork assises, not to come home without Mr. Cotter, he at once became jealous and did his utmost to have him convicted.[43]

The second Broderick was a Knight, Sir St. John. He died after Sir James Cotter was hanged in 1688 [sic]. He was a man of influence and a friend of Cotter's, but on his leaving home for the trial at

Cork his wife in the same friendly feeling desired him not to retum without saving Cotter. Her words however had a different effect on him. They filled him with jealousy and instead of befriending, he did his utmost in producing his condemnation on the trial. Sir St. John died in a few months after. His wife thereon quitted the house and went to reside in Kilkenny. A Broderick never after inhabited therin.[44]

An abortive rescue added to the public tension[45] and all attempts to have Cotter pardoned came to nothing. Indeed, it was believed by his followers that his pardon had been consciously thwarted by his enemies:

That one of the Barrys of Leamlara went to Dublin to obtain Mr. Cotter's pardon from the Lord Lieutenant, but that the Protestants of Cork were so much against him and hated him so much for his independent spirit and conduct towards themselves that he was executed before the usual time ... and thus the pardon was defeated ... That Mr. Cotter was executed about ¾ of an hour before the appointed time ... Old Mr. Barry had his pardon! Although he rode very fast from Dublin and changed horses several times on his arrival in Cork, the execution had taken place ... That the Protestants of Cork were so much against Mr. Cotter, that he was taken out and executed before the proper time.[46]

Dublin May 7th .... The time of Mr. Cotter's reprive being expir'd this day, and there not being any certainty of his pardon, it is disputable among the lawyers whether the sheriff to whom the warrant of his execution was directed will venture to put it in execution without another sentence ....[47]

An order is gone for Ireland for executing Mr. Cotter next Friday, upon being convicted for ravishig Mrs. Squib the Quaker, all endeavours for his pardon having proved ineffectual.[48]

The execution was particularly gruesome – even for such a barbaric ritual – in that, the gallows having been removed by his supporters, he was hanged 'on a single post at the Gallows Green, by a staple and ring'.[49] Being a nobleman, he was spared the ignominy of being drawn and quartered. After his execution he 'was brought to Ballinsperig to be waked and his funeral was so great, that it extended for two miles'.[50] He was laid to rest on Sunday night, 8 May 1720, in the family tomb at Carrigtwohill, beside the remains of his father:

Here lie interr'd the father and the son,
The former by his blade immortal honour won;
The latter in his life inferior was to none,
Till murdered by a plot as witnesseth this stone.[51]

Whatever the exact circumstances surrounding the alleged crime and the subsequent conviction,[52] the public perception, among the Catholic majority, was that an innocent person – because of his religious and political beliefs – had been hacked down in his prime 'by the Protestants of Cork'.[53] The public uproar was instantaneous and widespread:

All Cork and all the South of Ireland burst into a wail of rage, and the Friends were marked for retribution. Placards covered the walls. Quaker girls were mobbed in the streets of Cork, and threatened with being 'Cottered'. No Quaker could show in the streets. The mayor appealed to the Catholic clergy to restrain the people. The Catholic clergy either would not or could not. The passion spread to Limerick, to Tipperary, and at last over all Catholic Ireland. Quakers' meeting-houses were sacked and burnt. Quakers travelling about the country were waylaid and beaten.[54]

Corke, May 24, 1720
Sir – Since the execution of James Cotter, Esq., there has been so many persons insulted, assaulted, and abused, both in town and county, of Quakers, by others, that I could no longer withhold informing the Government thereof …. at which time said exam-inant and said Mary were followed by a crowd of little boys who cried out to them, viz., 'Two Quakers', and 'Will you be Cottered', and repeated the same words several times. Then a greater company gathered together, which increased at last to the number, as the Examinant believes, of about 200 men, women, and children … and then the mob, in a violent and insulting manner, abused the Quakers, and the said Joan swore that she would tear them to pieces, and that they should not go home alive ….

Examination of J. Leary, going to his lawful business to Loatah (Lota), was assaulted by a servant man, who swore 'his heart's blood was too little for him'. He was stopped by two persons, who assaulted him with a stick and sword, and swore that they would have his life, as he was the person who stopped Mr. Cotter when he had endeavoured to make his escape from the jail at

Cork ... They [the mob] got within the ditches, and not only call abundance of names, and say they will have the blood of thousands of us, but have in several places thrown abundances of stones after some that were travelling the road, especially at Mitchelstown ... I could give abundance more instances, etc. There is great danger of several of our friends being murdered ... and are now so bloodthirsty that they would murder us all if in their power.[55]

In Dublin a Quakers' meeting-house was attacked by a Catholic mob and as a result all Catholic churches were closed, 'excepting that in Cowlane, where its said the Chapple was hung in mourning and prayers offer'd up for the soul of Mr. Cotter'.[56]

The literary reflex of the general horror and outrage at Cotter's execution was no less pervasive. Among the 'placards' which, according to Froude, covered the walls of Cork city were the following specimens in prose and verse calling in no uncertain terms for revenge:

'Vengence belongeth to me; I will repay, saith the Lord.' Now look to it, ye hell-born crew. Cotter's life shall be a sting to your cursed carcases that shall be meat for dogs, and your cursed souls to burning Acheron, where they will burn in flames during eternity. Fenn, look sharp, and other bursengutted dogs besides, the which were instruments of taking Cotter's breath. Other blackguard dogs look sharp.

God save King James the Third, of England king, the whom will soon pay anguish and punish in this matter.

Poor grey-headed Ireland, with bloody tears,
Sharp revenge will seek in her antient years,
For being robbed of her famous peers.

Her drooping fabrics with grief opprest,
Her entombed heroes will take no rest,
Since Irish honour is a common jest ....

Or else old Ireland will resign her breath,
And lose her life by his too sudden death,
For seas of blood will overrun the earth.

Weep, mourn and fight, all you that can,
And die with grief for the unspotted man,
A loss to nations more than I will scan.

If dead by sword, or if in field was slain,
Although the loss was great, 'twould ease the pain,
And to his heirs leave neither spot nor stain.[57]

The female persona of 'poor grey-headed Ireland' was a central and ubiquitous image in Irish political poetry and it may well be that the verses in question were translated, although not very elegantly, from Irish. Whether original verse or a translation, some of its central sentiments are replicated in a series of laments in Irish written by the principal Munster poets of the day.[58] Although executed in the traditional modes, metres and diction of funereal elegy they are at one in proclaiming Cotter's innocence and in asserting that he was murdered by bribery, treachery and perjury:

I dteannta ag bathlachaibh mallaithe i bhfeighil corda/'s a cheann dá ghearradh aige madra feighleora ('entrapped by cursed boors in charge of a rope and his head being truncated by a watch-dog');

ó crochadh an laoch Séamus Mac Coitir le cleas ('Since James the hero was hanged by guile');

do mealladh an laoch le claoine an choiste go dian ... ó tachtadh le héitheach Séamus posta na gcliar ('the hero was betrayed by the deceit of the jury ... since James the prop of the poets was choked by perjury');

a ndóth níor cailleadh gur fealladh ar Shéamas ... ('They did not lose their hope until James was betrayed');

an t-óg nár mheata gur teascadh le héitheach ... ('The youth who was not cowardly until cut down by perjury');

cé gur fealladh le geallúin bhréige é ... ('Though he was betrayed by a false promise');

gur mheall feall na bhfealltach Séamus ... ('Until the treachery of the treacherous deceived James');

coiste na nGall nár mheabhraigh féile / ach breabaireacht fhallsa, feall is éitheach ... ('a jury of English who did not contemplate generosity, but false bribery, treachery and perjury');

Séamus Mac Coitir do crochadh i bhfeill ('James Cotter who was hanged in treachery');

do crochadh anois le munobar lucht fill is tnáith ... ('who was recently hanged by the plotting of the treacherous and envious crew');

dar crochadh flaith na gCoitireach le díoltas námhad ... ('by which the prince of the Cotters was hanged by the revenge of the enemy');

gur mhealladar le hairgead an croí as do chliabh ... ('so that they bribed with money the heart from your side');
arna dhaoradh chum báis / ag claonchoiste an Bhéarla / do léirscrios gort Fáil ... ('after he being condemned to death by a prejudiced English-speaking jury who have destroyed Ireland');
an uair chuala crochta tú in éitheach ('when I heard that you had been hanged in perjury').[59]

To his followers and admirers, James Cotter was a hero who had been murdered, not only for his standing in Catholic society, but also out of revenge and retribution for his political activities. There is, in fact, evidence to indicate that James Coter was indeed politically active, particularly after his father's death in 1705. Some of the evidence is merely suggestive, being anachronistic folklore, but which nevertheless reveals the popular perception of the local hero:

That she has heard her father say Mr Cotter used to hunt a fox with an orange lily fastoned to it, with hounds ornamented with white roses ... Mr. Cotter had the character of being a very disloyal person ... and made himself very obnoxious to the Government of George 1st. There is a very common tradition that his horses had frequently white roses attached to their heads and Orange Lillies to their tales, when drawing his carriage, etc.[60]

The official evidence is more substantive. On the day of his father's death in 1705, James Cotter was whisked away to London, to avoid being raised as a Protestant in Ireland, by 'the chief Papists of that province'. However he returned soon afterwards, married Margaret Mathews from Tipperary (another landed Catholic family) and legally inherited his father's title, lands and residence by circumventing the legal ordinances.[61] From then until his death he took a prominent part in public Catholic political activity, even in the capital, activity which drew on him the attention and retribution of the authorities:

25 July, 1707 ... Your committee have also taken into their consideration the matter ... And your worthy member Mr. Hyde[62] informed the committee, that the said Garret and Edmond Cotter about May was twelve months began to grub up trees, growing in your worthy member's lands, and to enclose the land into some land in their own possession ....

3 October, 1707 ... Ordered, that James Cotter, William Cotter, Dermot Riddane, John Clancy, William Shanaghan, John Carroll,

John Bowdrane, and Nicholas Browne, be all taken into custody of the Serjeant at Arms attending this House, for a breach of privilege by them committed in entring on the possession of Arthur Hyde, Esq. a member of this House ....

16 December, 1713 ... Resolved, that James Cotter Esq., an Irish Papist is guilty of the breach of the privileges of this house, in encouraging the disturbances of the election of citizens for the City of Dublin. Ordered, that the said James Cotter, Esq. be taken into custody of the Serjeant at Arms attending this House ....

16 November, 1715 ... And it further appearing to this House ... that Charles Pitts, John Simpson, James Tooley, Richard Mac-Gwire, James Agar, James Crofts, James Cotter, – Cooke, William Thwaites and Richard Jones, were ordered to be taken into custody the last parliament, for the riots by them committed at the election of Members for the City of Dublin, and that they absconded themselves, so as they could not be taken ....[63]

Mac Coitir's political activism

Grubbing up trees, enclosing land, encouraging disturbances, participating in riots do undoubtedly convey a certain image to twentieth-century susceptibilities and perceptions. It may be that image which has led one scholar to characterise James Cotter as a 'reckless Jacobite' who had openly adopted 'truculent and provocative' attitudes towards Protestants and to associate his character and activities with those of Morty Óg O'Sullivan (killed in 1754) and Arthur O'Leary (killed in 1773).[64] There is, perhaps, a superficial resemblance between the three; and there may be some grounds for such an identification and characterisation in the traditional accounts of James Cotter's public persona:

That he often heard Mr. Cotter used to go into Court with his hat on and with a sword at his side. That he was very active, taking great leaps,[65] etc. and used to drive six horses and two bullocks to his carriage .... That the Protestants hated him, he annoyed them in so many ways ... Both Sir James and his son were great shots. The Protestants were fonder of the father than of the son. The former was much a more sensible and sturdy man. He was very civil to the Protestants whilst his son annoyed them in many ways and was much disliked by the gentry who were much afraid of him ... Mr. Cotter, as well as his father Sir James, used to drive 4 and six horses to his carriage.[66]

> Cotter was hated by the faction of the day in Cork. He was a Catholic. Could not drive horses under his carriage. Used to ride into Cork, his carriage drawn by 4 bullocks. Around their fetlocks orange ribbons to trample. He was a handsome but foolish man. Boasted of favours from wives of many leading citizens and thus being obnoxious, some got hold of the story of the girl of Carnteerna and induced her to prosecute him for rape and robbery of a watch ....[67]

However, folklore characters are essentially prototypical and some of the heroic characteristics attributed to the culture hero may reflect an idealised type rather than historical fact.[68] Furthermore, it is salutory to remind ourselves that subjective evaluative characterisations like 'truculent' and 'provocative' reside ultimately in the eye of the beholder; to the beheld they may constitute nothing more than justifiable pride in one's lineage, an assertion of one's ancestral and legal rights or, perhaps, merely a reaction to the selfsame qualities emanating from others. Indeed, there was much more to James Cotter and his public activities than either truculence or provocation denotes; he was, it seems, a more sophisticated character than the official report suggests.

The 'riot' in Dublin in 1713 in which James Cotter took a leading part was not a mindless exercise in public protest but a conscious effort to influence voters' intentions; in particular an attempt to have Tory members returned. Such pre-election activity was common throughout Ireland and was the only means available to non-voters of influencing the outcome.[69] The context in which the election of 1713 took place was not only of local significance but one which was related to the general political climate of the time in the three kingdoms. James Cotter, it would seem, was not unaware of those circumstances. In an inventory of books belonging to him, drawn up 'at Cotters' Lodge, August 20, 1720' we find:

> An Irish Book handsomely bound,[70] The Hereditary right of the Crown of England, Ware's Antiquities of Ireland, A Diary of the Siege of Limerick, Whole Duty of Man, 50 Reasons why R.C. religion etc., Josephus 3 vols, Two great histories in French, Life of James 2nd, The present state of Great Britain 1718, Memoirs containing the affairs of Scotland, Fitzherbert Natura rerum, Quintus Curtius, Introduction to the principal Kingdoms and States in Europe, States of England in French, Trial of Dr. Sacheverelle, also some French, Classical and Law Books.[71]

The multilingual nature – Irish, French, Latin, English – of the library is in itself revealing as is the subject-matter: law, literature, politics, history, religion. Some of those books may have belonged to James Cotter's father; others, because of their date and/or subject-matter could not. Possessing a library does not in itself automatically allow one to infer a well-read owner, but given, again, the circumstances of time and place some of the volumes in James Cotter's library are of considerable significance: 'Life of James 2nd',[72] 'The present state of Great Britain 1718',[73] 'The Hereditary right of the Crown of England',[74] and particularly, 'Trial of Dr. Sacheverelle'.[75]

Henry Sacheverell[76] was an Oxford don and 'high-flying' Anglican divine who earned a place in political history as a result of a sermon he delivered in St Paul's Cathedral, London, on 5 November 1709, entitled 'The Perils of False Brethren Both in Church and State'. Rather than ignoring the sermon, the authorities decided to make a public example of the colourful preacher. He was accordingly impeached by parliament on the grounds that 'He, the said Henry Sacheverell, in his said sermon preached at St. Paul's doth suggest and maintain that the necessary means us'd to bring about the said happy Revolution, were odious and unjustifiable ... and to impute resistance to the said Revolution is to cast Black and Odious colours upon his late Majesty and the said Revolution'.[77] Sacheverell's impeachment and subsequent trial were matters of major public interest – in Britain and Ireland[78] – particularly as the sermon itself, the protracted trial and the accompanying public riots brought again into the public domain crucial political issues appertaining to the legitimacy of the 'Glorious Revolution', the morality of resistance to the rightful king and the hereditary right of succession. Indeed from then on the question of the succession assumed 'the proportions of a national crisis'.[79] Notions of 'hereditary right', 'legitimacy' and 'morality' would not be unknown concepts to James Cotter nor, most probably, would he be unaware of their contemporaneous implications. To what extent the text of the famous trial buttressed, paralleled or coloured his own inherited attitudes or even influenced his subsequent acitivity is undeterminable and, to a certain extent, irrelevant. Far more significant is the fact that James Cotter had access to and was exposed to material like *The tryall of Dr. Henry Sacheverell* and it suggests that he was indeed interested in and conversant with the political issues of his day. In fact, his subsequent political activities were not entirely unconnected with the sequel to the famous trial.

James Cotter came into his inheritance at a time of extreme tension and polarisation in Irish Protestant politics.[80] The lines between Whigs and Tories were now being sharply drawn and the ensuing conflict convinced Catholics that the Tories favoured a Stuart restoration. In

1709 the moderate Earl of Pembroke was replaced as Lord Lieutenant by Thomas Wharton, 'perhaps the most anti-Catholic governor since Orrery'.[81] He immediately re-introduced and strenuously promoted a lapsed Popery bill designed to close the many loopholes in previous legislation with unprecedented inducements for priest-catchers and discoverers of property illegally held by Catholics; tighter tests for conforming Catholics were proposed and registered priests were to be obliged to take an oath abjuring James III. The opposition of a large body of Irish Tories to new penal legislation and their willingness to mobilise Catholic electoral support gave the Whigs a propaganda ploy which they eventually came to believe themselves: leading Tories were but crypto-Catholics and covert Jacobites. In the aftermath of the Sacheverell fiasco, the Whig government in London was replaced by a largely Tory ministry, a change which precipitated further tension and conflict on the Irish political scene. Wharton, the Whig Viceroy, resigned and was replaced by the Tory Ormond who purged the Dublin administration and judiciary of Whig supporters. Sir Constantine Phipps, an English lawyer who had made his reputation as one of the counsel for Dr Henry Sacheverell, was appointed Lord Chancellor in 1711. Although an Englishman, Phipps had involved himself enthusiastically in Irish politics on the Tory side. As a consequence he was perceived as a hero by the Tories, while to the Whigs he was 'a deep-eyed villian, a secret Jacobite'.[82] His partisan administration but exacerbated a highly volatile situation. The Irish parliament was dissolved in 1713 and the ensuing election was fought in a most bitter and acrimonious atmosphere, one in which the election was presented as a struggle 'between the ideological heirs of king-killers and the friends of popery and the pretender'.[83] Phipps endeavoured to manage a Tory victory by appointing Tory sheriffs and by exerting influence on those who controlled the constituencies to return Tory members. A Tory government, it was generally believed, particularly while Queen Anne reigned, was liable to repudiate the Hanoverian succession and facilitate a Stuart restoration.[84] Accordingly, Catholics supported Tory candidates wherever possible and endeavoured to have them returned.[85] That was the context in which the Dublin riot took place in 1713, the aim of which was to influence the voters and 'encourage' them to return Tory members. James Cotter's leading role in that crucial election of 1713 has already been noted; the other leading instigator, it was claimed, was Thomas Harvey, servant to Sir Constantine Phipps:

> 16 December, 1713 ... Resolved that Thomas Harvey, gentleman, servant to the right honourable Sir Constantine Phipps, Knight, Lord Chancellor of Ireland, was a chief fomenter of, and

instrument in carrying on and putting in execution the riotous
design and force used to obstruct the poll at the Tholsel on the
sixth of November last.[86]

The death of Queen Anne in 1714 and the successful accession of
George I to the crown of the three kingdoms heralded the demise of
the Tories and the establishment of the Whig ascendancy. Sir Alan
Broderick's career blossomed: he was appointed Lord High Chancellor
of Ireland in 1714 and elevated to the peerage as Baron Broderick of
Midleton by George I in 1715; the title Viscount Midleton was conferred
on him in 1717. Tories were purged from public office and a conscious
policy of victimisation of those identified with the Tory cause ensued.
Although it may, perhaps, be an overstatement to claim that James
Cotter was henceforth 'a marked man',[87] he had come to official notice
and reprobation. Moreover his participation in the Dublin election of
1713 was all the more serious and portentous in that he was, after all,
his father's son:

> I shall only observe, that among these great number of Papists,
> and others unqualify'd to vote, it cou'd never yet be made appear,
> that there was any more than one of the latter, and two of the
> former; concerning one of them (whose name was Cotter), Coll.
> S[ou]th[we]ll thought fit to express himself thus, *This is the son of
> Sir James Cotter, famous for nothing but killing the Great Lord
> Lysle.* The reader will please to observe, that this *Great Lord Lysle,*
> was famous for nothing, but being a rebel, and a regicide, and yet
> tis made an aggravation of Cotter's supposed crime that he was
> the son of *him that slew the Traytor.*[88]

Conclusion

In the totality of available documentation appertaining to the career of
James Cotter one central voice is silent – his own. The views of teacher,
friends, detractors, admirers are reflected in contemporary sources, but
not his. His extant letters to his friends and solicitor,[89] written while
awaiting trial, deal primarily with his defence and other pressing
mundane matters. And although they do reveal a highly intelligent,
astute character, well-versed in points of law, they do not, naturally,
afford us any insight into his attitude to contemporary political affairs,
his beliefs, his values. The numerous laments in Irish, being written in
the traditional funereal modes, stress the aristocratic ideals of public
verse: his nobility, his courage, his liberality and so forth.[90] In that
regard an elegy written on his death and published as a broadsheet in
Cork in 1720 is more revealing. No matter how crude an exercise in

versification, it does bear what Erskine-Hill has identified as the main characteristic of the literary idiom of Jacobitism – 'apparently cryptic, yet openly evidence-bearing in historical context':[91]

Elegy

On the Unfortunate, tho' much Lamented Death of James Cotter Esq., who was Executed at Cork on the 7th of May 1720 for Ravishing Elizabeth Squib a Quaker

> And must he silent Dye, and Pitiless fall,
> No muse to Sum up now his Virtues all,
> He who the Poor's Chiefest supporter was,
> Supply'd their Wants, and Maintained their cause,
> Lo! tho' ingratitude's the basest Crime,
> That infects the most, in our Modern Times;
> His Manhood, I hope, no Man will deny,
> Nor dispute his Heroick Magnanimity?
> He ne'er was forward, but in a just cause,
> In which he acquir'd the great Applause;
> Of the Noble, Courageous and the Bold,
> Who does Assert his Virtues manifold?
> Unto all he behav'd himself Civil;
> Untill he met Squib the Quaker ---- l;
> Who's Yeas and Neas, and cunning smiles withall
> Wrought his, and his Families sad Downfall ...
> O! had I power, to withhold that Hand
> That Obey'd that Fatal and Dire Command.
> Who took away Hibernia's Heroe's Life,
> That was the Darling of 's friends and his Wife;
> His unparalleled patience in his Woe,
> And his Resignation did plainly shew
> But who is he, that Fortune can command,
> Or who can the Laws of this Land withstand,
> This is verified in great Cotter's Case,
> Whose Pardon, all his Friends could not Purchase ...

The Epitaph

> Beneath this stone, his body now does rest
> Whose Soul enjoys converse of death,
> Just, Prudent, Pious, everything that's Great
> Lodg'd in his Breast, and form'd the Man complete,
> His Body may consume, his Virtues shall
> Recorded be, till the World's Funeral.[92]

Undoubtedly, the telling phrases *Heroic magnanimity ... a just cause ... Hibernia's hero ...* conveyed in their own day – and thereafter – their own connotations and resonances to an understanding and sympathetic audience. More significant perhaps, are 'his virtues manifold', as ascribed to him by his anonymous laureate. These encompassed neither subersive concepts nor revolutionary principles, but the old traditional orthodox values which sustained Jacobitism and from which it drew its moral superiority – the selfsame values which Séamas Óg Mac Coitir imbibed at his tutor's knee in his father's house.

References

1. See, for instance, M. P. Hederman and R. Kearney (ed.), *The crane bag book of Irish studies (1977-1981),* i (Dublin, 1982), pp 13-89.
2. This article is an extended version of a paper read to the M.Phil. Seminar in Irish Studies in U.C.D., 26 Feb. 1992. I would like to thank those who attended the seminar and who contributed to the discussion.
3. L. Martines, *Society and history in English Renaissance verse* (Oxford, 1985).
4. B. Ó Cuív (ed.), *Párliament na mBan* (Dublin, 1952). Quotations from the text are hereafter referred to as *P.B.,* with line references. For the date of the text, see Ó Cuív, ibid., p. xxviii and below, note 18.
5. For the Cotters see B. Ó Cuív, 'James Cotter, a seventeenth-century agent of the crown' in *R.S.A.I. Jn.,* lxxxix (1959), pp 135-59; W. Hogan and L. Ó Buachalla, 'The letters and papers of James Cotter Junior 1689-1720' in *Cork Hist. Soc. Jn.,* lxviii (1963), pp 66-95; J. C., 'Notes on the Cotter family of Rockforest, Co. Cork' in *Cork Hist. Soc. Jn.,* xiv (1908), pp 1-12; Gibson, *Cork,* ii, pp 166-71, 449-50. Sir James Cotter's (*ob.* 1705) will is in P.R.O.I., Thrift Abstracts 1585: 1A/27/4; there is an account of the Cotter lands in a 'Petition of James Cotter' (19/1/1745-6) in P.R.O., SP 63/409/20 and of the lands in possession of James Cotter (*ob.* 1720) in N.L.I., MS 711, p. 156.
6. P. Ó Súilleabháin, 'Párliament na mBan' in *Catholic Bulletin,* ii (1955), pp 137-43; J. F. Killeen, 'Latin quotations in *Párliament na mBan'* in *Éigse,* xvii (1977), pp 55-60; J. Stewart, 'Párliament na mBan' in *Celtica,* vii (1966), pp 135-41; T. Ó Dúshláine, *'Párliament na mBan'* in *Léachtaí Cholm Cille,* xii (1982), pp 183-98.
7. *P.B.,* lines 240-50. The number thirty-two obviously corresponds to the number of counties in Ireland; see below, note 18. For the 'common good' see below, note 28.
8. T.C.D., MS 1172, p. ii.
9. *P.B.,* lines 1720-4; T.C.D., MS 1172, p. 42. In all probability these verses were composed by Ó Colmáin to whom is also accredited the composition of Irish verse in other sources. See below, note 11.
10. Ó Cuív, *Párliament,* pp ix-xviii, lists forty-two extant copies, not all of which contain the complete text; see p. xxvii; other copies have since come to light, R.I.A., MS 24 P 58, Cambridge University Library, MS Add. 6530; St Patrick's College, Maynooth, MS B 3a, C 87b and, most probably, several other copies existed. Two copies of an English translation survive (but neither of them is complete): T.C.D., MS 1172, pp 1-60; Belfast Public Library, Irish MS 36c.
11. The phrase used by Ó Colmáin, *P.B.,* line 24, is *teagasg flatha,* the Irish equivalent of *speculum principis.* Ó Colmáin also compiled, and perhaps

composed, collections of didactic and moralistic verse for his pupil. See N.L.I., MS 711, pp 181-90; N.L.I., MS G 353, pp 285-90, 294-304 where the verses are ascribed to Ó Colmáin. Other poems are also ascribed to Ó Colmáin in other MSS.

12.   I am not aware that this function of the Catholic clergy has been commented on or studied in modern Irish historiography. It seems to have been a common practise, as it was throughout western Europe.

13.   See Ó Cuív, 'James Cotter', pp 138-47; above, p. 5.

14.   I am grateful to Dr Kevin Whelan for pointing this out to me and for discussing other aspects of this paper with me. For the survival of a Catholic propertied class in eighteenth-century Ireland see K. Whelan, 'The regional impact of Irish Catholicism, 1700-1850' in *Common ground,* pp 252-77; L. Cullen, 'Catholics under the Penal Laws' in *Eighteenth-century Ireland,* i (1986), pp 23-36; G. J. Lyne, 'Dr Demmot Lyne: an Irish Catholic landholder in Cork and Kerry under the Penal Laws' in *Kerry Arch. Soc. Jn.,* ix (1975), pp 45-72.

15.   See D. Hayton, 'Tories and Whigs in county Cork in 1714' in *Cork Hist. Soc. Jn.,* lxxx (1975), pp 84-8. Alan Broderick (1655-1728), first Viscount Midleton, was in turn Solicitor-General, Attorney-General, Chief Justice and Lord Chancellor of Ireland and was one of the principal instigators of the penal laws. His name turns up fairly frequently in contemporary Irish poetry, but not in a very favourable light. According to the poet Piaras Mac Gearailt, Broderick used to knock down old churches and make walls for haggards, stables and orchards of the 'consecrated stones'; see St Patrick's College, Maynooth, MS M 58a, p. 39.

16.   The authors of the approbations were: Dr Donnagh MacCarthy (*c.* 1654-1726), who was consecrated Bishop of Cork and Cloyne in 1712 and was a brother of the Irish poet Diarmaid (mac Seáin Bhuí) Mac Cárthaigh; Fr Conchur Mac Cairteáin (Cornelius MacCurtain, 1658-1737), parish priest of Rathcooney, Cork; Fr Conchúr Ó Briain (Cornelius O'Brien, 1650-1720), parish priest of Castlyons and Irish poet; Uilliam Mac Cairteáin (1668-1724), Irish poet/scribe. For those authors see Ó Cuív, *Párliament,* pp xli-xliv; Ó Conchúir, *Scríobh. Chorc.,* pp 367, 368, 371.

17.   'James Cotter, eldest son of Sir James Cotter Knight, was born at Ballinsperig on Sunday the 14th day of August 1689, at 3 in the morning being St. Dominick's day and was christened the Thursday following by the Lord Bishop of Cork, Pierce Creagh who also was Godfather with the Lord Louth'; see N.L.I., MS 711, p. 127.

18.   See Ó Cuív, *Párliament,* pp xxiii-xxviii, particularly p. xxviii: 'We thus have ... hypothetical first edition composed in 1670, perhaps containing the didactic material only ... New Edition ... composed in 1697 in which previous edition was made topical by the addition of the later material ... including the preface to James Cotter ....' It is highly significant, as noted by Ó Cuív (p. xxvii, note 1), that though the final sermon is the thirty-third in the text, the number of women who originally met to contribute to the discussion is given (*P.B.,* line 241) as thirty-two.

19.   Ó Cuív, *Párliament,* p. 133, draws attention to the proverb *A Dieu, père, maître et patrie/Le semblable ne se rend mie.*

20.   The Cotters were related to the Butlers, the FitzGeralds, the Plunketts and, through the Mathews, to the Nagles, Ryans and several other prominent Catholic families; see Ó Cuív, *Párliament,* p. 133; idem, 'James Cotter', p. 137; *Cork Hist. Soc. Jn.,* lxviii (1963), p. 84.

21.   This translation of the address is taken from N.L.I., MS 711, pp 67-71. It captures

the tone and style of the original although in some passages it tends to paraphrase rather than translate.

22. Sir James Cotter spent a period in the Leeward Islands, West Indies and was Governor of Montserrat; see Ó Cuív, 'James Cotter', pp 150-51.

23. This claim has not been confirmed. Compare 'He was guaranteed his lands under the Treaty of Limerick but would have lost them were it not for the intervention of his powerful Protestant friends, especially, Sir Richard Cox'; see *Cork Hist. Soc. Jn.*, lxviii (1963), p. 67.

24. The original text reads *do chuir sé ar an náisiún Éirionnach* (*P.B.*, line 110), literally 'he rendered to the Irish nation'.

25. For Sir James Cotter's patronage of Irish learning see Ó Conchúir, *Scríobh. Chorc.*, pp 212-5; Ó Cuív, *Párliament*, p. 134.

26. This manuscript is now unfortunately lost; see below, note 70.

27. Ó Colmáin here relates a story of Cotter's unbounded charity to a French officer in the recent war.

28. The original text reads (*P.B.*, lines 2069-70) *sealbhann sí gach aontsórd maithios puiblíghe*, 'it possesses every kind of common good'. *Maitheas poiblí*, 'common good', was one of the new politico-religious concepts introduced into Irish discourse in the seventeenth century by the agents of the Counter-Reformation.

29. Translation taken from T.C.D., MS 1172, p. 52. It corresponds to *P.B.*, lines 2055-93.

30. The etymon *ceart* functions as both noun and adjective in Irish. See *D.I.L.*, s.v. *cert*, N. Ó Dónaill (ed.), *Foclóir Gaeilge/Béarla* (Dublin, 1977), s.v. *ceart*.

31. Compare the following exposition of righteous rule from an eighth-century Irish *speculum principis:* 'It is through the justice of the ruler that plagues and great lightnings are kept from the people ... that he secures peace, tranquillity, joy, ease and comfort ... that abundances of great tree-fruit of the great wood are tasted ... that milk-yields of great cattle are maintained ... that there is abundance of every high, tall corn ... that abundance of fish swim in streams ...' in F. Kelly (ed.), *Audacht Morainn* (Dublin, 1976), p. 7.

32. Literally 'since his right (claim) is right (lawful), to his right (entitlement, patrimony) may he come soon' in a poem written in 'praise of the Earl of Mar when the Pretender came to Scotland *anno* 1715' in R.I.A., MS 24 A 6, p. 367; see R. Ó Foghludha (ed.), *Carn Tighearnaigh* (Baile Átha Cliath, 1938), p. 29.

33. For this prelate's career and particularly his patronage of Irish learning see Ó Cuív, *Párliament*, pp xxxvii, 134, 144, 151; Ó Conchuir, *Scríobh. Chorc.*, pp 216-18. Dr Sleyne was imprisoned in Cork between 1698 and 1703 and then banished to Portugal where he died in 1712.

34. *P.B.*, lines 2078-86.

35. Another variant reading, *dá rí nach claon* in R.l.A., MS 23 B 38, p. 152, 'who is not disloyal to his King', renders the line even more political and suggests that *claon is* to be taken as an adjective, not a verb.

36. C. Tracy (ed.), *The poetical works of Richard Savage* (Cambridge, 1962), p. 17.

37. See, in particular, Ó Conchuir, *Scríobh. Chorc.*, p. 215; Ó Cuív, *Párliament*, pp xxviii-ix. In 1709 the scribe Conchúr Ó Corbáin transcribed a copy of Keating's *Foras Feasa ar Éirinn* now in Cambridge University Library, MS Add. 4181 for *An seabhac uasal Seamus Óg Mac Coitir*, 'The noble hawk ....

38. N.L.I., MS 711, pp 138, 154, 159.

39. Ó Cuív, 'James Cotter', p. 159.

40. Hogan and Ó Buachalla, 'The letters and papers', p. 66. While Professor L. Cullen, *Emergence*, p. 199, states that 'Cotter had probably ravished the

Quakeress Miss Squibb', he also admits that Cotter 'was executed in 1720 in reality for his political sentiments, but ostensibly for what seems the distinctly modern crime of raping his own mistress'; see *Eighteenth-century Ireland,* i (1986) p. 32.

41. N.L.I., MS 711, pp 145-53; *Cork Hist. Soc. Jn.,* lxviii (1963), pp 79, 82-90. See, for instance, 'I [Cotter] believe I shall be able to prove that indirect means were taken to procure examination against me' in N.L.I., MS 711, p. 139. 'From these letters it appears that some Quakers ... were very active aginst Mr. Cotter and that money was to be had and was applied to forward the prosecution' in ibid., p. 142. See also below, note 59.

42. Sir Alan Brodrick's eldest son (*ob.* 1728). As Sir Alan also died in 1728, the title Viscount Midleton passed to his second son Alan who, it is claimed, 'had different political views to his father and brother; he was a Tory and leader of a group of High Churchmen called "The Cork Squadron"'; see *Cork Hist. Soc. Jn.,* lxviii (1963), p. 91, note 36. According to James Cotter, he was befriended, while awaiting execution, by 'Mr Broderick', but he does not specify which one. See N.L.I., MS 711, p. 154; *Cork Hist. Soc. Jn.,* lxviii (1963), p. 91; below, note 44.

43. N.L.I., MS 711, pp 5-6. Similar anecdotes were prevalent throughout east Cork. See N.L.I., MS 711, pp 6, 8, 154; R.I.A., MS 12 I 3, pp 116, 118, 125. Compare 'That the people of Carrigtowhil and its neighbourhood, when they hear a noise at an unreasonable hour at night, are in the habit of saying that it is Cotter whipping or flogging Broderick and many assert that they have seen it on the public road' in N.L.I., MS 711, p. 5; 'But Broderick ... had been goaded into jealousy by his wife ... following him and admonishing him to bring back Sir James Cotter to dinner with him that evening' in R.I.A., MS 12 I 3, p. 118.

44. R.I.A., MS 12 I 3, p. 125. Compare 'That the Middleton family being afraid, in consequence of Mr. Cotter's popularity etc. left Ballyanan and have resided in England'; see N.L.I., MS 711, p. 8.

45. Several different versions of the rescue bid have come down, for instance N.L.I., MS 711, pp 5, 7, 138; *R.S.A.I. Jn.,* xxxiv (1904), p. 66. According to one version, the poet Liam Rua Mac Coitir 'exchanged dresses with him'; see N.L.I., MS 711, p. 5. According to another 'the younger daughter of the jailor' helped him; had he escaped 'at least 300 persons would have been in readiness to protect him'; see ibid., p. 7. See also F. J. Froude, *The English in Ireland,* i (London, 1881) p. 432.

46. N.L.I., MS 711, pp 5, 14, 425.

47. *Whalley's News-Letter,* 7 May 1720. Cotter's trial was postponed from August 1719 until the following year and on the 17 Mar. 1720 he was found guilty and sentenced to death. A reprieve of six weeks was granted but all efforts to have the reprieve extended failed.

48. *The Dublin Courant,* 9 May 1720.

49. T. A. Lunham, 'Some historical notices of Cork in the seventeenth and eighteenth centuries' in *R.S.A.I. Jn.,* xxxiv (1904), p. 66.

50. N.L.I., MS 711, p. 7. See 'Tradition says that he had an *immense* funeral' in ibid., p. 138.

51. N.L.I., MS G 353, p. 284; R.I.A., MS 23 E 12, p. 319; MS A IV 2, p. 58b. For another lament in English, *Here lies brave James in an open pasture dead,* see N.L.I., MS G 346. p. 26; for laments in Irish see below, note 59. The tombstone which once marked the Cotters' vault has since disappeared. It was apparently moved more than twenty years ago to facilitate an extension to the local Church of Ireland community hall.

52. According to James Cotter, Elizabeth Squibb 'among her friends in Cork, denied it'; see N.L.I., MS 711, p. 138, and according to a witness at the trial 'he heard on the road from the woman herself that no such thing had happened' in ibid., p. 154. See *Cork Hist. Soc. Jn.,* lxviii (1963), pp 73, 90. But popular tradition does record some encounter between them: 'He gave E. Squibb a watch, but took it away from her again, as it belonged to his wife and he did not wish to go home without it. He gave her however 15 guineas instead but she not being satisfied prosecuted him, having been strongly urged to do so by the Protestants'; see N.L.I., MS 711, p. 7; 'the legendary or more properly traditional story is that Cotter met at foot of Cairn Thierna a lady of great attractions who had been previously a kept mistress with whom he had intercourse having first given her what money he had together with his watch. On leaving her however he told her he did not wish to leave the watch but would shortly give her the value of it and took it from her partly by force'; see R.I.A., MS 12 I 3, p. 116). However, the charge, it is stated 'was deemed by himself and others a very frivolous one'; see ibid., p. 118. It was also recorded, in popular lore, 'that Mr. and Mrs. Cotter did not live happily together'; see N.L.I., MS 711, p. 14, and in a letter Margaret Cotter (his wife) states 'and because it was a general report that Mr. Cotter made a bad husband to me, I am brought in to have a hand in the plot against his life'; see ibid., p. 157.

53. Ibid., p. 415; see above, note 46. Compare *Marbhna Sir Séarnus Mac Coitir noch do crochadh le Gallaibh,* 'The elegy on Sir James Cotter who was hanged by the English', in N.L.I., MS G 101, p. 54.

54. Froude, *The English in Ireland,* i, pp 432-3. Compare 'It was easily the most traumatic political event of the first half of the century in Ireland, having no parallel in the rest of Ireland and providing in recollection on both sides the spark which set alight the sectarian tensions in Munster in the early 1760s', Cullen, *Emergence,* pp 199-200.

55. *Cork Hist. Soc. Jn.,* x (1904), pp 107-9.

56. *Whalley's News-Letter,* 19 May 1720.

57. Froude, *The English in Ireland,* i, p. 433.

58. These elegies are ascribed to Seán Clárach Mac Dónaill, Liam Rua Mac Coitir, Éamonn de Bhál, Piaras Mac Gearailt, Uilliam Mac Cairteáin. See, in particular, N.L.I., MS 711, pp 171-81; N.L.I., MS G 353, pp 249-84 ;R.I.A., MS A IV 2, pp 53-8; MS 23 E 12, pp 314-20 and below, note 59.

59. R.I.A., MS A IV 2, p. 55; P. Ua Duinnín (ed.), *Amhráin Sheagháin Chláraigh Mhic Dhomhnaill* (Dublin, 1902), pp 27-28; R. Ó Foghludha (ed.), *Cois na Cora: Liam Ruadh Mac Coitir agus a shaothar fileata* (Baile Átha Cliath, 1937), pp 30, 32, 33; R.I.A., MS 23 B 38, p. 49; R. Ó Foghludha (ed.), *Cois Caoin-Reathaighe .i. filidheacht Éamuinn de bhFál ó Dhún Guairne* (Baile Átha Cliath, 1946), pp 53, 54, 55; St Patrick's College, Maynooth, MS M 9, p. 343.

60. N.L.I., MS 711, pp 14, 137. The orange lily was not identified with Orangeism, however, until the end of the eighteenth century. Compare 'It was the newly formed Orange societies of the late 1790s who revived the practice of marching round William's statue in Dublin to celebrate his birthday and the anniversary of the Boyne. For these events the statue was painted white, the figure being decorated with orange lilies and adorned with a flaming cloak and sash, while the horse was trimmed with orange streamers, a bunch of green and white ribbons being placed beneath its upraised feet, to symbolise the crushing of the Jacobites'; see B. Loftus, *Mirrors: William III and Mother Ireland* (Dundrum, 1990), p. 28.

61. *Commons' jn. Ire.,* iii, p. 444; 'I must likewise observe that the Papists, by this alteration of the guardian, have not only the advantage of confirming the infants in the Popish religion; but have likewise prevented their sham settlement from being called in question in a court of equity'; see ibid., p. 445.

62. Arthur Hyde was M.P. for Tralee but the actual circumstances of the alleged offence are not recorded. Garret and Edmord Cotter were most probably relatives of James.

63. *Commons' jn. Ire.,* iii, pp 395, 476, 982; iv, p. 23.

64. Cullen, *Emergence,* pp 33, 199, 212.

65. Compare 'That Sir James Cotter Kt., was so very active a man that he took the famous leap, called 'Lame na Haiffey ...'; see N.L.I., MS 711, p. 6.

66. N.L.I., MS 711, pp 6-7. Compare above, notes 43-4.

67. R.I.A., MS 12 I 3. p. 116. Compare above, note 60.

68. The traditional accounts of Arthur O'Leary's and James Cotter's public behaviour are undoubtedly alike. In similar informal laments composed on their deaths, both of them wear a *claíomh cinn airgid,* 'a silver-headed sword'. See S. Ó Tuama (ed.), *Caoineadh Airt Uí Laoghaire* (Baile Átha Cliath, 1961), p. 34, line 23; *The Irish Press,* 27 Apr. 1936; R. Bromwich, 'The keen for Art O'Leary' in *Éigse,* v (1948), pp 236-52. Compare 'Suspicions should be aroused as soon as characters conform to ideal types'; see J. Vansina, *Oral tradition as history* (London, 1988), p. 107.

69. 'But there is one contested election deserves our peculiar notice ... and that is the election of the City of Dublin ... They call a disturbance that happened at the Tholsel on the Sixth of November last, about taking the poll a *riot,* before they so much as saw any examination relating to it ... scuffles of that kind were usual at elections'; see *A long history of a short session of a certain parliament in a certain kingdom* (Dublin, 1714), pp 25-6; 'Both sides in fact indulged in fairly crude electoral malpractise ... Dublin was not alone in having a violent riot during polling'; see D. Dickson, *New foundations: Ireland 1660-1800* (Dublin, 1987), p. 59; 'It was by no means uncommon for non-voters to participate in elections with the purpose of exercising pre-ballot influence on the voters'; see Cullen, *Emergence,* p. 198.

70. This is, most probably, the Irish manuscript referred to by Ó Colmáin, above, note 26, and now lost.

71. N.L.I., MS 711, p. 156.

72. Most probably D. Jones, *The life of James II, late King of England* (London, 1703); or, perhaps, *An impartial account of the life and actions of James the Second ...* (Dublin, 1701).

73. Most probably G. Miege, *The present state of Great Britain and Ireland ...* (London, 1718).

74. Most probably G. Harbin, *The hereditary right of the crown of England asserted* (London, 1713).

75. *The tryall of Dr. Henry Sacheverell, before the house of peers, for high crimes and misdemeanors ...* (London, 1710).

76. For Sacheverell and his trial see G. Holmes, *The trial of Dr. Sacheverell* (London, 1973); idem, 'The Sacheverell riots: the crowd and the church in early eighteenth-century London' in *Past and Present,* lxxii (1976), pp SS-85; G. V. Bennett, *The Tory crisis in church and state, 1688-1730* (Oxford, 1975), pp 98-118; J. P. Kenyon, *Revolution principles* (Cambridge, 1977), pp 128-46.

77. *The tryall,* p. 3.

78. For reports of the trial in Dublin newspapers see *Dublin Intelligence,* 4 Mar.,

14 Mar., 21 Mar. 1710; 1 Apr., 4 Apr. 1710. Compare 'We have the following account from Cork. That by order of our Mayor, a sermon preach'd by Mr. Tilly of Oxford ... was publickly burnt before the exchange and the cryer had orders to say that if there was any of Sacheverell's friends by, let 'em take the book out of the fire', *The Flying-Post,* 4 Aug. 1710. The significance of the trial is discussed by an anonymous Jacobite pamphleteer in N.L.I., MS 477, pp 1401-8.

79. Bennett, *Tory crisis,* p. 137.

80. J. G. Simms, 'The establishment of Protestant ascendancy, 1691-1714' in *New hist. Ire.,* iv, pp 1-30; Dickson, *New foundations,* pp 59-63; R. E. Burns, *Irish parliamentary politics in the eighteenth century,* i (Washington, D.C., 1989), pp 21-8.

81. Dickson, *New foundations,* p. 57. It was claimed of Wharton that, as Lord Lieutenant, he had achieved more 'towards rooting out Popery in three months than any of his predecessors in three years'; see *D.N.B.,* s.n.

82. Hayton, 'Tories and Whigs', p. 84. Compare 'In 1711, when the Tory ministers came into power, the Pretender's chances seemed again favourable. Rumours of a Stuart restoration were flying fast and thick in the Irish air'; see Froude, *English in Ireland,* i, p. 408.

83. Burns, *Irish parliamentary politics,* p. 27.

84. Compare 'It seems possible that ... Anne led the Stuart court at St Germain to believe that James ... would be restored in due course if her own accession after William's death were not threatened' in J. C. D. Clark, *English society 1688-1832* (Cambridge, 1985), p. 130. See also B. Lenman, *The Jacobite risings in Britain 1689-1746* (London, 1980), p. 112; E. Gregg, 'Was Queen Anne a Jacobite?' in *History,* lvii, no. 192 (October, 1972), pp 358-75.

85. 'The strong Tory showing ... suggests a positive correlation between Tory success and the relative survival of Catholic voters'; see Dickson, *New foundations,* p. 59; 'Catholics took a close interest in the elections, and there were complaints of the ways in which they helped the Tory candidates'; see Simms, 'Protestant ascendancy', p. 29.

86. *Commons' jn. Ire.,* iii, p. 982.

87. *Cork Hist. Soc. Jn.,* lxviii (1963) p. 69.

88. *A long history,* p. 41.

89. N.L.I., MS 711, pp 135-53; *Cork Hist. Soc. Jn.,* lxviii (1963) pp 71-95; his lawyer was Richard Burke, father of Edmund Burke.

90. Nevertheless they do carry a potent political message. See above, note 59.

91. H. Erskine-Hill, 'Literature and the Jacobite cause' in *Modern language studies,* ix, no. 3 (Fall, 1979), p. 18.

92. The only extant copy of this broadsheet is preserved inside the front cover of an Irish manuscript written by Tadhg Ó Neachtain, the Dublin scribe; see St Patrick's College, Maynooth, MS B 9. The text is faded at the edges and illegible in places and some of the readings are accordingly tentative. I am grateful to Professor Pádraig Ó Fiannachta for help in transcribing the text. Pasted to the back cover of the same manuscript is another broadsheet but as there is no title it is difficult to ascertain whether it also deals with Cotter's death or not. Some of the lines are indeed apposite: 'Firm to Religion, Truth and Loyalty/Knowing fulwell our Common Enemy'. For Ó Neachtain and his Jacobitism see B. Ó Buachalla, 'Seacaibíteachas Thaidhg Uí Neachtain' in *Studia Hibernica,* xxvi (1991-92), pp 31-64.

Plate 12.2   Blackwater Valley at Fermoy (Cambridge University Collection of air photographs).

Chapter 13

AN IRISH SCHOLAR ABROAD: BISHOP JOHN O'BRIEN OF CLOYNE AND THE MACPHERSON CONTROVERSY

DIARMAID Ó CATHÁIN

John O'Brien, bishop of Cloyne and Ross, 1748-69, has been identified as the author of a lengthy article or *Mémoire* which appeared in a French learned journal in 1764. This *Mémoire* was a contribution to a literary controversy then beginning, which would continue to engage the interest of the literati of Europe for a long time to come. In this work, O'Brien revealed himself as an able literary controversialist, a man of formidable erudition, and an urbane scholar with an extensive knowledge of Ireland's culture and history. The *Mémoire* has earned its own footnote in both French and German literary history and is deserving of more attention from the fellow-countrymen of the author than it has hitherto received as an instructive example of the culture and interests of an Irish intellectual of the time.

John O'Brien and his background

It may be appropriate, first, to present some account of O'Brien and his literary *milieu* in Ireland as revealed by the research of two contemporary Cork scholars, Dr Breandán Ó Conchúir and Fr James Coombes.[1] John O'Brien, or Seán mac Thomáis Ó Briain as he was known in Irish, was born at Ballyvaddy (Béal Átha an Mhadaidh), near Glanworth, county Cork, in 1701. Sometime after 1720 he went to France to study for the priesthood. He attended at the University of Toulouse and the Sorbonne in Paris, graduating as licenciate in theology and doctor in civil and canon law. Having been ordained sometime before 1727, he went in 1733 to Spain as a tutor to the son of the Connock family, an important expatriate Irish family. He was subsequently retained by other noble families in a similar capacity, travelling with them on the continent. In 1737 he was appointed tutor to the son of Thomas Geraldino (Fitzgerald), Spanish ambassador to the Court of St James in London.[2] About the beginning of 1738 O'Brien returned to Ireland as parish priest of Castlelyons and Rathcormac in the diocese of Cloyne, taking up residence at Ballinterry near

Rathcormac where he seems to have lived for most of the rest of his life.[3] In January 1748 he was appointed bishop of the dioceses of Cloyne and Ross. He is known to have visited Toulouse, Bordeaux and Louvain in 1756-57. As will be seen below, he was on the continent in 1764 also, and in September 1767 he travelled to Paris again via Dublin and London. O'Brien appears to have spent a total of at least eighteen years in France and Spain during his lifetime. He spoke and wrote English, Irish, Latin, French and Italian. His Spanish employments would indicate that he must have had a working knowledge of Spanish as well, and Greek and Hebrew words are sprinkled liberally through his *Irish-English Dictionary* (Paris, 1768), discussed in more detail below. He died on the 30 March 1769 at Lyons in France.[4]

Some sermons in Irish survive, ascribed in the manuscript tradition to Bishop John O'Brien, dating to about the time of his return to Ireland.[5] These and other items reflect his extensive and familiar connections with the culture of the scribes and hedge-school teachers, bishops and priests being not infrequently patrons of poets and copyists at the time.[6] O'Brien's connections with this tradition are also apparent from a number of poems composed in his honour on the occasion of his appointment as bishop of Cloyne and Ross in January 1748. One such poem beginning *Slán leat a litir bhig bhláith* ('Fare thee well, O little letter fair') was written by a Fr Pádraig Ó Broin, tentatively identified as a Franciscan of that name who died about 1777.[7] A namesake and kinsman, another Fr Seán Ó Briain welcomed him thus: *A chara 's a bhrathbáir, fáilte ó chroí rombat* ('My friend and brother, a welcome from my heart'). Fr Coombes tentatively identified the author of this poem as the Fr Seán Ó Briain referred to in the manuscript tradition as 'an Sagart Dubh' and the parish priest of Liscarroll near Kanturk from 1730 to 1750.[8] A third poem commencing *Táid uaisle Bhanba ag atal 's ag ádhbhacht le mian* ('The nobility of Ireland are rejoicing and celebrating with delight') came from Sean Ó Murchú na Ráithíneach of Carraig na bhFear, the last head of the Whitechurch/Carraig na bhFear *cúirt fìliochta* or 'poetic court', and a prolific minor poet and scribe.[9] Some seven years later in 1755 O'Brien presented him with a gold piece for which meeting Ó Murchú composed some further verses starting *Le cummann don easpog de mbaithibh na mileadh ngrádhach* ('With affection for the bishop of the noblest of the warriors in orders').[10]

Although there is some confusion between him and other writers of the same name, confusion which awaits clarification, Bishop John O'Brien was traditionally believed to have been a poet himself. One of the poems ascribed to 'An tAthair Seán Ó Briain', *Is tréith's is lag* ('Weak and weary...'), is a lament on an affliction which the writer

FOCALÒIR

GAOIDHILGE-SAX-BHÉARLA

OR

AN IRISH-ENGLISH

DICTIONARY.

Whereof the *Irish* part hath been compiled not only from various *Irish* vocabularies, particularly that of Mr. *Edward Lhuyd;* but also from a great variety of the best *Irish* manuscripts now extant; especially those that have been composed from the 9th & 10th centuries, down to the 16th: besides those of the lives of St. *Patrick* & St. *Brigit,* written in the 6th & 7th centuries.

Postremò, ad perficiendam, vel certè valdè promovendam litteraturam Celticam, *diligentiùs Linguæ* Hibernicæ *studium adjungendum censeo, ut* Lhuydius *egregiè facere cæpit. Nam, uti alibi jam admonui, quemadmodum* Angli *fuere Coloniæ* Saxonum, *&* Britanni *emissio veterum Celtarum,* Gallorum, Cimbrorum; *ita* Hiberni *sunt propago antiquiorum Britanniæ habitatorum, Colonis Celticis, Cimbricisque nonnullis, &, ut sic dicam, mediis anteriorum. Itaque ut ex* Anglicis *linguæ veterum* Saxonum, *& ex* Cambricis *veterum Gallorum; ita ex* Hibernicis *vetustiorum adhuc Celtarum, Germanorumque, &, ut generaliter dicam, accolarum Oceani Britannici Cismarinorum antiquitates illustrantur. Et si ultra* Hiberniam *esset aliqua insula Celtici Sermonis, ejus filo in multò adhuc antiquiora duceremur.* Leibnitzius Collectan. Etymol. *vol.* 1. *p.* 153.

PARIS,

Printed by Nicolas-Francis Valleyre, for the Author.

M. DCC. LXVIII.

BY ROYAL APPROBATION & PRIVILEGE.

Plate 13.1   John O'Brien's *An Irish-English dictionary* (Paris, 1768).

described as *an chrith*.[11] This may have been written by the bishop. In his *Irish-English Dictionary*, O'Brien translates *crith* as 'a fit of ague, the ague, a trembling'. It is known from a letter of his that the bishop suffered from a recurrent illness and that his final trip to the continent was partly occasioned by his doctor's instruction to him to change climate and visit a spa near Liège.[12] A manuscript compiled probably between 1762 and 1769 perhaps under the bishop's direction or for him, contains a poem described as 'Dr. Jeff Connell's prescription for the Rt. Revd. Dr. O'Brien's aguish disorder'.[13] If this poem was indeed written by the bishop then that would be additional evidence of familiarity with Seán Ó Murchú na Ráithíneach as the latter wrote a verse in reply, *A chléirigh chneasta, is a athair fhéil ghluin aoird* ('O gentle clerk, O generous pure and high father').[14]

Apart from his patronage of poets, O'Brien was an important patron of scribes.[15] Seán Ó Murchú na Ráithíneach has been noted. Another most important scribe who worked for the bishop was Mícheál (mac Peadair) Ó Longáin (*c.* 1693-1770). Ó Longáin was part of the *cúirt filíochta* at Carraig na bhFear and had close connections with the *cúirt filíochta* of 'Filí na Máighe' ('The Poets of the Maigue') at Croom, county Limerick.[16] Ó Longáin was employed as a scribe by Bishop O'Brien for periods between 1759 and 1762 as is testified by a number of manuscripts he wrote for him. These contain, amongst other matter, materials on the O'Briens, history, genealogies poetry and a list of books which may have been in Bishop O'Brien's library (see Appendix II).[17] A detailed study of Ó Longáin's surviving manuscripts would probably reveal more connections with O'Brien and with other scribes who worked for the bishop. In north Cork, the bishop is known to have had connections with members of a Mitchelstown Ó Dálaigh (or Daly) family, who at that time or soon after his death seem to have had possession of a number of valuable manuscripts, some of them vellum, connected with the bishop or formerly belonging to O'Brien, including the famous medieval codex, the *Leabhar Breac*.[18]

Another interesting but still somewhat obscure scribe/scholar who worked for O'Brien during the last ten years or so of the bishop's life was Rev. Seán Ó Conaire (1739 (?)–1773), who may have called himself 'Connery' in English, and was a priest of the Cloyne diocese. At least nine manuscripts written (in whole or in part) by Ó Conaire survive, and a not insignificant amount of other references to him have been traced also, though some confusion has been caused as well in this case by the fact that there were several individuals of the same name in the eighteenth century associated with the collection, transcription or study of Irish manuscripts.[19] It is clear that Ó Conaire was working with others in places linked with the bishop, with matter owned by the bishop or identical with that used in the bishop's *milieu*. As early as 1757 Ó Conaire is to be found transcribing in the diocese of Cloyne.[20] A number manuscripts were written by Ó Conaire himself, or jointly with Mícheál (mac Peadair) Ó Longáin, using material found in other documents associated with the bishop or owned by him, including one at least partly written by Ó Conaire in France in the mid-1760s.[21] Another of Ó Conaire's ('Joas. Connery') manuscripts (undated) contains extracts from the medieval *Annals of Tighearnach* and *Annals of Innisfallen*, and makes reference to 'Tighernach's continuator', texts O'Brien used, as will be seen. It also contains much matter relating to the O'Briens including the pedigree of ' an tAthair Seághan Ó Briain'.[22] According to a note by Mícheál Óg Ó Longáin, son of Mícheál (mac Peadair), 'John Conroy of the Diocese of Cloyne' made a copy of the 'Leabhar Breac Mic Aodhogain' about 1760.[23] This seems to refer to the famous codex already mentioned, which came into the possession of the bishop perhaps about 1760.[24]

Other transcripts of annals, historical and genealogical matter by Ó Conaire also contain copies of texts closely associated with the bishop, and his hand appears in manuscripts known to have belonged to O'Brien.[25] Ó Conaire transcribed from a *duanaire* or poem-book (now lost) of the seventeenth-century poet Piaras Feiritéar[26] and the bishop frequently quotes such a manuscript in his *Dictionary*. A note copied from a (now apparently lost) exemplar written by Ó Conaire indicates that in 1761 he was transcribing at Cloyne and in Ballinterry where the bishop resided.[27] A closer examination of Ó Conaire's work would probably reveal further connections with others in the bishop's circle. O'Brien stated of his dictionary that it had been compiled under his own supervision by persons 'learned in the language and antiquities of Ireland', and from the evidence of the manuscripts discussed it is probably fair to conclude that Fr Seán Ó Conaire and Mícheál (mac Peadair) Ó Longáin were two of these learned assistants.[28]

Dr Breandán Ó Conchúir and Fr Coombes have listed O'Brien's known published writings.[29] The most important of these was, of course, his Irish-English dictionary, *Focalóir Gaoidhilge-Sax-Bhéarla*. This was completed in 1762 but not published until 1768 because of scarcity of funds. O'Brien apparently started work on it sometime before 1760.[30] Charles Vallancey, the noted antiquarian and enthusiast for all things Celtic, published in volume one of *Collectanea de rebus Hibernicis*, in two parts, a treatise which is stated to have been written by O'Brien.[31] O'Brien perceived the practical use and necessity of the Irish language for priests in Ireland: this was an argument he used in his appeals to Rome for funding for his dictionary. He also stipulated that students who wished to avail themselves of bursaries he founded at Louvain and Paris would have to be able to speak Irish.[32] It is clear from his writings that Bishop O'Brien had an exceptional knowledge of, and acquaintance with, the literary tradition. This can only have been acquired by him through intensive contact with the hedge-school masters, scribes and poets who were its custodians, over a long period of time, possibly starting in his schooldays in Ireland.

As bishop, O'Brien seems to have been something of a confrontationalist, perhaps not the easiest person in the world to deal with. The approach to his house was known as *bóithrín an chrá* ('the avenue of torment') apparently because of the dread his priests had of visiting him.[33] He became embroiled in the late 1750s in a dispute between expatriate factions of the O'Brien family, rival claimants to the title 'Earl of Thomond'. O'Brien was a strong supporter of the faction headed by Colonel Daniel O'Brien (whom James II had created Earl of Lismore), and after his death led by his widow. The expert ranged against O'Brien on the other side was the Chevalier Thomas O'Gorman (1732-1809) from county Clare, that colourful antiquary, wine-exporter, intimate of Louis XV and friend and correspondent of eighteenth-century Ireland's greatest scholar-antiquary, Charles O'Conor of Belanagare (1710-1791).[34] The competing O'Brien faction was that of Charles O'Brien, 6th Viscount Clare, Maréchal de Thomond, who had commanded the Irish infantry at Fontenoy in 1745. An indication of the feelings generated can be gained from a comment in a letter written by O'Gorman in 1759, in which he speaks of the 'petulant pretensions of Lady Lismore', and says of Bishop John O'Brien and his Vicar-General, Fr Matthew McKenna, that they 'would sign the alcoran [The Koran] to please her'.[35] Incidentally, however, O'Brien was clearly held in high regard by Charles O'Conor of Belanagare, as is apparent from O'Conor's correspondence: O'Brien indeed may be perhaps reckoned as second only to O'Conor amongst Irish scholars at the time.[36]

John O'Brien's *Mémoire* and James Macpherson's *Ossian*

O'Brien's wide general erudition, his knowledge of the Irish tradition in particular, and his vigour in controversy are manifest in a lengthy *Mémoire* which appeared from his pen in 1764 in the prestigious *Journal des Sçavans*. This circumstance was brought about in the first instance by one of the great literary hoaxes of modern times, the poems of 'Ossian' written by a Scotsman, James Macpherson (1736-96). Macpherson, as is well known, caused a literary sensation all over Europe with his alleged translations from Scottish Gaelic of 'Ossianic' ballads, published between 1760 and 1763. These 'translations' into English, supposedly from Gaelic originals collected in the Highlands of Scotland, consisted of scattered shorter poems and two epics, *Fingal* and *Temora*, somewhat after the manner of Homer.[37] Macpherson constructed his works drawing material from the cycle of poems and tales known in Irish as *fiannaíocht* – now named 'Ossianic' in English thanks to Macpherson's 'translations' – dealing with the exploits of Fionn mac Cumhaill (Macpherson's 'Fingal'), his son Oisín ('Ossian'), and their companions.[38] Fionn mac Cumhaill and Fianna Éireann were, according to the tradition, a militia dedicated to defending the Irish shores against invaders and allegedly existed during the reign of Cormac mac Airt, placed in the third century A.D. A great body of prose and poetry, *fiannaíocht*, grew up from the twelfth century onwards dealing with the exploits of the *Fianna*, and this cycle of songs and tales was the raw material which Macpherson used for *Ossian*.

Macpherson was a native Gaelic speaker and *fiannaíocht* was part of his patrimony also. It should be borne in mind that *fiannaíocht* forms part of the common linguistic heritage of Ireland and Highland Scotland. In times gone by a cultural unity and common literary language extended from the south of Ireland to the north of Scotland, traversed in its length and breadth by the professional learned classes of medieval Ireland and Scotland, poets, doctors, harpers and the like. This common Gaelic commonwealth lasted for hundreds of years as long as the bardic order endured with its standardised literary language: in the seventeenth century *fiannaíocht* tales still circulated in manuscript 'from Co. Cork to the Hebrides'.[39] The traditions diverged increasingly after the decline of literacy in Irish at the end of the bardic order. But to this day ballads of Fionn and the Fianna are still sung in Scotland. Fionn and Oisín of course still live in the folklore of Ireland and traces have even survived into in English in places.[40]

Macpherson's versions of *fiannaíocht* ballads took the literati of Europe by storm, especially in Germany. 'On the continent, "Ossian" was welcomed with open arms by the precursors of the new Romantic period as the equal of Homer, and as a wonderful fount of original poetry. Translations abounded in Germany, France and Italy. Cesarotti (whose [Italian] translation appeared at Padua in 1763, and who was critic and commentator as well as translator) compared him enthusiastically with the Ancients; French translators found in him a new fount of inspiration ... and the influence of these "Gaelic" poems upon German literature is difficult to measure in its full extent and depth'.[41] Macpherson had effects as diverse as inspiring Mendelssohn to write *Fingal's cave* and causing a king of Sweden to be called 'Oscar'. Napoleon carried a picture of Ossian everywhere with him and in 1798 on his expedition to Egypt is said to have read *Ossian* in preference to Homer.[42]

As was immediately suspected and has since been proved, however, Macpherson in general changed his materials almost beyond recognition. His *Ossian* rarely approaches what would nowadays be termed a translation and, of course, there was no pre-existing epic. Doubt about the authenticity of the poems arose almost as soon as Macpherson's first book was published, but it was long drowned out by the reception accorded them. Bluffer though he may have been, Macpherson obviously had antennae for what the literary public all over Europe wanted to hear. The controversy about the poems had a strong Irish dimension naturally as Macpherson had taken the liberty of appropriating the *fiannaíocht* cycle in the cause of his 'translations' and had relocated Fionn mac Cumhaill and the Fianna in Scotland, in the process taking considerable liberties with Irish history and even geography. Macpherson was naturally attacked by Irish writers for this literary, historical and geographical piracy, quite apart from the question of the integrity or otherwise of his 'translations' from the original Irish/Gaelic.[43]

The controversy about Ossian's authenticity spread quickly to the continent. *Fragments of ancient poetry collected in the Highlands*, it will be recalled, had been published in 1760. Already in 1761 a note of hesitancy had been struck in France when in the *Journal Étranger*, reference was made to a seeming anachronism in Macpherson's work. In 1762 reservations were expressed in a notice of one of Macpherson's poems published in the *Journal des Sçavans*.[44] This prestigious journal had been founded in 1665 in Paris and is regarded as having been the first periodical in Europe other than a newspaper. The *Journal* 'enjoyed a long career ... under the editorship of learned Abbés ... Its issues were mostly made up of critical notes, which were precise and measured, on recently published books, and these ... were a great service, to judge by the journal's prolonged success and wide circulation all over Europe'.[45]

In June 1763, the *Journal* published an item on the topic of Macpherson's poems from an Irishman living in Brussels. This letter, signed by one Terence Brady who wrote on 3 May 1763, and described himself as 'Médicin', has been noted as the first Irish contribution to the Ossianic controversy in France.[46] Terence Brady can with reasonable confidence be identified as the Chevalier Terence Brady or de Brade, a distinguished Irish doctor then living in the Low Countries. The Chevalier de Brade had entered the service of the Austrian empire in 1734 and was ennobled in 1759. From 1755 until his death in Brussels on the 6 April 1770 he was *Proto-Medicus* or chief medical officer of the Austrian imperial armies in the Low Countries. He was, it appears, a man with a colourful turn of phrase: he is once recorded as having described a medical colleague as knowing as much about caring for the health of troops as 'I know about the Jewish Talmud'.[47] This writer does not impugn the authenticity of Macpherson's poems at all. He can clarify the matter, he states. *Carthon*, he says, was the work of 'des anciens *Bards* d'Irlande'. It is referred to in Irish authorities:

> ... The two chronicles of this country known as [that] of Tara and [that] of Cashel refer to it; Keating's History published in English in London in 1723 mentions it also ...'.[48]

Terence Brady assures the readers that many other such poetic works of bygone days survive in Ireland. M. Macpherson, he says, should have reflected on the name of his own mother-tongue, the language of the originals, *Goiligg*. This translates into English as 'Irish' and into French as *Irlandois*. If *Goiligg* had been correctly translated it would have cast light on the original language of the poem and on the part of the world where it was composed.[49] Brady's only criticism of Macpherson was that the matter was originally Irish, not Scottish: he does not engage in any analysis of Macpherson's fidelity to his sources. The Irish *chroniques* to which the Chevalier de Brade refers are *Saltair Teamhrach* (the 'Psalter of Tara') and *Saltair Chaisil* (the 'Psalter of Cashel'), both of them authorities often referred to by name in the manuscript tradition. 'L'Histoire de Keating' is of course *Foras Feasa ar Éirinn*, Keating's famous History of Ireland, written *c.* 1633 and published in English translation in Dublin and London in 1723.[50] Terence Brady makes reference to recitation of ancient poems by illiterate villagers and this, taken with his irregular spelling, might suggest that his own familiarity with such matter was acquired from hearing it recited or read aloud rather than from extensive acquaintance with the manuscript tradition such as that revealed, for example, by Bishop O'Brien, as will be seen below.[51]

As voices were also being raised in other quarters critical of aspects of Macpherson's work, the *Journal des Sçavans* decided to get to the root of the matter. It is clear that the person the editors approached with this aim in view was one known to them as a scholar of distinction. In the May 1764 issue of the *Journal* the editors published the first instalment of a lengthy paper entitled 'Mémoire de M. de C. a Messieurs les Auteurs Du Journal des Sçavans, au Sujet des Poëmes de M. Macpherson', introducing it in the following terms:

> Le Mémoire suivant nous a été adressé par un Sçavant respectable, qui a des connoissances très-étendues dans plus d'un genre, & principalement sur ce qui concerne les antiquités

d'Irlande & d'Ecosse. Nous l'avons prié de fixer nos doutes sur cette fameuse découverte de M. Macpherson, dont tant de Journaux ont retenti, & dont le nôtre a deja parlé plusieurs fois, sans oser rien decider. C'est à la solution de ce problême littéraire que le Mémoire est consacré.[52]

This substantial article of about forty thousand words extended over five issues of the *Journal des Sçavans* in 1764 and comprised, in effect, a small book.[53] Having first excused his own poor command of French, the author explains that what he proposes to do is 'perhaps a very daring enterprise on the part of one who has but a slight command of your language. One will however always excuse a stranger for this failing provided he makes himself understood and is essentially correct'.[54] The greater part of the *Mémoire* is a detailed attack on Macpherson's supposed underlying historical structure, dealing amongst other matters with the meaning of the Latin term 'Scoti'. To bolster his claim that his poems were translations of ancient originals, Macpherson had prefixed to *Fingal* (1762) an 'historical' introduction situating the *Gaeil* (Gaels) in Scotland first and only in Ireland later.[55] The writer of the *Mémoire* engages in a long and detailed *excursus* on Scottish and Irish history painstakingly dismantling and rebutting Macpherson's supposed historical framework and taking issue with other Scottish historians along the way. The latter part of the *Mémoire* is a trenchant attack on *Ossian*, whom he terms 'Cet Homere Calédonien'.[56]

The *Mémoire* is a very dense, closely argued and tightly documented piece of writing. M. de C. quotes over ninety different writers, many of them more than once.[57] The author cites continental, English, and Irish authorities, ancient, medieval and modern, Catholic and Protestant, secular and ecclesiastical, printed and manuscript, in refuting Macpherson and other Scottish historians. Amongst ancient and medieval authors he quotes Caesar, Gildas, Bede, Lucan, Pliny, Adamnan's *Life* of Colmcille and Notker Balbulus. Amongst the printed modern authorities he cites are John Lynch, Ussher, David Rothe (of Kilkenny), Thomas Innes (the Scottish historian), Edward Stillingfleet (the English ecclesiastical historian), Camden and John Colgan (the Franciscan), as well as Leibniz quoting the Welsh Celticist, Edward Lhuyd [58]

He refers regularly to a variety of then unpublished Irish authorities: he quotes *les anciens Regîtres des Généalogists Irlandois* ('The old records of the Irish genealogists').[59] Other (then) unpublished Irish sources he refers to are *le continuateur de Thigernach* and *Annal. Dungallen.*, namely the Annals of Donegal, otherwise known as the

Annals of the Four Masters [60] He cites the *Annals of Tigernach* stating that he possesses

> at the moment the same copy of the Annals of Tigernach which Mr O'Flaherty owned with an old transcript of the Chronicle of Clonmacnoise which is well known under the title of *Chronicon Scotorum Cluanense* and which belonged also to the same Mr. O'Flaherty ... I possess also a perfect and authentic copy of the Annals of Inisfallen [61]

'M. Ó Flaherty' is Ruairí Ó Flaithearta (1629-1718), author of *Ogygia* (London, 1685).[62] Some of M. de C.'s strictures against Scottish writers can probably be read as having Stuart overtones also. The writer can be seen in the tradition of Irish support for the Stuart claimants to the British throne, in common with Ruairí Ó Flaithearta and Matthew Kennedy, a prominent Irish Jacobite, whom he quotes as authorities [63] Referring to Charlemagne's relations with the Irish, he cites Matthew Kennedy describing in 1705

> an old piece of tapestry which was to be seen at Versailles in the Audience Hall of M. de Chamillart, in which Charlemagne was surrounded by various kings, allies of his, amongst whom appeared a King of Ireland with the harp, (the arms of that kingdom) at his side.[64]

M. de C. reveals a wide knowledge of historical sources, printed and manuscript, and handles them with remarkable facility. It is unlikely that such a large amount of research could have been done at short notice at the invitation of the editors of the *Journal* by a busy Catholic bishop in Ireland at the time.[65]

Having discoursed at length on Irish and Scottish history and on Macpherson's historical errors, M. de C. deals with *Ossian* in the last instalments. Here he reveals a high level of sophistication in the textual and source criticism he seeks to apply to Macpherson's poems. He attacks the latter's lack of clarity in his references to his originals: are they detached manuscript pieces found in different hands or what form do they take? What or where are the simple traditions collected from the mouths of Scottish Highlanders to which Macpherson refers? He quotes Macpherson as speaking of material about to be lost forever as much more allegedly was: what exactly does the Scotsman claim has been lost, or is about to be lost? Is he referring to written material or oral tradition? 'The vagueness which Mr Macpherson allows on this point has all the appearance of having been affected to mislead those who would demand to see the originals'.[66] He then refers to Macpherson's description of the lines and verses of these poems as being bound together by metre, rhymes and rhythm. The writer's observations again reveal a level of literary criticism strikingly sophisticated in the terms in which the origin of matter in hand is analysed:

> ... This multiplicity of rhymes as much in the middle as at the end of lines, and all this mechanical and frivolous artifice was only introduced into the construction of Irish verse since after the tenth century when Gothic taste, having spread throughout Europe finally reached the Irish either through their trade with the continent or through the great number of foreigners who came to the schools of Ireland since the reign of Brian Bóroimhe.[67]

He adds that he doubts if there are now fifty persons in the kingdom capable of explaining the Irish poetry which has come down from the fifth, sixth or seventh centuries for which one would need 'a very profound knowledge of the ancient Iberno-Celtic language'.[68]

In the December issue M. de C. finally comes to grips with Macpherson's treatment of *fiannaíocht* ballads and tales. He outlines the typical content of *fiannaíocht* material, having previously introduced Fionn as the general of the famous Irish militia called 'Fiana' or 'Phoenii'.[69] First he notes that in the Irish romantic tales or stories (*romans*) there is usually a king or son of a King of Lochlan [Scandinavia], who comes to invade Ireland and is engaged by the Fianna. Since the exploits of the Fianna under Fionn mac Cumhaill, whom he places in the third century, had been so greatly celebrated by Irish historians, he explains, 'les Bardes' of later times made up their compositions supposing the Viking invasions to have taken place in the third century. They then ascribed their compositions to Oisín son of Fionn who according to tradition survived to a great age, and having survived all the other heroes appeared 'the most appropriate person to perpetuate their memory'.[70]

M. de C. argues that Macpherson's *Fingal* is basically composed of elements taken from *Cath Fiontragh* and *Bruighean Caorthoin*, two of these tales and a third written in verse, *La guerre ou la descente de Dearg fils de Diric Roi de Lochlin* ('The war or the descent of Dearg, son of Diric, King of Lochlin [Scandinavia]'), and he proceeds to show Macpherson's dependence in particular on the third. The Scotsman, he says, has changed the names to conceal the sources from which he has drawn his productions.[71] A further episode, he claims,

... is taken from another romance which I have also cited under the title of *Cath Fiontragh*, which ... means, *the battle of the white strand* ... The heath or the plain of Lena, which Mr Macpherson chose for the scene of the action of his poem *Fingal*, he has borrowed from an historical account to be found among the ancient memorials of Ireland under the title of *Cath Maigh-Lena*, that is, the history of the battle of the field of Lena.

He states that Maigh Lena is in 'la Province de Midie', near Tara, not where Macpherson locates it, in the north.[72] Macpherson's geographical changes, as in the case of his altering of names, are part of his pattern of concealing 'the general plagiarisation through particular plagiarisations', but in fact 'the examination of the originals will confound him always'.[73] He says that 'Carton' is taken from *Bruion Chaorthainn*, already mentioned, the title of which properly translated into French would be *La Maison ou le Château du Bois d'enchantement* ('The house or the castle of the wood of enchantment'), *ou le Château enchanté* ('or the enchanted castle'). 'Darthula', he says, is also taken from an Irish 'Roman', *Oidle* [sic] *Clainne Uisneaice* [sic], namely *la mort tragique des fils d'Uisneach*.[74]

M. de C. finally observes:

We shall never finish if we wish to enter here into a detailed examination of all his other poems: it suffices to note that they are all drawn from the same source, composed in the same spirit, and the originals have all been falsified with the same skill.[75]

Concluding his lengthy criticism of Macpherson he describes the unfortunate lot of the Irish in latter days:

... so situated between certain Scottish antiquarians on one side and various English writers on the other. The former despoil them of their heroes and their great men in every field, the latter devote themselves to vilifying this worthy nation; they depict all the Irish as savages and wild beasts who did not deserve to possess the land which they have inhabited for such a long time.[76]

In a closing note the editors invite M. Macpherson or other 'partisans des Antiquités Ecoissoises' to reply if they should wish and state that they will give them a platform, but advise that unless such contributions are kept short, will they only be prepared to publish extracts from them.[77] It does not appear however that Macpherson or anyone of his supporters accepted this invitation.

M. de C. and John O'Brien

The editors give no further information about the author other than their introductory note, and the initials 'M. de C.' in the title of the *Mémoire*.[78] In 1933 M. de C. was identified as Bishop John O'Brien by Alexander Gillies in *Herder und Ossian*, a study of Macpherson's influence on the German writer, Johann Gottfried Herder. Gillies identified M. de C. as O'Brien from a note appended to a copy of the 1768 edition of O' Brien's *Dictionary*. This note identified the author of the *Dictionary* and the author of the *Mémoire* as the same person.[79] The author of the *Mémoire* was also independently identified as John O'Brien by Cormac Ó Cuilleanáin in 1947 in a detailed analysis of the sources of the text known as *The Dublin Annals of Inisfallen*.[80] Ó Cuilleanáin noted that 'M. de C.' used 'The Annals of Inisfallen' and Ruairí Ó Flaithearta's copies of *Annála Thighearnaigh* and *Chronicum Scotorum*, and that these manuscripts formerly the property of Ó Flaithearta are found amongst five manuscripts assembled and bound together by Bishop John O'Brien, and used by him in his *Dictionary* and in a treatise also attributed to him.[81] Principally on the basis of his employment of these and other sources, Ó Cuilleanáin identified M. de C. as Bishop John O'Brien.[82] Ó Cuilleanáin also noted that O'Brien in his *Dictionary* referred on more than one occasion to the *Mémoire*: there are at least four such references.[83]

O'Brien's authorship of the *Mémoire* may also be confirmed from internal evidence, in particular from repeated references to O'Briens both in the *Mémoire* and in the *Dictionary*. Different members of the O'Brien family are mentioned regularly in the latter, Brian Bóroimhe (*ob.* 1014) and his great-grandson, Conchubhar 'Slaparsalach', also known as Conchubhar 'na Cathrach', king of Munster (1118-1142), being referred to frequently.[84] In the *Mémoire* O'Briens also feature quite prominently, in particular in a number of lengthy digressions. Brian Bóroimhe is most prominent, but honourable mention is also made of Conchubhar 'Slaparsalach'.[85] According to a note in a manuscript written by Ó Longáin for O'Brien, John O'Brien traced his descent from this Conchubhar Ó Briain, *ré raidhtí Slapar Salach agus Conchubhar na Cathrach* ('who was called "Slaparsalach" and "Conchubhar na Cathrach"'). John O'Brien's epitaph, in fact, described him as being 'of the kingly and most ancient stock of the O'Briens through the direct line of Conchubhar O'Brien named Na Cathrach, known vulgarly as Slaparsalach, King of Munster ...'.[86] Furthermore in instructions for the administration of burses O'Brien founded in the universities of Paris and Louvain for the benefit of Irish students, he stipulated that preference was to be given to O'Briens of that branch 'descended from Conchubhar nicknamed "Macathrach" [*recte* "na cathrach", presumably] King of the Two Munsters in the 12th century ...'.[87] In the *Mémoire*, M. de C. refers to this Conchubhar 'na Cathrach' or 'Slaparsalach' O'Brien as the ancestor from whom the elder branch of the O'Briens is descended, 'which still subsists but in a state scarcely appropriate to the dignity of its origin having been despoiled of everything.'[88] These unnecessary references to O'Briens, parallelled in the *Dictionary*, are surely further evidence confirming the identity of John O'Brien as the writer of the *Mémoire* [89] It is clear that O'Brien traced his own ancestry to Brian Bóroimhe, and was very conscious of his own background.[90]

It is also evident that O'Brien was on the continent in 1764, the same year that the *Mémoire* was published, and in fact it appears that during that visit he founded the burses referred to above. On 12 August 1764 the bishop was in Brussels from where he wrote 'in excellent French' to Cardinal Castelli in Rome in connection with funding for his dictionary. As O'Brien states in this letter that he had just founded two burses for the Irish college in Paris, in addition to the Louvain burses, it is perhaps reasonable to assume that he had visited Paris also in the course of the same journey. Thus O'Brien is very likely to have been in Paris in summer 1764 when the *Mémoire* was first published.[91]

As the bishop spent about eighteen years all told during his lifetime on the continent, mostly in France, he must have built up a wide network of acquaintances. Such a network could explain his entrée to the *Journal des Sçavans*. Both O'Brien and his vicar-general and successor as bishop of Cloyne, Matthew MacKenna, for example, had good Jacobite connections and close ties with the Irish College in Paris.[92] Both O'Brien and MacKenna seem to have been associated with a fellow-Cork ecclesiastic with literary connections in Paris, David Henegan, who held positions of importance in the Irish College there for many years. Fr Henegan, a doctor of the Sorbonne who certified O'Brien's dictionary for publication, has been described as 'a facile writer of French [who] contributed a number of Irish biographies and articles of Irish interest to the "Dictionnaire de Moreri" – an important work which was published in Paris in 1759'.[93]

The reception of the *Mémoire*

Described by one critic as 'crammed with facts, names, titles, references of all descriptions', the *Mémoire* obviously generated comment in literary circles and has been noted as by far the most serious contribution up to that time to the Ossianic debate in France.[94] The *Mémoire* penetrated further however. The *Journal des Sçavans* itself was reprinted in an Amsterdam edition.[95] The *Mémoire* only was republished separately, in French, in 1765 in Cologne.[96] This Cologne reprint was in turn noticed in England in the *Monthly Review* in its 'Catalogue of foreign books'. In the course of this review, the editors remind their readers of their own scepticism with regard to the poems of Ossian and they continue:

> The reputation of this northern Moeonides was destined, however, to suffer a more formal and formidable attack, on crossing the British channel. Not that it had any thing to fear from the natives of France, the region of *poetry*, politeness and the Belles Lettres; it is well known that France abounds with foreigners, and particularly with the natives of a country, which, though subject to our own sovereign, furnishes our hereditary enemies not only with soldiers to fight their battles, but authors to write their books. In short, the Author of this memoir is an Irishman, who equally jealous of the honour and antiquity of his nation with the proudest Laird in Scotland, appears highly incensed at, what he calls, the pretended discovery of Mr. Macpherson ....

They then proceed to give a two-page summary of the *Mémoire*.[97]

The *Mémoire* seems to have attracted rather more interest in Germany where it was not only reprinted separately at Cologne, as stated above, but the parts dealing directly with Ossian were also published in German translation. Ossian had been received with particular enthusiasm in Germany where a generation of genius was about to burst into life. The writings of the youthful Johann Wolfgang von Goethe (1749-1832), Friedrick von Schiller (1759-1805), Gottfried August Bürger (1747-1797), Johann Gottfried Herder (1744-1803) and others were about to bring about a literary climate known to students of German literature as *Sturm und Drang* ('Storm and Stress') which lasted for perhaps twenty years from the mid-1760s.[98] A significant element in this intense and revolutionary interval was a reaction against the snob-value with which French literature and culture had previously been invested in Germany. Thus these young men turned to other sources of inspiration. In English literature they discovered Shakespeare, Percy's *Reliques of ancient English poetry* (1765), and in English they encountered *Ossian* also.[99] Ossian mediated through English was embraced as a source of inspiration independent of French neo-classical influence. Furthermore Ossian was 'Celtic' and at that time prehistory, archaeology and philology were still perceived in such a general confused jumble that Celtic and Germanic were regarded as akin. Furthermore, Ossian was primitive and primitivism was coming into vogue in Europe, in particular through the works of Jean-Jacques Rousseau (1712-78).[100]

504. **Vermischte Aufsätze.**

* * * * * * * * * * * * *

Beschluß
des
Aufsatzes
über Herrn Macphersons Gedichte.

Die Verse in diesen Gedichten waren, wie Hr. Macpherson sagt, durch Sylbenmaaß, Reime und Harmonie so mit einander verbunden, daß, wenn man eine einzige Zeile von einer Strophe wußte, man nothwendig auch die ganze Strophe behalten mußte. Das ist etwas, das über allen Begriff geht; denn daraus würde folgen, daß, wenn man einen Vers von einer Strophe gegeben hätte, alle übrige nothwendig seyn müßten, und daß die Strophe schlechterdings aus keinen andern Versen oder Worten zusammengesetzt werden könnte. Wer uns überreden will, daß es dergleichen Verse und Strophen gebe, der zeige sie. Uebrigens ist diese Beschreibung der Verse der vorgegebenen Originale hier nicht gleichgültig; denn sie beweiset, daß dieser erfinderische Schriftsteller niemals andere poetische Ausarbeitungen in der irländischen oder herfischen Sprache gekannt habe, als die aus den neuesten Zeiten. Erst seit dem zehnten Jahrhundert findet man wirklich solche Verse, die in Ansehung der Wortfügung so vielen Regeln, so vielen Reimen, so viel Accorden und Ton- Wort- und Sylbenspielen unterworfen sind. Man findet in den **tighernachischen** Jahrbüchern verschiedenen Stanzen alter irländischen Poeten über die großen Begebenheiten, die in diesem Lande im fünften bis zum zehnten Jahrhunderte vorfielen; aber in dieser ganzen Zeit findet man gar kein Exempel von einer so unbegreiflichen

Plate 13.2   Excerpt from the German translation of O'Brien's *Mémoire* (Staats – u. Universitäts bibliothek, Hamburg).

It was in such an atmosphere that Macpherson's *Ossian* was rapturously received. The influence of Goethe, then just emerging as one of the major figures in modern European literature, was of particular importance. Goethe made his own translations of Ossianic poems and used some of them in his best-selling novel *Die Leiden des jungen Werthers* ('The sufferings of young Werther'), published in 1774, thus magnifying the impact of Ossian across Europe. Werther, it is said, through his fictional suicide for unrequited love caused a rash of what would nowadays be termed 'copy-cat' suicides among earnest and love-stricken young men throughout Europe at the time, who, like their hero, drank too deeply at the springs of love and melancholy and Ossian: a phenomenon the French termed *Wertherisme*.[101] In such an atmosphere it was perhaps not surprising that John O'Brien's *Mémoire* should excite interest.

As was the case in France, the German translation of the *Mémoire de M. de C.* appears to have been the first significant attack on Macpherson in German.[102] The partial German translation was printed in the *Unterhaltungen* published in Hamburg in 1766, spread over three issues.[103] This translation omitted the historical section, reproducing only the portion dealing directly with Macpherson's poems. The *Unterhaltungen* introduced the essay ('Aufsatz') with a carefully neutral note, remarking that 'the erudition which prevails in this essay will make it valuable to some of our readers'.[104] Of the author, an Irish scholar ('ein irländischer Gelehrter'), the editors point out that while chauvinism must have some influence on his article, such accusations may only be entertained because nothing has been advanced to counter his serious historical arguments.[105] A further lengthy note reviews the doubts which had been cast on Macpherson's authenticity in England and France. This comments on the arguments for the Irish origin of Macpherson's poems advanced in Ferdinando Warner's *Remarks on the history of Fingal and other poems* (London, 1762) and also in another publication in English, *Fingal reclaimed*, for which a date of 1763 is given.[106]

The *Mémoire* appears to have stimulated the first doubts about Macpherson aired in public by a German critic. M. de C.'s arguments were taken up by Heinrich Wilhelm von Gerstenberg (1737-1823), a poet and commentator of significance in the *Sturm und Drang* movement. Gerstenberg was a German-speaking Dane, resident in Copenhagen. In the eighth of his letters on literary topics, *Briefe über Merkwürdigkeiten der Literatur* (1766), he refers to the 'Mémoire of an Irishman concerning the Ossianic poems newly received from Paris in recent days'.[107] This Mémoire was, of course, the M. de C. article. Gerstenberg explained that though hitherto he had had his suspicions about Macpherson from internal evidence, other proofs had been lacking. Now, however, he states 'The Irishman has plenty of them ... Through the fragments of the Irish romances the deception becomes clear'.[108] He refers the reader further to the *Mémoire* itself where, he says, the matter can not without pleasure ('nicht ohne Vergnügen') be read in detail.[109]

C. F. Weisse (1726-1804) a minor writer and critic, rejected M. de C.'s doubts *inter alia* in a review of the English edition of *Ossian* of 1765 in the *Neue Bibliothek der schönen Wissenschaften* (1766) and argued strongly for the authenticity of Ossian. Weisse based his arguments on the work of an intimate of Macpherson's and a strong supporter of his, Hugh Blair, sometime Professor of Rhetoric and Belles Lettres at the University of Edinburgh. An essay by Blair in support of Macpherson was appended to the 1765 (third) edition of Ossian, that reviewed by Weisse.[110] Blair's influential writings in support of Macpherson painted a picture of a primitive time when passion and poetry were unfettered and undulled by the influence of civilisation, 'where amidst the rude scenes of nature, amidst rocks and torrents, and whirlwinds and battles, dwells the sublime', a characterisation remarkably in tune with theories that Herder and others were working up to a climax in Germany.[111] Herder himself, in a review of the 1766 *Unterhaltungen* for the *Königsberger Zeitungen* of 7 December 1767, rejected the M. de C. article, also basing himself on Blair's essay. He did not consider the doubts maintained by M. de C. to be sufficient to disprove the authenticity of the poems. Some years later Herder returned to this theme, in 'Extract from an exchange of letters about Ossian and the songs of ancient peoples' ('Auszug aus einem Briefwechsel über Ossian und die Lieder alter Völker'), a piece he contributed to *Von Deutscher Art und Kunst*, an important collection of essays published in 1773 jointly with Goethe and others.[112]

Aftermath

Other German commentators seem to have shared Herder's attitude in rejecting the doubts caused by the *Mémoire de M. de C.* and it would be some time yet before the German critics accepted that Macpherson had falsified his 'translations'. This appears to have been the fate of the *Mémoire* in the French-speaking world also: in general, readers perferred to reject it without answering its criticisms, and so M. de C. did not succeed in shaking the credulous in the short term, it appears, in either country. Even the *Journal des Sçavans* seems to have reverted to a pro-Macpherson stance by 1765. The fashion was probably far too strong to be restrained by reasoned argument. The article being the first major attack on Macpherson to appear in French or German demanded also a far more detailed knowledge of Irish literature than was available in the late eighteenth century to any but a very few scholars. As one French critic observed: 'The *Mémoire* bristles with a scholarship so thorny that it is difficult to unravel with clarity the doctrine of the writer'.[113] One should perhaps recall that in the year 1760 as yet virtually nothing had been printed in Irish or Scottish Gaelic apart from religious matter. *Fiannaíocht* lore remained in manuscript or in oral form only, and no texts had been edited or published against which Macpherson's 'translations' could be measured. In France and/or especially in Germany, the *Mémoire* was probably also too early, too uncompromising and too detailed to be accepted in an atmosphere for which *Ossian* appeared to be tailor-made (as, in a sense, it was!).[114]

Such was the enthusiasm for Macpherson's poems however that, for example, both Goethe and Herder began to learn Irish in order to be able to read Macpherson's 'Gaelic sources'. Both made diligent translations from a 'specimen' Macpherson had published as an alleged example of one of these 'Gaelic' originals.[115] One of the books indeed that Herder employed in his study of Irish was John O'Brien's *Dictionary*. It was even mooted that as soon as Macpherson's 'originals' were published in full, Herder himself would translate *Ossian* directly from Gaelic into German.[116] This was not to be, of course: it gradually became apparent that there was no true Gaelic original underlying Macpherson's text.

In the long term the Ossianic controversy greatly encouraged interest in things Celtic in Europe, and the Romantic movement which it helped to create encouraged similar researches on a wider front. Under the influence of German scholarship in particular the systematic study of such disciplines as philology, archaeology and mythology emerged in Europe at this time and the vernacular languages, Irish included, became objects of academic study. This European trend was mirrored in Ireland in the increasing interest in antiquities and Irish-language culture on the part of the Anglo-Irish, but the matter was of course given added impetus in this country by the peculiarly Celtic and Irish dimensions of the Macpherson controversy.[117] The present writer has not noted any immediate reaction to the *Mémoire de M. de C.* in Ireland but it must have been read in Dublin at least as the *Journal des Sçavans* was taken by the Dublin Society's library in Grafton Street at the time.[118]

Whether or not John O'Brien made any other contribution to the Macpherson controversy is not known. His own energies were probably taken up with the publication of his dictionary which appeared in 1768 and shortly after that he died on 13 March 1769. The influence of the bishop's researches appears nevertheless to have filtered directly into the then awakening interest among the Anglo-Irish in Irish culture – a movement itself due in no small part to interest generated by the Macpherson controversy. On 4 January 1773 Fr Seán Ó Conaire ('Revd. John Connery of Cloyne') was appointed an honorary member of a Select Committee which the Dublin Society (now the R.D.S.) had established in 1772 'to enquire into the ancient state of arts and literature, and into the other antiquities of Ireland'.[119] This committee, established on the urgings of Charles Vallancey and others, was an important precursor of the Royal Irish Academy (established in 1785). Other honorary/corresponding members were the sometime scribe and archbishop of Dublin, John Carpenter, Sylvester O' Halloran, the distinguished doctor and historian from Limerick, and Charles O'Conor of Belanagare. The Select Committee also included Lord Charlemont ('the Volunteer Earl'), Sir Lucius O'Brien of county Clare, Lord Moira, the liberal (Church of Ireland) Bishop Frederick Hervey of Derry (formerly of Cloyne), Vallancey himself, Dr Thomas Leland sometime librarian of Trinity College, Dublin and, interestingly perhaps in this context, the Church of Ireland bishop of Cloyne, Charles Agar.[120]

Fr Seán Ó Conaire died very shortly after this in July 1773, but in May 1774 before the committee petered out, through the offices of Vallancey and the Bishop of Cloyne, some manuscripts which had belonged to Ó Conaire were purchased for the sum of £9. 2s. 0d., perhaps from a relation of his ('Mr. Connery').[121] These may possibly have included some codices of O'Brien's which reached Trinity College, Dublin about the second quarter of 1776, perhaps again through Vallancey's hands. Vallancey wrote to Charles O'Conor of Belanagare on 3 September 1774 advising him that 'The Leabhar Inse clain'h' Mhaol Conaire [sic], Magrath's Acta O Brienorum, the Annals of Tigheronac [sic], the Chronicon Scotorum and the Annals of Innisfallen are all come into my hands since I had the pleasure of seeing you'.[122]

The intellectual and other activities of the Irish in continental Europe in the seventeenth and eighteenth centuries are matters that still remain relatively unexplored and perhaps underestimated. Apart from trading contacts the linkage of the Irish-speaking and bilingual areas of Ireland with the continent was perhaps at its strongest in the presence of the Irish in continental armies and in the education of Irish doctors and priests on the continent, a linkage reflected, for example, in the Jacobite poetry of the poets and scribes of the time. Bishop O'Brien's career also illuminates this cultural and trading axis. John O'Brien/Seán Ó Briain was clearly a man of broad attainments: well-travelled, well-read, well-versed in European culture and well-versed in his own. The sources the bishop cites in the *Mémoire* (listed in Appendix I) form an imposing reading-list. If one adds to them the items identified by Ó Cuilleanáin as having been utilised for the 'Dublin Annals of Inisfallen', the sources O'Brien mentions in the introduction to his *Dictionary*, the manuscripts known to have belonged to him, and a list of books which Fr P. Ó Fiannachta has suggested may have been in the possession of the bishop (see Appendix II), one is confronted with a very formidable inventory indeed.[123]

Events in general, and in particular the Macpherson controversy, had by the 1780s brought about a situation where John O'Brien's *Mémoire* would have been enthusiastically seized upon and published by the new Royal Irish Academy, as other such matter was. Because of the way matters had unfolded in Ireland however, there was still no public forum in this country in the 1760s in which Irish studies were cultivated or indeed in which a Catholic bishop could take an active part. Thus both O'Brien's *Dictionary* and his *Mémoire* were published abroad. Although no doubt the impact of the *Mémoire* in Ireland was diffused because of its appearance overseas, it clearly generated significant comment and interest in a number of other European countries in its time. And for us, in retrospect, it surely remains an instructive witness to the erudition and culture of a distinguished Cork churchman of the later penal era.

Acknowledgements:
I should like to thank Ms Sharon Ryan who typed this article patiently. I am indebted to the following for help and advice: Professor P. Schäublin, Dr J. Beug, and in particular Professor Seán Ó Coileáin of U.C.C.; Rev. Stephen Redmond, S.J., Mr Éamonn Ó Cíosáin and the Librarians of Cork City Library, in particular Mr John Mullins. I am especially indebted to the library of the Goethe-Institut, Dublin, for generous facilities and for obtaining material on inter-library loan from Germany. Quotations from the German translation of the *Mémoire* are reproduced by kind permission of the Staats-u. Universitätsbibliothek, Hamburg.

Appendix I

The following specific sources are quoted by M. de C. in the course of the *Mémoire*, many of them more than once (sources are given here in the form in which they are cited by M. de C.):

Cambrensis Eversus
Usserius antiquit. Britan.
Messingamus Tract. de nominibus Hibernia
Rothic. de Hiberniâ resurgente, editionis Coloniae anno 1621
M. Innes ... son Essai Critique
Edouard Winton, Prieur de Lochlevin ... Chronique rimée ... 1408
Jacques Gray, Prêtre du Diocèse de Dublin ... un Chronique abrégée des antiquités

d'Ecosse ... avant 1447
Jean Fordun, Prêtre du Diocèse de Saint André *Scoti Chronicon* 1447
la Chronologie de Couper
Hector Boëce ... Histoire ... 1526
Lesly
Buchanan, *de iure regni apud Scotos*
Gordon de Straloch
Annales ... de Tighearnachus
Chronicon Scotorum Cluanense
Hollinghead
Ubbo Emius in Op. Chron.
Boxhor. Hist. Univers.
Evinius in vita S. Patricii
Jocelin [Life of St Patrick]
Jean Major abbréviateur de Fordun
... ouvrages historiques du Chevalier George Macenzie, & du Sieur Abercromby
Bollandus
la Chronique de Couper
Jo. Maior... de gestis Scotorum
Camb. Britt.
Ammien Marcellin
Bede, Histor.
Stillingfleet Brit. Antiq.
Claudien [dans son Panégyrique sur le ... Consulat d'Honorius]
Gildas, de *Excidio Britanniae*
Fabius Ethelwardus
Vit. 2 S. Patricii ... juxta Colganum
le quatrième vie de [S. P.] publiée par Colganus
le Sçavant O'Flaherty
Sabellicus
Beda in Chronico
Ado in Chron.
Paul. Diacon. in Continuat. Eutrop.
Henricus Huntingdon, Hist.
Florentinus Wigorn
Colgan Trias. Taumat.
les écrits ... de l'Evêque de S. Asaph
Stillinglfeet Antiquit.
Nennius Hist. Brit. Edit. Gal.
Sidonius Apollinaris
Lucan. Pharsal.
Plin. Hist.
Adamnan in vit. S. Colum.
la vie de S. Brendane
Comm. Caes de bello civil.
Agartharcides, Strabo, Virgile, Pline ... Herodote ... Keting
O'Flaherty Ogygia
Annal. Dungallen.
Thomas Dempster
Buchan. in Sylvis
Cambd. Hibern.

Notkerus Balbulus in vit. Caroli magni.
Vincent. *in spec. Historial.*
Antonin. *Cronic ... ex Cronicis Ecclesia Arelatensis*
Stepanus Vitus
Le Docteur Kennedy, dans son Traité de la Généalogie du Roi d'Angeleterre Jacques II
la vie de Charlemagne écrite par Eginard
Albinus, autrement Alcuinus, dans la vie de S. Willibrorde
la vie de Sulgenus qui fut Evêque de Meneve au päis de Galles
Guillaume de Malmesbury ... de gest. Regum Anglorum
Albinus, autrement Alcuinus dans sa Lettre a Calcus
Usserius *Sylloge Epistolarum Hibernicarum*
le continuateur de Thigernach
David Malcolme *Collection of Lettres* [sic] Edinburgh 1739
M. Lluyd *Archaeologia Britannica* ... Preface ... a été traduite & publiée en Anglois dans la Bibliothèque Irlandoise composée par l'Evêque Protestant de Derry
Loyd Evêque de S. Asaph.
Leibniz Collectan. Etymol.
Denis d'Halicarnasse
le Dictionnaire Anglois-Irlandois de M. Begly, Prêtre du College des Lombards
Diodor.
Valesius not. in Ammian.
Marcianus Héracloleota in periplo.
Tacite Agricola
Annales d'Innisfallen
Listes de tous les Rois de Suede, de Norvège & de Dannemark
Radulphus de Diceto, Doyen de Londres au douzième siecle
Reinerius Reinectus dans ses prolégomenes de l'Histoire Juliene
[M. Malcolme] ... en 1739 le *Prospectus* de deux Dictionnaires, l'un Irlandois-Anglois, l'autre Anglois-Irlandois
[le] Chevalier Newton
Cath Fiontragh
Bruighean Caorthoin
... Roman qui est écrit en Vers
Giraldus Cambrensis *De Expugnatione Hiberniae*
Cath Maigh-Lena
Oidle Clainne Uisneaice [sic]

Appendix II

In one of the bishop's manuscripts (I.L.l) now owned by the Society of Jesus, Leeson Street, Dublin, written perhaps about 1759 by Mícheál (mac Peadair) Ó Longáin, there is a three-page list of books which Fr Pádraig Ó Fiannachta suggested may have been in the bishop's library (Ó Fiannachta, *Mionchnuasaigh*, ii, pp 72-3). These items include scripture commentaries, works on canon law, church history, liturgy, patristics, apologetics, history and mathematics. There are perhaps fifty titles in Latin, approximately twenty-five in French and slightly fewer in English. There is at least one in Italian, and an Italian dictionary. There is also a Spanish dictionary and perhaps a work in Spanish if it is not a translation from Spanish. At least one of the books appears to be in Irish.

The following appear among the books in the list and are excerpted by kind permission. Those which could be identified with reasonable confidence are given with full titles and dates of publication:

[?] ... esy's Dictionary

Eusebi hystoria Ecclesiastica
Eusebius, *Ecclesiastical history*

[Acta] Sanctorum hyberniae Colgan
John Colgan, *Acta sanctorum veteris et maioris Scotiae, seu Hiberniae sanctorum insulae* (Louvain, 1645)

Stillingfleets antiquit. of the Brit. Churches
Edward Stillingfleet, *Origines Britannicae or the antiquities of the British churches* (1685). [This is quoted by M. de C., *Mémoire*, pp 354, 415, and 'Stillingfleet' on a number of occasions, e.g. ibid., pp 284, 290].

... ewparis hyst. of Enqld.
Matthew Paris (?), [*History of England*]

[Pol]idore Virgil Ditto
Polydore Virgil, *Anglica Historia*

... Boetius hyst. of Scotland
Hector Boece, *Scottorum Historae* (1527). [This is quoted by M. de C., *Mémoire*, p. 284].

Eusebi Cronicon

Irish missal

The New Testament in Irish. [This can only be Uilliam Ó Domhnaill, *Tiomna Nua* (1603), translated for the Church of Ireland]

Gibson's [?] Chronicon Saxonum [?]

florilegium Sanctorum seu vitae et acta Sanctorum hyberniae
Thomas Messingham, *Florilegium insulae sanctorum seu vitae et acta sanctorum Hiberniae* (1624) [M. de C. quotes Messingham, 'Tract. de nominibus Hibernia' in *Mémoire*, p. 278]

propugnaculum Cathol: veritatis Broudin
Anthony Bruodin, *Propugnaculum Catholicae veritatis* (1669)

hystory of Irland french by Gohogan
The Abbé James MacGeoghegan, *Histoire de l'Irlande ancienne et moderne ...* 3 vols. (Paris and Amsterdam, 1758-63)

hybernia Dominicana Bourke
Thomas de Burgo, *Hibernia Dominicana* (1762)

Saxonis Gramatici hyst. Danicae
Saxo Grammaticus

... french Geography with maps

... yra hybernica Carew
Thomas Carew, *Lyra, sive anacephalaeosis Hibernica* (1651)

[?] Dictionaries one Spanish the other Italian & French

[Ecclesi]astical hystory
Bede (?)

Bossuet's works french

hystory of the revolutions

Les interets presens [?] des puissance de l'Europe

hystoire des Juifes

hystorical collections on the changes of religion

The new odyssey by the Spanish Homer

[The] hystory of Mary Queen of Scots

The case of Irland by Mollineux
William Molyneux's *The case of Ireland's being bound by Acts of Parliament in England stated*

[Irela]nd's Case briefly stated
Hugh Reilly, *Ireland's Case briefly stated* ... (1695)

[Castl]lehaven's Memoirs
Charles O'Conor's edition of the *Memoirs of the Earl of Castlehaven* (1753)

... of the antiquity of royal line of Scotland
Sir George Mackenzie, *A defence of the antiquity of the royal line of Scotland* (1685)
[M. de C. refers to works of Sir George Mackenzie, e.g. *Mémoire*, p. 290]

References

1. Ó Conchúir, *Scríobh. Chorc.*, pp 218-222, 237-40; J. A. Coombes, *A bishop of penal tImes* (Cork, 1981).
2. Coombes, *A bishop*, pp 15-20, 101-5.
3. C. J. F. MacCarthy, 'The bishop's house at Ballinterry' in *Cork Hist. Soc. Jn.*, cxxiv (1969), pp 188-190; Coombes, *A bishop*, p. 24; Ó Conchúir, *Scríobh. Chorc.*, p. 322, note 78.
4. Coombes, *A bishop*, pp 9, 10, 17, 76.
5. Published in *Seanmóiri Muighe Nuadhad*, i (Dublin, 1906) pp 155-71, ii (Dublin, 1907), pp 23-37, and 144-74; *Má Nuad clár*, iv, p. 13. See also P. Ó Súilleabháin, O.F.M., 'Varia' in *Éigse*, ix (1960-1), pp 233-42, especially pp 233-4.
6. T. Ó Fiaich, 'Irish poetry and the clergy' in *Leachtaí Cholm Cille*, iv (1975), pp 30-56; Ó Conchúir, *Scríobh. Chorc.*, pp 211-26.
7. C. Mhág Craith, *Dán na mbráthar mionúr*, i (Dublin, 1967), pp 367-9, ii (1980), pp 312-3; Coombes, *A bishop*, p. 38.
8. This poem is part printed in Coombes, *A bishop*, p. 39, see also pp 102-5, 122; Ó Conchúir, *Scríobh. Chorc.*, p. 322, note 76. See also P. A. Breatnach, 'Dhá dhuain leanbaíochta' in *Éigse*, xxii (1987), pp 111-123.
9. Torna [T. Ó Donnchadha] (ed.), *Seán na Ráithíneach* (Dublin, 1954), pp 337-9; Ó Conchúir, *Scríobh. Chorc.*, pp 167-72. For the *cúirt filíochta* see also [T. Ó Murchú] (ed.), *Faiche na bhfilí* (Carraig na bhFear [?], 1962).
10. Ó Donnchadha, *Seán na Ráithíneach*, pp 337-9. Might *grádhach* also be translated as 'charitable'?
11. Ó Donnchadha, *Seán na Ráithíneach*, pp 352-3.
12. Coombes, *A bishop*, p. 92.
13. R.I.A., MS 23 C 23, cf. *R.I.A. cat. Ir. MSS*, p. 2081. 'Dr. Jeff Connell' is presumably the doctor referred to (with a colleague) in John Gilborne's poem *The medical*

review (1775) in the following terms: '... And Jeffry Connell has a Fortune made / in Cork a city of extensive trade. / These two physicians are so precious grown / They can't be spared one journey out of town', cited in J. F. Fleetwood, *The history of medicine in Ireland*, 2nd ed. (Dublin, 1983), p. 107.

14. Ó Donnchadha, *Seán na Ráithíneach*, pp 353-34. Ó Murchú lived in Carraig na bhFear. Dr O'Brien lived at Ballinterry near Rathcormac. Rathcormac is not much more than ten miles from Carraig na bhFear.

15. Ó Conchúir, *Scríobh. Chorc.*, pp 220-1.

16. Ibid., pp 88-91; [T. Ó Murchú], 'Micheál Ó Longáin (1720?1770)' in [Ó Murchú], *Faiche na bhfilí*, pp 49-52. For 'Filí na Máighe', some account of their poetic court and the connections of one of them, Aindrias Mac Craith, with the Chevalier O'Gorman, Richard McElligot and other Limerick Irish scholars and antiquarians see R. Hayes, 'Some letters of a Thomond antiquary' in *N. Munster Antiq. Jn.*, iii (1942-3), pp 162-8; R. Ó Foghludha, *Éigse na Máighe* (Dublin, 1952); B. Ó Madagáin, *An Ghaeilge i Luimneach* (Dublin, 1974), pp 35-37.

17. There are MS I.L.1 (Society of Jesus, Leeson St., Dublin) (1759-62); probably R.I.A., MS 23 G 2 (about 1760); T.C.D., MS H.I.7, part ii (1762), and possibly R.I.A., MS 23 C 23 with the Rev. Seán Ó Conaire (undated), from the evidence of the content. For this matter see Ó Conchúir, *Scríobh. Chorc.*, pp 88, 220; Ó Fiannachta, *Mionchnuasaigh*, ii (Dublin, 1980), pp 70-76.

18. Ó Conchúir, *Scríobh. Chorc.*, pp 58-9. See also Sir J. Gilbert (ed.), *Leabhar Breac*, (Dublin, 1876), pp x – xiii, and note 24 below.

19. Ó Conchúir, *Scríobh. Chorc.*, pp 51-53; R. Ó hÉanna, 'Alumnus de chuid Choláiste na nGael, Páras' in *Irisleabhar Mhá Nuad* (1989), pp 103-149. For references to the various different people named Seán Ó Conaire/John Conry see N. Ó Muraíle, 'The Manuscript annals of the Four Masters' in *Celtica*, xix (1987), pp 75-95, especially pp 88-9; C. Ó Cuileannáin, 'The Dublin Annals of Innisfallen' in S. Pender (ed.), *Féilscríbhinn Thorna* (Cork, 1947), pp 183-202, especially pp 187, 192, 193.

20. See the reference to 'Cluan Chollamaon in R.I.A., MS 23 C 12, *R.I.A. cat. Ir. MSS*, p. 1020. The historical and literary content of this manuscript reflects the bishop's milieu also.

21. R.I.A., MS 23 C 23, compiled between 1762 and 1769, which draws *inter alia* on manuscripts known to have belonged to O'Brien now comprised in T.C.D., MS H.I.18, see Ó Conchúir, *Scríobh. Chorc.*, pp 51; 219-220, 265, notes 336-7; *R.I.A. cat. Ir. MSS*, pp 2076-2085; and T.C.D., MS H.I.7, *T.C.D. cat. Ir. MSS*, pp 16-20, 64-6.

22. R.I.A., MS 23 C 11; see *R.I.A. cat. Ir. MSS.*, pp 2353-5. These sources were mentioned by O'Brien in the *Mémoire* discussed below. R.I.A., MS 24 K 22 is a copy of *Annála Thighearnaigh* made by Ó Conaire also apparently from T.C.D., MS H.I.18 which belonged to O'Brien; see Ó Conchúir, *Scríobh. Chorc.*, p. 51; Ó Cuilleanáin, 'The Dublin Annals', pp 198, note 70. Bound into this manuscript as it is today there is a bill and a receipt to 'Monsieur l'Abée Connery' from one 'Carsenac, marchand tailleur' dated 21 Feb. 1771 at Paris; see *R.I.A. cat. Ir. MSS*, p. 2959.

23. See N. Ní Shéaghdha, *Catalogue of Irish MSS in the National Library of Ireland*, iii (Dubin, 1976) p. 66.

24. Ó Conchúir, *Scríobh. Chorc.*, pp 242-3. Part of the *Leabhar Breac* was sold to the R.I.A. in 1789 by Conchúir Ó Dálaigh of the Mitchelstown family referred to above, note 18, for three guineas, who claimed his father had lent it to O'Brien; see Ó Conchúir, *Scríobh. Chorc.*, pp 58-9; Gilbert, *Leabhar Breac*, pp x-xiii.

However according to a note in J. Warburton, J. Whitelaw and R. Walsh, *History of the city of Dublin*, ii (Dublin, 1818), Appendix xii, p. lxxx, the 'Leabhar Breac mhic Eoghain [*sic*]', '... was found near Nenagh, in the County of Tipperary, by one Michael Longan [i.e. Mícheál (mac Peadair) Ó Longáin] a schoolmaster, and brought to Dr. J. O'Brian [*sic*], Roman Catholic Bishop of Cloyne, who used it to complete his Irish Dictionary published in France in 1767 [*sic*], whither he had retired from the disturbances in this country. The Leabhar Breac was left by Doctor O'Brien, at his departure, in the house of a relation, who brought it to Dublin, and disposed of it to the Royal Irish Academy for the trifling sum of three guineas'. This information was furnished to Warburton Whitelaw and Walsh by Patrick Lynch, the Clare scribe, scholar, printer and writer; see R. Flower and M. Dillon, *B. M. cat. Ir. MSS*, iii, p. 26.

25. R.I.A., MS 23 P 5 contains copies of the *Annals of Tighearnach* and the *Chronicum Scotorum*, contained in T.C.D., MS H.I.18 which also contains notes by Ó Conaire; see Ó Conchúir, *Scríobh. Chorc.*, p. 51, Ó hEanna, 'Alumnus', pp 107-8.

26. This transcript is found in the middle of part ii of T.C.D., H.I.7, written by Ó Longáin; see Ó Conchúir, *Scríobh. Chorc.*, pp 51, 221. Corrections from the hand of Ó Conaire appear in MS I.L.1 written by Ó Longáin for the bishop, Ó Conchúir, *Scríobh. Chorc.*, p. 51.

27. R.I.A., MS 23 K 34, *R.I.A. cat. Ir. MSS*, p. 1960.

28. F. M. Jones, 'The Congregation of Propaganda and the publication of Dr. O'Brien's Irish Dictionary, 1768' in *The Irish Ecclesiastical Record*, lxxvii (1952), pp 29-37, p. 32, cf. Ó Conchúir, *Scríobh. Chorc.*, pp 52, 237-41; Ó Cuilleanáin, 'The Dublin Annals', p. 192, note 40.

29. Ó Conchúir, *Scríobh. Chorc.*, pp 221-2; Coombes, *A bishop*, pp 79-84.

30. Coombes, *A bishop*, p. 82.

31. See Ó Conchúir, *Scríobh. Chorc.*, pp 222, 324, note 114. The copy of vol. i of the *Collectanea* available to the present writer was the second edition (Dublin, 1786) where the essay appears on pp 215-417 and 419-646. This was also identified by Ó Cuilleanáin from his study of O'Brien's sources as being by O'Brien; see 'The Dublin Annals', p. 189, especially note 24.

32. See his letter to Cardinal Castelli of Propaganda Fide (12 Aug. 1764) seeking financial assistance for his dictionary and advancing arguments of this nature quoted in Jones, 'The congregation of Progaganda', pp 32-3; cf. Coombes, *A bishop*, p. 75; L. Swords, 'Calendar of the Irish College, Paris' in *Archiv. Hib.*, xxxv, p. 109.

33. W. Holland, *A history of west Cork and the diocese of Ross* (Skibbereen, 1949), pp 400-401; Coombes, *A bishop*, pp 234, 33 ff., 65 ff.; Bolster, *Diocese of Cork*, iii pp 58, 67-70.

34. Coombes, *A bishop*, pp 72-74. The expatriate Irish aristrocracy on the continent frequently required certification from respected churchmen and scholars of their own ancestry to enable them to obtain access to positions of social status at continental courts: the Chevalier O'Gorman was recognised as an authority in this area; see R. Hayes, 'A forgotten Irish antiquary' in *Studies* xxx (December, 1941) pp 587-96. For a reference to what may be further documentation relating to this controversy see *R.I.A. Cat. Ir. MSS*, pp 2734-5. For O'Gorman see also Hayes, 'Some letters'; E. MacLysaght, 'O'Gorman Papers' in *Anal. Hib.*, vol. xv (1944) pp 382-3.

35. Coombes, *A bishop*, p. 74; see Hayes, 'A forgotten Irish antiquary', pp 591-2. In this connection it may be relevant that there is stated to be extant amongst the

Stuart Papers at Windsor Castle in England a 'manuscript history of the O'Brien's of Carrigogunell', written by the bishop. Some pastoral writings of the bishop for his priests and people survive also; see Coombes, *A bishop*, pp 73, 109-113.

36. Coombes, *A bishop*, p. 94; C. C. Ward and R. E. Ward, *The letters of Charles O'Conor of Belanagare* (Ann Arbor, Michigan, 1980), i, pp 221-2.

37. J. Macpherson, *Fragments of ancient Poetry collected in the Highlands of Scotland and translated from the Gaelic or Erse language* (Edinburgh, 1760); *Fingal an ancient epic poem* ... (London, 1762); *Temora an ancient epic poem* ... (London, 1763). He later published a history, *An introduction to the history of Great Britain and Ireland* (1771). His supposed Gaelic originals were published posthumously by the Highland Society of London in 1807.

38. For *fiannaíocht* generally see C. Ó Cadhlaigh, *An fhiannuidheacht* (Dublin, 1938); A. Bruford, *Gaelic folk-tales and medieval romances* (Dublin, 1969); G. Murphy, *The Ossianic lore and romantic tales of medieval Ireland,* revised ed., (Cork, 1971); B. Almqvist, S. Ó Catháin and P. Ó Héalaí (ed.), *The heroic process* (Dún Laoghaire, 1987).

39. A. Bruford, 'Oral and literary Fenian tales' in Almqvist, Ó Cathain and Ó Héalaí, *Heroic process*, pp 25-56, especially p. 27; K. Jackson, '"Common Gaelic": the evolution of the Goedelic languages' in *Brit. Acad. Proc.*, xxxvii (1951), pp 71-97, especially p. 77.

40. J. Mac Innes, 'Twentieth-century recordings of Scottish Gaelic heroic ballads' in Almqvist, Ó Cathain, Ó Héalaí, *Heroic process*, pp 101-130.

41. E. Purdie, *Von Deutscher Art und Kunst* (Oxford, 1924), pp 9-10. Partial translations of *Ossian* appeared immediately in various languages. The complete works appeared very quickly in Italian (1763), German (1768), French (1777), Spanish (1788), Danish (1790), Russian (1792), Dutch (1793), Swedish (1794), see *Celtica*, National Library of Scotland (Edinburgh, 1967), p. 17. Ossian would be translated in all into twenty-six different languages over the next hundred years; see F. J. Stafford, *The sublime savage: a study of James Macpherson and the poems of Ossian* (Edinburgh, [1988]), p. 2.

42. For the reception of and reaction to Macpherson generally see Stafford, *Sublime savage*, pp 163-80; P. J. deGategno, *James Macpherson* (Boston, 1989), pp 112-34.

43. On the geographical setting of the tales in Ireland, see Bruford, *Gaelic folk-tales*, p. 17. For some account of the controversy in Ireland see J. Th. Leersen, *Mere Irish and fíor-Ghael* (Amsterdam and Philadelphia, 1986), pp 400-3; C. O'Halloran, 'Irish re-creations of the Gaelic past: the challenge of Macpherson's Ossian', *Past & Present*, cxxiv (August, 1989), pp 69-95. See also note 106 below. The controversy is treated in J. S. Smart, *James Macpherson An episode in literature* (London, 1905; reprinted New York, 1973), pp 129-184; D. S. Thomson *The Gaelic sources of Macpherson's Ossian* (Edinburgh, 1952).

44. P. Van Tieghem, *Ossian en France* (Paris, 1917), pp 155-163.

45. R. Mandrou, *From humanism to science 1480-1700,* trans. by B. Pearse (Middlesex, 1978) p. 273. See also K. T. Hoppen, *The common scientist in the seventeenth century* (London, 1970), p. 90.

46. Van Tieghem, *Ossian*, p. 163.

47. Quoted in P. Logan, M.D., 'Chevalier Terence de Brade' in *Breifne*, iv (1970-75), pp 267-276, especially pp 275-6. The Chevalier de Brade died at Brussels on 6 April 1770. In his will he left bequests to the Irish Franciscan colleges in Prague and Louvain, the Irish Dominicans in Louvain and the Irish College of Antwerp; see ibid., pp 273-4.

48. 'les deux Chroniques de ce Pays dites de *Tara* & de *Casshel* en font mention: l'Histoire de Keating publiée en Anglois a Londres en 1723 en parle aussi ...'. Van Tieghem, *Ossian*, p. 164, refers to *Journal des Sçavans*, June 1763, p. 426. The copy of this issue of *Journal des Sçavants* to which the present writer had access appears to be an Amsterdam reprint in July 1763 of the Paris edition of June 1763, and in the Amsterdam reprint the letter appears at pp 84-88, and the present quotation on p. 85.

49. 'il auroit jetté des lumieres sur la langue originale du Poëme, & sur la partie du Monde où il fut composé ...' pp. 87-8.

50. For 'Saltair Chaisil' and 'Saltair Teamhrach' see P. Ó Riain, 'The Psalter of Cashel: a provisional list of contents' in *Éigse*, xxiii (1989), pp 107-30. Fr P. Walsh, *Irish men of learning* (Dublin, 1947), p. 244, says 'it was not unusual to give the name "Psalter of Cashel" to any book containing genealogies or other historical matter'. Brady also mentions *Bruin Chartuin* (Bruíon Chaorthainn), *Caha' Garve* (Cath Gabhra), *Fintraga* (Cath Fionntra), *Athra* [?], *Gilla d'Acre* (Eachtra an Ghiolla Dheacair), all well-known *fiannaíocht* tales; 'la mort de *Derdre*, & la catastrophe des enfans de *Usnach*', 'the death of *Derdre*, and the misfortune of the children of Uisneach' (p. 86).

51. For reading and recitation of tales see Bruford, *Gaelic folk-tales*, pp 55-64.

52. 'The following Mémoire was addressed to us by a scholar of merit who possesses very wide learning in more than one area of literature, and in particular in that which relates to the antiquities of Ireland and Scotland. We requested him to resolve our doubts about this 'famous' discovery of Mr Macpherson's which has been aired in so many newspapers and of which our own has already made mention several times without daring to reach a conclusion. To the solution of this literary problem this Mémoire is dedicated'; *Journal des Sçavans* (May 1754), p. 277; Van Tieghem, *Ossian*, pp 164-5.

53. May, 1764, pp 277-292; June, pp 353-417; Aug., pp 537-555; Sept., pp 604-617; Dec., pp 845-857.

54. '... peut-être une entreprise bien hardie de la part d'un homme qui a peu d'usage de votre Langue. Mais on excusera toujours un Étranger sur ce défaut, pourvû qu'il se rende intelligible & qu'il ait raison au fond', *Mémoire*, p. 279.

55. For Macpherson's treatment of material from Irish historians see Thomson, *Gaelic sources*, pp 69-72. For some account of the argument about the meaning of 'Scoti' between Irish and Scottish historians since the early seventeenth century see Leersen, *Mere Irish*, pp 303 ff.

56. *Mémoire*, p. 555.

57. A full list of the sources is given in Appendix I hereto.

58. *Mémoire*, p. 553: 'Collectan. Etymol. Vol. 1. page 152'. For Leibniz's acquaintance with Irish see E. Poppe, 'Leibniz and Eckhart on the Irish language' in *Eighteenth-Century Ireland*, i (1986), pp 65-84.

59. *Mémoire*, p. 609.

60. *Mémoire*, p. 548 and p. 541.

61. '... actuellement cette même copie des Annales de Tighernach que possédoit M. Ó Flaherty, avec un ancien Apographe de la Chronique de Clonmacnois, qui est bien connu sous le titre de *Chronicon Scotorum Cluanense* & qui appartenoit aussi au même M. Ó Flaherty. ... Je possede aussi une copie parfaite & authentique des Annalls d'Innisfallen', *Mémoire*, p. 607.

62. For Ó Flaithearta, a noted seventeenth-century antiquary in the Gaelic tradition, see T. Ó Raighne, 'Ruairí Ó Flaithearta' in *Dóchas*, ii (1964), pp 53-7

63. e.g. *Mémoire*, p. 286.

64. '... une ancienne piéce de Tapisserie qui se voyait a Versailles, dans la Salle d'Audience de M. de Chamillart, où Charlemange étoit entouré de différens Rois ses Alliés, parmi lesquels il paroissoit un Roi d'Irlande avec la Harpe (Armes de ce Royaume) à son côté', *Mémoire*, p. 543. This is quoted from 'Le Docteur Kennedy, dans son Traité de la Généalogie du Roi d'Angleterre Jacques II', presumably *A chronological genealogical, and historical dissertation of the royal family of Stuarts beginning with ... the Milesian Irish* by Matthew Kennedy (Paris, 1705). For some references to Kennedy (*ob.* 1735) see C. Mooney O.F.M., 'Manutiana' in *Celtica*, i (1946), pp 1-63, especially pp 2, 7, 10. This reference to the audience-hall of M. de Chamillart and the Irish association of the tapestry hanging there could conceivably have been the inspiration for the nom-de-plume 'M. de C.'.

65. C. Ó Cuilleanáin 'The Dublin Annals', p. 198, indicates that M. de C. may have consulted a manuscript of Micheál Ó Cléirigh then at St Anthony's College, Louvain, where one volume of the *Annals of the Four Masters* was at that time. O'Brien seems to have consulted Irish manuscripts in the British Museum (now the British Library) in London at some stage. In his *Dictionary* (second edition, p. 147) under 'Curmuc', he cites a manuscript 'in the British Museum at London ...'. [This in fact is B.L., MS Harley 1802.] He states that by virtue of the 'marginal remarks of the writer of that inestimable manuscript, I have been enabled to furnish the keepers and overseers of the British Museum with a note, whereby the antiquity of that manuscript is ascertained and fixed at the year 1138'.

66. 'L'obscurité que Macpherson laisse sur cette article, a bien l'air d'avoir été affectée pour dérouter ceux qui demanderoient á voir les originaux'; *Mémoire*, p. 614.

67. 'Cette multiplicité de rimes tant au milieu qu'au bout des vers, & tout cet artifice méchanique & frivole ne se sont introduits dans la construction des vers Irlandois que depuis le dixième siècle, lorsque le goût gothique s'étant répandu dans toute l'Europe, se communiqua enfin aux Irlandois, soit part leur commerce dans le continent, soit part le grand concours d'étrangers qui alloient aux Ecoles d'Irlande depuis le regne de Brien Borove'; *Mémoire*, pp 615. 'Brian Borove' is, of course, Brien Bóroimhe, Brian Boru (*ob.* 1014)

68. 'une connaisance bien profonde de l'ancienne Langue Iberno-Celtique'; *Mémoire*, pp 615.

69. *Mémoire*, p. 555

70. 'L'homme le plus propre à perpetuer leur mémoire'; *Mémoire*, p. 846.

71. Ibid., pp 846-7. Today *Cath Fionntrá* is known in many oral and written versions; see Ó Cadhlaigh, *Fiannuidheacht*, Bruford, *Gaelic folk-tales*, especially pp 118-22, 253; for *Bruíon Chaorthainn* see ibid, especially pp 115-6 251-2. One has not found *Dearg mac Diric*: there is an account in Ó Cadhlaigh, *Fiannuidheacht*, pp 170-2, of 'Dearg Mac Droichill, Rí Thíre na bhFionn' which may be it. See also G. Murphy, *Duanaire Finn*, iii (Dublin, 1953), p. 358. Professor Seán Ó Coileáin has suggested that 'Dearg mac Diric' could be a native speaker's corruption of Dearg mac Deirg. For the immediate sources of Macpherson's *Fingal* see Thomson, *Gaelic sources*, pp 13-41.

72. '... est tiré d'un autre Roman que j'ai aussi cité sous le titre de *Cath Fiontragh*, qui veut dire en Francois, *la bataille du rivage blanc* ... La bruyere ou la plaine de Lena, que M Macpherson a choisie pour le theatre de l'action de son Poeme de Fingal, il l'a empruntee dune relation historique qui se trouve parmi les anciens monumens d'Irlande sous le titre de *Cath Maigh-Lena*, c'est-a-dire, *l'Histoire de la bataille du champ de Lena*'; *Mémoire*, p. 850. The tale referred to here, *Cath Maighe Lena*, was edited by K. Jackson (Dublin, 1938).

73. 'le plagiat général par les plagiats particuliers' ... '... l'inspection des originaux le confondra toujours ...'; *Mémoire*, p. 851.

74. *Mémoire*, pp 852-3. The last reference is to *Oidhe Chloinne Uisnigh: the fate of the Children of Uisneach*; see J. E. C. Williams and M. Ní Mhuiríosa, *Traidisiún liteartha na nGael* (Dublin, 1979), pp 117-18.

75. 'Nous ne finirions pas si nous voulions entrer ici dans l'examen détaillé de tous ses autres Poëmes, il suffit d'observer qu'ils sont tous puisés dans la même source, composés dans le même esprit, et que les originaux y sont altérés avec le même artifice', *Mémoire*, pp 852-3.

76. '... ainsi plaéee entre certains antiquaires Ecossois d'un côté, & quelque Ecrivains Anglois de l'autre. Les uns lui enlèver ses héros & ses grands hommes en tout genre, les autres s'attachent a àvilir cette Nation respectable; ils peignent tous les Irlandois comme des sauvages et des bêtes féroces que ne méritoient depuis si longtems'; *Mémoire*, p. 854.

77. Ibid., p. 857.

78. Van Tieghem, *Ossian*, pp 165-166.

79. A. Gillies, *Herder und Ossian* (Berlin, 1933) p. 6, note 12. The note was apparently itself excerpted from a notice which appeared in a later issue of the *Journal des Sçavans* as follows: '"L'auteur du dictionnaire et du mémoire, très versé dans les antiquités celtiques, est le même sçavant irlandois dont nous avons inséré un mémoire sur les poëmes de M. Macpherson dans nos journax de mai, juin etc. 1764"' ('The author of the dictionary and of the mémoire, one very familiar with Celtic antiquities, is the same Irish scholar whose mémoire on the poems of Mr. Macpherson was published by us in May, June etc. 1764'). The present writer failed to find this note in a copy of the first edition of O'Brien's *Dictionary* consulted by him. Such an advertisement could perhaps however have been bound in with certain copies of the dictionary and not with others. It appears for example that O'Brien had had certain matter printed which he intended to include only in the copies circulating in France. Copies intended for circulation in Ireland bore no indication of authorship while those on the continent named the author as J. O'Brien; see Coombes, *A bishop*, pp 94-5. Similarly an advertisement in *The Corke Journal* of 23 Nov. 1768 gives no hint of authorship either; see Coombes, *A bishop*, p. 121.

80. T.C.D., MS H.I.7, part i; Ó Cuilleanáin, 'The Dublin Annals', pp 183-202.

81. Now T.C.D., MS H.1.18.

82. 'The Dublin Annals', pp 184, 188, 189, 194, note 50; 200. The treatise attributed to O'Brien was the article published by Vallancey in *Collectanea de Rebus Hibernicis*, see above note 31.

83. 'The Dublin Annals', p. 189; *Focaloir Gaoidhilge – Sacs-Bhéarla*, second edition, ed. by Robert Daly (Dublin, 1832), p. xii, and s.nn. *Caorthain, Conmaol, Dalrialda.*

84. For instance, s.n. 'Conchubhar' where he refers to the arms of 'the direct line of Conchubhar na Cathrach.' Under 'Curmuc' and 'Domhnal', the bishop again refers to Conchubhar na Cathrach. Under *slapar* we find: 'a skirt, or the trail of a king or nobleman's robe; hence the nick-name of a king of Munster of the O'Brien race in the beginning of the 12th century, called Conchur Slapar-salach, from his regal robes being often spattered with mortar by mounting on the scaffolds of masons in building his churches'. See also s.vv. *Clar, Comhluidhe, Cora Crotach* and so forth.

85. *Mémoire*, pp 278, 544-8, 615, 616.

86. 'ex regali et antiquissima O'Brienorum stirpe per lineam rectam Conchubari

O'Brien cognomento na catharach vulgo slaparsalach Regis Momoniae ...', the manuscript, T.C.D., MS H.I.7, part ii, is quoted in Ó Donnchadha, *An Leabhar Muimhneach* (Dublin, n.d.), p. 387, see also p. xxxii. The epitaph (now destroyed), is given in 'The last resting place of Dr. John O'Brien, bishop of Cloyne' in *Cork Hist. Soc. Jn.*, second series, i (1895), p. 188.

87. Fr L. Swords, 'Calendar', p. 109. It may also be worthy of note that M. de C. (*Mémoire*, p. 852) pays particular attention to the meaning of the name *Brian*.

88. 'qui subsiste encore mais dans un état peu convenable a la dignité de son origine, étant depouillée de tout ...'; *Mémoire*, p. 548.

89. Coombes, *A bishop*, p. 81, apropos of the nom-de-plume 'M. de C.', observing 'that writers rarely go far afield in their search for a pen-name,' suggests that 'Monseigneur de Cloyne' ('My Lord of Cloyne') is a likely interpretation. To this one might add that the Papal Nuncio in Brussels in a covering note in Italian to a lettter of O'Brien's which the Nuncio was forwarding to Rome also refers to O'Brien as 'Monsig.[nore] di Cloyne ...'; see Jones, 'The Congregation of Propaganda', p. 31. E. O'Curry *Lectures on the manuscript materials of ancient Irish history* (Dublin, 1878), pp. 66, 67, 120, believed that 'M. de C.' was a priest called 'Connery' whom he also called 'John Conroy', though he thought that 'M. de C.' might have been John O'Brien. This 'Abbé Connery' or 'John Conroy' may be identified as the Fr Seán Ó Conaire, referred to above. It can probably be safely said that if Seán Ó Conaire assisted in any capacity with the *Mémoire*, such assistance was under the direction of the bishop.

90. See Ó Conchúir, *Scríobh. Chorc.*, p. 218, p. 322, note 70, for further information supplementing and confirming Fr. Coombes's researches:

91. Jones, 'The Congregation', pp 30-31. He stated that he was to depart for Ireland the following day, and he was back in Ireland in November, 1764; ibid. While at Brussels he could have consulted Irish manuscripts at St Anthony's College, Louvain: see note 65 above.

92. L. Swords (ed.), *The Irish-French connection 1578-1978*, (Paris, 1978), Appendix 1, pp 160-1. See also Bolster, *Diocese of Cork*, iii pp 67-70.

93. R. Hayes, 'Biographical dictionary of Irishmen in France' in *Studies*, xxxii (Sept. 1943), pp 385-6. See also Swords, *The Irish-French connection*, pp 160-1; Coombes, *A bishop*, pp 94-6, 116.

94. 'bourré de faits, de noms de titres, de références de toutes sortes...'; Van Tieghem, *Ossian*, pp 165-166.

95. Amsterdam, June, July, Aug., Oct., 1764, and Feb. 1765; see R. Tombo, *Ossian in Germany* (New York, 1901), p. 5.

96. Tombo, *Ossian*, pp 5, 77-8.

97. *The Monthly Review*, xxxii (1764 [*recte* 1765?]), pp 558-60, especially p. 558.

98. See, for example H. B. Garland, *Storm and Stress (Sturm und Drang)* (London, 1952); L. R. Furst, *Romanticism*, second ed. (London and New York, 1976), pp 37-8; Ossian was also quoted enthusiastically by Gottfried Friedrich Klopstock (1724-1803) an early pre-romantic German poet; see Tombo, *Ossian*, pp 82-102.

99. L. Marsden Price, *The reception of English literature in Germany* (Berkeley, 1932). Thomas Percy (1729-1811), an Englishman, was a significant European pre-romantic figure: E. Legouis and L. Cazamian, *History of English literature*, revised ed. (London, 1971), pp 917-8. He was appointed to Ireland as Church of Ireland Bishop of Dromore in 1782 where he remained until his death. He corresponded with and influenced Charlotte Brooke, herself a pivotal figure in the rediscovery of Irish literature of the time, and he was a founding member of the Royal Irish Academy; see E. R. R. Green, 'Thomas Percy in Ireland' in *Ulster*

Folklife, xv-xvi (1970), pp 224-232; R. B. McDowell, 'The main narrative' in T. Ó Raifeartaigh (ed.), *The Royal Irish Academy: a bicentennial history 1785-1985* (Dublin, 1985), pp 1-92 especially p. 11; R. Flower and M. Dillon, *B.M. cat. Ir. MSS*, iii, p. 24.

100. For some account of the undifferentiated use of such terms as 'Celtic', 'Germanic' and 'Scythian' at the time see Van Tieghem, *Ossian* pp 193-201; Stuart Piggott, *Ruins in a landscape* (Edinburgh, 1976); pp 55-76; Leersen, *Mere Irish*, pp 337-8, For Germany see for example A. Gillies, *Herder und Ossian* (Berlin, 1933), pp 38-41; H. Schoffler, *Deutscher Geist im 18. Jahrhundert*, second ed. (Göttingen, 1967), pp 135-154.

101. See Van Tieghem, *Ossian*, pp 227-301.

102. Purdie, *Von Deutscher Art und Kunst*, p. 12.

103. 'Aufsatz des Herrn von C. über die Gedichte des Herrn Macphersons', 'Fortsetzung des Aufsatzes uber Herrn Macphersons Gedichte' and 'Beschluss des Aufsatzes über Herrn Macphersons Gedichte' ('Essay of M. de C. concerning the Poems of Mr. Macpherson'; 'Contination ...', and 'Conclusion ...'), *Unterhaltungen*, i, no. 4, (Hamburg, 1766), pp 329-40; no. 5, pp 420-36; no. 6, pp 504-23.

104. '... die Gelehrsamkeit, welche in diesem Aufsatze herrscht, wird ihn einem Theil unsrer Leser scätzbar machen,' *Unterhaltungen*, i, no. 4, p. 329.

105. Ibid.

106. p. 330. Warner may have based his pamphlet on information furnished to him by Charles O'Conor of Belanagare; see C. A. Sheehan, 'Some notes on the Ossianic controversy' in *Notes and Queries*, cxcv (1950), pp 300-2, and L. L. Stewart, 'Ferdinando Warner and the Ossianic controversy' in ibid., cc (1973), pp 4213. The other pamphlet was anonymous; see Stafford, *The sublime savage*, pp 165-6, where it is dated 1762.

107. 'Mémoire eines Irrländers über die Ossianischen Gedichte ... erst vor wenig Tagen aus Paris mitgetheilt' quoted in Purdie, *Von Deutscher Art und Kunst*, p. 12.

108. 'der Irrländer hat ihrer die Menge .... Der Betrug wird durch die Fragmente der Irrländischen Romanzen ... offenbar ...'; ibid.

109. Ibid., p. 12; Tombo *Ossian*, pp 6, 77-8, 106. For Gerstenberg see Tombo, *Ossian*, pp 103-119 and Garland, *Storm and stress*, pp 19-25.

110. Tombo, *Ossian* pp 6, 78-9; Gillies, *Herder*, p. 7,

111. H. Blair, 'A critical dissertation on the poems of Ossian' in *The poems of Ossian translated by James Macpherson Esq. with dissertations on the era and poems of Ossian; and Dr. Blair's critical dissertation*, ii (Glasgow, 1821), pp 152-254 (especially p. 246); see also M. Chapman, *The Gaelic vision in Scottish culture* (London and Montreal, 1979), p. 47, and Gillies, *Herder*, pp 25 ff.

112. Gillies, *Herder*, pp 8, 13, 15; Purdie, *Von Deutscher Art und Kunst*, p. 12; Tombo, *Ossian*, p. 78.

113. 'Le *Mémoire* ... est hérisse d'une erudition si epineuse, qu'il est difficile de démeler nettement la doctrine de l'auteur'; Van Tieghem, *Ossian*, p. 166.

114. Gillies, *Herder*, p. 7.

115. Gillies, *Herder*, pp 34-6, 90-1, 95; see also J. Hennig, 'Goethes Irlandkunde' in *Deutsches Vierteljahresschrift für Literaturwissenschaft und Geistesgeschichte*, xxxi (1957), pp 7083, especially pp 71-74. In an attempt to defuse the mounting criticism Macpherson had included in *Temora* (1763) the alleged Gaelic of the original of Bk. 7. This has been described as 'clearly a translation from Macpherson's English'; see *Celtica*, National Library of Scotland (Edinburgh, 1967), p. 16, and Thomson, *The Gaelic sources*, p. 86.

116. Gillies, *Herder*, pp 79, 90-92, 95, 146.

117. See, for example, P. Burke, *Popular culture in early modern Europe*, reprinted (Aldershot, 1988), especially pp 3-23, 287-8; R. H. Robins, *A short history of linguistics*, third ed. (London, 1990), pp 180-196. See also F. Shaw, 'The background to *Grammatica Celtica*' in *Celtica*, iii (1955), pp 1-16 and P. Ó Riain, 'An *Grammatica Celtica*: a cúlra agus a húdar' in *Capuchin Annual* (1970), pp 200-205.

118. See B. Traxler Brown, 'Three centuries of journals in Ireland : the library of the Royal Dublin Society, Grafton St' in B. Hayley and E. McKay (ed.), *Three hundred years of Irish periodicals* (Dublin and Mullingar, 1987), pp 11-28, especially pp 22, 25.

119. O Conchúir, *Scríobh. Chorc.*, p. 52.

120. Ibid., p. 52; For some account of the Select Committee see C. O'Conor, S.J., 'Origins of the Royal Irish Academy' in *Studies*, xxxviii (1949), pp 326-37, McDowell, 'The main narrative', pp 5-7, and the present writer's 'Charles O'Conor of Belanagare, antiquary and Irish scholar' in *R.S.A.I. Jn.*, cxix (1989), pp 136-163, especially pp 153-5.

121. Ó Conchúir, *Scríobh. Chorc.*, p. 53; see also Gilbert, *Leabhar Breac*, pp x-xiii, for a person of the same name.

122. Quoted in W. O'Sullivan, 'The Irish manuscripts in Case H in Trinity College Dublin' in *Celtica,* xi (1976), pp 229-50, especially p. 242. These were T.C.D., MS H.I.7. and H.I.18. Vallancey subsequently lent them to O'Conor; O'Sullivan, 'The Irish manuscripts', p. 243. See also Ó Cuilleanáin, 'The Dublin Annals', p. 189.

123. Ó Cuileannáin 'The Dublin Annals,' pp 193-199; Ó Fiannachta, *Mionchnuasaigh*, ii, pp 72-3 and Appendix II (page 522).

Plate 13.3   Gougane Barra (Cambridge University Collection of air photographs).

Chapter 14

THE BLACKWATER CATHOLICS AND COUNTY CORK SOCIETY AND POLITICS IN THE EIGHTEENTH CENTURY

L. M. CULLEN

The Blackwater valley and Cork politics

The Blackwater valley was noteworthy in many ways. Its very heart in social and political terms is the short stretch of six or seven miles from Mallow to Castletownroche with its Cotter/Nagle interface with the new political and landed interest now consolidated by the Williamite confiscation. Mallow was a large centre of English settlement, and its surroundings and the river to the east were characterised by many seats, a few great, many small. The immediate hinterland of this belt reached out to embrace Doneraile and Mitchelstown. The lands of the King family reached the parish of Clenor on banks of the Blackwater. The St Leger family at Doneraile played a role politically in Mallow, and Mallow itself was the social centre for life in the region. Indeed the resident gentry of north-east Cork even more than the spa accounted for the importance of Mallow and made it into a centre of winter social life. Within five miles of the town there were 'not less' than fifty seats.[1] Families moved within this region, and there was a drift at every social level towards the Blackwater and Mallow.

The region is also of interest because it had a strong Catholic presence. It is an irony that the largest gentry presence in the county surrounded a nucleus of propertied Catholics, largely in Clenor and Castletownroche, and beyond these, more thinly, towards Clogher and Doneraile. It was moreover the only rural group of rich Catholics in the county; the sectarian politics of the county in the 1730s and again in the 1750s and 1760s revolved around the interplay of interests and personalities in this region. It had other claims to note as well. While not the home of Eoghan Rua Ó Súilleabháin, he had resided there, perhaps as early as the mid-1760s, at a key time in his career, as a tutor to the Annikissy Nagles, and the politics and society of the region have strong re-echoes in his poetry. It was also the region of Edmund Burke. His mother was from there, so he spent much of his youth on the Blackwater and made the acquaintance of various Barretts, Nagles and

Plate 14.1   Blackwater Valley, Pallas Townland (Cork Archaeological Survey).

Hennessys whose contacts retained throughout his life. These nourished the loyalty which is one of Burke's most attractive features. Burke's writing too is in many ways a product of the region, not only indirectly but directly because of the political events of the 1760s: it is not an exaggeration to claim that his Irish politics and his writings on the penal laws all grew out of his stay on the banks of the Blackwater and happenings there.[2]

From the heart of this region too came Richard Hennessy. Burke and Hennessy knew one another as young men, and Hennessy was to spend a night with Burke in 1792 in Beaconsfield and to leave a letter describing the visit.[3] They certainly corresponded in the 1760s at the time when both were beginning to make their way in the world outside Ireland, and, though none of those letters survives, the names of common acquaintances, Nagles and Barretts especially, crop up then and later in the exchanges of both men. Far apart later, they no longer corresponded, though a common circle of relatives continued to appear in the dispatches of both men. To have provided a haven for Ó Súilleabháin, to have coloured indelibly the outlook of Burke and to have produced the founder of the famous brandy house is a large contribution by one small region to the story of the eighteenth century.

Richard Hennessy makes a good starting point, because the Hennessys resided at the heart of the region and they were related through marriage over several generations to the Nagles. The Nagles themselves were the most powerful of the Catholic families, indeed one of the greatest surviving Catholic families in Ireland, and marriages over the first half of the century to the Mathews in Tipperary, Frenches in Galway and Mapas in Dublin tell their own story of the family's social standing. In 1794 Edmund Burke reckoned of his kin that 'those who are so to me in the 4th and 5th degree are numerous indeed, not less, to be sure than 40 or 50 – of which but a small number are in good circumstances'.[4] The families connected to Burke included Nagles, Hennesseys and Sheehys and, in Burke's estimation, even distantly the FitzGibbon family. In the wake of the Nagle marriage to a French in the west of Ireland in 1758, Burke's sister Julia also married a French, of Loughrea. His mother visited the region in 1766 and was clearly impressed by the affluent lifestyle of Catholics in the tolerant western society.

That marriage too gave Burke an entrée to the county Galway circle in London and Paris. It was probably through the Frenches that he made the acquaintance of Thomas Sutton, Patrick Darcy and Isaac Panchaud. It was this circuit also that was relevant to the financial speculation in which Burke engaged centrally and which his admirers, rather like the admirers of Dickens in their difficulties in coping with his secret love life, have denied. Burke's actions in the late 1760s and early 1770s both in speculation and in East India affairs have to be seen not only in the web of Whig politics but in the context of the Irish interest in the French East India company which had close ties with the Colebrooke group in the English company (Colebrooke himself was already long connected with Irish families both through his wife and in his multiple business partnerships with the Nesbitts). When Burke described Paris society he was describing several weeks in Paris in early 1773 when he was taken in hand by Darcy and Sutton who introduced him to the salons.

As far as comfortable Catholics are concerned, the Blackwater was a land of Nagles and Hennessys [Fig. 14.1]. The Nagles resided in as many as five or six seats by the 1760s, the so-called 'seven houses' referred to by William O'Brien; the Hennessys in two more modest ones. The Nagles were at the pinnacle of their eighteenth-century standing in the 1750s. Though far less prominent, and apparently having moved down to the Blackwater some generations earlier from the Doneraile region, the Hennessys were also in a modest way rising in the world. Inevitably these families encountered the wrath of the politicised Protestants of the region, doubly so as in the course of the

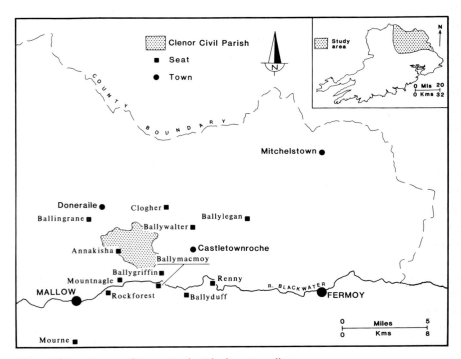

Figure 14.1   Seats and towns in the Blackwater valley.

first half of the century the centre of Protestant politics in the county moved north from the Brodrick region around Midleton to the Kings and St Legers and their satellites in the Blackwater valley and beyond it. Ó Súilleabháin was to recall with contempt *lucht dreadair bhriste meadrach do dhíol thar lear* ('those who sell the inferior products of churns abroad') in the Mallow area and he commemorated in alliteration the names of the political enemies of the Catholics.

In an earlier generation almost twenty poems had been written to commemorate the execution of Sir James Cotter in 1720. There was something of a repeat in the laments written in the 1760s, transcribed in some of the Gaelic manuscripts of the period, to record the execution of Nicholas and Edmond Sheehy, and in a more lowly fashion (lowly because it does not survive in any manuscripts transcribed contemporaneously in the county) in the great lament on the death of Art Ó Laoire in 1773. This is not a folk lament in its tone and attitudes, even if the surviving text was first written down *c.* 1800 from oral tradition. It almost certainly first made its appearance in a now-lost manuscript form and it may be seriously doubted whether it was the extempore composition it has been taken to be, or whether it was composed by O'Leary's widow at all. The surviving transcriptions of 1800 or later, moreover, are from Cork, not from Kerry, to which the widow retired. The poem has resonances of Cork, not Kerry, politics: that explains in all probability why, first, it was written, and why afterwards its combination of powerful emotional appeal and political undertone gave it a folk following. The lament on the death in 1754 of Morty Og O'Sullivan of Bearhaven is a further parallel. Collectively these laments provide a unique corpus of comment on a series of highly politicised tragedies in an entire county over half a century. Those relating to the Sheehys touch more directly on the Blackwater valley itself.

The events behind these laments make sense of course in the contemporary context of the individuals and regions described in them, but they gain wider and deeper significance as part of a greater story affecting the place of Catholics in what was politically the most powerful county in Ireland (county Cork provided 26 of the 300 members of the Irish House of Commons). The poems of Eoghan Rua Ó Súilleabháin and of Piaras Mac Gearailt, at any rate his later ones, have a new tone within them which is a somewhat coded response to the political events of the 1760s. The *Caoineadh Airt Uí Laoire* itself should be seen not in a folk context, but in a literary one, composed however at a time when literary communication was beginning to break down: declining circulation through poetic schools meant that literary composition itself was less likely to survive. Ó Súilleabháin himself it should be recalled was at the end of a tradition, and his involvement in the Blackwater valley and in county Cork embraced most of his active life. These traditions were declining rapidly in county Cork compared with more remote Clare, the residual centre of vitality, and the latter stages of the Ó Longáins' activity was urban in its patronage.

The story embraces Jacobitism, which is one way of looking at it (and one in which Protestants and Gaelic poets alike saw it), but more fundamentally the real issue was that of the place of propertied Catholics in local society and the extent to which they could use the law to protect themselves and to assert their position in society. Joseph Nagle was a lawyer. He and his brother Garrett were also lobbyists who used the system to influence legislation, and Garrett's daughter Nano in founding her schools in the 1750s was challenging the laws even more directly in the decade in which for the first time the question of the repeal of the laws became an issue.

The Hennessy family circle in county Cork

The Nagles are well-known because they were the most prominent Catholic family in Cork from the 1720s and because their Burke links made them famous. The Hennessys, the other landed family of the region, much smaller than the Nagles, are less well-known, or are remembered only in terms of the repute of Richard Hennessy after he went to Cognac or even of the mistaken belief that he had been a French officer at Fontenoy. Richard Hennessy arrived in Cognac in 1765 at the end of twelve years of frustration and failure. Who was he, or, as we know him quite well, who were his immediate forebears? His family was settled in county Cork and both his father and grandfather lived at Ballymacmoy on the Blackwater river in the north-east of the county. They belonged to a county Cork family which in the seventeenth century, so calamitous for many families, had fallen on evil days. In the 1691 Williamite dispossession of families who had fought against the English forces their names do not figure at all, which suggests that their landed substance was already slight. Indeed the Williamite confiscation, paradoxically perhaps, raised their status in the county by reducing to the same level hitherto more successful families who by marriage, friendship and business ties were later to feature in the Hennessy story at home and abroad. The Barretts, Nagles, Galweys, Sarsfields and Coppingers all lost land in 1691.

Of the Cork Catholic landed families the only one, apart from the Cotters, to survive relatively intact were the Nagles. In the Books of Survey and Distribution they remained in their native district, holding land both in their own name and under leases from more recent landowners. Moreover, though the pre-1720 Cotters lived at Ballinsperry, near Carrigtohill, the larger of their estates in extent was at Rockforest, less than two miles from Killavullen. Thus this enclave contained in 1720 the only large concentration of Catholic landed property in the county. Cotters and Nagles alike were also allied by marriage to the Mathews in Tipperay. Garrett Nagle of Ballygriffen, early in the new century, married a daugher of the Mathews of Thurles, the richest Catholic family in Tipperary. Such a marriage with a member of the leading Catholic family of Tipperary underlined their status and enhanced it. Along with the Cotters, they were the leaders of the Catholic interest. In turn two of Garrett's children made very good marriages. According to Richard Hennessy's brother James in 1753, one of Garrett's daughters had married Arthur French of Rahasane in county Galway, a gentleman with £2,000 per annum, and later in 1755 a son was also to marry a Kavanagh of Borris, county Carlow.[5] His information on the French marriage was somewhat premature as the Nagle wedding did not take place until 1758 (though the time-lag is interesting in illustrating the long deliberation in eighteenth-century marriage strategy), and the Kavanagh alliance in fact never eventuated: the marriage which eventually did take place several years later was to a Mapas of Dublin, a member of one of the surviving Catholic landed families who ironically ringed a Protestant capital.

These two marriages tell their own story of success. The Nagles, uniquely for Catholic landed families in the region, married, as one might expect from their wealth and status, far afield. Connected prior to 1758 to Tipperary's leading Catholic (or convert) family, and after 1758 both to the great Catholic landed circle of county Galway and to the venerable Catholic gentry of the Pale, they held a position to which no other Catholic family in Ireland could pretend, and its far-flung regional pattern was unique for its day. For the French marriage the reported dowry of the Nagle bride was £12,000, and the Nagle son in 1755 reportedly was to marry a lady with £3,000. Garrett's family was at its social peak in the 1750s. That added to the reasons which made them marked men in the political society of the region. Garrett's brother, Joseph, was famous as a lawyer, and given the penal laws that meant a role of devising methods of evading their impact. The Nagles were, after the death of Sir James Cotter in 1720, the perceived leaders of Catholic political society in county Cork. Both families were also identified with the church. A James Nagle was a priest in the 1704 returns[6] and John Hennessy had the daunting and dangerous position of parish priest of Doneraile at the outset of the 1730s. In the parish of Monanimy the church was sited on the Annakissy demesne, symbolising further the Nagle identification with the old order. In Cloyne diocese at large, a particularly repressive diocese in which few new mass houses had been erected, Castletownroche parish union in 1731 had three, one 'lately built'.[7] This was an assertion of Catholic determination in the key area of Catholic strength within the dioceses.

The Ballygriffen branch of the Nagle family was rich, the active spokesmen of the Catholic interest and not wholly intimidated by the hostile environment in which they lived. The success of the Ballygriffen Nagles created an environment in which lesser branches of the same family as well as related families including the Hennessys survived. The families also intermarried: in the mid-eighteenth century David of Ballygriffen for his second bride chose an Annakissy cousin. Small inherited patrimonies or more typically modest acreages rented from the new Protestant gentry and sublet to occupying tenants or farmers made it possible for the eldest son to live on a rental income, and thus to avoid slipping out of the gentry class. Marrying, if they married outside the county at all only in the border region of Tipperary which offered the comfortable Catholic class that county Cork lacked, they were a contrast to the Ballygriffen Nagles. Indeed, not only did they owe their survival to legal protection by Joseph Nagle who drew up their leases or defended them in the law courts but some of them held their land from the Nagles. With their diminutive properties the non-Nagle members recreated modestly a gentry style of life and perpetuated ties among themselves or with succesful kin who had moved into the freer and burgeoning world of business in Cork city. Blackwater Nagles apart, the unfriendly political and social environment of rural county Cork ensured that Catholics were already beginning to prosper more freely in the city than in its rural hinterland.

The Hennessys owed their land and probably their survival to the Nagles; as tenants of the Nagles they kept their place in the subdued Catholic world of north-east Cork. In 1758 James Hennessy of Ballymacmoy was one of twenty 'gentilshommes du comte de Cork' who certifed the gentility of an Irish colonel in French service; they in turn were certified by a Cork notary to be *tous et chacun d'entre eux des gentilshommes de famillies anciennes et respectables, et que toute sorte de croyance doit être ajoutée a leurs témoignages*.[8] Edmund Burke, hearing of the illness of James Hennessy (Richard's father) in 1767, wrote that 'he was as sensible and gentlemanlike a man as any in our part of the country – and I feel heartily for him and his wife'.[9] The Hennessy family moved in the circle of the surviving Catholic gentry families and of the rising business class drawn from the same background. Henry Galwey in 1797 reminded Richard that they had been at school together, and Antony Galwey, descended from a county Tipperary branch of the same family, noted in 1765 that he had in the past met Richard in Cork, and knew his family whom he regarded as *très braves gens*.[10]

James Hennessy, father of Richard, had married a Barrett. That family, which had lost more than other significant landed families in the county in 1691,[11] had been based like the Nagles and Hennessys on the north-east of the county, and one of the colonels of the Jacobite regiments of 1691 had been a Barrett. We know little of the family later, a circumstance which itself bears witness to their greatly reduced fortunes, though the fact that they could count on the friendship or support of Edmund Burke as late as the 1790s suggests that they had been members of his circle in his early days on the Blackwater. In the case of one member of the Barrett family, a daughter of James Barrett of Caronotta, county Cork, the contract for her marriage in 1758 to a nephew of James Hennessy of Ballymacmoy provided for a capital sum of £800, a modest but real competence, to finance her jointure.[12] Moreover, this sum was provided for the marriage of a daughter to a young man in the business house of his father in Ostend, not a great catch socially. It is probable that the earlier marriage of James Hennessy of Ballyymacmoy to a Barrett was a more advantageous affair. That probablity is also borne out in the very good marriage of his sister to Henry Goold, father of the George Goold who was to be the most successful Catholic merchant of the 1760s and 1770s in Cork. A brother of James Hennessy, Charles (hence an uncle of Richard), born around 1700, settled in Ostend probably in its boom of the 1720s when other Cork families like the Sarsfields had a stake in its business. He created the Ostend branch of the family, and it was probably the Barrett alliance of his older brother in Ballymacmoy that made possible a Barrett alliance for his son in 1758.

James Hennessy of Ballymacmoy would have been either the eldest or eldest surviving son. That was reflected in the fact that contrary to what has often been said he did not serve in the French army. In other words the inheritance to which he could aspire was attractive enough to keep him at home. In turn his own sons reproduced the same pattern. George (1725-76) succeded to Ballymacmoy in 1768. Richard, the second son, drifted into the French army in 1748 and out of it probably at the end of 1752 to his cousins' business circle in Ostend. A younger brother James was a merchant in Cork city, married to Ellen Nagle of the Ballylegan branch of the Nagle family. A sister, Biddy, in 1766 was to marry Callaghan MacCarthy, a member of one of the minor Catholic families of the county,[13] another sister married a Roche of Trabolgan, whose descendants married into the Spencer family and hence are distantly related to the current Princess of Wales. Another sister had married John Shea, a Cork city merchant in 1757; the eldest brother, George, had already married a daugher of John Comerford, another Cork merchant, in 1748, and the Comerford alliance was further cemented the following year by the marriage of a Hennessy sister to a son of John Comerford. The Hennessy links with the business world were close. Not only was one branch of the famly in business in Ostend, but a son of James of Ballymacmoy was a merchant in Cork. In turn they were related, apparently on the maternal side, to the Galweys, and recent marriage links had associated them with the Goolds and Sheas. Along with the Moylans, the Goold and Shea families were to be the dominant Catholic business interest in Cork in the 1760s and 1770s. Moreover the Hennessys and Comerfords were both related to the Kearneys of Tipperary, Bordeaux and Alicante, whose business rise was very much a feature of mid-century.

Thus, while conspicuously successful neither in land nor in trade, the Hennessys had some social and economic competence, reinforced by many ties with the successful Catholic interest of county Cork in the 1750s and 1760s. This group was at the pinnacle of its post-1720 standing at this time. The two Nagle marrriages in the 1750s had allied the county's leading family to families in Connacht and Leinster; the business circle which the various marriages in and near the Blackwater helped to nourish was at the same time about to reach its apogee. The Hennessys' own business ventures, whether that of James, Richard's brother in Cork, or the longer-standing one of the Ostend family, were not very rewarding. The Ostend boom of the 1720s had not outlived the effective demise of the Austrian East India Company in 1731. Charles' business there remained a modest one, the later short-lived prosperity of which was occasioned by the Austrian Lowlands' fleeting neutrality on the outbreak of war in 1756.[14] Some trade with Cork connections was certainly pursued by the house, not only with the Goolds, Galweys and Coppingers, but with their cousin James of Cork as well. Ostend provided little market for produce from Ireland, and after 1731 it ceased to be a useful peace-time source of goods in demand in Ireland either. Documents relating to the estate of Charles Hennessy who died in 1758 and of his son, James of Ostend, who outlived him only by four years, contain numerous accounts with houses in Ireland and with Irish houses abroad, but the sums are mostly very small and in all probability a residue of the hectic flourishing of Ostend in its short period of war-time neutrality in 1756-7.[15]

James, Richard's younger brother who was a merchant in Cork, did not really prosper either. His business, for what it was, was probably mainly with Ostend. Even a Nagle marriage, which should have been advantageous for him, may not have been, because of its circum-stances, of great help. The few references in his own letters make sense only if the marriage had been a runaway one in defiance of Nagle opposition or even an abduction, a not uncommon occurrence in Munster when the suitor was inferior in position to his prospective bride. The marriage must have taken place in 1753 or more probably a year earlier, as a child was born in February 1753.[16] However, the expected dowry failed to eventuate and in 1755 he was still in frustration:

> As to the old affair it is just in the same situation as when you left this. We had some meetings lately and have at length determined in God's name to let her father know how much we are engaged to each other. We were drove to this resolution from many declarations the father has made that if any of his children should attempt to marry without his consent that he would never given them a shilling, and knowing him to be a positive man, she would by no means consent to undertake anything more than she has done without his consent. How it will turn out God knows but I am determined he shall be made acquainted with all.[17]

It is not known whether he ever got his dowry. If he failed this might account for his poor circumstances. When he died, it was reported that 'his little accounts were in such confusion' and the widow and children were said to be 'very limited in their circumstances'.[18] However, circumstances were good enough to admit of the eldest son George appearing as captain of a constant trader on the Bordeaux run in 1788.

Careers and social mobility
For Irish families of respectability, as for comparable families in England or in France, an abiding problem was provision for sons. Hence while landholding, trade and church provided opportunities, the army was also a necessary outlet. In the middle of the century no fewer than six Hennessys, probably all from the family or from collateral lines, can be traced as holding office in the French army. Richard, himself a second son, combined in his career the interest in both army service and in trade. One of the children of Charles of Ostend, Thomas, was captain in the army at the end of the 1750s. The contemporary military prestige of the family – which was considerable – seems to have had an earlier Richard as its basis. The problem of accounting for the family's considerable military prestige has resulted in a spurious later history in which Richard of Ballymacmoy was given a distinguished career, fighting at Fontenoy (and according to some accounts being wounded), and the father and a son likewise have been

given in some accounts a military career. The reality however was that Richard had a short and undistinguished peace-time service, and neither father nor son served at all. While the Hennessy genealogy becomes very incomplete beyond the period of James, father of Richard of Cognac fame, the earlier Richard, if related to the family, would almost certainly be an uncle of James (that is of Richard's father), possibly carrying the hypothesis farther back having fought in Ireland in 1689-91 but certainly having entered the service in the 1690s. In all probability he would have been a younger son. Indeed, from the French records, he entered the service in 1695 and reached the rank of lieutenant-colonel in 1724.[19]

He can not be related on documentary evidence to the Ballymacmoy family. However, the evidence for a relationship to the Ballymacmoy branch, rather than to the more obscure family of John Hennessy of county Kilkenny, the only other Hennessy to reach high rank, is compelling. Richard Hennessy had entered Clare's regiment in 1695, commanded at the time by Lee because of Lord Clare's death in 1693, and though he transferred later to Bulkely's regiment, representations after his death in 1743 on behalf of his widow were made not only by the colonel-properietor Bulkely, uncle of Lee, but in 1744 by Lord Clare. When Richard of Ballymacmoy entered the service he entered Clare's. Needing a certificate of his service in 1757 for the purpose of proving a status as a French citizen in Ostend, overrun by the French, Lord Clare's son, colonel-proprietor and marshall of France, not only gave him a favourable one but blatantly misrepresented his record, stating that he had fulfilled 10 years' service (when the regimental records noted that he had already abandoned it), and giving a false reason for his leaving the service. A point was being stretched for Richard. Lord Clare's family recurs not only in the fact that the earlier Richard had originally entered Clare's regiment, but that two later Lord Clares obliged in 1744 and 1757 with actions in support of the family. In the case of Richard of Ballymacmoy only the standing of the family could have warranted the issue of an otherwise wholly unjustifiable certificate. Later accounts often refer to Richard as having served in Dillon's regiment. The statement is incorrect, and probably rests on the fact that Richard in 1777 secured a promise of places in the Brigade for his own sons. Clare's regiment had been disbanded in the aftermath of the Seven Years War, and its officers and men incorporated in the surviving regiments. In 1730 the earlier Richard Hennesssy had been entrusted with an extraordinarily difficult and unique mission of recruiting in Ireland, which had both high diplomatic and political significance. The family's military prestige rested on him, both through his lustre and its attainment in the early decades of the century when the size of the Brigade and within it its rank-and-file Irish membership were at their peak. He had became a lieutenant-colonel in 1724, and his service file hinted at the difficult missions he had undertaken. His two sons were also captains in the 1740s.

In terms of numbers serving in the army, the Ballymacmoy branch of the family itself was hardly prolific. Neither James nor, as far as can be judged, any of his brothers served. Of his sons, Richard was the only one to enter the Brigade, and his service was short and undistinguished. A large proportion of the identifiable Hennessys in the French army came from the Ostend branch. The comparative lack of service by the Ballymacmoy family reflects both a decline in the appeal of French service as promotional opportunities narrowed and the existence of a well-connected backing that made possible alternative careers for sons. A second-lieutenant earned no more than £25 a year; and progress to the rank of captain, the only level which provided sufficient competence for marriage, became progressively slower over time. The army was very much a career for younger sons and a confession of the lack of alternative resources. In France Richard Hennessy was very friendly because of family ties with one of the Nagles, at the time serving in Walsh's regiment. Stationed in the Rochefort military region in 1775, he was, like the other young Irish officers, fortune seeking, as John Saule, himself a mercantile fortune seeker, reported to his friend Richard: 'though I imagine Nagle to be as much in love as any of our countrymen, still I don't think he would chuse to embarras himself with a wife without a sufficient quantity of *gelt* [that is cash] to recompense for the want of it in him'.[20]

A career officer's complaints were almost monotonously the fewness of promotion prospects and the low salaries. Colonel Daniel O'Connell from a more army-oriented family in county Kerry, and a highly successful officer, is the most telling illustration of this litany of lamentations.[21] But the same complaints of his own early career by another member of the family, Captain Maurice O'Connell, were later recorded by James Roche,[22] and in 1776 and again in the 1780s the members of the Brigade at large were very restive. With rising rents (which enhanced landed incomes and made middle tenures profitable) and with more opportunities in the expanding trade of mid-century, the prestige of army service declined sharply. Few cases of two sons serving simultaneously now presented themselves; some generations missed out altogether and a higher proportion of officers came from within families living abroad who had become an emigré officer caste. Thus the Ostend Hennessys were far better represented in the Brigade than the Ballymacmoy family, whose service with Richard's departure in 1752 faded entirely. Their army service itself is a commentary on the modest success of the Ostend house. When Richard himself in poor circumtances in the 1770s envisaged army careers for his sons (and it is revealing that his thoughts turned to army service for his sons only when his own fortunes were at a nadir point), he had no difficulty in securing a promise of future places for them. It is worth noting too that his demarche was made in 1777 when war was in prospect, and career opportunities in the army were no longer the appallingly contracting ones of the mid-1770s. Moreover, he did not at first envisage the army for his eldest son. Promises of a place, while easily obtained with the right connections and valid in themselves, were hard to turn into reality without long delay in peace time. In the 1780s promotion prospects sank to their nadir for the entire century, and outlets existed only because second-lieutenants abandoned the career at an unprecedented pace. Quite simply, in contrast to the past, they no longer chose to remain in the army. The fact that Richard, at a low ebb in his finances, turned to the army for careers for his sons is itself telling of his plight, as is the fact that his hard-headed son James, from the outset, turned his face against an army career. Nor, beyond securing a promise of a place, did Richard push James, the only surviving son, hard in the direction of a military career.

The Ballymacmoy family's position, even if comparatively modest, was one of real social standing. In a modest way they were rising in the world. With small resources to start with, much depended on marriage strategy. On later – early nineteenth-century – evidence the Hennessy and Nagle family names alike concentrated in the baronies of Fermoy and Condons. However, while the Nagle concentration was most marked on the banks of the Blackwater, the Hennessy strength was slighly further north in three parishes on the King estate, with a secondary focus in a further three parishes in and around Doneraile, the estate village of another great landowning family, the St Legers. The pattern suggests that the Hennessys did not have a long tradition of residence on the Blackwater, and that the Killavullen branch was created by a Hennessy family moving south attracted by opportunities on the Blackwater, very probably in the wake of the marriage of Richard's great-grandmother to a Nagle, reportedly around 1670.[23] Logically of course the move could have been made either by Richard's father in 1718 when he married, or earlier by Richard's grandfather (presumptive elder brother of the celebrated Lieutenant-Colonel Richard Hennessy) in the 1690s when the Nagles sucessfully defended their position. In all probability either the original Hennessy marriage to a Nagle or in later times the good will created by an existing alliance to the Nagles provided the background to the acquistion of a beneficial tenure in the haven of the Blackwater. Given the fact that the head-rent of the Hennessy holder of the Ballymacmoy estate in 1775 was a mere £80, the lease should have been either an old one drawn up in the 1670s or 1690s, or a more roundabout one drawn up to evade the terms of the 1704 penal act. The balance of probability, given the simplicity of the later title, is that it was a pre-1704 lease.

The Hennessy situation in their original districts was modest: none arrived at a prominent position on the King lands, and only one in the Doneraile region. The few Nagles that far north fared no better, and like the Hennessys tended to drift out of the region. Even as far south as Annakissy, the original seat of the senior branch of the Nagles, the malign influence of the Kings may have played a role. Some of the parish of Clenor, in which Annakissy was situated, was in the hands of the King family even at the outset of the 1690s. Less favourable conditions of land tenure may in part explain why the head branch of the family ceased to be the prosperous one, and a cadet branch at Ballygriffen became the richest and most powerful branch in the eighteenth century. If there was already tension in the 1690s both casting a shadow over the Annakissy family and over their tenant relatives the Hennessys, that would help to account for the poisonous atmosphere which impregnated the region in the eighteenth century. Richard Nagle, head of the family in the 1680s, had been attorney general for the Jacobite government in Ireland, and the reputed progenitor in the Patriot Parliament of 1689 of the notorious act returning into the possesssion of the old owners the lands confiscated in the seventeeth century. The main estate of the Cotters (though not their original residence) adjoined the Nagle properties.[24] Sir James Cotter was Jacobite governor of Cork city and an active commander in the field in what was the most protracted scene of military action in Ireland in 1690-91. Thus the two key activist families of the county had interests on the Blackwater and the eighteenth-century tensions in many ways were a heady brew of fear and resentment originating in this period.

The Ballymacmoy Hennessys paled beside the Ballygriffen Nagles, or the urban Galweys, and could hardly hope to rival Henry Galwey, worth at least £10,000 'in a good and fine situation of business in Cork, if he minds it a little. He is amerous [sic] and I believe has a mistress'.[25] But if they could not compare either with the Nagles or with the Goolds, Galweys and Sheas whose urban wealth was increasing rapidly, the network created a promise of success, even if often illusory, in the changing world of rural Cork and the booming city. However, some economic competence combined with good connections and kinship enlarged the opportunities, and they could rise to positions which required trust. Thus, by 1788, proving the way application and backing could help, George, the son of Richard's brother, James, who had died in poor circumstances, had reached the respected position of master of a constant trader sailing between Cork and Bordeaux. An uncle of Richard's, who died in 1753, made a testamentary provision of £350 for his widow.[26] Another uncle who died in 1772, Christopher, was worth £1,000.[27] The possessor of Ballymacmoy, as an eldest son, of course fared much better. At the death of George, Richard's elder brother in 1775, his estate was worth £3,400 less £514 in liabilities. His net rental was £470 (rents of £550 less head rent of £80).[28] The head rent of £80 was very low, suggestive of a very old lease charged at seventeenth-century rent levels. His rents from occupiers suggest that he would have held not less than 500 acres, in other words the not-untypical acreage of the gentleman farmer or middleman of Irish society. The earliest known lease is a three lives renewable lease of 1786. This provided for a rent of £177 Irish for the townlands of Ballymacmoy, Killavullen, Shanballyduffe, Killisane and Rahatessenigg, the total acreage being 644 acres plantation measure (or approximately 1,000 acres statute measure). The unrealistic level of the increased rent itself suggests recognition of an existing Hennessy stake in the land, something which is borne out by the low level of fine – £40 – provided for the entry of a new life in the lease.

In foreseeing the 1778 relief act as likely to create estates running up to 'perhaps three or four hundred [pounds] a year',[29] Burke was in a sense generalising from what was already the case in the little enclave of Nagles and Hennessys on the Blackwater. A Nagle property which Burke acquired, probably in 1765, gave him £500 a year, and he attached importance to the income in the first decade of his political life. The rental of the Ballygriffen family alone among the Nagle and Hennessy households put that family in an upper reach of gentry affluence: David Nagle's rental in the 1770s was, on Arthur Young's authority, £2,000 a year.

Opting for the life of gentleman farmer or in emerging Irish parlance of the 1770s 'middleman', quite apart from its social appeal, was in economic terms a rational decision. The circumstances of such middlemen themselves, formerly marginal enough, improved rapidly once rents began to burgeon in the great economic uplift from the the 1740s onwards. The Hennessy house of the period at Ballymacmoy – which still survives – is a simple two-storey farmhouse, narrow in the vernacular fashion of the period and with low ceilings. However, there is a tell-tale symbol of status in the long avenue down the hill from the road to the house perched above the Blackwater. The seat is marked in Taylor and Skinner's *Maps of the roads of Ireland* in 1778, and Hennessy like the occupiers of all the other seats was conventionally given in the book the style of 'Esquire'. Moreover, however modest in both James's and Richard's generations the standing and success of other members of the family, a second 'Hennessy Esq.', according to Taylor and Skinner's maps, held a seat at Ballingrane just outside Doneraile: as it was beside a Nagle seat at Ballinamona, it seems likely that it was a Nagle-related Hennessy and hence either a member of the same Hennessy family or more probably a close cousin.

Thus the family were not going down in the world, even if the circumstances of individual younger sons were quite modest. With rising incomes already creating George's modest but real substance of 1775, greater pretensions were emerging, and the 1820s house on a new and commanding site overlooking the tiny village of Killavullen was firmly one of gentry scale and status. The position of inheriting eldest sons, whether Hennessy at Ballymacmoy or Nagles at Ballygriffen and other seats, was of course quite different from the lot of cadet sons whose gentry standing was harder to perceive in material terms, and harder to preserve. Ignoring both recent intra-family transfers of property and absenteeism, there were in this region in the 1770s two Hennessy and nine Nagle identifiable seats. The latter are in effect 'the Seven Houses' referred to by Willam O'Brien in his *Edmund Burke as an Irishman*. In its way the fact that only five of the houses find their way into Taylor and Skinner's atlas rather aptly illustrates the ambiguous position of many members of such families in or on the fringes of 'gentry' society. That is reflected also in the fact that they did not all assume the style 'Esq.', which originally designated landed income and high status, and which in the last quarter of the century began to be appropriated more widely. The heads of the Ballylegan and Renny Nagles together with George Hennessy as late as 1775 designated themselves as 'gent.', a term which indicated a gentlemanly lifestyle but in a modest fashion compared with the broad acres, advantageous land title and large rent roll which were once deemed necessary in order to earn the style 'Esq.'. The Ballygriffen Nagles securely fitted into the category of esquire; the other families, Nagles and Hennessys alike, hovered more ambiguously among the 'gentlemen' or 'gents', now beginning to be described as esquire. Their own reluctance as late as 1775, in a socially somewhat more indulgent world, to employ the term is a clear indication of where, in their own estimation, they stood.

The Nagles: patrons of Catholic society on the Blackwater

North-east Cork, in and around the extended Catholic parish of Monanimy (village of Killavullen, townland of Ballymacmoy, and seats of Ballyduff, Ballygriffen and Annakissy (Nagle) and Ballymacmoy

(Hennessy) on the Blackwater, was the only region in county Cork in which a group of comfortable propertied Catholics survived in the eighteenth century. The Nagles resided here, and just beyond it at Mourne had been the principal residence of the Barretts. No Barrett property however had recognition in the Taylor and Skinner maps. To the south of Killavullen the Nagle Mountains overhung the valley: below the mountains on both banks of the Blackwater stood the properties of the Nagle family. Monanimy Castle, abandoned by the Nagles for a better dwelling in the second half of the seventeenth century, was the centre of the district. In the shadow of the castle, perhaps even in it, was the school in which Edmund Burke made his first studies, and nearby is the graveyard in which the Hennessys and their Nagle relatives for generations have been laid to rest.

Remarkably, two of four Nagle families survived the vicissitudes of war in 1689-91 and of confiscation in its aftermath. Not only did some Nagles thus survive upheaval intact but members of the Nagle families seem after the Plantation to have occupied or rented even much of the forfeited lands.[30] Remaining secure in the district, younger sons were provided with estates (or rented land on advantageous terms) and continued to found landed collateral branches of the family. Given security and success, landed position created new branches of the family, all marked by estates and seats.[31] Other families such as the Hennessys had the same courtesy extended to them, and the survival and prosperity such as it was of the Hennessys depended on holding Nagle land. In 1786 the Hennessys held their land from David Nagle of Ballygriffen, and the lease of that year appears to be a renewal of an existing stake. The Ballygriffen Nagles' title seems to be uncomplicated, if we judge by the later evidence for the Hennessy title. But other Nagles, like the Annakissy Nagles, had fared less well, and new land-owners had been brought into the region by the Williamite settlement. The survival of the Annakissy Nagles and of other families on some of their old lands must have depended on complicated legal arrangements then and later when they had to cope also with the obstacles created by the 1704 act directed against a Catholic stake in property. The Annakissy Nagles lost their lands in the 1690s, though they later reoccupied them. The complexity of the situation can be sensed in the fact that, under the Ballygriffen Nagles, the Ballyduff Nagles were later, for their demesne, tenants to the Hennessys. What this suggests is that the Hennessys held an old (that is pre-1704) lease, and that under its convenient umbrella the Ballyduff family had been provided for collusively. It was not for nothing that Counsellor Joseph Nagle acquired his formidable reputation for ways around the penal code.[32].

Though part of the Nagle lands in the civil parishes of Monanimy and Clenor were forfeited, Nagle occupation reestablished itself. There was however a painful interlude in the 1690s when their right even to their surviving inheritance was challenged by Alan Broderick, leader of Cork Protestants, and their uncertain prospects are reflected in the fact that in 1704 none of the Nagles put up bail for the Catholic clergymen registered in that year. Thus survival itself involved a conflict whose detail is obscure, but it was to colour the future story of local society, Protestant and Catholic alike. The story also explains more obscurely why the senior Annakissy family, resuming occupation under less favourable circumstances, surrendered leadership of the family both economically and politically to the cadet Ballygriffen branch fortunate enough (precisely because of the lower profile of a younger son) to preserve its title in the 1690s, and to two determined sons. In essence the Nagle family can be seen as consisting in the eighteenth century of four main branches: Annakissy, Ballygriffen, Monanimy (or Ballyduff) and Clogher. The senior branch of the Nagles, the Annakissy branch, remained seated though less advantageously than in the past at its old residence: outshoots created seats for other members at Mount Nagle, Ballygriffen and in Tipperary at Garnavilla. The Ballygriffen branch may conveniently be regarded as a separate branch because of their wealth and status. Another branch of the family – the so-called Monanimy branch – was undisturbed in its small estate at Ballyduff in the 1690s: in the eighteenth century its seats were at Ballyduff (with which family Edmund Burke and the Hennessys were connnected), Ballylegan (again with a Hennessy connection) and Ballywalter. The fact that the Hennessys held Shanballyduffe (or Ballyduffe as the townland was also called) in 1786 suggests that at some time since the 1690s they had become immediate landlords under their head landlord, the Ballygriffen Nagles, by a sublease to the Ballyduff Nagles. While this might be regarded merely as the convoluted detail of Irish title, it gains added significance because it reinforces the ties between the Ballyduff Nagle and the Hennessys, and in turn further explains the friendship between Burke and Hennessy. Burke even gained his wife from his associations with the area. One of the Ballyduff Nagle girls was married to John Nugent, and Burke in 1757 married John Nugent's sister.

Another branch, the so-called Clogher branch, held seats close to Doneraile at Clogher and Ballinamona. The Clogher branch also held land at least as early as 1704 at Renny on the Blackwater, and in so far as sense can be made of events in badly-documented families, they seem to have transferred their seat to Renny on the Blackwater in the 1760s.[33] It has usually been said that the Nagle interest in the Clogher estate which Edmund Burke inherited from his elder brother had been tranferred to friendly Protestants – the Burkes (Edmund's brother and

Plate 14.2   Monanimy (Cork Archaeological Survey).

then Edmund himself) – in order to protect the Nagle ownership of the property.[34] This is however not the whole story. While it probably was the reason for the original transfer in 1757, letters from Burke from the mid-1760s show that, far from Burke holding the land to oblige relatives, he was instructing a relative as to how the land should be managed for him. A request by Burke in December 1765 that the stewart of the former owner of the estate should be treated favourably implies that effective change in management had just occurred.[35] The most likely explanation of the situation of Clogher is that Burke silently bought out the 'real' Nagle interest: the Ballyduff cousin who from 1765 acted as his agent is beyond ambiguity a man under instructions.

At the social centre of this little region, the only region in Cork dominated by propertied Catholics, stood the demesne and house of Ballygriffen, seat of the Ballygriffen branch of the Annakissy family, in the eighteent century, thanks to the business and legal acumen of its members, the richest branch of the numerous Nagle households. Just across the river from Ballygriffen stood Ballymacmoy, seat of the Hennessys. Social stautus, the politics of a common religion and proximity inevitably brought the Hennessys and the various branches of the Nagles together. They already held their land from them. Richard Hennessy's paternal great-grandmother had been a Nagle, and his own mother, a Barrett, was in all probability related in multiple fashion to the Nagles as well. Richard Hennessy's brother, James of Cork city, married Elizabeth Nagle of the Ballylegan branch which occupied a modest seat some miles to the north of Ballymacmoy. The widow of Richard's cousin, James of Ostend, Ellen ('Nelly') Barrett, was a niece of Patrick Nagle of Ballyduff. Edmund Burke's mother was a sister of Patrick of Ballyduff. In other words, Nelly Barrett, wife of James Hennessy of Ostend, was a first cousin of Edmund Burke, and it was this lady as a widow whom Richard Hennessy married in 1765. Friendship and existing links of remote kinship were thus cemented by the fact that Richard married a first cousin of Burke's.

Friendship between Richard Hennessy and Edmund Burke, it must be stressed, had long preceded the marriage. Ballyduff was only two miles from Ballymacmoy, and Edmund Burke spent 6 years from roughly 1735 to 1741 as a boy at his mother's home there. Given their ages – they were born within a year of one another – they grew up in daily contact, and Richard as well as Edmund Burke must have had their early lessons from the same schoolmaster, O'Halloran, at Monanimy. The two families remained very close, as Burke's mother kept up a close connection with the region: from her visit to county Galway in 1766 a long and chatty letter to the mother of Richard Hennessy survives.[36] Both men were also remarkably tall for the age;

Richard was six feet, and Burke was 5 feet 10 inches.[37] When Richard Hennessy in 1765 visited London in the course of making arrangements for his new business venture in Cognac, he saw Burke, and the meeting is mentioned together with news of Hennessy's wife's pregnancy in one of Burke's letters to Ballyduff.[38] That meeting would have been in September or early October. Having made arrangements with the Irish house of Isidore Lynch to handle his exchange business, Richard then went to Paris where he made similar arrangements with the house of Woulfe. At this time Richard was still keeping in touch with Burke (though unfortunately none of the letters survives), and complaints must have been made from Ballyduff to Richard's friend Burke that they had not heard from Richard. At the end of the year, Burke assured Patrick Nagle, his Ballyduff uncle, that 'Dick has been for some time past at Paris. It is true he has not wrote; but no man living loves and values you more; not even myself. He will make up for his neglect.'[39] Indeed by the time Burke's letter was written, Dick must have already been at least one week in Cognac.

Not only was Patrick Nagle of Ballyduff uncle of Nelly Barrett, but as a consequence of one of the many intermarriages within the Nagle families, the Ballylegan Nagle, whom Richard's brother, James, in Cork had married, was Patrick's niece. James' letters from Cork to Richard, of which a few survive, were full of news of relatives in the Blackwater valley. From what we can make out from this evidence, Richard, after he left his home district, can have visited it only twice, once in 1755 and a second time in a bitter-sweet stay in 1768, prolonged because of the final agony of his father. Mentally however, from the amount of Cork news which crops up in the surviving correspondence, his thoughts often dwelt on his home district (as did those of his boyhood friend Edmund Burke), and an avid interest prompted his correspondents to be generous with news. Precisely because of his knowledge of relatives, letters to him are allusive, and in letters from James or others we vividly but fleetingly glimpse the intense home life. An uncle took ill in 1753 on a visit to Ballymacmoy; setting out to visit the physicians in Cork, he stayed at George Goold's house on the way and died there. At the funeral – to the graveyard at Monanimy – 'the number that attended alone was sufficient to prove how sincerely the poor dear man was lamented. In my life I never saw such a concourse upon the like occasion.' A glimpse of Richard's father's attitude to financial affairs occurs in 1755 when Richard's brother sought to have a debt by the Ostend Hennessys to Richard discharged by their father out of funds he held on the account of the Ostend house:

I made application to our father for the money, but he excused himself by telling me he was out of cash, but would allow it you when the rents came in. I know how difficult it is to prevail on him to part with the cash. However I shall repeat my demand from time to time in hopes to shame him out of it.

The little family circle comes out more vividly still in a letter from Pat Nagle in 1772, describing visits not only to Ballymacmoy but to Ballylegan, a fact which suggests that he is probably a member of the Ballylegan branch. News was given of other relatives who can not be identified with certainty: 'Niet' [living at Castleterry] ... which farm he had taken during James Terry's life ... Athy ... who lives with his girl in Youghal. It is unworthy giving any further account of him; his poor wife keeps a poor shop in Fermoy.' Nagle at the time of writing was staying with his sister Jenny (Mrs Vaughan) and her two daughters and son at Tuckey Quay, Cork. Nagle was a medical doctor. In directing Hennessy to reply 'to doctor Nagle if you please,' the impression is given that he was newly qualified, and on his first visit home after long studies on the continent. His father seems to have provided in style for his return, giving him the use of two horses and a servant. The good doctor travelled widely among his relatives: 'I am partly in Corke, partly at Ballylegan, partly at Ballymacmoy, Ballyduff, Ballywalter, Ballynamona and many other ballies to tedious to mention'.[40]

This small enclave was gathered on the floor of the Blackwater valley at the heart of a region of intense English and Protestant settlement, in or close to the Blackwater river. Running north from Mallow and south of a wide arc sweeping across the foothills of the Ballyhoura and Galtee mountain ranges stood the estates of the St Leger family at Doneraile, and of the Kings, the richest and politically most conservative family in the region. The King estates stretched out over twenty miles (although not of course in continuous array). In the north-east of the county controlling the gap through the mountains into Tipperary stood their seat at Mitchelstown. Through the gap the little Catholic enclave on or near the Blackwater kept contact with the much larger and more secure Catholic society of south Tipperary. The Butler family at both Cahir and Kilcash, and further afield the Mathew family at their seats of Thurles, Thomastown and Annfield, provided the backbone of Catholic society in Tipperary. On the estates of the immensely rich and powerful Butler and Mathew families, lesser gentry Catholics, notably the Keatings, the McCarthys and Nagles, held large tenancies. Somewhat more modest families were to be found on Butler land close to the towns of Cahir, Clogheen and Ballyporeen. Catholics from Cork either married into this region or even migrated to it. One of the Annakissy Nagles, renting land from the Butlers a few miles south of Cahir, set up the Garranavilla branch of the family. Some of the MacCarthy-Reagh McCarthys had migrated from Cork in the politically troubled 1690s to the Mathew estate. They became the Springhouse MacCarthys, the main branch in Tipperary, but either descendants of the first migrants or other contemporaneous migrants from the same family created other households out of one of which came the MacCarthys who in 1748 created a Bordeaux business house, destined to become one of the largest in the city.

The resources of the families are strikingly illustrated both in the success of the Bordeaux MacCarthys and in the dazzling position of the Springhouse MacCarthys when they migrated, a generation later, to Toulouse in 1776:[41] they purchased the town's finest house then a building, and Justin MacCarthy, son of the Springhouse Justin of the 1760s, built up one of the finest private libraries in Europe. The MacCarthy marriages also illustrate the standing of the family. Justin MacCarthy, head of the Springhouse family in the 1760s, married a daughter of Nicholas Tuite, of Copenhagen and Saint-Croix, one of the handful of cosmopolitan Irish financiers overseas. Thomas Sutton de Clonard married a son to a MacCarthy daughter in Bordeaux: the Sutton family despite their Paris business interests later settled in the city. In the 1760s the Springhouse MacCarthys had become a butt of hostile comment because they had lent money to Protestant families. The hostile comment was made in the context of the troubles of the early 1760s, and prominence gained added relevance because of the proposal in parliament to make such lending easier. This hostility to MacCarthy was recorded by Sir James Caldwell in his book *Debates in the Irish parliament in 1764*: significantly Caldwell had been commander of a troop of soldiers there in the troubled year 1763-4, and was obviously repeating the lore picked up from the local gentry. The fact that the MacCarthy family had thrived in Tipperary, not in Cork, is also comment on the hostile environment in Cork for Catholics outside the enclave on the Blackwater.

Garrett Nagle of Ballygriffen, head of the most influential branch of the Nagle family, married Ann Mathew in the second decade of the century. The large gentry tenants below the Mathews and Butlers were frequently Catholic, and this was particularly the case on the Cahir state whose large tenants included the Nagles and Keatings. Richard Hennessy's paternal grandfather married an O'Phelan from Tipperary and his uncle Charles of Ostend had married a Mary Murphy of Clogheen. A younger sister of Richard also married into a Tipperary family (Burke of Curraghnabouly).[42] What all this all meant in the final analysis is that the success of the Catholic enclave in Cork depended not only on the presence of the Nagles but on their ties with the more secure and more numerous Tipperary Catholic interest. Marriage alliances across the county border were inevitable, because south-west Tipperary and the Monanimy regions represented in the eighteenth century a social pattern whose only parallel was in county Galway, of a successful Catholic landed interest. No other region in Munster or in Leinster had a comparable network of Catholic and crypto-Catholic landowners, creating with their protective umbrella a dense presence of numerous and from mid-century thriving middle interests.

The most public embodiment of the intercounty ties were the marriages between the Mathew family in Tipperary and the Cork families of Cotter and Nagle. The Mathews (even when, and indeed because, they ceased to be Catholics) remained leaders of the Catholic political interest in Tipperary. When James Cotter was executed in 1720, and his son was moved by judicial order to a Protestant family and brought up a Protestant, the leadership of Cork Catholics passed to the Ballygriffen Nagles, now the sole remaining rich landed Catholic family of the county. As James Cotter and Garrett Nagle had both married Mathew sisters this was inevitable, and it also helped to ensure that both families would be closely identified in the eyes of their political enemies. Garrett's brother Joseph was a counsellor-at-law, one of the surviving Catholic practitioners from before the time when entry to the law became closed to Catholics. He engaged in a series of sales and transfers of land from Catholics to Protestants: these seem to have been a smoke-screen of arrangements between Catholics and friendly Protestants to conceal the real ownership,[43] or more probably to give them more favourable leasehold terms than the penal laws permitted. Garrett's daugher, Nano, in a letter in 1769 was to recall that her uncle (who died in 1757) was 'I think, the most disliked by the Protestants of any Catholic in the kingdom'.[44] Nano Nagle, somewhat to the alarm of her counsellor uncle, set up Catholic schools, not as isolated ventures but in a network run by the religious order which she founded. The first was established in Cork city in either 1754 or 1755; by 1769 there were seven in all in the city. Catholic schools were in flagrant disregard of the penal laws, and doubly so when they were in the hands of a foundress of a religious order, entirely prohibited as such institutions were within the kingdom. Supported by her relatives, these schools represented the new-found confidence of Catholics and in their own way constituted a challenged to the status quo. Almost a generation earlier in 1731-2 the activity of the family in collecting money in support of parliamentary lobbying to protect the political interests of the Catholics had itself been one of the reasons justifying accusations against them: lists of subscribers seized in Joseph's possession were given a sinister meaning. Their role in funding the lobbying in the early

1730s in tandem with Thomas Woulfe in Dublin (doubtless also from his name a Munster-man) suggests that at that time the Nagles were in effect leaders not only of the Blackwater and Cork Catholics but of the Irish Catholics at large.

Colonel Richard Hennessy: the impact of his 1730 mission in the Blackwater valley

Colonel Richard Hennessy's recruiting mission to Ireland was catalyst of a political crisis between the London government and Dublin in 1730. While the authorisation of this mission created distrust by Protestants of the good faith of the Castle administration, Richard Hennessy's ties with the region inevitably highlighted the position of its Catholics, doubly vulnerable because of the Jacobite associations of their Cotter connection and their economic, social and political standing. Hennessy's mission had been drawn up in the honeymoon period of Anglo-French relationships under Fleury and Walpole, chief ministers of their respective countries. In return for French concessions to the English, the French would be allowed in a reciprocating concession to send Hennessy and six army officers to Ireland to recruit 750 men for the Irish Brigade. The purpose was at first sight a straightforward exchange of favours between two powers for the high diplomatic purpose of improving Franco-British relations.[45] Its underlying significance was wider, as tolerance of recruiting or arming Catholics for foreign service was also a response to French representations on behalf of Irish Catholics and implied an admission that they did not pose a threat: thus if it went ahead, the mission would challenge the entire underlying rationale of the penal laws. While the French had been told to recruit with discretion, it was impossible to keep recruitment on this scale secret. The officers had to be recalled, and Protestant anger in Ireland over the covert campaign boiled over. The political fall-out was the opposite of that intended. Far from the mission helping to ease the lot of Catholics, a nation-wide enquiry into the state of popery – the first sophisticated enquiry of the century – was launched in the next session of parliament. Projects of new legislation were also broached on the disarming of Catholics and on Catholics in legal practice, precisely the issues which the recruiting (in other words the arming) of Catholics and the Hennessy associations with the Nagle family raised.

Given Hennessy's family ties with north-east Cork, the mission was almost certainly the factor which revived the tensions simmering below the surface since the execution of Cotter in 1720. Rank-and-file recruitment for France had long been widespread in Cork and Tipperary, and younger sons served abroad as officers. Jacobite sympathies lingered on too, though more as resentment of defeat and as wishful thinking, measured for instance in the Gaelic poetry of east Cork, running from the laments for Cotter in the early 1720s to Liam Inglis's poems in the late 1750s, than as serious plotting. Stripped of their poetic imagery, they amounted to little more than idle pub talk. But fears existed in the Protestant establishment, whether genuine ones or simply politically-inspired fears intended to halt concession, it is impossible to say. From this region even before 1730 came repeated and exaggerated reports of the size of recruitment for foreign service. The fact that such complaints, and their most exaggerated tone, proliferated in the early 1720s in Cork and in neighbouring west Waterford, seems less a measure of recruitment itself than of the political fall-out over the Cotter affair.

The temperature of parliament was high when it met in the autumn of 1731. The House of Lords appointed its committee on popery at the outset of the session. It lost no time in seeking returns from around the country. With uncharacteristic speed they began to be put before the house from as early as 2 December, and the matter was a major issue among the several anti-papist ones that occupied the lords in the remainder of the session.[46] The speed ensured that the political purpose of enquiry could be maximised. It was supported by a census-type count of Catholics and Protestants based on the hearth money returns and compiled by the revenue officers. A parallel counting seems also to have been conducted by the clergy of the established church in at least some dioceses: it is not now well documented but its results survive for Ossory.[47] In the lower house legislation was proposed on arms and on Catholic practice as solicitors. But despite the political sound and fury in Ireland, the legislation made little progress in that session. This would appear to have been a result of the lobbying of the Privy Council in London organised by Thomas Woulfe in Dublin and by Joseph Nagle (and for which Nagle collected money in Cork). This activity (and its success, or possibly more accurately the success atttibuted to it) was what was in mind two years later when the two men were singled out in resolutions of the House of Commons prepared by a committee headed by a Cork politician, Sir Richard Cox, and denounced as having 'grossly misrepresented the proceedings of the House of Commons last session of parliament.'[48]

Even in the course of the earlier session of parliament events had acquired a momentum of their own in the Blackwater district. While the report to the Lords for the various dioceses was rather full, the county Cork thrust of the politics of the session can be seen in the fact that the account for the diocese of Cloyne, in which Doneraile and the Nagle region at large were incorporated, was one of the most comprehensive diocesan reports.[49] In Cloyne, very few mass-houses had been built since 1714, and the original report made a point of noting that they were 'mean thatched cabbins, many, or most of them, open at one end.' Moreover, within the diocese 'about three years ago' [1728], the finishing of several new mass houses had 'been prevented by the care of the magistrates of those places.' The politics of the session were also different in county Cork from the rest of Ireland. In public much attention was attracted by Stratford Eyre, high sheriff in county Galway, who not only conducted affairs in Galway but appeared before the Lords in early December and was finally commended by name in the report of 8 March. In Cork the issues were quite different. For one thing, while a major issue elsewhere was the presence of regulars, male or female, and Stratford Eyre had conducted raids on their monasteries in Galway, the issue in Cork related not to regulars but to raids on the abodes in Cork city of the bishop of Cork and one of the region's two premier lay Catholics, counsellor Joseph Nagle.

The raids had ulterior motives which were not present in other counties. They were conducted by the collector of Mallow, authorised by the grand jury at the spring assizes. Thus they took place outside the context of the Lords' enquiry, and as much as three months later than Eyre Stratford's well-publicised raids in Galway. They point to background machinations of a local interest group in Mallow and Doneraile, and while the events began in Cloyne diocese, the fact is that the collector's raids took place in Cork city, and the bishop raided was the bishop of Cork, not of Cloyne. The deposition by the parish priest of Doneraile, John Hennessy, which provided the justification for the raid, had been made before Lord Doneraile as late as 3 January 1732. The actions in county Cork, which contrasted with the routine information gathering by the clergy and bishops or action against regulars by sheriffs, harked back to events that had begun before parliament had met, and implied a hope of 'informations' [that is a case] against the two men could be put before the Grand Jury in due course. The fact that informations were not laid before the grand jury at the summer assizes meant that the evidence was too unconvincing even for local zealots, though it could still provide useful mileage, when parliament met again in 1733.

The political context of the Doneraile events has been somewhat obscured by the fact that a quarrel already existed between the lay Catholics of Doneraile and their priest, John Hennessy, either a member of the Ballymacmoy family or more probably a cousin from among the several Hennessy families near Doneraile. The quarrel had come to a head in a memorial of 20 March 1731 to his bishop by thirteen Catholics (including four Nagles) within the parish union who denounced the priest. The background to the quarrel between Hennessy and the lay

Catholics seems to have concerned relations with the Protestant interest, which is hardly surprizing given the still fresh memories of the Cotter episode. Hennessy's defects, in the allegations of the signatories, were compounded by the fact that 'when he gets any pence which heel seldom earn, thene [he proceeds] to hasten [*sic*] to the Protesdants of Donerail, and drink that in brandy and punch'.[50] Hennessy's obsequiousness, which contrasts with the more combative attitude of the laity, and his vulnerable position are a little more understandable when it is realised that all that he had was 'kind of shedd instead of a masshouse.'[51]

While these events had a context wider than a diocesan one, in Cloyne diocese itself, emphasising the reality of pressure on Catholic priests, effective Protestant activism was more marked than elsewhere: according to the report to the lords, 530 Catholic children were being educated in Protestant schools in the diocese, something that was not paralleled in information for any other diocese. In the St Leger and King lands moreover not as much as a single popish schoolmaster was identified. The later Commons report (of 19 December 1733) suggests that Hennessy volunteered his information. In fact the sequence of events suggests that it is more likely that Hennessy was leaned on in some form or other, though he did then oblige with allegations of a Jacobite plot. Because the session of parliament was prorogued on 10 March, the events could not be exploited for political purposes in 1732.

However no time was lost in constituting a parliamentary committee to enquire into the matter as soon as parliament reassembled in the autumn of 1733. While the evidence was vague, it could be used to support charges that Garrett and Joseph Nagle were the moving spirits in political conspiracy. Garrett (who sometimes visited the continent) was accused of being the Pretender's agent in Flanders and the bearer to the continent of funds raised in Ireland. No action other than the mock-serious step of ordering the arrest of Garrett Nagle and Thomas Woulfe, their Dublin agent, for insulting the dignity of the Commons was launched. This itself was no more than an ineffective and faintly ludricous gesture: Garrett Nagle was in all probability not in Dublin and known not to be in Dublin at the time, because no arrest was made and no fuss was created about the failure to arrest him, and Thomas Woulfe, who was arrested, was released the next day on making a very routine apology.[52] In other words the Commons did not take the charges very seriously. But they served their political purpose which was two-fold. First, the real objective was to cast doubt in London on the good faith of their role as lobbyists of the Privy Council: the proposed legislation which had made no progress in 1731-2 became law in this session. The second was that the committee called for the issue of a proclamation by the lord lieutenant enforcing the penal laws. This was duly issued in early 1734. The object of seeking such a proclamation was less added force for the implementation of the existing law than, after the recruiting debacle of 1730 in which the administration had connived with the French, of publicly identifying the lord lieutenant with the maintenance of the penal laws. The whole affair, which has merited little attention, was in fact a major political manoeuvre over the penal laws, orchestrated in parliament by the Cork interest, and for the Nagles their most unpleasant experience since the Broderick-driven attack on them in the 1690s. It was moreover both a sequel to the Cotter episode of 1720 and precursor of later events.

The St Legers (Lord Doneraile) at Doneraile, the Kings at Mitchelstown and the Bowens at Kildorrery, bitterly opposed to concessions to Catholics, presided over local society. In 1732 Lord Doneraile was the recipient of the charges against the Catholic lay interest, which conveniently surfaced in the course of a parliamentary session. In the next session the matter was on the agenda from the outset. The parliamentary committee was orchestrated by the Cork political interest, as its business was handled by Sir Richard Cox. Relative calm descended in Cloyne after 1734. It is tempting to find some role in this for Bishop Berkely's more enlightened presence as bishop from 1734 to 1751. His *Querist* written in 1735 has very positive expressions of toleration for Catholics, and it is easy to see the comments both as a re-echo caused by the unpleasant events in his own diocese on the eve of his elevation to the see, and as a fresh and more enlightened response to them.

Of course no region could be immune to external developments. Their role, or more accurately the matching rise and fall in the temper of the local gentry, can be measured in the Mayalow (or Mallow) Loyal Protestant Society, which was founded for defensive purposes in the political crisis of 1745, and became immediately the crisis was over a political drinking club of the local gentry. Significantly it barely outlived the parliamentary session of 1745-6; it revived again in the parliamentary session of 1755 to last until 1760.[53] Behind its reactivation was almost certainly the prospect of concessions to Catholics in the 1755-6 and 1757-8 sessions of parliament: the abortive registration bills of 1755 and 1757, which had they passed would have given the Catholic church a legal status by reviving on a more generous basis the legal machinery for registering Catholic clergymen. Resistance to the prospects of a conciliatory line towards Catholics was given an opportunity of expressing itself locally because of a quarrel within the Catholic clergy in 1758 in the King family's estate town of Mitchelstown. This was a very public event involving *inter alia* an interdict laid on the Catholic inhabitants of the town by the Catholic bishop of Cloyne.[54] While an interdict only directly affected Catholics, an ecclesiastical prohibition on Catholics going to the town, itself an archaic and in the eighteenth century outlandish measure, had much wider repercussions on local business and social life. The events prompted a call by King (Lord Kingston) for the enforcement of the penal laws, and for the apprehension of named (and unregistered) Catholic clergymen. This heralded a campaign reaching over the next five years from county Cork into county Tipperary, and in Tipperary largely confined to the lands between the Blackwater and Suir where the local Protestant interest faced a strong Catholic one with county Cork ties. Nicholas Sheehy, the priest at the centre of much of the later story of the region, first acquired notoriety in his role in enforcing the interdict. The Kingston response in Mitchelstown, while it helped to precipitate happenings in Tipperary, itself was prompted by recent events in Tipperary revolving around two clergymen. One had been proclaimed an outlaw by the grand jury in 1750 for atttempting to 'seduce' a Protestant; another, arrested in 1754 for marrying a Protestant abductor to his abducted lady, was rescued from the sub-sheriff and his forces by an armed mob; the sheriff himself was fired at later.[55] In a response to these challenges, Catholics carrying firearms were arrested from time to time and a number of unregistered clergy were apprehended.

The spread of tensions is made all the more comprehensible because of the pattern of Catholic intermarriage in the region. Apart from the Cork-Tipperary marriages facilitated by the Mitcheltown gap between the two counties, Limerick families like the Burkes and Sheehys and west-Waterford families on the lower course of the Blackwater formed connections as well. We are speaking in essence of a relatively compact region embracing propertied Catholics within a radius of ten to twenty miles around Mitchelstown. There was no comparable group elsewhere in mid-Munster. Political friction lay in the contact between this interest and a powerful Protestant one, based on Clonmel, Mitchelstown, Doneraile and Mallow. On both sides tensions communicated themselves throughout the region. The activities of the priest Nicholas Sheehy in the late 1750s and early sixties ran through three counties, Waterford, Tipperary and Cork, and his family background lay in adjacent districts in another county, Limerick, which formed part of the same network of family ties, intercourse and politics.

New plots in the 1760s: Edmund Burke and his Nagle and Hennessy relatives

Inevitably accusations of plots surfaced as well. In 1761 information was supplied to Dublin Castle of an alleged meeting in 1760 of which 'the Nagles and Hennessys were chief promotors'.[56] As in 1733 the allegation surfaced before the start of the parliamentary session. Given various intimations in the two preceding sessions (an abortive registration bill which had the Lord Lieutenant's support in 1757-8, and public acknowledgement in a friendly tone of an address from Catholics in 1759-60), the expectation that concessions would be made to Catholics in the course of the parliamentary session from the autumn of 1761 to spring of 1762 was strong. The misgivings of extreme Protestants were to prove only too well-founded in the course of the session. The formula, first associated with Richard Hennessy in 1730 of official support for recruiting Catholics under Catholic officers for service abroad, went a step further: a petition was put before the Commons ostensibly from several Catholic noblemen but in fact contrived by the administration. At the same time a mortgage bill (allowing Catholics to lend money on the security of land, which if the borrower proved insolvent would necessarily call in question the ban on Catholics securing fresh title to land) was put before parliament. Protestants, opposed to concessions, had already been expecting the worst. The fears of the hardline Protestant interest in Cork and south Tipperary were deepened by the fact that Edmund Burke was private secretary to the chief secretary in the new administration. Burke himself was of course the son of a Ballyduff Nagle mother, and hence a close associate of the detested Nagle circle.

The object of the allegations, raised at the outset of the session, was as in 1733 to provide material for an enquiry which would establish that Catholics were unreliable and hence that concessions could not even be contemplated. The lobby in parliament was conducted by what the Lord Lieutenant recognised as 'Lord Shannon's friends', and the circle was soon to widen from Cork, where the banner was first raised, to embrace the Protestant interest in south Tipperary. There the 1761 general election, in which a crypto-Catholic Mathew had pipped the Protestant Maude amid wild scenes at the hustings, had given a novel twist to events, and overt politicisation on this scale represented a progression beyond happenings in neighbouring north-east Cork, to which it was so closely linked by both Protestant and Catholic ties. The name Mathew was moreover resonant of associations of James Cotter and hence of past évènements.

As in 1730 when Colonel Richard Hennessy's mission had made the Blackwater a suspect region, Burke's position in 1761 ensured that the Blackwater was the starting point of counteraction (though it was eventually to be overtaken in public notoriety by south Tipperary). Burke, who had arrived in Ireland two months before the session, was the active lobbyist for the session's work, and both the plans and his support for them quickly became known. The events had the result of making the Nagles into marked men. If Burke started a process of lobbying friendly politicians, and in fact for a young man and mere private secretary he was remarkably close to many politicians, news of what might be proposed would have spreadly widely and quickly. If the alleged plot fixed on the little enclave on the Blackwater, long the sole centre of active Catholic opinion in county Cork, the point of the accusations gathered added force in the presence of a man related to the Nagles in the Halifax administration; and the letter of Fant, a county Limerick attorney to Halifax, dated 18 October, four days before the parliamentary session opened, was politically inspired and carefully timed.[57]

While the Cork interest did not feel strong enough to carry the house with them in a direct confrontation with a popular administration, they were able to prevail in the end. Defeated crushingly in the lords on 5 April 1762 in an effort to force a debate on the recruitment issue, they transferred their action to the Commons where their proposed address to the Lord Lieutenant was rejected on 12 April by a vote of 113 to 63, a result achieved apparently by a remarkable speech by Hamilton. This seems to have been drafted by Burke, and presumably it was the first public exposition of the powerful logic which underlay all Burke's future writing on the Catholic question. The address seems to have lasted near three hours. It was clearly to this speech and to Burke as an informant that Charlemont was referring when he wrote that 'an intimate friend of his [Burke] assured me that he had repeated to him no less than three times an oration which afterwards he spoke in the house, and which lasted near three hours'.[58] However, anticipating a favourable government outcome, the opponents had already prepared the ground for undoing the effects of a government victory by the simple device of proposing earlier the same morning in the house a committee of enquiry into the 'popish insurrections' in Munster. This committte was set up without a division, and when it reported its resolutions on 16 April, they were carried on a division by 58 votes to 44; the committee was recommitted, although it was the end of the session, to continue its work.[59] No administration could dare act in support of recruitment as long as a committee with such a serious remit was in being. All the work of the administration was now undone, and Halifax, writing to London on 17 April, revealed in a lame dispatch his awareness that he had been outwitted.[60] The opposition had already circulated scare stories in London, and even in reporting to London Halifax was on the defensive trying to deny their substance.[61] It had become impossible for the government to take the arming issue further.

At local level purely agrarian unrest, fuelled in a novel fashion by resentment of the restructuring of agriculture as much by Catholic gentlemen and middlemen as Protestant, set off by economic boom during the Seven Years War, proved a convenient pretext of action. Many arrests of Whiteboy suspects were made in the spring of 1762. By May some 237 suspects were in jail. A letter from Youghal at the outset of April had represented that 'our lads are as eagar to hunt them as ever a keen pack of dogs were to hunt a fox'. Those arrested included one of the several Garrett Nagles living in the Blackwater valley.[62] The scale and unprecented character of these arrests has not been given sufficient attention. To put them in context, they were probably far more numerous than the arrests in any Irish county in the troubled months of early 1798, with the possible exception of Carlow. The editors of the *Burke correspondence* expressed surprise, understandably enough, at finding among Burke's papers a letter addressed by Fant to Halifax which is actually endorsed in Burke's hand.[63] In fact, it simply illustrates Burke's central position in the matter. The survival of the letter in his papers, not in the state papers, shows that the matter had been handled by Burke. Addressed to Halifax, it must have been discussed in the Dublin privy council, and one suspects that lobbying by Burke is reflected in the fact that the issue was slow to come up in the Commons, and when it did in the form of the claim for an enquiry into the 'popish insurrections', many had stayed away from the house and the majority even among those present was small. Burke's pre-occupations are hinted at in a later reference in a letter from Charles O'Hara in August 1762 to the effect that 'you'd hardly expect this of a man you used to accuse last winter of being as bad as any Cromwellian'.[64] His savage comment on the temper of Munster gentry in another letter in the same month is likewise a telling indication of his state of mind and of its Cork focus.[65]

A search for firearms in the houses of Catholics in Cork city and county was organised, finding 'no more than thirty unserviceable firelocks and a few hangers'. This has been seen as a case of the enforcement of the penal laws.[66] The action had been authorised, however, by the Lord Lieutenant, prompted by Burke,[67] and its purpose was to disprove the assertions of the anti-Catholic interest in the Commons in their own political power base of county Cork. The action of overriding local interests by Dublin intervention could be repeated. In a response to the Commons' attempt to find a plot in Munster and to a local purge, the executive took the trials of the Whiteboys out of the hands of the local gentry and gave the task to a special commission of two law officers, John Aston, chief justice of the common pleas, and of all men Anthony Malone who, while as sergeant, one of the chief law officers, was the son of a convert. Again, the fact that Aston's much-quoted report has survived not in the state papers but in Burke's illustrates his crucial role.[68]

The commission itself took the form of an astonishing procession across Munster with crowds often heralding the two men as saviours. When leaving Cork, Aston was 'grossly insulted by the prosecutors of the Whiteboys for his lenity, or rather impartiality', and stones were thrown at his carriage.[69] However, the events made the Catholics more marked than ever, and in a sense these steps were the reason why in 1766 several were to pay a high price. Parliamentary action was orchestrated by Cork and Tipperary politicians, in concert with their local supporters. Arrests at local level and action in parliament occurred again in 1763-4, once more repeating the pattern in which charges were abroad by the outset of the session. In April 1763 reports that informations were to be lodged against 'men of property' were in the air.[70] Burke was alive to the issue immediately: 'I see by Williamson's last paper that they are reviving the rebellion stories; and have produced a second song, indeed more plausible as to the manner than the former; they asserted it was proved on the trial of Dweyr [sic] at Clonmel'[71]. On this occasion the opposition in the lower house was much better organised than in 1761-2 when it became effective late in the session. More seriously, the adminstration lost its ability to manage the Lords. On 11 February the Earl of Carrick (Lord Shannon's son-in-law) seems to have been the instigator of a Lord's committee appointed to enquire into 'the insurrections', and in the report he made on behalf of the committee on 14 February he implied criticism of the two judges' commission in 1762. Not only was the report agreed, but the Lords decreed the following day in an unprecedented order that it should be put up in market towns and public places throughout the kingdom. The Commons committee, in existence since the preceding session, also reported on 15 February and a motion against it was lost by 26 votes to 80. The Commons action seem to have been dominated by Lord Shannon's son for Cork and Maude and Bagwell for Tipperary.[72]

The parliamentary season in 1765 was preceded in now almost predictable fashion by a new wave of charges: in April 1765 32 men had already been indicted for high treason in Clonmel.[73] The focus centered more firmly on propertied Catholics, and in all about 40 Catholics were arrested over 1765 and 1766. Even Lord Kenmare, remote in the fastnessess of Kerry hitherto untouched by these events, was envisaged as a target.[74] Those arrested included James Nagle of Garnavilla in Tipperary. Garrett Nagle, the eldest son of the Ballylegan branch, apprehensive for his safety, conformed formally twice over to the established church inside seven months.[75] James Nagle of Garnavilla conformed in December 1765, no doubt in the vain hope of protecting himself, as did Robert Nagle at Clogher in the same month.[76] In all in these tense months no fewer than three Nagles at Ballylegan, Clogher and Garnavalla conformed. Burke's letters in the spring of 1766 are full of references to what was afoot in Ireland. His visit to Ireland in the second half of 1766, from August to October, is at first sight a little puzzling, as it occurred in a time of crisis in the career of his patron Rockingham, and its purpose does not clearly emerge in the few letters which survive. It was however to organise the defence of the Catholics. One of the persons he met was John Fitzgibbon:

> My last conversation with him was at Milltown in 1766 – we dined tête a tête, and he spoke to me like a good Irishman. Religion as such made no part of our conversation then, or at any former time – but the condition of his countrymen and blood, on account of that religion, from the insane prejudices, and furious temper then raging, in the lower part of the prevailng faction seemed to make a proper impression upon him ..... his mind was right, both as a lawyer, and as a man that wished well to his country.[77]

His mission was remarkably successful. He organised a powerful defence team and engaged in discreet lobbying of politicians in an effort to prevent any parliamentary action. Moreover, the day immediately after or before meeting Fitzgibbon (Burke did not recollect clearly 26 years later) he dined with the chancellor Bowes, obtaining an assurance that 'by no forwardness of his, any further mischief should be done by the penal laws'. The chancellor as chairman of the Lords and of the judicial machinery at large had of course a vital role in undoing both legal and political manouvres. Burke's activity reached beyond Dublin, and a letter in 1792 suggests that he may have visited in 1766 a Mr Butler, who was sub-sheriff of Tipperary in that year, and covered the ground from Limerick to Tipperary.[78]

His fears and concern for his relatives in this year of crisis come across in his lines to Garrett of Ballyduff:

> I am really solicitous for the welfare of all the people about the Blackwater, and most grateful for their friendship, in this I speak to all our friends, for I consider you all as one, and hope (as I am sure you do, if you are wise) that you consider yourselves in the same way.[79]

The reference to 'you all as one' hints at the fact that, drawing no doubt on his consultations with his political acquaintances, he saw the arrest of individuals as only part of the threat: Catholics needed to see themselves as a group with a common interest. When he had returned, well-briefed, to London, he hastened to advise his relatives that 'the plot is laid deep; and the persons concerned in it are very determined and very wicked'. Nagle was acquitted in 1767, as were the others. Significantly those who had been brought to trial in early 1766 before Burke organised the defence did not fare well. Three minor gentlemen and the priest Nicholas Sheehy were executed in the spring, and it was this turn of events which had brought Burke back to Ireland.[80] The defence council for the Catholics was remarkably talented, including among others Sir Lucius O'Brien, John Fitzgibbon, John Scott and Barry Yelverton, all young men destined to establish themselves as the greatest names at the Irish bar, or even to advance beyond it. In the surviving Burke correspondence the material has given the impression that Burke was concerned only with the defence of James Nagle of Garnavilla. This is incorrect, as James Nagle was the only Nagle facing an actual charge in 1766. Burke's self-appointed brief seems to have been much wider.

Edmund Burke was always to feel that Catholics should assert themselves. This belief may well have been acquired originally from his Nagle relatives, who had a tradition both of standing up whether in lobbying parliament as early as 1731 or in Nano Nagle's case in founding a religious order. It was Burke who organised the defence of Catholics in 1766 and who urged that they should not stint money on their defence. In 1777, when Catholic relief was in the air, his reaction to reports at the time of the visit to Ireland of Charles Fox, who met the Nagles, was one of pleasure that 'the old spirit and character of that country is fully kept up which rejoices me beyond measure'.[81] In retrospect he felt that his action had achieved a reversal of the menace threatening Catholics in the spring of 1766, and this belief that vigorous assertion was necessary was to remain the wellspring of his advice on Irish affairs right from his early unpublished writings to his dying days. It was these writings, or a further and now missing paper, which provided the material for the accounts of the Catholics and of the penal laws in Young's *tour*.[82] They are not, as they are often treated, independent corroboration by an Englishman of what Burke claimed. They are entirely derivative.

It was in this world that Richard Hennessy was born and grew up. A political threat hung over it from the time of the Cotter execution in 1720, and it certainly created fears. It also reflected a high-powered Protestant presence in Doneraile and Mitchelstown with a matching one in south Tipperary. The Kings were already identified with an anti-Catholic stance in the 1750s. When news of the Mitchelstown interdict

Plate 14.3   Nano Nagle (Crawford Municipal Art Gallery/Cork V.E.C.).

broke, Charles O'Conor somewhat unwisely discounted its significance because of the known outlook of the family.[83] A generation later the family were friends of George Ogle, and George King (Lord Kingsborough), as well as spearheading the opposition to political concessions in the Commons in tandem with Ogle in 1795,[84] was later the head of the North Cork Militia of '98 rebellion fame. The St Legers retained notoriety too. Lord Doneraile was tried for horsewhipping a priest in 1780, John Philpot Curran in one of his early cases appearing for the prosecution. Losing the case at the assizes, Doneraile was said to have issued an order to have every mass-house on his estate nailed up.[85] The region and its character seem to be obliquely hinted at in Curran's later speeches in the Commons. Significantly, dissent seems to have occured in the Doneraile Volunteer Rangers in which a number of Nagles and one Hennessy were enrolled, and the peremptory ending of the corps in December 1782 can be seen in the last entry, in Doneraile's own hand in the corps' order book, followed by the word 'finis'.[86] A re-echo of right-wing sympathies can be detected in the fact that Lord Doneraile had John Bagwell, a protagonist of the 1760s in Tipperary, as one of the M.P.s for his Doneraile borough in 1790. The rural focus of the interlinked gentry of this region had its urban counterpart in the two towns of Mallow and Clonmel which probably had, if their immediate environs are included, the largest Protestant populations of any towns, apart from the two cities of Dublin and Cork. More relevantly, they had better political connections than the servile towns of Bandon and Youghal which probably exceeded them in terms of the size of the Protestant population *intra muros.*

Cork alone in Ireland had a sequence of gentry episodes of blood in the century. The deaths of Cotter in 1720, Morty Oge O'Sullivan in 1754 and Arthur O'Leary in 1773 had no parallels elsewhere. French recruiting agents, usually officers from the Irish Brigade, were also executed on a number of occasions. While this occurred in Leinster as well as Munster, it was still anachronistically a live issue in Cork, post-1748, in peace time. In 1749 Denis Dunne was executed, and in 1752 Thomas Herlihy and Denis MacCarthy.[87] The death of Morty Oge O'Sullivan in 1754 was in essence another case, the most dramatic of all in fact involving a full-blown expedition from Cork to the Berehaven peninsula.[88] Such cases are all part of the bloodiest and most vindictive story of tensions in eighteenth-century Ireland. They were to last into the 1760s. As late as 1764 a recruiting agent, Dillon McNamarra, was sentenced to death in Cork, though, perhaps reflecting some effort by the liberal administration to hold out against the county's baying gentry, in May his execution was stayed for three months.[89] This may have been the last case brought against a recruiting officer, but it was over-shadowed by the more tragic events of 1766: the execution of Nicholas Sheehy and of three minor Catholic gentlemen in 1766 in the region of the Blackwater and Tipperary, the bloodiest episode of all. Burke was connected by marriage to Nicholas Sheehy: a cousin of Burkes had married, as far back as 1755 at least, a sister of the priest. As Edmond Sheehy, one of the gentleman victims, was related to Nicholas Sheehy, Burke would have been distantly connected with him as well.[90]

Burke grew up in the region in the key years of 1735-1741 and may well have visited the area on further occasions during his holidays from Ballitore and Trinity: his last identifiable visit at this stage of his career was in 1748. In 1744 a poem such as Séan na Ráithíneach Ó Murchadha's *Tá an bhliadhain seo ag teacht*[91], composed only nine miles south of Ballymacmoy, was well-informed and rather explicit, and re-echoed poetically a line of conversation which reached the ears of the region's managing gentry: fourteen miles up the Blackwater valley from Monanimy the agent of the Percival estate at Kanturk reported in the same year that the papists were greatly elated by prospects of invasion.[92] Awareness from Cork of the mood of expectation and foreboding in 1744 and 1745 must explain why as a student in Dublin Burke responded with sympathy and understanding to the '45. One letter was self-consciously dated with reference to the event, and commented on 'those unhappy gentleman who engaged in this affair' and who had thought their expedition 'a just cause'.[93] More strikingly still, as a result of awareness turning into intellectual curiosity, a letter of 12 July 1746 reveals that 'I have read some history. I am endeavouring to get a little into the accounts of this our own poor country'.[94] The Gaelic poet Eoghan Rua Ó Súilleabháin was later a tutor at Annakissy, once the main seat of the Annakissy branch of the Nagles, to the children of Pierce Nagle, brother-in-law to David of Ballygriffen. Burke and O'Sullivan could conceivably though improbably have met. It is very likely that O'Sullivan's awareness of political events was sharpened by his stay in the house of one of the families at the centre of Protestant accusations. He probably learned more from the Nagles than they did from him. His poetry would have been little understood by the Nagle circle itself. They were probably already English-speaking: according to James Roche, Richard Hennessy learned his Irish in the Irish brigade 'where the Irish was so generally spoken in the regiments'.[95] Burke's last visits were in the 1760s, and on the profile of both Pierce Nagle's and O'Sullivan's lives, O'Sullivan's tutoring should have occurred at about the same time. His poetry has a number of hints at the political storms in the region in the 1760s, and shows a dislike of the Protestant establishment of the Mallow region. His celebrated lines:

> Ní h-í an bhoichtineacht is measa liom,
> Ná bheith thíos go deo,
> Ach an tarcuisne a leanann í
> Ná leighisfeadh na leoin.

are almost a paraphrase of thoughts that come up in Burke's writings. His language and views are those of the Blackwater, as are Burke's own. Almost symbolically, the son of James Cotter, brought up a Protestant and a staunch loyalist who put his sympathies beyond doubt by sponsoring a charter school in the 1760s, resided on the Rockforest estate, on the road to Mallow only two miles beyond the abode of the Hennessys.

The events of the 1760s with their menace for propertied families caused more real fear than any occasion in the century so far, and inevitably fear lingered on beyond the decade. Even Mathew in Tipperary discretely left the country for a period in the early 1760s, while David Nagle of Ballygriffen, the richest of the Nagles, left his seat for good, first for Cork in 1762 and then for England where he lived out his days as a rich absentee in Bath. The Mountnagle family let their lands in 1773 and became absentee also, apparently moving to England like their richer relative David. The Clogher relative equally found discretion the better part of valour. Not only did a Clogher Nagle conform in 1765 but the fact that the Burke interest in the property was turned into an effective one seems to be associated with a move to a seat on their lands in the slightly more friendly athmosphere of Renny.

Tensions in the 1770s
The fears were still fresh in the county in the 1770s. The death of Art O'Leary on 4 May 1773 revived the memories. Though the tragedy happened further afield – O'Leary lived at Raleigh near Macroom on the Lee – the same political grouping in the county as in the early 1760s was behind the events. The story of O'Leary has been woven about both possible sexual misdemenour in 1771 and rivalry between O'Leary and the magistrate Abraham Morris in 1773, culminating in the famous offer of £5 for O'Leary's horse. In reality the background appears to be entirely political. The Muskerry Constitutional Society was founded in July 1771. After its next meeting on 7 August it published in the *Cork Evening Post* of 19 August a condemnation of O'Leary. The very issue contained a reply by O'Leary, which meant that the matter had been widely bruited. He declared his readiness to stand trial on the charges. Significantly, the dispute with Morris, high sheriff of the year, occurred on 13 July, according to a later Morris statement in the *Cork Evening Post* of 7 October. Thus the founding of the Society with the politically resonant term 'Constitutional' in its name and the O'Leary intervention with the high sheriff occurred in the assize month, and no less significantly, according to O'Leary's later declaration in the newspaper on 19 October, O'Leary had gone on 13 July 'to apply to Morris as magistrate relative to some law proceedings'. The balance of probability is that O'Leary had intervened in defence of some individuals who were being proceded against at the assizes, and that,

in a county already notorious for its magistrate readiness to keep the penal laws alive, Morris, possibly himself provoked by O'Leary and intending to put him in his place, demanded his horse in exchange for £5. Again Morris's offering of a reward for the apprehension of O'Leary on 7 October 1771 in the pages of the *Cork Evening Post* was followed by a reply by O'Leary dated 19 October, which also appeared in the paper. A sequence of two declarations, one by the Society in August, one by Morris on 7 October, both responded to by O'Leary, gave the dispute a remarkably public profile.[96]

The story reeks of politics. The resonances come through in the lines in the celebrated poem, *Caoineadh Airt Uí Laoire* ('The Lament for Arthur O'Leary') declaring that

> D'umhlaídís Sasanaigh
> Síos go talamh duit
> Is ní ar mhaithe leat
> Ach le h-aonchorp eagla

and in the much later tombstone inscription by the grandson that he 'had been outlawed and treacherously shot by order of the British government'. Significantly too, Colonel Daniel O'Connell, though opposed to the marriage in the first instance, in Ireland at the time seems to have followed the affair closely, noting in April with satisfaction that O'Leary had come safe. The wording is vague: what it implies is that he was at the time in Kerry, and the fact that O'Connell, who had already left Derryane on his way back to France, had made his acquaintance suggests that O'Leary made more than one visit to Derrynane. If so, he returned to Cork intermittently, and it was in the wake of doing so again that the final denouement occurred in May 1773. Very significantly, on receipt of news of his death, Daniel O'Connell observed that 'the short acquaintance I had with him gave me a more favourable opinion than I had at first conceived of him'.

The Muskerry Constitutional Society's declaration published on 15 August 1771 was signed by five clergymen, three Townsends (two of them clergymen), and Sir John Conway Colthurst, a rather cretinous parliamentary follower of Shannon, of whom it was noted in a 1773 list of M.P.s that 'he will always obey him [Shannon], a mere paltry fellow'.[97] In July 1773, after a shot had been fired at Morris in Cork, a subscription list setting out the sums put up by a large group of political worthies for a rewards fund was published. The county political backing was overt. The Earl of Shannon in person gave one of the three largest subcriptions, two other Shannonite M.P.s subscribed (one, the county member Richard Townsend, the other Riggs Falkiner).

The largest subscription was by William Tonson. His uncle, Richard, a sitting M.P., an elderly man who had been a 'bully' for the first Lord Shannon, had died in June; William Tonson himself acquired a borough seat the following year. Morris's brother Jonas, whose son was the Shannon M.P. for the county in 1791, was a subscriber. Two Devonshire relatives of another Shannon member also contributed. There was a Barnard signatory to the documents of both August 1771 and July 1773: the Barnard M.P. himself was a habitual absentee. The urban contributors were exclusively from the Shannon political and financial interests in the city (Riggs Falkiner, William Tonson, Francis Carleton, Walter Travers, Richart Hare). The list is as interesting for the names missing as for those on it.

Coming in the wake of the events of 1766, the case can only have added to the deep and abiding sense of fear and intimidation. In Tipperary the fears were further revived by the Whiteboy unrest of 1774-5 which seems to have created apprehension that a witch-hunt might be set up again. These fears explain why in his last will in January 1775 Thomas Wyse of Waterford (who already had painful memories of threat in 1765-6) referred to the events of the 1760s, and to plans he had in contemplation for his family leaving Ireland.[98] Most remarkably of all, the MacCarthys of Springhouse, although they did not sell up or alienate their lands, all moved to Toulouse by 1776.[99] Fear was deepened by the assassination in county Tipperary in November 1775 of Ambrose Power, one of the magistrate activists of 1765-6, and the declaration of sixty noblemen and gentry (including Kingsborough and Tyrone) in January 1776 which hinted ominously at violation of the penal laws by Catholics.[100] From the internal evidence it is clear that much of Eoghan Rua Ó Súilleabháin's poetry is much later than is often assumed, and was written in the late 1770s. In one of his poems, *A fhile chirt ghéir*, the alliterative list of names of poltical notables includes the names of Bagwell, Tonson and Townsend among others: they imply oblique reference to the events of the mid-1760s and of 1773.[101] The *Caoineadh Airt Uí Laoire* may itself lose some of its significance by being taken to have been written by his widow, and to have survived only in the folk tradition. However, the attribution of the poem to the widow (a poetess of whom no other known poetic composition survives) may be a convention, as it very obviously was, for instance, to attribute the dirge for Morty Og O'Sullivan to one of his companions on the eve of their execution in 1754. And while it has survived to modern times because it was written down from a folk version in 1800, it may have first appeared or been circulated in one or more manuscripts which are now lost. The poem seems to have had a predominantly Cork interest: of the nine sources which have provided much or little of the text, seven are from Cork, two from Kerry. If these speculations are correct, both the poem's appearance at all, and its circulation, may arise from the political tensions and resentments that the events of the 1760s and 1770s stirred up rather than from tragedy within a family. The fact that the piece did not acquire a literary permanence may itself reflect simply the end of the Gaelic world. Much of Eoghan Rua Ó Súilleabháin's poetry is itself remarkably late, and is no less significant as the last poetry by a poet-scribe firmly rooted in the now fading Munster classical tradition of poetic commentary.

The events and tensions of the mid-1770s explain Burke's renewed interest in the question of the penal laws in 1776. His concerns in turn explain why Young, in advance of his visit in 1776, was briefed by Burke (and, though purely coincidentally, Young came to know this region of Ireland more than any other). Burke's interest may explain too why David Nagle's large rental of £2,000, and Burke's own £500 for Clogher, featured in the list of absentee rents. Young did not report more directly on the Nagle family. On the other hand, Burke had not been been slow in ensuring that Fox, leader of the Whig opposition in the English commons, met his Irish relatives. The lack of mention of the family in Young's book may reflect the discreet spreading of Burke's protective mantle yet again across the Blackwater.

Unpleasant though life was (sufficiently so to cause three households in two of the richest families who bore the brunt of Protestant resentments, the Springhouse MacCarthys and the Ballygriffen and Mountnagle Nagles, to leave Ireland), local politics did not reach a stage of claiming victims other than O'Leary, even if the spectre was ominously present again in Munster in 1773 and in 1775-6. For those who remained, less important than such threats was the legal discrimination which excluded them from most public or professional careers in Ireland. That meant that the problem of providing for sons and daughters which affected all propertied families was a heightened one for Catholics. Younger sons had to make do with modest support to launch them into careers, and quite apart from the shortage of good suitors, small dowries narrowed further the prospects of suitable marriages for daughters. Most families married within their region, and often married cousins. Even in the case of a great family like the Ballygriffen Nagles, despite their brillant matches, a daughter married an Annakissy cousin. Such circumstances probably explain why Richard Hennessy's younger brother in difficult circumstances in Cork city had apparently abducted his Nagle bride. The problems are reflected too in the narrow circumstances of Richard, a second son. Apart from trade, the French and Spanish armies provided an outlet for such young men, especially for families like the Nagles or Hennessys which had a tradition of service and who therefore were well-recommended for the commissions that in peace-time were all too scarce. Moreover, in contrast to commerce, which for success required a real investment, and to the regular regiments of England or France which involved purchase, the outlay for commissions in the Irish Brigade was more modest: recommendation, though itself a scarce and prized asset, was sufficient. For comparatively modest families like the Hennessys trade was an important outlet. For the Nagles, there was greater ability to set sons up in status-conferring estates or seats, though for them as for others the fundamental dilemma of careers remained one for the younger sons. They were less evident in trade (only one Nagle can be traced in trade abroad, in Cadiz), and wealth and connection helped to ensure that while some had modest careers, they benefitted from a greater range of outlets. Burke's correspondence too bears witness to the advance of some of them in East India Company service and in British military or naval careers.

Legal acumen, middleman holdings, careers in army, trade and in the professions all helped to create a viable Irish society on the floor of the Blackwater. The pressures of the age did however tell upon the region. The absenteeism of two branches of the Nagle family is telling, itself a phenomenon anticipated at an earlier date in the migration of both one Nagle family and of the MacCarthys to Tipperary. Assertive Catholic leadership declined, the result of a protracted attrition, and it may be possible to cast O'Leary – on the fringes of this region – in the rôle of a victim of the extraordinary political circumstances of Cork. Some of this story was of course repeated across the border in Tipperay. The Springhouse MacCartys emigrated from Ireland in 1776, and the Cahir Butlers, so central to the story of Catholic society in south Tipperary, later conformed (and in their case socially as well as religiously). On the other hand, in Tipperary Catholic society itself remained vibrant. If some like the MacCarthys left, or like the Cahir Butlers conformed on all counts, other families like the Scullys were rising, and played a large part in supporting Catholic demands in the early nineeenth century. If Clonmel like a host of county Cork towns was Protestant, Carrick-on-Suir under the Butler umbrella was uniquely a thriving industrial town in which the main business interest was Catholic. Outstanding in this interest were the Galweys, who with the Tipperary MacCarthys also represented an extension of landed interest into high finance. The Galweys were agents for the Kilcash Butlers, agents also for the Dillon bank which was the first Catholic bank in Dublin, and had close ties with Martin Murphy, correspondent in Waterford for Edward Fitzgerald of London. Through that link they tied up with the rising Sutton empire, successor to the Fitgerald network after 1759. One of Galwey's sons, Anthony, was a brandy merchant at La Rochelle at the outset of the 1760s, married incidentally to a Madamoiselle Labadie, granddaughter of the richest and most aristocratic business house in that port, the La Rochelle Butlers. While there was a Galwey tie with McDermott in Dublin, the MacCarthys had widespread links also, and a Sutton-MacCarthy marriage in Bordeaux cemented relations at the time of the great wave of international speculation in 1771. The bride of Justin MacCarthy of Springhouse was a Tuite, of a Copenhagen-London-Saint Croix family that had formed part succesively of the Fitzgerald and Sutton circles. Thus south Tipperary from its Carrick and Springhouse axis was a central part of the richest single network of business Catholics. Some of its members were marked men in 1765-6; fears still affected them in 1775 as the story of the Waterford Wyses, who were part of this interest, and of the Springhouse MacCarthys shows.

The Tipperary high sheriff of 1798, Judkin Fitzgerald (Irish only in name as he was a Judkin, and had assumed the Fitzgerald name in response to a bequest), dimwitted, socially ambitious and probably semi-demented, represented in effect a futile challenge to this community in its latter days in an age of revolution and social upheaval. He had county Cork ties through his Uniacke relatives. These ties were themselves unhelpful, the more so as the murder of Mr and Mrs Uniacke in Araglin in what appears to have been an attack on their guest, the hardline magistrate Nicholas Mansergh St George, in February 1798, can only have reinforced his existing zeal to identify with government policy. Judkin Fitzgerald was overtly anti-Catholic, and was more active after the rebellion had occurred than in its course in May and June; the actions that earned him national notoriety moreover occurred in the south of the county in Clonmel and Carrick. In county Cork the Blackwater valley was remarkably undisturbed in the 1790s, and few letters from the valley reached Dublin Castle, even from Mallow, Doneraile or, despite the fanaticism of the Kings, from Mitchelstown. Unrest had shifted elsewhere in the county, and the growth of the United Irishmen caused disquiet mainly in Cork city and in the lands to the south of the Bandon river. The Blackwater valley was no longer at the centre of the political life of the county. The world of Eoghan Rua Ó Súilleabháin in the headwaters of the Blackwater, the turbulent life of the Millstreet hinterland where Arthur O'Leary died in 1773, and the assertive little milieu of Nagles and Hennessys had either faltered or faded away. The passing of the Nagle rôle in Irish Catholic society was the most striking change of the last quarter of the century on the banks of the Blackwater.

References

1. Lewis, *Topog. dict. Ire.,* ii, p. 341.
2. L. M. Cullen, 'Burke, Ireland and Revolution' in *Eighteenth-century life,* xvi (February 1992), pp 21-42.
3. Hennessy archives, Cognac, letter from Richard Hennessy to James Hennessy, Jan. 1792.
4. T. W. Copeland (ed.), *Correspondence of Edmund Burke,* viii (Cambridge, 1958) [hereafter *Burke Correspondence*], p. 99, Burke to Sir G. Colebrooke, 14 Dec. 1794.
5. Hennessy archives, Cognac, 23 Feb. 1753, 19 Nov. 1755, James Hennessy, Cork, to Richard Hennessy, Ostend.
6. 'A list of the names of the popish parish priests 1704 ... for the county of Cork' in *Irish ecclesiastical record* (May, 1876), p. 354.
7. 'Report on the state of popery in Ireland, 1731' in *Archiv. Hib.* (1913), p. 110.
8. Hennessy archives, Cognac, MS 'Extrait du dictionnaire historique de Morei, article O'Brien.' The certificate is dated 31 July 1758 and the notary's declaration bears the same date.
9. *Burke correspondence,* i, p. 329.
10. Augier archives, Cognac, Broussard papers, La Rochelle, Anthoine de Galwey to Broussard, Cognac, 15 Dec. 1765.
11. Excluding the huge Clancarty estate.
12. Hennessy archives, Cognac, marriage contract between James Hennessy of Ostend and Ellen Barrett. The jointure was for £500 in the event of issue, £800 in their absence.
13. Hennessy archives, Cognac, letter from Cork, 4 Mar. 1766. This marriage is not mentioned in the Hennessy genealogy in Cognac. There is a marriage of a Bridget Hennessy to MacWalter Burke. Either the first marriage did not occur or a widow later married a second time.
14. Hennessy archives, Letter book 1769-71, 27 Oct. 1770, to John Jennings, Dublin.
15. Hennessy archives, Inventory of estate of Charles Hennessy, 2 June 1759, 29 Nov. 1760.
16. Hennessy archives, Cork, 23 Feb. 1753, James Hennessy to Richard Hennessy, Ostend.
17. Hennessy archives, Cork, 19 Nov. 1755, James Hennessy to Richard Hennessy, Ostend.
18. Hennessy archives, Letter book, 1771-7, 22 Aug. 1772, to Connolly and Arthur; Cork, 18 Sept., Henry Galwey to Richard Hennessy.
19. Archives de la guerre, Paris, personal file of Lieut-Colonel Richard Hennessy.
20. Hennessy archives, La Rochelle, 20 July 1775, John Saule to Richard Hennessy.
21. M. J. O'Connell, *Last colonel of the Irish brigade* (1892, Cork reprint, 1977).
22. J. Roche, *Critical and miscellaneous essays by an octogenarian,* ii (Cork, 1851), p. 51.
23. Hennessy genealogy in *Burke family records.* One of Richard Hennessy's great-grandmothers was a Nagle.
24. 'Notes on the Cotter family of Rockforest, co. Cork' in *Cork Hist. Soc. Jn.,* xiv, no. 77 (Jan.- March, 1908), pp 1-12.
25. Hennessy archives, Bordeaux, 5 May 1772, John Galwey to Richard Hennessy
26. Hennessy archives, Cork, 23 Feb. 1753, James Hennessy to Richard Hennessy.
27. Hennessy archives, 18 Sept. 1772, Henry Galwey to Richard Hennessy.
28. Hennessy archives, 'A schedule of my bro. George's will'. George left five children (See Richard Hennessy to John Saule, 13 Jan. 1776). A daughter of George's in Cork in 1782 married Samuel Flanrey of the island of Tortola; see

Finn's Leinster Journal, 26-30 Oct. 1782. I am indebted to Dr Kevin Whelan for this reference. A Hennessy given employment in the island of St John's in the 1790s 'as he is without employment' may be a son; see *Burke correspondence*, ix, p. 110, 16 Nov. 1796.

29. *Burke correspondence*, iii, p. 438, to Edmun Sexton Pery, 16 June 1778.

30. J. G. Simms, *The Williamite confiscation in Ireland, 1690-1703* (London, 1956), pp 19, 33 note, 46, 54.

31. On the Nagles see B. O'Connell, 'The Nagles of Annakissy' in *Irish genealogist*, ii, no. 11 (1954), pp 337-348; idem.,'The Nagles of Mount Nagle' in ibid., ii, no. 12 (1955), pp 377-389; idem. 'The Nagles of Garnavilla' in ibid., iii, no. 1 (I956), pp 17-24; idem. 'The Nagles of Ballygriffen' in ibid., iii, no. 2 (1957), pp 67-73; T. J. Walsh, *Nano Nagle and the Presentation sisters* (Dublin, 1959).

32. The earliest legal title to Ballymacmoy in Hennessy possession is a fee farm grant of 1862: the light it throws on the past history of their interest is therefore limited.

33. E. O'Byrne, *The convert roles* (Dublin, 1981). In the convert roles a David Nagle in 1704 was of Clogher and Shannagh. As the surviving roles are copies of the lost originals, this must be a misreading of Rennagh, a 1778 Nagle seat noted by Taylor and Skinner. It is variously spelled Rennagh, Renny and Rinny. Garrett Nagle's residing in 1775 at 'Rinny' is confirmed in a marriage settlement for Nicholas Nagle, son of Athanasius Nagle of Ballylegan, of which he was a trustee; see Registry of Deeds, 309/260/205612, 28 Apr. 1775.

34. See W. O'Brien, *Edmund Burke as an Irishman*, second ed. (Dublin, 1926), pp 119-124. See also B. O'Connell, 'The right hon. Edmund Burke: a basis for a pedigree' in *Cork Hist. Soc. Jn.,* lx (July-Dec.1955), p. 73, and *Burke correspondence,* i, passim.

35. *Burke correspondence*, i, p. 228.

36. Earl Fitzwilliam and Sir R. Bourke (ed.), *Correspondence of the right Hon. Edmund Burke* (London, 1844), i, pp 111-14.

37. *Scots Magazine*, 1797, p. 795.

38. *Burke correspondence*, i, p. 217.

39. Ibid., i, p. 228.

40. Hennessy archives, Cork, 15 May 1772, Pat Nagle to Richard Hennessy.

41. Archives nationales, Paris, Oi 236, ff 40-1, Sept. 1776.

42. Hennessy archives, Hennessy genealogy

43. Walsh, *Nano Nagle*, p. 29.

44. Ibid., p. 345.

45. Archives de la guerre, A1 2770, nos. 76-83, 6 Aug.-28 Dec. 1730. See also personal file on Richard Hennessy, which hints at Hennessy's important missions.

46. *Journals of the House of Lords*, iii, pp 159, 167.

47. Bishop Tenison's visitation of the diocese of Ossory in 1731 is an example; see N.A., MS 2462.

48. *Journals of the House of Commons*, iv, p. 106.

49. *Journals of the House of Lords*, iii, p. 209. See also *Archiv. Hib.,* x (1913), pp 118-128, 354.

50. *Journals of the House of Commons,* iv, Appendix xlvii.

51. *Archiv. Hib.* (1913), p. 118.

52. *Journals of the House of Commons,* iv, pp 106, 107, Appendices xlvi-xlix.

53. E. Bowen, *Bowen's court and seven winters* (London, 1984), pp 132-141.

54. J. Brady, *Catholics and catholicism in the eighteenth-century press* (Maynooth, 1965), pp 94-95.

55. W. P. Burke, *The Irish priests in the penal times 1660-1760* (1914, reprinted Shannon, 1968), pp 360-362.

56. *Burke correspondence,* i, p. 147, note 8.

57. L. M. Cullen, 'Burke, Ireland, and Revolution' in *Eighteenth-century life*, xvi, no. 1 (Feb. 1992), pp 27-8.

58. H.M.C., *Charlemont papers,* i, p. 145. According to Charlemont 'all his speeches, however long, were written, and given by heart'. If the speech were written out, the likelihood that it was drafted by Burke becomes all the greater; it is also likely that it provided the first formulation of the ideas for his later unpublished papers in the 1760s on the penal laws. The speech made a large impact on Charlemont, and he refers to it elswhere (ibid., p. 19). This speech has wrongly been assumed sometimes to be the speech which earned Hamilton his nickname of 'single-speech', see *Scots Magazine*, 1797, p. 646.

59. *Journals of the House of Commons*, vii, p. 161.

60. *Calendar of Home Office Papers 1760-65*, p. 174.

61. *Calendar of Home Office Papers 1760-65*, pp 173-5, 14 Apr., 17 Apr. 1762.

62. *Glasgow Journal*, 11-18 Feb., 22-29 Apr., 29 Apr.-6 May, 6-13 May 1762. For details of local events see also M. J. Bric, 'The whiteboy movement 1760-80' in *Tipperary*, pp 148-184.

63. *Burke correspondence*, i, p.147, note.

64. Ibid., i, p. 146, Charles O'Hara to Burke, 10 Aug. 1762.

65. Ibid., i, pp 147-8, to O'Hara, ante 23 Aug. 1762.

66. W. Lecky, *History of Ireland*, ii, p. 31, note.

67. *Burke correspondence,* vii, p. 285, to Richard Burke, Jnr., 6, 7, 10 Nov. 1792. Burke gave the date as 1764, and this is the date followed in Cullen, 'Burke, Ireland', p. 41, footnote 26. A slip of memory citing 1764 in place of 1762 seems far more probable, doubly so in the context of the many actions in Cork that spring, and the administration's own intervention in the county.

68. Fitzwilliam and Burke, *Correspondence of Burke,* i, p. 38, Chief Justice Aston to Hamilton, 24 June 1762.

69. *Scots Magazine*, Oct. 1786, p. 512.

70. *Glasgow Journal*, 14-21 Apr. 1763.

71. *Burke correspondence*, i, p. 169, to Ridge, 25 Apr. 1763.

72. Cullen, 'Burke, Ireland', p. 31.

73. *Glasgow Journal*, 11/18 April 1765

74. See *Burke correspondence*, ii, p.143, to Charles O'Hara, 20 June 1770.

75. O'Byrne, *convert rolls*; *Burke correspondence*, i, p. 216; O'Connell, 'Nagles of Garnavilla', p. 22.

76. O'Byrne, *Convert roles*; *Burke correspondence*, i, p. 276, note; O'Connell, 'Nagles of Garnavilla', pp 21-2. James Nagle's conversion has sometimes been given incorrectly as Dec. 1766.

77. *Burke correspondence*, vii, p. 101, to Richard Burke. Jnr., 20 Mar. 1792.

78. Cullen, 'Burke, Ireland', p. 33.

79. *Burke correspondence*, i, p. 289, to Garrett Nagle.

80. Cullen, 'Burke, Ireland', p. 33. See also 0'Connell, 'Nagles of Garnavilla', p. 22.

81. *Burke correspondence*, iii, p. 391, to Garrett Nagle, 26 Oct. 1777. Burke's letter to Fox on 8 Oct. is immediately relevant and significant on this question at one point (ibid., p. 381).

82. Cullen, 'Burke, Ireland', pp 35-6.

83. H.M.C., Report on O'Conor MSS.

84. See reports of debate on Catholic bill in 1795.

85. Brady, *Catholics*, p. 210

86. O'Brien, *Edmund Burke*, pp 212-215.

87. Roche, *Critical essays*, ii, p. 49, note. Roche gives the date of MacCarthy and Herlihy's execution as 1751. While Herlihy was arrested in 1751, the execution of both men seems to have occurred in 1752. See R. Hayes, *Ireland and Irishmen in the French Revolution* (London, 1932), p. 255; Brady, *Catholics,* p. 317.

88. The importance attached by the authorities to O'Sullivan was quite disproportionate; his activities and tragic end fit into the obscure politics of the region at the time. Though he coloured the episode somewhat, Froude's interest in it and in its significance was by no means misplaced. He ended his justly famous novel, *The two chiefs of Dunboy,* with a translation of the lament.

89. B. O'Connell, 'The right hon. Edmund Burke: a basis for a pedigree' in *Cork Hist. Soc. Jn.*, lx (1955), p. xxx; idem., 'Nagles of Garnvilla', p. 22.

90. Brady, *Catholics*, p. 319.

91. Torna (ed.), *Seán na Ráithíneach* (Dublin, 1954), pp 255-7.

92. B.L., Add. MS 47009, pp 37, 43.

93. *Burke correspondence*, i, p. 63. The dating of the letter is 'April 26 (for fear I should forget) 1745'. This is a word play based on the fact that April under the was the first month of the old-style new year, and hence marked a break with the 'rebellion year'. The dating of the letter is rendered more intelligibly in Earl Fitzwilliam and Bourke, *Correspondence of Burke,* i, pp 16-17, 17 note.

94. *Burke correspondence,* i, pp 67-8.

95. Roche, *Critical essays,* ii, p. 51.

96. For the details, see J. T. Collins, 'Arthur O'Leary, the outlaw' in *Cork Hist. Soc. Jn.*, liv (Jan.-June 1949), pp 1-7; lv (Jan.-June 1950), pp 21-24; lxi (Jan.-June 1956), pp 1-6.

97. M. Bodkin, 'Notes on the Irish parliament in 1773' in *R.I.A. Proc.,* 48, section C, iv (1942), p. 182.

98. W. P. Burke, *History of Clonmel* (Clonmel 1907), pp 393-4.

99. Archives nationales, Paris, Oi 236, ff 40-1, Sept. 1776

100. J. S. Donnelly, Jnr., 'Irish agrarian rebellion: the whiteboys of 1769-76' in *R.I.A Proc.,* 85, section C, xii (1983), p. 330.

101. P. Dinneen, *Amhráin Eoghan Ruadh Uí Shúilleabháin* (Dublin, 1901), p. 48.

Chapter 15

GAELIC LITERATURE AND CONTEMPORARY LIFE IN CORK, 1700-1840

CORNELIUS G. BUTTIMER

The years 1700-1840 represent the final stage of Irish as a widespread vernacular in Cork and the country at large. Where and at what rate language transformation occurred are issues currently receiving attention for Ireland generally[1] and our county specifically, especially for the nineteenth century.[2] However, Gaelic maintained considerable vitality even in a changing environment.[3] More Irish manuscripts survive for the time-span discussed here than for any previous era.[4] Cork's share of pre-Famine Gaelic records in turn surpasses that of other regions. Dr Breandán Ó Conchúir has outlined the local scribal milieu at length, sketching the lives of copyists, providing inventories of their documents and identifying patrons and sponsors.[5] Building on this foundation the present chapter makes the Irish-speaking community's everyday life itself an object of enquiry as this life is revealed in written materials of the period for the Cork area.

Daniel Corkery's *The hidden Ireland,* sub-titled 'A study of Gaelic Munster in the eighteenth century', may be held to represent a similar undertaking.[6] Deficiencies in this work have been pointed out, such as its author's assumption of a uniformly impoverished contemporary Irish-speaking society.[7] Perhaps the most consequential limitation lies in the scope of the evidence used. Since the nineteen twenties noteworthy progress has been made in describing the major collections of Irish manuscripts, those of the Royal Irish Academy, the National Library of Ireland and other institutional and private holdings here and overseas.[8] Such accounts and the greater availability of the sources through microfilming enable a more detailed overview of the literature produced in the century and a half under consideration to be attempted than was possible in Corkery's day.

The hidden Ireland remains nonetheless a great achievement in that it drew attention to an important, overlooked dimension of the Irish past, highlighting the aesthetics of Gaelic literary composition in the process.[9] Curiously, however, many scholars concerned with the

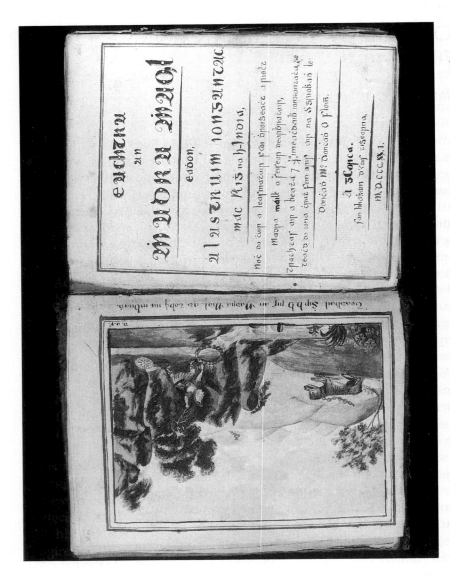

Plate 15.1   Scribe's illustration and title-page for *Eachtra an Mhadra Mhaoil* (U.C.C., MS Torna, T.i).

resources of pre-Famine culture still neglect the subject Corkery championed. Irish-language traditions scarcely figure in substantial works by historians like R. B. McDowell[10] or R. F. Foster.[11] These observations are not lightly made in an atmosphere which one commentator intimates has become excessively personalised.[12] Indeed *The hidden Ireland* is often marred by imperious attacks on other writers. Defects in recent publications may arise from a variety of causes, such as the weakness of formal structures of interdisciplinary cooperation between those working in the general domain of Irish studies.[13] Whatever their origins, shortcomings still persist in historiography from our own time, forming a serious obstacle to our understanding of Ireland and its constituent parts in the period reviewed.

When considered further one such deficiency paradoxically helps provide a framework for the remainder of this essay. Foster describes early seventeenth-century Gaelic Ireland as 'alien and bizarre'.[14] The connotations thereby established are not subsequently modified for the centuries after the seventeenth in his narrative. This negative representation of the Irish-speaking world recalls a debate on the supposed exotic nature of primitive tribes. Anthropologists have questioned whether the latter societies must be read in such terms, arguing rather that they have the features common to many cultures, relations with the outside world, internal configurations and other structures.[15] I believe the same observation applies to the era and the people of concern here, and that the framework of the presentation may be set out accordingly to reflect the primary concerns of any community.[16]

The paper is based on various forms of evidence. These include firstly the Gaelic texts themselves, whether previously edited or hitherto unpublished. Contemporary sources in English are also employed, particularly printed works, a type of material with which scribes and composers reveal themselves to be increasingly familiar.[17] Considerations of space prevent the citation of archival documents in English, but an extension of the enquiry in this direction would undoubtedly be fruitful. As the object of the exercise is primarily to make the Gaelic works known to the reader, the following approaches are employed to make Irish sources more accessible. A substantial proportion of the items cited are translated in the accompanying references. Gaelic compositions are often placed beside contemporary English matter with which they bear a close relationship. Particularly in the case of shorter passages, introductory remarks summarise the subsequent Irish-language originals. Finally, while Cork remains the primary focus, other Irish counties must also occasionally be explored, sometimes with the assistance of articles published in the present county history series.[18] Our region is no more set apart from other areas of the country than is Ireland as a whole from its Atlantic neighbours.

Foreign affairs

The epithet 'hidden' in the title of Corkery's work suggests an isolated and introspective Irish-speaking community. A sense of regression is reinforced when the volume describes Gaelic strongholds as lying 'far away beyond all the fat lands, beyond the mountain ranges that hemmed them in'.[19] The literature of the period shows matters in a different light. Contemporaries take a keen interest in events happening outside Ireland during the eventful one hundred and forty years in question here.[20] The eighteenth and early nineteenth centuries witnessed a series of confrontations which reshaped the balance of power in Europe and further afield.[21] Records from the Cork area are particularly valuable for certain of the more consequential moments. Two major phases of overseas activity at the time are analysed in what follows to illustrate the nature and scope of the evidence together with Gaelic speakers' attitudes towards the incidents examined. The section concludes with a summary of other potential lines of enquiry within this general topic for which an abundant local testimony is also forthcoming.

The Seven Years War

This was a European, a colonial and a naval struggle between Britain and Prussia on one side and France, Austria, Russia, Sweden and Saxony on the other.[22] It arose out of the Diplomatic Revolution, a reversal of previous international allegiances whereby a coalition of France, Austria, Russia and Sweden aimed at controlling the emerging Prussia, which had conquered Silesia from Austria in the War of the Austrian Succession (1740-48). The colonial and naval dimensions were a continuation of the long Anglo-French struggle for control of the seas and of North America, the West Indies, West Africa and India. Such was the extent of the Seven Years War that it is regarded as the first truly global war. The various conflicts were interdependent, as Britain was in alliance with Prussia and provided her with funding, while Prussian martial activity curtailed the deployment of French military resources elsewhere in the world. England maintained an Army of Observation in western Germany to protect its dependency of Hanover, together with Prussia, from French attack, while the British navy also assaulted the French fleet and the French coastline to reduce pressure on its European allies.

The initial years of the conflict are of most interest in the context of the present paper, as they form the subject-matter of the first Gaelic sources we shall examine. These are poems ascribed to the composer Liam Inglis (1708-78), edited by the indefatigable champion of pre-Famine Cork verse, Fiachra Éilgeach (1871-1957).[23] It is not certain whether Inglis was a native of Limerick or Tipperary, but he nonetheless spent most of his life in Cork, in the east of the county during his youth and subsequently as an Augustinian friar in Cork city. Upwards of thirty of his compositions survive, dealing with personal topics such as laments for friends, devotional verse to the Blessed Virgin, in addition to a large amount of witty and well-informed political commentary.

Inglis describes the outbreak of the Seven Years War in his best-known piece *Cré agus cill go bhfaghaidh gach bráthair*. The scene was set for this poem when, as the deteriorating Anglo-French relations of the mid-1750s in North America were soon thought likely to spill over into Europe, Britain and Prussia signed the convention of Westminster in January 1756. France and Austria responded by creating the defensive alliance known as the First Treaty of Versailles in early May. The war proper began a short few months later. In an apparent pre-emptive strike against his enemies' strengthening federation, Frederick the Great of Prussia invaded Saxony in August, a territory he is likely to have regarded as an Austro-Russian dependency and a probable base of attack against himself, thus precipitating the wider conflict.

The Gaelic text outlines the backdrop to these hostilities in terms which would have been familiar to residents of the Cork region. Inglis likens the engagements to a squabble over the division of a friar's keg of butter coming into the city's butter market. Various countries claim a section of the vessel's contents to match the colour of their national emblems, with Ireland seeking the green strips, Britain the red, France the white and so on.[24] Prussia alone is aggrieved at not having shared in the spoils and attacks its neighbour Austria to claim its due portion:

> Do thriall leastar don bhaile seo i dtáimse
> Go hÁrd an Gheata, 's is tapa do meádhadh é;
> Ní raibh cine 'san chruinne nach táinig
> Ag éileamh a ndathanna a' leastar an bhráthar.
> Na síoga uaine do buadhadh le Clár Luirc
> I dtaobh a harmais machaire is cláirseach,
> Na síoga dearga Sasana ráinig,
> Is rí na Fraíngce na síoga bána ....
> Do ghlac rí Pruise cnumh an lá san
> Ná fuair roinn den im seo an bhráthar
> Nochtann a cholg go hobann 'n-a láimh dheis
> Is cuireann cogadh go hullamh ar Mháire.[25]

The Cork market achieved prominence in the eighteenth century for its innovative grading system whereby butter was segregated into different categories according to quality. The metaphor of subdivision applied to Europe probably reflects this practice. Such is the visual, almost cartoon, aspect of the imagery that the latter is likely to have been inspired by its author's acquaintance with engravings or illustrations. I cite an account of one such item from the contemporary Cork press which speaks of reaction elsewhere in Europe to the start of the war:

> Amongst other whimsical prints, handed about at Amsterdam, there is one representing a French and a Prussian soldier fighting, while a Dutch boor is represented at a distance, sitting on a stool with a slice of bread and butter and ham in his hand, a large jug on one side, and a bottle of gineva on the other, with this motto in Dutch: 'While they fight who shall be our masters, let us make much of ourselves'.

Holland was anxious to remain neutral in the unfolding struggle, as its power had declined significantly in the preceding fifty years, reducing its capacity to confront more resourceful neighbours.[26] The tenor of the Gaelic composition may suggest that its author also views the beginning of hostilities with detachment. By likening Europe to the multicoloured components of a mendicant's butter-barrel, Inglis appears to propose that the continent deserves attention more for its humorous potential than as an object of serious reflection.

As the war progressed, however, a greater degree of partiality enters into the Cork Augustinian's verse, particularly in his reaction to the fortunes of the Anglo-Prussian alliance. We may follow these closely from the local journals, as Inglis himself possibly did.[27] Frederick won a spectacular victory against Austria in the neighbourhood of Prague in May 1757 and subsequently besieged the city. The following poem comparing the Prussian ruler to a wondrous natural occurrence conveys the spirit in which his allies applauded the achievement:

The COMET, for 1757

Sir Isazc foretold, I think, in this year.
A wond'rous Comet would somewhere appear:
Which Astronomers now begin for to doubt,
Because they, as yet, have not spy'd out
    His presence terriffic! there's nought can withstand,

A [sic] dreadful as Thunder in Jupiter's Hand!
Shot from Heaven's great Bow, he darts thro' the Skies
Looks Ruin below, and kills as he flies!
    No longer with Glasses, then, pore in the Sky,
This Comet, as yet, has not mounted too high,
On earthly Commission, at present, he's sent,
And PRUSSIA's the Comet which Sir Isazc meant![28]

This text is an example of the rich legacy of contemporary English and Anglo-Irish verse which includes satire as well as encomium.[29] It is not suggested that the Gaelic poetic heritage discussed here is derivative of the English tradition or that it lacks its own inherent strengths. One nevertheless wonders whether poetry in Irish might not owe much of its relevance to the act of replying in kind to material in the other vernacular.

Liam Inglis soon availed of an opportunity to celebrate a new twist to the campaign in his own particular idiom. William Augustus, duke of Cumberland and son of King George II of England, had set out for Hanover in mid-April 1757 as part of Britain's policy to assist its continental confederates.[30] Shortly afterwards the French advanced eastwards against Germany to counter these developments, in accordance with the terms of the Second Treaty of Versailles agreed with the Austrians on 1 May 1757. English reports seemed dismissive of French military capacity:

The Army of the Duke of Cumberland being joined by the Hessians, makes up 60,000 Men; and as the French Troops have not only the Badness of Provision, but also Sickness to fight with, (the Flux and the Small Pox having got into their Army), it is not doubted but this Campaign will ruin the French Army, by keeping them inactive, and confirm the long experienced Maxim, that Germany is the Grave of the French.[31]

Nonetheless the French consolidated their positions under the command of Louis-César Letellier, Comte d'Estrées, in early May, harrassing the duke of Cumberland's forces in June and finally inflicting defeat on him in the Battle of Hastenbach by the banks of the Weser on 27 July. The muted tone of the following account reveals English sentiment at the loss:

GERMANY. Harbourg ... Marshal Richlieu having advanced with his Army in such Manner that it almost surrounded the Army of the Duke of Cumberland and left it no other Resource but to retire

under the Cannon of Stade, which is a Post not tenable against a
superior Army, a Stop is just now put to all Operations of both
Armies by a Convention, by virtue whereof the whole Country of
Hanover, the Dutchy of Luneburg, the District of Zell, the Dutchy
of Brunswick, and Landgraves of Hesse, are to remain
provisionally in the Possession of the French, who will there fix
their Winter Quarters.[32]

In September Cumberland was obliged to make an embarrasing
peace treaty, the convention of Kloster-Seven, whose conditions are
foreshadowed in the above account. Details of the agreement were
fully reported in the Cork press in early October.[33]

The duke's defeat is related in Liam Inglis's poem *Mo ghearán
cruaidh le huaislibh Fódla*. In this piece the composer complains of the
theft of a pair of shoes, and tries to make out who stole them from
him. One possibility considered is that the malfactor may be none
other than Cumberland, now that his overthrow has deprived William
Augustus of the comforts of carriage and horse, obliging him to wander
about in desperation:

> Adeir cuid eile, agus creidim-se dhóibh-sean
> Nach é Pruise do rinn na gnótha
> Acht mac ár dtriaith-na Uilliam mac Sheóirse
> Atá fá chiach i ndiaidh Hanóbhar!
> Atá sé i dteannta ag Frangcaigh chródha
> In amhghar, in antart, i bpóna;
> Ní tualaing é ar ghluaiseacht i gcóiste
> Ná ar luath-each fá mhuar-phlaic a thóna.
> Do rug Huzzar do tháine ar neón dubh
> I ndáil an diúic mo chúpla bróg leis.[34]

Inglis speculates about the type of punishment his assailant deserves;
his suggestion is sufficiently vivid to allow one infer he may have
witnessed executions in Cork. The Englishman is to do 'the rope dance'
(Ringce ar gad), be hanged until his tongue sticks out, drawn, quartered
and his head set on spikes to feed flies. Rather than yield to his
imagination, however, the Augustinian concludes he will actually forgive
his adversary.[35] The poem's irony and sardonic satisfaction at the duke's
expense must have seemed adequate recompense for the earlier success
and ensuing triumphalism of the Anglo-Prussian alliance.

The close of 1757 appears to have caused dismay in the British
camp. Inglis speaks of King George II's despair at the vulnerability of
his European associates:

Is ró-dhian a screadann an sean-duine Seóirse
'Ó, a Dhia, cá rachad? níl agam Hanóbhar
Ná fós Hesse-Cassel, mo bhaile beag cómhghair,
Ná fód mo shean-athrach, táid airgthe dóighthe!'[36]

The despondency hinted at in the Irish text could reflect the suggestion that public immorality and vice are to blame for England's predicament:

The following pieces (from a late London Paper,) being applicable to the present Times, will we hope, be acceptable to our Readers.

To be sure this Age, and particularly this Nation, is come to the *Ne plus ultra* of all Wickedness. Drinking, Gaming, Whoring, and *Politicks,* are openly practised even upon the Sabbath, not only by the Nobles and Gentry of this Land, but even by the commonalty, without any regard to Subordination. Dutchesses are great with Squires; Dukes keep company with Drabs; and, if all that is said to be true, Men with Men, Women with Women, carry on a separate and exclusive Trade. This at least is certain, that, last Sessions at the Old-Baily, a Man was cast, *Horrendum Dictu!* for criminal Conversation with a real, live, Four-footed Mare. O *Tempora! O Mores!*

There is much anxiety to understand the origins of the conflict, as the reprinting in Cork of this work relating the history of recent continental conflict appears to argue:

An *Impartial Representation* of the CONDUCT of the several POWERS of EUROPE, Engaged in the late General WAR: including a particular Account of all the Military and Naval *Operations;* from the Commencement of Hostilities between the Crowns of *Great Britain and Spain,* in 1739, to the Conclusion of the General Treaty of Pacification at *Aix-la-Chapelle,* in 1748. To which are added, LETTERS between Monsieur *Voltaire* and the Author, relative to the Work, and to the Subject of History in General. By RICHARD ROLT.[37]

Readers of the foregoing treatise would undoubtedly have been moved to contemplate the possibility of renewed Jacobitism: assertion of the Stuarts' entitlements and defence of the Catholic cause.[38] Some likely domestic reverberations of the war around this time will be reviewed later in the present chapter.

Even as these matters were happening the campaign was about to take another of its many turns. In England, William Pitt the Elder assumed resolute control of the war effort in late 1757. He emphasised the North American dimension, increasing pressure on the French there in 1758 in a three-fold attack: up the St Lawrence via Louisburg and Quebec, along the Hudson valley via Ticonderoga and Crown Point and the Great Lakes, and into the Ohio valley against Fort Duquesne. From April of the same year onwards Britain began to pay Prussia an annual subsidy. Results soon flowed from the latter strategies with the capture of Louisburg in July and Prussia's defeat of Sweden and Russia at Zorndorf in August in the bloodiest battle of the war. Liam Inglis is silent on the these events but nevertheless continues keenly to observe the broader canvas on which they are taking place. This is evident from a poem *Atá an báire imeartha réidh,* dated in the edition of his works to 1757[39] but which internal and other evidence indicates belongs to the autumn of 1758 when the outcome of British plans for that year was not yet absolutely certain.

The poem's first line rather strikingly suggests the game is up for England and proceeds to give specific examples of recent British and allied discomfitures. It speaks, for instance, of the excellence of the Russians in battle *(Ní tláith na Ruisigh i siosma na bpléar).* There is likely to be an echo here of an incident reported in the Cork papers for early September:

> Vienna, Aug. 5. By an estafette which arrived on the 3rd from the Russian army, we hear, that a body of Russians having been sent against a Prussian regiment under the command of Count de Horn, a native of Sweden, 680 men of that regiment, on seeing this body arrive, threw down their arms, and went over to the Russians, crying out, 'God save Maria Theresa'. The colonel, and the remainder of the regiment saved themselves by flight.[40]

The poet has high hopes in the abilities of the French military leadership to win through:

> Contades glacfaidh an t-amas go cóir
> Is cionnárd a leanfaidh na danair sa tóir;
> Atá Brunswick i riocht puic gan treóir
> Is fágfaimid súd mar atá sé!

His view accords in substance if not in style with opinions expressed elsewhere: 'Hanover, Aug. 18. On the 16th, the Auxiliary Troops of Great Britain, joined the Army of Prince Ferdinand of Brunswick, on the Rhine, and consists of 50,000 Men. They write from Wesel, that the

French Troops under M. de Contades, were incamped near that place; and that they were disposing every thing ready for an Engagement with the allied Troops'.[41] An encounter with the forces of France surfaces in a later concise reference to significant British naval losses off the Brittany coast (*Féach ar an dteannta 'n-a raibh ag St. Cas*). In early September the Cork press noted the departure of the fleet and transports under the command of Lord Howe from Portland-Road for western France. In the second week of the month adverse weather played havoc with the expedition. Ships were obliged to take shelter in Breton bays in full view of a waiting enemy who inflicted significant casualties: 'We have lost between 6 and 700 Men killed, drowned and taken Prisoner .... The Officers missing or killed are about 10 .... The present State of the Troops makes it necessary to return to England'.[42]

The text ends with a sequence of New World defeats which may be briefly reviewed as follows:

> In Americe siar tá an diabhal ortha ar fad,
> Do fágadh 'san ngliadh iad fá chiach is fá cheas,
> Ní tháinig leath a dtrian as, acht iarmhar beag lag
>   An lá san do bhíodar ag Ticonderoga;
>
> Ag Fort Dhu Quesne ní léire bhí a mbail.

The Cork press reports succinctly on the first of these: 'We hear that upon Advice received at Louisbourg of the Repulse of the Troops under the Command of General Abercromby at Ticonderoga'. The fact that the initial English assault on Fort Duquesne was unsuccessful and repelled with heavy losses bears out the accuracy of Inglis's testimony.[43]

Even though the colonists and the English failed to take it in the first attack, Fort Duquesne was subsequently captured and renamed Pittsburg. Over time Britain gradually secured one of its major objectives by overcoming the French in North America. It proved equally difficult for the loose coalition of France, Austria, Russia and others to demolish the Anglo-Prussian alliance in Europe. The treaties following the Seven Years War constituted a major reversal for France. Its involvement in the conflict may be one of the factors leading to revolution there later in the century.[44] The peace agreements represented a substantial advance in world affairs for Britain, as the territories ceded to it in a variety of continents laid the foundation for empire (even if its American colonists would soon assert themselves with confidence based on the experience gained in what they termed the French and Indian Wars).[45] It seems unlikely that Liam Inglis could have imagined in 1758 that consequences so favourable to England

do lucht na Fraince fein, et e fein do dhul do lonúghadh go h-Oilean Elba. As ar an gcoiníolso, maille buain-chíos bliaghan-tabhall do thabhairt do, .i. xxxiu milleóin d'airgidd, tug suas í Luan Casgo na bliaghnaso an xi la d'Abrán.[53]

A full discussion of the information given here would take us beyond the confines of this chapter. However, its basic accuracy may be noted, even if it betrays its compiler's sentiments. Ó Floinn presents Napoleon in a sympathetic light, as the concern for the fate of Paris suggests. The Corkman may be reflecting Bonaparte's own view of matters as presented in the last bulletin before his surrender:

> The Bulletin, composed at Troyes, could not appear in the Paris Journals, the enemy's army having marched upon that city. The Emperor directed forced marches from Troyes on Paris. On the 31st March, his Majesty was at Fontainbleau; there he learnt that the enemy having arrived 24 hours before him, occupied Paris, after having encountered strong resistance, in which he suffer great loss.

> 'The occupation of the capital by the enemy is a misfortune which deeply afflicts the heart of his Majesty, from which however there is nothing to apprehend. The presence of the Emperor and his army at the gates of Paris, will prevent the enemy from committing his usual excesses in so populous a city.'[54]

The Corkman goes on to give his own explanation for the precise circumstances of the collapse:

> Do bhi Breatan, beg nach, a g-creathaibh eaga an tan so, nó gur rainig riu, mar raightear, TAILERAND .i. priomhthimpthire na Fraince do bhreaba ar d-tabhairt xxxi milleon airgid do féin et do lucht a chomhartha, agus uime sin do reic se a Impire agus a mhaighistir. Do bu e an T'ailearindso, an allod, easbog Auton 'san bhFrainc, no gur thréig se a chuing Chrabhuigh ar cheile etc an aimsir athrughadh seanriaghaile na tire sin.[55]

Here also the tense relationship between Napoleon and Charles Maurice de Talleyrand-Périgord (1754-1838), Bonaparte's erstwhile chief diplomat, would require further treatment. Both men were estranged in the years 1809-14, during which time Talleyrand was fully conscious of the inevitability of the Emperor's decline. The basic facts of his taking charge of the provisional government on Napoleon's defeat related in Donnchad's text are repeated elsewhere:

We are no longer without advice from Paris and advices from the most important description. – THE DECLARATION OF THE FRENCH SENATE DETHRONING NAPOLEON BONAPARTE . . . .

The Senate have declared against *BONAPARTE* – They have declared him deprived of the throne in a long decree, signed by about fifty Senators. TALLEYRAND is at the head.[56]

A concluding section of the text indicates why at this time Ó Floinn is likely to be particularly sensitive to bad news. Donnchadh is writing his composition as an appendix to a verse text which describes his misfortune on breaking his leg in January 1814, an experience from which one senses he had not yet fully recovered:

Ag seo dearbhairdídhe dearbhtha et treibhseacht oban seanmhar (má's seanmhar a chríoch) do phobal na Breataine, et míorbhuil as romhó et as marthaine tásg, na mo lurga chle-si do bhloghadh an aimsir duibh duibh-sheaca tre thuisleadh moir-eith. 'san amm chintesi do bhi mise go lan treórach, a bhuidhe re Dia, A g-COCHAL MO MHAIDIDHE CROISE. D. O' F.[57]

Again the information retailed is paralleled in contemporary sources which describe the harsh conditions obtaining in early 1814 at length. Accounts from the Cork region in late January, the time of Ó Floinn's mishap, speak of a 'great fall of Snow, which far exceeds any similar calamity within the memory of the oldest inhabitants of the country'. The 'singular state of the weather' is relayed in similar terms in other southern counties, being likened to the worst climatological disaster of the eighteenth century in the following Waterford report: 'In the second week of January, in a winter which had until then been distinguished for unexampled mildness, a sudden and very severe frost was accompanied with an unusual fall of snow. Indeed, the suddeness of the cold was not more remarkable than its intensity, which has scarcely been witnessed since the memorable winter of 1739'. While injurious to Ó Floinn, its severity would prove extreme to others, with one account citing 'A letter from Charleville, dated January 30', claiming '"The mortality in this neighbourhood is so dreadful, than one man has sold eighty coffins in one week"'.[58] Although the Shandon Street shopkeeeper did not meet a similar fate, it is nonetheless evident that the events of 1814 were for him physically and psychologically distressing.

The winter of 1814 witnessed the death of another Corkman whose demise attracted greater attention than the passing of the Charleville residents just noted:

> Captain O'Sullivan
> Died, on his passage from Bristol, where he had been for the recovery of his health, DANIEL O'SULLIVAN, of Cameatringane, in Beerhaven, County of Cork, Esq. Captain of the Bearhaven Loyal Infantry; and the first Roman Catholic appointed to the Commission of the Peace in the County of Cork, since the reign of Queen Ann.
> O'SULLIVAN it was, who, in 1796, when the French fleet were in Bantry Bay, and not a military man within forty miles of his residence, assembled upwards of 2000 of the Peasantry, principally his own Tenants, and watched the line of coast ... drove off into the interior all the cattle, secreted, or conveyed away, provisions, and took other precautions to harass the enemy, and deprive him of subsistence should he land. [O'Sullivan informs General Dalrymple of arrival of French and lends his 'pleasure-boat' to help capture them]. For these services, O'SULLIVAN, although a Catholic, was presented with the Freedom of the Corporation of Cork ... and Government gave him the command of a Yeomanry Corps. They, however, forgot to pay for his boat, although she was destroyed by the Enemy, and in public service.[59]

The event in question is the celebrated French expedition to Ireland under the direction of General Hoche and with the assistance of Wolfe Tone, the United Irish leader.[60] The accuracy of the 1814 report may be seen when compared with accounts of the news as soon as it became available in 1796:

> By a letter dated four o'clock on Sunday evening at Bantry, it is reported, that a fleet consisting of seventeen sail, eight of them two-decked ships, two frigates, two luggers, and three large ships, at a distance, were all at anchor off Bearhaven island. Those which could be best observed, were *certainly not English built* ....
> Accounts from General Dalrymple, dated Dunmanway, in the evening of the 26th, refer to the above report. It appears the cattle had been removed from the coast, that the people were well affected, and the army in high spirits.[61]

We have no clear confirmation of the fact that O'Sullivan or his followers were Irish-speaking, but, given the survival of substantial pockets of the language in the area down to this century and the tenor of both his obituary and the contemporaneous report cited above, the likelihood of the Gaelic community being involved is considerable. If so, the death-notice and related evidence recall the divergence in attitudes to France spoken of earlier.

Speculation about the precise nature and origins of O'Sullivan's anti-French sentiments may be helped when one considers the data set out in the second part of his obituary:

> This is no exaggeration. – He was descended from one of the branches of the Princly House of O'Sullivan Beare ... and he possessed, in an eminent degree, the Milesian virtues – he was generous, good-humoured, brave and hospitable. In him was exhibited the living model of the ancient Chieftains; and his afflicted Followers now mourn the hand that was never closed, and the heart that was never cold!
>
> O'SULLIVAN was first Cousin of Counsellor DANIEL O'CONNELL, the honest Advocate of his suffering Country.[62]

Mention of the O'Connell connection is interesting on a number of fronts. The O'Connells made their way in the world from their coastal trading activities, particularly in contraband. O'Sullivan may also have engaged in commerce, and been suspicious of any unwelcome disruptive developments to this enterprise. His reasons could have been ideological as well as practical. The O'Connell family was well known for its conservatism and political conformism, while Daniel O'Connell enrolled in the pro-government Lawyers' Auxiliary Corps in the immediate aftermath of the invasion.[63] Might his influence be felt here? Many of the Roman Catholic establishment were hostile to the invasion as the pastoral letter of the Catholic bishop of Cork concerning the event reveals:

> DUBLIN, DEC. 30
> DOCTOR FRANCIS MOYLAN,
> To his beloved flock
> *The Roman Catholics of the Diocese of Cork*

> 'At a moment of such general alarm and consternation, it is a duty I owe to you, my beloved flock, to recall to your minds the sacred principle of loyalty, allegiance, and good order, that must direct your conduct on such an awful occasion.– Charged as I am, by that blessed Saviour ... [it] is encumbent on me to exhort you to that peacable demeanour, which must ever mark his true and faithful disciples.

'Loyalty to the Sovereign and respect for the constituted authorities, have always been the pre-eminent features of the Christian character; and by patriotism and obedience to the established form of Government, have our ancestors been distinguished at times, and under circumstances very different from these in which we have the happiness to live. For, blessed be God, we are no longer strangers in our native land'.[64]

The O'Sullivan obituary has a further value in that its evidence recalls a pattern which has been identified in descriptions of Daniel O'Connell's background, namely its tribal character.[65] One senses that the latter is more often adduced for its colourful qualities than seriously investigated. There is rarely a discussion of the network of relationships and the hierarchy of command which underpin the clan-based structure. It would be important to treat these topics more carefully, because they impact on such factors as the control or limitation of the circulation of ideas within the society in question.[66]

It is accepted that Daniel O'Connell's feel for the essence of his community enabled him instinctively to shape the population into a political force, but that on the other hand he also rejected the Gaelic world. Whether his rejection is a complete abandonment rather than a subliminal or even conscious process of transmutation might be investigated further. The reference to Milesian virtues and the virtual medieval annalistic phraseology of his relative, Daniel O'Sullivan's, obituary are redolent of a redefinition of Irishness then under way, stressing its softer, more refined aspects. The newspapers for 1814 which report many of the incidents discussed here also note concerts of Irish harp music in Cork, meetings of the council of the Royal Irish Academy and the passing of the Thomond Gaelic scholar Theophilus O'Flanagan. The influence of the outside world is discernible in this formative process as well. The press remarks on the most favourable reception accorded to the works of Thomas Moore in England in publications like the *Edinburgh Review*. Warm sentiments were extended towards other Irish as well, it appears: 'Yesterday being the Anniversary of St. Patrick's Day, the Children of St. Gile's School, consisting of 125 boys, and 105 girls, were entertained with a dinner of roast beef and plum pudding, provided by the Committee, who distributed what has been so liberally contributed to the indigent Irish of that neighbourhood'.[67]

In meetings of the Catholic Board in early 1814 O'Connell was at pains to repudiate agrarian revolt and stress the more acceptable qualities of his people. One wonders what effect his awareness of an overseas audience may have had in this process of self-definition. Try as he might to argue his point on various fronts, the commencement of that year was not particularly happy for him. In late February his defence of John Magee, editor of the *Dublin Evening Post,* against the government's charge of publishing seditious sentiments expressed at a Catholic Board meeting in Kilkenny in the previous year was unsuccessful. Tensions within the Catholic organisation were evident when Board member Major Bryan of Kilkenny refused to offer testimony at the trial which might have assisted Magee's case.[68] While the latter defeat is not addressed in Donnchadh Ó Floinn's Gaelic composition, and even though the Corkman and O'Connell were unlikely to have shared the same political outlook, the reversal of this aspect of the Catholic cause in Ireland could nonetheless have contributed to Ó Floinn's palpable dejection.

New horizons

His losses in early 1814 were a temporary setback to Daniel O'Connell's pursuit of his objectives. While his career was to dominate public life in Ireland over the next decades, overshadowing international as well as domestic personalities, nevertheless a concern for the outside world remains noticeable. By the 1820s large-scale emigration had commenced. One of those to leave at this time was the Gaelic poet and scribe Pádraig Phiarais Cundún (1777-1857). His Irish-language letters to friends in east Cork are a mine of information on emigrant experiences in up-state New York.[69] The New World surfaces in other guises also, for instance in the curious transformation of the literature of the noble savage in the works of the east-Cork small farmer and scribe Dáibhí de Barra (1757/8-1851). One of his Gaelic verse compositions relates the dialogue of an Englishman and an American Indian as both are transported to the underworld following their deaths. Despite such habits as scalping and a taste for succulent French flesh, the Indian reveals himself to be a stalwart character who has expired in honourable combat with his enemies. His companion Pushwell on the other hand has led the life of a dissolute rake and dandy, and expired in ignoble circumstances.[70] Transportation of another kind features in a composition from the end of the eighteenth century in which Mícheál Óg Ó Longáin bemoans the banishment to Australia of his nephew Tomás for participation in United Irish activities.[71] From the very beginning of our period the works of Eoghan Ó Caoimh (1656-1726) reveal a fascination with the characteristics and climates of European peoples and countries.[72] This interest persisted while Irish remained spoken in the Cork area as many further unexplored compositions testify. The focus on overseas events may thus fairly be said to represent a sustained and influential component of the intellectual life of the region.

The urban experience

Although urban life has featured in the foregoing discussion, the *The hidden Ireland* may serve once more as the point of departure for this segment of the chapter. Corkery also gave some consideration to the role of Irish in cities and towns in pre-Famine times. He agreed that the language was found in an urban setting. With reference to rural journeymen and traders he noted 'Even in Dublin these traffickers were Irish speakers, if necessary; while in places like Cork and Limerick and Waterford their business was very often carried on in that language, as it is in Galway to this very day'. However he argued that 'For all this widespread use of their language ... the Gaels never made their own of the cities and towns', claiming they were 'little else than exiles among the citizens'.[73] I believe this aspect of Corkery's work requires the same degree of reassessment other features of his study have received. Irish-language evidence matches conclusions which may be reached about the presence of Gaelic in cities and towns from alternative sources.[74]

Cork city: landscape and life

Cork's urban topography appears in a composition of 1823 associated with the aforementioned Dáibhí de Barra from Woodstock, near Carrigtwohill. De Barra complained that a thief had stolen domestic items. It was suspected that the criminal fled to the city where a colleague of Dáibhí's, Risteard Mac Gearailt, claims to have gone to retrieve him. The pursuit began in the north side of town:

> Chuardaíos *Shandon Street* suas
> is ard an Gheata Nua
>   agus Bóthar na Blarnan.
> Chuardaíos fá thuirse,
> bun Ghabhal an Spurra
>   gach cúinne is lána.
> Chuardaíos go ceart
> Léitrim amach
>   is *Youghal Lane* dó.
> Ghabhas an Droichead Nua isteach
> 's an tSráid Mhór ó dheas,
>   gur chuardaíos *Cove Lane* dó.

From its northern precincts Mac Gearailt had advanced through the city centre, crossing the river Lee's second channel into the southern outskirts to continue the chase:

Plate 15.2   South Gate Bridge, c. 1796 by John Fitzgerald (Crawford Municipal Art Gallery/Cork V.E.C.).

Do chuardaíos go ceart
an *South Mall,*
   agus *Shitten Lane* dhó.
D'imíos ag rith
trí *Parliament Bridge*
is chuardaíos *Barrack Hill* go léir dhó.
Do chuardaios na *Flags*
agus an Leathan ó dheas
   agus an *Change* dhó.
Níor fhágas aon tigh,
i Lána na gCócairí 'stigh
   féachaint an raibh sé ar dinnéar ann.

Having explored in vain the Shambles *(an Seamblas Mór)*, the environs of the County Gaol north of the river *(an príosún ó thuaidh)* and the quays *(na céanna),* Mac Gearailt caught up with the fugitive at a public house *(Sign an Black Cock)*. From here he obliged the miscreant to return to east Cork and surrender himself to the victim of his crime.[75] The route of Mac Gearailt's search thus forms a miniature directory of Cork's streets and laneways in whose nomenclature either original Gaelic names or current *ad hoc* calques feature prominently.[76]

The range of urban edifices and structures mentioned in de Barra's composition can be extended when other similar sources are explored. St Fin Barre's Church of Ireland cathedral is mentioned in a Gaelic poem of about 1760. Its anonymous composer thanks one Uilliam Ó Ceallaigh, a city-centre tailor operating in Paul Street, for having made a bag for his pipes (probably uilleann pipes). The sound from the previously silent instrument is now likened to the cathderal's carillon played vigorously *(nó cloig Naoimh Barra 's a sealladh le téada righne)*.[77] Its Roman Catholic counterpart, St Mary's Cathedral in the city's north side, is the subject of verses ascribed to Labhrás Ó Séagha, a poet and schoolteacher from Dungourney near Castlemartyr in east Cork. Originally consecrated in 1808, the church was partially burnt in 1820 in a controversial fire. Contemporary sources claim the incident was accidental while Ó Séagha's piece describes it as deliberate and possibly sectarian. The work vividly portrays the conflagration's terrifying impact on the citizenry:

Bhí na flathasaibh go léir ar baillechrith le héacht
's an chathair seo go léir fá sceimhle,
'na lasaraibh nuair bhladhm an tigh beannaithe le taobh
an easpaig 's a chléir 'na thimpeall.[78]

A further Cork landmark from the same northern quarter is represented in an oral lament for Diarmaid Mac Eoghan na Tuinne Mac Carthaigh, a merchant from Claragh, near Millstreet. mac Carthaigh died at the city's butter market. His mother travelled to Cork for Diarmaid's body and mourned his demise amidst strangers gaping churlishly at her dead son (*gan éinne ag amharc ort / acht búir nú Sasanaig / nú clann ceannuithe!*). The lament refers to the market by its symbol, a cow's head (*sign na bó nár duireadh*).[79] A similar sign still survives on the present-day exchange building.

Construction of the Catholic cathedral underlined the strengthening position of the majority population in Cork's commercial life during the early nineteenth century. The provision in 1832 of a burial-ground chiefly for Catholics confirmed this trend. The opening of St Joseph's Cemetery at Ballyphehane towards the south of the city is celebrated in Is *aoibhinn ren' áireamh, a fhíorbhanaltra an Uain,* a Gaelic poem attributed to Dónall Ó Murchú, a scribe and schoolteacher, one-time resident of Mallow Lane and possibly a native of Grenagh between Cork and Mallow. Before their purchase the grounds had been the Botanic Gardens of the Royal Cork Institution, precursor of Queen's College, Cork. Ó Murchú's piece extols the excellence of the plant life which adorns the new cemetery. It thanks Fr Theobald Mathew and his charitable organisation, the Society of St Joseph, for their efforts in acquiring a site whose flora surpassed all others (*'s is fíor gur rug barr leo ó áitreabh na dtriúcha*). Catholics could now be interred with dignity.[80] Ó Murchú's sensitivity to human misery and squalor is clear from elsewhere. He copied a poem in which an unidentified man describes a distressful time spent in a House of Recovery recuperating from illness:

> Ba thláth do bhíos-sa, sínte ar leabaidh,
> lá agus míosa, gan intinn charaid,
> gan bháb dom dhíonadh ná gaoil im fharraid,
> ach gártha is bíog, sceimhle is peannaid.[81]

The location in question may be the insitution of the same name which functioned in the city from late 1802 onwards, or reflect structures like it elsewhere.[82]

In addition to its built environment other levels of city life also feature in pre-Famine Gaelic documentation. Aspects of Cork history and contemporary politics occur in a manuscript the greater part of which the scribe Séamus Ó Broin compiled in the city during 1736-9 and which would appear to have remained there throughout most of the rest of the eighteenth century.[83] The codex commences with a handwritten list, in English, of the mayors of Cork from 1333 to 1776, comprising a total of twenty-five pages (foliated 1-13 r° in catalogue). The inventory is probably drawn from a similar register printed in Charles Smith's *Antient and present state of the county and city of Cork,* first published in 1750.[84] Additional information regarding eighteenth-century urban affairs is supplied for fourteen years in the Ó Broin compilation, of which the following, for 1739, is a typical instance: 'The River Lee frozen from 29th December to ye 6th of January and walked over by ye People. That year thousands starv'd'. Similar annalistic-type entries relating to 1774 connect Cork with the broader international community:

> & on the 3ᵈ Of April 4 Regᵗ of foot & one of Horse marched from Cork for Cove to embark for Boston to quell the Rebellion of the Bostonians, as twas termed by the Parliamentary [*word erased*] villians [*sic*] because they wanted to free themselves from heavy Taxes Laid on them withouth their consent. by a villanous Parliment [*sic*] of Base [?] Cowards.

Nonetheless concerns closer to home remain paramount, particularly attitudes to the public officials listed. For 1775 one William Butler is described as 'a careless indolent Lucrative magistrate', while a passage of 1776 extols his successor, Hugh Lawton, in far more generous terms as 'a spirited active magistrate, he was the man who collected money for & sent the poor to the House of Industry – a doer of Justice & a lover of mercy'.[85] These data suggest a milieu in which civic affairs are actively observed, whether by the scribe or others in his general circle.[86]

Despite the fact that almost nothing is known of Séamus Ó Broin, circumstantial considerations enable parallels between him and other Gaelic composers in an urban setting to be drawn, on the basis of which a hypothesis about his life and work may be proposed. His manuscript of 1736-9 contains tracts on Irish orthography, grammar and a dictionary.[87] The record is reminiscent of documents associated with scribes based in Dublin around the same time, particularly Tadhg Ó Neachtain.[88] Among the latter's papers are extensive lexicograpical compilations and tracts on the preparations of inks and other writing materials. These items would have been of practical use as Ó Neachtain was a schoolteacher.[89] One wonders whether Ó Broin might not have followed the same profession in Cork. As regards this rapprochement between Ó Neachtain and Ó Broin it is interesting to observe that the latter's surname suggests a Leinster background while Leinster literature also appears among the Ó Broin material.[90]

Tadhg Ó Neachtain himself was not a native of Dublin but moved to the capital from Gaelic-speaking county Meath with his father Seán. The pattern of increasing interaction bewteen rural and urban Ireland reflected in this internal migration is well established for the seventeen hundreds.[91] Schoolteachers may have played a role in facilitating the transfer of country dwellers to cities and towns and their settlement in these new surroundings. Could the necessity to come to terms with linguistic barriers be at issue in the following mid-eighteenth-century advertisement for a teacher's services?

> By the Gentleman who keeps his Latin School on Farren's Quay Corke; the most corrupt Accent, hesitation, Stammering, or convuls'd stuttering, with every other impediment and deformity in the speech, are reclaimed and unquestionably removed and cured. English will be taught under his immediate Inspection.[92]

The air of anonymity and reticence in the item (no instructor's name is given, for instance) is noteworthy, hinting at the private Gaelic world as much as its more public English-speaking counterpart. While we may not now be in a position to determine the identity of the teacher in question, Irish-language scholars and educators bridging the rural-urban, Gaelic-English divide are known in Cork from the time. One thinks of the scribe Peadar Ó Féichín (Peter Fane), based in the Barrack Street-St Fin Barre's Cathedral area in the late 1760s and a one-time schoolmaster in the Blarney-Whitechurch district.[93] His background and experience and conceivably those of Séamus Ó Broin must have rendered them ideal mediators in assimilating the urban experience.

Whether settled in or near the city or visiting it for other purposes, it appears from the extant information that Gaelic speakers continued to employ Irish in undertakings which had a significant urban dimension. Politics is one such domain. The Ó Broin manuscript shows a lively interest in this subject for mid-eighteenth-century Cork. The topic increased in importance and relevance for the community at large with the turn-of-the-century enfranchisement of substantial numbers of Catholic voters. Electioneering was a regular facet of early nineteenth-century Ireland, comprising the formation of embryonic political parties, campaigning, canvassing, polling and vote-counting. Cities and towns played a major part in the these proceedings as the effective headquarters of party factions, the centres of publicity and the locations in which elections were held and decided.[94]

There is a rich store of evidence in Irish from the Cork region for various elements of the foregoing political activity. A number of these items will be considered here to demonstrate the nature of the material.

An early nineteenth-century document ascribed to Mícheal Óg Ó Longáin contains the following election oath in English and a parallel Gaelic version:

> I do Swear that I am the same whose name appears regestered in the Certificate or affidavit now produced & that my qualifications as such regestered Voter still continues [sic] and that I have not before voted at this Ellection and (in case of house holders) that not more than one half years Grand Jury or Municipal Cesses rates or taxes are now due or payable by me in respect of the premises in the Certificate mentioned.
>
> So help God.

> Mise a leitheid so do dhuine, dearbhuidhim gur mise an duine ceadna dá deasdeanan mo ainm, garadan anso deiminse no anso dearbhúgha anois a lathar 7 go seasuidhion an cailúidheacht céadna fos do graibh guth go bfuil se leanúmhnach, 7 nar thugas mo ghuth roibhe ag an ttogha so 7 (a ccás tigheasacha) na bfuil ni sa mho sraith leathbhliadna cochabhairtha ioca ráitúidhe na taxiona anois le heiliomh orm, deabh mo clú mo thighe is mo áit ansa deimhnúgha anso raite, mur is maith leat Dia do shlánúgha tanma.
>
> Póg an leabhar.[95]

A second related text is found in the same source in Irish only. This piece asks the voter to swear that he has not accepted or received bribes, favours or offices which would disqualify him from balloting, and also to confirm that he has not previously voted at the same election:

Leabar na Breibe

> Deárbhuidhimso nár ghlacas, is nár thalamhuidheas fein na aon duine uaim na air mo iontuídhibh na cum mo uasaide na tairbhe na cum usaide na tairbhe áon duine dom lín tíghe na dom gaodhalta cum mo thuigsiona na mo creidiomh, 7 dleaghthach na aindleaghtach aon suim na suimibh airgid, oifig, áit na feidhm gnotha aon airgid oigif na beart oibre toghbhrus an ordúgha cum mo ghuth do thabhairt aig an ttoghaso, 7 nar tugus mo guth roibhe so aig an ttoghad so, mur is maith leat Día shlánudha thanma.
>
> Pog an leabur.[96]

From the first section of the present chapter one may recall that in Mícheál Óg electors would undoubtedly have found a willing instructor. His involvement with Irish politics was well established, dating from his years as a United Irishman. His interest in this subject subsequently encompassed other affiliations. The manuscript containing the oaths presented above also includes a copy of a genealogy of the O'Connell family prepared in 1832 for 'Wm. O'Connell Esquire Rathcormack' in which Ó Longáin draws attention to the 'noble ancestors of our friend Danl. O Connell M.P.'[97]

O'Connell and his political objectives form the background to the final city-related composition considered here. The scenes described in the text convey the living reality of urban politics on the streets of Cork. The poem celebrates an election victory, as a result of which the Repeal cause under O'Connell's stewardship is felt to be about to succeed.[98] The tone of the piece and the identities of persons mentioned suggest the poll in question is that of early 1835. The election took place in the shadow of the ongoing campaign against tithe payments, which had witnesssed twelve fatalities in December 1834 at Gortroe in east Cork between Fermoy and Midleton. (In early 1835 the Cork public also learned of the recent death of Thomas Robert Malthus (1766-1834), that 'constant good Whig' and promoter of demography, much of whose work was based on the study of Irish population trends). Unionist candidates experienced reverses in the final count and in subsequent petitions:

Beagán tuarascála ar an guth agus ar an fuaimeant ar ghluais an t-election i gCorcaigh.

A chomharsana éistíg go neosad mo scéal díbh
mar tá Corcaigh ar tréan-lasadh i gcáilíocht;
Gallaphoic chréasacha dá gcartadh is dá dtraochadh
is go mbeidh a ngradam is a saoltacht ag Seán Buí.

Draw near to me neighbours, a few words I'll relate you
that will banish your pains and your whole grief,
that Cork is a-blazes this week by Milesians
to recover old Erin for Seán Buí.

Tá Chatterton tréithlag is crochta gan aon phreab
agus comhra dhó déanta de chrann truim;
do chnósamar déirc dhó do chlúdaigh a chréachta
is do bhí an tsailm dá léamh air ag Seán Buí.

611

> Poor Chatterton fainted when he was fairly defeated
> and could not get peace in the New Street.
> We hung him and waked him on a broken old table
> and his Creed was translated by Sean Buí.[99]

The dual-language nature of the text is characteristic of an age witnessing the increasing use of English, even though election poems still proliferated in Irish itself for the early nineteenth century.[100]

Cork towns and their hinterlands
Similar testimony to that examined for the city also calls into question Corkery's assertion concerning the tenuous links between Gaelic speakers and Cork's towns and villages. In 1737 the poet Liam Rua Mac Coitir bemoaned the fact that a friend of his, Pilib Doinneard, had fallen sick in Youghal in a piece commencing *Aréir is mé sealad ar mhaoileannaibh glasa*.[101] The theft of a pair of light shoes at a Cork city market in 1774 led to suspicion falling on residents of Clonakilty *(Atáid daoine / i gCloich na Coillte / 'na bhfuil amhras)*.[102] Natives of another west-Cork centre are also accused of misappropriation in a Gaelic text of later date. Dáibhí de Barra was informed that geese had been stolen from one Uilliam Ó Murchu from Killacloyne near Carrigtwohill. He instructed Mícheál Ó hArta to make a particular search of Bandon where despicable vagabonds might be found:

> Buail siar chum Bandan, is ann tá an gasra
> Is measa sa dúiche de chomplacht *Orangemen,*
> Paca gan riail, chuir an diabhal chum mearathaill,
> Do ghoidfeadh an iall, an scian 's a' meanaithe.[103]

Contemporary evidence allows one sketch the contact of Gaelic speakers with specific towns in greater detail, as the example of Kinsale suggests.[104] Its outskirts feature in a poem completed in 1777 and ascribed to one Donnchadh Ó Giollagain. This composer had received a complaint from a gardener named Ó Cinnéide that he had been robbed of his walking-stick. Ó Giollagáin instructs Baitéar Pipeard to pursue the thief and recover the missing item. He is to search the sea-ports in particular, for instance Cork and Dingle. At Kinsale he will require authorisation to be admitted to the heavily-armed fortifications, described thus:

> Ní foláir duit pas
> chun dul isteach
> *go fort* Chinn tSáile.

Plate 15.3   Kinsale Harbour and Charles Fort (Kinsale Regional Museum).

Tá gunnaí móra
is arm Sheoirse,
i bhfórsa ann láidir.[105]

References to Kinsale also occur in a manuscript Eoghan Mac Síthigh wrote there in the years 1786-1805. The document's contents are mainly late versions of early Irish sagas, contemporary poetry and some religious material. On a blank page in the middle of one story the scribe entered the following three notes concerning certain of Kinsale's ecclesiastical traditions. The first recounts the establishment by St Gobbán of a monastery in the town during the eighth century, the second the creation of St Mary's Carmelite foundation in 1334 and finally the thirteenth-century origins of the still extant church of St Multose:

> Ann sa mbaile seo do bhí Mainísdir bráithre, mar adeir Colgán, gurab e Náobh Góbán dísgiobal do Naomh Aolbhe, do bhí an abbo innte, an seachtmadh céad bliadhain do áois Chríost do bhí an fear so ann –

> Do Mháinistir Mhuire
> Do bhídh Máinisdir [do bhraithre *cancelled*] annso do Chairmélités – nó do bhráithre bánádh, do tógbhadh mar chuimhneadh míosa don Mhúire. le Róibeárt Mhuígh Risteárd Bálarín. an. bhliagháin dfaois [*sic*] Chríost – 1334.

> Do Theampoll Mbiltheóg
> Do tógbhadh an teampoll so mar chuimhniúghadh míosa do mheanaoímh ar a dtúgthar Múltósia no Náomh Multós. Mar adéir gurab é an bhlíaghain dfáois [*sic*] Chríost. míle et ii [?] ceathramadh chéad bliadhain da aois do togbhádh é.[106]

Mac Síthigh's concern with these matters may have been more than merely antiquarian. The Carmelites, for instance, remained associated with Kinsale down to the middle of the eighteenth century.[107] In the late 1750s the town's Calced Carmelite prior, Tadhg Ó Conaill, completed the adaptation into Irish of an early seventeenth-century French Catholic devotional work, *La trompette du ciel,* an undertaking examined in its proper religious context later in this chapter.[108] The work expresses unease at the fall in devotional practice among young Catholics and clearly targets itself at a fairly wide audience. The large number of extant copies of the piece from the Cork area suggests it went some way towards reaching a substantial readership.

The survival of a valuable body of municipal records enables one to explore some of the circumstances whereby Irish might have been present in Kinsale. If native Irish surnames, particularly those whose spelling closely reflects actual pronounciation, are taken as an approximate guide, then the Gaelic Irish certainly formed part of Kinsale's population in the late seventeenth century, the immediate background in time to the period under review here. In the 1650s and '60s this section of the community appears to have been monitored relatively closely. During the latter decades a greater than average number of persons with indigenous family names are cited for infringement of town rules. Two such violations in particular may be noted, lodging visitors without the necessary permits and erecting cabins unauthorised and in unapproved locations. Both of these factors point to migration from Kinsale's rural, arguably Gaelic-speaking, hinterland.[109]

Transgressions of this kind decline noticably in the 1680s in the extant documents, perhaps reflecting favourable attitudes to Catholics consequent on the accession of James II. In addition, more persons with native surnames achieve positions of responsibility in civic affairs during the period than in the preceding twenty years, roles for which certain of them reap increasingly generous rewards. Even after the Williamite wars and the establishment of the Hanoverian succession in the early eighteenth century, individuals of indigenous background (again using surnames to indicate this fact) seem to have retained a place in Kinsale town government and in the administration of its satellite hamlets and villages. Their employments are admittedly relatively unpretentious, as bailiffs for example. Modest though their conditions may have been, such a class of officer could nonetheless have made the town seem a less forbidding environment to actual and prospective dwellers. It appears not unlikely that kinship ties existed between minor officials and residents of the surrounding countryside, particularly officials on the fringes of the Kinsale. These functionaries may have used whatever influence lay at their disposal to establish their rural relatives within the town and its precincts.[110]

Over time the Irish language did not survive as a vernacular in any urban area. However the presence of Gaelic culture may be felt in certain centres even as the changeover to English was taking place. The scribe Pádraig Ó Mathúna from Manch near Enniskean copied a version of a debate between Dennis Morty O'Sullivan of Balteenbrack close to Manch and one Michael O'Donovan from Manch itself. The two differed 'on the pronunciation of the word Fault in an alehouse in Dunmanway on Sunday February 16th 1823'. They subsequently swopped mixed prose and verse epistles in which each castigated the other for his shortcomings.[111] Their correspondence matches in form and content many other such exchanges in Munster's Irish literary tradition, whether jovial or serious.[112] The fact that Ó Mathúna records English-language versions of Irish songs and other historical traditions from various areas of mid- and west Cork in the same manuscript argues for the influence of the Gaelic world here as well.[113] Poetry and singing in Irish are frequently encountered in the context of pre-Famine urban taverns.[114] This tradition must be echoed in the Dunmanway instance also. Residents of outlying townlands such as Ahakeera, Behagh, Shanlara were still frequently Gaelic-speaking even in the late nineteenth century. They must have brought their tradition as well as their commerce with them into the settler town.

The development of towns and their infrastructure may have had one final unexpectedly positive outcome for the Gaelic tradition in certain parts of Cork. Ó Conchúir has drawn attention to the paucity of Irish manuscript materials now extant for the county's western baronies from the seventeen hundreds. The picture alters noticably during the fifty years before the Famine as more scribes are recorded for centres like Ballyvourney, Clonakilty, Innishannon, Rosscarbery or their hinterlands, with Enniskean and its environs represented by the afore-mentioned Pádraig Ó Mathúna.[115] One wonders whether road improve-ments which were such a feature of Ireland generally and our region in particular towards the end of the eighteenth century may have played a part here. Enhanced transportation and postal networks linking towns are likely to have facilitated the regular contact Mícheál Óg Ó Longáin maintained with such copyists as Conchubhar Ó hIarluithe near Macroom, Seán Ó Coileáin in Carbery or Finín Ó hAllúráin in the Bandon area, as Ó Longáin sought to borrow their books and manuscripts. They were equally keen to request similar help from him.[116] Had these services not expanded (and the rise in literacy which must have accompanied them not been assisted), the corpus of west-Cork Gaelic writings might have been even more restricted than it now appears when compared with material from the east of the county where an urban culture was historically better established.

The evidence adduced here for Cork city and the county's towns helps in the assessment of scholarship to date on Irish urban life generally. It seems fair to say that the cultural and linguistic dimensions to this topic have been overlooked,[117] although there are recent indica-tions that such matters are receiving greater attention in, the identifi-cation of zones of ethnicity within town settlements, for example.[118] There is a danger that the employment of terms such as ghettoisation to describe concentrations of city-based Irish scholars will lead to the assumption that comparative material disadvantage may be taken as a barometer of intellectual impoverishment.[119] There is no reason to believe such a point of view is any more acceptable for Ireland than elsewhere.[120] I would argue the most valid approach to take is to treat the extant testimony with the application and sensitivity it deserves. Scholarship from other urban areas of the world suggests worthwhile insights into this important aspect of Irish regional and national experience may result from such an undertaking.[121]

Economy and morality

The third part of this chapter glimpses the efforts of Cork's Gaelic-speaking community to make a living in the period under review. Although various forms of agriculture, proto-industry or other kinds of work will therefore figure in the presentation, the technical aspects of these activities are not analysed as such. The overall ambition is to see what can be said about the nature of the society under discussion from a focus on employment or indigence. The famous article whose title is echoed in the heading to this section encourages one to attempt a similar, broadly-based investigation in an Irish context.[122] No innovative solutions are claimed in what follows for the questions raised. The data reviewed may simply be said to complement certain recently-established findings. Nonetheless, I would hope that by assembling evidence otherwise largely dispersed for one county, attention will be drawn to a rich vein of material on which further research into this important topic may draw.

Securing a livelihood

Use of the term manuscripts to describe pre-Famine Gaelic documents may convey the impression that these sources are exclusively literary or embellished in the medieval codicological style from which they ultimately derive. Many do appear well-wrought in design and penmanship. However, not all items could be described as ornate finished products, nor would their makers see them in this light. A number are collections of notes or jottings, some commonplace-books, others transcriptions begun but not completed. Such items are not to be disregarded for their rough-hewn condition, because scribes frequently enter in them revealing records of their circumstances. It can also be difficult for either copyists or later owners to resist annotating the better-executed codices in a similar way. The following sketch turns to these various resources in the quest for enlightenment on their compilers' lives.

The manuscripts show their writers attending to household requirements of a basic kind. Thus in one of his documents the scribe Mícheál Óg Ó Longáin enters the following calculations (denominated in shillings and pence) for the purchase of articles of clothing:[123]

Hat	–	2 - 6		2 - 6	Hat
Cloth	–	6 - 6		8 - 0	Coat
Shoes	–	2 - 6		2 - 1	trousers
		11 - 6		12 - 7	Peter
Paddy's	–	8 - 6 [*cancelled*]		11 - 6	Paddy
				21 - 4	
				30 - 0	
				5 - 11	left

It is not clear whether he acquired the items for or on behalf of the two sons mentioned, who, if the source for the accounts can be dated to approximately 1830, would themselves be in their twenties at that stage. We know the age of family members from a note their brother Seosamh penned in 1828.[124] Information of the latter type is frequently entered in contemporary sources, even if not all such inventories are as extensive as those of the Limerick scribe Nicholas Hayes who put down in tabular form the dates of birth and baptism of his eleven children born between 1815 and 1837, together with the names of the baptizing priest and sponsors, and other information relating to himself, his spouse and earlier generations of the Hayes family.[125]

Further on in the same collection of papers from which the clothing figures are taken Mícheál Óg estimates some likely farming expenses on 11 July 1829. Set against these is the income he expects to obtain from his scribal or possibly his teaching assignments, his other primary forms of support:[126]

Horse etc. —		12 - 0 - 0
To set the tillage		7 - 0 - 0
at the taking of yᵉ ground		6 - 0 - 0
500 copies at 1½ p	=	25 - 10 - 0
500 More at D°.	=	25 - 10 - 0
To pay our debts		6 - 4 - 0
To buy potatoes at		12 - 0 - 0
Christmas next		
Then for the Tillage [*cancelled*]		6 - 0 - 0
No but 6 Sheep		24 - 4 - 0
		25 - 10 - 0
		£1 - 6 - 0

We know from other codices that O Longáin kept a regular check on the use of writing materials, perhaps as a confirmation of his expenditure in this regard.[127]

The foregoing estimates reveal Ó Longáin to be clearly conscious of indebtedness, as were many of his contemporaries. The manuscripts are full of indications of sums of monies advanced on credit. These arrangements may be more than the inconsequential commitments they seem from their occurrence as casual annotations. The entry cited below reveals the apparent implications of failure to honour one agreement:

> County Cork to Will No. 4. You are herby required personally to appear before the said assist(an)t Barrester at Bantry on the 4th. day of February instant to answer the plaintiffs Bill in an action for the sum of 15 pounds tin shilleng and two pence sterling due for the defendant Promessariy note and also by an account stated and settled on demand we – or – either of us promsid to pay William Sullivan of Lishews the sum of tin pounds tin shilling and tin pence stirling value received this fourteenth day of August one thousand Eight hundred and forty three 184[...].[128]

Not all would have been in a position to fulfil their financial obligations or to sustain themselves or their dependents in a meaning-ful way, as the following nineteenth-century text reveals:

> To the Charitable and Humane –
> The petition of M.B. of Capagh in the parish of Myross –
>   Most humbly sheweth
>
> That, Petitioner is a very poor and truly distress'd widow, who has four young and helpless orphans, in a half-naked & famishing condition, destitute of all means of support or friends capable of yielding her the least help, which renders her a most miserable object of compassion, most humbly imploring the charitable con-tribution of all human and benevolent Ladies and Gentlemen for whom she will continually & gratefully Pray –[129]

Different forms of assistance were furnished to others. In a draft letter of reference for a female servant in his employ the scribe Seán Ó Súilleabháin (J. O'Sullivan) from Kanturk states: 'I do Herby Certifie that the Bear[er] Ellen Sullivan has served me these (twelve) Months Past faithfully and Honestly'. After paying her wages, her employer 'released her at her own Request' on 2 July, 1778.[130]

The examples so far investigated (apart from the foregoing) come from the early nineteenth century. There would appear to be a certain continuity if not necessarily an exact equivalence between them and evidence from one hundred years previously. We may observe the early eighteenth-century situation concerning making one's way in the world from the work of the Carrignavar-based poet and scribe Seán Ó Murchú na Ráithíneach (1700-62).[131] Ó Murchú completed a verse anthology between the years 1721 to 1744.[132] Into this collection he entered at regular intervals poetry in the Irish language on everyday events occurring around him, the death of his brother, contact with fellow poets and scholars such as that revealed by a request to his parish priest for the loan of a book or manuscript, defence of his pipe-playing and other topics.[133] The document is therefore effectively a diary of its compiler's life and times over the period covered. Its nature as a journal may be seen from its editor's observations on the dimensions of the codex, which he describes as pocket-sized, and the manner in which the texts appear, replete with corrections, sometimes written transverse, and showing signs of wear and tear.[134]

Concern for his own livelihood may be seen in *Greann dá gceapainn a seanchus dámh go gnaoi,* the humorous poem Seán na Ráithíneach composed against a colleague who suggested he would beguile him from his main activity of farming to devote more time to the composition of verse.[135] Matters became more serious shortly afterwards when the poet's wife was struck by smallpox. He presented a poem in the form of a petition *(peitision)* to St Gobnait to rescue his spouse from her distress, and a thanksgiving piece when he himself recovered from the same affliction later on.[136] An arguably more common use of this concept occurs in a verse petition *(petisiun)* made on behalf of a neighbour to a landlord, seeking the return of cattle seized in lieu of rent due on an applotment.[137] The establishment of a just rate for tithes is celebrated in a further text.[138] Ó Murchú composed a verse letter of reference *(Commendasion)* for one Stiabhna Ó Coileáin as he departed for the Roche country around Fermoy.[139] Seán na Ráithíneach may have been motivated to compose in this vein because he himself apparently acted as a bailiff in a local court.[140]

Social tensions

Contact with officialdom is echoed in other aspects of contemporary Gaelic literature where legal documentation surfaces in the genre known as *barántas,* emulating the warrant of Anglo-French tradition. Certain of these compositions are pastiches, in which for example writs are promulgated to restrain geese from attacking dogs, or summons issued for the capture of individuals who have stolen hats, sticks or shoes.[141] Others are in a more serious vein and offer a valuable perspective on the issue currently under discussion. The mid-eighteenth-century composer Éamonn de Bhál from Dungourney employs the form to recommend the apprehension and punishment of one Seáinín Rua Ó hEachiarainn for insulting the residents of Imokilly, but more importantly for raising the price of landholdings, presumably at auctions, to the disadvantage of small farmers and other renters. This complaint recalls the grievances which resulted in various forms of agrarian disorder in the period, both in tenants' reactions against landlords and in rivalries within the renting classes themselves.[142] Similar tensions may be observed in an early nineteenth-century warrant in which one Donnchadh Mac Giolla Phádraig from Ballynamona near Mallow castigates a certain Donnchadh Ua Muirriain for suggesting that he will break double the amount of stones at a lesser price than a companion of the poet's. The dating of the item to 1820 confirms the veracity of the information, as post-Napoleonic times witnessed a serious decline in labourers' wage rates.[143]

Such communal stress may be seen in full measure in a tract on weavers entitled entitled *Parliament na bhfigheadóirí*. This is the work of Dáibhí de Barra, the small farmer from near Carrigtwohill whose writings have previously engaged our attention. The composition requires a fresh edition to take account of its various manuscript recensions,[144] to deal with the complexities of the particular trade involved[145] and to establish a likely date for its first part in particular, so that the evidence presented on the evolution of the artisanal craft in question, for instance, may be estimated in its appropriate context.[146] It is also necessary to determine its composer's precise motivation in compiling the work, whether this arises from anti-combination or anti-unionisation sentiments and, if so, whether these are unique to him or shared by others of his calling. While it may not fulfil any of these requirements, the present discussion investigates the text for the outlook it affords on the interplay of class and economy in a still relatively differentiated Gaelic society.

The model for the weavers' parliament is the celebrated *Pairlement Chloinne Tomáis*,[147] a learned, aristocratic satire of the lower orders' rise to prominence during the upheavals of the seventeenth century. The composition falls into two parts, the first describing the underlings' demonic origins and invidious history in medieval Ireland. They begin to prosper in the reign of James I, and call contentious assemblies of their members for 1632 and 1645 where they attempt to better themselves by adopting noble surnames, refusing to pay rent and other measures. The second book details a similar parliament held in Cromwellian times, the Lord Protector having conferred great benefit on the Irish rabble. They elect to befriend the English, seek the removal in Rome of the malediction which has besmirched their ancestry, but break up in disarray when their innate fractiousness prevents them from adopting an agreed programme of action. Survival of the fittest will henceforth be the governing principle.

Parliament na bhfigheadóirí mirrors its predecessor in both form and content. In its opening section the weavers' leader, Séamus Caomh Ó hEachiarainn, gathers his colleagues from throughout Ireland to a meeting at a pub in the east-Cork town of Carrigtwohill. They complain about the material success of other professions as compared with their own; their neighbours appear to have little difficulty in enhancing their status in life by such means as making clerics of their children. The weavers thereupon convene a parliament at which they agree on steps to improve their circumstances, particularly inflating charges for their services and reducing the quality of goods produced. One Éamon Ó Dubhthaigh cautions against this strategy but Ó hEachiarainn angrily rebuffs his dissenting voice and rallies his followers by proposing to visit them regularly after their departure from east Cork. In the work's second part leadership has passed on to Tomás Fíréast but he too is concerned at his colleagues' plight. A parliament is again called for Carrigtwohill which passes similar measures concerning pricing and workmanship, adding to these better ways to deceive female customers and increase apprenticeship fees. Dissenting voices are again silenced. Despite their efforts, however, the composition concludes with the opinion that the weavers have not succeeded in fooling the public but are themselves worse off than before.[148]

The influence of *Pairlement Chloinne Tomáis* is also seen in the atmosphere and style of the later text. De Barra suggests the inferiority of the weaving fraternity by introducing the proceedings in an inauspicious, gloomy winter setting *(A ndeire an fhómhair sa ttosach an gheimhrigh, an tan do bhí an lonnra ag lagúghadh et an teas ag dul a luíghead).*[149] He shows examples of the weavers' churlishness, the sheepish manner in which their leader sets about his deliberations, pulling his cap down over his ears and his eyebrows,[150] or the tradesmen preparing themselves for their assembly, leaving their looms, bestirring sleeping cats and dogs out of their corners in which they then throw their shoes and aprons for safe-keeping.[151] The outlandish names frequently used to designate the weavers *(Siémon Smólsmáca, Domhnall an Díosgáin, Cormac Speisialta Ó hAlpacháin)* also reflect the seventeenth-century work.[152]

De Barra's powers of observation may be seen in the levels of information furnished on the social setting in which the weavers find themselves. They were particularly distressed at the capacity of other professions to make material progress, a pattern described thus:

Atá an donnus air phodátuídhe et air arbhar le daoíre, ba et

capuill et caoíre ag imtheacht chum ranngáis, feremúríghe ag
eirghe san Rématur et ag déanamh sagart et naómhchléir da
ccloinn, mar an ccéanna gaibhne ag árdúghadh *price* air gach uile
job, et gréasuithe ag mealla argid air ghiotanna et ar bhlúireacha,
et air dhroch-phaistáil et air leighbínídh leathair, gach fear
tabhairne ag méadúghadh a phrofit agus a fhághaltuis.[153]

The remedy they prescribe is to inflate charges for their own output,
set out in a manner which reveals the composer's understanding of the
specific processes involved:

Gan aon bhannlá do shúsa ná do shac dfhíghe gan pinninn, et trí
feóirlinnídhe air bhannlá fleannídhe et pinninn ar bhannla anairt
mhíne, tamídhe an nídh céanna. 5. cúig fheóirlinnídhe air an
mbannlá do anairt gharbh ... rael is leithphinne air shlait lin 7
cotúin, báinfíghe no fíghe carráin .... gan píosa anairte dá luíghead
do ghlaca o aon bheantíghe gan cárt mine coirce chum struisín no
Size, et dá ndeacha sé chum tríchad bannla, no 20 slat, pota mine,
7 mar sin d'réir méid gacha píosa, óir do thuigeadh dóibh dá
mbeadh an samhra gan [*sic*] gur mhaith an bilónus fíghdóra cúpla
béile maith leition san ló. Et do achtaíghdur easnamh do bheith
air gach abhras, et gan fuígheanna na fuíghiollach do chur tar
ais.[154]

In the conclusion to his work, de Barra indicated the weavers were
unsuccessful in implementing these schemes. By 1826, when second
part of the text at least was composed, the profession had in fact
experienced a steep decline, due to the decade's previously-mentioned
economic slump and competition from cheaper, imported goods.[155] The
craft nonetheless retained sufficient vigour for one of its members to
reply to de Barra's charges. In his spirited response to the Corkman's
allegations, the Kerry-born poet and weaver Uiliog Ó Céirín drew
attention to the plight which all the Irish suffer under foreign oppression. He argued for solidarity rather than dissent, particularly in light of
the efforts currently being made in the British parliament on behalf of
the distressed people of Ireland generally.[156] His reply appears to have
attracted a certain level of interest, as it circulated in manuscript in
areas of north Cork even in the decades after the Famine.[157]

The range of evidence
Mention of the post-Famine readership of texts on the weaver
controversy recalls a final aspect of the material discussed in the
present section. This is the existence of a substantial volume of later

data which helps round out the pre-Famine picture. It contains recollections of earlier procedures which can often be paralleled from contemporary eighteenth- and early nineteenth-century sources. We see this in the case of the Cúil Aodha *seanchaí* Amhlaoibh Ó Luínse (1872-1947), from whom folktales and traditional lore were taken during the recording campaign of the Irish Folklore Commission in the 1930s. One section of his published *Seanachas* deals with the subdivision of tracts of land whether for inheritance by a farmer's sons or for leasing. Leasing arrangements include allocations for a fixed term to a dairyman,[158] whom the lexicographer, Fr Patrick Dinneen, cogently describes as 'a small farmer or farm-labourer who rents a number of milch-cows, with grazing, house, facilities for crops, pig-raising, *etc.*, from a big farmer, the letting being called a "dairy"'. Dairymen, who may also be evicted tenants, pay 'an annual rent, with initial instalment', the payment being 'often made in kind – firkins of butter, *etc'*.[159]

Ó Luínse recalls various aspects of the latter practices in detail, commenting on the length of the agreement, the timing of transfers of property and payment and the ownership of usable by-products such as manure:

> 'Talamh a leogaint ar feag aon mhí déag' ('to let land'); 'Do leog sé a chuid talaimh ar feag aon mhí déag' – agus cé gur aon mhí déag an téarma, d'fhágtaí úsáid an tailimh ag an ndéirí chun go mbeadh an bhliain amù. Póinte dlí isea 'aon mhí déag': níl a thuille greama ansan ag an ndéirí. Ní bhfaighig an déirí an bhó ón bhfeirmeoir ach go dtí Lá Coille. Tógfaig an feirmeoir suas an bhó ansan. Beig an t-aoileach ag an ndéirí. Gamhnacha bheig ag an ndéirí ansan má thá sé chun imeacht sa Mhárta.

The informant distinguishes between dairying *(déiríocht)* and a second related practice of 'stewardship' *(reachtaireacht)*, the steward's *(reachtaire)* main function being to tend the farmer's stock, although he might also have other entitlements:

> 'Sé an saghas an rachtaire: fear a bheidh a' túirt aire nú a' féachaint i ndiaig stuic don fheirmeoir, agus bheadh cead aige cúpla bó leis féin a bheith ar a' dtalamh i n-aonacht le stoc an fheirmeora; agus 'na theannta san bheadh inead garraí aige, agus féar tirim dá bha féin, agus cúpla cuíora.[160]

Amhlaoibh recalls that dairying was especially counter-productive in that cattle were much reduced at the end of the year – whether through exploitation or neglect is not indicated. The Cúil Aodha *seanchaí* observes that these practices have completely disappeared from his area. In west-Cork English until relatively recent times the word 'dairyman' might still apparently designate a younger male as opposed to the eldest brother about to succeed to the family farm. During the early decades of the present century the former was assigned such chores as yard-work and the care of animals, while the latter's responsibilities included activities like tillage. The distinction between these functions ensured that when applied as a sobriquet the term 'dairyman' continued to convey connotations of inferiority of either status or capacity, whether justified or not as far as capability at least was concerned.

Ó Luínse speaks of these practices in Irish during the 1930s at a time when English had become the country's predominant vernacular. Somewhat paradoxically, perhaps, his conversation is echoed in English in a largely Irish-speaking pre-Famine context. The following record of a dairying contract survives in an eighteenth-century county Limerick Gaelic manuscript whose miscellaneous contents include mathematics lessons in English as well as Gaelic devotional verse, the Fianaíocht tale *Imtheacht an Ghiolla Deacair* and an Irish-language version of the Deirdre story:

> April 6th 1754 The under persons were by at a settlement of a Dearey sett by Richard Meagher at Bann Nouey to Patrick Whelan of the same place the said Meagher is to give the said Whelan seven in calfe cows over same land they graised on the yeare before and the same seven cows which said Whelan is now possest off to stand and hold in said Whelan's possession for 2 years provided the same be in calfe every year. If not the said Meagher is to give said Whelan a new milch's cow in the place of each such stripper if any there be and the said Whelan is to give said Meagher one hundred of butter out of each of the said cows and eight shillings horn money out of each of the said cows said Meagher is to give said Whelan half an accre of gardin freedom with said cows and 160 speads of new ground and addition to said halfe acre of gardin and said Meagher is to allow said Whelan ¼ of a hundred of butter to which he the said Whelan owes of the last years arrears to said Meagher. Present at this agrea[ment?] John Bourk.[161]

The existence of a range of sources, both written and oral, from alternative regions of the country and points of time, should allow for a more nuanced investigation of this way of life to be undertaken than has hitherto been attempted, at least as far as the Gaelic testimony is concerned.

Ó Luínse discusses other issues of farm and land management besides leasing, such as the problem of straying animals. He employs a specific term, *foghail,* to designate the damage wandering cattle may cause, and the word *scot* to indicate the fine for any resulting loss, particularly to cultivated ground or kitchen gardens. Arbitrators *(moltóirí)* may assess appropriate levels of compensation according to a system outlined at some length:

> Bhíodh molthóirí ann chun nithe don tsaghas so a shocrú: beirt, agus do ghlaofadh an bheirt seo ar an dtríú duine. Ba ghnáthach go mbeadh duine dosna molthóirí ag an mbeirt seo go mbeadh an t-achrann eatarthu: b'fhéidir duine múinteartha dhóibh féin age gach duine acu, agus do ghlaofadh an bheirt mholthóirí ar fhear iasachta éigint mar thríú duine: fear ná beadh aon bhuint aige le héinne don bheirt a bhí sa chlampar.
>
> 'Mola beirte' ba ghnáthaí thúirt air. Ach dá mbeadh a' teip orthu, nú dá mbeadh duine acu ró-bháigiúil, bheadh glaoite ar an dtríú duine. Don ph'róiste, nú b'fhéidir don bhaile, a b'ea iad so; nú do dhineadh sagairt an gnó san.[162]

This use of arbitration in land transactions is part of a more widespread pattern which also has eighteenth- and early nineteenth-century analogues. Thus in May 1758 one Charles McCarthy from Killarney placed a notice in Cork newspapers defending himself from allegations that he had selfishly attempted to enforce 'a Law made against Roman Catholicks holding Lands or Tenaments for a longer duration of Time than 31 Years', an ordinance which he denies invoking rashly against David Barry of Knockreen and another David Barry of Killarney to recover property from them. McCarthy claims that 'being unwilling to have any Difference [with the Barrys] (or any other Neighbours) I offered to leave the Dispute to the Decission [*sic*] of two Gentlemen, which was pitch'd upon'. When he found 'this Passive method to have no Force', he felt obliged in the interests of his family to have recourse to formal legal mechanisms.[163]

Traditional lore in Irish from west Kerry which explicitly claims to sketch life in immediate pre- and post-Famine times assigns a similar role to neutral adjudicators in overseeing the division of townlands among tenants in Ballyferriter parish. Lots are cast for the various applotments. *Moltóirí* draw from a bag of tokens *(cranna)* assigned one to each tenant, with each token in turn standing for an allocation of either good, middling or poor ground. This supervised method of distribution is intended to be unbiased:

Chuirtí an talamh ar crannaibh chun an roinnt a dhéanamh
cothrom, agus chun ná déarfaí go raibh lé le héinne ins an
roinnt.[164]

The procedure of casting for lots evokes a final Cork parallel in a realm
of activity which must have also been central to pre-Famine life but is
now best reflected in more recent sources. The Cape Clear *seanchaí*
Conchúr Ó Síocháin (*ob.* 1941) remembers from his apprenticeship
days on the island how a catch of fish was divided among senior
members of the crew of his boat. Six shares were made of the amount
in question and the allocations decided by randomly selecting tokens
hidden in one fisherman's hands, the tokens corresponding to the
portions. No one could them complain of the outcome (*sa chás ná
féadfadh béal cam ná díreach a bheith ag éinne nuair a bheadh
toradh a chrainn aige*).[165] Again this local practice may be associated
with more extensive provincial and national marine codes. In his
celebrated biography *An tOileánach,* Tomás Ó Criomhthain (*ob.* 1937)
of the Great Blasket records regulations concerning rights to shipwreck,
rules of behaviour on fishing banks (employing the term *dlí,* 'law', in
this regard), together with instructive cases related to him by his
parents' generation of such ordinances being infringed.[166]

Robin Fox has analysed a similar matrix of customary sea and land
law in Tory Island, highlighting complex interlinkages between
maritime, territorial and wider social provisions, such as marriage
arrangements.[167] His research provides evidence for reconstructing the
evolution of modern legal processes from dispute settlement
procedures in stateless societies and from obligations created by
communal sanction.[168] Pre-Famine Cork information of a similar type, its
legacy in twentieth-century traditional memory and its counterparts in
other areas of Ireland enhance the range of documentation available
for investigating the relatively neglected but patently critical system of
public values. It is easy to overlook the fact that regular modes of
conduct existed in the period under review. Contemporaries more
often than not describe the bulk of the population as being relatively
lawless, as did Horatio Townsend in his account of early nineteenth-
century Cork.[169] A more balanced opinion is now beginning to prevail,
which recognises the potential for strife but also focusses on the
existence and observance of basic norms of behaviour.[170] Testimony
from the Gaelic community considered in this section supports the
need for a more rounded interpretation.

Belief

The area of morality touched on in the preceding account matches the concerns of the chapter's fourth and final section. Its many and varied facets ensure that few subjects are as complex as religion. Christianity alone has experienced two millennia of doctrinal[171] and institutional[172] evolution. These developments may be observed in primary sources and a related secondary literature which for diversity and extent are scarcely equalled in western civilisation. Data on religion probably constitute the largest single category of material in Gaelic manuscripts generally and in pre-Famine documentation in particular. The subject is also dominant in written materials from the region and the period under discussion. In light of these considerations the following investigation of the question of belief cannot in any sense claim to be comprehensive, even for an area as restricted as an Irish county during one century and a half. The present part of the chapter will consequently be confined to an overview of the types of religious text found in Cork in these years and to a brief exploration of the works' direct contemporary setting. My comments are frequently a mere coda to the writings of other scholars who with greater learning and deeper appreciation have so signally advanced our understanding of this subject for Cork and Ireland generally in recent times.

The denominational orientation of county Cork's Gaelic religious literature and that of its compilers before the Famine is overwhelmingly Roman Catholic. The material explored below reflects that fact. However, in recognising this one does not thereby deny the existence of a Protestant aspect to religious traditions in Irish.[173] Church of Ireland clergymen, for instance, or members of other reformed faiths, employed the Irish language for devotional or instructional purposes during our time, either on an individual basis or as part of more organised effort. Thus earlier in his career Walter Atkin (1671-1741), treasurer of Cloyne, learned Irish when a vicar in the parish of Midleton and administered the rites of the Protestant faith with some success to the Gaelic-speaking population of his district.[174] The opening decades of the last century witnessed major proselytising efforts throughout the country in which substantial numbers of Gaelic instructors and scholars taught the Bible through the medium of Irish.[175] While it is not proposed to analyse the Gaelic religious materials of the reformed churches, Protestantism, or more accurately in this instance representations of Protestantism, will be treated below. An investigation of the latter topic highlights the significance of interdenominational relations in Cork as well as throughout Ireland in the post-Reformation age.

Texts, copyists and clerics
A random inspection of manuscript contents conveys an impression of the range of the religious compositions which survive for the Cork

area, county and city, on dates both within and after the era at issue here. In the 1860s Fr Muiris Paor (1791-1877), parish priest of Killeagh, wrote a Gaelic adaptation of the Old Testament for the benefit of his Irish-speaking flock, which he delivered in the form of sermons.[176] In Kinsale between the years 1788-90 the copyist Tadhg Ó Fearghaile completed a manuscript containing among other religious items a homily on St Patrick, a litany of the Blessed Virgin, the Acts of Charity, Contrition, Faith and Hope together with the *Salve Regina*.[177] In 1769 Muiris Ó Conchubhair, a shipwright living in Cork city, compiled for one Séamus Ó Dúgáin (whose relationship with the scribe is not stated) a prayer-book incorporating a version of the seventeenth-century Franciscan Bonaventura Ó hEodhusa's catechism, a work originally published in Louvain.[178] Similar catechetical material is found among the manuscripts of the west-Cork scribe Seán Ó Coileáin (*c.* 1754-1817), now best known for his lament on the decay of the monastery of Timoleague *(Oíche dhom go doiligh dubhach)*. Ó Coileáin's sources also include copies of the Lives of Saints Patrick and Margaret, renderings of which abounded in the period.[179]

For the majority of writers (who are in turn mostly laymen) recording religious matter is complementary to other forms of scribal activity. They may transcribe a collection of prayers, for instance, for personal devotional purposes while paying the greater part of their attention to alternative types of literature. By way of contrast, the production of religious traits predominates in the work of others. The documents of the early eighteenth-century scribes Seán Mac Cosgair,[180] who seems to have north-east Cork associations, or Seán Ó Dreada (*ob.* 1840),[181] originally from east Cork but who lived in Cork city in his latter years where he worked as a stonemason, reveal this trend. The fact that the latter received clerical patronage (Mac Cosgair from a local priest, Fr Richard Walsh, Ó Dreada from Dr John Murphy, bishop of Cork in the years 1815-47 and noted patron of Gaelic scribes)[182] may explain the abundance of the religious materials among their manuscripts. Alternatively their concern for this subject could reflect distinctive piety of a kind noted in other aspects of the culture. The Cork-based Gaelic poet Tadhg Gaelach Ó Súilleabháin, for example, is best remembered for the extent and intensity of his devotional verse,[183] while the county Waterford Gaelic enthusiast Pádraig Din (*ob.* 1828) is also renowned for the religious dimension to his *oeuvre*.[184]

The Cork evidence on scribal fondness for a religious output may also be considered in the light of recent reflections on specialisation in such matters, notably the obligation placed on schoolteachers to instruct their pupils in the catechism and other fundamentals. Such a pattern has been observed for the early seventeen hundreds[185] but is

Plate 15.4   Bust of Dr John Murphy, bishop of Cork, 1815-47 (Crawford Municipal
              Art Gallery/Cork V.E.C.).

also valid for the last century. A teacher proposing to set up a school in Midleton in 1825 placed religious matter to the fore in his curriculum:

> To children he will teach Our Father
> The Creed Hail Mary and Confiteor
> The Catechism he will rehearse
> And teach them psalms in prose & verse
> Grace before and after meat
> To shew their thanks for what they eat
> Prayers before and after bed
> With deprofundis for the dead.[186]

Both teachers and others lived in a community which witnessed various levels of religious leadership. Folk tradition retains the memory of the prominent part laymen played in ceremonies like wakes in the absence of the clergy.[187] Specialisation can be identified among oral tradition bearers in Gaelic-speaking areas down to relatively recent times. Much devotional matter was collected in the 1970s from Máire Bhreatnach near Murreagh in the West Kerry Gaeltacht. Her sobriquet, 'Máire na bPaidreacha', indicates the particular branch of the heritage in which she won acclaim.[188] One wonders whether compilers of religious manuscripts might not also have fulfilled such a guiding role in their localities in pre-Famine times. The materials instructors and others compiled in manuscript form deserve greater attention for the precise nature and sources of the religious message conveyed.

Primacy in matters of religion naturally resided with the clergy, and indeed their position in Gaelic Ireland has been the subject of substantial study.[189] Even here, however, the Cork evidence can offer insights into well-established issues. One of these is the representation of the priest as martyr figure. This phenomenon is seen most spectacularly in the case of Father Nicholas Sheehy, executed in 1766 following allegations of seditious conduct.[190] Sheehy appears first to have come to public notice when named in a newspaper advertisement of 1758, criticising him and a number of others, including Dr John O'Brien, bishop of Cloyne, for anti-establishment activities.[191] It is interesting to observe that this notice was issued at a time of particular sensitivity in the course of the Seven Years War, when in the autumn of that year English fortunes were at a particularly low ebb. The likely effect of the same war in Tipperary may be gauged from a journal account of the previous year celebrating the victory of Frederick the Great against the Austrians:

> We hear from Clonmell in the County of Tipperary, that on the 26th of this instant, in regular order, the regiment of dragoons

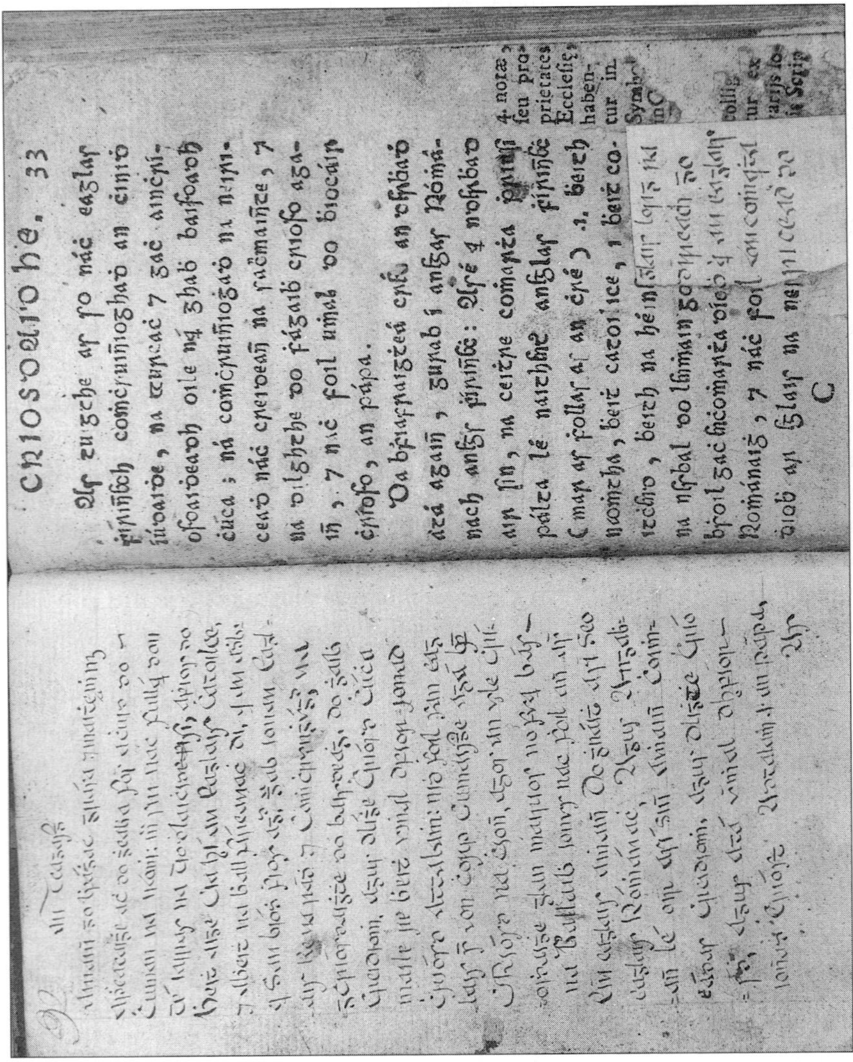

Plate 15.5 Script and print in Mathew Quaine's catechism (U.C.C.).

commanded by Lieutenant Colonel Wynn, in the absence of the Hon. Colonel Philip Honeywood, were drawn up before the Court house, and fired several volleys in honour of his Majesty the King of Prussia's gaining a victory over our faithless former ally, the Queen of Hungary, formerly supported by his present Majesty King George (whom and his allies may heaven support).[192]

Mr Kenneth Nicholls has suggested to me that Sheehy's sentence may have owed much of its harshness to the reaction against extreme anti-Protestantism in contemporary France. The execution of a Protestant minister, François Rochette, which occurred in Toulouse in 1762 in an atmosphere of public hysteria and suspicion of domestic adversaries, largely arose from French reverses in the Seven Years War.[193]

Fr Sheehy quickly became the subject of a considerable *corpus* of poetry in Irish. One of the most popular such texts commences *Ag taisteal liom fá smúit im aonar*, a lament attributed to one Seán Cúndún, a young poet from Kildorrery in north Cork.[194] His work is cast in the accentual verse form which in the seventeenth century became the vehicle for a remarkable series of texts bemoaning a declining Irish civilisation. One of these is by a namesake of our composer, Dáibhí Cúndún. The atmosphere of tragic loss and the feeling of victimisation characteristic of Seán Cúndún's work undoubtedly echo its predecessor's apocalyptic sentiments.[195] The coincidence of disaffection, Sheehy and Gaelic verse is seen in the case of other unpublished compositions, certain of which attain a hauntingly evocative poetic quality, such as *Is gearr do bhí mé im leabaidh im luí nuair a ghlaoigh amuigh*. Here the deceased clergyman is imagined to receive an armed deputation at night, addressing them in the first person concerning his understanding of contemporary English political fortunes and his own ambitions for Ireland.[196]

Clerics also attracted odium as well as praise. This is particularly the case as regards those who conformed and became Protestant ministers. One such was Dermot O'Hart, a native of Ross who was educated in France and served in Cloyne on his return to Ireland. He apparently sought a transfer to the diocese of Cork in the hope of advancing his ecclesiastical career, and subsequently became parish priest of Schull. He resigned from this position in 1774, becoming Protestant vicar of Killeagh in 1775.[197] Around this time a bitter Gaelic satire in the form of a prose and verse warrant was composed against him, castigating his apostasy, his betrayal of clerical orders and the taking of a wife.[198]

Local and universal
Even if it has taken second place to the understanding of church

structures and personnel, the subject-matter of religion has begun to receive attention for our period. Here also the contribution of the vernacular to an understanding of Irish spirituality is beginning to be more fully described.[199] The evidence from Cork and further afield suggests that additional insights may be gained into this question. In particular the testimony highlights the growing consciousness of the wider church in such matters as the regulation of religious practice. One aspect of the latter topic will be considered in what follows as it sets out patterns central to the conduct of everyday life.

Calendars present the framework of religious observance for the year at large, outlining tables of moveable feasts and indicating the annual liturgical high-points. They mark the anniversaries of the apostles, the martyrs, the saints and other holy persons who may be the object of especial veneration. An extensive calendrical tradition existed within the medieval Irish church,[200] and in certain circles the emphasis on indigenous hagiographical figures remained strong. This may be seen in the case of John Carpenter, archbishop of Dublin in the years 1770-86, a noted Gaelic scribe and scholar, many of whose manuscripts have survived.[201] One document, begun on 3 June 1746 and in its compiler's possession until his election to the see of Dublin, merits particular attention in this context. The work mainly consists of a selection of prayers for before and after mass, the Creed, the *Te Deum,* the Rosary and other forms of devotional matter. It is prefaced by a calendar of saints and list of church feasts *(Feilire na Naoimh, agas na Laethe Saoire),* particularly moveable feasts *(Na Saoire Aisdrightheacha).* The saints whose feast-days are recorded in the twelve months of the calendar are almost exclusively Irish. I give as an example the list for May *(Baltinne),* comprising entries for eleven days (no data are supplied for May 2, 4-6, 9, 11-13, 18-21, 23-24, 26-29, 31):

> 1 Philip et Iacob, aps. Macaoimh, ab. Tirdaglas. Ultan, ab. Brecain, C. 3 Conlaoch, ep. Cilledara. Lá na croiche. 8 Bearaidhe, ep. Athacliath. Odran, ep. Gibrian, C. 10 Comhghall, ab. Beannchor. Cathal, ep. 14 Carthach, nó Mochuda, ep. 15 Dioma, oigh, 7 M. Genebrard, M. 16 Breanain, ab. Clúain Ferta Breanain. Fidhmún, C. Maclaisre, ab Beannchor. Cairneach, C. 17 Silan, ep. 22 Conal, ab. Inniscoel. 25 Dúmadh, ab. 30 Maguil, C.[202]

Even if the archbishop may have moved among the Gaelic literati, a robust tradition of the veneration of local saints persisted in Leinster in both the manuscript and oral culture. Holy persons such as Moling are invoked to protect refugees in popular, politically-oriented poetry or are the objects of patterns and other cults at wells and shrines.[203]

Dr Carpenter's list contrasts with similar inventories elsewhere in which foreign rather than Irish saints predominate. This is evident from an early eighteenth-century mansucript (now in a Cork collection and which from the names of its pervious annotators or owners must have had Cork associations, particularly in the late eighteenth century) which prefaces its table of moveable feasts for the years 1747-60 with a twelve-month calendar of saints. The entries for May (with the exception of the thirteenth, the twenty-third and the twenty-fourth days of the month for which no data occur) are thus:

1 Lá Bealtuine .i. S. Philip ⁊ Jacob easbeil, 2 S. Atanasus easbog ⁊ confeasóir, 3 Faghail na croise naomhtha, 4 S. Monica mathair S. Augustin, 5 S. Pius an 5 Pápa confeasoir, 6 Lá féil Eóin roimhe an gheata laidneadh, 7 S. Stanislaus easbog ⁊ mart, 8 Taidhbse Mhichíl Arcaingeal, 9 S. Greagóir na siansanach easbog ⁊ conf, 10 S. Antónín easbog ⁊ confeasóir, 11 S. Nerius ⁊ a chommpanuigh. mart, 12 S. Peadair Regalat conf, 14 S. Bonifas mart, 15. S. Diompna óigh ⁊ mart, 16 S. Brandán. confeasóir, 17 S. Pascal. confeasoir, 18 S. Venantius mart, 19 S. Jobhán. confeasóir, 20 S. Bernardín confeasóir, 21 S. Félios confeasóir, 22 S. Peadair Celestín Pápa ⁊ coinf, 25 S. Augustín manach ⁊ conf, 26 S. Pilip Nerius confeasóir, 27 S. Eón Papa ⁊ conf, 28 S. Venansus mart, 29 S. Mhuire Mhagdalén ó Pairsi ógh, 30 S. Feardinand. confeasóir, 31 S. Petronell óigh.[204]

The paucity of indigenous personalities here is characteristic of the remaining months of the year and of similar enumerations in other documents.

The internationalisation evident in this calendrical source finds resonances in a further interesting range of compositions. These are eighteenth and early nineteenth-century translations into Irish of devotional works of continental provenance, particularly those with a French, Spanish or Italian background. While such tracts were composed at different points in time and in distinct locations (and were in turn adapted into Irish at equally varied dates and places) they nonetheless share a number of revealing characteristics. They are intended for the spiritual enlightenment of the public at large, not for the promotion of advanced ecclesiastical erudition among the few. They are attributed to individuals concerned with improving standards of church teaching generally, particularly clergy who founded religious orders for this purpose or had links with congregations associated with reforming tendencies within Catholicism. The compilers of the original French or Italian or Spanish sources were often persons of humble background who experienced hardship in their own lives or chose austere modes of living as a means of enhancing their religious sensibilities.[205]

Evidence from the Cork area for this type of literature is particularly rich. In Kinsale during the 1750s, as previously noted, a Calced Carmelite prior, Tadhg Ó Conaill (*ob.* 1779), completed under the title *Trompa na bhflaitheas* a Gaelic translation of a French pious manual *La trompette du ciel*. A Provençal clergyman, Antoine Yvan (1576-1635), compiled the original, issued posthumously in 1661. Yvan's peripatetic career included a period as a domestic servant and pedlar of his own art-work. Through contact with Pierre de Bérulle's (1575-1629) reformist Oratorian movement and by establishing his own Notre Dame de Miséricorde oder of nuns Yvan was motivated to compile pious manuals of self-improvement for lay people and clerics alike. Ó Conaill explains he made his translation due to the dearth of suitable devotional works in Irish, especially for the young, and to combat the drop in levels of religious instruction consequent on persecution. A Cork manuscript of the 1760s includes materials based on sermons by the bishop of Agen, Claude Jolie (1610-78). Jolie's career shows the influence of Jean-Jacques Olier (1608-1657) and indirectly that of St Vincent de Paul (*ob.* 1660) in its dedication to the amelioration of clerical training.

Similar trends may be observed in the early nineteenth century, particularly in the interaction between Dr John Murphy, bishop of Cork, and a circle of scribes to whom he offered extensive patronage as indicated earlier. The bishop entrusted Mícheál Óg Ó Longáin with the completion of Gaelic versions of a number of religious compositions or the transcription of works for which Irish-language translations had previously been provided. In 1819 Ó Longáin worked on an adaptation of *Guía de pecadores* (1567) by the Spanish Dominican spiritual writer Louis de Sarria, better known as Louis de Granada (1504-1588). De Granada became a Dominican in 1524 following an impoverished childhood after the death of his father. Extensive public preaching formed his main priestly activity. He also devised methods of prayer for the laity in which he emphasised the cultivation of virtue, contempt for the world, contemplation of God in nature, the practice of mortification and the imitation of the saints. His works were widely translated and his teachings influenced church figures similarly concerned with popular piety such as Charles Borromeo (1538-84), Francis de Sales (1567-1622) and Vincent de Paul.[206]

Already in 1817 Ó Longáin had transcribed for Bishop Murphy a copy of one of the works of Paolo Segneri (1624-94). Segneri, a Jesuit preacher and ascetical writer, is generally regarded as Italy's greatest religious orator after Bernardino of Siena (1380-1444) and Savonarola (1452-98). His preaching of Lenten sermons and conduct of missions were often accompanied by self-flagellation in the pulpit and penitential processions. Crowds of common people and more prominent public figures attended these occasions to hear an oratorical style which has been described as richly imaginative, rapid, fiery and impetuous in its delivery. The Gaelic item Ó Longáin copied in 1817 had earlier been adapted into Irish in 1739 based on an Italian version published in 1721. The translation is ascribed to a Fr John O'Brien. The latter may be the clergyman of the same name who later became the Catholic bishop of Cloyne. O'Brien had an extensive continental education resulting in a command of a number of contemporary European vernaculars and was a lifelong champion of the Irish language and its traditions.[207]

Works of the foregoing type are often read for the information they provide on the state of the Irish language, particularly when they exhibit dialect features. The manuals and the calendars also enable one to draw conclusions concerning forces at work in contemporary Gaelic spritual experience. They help fill out the picture which recent scholarship has been sketching of a renascent Catholicism whose focus is robustly on international religious sensibilities.[208] Indeed the extent and variety of the Gaelic evidence challenges the assumption that the Catholic missionary effort of the eighteenth century lacked drive.[209]

Alternatives

As well as offering a perspective on pre-Famine Catholicism, the international perspective helps one to some understanding of the sources of attitudes towards Protestants among certain contemporary Cork Gaelic speakers. One dominant strand is the interest taken in overseas works relating to various aspects of Protestantism, particularly compositions emanating from England or America. Just as Catholic friars and priests could conform to the Reformation faiths, the process might also work in the reverse direction. Richard Challoner (1691-1781) was one of the better known of such converts. Born a Presbyterian at Lewes, he became a Catholic at age fourteen and was subsequently educated in Douai. Consecracted bishop in 1741, he produced a number of pious works which enjoyed a substantial popularity in England, such as *The garden of the soul*. His devotional tract *Think well on it* was translated into Irish and circulated in the Cork region.[210] Motivations for conversion were explored in the Gaelic adaption of the accounts of the New England minister John Thayer.[211] The reasons for disaffection included unhappiness with the public and private mores of the established church. Similar criticism of establishment ecclesiastics and others politicians in the writings of dissenters, as in Daniel Defoe's (1659-1731) verse commentary *The true-born Englishman* (1701). It is interesting to note that a version of the latter work printed in Dublin in 1730 concludes the manuscript of Séamus Ó Broin discussed earlier in the present chapter. One can only speculate on the precise way the Cork Gaelic scribe might have read such a satirical trait.[212]

English Catholic commentary on contemporary Protestantism flourished on the accession of James II and generated a sustained interest in Ireland. John Gother (*ob.* 1704), who had earlier converted from Presbyterianism and whose works were read in Irish versions in the Cork area, exemplifies this trend.[213] One of the more popular compositions which emanated from this controversial period was *England's reformation (from the time of King Henry VIII to the end of the Oate's plot)*. Its author, Thomas Ward (1652-1708), was born a Calvinist, converted and received a commission in the Pope's guards. Returning to England from the continent in 1685, he also engaged in pro-Catholic polemics from which the foregoing work evolved.[214] *England's reformation* is divided into four parts. Canto I describes the foundations of English Protestantism under Henry VIII. Its opening lines convey the composition's flavour, quoted here from the Dublin edition of 1814:

> When Old King Harry youthful grew,
> As eagles do, or hawks in mew,
> And did in spite of Pope and Fate,
> Behead, rip, and repudiate,
> With axes, bills and midwives knives,
> Those too, too long liv'd things, his wives:
> When he the papal power rejected,
> And from the Church the realm dissected ...
> Then in the noddle of the nation,
> He bred the maggot *Reformation*.[215]

Cantos II-III deal with the furtherance of the Protestant cause under Elizabeth, while the concluding fourth section brings the narrative down to the author's own time.

The work was first issued in Hamburg in 1710 and subsequently in London in 1715, 1716 and 1719. One of the latter editions must have been the source of excerpts appearing in the writings of the Dublin Gaelic scribe Tadhg Ó Neachtain.[216] *England's reformation* continued to be read in Irish-speaking circles. The Carrigtwohill scribe Dáibhí de Barra drew extensively on it to a create an Irish-language poem regarding the proliferation of Protestant ministers in the time of Elizabeth and their settlement in this country. A citation from the original gives an idea of the flavour of the argumentation:

> Those Bishops as by Law Established
> For Villanies and Lies the ablest,
> And for true Cant and seeming Zeal
> The best in all the Common Weal;
> Ordain a Clergy like Themselves,
> And o'er the Flock they place the Wolves.
> A Clergy wed to Vice and Wives,
> And Doctrines impious as their Lives.
> Made up o'th basest sort of men
> The Nation had in being then;
> Bagpipers, Fidlers, Tanners, Tinkers,
> Cardmakers, Coblers, Common Drinkers,
> Carters, and Catchpoles, Chimney-Sweeps,
> Fishmongers, Butchers, Cattle-keepers,
> Bricklayers, Blacksmiths, Weavers, Taylors,
> Gold-finders, Scavengers and Jaylors.

De Barra is likely to have consulted the Dublin edition of Ward's publication which appeared at a time of growing controversy surrounding the activities of proselytising societies. The Carrigtwohill scholar was unremittingly hostile to their preaching and teaching in his area.[217]

Interdominational relations also feature in texts for which there are no demonstrable literary antecedents or models, works which in many ways succinctly capture the extent of the contemporary dichotomies. This may be seen in a piece attributed to one of the few women composers whose creations are examined in the present chapter. The poet's surname suggests a Cork origin for the item, as well as the fact that it is mainly attested in this county. The text deals with the suicide of a Protestant divine who apparently cut his own throat. The poem opens on a compassionate note, recalling the deceased's virtues, especially his neighbourliness and kindness to the poor:

> Máire Ní Mhurchú cct 1802
> ar mhinistir do thug anbhás dó fein.
>
> Ag Crosaire an Mhuilinn do bhí againn ministir
> Is ba ghrámhar soineanta an chomharsa é.
> Do bhí ró-thuisceanach don fhánaí dhona
> Do bhíodh gan costas an bhóthair.
> Do mhná is do leinbh do chíodh i n-uireasa

Is deimhin go bpiocadh sé a phóca,
'S an t-éadach go dtugadh dá chnámha mar fhothain
Don té bhíodh ar uireasa córach.

Partisan considerations soon gain the upper hand. The composer claims the minister's good deeds availed him nothing as he did not belong to the true faith. Had he placed himself under the protection of the Virgin, this clergyman would have been unlikely to end his life as he did:

Ní rinne a charthanacht ná a dhéirc aon tairbhe
Mar ná raibh a theagasc ar fónamh,
an tan nár baisteadh i dteampall Pheadair é
do ghein an Spioraid bheannaithe chumhachtach.
Dul ar tearmann réalta Pharathais
Níor bhaol go ngearrfadh sé a scornach,
Mar is mór é a caradas leis na trí pearsanaibh
Is aoirde i gcathair na glóire.[218]

Conclusion

Máire Ní Mhurchú's poem in its simplicity and yet stark clarity tellingly demonstrates the complexity of pre-Famine Gaelic Cork. I believe this is the type of conclusion to be drawn concerning the society in question from an analysis of the evidence presented for the period reviewed. Many more topics might have been investigated to colour the outline. Contemporary education is in urgent need of treatment if we are to understand the modalities of language change, the impact of literacy both on the promotion of English and curiously the survival and enrichment of Gaelic culture itself. If many Cork scribes had not first learnt to read and write in the other vernacular they would have been unlikely to acquire these competences in Irish proper. The fact that they did so has left a record of the first importance for describing this phase of their civilisation. It is of all eras the least studied in terms of the history of Celtic and Irish scholarship, whose exponents have been invariably attracted by the riches of the early and medieval literature. It is not an uninteresting or insignificant heritage. In the Gaelic writings of the Cork and other copyists we find an important window on a changing world, showing the growth of urbanisation, emerging industrialisation and other phenomena which would over time profoundly alter their way of life and ours. Those who would wish to explore the latter processes for either region or country will find in the documents of the period a resource equal to the challenge.

References

1. B. Ó Cuív, *Irish dialects and Irish-speaking districts* (Dublin, 1951; reprinted 1971), with a special emphasis on Cork; G. FitzGerald, 'Estimates for baronies of minimum level of Irish speaking amongst successive decennial cohorts: 1771-1781 to 1861-1871' in *R.I.A. Proc.*, lxxxiv (1984), C, pp 117-55, with the author's subsequent abbreviated version, 'The decline of the Irish language 1771-1871' in M. Daly and D. Dickson (ed.), *The origins of popular literacy in Ireland: language change and educational development 1700-1920* (Dublin, 1990), pp 59-69; M. Ó Murchú, 'The retreat from Irish: the statistical analysis and other aspects' in J. Dooge (ed.), *Ireland in the contemporary world: essays in honour of Garret FitzGerald* (Dublin, 1986), pp 112-21; R. Hindley, *The death of the Irish language: a qualified obituary* (London, 1990); G. O'Brien, 'The strange death of the Irish language, 1780-1800' in idem (ed.), *Parliament, politics and people: essays in eighteenth-century Irish history* (Dublin, 1990), pp 149-70.

2. M. Nic Craith, 'Staidéar ar mheath na Gaeilge labhartha i gcontae Chorcaí sa naoú haois déag', unpublished Ph.D. thesis, U.C.C. (1990).

3. C. G. Buttimer, 'Postclassical Modern Irish' in M. Ó Murchú (ed.), *School of Celtic Studies fiftieth anniversary report 1940-1990* (Dublin, 1990), pp 119-24.

4. For the fundamental guide to the location of Irish manuscript collections see P. de Brún, *Lámhscríbhinní Gaeilge: treoirliosta* (Baile Átha Cliath, 1988). Our period is also treated by B. Ó Cuív, 'Ireland's manuscript heritage' in *Éire-Ireland*, xix, pt. 1 (1984), pp 87-110, especially pp 104-110.

5. Ó Conchúir, *Scríobh. Chorc.*; see further N. Ní Shéaghdha, *Collectors of Irish manuscripts: motives and methods* (Dublin, 1985) and idem, 'Gairmeacha beatha roinnt scríobhaithe ón 18ú agus ón l9ú céad' in *Celtica*, xxi (1990), pp 567-75.

6. Citations here from the Gill and Macmillan edition (Dublin, 1967). For Corkery's background see P. Maume, 'Daniel Corkery: a reassessment' in *Stud. Hib.*, xxvi (1991-92), pp 147-66.

7. L. M. Cullen, 'The Hidden Ireland: re-assessment of a concept' in *Stud. Hib.*, ix (1969), pp 7-47, now published as a separate monograph incorporating some additional material (Mullingar, 1988); B. Ó Buachalla, 'Ó Corcora agus an Hidden Ireland' in S. Ó Mórdha (ed.), *Scríobh*, iv (1979), pp 109-37; idem, '*Annála Ríoghachta Éireann* agus *Foras Feasa ar Éirinn:* an comhthéacs comhaimseartha' in *Stud. Hib.*, xxii-xxiii (1982-3), pp 59-105.

8. P. de Brún, 'The cataloguing of Irish manuscripts' in *Newsletter of the School of Celtic Studies*, i (1987), pp 33-4.

9. S. Ó Tuama, 'Dónall Ó Corcora: fealsamh cultúrtha, léirmheastóir litríochta' in *Cúirt, tuath agus bruachbhaile* (Baile Átha Cliath, 1990), pp 57-83.

10. R. B. McDowell, *Ireland in the age of imperialism and revolution: 1760-1801* (Oxford, 1979).

11. R. F. Foster, *Modern Ireland: 1600-1972* (London, 1988). The topic is equally underrepresented in the same author's 'Ascendancy and union' in R. F. Foster (ed.), *The Oxford illustrated history of Ireland* (Oxford, 1989), pp 161-211.

12. T. Dunne, 'New histories: beyond "revisionism"' in *The Irish review*, xii (Spring/Summer 1992), pp 1-12.

13. C. Ó Gráda, '"Making history" in Ireland in the 1940s and 1950s: the saga of *The great famine*' in *The Irish review*, xii (Spring/Summer 1992), pp 87-107.

14. Foster, *Modern Ireland*, p. 3.

15. R. M. Keesing, 'Exotic readings of cultural texts' in *Current anthropology*, xxx, no. 4 (Aug.-Oct. 1989), pp 459-69, followed by colleagues' comments and author's reply on pp 469-79.

16. For other treatments of the period see R. A. Breatnach, 'The end of a tradition' in *Stud. Hib.*, i (1961), pp 128-50, B. Ó Cuív, 'Irish language and literature, 1691-1845' in *New hist. Ire.*, iv, pp 375-423, S. Connolly, 'Popular culture in pre-Famine Ireland' in C. J. Byrne and M. Harry (ed.), *Talamh an Éisc: Canadian and Irish essays* (Halifax, Novia Scotia, 1986), pp 1228 (for which reference I thank Professor Seán Ó Coileáin). See also the article cited below, note 119.

17. C. G. Buttimer, 'Manuscript and book in pre-Famine Gaelic Ireland' in *Newsletter of the School of Celtic Studies,* v (March, 1992), p. 23. Other dimensions to contemporary Gaelic literature are discussed by P. Breatnach, 'Oral and written transmission of poetry in the eighteenth century' in *Eighteenth-century Ireland,* ii (1987), pp 57-65.

18. B. Ó Buachalla, *I mBéal Feirste cois cuain* (Baile Átha Cliath, 1968), B. Ó Madagáin, *An Ghaeilge i Luimneach 1700-1900* (Baile Átha Cliath, 1974), E. Ó Néill, *Gleann an Óir* (Baile Átha Cliath, 1988), N. Ní Shéaghdha, 'Irish scholars and scribes in eighteenth-century Dublin' in *Eighteenth-century Ireland,* iv (1989), pp 41-54, together with E. Ó hÓgáin, 'Scríobhaithe lámhscríbhinní Gaeilge i gCill Chainnigh 1700-1870' in *Kilkenny,* pp 405-36, M. Nic Eoin, 'Irish language and literature in county Kilkenny in the nineteenth century' in ibid., pp 464-80 and E. Ó Súilleabháin, 'Scríobhaithe Phort Lairge, 1700-1900' in *Waterford,* pp 265-308.

19. Corkery, *Hidden Ireland*, p. 23.

20. For some discussion of this point see C. G. Buttimer, 'An Irish text on the "War of Jenkins' Ear"' in *Celtica,* xxi (1990), pp 75-99, especially pp 90-91.

21. D. McKay and H. M. Scott, *The rise of the great powers 1648-1815* (London and New York, 1983), offer a concise overview of the period.

22. In addition to McKay and Scott, *Rise,* pp 181-200, the subject is also cogently treated in R. Furneaux, *The Seven Years War* (St Albans, 1973), A. Seaton and R. Ottenfield, *The Austro-Hungarian army of the Seven Years War* (Reading, 1973).

23. R. Ó Foghludha, *Cois na Bríde: Liam Inglis, O.S.A.* (Baile Átha Cliath, 1937). In the absence of a fresh critical edition of the poet's works using all the manuscript sources made available since Ó Foghludha's time, the latter's presentation of texts is taken here at face value. For an assessment of Ó Foghludha (Fiachra Éilgeach) see D. Breatnach and M. Ní Mhurchú, *1882-1982 beathaisnéis a haon* (Baile Átha Cliath, 1986), pp 73-4.

24. N. J. A. Williams, 'Dermot O'Connor's blazons and Irish heraldic terminology' in *Eighteenth-century Ireland,* v (1990), pp 61-88 and idem, 'Irish heraldry: facts and fallacies' in [W. Nolan (ed.)], *The heritage business,* Centre for Local and Heritage Studies, U.C.D. [1992], pp 119-29.

25. Ó Foghludha, *Liam Inglis,* pp 26-28, citation from p. 27, lines 9-15, 25-28, trans. 'A vessel came into this town where I am to the North Gate, and quickly was it measured; not a race on earth but came to seek its colours from the friar's vessel. Ireland won the green strips by virtue of its heraldic arms, a field and a harp, the red strips went to England and to the king of France the white .... The king of Prussia took offence that day at not getting a section of this friar's butter. He bares his sword quickly in his right hand and readily makes war on Maria' .

26. *Corke Journal,* 30 May 1757; McKay and Scott, *Rise,* pp 184, 190, examine Dutch neutrality.

27. For the increasing availibility of the press from the early eighteenth century onwards see R. L. Munter, *A hand-list of Irish newspapers 1685-1750* (London, 1960), idem. *The history of the Irish newspaper 1685-1760* (Cambridge, 1967),

T. F. Sherry, 'The present horrid conspiracy: Dublin press coverage of two political trials in the early 1720s' in *Eighteenth-century Ireland,* vi (1989), pp 143-57, especially p. 143, notes 1 and 2.

28. *Corke Journal,* 2 June 1757.

29. R. Lonsdale, *The new Oxford book of eighteenth-century verse* (Oxford, 1984), P. Fagan, *A Georgian celebration: Irish poets of the eighteenth century* (Dublin, 1989). M. Peters, *Pitt and popularity: the Patriot Minister and London opinion during the Seven Years War* (Oxford, 1980), examines the extent to which various types of public opinion could influence contemporary government policy.

30. The Duke's impending departure is noted in the *Corke Journal,* 11 April 1757. For his and the English presence generally on the continent throughout the conflict see Sir R. Savory's excellent study, *His Brittanic majesty's army in Germany during the Seven Years War* (Oxford, 1966).

31. *Corke Journal,* 2 June 1757.

32. Ibid., 3 Oct. 1757.

33. Ibid.

34. Ó Foghludha, *Liam Inglis,* pp 30-32, citation from p. 31, lines 33-42, trans. 'Others say, and I believe them, that Prussia did not do the business, but the son of our leader William son of George, who is distressed after Hanover! The brave French have cornered him, disadvantaged, dessecated, impounded him; he cannot journey by a coach or swift steed under the soft expanse of his backside. A huzzar who came in the dark nones together with the Duke took away my pair of shoes'.

35. Ibid., pp 31-2, lines 52-63, for the punishment sequence and p. 32, line 64, for the suggestion of forgiveness.

36. Ibid., pp 35-6, lines 1-4 cited from p. 35, trans. 'Too harshly does old George shout "O God, where shall I go? I haven't Hanover, nor yet Hesse-Cassel, my adjoining homestead, nor my ancestors' homeland, they're plundered and burned!"'

37. For both citations see *Cork Evening Post,* 3 Nov. and 21 Nov. 1757 respectively.

38. This tradition in Irish political ideology is examined by B. Ó Buachalla, 'Irish Jacobite poetry' in *The Irish review,* xii (Spring/Summer 1992), pp 40-49.

39. Ó Foghludha, *Liam Inglis,* p. 38, title.

40. Ibid., line 5; compare *Corke Journal,* 4 Sept. 1758.

41. Ó Foghludha, *Liam Inglis,* p. 38, lines 13-16, trans. 'Contades will lead the attack fittingly, proudly will he pursue the barbarians; Brunswick is like a loose buck: let us leave things as they are!'; compare *Corke Journal,* 4 Sept. 1758.

42. Ó Foghludha, *Liam Inglis,* p. 38, line 24; compare *Corke Journal,* 28 Sept. 1758 which lists casualties in detail on its front page, particularly the vessel and status of each officer at or above the rank of major. For the important English maritime dimension to the conflict see S. F. Gradisch, *The manning of the British navy during the Seven Years War* (London, 1980).

43. Ó Foghludha, *Liam Inglis,* pp 38-9, lines 24-29, trans. 'West in America they are completely bedevilled, left distressed and debilitated in the fray, not one-sixth of them escaped but a tiny, enfeebled rump that day at Ticonderoga. No more wholesome was their condition at Fort Du Quesne'; compare *Corke Journal,* 4 Sept. 1758 and Fourneaux, *Seven Years War,* pp 82-85.

44. See J. C. Riley, *The Seven Years War and the Old Regime in France: the economic and financial toll* (Princeton, New Jersey, 1986) .

45. The background is discussed in E. Countryman, *The American revolution* (Harmondsworth, 1985), pp 3-40.

46. B.L., MS Add. 31877, f. 141 b. The document was written by Domhnall Ó Súilleabháin at Ballinleany and Liskennet, county Limerick, in the years 1755-62, see *B.M. cat. Ir. MSS*, ii, pp 214-21, especially p. 220 for our text. I hope to discuss the poem in greater detail elsewhere.

47. Ó Conchúir, *Scríobh. Chorc.*, pp 69-77.

48. Ibid., pp 91-133.

49. For which see M. Elliott, *Partners in revolution: the United Irishmen and France* (New Haven and London, 1982).

50. See C. G. Buttimer, 'A Gaelic reaction to Robert Emmet's rebellion' in *Cork Hist. Soc. Jn.*, xcvii (1992), pp 36-53.

51. C. G. Buttimer, 'A Cork Gaelic text on a Napoleonic campaign' in *Cork Hist. Soc. Jn.*, xcv (1990), pp 107-19, which discusses the Battle of Jena, with specific references to the correspondence on pp 111-12.

52. For a wonderfully succinct account of these events see F. Markham, *Napoleon* (New York, 1963), pp 208-220.

53. Maynooth, MS M 60, p. 15, *Má Nuad clár,* iii, pp 31-5, especially p. 31. The text is an appendix to a poem entitled (in the manuscript) *Do dhaoínigh Dia is me triall am aonar,* mentioned again below at note 57. The passage here may be trans. 'On 30 March of this year 1814 the many armies of Europe, together with the British forces, encamped beside Paris and occupy it on the thirty-first of the same month, as the Emperor Napoleon was in another part of the country at this time. After he returned to the city he made a treaty with them (to save the city from destruction): to surrender the crown of France to the French themselves, and to go to live in Elba. It is on this condition, together with the award to him of a yearly revenue, i.e. thirty-four millions of money, that he surrendered it on Easter Monday of this year, 11 April.

54. *F.J.,* 15 Apr. 1814.

55. Maynooth, MS M 60, p. 15, trans. 'Britain was virtually in the throes of death at that time until, as it is said, they succeeded in bribing TALLEYRAND, i.e. the French prime minister, having given thirty-one millions of money to him and his supporters, and it is thus he sold his Emperor and master. This Talleyrand was formerly the bishop of Autun in France, until he forsook his yoke of piety for a spouse etc. at the time of the change of the old rule in that land'.

56. J. F. Bernard, *Talleyrand: a biography* (London, 1973), J. Orieux, *Talleyrand: the art of survival* (London, 1974). The closing stages of the complex relations between Napoleon and his former minister are discussed in B. Norman, *Napoleon and Talleyrand: the last two weeks* (London, 1977); for press citation see *F.J.,* 12 April 1814.

57. Maynooth, MS M 60, p. 15, trans. 'Here is an accurate confirmation [?] and a swift auspicious change (if its end will be fortunate) for the people of Britain, and a greater and more lastingly famous miracle than the fracturing of my left leg in dark, black-frosted weather, through the fall of a great horse. And at that precise time I was fullly vigorous, thanks be to God. IN THE MANTLE OF MY WALKING STICKS. D. O'F.' For the poem see Buttimer, 'Napoleonic campaign', p. 115, note 38.

58. *C.M.C.,* 19 Jan., 2 Feb. 1814.

59. Ibid., 24 Jan. 1814.

60. P. B. Bradley, *Bantry Bay: Ireland in the days of Napoleon and Wolfe Tone* (London, 1931), pp 15-107, E. H. Stuart Jones, *An invasion that failed: the French expedition to Ireland of 1796* (Oxford, 1950), R. Harrison, *Bantry in olden days*

(Bantry, 1992), pp 8-9. M. Elliott, *Wolfe Tone: prophet of Irish independence* (New Haven and London, 1989).

61. *F.J.,* 29 Dec. 1796.

62. *C.M.C.,* 24 Jan. 1814.

63. For the O'Connell family's orientation in these matters see the chapter entitled 'The eighteenth century background' in M. O'Connell, *Daniel O'Connell: the man and his politics* (Dublin, 1990), pp 41-52. O. MacDonagh, *The hereditary bondsman: Daniel O'Connell 1775-1829* (London, 1988), pp 49-56, discusses his subject's motives in joining the auxiliary corps.

64. *F.J.,* 31 Dec. 1796.

65. G. Murphy, 'The Gaelic background' in M. Tierney (ed.), *Daniel O'Connell: nine centenary essays* (Dublin, 1948), pp 1-24, J. A. Murphy, 'O'Connell and the Gaelic world' in K. B. Nowlan and M. R. O'Connell (ed.), *Daniel O'Connell: portrait of a radical* (Belfast, 1984), pp 32-52, MacDonagh, *Hereditary bondsman,* pp 8-9.

66. Details enabling a richer family and regional history to be written are evident in O'Connell, *Daniel O'Connell,* especially in the chapters on 'Income and expenditure' (pp 13-29), 'O'Connell and his family' (pp 89-99), 'Lawyer and landlord' (pp 100-111). See also the chapters entitled 'Land and landlords' and 'The conditions of the people of Rossmacowen and Beara, 1758-1939' in R. S. Harrison, *Béara and Bantry Bay: history of Rossmacowen* (Rossmacowen, 1990), pp 3-23, 33-42 respectively.

67. For a treatment of O'Connell's dismissal of the Gaelic world see MacDonagh, *Hereditary bondsman,* p. 11. For the newspaper references see *C.M.C.,* 14 Jan., 9 Feb. 1814 (concert), 30 Mar. (R.I.A. meeting), 14 Jan. (O'Flanagan), 23 Mar. (St Patrick's Day).

68. MacDonagh, *Hereditary bondsman,* pp 126-27 for Magee case. For reports of speeches against illegal organisations see *C.M.C.,* 12, 14 Jan. 1814..

69. R. Ó Foghludha (ed.), *Pádraig Phiarais Cúndún* (Baile Átha Cliath, 1932); K. A. Miller, *Emigrants and exiles: Ireland and the Irish exodus to North America* (New York, 1985), pp 203, 216, 236, 270, 274-75, 277-78, 516.

70. I have consulted the copy of the work in R.I.A., MS 24 C 2, pp 273 ff., *R.I.A. cat. Ir. MSS,* pp 786-95, especially p. 792. For de Barra see Ó Conchúir, *Scríobh. Chorc.,* pp 8-13.

71. See the poem commencing *Ag taisteal seal im aonar le sleasaibh réidh' na Laoi* in R.I.A., MS 23 N 14, pp 175 ff, *R.I.A. cat. Ir. MSS,* pp 1325-54, especially p. 1340, where it is stated (erroneously I believe) that following the verse 'the author has written a long note on the place, date and circumstances of its composition'. Ó Longáin's life and work are examined in Ó Conchúir, *Scríobh. Chorc.,* pp 91-133. C. Costello, *Botany Bay: the story of the convicts transported from Ireland to Australia, 1791-1853* (Cork and Dublin, 1987) and R. Hughes, *The fatal shore: a history of the transportation of convicts to Australia, 1787-1868* (London, 1987) deal with the general area covered in the poem.

72. See Torna, 'An tAthair Eoghan Ó Caoimh: a bheatha agus a shaothar' in *Gadelica,* i, pt. i (1912), pp 3-9, especially pp 6-9; Ó Conchúir, *Scríobh. Chorc.,* pp 33-36.

73. Corkery, *The Hidden Ireland,* pp 22-3.

74. FitzGerald, 'Estimates for baronies ... of Irish speaking', pp 137-8, 143-50.

75. P. Ó Fiannachta (ed.), *An barántas 1: réamhrá, téacs, malairtí* (Má Nuad, 1978), text no. 27 (ii), p. 101, lines 169-80, p. 102, lines 181-95, 203.

76. Locations in these stanzas may be verified with reference to such cartographic productions as *A survey of the city and suburbs of Cork by Dan. Murphy architect*

[1789] or *A plan of the city and suburbs of Cork according to the latest improvements by Wm Beauford 1801,* where for instance Flag Lane is item 32. As we know from elsewhere that de Barra read widely in contemporary English literature, he may have been familiar with directories. For the latter see P. J. Cornfield with S. Kelly, '"Giving directions to the town": the early town directories' in *Urban history yearbook* (1984), pp 22-35; G. Shaw, 'Directories as sources in urban history: a review of British and Canadian material' in ibid., pp 36-44.

77. For both text and commentary see C. G. Buttimer, 'A Paul Street poem, *c.* 1760' in *Cork Hist. Soc. Jn.,* xciii (1988), pp 126-37. The citation is from line 26 of poem. Professor Pádraig de Brún points out to me that the Grange mentioned in this article (p. 130; see also note 23) is more likely to be in Limerick than Tipperary.

78. C. G. Buttimer, 'Early nineteenth-century Cork poems in Irish' in *Cork Hist. Soc. Jn.,* xc (1985), 158-85, especially pp 175-77. Lines 29-32 of poem cited here, trans. 'The heavens were all trembling with dread / and all this city terrorised/ when the sacred dwelling exploded in flames beside / the bishop and his clergy around him'. For Ó Séagha see also P. de Brún, 'Bíoblóir á chosaint féin' in *Éigse,* xxiii (1989), pp 80-82.

79. G. Ó Murchadha (ed.), 'Caoineadh Dhiarmad' 'ic Eóghain (a mháthair do chum)' in *Éigse,* i, pt. 1 (1939), pp 22-28, with citations from lines 31-33, trans. 'no one looking at you / except boors or Saxons/or merchants' children', and 153, trans. 'the sign of the unbulled cow', respectively. Alternative versions of the text are published in *Éigse,* i, pt. 2 (1939), pp 90-95, where the symbol for the butter market is rendered *sign na bó nár sniugadh,* with mention also of *Sign na Bó Brice* (p. 90). S. Ó Coileáin, 'The Irish lament: an oral genre' in *Stud. Hib.,* xxiv (1984-88), pp 97-117, discusses the background to compositions of this type, well attested in the Cork region.

80. See Buttimer, 'Early nineteenth-century Cork poems', pp 168-73, for the background to both Ó Murchú and the cemetery; the verse citation is from ibid., p. 179, line 4 of poem.

81. N.L.I., MS G 180, pp 239-40, *N.L.I. cat. Ir. MSS,* v, p. 37. Stanza 6 (MS p. 240) cited here, trans. 'Weak was my condition, / stretched on a bed, / for a day and a month, without a friend's company, / without a sweetheart protecting me or relations beside me, / but cries and fits, dread and torment', reading *dom dhíonadh* for MS *am dhíghinadh.* For a similar Gaelic reaction to the trauma of separation in a Waterford poorhouse see D. Ó Muirithe, A *seat behind the coachman* (Dublin, 1972), p. 120.

82. Pers. comm. from Colmán Uas. Ó Mathúna, Monkstown, county Cork. S. F. Pettit, *This city of Cork 1700-1900* (Cork, 1977), pp 68-81, 124-42 examines illness, impoverishment and relief measures in contemporary Cork.

83. B.L., MS Egerton 158, described in *B.M. cat. Ir. MSS,* ii, pp 221-29. For the scribe, concerning whom few biographical data are extant, see Ó Conchúir, *Scríobh. Chorc.,* p. 32.

84. Smith, *Cork* (1750 ed.), i, 'A list of the Magistrates of the city of *Cork,* from the earliest accounts to the present time' (pp 427-34), with the sub-title 'Protestant Mayors and Sherrifs' occuring from p. 431 onwards, possibly supplemented by data in ibid., ii, Book III, 'Containing the Civil History of the County' (pp 9-230) where the narrative is set out on a yearly basis.

85. B.L., MS Egerton 158, ff 9 v° (1739), 11 v°-12 r° (1774), 12 r° (1775) and 12 v° (1776). For the 1739 entry compare Smith, *Cork* (1750 ed.), ii, pp 229-30.

86. The apperance of the name 'Mary O Borne/O Birne' in the manuscript indicates a wider *cénacle* of readers, see B.L., MS Egerton 158, F. 65 rº.

87. B.L., MS Egerton 158, ff 41, 50 and 79 respectively, see *B.M. cat. Ir. MSS,* ii, pp 223-25.

88. For this Gaelic scholar and his family background see Buttimer, 'Jenkins' Ear', pp 85-6, B. Ó Buachalla, 'Seacaibíteachas Thaidhg Uí Neachtain' in *Stud. Hib.,* xxvi (1991-92), pp 3164.

89. Copies of Ó Neachtain's dictionary are in T.C.D., MSS H.4.20, pp 251 ff., see Abbott and Gwynn, *Cat. Ir. MSS T.C.D.,* pp 192-99, especially p. 198, and H. 1.16, catalolgued in ibid., p. 60. Tracts on ink and colouring materials among his writings occur in N.L.I., MS G 132, pp 4-15, see *N.L.I. cat. Ir. MSS,* pp 56-63, especially p. 57. A sample of Tadhg's other pedagogical matter, including geometric, geographical and literary texts, may be found in King's Inns, Dublin, MS 20, see P. de Brún, A *catalogue of Irish manuscripts in King's Inns Library, Dublin* (Dublin, 1972), pp 59-63.

90. See B.L., MS Egerton 158, f. 141, *B.M. cat. Ir. MSS,* p. 228, for an elegy on the death of Edmond Byrne, Catholic archbishop of Dublin (*ob.* 1723).

91. For a study of the process in a contiguous Munster county see P. J. O'Connor, 'The maturation of town and village life in county Limerick 1700-1900' in *Common ground,* pp 149-72.

92. *Corke Journal,* 6 Jan. 1757.

93. Ó Féichín is treated in Ó Conchúir, *Scríobh. Chorc.,* pp 66-7.

94. P. Jupp, *British and Irish elections 1784-1831* (Newton Abbot, 1973); K. Theodore Hoppen, *Elections, politics, and society in Ireland 1832-1885* (Oxford, 1984).

95. N.L.I., MS G 96, p. 79, *N.L.I. cat. Ir. MSS,* iii, p. 67.

96. N.L.I., MS G 96, p. 81.

97. Ibid., p. 176, cited in *N.L.I. cat. Ir. MSS,* iii, p. 69.

98. The poem of eight stanzas, inverted and reversed, is in MS Ó Tuama 1, pp 154-52; mention of repeal and O'Connell in stanzas 7 and 15. I am indebted to Professor Seán Ó Tuama for allowing me to consult his manuscript and publish the material quoted. For the manuscript's main compiler, Donnchadh Ó Murchú, and his interesting circle of mid-nineteenth-century scribal acquaintances in Cork city see Ó Conchúir, *Scríobh. Chorc.,* p. 167. D. Ó Muirithe, 'O'Connell in Irish folk tradition' in M. R. O'Connell (ed.), *Daniel O'Connell: political pioneer* (Dublin, 1991), pp 72-86, is the latest relevant discussion of Daniel O'Connell's association with the Gaelic-speaking community.

99. Title and first four verses (with Irish text standardised and punctuation supplied) cited here from MS Ó Tuama 1, p. 154. The 'New Street' is probably Great George's Street (now Washington Street), laid out in the 1820s and referred to colloquially by that name (pers. comm., Colmán Ó Mathúna). For the Gortroe incident see E. Garner, *Massacre at Rathcormac: last battle in the tithe war* (Fermoy, 1984). The obituary of Malthus is in *C.M.C.,* 5 Jan. 1835. M. Walker, *Parliamentary election results in Ireland, 1801-1992* (Dublin, 1978), p. 57, gives the outcome of the 1835 poll for Cork city and county.

100. See D. Ó Muirithe, *An t-ambrán macarónach* (Baile Átha Cliath, 1980), for an anthology of this type of composition. C. Ó Coigligh, *Raiftearaí: ambráin agus dánta* (Baile Átha Cliath, 1987), pp 99-102, has election verse related to Clare and Galway.

101. For one of many copies of this text see Maynooth, MS M 6, p. l0, *Má Nuad clár,* pp 49-60, especially p. 51.

102. Ó Fiannachta, *An barántas*, p. 115, lines 133-5.

103. Ibid., p. 142, lines 29-32, trans. 'Go west to Bandon, where there is the worst company of Orangemen in the region, an unruly pack who have deranged the devil, who would steal thong, knife and awl'. The town's settler background is discussed in O'Flanagan, *Bandon*. Centres in different counties become renowned for related features, such as the north-Kerry village of Ballylongford for faction-fighting; see Ó Fiannachta, *An barántas*, p. 62, lines 110-20.

104. For this location see M. Mulcahy, *A short history of Kinsale*, Cork Historical Guides Committee (1966).

105. Ó Fiannachta, *An barántas*, pp 116-19; lines 101-06 of text cited here, trans. 'You require a pass / to go into / the Kinsale fort. / There are great guns / and George's army / strongly in force there'.

106. St Patrick's College, Maynooth, MS M 51; the matter quoted occurs on p. 191, and is likely to be based on information given in Smith, *Cork* (1750 ed.), i, p. 227. Ó Fiannachta, *Má Nuad clár*, ii (1965), pp 99-104, catalogues the work, which would appear to be the scribe's only extant compilation; see Ó Conchúir, *Scríobh. Chorc.*, p. 29.

107. P. O'Dwyer, *The Irish Carmelites (of the ancient observance)* (Dublin, 1988), pp 127, 133, 136-7, 156-9.

108. C. O'Rahilly (ed.), *Trompa na bhflaitheas* (Dublin, 1955).

109. M. Mulcahy (ed.), *Calendar of Kinsale documents,* i (Kinsale, 1988), pp 16, item 20 (9 Oct. 1665), 17, items 9 and 12 (8 Oct. 1666), 20, item 2 (7 Oct. 1667), all grand jury presentments.

110. Mulcahy, *Calendar,* pp 73, item 3 (2 Oct. 1682), 80, item 25 (1 Oct. 1683), 82, item 14 (6 Oct. 1684), all grand jury presentments, Caulfield, *Kinsale,* pp 212 (2 Oct. 1710), 215 (11 Oct. 1714).

111. The texts are in R.I.A., MS 12 M 14, pp 462-63; see *R.I.A. cat. Ir. MSS*, pp 3068-73, especially p. 3071. Ó Conchúir, *Scríobh. Chorc.*, pp 162-63, sketches Ó Mathúna's life and work.

112. See R. Ó Foghludha (ed.), *Éigse na Máighe* (Baile Átha Cliath, 1952; reprint, 1970), pp 128-36, for the well-know dispute between Seán Ó Tuama an Ghrinn, innkeeper at Croom, county Limerick, Aindrias Mac Craith of the same area, and their colleagues concerning allegations that Ó Tuama sold inferior drink.

113. See R.I.A., MS 12 M 14, pp 425-427, *R.I.A. cat. Ir. MSS,* p. 3069.

114. B. Ó Madagáin, 'Limerick's heritage of Irish song' in *North Munster antiquarian journal,* xxviii (1986), pp 77-102, discusses this topic for a neighbouring county. I thank Professor Ó Madagáin for the reference.

115. See Ó Conchúir, *Scríobh. Chorc.*, pp 193-4, 199-201.

116. I am preparing a catalogue of Houghton Library, Harvard University, MS Ir 13 which, like other related codices, contains a substantial volume of correspondence in verse between the scribes mentioned here on the subject of loaning various kinds of documents.

117. This may be concluded on reading M. E. Daly, 'Irish urban history: a survey' in *Urban history yearbook,* xiii (1986), pp 61-69. The virtual ignoring of Ireland generally in such investigations as P. Bairoch and G. Goertz, 'Factors of urbanisation in the nineteenth-century developed countries: a descriptive and econometric analysis' in *Urban studies,* xxiii (1986), pp 285-305, does not help matters.

118. P. O'Flanagan, 'Urban minorities and majorities: Catholics and Protestants in Munster towns *c.* 1659-1850' in *Common ground,* pp 124-48. For other valuable recent work see K. Whelan, 'Town and village in Ireland: a socio-cultural

perspective' in *The Irish review,* v (Autumn, 1988), pp 34-43, and idem, 'Town and village in Ireland 1600-1960' in J. Vervloet (ed.), *Proceedings of the permanent European conference on the history of the rural landscape* (Wageningen, forthcoming). I thank Dr Whelan for allowing me to consult a copy of his paper in advance of publication.

119. M. O Riordan, 'Historical perspectives on the Gaelic poetry of *The Hidden Ireland'* in *The Irish review,* iv (Spring 1988), pp 73-81, especially p. 79.

120. See D. C. I. Okpala, 'Received concepts and theories in African urbanisation studies and urban management strategies: a critique' in *Urban studies,* xxiv (1987), pp 137-50; A. Manyne, 'Representing the slum' in *Urban history yearbook,* xvii (1990), pp 66-84.

121. For two stimulating accounts of multi-cultural urban situations see J. Dawson, 'Urbanization and mental health in a west-African community' in A. Kiev (ed.), *Magic, faith and healing* (New York and London, 1964), pp 305-42, for which reference I thank my friend Diarmuid Ó Giolláin, J. Quéniart, *Culture et société urbaines dans la France de l'ouest au xviiiè siècle* (Paris, 1978).

122. E. P. Thompson, 'The moral economy of the English crowd in the eighteenth century' in *Past and present,* l, (February 1971), pp 76-136.

123. N.L.I., MS G 99, p. 24, *N.L.I. cat. Ir. MSS,* iii, pp 79-86, especially p. 81.

124. See Ó Conchúir, *Scríobh. Chorc.,* p. 295, note 984.

125. N.L.I., MS G 494, pp 2-4, *N.L.I. cat. Ir. MSS,* x, pp 110-15, especially p. 111.

126. N.L.I., MS G 99, p. 38, *N.L.I. cat. Ir. MSS,* iii, p. 38.

127. See N.L.I., MS G 118, p. 16, *N.L.I. cat. Ir. MSS,* iv, p. 10.

128. The item is cited from Houghton Library, Harvard University, MS Ir 7, p. 49, a document which has associations with the Kealkill area of west Cork. I am preparing a catalogue of the manuscript.

129. N.L.I., MS G 95, p. 79, *N.L.I. cat. Ir. MSS,* iii, pp 52-64, especially p. 55.

130. U.C.C. Library, Torna collection, MS T.xii (b), p. 19, de Brún, *Cnuasach Thorna,* i, pp 47-8, especially p. 48. For the scribe see Ó Conchúir, *Scríobh. Chorc.,* p. 182.

131. Ó Conchúir, *Scríobh. Chorc.,* pp 167-72, gives an account of his life and works.

132. N.L.I., MS G 321, described in *N.L.I. cat. Ir. MSS,* vii, pp 62-73, for an edition of which see Torna [T. Ó Donnchadh] (ed.), *Seán na Ráithíneach* (Baile Átha Cliath, 1954).

133. Torna, *Seán na Ráithíneach,* pp 1-3, 1 1-19 and 43-46 respectively.

134. Ibid., pp xxiii, xxviii.

135. Ibid., pp 113-14.

136. Ibid., pp 136-37, 144-45.

137. Ibid., p. 210.

138. Ibid., p. 95.

139. Ibid., p. 160.

140. Ibid., pp xii-xiii.

141. Ó Fiannachta, *An barántas,* pp 58-9, 34-6, 42-6, S9-60 respectively.

142. Ibid., pp 94-5. For similar situations in the lattter half of the eighteenth century and into the early nineteenth in which Cork evidence is frequently to the fore see, *inter alia,* J. S. Donnelly, 'The Rightboy movement, 1785-8' in *Stud. Hib.* xvii-xviii (1977-78), pp 120-202, idem, 'The Whiteboy movement, 1761-5' in *I.H.S.,* xxi (1978), pp 20-54, idem, 'Irish agrarian rebellion: the Whiteboys of 1769-76' in *R.I.A. Proc.* 83 C (1983), pp 293-331, M. J. Bric, 'Priests, parsons and politics: the Rightboy protest in county Cork, 1785-88' in *Past and present,* (Aug. 1983), pp 100-23, J. S. Donnelly, 'Pastorini and Captain Rock: millenarianism and

sectarianism in the Rockite movement of 1821-4' in S. Clarke and J. S. Donnelly, Jnr. (ed.), *Irish peasants: violence and political unrest* (Manchester, 1983), pp 102-39, F. Whooley, 'The Rockite movement in north Cork 1820-25', unpublished M.A. thesis, U.C.C. (1986).

143. Ó Fiannachta, *An barántas*, pp 159-60; for observations on contemporary levels of pay see Donnelly, *Land and people*, pp 22-3.

144. Ó Conchúir, *Scríobh. Chorc.*, p. 251, note 74, gives references to the edition.

145. L. Hooper, *Handloom weaving*, paperback ed. (London and New York, 1979), and the related P. Baines, *Spinning wheels, spinners & spinning*, paperback ed. (London, 1982), introduce this topic.

146. M. Berg, *The age of manufactures: industry, innovation and work in Britain, 1700-1820* (London, 1985), provides relevant observations on the transitional nature of British industrialisation .

147. N. J. A. Williams (ed.), *Pairlement Chloinne Tomáis* (Dublin, 1981).

148. The present analysis is based on the copy of the work in N.L.I., MS G 656, pp 127-167, with part I on pp 127-45 and part II on pp 146-67. For the manuscript see *N.L.I. cat. Ir. MSS*, xii (1990), pp 49-52, especially p. 51.

149. N.L.I., MS G 656, p. 127.

150. Ibid., p. 128: Do shuigh air a bhínnse et do tharraing a chapín go portaibh a dhá mhalíghe agus go pollaibh a dhá chluas.

151. Ibid.: do sguireadur a seólta et chaitheadur a sbóil 's na cúinníghe. Tugadur tarraint fá na ccapínibh 7 do ruagadar as poill et as pórsíghe gadhair, et cait, agus coin-mhadraíghe, le tóirbasa et le fothram a seanabhróg et naparún dá tteilgion an áit nachar bhaoghul dóibh fán ná seachrán an tan dfhíllfidis o chómhluadar agus ó chuideachtannas an árdeasboig.

152. Ibid., p. 135.

153. Ibid., p. 131, trans. 'Potatoes and corn are terribly dear, cattle and horses and sheep going to the devil, farmers rising in the world [?] and making priests and clergy of their children, similarly smiths increasing the price of each job, and shoemakers seizing money for bits and pieces and bad patchwork and strips of leather, each publican expanding his profit and holdings'.

154. Ibid., pp 137-38, trans. 'Not to weave any cubit of a blanket or sack without a penny, and three farthings for a cubit of flannel, and a penny for a cubit of smooth homespun, patterned similarly. Five farthings for a cubit of coarse linen ... six-pence halfpenny for a yard of linen and cotton, plain or till-woven ... not to accept a piece of coarse linen however small from any housewife without a quart of oatmeal for weaver's paste or size, and if it goes to thirty cubits or 20 yards, a pot of meal, and thus according to the size of each piece, because they understood that if the summer was poor a few meals of porridge per day would be good sustenance [?] for a weaver. And they ordained that each yarn should be wanting, and not to return any remainders or remnants'.

155 . Donnelly, *Land and people*, pp 18-19.

156. R.I.A., MS 24 C 19, pp 132 ff., *R.I.A. cat. Ir. MSS*, pp 903-05, especially p. 904.

157. It occurs in a document compiled by Michael Lynch of Ballyhane in the early 1860s. This work forms part of the manuscript collection of Thomas Canon Wall, recently acquired by U.C.C. Library (items 176-87), which awaits precise numbering and cataloguing.

158. S. Ó Cróinín and D. Ó Cróinín (ed.), *Seanachas Amhlaoibh Í Luínse* (Baile Átha Cliath, 1980), pp 9-10.

159. P. Dinneen, *Foclóir Gaedhilge agus Béarla: an Irish-English dictionary* (Dublin, 1927), p. 883, s.vv. *reachtaire* and *reachtaireacht*.

160. Both citations and following summary from Ó Cróinín and Ó Cróinín, *Seanachas*, p. 10.

161. N.L.I., MS G 346, p. 88, cited in *N.L.I. cat. Ir. MSS,* viii, pp 23-29, at p. 27. For the scribe see Ó Madagáin, *An Ghaeilge i Luimneach,* p. 75.

162. Ó Cróinín and Ó Cróinín, *Seanachas,* pp 15-16.

163. *Corke Journal,* 25 May 1758.

164. T. Mac Síthigh, *Paróiste an Fheirtéaraigh: stairsheanchas an cheantair i dtréimhse an Ghorta Mhóir* (Baile Átha Cliath, 1984), pp 20-21, with citation from p. 21.

165. C. Ó Síocháin, *Seanchas Chléire,* eagrán nua (Baile Átha Cliath, 1970), p. 28. Fruitful lines of marine research are evident in M. McCaughan and J. Appelby (ed.), *The Irish sea: aspects of maritime history* (Belfast and Cultra, 1989).

166. T. Ó Criomthain, *An tOileánach* (Baile Átha Cliath, 1973), pp 57-58, 160-61.

167. R. Fox, *The Tory islanders: a people of the Celtic fringe* (Cambridge, 1978).

168. P. Stein, *Legal institutions: the development of dispute settlement* (London, 1984), especially pp 1-24.

169. Townsend, *Cork* (1810 ed.), i, pp 63-99.

170. C. Ó Gráda, *Éire roimh an nGorta: an saol eacnamaíoch* (Baile Átha Cliath, 1985), pp 32-42; S. J. Connolly, 'Violence and order in the eighteenth century' in P. O'Flanagan, P. Ferguson and K. Whelan (ed.), *Rural Ireland 1600-1900: modernisation and change* (Cork, 1987), pp 42-61. For an assessment of the difficulties inherent in measuring criminality, particularly in the early modern historical record, see J. A. Sharpe, *Crime in early modern England 1550-1750* (London and New York, 1984), pp 1-21 .

171. The five volumes published in Chicago and London by J. Pelikan, *The emergence of the Catholic tradition (100-600), The spirit of eastern Christendom (600-1700), The growth of medieval theology (600-1300),* and particularly for our period *Reformation of church and dogma (1300-1700)* and *Christian doctrine and modern culture (since 1700),* are a helpful introduction to this topic.

172 For canon law as a means of comprehending church structures (Roman Catholicism in particular) see J. A. Coriden, T. Green and D. E. Heintschel (ed.), *The code of canon law: a text and commentary* (New York, 1985), with copious references to the relevant scholarly studies, and a companion volume by J. A. Coriden, *An introduction to canon law* (London, 1991).

173. R. Giltrap, *An Ghaeilge in Eaglais na hÉireann* (Baile Átha Cliath, 1990).

174. Brady, *Clerical records,* ii, pp 389-90.

175. For his magnificent series of articles covering various aspects of this topic see P. de Brún, 'Scriptural instruction in Irish: a controversy of 1830-31' in *Folia Gadlica,* pp 134-59; idem, 'The Irish Society's bible teachers, 1818-27' in *Éigse,* xix (1983), pp 281-332, xx (1984), pp 34-92, xxi (1986), pp 72-149, xxii (1987), pp 54-106, xxiv (1990), pp 71-120, xxv (1991), pp 113-49, xxvi. (1992), pp 121-72.

176. B. Ó Madagáin (ed.), *Teagasc ar an Sean-Tiomna* (Baile Átha Cliath, 1974).

177. See N.L.I., MS G 70, *N.L.I. cat. Ir. MSS.,* iii, pp 1-5 and Ó Conchúir, *Scríobh. Chorc.,* p. 66, for the scribe.

178. U.C.C. Library, Torna MS T.lxxiv, pp 120 ff., de Brún, *Cnuasach Thorna,* i, pp 186-88; the scribe is discussed in Ó Conchúir, *Scríobh. Chorc.,* pp 53-4. W. Mahon, *Doctor Kirwan's Irish catechism* (Cambridge, Mass., 1991), especially pp xii-xxxiii, examines contemporary Gaelic catechetical literature and its background.

179. U.C.C. Library, Torna MS T.xliv, pp 204-223, 224-31 respectively, de Brún, *Cnuasach Thorna,* i, pp 117-121, especially p. 121. For Ó Coileáin see Ó Conchúir, *Scríobh. Chorc.,* pp 41-6.

180. Ó Conchúir, *Scríobh. Chorc.*, p. 25.

181. Ibid., pp 61-3.

182. Ibid., pp 222-24.

183. See R. Ó Foghludha (ed.), *Tadhg Gaedhlach* (Baile Átha Cliath, 1929).

184. Ó Súilleabháin 'Scríobhaithe Phort Lairge', pp 273-75.

185. J. L. McCracken, 'The ecclesiastical structure 1714-1760' in *New hist. Ire.,* iv, p. 95.

186. St Colman's College, Fermoy, MS PB 3, p. 169, lines 9-16, Ó Fiannachta, *Mionchnuasaigh,* i, pp 141-46, especially p. 146

187. T. de Bhaldraithe, *Seanchas Thomáis Laighléis,* an dara cló (Baile Átha Cliath, 1981), p. 136, for which reference I thank Gearóid Ó Crualaoich.

188. I am grateful to Pádraig Uas. Tyers for directing my attention to the existence of recordings he made from this informant which are now in the collection of Rannóg na Gaeilge Labhartha, U.C.C.

189. T. Ó Fiaich, 'Irish poetry and the clergy' in *Léachtaí Cholm Cille,* iv (1975), pp 30-56; S. J. Connolly, *Priests and people in pre-Famine Ireland 1780-1845* (Dublin, 1982), passim.

190. T. de Bhial, *Oidheadh an Athar Uí Shíthigh* (Baile Átha Cliath, 1954), P. O'Connell, *Proceedings of the Irish Catholic historical committee 1965-67* (Dublin, 1968), pp 49-61.

191. J. Coombes, *A bishop of penal times* (Cork, 1981), pp 67-8.

192. *Corke Journal,* 2 June 1757.

193. See D. D. Bien, 'The background to the Calas affair' in *History,* xliii, no. 149 (Oct. 1958), pp 192-206. I thank Mr Nicholls for this reference.

194. I have consulted the version of the text in R.I.A., MS 23 B 4, pp 9 ff., *R.I.A. cat. Ir. MSS,* pp 1151-53, especially p. 1152.

195. See C. O'Rahilly, *Five seventeenth-century political poems* (Dublin, 1952), pp 33-49. The works of both Cúndúns are found in close proximity in U.C.C. Library, Torna MS T.lii, pp 28-41, see de Brún, *Cnuasach Thorna,* i, pp 140-44, especially p. 141.

196. R.I.A., MS 12 E 24, pp 67 ff., *R.I.A. cat. Ir. MSS,* pp 2624-33, at p. 2627.

197. Bolster, *Diocese of Cork,* iii, pp 101-03.

198. Ó Fiannachta, *An barántas,* pp 46-50.

199. P. Corish, *The Irish Catholic experience: a historical survey* (Dublin, 1985), pp 123-37; D. Ó Laoghaire, 'Prayers and hymns in the vernacular' in J. P. Mackey (ed.), *An introduction to Celtic Christianity* (Edinburgh, 1989), pp 268-304.

200. For calendars see F. L. Cross and E. A. Livingstone (ed.), *Oxford dictionary of the Christian church* [hereafter Cross, *Dictionary*] (Oxford, 1978), s.v. calendar. My colleague Professor Pádraig Ó Riain of U.C.C.'s Department of Early and Medieval Irish is currently researching the Gaelic medieval calendrical tradition.

201. For a summary account of his work for the Irish language see Ní Shéaghdha, 'Scholars and scribes in Dublin', pp 52-53, L. Mac Mathúna, *Dúchas agus dóchas: scéal na Gaeilge i mBaile Átha Cliath* (Baile Átha Cliath, 1991), pp 48-49.

202. R.I.A., MS 23 A 8, pp i-xxv (pp x-xi cited here), see *R.I.A. cat. Ir. MSS,* pp 966-72, especially p. 967. The entire composition merits further comparison with such sources as Best and Lawlor, *Mart. Tallaght,* Stokes, *Mart. Gorman* and particularly Todd and Reeves, *Mart. Donegal.*

203. The saint is referred to in the text beginning *Codladh gan tsuan gan tsástacht* in T.C.D., MS H. 4. 20, p. 22, *T.C.D. cat. Ir. MSS,* pp 192-99, especially p. 193 where the work is it is stated to be 'On the hardships of Diarmid [*sic*] Kavanagh and Gerald O'Byrne when driven to wander in woods and mountains'; see also M. Mac Neill, *The festival of Lughnasa* (Oxford, 1962), pp 266-68.

204. U.C.C. Library, Torna MS T.xxviii, pp 3-13 (information from p. 6 cited here), de Brún, *Cnuasach Thorna,* i, pp 84-87, especially p. 85.

205. I have discussed issues of this type in C. G. Buttimer, 'The French influence on religious instruction in pre-Famine Gaelic Ireland' in the transactions of the Eighth International Congress on the Enlightenment (Bristol, 1991), forthcoming in *Studies on Voltaire and the eighteenth century.* The French evidence presented in the text following this reference draws on that account.

206. Maynooth, MSS M 36-38, *Má Nuad clár,* ii, pp 74-5. For de Granada see *Catholic encyclopaedia,* s.n.

207. Maynooth, MS M 27 (b), *Má Nuad clár,* ii, pp 64-5. For Segneri see *Catholic encyclopaedia,* s.n.

208. T. P. Power and K. Whelan, *Endurance and emergence: Catholics in Ireland in the eighteenth century* (Dublin, 1990), K. Whelan, 'Catholic mobilisation' in L. Cullen and P. Bergeron (ed.), *Politicisation in Ireland and France: a comparative perspective* (Paris, 1990), pp 235-38, T. Bartlett, *The fall and rise of the Irish nation: the Catholic question 1690-1830* (Dublin, 1992) .

209. L. J. Luzbetak, *The church and cultures: new perspectives in missiological anthropology* (Maryknoll, New York, 1988), p. 16.

210. See Maynooth, MS M 32, pp 1-235, *Má Nuad clár,* ii, pp 70-72, especially p. 70. For Challoner see Cross, *Dictionary,* s.n.

211. Maynooth, MS M 44, pp 123-210, *Má Nuad clár,* ii, pp 87-89, especially p. 88.

212. B.L., MS Egerton 158, f. 161 ff.

213. Maynooth, MS M 59 (d), pp 349 ff., *Má Nuad clár,* iii, p. 30. For Gother see Cross, *Dictionary,* s.n.

214. For Ward see *D.N.B.,* s.n.

215. Vol. i, p. 1.

216. See N.L.I., MS G 132, p. 21, *N.L.I. cat. Ir. MSS,* iv, p. 58.

217. *England's Reformation,* i, pp 212-13; for de Barra's work see St Colman's College, Fermoy, MS PB 6, p. 77, Ó Fiannachta, *Mionchnuasaigh,* i, pp 148-52 at p. 150.

218. R.I.A., MS 24 M 4, pp 271 f., *R.I.A. cal. Ir. MSS,* pp 19041-11, especially p. 1910, trans. [1] 'At the Mill Cross we had a minister who was a loveable, innocent neighbour. He was quite understanding to the wretched wanderer who had not the cost of his journey. For women and children he would see in want he would pick his own pocket, and would take the clothes from his own bones to shelter any who lacked raiment'. [2] 'Neither his charity nor almgiving were of any benefit because his teaching was not proper, since he was not baptised in Peter's church which the blessed powerful Spirit created. Under the protection of the Star of Heaven he would scarcely have cut his throat, because great is her friendship with the three persons who are highest in the glorious city'.

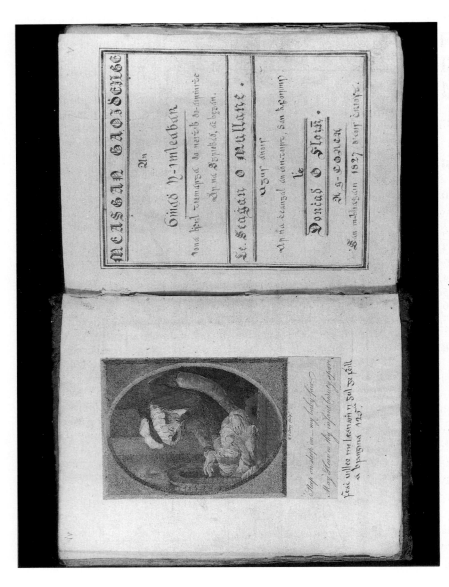

Plate 15.6   Donnchadh Ó Floinn's title-page for Seán Ó Mulláin's manuscript (U.C.C., MS Torna, T.i).

Chapter 16

SOCIAL, ECONOMIC AND LANDSCAPE TRANSFORMATIONS IN COUNTY CORK FROM THE MID-EIGHTEENTH TO THE MID-NINETEENTH CENTURY

WILLIAM J. SMYTH

Introduction

The central issue addressed in this paper is the assessment of levels of transformation and continuity in the social structures and settlement patterns of rural county Cork between the mid-eighteenth century and the onset of the Great Famine. When looking at the relationships between social and agrarian structures and patterns of settlement and landscape transformation in this region one is faced with at least three major problems: (i) the complex structure of county Cork's physical and human topographies, (ii) the dynamism in its economy and the rapidity of its population growth between 1750 and 1845 and (iii) the variable character of the documentary source materials available to the researcher for the same period. Given its highly varied character both in terms of its physical morphology and its social and settlement history, county Cork presents special problems when one attempts to generalise across such a diversified topography and heritage, particularly during a period of rapid economic and cultural change.

A massive county by Irish standards, Cork stretches along 1,094 km of a highly irregular coastline (15 per cent of the national total) and yet penetrates deep into the inland heart of Munster. Its complicated physical make-up incorporates the steep-sloped peninsular/insular world of the south-west, the wet carboniferous shale uplands of the north-west, the Old Red Sandstones of the western mountains and interior hill ranges with their reclaimed podzols, peaty gleys and climatic peats, the rich, extensive and flexible limestone lowlands and valleys of the north and east and the drowned valleys of the sun-warmed shales and slaty soils of the southern coastal zone.[1] County Cork, therefore, exhibits a great variety of scenery, slope, altitude, soil structure, drainage patterns and exposure to wind, rain and sun. It is relevant to note that its ridge and valley character and its exceptionally mild Atlantic climate have traditionally provided rich sheltered environments for the out-wintering of cows and cattle. Over the March-September period, the county has a ten per cent advantage in grass growth potential – as defined in degree days – over the midland counties of the country. Yet within the county area as a whole, potential grazing capacity in north-west and south-west Cork is still less than half that of the rich lands of Imokilly, north-east Cork and the two Bride valleys.[2]

Interwoven with the varied habitat is the diversity of many societies' imprints and adaptations through time. The map of mid-nineteenth century land values highlights just one dimension of this varied human and physical legacy (Fig 16.1). Griffith's valuation fused together the two powerful geographical measures of quality of land and degree of accessibility to market towns and port cities. The land values map pinpoints the massive variations in the land productivity and related levels of rural wealth in mid-nineteenth century county Cork. The strong local impact of urban spheres of influence is a striking feature. If one were to include the additional valuations of buildings and infra-structure to the land values *per se*, the contrasts locally and regionally would be even stronger. Apart from this great variety, Figure 16.1 emphasises the exceptionally rich endowment of much of north and east Cork with extensive areas valued at more than £1 per acre in the mid-nineteenth century. Equally revealing are the extensive areas of relatively poor land (valued at less than forty pence per acre) which are located throughout the county, including the north-east corner but which are particularly characteristic of the north-west, west and south-west. One thinks also of the different human heritages of the coastal maritime regions as opposed to the interior lands with their long-established contrasting life-styles and varying levels of accessibility to a range of other places, peoples and experiences. In particular, the contrast between a great Atlantic port city and its immediate hinterland and remoter, utterly rural peripheries is also very sharp.

Woven into this already complex heritage is the enduring legacy of a hybrid Irish/Cambro-Norman cultural world, particularly in the northern and eastern half of the county, a pattern emphasised by the far greater temporal depth of urban and village life in these regions, strongly opposed to the very late urbanised worlds of the north-west and south-west.[3] These latter stand out as one of the most striking indigenous surname regions in the whole of Ireland. Dominated by the McCarthys and O'Sullivans and flanked by the Crowleys, O'Donovans, O'Driscolls and O'Keeffes, the western half of Cork constitutes a wider maritime cultural domain together with south Kerry that seems to stand apart not only from the rest of Ireland but also the rest of Munster.[4] This regional heritage was to be further complicated by the establishment of a new layer of landowners and settlers from the late sixteenth century

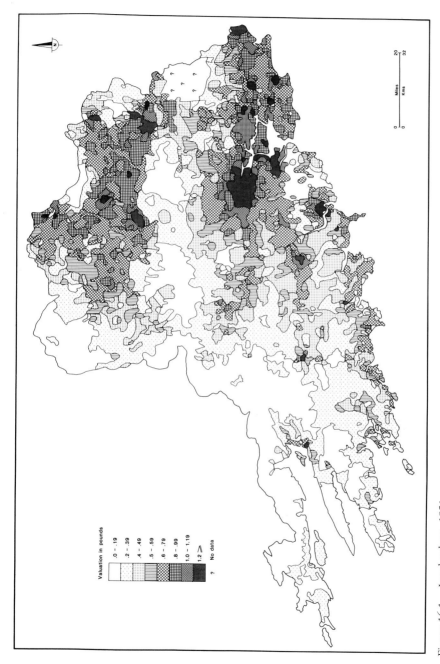

Figure 16.1 Land values, 1851.
Source: Griffith, *Valuation*.

657

onwards – this was particularly the case in the harbour area and the south-western baronies of the county which witnessed the cumulative processes of colonisation, settlement and development by not just a land-owning élite but also the full spectrum of a colonial society.[5] In the south of Ireland, south-west Cork comes closest – if in a more isolated fashion – to replicating the settlement experiences of much of Ulster. Culturally, therefore, Cork is characterised by at least three great regions – a deeply feudalised and urbanised world in the south-east which is centred on the city, the harbour region and Imokilly, a hybrid world running north-east to south-west across the broad middle of the county, characterised by complex and long-term fruitful exchanges between Gael and Cambro-Norman and thirdly, in the far west and south-west, one of the great long-lasting outliers of essentially Gaelic culture which was in turn to be transformed by the Munster plantations and their consequences.

In land-use terms there have also been oscillations in different eras and in different regions in the extent to which the local economy was more strongly pastoral or tillage-oriented; the development of an intensive mixed dairy-farming tradition in the region can be seen as a rich fusion between these two extremes of land use and adds further emphasis to the transitional-hybrid character of the peoples and landscapes of county Cork in an island-wide context. Cork city itself, the central hinge of this large county – with its port linking the region to the outside world – also exhibits such a complex hybrid structure. On the pastoral side of the city's heritage – apart altogether from the fact that the rapid growth of the eighteenth-century city itself is specifically founded on the pastoral produce of the region – it is unlikely that any other west European city has as high a density of dogs, dog-walkers and hound/beagling associations. On the other hand, Cork city is alone amongst other Irish cities in seeing the transfer of the skilful field-game of hurling (traditionally nurtured in the mixed tillage regions of the east and south of the country) into the narrow streets of its old inner-city parishes.[6]

The second major problem of analysis relates to the dynamic character of the region's economy and the substantial growth of its population in the period under review. When we look at central government grants of patents for fairs and markets in Ireland we find that over much of the island the greater proportion of fair and market centres was formally recognised during the seventeenth century; when however we look at the Munster region, we see that despite a large number of seventeenth-century grants, an even higher proportion of fairs and markets was approved for the eighteenth century.[7] In this context county Cork has a clear lead over the other Munster counties –

the central lynchpin, then, in the buoyant pastoral economy of the region in that crucial century. Within the county the distribution of fair sites both intensified locally and spread to remoter regions during the eighteenth century. Ballyvourney's right to hold a fair was granted in 1756, Milford's and Lisgoold's in the 1760s and places like Cahermee, Knocknagree and Shanballymore were granted their fairs in the later eighteenth century. It is also worth noting that the yearly *number* of fairs held in the county doubled from *c.* 100 in 1740 to over 200 by 1760 and was to treble by 1790 to reach a total of 335.[8] Fairs and markets thus provide one index of both the dynamic and relatively distinctive character of this south-Munster region.

A second indicator which emphasises the regional distinctiveness of the Munster economy – particularly that of counties Cork, Tipperary and Limerick – is the varying county trends in tenant-tree planting over the period 1765-1850 (Fig. 16.2). From 1765 – unlike previously – a tenant with a lease of 12 years or longer was entitled to own all his/her tree-plantings, provided these were registered with the Clerk of the Peace of the county within six months.[9] Looking at trends in tenant tree-planting over the island from the mid-eighteenth century, it would appear that western counties show a much reduced general rate of such planting. Eastern and northern counties display a stable normal distribution over the whole period. In contrast, there was a boom in tree-planting in Munster counties (excluding county Waterford) in the late eighteenth and early nineteenth centuries; this phase then dipped very sharply from 1815 to 1820 and revived dramatically again from the 1820s on. It may well be that changes in agricultural conditions and prices may have bitten deeper into the fabric of this south Munster regional economy; adaptations to post-war agricultural conditions may have, therefore, expressed themselves earlier and more sharply in the southern part of the island. However, as Figure 16.3 indicates, county Cork itself – given its size and varied character – reflects a similar range of experiences in the timing and spread of tree-planting to that orchestrated over the island as a whole.

In population terms, the dynamism in the region is also suggested by what appears to be a dramatic increase in the late seventeenth and early eighteenth centuries; the city was possibly to quadruple its population between 1700 and 1821 when it reached a total of over 71,000, while in the remainder of the county, despite the severe setback of the 1741 famine, the number probably more than doubled between 1766 and 1821 when it reached a total of 0.63 million. By 1841 the population of the county as a whole was 854,118.[10] However, population increases were not shared equally across the county – there are sharp differences in the settlement and population histories of

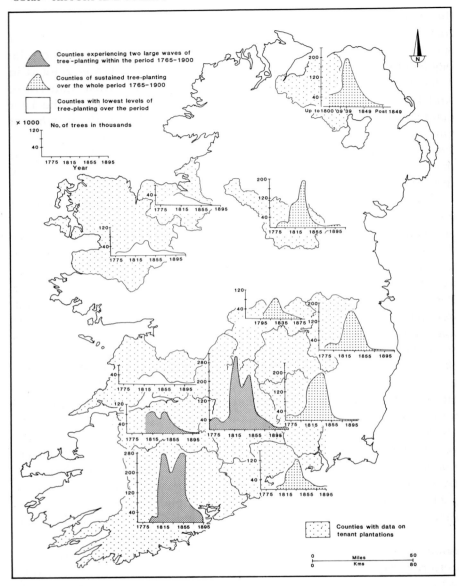

Figure 16.2   Tenant tree-planting by county, 1765-1900.
Source: N.A., 'A register of trees'.

different sub-regions over the period. In the 1820s some regions were still witnessing significant expansion while in other areas both declining populations and substantial emigration were already characteristic features. It is very difficult, therefore, to interpret how these varied demographic, social, economic and cultural processes, operating between *c.* 1750 and *c.* 1845, were married in such complex combinations to the diverse human and physical topographies of the region.

The third problem relates to the limited range and areal incompleteness of the source materials used in this chapter. As compared with the rich central government-sponsored data-sources of the nineteenth century – including the detailed reports of government commissions, census information, valuation records and the six-inch and other Ordnance Survey maps – the eighteenth century presents a more varied, fragmented and localised range of evidence. The geographer finds it particularly difficult to obtain a detailed comprehensive set of relevant source materials which cover the county as a whole. Likewise, in the absence of detailed fieldwork, one can only explore the county via the published maps – stumbling across Cork's townlands as they are revealed on the numerous Ordnance Survey sheets. Cartographic and other documentary evidence likewise cannot fully illustrate the largely unwritten processes of cultural adaptation and adjustment that accompanied this critical 100 years. Documents too are never neutral. They generally reflect the goals and interests of their compilers; the attitudes and values of some of the more important sections of society may not be represented at all in such sources. There is still much hidden of the reactions, activities and experiences of the great majority of Cork's eighteenth and early nineteenth-century populations. There are, therefore, still many 'geographies' to be explored, particularly in terms of the varying perceptions, needs and goals of the different social groups who worked, loved, struggled and died in the shaping of Cork's society, economy and settlement between 1750 and 1845. However, the county has been well served by earlier topographers such as Smith and Townsend and in more recent years by the exhaustive studies of Burke, Deady, Donnelly and in particular the outstanding work of Dickson on the economic history of the wider Cork/south Munster region in the eighteenth century to which I am greatly indebted.[11]

Ascendancy, reorganisation and relocation: mid-eighteenth-century county Cork

While recognising continuities in townland names and settlement sites, the great differences between Smith's mid-eighteenth-century map of county Cork and Petty's earlier survey is the superimposition on the latter's mid-seventeenth-century map of a more complex array of towns and villages and, in particular, a far denser network of roads.[12] Many of these new roads radiated out from Cork city – symbolising the intensification of inland trade on the one hand and its concentration on the great port city on the other. The period from 1730 to 1770, particularly, witnessed the continued evolution in the lower-order

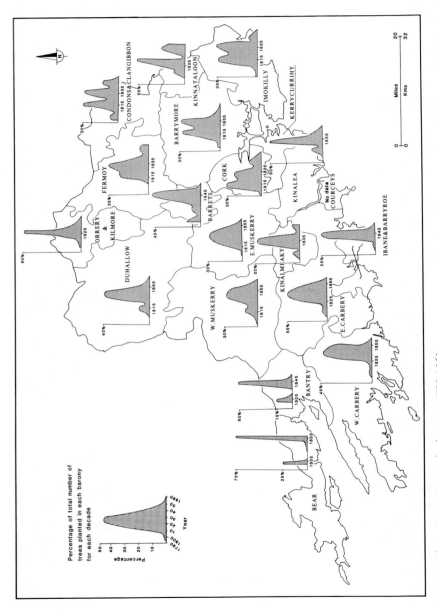

Figure 16.3 Tree-planting by barony, 1790-1860.
Source: N.A., 'A register of trees, county Cork'.

central-place structure as the creation/embellishment of estate villages and the spread of fairs and markets into both older and newer settlements increased. The old and newly-established nodes played an important role as gathering points for the cattle, sheep, butter (and sometimes wool) destined either for the English or the Atlantic trade. Emphasis on commercial tillage crops was probably at its lowest for the third quarter of the eighteenth century.[13] Dairying and grazing farming systems were still expanding in scope and area in the 1760s; the Whiteboy reactions along the foothills of the mountains of the north-east of the county reflected in part the response of small-holding tillage families to displacement as a commercial grazing economy lapped up around these former subsistence zones. Even as late as the 1770s, corn-producing partnership tenants in the Mallow region were being replaced by sheep and cows – a process of territorial, social and land-use organisation which had been accelerating from the seventeenth century onwards.[14]

The geographical spread and intensification of the distribution of fair sites provide good clues to the areal expansion of a commercial cattle economy, while also suggesting the areas where the creation of newly-enclosed landscapes of compact independent farms was nearing completion. In the 1690s, the limited number of fair sites was for the most part evident in both the old and new market towns of the county. These were obviously the primary zones for the diffusion of a more commercialised pastoral economy and the modern enclosure network. By the late 1730s and early 1740s these market towns still dominated the trading patterns, although quite a number of secondary fair locations were then emerging, especially in the barony of Imokilly but also in places as far afield as Killcummer near Fermoy, Burnfort near Mourne Abbey in the barony of Barretts, Shandrum in Orrery and Kilmore and Rockhill in Duhallow.

The most critical phase in the diffusion of fair sites was clearly in the 1740s and 1750s. Both the number and location of fairs had increased dramatically by the early 1760s. There was an intensification of the number of fairs in the established market towns but equally there was a massive expansion of new fair centres right across the county. In north Cork, Ballyclough, Bartlemy, Brigown, Castletownroche, Cecilstown, Conna, Fermoy, Liscarroll, Nadrid and Rathcormack all emerge as significant new fair centres. In the immediate Cork city hinterland region, Ballinhassig, Ballinspittle, Blarney, Castlemartyr, Crookstown, Donoghmore, Dunderrow, Killeagh, Kilmurray and Innishannon grew in importance, while in the west and south-west Ballyvourney, Ballydehob, Kilbrittain, Inchigeela, Leap and Newcestown were added to the now dense network of fair sites.[15]

This mid-eighteenth-century fair pattern was to provide the basic marketing network for the remainder of the eighteenth and early nineteenth centuries. By the 1790s the pattern which emerged was a significant expansion in the number of fairs at *existing* sites rather than much geographical expansion in fair locations. True, there was some in-filling of the pattern as at Passage West, Annesgrove, Massystown and Rostellan, and some expansion on the edges as at Lisgoold, Glenville, Grenagh and Milford, but overall the dramatic foundations laid down in the early and mid-eighteenth century sufficed for the remainder of the century.

Cork city's colonial provisions trade dominated this whole pattern of fair activity. Youghal in 1750 was stagnant while Kinsale's maritime role (apart from its fishing) was very much reduced; Baltimore and Crookhaven were no more than shrunken villages, while as late as 1780 Bantry is described as a 'poor insignificant village'.[16] Much of this south-western coastal zone was still in decline after the disappearance of the great pilchard fishing industry. In contrast the more centrally-located towns of Skibbereen and Clonakilty were just beginning to revive as market centres, especially for the developing linen trade. This latter industry was also significant in the revitalisation of the urban order inland and westwards as in the case of Dunmanway, a smaller and reconstituted version of the earlier industrial plantation towns of Bandon and Mallow. Deliberate encouragement of the textile industries was also reflected in the newly-designed villages of Blarney and Castlemartyr and a rebuilt Innishannon with their often recently-established charter schools providing, amongst other features, a training ground for young spinners and weavers.[17]

Infrastructural investment was not obviously confined to the settle-ment nodes but also appertained to the road network. There was a greater elaboration of the lowland routes – including the building of many new bridges along the new roads converging on such centres as Dunmanway and Castlemartyr. However, many of the great road developments of the early and mid-eighteenth century were bringing the great cattle/dairying regions of west and north Cork closer to Cork city. It is interesting to compare the linear structure of the frontier towns of Macroom, Millstreet and Newmarket – all drover towns, funnelling the cattle, butter and sheep from points further north and west on to Cork markets and thence to the British, French, Spanish and Portuguese colonies. From Smith's descriptions one also catches a glimpse of the booming dairy/cattle economy in the north-Cork lowlands and the richness of life for some in the towns and villages. Kanturk was then thriving on its fairs; Charleville, located between Cork and Limerick, was one of the great thoroughfares for cattle and butter, as was Mallow. Apart from such larger urban centres, this zone was also characterised by a number of revitalised or newly-established estate villages. In the traditional tillage region around 'Roches county', the old centres of Castletownroche and Glanworth were to slumber until the flour milling revival of the later eighteenth century; further north-east both Mitchelstown with its fairs – and Kilworth along the busy Dublin coach route – were also thriving, while at the bridge of the Blackwater Fermoy was still a small posting village.[18]

Thus the expanding economy of mid-eighteenth-century Cork was to enhance the centrality of some locations while others were to stagnate. The shifting centres of power and patronage added further variety to the evolving pattern, as landowners sought to maximise advantages for their estate towns. The old episcopal seat of Cloyne was losing out to Castlemartyr and particularly Midleton; Buttevant languished even further, caught between Charleville and Mallow; Castletownroche was affected by Doneraile's development while Timoleague and Rosscarbery may have declined even more in the face of Bandon's, Clonakilty's and Skibbereen's growth. In this western region a series of new or reconstituted urban centres were still frontier towns in an old rural world. Vallancey's survey allows us an additional glimpse of the completion of these processes of commercial expansion as well as pin-pointing the distribution of power and wealth in the countryside – then dominated by the landlords and a galaxy of middlemen (Fig. 16.4). In estate terms, the early and mid-eighteenth century can be distinguished as a phase in which the 'improving' landlord was generally only in indirect control of territorial, social and landscape structures. In using the term 'improving' for the period, one is talking about improvements not only in plantations and ornamented demesnes but more funda-mentally about the reorganisation and further commercialisation of agriculture. By the third quarter of the eighteenth century this process was now in its penultimate stage, following more than a century of transformation which saw the completion of the process of enclosure and the supremacy of compact farms and fields in lowland areas. Dis-placement of local villages and populations was obviously a feature of this process of reorganisation. Intensification of land use, relocation of some lowland populations and the piecemeal reclamation of poorer lowlying and upland soils were also features of this era. As Dickson has outlined elsewhere, the landowners main ally in making and supervising such investments was the 'residing, improving industrious' and hopefully, 'Protestant head-tenant' who was granted a long lease of one or more townlands in exchange for carrying out the necessary infrastructural changes.[19] As indicated for the adjoining areas of south-west Tipperary, head-tenants – particularly from the 1730s onwards –

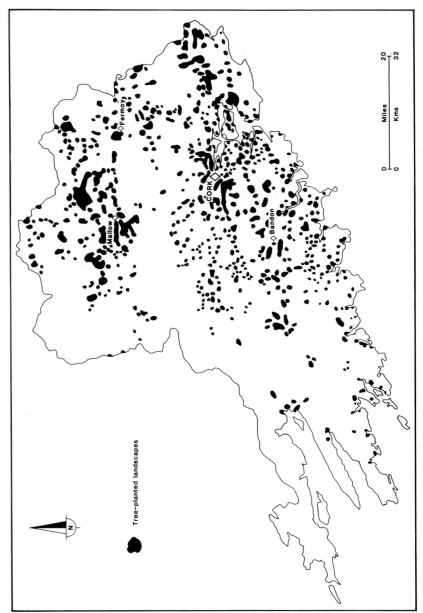

Figure 16.4   Gentleman's seats and tree-planted landscapes, c. 1788.
Source: B.L., 'A military survey of the south part of Ireland'.

were being required to build good farmhouses, plant orchards and set out farm and field boundaries with proper quick-setted ditches.[20]

Figure 16.4 highlights what could be described as the climax of a more strictly defined 'colonial' landscape of county Cork. Vallancey's detailed military survey reveals over 350 gentry homes and associated landscapes for 1780-82.[21] Characteristically the crucial contexts of concentration are the long-settled lowland river-valley zones. Excluding Cork harbour, if one were to pinpoint the core area of rural development elaboration at this time, one would have to settle for the Mallow-Doneraile region, then characterised by what must have been one of the most highly embellished landlord and middleman landscapes in the whole island. It is also striking how many of the extensive demesnes dominate the richer lowland valleys, while smaller demesnes are sprinkled in less-well-endowed foothill regions.

Figure 16.5, representing the estate distribution in mid-nineteenth century county Cork, can be used retrospectively to modify and augment Vallancey's picture of the cores of the estates in the late 1770s. Clearly there had been some changes in both the distribution and size of estates between c. 1770 and 1850, most specifically the break-up of the great Barrymore estate in east Cork.[22] Nevertheless the general patterns outlined in Figure 16.5 were of such duration as to be also clearly relevant to the 1760s and 1770s. Examined geographically, the pattern is clearly one of much complexity, involving estates which greatly varied in size, level of fragmentation, quality of land and a whole host of other criss-crossing variables.

The great estates clearly stand out on the map – those of the earls of Bantry and Kenmare and of R. E. White in the far west, as well as the lands of the web of Townsends and Beamishes, who almost reconstructed themselves as clans in the former Gaelic lands of Carbery. The Freke-Carbery estate is noticeable for its high level of fragmentation, a feature indeed of many other Cork estates including those of the Colthursts of Blarney and Ballyvourney, the Bernard earls of Bandon and Connors of Manch House beside Ballineen.

These fragmented estate units were all partly a product of far-flung purchasing patterns.[23] In the baronies of west and north-west Cork, there are other long-established patterns of fragmentation between the lowland and upland segments of estate units whose roots go deeper than the seventeenth century and which require further study as to their relevance to the types of farming and internal migration systems which they helped sustain. Across the north of the county the great estates of the Aldworths of Newmarket, the St Legers of Doneraile, the Percivals of Kanturk, the earls of Kingston and Mountcashel at Mitchelstown and Kilworth, the Hydes and Roches of Fermoy, stand

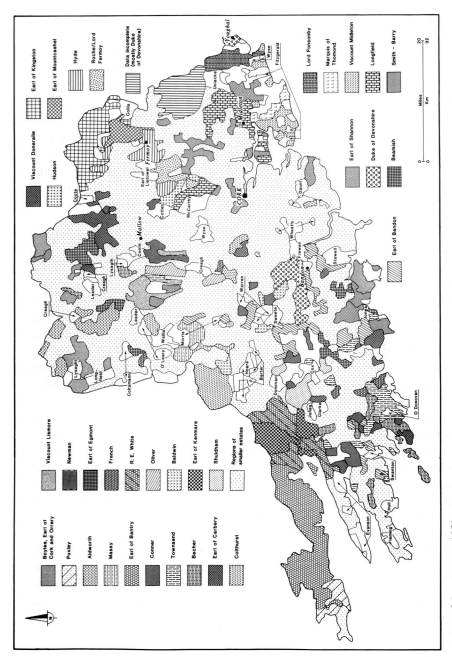

Figure 16.5   Estates, 1851.
Source: Griffith, *Valuation.*

out. The Duke of Devonshire dominates the northern half of Kinatalloon as well as holding one of the largest, most improved and most compact blocks of land in all of county Cork in the Bandon region. East Cork has a greater share of old estate families such as the Smith-Barrys, the Uniackes, the Fitzgeralds, the Inchiquin O'Briens, the Roches and the Wyses. In the heart of Barrymore and Imokilly the great estates of Viscount Midleton and the Earl of Shannon, centred on Midleton and Castlemartyr, dominate the landlord estate system.

However, equally relevant to an assessment of county Cork's estate system is the numerical strength and regional dominance of estates of less than 2,500 acres. Figures 16.4 and 16.5 also provide a rough guide to the distribution of the smaller estate units. The Cork city region is emphatically the focal point of these estates which also extend north eastwards to Fermoy, northwards to Mallow and westwards north of Macroom. Smaller estates are also strongly represented on the map along the ridges south of the Bandon river from Kinsale onwards to the Mizen peninsula. The ancient arable core of the 'Roches county' retains what appears to be an older smaller landowning system, a pattern replicated in other pockets of lowland north Cork.

As with everything else in county Cork, there is no simple correlation between size of estate and quality of land. The richest lands of Imokilly and south Barrymore are dominated by large estates while the fertile lands of the Cork city region and the Lee valley are full of smaller land units. Big estates dominate the fertile lands along the Bandon river. In contrast west Muskerry, Beara and Bantry form a region of big estates on very poor land, while the poorer lands of Mizen and Carbery constitute a region of smaller estates. On the other hand some of the best land of north-east Cork also constitutes a zone of smaller estates. Orrery and Kilmore is transitional in estate size while the estate structure of the uplands of Duhallow (that is, if the term 'estate structure' has any great validity in these remoter regions) defies easy description, given the levels of estate fragmentation, absenteeism and the juxtaposition of large and small land entities which characterise these wet rugged areas.

It is also relevant to note that much estate reorganisation and development took place within the long-established frame of the older townland network and we are still unsure of the extent to which new field and farm patterns were to incorporate previous territorial units within the townland frame. Likewise, there were significant regional variations in the degree to which landowners were attracting model Protestants as head-tenants. There is a strong probability that on the majority of eighteenth-century Cork estates a substantial number of head-tenants bore Irish names. This was particularly true of Imokilly and Barrymore and to a lesser extent the north-Cork lowlands. The Barrys were the leaders amongst the great middleman families here, followed by the Murphys, Ahernes, Coppingers, Creaghs, Fitzgeralds, Galweys, Longs, Roches, Walshes and Wyses. The areas of greatest change in middle management were on estates in the Muskerry, Bandon and East Carbery regions. Again the Townsends and Beamishes had important middlemen families here, while the Warren, Smith, Swanton, Bennet, Clarke, Daunt, Robert, Leader, Meade and Evans families were also conspicuous. In the extreme western and south-western regions of the county, older and probably more cumbersome patterns of estate management persisted, involving long-established old Irish families who remained dominant in those areas for much of the eighteenth and in some cases survived well into the nineteenth century.[24] The O'Sullivans, McCarthys and O'Callaghans were clearly the dominant family groups at this level, followed by the Collins, the O'Donovan, O'Mahony, Regan, O'Riordan and McSweeny families. It is clear, therefore, that we have to be somewhat cautious in accepting the view that we must look to 'innovative outsiders' for all the impetus to change and development that characterised the county in the eighteenth century.

This is not to say, however, that the great majority of the larger gentry mansions were not occupied by settler families, however diverse their backgrounds; but change in the composition of élites does not necessarily involve as radical a transformation in settlement and social structures as has been suggested in much of the literature. An analysis of the character and siting of the bigger gentry houses which Smith describes for each barony in the mid-eighteenth century is revealing in this respect. In the baronies of Imokilly, Kinnatalloon, Barrymore, Fermoy, Condons and Clangibbon (the eastern half of the county), at least half of the big houses are sited on or near (or in a few cases actually are) the castles or tower-houses of the previous era. Significant continuities, therefore, characterise the occupation of key sites even if changes have taken place in the actual occupiers themselves and in the settlement structure. The big house, however, was replacing the medieval village as the great power centre of rural life in both north and east Cork and in south-east Ireland as a whole by the mid-eighteenth century. In the north-Cork barony of Orrery and Kilmore, more than half of the big houses reflected this kind of continuity in the use of all their sites; Duhallow is also transitional in this respect. In contrast the ratio of new big house sites to old in Muskerry is three to one; here Smith notes that since the Earl of Clancarty's forfeiture in the early eighteenth century '200 good slate houses have been built ... also 7 new churches and several stone bridges'.[25] Likewise west and south of Cork city, in Kilnalea, Kerrycurrihy, Ibane and Barryroe, there is a two-to-one ratio in favour of new big house sites. In Carbery barony – its landscape littered with the deserted castles of the old families (the latter ruined both by the plantations and the disappearing fish shoals) – the ratio is three-to-one in favour of new big house developments. It is, therefore, critical to recognise that in some regions of county Cork the colonial culture of the landlord and the lesser gentry was solidly built on the ruins of the medieval (and indeed pre-medieval) settlement pattern and pivoted around a much older territorial and social structure. The zones of sharpest cultural conflict and change were to the west and south-west.

Materials from diocesan and hearth-tax returns for 1764-1766 demonstrate the high-point in the distribution and density of the rural Protestant community in county Cork.[26] The Cork city and harbour region, with a weak and narrow extension to the now strongly Protestant town of Youghal, constituted one important and durable area of planter settlement by the mid-eighteenth century. The second and more extensive settlement of rural Protestants stretches inland from Kinsale along the Bandon valley, peaking in the hinterland of Bandon town itself and then expanding solidly westwards through Dunmanway, before bending southwards before O'Donovans' country to join up with a coastal concentration from Skibbereen south-west-wards. A ragged frontier of poorer Protestant settlers was then colonising the difficult lands of the Mizen peninsula.

This second region in west Cork was clearly the focal point of the most dynamic expansion of Protestant settlement, eventually running up against long-established Irish-speaking communities to the north and to the west and marking, as Cullen has noted, one of the sharpest cultural frontiers in all of eighteenth-century Ireland; levels of ethnic segregation in the associated towns of Bandon and Youghal were extraordinarily high in mid-eighteenth-century Cork.[27] In the rest of the county, with the exception of the heavily gentrified worlds stretching from Mallow to Doneraile, Protestant concentrations were mainly in the urban zones, as in the vicinity of Charleville, Kilworth and Kanturk. In these baronies of Fermoy, Orrery and Kilmore and Condons and Clangibbon, small Protestant congregations of thirty to sixty families were the norm, while in Muskerry, Carbery and Imokilly more vibrant Protestant communities often exceeded 200 families per local Anglican church.

In contrast there were great areas of essentially local and Catholic populations in mid-eighteenth-century Cork, particularly in coastal Imokilly, the uplands of Imokilly and Barrymore, parts of the south coast and especially in the vast interior foothills and uplands which run across the middle and north of the county. Although the Catholic church was still not fully reorganised at this stage – the number of parish registers, apart from those in the city and other urban centres, was yet few and far between in rural areas – there was by 1766 a solid distribution of chapels/mass-houses right across the county.[28] Baronies such as Orrery and Kilmore and Imokilly were best served with churches having congregations averaging 170 to 200 families, while other baronies – Condons and Clangibbon, Fermoy and Muskerry – had much larger congregations (350-400 families) – and a less dense distribution of chapels. Both friars and diocesan priests were also well distributed across the county, the secular clergy trained on the continent in places as far afield as Antwerp, Avignon, Bordeaux and Sarlat.

However, the still subservient position of the Catholic church in the wider political order is well-attested in the letter of the Bishop of Cloyne and Ross advising his 'frontier priests' during the Whiteboy era:

> To exhort and admonish the good people of the respective congregations against having any hand, or taking the least part, directly or indirectly, in any illegal practices, or holding any sort of conduct, that may give offence to the government, especially in the present general conjuncture of troublesome times, when all the Roman Catholics of this kingdom should rather be more attentive than ever, to manifest their unfeigned dispositions of giving our most excellent and noble minded Lord Lieutenant, Lord Halifax and all our other great and good governors, the best and most solid proofs in our power, of the just and grateful feeling we have, and always should have of their lenity and indulgence towards us in our unhappy circumstances subjected as we are, according to the disposition of Providence not only by legal restraints and incapacities, but also to penal laws, whose might and severity we already find to be alleviated in great measure, through the goodness and clemency of our most gracious rulers.[29]

It was truly the high-point of the Protestant ascendancy in Cork as in Ireland as a whole. The critical period from 1775 to 1815 was radically to alter the shape of Ireland and the shape of Cork – economically, socially, culturally and politically.

The observant Vallancey provides a bridge into the 1780s as he comments on the opening up of west Cork at this time. He notes that formerly

> ... there was only one road leading from Cork to Bantry; you now may proceed by eight carriage roads besides several horse tracks

branching off from these great roads ... from Bantry to
Dunmanway the country is mountainous and from the high road
has the appearance of being barren and very thinly inhabited; yet
the valleys abound with people, corn, and potatoes and the
mountains are covered with black cattle ... Twenty years ago
[c. 1760] it was so thinly inhabited, an army of 10,000 men could
not possibly have found subsistence between Bantry and Bandon.
The face of the country now wears a different aspect: the sides of
the hills are under the plough, the verges of the bogs are
reclaimed and the southern coast from Skibbereen to Bandon is
one continued garden of grain and potatoes except the barren
pinnacles of some hills and the boggy hollows between which are
preserved for fuel.[30]

Vallancey gives glowing descriptions of the now completely enclosed
world around Bandon where east of this town and the towns of
Macroom and Clonakilty ' the country opens out in avenues to Cork
city'.[31] He also provides a benchmark against which to measure the
changes that were still to come; the road from Bantry to Cork through
Inchigeela was still to be built, the farmers of west Cork still continued
to use small horses rather than wheeled vehicles for carting both grain
to the market and sea sand as manure many miles inland. The towns of
Skibbereen and particularly Bantry and Rosscarbery had yet to undergo
the later eighteenth- and early nineteenth-century transformation. And
all along the south of the county the estate maps of the Freke estate,
from the parish of Athnowen on the Lee to Baltimore in the south-west,
displayed compact agricultural villages locked within the townland
frame as still being the norm of rural living as late as 1788.[32] The juxtaposition of alienated and appropriated landscapes on the one hand and
old agricultural villages and townland communities on the other is still
very much a feature of late eighteenth-century Cork.

Elaboration, diversification and marginalisation: late eighteenth- and early nineteenth-century county Cork

'The only purpose that Smith's description of 1750 can now serve is as
a monument to the improvements that have been carried out since his
time'.[33] Such was the comment of the French consul about Cork in the
1790s. The later eighteenth and early nineteenth century is one of the
great boom periods of Cork's agricultural history. It was a golden age
for many elements in society but not for all. The major components in
this dynamic situation were firstly a significant relative shift in market
prices which favoured tillage farming and intensive dairying at the
expense of the formerly dominant system of extensive stock-rearing

and dairying. This change is above all symbolised by the relatively rapid diffusion of large flour-milling establishments across the eastern and south-eastern half of the county. In addition to the long-established provisions industry, a substantial expansion in other agriculturally-related industries such as brewing and distilling was also significant in the area.[34] A third element was the growing attempts by landlords and by a developing estate bureaucracy to supplant the intermediate head-tenants or middlemen and deal directly with the full array of hard-working tenant farmers.[35] The main goal of the landlord here was to reap the benefits of the enormous increase in rents which accompanied this agricultural boom. This, however, was a long-drawn-out process and was complicated by the ease with which larger farmers and lease-holders could benefit from sub-letting at the sub-townland level in the era of rapid population growth. Nevertheless, it is not surprising that there was a rapid increase in the number of estate surveys during this period, revealing for the first time the internal arrangement of farm units within the townland, tenurial units which had previously been left to the management of a hierarchy of middle tenants.[36] A fourth element woven into this complex system of changes was the phenomenal, if uneven, expansion in population in this brief period. This process alone powerfully influenced the shift to intensive forms of tillage farming. It also helped to prompt changes in estate administration, given the high rents which could be acquired in this world of pro-liferating farmers and 'cottiers'. Population increases were also inter-woven with substantial changes in the relative significance of different social groups at both sub-regional and county levels. Significant alterations in religious, social and political organisations were also characteristic of this extraordinary fertile period.

We are dealing then with an expansive age, an age of significant transformation in settlement and land-use patterns and in com-munications generally, as the already basic design of roads was further elaborated upon. Politically and culturally there were changes too. The greater visibility of the Catholic middle classes was expressed not just in the landscape and in levels of social mobilisation but also in amending legislation which expanded their leasing and electoral rights. The surplus accumulated in this exceptional phase is still written into today's landscapes – in the wealthy suburbs of Cork city and the villas that stretch from Glanmire to Blackrock. This era saw the building of new towns like Cobh and Fermoy; older towns such as Mitchelstown were completely reconstructed as were smaller centres such as Buttevant, Castletownshend and Liscarroll. All of these growing centres were to acquire an increasing range of market and industrial functions and indeed other retailing services. The Vallancey map of gentry houses was also to be dramatically transformed as the countryside witnessed a burst of both new house building and the redesigning of many of the older houses (Fig. 16.4). Not unlike the 1960s and 1970s, this great building boom of the late eighteenth and early nineteenth centuries saw exceptional growth amongst the master builders and artisans generally. This latter group may have come to comprise up to ten per cent of the total population in the parishes most exposed to new developments – thus adding further diversity to the social structure and cultural milieu of such communities. But this expansive period was also one of contraction in the status of some elements in society – the proliferation of the rural labouring class in an inflationary era saw a gradual reduction in their living standards, a process which was exacerbated still further in the decades after 1815.

In terms of estate administration, it has been demonstrated elsewhere that the more progressive landlords moved to lease land in much smaller units – a strategy facilitated by the long-run expansion of the more comfortable tenant farming class.[37] Here it is relevant to note that some eastern and particularly south-eastern estates such as those of Midleton and Barrymore were earliest in moving towards direct tenancies of smaller units and a preference for hardworking under-tenants as against the now often absentee head-tenant. By the end of this phase, it would appear that within the townland smaller tenancies for one life of 21 years were already characteristic of much of Ibane and Barryroe, Imokilly and Fermoy, Condons and Clangibbon and parts of East Carbery, whereas in baronies such as Duhallow, West Muskerry and the south-west generally, a looser and more flexible system of estate management still prevailed.[38]

This greater emphasis on smaller tenancies did not always involve a single tenant; it could also involve – particularly on the remoter estates, or in areas where traditional systems of tillage farming had not been eroded – leasing to a joint group of partnership tenants (Figs 16.10 and 16.11). Overall, however, new landlord leases were given to individual tenants who were required to carry out a whole range of improvements on their holdings. These new farm leases now included regulations relating to tree-planting, quick-setting, better rotations and better manuring. In the absence of comprehensive county-wide data on tenurial and farming changes, the diffusion of tenant tree-planting within the county between the years 1790 and 1825 is used to provide a geographical indicator for evaluating the progress of 'improvements' along this one dimension. Over the period of registration from 1790 to 1860, c. 9.5 million trees were planted by county Cork tenants in a variety of situations. Some trees – perhaps two-fifths of the total – were planted in compact blocks for strictly commercial purposes. Tree-planting for (i) shelter belts along the side of the fields, (ii) gardens, avenues and parklands around dwelling-houses and (iii) in hedgerows and ditches each accounted for a further one-fifth of the total. Although ten timber merchants accounted for 14 per cent of the total number of trees planted, 70 per cent of tenants planted fewer than 5,000 trees each. These, then, were the small-scale planters, the people who laid the basis for the present-day farm landscape of hedgerows, shelter-belts, avenues and groves. The evidence is inconclusive about the types of tenant planters involved; work on equivalent sources for south-west Tipperary would suggest that c. 50 per cent of the total number of tenant tree planters were 'working' tenant farmers, c. 25 per cent lesser gentry/middlemen, and c. 25 per cent involved other middle-class rural dwellers such as doctors, parsons, priests, millers and merchants.[39] County Cork probably reflects the same kind of social range, although given the importance of Cork city's merchants in the countryside the proportion of tree planters from this class may have been somewhat higher. In terms of ethnic background, settler names comprise just over 50 per cent of the total. We are, therefore, dealing with a relatively small, well-to-do segment of rural society beneath the landowning class. However, it may well be that the patterns of tree planting revealed in Figure 16.6 may tell us more than might appear at first glance.

This evidence of the distribution and volume of tree-planting can also be used to analyse some other aspects of the geography of rural change in county Cork for this period. Since investment in tree-planting was very much a long-term one, the diffusion of tree-planting is not only an index of landscape change but also provides an indirect measure of the geographical distribution and expansion of rural wealth over the period. The diffusion pattern also no doubt reflects the social aspirations of tree-planting tenants as the fashion of demesne land-scaping was imitated at a different social level and amongst a wider spectrum of society. These patterns also reveal something of the slow evolution of a more comfortable farming class. Such tree-planting records, therefore, provide us with clues to the timing and distribution of new house building and the spread of ornamental gardens and avenues amongst such a comfortable tenant-farming group. It is probably safe to assume that these ornamental patterns may have also been accompanied by internal changes in farm-home arrangements as in the emergence of a separate kitchen area, the development of the kitchen/vegetable garden and the building of barns and stables.

The actual diffusion pattern from 1790 to 1825 is linked to a variety of factors such as varying tenurial structures, landlord patronage, quality of land, size of farms, proximity to towns, access to a range of

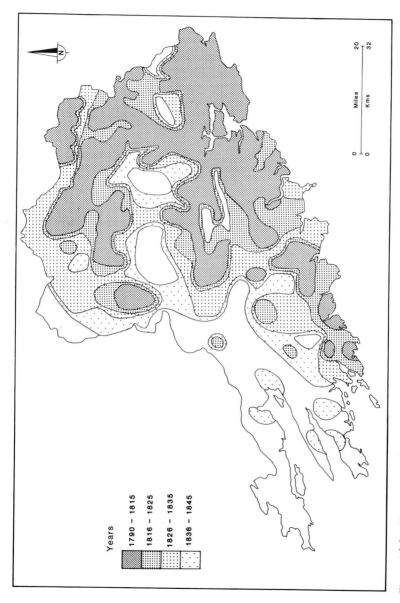

Figure 16.6   Tenant tree-planting, 1790-1845.
Source: N.A., 'A register of trees, county Cork'.

communications, together with physical factors such as altitude and exposure. Yet the picture emerging is not an unsurprising one. The core area is the great mixed-farming/tillage region of Imokilly, flanked by the eastern and south-eastern lowland regions – highlighting that while all Cork regions may have shared in the general upsurge of economic activity for the period, it is probable that the most commercialised tillage areas benefited most. These were the zones of most advanced farming systems and the most stratified rural societies. Other evidence indicates that the immediate Cork city region and the baronies of Imokilly and Barrymore comprise the core zone of the diffusion of cow-house building in the county.[40] The spread of innovating farming societies is also relevant to these processes: Castlemartyr had such a society as far back as the mid-eighteenth century and by the first decade of the nineteenth at least six such societies had emerged in the Carrigaline, Barrymore, Fermoy, Kerrycurrihy, Imokilly and Bandon regions. These societies sought to encourage amongst other matters better-managed farms, better rotations and better ploughing techniques. Although the majority attending an Imokilly Farming Society dinner on 7 December 1813 belonged to the local gentry, a sizeable minority originated from what were called 'working farmers'.[41] The most innovative areas may, therefore, have been the longer-settled zones with the oldest place-names. Imokilly was the most adaptive tillage region, therefore, while the north-Cork lowlands, given their long-distance interaction with the midland grazing areas, were probably leaders in the introduction of new improved cattle breeds; Orrery and Kilmore and Duhallow were also reasonably innovative and whilst slow in the use of cow-houses and stall feeding were also noted for the number of good farmhouses being built in the decade before 1815.[42] The remoter parts of Muskerry were generally later with only the gentry apparently involved in introducing new farming techniques by 1815. The south-coast region – centred on the barony of Ibane and Barryroe – was to retain a highly commercialised yet strongly traditional small-farm ecology with its hard-working and skilful farm populations exhibiting a classic seasonal rhythm in their exploitation of the joint resources of land and sea. Carbery too was certainly to be revitalised during this period via fishing, corn and potato cultivation and flax, pig and poultry production.

These generalisations over-ride, however, the contrasts that existed locally and regionally in both the composition of the farming classes and between the farming and landless elements.[43] For the late eighteenth century had its hidden worlds too; tenant tree-planting zones were almost certainly the areas where the highest proportion of landless labourers were available to provide the necessary muscle power for these and other major transformations in the material landscape. These were also the zones of 'improved' crop rotations and proliferating lime kilns. The lime-burners and the sand-carriers were now – like the craftsmen – adding to the teeming diversity of this colourful world. Likewise improvements in tenant tree-planting may not have been a priority for a majority of tenant farmers – including many comfortable ones – who might have preferred to invest their profits in purchasing more cows than improving the material living conditions in and around the dwelling-house. The growing power and stability of the farming class is perhaps best epitomised by the agrarian 'Rightboy' movements of the 1780s. These more elaborate and sophisticated protest movements which originated in mid-Cork do not reflect the problems of marginalisation but, for the most part, reflect the efforts of a growing tenant farming class to consolidate their hard-won leaseholding positions. In part the movement is also a reaction to the windfall of tithe incomes accruing to the parsons of the established church, their wealth reflected in the proliferation of new glebe houses throughout the region in this expansive era.[44]

The establishment of parish registers across the county is, likewise, a key indicator of the success of the new Catholic church in reorganising its parishes and congregations in the same period.[45] Only 6 per cent of the registers, these mainly in Cork city and other urban parishes, were in place by 1780. By 1815, however, a further 31 per cent of all parish registers in the county had been initiated, along three major axes of development, firstly from the Cork city region north-eastwards through Fermoy to Mitchelstown, secondly all along the south coast from Youghal to Bantry and thirdly extending inland along the Lee Valley in Muskerry. The post-1820 expansion of Catholic parish registers took place in the more upland areas of east, mid- and north Cork as well as in the mainly insular/peninsular worlds of the south-west. The Cork city hinterland and the south coast also led in early big-chapel building with a secondary axis extending north-east to Mitchelstown and outliers in pockets near Charleville and Millstreet. This pattern was not dissimilar to the zones of wealthier mixed/tillage farming reflected in earlier patterns of tenant tree-planting. Other aspects of the cultural geography of the area still remain hidden; further research may reveal the significance of the period for the final crystallisation of the reconstituted parochial territories of a revitalised Catholic church which were so critical in influencing attitudes and behaviours, especially after 1820.

Figure 16.7, although reflecting mid-nineteenth-century patterns, also suggests how literacy in English was advancing not only in the urban centres but also among the more stratified rural populations during the eighteenth century. This may have been particularly characteristic of the more mobile, more leisurely fair-going populations of the commercialised pastoral zones of the interior.[46] English literacy is matched in some areas by the clear emergence of a strong manuscript tradition in Irish. Dr Brendán Ó Conchúir has researched much about the composition, motivations and traditions of these scribes.[47] In distributional terms, the main centres of manuscript activity – apart from some western outliers around old and monastic centres such as Rosscarbery and Timoleague – were to be in mid-Duhallow, much of Orrery and Kilmore, Fermoy, Barrymore and Imokilly baronies with small clusters around the towns of Bandon and Innishannon. Varying rates for manuscript compilation existed for different areas as between the second half of the eighteenth and the first half of the nineteenth centuries and these may reflect space/time variations in levels of literacy and frontiers of contact between English and Irish speakers. It may be relevant to note here that it is again the old settled areas which provide this cultural response – with the scribes generally originating not from the richest or poorest areas but often from the foothills – along the boundary zone, for example, between Imokilly, Kinatalloon and Barrymore baronies in parishes such as Dungourney and Clonmult. The roots of these patterns may be very old indeed but the pattern clearly reflects the response by Irish scribes located along critical cultural frontiers – scholars aware of the need to conserve a literary and linguistic heritage in the face of a rapid process of erosion, poets under pressure, sensing change.[48]

Many of these poets and scribes, however, did not belong to the well-to-do farm families, although in some cases they were patronised by members of this group as well as by some gentry families. Their foothill location and hinge function culturally, however, open the door to another social geography of late eighteenth- and early nineteenth-century Cork – that of population growth, marginalisation and settlement intensification and expansion. Figure 16.8 provides a rough guide to the changing distribution of population between c. 1766 and 1821. Compared to the land values map, it is clear that the poorer areas valued at less than 10 shillings and especially less than 3 shillings per acre bore the brunt of population expansion in this period (Fig. 16.8).

The whole process by which families proliferated, subdivided land, colonised both old grazing lands and new frontier lands still remains to be documented at the intimate local scale. Likewise the significance of both the extent and the often highly fragmented character of individual estate units in understanding the internal migrations of colonising populations also requires attention. Certainly the latter half of

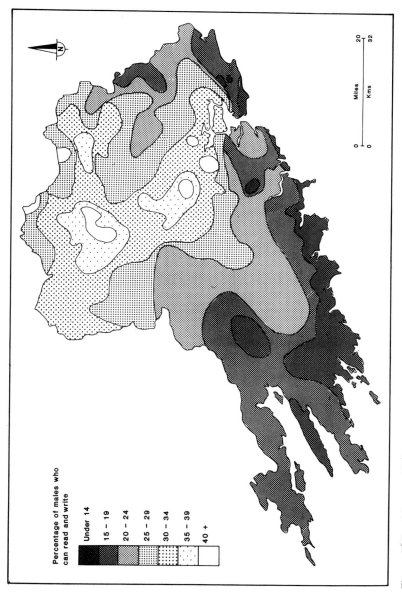

Figure 16.7 Literacy, 1841.
Source: Census.

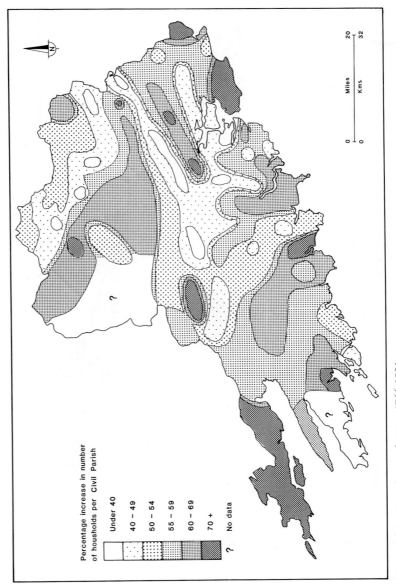

Figure 16.8   Population change, 1766-1821.
Source: reference 26 [1766] and Census [1821].

eighteenth- and the early part of nineteenth-century Cork not only saw such intensification of settlement in the lowlands but also a powerful assault on former upland grazing areas as well as on the remaining boglands and moorlands. The schemes of 'improving' landlords and the collective efforts of kin and neighbourhood groups both played a significant part in the process of land reclamation and the extension of the settlement frontier. For the landlord, population increase and land reclamation were a boon for they augmented the value of his property, while much of the capital needed for colonisation derived from the labour power of the poorer sections of the population – the builders of new roads, ditches, houses, drains and fields. The role of kin and neighbourhood groups in the process may have been particularly important. Here again, the long-established, densely-settled farming communities in *foothill* locations may have provided the crucial resources for permanent as opposed to seasonal utilisation of the uplands, the bogs and indeed in some cases of the coastal zones.

The territorial structures provided by the often scattered estate units and by community networks were of course building on both old and new technologies. The spade was old as were some of the roads. Other roads were new and the potato was relatively new as a field crop; the latter was both the instrument for and the crucial objective in colonising new land while the new roads brought remoter areas nearer to manures, building materials and markets.[49] In summary then, kinship structures and the emphasis on sub-division, landlord initiatives, the centrality of expanding corn/potato rotations, the facility for early marriage in a non-capital intensive economy, the widespread availability of extensively underutilized land or 'wasteland', smallpox inoculation (perhaps) and in some cases, as in the south and south-west, increased flax production and a cottage textile industry and in the coastal zones, the fishing industry – all combined in varying ways in different regions to produce the complex formulae for both the internal expansion and geographical spread of the rural population.

It is not surprising to note that the populations of many urban centres increased (Fig. 16.8). This is especially characteristic of the towns in the most commercialised tillage areas such as Mallow, Fermoy, Youghal, Clonakilty and Kanturk; on the other hand the relatively large industrial town of Bandon was in decline by the 1800s. Secondly, the greatest stability in rural population densities was generally in the long-established farming zones with already complex rural structures – as in the barony of Fermoy, Orrery and Kilmore, the east and west Bride valleys, the Cork harbour region and the inland areas of East Carbery. There is a strong possibility that the major impetus to population increase in these areas derived from the expanding cottier/landless population. Thirdly, significant increases are demonstrated for some of the lowland areas which were broadening their tillage orientations, as for example, east Duhallow, and also the old tillage regions of the southern coastal zone, in particular Imokilly. In this latter zone the more intensive use of marine resources saw both further subdivision and fragmentation in the coastal parishes – already densely populated in the mid-eighteenth century – and this led to population overspill into inland parishes.[50]

Fourthly, the greatest increases were focused on upland regions in west Duhallow, in the mid-Cork uplands and Muskerry and particularly in the West Carbery, Bantry and Beara regions. Expansion here was particularly characteristic of the zone west of Dunmanway, while here again as in Imokilly there is also clear evidence of the expansion inland from the coast as sea-sand carried inland by boats along the Bandon River facilitated and intensified tillage farming as far inland as Innishannon.[51] Up to the 1820s, people were still migrating inland from these densely-settled coastal parishes. Similarly in the Clonakilty-Carbery region, both Townsend and the local parish priest noted the contrasts in population densities in the region thirty/forty years before as compared with the situation *c.* 1810. 'Both furze and heath have fast disappeared and hills deemed unfit for anything but coarse grazing are now cultivated to their very tops'.[52] Yet in this area as in many others further west and north-west there were still extensive tracts of uncultivated land. Some of these virgin lands would also feel the pioneer thrust of the spade when the cruel and turbulent decades of the post-Napoleonic era would drastically affect agricultural conditions – particularly in the lowlands – and bring further pressure and further displacement to bear on the upland edges.

Retrenchment, consolidation and impoverishment: pre-Famine county Cork

After the post-war depression of 1815-20 the days of both sustained and broadly-based economic development and dramatic population growth were coming to an end. The three decades preceeding the Great Famine were a period of often painful adjustment for many sections of society. Most landlords, now often deep in debt, finally gained direct control of all their properties; conversely the long-established intermediate landlord or middleman class was virtually eclipsed. So ended in conflict the relationship between two elements of society whose fortunes and whose territorial powers had been so interlocked over most of the eighteenth century. Tensions also developed between the now substantial section of comfortable tenant farmers and the far greater number of smallholders as an era of farm consolidation was initiated. Above all there now crystallised further divergence and sometimes violent conflict between the interests of the farmers and the cottier/landless labourer class who were dependent on the former for either employment or the letting of potato ground or both. Labourers comprised 60 per cent of the total agricultural population in county Cork by 1821.[53] The origins of sections of this servile class stretch back into the medieval period but there is no doubt that their numbers increased disproportionately from at least the mid-eighteenth century on. Now as agriculture swung away from highly intensive tillage/dairying farming and back to more extensive forms of dairying and stock-rearing, the actual number of job opportunities available to labourers declined precisely at the time when their numbers were increasing most dramatically. These were the general post-war trends, but as one might expect from county Cork such trends worked their way with varying intensities and in varying directions throughout the sub-regions of the county.

In terms of economic change the fairly rapid contraction in overseas markets from 1815 onwards saw significant decline in Cork city's role as a provision centre.[54] In the countryside there was a slow but significant shift in response to these and other market trends favouring beef and sheep rather than over-concentration on tillage farming only. This was of necessity a long-drawn-out process since, amongst other things, the existing population densities and complicated farm structures did not easily facilitate rapid adaptation to the changed economic environment. However, it would appear that by the late 1820s and certainly by the early 1830s the shift to a more extensive farming system was already taking place, particularly on the large mixed farms, which – endowed with ready capital – could operate at a scale which facilitated innovations such as intensifying stock levels through better stock breeding and better systems of tillage cultivation.

At the landlord level, Donnelly describes the era as one of reform in estate administration.[55] This was certainly true of many of the western and northern estates but, as as we have seen, estate reform and a developing estate bureaucracy were already characteristic of many of the larger eastern estates since at least the 1790s. The post-1815 period was above all one of belt-tightening in estate administration – the making of economies in a whole series of areas. Now one sees the emergence of a more vigorous implementation of specific estate policies – firstly the abolition of the remaining intermediate landlords, secondly the consolidation of farm-holdings and related stringent controls attempting to prevent further sub-division and sub-letting, and thirdly the carrying out or the encouragement of the necessary improvements in the infrastructure of the reconstituted tenant farms. By 1851 one can analyse (courtesy of Griffith's valuation) the residual distribution of immediate lessors of land who were not head landlords – providing us with one final snapshot of a highly dynamic middleman leasing pattern which had been changing in form and character throughout the eighteenth and early nineteenth centuries (Fig. 16.9).

The distribution of surviving middlemen in the mid-nineteenth century throws up some surprises. Their expected relative sparsity in the eastern half of the county (although even here it is relevant to note that quite a number of Barry, Coppinger, Power, Wyse and other old families still survived at this middle level)[56] would seem to reflect the trend by landlords of not renewing leases to existing middlemen at an earlier period. However, a great diversity of both estate structures and estate policies could co-exist in close proximity. For example, middlemen were still hanging on in parts of the Midleton estate in the 1840s. The relative sparsity of large leaseholders in the western and north-western half of the county seems more surprising – the progressive elimination of middlemen as leases fell in the 1830s and indeed as late as the mid 1840s saw, as Donnelly has documented, the virtual eclipse of the system on such large estates as those of Kenmare, Bantry, Lisle, Cork and Orrery, Burlington/Devonshire, Colthurst and Aldworth and on smaller estates too as on Benn/Walshe's and the Crownlands'.[57] On the other hand, a landlord like Viscount Lismore, residing on a much larger estate in south-west Tipperary, was still letting his Banteer lands to one intermediate head-tenant.[58] Overall the rapid decline of the middle landlord reflected the emergence of tighter systems of estate administration combined with the traumatic effects of the agricultural depressions of the 1820s and 1840s on the fortunes of the residual middlemen.

Although many large leaseholders had disappeared by the mid-eighteenth century in the central part of the county, their greater relative strength here is also initially surprising. There is no doubt that this group survived and resided in larger numbers and invested more in the larger towns, as at Mallow – and especially in Cork city. Not surprisingly, this city hinterland was also characterised by complex tenurial structures. Property units were generally smaller in the middle zone also (Fig. 16.5). It may well be that unlike the more effective and highly-centralised administration systems of the larger estates, the smaller property owner may have been less able or willing to effect radical changes in their tenancies, and a higher rate of absenteeism may also have characterised this kind of property owner. It may also be possible that in this middle zone of mixed farming par excellence in county Cork – of intensive cattle/dairying/tillage farming – middlemen may have been better able to withstand the shifting economic

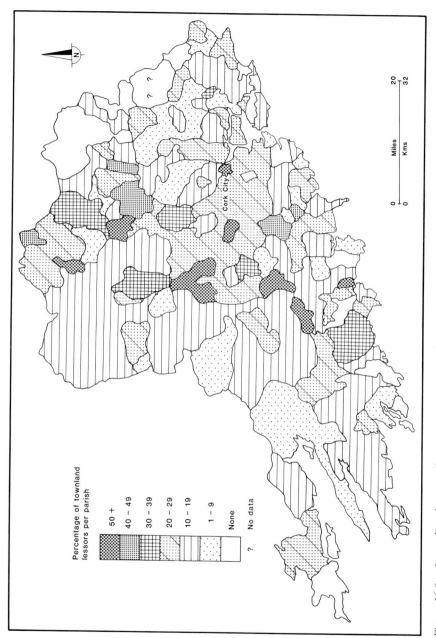

Figure 16.9   Immediate lessors who were not owners in fee, 1851.
Source: Griffith, *Valuation.*

Percentage of townland
lessors per parish

50 +

40 – 49

30 – 39

20 – 29

10 – 19

1 – 9

None

? No data

conditions after 1815. Arthur Young and others were to characterise the middlemen as hard-drinking, fox-hunting squires. It would be interesting to ascertain whether the continued strength of the horse culture and hunting tradition in the central region of county Cork today has anything to do with the life-styles of this middlemen/lesser gentry culture which survived strongly here as late as 1851.

Over the country as a whole, therefore, there is no doubt that the large middle tenant had become a vanishing breed, their substantial farms now often colonised by powerful local families who had adapted most successfully to the changing social and economic climate. It should also be remembered that sub-letting within the townland could and did continue. Quite a number of farmers, both large and small, compensated for falling agricultural prices by renting to the labourer his miserable cabin and his life-sustaining acre of potato ground at exorbitant rates.[59]

Other dimensions of the estate policy involved the consolidation of smaller and sometimes fragmented farms into a series of larger and improved compact holdings run by hard-working tenants with the drive and capacity necessary to innovate – and so provide a landlord with an assured and comfortable income. This programme of con-solidation was often a piecemeal process and was usually carried out with a fair degree of diplomacy, given its mortal consequences for some smallholders. A number of strategies – sometimes in combination – were involved in restructuring farmholdings. The introduction of assisted emigration and the relocation of excluded tenants onto the poor lands within an estate were both characteristic of this period. The remaining sitting tenants were given enlarged reconstituted farms while some of the former tenants remained on, further augmenting the labourer class. Similar processes of reorganisation may well have been operative in the boom period of the grazing economy over the middle half of the eighteenth century. Other displaced tenants were gravitating towards the now bloated villages and towns whose back-lane pauper populations increased at a dramatic rate between the 1820s and the famine. Others were augmenting the ragged band now establishing frontier upland and peninsular settlements on some of the poorest lands in Europe.

The incidence of partnership and non-partnership farming regions shows, in part, how successful landlords and their agents had been in creating and/or maintaining viable farm structures in the better lands of the county (Fig. 16.10). However, there is little doubt that these extensive regions of viable compact holdings and more stable social structures developed over a much longer period. Whatever about their origins, it is also clear that these farms witnessed a continued acceleration in farm improvements relating to rotations, farm buildings and hedging, including greater use of central chimneys, bed-chambers, more comfortable rooms, good glass windows and more slated roofs.[60] The diffusion of tenant tree-planting for the period 1825-1845 highlights the renewal of processes begun in the late eighteenth century and hints again at both the continuing numerical and geographical expansion in the power and wealth of a more comfortable lease-holding farming class (Fig. 16.6).

In this later phase we now see a gradual but significant shift in the location of tree-planting and landscape embellishment to the middle-western and more upland parts of the county. In part this changing pattern is a product of distance-decay factors operating on the spread of information relating to the registration and planting of trees. Secondly, tree-planting among the better-off leaseholding farmers in most of the north-east and south-east had already reached saturation stage by the 1820s. But it is also tempting to see it as illustrating the greater prosperity of the beef cattle/dairying regions, when the swing in farm prices came to favour these producers, particularly after the 1820s. Whatever the process at work, we have further evidence of material and structural consolidation of rural middle-class farmers – a class considerably influenced by the life-styles of the lesser gentry and who are now often building smaller replicas of their houses and avenues. We have here a hybrid cultural group who are also associated by marriage ties, social context and life-styles with the now more powerful native shopkeeping and professional classes in the town. Here too we have the backbone of a resurgent Catholic church in Cork which in these decades saw c. 70 per cent of its nineteenth-century parish churches built or rebuilt and which saw 53 per cent of its parish priests organise detailed parish registers for the first time.

Other innovations were also beginning to characterise these well-to-do farming regions in pre-famine decades which also threatened the whole balance of the traditional social structures. The use of artificial grasses and clover, the intensification of pastoral production, the replacement of the old spade/ridge culture by drilling methods, the improvement of grain output by better ploughing and tilling techniques now all became more characteristic.[61] The scotch-swing plough and the scythe represent only two of the many new kinds of farm equipment that were creeping in. All of these innovations were to threaten further the livelihoods and in the long run the lives of the labouring and cottier classes. There were 141,000 agricultural labourers in county Cork in 1841 as compared with a total of 41,000 farmers. As Burke has illustrated, the great concentrations of this class (that is, the areas where labourers came to comprise more than 60 per cent of the total male

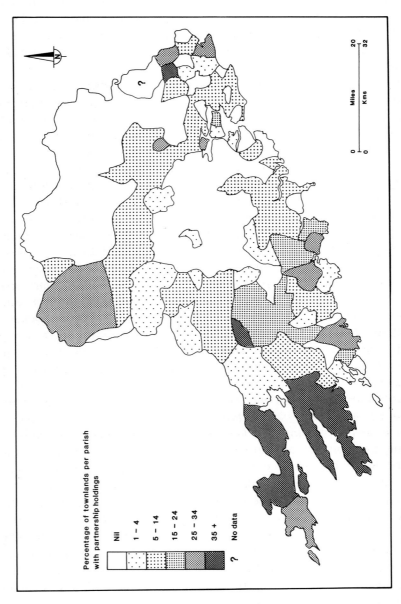

Figure 16.10 Fragmented farms, 1851.
Source: Griffith, *Valuation.*

working population) were for the most part in the long-settled commercialised farming regions in Orrery and Kilmore, the western part of
Fermoy barony, around Fermoy town and the east Bride valley, the
central and northern part of Imokilly, East Muskerry south to the
Bandon and Clonakilty areas with an outlier of labourer concentrations
centred on Millstreet and Kanturk.[62] Apart from this latter region, where
it would appear that the tillage economy was still expanding at the
expense of a grazing one in the 1830s, all these zones were areas of
population stabilisation or decline in the two decades before the
famine and also areas of great social extremes. The comfortable farmers
of these regions – who provided different categories of labourers with
either permanent or seasonal employment – were characterised by
marriage and inheritance patterns which stressed foresight, thrift and
the maintenance of both viable farm entities and family status. In
contrast, previous decades had seen the numbers of the labourer
classes augmented both from within and through the de-classed sons
and daughters of smaller holders. In these long-settled zones, there was
no opportunity for colonising marginal lands. The shift towards more
extensive pastoral farming was not only curtailing employment opportunities but was also leading to the shrinking of the area of potato
ground available as the corn acre/potato rotation now became less
relevant to the farming community. Competition within this class and
conflict with the farming world therefore became increasingly fierce
and endemic. As a consequence of all these processes, there is a strong
possibility that mortality rates rose and fertility levels were reduced
amongst underemployed labourer families who were now often on the
verge of starvation.[63]

There were, however, regional differences in living conditions
amongst the labouring population. In the traditionally strong tillage
regions as in the Fermoy, Castletownroche, Bride valley and Imokilly
areas, the labouring population was in a somewhat more secure and
stable position.[64] In contrast desperate living conditions often characterised this group in the traditional pastoral zones which had been
slowest to shift towards a commercialised tillage economy during the
buoyant years of the revolutionary Napoleonic wars – and who were
now swiftly reverting to traditional pastoral pursuits and ruthlessly
jettisoning their tillage labourers in the process. This was particularly
the case in the north-Cork lowlands of east Duhallow, Orrery and
Kilmore and parts of the Fermoy, Condons and Clangibbon baronies
with their highly-stratified rural societies and with towns in 1841 which
were characterised by the highest proportion of under-employed
agricultural labourers in the whole county, characteristics shared with
similar pastoral regions in east Limerick and central county Meath.[65]

There was always a substantial overlap between the areal concentration of well-to-do lowland farmers and landless labourers. In
contrast, Figure 16.10 also highlights farming regions where landless
labourers were much less conspicuous and where the working of the
land (and the sea) was dependent on the cooperation of kin and
neighbourhood groups. Partnership farming is here defined as where
the Griffith valuation entries indicate that a joint return is made by a
group of farmers – usually smallholders – of the rateable valuation (and
presumably the landlord's rent). These partnership groups may
encompass a townland or part of a townland. The actual working
patterns associated with these units might involve joint arrangements
for the common utilisation of certain resources such as grazing or bogland (or those of the sea), while also involving agreed systems of
cooperation in the working of the individually-held, if often scattered,
tillage plots. Some of these territorial arrangements in the working of
the land may have been quite old, but a comparison of partnership
farming areas with the zones of Ireland's population increase from the
second half of the eighteenth century would suggest that many of these
partnership groups developed as a product of the excessive population
pressure on limited land resources over this exceptional period. These
too were the zones which over the eighteenth and early nineteenth
centuries were still characterised by traditional estate structures
involving a hierarchy of middlemen – often local in origin – and a less
commercialised farming ethos. The north-western and particularly the
south-western distribution is therefore a predictable one. However,
estate policies elsewhere may also have contributed – the Midleton and
Inchiquin estates long tolerated partnership-farming systems in this
world of skilled tillage farmers.[66] Likewise along the southern coastal
zone generally, sharp contrasts exist between the policies of different
adjacent estates; on the Becher estate (including Cape Clear),
partnership-clustered settlements were reorganised in the 1830s[67] while,
close by, other estates were far more tolerant and/or more neglectful of
these systems of farming. Above all, it is the insular-peninsular world of
the Skull-Kilcrohane-Beara region which displays the most densely-
populated clustered settlements and the most complex partnership
arrangements in the organisation of land-use and work rhythms. This
was the only real small-farming culture zone in the whole county. Joint
farming (not always necessarily by the extended kin group) was
therefore most deeply embedded in this world where marine resources
were most extensively used. Mining developments were also to swell
further many of these larger, clusters while seasonal migration to the
richer areas of east Cork and Munster offered an additional source of
income which further sustained these extraordinary population

densities up to the famine years – densities of south-east Asian rather than west-European proportions.

The distribution of individually-held farms which were, however, worked in fragmented lots mirrors the partnership pattern (Fig. 16.11). It is more extensive in distribution, since this category may also include groups of individually-held compact farms which, given their location, also involve joint sharing in the non-adjacent resources of sea, bog or mountain. Consequently this distribution extends more deeply inland along the upland ridges and is even more conspicuous along the coast. Here, as with quite a number of partnership arrangements, we have some examples of peripheral colonisation and enclosure of former open grazing lands and, like the surviving examples of partnership farming, some of these zones may also have depended on cooperative farming groups whose labour was the most critical asset in colonising some of these areas of difficulty. Others, especially along the south coast, reflected older tenurial arrangements with their roots in the medieval period.

Pre-Famine Cork was therefore characterised by great variations and extremes of settlement and social structures – patterns, as we have seen, which had been much influenced by the age and density of settlement. Not only were there contrasts in the arrangement, size and structure of rural settlements in the different regions of the county but there were also significant regional differences in the demographic structures and rates of population change in this period. Deady has analysed population changes in the county between 1821 and 1841.[68] Much of the population growth is focused, as one would have predicted from Figure 16.8, on the upland mountain districts, including the mountains to the north, but there is no simple correlation between patterns of population change amongst lowland rural cultures. Population densities were relatively low and population changes negligible in the Bandon, Fermoy and Orrery and Kilmore regions but there was still high population growth in the rich lowlands of Roches county, south Imokilly and east Duhallow. Likewise, there was no simple correlation between farm size and population growth. The populations of small farm areas along the south coast and around Fermoy were stabilising while those of south-west Carbery and south Imokilly were still increasing. Equally the large-farm regions of Duhallow and West Muskerry exhibited rapid population growth while stability or even decline had now come to characterise the bigger-farm regions of Bandon, Kinalea, East Carbery, Barretts, north Imokilly and the Orrery and Kilmore regions.

Overall, the most dramatic increases were still taking place in upland and coastal peninsular areas – in the upland north-east, in the north-

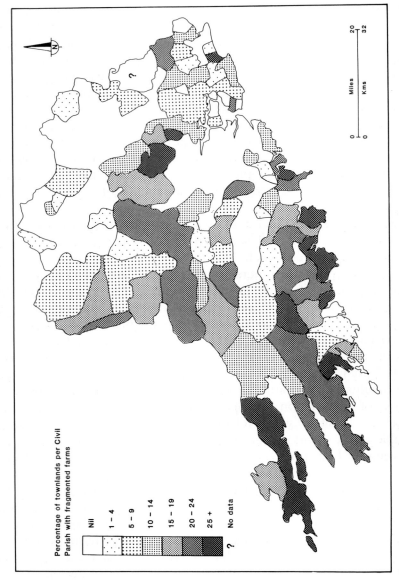

Figure 16.11 Partnership farming, 1851.
Source: Griffith, *Valuation.*

west and west and in some of the central upland ridges but in particular in the lands of south-west Cork. It is relevant here to refer back to the maps of partnership and fragmented farming systems (Figs. 16.10 and 16.11) and to note how closely they compare to these zones of late high population growth, reflecting the vitality of the twin processes of sub-division and joint reclamation in the poorest lands of the county. These were the areas where there was it much unenclosed land, however marginal in quality, which could still be colonised. Such opportunities for colonisation were no longer available in the longer-settled regions of the county. This final settlement frontier was built on the momentum of population growth from previous decades, on the availability of land to be colonised and it took place among the communities where property controls were much less powerful and where checks on the age at marriage were not an inbuilt feature of the culture. In short, these were the zones of the most youthful populations in all of Cork. This youthful population was a colonising one and the colonial frontier was full of young people.

There was one further crucial technological factor in the 1820s. These late colonial zones often had been neglected by absentee land-lords, middlemen and grand juries. Now the central state and its engineers like the young Griffith intervened in the turbulent 1820s to drive a new series of roads through such remote and unsettled areas, as in the extensive areas of west Duhallow.[69] This process was complemented by the greater elaboration of the secondary and tertiary road systems in the far west, the south-west and south coasts as new lines were forged between the central spine of roads created or improved in the second half of the eighteenth and early nineteenth centuries. Mizen Head was connected to the main road network by 1835 and Allihies on the Beara peninsula by 1837.[70] Along the coast many new minor roads were driven into the interior – into parishes like Ballyvourney, Drinagh and Kilmeen – and so helped to transport the lime-rich sea sands inland to the sour acidic slopes of these parishes.

These wedges of new roads breaking into formerly unenclosed or sparsely populated regions provided the impetus for continuing colonisation which saw more of county Cork's territory enveloped by permanent settlement than had ever been witnessed before or since. The lithographs of the *Illustrated London News* with their tragic and graphic portrayals of famine deaths around Skibbereen and the Mizen brought England's and Europe's attention to the enormity of the tragedy unfolding in Ireland and in Cork in particular.[71] These awful events also marked the end of the explosive population and settlement expansion into the most marginal lands of the county. The traumatic processes of the Great Famine were to work their way across the highly diverse social and physical topographies of county Cork with varying levels of intensity. That is another and very complicated story.[72]

References

1. *West Cork resource survey*, An Foras Talúntais (Dublin, 1963).
2. J. Lee and S. Diamond, *The potential of Irish land for livestock production*, An Foras Talúntais (Dublin, 1972).
3. G. Martin, 'Plantation boroughs in medieval Ireland, with a handlist of boroughs to *c.* 1500' in Harkness and O'Dowd, *Town,* pp 23-54; B. J. Graham, 'The towns of medieval Ireland' in Butlin, *Town* pp 28-57, especially pp 56-57.
4. W. J. Smyth, 'Society and settlement in seventeenth century Ireland – the evidence of the "1659 Census" ' in *Common ground*, pp 55-62.
5. MacCarthy-Morrogh, *Plantation,* especially pp 244-286; idem, 'The English presence in early seventeenth century Munster' in Gillespie and Brady, *Natives and newcomers*, pp 171-190.
6. W. J. Smyth 'Exploration of place' in J. J. Lee (ed.), *Ireland: towards a sense of place* (Cork, 1985), pp 8-12.
7. N.A., Chancery Rolls, 1293-1773 (for county Cork), Abstract of grants of fairs and markets in Ireland.
8. Watson, *Almanack*, 1734-39, 1760-64, 1790 and 1814.
9. N.A., MS I.D.I.25, A register of trees, county Cork (2 vols). See also D. P. McCracken and E. McCracken, 'A register of trees, Co. Cork 1790-1860' in *Cork Hist. Soc. Jn.,* xxxi (1976), pp 39-60, (hereafter, 'Register of trees').
10. Dickson, 'Cork region', chapter 8; *Abstract of answers and returns, county of Cork under the Regulation Act of Ireland 1821* (Dublin, 1821), pp 148-180; *Census of Population*, Ireland, 1841.
11. Smith, *Cork* (4th ed., 2 vols); Townsend, *Cork*, (2nd. ed., 2 vols); Burke, 'Cork'; Donnelly, *Land and people*; J. Deady, 'Population growth in county Cork 1815-45', unpublished M.A. thesis, U.C.C. (1974); Dickson, 'Cork region'.
12. Smith, *Cork*; Petty, *Hib. Del.*
13. D. Dickson, 'Eighteenth-century county Cork', unpublished lecture to Cork Historical and Archaeological Society, 30 Jan. 1979; Dickson, 'Cork region', chapter 5.
14. Anon. [J. Mockler], 'A report on the state of the district around Mallow in 1775' in *Cork. Hist. Soc. Jn.,* xxi (1918), pp 17-29; Burke, 'Eighteenth-century Cork'.
15. Watson, *Almanack*.
16. C. Vallancey, 'A military survey of the south part of Ireland, part I, 1778', B.L., Map Division, M. 51, 31-2, and accompanying report, p. 8. See also J. K. Hourihan, 'Town growth in west Cork: Bantry 1600-1960' in *Cork Hist. Soc. Jn.,* lxxxii (1977), pp 83-97.
17. Smith, *Cork*, pp 87-89, 152-153, 202-3; Cullen, *Emergence*, chapter 9 and especially pp 194-198.
18. Smith, *Cork*, pp 319-20.
19. D. Dickson, 'Property and social structure in eighteenth-century south Munster' in Cullen and Furet, *Ireland and France,* pp 129-138; Cullen, *Emergence*, pp 83-108; Dickson, 'Cork region', chapter 3.
20. W. J. Smyth, 'Estate records and the making of the Irish landscape: an example from County Tipperary' in *Ir. Geog.*, ix (1976), pp 29-49.
21. Vallancey, 'A military survey.'

22. Dickson, 'Property', pp 129-131; see also his 'Cork region', chapter 2.

23. Griffith, *Valuation* (barony volumes for county Cork); D. Dickson, 'Cork region', chapter 2; J. O'Shea, 'The historical geography of the Kenmare estate', unpublished M.A. thesis, U.C.C. (1990).

24. J. O'Shea, 'Kenmare estate'; Dickson, 'Middlemen' in T. Bartlett and D. W. Hayton (ed.), *Penal era and golden age: essays in Irish history* (Belfast, 1979), pp 162-185.

25. Smith, *Cork*, pp 158-161.

26. The following discussion is based on (a) N.A., MS M2476, Hearth tax returns, 1764-5 for county Cork and (b) N.A., MS M4921, Revd B. O'Keeffe manuscript returns (1904) of diocesan census Cork, Cloyne and Ross (1766).

27. Cullen, *Emergence*, pp 193-209 and pp 199-202; P. O'Flanagan, 'Urban minorities and majorities: Catholics and Protestants in Munster towns *c.* 1659-1850' in *Common ground*, pp 124-148.

28. N.A., MS M2476, Hearth tax returns, 1764-5.

29. N.A., MS M4921, O'Keeffe manuscript returns, part iv, A pastoral letter of the Most Revd John O'Brien, D.D., Lord Bishop of Cloyne and Ross, p. 545. See also list of registered priests of diocese of Cloyne, pp 523-528.

30. Vallancey, 'A military survey', introduction, pp 11-12.

31. Ibid., p. 20.

32. T. Sherrard, Manuscript survey of the estate of Sir John Freke 1787-88 (Church of Ireland, Rosscarbery, county Cork).

33. S. Ní Cinnéide, 'A new view of Cork city' in *Cork. Hist. Soc. Jn.*, lxxvii (1973), pp 1-13 and pp 117-123; see also idem, 'A Frenchman's impression of county Cork in 1790' in *Cork. His. Soc. Jn.*, lxxix (1974), pp 14-25.

34. Dickson, 'Cork region', chapter 7; see also his 'Property'.

35. Smyth 'Estate records', pp 38-47; Dickson 'Middlemen', pp 181-185 and idem, 'Cork region', chapter 4.

36. Sources for list of late eighteenth- and early nineteenth-century estate surveys for County Cork in Hayes, *Sources*, vii, pp 207-217.

37. Dickson, 'Cork region', chapter 4; Smyth, 'Estate records', pp 38-47.

38. Donnelly, *Land and people*, pp 12-13. See also his *Landlord and tenant in nineteenth-century Ireland* (Dublin, 1973).

39. 'A register of trees, county Cork'; W. J. Smyth, 'The greening of Ireland – thoughts on the diffusion of tenant tree-planting 1765-1900', unpublished paper to Conference of Irish Geographers, Galway, 1977.

40. Townsend, *Cork*, i; pp 187-230.

41. *The Munster farmers magazine* (Cork, 1813-14), pp 252-60.

42. Townsend, *Cork*, pp 396-445; Dickson, 'Cork region', chapter 5.

43. Cullen, *Emergence*, pp 104-108.

44. J. S. Donnelly, Jnr, 'The Whiteboy movement 1761-5' in *I.H.S.*, xxi (1978), pp 20-54. See also his 'The Rightboy movement 1785-88' in *Stud. Hib.*, xviii (1977-8), pp 120-202; Townsend, *Cork*, pp 169-186.

45. The following interpretation is based on an analysis of the manuscript index to register of parishes for Catholic dioceses of Cork, Cloyne and Ross, in N.A., MS M4921.

46. Townsend, *Cork,* p. 8, and pp 269-270.

47. Ó Conchúir, *Scríobh Chorc*, especially pp 192-229.

48. S. Ó Tuama, *Filí faoi sceimhle* (Baile Átha Cliath, 1978). See also L. M. Cullen, *'The hidden Ireland' – reassessment of a concept* (Mullingar, 1987).

49. Burke, 'Cork'.

50. A. Power, 'Agricultural geography of the barony of Imokilly in the nineteenth

century', unpublished B.A. dissertation, U.C.D. (1972); see also T. Jones Hughes, 'Society and settlement in nineteenth-century Ireland' in *Ir. Geog.*, v, pt. 2 (1965), pp 79-96.

51. Townsend, *Cork*, i, pp 360-61.

52. Townsend, *Cork*, i, pp 266-268.

53. *Census of Ireland*, (Dublin, 1821).

54. J. O'Brien, *The Catholic middle classes in pre-famine Cork* (Dublin, 1980); J. Keane, 'A tale of four cities – social, economic and political geography of Cork city 1780-1846', unpublished M.A. thesis, U.C.C. (1990).

55. Donnelly, *Land and people*, pp 9-14, 52-72.

56. See Griffith, *Valuation* (barony volumes for Barrymore, Fermoy and Imokilly).

57. Donnelly, *Land and people*, pp 50-63. See also his 'The journals of Sir John Benn-Walsh relating to the management of his Irish estates 1823-64' in *Cork Hist. Soc. Jn.*, lxxix (1974), pp 86-123.

58. Smyth, 'Estate records', pp 29-49.

59. Donnelly, *Land and people*, pp 26-44.

60. Cullen, *Emergence*, pp 29-50, 99-113; see also *Life in Ireland*, (London, 1968) and Dickson, 'Cork region', chapter 5.

61. T. P. O'Neill, *Life and tradition in rural Ireland* (London,1977); Donnelly, *Land and people*, pp 19-22; Smyth, 'Estate records', pp 39-49.

62. Burke, 'Cork', especially chapter on 'The mid-nineteenth century'.

63. Burke, 'Cork', pp 167-181; S. Ó Tuama, 'Dánta droch-shaoil 1800-1845', unpublished M.A. thesis, U.C.C. (1946).

64. Burke 'Cork', chapter 5; Donnelly, *Land and people*, pp 26-44.

65. H. Mason, 'The development of the urban pattern in Ireland, 1841-81' (3 vols.), unpublished Ph.D. thesis, National University of Wales (1969).

66. Donnelly, *Land and people*, pp 12-16; Dickson, 'Cork region', chapter 5.

67. C. Ó Síocháin, *The man from Cape Clear*, translated from the Irish by R. P. Breathnach (Dublin, 1975), pp 1-24 and especially pp 23-24.

68. Deady, 'Population growth'.

69. J. H. Andrews, 'Road planning in Ireland before the railway age' in *Irish Geog.*, v, pt. 1 (1964), pp 17-41.

70. J. J. Hourihan, 'Migration and settlement on the Muintervarra peninsula', unpublished M.A. thesis, U.C.C. (1974); Andrews, 'Road planning'.

71. C. Woodham-Smith, *The great hunger – Ireland 1845-49* (London, 1965), especially pp 418-422.

72. Donnelly, *Land and people*, pp 73-131; Woodham-Smith, *The great hunger*.

Chapter 17

POPULATION, POLITICS AND SOCIETY IN CORK, 1780-1900

JOHN B. O'BRIEN

The population of Cork city did not change much between 1821, the year of the first census, and the end of the century. It oscillated around 80,000, rising in the 1840s and again in the 1880s, but even then the increases were not spectacular.[1] This was in stark contrast to the striking 250 per cent increase during the eighteenth century.[2] Still, in the national context Cork more than held its own in the nineteenth century. While Ireland's population dropped by more than 40 per cent between 1841 and 1891 Cork's declined by only 6 per cent and in fact was still ahead of Belfast until 1841 but, of course, was far outstripped by the latter city in the second half of the century when, against the national trend, Belfast more than trebled between 1841 and 1891.[3] However, the apparent stability of Cork's population throughout the nineteenth century conceals the fact that, in terms of natural increase, Cork was declining from at least 1841 onwards. Had it not been for the influx of people from elsewhere in Ireland and abroad it undoubtedly would have registered a substantial population drop in the second half of the century.

Regrettably, the census enumerators did not distinguish between Cork city and Cork county so that we do not know the extent of migration from the county into the city. In the light of the consolidation of rural holdings in county Cork, where the percentage of those over thirty acres in 1841 was nearly double that of the national average,[4] and due to the more extensive grazing which accompanied those structural changes, there is no reason to doubt that a substantial number of these dispossessed country people found their way into the city. For many it would have been an alternative to emigration. In the city they would have joined those born elsewhere in Ireland and abroad, 5,224 in 1841 rising to 10,930 by 1901, or from 6.5 per cent of the population to 14.4 per cent.[5]

During the nineteenth century migration into Cork owed less to the city's economic prospects that it did to the depressed rural situation which forced people to leave. Further, because of the prevailing prosperity within the city, especially in the second half of the eighteenth century and up until the 1820s, Cork was attractive for prospective migrants. Dr Dickson, the historian of eighteenth-century Cork, has concluded that the 'most plausible explanation of the region's demographic transformation is that a traditionally high birth rate was accompanied by a fairly low death rate over long periods of time. The rarity of subsistence crises in the eighteenth century does not mean that the general level of health was particularly satisfactory or that the adult life expectancy was great, only that with one exception major reverses were absent'.[6] From around 17,500 in 1706, Cork's population had grown to 41,000 in 1750 and then to a striking 80,000 by 1821.[7] While that population was a major influence in Cork's development, it in turn benefitted from the city's growing prosperity, especially in the later eighteenth century.

The area contiguous to Cork city is not blessed with natural resources; it has no coal, no iron ore, nor has the city ever been an administrative centre of consequence. For these reasons it has had to rely on its harbour and on its hinterland for its economic momentum, though once growth was under way the city's prosperity was enhanced by the range of the commercial and professional services which it then provided. It was indeed fortunate for Cork that its commercial development, especially external, in the eighteenth century was matched by a corresponding expansion in domestic production. It was this feature which distinguished Cork from its northern rival, Belfast, and from its southern neighbour, Waterford. The latter averaged 38,302 tons of shipping per annum through its port between 1776 and 1800 compared with 96,680 tons for Cork during the same period.[8] Still, Cork's population was more than treble that of Waterford when comparable figures became available for both cities in 1821.[9]

But these factors do not in themselves explain the dramatic improvement in Cork's fortunes relative to Waterford from the middle of the eighteenth century. It could be argued that Waterford with its excellent harbour and its fertile hinterland should have equally prospered; it also had the advantage of being closer to Britain, of possessing an extensive estuary stretching far inland due to the confluence of the Rivers Suir and Barrow, while in medieval times it had been the second city in the country.[10] Why the difference then between the two cities?

Growth
Cork's ascendancy was due to a combination of factors: human, institutional, geographic and traditional. Waterford may have been closer to Britain but its proximity to Dublin, equally close to Britain, placed a formidable competitor in the way of its development. Cork

Plate 17.1   Cork Harbour, c. 1840 by G.M.W. Atkenson (Crawford Municipal Art Gallery/Cork V.E.C.).

had little to fear from that quarter since it was further away and because of the nature of its hinterland it was shielded from Dublin competition. Cork's agricultural catchment area was more geared to pasture than to tillage. Being deep-soiled and so well suited for grass, it was ideal for cattle rearing, both dry and dairying, whereas the lands adjacent to Waterford, in that county and in Wexford, being light-soiled, were best tilled. Corn prices were admittedly buoyant in the second half of the eighteenth century, but because of transport difficulties much of the corn grown in Waterford's hinterland was milled in rural flour mills, ultimately finding its way to Dublin bakeries. It was otherwise with Cork's agricultural staples. Cattle could be moved even on foot, despite the bad roads, allowing Cork abattoirs to draw supplies from as far north as Tipperary, as far west as Limerick and also from parts of county Kerry. The dairy herds of the Lee and the Bandon valleys ensured a steady supply of butter for the Cork Butter Market as well as an ample supply of pigs for Cork pork butchers. In the course of the eighteenth century Cork merchants recognised these natural advantages and were not slow in exploiting them. The Cork Butter Market, a traditional dealing market, was reorganised in 1769 in response to complaints about the quality of Cork butter, and a Committee of Merchants was established which for a hundred years maintained strict control over the running of the market, especially the grading of its products.[11] By 1789 the Cork market accounted for nearly 50 per cent of all Irish butter exports.[12] In the case of beef, exports through Cork reached a peak of 58.6 per cent of the Irish total in 1789 though the decline after that date, especially in the late 1790s, conceals the fact that the provisioning of the British fleet in Cork harbour was not recorded in the export figures[13] (they still need to be extracted from Admiralty records in London). Pork exports reached their peak in 1784 with 59.1 per cent of Irish exports passing through Cork in that year[14] but, as in the case of beef, the decline in pork exports in the 1790s may well be attributed to the demands of the fleet in Cork port for provisions which means that output was well maintained.

However striking the advances made in the provisioning trade and in exports, it was Cork's eminence in textiles which especially distinguished her from her southern neighbour in the last quarter of the eighteenth century. The employment opportunities provided in the textile industry were the main outlets for Cork's growing population. Food processing had less employment potential. In the yarn-spinning sector of the industry Dr Dickson has calculated that between 15,000 and 20,000 spinners were employed in the Cork region catering for the export market, and he suggests that another 4,000 to 5,000 were working for the home market.[15] Developments in that industry at the end of the eighteenth century were able to build on a textile tradition in the Cork region extending back into the seventeenth century or earlier. It was a feature of the genius of Cork, at least until the end of the eighteenth century, that producers were able to move from one line to another, depending on the state of the market; in the early eighteenth century the emphasis was on the production of frieze and worsted yarn, but when that trade declined 'some of the displaced wool spinners became hand spinners for cotton, others found more enduring employment as cotton weavers, and former combers were able to work in jenny-shops instead'.[16] The same was true of the linen industry. That industry found a ready outlet in the sail-cloth required by visiting vessels in need of an overhaul, but it was not confined to them. Exports of linen cloth rose dramatically at the end of the eighteenth century, increasing from 280,000 yards in 1780 to 1,540,000 yards in 1816.[17]

But these spectacular endogenous developments cannot be isolated from the impact which foreign trade had through the port of Cork. Custom receipts grew from about £50,000 per annum in the 1750s to over £200,000 by the end of the century.[18] While this was so, it was indeed paradoxical that the local agents engaged in the export trade were far more passive than their domestically-orientated counterparts. Exporters responded to demand; they seldom created it, nor for that matter did they risk their capital in foreign ventures. Unlike their fellow merchants catering for the local market who were prepared to lend money to their farmer suppliers during the growing season, the exporters were invariably commission agents, engaged by principals in England, France or even further afield. Their most important client was the British government, in particular the Admiralty and the Treasury. Up until 1782, Cork was the sole centre for provisioning navy and army supply ships and even after that concession was withdrawn Cork still supplied nearly two-thirds of the wet provisions. Dr Dickson attributes that monopoly to the fact 'that Cork absentee landowners – the Southwells and the second Earl of Egmont – held high office in the Admiralty'.[19] In fact the 'Navy Board opposed the lobby by other ports to become supplementary provisioning agents'. But Cork was not entirely dependent on military provisioning; its worldwide export trade, built up in the course of the eighteenth century, ensured that Cork had alternative outlets for its products should its Admiralty contracts fail. The success of that business can be attributed to Cork's strategic location for ships employed in the Atlantic trade, especially the American trade.[20] In 1794 Cork exported 80 per cent, or 22,500 tons, of all Irish beef going to America. In 1795 it supplied the countries on the American continent with 91.5 per cent of their Irish butter, or 20,101[21] tons, while in 1799 Cork provided nearly 100 per cent of (redundant) Irish pork going to America, or 15,000 tons.[22] In addition, it had a lucrative trade in butter with Portugal, amounting to an average of 24,000 tons per annum between 1783 and 1800.[23]

Decline

But it was not to last. The future which had looked so assured at the turn of the nineteenth century was soon to give way to one of the most depressed eras in Cork's history. Factories were to close, trading was to decline, unemployment was to rise, living conditions were to deteriorate, disease was to become rampant with one major outbreak in 1832 sweeping away hundreds of Cork's inhabitants. The bonanza of the late eighteenth century was to prove ephemeral.

A number of processes can be cited for this decline, any of which would have adverse effects but the combination of all in so short a time was to prove disastrous. Perhaps the most important of these was the depression which beset Cork's agricultural hinterland after 1818 when prices in Britain for agricultural produce dropped sharply. Between 1818 and 1822 grain prices were halved,[24] while prices of beef and pork fell by about one-third between 1812-15 and 1821-25.[25] A depressed agricultural hinterland inevitably had adverse repercussions for Cork; the fall in farmer demand inevitably led to a contraction of the textile, leather and even liquor industries. But this was compounded by the collapse of British demand, especially for Cork provisions. With the ending of the Napoleonic wars and the dispersal of the British navy the provision trade of Cork declined. The growing export trade in live cattle was slight compensation, as it contributed little to the local urban economy; while the sales yards may have been throbbing with life, the butchers, the packagers, the provision merchants and even the coopers suffered because of the demise of the meat trade. These also suffered from the return to gold in 1819 and the re-establishment of the convertibility of Irish bank notes into gold. A contraction of credit ensued especially among those banks which had over-extended themselves during the heady days of the Napoleonic wars. The banks that were unable to accomplish this adjustment invariably failed, with seven of the fourteen Munster and Kilkenny banks closing their doors during those years. According to L. M. Cullen, 'from a peak of between £1.3 to £1.5 million in 1813, the circulation of private bank notes in the south fell to between £400,000 to £500,000 in 1823'.[26] When the Irish pound was raised to parity with sterling in 1826, the impact was exceptionally deflationary because of the apparent 20 per cent overvaluation of the Irish currency. The most telling blow had fallen in 1824 when, after a respite of twenty-four years, Irish industry was at last exposed to the full brunt of the commercial clauses of the Act of Union. It then experienced the full blast of British competition and as this unfortunately coincided with a sharp and severe slump in Britain, following the repeal of the Bubble Act in 1825, more than the usual quota of British manufactured goods were dumped on the Irish market at ruinous prices.

The impact of these developments on Cork was devastating. The textile industry suffered most; in fact it was all but decimated. By 1833 there was only one manufacturer of woollens and only two worsted-spinning and stuff manufacturers of any consequence in the city.[27] This rout had particularly serious repercussions for Blackpool, the traditional textile centre in Cork. It led to an era of unprecedented poverty and destitution in that area of the city and eventually to the clearing of many of the unsanitary hovels located there. The linen industry suffered from the reduced number of fleets using Cork harbour. Soap manufacturers were also hit by the decrease in the slaughtering of cattle while the manufacturers of candles were adversely affected for the same reason.[28]

Of the industries to survive, by far the most significant was tanning. Cork leather was of high quality and was readily exported. In 1835 there were possibly forty-six tan yards in various parts of the city, the most extensive being located in the North Gate vicinity where there were 615 tanners in constant employment.[29] The average number of hides tanned annually amounted to 110,000 and from 1835 onwards tanners found it necessary to import hides from as far afield as Montevideo and Gibraltar in order to supplement local supplies.[30]

Brewing and distilling could still call on the abundant corn crops for their raw materials and like the leather industry these continued to prosper, as yet unhampered by Father Mathew's temperance campaign. In 1835 Cork city distillers were producing 1,400,000 gallons of whisky annually. They were processing 268,000 barrels of corn and were employing about 1,000 men. The quantity of whisky shipped at the port in that year was 1,279 puncheons. Among the twenty-eight breweries found in the city and county of Cork in 1835, by far the largest was Messrs Beamish and Crawford, which brewery had also been the leading one in Ireland up until 1833. Henry Inglis, who visited Cork city in 1834, wrote that 'of the concerns of Beamish and Crawford, in breweries and flour mills, some idea may be formed from the circumstance that one-eighth of the whole rate of the city of Cork is paid by that firm'.[31] However, the advent of Fr Mathew severely damaged the prosperity of the drink industry and also that of barley growers. Professor J. S. Donnelly, Jr, claims that 'Brewing was less hard hit than distilling, but during the decade following the start of the temperance campaign in 1838, the number of bushels of malt upon which the required duty was paid, fell from over 2,000,000 to only about 1.5 million or by about 25 per cent'.[32] In fact in Ireland as a whole domestic consumption of grain spirits fell from nearly 12.3 million gallons in 1838 to only about 6 million gallons in 1848 or by more than 50 per cent.

Shipbuilding was an industry in which Cork played a prominent part; the first paddle-steamer made in Ireland was built in Cork in 1812 while the Cork and Waterford yards were the pioneers in the 1840s of iron shipbuilding in Ireland. In 1836 there were 302 ships grossing 21,514 tons registered in the port of Cork while the two shipbuilding yards, each having a patent slip in which vessels of 500 tons could be hauled up and repaired, also provided valuable employment, with at least 1,600 men working in the shipbuilding industry. While obviously not as busy as during the heyday of the Napoleonic wars, Cork harbour still bustled in the first half of the nineteenth century. In 1835, for example, 141 vessels of 27,571 tons left the harbour for foreign ports while 167 vessels of 30,191 tons arrived; coastal trading was even more extensive with 1,844 vessels of 235,912 tons arriving and 1,422 vessels of 138,767 tons departing. In addition to the passage of the merchant fleets of the world through its port, Cork had by 1825 its own line of packets owned by the St George's Company which traded on a regular basis between Cork and Liverpool and afterwards between Cork and Bristol. In the 1840s the capital of that company according to Lewis '... amounted to £300,000 subscribed in shares, of which one-third were held by Cork proprietors'. It employed seven vessels of about 500 tons burden and 250 horse power each; two of these plied to Bristol, one to Liverpool, three to London and one to Dublin and all carried passengers, goods and cattle.[33]

The impact of the depression was unevenly spread; manufacturing suffered most and except for tanning, brewing, distilling and ship-building it was nearly wiped out. Regrettably the new industries were not yet capable of absorbing the employment fall-out of the traditional textile-based ones, with the result that for most of the first half of the nineteenth century unemployment was excessively high in Cork. Trading was far less affected by the slump and, in fact, the port on this occasion came to the rescue of the hinterland and city, but because of the shift in exports from beef to cattle on the hoof it was no substitute, especially in employment terms, for the collapse of the textile industry.

Cork's primary commercial activity, butter marketing, prospered during those years; the average annual number of firkins passing through the weigh-houses of the butter market rose from 209,000 between 1800 and 1809 to 260,000 between 1830 and 1839.[34] As has already been observed, port activity was equally buoyant while the range of the city's imports is also indicative of the wealth of the fortunate few still in employment in the surviving industries or of those engaged in commerce. For example, wine imports still remained high despite the challenge from home distilled spirits; the quantity of tobacco on which duty was paid annually at the Custom House in 1835 was 647,000 lbs.[35] Herrings, linseed oil, raw sugar and many other such items were all imported in large quantities. It is apparent that certain sections of Cork society continued to enjoy a high standard of living despite the fact that the quality of life of their less fortunate neighbours continued to deteriorate.

Social and political conditions

Despite these oscillations in Cork's economic fortunes, its inhabitants were reluctant to change their life-styles. This may have been due to the city's origins on a group of marshy islands in the lower reaches of the river Lee. Until 1750 the present main street was still a channel of the river, and not until the beginning of the nineteenth century were all the little channels that criss-crossed the main island (Morrison's Island) filled in or bridged over. This meant that even when Cork's population began to grow rapidly in the eighteenth century access to and from the main island was confined to two bridges, North Gate and South Gate. Movement was accordingly restricted; people stayed put, ignorant of the surrounding countryside but apparently content with their circum-scribed horizons. This left an enduring mark on attitudes in Cork, because even when seven more bridges, including a major one leading off Patrick Street, were constructed during the fifty years after 1774, the people were slow to move from the congested original island to the more spacious liberties.

The first available figures from the 1841 Census point to an average population density of 35.7 persons per acre for the seven parishes of the city, ranging from 18 persons per acre in St Anne's, Shandon, to 219 in St Peter's.[36] There was little change until the late nineteenth century, despite the exodus which took place during the Famine; it would appear that the tenements vacated were promptly filled by recently-arrived migrants in the city.[37] This concentration is also apparent from the occupancy of houses where, on average, there were two families per house in 1831 and 1841.[38] Dr Murphy has calculated from census returns that 72.3 per cent of all families were living in slum accommodation in 1841 and that there was no appreciable change in that situation until the 1890s.[39] Even when in the 1870s, the corporation, acting under Crosses Act, embarked on a systematic scheme for slum clearance and re-housing, they encountered much resistance from those who were not prepared to move the one mile from the city centre to the new houses.[40]

The suburbs were slow to develop in Cork. In fact the liberties containing 42,621 acres in 1831, had only 22,000 inhabitants, or approximately 0.51 per acre.[41] This concentration of population is all the more remarkable when placed in the context of the evolution of European cities. Roger Mols has shown how the population densities of towns in Europe before the Industrial Revolution were particularly low; for example Rome in 1526, with a population of nearly 54,000, averaged only 15.5 people per acre, while the range over its vast surface of 5.27 sq. miles varied from 125 persons (approximately) in its most crowded area, Rioni, to no more than 3 or 4 persons per acre in its least crowded.[42] Cork could never be described as an industrial city. Even at the peak of the late eighteenth-century industrial boom trading was still the dominant activity and the one that endured into the nineteenth century. It is all the more surprising, then, that its population should have been so concentrated for so long.

It also provides some explanation for the bitterness of urban politics in Cork before the move to the suburbs and elsewhere in the later nineteenth century. In pre-Famine Cork people of all classes lived out their lives in close proximity to one another, without much privacy and in an atmosphere bordering on the claustrophobic which left an indelible stamp on their social relationships, their power struggles and their cultural pursuits. As the Commission on Municipal Corporation Boundaries observed: 'It is difficult to particularise on any quarter of the city; St. Patrick's St., the Grand Parade, the South Mall, Great George St., St. Patrick's Hill etc. are inhabited by persons of wealth and respectability or occupied by warehouses; but many of the streets, and nearly all the lanes branching off from these main streets and places, are occupied by numerous families of the lower classes, and many apparently in the lowest state of destitution.'[43] Thus, within the confines of the city centre all the classes shared the limited space available; merchants rubbed shoulders with artisans, artisans with labourers, Protestants with Catholics and all with the vast army of destitutes who, impervious to the fading employment opportunities in the nineteenth century, squatted in central Cork.

The wealthy were, of course, outflanked by the poverty-stricken; even in 1832 the propertied classes did not account for more than 7,000 of the city's 80,000 citizens.[44] But it was a measure of the former's astuteness that, even within that confined space, they successfully contained the masses. This was no mean feat because, as a police official reporting to Dublin Castle in 1870 observed, 'the Cork masses can be collected in an incredibly short time — ripe and ready for

Table 17.1

Density of population in Cork city parishes, 1841-91

Parishes	1841		1851		1861		1871		1881		1891	
	No.	Per acre	No.	Per acre	No.	Per acre	No.	Per acre	No.	Per acre	No.	Per acre
Holy Trinity	8,338	102	10,920	133	8,687	106	8,090	99	7,104	86	6,198	75
St Anne's, Shandon	23,087	18	24,560	19	25,600	20	25,793	20	27,113	21	26,698	21
St Finbar's	6,207	32	6,119	32	5,678	30	6,090	32	7,057	37	6,986	37
St Mary's, Shandon	14,149	52	14,212	52	12,893	48	12,106	45	13,488	50	11,331	42
St Nicholas'	16,273	44	13,860	37	14,622	39	15,326	41	15,247	41	15,228	41
St Paul's	4,563	207	4,468	203	4,147	188	3,752	170	2,967	134	2,245	102
St Peter's	8,103	219	8,809	238	7,966	215	7,482	202	7,148	193	6,659	179
TOTAL	80,720		82,948		79,594		78,642		80,124		75,345	

Sources: Censuses 1841-1891 .

mischief —— perhaps in no other part of the country is there so formidable and so disaffected a mob as that of Cork'.[45] However, success in that respect conceals deep internal animosities. Cork middle-class cohesion was deceptive; they closed ranks when confronted by the masses or when their own economic well-being was at stake. On all other occasions the divisions among themselves were openly manifest and, on balance, the fissures within their own ranks were greater than those between themselves and the poorer classes. The fact that before the Famine most propertied classes of all religious per-suasions lived, worked and socialised within the city centre accentuated the differences, especially political, which divided them.

The main focus for discontent was the corporation from which most Catholic merchants were excluded before 1841. Of course, the 73,000 citizens disenfranchised at parliamentary elections were also debarred from the corporation, but in pre-Famine Cork they voiced few objections; they apparently knew their place! With the Catholic merchants it was different; these were at least the economic equals of their Protestant counterparts, and also there were far more of them.[46] After 1841, the composition of the corporation was closely to mirror the balance of wealth in Cork with merchants dominating proceedings throughout, winning an average of twenty-three of the twenty-five seats, and with manufacturers gaining a declining number of seats in accordance with their diminishing importance. Both Catholics and Protestants were included amongst these groupings, but now in pro-portion to their numbers and standing in Cork society, as Table 17.2 illustrates.

Table 17.2

The politico-religious composition of Cork Corporation, 1841-99

	R.C./Liberal		Unionist	
	Members	**per cent**	**Members**	**per cent**
1841	44	69	20	31
1853	29	52	27	48*
1863	33	59	25	41
1871	38	68	18	32
1883	39	70	17	30
1891	38	68	18	32
1899	36	64	20	36

*The corporation membership was cut from sixty-four to fifty-six in 1852.

'Economic and religious composition of Cork Corporation' quoted by M. Murphy, 'Cork commercial society 1850-1899' in Butel and Cullen, *Cities and merchants*, p. 237.

However, Protestant wealth still ensured that they got a higher proportion of the seats than their numbers warranted.[47] Because Catholic wealth failed to achieve similar representation before the Famine, due to the skill with which a Protestant clique manipulated an undemocratic system to their own advantage, the Catholics were understandably aggrieved. In pre-Famine Cork, the political and the economic élites did not overlap at a time when the franchise was property-oriented. That disjunction accounts for the bitterness of the struggle between the two groups for political ascendancy in the 1830s. It also heightened social tensions.

In the claustrophobic atmosphere of pre-Famine Cork few occur-rences went unnoticed, not least the provocative displays of exclusive-ness by the corporation clique. With their glittering receptions in the Mansion House, the balls on royal occasions, their ceremonial opening of the corporation and a host of other semi-private functions obliquely linked with public office, they reinforced the barriers between themselves and their Catholic rivals, who could not avoid these mani-festations of their own ostracisation.[48] Chamber of Commerce dinners and parades for the 'Liberator' were no substitute for the panache associated with the trappings of state, albeit at the local level. It also meant that the many business dealings of the two communities could not allay the resentment of the Catholics at their political isolation.

The enactment of the Municipal Reform Act in 1840 changed all that; now both merchant communities had equal access to local power and as a result the close correlation between creed and politics no longer evoked the same animosities. While the Protestants still, in general, held to their Unionist commitments and the Catholics to their Repeal aspirations, they were quite prepared to cooperate on local issues, ensuring that between them they retained a monopoly of power. Membership of the corporation was still mainly restricted to merchants, manufacturers and professionals, while Cork's representatives at Westminster were also confined to merchants, preferably native born, although with the arrival of C. S. Parnell, M.P. for Cork in 1880-90, outsiders got a foothold, though all were expected to place local issues before national and imperial.

This continuity in the character of the membership of Cork corporation tends to conceal the frequent changes which occurred both in the composition of that body and also of the merchant community itself. In general these closely paralleled changes in Cork's economy. From my examination of merchant life in pre-Famine Cork[49] I found that few of the merchants cited by Dr Dickson as being prominent in the 1780s were still in business in the 1840s; these according to Dickson were 'all descendants of families who had owned much of the city and administered trade and society before 1641'.[50] Change was much more rapid in the nineteenth century, with many of these general merchants disappearing and their places being taken either by the butter merchants or by textile manufacturers or by meat processors and, later, by the tanners. The Goulds, the Roches, the Terrys, the Meades, and the Coppingers had to give way to the Murphys, the Lyonses, the Hacketts and the Beamishes. Some of these were to survive into the twentieth century, especially those associated with brewing and distilling, but for the rest their fortunes were to ebb like those of their respective industries in the last quarter of the nineteenth century. Cork's butter market succumbed in the 1870s to continental competition in the British market, to the growing popularity of butterine and to the increasing number of fresh butter outlets in the Munster region, before finally closing its doors in 1884.[51] In the case of tanning the 1870s heralded its decline because of competition from more highly mechanised British leather products, especially purpose-made footwear, so that those families engaged in that trade went out of business. The only remaining testament to their and to the butter merchants' former prowess were the substantial monuments erected to their memories in better times in St Joseph's Cemetery.[52] From an examination of the Cork trade directories at approximately ten-yearly intervals beginning in 1824 and continuing to the end of the century, Dr Murphy has concluded that 'though certain large city business concerns like the brewers, distillers and provision stores remained in the same families for generations, the smaller concerns remained in individual families for much shorter periods, that is, from one to three generations'.[53] She also found that the same pattern was reflected in the composition of the corporation in the latter decades of the century. In the 1880s and 1890s the former merchants of the butter market and of the leather industry had their places taken by retailers and vendors and those within the general classification of dealers, still men of property but those whose forbearers would have been associated with the excluded Burgesses Association of the 1840s (certainly not in the same category as the dethroned merchant princes).[54] Nevertheless they shared the socially conservative attitudes of their more wealthy predecessors.

For the most part they operated within the constraints of the existing system, seldom questioning the wisdom of the prevailing orthodoxy. They responded to acute urban distress with piecemeal palliatives, without ever ascertaining the causes of these problems. In 1831 they made no provision for the cholera epidemic that was sweeping Europe and which reached Cork in April 1832;[55] in the first few months of that epidemic they moved the sick and the dying from one improvised hospital to another in response to a public anxious to distance itself from the infected. As a remedy for the ensuing depression they merely campaigned for the promotion of Irish manufacturers or a 'buy Cork' campaign, without ever considering the level of wages, the wider market for Cork goods or even the living and working conditions of their operatives.[56] Their criteria were essentially parsimonious, so that even in the economic sphere they were not prepared to spend more than they had to on the city; instead they pressed Westminster to create a suitable environment in which Cork business would flourish. In 1836, for example, they sought to convince the British government that they should purchase Portuguese wines in order to prevent the Portuguese from raising duties on Irish butter.[57] In 1839, thirty Protestant and eleven Catholic merchants combined to oppose the Poor Law Commissioners' plan to build a new Poor House for the city;[58] nor did the town council as a body give any aid to the Irish manufacture movement of the early 1840s, that is after reform, though a deputation of tradesmen had especially requested the council to help in the establishment of an Irish manufacture market on the North Main Street.[59] When under the 'Act for the Improvement of the Borough of Cork' (15 and 16 Victoria c. 145) in the early 1850s the corporation built a number of new streets and accompanying new houses, '... the changes were geared to improving the appearance of the city rather than bettering the conditions of the slum dweller'.[60]

The surprising feature of Cork in the nineteenth century is not that the propertied classes held these views but that, on the whole, these were shared by many of the distressed majority. The latter had far less to be complacent about, especially the unemployed and those living in sub-human conditions. Still, in the course of the nineteenth century, in spite of their proclivities to riotous behaviour, their demands were essentially for more bread and more work, seldom for a reconstruction of the productive system.

As has been already noted, distress stemmed mainly from the collapse of the textile industry in the 1820s and from the contraction of the provision trade after the Napoleonic wars. Those employed in the leather industry, in brewing and distilling and especially in the butter market, could still count on secure employment and on liveable wages. However, these openings fell far short of Cork's employment require-ments. Even in the second half of the century when new textile factories were built, utilising more modern equipment,[61] and when the transport and building sectors of the economy prospered,[62] there was still high unemployment.[63] Because of falling prices and stable or even rising wages in some spheres[64] those in employment actually experienced an improvement in their standards of living. But even for the latter the seasonality of much of their work, the existence of a large residual labour force only too willing to take their places and the blurring of the distinctions between skilled and unskilled which the new machinery, especially in textiles, effected, emphasised the precariousness of the situation also. Why then did they conform?

They had to conform because they believed that they had no other choice. They were encouraged in that belief by those who considered that they themselves had much to lose from changes in the social structure and the economic system. These included not only the propertied but also those workers in gainful employment who were not prepared to risk their precarious positions for an economic or a social unknown. By skilful manipulation, they deflected the hungry masses from radical or revolutionary agitation, holding out the possibility of a better future within the existing system that might be jeopardised by precipitate action. If such an appeal did not convince, they invariably embellished it by invoking Repeal as a panacea for all Cork's troubles. The Catholic clergy and the local press were welcome allies in that deception.

Until the end of the nineteenth century the masses and the general or unskilled workers lacked any type of organisation through which to vent their economic and social grievances; in the 1830s, they may have swelled the ranks of the Trades Associations' parades in Cork but these were controlled from the very beginning by the Catholic merchants.[65] Even 'as late as the 1830s', according to Dr Murphy, 'perhaps only about three in every ten unskilled labourers in Cork were unionised'.[66] The craftsmen were better organised but, as elsewhere, they were loath to share their organisation with others; they resented the presence of skilled labourers from outside Cork entering the city and were particularly suspicious of talented general labourers, the so-called 'handymen', who might threaten their own exclusiveness. They were not prepared to risk their security either by opening their ranks to others or by engaging in unacceptable public agitation. The irony was that, in spite of their best efforts, they too found themselves by the 1870s with a skeleton organisation because of the decimation of many of the trades due to the collapse of their respective industries. In the 1830s as many as forty separate trade societies marched behind their colourful banners in public demonstrations, but by 1900 the maximum number participating was nineteen.[67] By then the survivors identified more with political groups like the Fenians than with their traditional vocational organisations.

The merchant classes capitalised on these deficiencies. By the unusual expedient of encouraging the masses in their belief that the root of all their troubles was British misrule in Ireland rather than the

propertied classes own economic shortcomings, they erected a political
smoke-screen around a conflagration that was essentially economic. A
Cork ballad of the 1830s[68] succinctly captures these hopes:

> The tradesmen and labourer that's now in poverty
> Will sit in their parlour and sing melodiously
> We'll have mutton, beef and bacon with butter eggs and veal,
> And religion will come again to welcome the Repeal.

As a result, the unemployed and the unskilled workers channelled their
discontent through nationalist rather than through vocational organisations; for example, the mobs gave vocal support to nationalist candidates in the 1832, 1835 and 1841 elections,[69] the latter being the most
violent election in nineteenth-century Cork when men and their
womenfolk conducted a campaign of open agitation against the Conservative voters. In the election of 1852 similar scenes took place. Any
wonder, then, that the ever-vigilant *Cork Constitution*, the Tory paper,
should have observed in 1832 that 'while men anxiously search for the
means of employing the industrial tradesmen, it is not seemly that
others should labour to turn him into a party tool, to be employed for
ends that will ever be contested while attempted by a party'.[70] By the
1860s the disenfranchised were swelling the ranks of the Fenians. As
Table 17.3 indicates, the Cork Fenian movement was drawn from
amongst the lower-ranking groups in Cork, in contrast to O'Connell's
movements of the 1830s and 1840s when merchants, manufacturers and
professionals had dominated events. Nevertheless, even with the
Fenians, it was still the small shopkeepers and small masters that
supplied the leaders, for example Brian Dillon who was a publican and
William O'Carroll who was a master baker.

Table 17.3

Social composition of the Cork Fenian movement, 1865-1870[71]

Occupational group	Per cent of rank-and-file	Per cent of leadership
Artisans	46	32
Unskilled labourers	20	–
Drapers' assistants	8	7
Clerks	3.5	14
Publicans, shopkeepers	3	3.5
Merchants, dealers	3	–
Others	5.5	–
Unidentified	14	11

But the appeal of nationalism does not completely explain why peculiarly working-class movements had such little support in the depressed conditions of nineteenth-century Cork. For example, the Chartists and the Fabian society had few adherents in Cork, while trade unions were dominated by craftsmen whose conservatism ensured that these remained firmly within the existing structures and reflected prevailing values that were essentially bourgeois. Even though Fergus O'Connor, founder of the Chartists, was born near Cork, that movement generated no enthusiasm in his native county. It was likewise in the case of the Fabians. An English coach-maker who came to Cork failed in his attempt to establish a branch of that society in the city. He concluded that the Cork tradesmen were '... far from fit subjects for a Fabian society — scratch them, and you find a conservative of the crudest type'.[72] The Internationale in 1872 met a similar reception while Connolly's Republican and Socialist Party in the early 1900s evoked much the same response.

A possible explanation of this conservatism is to be found in the general structure of Cork industry and trade throughout the nineteenth century. In contrast to large British cities, dominated by a single industry, there was far more fragmentation and diffusion in Cork. Further, production and trading units were, on the whole, small, ensuring close contact between employer and labourer, so that the conservatism of employers percolated through the ranks of the work-force. Outside of shipbuilding, where in the 1850s and in the 1860s between 300 and 800 men were employed in each of the two local shipyards,[73] the average work-force was much smaller. Among the bigger tailoring establishments, up to fifty men worked together on the employers' premises, but in the case of smaller firms, between ten and fifteen men worked on the premises, a large part of the work being done by male and female outworkers in their own homes.[74] In the case of the printers, between twenty and forty men worked in each of the newspaper offices, while among coopers, individual workshops could accommodate between ten and forty men.[75]

Two influences against the growth of radicalism in Cork came from outside the working classes: from the press and the clergy. The local press, liberal as well as Tory, adamantly opposed any movement seeking social change and successfully blocked local advance of any such movement by the simple expedient of ignoring its existence. Thus the short-lived Irish Democratic Association of 1849-50 was ignored by the *Cork Examiner*, the local liberal newspaper. But perhaps more powerful than the press in discouraging the development of social radicalism was the influence of the Catholic clergy. The Democrats, the Internationale classes of 1872 and the Irish Republican and Socialist

Party of the early 1900s all came under the lash of clerical opposition, with a consequent decimation of membership.[76]

The clearest indication of the absence of any desire for social change was the reluctance by labour to enter local government before 1898, or to group behind a merchant with socialist commitments. In 1898, in the election for the corporation under the Local Government Act of that year which increased the municipal electorate fourfold, Labour candidates won 7 of the 56 seats but, true to form, not one of these was a skilled labourer.[77] Moreover they entered the town council without any social or political programme whatever. They appear to have made no pre-election pledges and were obviously more anxious to prove the strength of their nationalism than of their 'Labourism'.

While population was a significant factor in determining the course of social and economic development in Cork, it was not the dominant one. In the eighteenth century when economic progress was rapid the strategic situation of Cork harbour, the character of the city's hinterland and the quality of its entrepreneurs were as important in that respect. However, in the nineteenth century the size of the population bore little relation to the level of economic activity, mainly because of the alacrity with which migrants moved into the city to fill the places of the voluntary and involuntary emigrants. In fact, the presence of a surplus population and the ensuing high level of unemployment may well have impeded the emergence in Cork of a distinctive working-class consciousness and of working-class policies. The employed were intimidated by the reservoir of potential workers from overtly criticising the existing system in case they might also find themselves redundant, while the unemployed did not rise above the occasional riot, certainly never to demanding a radical restructuring of the existing system. These were duped by their expectations of a repeal of the Union, which the property owners and craftsmen did nothing to dampen; if anything, they encouraged such fallacious beliefs. In one respect however, population did have a dynamic role to play in nineteenth-century Cork. Because of its concentration within narrow confines, it tended to sharpen divisions between people, especially within the merchant classes. The ensuing clashes may not have concerned economic fundamentals and were in most respects removed from Cork's real problems; nevertheless, because of the claustrophobic atmosphere in which they took place they were very bitter and perhaps even deflected the conflicting parties from attending to Cork's real needs. Thus while population in the eighteenth century contributed to economic development, in the nineteenth century it had a greater impact on social attitudes and on local politics.

References

1. *Censuses of Ireland 1821-1891*. See Table 1.
2. D. Dickson's revised estimates for eighteenth-century population where he calculates the population in 1706 as 17,595 and that in 1796 as 57,033. See Dickson, 'Cork region', Appendix Table xxii.
3. H.C., *Report from the select committee on the financial relations* (England, Scotland and Ireland), (London, 1891) reproduced by Irish University Press (1970), p. 535 (hereafter *Report ... on financial relations*).
4. Donnelly, *Land and people*, p. 15.
5. *Censuses of Ireland*, 1841-1901.
6. Dickson, 'Cork region', p. 638.
7. *Census of Ireland*, 1821; Dickson, 'Cork region', p. 420.
8. P.R.O., Customs 15: figures derived by author from table cited in D. Dickson, 'Large-scale developers and the growth of eighteenth-century Irish cities' in Butel and Cullen, *Cities and merchants*, p. 109.
9. *Report ... on financial relations*, p. 535.
10. J. Walton, 'The merchant community of Waterford in the sixteenth and seventeenth centuries' in Butel and Cullen, *Cities and merchants*, p. 183.
11. J. S. Donnelly, Jr., 'Cork market: its role in the nineteenth-century Irish butter trade' in *Studia Hib.*, xi (1971), pp 130-63 (hereafter 'Cork market').
12. O'Sullivan, *Econ. hist. Cork city*, Appendix 32, p. 334.
13. Ibid., Appendix 31, p. 326.
14. Ibid., Appendix 33, p. 341.
15. Dickson, 'Cork region', p. 563.
16. Ibid., p. 597.
17. Ibid., Table xix.
18. Ibid., Table viii.
19. Ibid., p. 488.
20. O'Sullivan, *Econ. hist. Cork city*, Appendix 31, p. 333.
21. Ibid., Appendix 32, p. 340.
22. Ibid., Appendix 33, p. 347.
23. Ibid., Appendix 32, p. 337.
24. B. R. Mitchell and P. Deane, *Abstract of British historical statistics* (Cambridge, 1962), p. 488.
25. Crotty, *Ir. agric. prod.*, Table 68C, p. 284.
26. L. M. Cullen, *An economic history of Ireland since 1660* (London, 1972), p. 103.
27. *Parl. gaz.*, p. 528.
28. Lewis, *Topog. dict. Ire.*, i, p. 417.
29. Ibid., p. 416.
30. Ibid., p. 416.
31. H. Inglis, *A journey throughout Ireland during the spring, summer and autumn of 1834*, i (London, 1834), p. 187.
32. Donnelly, *Land and people*, p. 35.
33. Lewis, *Topog. dict. Ire.*, p. 415.
34. Gibson, *Cork*, ii, pp 379-380.
35. Lewis, *Topog. dict. Ire.*, p. 414.
36. *Census of Ireland*, 1841. See Appendix 1.
37. Constructed from figures extracted from *Censuses of Ireland*, 1841-1891.
38. *Census of Ireland*, 1841.
39. M. Murphy, 'The working classes of nineteenth-century Cork' in *Cork Hist. Soc. Jn.*, lxxx (1980), p. 27 (hereafter 'Working classes').

40. Murphy, 'Working classes', p. 30.

41. *Census of Ireland*, 1841.

42. R. Mols, 'Introduction à la demographie historique des villes d'Europe du xive au xviiie siècle' (Louvain, 1954-6), quoted by E. E. Lampard in D. Fraser and A. Sutcliffe (ed.), *The nature of urbanization* (London, 1983), p. 33.

43. *Parl. gaz.*, p. 520; See also A. M. Fahy, 'Residence, workplace and patterns of change; Cork 1878-1863' in Butel and Cullen, *Cities and merchants*, p. 47.

44. J. B. O'Brien, *The Catholic middle classes in pre-Famine Cork* (Dublin, 1980), p. 4.

45. S.P.O., C.S.O., R.P., 1870: nos. 12819, 12956, 13023, 16317.

46. O'Brien, *Catholic middle classes*, pp 6-7.

47. Ibid., p. 11.

48. Ibid., p. 9.

49. J. B. O'Brien, 'Merchants in Cork before the Famine' in Butel and Cullen, *Cities and merchants*, p. 225; idem, 'The Hacketts: glimpses of entrepreneurial life in Cork, 1800-70' in *Cork Hist. Soc. Jn.*, xl (1975), pp 155-6.

50. Dickson, 'Cork region', p. 753.

51. Donnelly, 'Cork market', pp 154 and 160.

52. O'Brien, *Catholic middle classes*, p. 8.

53. M. Murphy, 'Economic and social structure of nineteenth-century Cork' in Harkness and O'Dowd, *Town*, p. 132.

54. See Table 2 in M. Murphy, 'Cork commercial society 1850-1899' in Butel and Cullen, *Cities and merchants*, p. 234.

55. J. B. O'Brien, 'Cork, its people and environments, 1800-45' in *C.E.*, 13 May 1985.

56. O'Brien, *Catholic middle classes*, pp 17-18.

57. George Atkins, secretary of merchants, to all M.P.s for Cork, 8 Feb. 1836 in Cork Public Museum, Committee of Merchants' Records.

58. *C.C.*, 4 July 1839.

59. *C.E.*, 20 Dec. 1841, 3 Jan. 1842.

60. Quoted in Murphy, 'Working classes', p. 30.

61. *C.E.*, 5 Aug. 1850, 27 Nov. 1850.

62. *Censuses of Ireland*, 1841-1901. In 1841 there were approximately 8,000 men engaged in manufacture in Cork; in 1901, there were a little over 4,000. The number of skilled men in the building trade rose from approximately 1,400 in 1841 to over 1,600 in 1901 and the rise in the transport section was particularly striking with the number of men employed rising from 315 in 1841 to 3,423 in 1901.

63. Murphy, 'Economic and social structure', p. 128, where she writes that 'between 40 and 70 per cent of Cork's male population was engaged in gainful employment during the nineteenth century while among females the proportion so employed varies between 34 and 40 per cent'.

64. J. B. O'Brien, 'Agricultural prices and living costs in pre-Famine Ireland' in *Cork Hist. Soc. Jn.*, lxxxii (1977), p. 9.

65. O'Brien, *Catholic middle classes*, pp 17-18.

66. Murphy, 'Working classes', p. 42.

67. *C.M.C.*, 21 Mar. 1832 and 9 June 1832, and *C.E.*, 8 Oct. 1898.

68. Quoted in Murphy, 'Economic and social structure', as 53 plus 63.

69. O'Brien, *Catholic middle classes*, pp 16-17.

70. *C.C.*, 14 June 1832.

71. Murphy, 'Working classes', p. 47.

72. Ibid., p. 44.

73. *C.E.*, 8 Oct. 1852, 28 Apr. 1854, 29 Feb. 1860, 8 Oct. 1864.

74. *C.E.*, 28 Aug. 1892, 3, 4, 8 Apr., 31 May, 25 Aug., 1893.
75. Ibid., 4 Sept. 1888.
76. Murphy, 'Economic and social structure', p. 153.
77. *C.C.*, 18 Jan. 1899.

Chapter 18

WORK AND WORKERS IN CORK CITY AND COUNTY 1800-1900

MAURA CRONIN

> And many's the time late and early
> I wished to be landed again,
> To see the sweet Watercourse flowing
> Where the tanners their glory maintain ...
> ... Success to the jolly hoop coilers,
> Likewise to the shuttle and spool,
> To the skinners and worthy glue boilers
> That live in the Groves of Blackpool.
>
> *The Groves of Blackpool.*[1]

The Groves of Blackpool, known more commonly as the Glen, stretch for about a mile along the course of the Glen river on the north-eastern corner of Cork city. When the song was written in the early nineteenth century, this glen, with its ready supply of water power, provided a site for a multiplicity of small-scale industries, and as late as the 1840s housed a distillery, a malt mill, a rope walk, an ironworks and a small sailcloth factory.[2] By 1900 nothing remained except a fertiliser factory on the site of the distillery, the other buildings being in ruin and the mill ponds used as swimming pools by the youngsters of the area. By the 1970s the Glen had been developed as an amenity area, the over-grown mill-ponds cleaned to make a lake for wildfowl, swings and slides erected for the children and the old pathways opened for walkers.[3] The series of transformations of the Glen from rural area to industrial enclave back to rural area presents a microcosm of Cork's changing patterns of industrial and working life during the nineteenth century: the advent of machines, the establishment of a factory-based production system in competition with the traditional trades, then finally the demise of both the craft and factory-based industries and with them the communities which had centred round them.

However, this change from tradition to modernisation was erratic. Attitudes altered little over the period: localism gave way very slowly to a more outward-looking approach to labour organisation. If women entered the labour market in increasing numbers, their presence there continued to be viewed with suspicion by male workers. Though mechanisation and large-scale production spread from the 1850s onwards, the city's craft trades continued to dominate the organised labour force well into the twentieth century.

The nature of the work-force

The working milieu in nineteenth-century Cork was characteristically small and intimate. Though by the 1890s few artisans except the nailers lodged with their masters, workshops were based on a single trade and run by a working master. The master had frequently risen from the ranks of the journeymen and was liable to fall to that level again with the uncertain fortunes of trade. It is not quite accurate to label these concerns as 'small-scale', for though many employed a handful of workers, others had a work-force of up to sixty. Into the 1900s most of the casks for the breweries, distilleries and city butter trade were produced in coopering shops employing between ten and forty men. Similarly, cabinet-making was carried on in establishments employing six to forty journeymen, and while some tailors' shops employed up to fifty men, the average work-force in a single shop was less than fourteen. In the baking trade the same variation was evident: the bigger city bakeries employed up to sixty men, but the average small urban bakehouse had a work-force of less than a dozen – possibly four bakers, two apprentices, two labourers and two women as general dogsbodies – while bakeries in the county towns ran on the labour of one or two journeymen.[4] In the building trades, too, the small business was the norm. Early in the century individual master carpenters and slaters ran their own workshops, a practice continued by many plumbers and painters into the twentieth century. By the 1870s however, to meet the rising demand for housing, the more prosperous masters had expanded their businesses to become building contractors. A clear distinction grew between the small builders who employed a handful of men and the big builders of the Master Builders' Association who each employed up to twenty carpenters, an equal number of masons and plasterers and almost twice that number of builders' labourers.[5]

Petty squabbling and introversion were an integral feature of the small-scale workplace. Tradesmen long established in a particular workshop identified with that shop more than with their trade as a whole – a factor causing many headaches for trade-union committees. The local coopers' union, for instance, had constant struggles with many of its constituent workshops over the payment of union dues and adhesion to union rules, while the printers' society had to compete with the traditional 'chapel' system which left considerable authority in

Plate 18.1   Glanmire Mill (M. Cronin).

the individual printing offices.[6] The prevalence of small masters, too, led to economising on wages, dodging of apprenticeship rules and general penny-pinching which strained labour relations considerably. Struggling employers in the tailoring and baking trades were notorious in this regard, as were the 'men of small or equivocal capital' who ran many of the coopering shops in both city and county.[7]

However, it was the variety of the work-force rather than the numbers employed which marked the essential difference between small and large-scale concerns in nineteenth-century Cork. While the small workshop was generally staffed by men of the same trade, helped, perhaps, by a handful of labourers, the larger concern was multi-occupational. The breweries and distilleries of the city, which in 1837 employed between them something under two thousand men (a figure reduced by fifty per cent in 1900), had a work-force consisting of maltsters, coopers, coppersmiths, carpenters and wheel-wrights with their respective semi-skilled assistants, as well as watchmen, carters and labourers assigned to the yards, mash-rooms, kilns, lofts and stores. In mid-century, the three shipbuilding yards in the harbour (at Passage, Queenstown and Tivoli) together employed between them 300 and 800 men, figures fluctuating according to the availability of contracts. Between 1871 and 1874 the Cork Steam Packet yard employed a total of 337 men, comprising sixteen different skilled categories, to a total of 167 journeymen, their forty-six apprentices, eighty-five semi-skilled helpers and thirty-nine labourers.[8]

The proportionate distribution of the work-force between small and large-scale concerns is almost impossible to calculate, but by 1901 apparently less than eight per cent of the city's skilled workers were employed in large-scale manufacturing concerns. If to this is added the two other large-scale employment categories of labouring and transport, we find that by 1901 less than thirteen per cent of skilled men and less than half of the total male work-force were employed in large establishments.[9] In general, the skilled tradesmen were more likely to work in small workshops on the traditional model, while the unskilled worked for larger concerns. However due to increasing mechanisation the lines of demarcation became blurred, with unskilled men and low-paid female employees doing the work which was traditionally the preserve of the skilled trades.

Labour relations

The defence of the craft trades' livelihood in the face of inexorable modernisation fell to the trade unions. At least eight of these unions dated from the mid-eighteenth century while a number of others emerged in the early nineteenth century.[10] Regarded in these early days as subversive, these clandestine organisations frequently sought their objectives through violence. The greatest wave of violent trade-union activity in the city began in 1817 when widespread distress led to several food riots as local industry collapsed and unemployment spread. By the early 1820s attacks on the persons and property of unpopular employers and blacklegs increased, accelerating in 1826 when the English and Irish currency assimilation resulted in the reduction of one penny in the shilling in the nominal value of wages.[11] In 1833 further attempted wage cuts led to a new wave of disturbances in which, as the mayor reported:

> our city, hitherto so peaceable, has become lately, and yet is, almost every night, greatly disturbed by persons calling themselves 'the Union of Trades', who assemble by night, break into the houses of tradesmen not belonging to their illegal body, and beat and otherwise illtreat them, so as in several cases to endanger life. They have also committed many outrages by breaking the windows or otherwise damaging the houses of citizens and traders who venture to employ persons contrary to the will of the combinators, and these offences are now become so frequent and alarming that we much fear murders may be committed.[12]

Particular localities in the city were closely associated with specific trades. This close intermeshing of local community and workplace produced its own problems as, in the crowded and squalid lanes where the artisans and labourers lived, labour grievances affecting the few became the concern of the many, throwing entire localities into chaos. In 1822 when the authorities interrupted a meeting of 300 journeymen coopers in the city's north liberties, and arrested ten of their number, a huge mob gathered to rescue the captives. Two decades later a number of strike-breaking country coopers were set upon by a 'vast number of city coopers, their wives, sons and others' so that the streets around the Butter Market 'soon became the scene of riot and tumult'.[13]

A hostile press refused to acknowledge the source of this violence as the desperate response of traditional workers to accelerating change. The press preferred to ascribe it (perhaps with some reason) to the rowdy habits of the lower classes, and accusations of drunkenness continued as an anti-trade union theme right through the century. In 1829 the hatters were criticised for their 'habits of intoxication and tendency to combination'. As late as 1870 this accusation was repeated by a meeting of master tailors involved in a lockout with their men:

> When it was complained that the men could not get sufficient food for their stomachs, it should be remembered that if they kept more whiskey out of them, they could have more food to put into them.[14]

By the 1870s, however, reflecting the growing respectability of trade-unionism throughout the British Isles as a whole, the Cork unions generally avoided violence and increasingly used newspaper advertisements as a means of publicising their case. Yet wage grievances, employment of non-union labour and the displacement of men by machines continued as sources of labour conflict into the twentieth century.

The most serious problem facing both skilled and unskilled workers in the city was the flooding of the local labour market by agricultural labourers and small-town artisans who, increasingly displaced by changing work patterns and over-supply of labour, came to the city for employment at a higher rate of wages than at home. Particularly acute for the unskilled, this question of displacement by country labour reached its peak in the 1890s. In 1894 agricultural labourers in Skibbereen Union, paid only four shillings a week without food, and Kanturk labourers with an unemployment rate of over sixty per cent, flooded into the city in search of work, acting as blacklegs in labourers' strikes and doing the work of skilled men at a lower rate of wages.[15]

The skilled trades were equally susceptible to the incursions of, as they put it, 'barbarian hordes of rustic mechanics'. The most vulnerable were the bakers with their notoriously bad working conditions and inability to organise effectively. In Cork they began work at five in the evening. They worked through the night until the delivery vans set out in the early hours of the morning, snatching short periods of sleep between the processes of mixing, proving, kneading and baking the bread. The bakers received no overtime pay, worked in unhealthy and cramped conditions and frequently spent half the year on sick-pay from their union, a rate less than forty per cent of their normal pay.[16] Their problem was that the trade was easily learnt, so that labourers could be trained in a matter of weeks to replace strikers. Furthermore, every small town had its supply of surplus journeymen bakers willing to strikebreak in the city for rates which, though low by union standards, were far higher than those paid in the smaller towns.[17]

The city's highly-skilled coopering and printing trades, too, though not as vulnerable as the bakers, were also susceptible to the competition of country tradesmen. Almost every town in the county during the course of the century had two or three coopering shops whose fortunes rose and fell with those of the butter, provision and liquor trades, and whose employees eagerly answered the types of advertisements appearing in the Limerick press in 1828:

> Country Coopers!!!
>
> Now is your time! The City of Cork is open to you. Employment will be given to thirty or forty Country Coopers in Cork and Fermoy at the rate of 3s. 4d. a day. Apply to James Keppel at my Cooperage in Fermoy or at my home in Cork, St. Dominick Street.
>
> – James Noonan.

As late as the 1880s and '90s many city employers ran their cooperages entirely on country labour, while in the case of the printers the county towns provided a fund of blacklegs for city employers in dispute with the union.[18]

Closely tied to the issue of country labour was that of the over-supply of apprentices. The hallmark of the skilled worker was his claim to be a 'seven years' man', to have served a seven-year apprenticeship before being recognised as a journeyman. As it was this apprenticeship which distinguished the skilled man from the unskilled and casual labourer, it was considered essential that the control of apprenticeship numbers and training should remain in the hands of the organised journeymen.[19] In the 1820s and '30s the rope-makers had allowed only members' sons to enter the trade. The slaters and hatters permitted only two apprentices to each master, while the shoe-makers limited each journeyman to one apprentice, preferably his son. From the 1870s the coopers allowed a maximum of three boys per master, maintaining a preference for members' sons into the 1890s. By this time, too, the seven-year indentured apprenticeship continued in the building trade, although a man could teach his own son the trade without an indenture. The boy so trained was called an 'improver' and not being directly bound to any master could move from shop to shop to get a wider knowledge of the trade.[20]

Considered by the unions as essential for survival, these rules were seen by outsiders as an outdated block on the natural process of supply and demand, as an impediment to cheapening labour and as an unfairly exclusive measure against boys eager to enter a trade with which they had no family connection. On this issue the skilled union on the one hand and employers and middle-class opinion on the other were bound to clash. In the 1820s the trades condemned the Cork Foundling Hospitals' practice of apprenticing hospital boys to city tradesmen. From the 1850s onwards the industrial schools' training of boys, mostly as bakers, met with the same response.[21] The most severe criticism of incursions into the trades' apprenticeship preserves was meted out in

1857 to the Benevolent Apprenticing Society, a body of philanthropic local gentlemen headed by John Francis Maguire of the *Cork Examiner*, which unwittingly roused the ire of the trades by apprenticing workhouse-trained boys to 'respectable master tradesmen', mainly in the baking trade. The scheme collapsed after about a year, but the 'illegal apprentice' problem continued.[22] By mid-century, many of the city's smaller cabinet-making houses were run exclusively on boy labour. In the printing trade over half the jobs were in the hands of apprentices, while one of the biggest printing houses in the city, Guy and Company, was run entirely on boy labour. Similarly, as late as the 1890s the plumbers and carpenters had a considerable struggle to enforce rules on apprentice limitation and maintain the wage levels of the skilled men.[23]

Wage rates

Wages in the county towns are very difficult to assess due to the absence of records. However, the available figures show that while wages in Cork city were generally lower than those of Dublin, they rose considerably in all occupational sectors over the years from 1820 to 1900. This overall increase in wages occurred in spite of an initial decrease in the 1820s, consequent upon the breakdown of traditional wage regulation machinery. From the mid-eighteenth century wages in Cork city had been determined by an Act of Parliament which directed that at the Easter Quarter Sessions yearly the local Justices of the Peace, in the presence of the Recorder or his deputy, should ascertain:

> what wages or sum of money every mason, carpenter, slater, cooper or other artificer shall take and be paid by the day or by the certain denomination, piece or parcel of work, or job, either with or without meat or drink, during the year following.[24]

While this act provided for the maintenance of wages at the customary level, and for pre-settlement consultation between magistrates, masters and journeymen, the journeymen were at a disadvantage. Once the settlement had been made they were prohibited from asking for any further rise of wages during the ensuing year, though the masters were entitled to force a reduction. From the early 1820s, however, there was a move away from the 'Court Settlement' of wages, as masters now regulated rates without reference to either magistrates or journeymen. Wage levels consequently fell, so that by the 1840s the city's coopers were earning an average seven to ten shillings per week, in contrast to the 1821 'Court Prices' of twenty shillings, while in the cabinet-making trade earnings were between eight and eighteen shillings lower than they had been before 1820.[25]

However, though the incomplete nature of figures available makes precise assessment difficult, the following table²⁶ attempts to show that the trend in wage-rates from 1820 to 1900 was generally an upward one. Wage rates in the building industry rose some fifty-six per cent between 1830 and 1900, cabinet-makers' rates rose by sixty-one per cent in the eighty years after 1820, engineering workers' wages rose by between twenty-five and forty-two per cent in the second half of the century, and in shipbuilding wages rose between twenty-eight and fifty per cent over the same period.

A low rate of unionisation and a consequent lack of records make wage rates among the unskilled the most difficult to document. Moreover, the term 'labourer' hides more than it reveals. It covers a number of different occupations whose working conditions, levels of skill and pay rates were far from uniform – builders' labourers, foundry workers, dock labourers, brewery workers, corporation labourers and casual labourers unattached to any particular business or industry. Over the course of the century the wage rate for unskilled labourers generally ranged between one-quarter and one-half that of skilled workers. For instance, while the weekly rate for skilled city workers in the 1820s and '30s was between eighteen and twenty shillings, that for an unskilled labourer was between five and six shillings, although the better-paid brewery and distillery workers received nine shillings and fourpence.²⁷ By the 1870s the wages for unskilled men averaged thirteen shillings, although the internal variations even within a single establishment make all generalisations meaningless. In the Watercourse Distillery in 1871, yardmen, coopers' helpers and cornstore men earned thirteen shillings a week, while watchmen, carmen and kilnmen earned fifteen shillings. Three years later, unskilled and semi-skilled workers' wages in the Cork Steam Packet Company's yards varied from thirteen to thirty-five shillings weekly, though some wages – probably those of young boys beginning work – were as low as six shillings.²⁸ By the end of the century the conditions of unskilled labourers in Cork were described as better than in other centres. Indeed, the labourer's weekly wage rate, standing at between fourteen and seventeen shillings, had risen proportionately higher over the previous sixty years than a skilled tradesman's wage which now averaged twenty-eight to thirty-five shillings.²⁹

However, theoretical wage rates like those described above did not necessarily coincide with real income. Real wages for a labourer in the early 1890s were nearer twelve shillings than the official level of fifteen shillings.³⁰ In the case of the skilled trades, moreover, theoretical figures were modified in some cases by the prevalence of piece-work and in others by the erosive effects of unemployment. In coopering, for example, piece-work and time-work were combined, different

Table 18.1
Daily wage rates in Cork city 1800-1900

	1820	1830	1840	1850	1860	1870	1880	1890	1900
Masons	3s.-3s. 6.d.		4s.	4s.	4s. 2d.		5s.	5s. 6d.	5s. 9d.
Bricklayers				4s.					
Plasterers		3s.	4s.	4s.			5s.	5s. 6d.	5s. 9d.
Carpenters	3s.-3s. 6d.			4s.	4s.	5s.	5s.	5s. 6d.	5s. 9d.
Plumbers				4s.	5s. 4d.	5s. 8d.	5s. 8d.	6s. 6d.	
Painters				4s.		5s.	5s.	5s. 6d.	5s. 9d.
Paperhangers						4s. 8d.-5s. 10d.			
Stonecutters			3s. 6d.	4s.					
Builders' labourers							2s. 2d.-2s. 4d.	2s. 6d.-2s. 8d.	
Boilermakers				5s.					
Engineers				4s.-10s.	4s. 6d.-4s. 8½ d.			5s. 8d.	
Millwrights				4s.-10s.				5s. 8d.	
Gunsmiths				4s. 5d.					
Ironfounders				4s. 5d.			4s. 5d.	4s. 8d.	5s.
Nailors				4s.					
Cabinetmakers	3s.-3s. 4d.			4s.	4s.	4s. 4d.		4s. 6d.	4s. 10d.
Coopers				3s.	5s.				
Sawyers						3s. 4d.-5s.	3s. 4d.		
Corkcutters				4s.					
Paperstainers				3s.-4s.					
Chandlers				4s.-10s.					
Shipwrights (iron)				4s.-6s.					
Shipwrights (wood)				3s.-4s.					
Sail & rope makers									
Printers		3s. 6d.		3s.-5s.	4s.-5s. 4d.	7s.		5s. 5d.-7s. 1d.	

	1820	1830	1840	1850	1860	1870	1880	1890	1900
Litho printers							5s. 6d.	5s. 6d.	
Millers		2s.-3s.							
Bakers				3s.-4s.	3s. 4d.		4s. 8d.-6s.	2s. 5d.-2s. 10d.	
Butchers				3s.-5s.				5s.-6s.	
Tanners		10d.-1s. d.		2s. 6d.-3s.					
Weavers				1s.-3s.					
Tailors				4s.		4s.			
Shoemakers				3s.-4s.		6s.			
Bootrivetters		10d.-1s.	1s. 4d.-2s.	1s. 4d.-2s.		2s. 2d.-2s. 6d	2s. 10d.-4s. 4d.	2s. 10d.-4s. 4d.	2s. 6d.-2s. 8d.
General labourers						4s. 4d.	2s. 6d.	2s. 6d.	
Firemen						2s. 6d.			
Lamplighters									
Brewery workmen				2s.					

Source: See reference 26.

processes being paid at different rates. From the 1870s the city coopers' society tried to substitute time-work for piece-work, especially in brewery overtime work, so that by the 1890s some men in the trade worked exclusively on time-work. Considered the best off in the trade, they were required to pay double the contribution of the piece-workers when any collection was made in their union.[31] Piece-work was the norm in shipbuilding where caulking and coppering work were the exceptions. Shoe-makers' earnings were also calculated on a piece-work basis: in mid-century, boots and shoes of different styles earned the maker from two-and-twopence to two-and-sixpence a pair, and this piece-work still continued into the early 1870s. The average earnings of the shoe-makers, however, remain unclear. It was calculated that the weekly income of a city shoe-maker in the 1830s was between twelve and fifteen shillings, rising by the 1870s to around thirty-six shillings. These figures, however, appear to apply to times of full employment; average earnings over the whole year were probably much lower.[32]

Among the city tailors daily earnings averaged from two to four shillings in the 1850s and four shillings in the 1870s. This average continued for the rest of the century, though in a busy season men could earn up to ten shillings a day.[33] Tailors' earnings are difficult to calculate, based as they were on the 'log' system. Introduced in the 1830s, this combination of piece- and time-work was described in the 1890s as:

> the printed statement of times allowed for making garments ... agreed upon between employers and employed. The number of hours allowed to a garment multiplied by an agreed price per hour fixes the remuneration to be given to the workman.[34]

Standing at threepence-halfpenny since the 1840s, the log was raised to fourpence in 1870 and in 1878 to fourpence-halfpenny. However, in 1886 the journeymen's society agreed that some less prosperous employers could return to the fourpenny log, a gesture designed to allow small struggling masters to establish themselves in business and encourage them to use unionised labour.[35] From 1886, therefore, the calculation of Cork city tailors' wages is further complicated by the concurrence of two logs. These were the fourpence-halfpenny or first-class log, paid by the three well-established and thriving employers who together directly employed some 150 union members, and the fourpenny or second-class log, paid by the smaller employers who each directly employed from seven to nine society members but who were largely dependent on sweated outworkers and machinists.[36]

Cyclical and seasonal fluctuations in income also obscure the actual earnings of many trades, particularly in the clothing and footwear sectors. A witness before the Royal Commission on Labour in the early 1890s claimed that a tailor's working time could range from two days per week in winter to a full week of twelve- to fourteen-hour days in summer. In Cork, the tailors working on the first-class log depended for a great deal of their custom on the gentry's requirements during the autumn fox-hunting season. They did so to such an extent that the Land League's repeated bans on fox-hunting in the 1880s caused unemployment levels to rise among the city tailors and wage levels to fall as much as fifty per cent. The boot-makers, too, were largely dependent on gentry custom, the poorer classes in general buying cheaper factory-made footwear, either locally made or imported. Even the factory-based footwear trade in the city had a seasonal nature, with the winter months tending to provide fuller employment than the summer, since the Cork factories manufactured little in the way of light summer goods.[37]

The shipbuilding industry, in Cork as elsewhere, was marked by extreme fluctuations between boom and slump. Flourishing in the 1850s, the industry declined rapidly from the 1860s. This was partly due to lack of capital and partly through the failure, until the '80s, to adapt the local wooden shipbuilding skills to the newly-developing methods of iron shipbuilding. Moreover, the local yards failed to compete with English and Scottish concerns, and although Cork won a number of Admiralty contracts in the late 1880s and '90s, this did little to boost the industry in the long term.[38] Even under the best conditions the shipbuilding industry was, of its nature, subject to violent fluctuations. In Britain these led to fourteen major wage adjustments in the fourteen years from 1879 to 1892. In Cork the boom-slump pattern was even more apparent as the local yards' fortunes rose and fell with the availability of contracts, affecting not just the shipwrights but also the engineering workers and the unskilled dockyard labourers. In busy times in the early 1870s shipwrights and their apprentices in the Cork Steam Packet yards worked a minimum of ten hours a day, and sometimes over-ran into the next day, to reach a total of twenty-five hours. In such times shipwrights' weekly wages ranged between thirty-four and fifty-one shillings when the contemporary average rate for skilled workers was thirty shillings. In 1893 and 1894, on the other hand, severe depression led to an unemployment level of 100 per cent among the unionised shipwrights. Although this was followed by a boom in repair contracts which increased the dock work-force from 100 to 250, the latter increase mostly comprised unskilled labour and the shipwrights' unemployment level remained as high as seventy per cent.[39] Such seasonal variation was also a feature of the building trades, where bad weather could halve wages and throw fifty to sixty per cent of workers out of employment. In coopering the firkin trade almost came to a standstill in the months of low butter production between November and April.[40]

The impact of mechanisation

The decline of the coopers' fortunes may be viewed as a microcosm of the fate of many local skilled crafts during the course of the nineteenth century. In its heyday during the Cork provision trade's zenith in the late 1700s, the trade of the 'jolly hoop coilers' stagnated from 1815 onwards. Partly due to the collapse of the wartime trade, this was also occasioned by the raising of import duties on salt, making the Cork provision trade less competitive in the face of English rivals. Further setbacks occurred from 1827 onwards when Cork lost its near-monopoly of the Newfoundland and West Indies trade. By early 1832 only 200 of the city's 700 coopers were working, and then only for an average of four months per year, with weekly earnings of one-and-sixpence each.[41] From this time onwards, the coopering trade became increasingly dependent on the butter trade and on the brewing and distilling industries centred on Cork city, Bandon and Midleton. As the century passed, however, the Cork butter trade went into decline. In the late 1870s a number of bad seasons – wet weather followed by very cold dry weather – cut dairy yields and butter production. From 1887 the Cork trade was hit when the British market opened up to butter imports from the continent, while in the 1890s the introduction of margarine (initially called butterine) further damaged the Cork butter trade and severely affected the employment opportunities of the coopers.

Around the same time, the erosion of the Cork provision trade monopoly on the navy pork contract was a further blow. This was compounded by the Dublin-based Guinness company's pre-eminence in the brewing industry and by the amalgamation of a number of Cork-based distilleries.[42] The ultimate disaster hit with the increased importation of casks and machine-made timber boxes by the butter trade, breweries and fish curers. The immediate effects of this were apparent when one city firm, Londsale and Company, changed over from hand-coopered firkins to butter boxes, and forty coopers were immediately thrown out of work. By the eve of the twentieth century most of the traditional employment areas of the coopers had seriously contracted: the numbers in the trade had fallen by fifty per cent since the 1840s and the number of masters listed in the trade directories had fallen from seventy-one in 1870 to ten in the 1880s.[43]

It is understandable, then, that the skilled trades were highly suspicious of mechanisation and large-scale production which tended to displace skilled workers and undercut the wages and bargaining power of the traditional trades. This was most obvious in the case of the sawyers, a great number of whom were replaced by labourers when the local sawmills changed over from manual labour to steam power in the late 1820s. Violent and futile attacks on modernising employers, culminating in 1842 in the serious injury of a sawmill owner through vitriol burning, resulted only in the transportation of the perpetrators. The issue of sawmill mechanisation continued to dog labour relations into the 1880s, but the handsawyers were doomed. In the early 1870s the Cork Steam Packet Company's sawmill was operated by a single sawyer helped by seven labourers, and the number of sawyers listed in the census fell from 207 in 1831 to 93 in 1901.[44]

This active hostility towards machines gradually changed over the course of the century to periodic muted complaints. By the 1880s it was generally accepted that while mechanisation could prove detrimental to one sector of a trade, it was essential to save the trade as a whole, particularly in the face of foreign competition. Thus in the printing trade of the 1880s and '90s the increased use of machinery led to an expansion in the numbers employed and to a rise in wages. Though it also hastened the phasing out of the pressmen who were never re-absorbed into the trade, it was not generally objected to by the printers' union.[45] Some trades like the stonecutters actually pressed for mechanisation to make their work easier, although in their case the employers had insufficient capital to comply. Other trades like the coopers very reluctantly approved the production of machine-made herring barrels in one city cooperage, and then only in the face of insurmountable competition from imported casks and boxes.[46] Such eleventh-hour concessions to mechanisation were based on the awareness that inability or reluctance to adapt could destroy a trade, as shown by the near extinction of some occupations. Between 1831 and 1901 the weavers disappeared from both the city and county census, glovers' numbers fell by ninety-five per cent and nailers, hatters and brushmakers by ninety-one, eighty-one and fifty-eight per cent respectively.[47]

In rope-making and cork-cutting the same situation prevailed. In the 1820s rope-making had been carried on in small city establishments employing an average of ten men each. In the 1850s a major sailcloth and rope factory re-opened at Douglas village, some three miles from the city centre, where it continued in operation until the early 1880s, by which time the seven remaining small rope-works were on the verge of collapse. Mostly men of limited capital, the proprietors lacked the means of establishing a large-scale modern rope factory able to compete with the imported goods which were then flooding the market. The demise of the trade was therefore inevitable: in 1881 only three rope factories remained in the city and by 1901 this was further reduced to two.[48] The experience of the local cork-cutting trade proved no better. Moving towards the factory system since the mid-1870s, the number of mechanised concerns rose from four in 1875 to ten in 1900, employing unskilled labourers at rates cheaper than those paid to the skilled cork-cutters. Sufficiently mechanised to destroy the traditional craft, these factories were not mechanised enough to compete with importations from Spain, Portugal and France. By the early twentieth century the number of firms in the city had fallen to eight, two of these being importers rather than manufacturers.[49]

The textile trade was the first area of manufacture attempting to boost output and competitiveness through what Cullen calls 'factory-type firms', that is firms using some degree of mechanisation and a large number of well-organised outworkers.[50] As early as 1711 the Linen Board was established to encourage the Irish linen industry, and though most of its success was in the north-east, it also helped to sponsor the enterprise of Sir Richard Cox at Dunmanway and Thomas Adderley at Innishannon. In 1794 there were 230 flax wheels in production around Dunmanway and sixty-six looms working around Innishannon, while by the 1820s some 10,000 of the peasantry in Ross and the surrounding areas reputedly worked on the production of coarse linens which were sold weekly in the Clonakilty market-hall erected for the purpose by the Earl of Shannon.[51] By the 1820s, in fact, the upsurge in linen production was county-wide, from Bantry in the west to Castlemartyr in the east. Though patronised in places by local and English entrepreneurs, the industry was generally 'carried on by persons of small capital who employ from one to four looms', the main exception being the Douglas sailcloth factory (precursor of that established in the 1850s) which in 1809 employed some 300 hands.[52]

The woollen industry, for its part, had been in decline over most of the country during the last two decades of the eighteenth century. By 1815 the Bandon woollen trade had collapsed, reputedly because of the pressure of continued strikes, but more likely because of the out-dated production methods, high transport costs and changing demands of fashion. There was a consequent exodus of Bandon weavers to Canada and to the textile centres of England, while others moved to Cork city to swell the ranks of the under-employed weavers in the north-side Blarney Lane area.[53] By the early 1820s, though small-scale woollen production and wool-combing continued as a source of employment in many county towns and on Cork city's north side, the industry was failing as that of Bandon had done. However, in some places the remnants of the old woollen production skills enabled a new textile industry to be established on the ashes of the old. In Bandon a new cotton mill was opened in 1810 which, with 10,000 spindles and a work-force of some six hundred in 1825, was capable of producing 3,000 pounds of cotton weekly. This industry and the associated corduroy manufacture promised by the mid-1820s to 'undoubtedly make Bandon one of the most flourishing towns in this part of the kingdom'. The trade directory for 1824, in fact, listed fourteen cotton manufacturers for Bandon, possibly employing a total of 2,000 weavers, mostly outworkers, ten for Cork city and one for Youghal.[54]

This attempted expansion of the textile trade, however, ironically coincided with its demise. Reflecting an overall depression in the economy of the British Isles, unable to keep pace with the British-based textile industry once protective duties had been removed in 1824, and apparently lacking the capital and enterprise to achieve competitiveness through mechanisation, the Irish textile trade outside Ulster went into rapid decline. The first signs of slump appeared in 1825 and by 1826 collapse was reported from centres as far apart as Drogheda, Dublin, Bandon and Cork itself.[55]

In 1826 one Bandon weaver wrote to his uncle in British North America describing how, in spite of his family's success in keeping three looms at work:

> very few looms in this whole town are going ... the price of provisions is very high and the price of labour very low. Great numbers are leaving this poor kingdom for the United States and the British Settlements.[56]

A year later the writer had abandoned weaving and moved to Ballinadee near Kinsale to teach in the parish school. However the correspondence was kept up by another relation still involved in the trade and trying to supplement his livelihood by cultivating a few fields under potatoes and barley. Attempting unsuccessfully to scrape together enough money to pay the family's passage to Canada, he told how he had been idle:

> since last Christmas was twelve months – only [for] the bare weaving of three cuts of cord which came to very little to support the family ... The chief part of the weavers of Bandon are in a state of beggary and many of them turned begging entirely.[57]

By 1830 a modest estimate showed between six and eight hundred textile workers in the Bandon area as unemployed. Ten years later a witness before a parliamentary committee described how only 150 weavers were employed in Bandon and then only for ten months of the year at three-and-sixpence per week. No able-bodied weavers remained in the town: only old men and boys worked at the loom and the young men had either taken to labouring or enlisted in the army.[58]

The experience of the city textile workers was no better: small masters were reduced to working as journeymen, undertakers who had hired out houses and looms fell into destitution, and as distress spread in the textile areas of Blarney, Glasheen and Blackpool, the unemployed weavers and combers were employed on a relief scheme as stone-breakers for a shilling a day. A scheme of subsidised emigration attempted to relieve the situation and a number of unmarried weavers emigrated to Manchester in 1826. Such emigration among weavers had been continual since 1810, between which date and 1833 over 4,000 families reputedly left Cork for the textile areas of England.[59]

Women in the workplace
Attempts over the following two decades to revive the textile trade through movements for the promotion of local manufacture proved futile. The city's 463 weavers in 1831 had fallen in numbers to 160 by 1851, to 25 by 1871 and had disappeared from the census by 1901, while in the county numbers fell over the same period from 2,409 to fifty-seven. However, as the male-dominated domestic textile industry flickered out, there emerged a female-based domestic manufacture movement producing knitted goods, sewed muslin, gloves, lace, crochet and embroidery. This movement to employ the female poor had begun in the 1820s but took off with a new urgency in the crisis years of the mid-forties, with at least a dozen agencies to promote female employment set up in the city between 1845 and 1851. One such training scheme was directly connected with the Established Church. Five others were run by the city's convents, where girls were trained and subsequently employed in the making of crochet-work, silk hair-nets, shirt-fronts and general needlework. Four schemes were run by the combined efforts of benevolent ladies of both major religious persuasions, teaching embroidery, crochet and knitting to girls who in turn trained and employed others on a sub-contracting basis. The remaining schemes were connected with large commercial establishments whose industrial schools-cum-factories employed several hundred female shirt-makers and a small number of children making silk net.[60]

The work-force ranged from ten-year-olds to those described as 'elderly', but most were young women, the daughters and wives of unemployed labourers and tradesmen. Frequently these female workers were the sole earners for their families, bringing in from as little as one shilling to as much as twenty shillings per week, though the average wage appears to have been between three and seven shillings, usually calculated on a piece-work basis.[61] The co-ordinating Irish Manufacture Board in Dublin periodically received complaints regarding the unwillingness of women to work for these low rates, particularly in rural areas where seasonal agricultural work proved more remunerative. The replies to such complaints, however, revealed that much of the movement's motivation was benevolently moralistic rather than purely economic, providing:

> a means of improving and remunerating employment for women and children, and of raising the peasant family from those habits of indolence, and that contentment with privation, dirt and misery which so lamentably characterise it in most parts of Ireland.[62]

Similarly, striking a dual blow for home industry and that cleanliness which is next to godliness, the Cork Ladies' Clothing Society in 1854 had a locally-made blue smock introduced as uniform to neaten the workmen of the tanneries and Butter Weigh-House. A decade later, with the same moral intent, the industrial school connected with the Confraternity of the Holy Family provided that its trainees listened while working to 'instructive and entertaining readings, obviating the worst dangers of association'.[63]

Most of the women employed through these schemes worked either as outworkers or in small groups under the supervision of their patrons. However, from this period too the direct employment of women in large manufacturing establishments became increasingly common. This was particularly true in the city's revived textile trade where the female share of the work-force rose undramatically but steadily from eight per cent in 1851 to thirteen per cent in 1901.[64]

Cotton-spinning briefly employed a work-force of 120 girls and twenty men when Nash and Harty's factory operated on Albert Quay between 1868 and its collapse in bankruptcy in 1871.[65] The area of textiles first to see the real potential of cheap female labour, however, was the linen trade. From 1850 onwards the growing of flax was enthusiastically patronised by improving landlords and aspiring entre-preneurs. In 1851 the Cork Flax Association was founded with the objective of increasing the acreage under flax and setting up scutching and spinning-mills to boost prosperity among the tenant farmers and the labouring classes of city and county. Several scutching-mills were established throughout the county, sometimes building on an area's earlier textile tradition as at Bandon, Drimoleague, Rathcormac and Youghal. In 1864 the Cork Flax Spinning and Weaving Company was established, procuring a mill site and premises for a spinning factory at Millfield near Blackpool.[66] The linen trade weathered the depression of the 1870s badly: by the early '80s it had disappeared from the neighbourhoods of Bandon and Clonakilty while the city experiment met mixed fortunes. The Blackpool mill closed down for a time in the depression of the early 1870s, but opened again in the late '80s to employ a total of 800 workers, mostly women. By 1919 its female work-force had risen to one thousand, one of the largest concentrations of female labour in the county. Another smaller linen-spinning factory operated in conjunction with the sailcloth factory in Douglas from 1866 until it was converted to woollen spinning in the early '80s.[67]

This change-over to woollens was typical of the general trend in textiles from the early 1870s onwards. The oldest woollen manu-facturing firms in the city, at least, had operated in the traditional textile areas within the municipal boundaries: around Blarney Street, Shandon Street and the Watercourse. An early example of a textile concern established in the rural hinterland of the city had been the Glasheen cotton factory of 1779,[68] but the tendency to move out to rural areas was most noticeable from the 1840s when paper mills were established at Trantsbrook near Watergrasshill and at Glanmire, two miles north-east of the city. Glanmire, with its ready supply of water power from the Glashaboy river, remained one of the centres of greatest factory concentration until the twentieth century. Woollen-mills, in particular, were a feature of the area, operating beside bleaching, dyeing and starch-works, though no evidence survives of the numbers employed or of their working conditions.[69] Five miles away on the north-west of the city, the Blarney woollen-mills were established in the 1850s by the Mahoney family; employing some 300 hands by the mid-sixties, this concern continued to operate until the 1970s. It was in the 1880s, however, that the organisation of the woollen industry on a factory basis accelerated. The work-force of the Blarney mills rose to 600; the Dripsey mills, established in an old corn-mill in the 1830s, were reorganised and modernised in 1883. The O'Brien Brothers' mill was opened in Douglas in 1882, employing 450 workers by the end of the century; in 1882 also the linen and sailcloth factory of Wallis and Pollock in the same locality changed over to woollens and in 1890 was bought and modernised by Murrough and Company who thenceforth employed some 300 hands.[70]

By the 1890s, then, the main factory-based employers of female labour were the woollen-mills, the Cork Spinning and Weaving Company, and the readymade clothing firm of Thomas Lyons and Company in the city's South Main Street. Involved directly in cloth manufacture in the 1840s, this firm had by the 1870s moved away from manufacture and into the wholesale business. In 1833, however, it opened its own readymade clothes factory to cater for the working-class and rural markets, and employed some 200 women for the remainder of the century.[71]

The vast majority of women working in these factories were young: over the period 1871 to 1901 from sixty-four to seventy-seven per cent were aged between fifteen and twenty-five years. Because of their youth, their sex and their total lack of unionisation, these factory workers showed little or no militancy. The only recorded instances of strikes were in 1870, 1891 and 1894, while the paternalistic attitude of the employers manifested itself in periodic picnics and entertainments staged for fulsomely grateful employees.[72] Paternalism, female labour and low wages went hand in hand. Female factory-workers' wages were considerably lower than those in the unskilled and semi-skilled male sector, though lack of consistent documentation precludes any real assessment. Piece-work was apparently the norm in the textile and clothing factories: in the early 1870s this seemingly meant an average weekly income of six shillings, rising by the '90s to something under fourteen shillings in the spinning mills and from fifteen shillings to a pound in the clothing factory, although some wages were reputedly as low as half-a-crown a week.[73]

The skilled trades' attitude to large-scale production and female labour remained equivocal: where it did not substantially injure the employment prospects of the existing craft trades it was at best welcomed, at worst tolerated. The spread of the textile factories, for instance, was not apparently objected to, since from the 1830s onwards it was obvious to all that the domestic textile trade was past resuscitation. On the other hand, where large-scale production was accompanied by sweated labour, largely female, it led to bitter conflict in which the craftsmen generally lost out to the forces of modernisation.

As early as 1841, the leaders of the local manufacture revival movement had pressed the hatters' union to admit women to the trade 'in order to cheapen labour'. The move, though predictably rejected by the union, was apparently successful, as the census for the rest of the century shows female workers accounting for twenty-five to thirty-three per cent of the work-force in the city's hat-making industry.[74] With the introduction of the sewing-machine into tailoring, shoemaking, book-binding and upholstery in the 1850s, sweated female labour became increasingly common. The number of female workers rose from fourteen per cent to sixty-six per cent of the city book-binding work-force between 1841 and 1901, and in upholstery the female share of the trade rose from eighteen to thirty per cent in the same period. The

city census for 1851 and 1861 listed some 330 female shoe closers
(thirty-five per cent of the trade), and though this precise category
disappeared from the census thereafter, females continued to account
for between thirteen and nineteen per cent of the footwear trade
labour force until 1901. In tailoring, sweated female labour was
employed from the 1850s, especially in vest-making and in machining
garments cut out by the skilled tailors.[75] Census figures here, however,
hide as much as they reveal, for while the number of females involved
in the combined areas of tailoring, dress-making and shirt-making in
the city averaged some 2,200 over the period 1841 to 1901, it is
impossible to distinguish between factory workers, sweated outworkers
and those self-employed dressmakers who dealt directly with the
public.

The problem of sweated labour in the clothing trade was, however,
sufficiently serious to lead to a protracted strike in 1870, when the city's
unionised tailors attempted to safeguard their position by imposing a
fine on all employers using sewing-machines. The masters claimed that
mechanisation would actually give increased employment by enabling
the manufacture of cheap readymades in otherwise slack periods, and
considering that the 'working tailors of Cork were so obtuse that the
benefits of machinery in their trade would have to be beaten into their
heads' they brought in German strike-breakers, eventually forcing the
journeymen back to work.[76] The outwork controversy continued,
however, and in the 1890s led to a brief ripple of anti-semitism among
the city trades, which condemned the production of 'slop' clothes and
furniture by immigrant Jews as undercutting the livelihood of the
established cabinet-makers and tailors.[77] A more bitter controversy
erupted in 1899 when the tailors' union pressurised the local Harbour
Board to refuse the clothing tender of Thomas Lyons and Company,
arguing that this firm operated on 'unfair' labour, that is unorganised
female labour working under union prices.[78]

Organising the workers
Such undercutting of wages was inevitable while unskilled workers,
both male and female, remained unorganised. In the summer of 1870
some moves towards organisation were apparent when the ten-week-
long tailors' strike generated a wave of popular unrest which
culminated in what the press described as 'the most extraordinary
movement that has yet occurred in our experience' – a wave of strikes
among the unskilled and semi-skilled workers of city and county. The
disturbances began in the Cork Steam Packet Company's yards,
spreading within a matter of hours to the timber yards, salt and lime-
works, provision stores, gas-works and factories. As a band of strikers

led by the flax-mill workers and the notoriously badly-paid foundry labourers paraded from one concern to the next, even the factories employing mainly boy and female labour were drawn in. The feather-dressers, paper-factory women, cotton-mill and flax-mill women and the newspaper boys and tobacco-factory boys all turned out for a uniform rise of two shillings weekly over the then current rates which varied from half-a-crown to six shillings. Within two days the grocers' porters, sailors and coal heavers had joined in, demanding a minimum weekly wage of fifteen shillings.[79] The labour unrest spread to the county towns during the following month: in Mallow strikes of short duration occurred in tan-yards and factories, in Youghal the brickyard labourers struck for a wage rise, and further strikes were reported from Charleville, Kanturk, Fermoy, Queenstown and Kinsale.[80]

General unrest and wage rise demands continued among the city's unskilled over the following two years, but after their initial capitulation employers launched a concerted offensive against the demands of the unskilled. Many of the wage gains of 1870 were eroded in the succeeding decade. By the late 1870s the Butter Market labourers' wages had been reduced to thirteen-and-sixpence to meet a low ebb in the trade, and in the early '80s the Passage dock labourers' wages were similarly cut from eighteen to sixteen shillings.[81]

Yet the consciousness of unskilled labour had been raised and rudimentary unionisation emerged. In the immediate aftermath of the 1870 strike the Butter Market porters established the short-lived Saint Dominick Society, while the grocers' and wine merchants' porters established their own society which lasted into the 1890s. The following twenty years saw the formation of a number of societies catering for the semi-skilled in the city – the Coal Carriers' Union, the Cork Carriers' Society, the City of Cork Quay Labourers' Society and the Builders' Labourers' Society.[82] These local societies were supplemented from 1889 onwards by the organisational drives of the British-based 'New Unions', including the Sunderland-based Sailors' and Firemen's Union and the Merseyside-based National Union of Dock Labourers, both organising from 1889 among the Steam Packet Company employees. Also active was the Amalgamated Society of Railway Servants which organised in the city from 1890 and established branches in Mallow, Queenstown, Fermoy, Skibbereen and Bandon over the following decade.[83]

It was in the 1870s, too, that the first attempt was made to organise the county's agricultural labourers with the establishment of the Kanturk branch of the National Agricultural Labourers' Union in 1873. Though this union's quest for better wages and housing for agricultural labourers made little headway before it was subsumed in the Land

League, it did give some experience of labour and political agitation to the agricultural workers of Kerry and north-east Cork. It was on this earlier foundation, moreover, that in 1881 the labourers and tradesmen of Kanturk organised themselves into a short-lived trades council which was to become the model for the city's first effective trades council.[84]

In the summer of 1881 also, a further wave of militant action erupted among the farm labourers of county Cork. Following a meeting at Limerick at which the Land League urged labourers to join its ranks, a movement began for the improvement of labourers' housing and working conditions. Moving out of Land League control, the labourers in areas as far apart as Kanturk and Millstreet in the north of the county and Carrigaline and Whitechurch in the south struck for wage rises, while around Charleville ricks were burned on the lands of farmers who had displaced labourers by hiring mowing machinery.[85] Though this movement had petered out by the autumn of 1881, it had some repercussions among the city's unskilled when a band of thirty striking farm labourers from Castletown-Kinneigh, some twenty miles north-west of Bandon, came to the city and called on the urban labourers to strike for a wage rise. As in 1870, the call met with an enthusiastic response from the corporation workers, the foundrymen and the tan-yard and factory workers. However, the movement lacked direction and the initial wage rises which some gained were eroded within a year, so that by 1890 the average weekly wage for the city's unskilled was still between twelve and fifteen shillings.[86]

The problem was one of organisation: though unionisation had been slowly spreading outside the traditional craft trades since the 1870s, it failed to reach a really wide spectrum of the unskilled. Hardly any of the newly-formed unions of the 1880s and '90s recruited among either the unskilled or (with the possible exception of the builders' labourers' and railwaymen's unions) among the lowest-paid wage earners. While the builders' labourers earned an average weekly wage of fourteen shillings and the railway porters and signalmen from sixteen to twenty-one shillings, seamen earned between seventeen-and-sixpence and twenty-eight shillings and dockers an average of twenty-three shillings, rates not much lower than those earned by most skilled trades.[87] The majority of these newly-unionised workers, moreover, though generally referred to as 'unskilled', did possess considerable skill and experience in their work and considered themselves far superior to the truly unskilled casual labourer.

In the early 1870s two short-lived societies attempted to unionise the unskilled of the city. These were the Cork Labourers' Society which catered for the general labourer and the Cork Workingmen's Association, originally a Fenian front group but later concentrating on the problems of the agricultural workers and casual dock labourers.[88] By the 1890s, however, these bodies were defunct. The defence of the unskilled fell to the South of Ireland Labour Union, which emerged from obscure origins in 1890 and began recruiting among the labourers of the mills, foundries and factories, claiming within a few months a membership of some 300 drawn from fourteen different categories of labour.[89]

The craft unions regarded these bodies with considerable suspicion and with the snobbery of the skilled towards the unskilled.[90] But this attitude was also based on reluctance to strengthen the bargaining power of workers who, by working as handymen and blacklegs, frequently undercut the wages and employment prospects of the skilled trades. Thus, the Cork trade unions gave no help whatever to the South of Ireland Labour Union's organising drive and, in fact, actively opposed its recruiting efforts,[91] while an equally frosty reception was given to Michael Davitt's Labour Federation of 1890 and to its successor, the Land and Labour League of 1894.[92] This hostility of the skilled towards the unskilled, combined with the oversupply of unskilled workers and the lack of a real activist tradition in their ranks, delayed unionisation of the unskilled into the new century. By 1900 it can be roughly calculated that while some seventy per cent of all skilled men in Cork city were unionised, the level of unionisation among the unskilled and semi-skilled was probably as low as thirty per cent, while in the county the degree of unionisation – skilled and unskilled – was negligible.[93]

Even apart from their shunning of the unskilled, the attitude of the city trade unions remained insular in other respects. Attempts to set up arbitration machinery for the settlement of industrial disputes repeatedly perished on the rock of trades' suspicion of outside intervention in trade matters. Even when the local trades council succeeded in establishing an arbitration board in 1894[94] it was considerably weakened by the constituent unions' fear that publicly-acceptable arbitrators (usually drawn from the business, professional and ecclesiastical circles of the city) would prove favourable to the employer. Most trade societies preferred disputes to be settled within the trade, by a general conference between masters and men, at which all questions could be fully discussed before the imposition of any solution by an outside body.[95] The same caution was evident in the trades' attitude to the question of state regulation of working hours. Agreeing with the principle of an eight-hour day, they considered that any attempt to legislate for such a measure could only succeed if enforced internationally, and in the meantime they preferred to rely on local bargaining between employer and employee.[96]

Localism was even more evident in the Cork city unions' attempts to limit admission of non-local tradesmen to the city labour market. The Ballincollig coopers (a unionised body) who worked in the gunpowder mills five miles from the city centre, were allowed to work beside the city's unionised coopers only under stringent conditions, while the city's unionised painters blithely blacklegged on the Fermoy painters' union, defending their action on the grounds that 'their society had nothing to do with men of other towns, and only looked after its own members'.[97]

Cork workers' external links

The story, however, was not one of unmitigated isolationism. Connections between the Cork city unions and those of other Irish towns had long existed, though it is not clear whether these were formal amalgamations or simply *ad hoc* informal contacts. In the early 1830s, for instance, the Cork brushmakers, hatters and glovers were in contact with their counterparts in Dublin, and in 1845 the Cork stonecutters were described as being 'in union with' those of Youghal. On the occasion of public parades in the same period, local societies borrowed the trade banners from other centres, the Cork societies lending banners to the Mallow and Cahir unions in the mid-1840s and borrowing those of the Limerick tailors in 1862.[98] Later in the century more formal amalgamations were forged with trade unions in other Irish centres. In 1873 the Bakers' Union of Ireland, founded after a successful strike by the journeymen bakers of Dublin, began to organise in the provinces, including Cork city and fourteen county Cork towns.[99] Seeking a wage rise and the abolition of night-work, the union was only temporarily successful and by the mid-seventies any gains it had made were undone.[100] When the Cork bakers next joined an amalgamation in 1890, it was the Belfast-based Irish Bakers' Federal Union which again sought wage rises and the abolition of night-work in resurrected branches at Cork, Midleton, Cloyne, Castlemartyr, Aghada, Carrigtwohill and Whitegate. Again, the gains proved short-lived: a major anti-night-work strike in the city collapsed within six weeks and many of the county branches – the largest of which cannot have numbered more than twenty members – relapsed into obscurity.[101]

Links with other Irish-based amalgamations were attempted by the city's stonecutters and coopers, and by the pork butchers. The stonecutters joined with the Operative Stonecutters of Ireland in the early 1890s, but no details of the nineteenth-century history of this union have been found. The pork butchers of the city joined with the Amalgamated Society of Pork Butchers of Cork, Limerick and Waterford in 1890, while the coopers attempted an even more limited organisation, establishing a Bantry branch of the city society in 1887.[102] In 1881, an attempt at wider labour co-operation was made with the establishment of the city's United Trades Association, whose ultimate objective was to form the nucleus of an all-Ireland body, geared to protect home industry and establish a dispute-free industrial climate. By late 1881 Cork had co-operated with the trades of other centres to establish branches at Skibbereen, Queenstown, Mallow, Bantry, Fermoy, Youghal, Clonakilty, Passage, Mitchelstown, Kanturk and Millstreet and with two county Tipperary branches at Clonmel and Tipperary town. However, between 1882 and 1884, although the county branches continued to function, the disturbances accompanying the land agitation prevented further organisation outside Cork city. By 1884 all links with the county branches were severed while the city body independently developed into the Cork Trades Council of the twentieth century.[103]

The most successful attempts to co-operate with organised labour outside Cork city were, in fact, made with British-based rather than Irish organisations. This trend dated from at least as early as the 1830s when the Manchester-based Friendly Society of Journeymen Cabinet-makers, Carvers and Wood-turners established a twenty-six member Cork branch. At the same time the Birmingham-based United Operative Stonemasons' Society began organising branches in Ireland, radiating south from Belfast and reaching Cork in 1837. Active for a number of years, the Irish branches distinguished themselves by a consistent reluctance to obey the rules and pay union dues, and were eventually cut off, to lapse into localism for the rest of the century.[104] The Cork printers, too, had a brief affiliation with the British-based National Typographical Association between 1845 and 1849. However in their case the separation was amicable and they continued to co-operate with the British society, sending trade reports to the executive, supporting strikes in other centres in the two islands and arranging for the mutual relief of members on tramp.[105] The local Coachmakers' Society, in existence since 1812, joined the Liverpool-based United Kingdom Society of Coachmakers in 1851, followed sometime between 1852 and 1860 by the coachmakers of Fermoy. Though the small Fermoy branch had apparently lapsed by 1870, that of Cork maintained a membership of between fifty and one hundred for the rest of the century.[106]

This move towards amalgamation on the part of the coachmakers reflected the rise of the 'new model' unionism in the British Isles: a unionism distinguished from earlier movements by its efficiency, respectability, centralisation and comprehensive benefit schemes. Also part of the same development were the new and reorganised engineering unions towards which some Cork workers gravitated from the late 1840s. The Manchester-based Ironmoulders' Friendly Society

Plate 18.2   Unidentified Cork tailors' workshop c. 1890 (M. Cronin).

had a short-lived Cork branch from 1840 to 1852, while the United Society of Boilermakers and Iron Shipbuilders maintained a branch in the city from 1847 to the end of the century. In 1851 the Amalgamated Society of Engineers established a thirty-six member branch in Cork, based probably on the pre-existing local Society of Machine Smiths. Including turners, fitters, millwrights, pattern-makers and smiths, the Cork membership numbered 102 by 1867, and fluctuated between this and 150 for the rest of the century.[107]

By 1855, then, Cork unions had experienced official links with labour organisations in several British centres, but it was really from the late 1860s that the greatest drive was made towards unity with British trade-unionism. In 1868 the Liverpool-based United Operative Plumbers' Association established a Cork lodge which continued to function for the rest of the century. In 1873 the Amalgamated Society of Tailors began to admit the various local societies in Ireland, Cork being one of the first to join, followed by Queenstown, Fermoy, Midleton, Kanturk and Skibbereen between 1875 and 1889.[108] Ironically, this increasing co-operation between Cork organised labour and that in Britain coincided with the growth of nationalism in the shape of the separatist Fenian movement and the more moderate Home Rule campaign. At times, indeed, the move towards labour solidarity was destined to clash with a combination of new nationalism and traditional localism. Thus, from the establishment of its Cork branch in 1871, the Manchester-based Amalgamated Society of Carpenters and Joiners met continued fierce opposition from the local carpenters' society which dismissed the amalgamated men as 'English dupes' and described its own continued independence in the political terminology of the day:

> With an unsullied record of two-hundred years, we decline to sell our birthright, and on the principle of Home Rule, prefer to govern ourselves.

Twenty years later the recruiting efforts of another British-based body, the General Union of Friendly Operative Carpenters and Joiners, met with similar hostility: deputations were sent to local builders to prevent the employment of the General Union members, their meeting rooms were picketed and their attendance at the Irish Trades Union Congress caused a major furore.[109] Similarly in 1894 when an internal dispute among the local Plasterers' Society led to the defeated group establishing a branch of the English-based National Union of Operative Plasterers in the city, the continued opposition of the local body led to the collapse of the amalgamated branch by 1899.[110]

Even where amalgamation was accepted at local level, considerable friction ensued between executive and local branch, the practice of equalisation being the source of much irritation to prosperous local branches. The Cork branch of the Amalgamated Society of Engineers, for instance, had its funds cut by almost £200 in 1894 to meet the equalisation requirements of the union.[111] But the irritation was more frequently felt by the executive than by the local branch. Financial issues were a major irritant: the Amalgamated Society of Tailors' executive was annoyed by the unsatisfactory nature of the Cork city branch's financial reports and by its high room rents. Moreover, when the Cork secretary drank the funds in 1887, the local branch stood by him for four years and refused to reimburse headquarters.[112] Besides, union aid for local strikes was often given grudgingly when it was felt that action had been hasty. In 1872, the coach makers' union sharply criticised the Cork branch for striking for a cut in hours, while the local branches of the seamen's and dockers' unions received severe censure from their respective executives for strike action taken in 1890-91. Although the executive stood by the men in the settlement talks, several of the offenders received no strike pay.[113]

Nonetheless, despite these frictions and the continued preference of some trades for locally-based societies, the move towards British-based labour organisations continued. By 1880 there were six branches of British amalgamated unions and sixteen local bodies in Cork city; the following fifteen years brought a further rise in amalgamation. Six new union branches were established on the amalgamated principle in Cork in the 1880s and eight in the 1890s, either fusing or co-existing with local societies or starting from scratch where no previous union had existed. In 1880, over seventy-five per cent of all unionised workers in Cork city had belonged to locally-based societies; by 1895 over seventy per cent belonged to amalgamated union branches, twenty-one of which operated beside the nine local societies.

Continuing contact between the trades of Cork city and county and those of other centres was ensured by the prevalence of the traditional 'tramping' system whereby most trade societies used part of their funds for the relief of visiting tramps. The tramp system long predated the amalgamated unions, but the existence of an amalgamated society branch in a town guaranteed the survival of the tradition by ensuring a constant stream of tramps, not alone from other Irish towns but also from Britain. Between 1865 and 1877 the Cork branch of the Amalgamated Society of Engineers relieved an average of ten tramps per year. These men passed through Cork *en route* to and from Britain and America as well as between Cork and other Irish towns. So great was the tramp traffic in the trade in general that in 1866 it was found necessary to prevent frauds by tightening up the regulations governing the issue of travelling cards. The local branch of the Ironfounders' Society also catered for tramps, providing them with beer, bed and supper together with payment at the rate of one penny per mile tramped. Between 1840 and 1852 the Cork branch catered for 1,160 tramps – an average of ninety-six per year, with the greatest influx (844) in 1847 and 1848.[114]

Not all trades favoured the tramping system: the Amalgamated Society of Tailors, whose Cork branch was set up in 1873, catered little for tramps. Between 1874 and 1893 the Cork branch issued very few travelling cards to its members and spent only £7. 5s. on relieving tramps. During the same period £266. 8s. was spent by the local branch of the United Kingdom Society of Coachmakers, that society generally preferring tramp relief to the 'stationary' relief favoured by the tailors. In the coachmakers' case tramp traffic through Cork continued steadily from 1850 to 1880, reaching its zenith in the latter half of the 1870s and declining to a trickle from 1880 onwards with the shrinking of employment opportunities in the city.[115]

For the nineteenth-century workman, the tramping system opened up a window to the outside world in a society which is often seen as insular and introverted. In 1833, an unemployed Cork baker, appearing in court on a combination charge, gave an account of his travels. He had tramped in three weeks from Cork to Macroom, thence to Killarney, back to Passage West and Cove, on to Fermoy and back to Cork city, a distance of well over 160 miles, getting threepence relief from the bakers' society in each town *en route*.[116] Three decades later the records of the Amalgamated Society of Engineers show this rather limited circuit had been greatly widened by the experience of amalgamation. In 1865 one member left Cork in November, and travelling through Bristol, Newport, Plymouth, Stockport, Highbridge and Manchester, was relieved by the union branch in each centre, finally arriving in Worcester in December. In March 1870 another member who left Cork made an even longer circuit to Burnley, back to Waterford, cross-channel again to Middlesborough, York, Jarrow, Gateshead, Newcastle-on-Tyne and Sunderland, back to Jarrow and on to Ayr, Dumfries, Kilmarnock, Johnstone, Dumbarton, Dunfermline, Edinburgh, Greenock and Leith.[117]

This increasing mobility of tradesmen was greatly facilitated from the 1840s onwards by the development of both the railways and the cross-channel steamers, but Cork's proximity to the British ports was a mixed blessing. Since access to Cork from inland Irish towns was less easy (even when the railway system had long been established) than Britain's access to Cork, the southern city frequently received an influx of tramps from Britain who, instead of passing through *en route* to other Irish towns, stayed in the city to add to the already overstocked labour market. In 1896 favourable reports of the Cork printing trade by the *Labour Gazette* and *Print* led to a great influx of tramps to Cork, much to the disgust of the local printers' society, while the boot and shoe rivetters faced this same problem during the 1880s and '90s.[118]

Nineteenth-century work and workers in Cork: a reappraisal

In 1893 the *Cork Examiner* commented on the:

> growth of sympathy between workingmen of the two countries [i.e. Ireland and England]. The quay labourers in Cork or in Waterford, in Belfast or Dublin, have today a keener personal interest in the fate of the workmen in Bristol or in Hull than their fathers had in the neighbouring county.[119]

While this assessment was basically accurate, such neat conclusions, tempting though they may be, impose an artificial sense of progression on what was a halting and sporadic development. If a more outward-looking labour consciousness grew among Cork workers, it was not totally new, as the experience of amalgamation with British trade-unionism had shown as early as the 1830s. Neither did this growing awareness of the outside world fully displace the traditional isolationist tendencies of the skilled workers, or change their antipathy towards the unskilled labourers.

Similarly, while working conditions generally improved over the course of the century, many earlier features remained unchanged. If unionisation spread among the skilled and semi-skilled male workers, the ranks of the unskilled casual labourers and the female factory and sweated workers remained largely unorganised. If wages rose in many sectors, such advances were frequently eroded by the effects of unemployment. Finally, if modernisation and mechanisation provided increased employment and better conditions for many workers, they threw many others onto the refuse heap of redundancy and eventual oblivion.

Writing in the 1960s, the Cork sculptor Séamus Murphy voiced in perhaps over-romanticised terms what some workers of the late 1890s might have thought as they looked back at the combined course of progress and decline over the preceding decades:

> I am always deeply moved when I meet some of the old men I have worked with, standing idle at street corners with their lumpy hands awkwardly by their sides – always hoping things will improve. There is something about men with whom you have

done many a hard day's work that makes them very dear to you. I don't know what it is, but it can be conveyed by a look in the eye, and one feels the bond is strong. They have meant much to me. From them I have got companionship and friendliness and the respect for a job well done. They put me on my road. But it is a lonely road now. Every year there are bigger gaps in the ranks, and no one to fill them. We will go on till we become just a memory for another generation, and perhaps they will think of us occasionally, maybe honour us with a little study.[120]

References

1. Text from D. Casey (ed.), *Cork lyrics; or scraps from the beautiful city* (Cork, 1857), pp 125-27. The *Groves of Blackpool* was again popularised by Cork folk-singer Jimmy Crowley in the 1970s.

2. See Moore's *National Exhibition map of the city, river & harbour of Cork* (June, 1852) in Cork City Library, map collection, map no. 30.

3. Pers. comm. in 1978 from Mr Thomas Murphy, longtime resident of the area.

4. C.A.I., Cork Coopers' Society minutes (hereafter Coopers' mins.), 4 May 1886-12 June 1895, 6, 20 May 1896; *Reports of strikes and lock-outs by the labour correspondent of the Board of Trade* [hereafter *Reports of strikes*], 260 [C 7901], H.C. 1895, xcii, 211; ibid., 441 [C 8231], H.C. 1896, lxxx, 228; *C.E.,* 11 Nov. 1850.

5. *C.C.,* 27 Feb. 1829, 9 Mar., 1834; *C.E.,* 9 June 1845; Census, Cork city, 1871-1891; *Reports of strikes,* i, 423 [C 7566], H.C. 1894, lxxxi, 42, 63, 65; ibid., 211 [C 7901], H.C. 1895, xcii, 82-3; ibid., 239 [C 8643], H.C. 1896, lxxiv, 20-21; ibid., 423 [C 9012] H.C. 1898, lxxxviii, 20-21; *Minutes of evidence before the Royal Commission on labour* [hereafter *Royal Commission on labour,* 1892], ii, [C 6795-vi], H.C. 1892, ii, q. 16969 (hereafter references to question numbers only).

6. C.A.I., Coopers' mins., 19, 25 Jan. 1883, 30 Sept. 1886, 8 Aug. 1888, 30 May 1889, 6, 15 July 1896; C.A.I., Cork Typographical Society minute book (hereafter Typographical mins.), 21 Apr. 1888, 17 Dec. 1891, 23 April 1892, 25 Feb. 1893, 1 8 June 1895.

7. *C.E.,* 19 Jan. 1855, 21, 28 Oct., 25 Nov. 1886, 18 Nov., 2 Dec. 1892.

8. Lewis, *Topog. dict. Ire.,* i, pp 416-17; *Report on changes in the rate of wages and hours of labour in the United Kingdom: second report,* i, 225 [C 8075], H.C. 1896, lxxx, 104-5; *Reports of strikes,* 239 [C 8643], H.C. 1897, xcix, 275; C.A.I., British and Irish Steam Packet Company records, City of Cork Steam Packet Company wages books, 1871-74; ibid., Watercourse Distillery labour lists, 1830, 1871, 1881, 1889, 1893-98.

9. Census, Cork city, 1841-1901.

10. J. D. Clarkson, *Labour and nationalism in Ireland* (New York, 1925), pp 40-42; A. Boyd, *Rise of the Irish trade unions 1729-1970* (Tralee, 1972), p. 14; S. Daly, *Cork: a city in crisis* (Cork, 1978), pp 281-310, 383-5.

11. S.P.O., S.O.C.P., 1817: 1835/1; 1822: 2344/5, 2345/81; *Cork Morning Intelligencer,* 16, 18 Jan., 8 Feb., 13 Mar., 12, 26 May, 19 June 1821; *Freeholder,* 12, 21, 29 June 1822; *Southern Reporter,* 10, 12, 15, 19, 24 Jan., 1826.

12. S.P.O., O.P., 1833/5859.

13. S.P.O., S.O.C.P., 1822: 2435/81; *S.R.,* 10 Sept. 1840.

14. *C.C.,* 23 April 1829; *S.R.,* 21 July 1840; *C.E.,* 11 June 1870; *Royal Commission on the state of the poorer classes in Ireland: first report* [hereafter *Royal Commission ... poorer classes,* 1836], [C 35], H.C. 1836, xxx, 25, 89, 90, 100.

15. *C.E.,* 25 Sept. 1891, 4, 17 May 1893; *Labour Gazette,* June 1894, *Limerick Reporter and Tipperary Vindicator,* 18 Nov. 1890. This pattern was common to all big towns: in 1890 a strike by Limerick dockers was broken by the employment of agricultural labourers specially brought in from Portlaw in county Waterford.

16. *C.E.,* 6, 10 Mar. 1883; *Royal Commission on labour,* 1892, qq 16576, 16581-5, 28952-3, 29006. Average Cork rates in the baking trade by the 1890s were 28*s.* for a 76 to 90 hour week; bakers in some provincial towns throughout the country worked a 105 hour week for 18*s.* while those in Dundalk were expected to act also as deliverymen.

17. *Royal Commission on labour,* 1892, qq 17042-6, 28811, 28969, 29006, 29037-38.

18. *Limerick Evening Post,* 11 Jan. 1828; *C.E.,* 12 Jan. 1853, 19 Jan. 1855, 1, 2, 3 July 1863; C.A.I., Coopers' mins 4, 5 May 1886, 6 Sept. 1898.

19. *C.E.,* 7 Mar. 1851, 24 Jan. 1855; Modern Records Centre, Warwick University (hereafter M.R.C.), *Typographical Circular,* July 1853, 18 Oct. 1887; *Typographical Society monthly report,* Feb. 1860, p. 2, Sept. 1860, p. 1; *Royal Commission on labour,* 1892, q. 22799.

20. *C.M.C.,* 13 Feb. 1828, *C.C.,* 1 July 1834; *C.E.,* 23 Oct. 1850, 20, 23 Apr., 7 May 1855, 29 Apr. 1859; *Royal Commission ... poorer classes,* 1836, Appendix C, p. 27; C.A.I., Coopers' mins., 7 Jan. 1875, 21 Apr. 1887, 27 Sept. 1898.

21. *C.E.,* 20 July, 23 Sept. 1881.

22. *C.E.,* 23, 28 Jan., 11 Feb., 4 Mar., 1 July 1857, 2, 16, 26 April 1858.

23. M.R.C., *Typographical Circular,* Feb. 1850; Webb Trade Union Collection, London School of Economics (hereafter L.S.E.), *Half-yearly report, National Typographical Association,* 1861; *C.E.,* 15, 18 Mar. 1882, 30 May 1894, 19 Sept; 27, 30 Oct. 1896, 7 Sept. 1897.

24. Clarkson, *Labour and nationalism,* pp 40-42 quoting Act for Regulation of the City of Cork, 11 & 12 Geo. III, c. 18.

25. *Cork Morning Intelligencer,* 1 Oct., 31 Dec. 1802, 8 March, 15, 17, 19, 29 May 1821; *C.E.,* 4, 11 Feb. 1846, *S.R.,* 2 Feb. 1826, 27 Feb. 1841.

26. Daily wage rates compiled from evidence in contemporary newspapers, trade-union records and parliamentary reports.

27. *C.C.,* 18 Feb., 1830; C.A.I., Watercourse Distillery wages book, 1830-1834.

28. C.A.I., Watercourse Distillery wages book, Dec. 1871; ibid., City of Cork Steam Packet Company wages books, 1871-1874.

29. *Royal Commission on labour,* 1892, q. 17143.

30. Ibid., q. 16960.

31. *C.C.,* 23, 26, 30 Nov. 1855; *C.E.,* 11 June 1855, 29 June 1870, 21 July 1887; C.A.I., Coopers' mins., 13 Dec. 1871, 9, 16, 23 Sept. 1896, 6 July 1898.

32. *Royal Commission ... poorer classes,* 1836, Appendix C, p. 28; *C.E.,* 23, 26, 30 Nov., 2 Dec. 1855, 29 June 1870.

33. *C.E.,* 25, 27 May 1870, 6 June 1893; National Union of Tailors and Garment Workers, Radlett House, West Hill, Aspley Guise, Milton Keynes (hereafter N.U.T.G.W.), *Yearly financial report of the Amalgamated Society of Tailors,* 1868-1900; *Return relating to wages in the United Kingdom, 273* [C 5172], H.C. 1887, lxxxix, 410.

34. *Royal Commission on labour,* 1892, pp 82-3.

35. *C.E.,* 2, 4 Aug. 1870, 6 Feb. 1886, 10 Apr. 1893, N.U.T.G.W., *Yearly financial*

report of the Amalgamated Society of Tailors, 1878, 1887.

36. *C.E.,* 23 Aug. 1892, 3, 4, 8 Apr., 31 May, 10 June, 25 Aug., 1893, 17 Nov., 1896.

37. *Royal Commission on labour,* 1892, qq 14641-2; *C.E.,* 1, 10 Nov., 11 Dec. 1882, 10 Mar., 23 Nov. 1887; *Cork Daily Herald,* 18 Nov. 1887; National Union of Footwear, Leather and Allied Trades, The Grange, Earl's Barton, Northampton (hereafter N.U.F.L.A.T.), *National Union of Boot and Shoe Rivetters and Finishers' monthly report,* 1885-1900.

38. *C.E.,* 24 Apr. 1882, 21-27 Jan. 1877, 26 Feb., 10 June, 26 Aug., 8, 9 Sept., 17 Oct., 29 Nov. 1893, 16 Nov. 1896.

39. *C.E.,* 4 Feb., 8 May, 20, 27 Sept. 1895; C.A.I., Cork Steam Packet Company wages books, 1871-74; Bishopsgate Institute, London (hereafter B.I.L.), *Quarterly report of the Amalgamated Shipwrights' Society,* June 1893 – June 1894, Sept. 1894, Mar. 1895; *Labour Gazette,* May 1894, pp 138-9, Sept. 1894, p. 266, Nov. 1894, p. 331.

40. Donnelly, *Land and people,* p. 139; C.A.I., Coopers' mins., 3 Mar. 1887, 2 Feb. 1888, 6 Feb. 1889; *C.E.,* 5 May 1843, 6, 20 May, 21 Sept. 1846; *Royal Commission on labour,* 1892, q. 16969.

41. *C.M.C ,* 1 Feb. 1832; Census, 1831; E. J. Riordan, *Modern Irish trade and industry* (London, 1920), pp 31-2. Before 1815 salt import duties were £4 per ton but in that year were raised to £40 to equal those paid by English importers.

42. *C.E.,* 19 Sept. 1891, 8 Dec. 1893, 14 Dec. 1894, 15 Nov. 1895; C.A.I., Coopers' mins., 14 Sept. 1895.

43. C.A.I., Coopers' mins., 12 Mar. 15 Aug. 1883, 8 June, 10 Aug. 1886, 17 May 1888, 7 Dec. 1892, 17 Jan. 1899, *C.E.,* 6, 12 June 1896; *Guy's directory of Munster 1886-1900* (Cork, 1886); A. Aldwell, *County and city of Cork directory 1844-45* (Cork, 1844).

44. *C.C.,* 7 Feb. 1829; *C.E.,* 15, 19 Aug. 1842, 5 Dec. 1888; Census 1831-1901; C.A.I., City of Cork Steam Packet Company wages books, 1871-74.

45. *C.E.,* 15 Dec. 1829, 3 Mar. 1885, 13 Jan., 27 Mar. 1886, 12 June 1896.

46. *Royal Commission on labour,* 1892, q. 16973-5; C.A.I., Coopers' mins., 18 Jan. 1898, 26 Jan. 1899.

47. Census, 1831-1901.

48. *Slater's royal national commercial directory of Ireland* (Manchester, 1856), p. 208; *Guy's directory of Munster,* 1881, 1884, 1907; *C.E.,* 23 Sept., 19 Oct. 1881, 24 Apr. 1882.

49. *C.E.,* 19 Oct. 1881, 2, 6 Nov. 1883, 29 April 1884, 12 Aug. 1886, 17 June 1895, *Guy's county and city of Cork directory 1875-6* (Cork, 1875), *Guy's directory of Munster 1886-1907.*

50. L. M. Cullen, *Economic history of Ireland since 1660* (London, 1972), p. 105.

51. W. Crawford, *Domestic industry in Ireland* (Dublin, 1972), pp 3-5; *Pigot and company's city of Dublin and Hibernian provincial directory* (London, 1824), pp 232-4, 307; *Slater's royal national commercial directory of Ireland* (London, 1870), p. 100; Bennett, *Bandon,* p. 314.

52. Cork Chamber of Commerce, *Cork industrial and commercial* (Cork 1919), p. 56; *Guy's directory of Munster,* 1881, 1884; *Pigott's directory 1824,* pp 232-4.

53. Cullen, *Economic history,* p. 105; Bennett, *Bandon,* pp 314-315, 370-373.

54. *Pigott's directory 1824,* p. 222; Riordan, *Modern Irish trade,* p. 23.

55. Cullen, *Economic history,* pp 105-109; *S.R.,* 16 Mar., 29 April, 9, 16 May, 15 June, 15 Aug., 19 Nov. 1826.

56. J. Huston to his uncle, 24 Mar. 1826 in C.A.I., Bandon File, MS U 9 (5).

57. C.A.I., Bandon File, MS U 9 (5), W. and L. Anstis to R. Cody, 29 July 1826.

58. *C.C.,* 10 Dec. 1830; *Report of the Royal Commission to enquire into the condition*

of the handloom weavers, iii, [C 43-11], H.C. 1840, xxiii, 658.

59. *C.C.*, 5 Jan. 1825, *S.R.*, 15 June, 4, 9, 11 Nov. 1826, 10, 15, 20, 25, Feb. 1827; *C.C.*, 6, 17 Apr. 1830; *Royal Committee ... poorer classes*, Appendix C., pp 27-28.

60. J. F. Maguire, *The Irish industrial movement* (Cork, 1853), pp 185-92, 203-09, 214-22, 234-46; *C.E.*, 12 Feb., 16 Oct. 1850, 15 June 1857.

61. Maguire, *The Irish industrial movement*, pp 203-09, 219-22; *C.E.*, 31 July 1850, 5 Feb. 1851, 26 Jan. 1853.

62. *Irish Trades Advocate*, 25 Oct. 1851.

63. *C.E.*, 26 July 1854, 28 May 1862.

64. Census, 1851-1901: the percentages were 8.10 (1851), 9.09 (1861), 11.70 (1871), 9.18 (1881), 10.63 (1891), 13.09 (1901).

65. *C.E.*, 1 July 1871.

66. *C.E.*, 24 Jan., 7 Feb. 1851, 23 Nov. 1853, 1 Jan. 1864, 10 July 1866.

67. *Guy's directory*, 1875-1886.

68. M. J. Gough, 'History of the physical development of Cork city', unpublished M.A. thesis, U.C.C. (1973).

69. *Cork industrial and commercial*, pp 200-201.

70. *Guy's directory of Munster*, 1881-1900; C.A.I., Murrough Mills sundry books; *Cork industrial and commercial*, pp 171-3.

71. *Aldwell's Directory 1844-45;* C.A.I., Thomas Lyons and Company minute books [hereafter Lyons, minute books], 30 Sept. 1873, 27 Feb; *C.E.*, 14 April 1896.

72. *C.E.,* 28 Dec. 1869, 28 June 1870, 7 Apr. 1891, 22 Apr. 1896; C.A.I., Lyons, minute books, 15 May 1894.

73. *C.E.,* 28 June 1870, 1 May 1890, 26 Aug. 1899; Census, 1871-1901.

74. *S.R.,* 15 May 1841; *Royal Commission ... poorer classes*, 1836, Appendix C., p. 27; Census, 1841-1901.

75. Census, 1841-1901; *C.E.*, 22 Aug., 10 Sept. 1855, 16 Feb. 1857, 11 Nov. 1872, 24 Jan. 1894.

76. *C.E.,* 27, 30 May, 11 June, 6 July 1870; Daly, *Cork: a city in crisis,* pp 144-5, 153-4.

77. *C.E.,* 2 Mar. 1888, 22, 24 Aug. 1894, 10 May 1895.

78. C.A.I., Lyons, minute books, 1 June 1899; *C.E.*, 26 Aug., 2 Sept. 1899.

79. *C.E.*, 28, 29 June 1870.

80. 6, 7 July 1870; C.S.O., R.P., 14005, 15232.

81. *C.E.*, 1 Jan., 26 Oct., 9 Nov. 1871, 10, 29 Aug., 2 Sept., 28 Oct. 1872, 7, 10 Nov. 1881, 4 Apr. 1882.

82. *C.E.*, 28, 29 June 1870, 12 Dec. 1889, 18 March 1890; *Reports of strikes,* 277, [C. 7901], H.C. 1895, xcii, 60; ibid, 239 [C. 8643], H.C. 1897, xcix., pp. 16-17, 132-22.

83. *C.E.*, 2 Mar. 9 Dec. 1889; *Seafaring,* 20 Mar. 1889, p. 8; L.S.E., *National Amalgamated Sailors' and Firemens' Union of Great Britain and Ireland annual report*, 1889, p. 111; B.I.L., *Amalgamated Society of Railway Servants report and financial statement*, 1889-1899.

84. P. L. R. Horn, 'The national agricultural labourers' union in Ireland 1873-79' in *I.H.S.*, xvii, no. 67 (Mar. 1971), pp 350-51; *C.E.*, 21, 25 Feb. 1881.

85. D. Keane, 'Agricultural labourers in north Cork, 1870-1890', unpublished B.Ed. dissertation, Mary Immaculate College, Limerick (1983), pp 10-12.

86. *C.E.*, 18, 19, 20, 22 July, 2, 3, 5, 9, 16 Aug. 1881, 13 Sept. 1882, 6 May 1890; Donnelly, *Land and people,* pp 238-40.

87. *C.E.,* 12 Dec. 1889, 31 Mar., 9 Nov. 1890; *Seafaring,* 6 Apr. 1889, p. 13, 1 June 1889, p. 12, 7 June 1890, p. 13.

88. Daly, *Cork: a city in crisis,* pp 5, 90, 214, 314; *Cork Daily Herald,* 13 Oct. 1875.
89. *C.E.,* 3, 24 Feb. 1890.
90. A Dublin artisan giving evidence before the Royal Commission on Labour in 1892 stated his conviction that no artisan 'should resort to such a lot' as to become a labourer, and described how artisans taking up unskilled work moved to avoid embarrassment to areas where they were not previously known; see *Royal Commission on labour,* 1892, qq 16858-9, 16862.
91. *C.E.,* 31 Jan., 3, 4, 8, 14, 17, 19, 28 Feb., 2, 4, 8 Mar. 1890.
92. *C.E.,* 19 Oct., 9, 12 Nov. 1890.
93. Percentage unionisation is calculated on the basis of evidence in the surviving trade-union records and census reports.
94. *C.E.,* 24 Feb., 24 Mar. 1893, 14 Dec. 1894.
95. *C.E.,* 31 May, 1 June 1893, 12, 14, 25 May 1894.
96. *Royal Commission on labour,* 1892, qq 17000-01, 17147-8.
97. B.I.L., Webb Trade Union Collection, Sec. A, iii, ff 46-7.
98. *C.M.C.,* 12, 13, 16 Mar. 1832; Clarkson, *Labour and nationalism in Ireland,* pp 110-113; *C.E.,* 5, 9, 12 June 1843, 9 June, 22 Sept. 1845; *Cork Daily Herald,* 2 Jan. 1862.
99. *C.E.,* 1, 25, 26 Aug. 1873. The towns were Midleton, Kinsale, Dunmanway, Clonakilty, Bantry, Rosscarbery, Fermoy, Mallow, Kanturk, Macroom, Charleville, Mitchelstown, Millstreet and Youghal.
100. *C.E.,* 4, 5, 15 Dec. 1876.
101. *Bakers' Record and General Advertiser,* 19 Apr. 19 July, 6, 16, 30 Aug., 13, 20 Sept. 1890; *C.E.,* 11 Aug., 8, 10, 17, 29 Sept., 9 Oct., 15 Nov. 1890, 1 June 1892; *Royal Commission on labour,* 1892, qq 28862-5.
102. C.A.I., Bantry coopers' book, 1887.
103. *C.E.,* 1 Jan., 21 Feb., 10 Mar., 11 July, 2, 3 10 Sept., 17, 18 Oct. 1881, 31 Jan., 23 May 1884.
104. M.R.C., *United Operative Stonemasons' forthnightly report,* June 1835-Mar. 1840.
105. *Half-yearly report of the National Typographical Association,* January-June 1845, Jan.-July 1846; *Provincial Typographical Association half-yearly report,* 1860, 1867, 1870, 1871.
106. Vehicle Building and Automotive Museum, Coventry, *United Kingdom Society of Coachmakers, first quarterly report; Quarterly report of the United Kingdom Society of Coachmakers,* 1851-1900.
107. D. C. Cummings, *A historical survey of the boilermakers and iron shipbuilders' society 1834-1904,* (Newcastle-on-Tyne, 1905), p. 38; Amalgamated Union of Engineering Workers, 110, Peckham Road, London, *Annual report of the Amalgamated Society of Engineers,* 1851-1900.
108. N.U.T.G.W, *Quarterly report of the Amalgamated Society of Tailors,* Nov. 1873, pp 1-7, 12 Apr. 1875, p. 8, Jan. 1885, p. 4; *Yearly and financial report of the Amalgamated Society of Tailors,* 1874-1889.
109. *C. E.,* 12, 18 Apr. 1875, 22 Mar. 1877, 15-28 Mar. 1887; *Cork Daily Herald,* 11, 12 Apr. 1873; B.I.L., *Annual report of the Amalgamated Society of Carpenters and Joiners,* 1871, 1877; *Report of the second Irish Trade Union Congress,* 1895, pp 17-20.
110. *C.E.,* 16 Oct., 19 Nov. 1894; M.R.C., *Monthly report of the National Association of Operative Plasterers,* Nov. 1894, p. 16, Sept. 1897, p. 17, *National Association of Operative Plasterers auditors' report 1894-99.*
111. Equalisation enabled the union executive to appropriate local branch funds which had risen above a certain level for distribution among branches whose

funds were below that level; see *Annual report of the Amalgamated Society of Engineers,* 1894.

112. *Quarterly report of the Amalgamated Society of Tailors,* July 1874, Apr. 1875, Feb. 1887, Feb. 1891.

113. *Quarterly report of the United Kingdom Society of Coachmakers,* June 1872, p. 1; *Seafaring,* 8 Nov. 1890, p. 3, 4 July, 22 Aug. 1891.

114. *Annual report of the Amalgamated Society of Engineers,* 1865-1871; *Half-yearly report of the Ironfounders' Society of England, Ireland and Wales,* 1840-52.

115. *Yearly and financial report of the Amalgamated Society of Tailors,* 1874-1894; *Quarterly report of the United Kingdom Society of Coachmakers,* 1874-1900; *C.E.,* 28 Sept., 7 Oct. 1881, 24 Apr. 1882.

116. *C.C.,* 30 Nov. 1833.

117. *Annual report of the Amalgamated Society of Engineers,* Travelling Accounts, 1865-71.

118. *Monthly report of the National Union of Boot and Shoe Rivetters and Finishers,* Aug. 1888, p. 5, July 1890, p. 7, May 1898, p. 5; C.A.I., Typographical mins., 12 Sept. 1896; *Labour Gazette,* April – Dec. 1896.

119. *C.E.,* 16 Oct. 1893.

120. S. Murphy, *Stone mad* (London, 1966), p. x.

Chapter 19

KEEPING FAITH: AN EVOCATION OF THE CORK PROTESTANT CHARACTER, 1820-1920

IAN d'ALTON

'Not of the Irish best'?[1]

The High Sheriff of Cork for 1843 was in no doubt. Protestant morale in the city was low:

> ...the party here attached to the British
> connection have not the same confidence
> in themselves which they formerly had.[2]

Sixty-four years later the same sense of pessimistic perplexity was expressed in the doggerel of a county Clare Unionist:

> I am only a poor West Briton
> And not of the Irish best
> But I love the land of Erin
> As much as all the rest.[3]

On the face of it, one might be tempted by these sentiments to view a unilinear descent by southern Irish Protestants into what has been described as their modern-day 'acceptance of the need to live quietly and passively in their dying culture'. Their history is, however, more complex than that: so complex, indeed, that another observer, writing of the late 1970s, can reach a diametrically opposite conclusion, and suggest that 'the prospects for Protestant survival seem much brighter than at any time since 1922'.[4]

The elements which went to make Cork Protestant society in the last century of the Union can perhaps be best illustrated through the lives of those who were amongst its most influential members. In this paper short biographies will be used to illuminate important themes within, and influences upon, Cork Protestantism and its political, social and economic structure over the period. Cork, with its strong regional identity, is particularly well suited for a study designed to evoke a close-knit community through its local leadership.

The major thread which runs right through the period and impinges upon all facets of life is the tension between town and country. Protestantism, in its urban manifestation, often offered an inventiveness, freshness and a vitality that could put the 'tea-and-cakes' unionism of the landed classes to shame. Perhaps this was because, rather than in spite of, the occasional indifference and often hostility, of country to town Protestantism. A minor Cork landlord writing to W. H. Lecky in 1895 could not really say why: but he knew in his bones that 'we of the country have a standing grievance against the towns – they are ruining the country'.[5] Perhaps it was because, in Oliver MacDonagh's striking phrase, '...the cash economy was slowly advancing into the countryside'[6] followed in its wake by urban and suburban *petite bourgeoisie*. This was socially unsettling to the gentry, and their attitudes did not change much over the century. The blackballing of the city merchants' attempts to join the Cork County Club in the 1830s (see p. 765) was mirrored in the prohibition in the early 1900s on anyone 'in trade', whether Catholic or Protestant, joining the local tennis club in the tiny west-Cork village of Timoleague and in the establishment of the Munster Model Yacht Club in 1872 for those not socially elevated enough to be members of A. H. Smith-Barry's Royal Cork Yacht Club.[7]

By 1881, Cork Protestantism, treated as a community, was as much an urban as a rural phenomenon. Of the 45,000 Protestants in the city and county nearly half could be classed as town-dwellers.[8] Moreover, land as a business was in trouble. In particular, unwise family settlements (as in the case of the earls of Kingston, see below, p. 767), the famine of 1845-47 and Gladstone's first attempts to settle the land question had left the gentry crippled by the twin diseases of over-mortgage and insecurity. In general, in the period of relatively buoyant agricultural prices between 1850 and 1875, landlords neither took immediate cash advantage by maximising rentals nor set a store of value for the future by investing in improvements.[9]

All this was by way of sharp contrast with urban Protestantism. The landlords who should have capitalised industrial and commercial concerns could not and did not. In 1899 eight railway, two steamship and four town gas companies based in Cork city boasted of a small number of landed gentry on their boards. But of the fifty-seven or so other major commercial enterprises in the city, only two had landed representatives amongst their directors.[10] Capital realised by the resident gentry from inheritances or from the sale of land was usually invested in British gilt-edged stock or sound Irish securities.[11] By the end of the century urban and landed Protestants were heading in economically different directions. On the one hand, the economic interests of the urban classes had perforce to lie with Ireland; on the other, the centre of economic gravity of the dispossessed gentry, especially after the 1903 and 1909 Land Acts, increasingly lay with Great Britain. It is hardly surprising that this led to a clear divergence of political attitudes, actions and aspirations as well. My two final biographical essays, covering secondary education and local politics, demonstrate this development.

Just as Cork Protestantism was not socially united, neither was it politically monolithic. A streak of liberalism and political dissent, admittedly never very wide or deep, runs from F. B. Beamish and the anti-corporation men of the 1830s to Revd R. Anderson and the Protestant Home Rulers of the 1880s. Its significance lies not in itself particularly, but rather in the contrast it offers to the actions and attitudes of the vast majority of Protestants. Their supersensitivity to a fully realised minority position explains, in large measure, the almost violent reaction to those whom they saw as political renegades. They may have been, in the words of a contemporary, 'socially proud' because of possessing 'all the landed property of the country',[12] but the sense of being a minority pervaded and shaped their political activities, especially after the 1880s. Organisations ostensibly political, like the Primrose League, were really social buttresses for an isolated community. This also meant that the political influence of women like Lady Mary Aldworth and the Countess of Bandon was correspondingly more powerful than that of their nationalist counterparts. But if, from as early as the 1840s, Cork Protestants began to feel a wall behind their backs, this did not mean submitting to the blindfold and the last request. Men like A. H. Smith-Barry, Sir John Scott and Revd R. Harvey all fought back in their different ways, and all with a measure of success.

It is perhaps fitting that the series of biographies begins with the third Earl of Kingston and Gerard Callaghan. Both, in many senses, bridge the eighteenth and nineteenth centuries. Kingston, straight out of the pages of Jonah Barrington's *Personal sketches of his own time,* based his politics on the certainties of the earlier century, as his sad decline, financial and mental, sprang from the upheavals of the later. Callaghan's was new money, trying to buy respectability and the power which wealth should properly have. They were political opponents, yet each wielded power and used it in similar fashions and in ways instantly familiar to modern Irish politicians. To each, dynastic interest and patronage considerations were paramount, and to excess. They used the rhetoric of the same abstract cause – Catholic Emancipation – to further obsessive personal ambition. Callaghan, a convert from Catholicism, whipped up anti-Catholic sectarian politics in the 1820s, though quite prepared to switch his alliances for personal ends. Kingston, on the opposite side, was a self-confessed 'advocate for Emancipation, [not] from liberality but from necessity'.[13]

The decay of aristocratic power: George King, third earl of Kingston (1771-1839)

The Kingstons were great landowners, and their estates, centred on the town of Mitchelstown, amounted to nearly 75,000 acres in Cork and Limerick, with a nominal rental of about £40,000 per annum.[14] The first and second earls died within two years of each other, leaving combined debts of £90,000 and a £28,000 annual charge on the estates. This crushing burden was to be further added to by the third earl, George, who was born in 1771. He succeeded to the title in 1799. 'He was a tall, strongly-built man of handsome and commanding appearance and of an imperious temper' wrote one observer.[15] In Elizabeth Bowen's words, he had 'entered on life young'.[16] While still in his teens he witnessed the killing of his sister's lover by his father, as she attempted to elope. In 1798, as a young militia officer, he was captured by rebels during the insurrection and narrowly escaped death. Until his mother's death in 1823, George had to be content to have the use of a pretty, if isolated, house at Glandore in west Cork.[17] This was not overburdensome. He had become an intimate of the Prince Regent and tended to spend a significant proportion of his time in London.[18] But George's father had not just kept him out of the Mitchelstown residence; he denied him control over the estate's revenues as well, so long as his mother remained alive.[19]

Perhaps he had prescience of his son's potential profligacy. As a descendant has rather ruefully put it '... the year 1823 ushered in an era of folly and disaster which led finally to the ruin of the great Mitchelstown inheritance of the Kings'.[20] As soon as George got his hands on the money (or, more accurately, on a security for vast borrowings) he set about building a seat to match his pretensions. Mr and Mrs Hall may not have been overly impressed by what they described as a 'modern castellated mansion', but they were in the minority. Designed by the Pain brothers, it was a neo-Gothic fancy of immense proportions, consciously modelled on Windsor Castle. Everything about it was on a grand scale. The cost was enormous, variously estimated at between £100,000 and £220,000. It was erected in two years, with the employment of hundreds of workmen.[21] The castle was run lavishly, even for the importune aristocracy of the south of Ireland. There were parties, balls, vast quantities of plate, liveried footmen, large chandeliers and great chefs (one was young Claridge, later of London hotel fame).[22]

George King careered on as if there was no tomorrow, which, in a sense, there was not. The debts continued to pile up. His son's literary equivalent to Mitchelstown Castle was an esoteric work on Mexican history, published at a cost of some £32,000 to the estate.[23] De

Plate 19.1   Mitchelstown Castle (Lawrence Collection, National Library of Ireland).

Tocqueville said that by the 1830s the earl 'found himself burdened with £400,000 of debts without hope of ever being able to pay them off'.[24] Eventually Kingston broke down under, it is said, the financial strain. He was declared publicly insane in 1833, his affairs were put in the hands of the court of Chancery and he died in London in 1839.[25] While the proximate cause of George King's lunacy may have been his impossible financial affairs, Elizabeth Bowen might have divined the real reason:

> ... he epitomises that rule by force
> of sheer fantasy that had, in great or
> small ways, become for his class the
> only possible one. From the big lord
> to the small country gentleman we were,
> about this time, being edged back upon
> a tract of clouds and obsessions that
> could each, from its nature, only be
> solitary. The sense of dislocation was
> everywhere. Property was still there,
> but power was going. It was democracy,
> facing him in his gallery, that sent Big
> George mad.[26]

The earl of Kingston saw his role as an amalgam of the feudal baron and the great Irish chieftain; he was popularly known as 'The Chief of the Galtees' in Cork in the early 1820s.[27] He hankered after the title of White Knight borne by his mother's Geraldine ancestors and regularly badgered Robert Peel for its royal recognition.[28] On receiving a final refusal from Peel in 1823, he imperiously claimed 'I shall be satisfied with a recognition of the people and *that* nothing can deprive me of – I am proud of the title and of the affection the ... people bear to it'.[29]

Lord Kingston also ran county politics like a great feudal lord. The Kings' political philosophy was openly dynastic. They controlled almost ten per cent of the county Cork freeholder votes before reform in 1832, and they '... would never give their interest to any but a good Protestant'.[30] To the great political families in Cork – Barnards, Boyles, Cavendishes, Hares, Hedges, Longfields, Hydes, Smith-Barrys – power was all about patronage.[31] The amoral nature of this policy significantly retarded the development of a specifically Protestant political consciousness in Cork. Paradoxically, while Catholic Emancipation and parliamentary reform meant a quantum leap forward for political Catholicism, it also had the same effect on political Protestantism. This was particularly evident in the small parliamentary boroughs of Bandon, Mallow, Kinsale and Youghal, where a new aggressive sectarian Protestantism was freed from the lordly arrangements of the great landed proprietors.[32]

Developing urban sectarian politics: Gerard Callaghan (1796-1833)

One of Kingston's fiercest opponents in Cork city was Gerard Callaghan. Gerard was the third son of Daniel Callaghan, a Catholic merchant who had ridden to prosperity on the back of the Cork victuals trade during the wars in America and with France. The family owned city land as well as the largest distillery. Gerard's background was thus similar to many of the men who later supported O'Connell. He was educated in England. In 1811 he was described as 'a slight young man, rather elegant in his appearance, affected in his manners, and anglicised in his accent'.[33] He became a Protestant convert and with family money procured a seat in parliament for Dundalk, remaining as M.P. for two years until 1820. Callaghan can lay claim to the creation of an urban Protestant political consciousness in Cork in the 1820s. What he first had to overcome were the grandee dynasties that had controlled city politics, on and off, since the 1750s. These great landed families – the houses of Cork, Kingston, Donoughmore, Colthurst, Warren, Longfield, Hare *et al.* – used the city as a convenient political battle-ground for their own inter-family warfare. The poor Protestant freemen in the city and the Catholic forty-shilling freeholders in the liberties were equally expendable cannon-fodder.

The aristocrats and leading landed families patronised the city in every sense in the 1820s. They were often gratuitously offensive to the inhabitants, as when in 1828 they resolved to set up a 'County Club' with membership restricted to 'gentlemen of the county only'. When some prominent city merchants had to be admitted in order to maintain the financial viability of the venture, a large number of these 'gentlemen of the county' resigned *en bloc*.[34] Gerard was one who felt such social slights keenly, precisely because he was excluded from the social set. This, however, in no way diminished his own pretensions; in fact it was a matter of local comment that, at a dinner he hosted in 1826 for the assize judges, all the dishes were named in French to the obvious incomprehension and discomfort of the provincial plutocracy present.[35]

Breaking the political back of the grandees required allies and Callaghan was not averse to using the combined power of Catholic and Protestant merchants to achieve this end. He had already foreshadowed this in 1820 when he stated that 'neither in the Irish parliament, nor the imperial parliament since the Union, were the commercial and manufacturing interests of Ireland represented'. As president of the city's Committee of Merchants in 1815-1816 he also acted as a lobbyist

Plate 19.2   County Club (Crawford Municipal Art Gallery/Cork V.E.C.).

on behalf of all the merchant classes.[36] Callaghan tried to mobilise this Catholic support in 1820, when he stood for election against the sitting M.P., Sir Nicholas Colthurst and the Hon. C. H. Hutchinson (a member of the Donoughmore family).[37] The attempt failed, however, and from then it was an increasingly sectarian Callaghan who (with his brother, Daniel) spent an estimated £30,000 on contests in Cork city between 1820 and 1830.[38]

The tenor of the times, with Catholic emancipation and the rural agitation of the 1820s, favoured a sectarianisation of society at all levels. By the time of a city by-election in 1826 Callaghan's claims to the representation had been accepted by a significant proportion of those lesser landed gentry that possessed votes as freemen, and by influential elements in the corporation.[39] The Brunswick Club movement (a sort of semi-detached Orangeism) between 1826 and 1829 further pushed the corporation men and Protestant middle classes into Callaghan's camp.[40] In 1829 the Club helped Callaghan to achieve his ambition. After an expensive and keenly-fought contest he was elected M.P. at a city by-election, but his moment of triumph was short-lived. The occupational hazard of running a campaign on money rather than morals asserted itself, and he was unseated on petition.[41] If the aristocratic faction thought it had routed the upstart, it was quickly disabused of the notion. Callaghan promptly had his brother Daniel (a Catholic) nominated as the candidate of the Brunswick ultra-Protestant faction. The grandees, backed by the political Catholics, had as theirs a prominent Protestant landowner, William Newenham. When Sir Thomas Deane (a leading member of the corporation) wrote that 'he was most awkwardly placed between family connection, friendship and Protestantism'[42] he was only expressing a degree of confusion felt by many. The issue was that 'Cork shall never be made a borough', and the aristocrats were narrowly, but decisively, beaten.[43]

Gerard Callaghan was successful in creating a sectarian polity by loosening a lower-middle-class urban Protestantism from the shackles of a patronage-dominated aristocracy and gentry. By 1830 the bulk of the grandees had been tamed. No longer was there talk of 'the scandalous coalition of the nobles, forcing into the heart of the city, county speculations'.[44] By then the *Cork Constitution* newspaper, the mouth-piece of Cork Protestantism, would 'not think it altogether just to proscribe the youth of proud and distinguished families, from representing places which would call themselves *independent*'.[45]

The difficult path of a Protestant liberal: Francis Bernard Beamish (1806-1868)

The 1830s may have witnessed the growth of a sectarian cleavage in

Irish politics but there were those who still crossed the line or affected not to recognise its existence. If, as one observer has stated, 'fragmented localism'[46] is the dominant political and social reality of Ireland in the nineteenth century, then the career of Francis Bernard Beamish, M.P. for Cork city from 1837 to 1841 and from 1853 to 1865, is comprehensible. The Beamishes had become one of the great mercantile families of Cork. Originally minor gentry from around the west-Cork town of Bandon, in 1792 William Beamish had, with William Crawford, entered into a partnership with Messrs Allen and Barrett and founded a major brewery. One of Cork's principal firms, it employed 350 men by the 1860s. Well-managed in its early years, it was fortunate in the fecundity of one of its founding families. Of William Beamish's eleven sons, no fewer than five became partners on his death.[47]

Francis was the eighth son. His eminence in city life was entirely predictable. He was a magistrate and a deputy lieutenant and was elected a freeman in 1827. He became mayor of Cork in 1843 and high-sheriff in 1852. What may not have been predictable was his political outlook. 'A moderate liberal and supporter of Lord Palmerston' was the description given of him by a descendant.[48] He was a little more than that, however. Beamish was one of the few Protestants openly to support O'Connell in the 1820s and 1830s. He was prominent as one of the 'Friends of Civil and Religious Liberty', a pro-Catholic emancipation group in Cork in 1829,[49] and there is little doubt that he felt that Catholic political aspirations should have been largely satisfied by the grant of emancipation and the reform of municipal government. An enthusiast for repeal of the Union he was certainly not.[50] The radical O'Connellites admitted as much at the election of 1837 when Beamish was chosen as a candidate. He would be expected to attend parliament only on the municipal and tithe questions.[51]

Beamish had few public political skills: '... a bad speaker, he was not able to aid the cause much but he always attended [meetings] and did his best ...'.[52] 'His best' was largely given to the effects of national measures on his local world. Repeal was never a real political concern, but the imposition of stamp duties (April 1830) was, as were the coal tax (March 1832) and the tithe question (January 1834).[53] Above all, it was in Beamish's attitude to the unreformed Cork corporation that his political, economic and social views came together. The corporation was an edifice of seemingly sectarian privilege founded in fact on a base of economic monopoly and financial corruption. Throughout the 1820s and 1830s Beamish was amongst those Protestant liberals that snapped and snarled at its heels.[54]

By the 1830s, however, the liberal Protestants were starting out on a lonely and dangerous journey. The pustule of sectarian politics was irritated on the one hand by evangelical Protestantism and rural agitation, and on the other by the increasing influence of the Catholic priesthood at local political level.[55] This at once created a permanent minority/majority axis and led inevitably to the charge that the liberal Protestants were either dupes or decoys.

It is rather piquant that Gerard Callaghan had tried to use the Catholic city plutocracy as precisely similar bait in his struggle with the Protestant aristocracy in the 1820s. The O'Connellite party in Cork was much more successful in its mirror-image operations throughout the 1830s and 1840s. The mainstream of Protestant opinion was well aware of the dangers. 'Let every Conservative elector be ... on his guard against the canvass of Mr Beamish' warned the *Cork Constitution* newspaper at the 1837 city election.[56] And Beamish's vote-pulling power was revealed at the first elections for the reformed Cork corporation in 1841 when, in the most Tory ward, he easily topped the poll.[57]

The social dimension of Cork unionism: Lady Mary Aldworth (1840-1920)

The organic interaction between the social and political sides of the mid- and late-nineteenth-century Cork Protestantism is epitomised by Mary Catherine Henrietta Bernard, first daughter of Francis, third earl of Bandon. Like most of the Cork gentry, she married within her own local set. Her husband, Richard Aldworth, owned about 8,700 acres in counties Cork and Limerick, producing a modest gross rental of some £2,600 in 1882. In common with many of her class and gender, Mary Aldworth led a busy and varied life. She was involved in local politics (as a Poor Law guardian), amateur theatricals and the promotion of agricultural education,[58] and all this while managing the domestic intricacies of a Big House. Elizabeth Bowen has perhaps best caught the extent to which these houses and their ancillary activities literally dominated the lives of those who loved them and lived in them. For instance, in the late 1890s Edith Somerville inherited her family home at Castle Townshend, county Cork. She set about reorganising the garden, renovating the house, running the demesne farm, introducing Friesian cattle, buying, training and selling horses in America, designing and supervising the building of a cottage, caring for Violet Martin after her riding accident, becoming M.F.H. of the West Carbery hunt and writing hundreds of letters to her brother Cameron.[59]

Given the relative isolation of the Big Houses and the sectarian axis of Irish politics, it behoved southern unionists to find an organisational form that would best marry the social and political necessities of the age. They found that form in the Primrose League. Throughout the late nineteenth century the unionist counterpoint of the ideological kind to Irish nationalism was the Empire and the imperial dream. The League allowed a celebration of this idea, and with its habitations (as branches were styled), knights and dames of several grades, it appealed strongly to a caste becoming more and more obsessed with the minutiae of its own social gradations.[60]

The growth of the Primrose League was phenomenal. In 1885 there were 11,000 members in the United Kingdom. Five years later membership had almost reached one million. Of equal significance was the growth in women members. In 1885 they accounted for one in six; by 1890 over one in two.[61] In Cork the League took root in 1884. By 1891 it had over 4,000 nominal members, and the branch had to split into four – Bandon and west Cork; Mitchelstown, Fermoy and Castlelyons; Kinsale and St Patrick's (Cork city and environs).[62] Lady Mary Aldworth was nominated ruling councillor (convenor) of the Mitchelstown habitation, while her sister-in-law, the Countess of Bandon, performed a similar function in Bandon. Mary Aldworth was an accomplished and fluent speaker, much in demand at Primrose League gatherings.[62]

In the context of how the Primrose League worked within practical politics, this is best demonstrated during the 1893 Home Rule crisis. Under the leadership of Lady Bandon the League in Cork constituted itself as the 'Cork Loyal Women's Committee' with its own offices, responsible for the collection of unionist newspapers and the raising of funds.[63] Channelled into political modes, the relatively strong sense of caste amongst the landed classes might have been a bulwark for southern Irish Protestantism. But in Cork, as elsewhere, organisations like the Primrose League always had an in-built propensity to degenerate into 'tea-and-cakes' conservatism. If, as Lionel Fleming averred of his Drimoleague childhood, 'nothing counted for about three miles on any side of us because there were no Protestants until then',[64] politics offered an excuse, no more, for social intercourse. This, for instance, explains why a purely political meeting of the League in Cork city in January 1891 (at the height of the Parnellite agitation) could attract only about 60 people,[65] while ten times that number turned up at a League garden-party in the hot August of that year.

The flavour of that August meeting of St Patrick's habitation held in the grounds of Sir George Colthurst's (landlord, railway investor, cricketer, *çi-devant* liberal unionist) Blarney Castle, was distilled thus by the nationalist *Cork Examiner*.[66] The event was extraordinarily well-organised; in the social sphere, if not in the economic or political, the gentry could be relied on to put on a good show:

> The open-sesame to the proceedings was a
> perforated ticket, one part of which
> carried the holder over the Cork-Muskerry
> line, another admitted to the grounds, and
> the third entitled to refreshments.

The ladies outnumbered the gentlemen ten-to-one, we are told. There was a band, dancing, stalls, side-shows and the minimum of political speeches. The conclusion from this example of social unionism, at any rate, is that the unionism was the veneer, and the socialising the underlying necessity, within the Cork landed Protestant community.

Orderly retreat: Arthur Hugh Smith-Barry, Baron Barrymore (1843 – 1925)

Like Lady Mary Aldworth, Arthur Hugh Smith-Barry is one of comparatively few southern unionists to justify the description (in Patrick Buckland's rather misleading phrase) of being in 'confident opposition' in the generation after 1884.[67] Smith-Barry stands out, not for his inherited position or his wealth, but rather for his competence and efficiency, qualities in short enough supply within the Cork unionist nexus. The Smith-Barry family straddled a Hiberno-English, rather than Anglo-Irish, world. The family owned 22,000 acres in counties Cork and Tipperary, and over 5,000 in Cheshire and Huntingdonshire. Arthur Hugh was educated at Eton and Christ Church, Oxford, and succeeded to the estates in 1856 while still a minor.[68] His political career started at the age of twenty-four when he was elected a Liberal M.P. for Cork county in 1867. Much later, in 1886, he could only excuse this interlude by reference to his extreme youth at the time.[69] History has remembered Smith-Barry not as an improving landlord, nor as a supporter of the extension of the franchise, nor as one in favour of Irish Church disestablishment, nor of denominational education,[70] but rather as the prime mover in the most efficient landlord combination that Ireland was to see in the 1880s.

The Cork Defence Union (hereafter C.D.U.), as that combination came to be known, was not the first of its kind.[71] But it certainly was the most effective. The C.D.U. was founded in October 1885. Smith-Barry was chairman, setting out its objectives in a letter to *The Times*:

> It [the C.D.U.] is not in any respect an
> organisation for the purpose of
> enforcing the payment of rents, or for
> the especial defence of land-owning
> interests. The system of boycotting

Plate 19.3   Arthur Hugh Smith-Barry (R. Wood/Fota House).

> and intimidation ... affects the liberty
> of not only land-owners, but also
> merchants, farmers, shopkeepers, artisans
> and even labourers ... The aim of the C.D.U.
> is to afford such persons an organised
> assistance, so that they may carry on
> their occupations unembarrassed by
> illegal interference.[72]

The C.D.U. provided labourers and machinery for boycotted persons and organised sales outlets for produce and cattle. Its relative success was mainly due to avoiding the minefields of rent disputes, evictions and forced sales.[73] It was kept busy during its first months. The executive committee met four times each week and the general committee once a fortnight.[74] Winning moral and material support outside Ireland was one of its prime aims and it soon had a permanent office in London. Smith-Barry's foresightedness was evident in the precautions taken by the C.D.U. against legal attack from the nationalist side. The C.D.U.'s trustee status (trustees: Smith-Barry, P. S. French, J. Penrose-Fitzgerald, D. P. Sarsfield and J. H. Bainbridge) protected its funds and individual members, and it was deliberately reticent about its financial affairs.[75]

The landlords may have ultimately lost the war to hold onto their land but Smith-Barry was associated with two of their successful battles in the 1880s. First, a dispute broke out in the winter of 1885-86 between the South of Ireland Cattle Dealers' Association (nationalists) and the City of Cork Steam Packet Company (largely controlled by unionists). The cattle dealers insisted that the company should cease carrying cattle from the herds of boycotted persons. The company refused. The C.D.U. then became its sole supplier. Eventually, as all parties were losing money heavily, a compromise was agreed. It was generally accepted, however, that the C.D.U. had achieved a moral victory.[76] Secondly, Smith-Barry was reputed to have bankrolled C. W. T. Ponsonby during the latter's resistance to the Plan of Campaign. He was certainly one of the syndicate that purchased the Ponsonby estate in February 1889 and which successfully fought off attempts to make the Plan stick there.[77]

While landlordism was sputtering on in the 1880s and 1890s, Cork unionists were retreating from the high ground of parliamentary electoral politics. Only in times of relative political quiescence could Irish conservatives outside Ulster put up a decent fight. Even under the pre-1884 restrictive franchise they mustered a majority of Irish seats only once, in 1859.[78] The stark result of the 1884 Parliamentary Reform

Act was to destroy any sustained base for Protestant/unionist electoral politics outside the north-east. This was powerfully brought home at the 1885 general election. The newly-formed Irish Loyal and Patriotic Union (hereafter I.L.P.U.) contested 52 seats in the south only to be comprehensively defeated in all but two.[79] Henceforth, if southern Irish unionism wanted a voice at parliamentary level, it had to rely on the House of Lords, or on the forbearance of English electors.

Their tolerance appears to have been generous. Over a dozen of the 'Anglo-Irish' sat for the British constituencies between 1886 and 1918. Cork was well-represented, with (Sir) Robert Penrose-Fitzgerald (Cambridge city, 1885-1906), J. R. B. Pretyman-Newman (Enfield, 1910-1918) and Smith-Barry himself (South Huntingdonshire, 1886-1900):

> Although Mr Smith-Barry has not been
> elected for an Irish division

claimed the *Cork Constitution* in 1886,[80]

> We have no doubt that the many thousands
> in the county and city of Cork, who have
> no direct exponent of their views in
> parliament, will feel that in him and in
> Mr. R. U. Penrose-Fitzgerald they have fast
> and firm friends, who know of their wants
> and who will not be unwilling to advocate
> their interests.

To their English constituents, however, it sometimes seemed that these M.P.s were more preoccupied with Irish concerns; it has to be said that the interests of Cork were as removed in kind as they were in space from those of east Anglia.[81] Smith-Barry (created Baron Barry-more in 1902) remained prominent in the Irish Unionist Alliance (hereafter I.U.A., the successor to the I.L.P.U.), acting as chairman between 1911 and 1913. Like the 'Anglo-Irish' M.P.s, the I.U.A. concentrated upon influencing British, rather than Irish, public opinion. Copies of Irish unionist newspapers (prominent among them the *Cork Constitution*) were dispatched to puzzle the users of English public libraries and perplex workingmen's clubs. Speakers were sent to marginal constituencies; in 1892, Edith Somerville and Violet Martin toured east Anglia for the I.U.A.[82] All this activity may have satisfied the immediate necessity of fighting where it was most useful. In a sense, however, it begged the very question which it purported to answer. If the cause of the union could not be advanced in three-quarters of

Ireland, where was its *raison d'être*? Furthermore, the drift of politically-minded Irish unionists to English constituencies indicated, with great clarity, that the leaders of landed society, at any rate, had already packed their political belongings.

Protestant home rule in Cork: Revd R. Anderson (1849-1890)

While the grip of sectarianism upon politics tightened perceptibly from the 1850s, it did not squeeze out all non-conformist political thinking. But as the careers of Rev Robert Anderson and his friends show, difficult as it was to ride different political and denominational tigers in the 1830s, it was practically impossible by the 1880s. Anderson's was a conventional clerical career. Following curacies in various west-Cork parishes from 1870, he was appointed to the living of Drinagh, Dunmanway in 1875, an area with a relatively numerous population of Protestant farmers.[83] In every way Anderson was unexceptional, except in one regard. He was a convinced and public advocate of Home Rule. He had arrived in Cork at a time when political and economic sensitivities had been greatly heightened by land agitation, widening of the franchise, the coherence of Parnellism and the imminence of a general election. There was a sense of apocalypse, then, when it was announced that a Protestant Home Rule Association (hereafter P.H.R.A.) had commenced in the city. The initial reaction of the unionist establishment was to ignore the phenomenon. But when the *Irish Times* reported a Protestant meeting in Cork in November 1885 at which '... a series of resolutions ... containing pronouncements on home rule, and other planks on the national platform' had been discussed, the local unionists had to take notice.[84]

A week after the *Irish Times* report the 'new departure' – so styled sarcastically by the *Cork Constitution* – had been flushed out of the city's political undergrowth. The movement published a statement of aims on 19 November 1885.[85] Its position on Home Rule was markedly moderate:

> While we shall endeavour to uphold the
> integrity and unity of the Empire, we
> see no reason why the legitimate demand
> of the Irish people for the management
> of purely Irish affairs in their own
> country should not be conceded ....

They also favoured a reasonable settlement of the land question, encouragement of trade on protectionist lines and reform of local government. In these latter issues they were not far removed from the positions occupied by moderate unionists like Horace Plunkett at a national level and Sir George Colthurst at a local. What really set Cork unionists ablaze, however, was the Protestant Home Rulers' perceived 'abject surrender'[86] to majority feeling on Home Rule:

> We deprecate the proposal to contest every seat
> at the coming election, regarding opposition
> of this character as calculated to intensify
> and increase the feelings of irritation which
> unhappily exist ....

This 'cringing' rather than their support for Home Rule *per se* unleashed a storm of vituperation about the Protestant Home Rulers' heads. The *Cork Constitution* tried ridicule: '... during the summer holidays, and when excursion tickets are available at a cheap rate, it is not surprising that the members of the "Irish P.H.R.A." should pay a visit to Dublin', while an anonymous letter-writer in the same paper showed how inconceivable a separation of political and religious feeling could be by posing the question whether R. A. Atkins, one of the movement's leaders, was 'really a Protestant at all'.[87]

As a concerted political movement the 'new departure' in Cork was neither influential nor long-lasting: but its demoralising and destabilising defections from the unionist cause were keenly felt. Its period of greatest public activity was between the general elections of 1885 and 1886. Local meetings were held; delegations, despite the ribbing of the unionists, were sent to P.H.R.A. gatherings in Dublin; resolutions in favour of Home Rule were moved by its members in Cork corporation; and members filled one of Parnell's nomination papers at the 1886 election.[88] What were the movement's characteristics? First, despite the innuendoes of the *Cork Constitution,* it was 'respectable': that is to say, it was composed largely of men of property and commercial standing. Of the leaders, Henry Dale, J. C. Leslie and B. J. Alcock were prosperous merchants; R. H. Rutter and G. J. Roche were wine merchants; Richard Martin, a hotel proprietor; Revd R. Anderson and Revd M. Kerr, clerics (the latter a Presbyterian); and R. A. Atkins a newspaper proprietor, company secretary, insurance agent and landowner.[89] Secondly, the movement was youthful; the vast majority of members were under forty. Thirdly, while economically conservative, it had been spawned from an unlikely source, the Cork Church of Ireland Young Men's Association, whose radical credentials included a debate in 1891 as to whether the unionist or Parnellite candidate should be supported at a by-election and which in 1893 discussed the women's franchise.[90] Fourthly, it was overwhelmingly

Anglican in the character of its membership. Finally, it espoused a wholly materialistic and imperial view of nationalism, seeing Home Rule purely as the means-to-an-end to poverty, disorder and disunity. The transcendental aspect to Irish nationalism seems to have passed the 'new departure' by.[91]

The difficulties of Gerard Callaghan in being accepted into the Tory gentry camp in the early years of the century were mirrored by the uneasy relationship between the Protestant Home Rulers and nationalists. As Alderman John O'Brien of Cork claimed in 1886: 'we don't seek the support of the "New Departure" gentlemen: we only seek honest support'.[92]

The fate of Anderson typifies the even more virulent reaction of Cork Protestantism to any hint of public political apostasy. Anderson was in an exposed position. His parishioners, a vindictive lot, taking a leaf out of their nationalist neighbours' books, boycotted him. A charge he rashly made against the Cork Defence Union of circulating defamatory literature about him had to be publicly retracted. Reduced to near-destitution, he was forced to rely for bodily support on the proceeds of public lectures given on nationalism.[93] He died of lung cancer in 1890, leaving a penniless young family. It remained for the nationalist *Cork Examiner* to set up a fund for their relief.[94] The unionists' violent response to Anderson may have been because, of all things, he was a clergyman of the recently disestablished Church of Ireland. But worst of all, he saw nationalism in terms of something more than a balance sheet.[95] This, above everything, made him incomprehensible to most unionists and, ultimately, more subversive.

The adaptability of urban unionism: Sir John Scott (1849-1931)

In his own way, John Harley Scott was as radical as Anderson, in a period of vital transition and transformation for Cork Protestants. Son of an architect, he rapidly rose to commercial eminence to become chairman of a major shipping company, trustee of Cork Savings Bank and president of the Chamber of Commerce. In public life he was a justice of the peace and sometime high-sheriff and lord mayor of Cork.[96] His particular political genius lay in exploiting the fault-lines of local nationalist politics in the city, broadening and deepening the fissures wherever he found them. On at least three occasions between 1890 and 1918 – during the Parnellite split in the early 1890s, at the time of the first local government elections in 1899 and during the O'Brienite phase of the early 1900s – he worked to ensure that Cork unionists would play a pivotal role in local politics.

The gladiatorial circus was provided by Cork corporation. The results of the 1885 general election merely confirmed the primacy of local over parliamentary electoral politics, as far as Cork unionists were concerned. At local level, the combination of a substantial property franchise with concentrations of Protestant voters in small areas meant that the 'Protestant vote' could be of significance if marshalled and motivated. Just how significant was clearly shown in Cork where, with fifteen per cent of the population, the unionists in the 1880s and 1890s were able to control up to one-third of the seats on the corporation.

The first reaction of many Cork unionists to the Parnellite split was unfortunately (for the local Parnellites) ill-thought-out and counter-productive. Just as Parnell, a landlord, could not entirely reject his own class, so Protestants could not equally spurn his claims on their indulgence.[97] Besides, here was a golden opportunity to engage in a little priest-baiting, with the unexpected bonus, for once, of a substantial portion of the Catholic population in the van. The nationalists, then, should be left to tear themselves to pieces, and an ideal chance occurred when the death of Parnell in 1891 created a parliamentary vacancy in one of the two Cork city seats. The advice of the chief secretary, Arthur Balfour, and the Castle administration was to let nature take its course.[98] The local unionists could have created mayhem through the confusion of the ballot-box. But the gentry, largely dormant in city politics since Gerard Callaghan's time, sprang into life and ambushed a surprised city unionism. They imposed an Orange landlord, D. P. Sarsfield, as unionist candidate; the liberal unionists, the Methodists, even the Church of Ireland Young Men's Association, revolted; and the anti-Parnellites were encouraged to vote in numbers greater than otherwise might have been the case. Even if Scott had stood (and city unionists, when they realised what the die-hards were up to, attempted to draft him in to limit the damage) little would have been achieved.[99]

Parallel to head-on confrontation, a new (and ultimately more productive) tack was tried. Between 1891 and 1895 the unionists moved forward politically by means of a tacit alliance with the Parnellite forces, increasing loyalist representation substantially on the city corporation. The Parnellites however were unwilling, at the last, to allow the unionists to have the prize they so badly wanted: the mayoralty. They threw the bone of high-sheriff to Scott in 1892, which netted him a knighthood. But no more than that. By 1895 unionist patience was exhausted. Not without much agonising, the majority of unionist councillors decided to switch their support to the anti-Parnellites. As part of the deal, Scott was elected mayor for 1896. Not all anti-Parnellites could swallow such bitter medicine. The influential *Cork Examiner* was outraged. 'Our counsels have been disregarded', it thundered, 'and we have for the ensuing year, as a consequence, a

Unionist Mayor and a Unionist Sheriff to speak for the Catholic and National city of Cork.'[100]

The Parnellite split revived Cork unionism. Scott converted the old, moribund Parliamentary Registration Society into a vehicle unashamedly more modest in its aspirations: the winning of municipal seats. A 'Unionist Hundred', elected by city rate-payers only, was set up, with eleven representatives from each of eight municipal wards, and twelve for the city liberties. Scott ensured his control by the election of his father-in-law as president of the new body.[101] The price of such political activism was, however, a sometimes dangerous visibility, often exacerbated by sectarian tensions just below the surface in other forums.[102] Cork unionism reacted in two ways in the 1910s to reduce this visibility. When William O'Brien made a pitch for Protestant participation in his All-for-Ireland League, Cork Protestants happily supported him in the secrecy of the ballot-box. No longer was there talk of unionist parliamentary candidates. Lord Castletown might rail against such closet O'Brienites as 'a nice lot of cowards', but the lessons of the Parnellite period had been well learnt, and Cork unionists now knew how to use their electoral muscle to maximum advantage. The strategy thus adopted worked. It is doubtful whether O'Brien and Healy would have been elected as M.P.s for Cork city in either 1910 election if the Protestant vote (numbering about 1,500) had not almost solidly plumped for them.

The second unionist response was to imitate the chameleon. By 1911 a unionist party by that name had all but ceased to exist within municipal politics. This did not mean that Cork unionists had opted out. Quite the converse: they were still well represented in local government, but under the banners of 'independents', 'commercial candidates', or tangential supporters of the All-for-Ireland League. It is significant that this represents integration rather than assimilation; it marks the most startling cleavage with the remnants of landed ascendancy politics.[103]

Protestants in the new century: Revd Ralph Harvey (1851-1925)

Sir John Scott represented the political resilience and adaptability of a generation of Cork Protestants that had had its formative years in the immediate post-famine era, at a time when Irish Protestantism was visibly on the defensive. So in his turn was Ralph Harvey, one of those who were instrumental in equipping the generation that would have to face living in the Free State with as much competitive advantage as possible.

Protestant economic power in Cork city may have still been formidable in the 1880s, but its relative position had been considerably eroded over the previous half-century.

Plate 19.4   Revd Ralf Harvey (Ashton Comprehensive School, Cork).

Table 19.1
Selected occupations, 1833 and 1881 (percentage)[104]

	1833		1881	
	Protestant	Catholic	Protestant	Catholic
Legal profession	81	19	38	62
Medical profession	57	43	36	64
General merchants, bankers	59	41	44	56
Insurance agents	82	18	40	60
Refuse disposal	not given		4	96

Two significant processes had taken place within Cork city Protestantism between 1833 and 1881. The denominational balance within many of the more prestigious and lucrative occupations had almost been reversed. And within Protestantism itself there was a substantial change in class balance. In 1881 two-thirds of Protestant males could have been described as being in skilled occupations. The 'hundreds' of Protestant inhabitants 'in greatest distress' graphically described by a city parish rector in 1845 were no longer much in evidence.[105] Increasingly city Protestants were being forced to slog it out with their Catholic neighbours on a rapidly-levelling playing-field. Lacking the network of large, Protestant-controlled firms, which in Dublin acted as an employment reserve, Cork Protestants needed to be equipped to compete on home – and foreign – territory. This was principally to be delivered through an aggressive and relevant education system.[106]

It is in education that a further clear distinction between landed and city/small-town Protestants was evident. From the early nineteenth century at least, the landed classes, especially those with decent incomes, were educationally abandoning Ireland. In 1833 the thoughts of Captain Otho Travers, a recruiting officer for the East India Company in Cork, '... were greatly occupied in fixing upon some English school for my boys the advantages of which I see more clearly every day'. Lionel Fleming's grandfather had been educated at Kilkenny College, but his father had been sent to school in England. Likewise, Henry Cole Bowen's sons went to Midleton College in the 1780s and their sons, in turn, were given an English education. The list can be made much longer. An examination of Bateman's *The great landowners of Great Britain and Ireland* reveals that a majority of the indigenous Cork landlords listed therein (most of whom underwent their formal education before 1850) attended English schools and Oxford and Cambridge.[107]

For those who could not afford, or who did not care for, an English secondary education, there existed prior to the 1870s a plethora of small schools in Cork; for example, Bishop Crowe's school at Cloyne, the venerable foundation of Midleton College, Fermoy College, Bandon Grammar School, and St Edmund's College, Dunmanway, whose '... situation is unrivalled for healthiness and beauty of scenery, and, being completely in the country, is removed from the vices and temptations incident to towns and villages'.[108] Most of these schools provided, at best, an indifferent education. The situation was somewhat better in Cork city, where schools such as Dr Porter's and Mr Hamblin's and Mr Knapp's Academy had high standards and good reputations. Curiously, perhaps, for the times, girls were excellently served by Rochelle seminary (founded 1829) and The High School and Kindergarten (founded 1876).[109]

Amongst the founders of the latter was William Goulding, Conservative M.P. for Cork city in 1876-1880, who, with Thomas Osborne, a city merchant, and the Anglican archdeacon of Cork, was instrumental in establishing a new city school for boys in December 1881. The resurgence of Home Rule sentiment had not blunted Osborne's desire to see an 'Irish' education for Cork Protestant boys:

> The school was simply set on foot ...
> with the object of inducing persons
> who had been sending their children to
> England, to educate them at home[110]

he stated.

> It is a great pity that Irish parents who labour at
> home and expect their sons will live in the country for
> wear or woe, will not see how desirable it is to keep up
> the connection during the time of their
> education with the people amongst whom
> they are to live subsequently ... they did
> not want to make Englishmen of their boys
> There was much to admire in the Irish
> character and they wanted to maintain it.

It was not enough, however, to sit back and let the pupils drift in, which is what the school's management seems to have done. While the school was itself a product of the revolutionary change effected in Irish secondary education by the 1878 Intermediate Education Act, the highly competitive atmosphere engendered by the Act meant that schools had to be promoted and well-run. In its first flush, Cork Grammar School attracted forty-nine pupils; this number then proceeded to drop every year from 1884 to 1887. Under the incompetent headmasterships of Edmund Arblaster (1881-84) and John Berry (1884-87), the school neared collapse. Results – on which a successful use of the 1878 Act was predicated – could not be achieved without numbers. Numbers could not be kept up without results. Drastic action was needed by 1887 to ensure that the school would have a future. Salvation, as it turned out, appeared in the unlikely form of Ralph Harvey.[111]

Harvey was a bluff, tough, Yorkshireman who had come to the school as a junior assistant master in 1893. Educated at the universities of Leeds and London, he was a classicist and historian. He was ordained an Anglican priest in 1893. From then on he followed a church career in tandem with his headmastership, which he held until 1908. In that year he resigned and accepted nomination to the north-Cork parish of Charleville, where he remained until his death in 1925.[112] Stephen Farrington, later Cork city borough engineer and one of Harvey's star pupils, was singularly unimpressed. He tells us that Harvey was tall and broad, with a square cut, rust red beard. The beard would have done justice to a South Sea pirate and should, according to Farrington, have been accompanied by a sun-burnt, cutless-carved physiogonomy. Instead Harvey sported a pink and white 'Dresden china complexion', giving him an alien and rather terrifying appearance, especially to small boys. Farrington maintained that Harvey instituted a reign of terror which was immoral, 'having no relation to conduct', and unpredictable, 'having no relation to cause and effect'. Farrington admitted that, overall, this might have been no bad thing: '... thriving communities are known to have lived on volcanoes ...'.[113]

Whatever about Harvey's general demeanour, there is little doubt that he created a successful school, as measured by his own (and many others') lights. He concentrated on five areas of activity: the achievement of examination successes within the intermediate system; a bias towards the Royal University rather than Trinity College, Dublin; an emphasis upon applied science and practical entrance to the civil service and mercantile careers; an improvement in the physical premises of the school; and a further cementing of Anglican influence over management and teaching.

The Church of Ireland's extension of control over Cork Grammar School reflected what was happening on the Catholic side.[114] In 1889 the City of Cork Church School Board was established to manage Anglican primary schools. Following some discussion, the Grammar School was brought within the board's sphere in March 1890, under the provisions of the 1885 Educational Endowments (Ireland) Act.[115] This was just one of the local instances of the increasingly vertical denominational control of education that the 1878 Act did nothing to hinder, despite the provisions designed to avoid such a danger.[116]

School premises were never to Harvey's satisfaction. Despite his alleged toughness, he saw no educational merit in imposing Dickensian physical conditions upon his boys. Management, however, took a somewhat different view, and dissension over premises was to be the proximate cause of Harvey's resignation. From the first, the school was located in a cramped and unsuitable inner-city location. It took Harvey nine years to obtain a modest extension to the premises, and it was a further six before substantial alterations were completed. 'Personally', said Harvey in 1901, 'this fact of improved premises is more satisfactory to me than all our long list of successes.'[117] By 1908 increased numbers were again putting considerable pressure on resources. At that stage Harvey felt that only new school buildings would fit the bill. But the bill – in this case £20,000 – was too high to pay.[118] The failure of a scheme to raise funds for a new school bitterly disappointed Harvey, who saw the institution condemned for the foreseeable future to an overcrowded and inadequate existence. He resigned as headmaster shortly afterwards.

Harvey's principal educational achievements were to equip his pupils with serviceable academic qualifications; involve the school more with Queen's College, Cork; and use the intermediate system to maximum financial advantage. In these limited aims he was successful. Given the small size of the school, it provided for a surprisingly wide range of careers and further education. Pupils were prepared for a plethora of universities, English and Irish. Entrance examinations for the home and colonial civil services, the armed forces, the Royal Colleges of Surgeons and of Science, the banks and accountancy were also taken. Pitman courses in typing and book-keeping were taught, as were 'city and guild' vocational and technical subjects. Less frequently, entrance scholarships for other schools – principally English public schools – were competed for.

The bias towards the Royal University, rather than Trinity College, Dublin, appears to have had the support of a surprising number of parents. Twice as many pupils took the examinations of Queen's College, Cork than attended T.C.D. during Harvey's headmastership, and in 1896 it was said that more pupils from the Grammar School passed into the Royal University than from any other Protestant school in the south of Ireland. This was, in turn, reflected in the high percentage – twenty-five – of Protestant students at Q.C.C. by the turn of the century. The bias against T.C.D. seems to have troubled some of the more conservative church elements. This cut little ice with Harvey: 'Ireland was not the richest country in the world', he brusquely asserted, 'and the fees of Trinity College compared unfavourably with the R.U.I.'

In general, Harvey was a staunchly unfashionable proponent of Pearse's 'murder machine'. Under his control the intermediate examinations became the very *ne plus ultra* touchstone of the Grammar School. Its resources were single-mindedly focused upon the examinations, so that in 1898, 1900 and 1901 it was adjudged to be, respectively, the third, fourth and sixth most successful Protestant school in Ireland. Nothing could be further from Harvey's attitude than that of his predecessor, who in 1886 declared that 'the preparation for this examination [the intermediate] was so arranged as not to interfere with the regular work of the school.' Early into Harvey's headmastership the intermediate was the 'work of the school', so much so that external examiners were dispensed with in 1893 and internal school examinations after 1898.[119]

This heavy emphasis on the intermediate examinations made many members of the governing body uneasy. The bishop of Cork timidly suggested in 1907 that, for pupils, 'The real object [of education] was that their characters might be formed, and that they might learn to be earnest, faithful, true and diligent'.[120] Harvey clearly felt this to be nonsense. He always maintained that the intermediate system *was* sound in principle, if somewhat capricious in practice.[121] He denied that the system led to cramming, though it is not surprising to find that the intermediate inspectors uncovered clear evidence of it going on in the school.[122] To the last, Harvey asserted that the intermediate system was vital to the school's continued existence: '... if he [Harvey] did not produce examination results quickly there would be no school – nothing left but the four walls ... Except for the Intermediate system of payment of results the Cork Grammar School would not live six months'.[123]

'A scribble in the margin of history'?[124]

Pattern and process are the staple of the historian. At a distant glance, the final century of 'political' Protestantism seems to offer a surfeit of coherence in this regard. Analysts have duly risen to a tempting bait. The conventional wisdom persists in setting southern Irish Protestantism in a tragic mode almost before the ink was dry upon the Act of Union. 'Twilight' is the dominant image used by many observers, from F. S. L. Lyons aiming it at a predominantly academic audience, to Mark Bence-Jones and Jack White at a more popular one. Twilight as transition, perhaps; as finality, darkening towards oblivion, no.

That image of twilight applied virtually indiscriminately to southern unionism is largely due to the almost irresistible urge to concentrate on the landed gentry as its true (often its only) representative. But even as applied to the landed classes, the inevitability of tragedy has been overblown.[125] Hindsight, literary artifice and the need for personal explanation led writers like Elizabeth Bowen and Lionel Fleming to see in the gentry the introverted integrity of a lost cause. However, most of the time, the bulk of that class simply had a 'cyclically static' view of itself. Right through to 1920, if something untoward happened, they had been there before. 1919 was a re-run of 1798. Land war in the 1880s echoed the 1820s rural agitation. Relative political quiescence in the early 1900s mirrored the post-famine years. Granted, a secular trend established itself during the century, as power and privileges were gradually eroded in the face of advancing democracy.

Dr Theo Hoppen writes:

> What is in the end remarkable about
> the landed gentry of nineteenth-century
> Ireland is not the fact that its power outside
> Ulster fell into ruins during the 1870s
> and 1880s, but that, by a generally acute
> maximisation of advantages, it was able to
> retain a strong voice in political and
> electoral affairs for as long as it did.[126]

But from an insular perspective placed into a wider context it is not really remarkable at all. The integration of even the most *haut* of the Irish aristocracy into the life of the people around them was greater than that of their counterparts in much of continental Europe. The Catholic bourgeoisie may have been few in numbers; the landed classes may have been intensely suspicious of the towns; but there was a sufficient, if narrow, bridge of shared Victorian culture joining the two. And while the gentry's power in parliament, local justice and local government may have waned over the nineteenth century, its prestige remained largely intact. Conor Cruise O'Brien's 'Indian summer'[127] rather than Lyons's 'twilight' is perhaps more appropriate as a metaphor for those who pioneered motoring, flying, photography, typewriters and telephones. At the end of the century, the gentry was still setting the style, even if that style was brittle and often vacuous. Lord Barrymore in 1920 was at the apex of Cork county society, just as Lord Kingston had been a century earlier.

There was a kind of constancy about the Irish unionist Protestant landed classes through the century. What changed was the world outside. By 1920 'Ireland' as a political entity no longer existed; the union was all but dead; their landed base had gone. All that most of them were left with were their Big Houses, a sort of social fig-leaf, out of scale and out of time with their surroundings; and, of course, their Protestantism. Much more intriguing in the century from 1820 to 1920 are the Protestant urban and suburban classes, and the minor clergy, the political dissenters, represented by such as Gerard Callaghan, F. B. Beamish, Sir John Scott and Revd R. Anderson – the people of Shaw, the people of Hyde, the people of Yeats. Somerville and Ross may have accused the town of being 'full of second-hand thinking',[128] but the fact is that even in their most vibrant novel, *The real Charlotte*, town and city, though remote and threatening, are the ultimate arbiters of life outside them.

Furthermore, it is clear that the townsman's perception of place in his community was anything but 'cyclically static'. Free trade in religion (after 1829), in municipal government, in the post-Northcote/Trevelyan imperial and home civil services, left Cork urban Protestants with a fight on their hands. As a result they had to become better equipped to meet the challenges of the day. Often prosaic, their tendency to go with the flow may have been their saving grace. Beamish's commercial interests gelled with his liberal leanings. Callaghan's dynastic ambitions grafted themselves onto a sectarian and anti-aristocratic root. Scott pragmatically exploited cracks in the nationalist façade. It is perhaps a measure of the relative strengths of survival of urban and landed Cork Protestantism that while Lord Kingston's fantastical imagination has left no permanent mark upon the landscape, Ralph Harvey's pedagogic utilitarianism has a living and lively descendant.[129]

References

1. I wish to express my thanks to Mr Felix Larkin, one of the 'Irish best', for his lucid and useful comments on an earlier draft of this paper. The finished product is, of course, my own responsibility.
2. B.L., Add. MS 40537, pp 298-9, James Morgan to Sir R. Peel, 27 Dec. 1843.
3. Anon., *Poems by a county Clare west Briton* (Limerick, 1907), p. 7.
4. D. Bowen, *The Protestant crusade in Ireland 1800-70* (Toronto, 1978), p. 314; K. Bowen, *Protestants in a Catholic state* (Quebec, 1983), p. 217.
5. T.C.D., Lecky papers, MS 1113, A. Daunt to W. E. H. Lecky, 9 Dec. 1895.
6. O. MacDonagh, *The nineteenth-century novel and Irish social history: some aspects* (Dublin, 1970), p. 11.
7. L. Fleming, *Head or harp* (London, 1965), p. 36. 'Corinthian' [H. P. F. Donegan], *History of yachting in the south of Ireland 1720-1908* (Cork, 1909), pp 70, 85, 98, 102.
8. *Census of Ireland*, 1881, vol. ii, no. 2.
9. W. E. Vaughan, 'An assessment of the economic performances of Irish landlords, 1851-81' in F. S. L. Lyons and R. A. J. Hawkins (ed.), *Ireland under the union:*

varieties of tension (Oxford, 1908), p. 199; M. Bence-Jones, *Twilight of the ascendancy* (London, 1987), p. 20.

10. F. Guy, *Directory of Cork, 1899* (Cork, 1899), pp 191-5.
11. A sample of Cork estate papers which I have examined for the period 1900-12 (Conner, Ballineen; French, Queenstown; Evans, Doneraile; Newenham, Carrigaline) has numerous receipts for and references to such securities, together with applications for gilt-edged and particularly mining, stock. See also Bence-Jones, *Twilight of the ascendancy*, pp 191-3.
12. D. O. Madden, *Ireland and its rulers; since 1829. Part the first* (London, 1843), p. 4.
13. P.R.O.N.I., T3030/10/22, Kingston to Lord Redesdale, 21 Dec. 1824; B.L., Add. MS 40276, p. 384, Lord Carbery to Peel, 28 Nov. 1817.
14. Donnelly, *Land and people*.
15. R. D. King-Harman, *The Kings, earls of Kingston* (Cambridge, 1957), p. 79.
16. E. Bowen, *Bowen's court* (London, 1984), p. 255.
17. H.C. 1825 (81) ix, i, *Minutes of evidence taken before the select committee of the House of Lords, appointed to inquire into the state of Ireland*, p. 434, 1, evidence of Lord Kingston; Madden, *Revelations of Ireland*, pp 85-107.
18. Bowen, *Bowen's court*, pp 255-56.
19. Ibid., p. 255.
20. King-Harman, *The Kings*, p. 81.
21. Mr and Mrs S. C. Hall, *Hall's Ireland*, ed. M. Scott (London, 1984), pp 1, 40; King-Harman, *The Kings*, p. 82, Donnelly, *Land and people*, p. 70; [N. L. Beamish], *Peace campaigns of a cornet*, ii (London, 1829) p. 33.
22. *C.C.*, 12 Dec. 1829; King-Harman, *The Kings*, pp 82-3.
23. Donnelly, *Land and people*, p. 70.
24. A. de Tocqueville, *Journeys to England and Ireland*, ed. J. Mayer, trans. G. Lawrence and K. Mayer (London, 1958), p. 158.
25. *C.C.*, 27 July 1833.
26. Bowen, *Bowen's court*, p. 258.
27. *The Freeholder*, 29 Sept. 1827.
28. B.L., Add. MSS 40353, pp 174, 203, 243, 245; 40354, p. 124; 40355, pp 90, 92: Lord Kingston to Peel, 10 Jan., 10 Feb., 14 Dec., 30 Dec. 1822; 29 Jan. 1823; Peel to Kingston (copies), 19 Dec. 1822, 20 Jan., 13 Mar. 1823,
29. B.L., Add. MS 40355, p. 91, Kingston to Peel, 12 Mar. 1823.
30. Quoted in P. Jupp, 'Irish parliamentary elections and the influence of the Catholic vote, 1801-20' in *The historical journal*, x, pt. 2 (1967), p. 185.
31. For a fuller treatment of this point see d'Alton, *Protestant society*, pp 124-5.
32. See *C.C.*, 6 Aug. 1829, editorial; B.L., Add. MS 40379, p. 119, W. Johnson (Youghal) to Lord Liverpool, 12, 13 June 1825; K. T. Hoppen, *Elections, politics and society in Ireland 1832-1885* (Oxford, 1984), pp 309-10. In relation to Kinsale, Dr Hoppen's contention that J. I. Heard's domination of the borough was 'extremely brief' does not withstand detailed scrutiny. At elections in 1837 and 1847 Heard, as the power behind the throne, proposed the winning liberal; in 1848 the victor, Hawes, acknowledged that he won only with Heard's support; and Heard himself was M.P. for over seven years, 1852-59.
33. Madden, *Revelations of Ireland*, p. 187.
34. *The Freeholder*, 14 Apr. 1828: The Cork and County Club, MS volume, general committee minutes, 29 July 1837 and 11 Mar. 1840, in the possession of the Cork and County Club, South Mall, Cork.
35. *The Freeholder*, 21 Apr. 1826.

36. Anon., *A full and accurate report of the proceedings at the election for the city of Cork which commenced on Friday the 17th and terminated on Friday the 24th March, 1820* (Cork, 1820), p. 9; B.L., Add. MS 40253, pp 15-16, Callaghan to R. Peel, 21 Feb. 1816.

37. Anon., *A full and accurate report*, passim. Callaghan's attempts to unite Catholic and Protestant voters against the grandees in 1820 was a continuation of C. H. Hutchinson's similar attempts in 1818; see P. Jupp, 'Urban politics in Ireland, 1801-1831' in Harkness and O'Dowd, *Town*, pp 116-7.

38. *C.C.*, 4 July 1829; Madden, *Revelations of Ireland*, p. 219.

39. *The Freeholder*, 9, 30 Dec. 1826. Cork City Library, Croker papers, ii, p. 2, R. Sainthill to T. C. Croker, 30 Nov. 1826.

40. *C.M.C.*, 21 Feb., 10 Apr. 1827; *The Freeholder*, 21 Apr. 1827; N.L.I., MS 5017, p. 1, letters ... relative to the Brunswick Constitutional Clubs, 1828.

41. See P. Madden, 'Unseating a Cork MP' in *C.E.*, 30 Aug. 1976; Anon., *A full report of the proceedings at the election for the city of Cork, 7th-9th July 1829*, 2nd ed. (Cork, 1829), passim.

42. Cork City Library, Croker papers, iii, item 175, Deane to Croker, 18 Apr. 1830.

43. Anon., *The entire proceedings of the election for the city of Cork, which commenced on Saturday the thirteenth, and terminated on Monday the twenty-ninth of March, 1830* (Cork, 1830); *The Freeholder*, 13 Nov. 1830.

44. Anon., *A synoptical exposé of the proceedings of the late city election ...* (Cork, 1818), p. 34.

45. *C.C.*, 3 Aug. 1830.

46. Hoppen, *Elections, politics and society*, p. 485.

47. B. M. Walker (ed.), *Parliamentary election results in Ireland, 1801-1922* (Dublin, 1978), p. 264; C. T. M. Beamish, *Beamish* (London, 1950), pp 13-15.

48. Beamish, *Beamish*, p. 133.

49. *C.C.*, 4 Apr. 1829.

50. For a report purporting to demonstrate that Beamish was against repeal see *C.C.*, 20 July 1841. But see Walker, *Parliamentary election*, p. 264, where he is classed as repealer, and M. Murphy, 'The economic and social structure of nineteenth-century Cork' in Harkness and O'Dowd, *Town*, p. 148, describes him as 'among the foremost adherents of O'Connell in Cork'.

51. W. Fagan at a Cork meeting, *C.C.*, 22 July 1837.

52. N.L.I., mic. p. 3064, diary of Capt. O. Travers [hereafter Travers' diary], Feb. 1832.

53. *C.C.*, 29 Apr. 1830; 15 Mar. 1832; 4 Jan. 1834.

54. J. O'Brien, *The Catholic middle classes in pre-famine Ireland* (Cork, 1979), pp 14-5; *C.C.*, 1 July 1837; d'Alton, *Protestant society*, pp 100-1.

55. For sectarianism see Bowen, *The Protestant crusade in Ireland*, especially pp 83-192.

56. *C.C.*, 18, 22, 25 July 1837; Travers' diary, Jan. 1835.

57. *C.E.*, 25 Oct. 1841; *C.C.*, 30 Oct. 1841.

58. J. Bateman, *The great landowners of Great Britain and Ireland* (London, 1883), p. 6; *Burke's Peerage*, 82nd ed., p. 194; *C.E.*, 1 May 1895; *C.C.*, 28 Mar., 16 May 1898.

59. E. Bowen, *Collected impressions* (London, 1950), pp 195-200; H. Mitchell, 'Somerville and Ross: amateur to professional' in E. E. Evans (ed.), *Somerville and Ross: a symposium* (Belfast, 1968), pp 21-22; T.C.D., MS 4261-70, West Carbery Hunt papers.

60. For an atmospheric evocation of the ascendancy's *fin-de-siècle* see Bence-Jones, *Twilight of the ascendancy*, passim.

61. J. H. Robb, *The Primrose League, 1883-1906* (New York, 1942), p. 228.
62. *Notes from Ireland*, 1894, no. 49, p. 214; P.R.O.N.I., MS D89C/3/22; *C.C.*, 20 Apr. 1891, 20 Apr. 1892, 27 July 1898.
63. *C.C.*, 14, 20 Mar. 1893.
64. Newenham papers, anon., diary for 1898 (in the possession of the Newenham family, Coolmore, Carrigaline, county Cork); Fleming, *Head or harp*, p. 36; Bowen, *Bowen's court*, pp 344-5.
65. *C.E.*, 30 Jan. 1891.
66. P. Ó Maidín, 'The Primrose League at Blarney 1891' in *C.E.*, 18 Aug. 1971; *C.E.*, 19 Aug. 1991.
67. P. Buckland, *Irish unionism 1: the Anglo-Irish and the new Ireland 1885 to 1922* (Dublin, 1972), p. 1.
68. Bateman, *Great landowners*, p. 27; *Burke's Peerage*, 82nd ed., p. 214.
69. *Cambridge Chronicle*, 30 Apr. 1886; Walker, *Parliamentary elections*, pp 106, 266.
70. *C.C.*, 13 Feb. 1867, 24 Sept. 1868; Donnelly, *Land and people*, p. 168.
71. The Property Defence Association was founded in 1880. It involved itself in execution sales and supplied labourers to work on boycotted farms, cf. Donnelly, *Land and people*, p. 276; Evans papers, Carker House, Doneraile, county Cork. Few Cork landlords were members, see P.D.A. circular and list of subscribers.
72. *C.C.*, 16 Oct. 1885, reprint of a letter to *The Times*.
73. G. Pellow, *In castle and cabin* (New York, 1887), p. 83.; *C.E.*, 9 Oct. 1885; *C.C.*, 16 Oct. 1884; *C.C.*, 16 Nov. 1886, first annual C.D.U. report.
74. See periodic reports in *C.C.*, Oct.-Dec. 1885; also ibid., 25 Oct. 1886, editorial.
75. Donnelly, *Land and people*, p. 329.
76. *C.C.*, 14 Nov. 1885, letter from Smith-Barry.
77. Donnelly, *Land and people*, pp 358-60.
78. Hoppen, *Elections, politics and society*, p. 165.
79. Buckland, *Irish unionism*, pp 2-3; for a description of the 1885 I.L.P.U. activities in Cork city and county see I. d'Alton, 'Southern Irish unionism: a study of Cork city and county unionists, 1885-1914', unpub. M.A. thesis, U.C.C. (1972), chapter 3.
80. *C.C.*, 15 July 1886.
81. See, for instance, an editorial in *Cambridge Independent Press*, 21 Nov. 1885; also Smith-Barry's remarks at Huntingdon, *Cambridge Chronicle*, 7 May 1886.
82. *Notes from Ireland*, i, no. 50, 16 Dec. 1893, P.R.O.N.I., D/1327/2/4, I.U.A., register of speakers; P.R.O.N.I. D989A/1/6; 1908, speakers' committee minute book, *C.C.*, 10 Mar., I.U.A. reports for weeks ending 14, 21 Dec. 1893, Apr. 1893.
83. *Crockford's clerical directory 1890*, p. 23.
84. *I.T.*, 12 Nov. 1885.
85. *C.C.*, 19 Nov. 1885, letter.
86. The phrase is Arthur Patton's, I.L.P.U. candidate for mid-Cork, at the 1885 general election, *C.C.*, 20 Nov. 1885.
87. *C.C.*, 1 Mar., 24 June 1886.
88. *C.E.*, 27 Feb. 1886; *C.C.*, 11, 23 June, 3 July 1886. Maurice Healy (the other Home Rule candidate) went out of his way to thank Cork P.H.R.A. for its assistance.
89. F. Guy, *Directory of Munster 1886* (Cork, 1886), pp 364, 371, 381, 391, 400.
90. *C.E.*, 27 Oct. 1891, editorial; *C.C.*, 7 Mar. 1893.
91. See, for example, the remarks of R. A. Atkins at Cork corporation, when he concentrated exclusively on the material advantages of Home Rule, *C.C.*, 27 Feb. 1886.

92. J. Loughlin, 'The Irish Protestant Home Rule Association and nationalist politics, 1886-93' in *I.H.S.* xxiv, no. 95 (May 1985), pp 341-60; *C.E.*, 16 Jan. 1886.

93. *C.C.*, 17, 25 June 1886.

94. *C.E.*, 9 Jan. 1891.

95. See a report of his lecture 'The survival of Irish nationalism' in *C.C.*, 17 June 1886.

96. *Burke's Peerage*, 82nd ed., p. 2642; Guy, *Directory of Cork, 1899*, pp 193-5.

97. P. Bew, *Conflict and conciliation in Ireland, 1890-1910* (Oxford, 1987), pp 15-6; J. Loughlin, *Gladstone, Home Rule and the Ulster question 1882-93* (Dublin, 1986), p. 23.

98. A. Jackson, *The Ulster party. Irish unionists in the House of Commons, 1884-1911* (Oxford, 1989), p. 213. L. P. Curtis, *Coercion and conciliation in Ireland* (Princeton, 1963), p. 321.

99. *C.E.*, 8, 10, 24, 27 Oct. 1891; *C.C.*, 24, 29 Oct., 6 Nov. 1891; *C.C.*, 24 Aug. 1891 (letter from 'an old Cork tory'); *C.E.* 20 Oct. 1891, editorial.

100. *C.C.*, *C.E.* Oct.-Nov. 1891-95; *C.E.*, 3 Dec. 1895; d'Alton, 'Southern Irish unionism', chapter 3.

101. P.R.O.N.I., D989A/8/2, I.U.A. letters, 1893, J. H. Scott to G. Cox (secretary, I.U.A.), 24 Feb. 1893.

102. For examples of incidents sparked by sectarian attitudes and actions see *C.C.*, 6 Apr. 1886, 3, 10 Mar. 1893 (sectarian tensions in Cork workhouse); *Report of the unionist convention for Munster Leinster and Connacht* (Dublin, 1892) (allegedly sectarian remarks made by J. H. Scott); *The Times*, 29 Jan., 1, 4 Feb. 1894 (riots started by aggressive Protestant street-preaching in Cork city); *C.E.*, 7 May 1895 (use by the Gaelic Athletic Association of Cork Agricultural Society's showgrounds on Sundays).

103. U.C.C. Library, O'Brien MSS AR, 91, 76, Castletown to W. O'Brien, 15 Apr. 1910; R. M. D. Sanders (a Cork landlord) to O'Brien, 12 Feb. 1910. The 1910 municipal elections saw 16 Protestants standing under various labels, *C.C.*, 29 Nov. 3. Dec. 1910, editorials; *C.E.*, 7 Jan. 1911; Bowen's *Protestants in a Catholic state* is a sociological study of southern Protestants since 1922. Much of the 'integration' which he professes to identify as occurring in the post-independence period was already in evidence in Cork by the 1910s.

104. Evidence of J. Hayes to the commissioners appointed to inquire into the Irish municipal corporations, *C.C.*, 24 Oct. 1833; *Census, 1881*, xixa, pp 296-302.

105. B.L., Add. MS 40558, p. 307, Rev. W. Neligan to Peel, 28 Jan. 1845.

106. For a discussion of the competitive effects of the ten-fold increase in the numbers of the Irish civil service between 1861 and 1911 see J. Hutchinson, *The dynamics of cultural nationalism: the Gaelic revival and the creation of the Irish nation state* (London, 1987), pp 258-62; White, *Minority report*, p. 159; Bowen, *Protestants in a Catholic state*, pp 91, 93.

107. Travers' diary, Dec. 1833; Fleming, *Head or harp*, p. 17; Bowen, *Bowen's Court*, pp 192, 281, 293, 368; Bateman, *Great landowners*, passim.

108. *C.C.*, 20 July 1881, advertisement.

109. Ashton School archives, Cork, sec. of the Irish Society for Promoting Protestant Schools in Ireland to J. V. Bond, principal of Ashton School, Cork, 28 May 1975; I am grateful to Mr Bond for permission to consult the archives. See also D. Rudd, *Rochelle, the history of a school in Cork, 1829-1979* (Cork, 1979).

110. Speeches at the school's first prize day, *C.C.*, 21 July 1882.

111. Prize day reports in *C.C.*, 24 Dec. 1883, 23 Dec. 1885, 23 Dec. 1886, 24 Dec. 1888.

112. *Crockford's clerical directory, 1911*, p. 666; ibid., 1920 p. 668.

113. S. Farrington, 'The Grammar School under Harvey' in The Grammarian [the past pupils' magazine], i, pt. 4 (1953), p. 10.

114. T. J. McElligott, *Secondary education in Ireland 1870-1921* (Dublin, 1981), pp 168-9; K.T. Hoppen, *Ireland since 1800: conflict and conformity* (London, 1989), pp 155-80.

115. 49 and 49 Vict., *c.* 78. The C.G.S. scheme was number 47 under the act: a copy is in the Ashton School archives.

116. J. Coolahan, *Irish education: its history and structure* (Dublin, 1983), p. 63. McElligott, *Secondary education in Ireland*, pp 28, 45.

117. *C.C.*, 18 Dec. 1895, 23 Dec. 1898, 23 Dec. 1899, 19 Dec. 1901. A detailed description of the premises is in the Intermediate Education Board for Ireland, *Reports of inspectors* (1901-2 and 1909-10).

118. Ashton School archives, printed list of potential subscribers; *C.C.*, 23 Jan. 1908, report of a public meeting.

119. Prize day reports, end Dec. each year, 1888-1908, in *C.C.*

120. *C.C.*, 21 Dec. 1907.

121. *C.C.*, 21 Dec. 1906.

122. Intermediate Education Board for Ireland, *Reports of temporary inspectors* (Dublin, 1903), i, p. 163.

123. *C.C.*, 24 Dec. 1894.

124. The phrase is Jack White's, *Minority report*, p. 69.

125. For a balanced overview of the Anglo-Irish as portrayed by historians over the last 150 years, see G. C. Bolton, 'The Anglo-Irish and the historians 1830-1980' in O. MacDonagh, Mandle and Travers (ed.), *Irish culture and nationalism*, pp 239-57.

126. Hoppen, *Elections, politics and society*, p. 170.

127. Quoted in J. Cronin, 'Dominant themes in the novels of Somerville and Ross' in *Somerville and Ross: a symposium*, p. 9.

128. E. Somerville and M. Ross, *Irish memories* (London, 1925), p. 324.

129. Mitchelstown Castle was burnt down during the Irish war of independence, 1920-21, and the site was purchased by a dairy co-operative society. Cork Grammar School still flourishes as Ashton School, a state-funded 'Protestant comprehensive' secondary school.

Chapter 20

PLACE AND CLASS IN CORK

A. M. FAHY

By the first decade of the twentieth century, Cork city had acquired many of the spatial and social characteristics of the modern European and North American city. The city centre was dominated by business activities, such as shops and offices: each having special zones of concentration. Residential areas near the centre were generally poor, insanitary and overcrowded. Members of the predominantly Catholic middle classes lived in the suburbs in substantial terraced and detached houses, set in neat gardens behind walls, safe, they hoped, from the poverty, crime and ill-health associated with much of the city's population. Yet one hundred years before Cork was different in many important ways. Most of its inhabitants, rich or poor, lived in or near the city's old medieval core. Homes, offices, shops, warehouses and workshops were often side-by-side. Its commercial, professional and political life was dominated by a small Protestant élite. Cork's economy was flourishing, due largely to its extensive port activities which generated substantial family fortunes in the wholesaling of agricultural products for export.

In the intervening century many changes occurred. Cork was affected by economic, political and social forces which were both local, national and international in their origins.[1] Transformation in the fabric of the city – the location, function and style of buildings; the residential preferences of the middle classes; the development of roads and public transport, all expressed conscious and subconscious responses to these changes. The present essay concerns itself with the evolving social geography of Cork city in the nineteenth century, with particular emphasis on the impact of the growth of a large Catholic middle class on the physical fabric of the city. The most important expression of the development of this social group was the growth and expansion of middle-class suburbs. However, in order to understand the timing, nature and scale of changes in the city's social geography it is necessary first to review the economic, political and social development of Cork in this period.

Background
By the late eighteenth century Cork had become a prosperous and

significant Atlantic port city exporting the agricultural products of its rural hinterland. A range of manufacturing activities such as tanning and textile production had also emerged.[2] Its economic growth led to physical expansion, especially in the area beyond the North and South Gate bridges. In 1750 Smith remarked that the city was now 'thrice as large as it was forty years ago.'[3] Shortly after this Parliament Bridge was built to improve the flow of traffic in and out of the city. At the same time areas were opened up on the south bank of the river for development.

The profits of trade were enjoyed by a merchant class which was predominantly Protestant, Catholics being barred by law from many realms of business. Some Catholics became wealthy through the provision trade, such as in the packing and wholesaling of butter. By the 1820s thirty-five per cent of merchants were Catholic.[4] As David Dickson has shown, neither Catholic nor Protestant merchant families remained in these trades for more than two generations; they chose instead to invest in land and place their children in the legal and medical professions.

The provisioning of British naval vessels during the revolutionary and Napoleonic wars buffered many merchant fortunes. But after 1815 this business contracted rapidly. The increased self-sufficiency of North America reduced the market for imported goods there. Simultaneously, the volume of cheaper, factory-produced goods from England under-mined Irish industry. In the opening decades of the nineteenth century, Cork's economy was in an uncertain state. The provision trade had seriously weakened and the local textile industry was in decline. To some extent the expansion of brewing and distilling cushioned the labour market. So too did the fact that the previous decades of prosperity had established the city as a regional provider of banking, retailing and professional services. In these aspects Cork's important regional role was maintained and even strengthened.

For most of Cork city's population the first half of the nineteenth century was difficult. Destitution prevailed in the suburbs of Blackpool and Glasheen due to the decline of the textile industry. In 1839 Windele wrote that in Blackpool 'its once numerous and respectable inhabitants have given way to a poor and ill-employed population'.[5] Those affected most by the early advances of the industrial revolution were the hand-loom weavers. Daily earnings for workers in Cork fell from five shillings in 1820 to one shilling in 1850.[6] Throughout the nineteenth century artisan production declined steadily, leaving only street names such as Weavers' Alley, Tanners' Row, Nailers' Alley and Combmakers' Lane as testaments to former activities.[7]

Poverty was concentrated in the medieval core and in the Shandon

Street and Bandon Road areas. The distribution of charity schools in 1830 confirms this observation.[8] In 1841 the census recorded that seventy-two per cent of families in Cork inhabited slum accommodation.[9] On the eve of the Great Famine the population of Cork had reached eighty thousand; the years which followed would witness a further increase as country people flooded to the city seeking assistance or to await passage to America. By 1851 there were almost eighty-six thousand people in the city.

The impact of population growth was not uniform.[10] The overall increase was 6.2 per cent between 1841 and 1851, but some parishes experienced much more dramatic expansion. Holy Trinity, a centre city parish, for example, recorded a population increase of over thirty per cent. Other city centre parishes of St Peter and St Paul had 11.6 and 10.2 persons per house respectively in 1851. In each case this represented an increase in density since 1841. The southern parishes of St Nicholas and St Finbar had 7.6 and 6.5 persons per house; while the northern parishes of St Anne and St Mary's Shandon had a density of 7.2 each. In St Finbar's, St Anne's and St Mary's the population had increased but so too had the number of houses. These general figures, of course, conceal the important internal differences in each of the suburban parishes where pockets of poor and overcrowded housing existed in the streets nearer the city centre and in the Blackpool area. The contrast between poverty and wealth in Cork had been identified by Townsend in 1810 when he wrote that:

> with respect to modes of living the fault imputable to many cities is too observable in this; luxury and want exhibit a melancholy and mortifying contrast. The middle classes are frugal enough, the lowest very indigent; the highest often profuse. In a town of gay and fashionable resort parade and profusion form an expected, if not a commendable, part of its character. To a commercial city, like Cork, they are altogether inappropriate.[11]

By the mid-nineteenth century substantial disparities in standards of living were characteristic of most large European towns. This provoked, for various reasons, great concern amongst the middle classes. As crime, drunkenness and immorality (as defined by the middle classes) increased among the working classes causes and solutions were sought. In England the Industrial Revolution was judged to have occasioned profound changes in the structure of society. Those concerned about its negative effects included the future British Tory Prime Minister Benjamin Disraeli. In his novel *Sybil*, published in 1845, he advocated social and political reform to bridge the division between

the 'two nations' of the rich and poor.[12] In the same year Friedrich
Engels published, in German, *The condition of the working class in
England*, in which he documented the plight of workers in Manchester.
He proposed the more radical solution of a proletarian revolution.[13] In
Cork industrialisation had only a limited impact, yet many of the
problems to be found in Britain and French industrial cities were also
evident. However, unlike in those countries unemployment, low wages
and poverty did not spawn working-class radicalism. Nor did fear of
social disorder produce political unity amongst the middle class. The
people of Cork had other types of concerns; these included issues of
religion and nationalism, which gave its political, social and cultural life
distinctive qualities.

The growth of nationalist sentiments, led by Daniel O'Connell, cut
across social boundaries in Cork. Middle- and working-class Catholics
joined local nationalist societies. Some members of wealthy Protestant
merchant families, such as the brewing families of Beamish and
Crawford, supported the Repeal movement. One of the Beamishes had
written a novel in 1829, set partly in Cork; it was sympathetic towards
Catholic Emancipation, which is perhaps why it was suppressed by the
publishers.[14] Common interest in the nationalist question diverted the
attention of the Cork working classes away from any political activities
directed against their employers or against the middle classes.[15]

Morphological change

One of the most obvious expressions of the transformations taking
place in Cork, as in many European and North American cities in the
nineteenth century, was the increasing tendency for the middle classes
to live in suburban homes and for work-place and home to be
separate. While innovations in transportation obviously played a part in
allowing easier, reliable and economical travel into the city, the
development of suburbs was not simply an expression of the increased
mobility of those who could afford to pay for railway and tram tickets,
or even their own horse-drawn carriages. Middle-class suburbs were
also the expression of a complex set of values and aspirations surrounding the family, the role of women and children and the relationship between social classes.[16] This was no less the case in Cork where,
as the ranks of the middle classes widened and members were drawn
from more diverse religious and social backgrounds, social status was
no longer determined exclusively by family name or mode of dress, but
also by address.

Many middle-class men looked approvingly on progress, especially if
it generated new business opportunities, but uneasily watched the
increased disorder which it seemed to bring in its wake. Reports of

strikes, protests and new popular political movements in England, such as Chartism, reached the Cork middle classes through the pages of the *Cork Examiner* and the *Cork Constitution*. Meanwhile the increasing complexity of business organisation, be it retailing or manufacturing, caused the displacement of middle-class women from work alongside their husbands, where they were replaced by men trained as book-keepers, foremen, salesmen, accountants and engineers. The link between family and the day-to-day operation of business was severed, making residence near the place of work unnecessary. Therefore many fundamental changes in the organisation of nineteenth-century urban society were expressed in the development of Cork's middle-class suburbs.[17] There the family lived amongst others of the same kind, safe (it was hoped) from disorder, disease and moral corruption. The husband would venture forth to the city, to return before dark, while his wife was immersed in the cult of domesticity. She supervised children and servants, ensuring order in the ornately and densely-furnished rooms. Here was the refuge from the pressures of a rapidly changing world, a guarantee of tranquillity, order and 'respectable' values.[18] The cultural historian Peter Gay has remarked that 'the suburbs, creatures and creators of change, loomed large in that [middle-class] experience as defences from anxiety no less than realisations and wishes'.[19]

Social behaviour was also influenced by fashions outside of Ireland. In 1841 Mr Brennan advertised classes in 'fashionable modern dancing' and announced that 'having visited London and Paris, [he had] returned with all of the novelties of the fashionable world'. He welcomed appointments for classes and cited recommendations from various satisfied clients including Mrs Morgan of Tivoli House, Mrs Hamilton of South Terrace, Mrs Cummins of Silver Spring and Captain Westropp of Adelaide Place.[20]

By the late nineteenth century suburban residence was probably typical of most of the middle class in Cork. The movement out of the island city began in the mid-eighteenth century when some of the wealthiest merchants invested in country estates in areas which would later become fashionable middle-class suburbs. These families – the Rogers, Dunscombes and Newenhams – built rural retreats at Lotabeg in the north-east, Mount Desert in the north-west and Maryborough in the south-east.[21] Hence they could enjoy the life-style of the landed gentry but still be close to the merchant city, since they could afford private carriages to travel the narrow roads. For most Corkmen such a life would be neither affordable nor practical. They chose instead to invest in their businesses and in homes in the newly-reclaimed marsh areas east and west of the medieval core of the North and South Main Streets.

Visitors to Cork remarked on the deteriorating condition of the medieval part of the city centre. Chief Justice Wallis, in about 1750, compared Cork to Dutch cities with the exception 'that it does not partake of their cleanliness and neatness, some gentlemen's and merchants' houses are new built, and tolerably handsome, but in general [they are] very bad, much like houses in St. Giles and the worst parts of Holborn'.[22] In 1776 Arthur Young was equally unimpressed with the city: 'the best built part is Morrison's Island which promises well; the old part of the town is very close and dirty'.[23] The deteriorating condition of the old part of the city centre no doubt acted as a strong encouragement for those who could afford it to build their homes elsewhere, though for many years yet it would only be the lucky few who could afford to move immediately outside the river valley. Smith described these early suburban pioneers in 1750. Of Sunday's Well he noted 'on the north bank of the river are several pretty improvements and country houses of the citizens; and to the north west of the city several houses and pleasant gardens, which form the pretty hamlet of Sunday's Well'. He went on to write that 'here are very great plantations of strawberries of the largest and finest kinds. The planters of those fruit pay considerable rents for their gardens, by the profits arising from them alone.'[24]

The residents of Sunday's Well seem not to have been considered noteworthy by Smith since he did not provide any more detail on their identity or the delights of their houses and gardens. It was the families who lived in the areas which would later be known as Montenotte, Tivoli and Blackrock who were so favoured. He described the north-eastern ridge as

> a most charming outlet; upon it is Lota a pleasant seat, with gardens, plantations and waterworks, inhabited by Alderman Bradshaw; and near it the late Joseph Bennet Esq., recorder of Cork had a pretty villa; also nearer Cork, Mr. Richard Dennis, merchant has a good house and neat gardens, with an aviary; the gardens afford a fine view of the harbour and opposite country. Nor ought I to forget a neat garden and improvement of Mr. Daniel Foster, with fountains, statues and canals and a pretty house seated on a hill, half a mile from the city.[25]

This area would in later years become a large and fashionable suburb, as would the south-eastern suburbs of Blackrock and Douglas. Here, in 1750, lived the merchant Richard Newenham, whose house was adorned with a cupola. Other residents were Boyle Davis, Swithin White and Emmanuel Pigot who had 'a pleasant place with good gardens, fine canals and waterworks well stocked with carp'.[26]

By the first decade of the nineteenth century the construction of the fore-runner of the present St Patrick's Bridge had given the development of the north-eastern suburbs a new impetus. While previously the only entrance to the city from the north bank was across the North Gate Bridge, and through the poor, crowded lanes around it, the new bridge gave access to another part of the city centre where most of the Cork's merchants and professional people did business. In 1810 Townsend wrote that the bridge had encouraged the building of many excellent houses on the north side of the river which has lately become one of the most fashionable places of residence: these included houses on Camden Place and Patrick's Hill.[27]

While the attraction of the north bank lay in its elevated position and proximity to the city, Blackrock became popular as a place of weekend and summer retreat. Townsend noted that the road to Blackrock was 'almost converted into a street from the number of summer lodging houses which were erected in the previous twenty years'.[28] The status of these early residents, people who could afford large houses with gardens, as well as private carriages, endowed these incipient suburbs with a social cachet which ensured their continued popularity for decades.

Up to 1815 the mercantile economy in Cork was generating handsome profits, thereby making capital available for investment in houses and land. Greater demand for property had the effect of increasing land prices and reducing plot size. Smaller detached houses and terraces began to appear in between the large detached villas described by Smith in 1750. Townsend wrote of the suburban houses that 'the great value of ground necessarily reduces their demesnes to a small compass so that though there are many pretty, there are hardly any fine places. The general effect, from such a number of villas, is lively and pleasing, but would be agreeable to the eye, if there were more of hedge and less of wall'.[29] These houses were built close to the roads leading to the city for 'the townsman does not like to rusticate too much. With his relish for the country he mixes his love of the town and plants himself on the side of the dusty road for the pleasure of seeing folks pass'.[30]

These comments point to two of the most important characteristics of nineteenth-century suburban development. First was the retreat of the middle-class family into a formally-bounded privacy, behind a wall, where the domestic world was safeguarded from the public world. Second, there was the search for the 'bourgeois utopia', a perfect world in which the pleasure of the countryside was enjoyed and middle-class values nurtured without loss of contact with the town from which wealth was derived.

The point at which suburban residence became the norm for the Cork middle classes is difficult to assess, in the absence of detailed census returns. However, some alternative methods can be used to reconstruct the evolving social geography of the city. These include analysis of street directories and Griffith's valuation of 1852.[31] Directories usually contain a listing of business addresses for each occupational group, a street directory giving the names of residents in each street, and sometimes also an alphabetical directory of residents. Cross-comparison of trade and alphabetical lists allows the determination of whether particular individuals had separate addresses for business and residence, and thus the nature and direction of suburbanisation can partly be revealed.

Some directories also contain lists of a category called the nobility, gentry and clergy of the city. Though the definition of the nobility and clergy was obvious, the bulk of people belonging to groups were the gentry: people living off private means. The distribution of nobility and gentry in the nineteenth century acts as an indicator of the relative status of different areas of the city as places of residence. For example, in 1824 members of this group were found both in the island city, around the Mansion House[32] (now the Mercy Hospital) and the South Mall as well as on St Patrick's Hill and Sunday's Well.[33] The latter area was described in Pigot's *Directory* as having 'country seats' which were 'tastefully arranged and well wooded'. Of most interest is the continued popularity of the island city amongst a group who did not need to live close to the commercial centre of Cork. Residence there in 1824 still carried with it a certain social status. The most popular area of suburban residence for the nobility and gentry was Sunday's Well, while there was a further concentration in the Patrick's Hill area, nine residents in Sidney Place alone. Several of the gentry listed were from merchant families, such as Daniel Callaghan in Lotabeg, and Mrs Leahy in Sunday's Well.

It was in the north-east that suburban growth focused in the 1830s. In 1839 Windele described this area, saying that:

> east of the Kiln river ... has quite a new and suburban aspect. The streets are less continuous and connected, and open spaces are frequent between the houses. To one returned after an absence of a few years, Summerhill must be regarded with surprise and pleasure ... a suburb has grown up full of beauty and teeming with population ... the Lower Glanmire Road has been greatly extended, and wide vacant intervals filled up, whilst, on the long line of the hill to the rere, innumerable villas have been raised, pressing on each other, and vieing in their ornamental feature ...

Ballinamought, i.e. the townland of the poor is now a misnomer; poverty has been replaced by affluence.[34]

He went on to record the principal residents of the area. These were J. Morgan at Tivoli; J. Leycester (a former M.P.) at Eastview; Daniel Callaghan (butter merchant and M.P.) at Lota; William Green (grain merchant) at Lotamore. The residents of the south-eastern suburbs were a diverse group including several merchants, Sir Thomas Deane, Sir William Chatterton, the Quaker merchant Ebenezer Pike and the brewery owners Beamish and Crawford. Clearly the focus of high-status suburban residence had now shifted to these two areas, while Sunday's Well was in decline. In 1837 Tuckey noted that Sunday's Well 'is now out of fashion and has lost its reputation for superior salubrity'.[35] Windele asserted that 'in the last century, it was, what the eastern suburbs are now, covered with the "boxes" and pleasure of the more substantial citizens; Smith called it a "pretty hamlet", but the tide of fashion has set against it and Sunday's Well has been rather on the wane'.[36]

The declining popularity of Sunday's Well had been symbolically expressed in the construction of the City Gaol there in 1824. The building of large public institutions was only possible if the price of land was reasonable. Also the construction of a gaol, because of its obvious association with undesirable and illegal behaviour, would be effectively resisted by a social élite well connected with the city fathers. Clearly this did not happen in Sunday's Well. Unfortunately the destruction of the Grand Jury records (which covered the period before 1853), and of many of the corporation minute books (which dealt with the years after 1853), prohibits any detailed revelation of the decision-making behind the erection of the goal.

Nevertheless some prominent Corkmen were still attracted to the area. In 1831 the writer, philanthropist and manufacturer Richard Dowden built his home there. Overlooking the river, this tall, square, weather-slated house was unusual in design and name. He called it Rathlee, an act not in conformity with his peers who designated their homes by English names such as Chiplee and Woodhill. He was active in Cork cultural and political life, and showed concern for diverse issues. In 1848 he wrote an article condemning the closing off of public paths by the owners of large houses in the suburbs.[37] When he died his obituary described him as 'the strongest pillar of the Temperance movement' and declared that as a member of the Cork Literary and Scientific Society 'he shone not like a star, but like an entire constellation'.[38]

Some indication of the changing fashions of residential choice can be found in newspapers of the period. In the 1840s houses in Summerhill were frequently advertised and the same phrases were always used, for example 'desirable residence ... suited for the accommodation of a respectable family'.[39] But even the most respectable suburban residents were not insulated from the dangers of life as Mr James Murphy of Ringmahon Castle was to discover. In September 1841 he advertised a reward of £50 for the capturing of thieves who, he wrote, 'feloniously broke into the front hall of my Dwelling House ... and carried away a large Chased Silver Coffee Pot, a Chased Silver Sugar Bowl, and some small articles of Plate'.[40] Further misfortune was to befall Mr Murphy, who was a brother of the Catholic bishop of Cork, when travelling on the mail coach to Dublin. While stopped at Caher (Cahir), the *Cork Examiner* reported, 'one of our most worthy, charitable and independent merchants was set upon by a band of ferocious Orangemen'.[41]

Suburban development was accompanied by a decline in the city centre as a place of middle-class residence. Houses on the South Mall had been built in the late eighteenth century to serve multiple purposes – home, warehouse and office were found under the same roof. By the mid-nineteenth century this was less often the case. Some buildings were given over entirely to offices. In 1850 there was advertised 'to be let, the offices No. 93 and 94 South Mall ... They are particularly well adapted for gentlemen of the Legal Profession, or for merchants not requiring Warehouses attached'.[42] In the South Mall offices and banks replaced homes. By 1852 fifty-four of the one-hundred and four lawyers (including attorneys, barristers and solicitors) in Cork had offices on this street, at Nos 3-4, 8, 10-13, 17-18, 23, 26, 37-40, 43, 45, 48, 58-60, 62, 64-5, 69, 72, 74-5, 78-80, 83, 95 and 96. Of these, four buildings had more than one lawyer's office; an additional fourteen lawyers had South Mall addresses with no number given.[43] The 1852 directory does not have an alphabetical listing for city residents, so it was not possible to determine whether these men had homes elsewhere in the city. An analysis of the directory of 1863[44] indicates that sixty-nine solicitors were listed for Cork. Of these, forty-six had offices on the South Mall (the remainder were to be found in the adjoining side-streets) and forty had separate residences. These were divided almost equally between the Patrick's Hill/Summerhill/Montenotte area, and the road to Blackrock. In contrast, the alphabetical directory of 1844 had listed only thirteen of the ninety-eight lawyers with suburban homes.[45]

Transportation change and its influence

Up to the 1850s there was no public transport in Cork. Those who wished to live outside the city centre had to either own a carriage, rely on hiring a hackney carriage or walk. Notices of houses to be sold or let often specified the walking distance to the city. In 1845 a house in Sunday's Well was advertised as having a 'delightful situation, southern aspect. Janeville, Sunday's Well, near Wellington Bridge (within twenty minutes walk of the city). To be let ... a few neatly finished and substantially built houses, with flower gardens in front and every accommodation, fit for the immediate reception of respectable families.'[46]

While there were many substantial houses much closer to the city, particularly in the area of the Mansion House (by 1861 the Mercy Hospital), they were rejected by suburban-bound Corkonians. In 1861 Gibson noted that

> the tide of population and the hum of business do not extend west of Duncan Street. Here was once the fashionable end of town. Here we still have the old Mansion House, which is now used as a hospital ... the fine houses of the Mardyke have a faded and antiquated appearance, the Mardyke itself has lost *ton*. Bachelor's Quay is no longer a promenade; Prospect Row has lost its pleasant look; Nile Street and Henry Street are wide and deserted thoroughfares; Francis Street and Thomas Street and Devonshire Street have their names recorded in this history out of pure respect for their by-gone grandeur and gentility.[47]

The process of abandonment of the city centre by the middle classes was gradual. The expense and inconvenience of commuting ensured that buildings on the newly-constructed Great George's Street (now

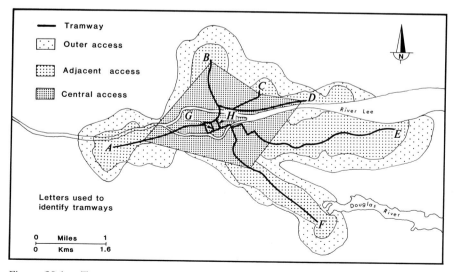

Figure 20.1   Tramway access zones.

Washington Street) would still retain a partly residential use. In 1850 the upper part of No. 30 on this street was advertised to be let 'near the Court House ... from the airy situation of this house and the spaciousness of the rooms, it would be a very desirable residence for a respectable family; or from its nearness to the Colleges, it would make an excellent Boarding House'.[48]

For the richest citizens of Cork private carriages were increasingly necessary as the residences of the élite became more dispersed. Meanwhile for businessmen living in the expanding suburbs carriages were needed to reach the city centre. Thus many houses, both in the city centre and suburbs, continued to be advertised as having coach-houses and stables. In 1850 a house called Bellevue 'one and a half miles from Cork' was advertised for sale with the desirable features of six excellent and airy bedrooms, two dressing-rooms, water closets' and stabling for five horses.[49] In September of the same year the home of William Deane, Esq., at No. 87, South Mall was advertised to be let 'with stable and coach-houses'.[50] By 1863 this property was occupied by a solicitor and a private school.[51] Other properties on the South Mall more clearly demonstrated the increased intensity of commercial uses in this street. In 1855 No. 51 was advertised to be let, at £90 per annum, and was stated to be 'well adapted for any extensive trade or for professional chambers' as it had a shop on the ground floor and residence above with 'eleven bedrooms and patent water closet set in mahogany'.[52] Perhaps it was the water-closet advertised as 'most severely tested at the Great Exhibition of 1851 ... and least apt to become deranged'[53] which attracted attention.

The construction of suburban railway lines, such as the Cork, Passage and Blackrock railway, also produced important spatial responses in the city. These railways were built to serve the growing middle-class appetite for leisure, especially for recreation in or near the sea. In addition, they also made the south-eastern suburbs accessible to a larger section of the middle classes since private carriages were no longer necessary to get to the city centre. The effect on housing development was immediate and land was quickly offered for sale near the railway. In 1855 building land was advertised 'within five minutes walk of the railway' and buyers encouraged by offer of 'a free ticket for three years on the Cork, Blackrock and Passage railway, to the head of family occupying every newly-built house, of an annual value of £25 and upwards'.[54] The construction of the railway not only offered a business opportunity for landowners, builders and railway shareholders but also for those aware of Cork people's suspicion about this new form of transportation. In the same issue of the *Cork Examiner* an agent offered insurance for railway passengers, citing loss of limbs by various commuters on English railways.[55]

Residence in the south-eastern suburbs had a further advantage in this period – these suburbs were located outside the municipal boundary and were exempt from city taxation. Thus No. 1, Ashton Place was advertised in 1860 as 'most desirable residence ... free from city taxation ... within three minutes walk of the Cork and Passage Railway Terminus and six of the South Mall'.[56]

In 1865 incentives were still being offered to potential Blackrock residents. Blackrock Villas were 'close to the pier ... and within five minutes walk of the railway station'. A free first-class railway ticket was offered for purchasers of these houses. The houses provided 'first class accommodation for a Gentleman's family'. Each villa had 'a private walled-in garden', stables and coach-house.[57] This single advertisement expressed the most important characteristics of suburban development in Cork. In the case of the newer areas like Blackrock, residents were wealthy – able to afford both first-class railway travel and a private carriage. In their homes they clearly separated the private and public world, by surrounding themselves with walls. Even when travelling to and from the city, they ensured isolation from less-well-off Corkonians by using the first-class railway carriage.

Suburban areas closer to the city, especially in the north-east, continued to offer many advantages. Houses on Wellington Road were substantial and within walking distance of the city. In 1870 a 'first-class dwelling house at St. Patricks Place' was advertised as being 'in the most fashionable and convenient part of the City'.[58] Even the most exclusive houses, with large gardens, were advertised with particular mention being made of their proximity, in walking time, to the city. In St Luke's in 1880 'a most desirable suburban residence ... on eight acres' was '10 minutes walk from St. Patricks Bridge'.[59] In 1890 Arbutus Lodge was advertised as being fifteen minutes walk from the city.[60] This suggests that even for suburban residents of considerable wealth, certainly able to afford private carriages, quick access to the city on foot continued to be a consideration in the selection of a home. The further reaches of the north-eastern ridges were now accessible from the Tivoli railway line. Woodhill and Bellevue Terraces were advertised in 1890 as 'a few minutes walk from Tivoli station, fine houses ... for a gentleman's family'.[61] To the west of the city, near the Queen's College, suburban development was facilitated by the extension of the Western Road. In 1890 Nos 3-6, Brighton Villas were for sale as 'a splendid investment ... newly built and most fashionable villa residences ... outside city taxation'.[62]

Up to this time, suburban residents used private carriages, hackney carriages, walked or commuted on the limited suburban railway lines in order to travel to and from the city centre. Many encountered difficulty in their journeys, evidenced by frequent complaints to the corporation about the condition of the roads, as the surviving minute books of the Cork corporation Improvement Department record.[63] In October 1886 James Penrose of Woodhill complained about the state of the road between Tivoli Station and his home.[64] Frequent requests for the lighting of suburban roads were also recorded. While suburban dwellers were clearly concerned about the general safety of the roads along which they and their families travelled, the city centre and poorer residential areas had more serious problems. The records of complaints concerning those areas provide colourful evidence of the conditions which further encouraged the middle classes to abandon the city centre. In 1886 Matt Rearden sought compensation of £6 from the corporation after his horse, cart and self had fallen into an open sewer in Gilabbey Street.[65] A city centre resident, Mr William Bishop, complained of 'annoyance occasioned by the misconduct of disorderly women, and by springless carts and droves of pigs driven through the streets at night'.[66] Other residents appealed for more public lighting to prevent immorality at the Turkish Baths near Bachelors Quay,[67] and to prevent noise and bad language on Patrick's Street.[68] Even the Mardyke, once fashionable as a promenade for the middle classes, had become a

Plate 20.1   Minute-Book of Cork Corporation Hackney Carriage Committee (Cork Archives Institute).

troublesome spot. A caretaker complained of cyclists travelling too fast, or 'scorching'.[69] Seats which had been installed there were the subject of complaints from several residents whose gardens backed onto the Dyke because they were 'frequently used by objectionable characters'.[70]

For many who had abandoned the city in favour of the more salubrious suburbs, hackney carriages were a frequently-employed means of transportation. The behaviour of the carriage drivers often gravely offended their middle-class passengers, as the minutes of the Corporation Hackney Carriage Committee recorded.[71] The relationship between drivers, passengers and the Committee became more tense as attempts were made to enforce standards of 'respectable' behaviour on the drivers, especially as their business was increasingly undermined by the development of the tram system after 1898. The most frequent complaints concerned drivers guilty of drunkenness and of the use of bad language. Punishment usually consisted of suspension of the driver's licence for a specified period. Gerald Penrose of Woodhill, Tivoli, complained that a driver 'was drunk, and assaulted him and demanded more than his legal fare'.[72] Mr McNamara of Dundanion, Blackrock, wrote that a driver 'having been hired to convey his sister and self from the Opera House to their residence refused to drive them beyond Dead Woman's Hill, and compelled them to alight in the midst of heavy rainfall'.[73] Another driver was reprimanded for what was, in the eyes of the Committee, one of the most serious offenses when 'he used abusive language towards a woman passenger, whom he drove to Ballintemple, and detained a parcel of groceries, in lieu of the fare which she at the time was unable to pay'.[74]

It was not only their treatment of middle-class passengers which was of concern to the Committee. Frequent complaints were made about the 'immoral' behaviour of some passengers, for which the carriage drivers were punished. A policeman reported that 'he had seen prostitutes in the car of William Nagle, ... in Patrick's Street at four o'clock in the morning ... and had seen a man emerge there from and make off'.[75] Another complaint alleged that a driver 'had two navy seamen and a prostitute in his car with the curtains drawn on the Lee Road'.[76]

The stern dealings of the Committee with drivers did not endear members of the corporation to those men whose livelihoods depended on the plying of hackney carriages. In 1890 one driver 'attempted to run down any member of the corporation that came in his way'.[77] This relationship further deteriorated when the corporation agreed to the establishment of a horse-drawn omnibus service in 1897. The drivers engaged a solicitor to represent them and objected to many aspects of the omnibus system – the location of stops on Patrick's Street, for example. Once the omnibus was in operation some drivers were openly hostile. A certain omnibus driver complained of a hackney driver 'shouting at ladies getting on his buses, and so driving his hackney car as to impede the passing of the horses and try to throw down the horses'.[78] The chairman of the Committee complained of a hackney driver threatening him 'which he could only account for by his having voted for the omnibus licenses'.[79]

Another increasingly popular form of middle-class transportation also antagonised the hackney carriage drivers. This was the bicycle. By 1884, a Bicycle Club was already established in Cork.[80] In 1885 a deputation of cyclists had asked for permission to ride on the Mardyke and Marina walks.[81] As bicycles became more common so did conflict with the hackney drivers. In 1896 a lieutenant in the Royal Irish Fusiliers complained of a driver 'having deliberately attempted to drive over [his] bicycle on the Douglas Road ... and violently assaulted him'.[82] Of course there may also have been an element of political conflict in this particular encounter. More common complaints were those such as that of Mrs Yourdi who was the victim of 'furious and negligent driving' on the South Mall,[83] and of Dr D. J. O'Connor who was injured while riding his bicycle.[84]

In 1898 the first relatively cheap form of public transportation, serving the suburbs, was introduced in Cork. This was an electric tramway system.[85] There were six suburban lines, leading to Summerhill, Tivoli, Blackrock, Douglas, Sunday's Well and Blackpool. Trams ran every ten to twelve minutes and fares ranged from 1d. to 3d.[86] Hackney drivers protested frequently, especially when their stands at Father Mathew's Statue were moved to make way for the tramcars.[87]

The public was also critical of trams and complained about their speed. It was proposed that they should not exceed nine miles per hour.[88] Conflict between new and traditional forms of transportation became more common. The owners of the Munster Arcade complained that the trams interfered with delivery of goods to their shop, which delivery was by horse-drawn van. In 1898 Mr Lester of Patrick's Street reported to the Hackney Carriage Committee that 'while his son was riding a bicycle the driver of an outside car swerved his horse so quickly towards him as to force him towards the electric tramcar from under which he was afterwards taken out'.[89] Before 1900 no complaints were received from suburban residents about the electric trams, which now provided a reliable, frequent and economical means for them to enjoy residence in the suburbs, while continuing to work and shop in the city centre.

The construction of the tramlines would initiate the final wave of nineteenth-century suburban growth in Cork. Suburbs, such as Blackrock, which had been scattered with a few large houses surrounded by extensive estates, now entered a period of redevelopment. The land attached to early nineteenth-century residences was often sold for the construction of terraced houses. Solicitors, bankers, managers and office workers could now live in suburbs previously occupied only by the wealthiest merchants, industrialists and gentlemen. In the *Cork Examiner* advertisements such as this became common:

> Auction. Grange View, Douglas Road. Beautifully situated and convenient suburban residence ... having a frontage of 550 feet to the road ... giving a splendid building site in a locality where every day the demand for houses is becoming greater and the opportunities for acquiring building sites fewer.[90]

By 1900 the suburbs of Cork city expanded far beyond the municipal boundary, which had been established by the Cork Improvement Act of 1853. Since that time the areas which fell outside the boundary included Tivoli, Douglas, Blackrock, Ballintemple and Sunday's Well west of Shanakiel. A substantial extension, to include all of these areas and more, had been proposed by the Municipal Boundaries Commission in 1882 but had not been put into effect.

Conclusion

Cork's physical fabric had undergone major change since 1800, as had its economic, political and social organisation. At the beginning of the nineteenth century most Corkonians lived and worked in the island city which lay between the two branches of the Lee. This area contained within it some newly-built and fashionable streets, such as the South Mall, North Mall, Dyke Parade and Grenville Place. Here were to be found the homes of the city's economic and social élite. Those few who could afford to live on the northern ridge overlooking Cork, or in the south-east overlooking the harbour, had already built fine houses there. In doing so they endowed those areas with qualities which would attract successive ranks of the middle classes. First came those who could afford to travel by private horse and carriage. They were followed by families who chose to live in an intermediate location between the exclusive villas of the very wealthy and the island city. Husbands could walk to the city from Wellington Road, Summerhill and Sunday's Well, and the cost of engaging a hackney car in inclement weather or for a social outing was not excessive. Clearly the flow of the Cork middle classes to the suburbs was well under way before there were any substantial innovations in public transport, before the construction of the Blackrock and Passage railway or of the electric tram. The desire of the middle classes to declare their economic and social status by taking up residence in socially exclusive areas determined the timing and direction of improved transportation.

For the growing middle class of Cork the quest for the suburban utopia would continue. This search had been responsible for the most noteworthy changes in the physical fabric of the city during the nineteenth century. The existence of clearly differentiated middle-class residential areas was firmly established by 1900. They were the spatial expression of changing social values and aspirations within the middle class and of changing relationships between social classes in Cork.

References

1. For a broad and stimulating discussion of this period in European history see E. J. Hobsbawm, *The age of revolution 1789-1848* (London, 1962), *The age of capital 1848-1875* (London, 1975), and *The age of empire 1875-1914* (London, 1987).
2. Dickson, 'Cork region'.
3. Smith, *Cork*, p. 370.
4. D. Dickson, 'The Cork merchant community in the eighteenth century: a regional perspective' in L. M. Cullen and P. Butel (ed), *Négoce et industrie en France et en Irlande aux xviiᵉ et xixᵉ siècles* (Paris, 1980), p. 47.
5. Windele, *Cork*, p. 43.
6. M. Murphy, 'The working classes of nineteenth-century Cork', in *Cork Hist. Soc. Jn.*, lxxxix (1980), pp 26-51, especially p. 28.
7. Griffith, *Valuation* (Cork).
8. Finny's *Royal Cork Almanac* (Cork, 1830).
9. *Census of Ireland: 1841* (Dublin, 1841).
10. All data for housing and population are derived from the *Census of Ireland* for 1841 and 1851.
11. Townsend, *Cork*, pp 655-6.
12. I have consulted the Oxford, 1981 edition.
13. F. Engels, *The condition of the working class in England*, translated by W. O. Henderson and W. H. Chaloner (Stanford, California, 1958).
14. N. L. Beamish, *Peace campaigns of a cornet* (London, 1829).
15. M. Murphy, 'The working classes'; idem, 'The economic and social structure of nineteenth century Cork' in Harkness and O'Dowd, *Town*, pp 125-54.
16. For discussion of the development of suburbs in Britain and North America see R. Fishman, *Bourgeois utopias: the rise and fall of suburbs* (New York, 1987).
17. Any estimate of how large the middle-class population of Cork was depends on the manner in which class membership is defined. It is most commonly considered to be determined by occupation or income, because these are easily quantified characteristics. However, it can be argued that middle-class values may not be confined to those of particular occupations or incomes; nor indeed did having a particular occupation or income always dictate that one had such values. Using occupation as a broad indication of class affiliation Murphy has suggested (in 'The working classes') that eighty per cent of the population of Cork belonged to the working class in the mid-nineteenth century. By inference one can therefore argue that twenty per cent were middle class – though this group was internally diverse, containing a wide range of occupations and incomes.

18. For a discussion of the role of women and the family in middle-class Victorian society see L. Davidoff, *The best circles: women and society in Victorian England* (Totowa, New Jersey, 1973); J. M. Peterson, *Family, love and work in the lives of Victorian gentlewomen* (Bloomington, Indiana, 1989); and B. G. Smith, *The bourgeoises of northern France in the nineteenth century* (Princeton, New Jersey, 1981).

19. P. Gay, *The bourgeois experience: Victoria to Freud; volume 1, the education of the senses* (Oxford, 1985), pp 51-2.

20. *C.E.*, 30 Aug. 1841.

21. Dickson, 'Cork region', p. 90.

22. Quoted in Smith, *Cork*, p. 419.

23. Young, *Tour.*

24. Smith, *Cork*, p. 355.

25. Ibid., p. 357.

26. Ibid., p. 359.

27. Townsend, *Cork*, p. 699.

28. Ibid., p. 699.

29. Ibid., p. 700.

30. Ibid., p. 701.

31. For a detailed examination of these sources, see A. M. Fahy, 'A social geography of nineteenth-century Cork', unpublished M.A. thesis, U.C.C. (1981).

32. The Mansion, or Mayoral, House was built in 1773.

33. *Pigot and Co.'s Munster directory* (Cork, 1824), pp 243-4.

34. Windele, *Cork*, p. 45.

35. Tuckey, *Cork remembrancer* (Cork, 1837), p. 24.

36. Windele, *Cork*, p. 52.

37. *Cork Magazine*, June 1848, pp 484-8.

38. Quoted in 'Cork worthies of old' in *Cork Hist. Soc. Jn.*, xxii (1916), pp 21-4.

39. Ibid., 3 Sept. 1841.

40. Ibid., 3 Sept. 1841.

41. Ibid., 1 Nov. 1841.

42. Ibid., 1 Mar. 1841.

43. *Purcell and Co.'s commercial almanac* (Cork, 1852).

44. *Robert H. Laing's Cork mercantile directory* (Cork, 1863).

45. *County and city of Cork Post Office and general directory,* (Cork, 1844).

46. *C.E.,* 1 Feb. 1845.

47. Gibson, *Cork*, p. 315.

48. *C.E.*, 1 May 1850.

49. Ibid., 3 June 1850.

50. Ibid., 3 Sept. 1850.

51. *Laing's Cork directory* (Cork, 1863).

52. *C.E.*, 2 Feb. 1855.

53. Ibid., 2 May 1855.

54. Ibid., 1 Aug. 1855.

55. Ibid., 1 Aug. 1855.

56. Ibid., 2 Jan. 1865.

57. Ibid., 2 Jan. 1870.

58. Ibid., 2 Jan. 1870.

59. Ibid., 1 Dec. 1880.

60. Ibid., 7 June 1890.

61. Ibid., 18 Jan. 1890.

62. Ibid., 3 May 1890.
63. C.A.I., Cork Corporation Improvement Department Minute Books (hereafter Improvement Department), 11 Feb. 1881-24 Apr. 1891.
64. Ibid., 15 Oct. 1886.
65. Ibid., 5 Feb. 1886.
66. Ibid., 8 July 1887.
67. Ibid., 7 May, 1886.
68. Ibid., 2 Nov. 1888.
69. Ibid., 24 June 1898.
70. Ibid., 24 Mar. 1899.
71. C.A.I., Cork Corporation Hackney Carriage Committee (hereafter Hackney Carriage Committee), 1890-1900.
72. Ibid., 27 Mar. 1893.
73. Ibid., 22 Oct. 1894.
74. Ibid., 10 June 1895.
75. Ibid., 13 Feb. 1890.
76. Ibid., 26 May 1896.
77. Ibid., 13 Mar. 1890.
78. Ibid., 12 July 1897.
79. Ibid., 11 Oct. 1897.
80. *Francis Guy's almanac* 1884, p 99.
81. C.A.I., Improvement Department, 12 June 1885.
82. C.A.I., Hackney Carriage Committee, 27 Apr. 1896.
83. Ibid., 27 Sept. 1896.
84. Ibid., 27 Sept. 1897.
85. Plans for the proposed system survive in the C.A.I. Initial plans, in 1896, were for lines from the city centre to the Gaol Cross, and also to Victoria Road, to the Lower Glanmire Road (Myrtle Hill Terrace) to Blackpool (junction of Great Britain Street and York Street), to Adelaide Place, to Douglas Village. In 1897 extensions were proposed from the Gaol Cross to Wellington Bridge, from Victoria Road to Ballintemple, from Patrick's Bridge to the North Mall (via Camden Quay), from Patrick's Street to North Gate Bridge (via Cornmarket Street), from Albert Quay to the Marina. The tramway system was also discussed in detail by the Hackney Carriage Committee in 1897 and 1898.
86. W. McGrath, *Tram tracks through Cork* (Cork, 1981).
87. C.A.I., Hackney Carriage Committee, 2 Jan. 1899.
88. Ibid., 20 Mar. 1899.
89. Ibid., 28 Dec. 1898.
90. *C.E.*, 6 Jan. 1890.

Chapter 21

ART INSTITUTIONS IN NINETEENTH-CENTURY CORK

PETER MURRAY

The history of art in nineteenth-century Cork may be traced through biographies of individual artists, most notably Professor John Turpin's monographs on John Hogan and Daniel Maclise, as well as through a number of recollections of artists and their works, generally written by local historians and antiquarians.[1] There have also been published comprehensive accounts of the Royal Cork Institution (R.C.I.), which played an important role in art education up to the mid-century.[2] However significant gaps remain. Apart from the above-mentioned sources, few descriptions exist of those Cork societies and schools which trained and supported artists, or exhibited their paintings, prints and sculptures. The story of these successive endeavours forms a continuous thread through the nineteenth century. This article attempts to examine four such institutions active in Cork in the period: the Cork Society for Promoting the Fine Arts (hereafter generally referred to as the Society of Arts), active between 1815 and 1833; the Cork Art Union, founded in 1840, and the Cork School of Design, established in 1850, which subsequently evolved into the Crawford School of Art.

Their activities may be summarised as follows. The Cork Society for Promoting the Fine Arts organised the first of a series of annual exhibitions in Cork in 1815 and was formally instituted the following year. It was presented with a collection of sculpture casts in 1818, which enabled the setting up of the first Cork School of Art. Financial difficulties in 1825 forced the Society of Arts to give over its headquarters on Patrick Street to the newly-founded Mechanics Institute, and obliged the sale of its cast collection to the Royal Cork Institution (the precurser of Queen's College, now University College, Cork). In the event, the Mechanics Institute did not survive long, and the R.C.I. took over their art classes, moving both these and the cast collection into the Old Custom House in 1832. The Society of Arts revived briefly in the early 1830s, but was effectively supplanted by the Cork Art Union from 1840 onwards. The Art Union was founded by local artists and based on similiar organisations in other British cities. Like the Society of Arts, the Art Union mounted a series of annual exhibitions, although its main purpose was the selling of works of art through a lottery system and the wider dissemination of contemporary art through engravings. By the time the Government School of Design replaced the R.C.I. in the Old Custom House in 1850, neither the Society of Arts nor the Art Union remained in existence. Supported by local rate-payers and central government, the Cork School of Design went from strength to strength, although its original egalitarian aims were progressively diluted by social pressures. In 1884 it emerged as the Crawford School of Art, with magnificent new studios and galleries added to its home in the Old Custom House. It is worth noting that of these four institutions it was only the School of Design, later School of Art, which was to flourish in the long term. For an age which prided itself upon the effectiveness of philanthropy, the failure of the early privately-supported ventures raises questions which this paper attempts to address.

The economic and cultural background

Before embarking on a detailed look at the histories of the Society of Arts, the Art Union and the School of Art, it is necessary to outline the social and economic contexts which controlled the arts during these years and, in passing, to examine the relationship between Cork artists and their patrons. During the course of the eighteenth century the population of Cork city had grown to 60,000, supplying labour for brewing, flour-milling, shipbuilding, textiles and other industries, based either on the rich agricultural hinterland of Cork or on the strategically important harbour, which was Ireland's main Atlantic port during this period and the source of much of the city's wealth. Whether used for assembling fleets of convict ships for Australia, warships for the American War or flotillas of troopships for the Peninsular War, the harbour's size and security made it one of the busiest ports in the world at the time. Its key location on the Atlantic rim ensured continuing contacts with the New World: much of the export trade was in agricultural produce, although decorative glassware from Cork was highly prized in America. Reflecting the importance of the harbour, Cork's wealth was based more on commerce than on manufacturing; the municipal council and corporate life were dominated by a commercial merchant class which also controlled the city's cultural life and remained a potent force throughout the period considered here.

The trans-Atlantic trade was not only in goods. Over the course of the century tens of thousands of people embarked at Cork Harbour for the New World. Many were unskilled and poverty-stricken, but by no means did all emigrants fit in this category. Several of America's notable nineteenth-century artists and architects, including William Harnett and

Thomas Hovenden, were born or trained in Cork. One of Abraham Hargrave's assistants, the architect Henry Howard (1818-1884), emigrated from Cork to Louisiana where he designed some of the South's finest ante-bellum mansions, such as those at the plantations of Belle Grove, Woodlawn and Madewood.[3] The construction of the Cathedral of St John and St Finbar (the founder and patron saint of Cork) in Charleston, South Carolina, in 1850 necessitated a number of skilled Irish stonemasons and carvers emigrating to that city.[4] Significantly, census returns in the United States around mid-century record a considerable number of Irish engravers and skilled artisans pursuing their trade in New York, Philadelphia and other cities of the eastern seaboard.[5]

This emigration was caused mainly by economic factors. In the period immediately following the Act of Union in 1800 Cork had experienced a fairly steady growth in manufacturing industries and commercial life. However this prosperity was seriously affected by the post-war recession of the mid 1820s. In Ireland, as in England, an economic slump followed the Allied victory at Waterloo, caused largely by the heavy taxation imposed by the government to pay for the expense of twenty years of war. Many English manufacturers who had thrived on military contracts went bankrupt, while Cork farmers who had grown wealthy supplying the army and navy suffered equally. Rates and taxes rose, wages fell and unemployment, particularly in England, soared. Cork's economic fate was not only linked to Britain; by 1830 the 2,500 linen looms of west Cork had been devastated by cheap Continental textile imports into Britain and the consequent dumping of inexpensive English factory cottons in Ireland.

Economic uncertainty gave rise to political change. The newly-risen English middle class and a new working-class consciousness combined against the traditional structures of English landed society, causing a decline in established patronage of the arts, a pattern repeated in Cork. The passing of the Reform Bill in 1832 has been traditionally identified as marking the decline, in England at any rate, of the old aristocratic system, a system which had expressed itself publicly through the refined taste of the Georgian period, especially in architecture. Initiatives to help alleviate the recession were to include setting up in the 1830s an extensive system of Government Schools of Design. These Schools, based on successful French and German models, were intended primarily to teach industrial design to workmen and artisans and thus improve the quality of manufactured goods in Britain.

The early years of the century were kind to Cork as firstly the American War of Independence and later the Napoleonic wars brought prosperity to its farmers, tradesmen and merchants. Life was comfortable for the wealthy, and tolerable for many. Some of Cork's finest houses, such as Lota Beg, Lota Park, Castle Hyde, Dunkathel, Castle Bernard and Hoddersfield were constructed at this time. The wooded banks of the river Lee and the shores of the large harbour were increasingly dotted with fine villas and mansions, while the skill and sophistication of architects like Abraham Hargrave, Thomas Deane and Richard Morrison indicate a fairly wide appreciation for the visual arts, albeit amongst an audience that was restricted to the middle and upper classes. Houses like Coolmore, Dandanion, Convamore and their owners, Robert O'Callaghan Newenham, Thomas Deane and Lord Listowel, formed the cultural context within which the Society of Arts emerged, and so it is worth pausing briefly to examine the symbolic values expressed in their residences. By and large they followed the Palladian type so notably established in eighteenth-century Cork by Davis Ducart, but it was a Palladianism pared down to essentials. Unlike their ebullient counterparts in the American deep South whose Grecian features have been claimed to denote 'a persuasive ideal of Greek democracy', these Cork houses hardly even attempted to dissemble.[6] Although classical in general form and detail, they were plain barns for the most part, built on a gigantic scale chiefly to stimulate and accommodate proper social intercourse amongst their inhabitants. Ideological classicism, perhaps held in restraint by the strong Quaker influence in Cork, could follow on later.

The interiors of houses like Dunkathel and Coolmore were generally quite plain. The staircases were typically cantilevered, with slender iron balusters and mahogany rails. Apart from their Adamesque stuccoed ceilings and carved mantlepieces a number of these homes had good art collections, particularly those of George Newenham and Cooper Penrose. A purpose-built gallery in a wing of Penrose's Woodhill residence contained works by James Barry, Angelica Kaufmann and Jacques Louis David, while classical casts were displayed in niches in a series of octagonal and cube-shaped rooms. The house was also adorned with decorative shell-work and feather-work, executed by Penrose's mother. Not far distant, Newenham's villa at Summerhill, with its collection of paintings by Nathaniel Grogan, was frequented by Daniel Maclise, who described it as

> a residence entirely congenial ... For Mr. N. had a gallery of pictures very well selected and, besides being the resort of all who could at all pretend to taste, there was in the house, carried on by the daughter and the father, the actual exercise of the arts of Painting and Modelling. Colours, canvas and the easel, the model stand and clay were familiar objects.[7]

As the century advanced and new money became consolidated there emerged a renewed appreciation of the symbolic value of architecture. The 'battle of the styles', Classical versus Gothic (with Tudor riding on the coat-tails of the latter), was fought in Cork as in other cities, but with consummate architects like the Deanes, the Morrisons and the Pain brothers switching easily from one style to the other it cannot be said that there was much heart in the fight. The ambivalence was neatly expressed in the gardens of James Morgan's house at Tivoli where a scaled-down version of the Temple of Vesta happily co-existed with a Gothic temple.

While most of the great houses around Cork were variants on Hargrave's Palladian style, their owners vied in embellishing them with Gothic accessories such as turrets and castellated gateways. Blackrock Castle and the tower at Fota date from this period. These medievalising gentlemen were seeking an air of antiquity as much as responding to fashion, endeavouring to give the impression that their houses – and their money – had been there for centuries. Not all householders of this period succumbed to the Romantic charm of battlements and bartizans. Indeed one of the finest Regency villas in Ireland was built near Cork in the 1820s, when Richard Morrison was comissioned by John Smith-Barry (1793-1837) to remodel an old hunting lodge on Fota Island. Morrison, working with his son, enlarged the house by adding pedimented wings onto either side of the original structure and showed that he was equally at home with a gentle Regency style as he was with the Gothic excesses of Castlefreke. Morrison extended his interest in the Classical orders by naming his son and assistant William Vitruvius, and between them they embellished the interior of Fota House with Ionic and Corinthian scagliola columns and a host of erudite and delicate classical references.

The construction and fitting out of Cork's great houses determined to a large extent the economic background to the arts in the city. While there was plenty of work for masons, carpenters and stuccodores, life could be hard for the journeymen-painters, like scene-painter James Coyle, brought to work in the theatre in Cork by Henry Johnston, who subsequently failed to pay him. The unfortunate artist was described in 1811 as being 'in a most forlorn situation in Cork with a large and helpless family' although he afterwards found employment for a short time at the Fermoy Theatre, before making his way back to Dublin.[8] Coyle's difficulties were not untypical. Artists also supplemented their income through private classes. In 1812, Mrs Fenwick (familiar to readers of the essays of Charles Lamb), who was then a tutor to the Honner family at Lee Mount, commented that Nathaniel Grogan, Jnr, was one of the few masters in Cork who was willing to venture outside the city: '. . . with these roads & wet Climate to go in in all weathers was misery & endless consumption of time'.[9]

The difficulties experienced by artists often stemmed from differing perceptions of their social standing. A dispute between architect Thomas Deane and sculptor John Hogan illustrates this point. After completing his apprenticeship, Hogan was paid 13 shillings a week by Deane to draw plans, make architectural models and carve 'balusters, capitals and ornamental figures'.[10] The disagreement was caused by Hogan's refusal to carry out architectural embellishments to the dining-room of Deane's new house at Dundanion, although the artist was happy to carve a statue of Adonis to stand in the hallway, as well as a figure of Minerva for Thomas Deane's new insurance offices in the South Mall. But while Hogan may have aspired to be a worthy successor to the sculptors of the Renaissance, as far as Deane was concerned he was an exceptionally skilled tradesman. Deane's previous decorative carver had been the sculptor Thomas Kirk, of whom Hogan wrote:

> During the first and second years of my apprenticeship there was a woodcarver of the name of Kirk employed by Mr. Deane, whenever he wanted capitals, pateras, lyons heads etc. for his buildings in Cork. This man finding that he had more work than he could conveniently execute set up a high price upon it which so much provoked Mr. Deane that he said he would sooner be satisfied with whatever might come from my hands than employ Kirk again.[11]

And in turn Deane was so provoked by Hogan's demands that when the sculptor elected to leave Cork his erstwhile employer commented: 'It is high time that he should quit the country and see if there are as talented persons elsewhere. Arrogance has got the better of him and until he is more humble, he will never be an Artist'.[12]

Although the Fine Arts were by all accounts in a relatively healthy state at the beginning of the century there were few opportunities for people in Cork to learn about painting or sculpture. There was no municipal art school or museum. The lack of educational opportunities is confirmed by the writer of a memoir on the ill-fated artist Samuel Forde, born in Cork in 1805:

> There were at that period, when he was between eight and ten years of age, only two portrait painters in Cork, of very limited practice – no very eminent teacher. Amateurs, there were several, but to these he does not appear to have had access. There was

but one print-shop where the eternal, but not immortal Warmsly landscapes, and Bartalozzi's red round, Angelica Kaufmann's prints, stood waiting in the window to be framed and glazed . . . Sometimes a roving auctioneer would bring a 'rattling print or two', that astounded him.[13]

Most art education was conducted through the time-honoured system of apprenticeship or in private schools such as those run by Mrs Bolster and Mme de Lestang. Painters in Cork might enjoy some years of comfort if their ability to capture a likeness met with approval, or if their talents were sufficiently adaptable. John O'Keeffe, born in Fermoy around 1797, was successively coach painter, herald painter, theatre set painter, before finally exhibiting biblical scenes in the 1822 Society of Arts' exhibition.[14] Portraitists abounded at this time: the names Ronan, Leahy, Gibbs, Corbett and Parks recur frequently in accounts of the period, but their paintings are nowadays either unidentified or scattered and lost. Miniaturists Henry Kirchhoffer and Frederick Buck were kept busy painting keepsake portraits as thousands of military men departed for the Peninsular war and other campaigns overseas, while Daniel Maclise is recorded as producing a great number of miniature portraits in Cork in the years preceding his 1827 departure for London.

Apart from such portrait paintings and sculptures as they might encounter in municipal buildings, the vast majority of the citizens would have been familiar with art only through engravings in periodicals, painted shop signs or prints on sale at shops such as William Davis's, on Mardyke Street, Michael Mathews' on Patrick Street, Del Veccio's on Georges Street or the bookshop run by William West. The prints produced in Cork were generally not of great quality; the engravers, including James Green and Frank Lewis, tended to specialise in the fairly pedestrian work of book-plates and seals.

The Society of Arts: concept and foundation

The founding of the Cork Society for Promoting the Fine Arts in 1815 was an attempt to draw together the various artistic strands in the city. The idea was not original to Cork. A number of similiar organisations had been formed in cities throughout Britain in the late eighteenth and early nineteenth centuries. In most cases, as in Cork, these societies were broadly philanthrophic, aiming to improve the standard of 'Taste' in society. Many were used by radical non-conformists like the Revd Thomas Dix Hincks, who in 1803 founded the Cork Institution (awarded its royal charter in 1807), to help achieve political change through promoting the concept of specialised education for carpenters, carriage-makers, masons and other artisans. There was a rising middle class in Cork that saw education as the key to social improvement. However, most of the arts societies founded in British towns and cities did not survive. Established for professedly egalitarian reasons, they were quickly monopolised by sectional interest groups. The artist members, who frequently maintained their own private drawing schools, regarded the societies mainly as vehicles for selling works of art. This went against the desires of merchant and industrialist members who wanted to improve design in manufactured goods through educating artists and artisans. Some enlightened members saw art education as a means of social progress, but the majority more likely regarded the societies as a means of promoting their own personal social advancement, or at best, as setting an example of civilised life to which the lower orders might aspire, having paid their admission fee.

The societies' erratic histories tell their own story. The earliest, at Liverpool, lasted only from 1769 to 1774, although it was revived briefly in the following decade. Manchester saw the rapid failure of William Craig's 'Academy for Drawing and Designing' which had opened in 1804, and it was not until 1823 that the Associated Artists of Manchester was formed.[15] Similarly in Birmingham the fledgling Academy of Arts, founded in 1814, was supplanted by the Birmingham Society of Arts of 1821, which in turn was undermined by disagreements between members. In 1828 the Norwich Society of Arts, established in 1803, changed its name to the Norfolk and Suffolk Institution for the Promotion of the Fine Arts and ultimately emerged as the Norwich School of Design.[16] These societies were manifestations of both a new confidence and a new uncertainty. The new confidence was that of money no longer confined to the narrow eighteenth-century aristocratic channels which had long dictated style and taste; the new uncertainty was what forms should culture then adopt in this partly-revolutionised system. The societies were founded to provide cultural guidance and to solve this dilemma. Their histories demonstrate how effective they were in achieving this aim.

The first recorded art exhibition in Cork in the nineteenth century was held in 1815, at 'Dean's Buildings' on the South Mall. Entitled 'The First Munster Exhibition', it was organised by a group that was to become the 'Cork Society for Promoting the Fine Arts'. Little today remains to document the precise aspirations of the founders of this Society who set out in 1815 to transform Cork into a city of culture. A few catalogues (none for the exhibitions in 1830 and 1831) and pamphlets, some newspaper reviews and probably no more than a hundred paintings, prints and sculptures survive, a scant record of a buoyant period. The poet Richard Alfred Milliken, born at Castlemartyr in 1767, founded this group. Milliken is best remembered for his popular songs, such as *The groves of Blarney*, although he was also a set designer for the Apollo Society of Amateur Actors, whose theatre in Patrick Street (now the *Cork Examiner* building) was used for subsequent exhibitions of the Cork Society of Arts. Little seems to be known of the Apollo Society, but it may be supposed that amongst its members were some of the more active literary and artistic minds in the city. For Milliken it was a short step from being set designer for an amateur theatre company to establishing the first society for artists and their patrons in the city. He was not destined to see his initiative flourish as he died on 16 December 1815, the year of the first exhibition of his fledgling society. At the outset the Society of Arts planned to have an annual art exhibition in Cork, and also to show the work of old masters so that students would obtain a 'correct taste for coloring', while casts from the antique would be provided for the improvement of drawing. In fact only seven annual exhibitions were held. However enlightened its first principles, the subsequent history of Millikin's enterprise was not destined to be all sweetness and light. Nonetheless it would be no better or no worse than many of its counterparts in English cities.

The introduction to the catalogue of the *First Munster exhibition* describes how barely thirty years had passed since the introduction of art exhibitions of any kind in Ireland and how such exhibitions had gradually 'exploded the insignificance of French taste'. High hopes indeed, although as the writer (possibly Milliken himself) recorded, Cork had already established something of a reputation as a city graced with artists of note, even if they did not always flourish on home soil:

> Unfavourable circumstances ever await the talents of our country; and while we congratulate ourselves on the transcendent talents of Barry, they are scarcely preserved to the age and country to which they belonged. The luxuriant and glowing pencil of Butt was retained, but not rewarded at home. The playful fancy, and native humour of Grogan, surmounted professional disadvantage – displayed and wasted itself for the applause of a few; ... Mr. Corbet, whose recent loss we have so much to lament, was one of those in whom nature mingled those contrarieties which so frequently characterise genius; bestowing much talent, where she denies the industry to improve it.[17]

This refrain was to echo through the nineteenth century.

In all, 143 works were exhibited at the First Munster Exhibition, by 25 artists; some professional, some amateur, some, like John Corbett and Nathaniel Grogan the Elder, deceased. A total of 25 paintings are listed as being by Nathaniel Grogan, Snr, amongst them several views of the Cork harbour area and bucolic scenes of city and rural life, like *Return from hay-making*, *The forge*, *Whipping the herring out of town*, *Powdering the mayor* and *Breaking up of the fair*. 'Baiting the herring' was apparently an old Cork tradition where crowds thronged the streets, singing 'Herring our King', while 'Powdering the mayor' was another Cork custom which involved the newly-elected mayor being pelted, and frequently half-blinded, with flour or bran. Grogan's paintings often featured the poorer classes of society, depicting them generally as a rollicking, feckless, gullible or drunken. His style was borrowed from Hogarth or ultimately from Hobbema. There was nothing personal in it. Most of northern Europe's bourgeoise delighted in these scenes which provided humour in the home and reinforced a sense of social superiority. Richard Millikin had sixteen landscapes on show, views of scenery in Glengarriff, Killarney, Glandore and Glanmire, as well as a view at Convamore. Henry Kirchhoffer was represented while James McDaniel showed several of his wry and witty drawings. Another participant, William Willes, afterwards became a student in the Royal Academy (R.A.) and on the foundation of the School of Design in Cork in 1849 he was appointed the first Headmaster.

'Dean's Buildings' on the South Mall, where the exhibition took place, had been designed and built by Thomas Deane just two years before. Now the Imperial Hotel, it is a large square building adorned with Neo-classical Ionic pilasters. Deane himself was represented in the exhibition with *A design for a Gothic entrance to a gentleman's demesne*. The Deanes were an enterprising family of builders and architects. In the late eighteenth century Mrs Deane had taken over the family firm on the death of her husband and had run it with consider-able acumen, being responsible for, among other major works, the naval base and stores at Haulbowline. Mrs Deane's son Thomas became one of the city's most successful architects. As his wealth increased he moved to a house at Dundanion near Blackrock, which he renamed Herculaneum after a statue of Hercules purchased at the sale of old Blarney Castle and placed on the lawn. His pretentions did not escape the gentle satire of Father Prout:

Who bought the castle, furniture and pictures, O!
And took off in a cart,
('Twas enough to break one's heart),
All the statues made of lead and the pictures, O![18]

Thomas Deane's younger brother Kearns Deane became an architect; their cousins, David and Alexander, were also architects or builders.

Thomas married three times; the son of his second marriage, to Eliza O'Callaghan Newenham, was the architect Thomas Newenham Deane. Eliza's father, Robert O'Callaghan Newenham (1770-1849) of Coolmore, was a founder of the Society of Arts, at which both he and Eliza regularly exhibited.

The presidents of the Society, formally instituted the following year, 1816, were the Earl of Shannon and Viscount Ennismore (Lord Listowel). There were no fewer than eighteen vice-presidents, including the Duke of Devonshire, the Earl of Kenmare, Sir Nicholas C. Colthurst, Colonel Longfield, Daniel Callaghan, members of the Crawford, Roche, Penrose and Beamish families and Robert O'Callaghan Newenham. There were 184 works in the 1816 exhibition. Along with a memorial exhibition of twenty-four works by Milliken, the artists again included Henry Kirchhoffer and Grogan, Martin Archer Shee, R.A., and John Corbett. The amateur artist James Beale was represented by a large scene of revelry on the streets of Cork entitled *Skellig night on South Mall.* The recently-deceased James Cavanagh Murphy (1760-1814), author of *The Arabian antiquities of Spain,* had two works shown, both entitled *Interior of a palace.*[19]

The year 1816 was also notable in that the architects James and George Richard Pain, pupils of John Nash in London, settled in Cork. One of the first commissions James Pain received was the total rebuilding of Convamore, home of Viscount Ennismore (Lord Listowel), one of the presidents. Its owner, himself once plain Mr William Hare (1751-1837), was M.P. for Cork in 1796. After voting for the Act of Union he had been rewarded with the title Baron Ennismore in 1801 and purchased Convamore from the Callaghan family that same year. The Hares, although 'improving landlords', were regarded as *arrivistes* by the older families of the Blackwater Valley; one of their neighbours, a Captain Roberts, unkindly referring to Lord Listowel as 'Lord Candlegrease'.[20] Convamore was rebuilt as an extremely large and quite plain house with restrained classical detail, very much in the spirit of Nash's Carlton House Terrace which had recently replaced the Prince of Wales' Carlton Palace. Lord Listowel also kept an important collection of paintings at Convamore, including Nathaniel Grogan's *The itinerant preacher* and *The wake.* These works survived the burning of the house in 1921 and are now in a private collection in England.

Neither Grogan nor Deane was represented in the Society of Art's 1817 exhibition, and apart from the familiar names of Edwards, Parks, Milliken, Kirchhoffer, Corbett and Beale, many of the artists listed in the catalogue were exhibiting in Cork for the first time.[21] John Brenan (c. 1796-1865), who had moved to Cork some years before, showed four 'landscape compositions'. Brenan had been born in Fethard, county Tipperary and had studied at the Dublin Society's schools before settling in Cork. He worked initially painting heraldic devices before achieving some success as a landscape painter. A newcomer at the 1817 exhibition was the aspiring young artist and author Thomas Crofton Croker, who held a customs post in Cork and lived at Blackrock. In the years that followed Croker did not persevere as an artist, concentrating instead on writing, although he did contribute sixteen sketches to Hall's *Ireland, its scenery and character*, published over twenty years later. He is best remembered today as the author of *Fairy legends and traditions in the south of Ireland*, published in 1825, which was illustrated with drawings by Maclise. Croker was friendly with the English watercolour artist Francis Nicholson and his son Alfred. The Nicholsons were well represented in 1817, contributing eighteen views of England, Ireland, Scotland and Wales, as well as one of Lake Albano. Croker was to move to London in 1818 to take up an appointment at the Admiralty. There he met, and later married, Marianne, the daughter of Francis Nicholson. Three years later, in company with Marianne and her brother Alfred, he returned to Munster for a visit and began work on his *Researches in the south of Ireland*, published in 1824 and illustrated by the Nicholsons.[22]

The Society of Fine Arts' third exhibition, held in 1818, was characterised by the presence of works by old masters, calculated to 'add to the refinement of public taste'. Among the lenders were James Penrose, Dr Woodrooffe, William Carleton and the Earl of Besborough, who had a number of valuable paintings at his house near Carrick-on-Suir.[23] The inclusion of pieces by old masters greatly changed the nature of the Society's exhibition for now Croker, with his flower and landscape pen sketches, found himself surrounded by paintings ascribed to Rembrandt, Ruysdael, Berghem and Hobbema. Local exhibitor M. Crosbie attempted to rise to the occasion by exhibiting his *Woman taken in adultery copied from the picture by Rubens*. But this assemblage of paintings did not impress everyone, least of all Croker, who later wrote:

> Instead however of progressing from the first exhibition of the Society, the annual assemblage of performances declined in number as well as quality ... in 1818, of a total of 114, but forty four were the productions of residents of Cork, the remaining seventy being an incongruous collection. The injudicious exhibition of 1818 placed the existence of the Society in a critical position.[24]

Even by the standards of the day the Society of Arts' 1819 exhibition must have been a dull affair, with views of Dutch seaports, eruptions of Vesuvius, landscapes with cattle, sheep, ruins or figures, enlivened perhaps by the occasional drunken cobbler; or a sea view, with a brisk gale. There were few enough works by contemporary Cork artists; notable amongst them was Chalmers' view of the New Cork Custom House which had been designed by William Hargrave.

The Canova casts and the development of a school of art

The character of the Society of Arts had changed substantially in the intervening year with the arrival in Cork of the celebrated Canova casts. These had been made under the direct supervision of the famed Italian sculptor Antonio Canova in Rome from works in the Vatican collections. They were prepared on the orders of Pope Pius VII for presentation to the Prince Regent of England, later King George IV, in recognition of British help afforded the Vatican in the return of treasures looted by Napoleon. Apparently the Prince Regent was not entirely enamoured of his gift and for some time after their arrival in London the casts languished at his residence in Carlton Gardens.[25] The pieces were housed by the prince in a large tent. The scene was described as follows by a contemporary writer:

> They surrounded the interior base of that prodigious tent-room, erected in the gardens of what was once Carleton palace. There, as if beneath an ample awning, were assembled, amidst the blaze of chandeliers and regal stars, at one period, the allied sovereigns, princes, and chiefs from the Steppes of Tartary, warriors, states-men, 'fair women, and brave men', to celebrate the conclusion of that heroic period which had just terminated in the battle of Waterloo.[26]

The casts had come to Ireland through the efforts of Viscount Ennismore (Lord Listowel) of Convamore, who was a friend of the Prince Regent. On 7 November 1818 the *Southern Reporter* informed its readers that conversion work on the Apollo theatre on Patrick Street which had been taken over by the Society of Arts, with a view to converting it into a 'saloon of sculpture', was nearly complete. By 26 December Mr Cockaine, 'Moulder and Figure Caster to the Royal Academy', had finalised the arrangements and the exhibition of over two hundred sculpture casts was then opened to the public.[27]

Daniel Maclise would have been a mere ten or eleven years of age when the casts were first exhibited in Cork, yet he became on of the first students at the school of art which was quickly established in the former Apollo Theatre. In his manuscript biography he describes the

Plate 21.1   Laocoon Group, one of the 'Vatican casts' presented to Cork by the
Prince Regent in 1818 (Crawford Municipal Art Gallery/Cork V.E.C.).

elaborate steps taken to display the works: '. . . the stage was screened off by a well-painted scene of the interior of a Greek Temple. The Pit was boarded over, the Gallery was partitioned off. The boxes remained nearly as they were, and the Statues were arranged around the Parterre with much taste.'[28] With the sculptures on display in the Society of Arts' theatre, the first proper school of art in Cork was now a reality. J. Chalmers was the Headmaster of this important venture which was launched with great optimism. Under his tuition students such as Maclise, John Hogan and Samuel Forde drew from the casts in this improvised but effective setting. Maclise and Forde, then in their mid-teens, were close friends at this point; apart from studying the Canova casts they attended demonstrations in anatomy given by Dr Woodroffe at the South Charitable Infirmary and made sketching tours in the surrounding countryside. Croker mentions Forde, an artist of consider-able talent who was to die of tuberculosis some years later, going through the unfrequented back lanes of Cork, avoiding crowds and seeking the shade: 'his mode of walking has been described to me as "slipping along by the wall like one afraid of his own shadow"'.[29]

The initial enthusiastic support amongst prominent citizens for the school proved to be short-lived and a contemporary recorded how 'these Maecenases and Medici "of the hour" fled to their villas and their counting-houses' when they realised that founding and supporting an academy of Fine Arts took more than fine words and flowery phrases.[30] Amongst the general public too there was concern, but this was for the morals of the innocent citizenry exposed to the undraped figures. In 1819 George Bolster, who ran a famous bookshop on Patrick Street, published a pamphlet describing the benefits of the casts and how the development of a school of art in Cork would save young art students from the trauma of having to go to London, where '. . . in addition to the temptations with which every young person there is surrounded, an additional and great one, occurs in drawing from living models, before the morals are matured, and the mind annealed, so as to endure without warping or cracking, the ordeal to which it must be thus necessarily exposed.'[31] In 1826, the Society of Arts having fallen on hard times, the casts were transmitted to the care of the Royal Cork Institution where they were housed, as Maclise recorded, 'in an attic of the old custom house where they are effectually preserved from intruders or admirers, as if surrounded by a cordon sanitaire'.[32]

The Society of Art's 1820 exhibition was significant in that for the first time it included works by students of the new art school. Daniel Maclise, J. Kelleher and Samuel Forde were each represented by drawings made from the antique sculpture casts which themselves formed an important part of the 1820 exhibition. In other respects the enterprise differed little from those of the two previous years, with a preponderance of works ascribed to Canaletto, Cuyp, Teniers, Veronese, Guercino, Poussin and other old masters. Over one-third of the 155 works shown in 1820 were from the private collection of James Roche.[33] The sixth annual exhibition of the Society of Arts held in 1821

Plate 21.2   Samuel Forde – self portrait (Crawford Municipal Art Gallery/Cork V.E.C.).

repeated this formula in that a great number of works came from one private collection. The paintings were mainly by Dutch old masters, or British artists such as Wilson, Lely and Morland, although in addition there were a good number of pieces by Irish artists such as Hogan, George Barrett, William Ashford, James Arthur O'Connor and Francis Danby. George Newenham loaned several works, including a landscape by the eighteenth-century Cork artist, Butts.[34]

By 1822 the Society of Arts had over one hundred yearly subscribers, but as its operations expanded it became evident that their annual subscription of one guinea per person was not sufficient to sustain the Society. In spite of the financial difficulties the yearly exhibitions continued, albeit intermittently. In 1828, apart from Samuel Forde, there were 34 artists represented, with a total of 113 works exhibited.[35] There were no paintings by old masters and only a few by English artists such as Copley Fielding. Among the local artists were Charles Skottowe, John Noblett and John Brenan who showed watercolour views of *Ballyhooly Castle, Killarney* and *Glengarriff.* The designs of architect Kearns Deane for a new chapel in Patrick Street 'of a Grecian Order' were on display and considered 'exceedingly grand and beautiful'. He also showed a model of the front of the Agora in Athens, which was a proposal for the façade of the new Cork Markets. Kearns Deane, brother of the first Sir Thomas Deane, was the architect of St Mary's Dominican Church, construction of which was to begin in 1832. Other architects in the 1828 exhibition were William and Henry Hill, G. H. Buckley and George Richard Pain, whose elegant designs for the complete remodelling of Christ Church's interior and portico were occasioned by a disastrous outbreak of dry rot in the building.

Robert Richard Scanlan, a fashionable Dublin portrait painter (he painted portraits of horses and dogs as well as people), showed some fourteen works in Cork in 1828, including five miniature portraits of members of the Smith-Barry family. Scanlan afterwards moved to London where he remained until 1853 when he was appointed Headmaster of the Cork School of Design. Amongst the amateurs who submitted works was a William James Morgan, recorded as 'a Cork artist of much natural talent' whose career was marred by 'intemperate habits and irregular life'.[36] Miss N. Newenham showed six landscapes, while Robert O'Callaghan Newenham was represented by four landscapes and architectural views. This exhibition closed its doors to the public on 10 July 1828 after having attracted considerable attention, not least from visitors anxious to see the death mask of Napoleon 'taken the morning after his decease' which had been placed on exhibition for the 'gratification of the public curiousity, so naturally excited by it'.[37]

There was to be a two-year gap before the next exhibition which contributed to its success. News of the successful sales from the 1830 show obviously filtered through to the English art world, because when the time came for the 1831 event no fewer than one hundred and twenty-seven works by 'the best Masters in England' had been submitted by the opening date of 9 August, although to their credit the 'Artists of London' had donated some works to be sold for the 'relief of the suffering poor in Ireland'.[38] The cholera epidemic referred to here continued through the following year, and when the Society's exhibition opened in 1832 it was decided to donate half its profits towards the relief of the 'present prevailing Malady'.[39] This exhibition contained English and Continental artists, as well as the usual representation of local ones, both amateur and professional. The 1833 event continued this format. The exhibition was shown in two rooms; the first contained 135 works by 43 artists, mostly living, while the second room contained a further 73 works by old masters and eminent Cork painters such as Grogan, Butts and Barry. In the first room the familiar names of Hogan, Forde, Maclise, Beale, Brenan, McDaniel, Hill, Morgan, Penrose and Carleton were added to by relative newcomers Richard Dunscombe Parker, Louis K. Bradford, James Mahoney and Robert Lowe Stopford (1813-1898) who showed four works, amongst them *Blackrock Castle*, *View of Rostellan Castle* and *Carrigrohan Castle*. Stopford, a Dublin-born topographical watercolourist, settled in Cork while a young man and worked successfully there until his death in Monkstown, county Cork, in his eighty-fifth year. Many of his works were lithographed, such as *Cork Harbour, Queen's College, Cork* and *The Evening gun, Haulbowline Island*. He was for a number of years art correspondent in the south of Ireland for the *Illustrated London News* and other journals.

With the transfer of the Royal Cork Institution to the Old Custom House in 1832 the activities of the Society of Arts seem to have gone into a decline, probably because the well-established R.C.I. formalised the teaching of art in Cork a further step. This marginalised the largely amateur efforts of the Society of Arts, which in any case was largely a legacy of late eighteenth-century social aspirations. In his 1846 *Guide to the south of Ireland* Windele had some scathing remarks to make about the defunct Society of Arts:

> It was at best, but a flickering affair, at one moment apparently extinct, and in the next, again revived; having never received much encouragment from the wealthy and influential. Professional jealousies and bickering, ultimately weakened its efforts; divided into sections, its members ceased to coalesce. Its exhibitions were usually held in the old theatre in Patrick's Street; but it had often been objected against the Society, that its benefits had been more

generally bestowed on strangers, than on the productions of native artists; there certainly has been no real fostering of any eminent genius, into note or eminence through its aid or patronage.[40]

Windele's objections are an over-simplification as the annual exhibitions varied considerably in their representation of local artists, English artists, and 'old masters'. The influx of opportunist English painters that he refers to did not take place until 1831, some fifteen years after the first exhibition. It seems unfair to say that the Society did not foster genius as both Hogan and Maclise were amongst the initial students at its school. Nontheless Windele in these few lines gives probably a better insight into the Society's history than any other source.

The Cork Art Union

The demise of the Society of Arts did not mean the end of institutional support for painters and sculptors in Cork, although it was some time before a fresh initiative appeared in the person of artist James Mahoney. In 1841 Mahoney, who had been born in Cork in 1810, returned to Ireland after a number of years studying in Rome and travelling on the Continent. He settled at the home of his father, a carpenter, at 34 Nile Street.[41] Mahoney came back to his native city brimming with energy and new ideas and immediately commenced organising a Cork Art Union. The concept of the Art Union, where outstanding works of art from an annual exhibition were purchased by a panel of experts and distributed by lot amongst a group of sub-scribers, had already been put into operation in London and in other British cities. There was an Art Union in Dublin which had been founded two years previously and one in Belfast. James Mahoney joined with Samuel Skillen (c. 1819-1847) in setting up the Cork Union. Each member of the Union paid an annual subscription of one pound. This gave the subscriber (and up to three friends) free admission to the exhibition as well as participation in a lottery of paintings. In the first year of the Art Union's operation in Cork it was reckoned that more than £100 would be spent on the purchase of paintings, to be distributed to the subscribers by lottery.[42]

The first Cork Art Union Exhibition was held in September 1841 at Marsh's Rooms on the South Mall and in spite of the bad weather was an immediate success. Although British painters were included, attention was focused on artists from the locality, not least the organisers Mahoney and Skillen, as well as James Brenan, William Roe and the local maritime painters George Hayes and George Mounsey Wheatley Atkinson (the latter showing no fewer than five works).[43] A

Plate 21.3   Bowling match at Castle Mary, Cloyne, by Daniel McDonald (Crawford Municpal Art Gallery/Cork V.E.C.).

second Art Union event was held in 1842 and while again substantial in scale, reports in the press were largely confined to local artists such as William Fisher, John Connell, the miniaturist Edward Harding and Daniel MacDonald, son of James McDaniel. *The Cork Examiner* critic devoted some time to describing the Daniel MacDonald painting, which depicted a bowling match at Castlemary, Cloyne, county Cork:

> No. 41 Demands our attention. It is *Bowling* by Mr. D. Macdonald. Its characteristic is floridness. It seems, in scenery and coloring, too fine for its subject. But when the artist's judgement shall have been sobered down, somewhat, to the forcible simplicity of things as they are, we think he will be capable of a great deal. His figures on the left are well disposed, though rather too crowded, and too freshly tinted. Those on the right are very expressive and very good. The squire, or well-dressed young farmer, leaning forward, less to mark the chances of the bowl, than to put his 'commether' on the coquettish little peasant girls before him, is very well imagined and executed. The principal figure – yes, really, we should be much better pleased if that principal figure was left out altogether, by particular desire. The head seems arranged for an appearance on the stage, and it wears pumps – the figure, we mean. Moreover, the face is the very facsimile of a portrait in the room by the same artist. Mr. MacDonald has much to unlearn.[44]

The distribution of the 1842 Art Union Prizes took place at Marsh's Rooms on the South Mall under the chairmanship of Lord Bernard. The secretary, John Windele, reported that at the close of the previous year the Cork Art Union had attracted 120 members, amongst whom 24 pictures (purchased for a total of £140) had been distributed. However, in the present year membership had risen to 300, amongst whom 38 paintings were to be allocated by lot. Lest there be any feelings of disappointment at the slow but steady growth of the Cork Union, Windele recollected that the giant London Art Union which at that point consisted of over 20,000 subscribers, had a mere 400 members in its first year. It was to be regretted, he added, that practically all support for their organisation had come from the city of Cork, in spite of its avowed aims to encompass the entire south of Ireland. Nonetheless, the whole enterprise was judged a great success, both from the point of view of the public and the artist. A good many artists had participated in the second exhibition who had 'kept aloof' in 1841, but many of them had placed what were felt to be unreasonably high prices on their works. After some negotiation most of these prices had been reduced in order that the Art Union could afford to buy the 37 works for distribution. Windele commented:

> That some such mode of fostering Art in Cork as that which characterizes the Art Union principle, is absolutely necessary, is manifestly shown in the scarcely credible fact – ascertained, however, upon sufficient enquiry – that neither in the last nor in the present Exhibition, have more than one or two single orders, for the purchase or painting of pictures been given to any of the numerous artists whose productions grace your walls. Apart, therefore, from that employment which teaching, or the execution of portraits gives, there remains scarecely any other market for artistic talent.[45]

Art Unions in other cities had attracted subscribers with the promise of an engraving each year in addition to the possibility of winning a painting by lottery. The Cork Art Union, having examined the costs involved in producing an engraving, had concluded that it would absorb almost half their available income and had decided to concentrate their spending on acquiring works of art. Their policy in acquiring works was to try to aim for a wide representation of artists rather than concentrating on the 'very best, from a few'. There was nonetheless one aspect of the Cork Union which Windele felt needed to be addressed:

> . . . the question, which has been often raised, and which ought to be disposed of – the exclusiveness of this society – shutting out, as it does, from the advantages of its funds, all non-subscribing artists. This principle is, on the face of it, narrow, and with the exception of Glasgow, dissimiliar to that of all other Art Unions, whilst in truth it is also injurious to the artists themselves. It shuts out the works of men who have attained eminence in the profession elsewhere, and excludes the means of improvement which should be open to our students, and even to our more experienced professors.[46]

After Lord Bernard delivered a speech in which he touched on the importance of Cork artists striving to gain commissions for the new Houses of Parliament, Sir Thomas Deane moved that the report of the secretary be adopted. He also moved that the 'gentlemen scrutiners and conductors of the ballot' be Messrs Bagnell, Willis and Parker, who duly conducted the lottery. Slips of paper bearing the names of each subscriber were placed in a hat on the table. In another hat alongside were placed thirty-eight numbered slips, one for each work of art to be included in the lottery. The hats were covered with handkerchiefs so that no one could see the names on the tickets, and as the draw commenced ' . . . the greatest possible excitement pervaded the room, all pressing forward with a kind of instinctive movement towards the mysterious hats, in which success and disappointment were unconsciously buried'.[47] These simple precautions did not prevent the secretary, John Windele, from doing well: his name was drawn along with the slip for Samuel Skillen's painting the *King of the Munster beggars*, which was generally agreed to be the masterpiece of the exhibition.

The Cork Art Union may have been thriving in 1842 but it escaped the notice of William Makepeace Thackeray who visited the city that year and commented on the conditions under which art was taught at the R.C.I.:

> There is an institution, with a fair library of scientific works; a museum, and a drawing-school with a supply of casts. The place is in yet more dismal condition than the library. The plasters are spoiled incurably for want of a sixpenny feather-brush; the dust lies on the walls, and nobody seems to heed it. Two shillings a year would have repaired much of the evil which has happened to this institution; and it is folly to talk of inward dissensions and political differences as causing the ruin of such institutions. Kings or law don't cause or cure dust and cobwebs; but indolence leaves them to accumulate, and imprudence will not calculate its income, and vanity exaggerates its own powers, and the fault is laid upon that tyrant of a sister kingdom. The whole country is filled with such failures; swaggering beginnings that could not be carried through; grand enterprises begun dashingly, and ending in shabby compromises or downright ruin.[48]

Thackeray was not alone in his opinions. At a meeting of the Cork Art Union held in May 1843 Mr Keleher had commented on the 'wretched condition' of the casts in the Institution's building and had requested that a new gallery be constructed for their display. Sir Thomas Deane was not sanguine about this possibilty and commented: 'The people of Cork did nothing but talk – they were proficient at filling up a newspaper with their speeches, but they did not put their hands in their pockets'.[49] Deane was gentleman enough to admit that he himself was probably one of the greatest talkers in Cork, 'but it was to abuse them'.

The Cork art world was active the following year. The third Art

Union Exhibition opened on Monday 14 August 1843 at 'the Saloon of the late Society of Arts on Patrick Street' (also referred to by then as 'McDonnell's Mart'). The main gallery with its central door was closely hung with a large number of paintings and drawings, mostly by Irish artists. This was in contrast with earlier years when a substantial number of British artists had been represented. It was an oft-repeated criticism that many of the English and Scottish artists who had been shown in the Union's previous exhibitions were well supported in their own part of the world and had no real need to solicit new patronage in Ireland, to the detriment of Irish artists' livelihoods. Nevertheless, the sophistication and acceptability of the imported paintings had made the argument in support of native artists difficult to put across to the public, who were apt to buy pictures they liked. Moreover, the picture-buying public in Cork were also inclined to want paintings by English artists for reasons of snobbery and social prestige, a prejudice by no means confined to Cork. Earlier that year, at a meeting of the Cork Art Union held in May, the painter Henry Brocas had spoken of the unfortunate decision of a 'certain Northern Ireland Art Union' which,

> having collected a sum of Two Hundred Pounds for the avowed purpose of encouraging Irish Art, paid away one hunded and sixty pounds for freightage and coach-hire for pictures brought from different parts of Enlgand and Scotland, and then turned round upon their disappointed townsmen and told them that the residue of the fund was little enough to pay the incidental expenses of the Exhibition and that they were too poor to buy any of their pictures.[50]

Brocas observed that this was a rather awkward way of encouraging Irish art, and he noted that the total contribution from England and Scotland the previous year to the Cork Art Union had amounted to one pound.

As a result of his entreaties, the committee agreed to include only 'Pictures of Irish Artists generally, but more particularly those of the Cork School of Art' in the forthcoming exhibition, and as the opening day approached the *Cork Constitution* was please to report that nearly all the paintings were by 'native artists'.[51] Although there was dismay at the delay of six days in opening the exhibition, the writer congratulated the 'projectors and perpetuators' of the Cork Art Union on the work: 'All our artists are here; the dead, the expatriated and the living, and local; and they form a distinguished and a goodly company. Saluez les!'[52] Delegates of the British Association, who were then meeting in Cork, were invited to attend the exhibition free of charge. The members of the Union were keen that the visiting dignitaries should be given the opportunity of purchasing works by local artists, while the chairman, Sir Thomas Deane, continued to hope that through this exposure Cork artists might be given the opportunity of working on the new Houses of Parliament, then under construction in London.[53]

Early in 1844 a dispute developed about the legality of the Art Union organisations, which at that point had been established in England for over eight years and had grown steadily in importance. A date in April had been fixed for the London Art Union draw, but one week before this was due to take place, a notice from the Attorney-General was issued stating that Art Unions were illegal. Although this official disapproval was ostensibly in relation to the operation of the art lottery by the unions, it was seen by some radicals as a reflection of the success of the Art Union movement which had eroded the monopolist position of established artists. A writer in the *Cork Examiner* was unequivocal in attributing blame for the suppression:

> The same class of gentry who attempt to put down the school of design at Somerset-house, because it would ruin the monopoly of artists, now seek to stop the unions because they give cheap prints to the public. Monopoly is the curse of this country, whether in the print-sellers, who make the people pay dear for their prints, or the landlords who would make the people pay dear for corn.[54]

The Art Unions happily survived the Attorney-General's pronouncement as to their doubtful legality and a subsequent Act of Parliament confirmed their legal validity. Unfortunately, the uncertainty had resulted in the Cork Art Union's fourth annual exhibition being delayed, so much so that on 10 December 1844 the secretary, James Tobin, placed an advertisement with the *Cork Examiner* stating that their annual exhibition in Marsh's Rooms would remain open through to mid-January 1845, when the distribution of prizes would take place.

At one o'clock on Saturday 18 January of that year, the friends and subscribers of the Cork Union assembled at Marsh's Rooms on the South Mall under the chairmanship of Viscount Bernard, their president. The purchase funds at their disposal had dropped from £250 in 1843 to £120, largely as a result of the uncertainty generated by the legality issue, but the secretary also attributed some fall in support to '. . . the unaccountable and mysterious opposition offered to it by parties from whom it may reasonably have expected support'.[55] Apparently a 'serious division' amongst committee members had resulted in some not only resigning but also actively discouraging others from subscribing.[56] However, in moving the adoption of the secretary's report Major Beamish did not equivocate in directing criticism, referring to the 'unfortunate differences' which had arisen between the artists and the previous board of management. Beamish felt that the Art Union would not thrive until a 'constellation of all the aristocracy' joined in support of the enterprise, but he was heartened to at least see 'several new stars twinkling in the subscription list'.

Referring to the recent death of Bertel Thorwaldsen, the Danish neo-classical sculptor who had been so supportive of John Hogan in Rome, Beamish commented on the reverence paid him by the people of Denmark and the fact that princes and lords had attended his funeral, the way to the burial place being 'strewn with white sand and juniper, according to the ancient scandanavian custom'. Beamish looked forward to such a time in Ireland when the struggling artist would be 'treated as something better than a mere mechanic', and evinced the hope that Hogan might fill Thorwaldsen's place (Hogan at this time was working on a bust of Beamish's friend and business associate, William Crawford).[57] Beamish also alluded to one of the perennial problems associated with the support of young artists in Cork:

> . . . the utility of the Cork Art Union has been questioned upon the ground of our inability to retain the genius which we may happen to evoke, but which the want of encouragement sends to . . . the English capital. But admitting the fact of this migration, is it nothing to scatter the seed which others reap, to kindle the flame which others feel, to warm into life the embryo of genius which in other lands is destined to bloom to eminence and distinction.[58]

Beamish's eloquent appeal was spurred by the knowledge that a number of subscribers had withdrawn from the Art Union on the grounds that the artists being supported were not remaining in Cork.

The founder of the Art Union, Mahoney, resumed his travels in 1846, spending a number of years in Spain before returning to Ireland in the 1850s. He settled for some time in Dublin, was elected an Associate of the Royal Hibernian Academy (R.H.A), but was to resign his associateship in 1859 and move to London where he worked as an illustrator until his death in 1879. The Cork Art Union seems to have lapsed upon his departure. Samuel Skillen, co-founder of the Cork Union, died young in 1847, probably in one of the cholera epidemics that accompanied the Great Famine. This effectively brought a halt to the rapid progress in the Fine Arts in Cork which had been evident up to that year.

The Government School of Design

The departure of Mahoney from Cork left a vacuum that was not long in being filled. Even as the Cork Art Union was in decline, moves were afoot in the late 1840s to establish a municipal school of art – or Government School of Design as it was called – in the city. The School of Design system in Britain had come about largely through the efforts of William Ewart, M. P. for Liverpool. In July 1835 he persuaded the government to appoint a Select Committee 'to enquire into the best means of extending a knowledge of the arts and principles of design among the people (especially the manufacturing population) of the country; also to enquire into the constitution of the Royal Academy and the effects of institutions connected with the Arts'. Ewart had been subject to the powerful influence of history painter Benjamin Robert Haydon, who passionately advocated a new system of public art education to counter the restrictive influence of the Royal Academy, an independent body of artists established under royal patronage in 1768.[59]

In France, drawing was commonly taught in state schools and the public were accustomed to visiting museums and galleries. Colbert had established his Manufactures Royales as far back as the seventeenth century, while in 1762 Jean-Jacques Bachelier founded in Paris the École des Arts Decoratifs, a school devoted to industrial design. That same year Matthew Bolton founded his School of Industrial Design in Birmingham, but only the military academies of Woolwich and Sandhurst could claim to provide full government-subsidised art training in Britain. In the English provinces the only towns to have set up drawing schools were Birmingham, Liverpool and Carlisle, while the Drawing School of the Dublin Society was for many years the sole art academy in Ireland. The Mechanics Institutes, spreading throughout Britain in the years following 1823, did provide some instruction in drawing; this was certainly the case in Cork, but such instruction depended largely upon the availability locally of suitable teachers. In Britain the first National Gallery was founded in 1824, but only through the munificence of a private benefactor, while provincial British museums were independent bodies supported by voluntary sub-scribers. The Select Committee concluded: 'from the highest branches of poetical design down to the lowest connexion between design and manufactures, the Arts have received little encouragement in this country . . . Art is comparatively dear in England. In France it is cheap, because it is generally diffused'.[60]

Although impressed by the successes of the French provincial school of art system – there were over eighty such schools in 1836 – the Select Committee decided instead mainly to follow the German 'Gewerb-Institut' structure, where art was more directly linked to industry. The

Whig administration of the day concurred and in 1836 the House of Commons voted £1,600 for the Board of Trade to set up a Central School of Design. On 1 June 1837 the Government School of Design opened in Somerset House, London. Underwriting the distinction between these Government Schools of Design and the Royal Academy, the syllabus expressly forbade the study of the human figure. The School was to educate artisans for industry, not the Fine Arts. It was also to supply teachers to the provinces where provincial branch schools were to be set up.[61]

In 1849 a group of leading citizens in Cork, including Horace Townsend, Colonel Ludlow Beamish, Sir Thomas Deane and R. O'Callaghan Newenham, appealed to the Board of Trade for the establishment of a Government School of Design in the city. The secretary of the Cork committee was Mr W. Keleher and, as a result of his efforts, Charles Heath Wilson was sent over from the School of Design at Somerset House in London to discuss the opening of a school in Cork. Cork was rather late in making its representations. Coventry had applied for a School of Design before 1835 and several other application were received in 1838 by William Dyce, Superintendent at Somerset House. The expanding manufacturing towns of Manchester, Nottingham, Sheffield, Birmingham and Newcastle had Design Schools operational by 1842, and more were set up that year at Norwich and York. On his visit to Cork in 1849 Charles Heath Wilson pointed out to the School of Art committee that, in line with other regional schools which had been established, before a government grant could be given an equal amount would have to be raised locally. A deputation of gentlemen was therefore dispatched off to Cork corporation to ask for a grant of £200 per annum. The delegation was 'received with the greatest enthusiasm' and the required sum was unanimously voted. The directors of the Royal Cork Institution then 'cheerfully expended' £500 on the renovation of the Institution's building and its transformation into a School of Design.

Beginnings: promise and achievement

The *Cork Examiner* of 4 January 1850 announced that the new Cork School of Design would be open 'for the reception of Pupils' on Tuesday, 8 January 1850. The formal opening of the School took place three days later on 7 January with the Lord Mayor, Mr Shea, officiating. 'From noon until one o'clock the visitors promenaded the Museum Rooms, Library, East Rooms, Drawing Rooms, &c and at that hour the Lecture Theatre was thrown open and immediately filled'. Amongst those who crowded into the lecture theatre were Viscount Bernard, William Fagan M. P., Colonel Chatterton, Sir Thomas Deane, Sir William and Lady Lyons and Horace Townsend. The Headmaster of the new School of Design, William Willes, then delivered a 'voluminous but exceedingly detailed' address on the importance of such schools. James Roche, president of the School committee, promised the assembly that the sculpture cast room would be open to the public for viewing each afternoon. Roche was followed as speaker by Sir Thomas Deane who presented a bust of his 'beloved and departed' father-in-law' (Newenham) as a stimulus to others to do likewise.[62] Deane had very specific notions of the role of the new School:

> For forty years he (Sir T. D.) was acquainted with the tradesmen of this city, who laboured under the great disadvantage in the want of a School of taste, though no more naturally talented men could be found anywhere. He recollected when the Cork Court Houses were building, and that terra cotta capitals were brought over for the portico columns, a jealousy sprung up amongst the masons, who insisted that they ought to be stone, but the answer was that no one in Cork could be got to chisel them. They besought a trial, and one of the imposed capitals was given to them, and immediately all the apprentice boys of Cork were copying and in six weeks the public was presented with the fine Corinthian capitals which now adorned the building. (Hear, hear).[63]

Sir Thomas pointed to the successful embroidery schools which had been set up in Cork to help relieve the distress caused to many women by the potato Famine. (The best-known of these schools had been established by Mrs Sainthill and Mrs Paul McSwiney). Deane referred to fifty families being supported in Cork through the production of fabric which imitated point lace. Other speakers put forward similiar arguments in favour of the new School as the enthusiastic inaugural meeting drew to a close.

After several days of operation the *Cork Constitution* reported that about one hundred students were attending the new School of Design. A separate morning class had been established 'for the ladies' and this was attended by sixteen students, all engaged in the first division of the government lessons: 'Drawing outline from the flat'.[64] In July 1850 the Cork School of Design closed for the summer vacation, after a successful first six months' operation. There were many optimistic predictions for the future development of the Fine Arts in Cork, for the emergence of a generation of artisans who had been educated to a high degree and who had developed an awareness of the canons of design which were, at that time, taken as a standard. The majority of the pupils at the School of Design were from the 'artisan and mechanic' classes, and it was perceived as a fundamental role of the School that the various trades and crafts operating in Cork would benefit directly from the 'cheap and valuable' art education enjoyed by their members '. . . correcting that want of taste and elegance of finish which has been well pointed out as a principal cause of the deplorably backward and languishing condition of several local trades'.[65]

Alongside the teaching role of the new School of Design the formation of a permanent art collection was also seen as a priority. While there is ample evidence that the Vatican sculpture casts had been publicly exhibited since their arrival in Cork in 1818, which year can therefore be taken to constitute the true birth of Cork's municipal art gallery, it was really with the formation by Willes in 1850 of a 'memorial-room' for the exhibition of works by Cork artists that the deliberate foundation of a civic art collection for the city may be dated. Apart from Heffernan, the artists Barry and Forde were represented in this small art collection. The *Cork Constitution* of 8 January 1850 reported that James Heffernan's sculpture group *The distressed mother,* presented by the sculptor's widow, had been placed on exhibition in the School.[66] The R.C.I. presented the new School of Design with two other works by James Heffernan, which they had received from the sculptor's widow, *Susannah at the bath* and *Mother and child.*[67]

A graphic description of the Cork School of Design during this period is given by the Cork historian Michael Holland:

A School of Design was established in 1850 under the auspices of the Cork Institution, whose premises were then in a dilapidated state. The entrance was through a doorway on the southern side of Nelson's Place. A staircase required cautious negotiation to the first floor and the Headmaster's room.

This apartment, used as a library, had a curious clock, presented by Ben Deeble; its dial had one hand indicating both the hour and minute. On the chimney-piece was a pencil portrait of Charles Dickens, one of several made of the artist when he visited and lectured in Cork.

The original purpose of the schools of design was to educate original designers – not mere copyists or rule and compass draughtsmen. The branches of instruction were: ornament – outline drawing from the flat and round, shading, painting and modelling; geometrical and perspective drawing; drawing, painting and modelling figures from the cast; painting in watercolours, tempera and oil; plants, fruits and flowers drawn, painted or modelled from nature; and composition as applied to design.[68]

The newspapers were keen to report on the success of the new Cork Design School, students of which in 1853 obtained ten prizes at the art schools' exhibition at Gore House in London. The report of the 'Government School of Art' committee for 1853 also listed the earlier successes of William Heazle, William L. Casey, John J. Brennan, Huldah Beale and Eliza Olden, this last pupil receiving praise for her compositions of fruit, flowers, birds and shells. Most of the prizes were awarded for shaded or line drawings of ornamental devices, and drawings from the casts.

However, less than four years after the opening of the School, problems had arisen in relation to the student intake. The high fees of five shillings a quarter prevented most children from artisan and working-class families from attending, whereas the offspring (mainly girls) of wealthy Cork families who could well afford this fee were flocking to attend the increasingly fashionable School. In an attempt to broaden the student intake the committee decided to impose a new fee of a guinea a quarter for a select class of pupil who would attend twice a week and be allowed to deviate from the strict system laid down by the government, concentrating on landscape and figure drawing. A more moderate charge of ten shillings a quarter would apply to those who were unable to pay the first-class fees, while a third fee of five shillings was designed to enable the mechanic and artisan classes to attend.[69]

At the annual awards ceremony in 1853 the Lord Mayor, John Francis Maguire, responding to these complaints about the School of Art's middle-class bias, was at pains to point out that successful students were not just drawn from the privileged classes of the city: Francis Cunningham, 'the son of a mechanic', had obtained a medal, while a prize-winning pupil of the previous year, who now worked as a lithographer, was paralysed from the waist down and had previously been confined in an institution. Another former student, a deaf and dumb boy, also worked as a lithographer. Maguire cited further cases of 'Art-Workmen' improving themselves through diligent study at the School of Art. The mayor also listed the career successes of former Cork students John J. Drummond, who had been appointed Master at Llanelly School of Art in Carmarthen in Wales, William L. Casey, who was now Second Master at the Limerick School of Art and John J. Brennan, a Scholar at Somerset House, London (the Royal Academy), while John Kemp was training as an art master at the same establishment. Frederick Hosford had won a scholarship to Somerset House as well.

A soirée was held on Thursday 11 October 1853 for the purpose of presenting the prizes and medals to the successful students. The Mayor was unhesitant about promoting the objectives of the School:

Your firegrate must now do something more than answer its main purpose, of diffusing heat through your apartment; and whether it be of iron, of brass, or of steel, it must gratify the eye, if not satisfy the taste, by the appropriateness and elegance of its decoration. Your fender must now be an article of ornament as well as use. The chandelier which lights your room, the candelabrum which crowns your table, must be something more than serviceable and enduring – it may be graceful – it may be fanciful – it may be classical – but it must be beautiful.[70]

Although staffing at the School of Design had improved it continued to be a problematical issue. The landscape painter Thomas Frederick Collier had been appointed Second Master under Richard R. Scanlon, who had recently replaced William Willes. In 1854 Collier exhibited several landscapes at the Royal Hibernian Academy – he specialised in autumnal, twilight or moonlit scenes – and again in 1860 he exhibited eleven works at the Academy. Collier was appointed Headmaster some years later, replacing Edward Sheil, but held the position for only a few months due to his being continually drunk.[71] He was found by his pupils one morning, at the opening of the school, surrounded by the wrecks of plaster casts, which, as Strickland relates, 'he had smashed in a drunken fit'. After his removal from the School he left Cork, abandoned his wife and children and was 'not heard of afterwards'. But he reappeared as an exhibitor at the R.H.A. twenty-eight years later, with an address in Hampstead Hill Gardens, London.

In December 1854 the Cork School of Design was forced to close, due to the cessation of government funding, and the pupils were 'scattered'. At a meeting of the committee held on 28 August 1855 Richard Dowden outlined a new financial proposal for funding the School. If the new rating proposed by the committee raised £200, then the Board of Trade would pay the salaries of the masters. The Headmaster would receive £250 a year, while his two assistant masters would receive £20 per annum each 'and a promise of promotion'. The Board of Trade would also pay a small materials grant, about £50 a year, which would bring their total contribution to around £350. That would give the School committee a budget of over £500 which would amply cover their outgoings of £300 for salaries, £50 a year rent, £30 for fire and light, £20 for printing and advertising and £20 each for a secretary and attendant. Dowden was not sanguine about raising much money from fees; what he was concerned with was ensuring that the children of tradesmen could get a better education, thereby increasing their capacity to earn a living.

Colonel Beamish expressed support for the rating proposal, in spite of the 'general horror of taxation' amongst the citizens of Cork who were already being taxed to a punitive degree. Beamish himself had been instrumental at parliamentary level in laying the foundations for this rating proposal. At the passing of a bill for the establishment of libraries and museums in Ireland he had had inserted the words 'Schools of Science and Art', thus enabling the burden of support for the Cork School to be legally transferred to the rate-payers of the city. John Francis Maguire then spoke strongly in support of the proposal, stressing the beneficial effects of the new system which, being instituted through Act of Parliament, would ensure that the children of the poorer classes in national schools would receive art education from the School of Design masters, while the School itself would cater for the artisan and middle classes. Committee member Dr O'Connor picked up on this last point, noting that children from well-off families had attended the School on reduced fees when they could well afford to pay the full rate. However, both O'Connor and Beamish were at pains to point out that the attendance of these middle-class children at the School did not interfere with 'the general instruction'.

Dowden then spoke again, commenting that in the two years he had been involved in the School's administration there had been no 'jobbing or mismanagement', or if there had, it was since he had left:

> He was aware that a few of the Corporation who did not know the rules, had sent in lads who could afford to pay, but the Committee sent them back again. It was a rule that no boy should be admitted that the entire committee did not agree to. As to the additional class, those who paid a guinea a quarter did not receive a bit more attention than those who paid 10s, or 2s. 6d., or nothing at all.[72]

The 'rules' that Dowden alluded to were in fact a sort of compact between the committee of the School and the Corporation, whereby the members of the Corporation were given the right to nominate 20 free students a year to the School in return for their grant of £200. The Corporation members were evidently abusing this privilege by nominating well-off children. The motion was put to the vote, carried, and the Cork School of Art re-opened on Thursday 8 January of the following year, 1856.

The School re-commenced with David Wilkie Raimbach (godson and pupil of the well-known British artist Sir David Wilkie) as Headmaster. Raimbach was no stranger to schools of art in Ireland, having already served as Second Master in Belfast and head of the Limerick art school. By Friday evening, 9 January, there were 71 students attending. The gallery and drawing schools had been redecorated and the casts rearranged. In addition, pupils were offered the treat of free admission, 'through the kindness of Mr. Hampton', to the Diorama of *Napoleon's campaigns* and the *War in the Crimea* which was then on exhibition in Cork.[73] Less than two weeks later the number of students had risen to 89, and the *Cork Examiner* expressed satisfaction at the high proportion of pupils from the artisan class, '. . . the class of all others on whom art education is capable of conveying the largest amount of practical good'.[74] The student numbers were rapidly built up, so that by March 1856 there were 156 paying pupils in the School. Included amongst these were 30 engineers, 8 carpenters, 4 cabinet-makers, as well as carvers, gilders, modellers, photographers, lithographers, Japanners, decorators and house painters. There were four architects, six builders and ten female trainee teachers. In addition to the various scholarships awarded by the School through the Department of Art (under which, in 1855, eight Cork students were studying in London or Paris), no fewer than three local scholarships had been instituted, one from the School committee and three from the Mayor. Avanced students were allowed to study 'practical anatomy' in the dissecting room of Dr Caesar's School of Medicine, while one of the committee members made his extensive gardens available to the pupils twice weekly. The spring term of the School of Design commenced on 1 April 1856, and two days later the committee met to debate progress. There was laughter when the poor remuneration offered by the 'liberal Board of Education' was discussed. The Board expected national schools in the area to employ art teachers from the School of Design on salaries of a mere £5 a year.[75]

The annual examinations, although intended primarily for pupils of the School, were also open to interested amateurs. In October 1856 Mr Bowler of the Department of Science and Art in South Kensington held examinations in freehand and mechanical drawing. At the same time an exhibition was mounted in the Rotondo room of the newly-built Athenaeum theatre, beside the School, to coincide with this important event, with works being borrowed from committee members and Cork collectors including William Crawford, Francis Sealy, Cooper Penrose and James Lambkin.[76] The exhibition was opened on a Friday evening, the day after the examinations took place, with a gala reception attended by over four hundred people, prizes to the students and a band in attendance. The Mayor of Cork, Alderman Scott, spoke at length about progress in the School; how student numbers were approaching 200, while another 450 pupils in various national schools were benefitting from art classes run by Mr Sheil. After a speech by Mr David Urquhart, the representative from the central School in London, in which he expressed considerable surprise in finding a thriving art establishment 'in such a remote corner of the British Empire', Mayor Scott awarded medals to prize-winning students, glossing over the slightly awkward fact that the medals had not been completed in time for the presentations. Award winners in 1856 included Michael O'Leary and Henry O'Shea for their medal designs, Jane Morgan and Fanny Harrington for their lace designs and William H. Hill of the famous Cork architectural dynasty.

Like his predecessor Scanlan, Headmaster David Raimbach was destined to remain in Cork for less than a year. He resigned in July 1857 and was appointed principal of the Bermingham School of Art the following year. He was succeeded by Edward Sheil, who taught mechanical drawing.[77] The award-winning students of 1877 included Jane Morgan, Margaret Hill, Richard West, and John O'Hea, who spent much time sketching the environs of Cork Harbour along with Henry Albert Hartland. Prizes also went to William Stopford and Henry O'Shea, who exhibited two large sepia drawings, based on photographs, of the 'Emperor and Empress of the French'.[78] The awards ceremony had become one of the leading events in Cork's cultural calendar:

> The number of ladies present was very large and the attendance was exceedingly fashionable ... Mr. Bowler, the government inspector ... congratulated the public of Cork on the growing taste for art, in which it was one of the most forward cities in the United Kingdom. The largest number of medals that he was entitled to award to any school was thirty, and theirs had got 21 ... After the business of the evening had concluded, M. Roeckel favored the audience with some admirably performed airs on the organ.[79]

The following year, 1858, was not an auspicious one for the School of Design. In February the press reported that the roof of the School had fallen into such disrepair that whenever there was heavy rain the sculpture casts had to be moved backward and forward to prevent them being destroyed: 'During the late heavy rain the Adonis, one of the noble casts from the antique which have come from the hand of no less an artist than Canova, has become irreparably damaged'.[80] Rain was not the only problem afflicting the institution. A leading article in the *Cork Examiner* in June 1858 described the Department in London as an autocracy which promoted 'quackery in art instruction, dissatisfaction amongst teachers and discontent amongst pupils'. The chief reason for this outburst was the recent issuing of a directive which required that the School of Design should endeavour to take under its wing no less than one per cent of the population of the city. In 1858 one per cent of the population of Cork would have amounted to over 800 persons!

> Instead of a great system of art education, Parliament and the country will see in it a gigantic sham, and in all probability will be inclined to class the department in the same category as its work. Undoubtedly it must awaken the anger of masters to find them-selves obliged to convey art teaching to pupils in hundreds, and never to hope to have an eleve capable of going beyond his pot-hooks and hangers.[81]

As further evidence of stinginess the same correspondent quoted the case of three silver medals which had been awarded to pupils from the Cork School some time past. As weeks drew into months, the pupils anxiously awaited the arrival of their silver medals. Two years passed, and finally the medals arrived. Unfortunately, they had been trans-muted into copper! Describing this as 'the alchemy of the department', the writer criticised the 'awkward apology' which had accompanied the medals, and commented that the Department of Art would have been better to have 'brazened it out'. The appearance of the medal also came in for criticism:

> . . . the design is bad, comprising only broken-necked figures, such as Justice leering like a harlot, or Genius, recognisable only by the indications of the poverty which is so often his fate – especially when he has had to deal with departments – or the effigy of Queen Victoria, that could not bear comparison with the head upon a penny.[82]

To assist in fund-raising, a 'Soirée and Promenade' was held on 12 October, when the School as well as the rooms of the Cork Institution were thrown open to the public. The works of local artists and of students were exhibited along with some 'splendid specimens of Photography and Chromolithography'. In contrast with previous years, there were few items from outside collections or from professional artists included in the annual exhibition of students' pieces held in the Athenaeum early in November. Richard Lyster contributed one small portrait of a very young man in oils and a pupil named Casey showed some sketches. Amongst those works that had received medals were three designs for carpets. There were also designs for lace and wallpaper on exhibition.[83]

The later years: problems and transformation
After a succession of short-lived and occasionally disastrous appoint-

ments to the Headmastership, the advent of James Brenan, R.H.A., to the position in 1860 (Edward Sheil having resigned in order to travel to Rome) must have come as something of a relief to the committee and students. In spite of his tender years – he was twenty-three when appointed – Brenan had had considerable experience both as an artist and educator. At an early age, after studying art in Dublin, he had assisted Owen Jones and Matthew Digby Wyatt in the decoration of the Pompeian and Roman Courts in the Crystal Palace. Returning to Dublin he taught for a period at the Dublin Society's schools. In 1857 he was assistant at the Bermingham School of Art but returned to the training college at South Kensington to further his education. After some short spells in charge of arts schools at Liverpool, Taunton and Yarmouth, he was appointed Headmaster of the Cork School, a post he was to hold almost thirty years. Brenan's interest in art and industry, founded in the Great Exhibition of 1851, resulted in his working to revive the lace industry in the south of Ireland in the 1880s.[84] In August 1860, under its new Headmaster, the annual exhibition was opened to the public. Receiving most attention was a series of photographs, each measuring three feet by two feet, by Colnaghi & Co., of Raphael's cartoons. A marble copy, by Jane Morgan, of *Ariadne abandoned* was also applauded, as were a series of studies by Thomas Frederick Collier, described as 'late head master'.[85]

The School re-opened for the 1860 winter term on 15 October and four days later the annual inspection of the students' work by the government inspector, Mr Wylde, took place at the Athenaeum, next door. Jane Morgan's life-size sculpture *'Nourmahal' – the light of the harem* (which had won a prize in the prestigious Taylor competition in Dublin that same year) gained a medal for the artist, as did drawings by Fanny and Maria Thorpe, Helen Barry and Miss Dorcas McMullen. Medals were also awarded to Sarah Gibbings and Sarah Barry as well as to the two Strangman sisters, Elizabeth and Kate, the latter receiving an award for her drawing of the Parthenon frieze. Jane White and Sarah White won medals for their carpet designs. An oil painting of ferns, by Miss Max, got a medal and was also selected for the national competition. Two members of the Hill family, Arthur and Margaret, received prizes in 1861, Margaret for her painting of *Cactus* and *Tiger Lily* and Arthur, later to be the architect responsible for the 1884 rebuilding of the School and galleries, for his outline drawings. Of the men, Thomas Hawarden (probably a misspelling of Hovenden, who was to be awarded a medal two years later) received praise for his landscape drawings, as did William Stopford for his drawing of the Discobolus, which had been selected for the national competition, while Francis Kemp and James Philips won medals for their mechanical drawings. Otherwise, even allowing that the newspaper reports would have focused on the names of prominent families, practically all the prizes and honours went to female middle-class students, a predictable development but sad in terms of the idealism for the School's egalitarian aims which had been expressed as recently as 1854.[86]

In this the School of Design in Cork followed a common pattern. Throughout Britain, economic and philanthrophic pressures to provide art education primarily for artisans had led to the founding of provincial Schools of Design. However, in most such Schools these early objectives subsequently became blurred with the swing from Design to Fine Art caused by the influx of the middle classes, especially well-heeled women students, and later by the effects of Cole and Redgrave's National Competition and the rigourous examinations of the 'South Kensington System'. These disadvantaged the less-well-educated students and provided a strong middle-class bias to government-funded art education in Britain. A utilitarian philosophy of art education was to come into prominence again at the end of the nineteenth century through the influence of the Arts and Crafts Movement and the rise of technical education, but for the Government Schools of Design this was too late. Even as the School of Design in Cork was becoming established in the years after 1850 a new parliamentary Select Committee was preparing the report that would lead to the establishment of the South Kensington 'system'.[87]

These issues, and the direction which art education was taking, were the subject of much discussion and comment. In spite of the fact that in 1861 the Cork School carried off no fewer than twenty-one medals, while in the same year the Metropolitan School in Dublin gained only seventeen, it was noted in the *Cork Examiner* that there was a paucity of examples of applied art: 'Unfortunately, the school is not as much frequented as it ought to be by the young artisans of the city . . . mere study . . . surely will be found a better mode for passing a tradesman's idle evening than the public house'.[88] This complaint was also heard in the speech given by the Lord Mayor-elect, Alderman Maguire, during the presentation of prizes just before Christmas 1861. Maguire commented on the large numbers of artisans working in the city, fewer than fifty of whom had chosen to enroll in the special Artisans Class at the School of Art. 'One feels that it is well to have even so many of this interesting class, while one is ashamed at having so few'.[89] The annual fees for the class were only five shillings: 'Why this trifling sum would be spent by almost any one of them in the enjoyment of a single day, or the indulgence of a single night'. Continuing difficulty in recruiting male students from amongst the industrial working classes meant that the School appeared to favour the admission of women from more prosperous backgrounds, a fact that did not escape public attention:

> Cork School of Art: This institution is now very fully attended, and all the classes and lectures are in active operation. There is a considerable increase in the numbers of pupils from National Schools at the evening classes; but it is to be regretted that, in a city which boasts of extensive dockyards, iron foundries, and other public establishments, which require and employ skilled workment, a greater number of the artisan and mechanic classes do not avail of the great advantages to be derived from the knowledge of Mechanical Drawing, Perspective, and Orthographic projection.[90]

This imbalance was partly due to the high status associated with English art schools, which had a number of Irish artisans to travel to England for their education, combined with the economic reality that Irish women did not have the financial independence to travel abroad in this way for their instruction. Those manufacturing industries which most needed the services of designers tended to be located in England, and would conveniently draw their designers from local art schools. It was this factor that led aspiring, and financially independent, male Irish artisans to move to English art schools and from thence into English industry. The result was that a significant proportion of the English creative and design talent was in fact Irish. Schools of Design in Ireland were thus placed at a double disadvantage, their local industries being unused, or unwilling, to employ skilled designers and a base of local talent that was continually draining away to England, or indeed to the United States. In the latter country census returns from this period show that a very large number of engravers, lithographers and other skilled artisans were from Ireland. The situation was summed up in a letter to *The Times*, written in 1865:

> Employers of artists do not echo the sentence, 'No Irish need apply,' for they encourage them extensively, and notwithstanding the immense competition caused by the demand for their service the art-facility will command its price, and the market is not overstocked with good artistic labour. The popular rage for illustration alone opens a great field for it, and the increasing application of design to structures and textures affords it promise of a vast future. Men and women from Ireland throng the brances of work connected with the first of these particularly, and, as these branches multiply, it is probable that Irish artists will avail themselves of them even more intensively. The employment is peculiarly congenial to their tastes, and the remuneration they will

be likely to yield will be more acceptable to them then to people of a more money-getting spirit.[91]

While it was acknowledged that art schools in Ireland gave an excellent basic grounding in art and design, they were criticised for providing a limited education to their students, stopping short in support at the point when pupils needed it most and forcing the more talented to seek further specialised education abroad. This was evidenced by the meeting held at the end of February 1863 to say farewell to a student of the school, a Miss Harrington, who was emigrating to Australia. The Headmaster, Brenan, referring to Miss Harrington as 'so bright an ornament of the school', presented her with an inscribed silver 'porte crayon' on behalf of the staff and students. Miss Harrington replied courteously: 'I am leaving Ireland for a distant land, but Cork and the old school shall always find a place in my memory'.[92] Another pupil of the Cork School who emigrated around this time was Thomas Hovenden, later to achieve fame as a painter in the United States, while student Jane Morgan also subsequently gained some prominence as a painter in New York.

The 1869 examinations exemplified the strict and unrelenting attitude of Redgrave's South Kensington System. Students' works from Schools of Art throughout the United Kingdom were dispatched to London to be examined. The paintings and other works of art were then returned to the schools, with small gummed labels attached, giving the judges' marks. 'Satisfactory' was marked on the work of Cork pupils Jemina Burrows, Luke Franklin, Fielding Lloyd, James Perry, Adelaide Skuse, James Griffin and Samuel Hynes. The distinction of having their work selected for 'national competition' was achieved by Henry A. Hartland, Samuel Hill, Jeremiah Mullins, Patrick Meade, Patrick O'Keefe, Anne Baker, Kate Craig, Emma Gregg, Margaret Hill, Fanny N. Thorpe, Maria J. Thorpe and Sarah E. Wood. Free studentships (exemptions from paying fees for one year) were awarded to Stephen Hennessy, Samuel Hill, Jeremiah Mullins, Patrick Meade, Patrick O'Keeffe and Samuel Walsh. Students at this time were encouraged not to use expressive draughtsmanship of any kind, but rather to build up images gradually and precisely, using pencil, conte and the 'stump' (a tight roll of paper which enabled subtle gradations in tone to be achieved in drawings). Thus was encouraged a rather pedantic and leaden approach to the teaching of Fine Art. The system was therefore failing on both counts. In rejecting the primacy of design education and professing to favour aesthetic sensibility, it might have been hoped that individual creativity would at least have been nutured.

While design as a concept may have been suppressed, the actual means of teaching design were eminently suitable for assessing in a competitive examination system. There was no deviation from this canon, for students at Cork or at any other art school in Britain. Prizes were awarded to Samuel Hill and Patrick Meade ('ornament modelled from the cast'), Joseph P. Addey ('ornament shaded from the cast'), William C. Cummins ('ornament outlined from the flat'), James Demery ('ornament shaded from the flat'), George Griffin ('figure shaded from the cast'), Richard Willis ('capital shaded from the flat'), Jeremiah Mullins ('arabesque painted in oil'), Kate Craig ('flowers painted from nature') and Maria Thorpe ('head from nature, shaded, in chalk'). Finally, 'Patrick O'Keeffe, carpenter, was awarded the bronze medallion, for ornament modelled from the cast, and design for Spandrel modelled in clay'.[93] Of these pupils Joseph Poole Addey and Richard Henry Albert Willis later went on to achieve prominence as artists. The Mayor commented that art students in Cork 'had a great many more disadvantages to labour under than those attending schools in other cities, which possessed picture galleries in which the pupils could instruct themselves.'

The condition of the School building remained a cause for concern in these years mainly because the 'absence of well-lighted, or comfortable, apartments, in which one would go with feelings of personal comfort, and apply himself to study'.[94] In December 1874 the correspondent of the *Cork Examiner* remarked that, exhibited anywhere else, the School of Art collection would have excited 'interest and admiration', but 'when one has scrambled up several flights of stairs to a dim and dusty attic, the very dinginess of its surroundings makes him dwell with the greater pleasure upon the freshness, beauty and vitality of mind with which the works impresss him. Here, in company with a unique series of casts, which many a city would gladly build a palace for, is found such evidence of the prevalence of a vigorous artistic faculty.'[95]

A description of what it was like to attend the Cork School of Art in 1876 was given by Henry Jones Thaddeus twenty years after while sitting on the terrace of the Casino at Monte Carlo. Thaddeus, by that time a highly successful portrait painter, recalled his student days in Cork for a correspondent of the *New York Herald*:

'It was a funny experience,' said Mr. Thaddeus, referring to his early artistic training. 'There was divil a thing in the place except a lot of plaster casts that had been sent to George IV by the then Pope. This collection was all we had to draw upon and to draw. And dirty! . . . The very size of the muscles was increased and the shapes of the faces altered by the thick layers of dust.

'Such a crazy place as that old building was. There was a staircase in it that trembled for its life every time you put a foot on it.
It was a standing danger for a long time until some genius hit
upon a way of putting everything right without any expense. He
just stuck up a notice that was there for years, reading – 'Do not
run down the stairs as they might give way'.

After several years of this training – which, notwithstanding
limitations, had its good points, as, by dint of drawing and
redrawing the George IV collection of casts, Mr. Thaddeus
acquired a facility and surety of draughtmanship that has stuck to
him to this day – he went to Paris and studied with Julien . . . 'I'd
like to know who didn't,' he added drily.[96]

Even while Thaddeus was still a student, moves were afoot to
improve conditions in the Cork School of Art. On 24 March 1876 a
committee was appointed at a public meeting held in the Royal Cork
Institution to seek to establish Schools of Science, Art and Music in
Cork. School Headmaster James Brenan and architect Arthur Hill were
the honorary secretaries of this Committee. Also in March a petition,
signed by the managers of the R.C.I., was forwarded by the Earl of
Bandon to the Committee of the Council on Education at the Department of Science and Art in London. In January 1878 Brenan's
committee presented its findings in a report which reviewed the
changing nature of government support for art education throughout
the British Isles. Their submission referred to the Great Exhibition, held
in London in 1851, which had revealed the differences in technical
education between Britain and other industrialised nations, and which
had highlighted the 'poverty of design, inelegance of form and glaring
contrasts of colour' which were characteristic of goods manufactured in
Britain. To remedy this, the Department of Science and Art had been
set up, at first under the administration of the Board of Trade, but
latterly under the direct control of the committee of the Privy Council,
which was charged with the administration of education. The Privy
Council was in a position to grant-aid local initiatives in art and science
education and, in addition, the amending of the Public Libraries Act in
1855 also enabled towns and cities to raise money from their own rate-
payers for the support of schools of science, art, museums and public
libraries. In Cork advantage had been taken of the amended act in 1855
to raise money for the support of the School of Art. In England, a
subsequent Public Libraries Act gave power to local authorities to raise
bank loans 'on the security of the rate' for the construction of schools
of science and art. However, by some oversight Irish local authorities
were not enabled to take advantage of this provision, a position which

was rectified in the last parliamentary session of 1855 through the efforts of Cork M P., Mr N. D. Murphy, with the passing of an amendment to the Irish Public Libraries Act. This amendment gave a significant advantage to Irish local authorities: by including music in its provisions, it enabled schools of music to be set up along with schools of science and art.

In Cork in 1878 the School of Art had 220 pupils. It was supported by an allocation from the city, by a share of the annual Parliamentary grant for the various art schools of the United Kingdom and by the fees of the pupils – all of which, taken together, were just sufficient to meet ordinary working expenses. The report of the committee outlined the deficiencies of the School of Art:

> But although Cork deserves credit for being one of the first towns in the Kingdom that endowed its Art School out of the public taxes, and is still the only town in Ireland that does so, it has performed but half its duty, for it has yet to provide a building suitable for an Art School, and affording sufficient accommodation for the increasing number of pupils. The building in which the school is conducted, and which is held from the Royal Cork Institution at a rent of £60 a year, was built for a custom house in the last century, and is badly adapted for art teaching. The class rooms are not spacious enough for the large classes now attending, and the light from the windows is so defective that the pupils, especially the advanced ones, labour under serious disadvantages. Add to this that the premises are very much out of repair.
>
> Again the school has no art gallery, in which to exhibit the work of the pupils, or loan collection of pictures, and other works of art, and in which the nucleus of a permanent art collection might be gradually gathered . . . Art can only flourish in an atmosphere of art – in other words art can only make progress where true taste is spread among the public at large. One of the best ways of doing this is to accustom the people to the sight of works of fine art in a public gallery. As regards painting this is difficult; but although we cannot hope in Cork to possess masterpieces, many fine examples may from time to time be borrowed . . . The fine collection of casts in the School of Art, and which the Royal Cork Institution hold in trust for the people of Cork, would form the beginning of a great gallery of casts, which might be made in a short time an object of which the city of Cork might feel justly proud. At present, these casts cannot be properly used for study by art students, and are not at all available for the

education of the general public. They are also in continual danger of receiving irreparable injury, owing the character and state of the building in which they are.[97]

The committee's report dwelt not only on the School of Art but also on the possibility of opening new schools of Science and Music in Cork. In order to move the whole project forward it was decided to send a deputation to the corporation to ask it to take advantage of the powers granted by the fourth section of the amendment of the Public Libraries Act (Ireland) which related to building grants. If the corporation were willing to act, it would have to set up its own committee and make application to the Commissioners of the Treasury for funding. At this point James Brenan's group would be wound up, and the corporation's committee would take over the task of acquiring the old houses which stood between the School of Art and Half-Moon Street, in order to construct a new building adjoining the Old Custom House which would accomodate the Schools of Science, Art and Music together on the one site. Brenan believed that the necessary alterations and additions would cost about £6,000, of which he hoped £2,500 would be raised through public subscription. He expressed the hope that the county gentry would contribute generously towards the cost of building the proposed schools, on the basis that the city tax-payers would look after their subsequent maintainance.[98] The pressing need for improvement was highlighted by the visit in November 1880 of Edward J. Poynter, Director for Art in South Kensington. He was met by Robert Scott, chairman of the School of Art committee, George Adams, and James Brenan. Poynter spent some time looking around the building and before taking his departure for Dublin on the 12.30 train observed that it was a most uninviting edifice in appearance and that the arrangements for lighting were 'by far the worst' he had ever seen.[99]

The Crawford School of Art

It must have been largely through Headmaster Brenan's efforts that one of Cork's merchant princes, William Horatio Crawford, was induced to help remedy the shortcomings of the old School buildings. Although involved in many areas of the city's business life, the Crawford family fortune stemmed mainly from the brewing firm Beamish and Crawford. William Horatio was to eventually donate £20,000 towards the complete remodelling of the Old Custom House and construction of a magnificent new extension. This latter was designed by Arthur Hill of the architects firm of Hill & Co., whose practise extended through several generations and three centuries in the city of Cork. Hill & Co. are responsible for much of the better quality Victorian building work in Cork, and their characteristic use of red-brick with white limestone trim is sympathetic and attractive in an urban context.

Judging from architectural drawings submitted by the Hill firm, it had originally been intended that the extensions and additions to the Old Custom House in 1884 would include a School of Art and Science, and indeed the wrought-iron gates at the entrance to the present Gallery do bear the inscriptions 'Art' and 'Science', but in the event these proposals were scaled down. The architect's model of the original proposed building survives in a private collection in Cork and is considerably more ambitious in scale and treatment than the actual extension. This model, and the ground plans associated with it, show that the initial intention was to have had art and technology taught under the one roof, with both an art museum and a science museum enhancing the building. The Crawford School of Science and Art was to be replete with several turrets, not just the one octagonal tower which graces it today, and if it had been so constructed the proposed school would have put a good number of major metropolitan buildings to shame. As with many such ambitious architectural proposals, the edifice which was eventually constructed reflects a keener awareness of budgetary constraints, although even in its abbreviated form by any standards the new Crawford School of Art was magnificent.

Arthur Hill successfully blended in the new extension with the old 1724 Custom House edifice. It seems that he went to the trouble of re-facing the entire existing building with the same new brick in order that the two parts would harmonise. The octagonal tower (a feature characteristic of Hill's architecture) marks the joining of the old Custom House/School of Design with the new School of Art and Gallery extension. The extension more than doubled the size of the building, providing two sculpture galleries, a life-drawing room and workshops on the ground floor, while on the first floor were five large studios for the teaching of painting and other activities. A fine mahogany staircase, appropriately embellished with carved wooden sheaves of barley, leads to the panelled main landing and to three impressive exhibition galleries in which are currently displayed the more important nineteenth-century paintings in the Crawford's collection. On this floor also is a magnificent library, entirely panelled in wood, with brass light fittings and glazed bookcases. Many of the volumes from this library were transferred to the new College of Art library when the School of Art moved to Sharman Crawford Street in 1979. Those that remain bear mute testament to the history of the building, many of them carrying the imprint of the Royal Cork Institution or the Government School of Design. Th extension gave Cork what must have been the finest art school in Ireland at that time. As a consequence of Crawford's

Plate 21.4   Exterior Crawford Gallery, Cork (Crawford Municipal Art Gallery/Cork
              V.E.C.).

Plate 21.5   View of Sculpture Galleries *c.* 1890 (Crawford Municipal Art Gallery/Cork
              V.E.C.).

generosity the new building was to bear his family name, as it still does to the present day. The technical school which was also named after the family was not completed until 1911, and was located on Sharman Crawford Street, near St Fin Barre's Cathedral. It is no longer used as a technical school but now houses the newly-styled Crawford College of Art and Design, which, as has been mentioned, transferred from Emmet Place in 1979.

The wrought-iron gates at the entrance to the new School of Art and gallery building bear the date 1884, the year the extension and renovation were completed, but the official opening ceremony was not held until April 1885, when the Prince of Wales (later King Edward VII) formally opened the building. A report in the *Cork Examiner* for 16 April of that year gives a graphic account of the event:

> Long before the hour appointed for the visit to the new School of Art, crowds of people assembled in Academy-street and Nelson's Place. They lined the footpaths, and where practicable, the centre of the streets, but as a rule the latter was taken up by a troop of the 11th Hussars and a body of police . . . All the members of the committee of the School of Art were in the building making arrangements for the reception from an early hour in the morning. A carpet was laid down all the length of the entrance hall . . . the exterior was tastefully decorated with flags. At a quarter to twelve o'clock, the Royal carriage rolled up to the main door amid the music of the Hussar's band and the cheers of those within the building. Some handkerchiefs were waved from the windows, but all the demonstrations of welcome were completely drowned by the storm of hissing that burst from the large crowd in the street. Dr. W. K. Sullivan (president of the building committee) received their Royal Highnesses at the entrance, and the members of the committee were ranged along the hall . . . The Princess of Wales led the procession through the building, leaning on the arm of Mr. James Brenan. The male students of the school cheered the Royal party as they visited the old portion of the building, while the lady students were also cordial in their demonstration of welcome, and at one period of the visit they sang 'God Save the Queen'. The crowd in the street kept hissing all the time, except when they varied the sibilant expressions of disapproval by cheering for Parnell and singing 'God save Ireland'.[100]

Miss Beamish presented a bouquet to the Prince on behalf of the lady students. The Royal party were then conducted downstairs to the new exhibition room for casts where Mr George Adams read an address, after which the Prince of Wales formally named the new building the 'Crawford Municipal School of Art'.

A year after the opening of the new School of Art in February 1886, James Brenan noted that 235 students were now attending. Of these only 19 were described as being in the 'Science Classes', while just two pupils obtained results in building construction examinations. He regretted that more students did not attend 'this useful class', and went on:

> It is true that close study and earnest work are required by those who do attend, but when the utility of these subjects is considered, it cannot but appear strange that in a city like Cork, where technical education is so much spoken of, such subjects as descriptive geometry, machine drawing, etc., which form the foundation of a great deal of technical knowledge, should not attract more than 19 students, of whom only five or six attended to the end of the course.[101]

Brenan was to repeat these observations ten years later when, as Headmaster of the Metropolitan School of Art in Dublin, he remarked on the dominance of women students who were more interested in 'picture painting' than in following technical courses.[102]

Around this time also initiatives which Brenan had undertaken in 1884 regarding the teaching of lace-work, crochet and embroidery began to bear fruit. These skills were imparted in classes set up by Brenan in the convents of Kinsale, Kenmare and Killarney, extending the network of the South Kensington Schools system. An important branch class of the School of Art which was held in Convent of the Poor Clares, Kenmare, concentrated on teaching nuns and students the art of lace-making. Prizes were awarded to M. Courtenay, B. Courtenay, G. Smith, L. Trappes and L. Guisani, whose designs, mainly for Irish point lace handkerchiefs, were forwarded to South Kensington for the national competition.[103] The first of these, Mary Courtenay, was a fashionable lady from The Square in Kenmare, who had joined the Convent of the Poor Clares shortly after its foundation in 1861. The abbess of the convent, Mother O'Hagan, was an enthusiastic promoter of needlepoint lace-work as a means for women to gain a measure of economic independence.[104] The classes in lace design at the convents at Killarney and Kinsale were also proving very successful – the Kinsale class had been founded as far back as 1847, but it was only in 1885 that it was brought into association with the Department of Science and Art at South Kensington. Alan S. Cole of South Kensington in that year had succeeding in obtaining a prize fund of £73 which was awarded in

43 different prizes in an open competition for the design of Irish lace. Students at the Cork School and its branches had succeeded in winning ten of these awards, with other prizes going to lace designers in places as far afield as Hamburg and Karlsruhe. Cole had been given £200 to collect examples of Irish lace for the Victoria and Albert Museum after the Cork Industrial Exhibition of 1883, and he had worked closely with James Brenan in promoting the lace-making industries of county Cork. From the central School in Cork T. Scott, L. Perry and E. Anderson won prizes for their designs for dress trimmings, antimacassars and chalice veils.

During the previous September (1884), the national competition drawings, which included works from all the Schools of Art in the United Kingdom, had been exhibited in the new galleries of the Cork School of Art with over 4,000 people attending. The exhibition of national competition drawings had also been shown in Cork in 1883. Brenan emphasised to the pupils that he had requested the competition drawings for a second showing in order to inspire work befitting their fine new school: 'This gratification the students can give Mr. Crawford, and at the same time, benefit themselves.'[105] In moving the adoption of Brenan's annual report, Mr R. Scott expressed satisfaction with the new school building. He recalled how students in the old 'dilapidated' school had been hard put upon to produce art under difficult conditions: '. . . some of them were obliged to hold umbrellas over their heads whilst at work to prevent the rain from descending upon them through the old worn-out roof of the building (laughter)'. He also praised the generosity of William H. Crawford:

> Fortunately for them, Mr. Crawford was himself a man of taste, a lover of fine arts; and he had the means – the money in his pocket – and he did lavish it with an unsparing hand in order to provide for them one of the best establishments of its kind . . . .[106]

Alan Cole of the Department of Science and Art in South Kensington paid two visits to Ireland in 1886, inspecting the lace class at the Convent of the Poor Clares in Kenmare on 29 January and again later that year in November. He was impressed with the work he found, particularly with the design for a large quilt, valued at £300, which had been commissioned by the wife of an American millionaire named Winnaces.[107]

The new School of Art buildings were convenient for a wide range of social events. A long-promised *Conversazione* took place at the School on three evenings, from Tuesday 27 to Thursday 29 April, 1886. The first evening of exhibitions, concert recitals and other entertainments was followed by a second night devoted to a concert given by the School of Music: 'It was a real pleasure to hear Miss O'Callaghan's beautiful contralto once again. Her singing of the song "Should he Upbraid" was exquisite, and proved abundantly her rare gift of voice'.[108] The crowds were also excited into admiration by Miss Lambkin's piano playing, while the rendering of Beethoven's 'Sonata in D' by Miss Reynold, 'of tender age', was considered 'a most creditable effort', as was Mr McCarthy's singing of the melody 'Erin, the Tear and the Smile'. The crowds were also entertained throughout the evening by the band of the Queen's Regiment, which played 'a fine selection, irreproachably'. On the final evening of the Conversazione, Professors England, Hartogg and Pearson of Queen's College, Cork demonstrated the use of the microscope and other scientific instruments.

In 1887, with 268 students now attending the School, James Brenan took particular pride in the awards which had been won by members of the lace classes, notably Bridget Moran of Killarney, Margaret O'Sullivan of Tralee, Emily Anderson of Cork and both Bridget and Mary Courtenay of Kenmare. Caroline C. Beatson received a silver medal for crochet design. There were now seven branch classes in lace design affiliated to the School in Cork. These were held at the Convents of the Poor Clares, Kenmare; Presentation Convents, Killarney, Tralee and Youghal; the Convent of Mercy, Kinsale; St Vincent's Convent, Cork, and the Ursuline Convent, Blackrock. Kenmare and Youghal specialised in point lace, while Killarney concentrated on reticella and embroidery. Limerick lace and crochet were taught at Kinsale, Tralee and St Vincent's in Cork. It was intended to establish further branch classes at Thurles and Parsonstown, pillow-lace making being already well established in the latter town. Brenan was pleased to report on the commercial success enjoyed by these classes in lace design: students at the Cork School of Art had prepared designs for a Mrs O'Brien in Limerick, for the firm of Biddle Brothers in London, and for Todd & Co., also in Limerick. It was intended to hold an exhibition of lace design at the Cork School in April 1888. Alan S. Cole of South Kensington, who had provided much of the impetus and support for this revival of lace-making, had visited Cork twice in the past year, and had given much valuable advice to the teachers and students of the lace-making classes. Cole had also lectured to the students at Kenmare, Tralee and the other branch schools, who subsequently applied to the Treasury for support for the continuation of his visits and lectures. Brenan worked closely with Cole on the development of this Irish lace revival and had himself in the past year visited lace-making centres in Belgium and France. A recent article in The *Illustrated London News* had reproduced a design for a piece of Irish lacework, which was to be presented to the Pope by the bishops of Ireland, and which had been designed in Kenmare and executed in the Presentation Convent at Youghal.[109]

For the first time in 1888 a student from Cork was awarded the National gold medal, the highest honour granted by the Department in London. The student, Caroline Beatson, had also won the £25 Princess of Wales' Scholarship, for her lace designs. Beatson and another member of the lace classes, Emily Anderson, were invited to London to attend lectures on design. The lace classes generally were thriving, with the convent at Tralee spending £1,000 on the construction of a small Art School for their classes. A new class had been opened at the Presentation Convent in Skibbereen. These branch classes were being attended by many national school teachers, who in turn were passing on the instruction to their pupils. Brenan complimented the class at Youghal on their completion of a lace-work fan for Mrs Alfred Morrison, while students Mary Hennessy and Edith Breton of the lace class in Kinsale had won prizes offered by the Society for the Promotion of Home Industries in Dublin. The exhibition of lace-work held at the School of Art in April 1888 under the auspices of the 'Ladies' Committee of the 1883 Cork Exhibition' had been successful, although the amount of money raised from the public for future prizes had been disappointing.[110]

James Brenan was not destined to remain in Cork for much longer to enjoy the facilities at the new School. The *Cork Examiner* in its edition of 30 March 1889 records the 'gloom over the entire establishment' at his departure to take up a new post as Headmaster at the Metropolitan School of Art in Dublin. Brenan's own theories were very much those of Ruskin and William Morris: 'He believed firmly, from the day the Cork Exhibition was opened [1852], that they could do nothing better than add art to industry. He belived in that firmly, and it was the one hope he had in going to Dublin, to apply some of the principles there he had endeavoured to carry out in Cork'.[111] Brenan was to remain at the Metropolitan School until his retirement fifteen years later.

However, there were inbalances in the School's operation that even Brenan with his 'commensense shrewdness and tact' was unable to redress. Student Kate Dobbin, married to wealthy merchant Alfred Graham Dobbin, may have represented an extreme in the social divide that existed in the Cork School of Art, but she was not untypical. Since its foundation, the institution's intake tended towards the more affluent and educated families, and realisation of this social imbalance led to initiatives such as the 1891 scheme for admitting apprentice plasterers, stone-cutters, carpenters and masons at half-fees. This initiative did not come from the School of Art committee but rather from an amalgamation of unions known as the United Trades, which offered to pay the balance of the apprentices' fees. The art master Mr Maguire, 'himself a member of one of the trades', was to teach the class. The Art School committee also agreed to give two free studentships to each national school in the city in addition to the studentships they already offered at the Christian Brothers' schools.[112]

Other initiatives to help broaden the student intake at the School included the scheme, instituted at the beginning of the 1893 term, whereby an examination was held to select eight free pupils who would attend the School of Art without paying any fees until 30 June the following year. The only condition was that candidates should be under twenty-one years of age and not have attended the School of Art previously. This scheme was funded privately by philanthropist Sir John Arnott, who subscribed £25 annually to support it. In addition, another examination was to be held on 28 September to select the ten free pupils from the national schools of the city, thus enabling a total of eighteen free students to attend the Crawford School of Art in the coming year. The *Cork Examiner* commented 'this should tend to make our School of Art a thoroughly popular institution', although in the event only thirteen free pupils were admitted to the school in 1893.[113]

In the latter year, under the Headmastership of W. A. Mulligan, pupils attending the School numbered 258; just over a third of these were day students. The number of evening students had more than doubled over the previous four years and now stood at 158, while day pupils had decreased in the same period, but Mulligan commented 'it is clearly much more important that the artizan classes should flourish than that there should be a large number of ladies attending in the day time'.[114] The 1895 winter session at the Crawford School commenced on Monday 2 September and continued until 31 January the following year. In keeping with the policy of trying to promote technical education, students at the School were now segregated into 'Industrial' and 'Non-Industrial'. There was an emphasis on teaching technical drawing, with geometry and perspective now vying with artistic anatomy and historic ornament. Classes for machine and building construction had also been established at the School; there was no mention of 'Drawing from the Antique', although presumably this still formed a significant part of the curriculum.[115]

In 1896 the number of students had remained unchanged from the previous year, at 223. In addition, there were 23 pupils 'from the artizan classes' studying building construction, and 24 studying machine construction, but presenting the annual report, the Headmaster wondered if some arrangement could not be made whereby 'apprentices and others might be induced to attend regularly and punctually during the session'. Mulligan noted that only 37 of these artisan pupils had not attended any art classes, and so were not included on the register of art students. A student teacher from the Crawford School, Patrick O'Sullivan, who had consistently won prizes in previous years' examinations and who had also served for a time as art master in Galway, had been admitted in 1896 as 'a Master in Training' at the Royal College of Art in South Kensington. He was replaced as teacher in the Elementary Room in the Crawford by John Roberts. Another talented student teacher, Michael McNamara, had received a two-year scholarship to attend the Royal College of Art from the committee of the 1883 Cork Exhibition, while a similiar scholarship was awarded to Miss Albina Collins of the Kinsale art class. McNamara was replaced in the Modelling Room in Cork by Hugh Charde. The two most recent recipients of these Cork Exhibition scholarships were Madeline Le Mesurier and Denis Santry, the latter also winning the Queen's prize for 'freehand drawing' and being placed joint first in the United Kingdom in this section.[116]

Conclusion

By the end of the century the Crawford School of Art was therefore well established and played a prominent role in education in the city. However, imbalances in student intake which had manifested themselves in the early years persisted. It is perhaps being over-dramatic to claim that the history of art in nineteenth-century Cork is thus a succession of lost ideals, but to some extent the progress of the arts that city cannot be read in any other terms. The stratification of Cork society and its fragmentation in terms of religion and politics formed, as was usual in Ireland, a rather heavy brew which befuddled even the most enlightened of social or economic entrepreneurs. The core of the problem lay in the development of a cultural attitude which regarded Fine Art and the Decorative Arts as being mutually exclusive and distinct in terms of class. That these same factors were at work throughout Britain is apparent, and the similiarity of patterns in art education encountered in towns and cities throughout these islands is often striking, so it is unwise to assume that Cork's difficulties were unique. Cork did not lag significantly behind other British cities in establishing its Society for the Promotion of the Fine Arts to exhibit the work of talented local artists, or its Cork Art Union, or indeed its School of Design for the instruction of local artisans and workmen. When the Cork School of Design was derailed from its original intentions by an influx of middle-class women students, this again was only a reflection of what had already been seen in other cities.

Although the histories of the main art institutions in nineteenth-

Plate 21.6   Cork College of Art students *c.* 1893 (Crawford Municipal Art Gallery/ Cork V.E.C.).

century Cork have been elucidated in some detail in the course of this chapter, giving an objective assesment of their success or failure is more difficult. Much depends, even today, on the criteria employed to gauge their performance. One of the dilemmas which arose as a result of the activities of the Society of Arts, and later the Cork Art Union, related to the issues of nationality and independence. After the Act of Union there was a close relationship between Cork and London, which gave opportunity to ambitious young writers and artists to move readily into positions in the English capital. Daniel Maclise, equipped with letters of introduction, emigrated to London in 1827, while the collection taken up to send Samuel Forde in the same direction was terminated only by the artist's untimely death. With the establishment of a Government School of Design in Cork in 1850, this process was simply accelerated and institutionalised. It was a relationship between region and centre that was held by many to be an admirable one. But there was also the opposing view, which argued that it was nonsense for people thus to contribute time and money towards simply depleting the city's stock of artistic talent. With the same uncertainty of purpose the annual exhibitions of the Society of Arts vacillated between pro-moting local artists and importing, generally from London, works of art calculated to inspire new standards of taste amongst the Cork bourgeoise. In the main, however, a cordial diplomatic balance was struck. Maclise remained in London, but remained 'loyal' to Cork as did Hogan in Rome.

That Cork produced many artists of considerable talent has long been acknowledged. So also has the fact that they found fame overseas. What is less generally realised is that this flow acted in both directions, with immigrant portrait and topographical artists easily balancing the outflow from the city. The incoming painters, John Henry Brocas, Robert Lowe Stopford, William Roe, Augustin Edouart and others, were obviously attracted by the economic vitality of Cork. They occupied comparatively specialised niches, either as portrait or topo-graphical artists. Sometimes, as with Barter, Sheil, Lyster and Mahoney, artists were drawn back to their native city after years of travelling, while Scanlon, Brenan and others came to Cork when appointed to teaching positions. Local Cork artists catered successfully to local taste, recording the agreeable faces of steamship owners, landlords, and their wives, the construction of new railway viaducts, distilleries and harbours and beauty spots such as Blarney and Gougane Barra. Their occasional ventures into the political arena were almost invariably only to support the status quo. With a similar regard for local sentiment, the English artists invited to show in the 1832 Cork exhibition donated part of their profits to cholera victims in the city. It must be admitted therefore that the stereotypical Cork artist, weaned in the midst of encouragement but starved of opportunity, as embodied in the romantic and frequently dramatic lives of James Barry, John Hogan and Daniel Maclise, disguises the fact that the city of Cork was prosperous enough to attract in a fair number of artists and provide them with a certain market for their work. These were not artists of genius, but were certainly talented enough to warrant attention in any history of Cork during this period.

Apart from those sufficiently lucky and gifted to secure teaching positions, those professional artists working in Cork nonetheless faced the economic reality that they were competing in a limited market. After the close of the second Art Union exhibition, John Windele bitterly recounted the 'scarcely credible' fact that only one or two single orders for the purchase or painting of pictures had resulted from the exhibitions, while summing up after the 1845 Art Union exhibition, John F. Maguire commented that the star of the exhibition, marine artist George Atkinson, had earned a 'wretched sum' over the previous twelve months. Lotteries became common in nineteenth-century Cork as a means of inducing people to purchase works and Atkinson resorted to this method on several occasions, as did the sculptor Edward Ambrose.

Broadly speaking, the pattern of the nineteenth century in Cork was one of increasing state control in art education. Before 1850 and the establishment of the School of Design, the initiatives had tended to come from individual artists. In spite of the support of influential patrons like Cooper Penrose and Lord Listowel, such undertakings enjoyed a fragile existence. Inertia, snobbery and social divisions rapidly untied the ideals of these worthy local enterprises, and even in time quite seriously affected the state-funded School of Design. The history of the Cork School of Art is of successive Lord Mayors bemoaning, at the annual prize-giving ceremonies, the lack of interest evinced by the artisan classes in an educational institution that had been set up for their particular benefit. Things were not so different in London either, but the founders of the original School of Design at Somerset House attempted through their teaching policies to forestall any takeover by the middle classes. At the outset, students at Somerset House were forbidden to draw from the casts or from the live model and compelled instead to learn mechanical drawing and the techniques of the decorative arts. It was a valiant attempt that lasted several terms before succumbing to the scorn of the middle class.

Rigid divisions of class were imposed on the arts both in terms of instruction and appreciation, and the imposition nationally of the South Kensington system of art education after the mid century codified these divisions as an arm of government policy. This system worked better in

England where manufacturing industries were located close to the Schools of Art, so at least there were some job prospects for artisans who could draw. But in Cork the massive exports of meat, butter, linen and other staples required only casks, boxes or bales to see them on their way. The basis of Cork's wealth throughout the century remained in agriculture, and with the progressive decline in manufacturing industry there was little future in the region for an aspiring artisan or mechanic, with or without the skills of the draughtsman.

The last act of the nineteenth century was played out in the first decades of the twentieth when the deliberate burning of many great houses in county Cork – the final betrayal of a landlord class by a population that felt itself betrayed – destroyed a great deal of the material evidence of the arts in nineteenth-century Cork. However, the works of art and artifacts that survive in houses such as Fota, Bantry, Dunkathel and Doneraile, as well as in the growing collections of the Crawford Municipal Art Gallery, do at least form a partial basis on which to evaluate the achievement of the artists and artisans of Cork in the last century. Nontheless much work remains to be done in the identification of works of art from the period which have been dispersed and on the identification of sources of information concerning the individuals and institutions which shaped the art of that time. It hoped that the present paper has made some contribution towards this end.

Acknowledgment

I am indebted to Dr Neil Buttimer for his assistance in preparing this paper for publication.

References

1. J. Turpin, 'Daniel Maclise and Cork society' in *Cork Hist. Soc. Jn.*, lxxxv (1980), pp 68-69; idem, *John Hogan, an Irish neo-classical sculptor* (Dublin, 1984). For supplementary references to art and artists in Cork see P. Murray, *Illustrated summary catalogue of the Crawford Municipal Art Gallery* (Cork, 1991). The present chapter derives much of its information from the data presented in this catalogue.

2. M. McSweeney and J. Reilly, 'The Royal Cork Institution, part 1: 1803-1826' in *Cork Hist. Soc. Jn.*, lxii (1957), pp 26-36; 'The Royal Cork Institution, part 2: 1826-1949' in ibid., pp 77-94; S. F. Pettit, 'The Royal Cork Institution' in ibid., lxxxi, (1975), pp 78-9.

3. A. K. Placzek (ed.), *Macmillan encyclopedia of architects* (New York, 1982).

4. K. Severens, *Charleston, antebellum architecture and civic destiny* (1985), pp 176-8.

5. G. C. Groce and D. H. Wallace, *The New York Historical Society's dictionary of artists in America 1564-1860* (New Haven, 1957), passim.

6. R. G. Kennedy *Architecture and money in America 1600-1860* (New York, 1984), p. 339.

7. Royal Academy of Arts, London, MS 5630, 22A (1), Daniel Maclise autobiography (1846), [hereafter 'Maclise autobiography'], quoted in Turpin, 'Daniel Maclise', p. 68.

8. *F.J.*, 8 Oct. 1811, quoted in W. G. Strickland, *Dictionary of Irish artists,* i (Dublin, 1913), p. 217.

9. A. F. Wedd, *The fate of the Fenwicks* (London, 1927), pp 117, 149.

10. Strickland, *Dictionary*, i, p. 490.

11. Turpin, *John Hogan*, p. 23.

12. Ibid., p. 29.

13. Anon, 'Memoir of Samuel Forde – A Cork Artist' in the *Dublin University magazine*, xxv (March, 1845), p. 338.

14. Strickland, *Dictionary*, ii, p 193.

15. S. C. Hutchison, 'The Royal Academy Schools 1768-1830' in *Walpole Society*, xxxviii (1960-62), pp 157, 162, 170.

16. M. Allthorpe-Guyton and J. Stevens, *A happy eye: a School of Art in Norwich 1845-1982* (Norwich, 1982), p. 26.

17. *Catalogue of the first Munster exhibition of original pictures, at Deans's Buildings, South Mall* (Cork, 1815), Introduction, p. iii.

18. 'The powers of hot water, or the new Kerry steamer' in Bolster's *Quarterly Magazine*, i (1825) p. 182.

19. *Cork Society for Promoting the Fine Arts: catalogue of first exhibition* (Cork, 1816), passim.

20. C. Roche (ed.), *The Ford of the Apples: a history of Ballyhooly* (Fermoy, 1988), passim.

21. *Cork Society for Promoting the Fine Arts: catalogue of exhibition, 1817* (Cork, 1817), passim.

22. D. and M. Coakley, *Wit and wine* (Dublin, 1985), p. 32.

23. It is unlikely that this William Carleton was the well-known Irish novelist.

24. T.C.D., MS 1206, T. C. Croker, Recollections of Cork (*c* .1833), p. 260 [hereafter Croker, 'Recollections'].

25. Pettit, 'The Royal Cork Institution', p. 82.

26. 'Memoir of Samuel Forde', p 343.

27. *S. R.*, 7 Nov. 1818, 22 Dec. 1818.

28. 'Maclise autobiography', pp 11-12.

29. Croker, 'Recollections', p. 270.

30. 'Memoir of Samuel Forde', p. 344.

31. G. Bolster, *Considerations on the utility of the casts presented by H.R.H. the Prince Regent* (Cork 1819), p. 12.

32. 'Memoir of Samuel Forde', p. 344.

33. *Cork Society for Promoting the Fine Arts: catalogue of exhibition, 1820* (Cork 1820), passim.

34. *Cork Society for Promoting the Fine Arts: catalogue of exhibition, 1821* (Cork 1821), passim.

35. *Cork Society for Promoting the Fine Arts: catalogue of exhibition, 1822* (Cork 1822), passim.

36. Strickland, *Dictionary*, ii, p. 129.

37. *C.C.*, 1 July 1828.

38. *C.C.*, 25 Aug. 1831.

39. *C.C.*, 20 June 1832.

40. Windele, *Cork,* p. 131.

41. Strickland, *Dictionary*, ii, p. 88.

42. *C.E.*, 10 Nov. 1841.
43. Ibid., 26 Sept. 1841.
44. Ibid., 3 Oct. 1842.
45. Ibid., 4 Nov. 1842.
46. Ibid.
47. Ibid.
48. W. M. Thackeray, *An Irish sketchbook, 1842* (London, 1843), p. 83.
49. *C.C.*, 6 May 1843.
50. Ibid.
51. *C.C.*, 10 Aug. 1843.
52. Ibid., 22 Aug. 1843.
53. Ibid., 10 Aug. 1843.
54. *C.E.*, 24 April 1844.
55. Ibid., 20 Jan. 1845.
56. Ibid., 22 Jan. 1845.
57. C. Fitz-Simon, *A chronology of art in Ireland* (Dublin, 1982), p. 136.
58. Ibid.
59. Allthorpe-Guyton and Stevens, *A happy eye*, p. 29.
60. *Report from the select committee on arts and their connection with manufactures* (1836), pp iii, iv, quoted in Allthorpe-Guyton and Stevens, *A happy eye*, p. 29.
61. Ibid, p. 30.
62. *C.C.*, 8 Jan. 1850.
63. Ibid.
64. Ibid.
65. *C.C.*, 11 July 1850.
66. For *The distressed mother*, also known as *The deserted mother*, see Murray, *Catalogue*, no. 721.
67. *C.E.*, 15 July 1850.
68. M. Holland, 'Culture and customs: a Cork miscellany' in *Cork Hist. Soc. Jn.*, xlvii (1943), pp 99-105. The clock Holland refers to was probably made by Richard Deeble, a clock-maker working in Cork in 1709, or one of his descendants.
69. *C.E.*, 27 Sept. 1854.
70. *Report of the Cork Government School of Art, Royal Institution, Nelson's Place, Cork* (Cork, 1854), p. 8.
71. Strickland, *Dictionary*, i, p. 187.
72. *C.E.*, 29 Aug. 1855.
73. Ibid., 14 Jan. 1856.
74. Ibid., 18 Jan. 1856.
75. Ibid., 4 Apr. 1856.
76. Ibid., 22 Oct. 1856.
77. Strickland, *Dictionary*, ii, p. 272; *C.E.*, 31 July 1857.
78. *C.E.*, 3 Aug. 1857.
79. Ibid., 6 Nov. 1857.
80. Ibid., 26 Feb. 1858.
81. Ibid., 21 June 1858.
82. Ibid.
83. Ibid., 6 Sept. 1858, 25 Oct. 1858.
84. Strickland, *Dictionary*, i, p. 77.
85. *C.E.*, 24 Aug. 1860.
86. Ibid., 19 Oct. 1860.
87. Allthorpe-Guyton and Stevens, *A happy eye*, p. 26.

88. *C.E.*, 22 Oct. 1861.
89. Ibid., 20 Dec. 1861.
90. Ibid., 14 Nov. 1864.
91. Reprinted in ibid., 3 Jan. 1865.
92. Ibid., 26 Feb. 1863.
93. Ibid., 14 Aug. 1869.
94. Ibid., 21 Dec. 1872.
95. Ibid., 31 Dec. 1874.
96. Ibid., 7 Apr. 1896.
97. Ibid., 26 Jan. 1878.
98. Ibid.
99. Ibid., 11 Nov. 1880.
100. Ibid., 16 Apr. 1885.
101. Ibid., 24 Feb. 1886.
102. J. Turpin, 'The RHA schools 1826-1906' in *Irish Arts Review 1991-1992*, p. 205.
103. *C.E.*, 4 Sept. 1885.
104. P. O'Sullivan, 'Kenmare lace' in *Irish Arts Review 1991-1992*, p. 106.
105. *C.E.*, 4 Sept. 1885
106. Ibid.
107. O'Sullivan, 'Kenmare lace', p. 107.
108. *C.E.*, 29 April 1886.
109. Ibid., 19 Jan. 1888.
110. Ibid., 24 Dec. 1888.
111. Ibid., 30 Mar. 1889.
112. Ibid., 6 Oct.1891.
113. Ibid., 22 Sept. 1893, 19 Feb. 1894.
114. Ibid., 19 Feb. 1894.
115. Ibid., 3 Sept. 1895.
116. Ibid., 12 Jan. 1897.

Chapter 22

FAMINE, MORTALITY AND EMIGRATION: A PROFILE OF SIX PARISHES IN THE POOR LAW UNION OF SKIBBEREEN, 1846-7

PATRICK HICKEY

> The time will come when we shall know what the amount of the mortality has been; and though you may groan, and try to keep the truth down, it shall be known, and the time will come when the public and the world at large will be able to estimate, at its proper worth, your management of the affairs of Ireland. [Lord George Bentinck, leader of the Tories, in the House of Commons, 1847]

'Every civilized nation, aye, savage nation on earth is familiar with Skull, the place of the Skulls', so exclaimed the Cork newspaper, the *Southern Reporter*, at the end of 1847. Schull and Skibbereen had become synonyms for famine. One writer called them 'the two famine slain Sisters of the South'.[1] Both were located in the region which was the focus of the vivid and famous illustrations by James Mahoney in the *Illustrated London News* in February 1847. All this is reinforced by the song *Dear old Skibbereen*. The full story of the famine in west Cork and in Ireland remains to be told. This study is concerned with the famine in 1846 and 1847 in a region encompassing six parishes in the Poor Law Union of Skibbereen (Fig. 22.1). These six parishes are Drimoleague, Drinagh, Caheragh, Kilcoe, Schull, and Kilmoe or Goleen which includes the Mizen Head in the extreme south west of the county. All are in the diocese of Cork except Kilcoe which is in the diocese of Ross. Kilcoe is a civil parish forming part of the Roman Catholic parish of Aughadown. Drinagh is a civil parish and part of the Roman Catholic parish of Drimoleague. The eastern part of Drinagh including the village belongs to the Union of Dunmanway but it falls within the remit of this work unless otherwise stated. Although Skibbereen itself is not within these parishes it was the Union town so a close watch is kept on it. The impact of the potato disease and of the relief measures is first discussed. The second part of the chapter analyses excess mortality and emigration from the region detailed in a rich but neglected source.[2]

Part I   The blight: impact and relief

The rapid spread of the devastating potato disease in the summer and autumn of 1845 caused alarm in west Cork. Members of the Carbery Agricultural Society discussed it at the dinner held on the night of their show in Skibbereen in October 1845. John Limerick, a landlord of Schull, was pleased that butter was making more that £3 a hundredweight in the Ballydehob market and felt sure that the pit specially designed by his rector, Dr Traill, would save the potato crop. But Dr Donovan, dispensary physician at Skibbereen, found that the wail all around him was that the potatoes were rotting everywhere. The discussion ended at 11.00 p.m.[3] It was also the eleventh hour of a period of Irish history.

In summer 1846 the potato disease struck even more severely. In August Captain William Thomas of Coosheen near Schull, a Cornish miner, warned the chairman of his mining company, Ludlow Beamish, that 'Small farmers ... are as badly off now as the poorest labourer ... Whatever is done by the government or public works will be too late, after the people are driven to despair by hunger'. He wrote again: 'The whole country is nothing but a slumbering volcano. It will soon burst'. Beamish forwarded Thomas's letters to Charles Trevelyan, assistant secretary to the Treasury, in London. Beamish believed that in the city competition among the merchants would control prices but that the poor would be at 'the mercy of the griping and the covetous' in the small towns. Trevelyan replied that it had already been decided to establish a reserve depot of Indian meal around Schull but made it clear that he relied on the merchants of Cork to supply the eastern part of the county.[4]

Relief works under the Labour Rate Act[5] were to be supervised by the geologist, engineer and land valuer Richard Griffith together with Thomas Larcom of the Ordnance Survey. Presentment sessions under this act for a division of the Barony of Carbery were held in the chapel at Ballydehob. Many local people present would have remembered the making of the Skibbereen-Crookhaven road under Griffith himself during the famine of 1822-23, which had been a highly successful scheme both as a relief measure and as a public work.[6] Landlords, ratepayers and clergy, both Catholic and Protestant, attended. Several road proposals were passed 'through a spirit of charity under the affliction of providence' but others called it 'presentment mania'.[7]

The Board of Works responded quickly and within four weeks there were at least 1,300 men employed in the Mizen Peninsula alone.[8] When

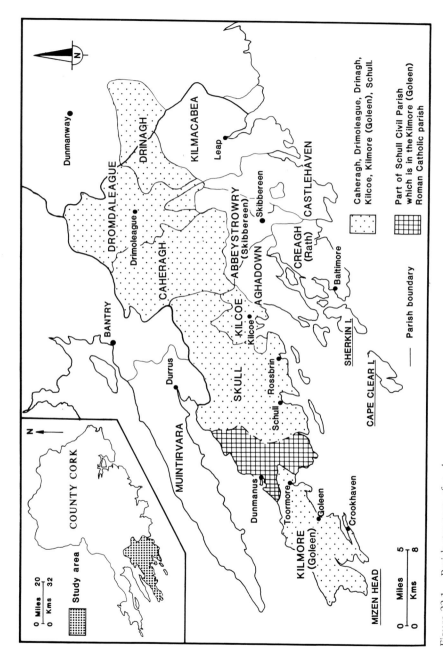

Figure 22.1 Parish structure of study area.

the hungry men on the Caheragh roads heard a rumour that their scheme was going to be stopped, a thousand of them marched into Skibbereen with spades and shovels on 30 September. Confrontation with the military was just avoided when the road-workers were allowed to buy some food from the government depot.[9]

On 24 October Denis M'Kennedy, who had been owed two weeks wages, died on the Caheragh road. At the inquest the jury, which included Dr Donovan, gave the verdict that he had 'died of starvation, owing to the gross negligence of the Board of Works'.[10] In November another Caheragh road worker, Jeremiah Hegarty, died. He had had some barley in his haggard but the landlord had confiscated it. Hegarty had not been paid for eight days.[11]

By now the district of Skibbereen was becoming notorious for famine. J. H. Marmion explained that a 'superabundance of sea manure' enabled the inhabitants to grow large quantities of potatoes. The markets of Cork and Waterford were 'principally supplied' with potatoes from this region and he himself had exported 2,000 tons of them in one season. The crop 'induced a superabundance of population, contrary to the wishes of the proprietors'. However, when the crop failed the labourers went hungry.[12] Public attention was directed at the horrors of famine in Skibbereen by the open letter of the Cork magistrate, Nicholas Cummins, to the duke of Wellington, published in *The Times* on 24 December 1846.

Further presentment sessions had been held in Ballydehob on 23 December. Some new road proposals were passed but many people were now disillusioned. Limerick agreed that they were only cutting their throats by concentrating on transport infrastructures. Another wanted to enlarge the work house. The reporter who attended these sessions in Ballydehob described misery and death in Dunmanway and Skibbereen, but he then announced:

> Greater misery was reserved for me in Ballydehob. Here they are in a deplorable state dying in all directions ... The people are living on seaweed and cattle they steal. On Sunday night they broke into the foodstore and stole all that was in it ... There were thirteen burials in the Schull churchyard yesterday; not one of them had got a coffin. It is cruel to insist that these wretched skeletons go miles to and from work to earn a few pence: it would be much wiser to give them a little food and permit them to remain within doors.[13]

In early January 1847 another reporter visited the Ballydehob district. An overseer told him that one man had collapsed and died from

Dr Donovan   Dr Traill

Richard Trench

Plate 22.1   Richard Trench (Trench, *Letters*); Dr Donovan (W. P. Pike, *Cork and county in the twentieth century:* contemporary biographies); Dr Traill (R. Skelton, *J. M. Synge and his world* (London, 1971)).

877

exhaustion and hunger and that he had been the fifth to meet this fate since 14 November last. This reporter protested: 'The total extermination of the labouring classes is inevitable. Lord Russell looks on with folded arms while her Majesty's Irish subjects are dropping in hundreds'.[14]

On 31 December 1846 Major Parker, an Englishman and an inspecting officer of the Board of Works, had sent Colonel Jones, its chairman, the following account of the prospects for the new year:

> A great number of people must inevitably be swept off by starvation and by diseases. Food is daily becoming scarcer and much dearer and where are future supplies to come from? Hitherto, Skibbereen has been the peculiar object of solicitude but Schull and Kilmoe [Goleen] are equally as badly off. Traill has soup-kitchens constantly at work, ... but all will not do. Individual charity will not go far.

Jones immediately forwarded this letter to Trevelyan who then wrote to Randolf Routh, chairman of the Relief Commission in Dublin, describing the correspondence as 'the most awful' he had yet seen. He wanted to know from Routh what progress the commissary, Mr Bishop, had made for the extension of soup-kitchens. Routh was annoyed at Major Parker's allegation that there was a scarcity of food. He claimed that there was plenty of food in the market at Skibbereen. He further stated that J. H. Swanton's two large mills at Skibbereen were full of meal for sale and that the government depot was also open. His explanation for the famine was that 'food is not lacking but rather the money to buy it'. This was a counter-attack on Parker's Board of Works which was supposed to provide employment and money. Money was indeed lacking, not only on account of the low wages of the board but also due to the high cost of meal. It was impossible for a man to support himself and his family on eight pence a day when meal was 2s. 6d. a stone. Routh also blamed the Skibbereen landlords who had an annual income of £50,000. 'Ought such destitution prevail with such resources?', he asked. Trevelyan's failure to respond was summed up in a Treasury minute stating that the local committees should do more, gather more subscriptions and open more soup-kitchens.[15]

In Skibbereen the workhouse was 'full to suffocation' and by the middle of January 1847 was closed to further admissions. It had been built to accommodate 800 but now held 1,169, of whom 332 were in fever.[16] On 1 February the Skibbereen soup committee reported that in one week forty-six died and on a single day, on 30 January 1847, deaths had numbered sixteen. Famine and pestilence prevailed in every parish in the Union and were causing 'a mortality proportioned to the destitution'. The average mortality per day in Schull was estimated at twenty-four while in Kilmoe (Goleen) twenty died on one day and eighteen on another. The same committee asserted that 'deaths which have already taken place should be numbered by thousands'.

The workhouse was £1,300 in debt; £1,400 was due in rates which were often impossible to collect. Some ratepayers were in the work-house themselves, others were dead or had emigrated or were on the public works.[17] A rate collector entered the house of Patrick Regan of Rossbrin near Ballydehob only to find the man, his wife and their son apparently dead. James Barry, the parish priest of Schull, soon determined that the man was actually alive. His wife died almost immediately; their son had been dead for five days.[18]

On 19 January 1847 Stephen Sweetnam, the dispensary physician at Schull, informed John Limerick that the daily average mortality in the parish was not less than twenty. 'I fear', he added, 'all your trouble and exertions ... are but as a drop in the ocean if some *gigantic* measure of relief is not *immediately* carried out by the government'. Limerick was also told by the priest that for the previous six weeks he had given the last rites to at least fifteen persons a day, not including children, 'numbers of which are perishing'.[19]

The Revd Barry described his visit to 'the village of Kilbronogue' near Ballydehob: 'Fever consequent upon starvation', he wrote, was spreading among the clusters of cabins. Barry regretted that the townland would 'soon be at the immediate disposal of the head landlord, Lord Bandon. There will be no need of extermination or of migration to thin the dense swarm of poor people ...; this will take place without his lordship's intervention or agency, I hope, to a better world'.[20] Revd. John Kelleher who succeeded Barry as parish priest later in the year told a public meeting in Dunmanway in 1850 that in the two months after the potato rot 120 persons died of starvation on Lord Bandon's property in the parish of Schull.[21]

A soup-kitchen was opened in Kilcoe as early as September 1846 and one in Skibbereen on 7 November and by the end of January 1847 they were replacing the road-works as the chief means of famine relief. There were two each in Aughadown, Caheragh, Crookhaven and Schull, and one each in Ballydehob, Drimoleague and Kilcoe. A soup-kitchen was only 'proposed' for Drinagh. Nevertheless Bishop admitted to Routh that it was but 'a drop in the ocean': 'Hundreds are relieved, but thousands still want'.[22]

Parliament met towards the end of January 1847. Lord Bandon told the House how the people were dying and quoted from a letter of Dr Traill's. Bandon reminded the government of its promise to supply food to the remoter districts, but such relief was 'tardy and hardly felt until the present time'.[23] Daniel O'Connell, M.P. for county Cork, predicted that unless England came to his country's rescue a quarter of her people would perish.[24] The response of the government was the Temporary Relief Destitute Person's Act, better known as the Soup-Kitchen Act, introduced by prime minister Lord John Russell on 25 January.[25] This act sought to bridge the gap until the harvest in September. It was, however, a long way from parliament to parish.

On 29 January relief commissary Bishop informed Trevelyan of the Treasury that 'the floating depot for Schull arrived yesterday and has commenced issues; this removes all anxiety for that quarter'.[26] But he seems to have been the only one without anxiety. Laurence O'Sullivan, parish priest of Kilmoe (Goleen), reported how his people were dying at a rate of 100 a week and that the rate was rapidly increasing. His parish had received less aid than others because of its remoteness. O'Sullivan claimed that the 'tardy relief' contemplated by the government would not come into operation until some additional hundreds were added to the victims and even then it would be 'totally inadequate'.[27]

Schull's rector, Dr Traill, wrote: 'Frightful and fearful is the havoc around me'. Sweetnam, the local doctor, had told him that the mortality in his parish was now 35 daily. Traill continued: 'The children in particular were disappearing with an awful rapidity, and to this I add the aged who ... are almost without exception swollen and ripening for the grave'.[28] The Ballydehob Ladies' Association distributed food and clothes to 130 families but many were denied. Jane Noble, its secretary, appealed to commissioner Routh: 'The young mothers and their famished infants ... present scenes of distraction, ... far beyond my powers of description.'[29]

These horrors of the famine were by then not only described but vividly portrayed by the artist James Mahoney of the *Illustrated London News*, who visited west Cork early in February. At Schull he saw 300 to 400 women with money in their hands being doled out 'miserable quantities' of food at 'famine prices'. Food had recently arrived in a government ship but it was totally inadequate for a population of 27,000. Mahoney drew a sketch of the hut of a poor man who lay dying on a bed of straw. Traill was the visitor depicted in the sketch. The dying man's wife had passed away some days previously and their three wretched children lay beside a smouldering fire. This artist also saw the rector's daughters distributing food.[30] At Caheragh Mahoney drew his celebrated representation of the forlorn boy and girl searching for potatoes. The curate of Drimoleague, Revd Creedon,[31] guided him to the village of Meenies.[32] Like the village of Kilbronoge near

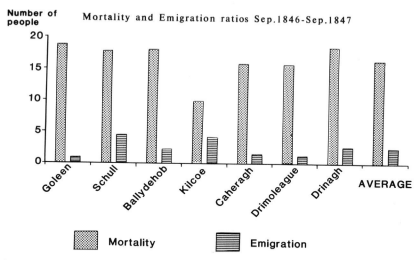

Figure 22.2   a   Mortality and emigration, 1846-47.
Source: reference 61 ('Marshall's return').

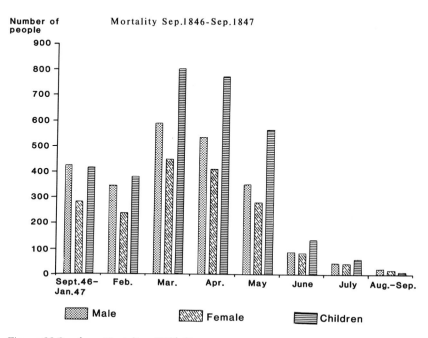

Figure 22.2   b   Mortality, 1846-47.
Source: reference 61 ('Marshall's return').

Ballydehob, Meenies was one of west Cork's many 'grave-yard villages'.[33]

The rector of Caheragh, Francis Webb, received the following report on Toureen:

> I saw the bodies of Kate Barry and her two children very lightly covered with earth ... the flesh completely eaten by dogs ... Within about thirty yards ... are two most wretched looking old houses, with two dead bodies in each, Norry Regan, Tom Barry, Nelly Barry (a little girl), and Charles McCarthy (a little boy), all dead about a fortnight, and not yet interred.

The Revd Webb published the above account in the *Southern Reporter* and asked in disbelief 'Are we living in a portion of the United Kingdom?'[34] Commissioner Bishop sent a copy of this piece to Trevelyan stating that the natural conclusion was 'that food could not be found'. Bishop however also enclosed a letter from the miller J. H. Swanton, reporting that he had 100 to 200 tons of Indian meal and other flour, but that he had difficulty in disposing of it as the Skibbereen Relief Committee was selling meal '*indiscriminately* for as little as 2*s*. 2*d*. a stone. If the government bought it, Swanton asserted, it would save him 'the freight of shipping it to another market'. Bishop pointed out that this meal is to be found within *two* miles of the parish of Caheragh and asked indignantly: 'May we not conclude with the rector, "Are we living in a portion of the United Kingdom?"'[35]

Thomas Tuckey, rector of Drimoleague, recited how faction fights were laid aside, and how the people had grown so accustomed to death that the *caoineadh* was never heard.[36] George Robinson, treasurer of the local relief committee, gathered many subscriptions. He hoped to obtain a grant of funds sufficiently large to enable him to establish a soup-kitchen in Drinagh as well as in Drimoleague. He made a special appeal for Drinagh as it had no resident rector or gentry; its situation was remote and it was 'the most neglected part of west Carbery'. His responsibilities consisted of the parish of Drimoleague and most of Drinagh, containing 6,000 persons in all, of whom the labouring class numbered about 5,000. 'This class in this district', he stated, 'have always been miserably poor'. Now they had been thrown on the public works or on charity, the large farmers with rarely an exception '*not having retained in their employment a single labourer*'. There were about 150 small farmers but they were reduced by the failure of the potato 'to abject misery'. Five-sixths of the population, that is all those categorised as labouring class, felt 'the gnawings of intense hunger every day'. He maintained that the population of his own area contained a higher proportion of poor than the parishes in which the town of Skibbereen was situated.[37]

In mid-February 1847 commissary Bishop went on a tour of inspection of the parishes under study and reported to Trevelyan. At Schull he found that 'mortality had greatly increased'. When fever attacked the inhabitants of a cabin nobody would dare help them, not even a parent or a child. So many died from 'positive neglect'. In Goleen he found that:

> Fever, dysentery and consequent death have greatly increased ... The relief committee of Schull and Kilmoe [Goleen] exert themselves greatly to the benefit of the poor. There is an ample supply of provisions in both places.[38]

Once again food and starvation were side by side. No wonder Canon O'Rourke asked: 'How did they manage to die of starvation in Schull?'[39] The answer had been given by the artist Mahoney: provisions were not ample and were at inflated famine prices.

More publicity was given to Schull by Captain Caffin of H.M.S. *Scourge* in his letter of 15 February, written the day after Bishop's report. The captain had landed 96 tons of food in Schull on behalf of the British Relief Association. Dr Traill drove him around to visit some of his Protestant parishioners and in every house they visited they found the sick, the dying and the dead. 'Famine exists to a frightful degree, with all its horrors!' he exclaimed. 'Fever has sprung up in consequence upon the wretchedness; the swellings of limbs and the body, and diarrhoea, from the want of nourishment, is everywhere to be found'. This letter was soon published in Irish newspapers[40] and shortly afterwards in *The Times* in London on 26 February.

Caffin's report shocked Trevelyan. He wrote to the new chairman of the Relief Commission, John Borgoyne, describing the correspondence as 'awful'. He suggested some little extra aid for Schull, but he admitted that relief could only be carried out to a limited extent, concluding: 'Let us save as many as we can'. Burgoyne replied thus: 'Terrible as are the accounts from Schull, it is, I fear, too certain many other districts suffer in the same degree from want of food, some of them in the interior'. A Treasury minute of 23 February 1847 confirmed 'the dreadful state of destitution in the parishes of Schull and Caheragh' and stated that the Lords of the Treasury desired that the Relief Commission and the relief committees do more for the district.[41] But no special aid was forthcoming from the Treasury.

Traill wrote that Caffin had been 'shocked beyond measure at what he witnessed', but insisted that 'verily the half was not shown him.

Farther up among our rocks and fastness, he might have seen hovels filled with the dying and the dead'.[42] Caffin continued to deliver food along the west coast of Ireland. On 10 March 1847 he wrote from Belmullet, county Mayo, describing the famine in Erris but concluded that starvation was 'getting worse as you go south, and at Schull and its neighbourhood the very climax of misery finds its resting-place'.[43]

A woman begged John Limerick to bury her husband and family. Revd Barry praised him as 'a good magistrate ... unsparingly devoted to deeds of benevolence'.[44] Tuckey, the rector at Drimoleague, met a woman on the way to the graveyard to bury her seventh and last child.[45] Thomas Beamish of Kippagh Lodge, secretary of the Drinagh Relief Committee, gathered £48 but complained to the relief commissioners that they had received 'no aid' and pleaded for this 'extensive and mountainous' district.[46] Thomas Swanton of Cranliath near Ballydehob, landlord and Gaelic scholar, became so disillusioned that he announced his conversion to Repeal and even declared that 'murder is going on for the benefit of Manchester and Liverpool'.[47]

The Church of Ireland burial records for Drimoleague and Drinagh have fortunately survived:

Table 22.1

Burials

Year	1845	1846	1847	1848	1849
Burials	3	6	23	5	3

Source: N.A., Church of Ireland parish registers, 1845-1849.

The huge increase in the number of burials in 1847 is evident. Among them were members of a Stout family; the youngest, John (2) and his sister Mary (7), were buried on 9 April. Their brother, Michael (10), was buried the next day. Their parents John (45) and Mary (47) joined them on 23 April. John was a labourer. Here we see famine mortality at family level: the children died first, beginning with the second youngest if not the youngest.[48] The Stouts shared the fate of many of their class.

Trench's relief scheme

The urgent response which Parker, Sweetnam and Caffin had called for came not from the government but from a Protestant clergyman, Frederick F. Trench, curate of Cloughjordan, county Tipperary. His attention was drawn to the area by Caffins's letter and he 'volunteered to come out of charity'. On Sunday 14 March 1847 he met the

Plate 22.2   Meenies (*Illustrated London News*, 13 Feb. 1847).

Ballydehob Relief Committee and outlined his plan of establishing 'eating-houses' at various places. He set up a sub-committee consisting of, amongst others, John Barry[49] and John Triphook, the Catholic and Protestant curates respectively.

At Schull Trench met Dr Traill, his curate Alexander McCabe and Sweetnam, the local physician, who described many adults as 'delirious with fever and hunger'. McCabe remarked to Trench that 'he had altered in the course of the last eight days in a hundred instances the names of the men who had died to the names of their wives and that in that space of time there had been six cases in which he had altered the name from the father to the son, and from the son to the widow, and from the widow to the daughter, all having died'. Trench and McCabe went to Kilbronogue south of Ballydehob where they met Revd John Barry and together they visited nine houses. Out of forty-three inhabitants they found eight who were apparently healthy enough, twenty-five in fever, eleven starving, three dying. Barry remarked that the people of one house had been decent farmers. Trench presented his urgent plan:

> ... the establishment of eating-houses within reach of those upon whom disease has not as yet made mortal inroads.
> ... the sending of a sufficient number of suitable agents to manage those eating houses; and physicians should be sent to prescribe the food and medicine.

Trench's aim was to give 'a meal of substantial Indian meal stirabout or porridge' a day to each person in danger of perishing rather that just soup. The meal would cost only one and a half pence per day. His comment on the vital question of the availability of food deserves attention:

> There is no want of food in any place (delightful consideration) but there is a most deplorable want of *available agencies, and a consequent want of suitable measures to bring the food and the medicine within the reach of the people.*

The Tipperary curate appealed for a 'sufficient staff of fit men' to prescribe for the sick and to put a cooking place within reach of the poor. He also asked an eminent physician, Dr Kennedy of Merrion Square, Dublin, to select a doctor to send to Schull and to accept the services of any other gentlemen. Trench held that the arrangements concerning the Soup-Kitchen Act were 'complicated, and the lives of thousands depend on what is done *now*'.[50]

Major Parker of the Board of Works died of fever on 23 March 1847 and was buried at Creagh near Baltimore. The Board of Health sent a Dr Lamprey to Schull. He placed the sick in army tents and visited Dunmanus where he found one of Trench's agents feeding 600 people and praised the system as 'the only means yet devised to stay the famine'.[51] One man who answered Trench's call for volunteers was his cousin, the Revd Richard C. Trench, Professor of Divinity at King's College, London,[52] who arrived in Dublin on 6 April and went to Ballydehob with two helpers. He considered that 'Skibbereen had the appearance of a flourishing place' compared to Ballydehob and Schull and discovered that his cousin's five eating-houses were not one-tenth of what was necessary and two more were started in Ballydehob. There was now a total of nine eating-houses in the parish and new ones were still being opened. From each about 500 people were fed every day. Professor Trench and his helpers had given out 10,000 meals at less than a penny farthing each and were thus encouraged at 'the trifling cost of food'. He held that what cost much was 'the agency which is essentially necessary and for want of which, more than for want of food, life is lost'. Still Trench had to admit that in spite of all their efforts there were 'vast regions yet untouched'. He claimed, however, that 'the mortality, though it had not ceased yet it had been arrested'. This was 23 April 1847.[53] The tide of famine and fever was at last beginning to turn. Trench could speak of the 'trifling daily cost of food' partly because, as Fr Mathew had announced in March, 'The markets are rapidly falling; Indian corn from £16 to £15 a ton' due to 'vast importations'. Indian meal had been £19 a ton in February.[54]

Among Lamprey's patients was Traill himself who died of fever on 21 April and was buried in Schull.[55] A new Fever Bill became law on 27 April.[56] Temporary fever hospitals were then set up in Skibbereen, Ballydehob, Schull, Kilcoe, Caheragh and Drimoleague in May and June.[57] By the middle of May 1847 famine and fever had at last been brought under some sort of control, but casualties were already heavy. The editor of the *Cork Examiner*, J. F. Maguire, protested; his informant was a Catholic clergyman, probably the Revd James Barry. Maguire claimed that disease and mortality had increased due to 'the reckless dismissals of labourers from the public works'. He wrote that the population of East Schull or Ballydehob had been 8,000:

> It is now reduced to about 6,000 – that is to *three-fourths* of what it was less than one year since. It is computed from accurate data that, from the end of October 1846 to the beginning of May 1847 – a period of six months – *ONE-FOURTH of the entire population of East Schull has been swept away by famine and disease.*

This did not surprise Maguire when he was informed that from 17 March to 17 April 1847 200 bodies were buried by the relief committee with sliding coffins and another 100 received a decent burial, a total of 300. Maguire was also told by the same clergyman that this mortality would perhaps have doubled were it not for 'the noble and God-like exertions and benevolence' of F. F. Trench who had 'not made the least attempt to interfere with the religious faith' of the people. Maguire declared that 'work, work' was the constant cry of the people of Ballydehob.[58] The days when the government would provide work were over. It would now be cheaper, easier – and ultimately more humane – to dole out soup. Some people, however, regarded the public works as being just as much a form of dole as the soup. One famine road in Castledonovan near Drimoleague is still called *Bóthairín na déirce* or 'The little road of the alms'.

Accordingly, as the Soup-Kitchen Act was coming into operation the road-works were to be phased out. The relief commissioners directed that from 20 March the numbers employed in them should be reduced by 20 per cent and a further 10 per cent by 23 April. Thomas Gibbons, financial officer for the Skibbereen Union under this act, reported that when the 10 per cent were dismissed in Schull it led to outrages.[59]

The new act was slow in taking effect. As late as 15 May 1847 only 1,250 electoral divisions out of almost 2,000 had been brought under it. Professor James S. Donnelly, Jr, states that the preparation of sheets and tickets consumed valuable time.[60] The Soup-Kitchen Act came into operation in the six parishes on 10 May except for Goleen where it was delayed until 24 May. The government inspector introducing the measure was named J. J. Marshall. The following table shows the number of rations distributed on 19 June.[61]

The population receiving rations – an average of 52 per cent – is

Table 22.2

Rations

Parish	Rations	Population 1841	Percent dependent on rations
Goleen	4,942	7,234	68.32
Schull	4,918	8,604	57.16
Ballydehob	4,612	8,710	52.95
Kilcoe	1,074	2,339	54.47
Caheragh	3,272	8,375	39.07
Drimoleague	2,520	5,501	45.81
Drinagh[62]	1,296	2,503	51.78
Total	22,634	43,266	52.31

Source: Marshall's return. See reference 61.

indeed high but not as elevated as in the neighbouring parish of Muintirvara (Durrus) near Bantry (60 to 70 per cent), or parts of Connaught (70 to 100 per cent).[63] Children received only a half-ration and they were estimated as still numbering 20 per cent of the population in need.[64] To sum up, the 22,634 rations distributed under this act in the six parishes fed about 27,160 persons out of a total population of 43,266 or 62.77 per cent. This percentage was high but in reality it must have been greater as the population was now lower than it had been in 1841 owing to death and emigration.

The results of these great efforts made by the Trenches and also of the Soup-Kitchen Act were recognised at a meeting of the Ballydehob Relief Committee held on 20 June. A resolution was passed expressing gratitude to Revd F. F. Trench and his agents for their work. In the covering letter Revd Barry told how deaths were now so few that the slide-bottomed coffins[65] were no longer in use. He was confident that the Soup-Kitchen Act, under the guidance of a 'wise and indefatigable inspector', J. J. Marshall, afforded a hope of 'few deaths from dire want'.[66]

The Soup-Kitchen Act was due to expire in September. The Irish Poor Law Extension Bill which transferred the responsibility of Irish destitution to the Irish poor rates became law in June.[67] A meeting of landowners was held in Ballydehob on 10 September 1847 which declared that the local property could not support the paupers and that if they were to depend solely on the rates, 'thousands of lives must be lost'. A resolution to this effect was sent to the prime minister, Lord John Russell. His reply was cold, curt but crystal clear:

> I am deeply concerned at the prospect of distress in East Schull [Ballydehob] ... It appears to me that the owners of property in Ireland ought to feel the obligations of supporting the poor, who have been born on their estates, and have hitherto contributed to their yearly incomes. It is not just to expect the working classes of Great Britain should permanently support the burden of Irish pauperism.[68]

Such sentiments foreshadowed the Encumbered Estates Act. Nationalists saw this answer as proof of England's failure to take responsibility for Ireland's problems and a new argument for Repeal. But it was only in dealing with its own poverty that Ireland was to be granted Repeal.

Part II   Mortality and emigration
(i) Mortality

The Soup-Kitchen Act was relatively successful as far as it went. But more lives would have been saved if it had been brought into operation with the same haste as it was terminated. Trevelyan boasted that 'the famine was stayed ..., upwards of three millions of persons were fed every day'.[69] Many hard-pressed relief committees were grateful for this provision. The Revd David Dore, parish priest of Caheragh publicly praised J. J. Marshall. The Schull and Ballydehob relief committees held a joint meeting on 28 September 1847. John Limerick was chairman of the Schull committee and Revd Barry acted as chairman at Ballydehob. These committees declared that the Soup-Kitchen Act had done 'great good' in their own districts, and as 'a criterion by which the public may judge the good results of that act generally' they adduced the following:

> a copy of the statistical return made out with scrupulous exactness under the directions of J. J. Marshall, inspecting officer for this district, shewing at one view the very great mortality which preceded, and the equally great decrease of such mortality which followed, the introduction of that measure.

The 'statistical return' presented to the public was entitled *A return of deaths and emigrations in the western division of the Skibbereen Union, from the 1st September 1846 to 12 September 1847*.[70] This dossier gave the numbers who died in each parish, whether men, women or children under fifteen, on an almost month-to-month basis and also the causes of death. Marshall's return is particularly rare and valuable because the information is community based. Data on mortality rates in institutions are less difficult to obtain. Estimates of the number of people who died during the famine are extremely varied: they range from as low as 800,000 to as high as 1,500,000. Mokyr has advanced a figure of at least one million: Professor Ó Gráda and Dr P. P. Boyle have suggested a similar figure.[71] Part of the reason for the wide range of those estimates was given by the census commissioners of 1851, one of whom was William Wilde (father of Oscar Wilde), regretted that 'No pen has ever recorded the numbers of the forlorn and starving who perished by the wayside or in the ditches, ... whole families lay down and died'.[72] Evidently Marshall and those who worked under his direction attempted to do precisely that. It has already been shown how from January 1847 onwards John Limerick, Sweetnam and Barry were trying to count the numbers who had died. As already stated, J. F. Maguire of the *Cork Examiner* maintained that his figures for mortality in Ballydehob had been 'computed from accurate data'. On 20 March Dr Traill wrote that it had been 'computed' that 2,000 of his parishioners had already fallen victim.[73]

Marshall's digest was presented in a calm, matter-of-fact manner, no attempt being made to politicise the famine dead. The same cannot be said of the 'death census' published by the *Nation*[74] whose editor, Gavan Duffy, described the famine as 'a fearful murder committed on the mass of the Irish people'.[75] In any case this death census is only a random spatial simple count of fatalities and has none of the detail and analysis of Marshall's return. When the Revd Kelleher told the political meeting of landlords in Dunmanway that 120 persons had died on Bandon's property in Schull the response was 'shouting'. Dr Donovan published Marshall's return in the *Dublin Medical Press* as will be seen later. This report therefore has good authority, as it was also accepted by Limerick and Barry. It was not on every subject that the doctor, the landlord, the parish priest and the government official would have agreed!

Derived from Marshall's return, Table 22.3 represents mortality in the six parishes from 1 September 1846 to 12 September 1847. It is clear from the causes of death which are given below that it concerns excess famine mortality [Fig. 22.2].

Table 22.3 shows the dramatic mortality of 1,125 persons for the period September 1846 to January 1847. The highest number of deaths was for adult males, 424, which was greater than even for children, 418. The casualties among the road workers must account for some of these men. In February 1847, 962 persons died; this figure was made up of children, 378, followed by males, 345, and females, 239. This pattern of change held for the rest of the year. Mortality reached its climax in March, when 1,838 perished. In April mortality decreased only slightly to 1,710.

There was now a significant difference between the peninsular parishes, Goleen, Kilcoe and Schull and the inland ones, Caheragh, Drimoleague and Drinagh. Mortality peaked in the peninsular parishes in March at 1,372 and fell in April to 1,067 and in May to 670. In the inland parishes, however, mortality reached its zenith not in March but in April and continued at this level even in May when it was higher than it had been even in March. In March there were 466 deaths, in April 643 and in May 524 – in spite of the Soup-Kitchen Act. The arrival of the Trenches in the peninsular parishes in the middle of March is no doubt the reason why mortality was prevented from continuing to rise and peak there also in April. We have seen how Professor Trench stated that by 23 April mortality had been 'arrested' although it had not ceased. The efforts of the Trenches were such that even in all six parishes taken together mortality peaked in March and not in April; 1,838 died in March and 1,710 in April. In the workhouses all over the country it was around the middle of April that mortality peaked and

Table 22.3
Parish mortality, 1 September, 1846 to 12 September, 1847
(M. Males; F. Females; C. Children)

Parish	Sept '46-Jan '47 M	F	C	February M	F	C	March M	F	C	April M	F	C	May M	F	C	June M	F	C	July M	F	C	Aug - Sept M	F	C	Total	1841 Population	Percentage Mortality
Goleen	77	69	90	70	58	83	114	84	129	82	76	145	54	68	73	21	17	15	8	7	15	4	2	2	1,363	7,234	18.84
Schull	63	44	86	76	53	90	139	106	191	109	98	170	50	54	107	16	14	11	11	14	15	4	3	1	1,525	8,604	17.72
Ballydehob	67	36	53	75	44	111	155	121	233	112	72	166	60	52	124	12	12	31	8	6	9	3	5	2	1,569	8,710	18.01
Kilcoe	14	6	6	7	7	8	29	30	41	14	12	11	7	6	15	2	2	3	1	1	3	2	1	0	228	2,339	9.75
Caheragh	113	60	117	46	25	36	57	36	60	120	77	178	87	51	162	7	21	41	5	7	10	3	2	0	1,321	8,375	15.77
Drimoleague	43	36	44	40	37	42	69	58	100	76	44	69	65	23	49	17	10	15	11	6	4	2	3	2	865	5,501	15.72
Drinagh	47	32	22	31	15	8	25	13	48	21	28	30	27	25	35	13	8	19	1	2	4	4	1	2	461	2,503	18.42
Totals	424	283	418	345	239	378	588	448	802	534	407	769	350	279	565	88	84	135	45	43	60	22	17	9	7,332	43,266	16.95
Grand Total	1,125			962			1,838			1,710			1,194			307			148			48			7,332		
	15.34%			13.12%			25.07%			23.3%			16.28%			4.19%			2.02%			0.65%					

Source: Marshall's return. See reference 61.

then gradually decreased. To a certain extent this was due to the opening of fever hospitals. In the week ending 17 April 1847 deaths numbered 2,551 in the workhouses and in the following week 2,330.[76]

In the Bantry workhouse mortality peaked with 70 dead on the week ending 27 February 1847 (the Skibbereen workhouse minute books have been lost). Mortality was at its highest level in the Dunmanway workhouse on week 20 March with 76 deaths, 16 men, 21 women and 39 children. The greatest number of deaths in the Bandon workhouse was 59 in the following week.[77] So in the workhouses of much of west Cork and in six specific parishes the number of deaths was at its highest in March rather than in April, although both were dreadful months.

In all six parishes March and April accounted for 48.4 per cent (3,548) or nearly half of the total deaths (7,332). Mortality decreased in May, from 1,710 to 1,194, thanks to the Soup-Kitchen Act. Famine and fever had already held too many in their fatal grip. In spite of all sorts of relief measures mortality remained higher in May than it had been even in February, that is 1,194 or 39 per day as against 962 or 34 per day for February. A drastic change happened only in June when mortality fell from 1,194 to 307. In July it continued to fall to 148 and finally in August-September to 48. This drop in mortality in June is confirmed by Revd Trench's letter.

The total mortality of 7,332 from a population of 43,266 is of course extremely high. According to this census the population of Schull was 17,314; Dr Traill gave it as 18,000 in 1846.[78] Professor Joseph Lee has argued that the census suffers from adult undernumeration by at least one per cent.[79] As will be apparent later emigration was already increasing in the early 1840s. The 1841 census however must remain the base from which mortality and emigration rates can be calculated as these figures were given in Marshall's return itself.

Marshall's data are not in the least exaggerated and may even be conservative; as a government inspector and a landlord like Limerick were likely to exaggerate mortality or emigration. The Skibbereen Soup Committee reported that deaths in the parish of Schull averaged 24 per day in January 1847, which would mean 744 for the month. But Marshall's return gives 'only' 349 for the whole period from September 1846 to the end of January 1847. In February Revd O'Sullivan of Goleen told how his parishioners were dying at a rate of 100 a week, but according to the return there were 'only' 211 deaths for that month, even granting that the census was based on the civil parish which is smaller than the new Catholic parish. Dr Sweetnam estimated that the average daily mortality in the parish of Schull in early February was thirty-five a day, which would mean a total of 980 for the month, but for which Marshall's return shows as 'only' 449. Dr Traill reported on 20 March how 2,000 of his people had died. The return gives the figure of 'only' about 1,407 up to that date. J. F. Maguire claimed that 2,000 or a quarter of the people of Ballydehob had perished by the beginning of May. The return puts it at 'only' 1,245 or 14.3 per cent.

A mortality rate of 16.3 per cent in the study area from September 1846 to September 1847 was very high by any comparison in either county or country. Dr S. H. Cousens calculated that mortality in the county of Cork for 1847 ranged from 5 to 5.9 per cent, which with county Leitrim's was the highest in the country, for which he gives an average mortality of 3 to 3.9 per cent. It must be recalled however that Cousens' estimate of 800,645 famine deaths for Ireland is probably too low.[80] Of the 7,332 persons who died in the six parishes men totalled 2,396 or 32.7 per cent, women 1,800 or 24.6 per cent and children 3,136 or 42.8 per cent. The high casualties among the roadworkers must account for some of the male deaths but not for others. By May 1847 the public works were stopped, while the men still had a lethal lead on the women in the race to the grave, 350 as against 279, and they still held on to their lead until September when it became twenty-two to seventeen. It is surprising that more men should have died than women. In modern famines it is usually the reverse. Fr Jack Finucane of the relief agency *Concern* has written that in the recent famines in Sudan and Ethiopia the highest mortality was among children followed by women, both of whom were more vulnerable than men.[81] Dr Mary Daly points out that in pre-famine Ireland and indeed up to the 1930s normal mortality was higher among women. Yet in famine conditions men are often more vulnerable as they need more calories. In the famine in West Holland in 1944 male mortality rose by 16 per cent and female by 7 per cent.[82] In the Irish famine men were also more vulnerable to disease. In the fever hospitals in the six parishes 196 men died compared to 193 women, but in all west Cork 674 men and 604 women died.[83]

Dr P. P. Boyle and Professor C. Ó Gráda have estimated that 'there were slightly more excess deaths among males than females', 511,000 males as compared to 474,000 females. As already stated, significantly more men died in our parishes than women, 2,396 men as against 1,800 women. This is clearly a far larger proportion than the estimate of Boyle and Ó Gráda for the whole country. These authorities argue that famine excess mortality was very close to a simple multiple of normal pre-crisis mortality, that is almost double. They show that in pre-famine times the death rate was higher among females than males.[84] This must have been true in our parishes as well. Yet in these six parishes during the famine the situation was reversed; male mortality was significantly

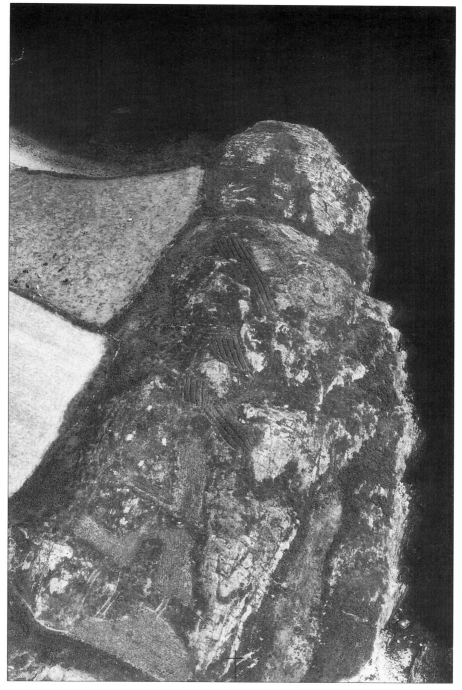

Plate 22.3   Rundale near Ballydehob (Cambridge University Collection of air photographs).

higher than female mortality although males and females were in equal numbers. So here at least famine mortality does not seem to have been a simple multiple of pre-crisis normal mortality. There was something less straightforward and more complex about it. Male mortality both increased and multiplied. Child mortality, 3,136 out of 7,332 or 42.3 per cent of the total, was very high. An unusually high infant mortality is indicated by the Catholic and Church of Ireland baptismal records.

These figures show that with the ominous exception of Goleen[85] there was no decrease in the number of baptisms as a result of the arrival of the potato blight. In the parish of Schull in the 1820s the number of baptisms was in the 200s; in the 1830s in the 300s and in the 1840s in the 400s and heading rapidly for the 500s. Then suddenly in 1847 the numbers dropped to 194; the decline was 60.7 per cent. The average decrease for all six parishes is 60.9 per cent based on the 1846 total or 65.7 per cent on the 1845 total.

Fortunately, Church of Ireland baptismal records for the Ballydehob side of Schull parish, Caheragh, Drimoleague and Drinagh, have survived:

Table 22.4
Catholic Baptisms, 1843-47

Parish	1843	1844	1845	1846	1847	Decrease percentage
Goleen	394	418	418	196	62	68.4
Schull	409	450	466	494	194	60.7
Aughadown/Kilcoe	219	257	225	301	119	60.5
Caheragh	344	316	328	348	152	56.3
Drimoleague/Drinagh	301	378	359	373	143	62.5
Total	1,667	1,819	1,796	1,712	670	60.9

Source: Parish records.

Table 22.5
Church of Ireland Baptisms, 1843-47

Parish	1843	1844	1845	1846	1847	Decrease percentage
Ballydehob	33	39	40	43	16	62.8
Caheragh	3	5	4	0	0	100.0
Drimoleague/Drinagh	—	—	20	17	14	17.6

Source: N.A. Church of Ireland parish registers, 1843-47.

One is surprised to find that the Protestant birth rate in Ballydehob was affected just as severely as the Catholic one; many Protestants however were just as poor as the Catholics. Dr Traill related how he had the charge of a 'Protestant population one of the largest rural ones in the kingdom'. It numbered 2,000 and was one whose 'destitute condition' weighed heavy on his heart.[86] Triphook visited thirteen Protestant families with dysentery near Ballydehob.[87] The lowest decrease in birth rate was among the Drimoleague and Drinagh Protestants. Many of these people would have been the larger farmers who – whether Catholic or Protestant – had more resources to weather the storm. It was this of course which was crucial rather than religion as the case of the Stout family showed.

The Goleen Catholics and the Caheragh, Drimoleague and Drinagh Protestants were the only people to reduce their birth rate after the arrival of the blight. It is strange to find no Protestant baptism for Caheragh in 1846 or 1847. The records are complete and were carefully collated by Webb. There is one baptism for 1848 and another for 1849. The Protestant population however was only 131 in 1834.[88] Yet a zero birth rate for two years tells its own story.

How many missing baptisms were there? It is possible to answer this for Catholics since their records are complete. If there had been no blight and if the number of baptisms increased from 1846 to 1847 at the same rate as it had been increasing since 1842 we can calculate that the figure would have been about 2,000 for the Catholic parishes for 1847. As it actually happened there were only 267, so the number of missing baptisms is about 1,733.

There was a corresponding number of averted marriages. In the marriage register Revd Troy annotated 'A frightful famine and fever year, alas! no marriages'. Alexander Hallowell, the Protestant curate of Bantry, could see only one couple in Bantry on Shrove Tuesday. Many women young and old came to him looking for work on the roads.[89]

The number of baptisms in the study area may be taken as roughly equivalent to live births. Why were there so many averted births? Many babies and their parents were dead. There were some abortions too. Dr Donovan observed that starvation provoked abortion and asthenic sterility, that is caused by debility.[90] In February 1847 the North Infirmary in Cork opened its door to hundreds of fever patients. Dr Popham, its medical director, reported that 'in females who are pregnant, abortion commonly took place'.[91]

The sharp decline in the number of baptisms in 1847 is of course significant but what must also be noticed is the time of the year in which most of this decrease happened. It was not so much in the spring as in the autumn and winter. For example in Caheragh parish in

March 1846 there were thirty-eight baptisms and in March 1847 only twenty-six. In December 1846 there were twenty-four births[92] but in December 1847 only three. The figures for Drimoleague are similar. This drastic decline in the number of baptisms in the autumn and winter was even more pronounced in Aughadown. In the August-October period of 1846 there had been sixty-one baptisms but in the same period of 1847 only two. In March and April 1847 there were twenty-eight baptisms but in August only one single baptism; in September there was just another one but in October none at all. The Revd Troy again gave the reason in an annotation: '*A dreadful year of Famine*, all dying of starvation, no baptisms'. It was a sign of the times that there should have been no baptism in a Catholic parish for a month and in a Protestant parish for two years.

The children that would have been born in the autumn and winter of 1847-8 would have been conceived in the winter and spring of 1846-7, but either such conceptions did not take place, or at least not nearly as frequently as hitherto. Dr Donovan noted that there was a sharp decline in fertility due to debility. Women's menstrual cycles may have often been interrupted as may happen when females suffer from starvation or trauma.[93] People must also have simply either abstained from procreation amid scenes of death or they may have been considering emigration. For these reasons then, both voluntary and involuntary, there was a severe decline in fertility and in births in 1847. Our findings are in line with the conclusion of Boyle and Ó Gráda, namely that there was a fall of 25 per cent in the fertility rate during the famine and that this translated into 315,000 averted births for the whole country.[94]

The plight of children is clearly shown by poor attendance at school. Dr Sweetnam reported in February how the national schoolmaster in Schull had told him 'that this time twelve month, he had *one hundred and forty* school children; this day he has not one. Half, he said are dead and the remainder are unable to attend for want of food and raiment, and he himself is obliged to get some situation on the roads'.[95] In March 1846 there were 123 pupils on the roll in Schull school (male) but only 14 in March 1847. In the female school there was a dramatic decrease from eighty to eleven. Out of ninety-one on the roll in Crookhaven only eight were left. In Caheragh parish the total number on the roll fell from 441 to 85 and in Drinagh from 330 to 125. Some children had been sent to work on the roads.[96]

Boyle and Ó Gráda give figures for mortality among children in Ireland as a whole from 1846 to 1851. They estimate that 472,000 children under 10 years died or 24 per cent of total mortality: children amounted to only 13 per cent of the total population. In the six parishes the number of deaths given for children is for a wider age bracket, that is under 15. Their number, 3,136 (42 per cent) out of a total of 7,332 persons dead, is extremely high compared to the rest of the country. The census commissioners of 1851 found that famine mortality was usually higher among men than women and that many children died, a fact confirmed at the local level.[97] To sum up in round numbers for the six parishes: the ratio of deaths between men, women and children was as 3:2:4. Out of every nine persons who died, three were men, two were women and four were children.

(ii) Who died and how?

Having attempted to find out how many died in the famine the next question to ask is 'Who died?' The increasing poverty of the masses of the people rendered them very vulnerable to disease. The census commissioners of 1851 wrote that fever was 'lurking in hovels and corners ..., but ever ready like an evil spirit to break out at the slightest provocation'.[98] And *phytophthora infestans* was no slight provocation.

At a hearing of the Poor Inquiry held in Ballydehob in 1833 nobody noted anybody dying of 'actual starvation' but Revd Barry had often seen cases where 'the ordinary necessaries of life would have prolonged the existence of people'. When a labourer got sick he went to his neighbours for assistance, or sometimes the farmers would send food to the sick-house. But one farmer admitted that hundreds would die before the farmers could send them anything because they were 'too much taxed and strained and troubled themselves'. Several labourers cried out in unison: 'that is the truth you are telling!' – more truth than they realised.

Those who presented Marshall's return had good reason to know of the nexus between poverty and mortality. They gave the Poor Law Valuation for each parish. Property or lack of it was a vital or mortal factor. The Poor Law Unions, the parishes of Goleen and Schull/Ballydehob are in the worst category in the country while Caheragh, Drimoleague, Drinagh and Kilcoe are in the second poorest.[99]

The highest rate of mortality (18.8 per cent) and the least amount of property per person were to be found in the most westerly or remotest district, namely Goleen. This was the last place too in which the Soup-Kitchen Act came into operation, 24 May 1847 instead of 10 May as in the others. It would however be an oversimplification to conclude that the further west the more intense was the impact of the famine. Schull and Ballydehob show very high mortality rates and a very low valuation. Kilcoe had the lowest mortality rate (9.8 per cent) and a high valuation (£1 0s. 3d.). Drimoleague and Caheragh show a high mortality rate and low valuations. One is almost ready to conclude that

Table 22.6

Mortality and property/poverty

Parish	Mortality per cent	P.L.V. (per person) £ s. d.
Goleen	18.8	11 10
Schull	17.7	12 07
Ballydehob	18.0	14 07
Kilcoe	9.8	1 00 07
Caheragh	15.8	19 02
Drimoleague	15.7	18 05
Drinagh	18.4	1 04 00

Source: Census.

mortality varied neatly in inverse proportion to valuation: the lower the valuation the higher the mortality. But the famine was seldom straightforward. Drinagh recorded a very acute mortality rate (18.4 per cent), practically as severe as the worst, Goleen, but this was combined with a valuation, £1 4s. 0d., which was the highest of all. In addition, Drinagh is located at the eastern end of the whole area so the severest mortality rates were to be found in the most easterly and the most westerly parts. But both were at the Poor Law Union extremities of the union and remote from centres where food was available. The high valuation of Drinagh is explained by Lewis who wrote that 'great improvements have been made recently in agriculture by the opening of new lines of roads' while he reported agriculture in Drimoleague was 'in a very backward state'.[100] Yet such improvements need not have greatly bettered the lot of the labourers which was invariably severely deprived.

The reasons for a high mortality rate come as no surprise in Drinagh. They had already been noted by Mr Robinson of the Drimoleague Relief Committee. Drinagh was remote, had no resident rector or gentry, no soup-kitchen had been set up there by February 1847 and it had a high proportion of labourers who were particularly poor. Now in time of crisis nearly all the large farmers dismissed them, which of course happened all over the country. Nor were the farmers well off either, the poor rate levied there in May 1847 was 10 pence in the pound while in Schull and Goleen it was a shilling and in Caheragh, Drimoleague and Kilcoe 1s. 3d.[101] Drinagh may not have paid even that much. In the part of this parish which was in the Dunmanway Union only £4 10s. 0d. had been collected by the end of 1847 and arrears amounted to £293.[102] So ultimately the case of Drinagh clearly serves to reinforce the definite correlation between poverty and mortality. This corroborates the statement of the Skibbereen Soup Committee that the famine was causing 'a mortality proportioned to the destitution'.

In addition to the number of deaths, Marshall's return categorised the causes of death under the headings of 'fever', 'dysentery' and 'destitution and other causes'. As regards what exactly 'destitution and other causes' means, the census commissioners of 1851 asserted that they are 'synonyms', that is 'want, destitution, cold and exposure, neglect ...; in Irish it is *gorta*, starvation'.[103] The following table gives the causes of death in the study area:

Table 22.7
Post-mortems (1846-47)

Cause	Number	Percentage
Fever	3,191	44
Dysentery	1,626	22
Starvation	2,515	34
Total	7,332	

Source: Marshall's return. See reference 61.

The results of these post-mortems were no doubt the opinions of lay persons rather than professionals, but one must allow that such lay persons had their own experience of fever. Dr Donovan held that the effect of food in curing fever was 'clearly proven' by this table 'drawn up by a most intelligent and zealous public officer, Mr Marshall'. The doctor further observed:

> This document shows the dreadful waste of life that occurred in this neighbourhood in the early part of 1847, exhibits the sudden falling off in mortality, even from fever, that took place on the introduction of the temporary relief act that came into operation on 10 May, and establishes the fact, that food is the best cure for Irish fever; and there is no doubt but that employment would be the best preventative.[104]

At that time, of course, the existence of microscopic organisms, *rickettsia* causing typhus and *spirochaetes* causing relapsing fever, plus the role of the louse in their transmission, had not yet been discovered.[105] Some of Ireland's leading physicians such as Dominic Corrigan held that famine and fever were simply cause and effect.[106] Dr Donovan was of the same opinion and estimated that a million people died in 1847 'from *fever, dysentery and starvation*'. He granted that at all times a large number of the poor and labouring classes fell victim to malnutrition but that until the previous year few had seen human beings die from 'absolute want of food'. He observed that the majority of those who had perished of starvation were able to provide some food which preserved life for a while, but exposure to cold or some accident 'extinguished the faint spark'. Then diarrhoea or asphyxia often preceded the fatal attack so that many attributed the resulting death to disease, whereas in reality it was the result of hunger.

Dr Donovan pointed out that starvation 'induces dysentery', and now caused 'immense mortality'. From September to October 1847 dysentery prevailed but only to a trifling degree although the poor were subsisting on diseased potatoes. But as soon as that crop was all eaten and Indian meal became the almost exclusive food of these poor people 'dysentery broke out generally and raged to a frightful extent until the spring of 1847, when the virulence of the disease began to decline in proportion as the supply of milk increased'.[107] Farmers had turnips and vegetables which lasted up to December, but from then onwards they were also obliged to eat maize and fell victims to dysentery. This doctor remarked that diarrhoea was aggravated by the 'soups (or rather slops) with which the poor were drenched'.

Dr Donovan mentions that scurvy due to lack of vitamin C resulted from exclusively eating meal. Dr M. Crawford concluded that this deficiency combined with exertion caused scurvy and sudden death due to cardiac failure among road-workers: the death of M'Kennedy of Caheragh fits into this scenario.[108] 'Dysentery was far more prevalent than fever' around Schull and Ballydehob, Dr Lamprey reported. This was because people resorted to seaweed and shellfish but more particularly to Indian meal which they could not cook properly and often had to eat raw for want of firing.[109]

Donovan also described cases of typhus where the skin had 'a dusky hue', in Irish *fiabhras dubh* or 'black fever'. Others contracted jaundice or *fiabhras buí*, 'relapsing fever'. As a rule typhus was the more fatal. Lamprey was surprised to notice that among 'the several thousands that suffered from starvation ... how comparatively rare' were cases of typhus or relapsing fever. These were more inclined to strike better-off persons; he mentioned in this context his patient Dr Traill. Lamprey considered that, regardless of the kind of famine fever that struck, medical treatment was not usually of great significance; the result depended on whether 'the individual could obtain sustenance or not'. Both doctors, Lamprey and Donovan, agreed that the principal causes of death were starvation and dysentery. Children were inclined to fall victims to dysentery. For example in the workhouse in Kilrush, county Clare, in 1850-1, 60 per cent of the children who died suffered from dysentery and diarrhoea or died of these combined with other illnesses; only 2.4 per cent died of fever.[110] Donovan concluded his 'Observations' by stating that in relation to dysentery a physician was forced to 'admit that his art can by itself do little in a disease that owes its origin to squalor, misery and starvation'.

It has already been demonstrated that of those who perished in the study area 43.5 per cent died of fever, 22.2 per cent of dysentery and 34.3 per cent of starvation. If fever and dysentery are put together to designate famine fever it would mean that 65.7 per cent died of famine fever and 34.3 per cent of starvation. The commissioners admitted that their mortality figures were only the officially recorded ones and they are far too low. For starvation in 1847 they give only a total 6,058 people. If the figure for dropsy or hunger oedema, 5,246, is added this totals 11,304. They reported that 57,095 died of fever, 25,757 of dysentery and 10,717 of diarrhoea. As the latter two were often confused it is perhaps as well to combine them and call both dysentery, so the total figure is 36,474. In 1847, 11,304 died of starvation, 57,095 of fever and 36,474 of dysentery, making a total of 104,873 in the whole country.[111] Although these figures are far too low in absolute terms the ratios may well have a certain validity:[112] 10.7 per cent died of starvation, 54.4 per cent of fever and 34.8 per cent of dysentery.

The main difference between Ireland in general and the study area specifically lies in the figures of starvation, 10.7 per cent for the country as against 34.3 per cent for the parishes. Since deaths from starvation were less likely to take place in institutions the commissioners' figures must be too low. The west-Cork data may be more representative of the country in general. To sum up for the six west Cork parishes: in round figures the ratio of the number of deaths from starvation, fever and dysentery is as 3:4:2. Out of every nine persons who perished, three died of starvation, four of fever and two of dysentery. If fever and dysentery together designate famine fever then six died of famine fever and three of starvation.

(iii) Emigration

Professor Kerby Miller estimates that between 1815 and 1844 nearly a million people left Ireland for America.[113] Such substantial emigration is reflected in west Cork. Dr Traill reported to the Poor Inquiry that 90 persons departed from his parish in 1831 and 40 in 1832; they were mainly Protestants in comfortable circumstances. The Revd Barry described the emigrants as 'tradesmen, hardy labourers and farmers with £20 to £60 capital. Others were evicted tenants or young married couples'. They went 'almost universally to Canada'. Richard Notter of

Goleen claimed that most of the people 'who could afford to emigrate would do so'.[114] Among those who left from Schull parish in 1832 were Dennis Harrigan, his wife Catherine Driscoll, and nine of their ten children. They arrived in New Brunswick, Canada, no doubt in the hold of a ship from Crookhaven or Bantry engaged in the timber trade. This Harrigan family was a link in 'chain emigration' involving many relatives. The Harrigans became lumbermen and farmers or 'sodbusters' or worked on the highways. A grandson wrote 'Grandpa Harrigan was poor but far from illiterate'.[115]

The timber trade with Canada became very important when the Scandinavian routes were blockaded during the Napoleonic wars. Arthur Lower maintains that until about 1835 conditions for passengers on the lumber ships were 'abominable' and 'probably worse than in the slave trade'. Deaths from fever and dysentery were commonplace. In 1834 alone thirty-four of these ships, carrying 731 emigrants, sank. But fares were very cheap, as little as thirty shillings from Ireland in 1835.[116]

In 1844 Revd Barry informed the Devon Commission that if locations were provided for people in the colonies or if they could pay the fare they would emigrate. There were 'very many people' who had sold their interest in the land and gone to America. They wrote letters to their friends who brought them to him to read. Accounts were 'very flattering'; they told of 'no tyranny, no oppression from landlords and no taxes'. At Ballydehob a ship or two had been freighted each of the previous five years and if they had been larger they would have been filled.[117]

Such a volume of emigration was new – some straws which showed which way the wind was blowing. Daniel Corkery wrote of the people of west Cork and of the west of the country in the following way:

> ... the natives being home-keeping to a fault: They seem not only tied to the country, but almost the parish in which their ancestors lived', Arthur Young wrote of the Catholics who had not yet learned to emigrate. Among themselves they had a proverb: 'Is maith an t-ancoire an t-iarta' (The hearth is a good anchor).[118]

Emigrant letters however like those mentioned by Barry and no doubt remittances were now pulling this anchor and the 'push' was now to come from the fear of famine as the potato rotted.

In 1845, 901 persons emigrated from Baltimore and 2,122 in 1846. In October of the same year the merchant Swanton announced that he had a boat going empty to Newport in Wales for corn and that he would give 100 free passages. Donovan soon had 80 applicants. They had no food or clothes for the voyage but the doctor got two shillings for each from the relief committee for 'sea stock'. The peculiar welcome the emigrants received at Newport comes as no surprise: they were accused of 'bringing pestilence on their backs, famine in their stomachs'. The colonial officer complained to Trevelyan who asked Routh to investigate the matter. The latter was informed that Donovan and Swanton were applying funds intended for the relief of the poor 'to shipping the wretched and naked creatures to England and Wales' and that the mayor of Newport had detained a vessel belonging to Swanton on the charge of landing paupers.[119]

Donovan held that overcrowding on ships was a 'preeminently pest-generating agent'. He related how he embarked about a hundred healthy persons on board a collier bound for Newport but it was detained by contrary winds. Fever broke out, some passengers died and many others became infected.[120] This doctor was later accused of 'shovelling paupers' into England. A woman and her son were brought before a London magistrate for begging. She said that she had come from Skibbereen and that Donovan had paid their passage. The magistrate indicated a desire to punish that doctor. The woman and child were given some bread and dismissed.[121]

Already in the spring of 1847 some people were preparing to emigrate – if they had the money 'to pay for the steam'. The Revd Triphook told Mahoney, the artist, that anybody in Ballydehob who could command £5 was emigrating in dread of fever.[122] Fares to Canada were lower than to the United States because any regulations for the safety of passengers were often not enforced. Passages to Canada cost officially from £2 10s. 0d. to £3 0s. 0d. but the United States from £3 10s. 0d. to £5 0s. 0d. But passengers could sometimes strike bargains. Ships Canada-bound, however, were more inclined to be overcrowded, fever-filled and even unseaworthy; in short, they were coffin-ships. Yet for many it was a stark choice between the coffin-ship or the hinged-coffin. William Justin Dealy of Bantry owned a ship, *The Dealy Brig* which had made at least thirteen trips to America, two per year, bringing passengers out and timber back. The following advertisement for it appeared in the *Cork Constitution* of 9 February:

> The 'Dealy' of Bantry, 400 tons, is now fitted out in a very comfortable manner for the reception of passengers and, wind and weather permitting, she will sail from Bantry for St John's, New Brunswick, about 25 March.

Cornelius Harrington of Castletownbere publicised in the same newspaper of 8 March:

> To sail direct from Berehaven, Bantry Bay, convenient to
> Skibbereen, Ballydehob, Dunmanway, for St John's, New
> Brunswick, convenient to Boston, on or about 1 April next, the
> well known fast sailing clipper barque, 'GOVERNOR DOUGLAS',
> 1,000 tons burthen; the splendid clipper ship, 'OCEAN', 400 tons.
> The above ships will be fitted up in a superior manner for the
> accommodation of passengers.
> N.B. Passengers by these ships will be supplied with one pound
> of biscuit, daily during the voyage according to the Act of
> Parliament.

Interestingly, St John's is described as 'convenient to Boston'. Up to
now about a third of the Irish emigrants crossed into the United States,
getting in by the 'back door'. This was becoming all the more
necessary because Congress wanted to know nothing of Irish Catholic
paupers and was already passing even stricter passenger acts.[123]

We shall now follow these good ships *Dealy, Governor Douglas* and
Ocean to see how they fared. An emigrant agent reported that they
were in quarantine in Partridge Island in the Port of St John's, New
Brunswick on 31 May. The passenger list of the *Dealy* numbered 169 of
whom twenty-two had died at sea, forty were sick on landing and
three had since died 'like fish out of the water'. The number of passage
days is not given. The *Dealy* was something of a coffin-ship. The
Governor Douglas carried 261 passengers in thirty-two passage days
which was normal and the *Ocean* had eighty-nine on board for thirty-
one days. Nobody from either ship had died at sea or since landing.
The *Ocean* was among the ships whose passengers were satisfied with
food and water and general conditions aboard although she had only
temporary decks of uncaulked planks. The medical officer for the
quarantine station in Partridge Island reported early in June how she
had been discharged. The *Governor Douglas* and the *Dealy Brig*
however were still detained:

> These cases have been severe, the fever having returned, and the
> greater number of the passengers have suffered from the disease
> after landing the sick; many of the others on board in a day or
> two would be attacked, and it was impossible to land all the
> passengers from the fever vessels for purification for want of
> accommodation, as the tents would only contain the sick.

There were 450 sick on the island at the time. Nevertheless, the
medical officer stated that our ships were undergoing purification and
would shortly be released.[124]

As the summer approached more and more emigrants rushed towards the ports, indicating almost panic emigration:

> Their only anxiety seemed to be to leave Ireland. ... the United States, or the British Colonies – they cared not which ... a convenient ship was their only object – hence ships calling at Baltimore, Crookhaven and Bantry took off large numbers who had not the means of proceeding to Cork.[125]

Although it was a precipitative emigration it was not by any means all pauper emigration. The Revd FitzPatrick of Skibbereen noted that a good many 'substantial farmers' were leaving.[126] Thomas Swanton of Cranliath complained that 'some of the best tenants were going off with three years' rent'.[127] Thomas Gibbons also reported that tenants were using the rent as passage money, leaving 'the dregs' behind. Others would make a deal with the landlord knowing that it would cost him money to evict them legally: 'I go out quietly if you give me £2'.[128] There must have been many labourers among these emigrants too as Dr David FitzPatrick has shown for the rest of Ireland.[129] This emigration may have been similar to that of the 1830s which Barry described as being composed of tradesmen, hardy labourers and farmers with capital rather than 'the dregs'.

The emigrants from the six west-Cork parishes who left from Cork are among the thousands whose surnames are on the ship lists of passengers.[130] One vessel leaving Baltimore was the *Malvina*. On board were 183 passengers and she arrived in St John's on 9 May, only one man dying aboard.[131] The *Leviathan* also left Baltimore and arrived, only two persons having died at sea.[132] The *Margaret Hughes* of Sherkin Island no doubt took islanders and others to Liverpool. On 7 May she sailed back to Sherkin and then westward to St John's with a complement of emigrants.[133] By August the *Dealy Brig* had returned from New Brunswick with cargo and would soon sail again for St John's.[134]

Grosse Isle below Quebec quickly became notorious. The *Sir Henry Pottinger* left Cork with 399 passengers; on arrival at that island 112 were sick and ninety-eight had died.[135] In September the names were published of 300 persons who had left Cork and died there between 8 May and 3 July.[136] On ships bound for Canada from Liverpool and Sligo one passenger in fourteen died at sea but on ships from Cork it was one in nine.[137] Although mortality was not quite so horrific at St John's in New Brunswick it was still high. The official figures for 1847 are as follows: of the 17,074 who landed or hoped to land in New Brunswick, 823 died at sea, 697 died in quarantine and 595 in hospital.

Mortality was 12.4 per cent.[138] Others must have died but there is no record. Mortality could have been almost as high as in the study area. Many others were inevitably left behind. The parents of Thomas Sullivan (13) from Schull may have died on Grosse Isle. He was placed in a Quebec Catholic orphanage in November 1847. Such children were usually adopted but he 'went into service'.

We can trace two of the emigrants who went to Canada at this time. Henry Field and his wife, Mary Driscoll, and their five or six children left Dunbeacon between Ballydehob and Bantry. They landed probably at Quebec around the time of the famine. By 1850 their names appear in church and civil records. They are clearing 'stony farm-wood lots' high in the Gatineau Valley, thirty-five miles north-east of Ottawa. Their settlement, now a village, was called Fieldville.[139]

Many emigrants departed from Cobh to America, for example the mother, brother and sister of Jeremiah O'Donovan Rossa from the neighbouring parish of Rosscarbery in 1848. His father had died as a result of working on a famine road. His mother and family were evicted. A brother who had already emigrated to Philadelphia sent the passage tickets – a classic example of the operation of 'push' and 'pull' forces. Rossa was left alone in Ireland, he recalled:

> At Reenascreena cross we parted ... Five or six other families were going away ... The cry of the weeping and the wailing of that day rings in my ears still. That time it was a cry heard every day at every cross-road in Ireland.[140]

The last part of Ireland most of them would ever see again was the Fastnet Rock which came to be called *deor Éireann*, 'Ireland's tear'.

Marshall's return provides not only figures for emigration from each parish for the period 1 September 1846 to 12 September 1847 but also the destination, either England or America, and are tabulated as follows:

Table 22.8
Emigration

Parish	North America	England	Total	Percentage
Goleen	22	45	67	0.9
Schull	225	155	380	4.4
Ballydehob	105	96	201	2.3
Kilcoe	78	17	95	4.1
Caheragh	38	85	123	1.5
Drimoleague	54	12	66	1.2
Drinagh	13	52	65	2.6
Total	535	462	997	

In all 535 persons left the six parishes for America and 462 for England, the total being 997. As in the case of mortality there is a difference between the peninsular parishes, namely Goleen, Kilcoe and Schull, and the inland ones, Caheragh, Drimoleague and Drinagh. In the peninsular parishes the majority of emigrants went to America, 430 and 313 to England. In the inland parishes, however, more went to England, 149 as compared to 105. There are two exceptions: in Goleen twenty-two went to America and fifty-four to England while in Drimoleague fifty-four went to America and twelve to England. Many of those who went to England must have travelled via Cork and must be among the people from the western districts who, according to Dr Popham, brought fever with them to the cheap lodging-houses from where it spread everywhere.[141]

(iv) Relation between mortality and emigration

As Miller and Donnelly found, the relationship between mortality and emigration is usually inverse, that is the higher the mortality the lower the emigration and vice versa. Donnelly states that this pattern is perhaps clearest in Galway, Clare and west Cork where excess deaths were high and emigration relatively low.[142] The study area conforms to this pattern.

The average mortality rate of 16.3 per cent was high compared to the rest of the county and country. The average emigration rate of 2.4 per cent was correspondingly low. Cousens estimated that emigration for county Cork in 1847 was from 10 per cent to 12 per cent and in north Connaught, south Ulster and Leinster around 20 per cent.[143] Within our area alone there were local variations at parish level and they were most pronounced in the cases of Kilcoe and Goleen. Kilcoe has by far the lowest mortality rate and highest emigration rate while Goleen recorded the highest mortality rate and the lowest emigration rate. Schull and Ballydehob show a similar mortality rate, and an average

Table 22.9
Mortality and emigration

Parish	Mortality (percentage)	Emigration (percentage)
Goleen	18.8	0.9
Schull	17.7	4.4
Ballydehob	18.0	2.3
Kilcoe	9.8	4.1
Caheragh	15.8	1.5
Drimoleague	15.7	1.2
Drinagh	18.4	2.6
Average	16.3	2.4

low mortality rate for the parish. Caheragh and Drimoleague indicated the same high mortality rate and also coincided in their low emigration rate. Drinagh's mortality rate was practically as high as that of Goleen, 18.4 per cent compared to 18.8 per cent, yet Drinagh's emigration rate is not nearly as low as Goleen's, 2.6 per cent as compared to 0.9 per cent. No doubt Drinagh was not quite as remote from Cork city but Goleen had a port of its own at Crookhaven and Bantry too was nearby. The differences rested not so much in remoteness but more in the incidence of small holdings. Drinagh had £1 4s. 0d. to support each human being whereas Goleen had only £0 11s. 9d.

A clear correlation between mortality, emigration, and also between poverty and geographical location or remoteness is evident. Kilcoe parish recorded of the lowest mortality rate, the highest emigration rate, the second highest Poor Law Valuation and the least remote location (being towards the centre of the Union). Similarly, the highest mortality rate, the lowest emigration rate, the lowest Poor Law Valuation and the remotest location were all characteristics of Goleen parish.

Marshall's figures for the famine of 1846-47 in the six parishes are solid and revealing: out of a population of 43,266 persons 7,355 died and 997 emigrated. In round figures for every forty-three persons seven died and only one emigrated. For many of the destitute it was, as the Revd Webb remarked, simply a matter of 'an awful mode of emigration – emigration to the next world, without even the expense of a coffin'.[144]

It has already been demonstrated how, by September 1847, famine mortality had decreased to a minimum. There were fears that it would rise again as winter approached, but such fears were mercifully not realised. Marshall was introducing the Poor-Law Extension Act with the same efficiency with which he had put the Soup-Kitchen Act into operation in the Skibbereen Union. By December upwards of 7,000 persons were on the out-door relief lists and there was room in the workhouse for 200 more. Forty tickets to the poor-house were offered to people on the outdoor relief lists; refusing them meant that they were removed from the lists. Such was 'the workhouse test'. The poor rates were being payed reasonably well. More that 15,000 children in 100 schools were being fed by the British Relief Association under the direction of Count Strzelecki. However, Marshall reported that fever and dysentery prevailed in some parts of the union and that the hospitals were full. Yet in January 1848 he noted 'very few deaths' occurred. In Ballydehob and Kilcoe only four persons who were on outdoor relief had died during the previous three months.[145] Any deaths that were now taking place were mainly in the fever hospitals. These had been opened in May 1847 and were all closed by June 1848, except the one at Schull which remained open until 1850. The total number of deaths in these hospitals was 413 as already given, but those which had occurred between May and September 1847 were undoubtedly already counted in Marshall's return.

In parts of the west of Ireland the famine conditions of 1847 deteriorated. Ignatius Murphy in referring to west Clare noted: 'What happened in the next three to four years made 1845-7 look like the good times of the past'.[146] Mercifully this was not to be the case in the Skibbereen Union or in west Cork. But it does seem that, as Captain Caffin confirmed, the famine was more severe in west Cork in 1847 than in the west of Ireland. One of the few deaths which Marshall had to report was that of Dr Brady of the Caheragh fever hospital. He had replaced Dr McCormick of Goleen who was on duty in the Kilcoe fever hospital; the latter became ill with fever but recovered.[147] Brady was one of the 36 casualties among the 473 medical men appointed to special fever duty by the Board of Health – an unlucky one in thirteen. In all, 123 doctors died of fever in 1847.[148]

Forty Church of Ireland clergymen experienced fever-related deaths in 1847.[149] In 1850 R. B. Townsend, rector of Abbeystrewary or Skibbereen, died of fever caught in the workhouse,[150] 'a magnet for misery', where 3,909 died between 1842 and 1851. In the Schull workhouse 165 died during 1850-51 making a total of 4,074 for the two workhouses.[151] The *Catholic directory* lists the names of thirty-five priests who also died of fever in 1847 but it is by no means complete. Twenty-six priests fell victims in England including ten in Liverpool alone.[152] At least eleven priests died in the dioceses of Cork and Ross during the famine period; the list includes D. McSwiney, Bandon; P. Walsh, Sherkin Island; M. Ross, Castlehaven. Laurence O'Sullivan of Goleen went down with fever in 1847 but survived.[153] Professor Trench also survived an attack.[154] Workhouse staff and government inspectors died at their posts. Early in 1849 Marshall himself joined the famine victims he had so well enumerated. Fever or cholera claimed him as well as fifteen other inspectors including Captain Lang of Bantry.[155]

Conclusion

As regards responsibility for the catastrophe, attitudes of those who lived through it have been diverse. The Revd Kelleher maintained that a 'great distinction' should be made between the 'crimes and cruelties' of the Irish landlords and English statesmen on the one hand and on the other 'those generous hearted Britons who have made sacrifices to stay the steps of famine'.[156] Some were offended by the anti-Irish feelings of *The Times*. Revd Webb, like Revd Kelleher, recognised English generosity and exclaimed: 'Thank God, England is not *The Times*'.[157] But it 'sickened' the heart of O'Donovan Rossa to think of the 'starved and the murdered of Schull and Skibbereen'.[158]

According to the principles of Malthus 'pestilence and plague' and 'gigantic and inevitable famine' are nature's most radical corrective to severe overpopulation.[159] Was Malthus right in the case of Ireland? Karl Marx lamented that the country was viewed as 'the promised land', as it exemplified the fulfilment of some Malthusian prognostications.[160] The six parishes would indeed seem to be part of that 'promised land'. Yet Malthus was only partly correct. There were indeed plague and famine but these were not inevitable. No doubt a certain amount of mortality would have been difficult to avoid; in our own time we are not always able to prevent deaths when ecological disasters strike poor, stressed and densely-populated regions. Yet the magnitude and duration of the Irish famine mortality is another matter. Many maintained that Westminster could have done more. Those who expressed such views would not have been extreme Repealers either, for instance Hugh Parker from Yorkshire, a major in the British Army, and William Thomas from Cornwall, a mining captain. The latter was scandalised to think that 'in a Christian country, in a time of profound peace' people should be left to live or die 'on political economy'.[161]

Apart altogether from England could not the east of Ireland have done more to help the west? Why were there not a few others like the Trenches? Many landlords, large farmers and the rich in general could have given greater succour to the poor. McCarthy Downing, the solicitor, said that the farmers 'dealt more hardy' with the labourers than the landlords did with themselves.[162] As A. M. Sullivan witnessed: 'sauve qui peut had resounded throughout the country ..., human nature had become contracted in it sympathies'.[163] The annals record a famine in the summer of 1433 which was called 'a greedy summer', samhradh na mearaithne, 'the summer of the slight acquaintances',[164] as nobody would recognise friend or relative. The great famine saw a succession of such summers.

The churches emerge with fair credit from this famine. The number of victims among their clergy testifies to their efforts. But it was only a small part of what Canon O'Rourke called 'the bright and copious fountains of living charity which gushed forth'[165] in spite of the indifference of some. No doubt the controversy about souperism was unedifying, the case of William A. Fisher, rector of Kilmoe or Goleen, was a classic example.[166] Worse still, souperism – both myth and reality – distracted attention not only at the time but ever since from the heroic charity of men such as Traill, Townsend, Webb and the Trenches. There is much truth in Professor Louis Cullen's claim that 'The Famine was less a national disaster than a social and regional one'.[167] In the study area this subsistence crisis was indeed a social disaster, *gorta dubh*. We have seen how those who presented Marshall's return declared that it was 'a criterion by which the public may judge the good results of that [Soup-Kitchen] act generally'. The return is, however, a two-edged sword. It can also be used as a criterion by which the public may judge the bad results of the other relief acts generally. The amount of the ensuing mortality has been made known for the six parishes at least, as Lord Bentinck foretold that it would be for the whole country. He was right too in warning the members of the House of Commons that it was on this mortality that the public and the world at large would 'be able to estimate at its proper worth' their management of the affairs of Ireland. Already he had a presentiment that one day there might be people whose estimate would provoke them to raise such a cry as 'Revenge for Skibbereen!'.

Acknowledgment
I wish to thank Professor C. Ó Gráda, U.C.D., and Dr R. V. Comerford, Maynooth, for comments on an earlier draft.

References
1. *S.R.*, 29 Nov. 1847, 4 Mar. 1847.
2. In this chapter 'mortality' always designates 'excess or famine mortality'.
3. *C.C.*, 1 Nov. 1845.
4. Thomas to Beamish, 21, 22 Aug. 1846, Beamish to Trevelyan, 24 Aug. 1846, Trevelyan to Beamish 28 Aug. 1846 in *Correspondence from July 1846 to January 1847 relating to the measures adopted for the relief of distress in Ireland (Commissariat series), Famine, Ireland, Irish University Press series of British Parliamentary Papers*, v (Shannon, 1970), pp. 450-1 (hereafter *Comm. corr.*).
5. 9 and 10 Vic., c. 107 (28 Aug. 1846).
6. P. Hickey, 'A study of four peninsular parishes in west Cork, 1796-1855', unpublished M.A. thesis, U.C.C. (1980).
7. *C.C.*, 17 Sept. 1846; *S.R.*, 17 Sept. 1846; *C.E.*, 19 Sept., 1846.
8. Hickey, 'Four peninsular parishes', p. 341.
9. Dr Donovan, 'Memoir of his experience during the Famine written for the author' in J. O'Rourke (ed.), *The history of the Irish famine of 1847, with notices of earlier famines* (Dublin, 1875), pp. 233-5.
10. *S.R.*, 5 Dec. 1846; O'Rourke, *Famine*, pp. 145-6.
11. *C.E.*, 30 Nov. 1846.
12. *S.R.*, 1 Dec. 1846.
13. *C.C.*, 29 Dec. 1846.
14. *C.E.*, 6 Jan. 1847.
15. Parker to Jones, 31 Dec. 1846, Trevelyan to Routh, 5 Jan. 1847, Routh to Trevelyan, 7 Jan. 1847, Treasury Minute, 8 Jan. 1847 all in *Comm. corr.*; O'Rourke, *Famine*, pp 877-81.
16. *S.R.*, 14 Jan. 1847.
17. N.A., *Statement of the present condition of the Skibbereen Poor Law Union District*

to the Relief Commissioners, Skibbereen, February 1 1847, pp 2-3; 13014, Relief Commission (hereafter R.C.).

18. *S.R.*, 28 Jan. 1847.
19. Sweetnam to Limerick, 19 Jan. 1847, Limerick to Relief Commissioners, 19 Jan. 1847 both in R.C. 9360.
20. *C.E.*, 3 Feb. 1847.
21. *C.C.*, 5 Jan. 1850. He was now parish priest, Dunmanway, after Revd M. Doheny.
22. Bishop to Routh, 27 Jan. 1847 in *Comm. corr.*, i, vii, pp 397-98.
23. *C.C.*, 6 Feb. 1847.
24. 8 Feb. 1847, *Hansard*, 3rd series, lxxxiv, cols 944-45.
25. 10 and 11 Vic., c. 7 (26 Feb. 1847).
26. *Comm. corr.*, i, vii, p. 388.
27. *C.E.*, 8 Feb. 1847.
28. *C.C.*, 7 Feb. 1847.
29. Noble to Routh, 2 Feb. 1847 in R.C., p. 10151.
30. *Illustrated London News*, 13 Feb. 1847. One of these girls later married a John Synge and became the mother of John Millington Synge; see R. Skelton, *Synge and his world* (London, 1973), p. 9; P. Hickey, 'The visit of the artist, James Mahony, to west Cork in 1847' in *The O'Mahony Journal*, xii (1982), pp 26-32.
31. A predecessor of the present writer.
32. *Illustrated London News*, 20 Feb. 1847.
33. *C.E.*, 3 Feb. 1847.
34. Also in *C.C.*, 18 Feb. 1847. Italics in this chapter always denote original text.
35. Bishop to Trevelyan, 19 Feb. 1847 in *Comm. corr.* ii, vii, p. 552.
36. *C.C.*, 26 Jan. 1847.
37. Robinson to Bishop, 12 Feb. 1847 in R.C., 9842.
38. Bishop to Trevelyan, 14 Feb. 1847, *Comm. corr.*, ii, p. 486.
39. O'Rourke, *Famine*, p. 408.
40. *C.C.*, 18 Feb. 1847; *C.E.*, 19 Feb 1847; *F.J.*, 19 Feb. 1847.
41. Trevelyan to Burgoyne, 18 Feb. 1847 Burgoyne to Trevelyan, 22 Feb. 1847 in *Comm. corr.*, ii, vii, pp. 518-23.
42. *C.C.*, 18. Feb. 1847.
43. Ibid., *C.C.*, 18 Mar. 1847.
44. *C.E.*, 3 Mar. 1847.
45. *C.C.*, 3 Mar. 1847.
46. R.C., 13369.
47. *The Nation*, 13 Mar. 1847; *C.C.* 3 Apr. 1847.
48. N.A., Church of Ireland parish registers (microfilm).
49. All other references are to Revd James Barry.
50. Trench to *Saunder's News Letter*, 22 Mar. 1847 in W. S. Trench, *Realities of Irish life* (London, 1868), pp 389-397; *C.C.*, 27 Apr. 1847; *S.R.*, 29 Apr. 1847.
51. *C.C.*, 27 Apr. 1847.
52. He became the next Archbishop of Dublin (1864-84) after Dr Whately, see *D.N.B.* xix, pp. 1118-21.
53. R. C. Trench, *Letters and memorials ed. by the author of Charles Lowder*, i, (London, 1886), p. 286; R. C. Trench to F. F. Trench in Trench, *Realities*, p. 406.
54. *Census of Ireland 1851* (Dublin, 1853), pt v, i, pp 287.
55. *C.C.*, 22 Apr. 1947.
56. 9 Vic., cap. 6.
57. *Third report of the Relief Commissioners with appendix, 1847* in *Comm. corr.*, viii, p. 124.

58. *C.E.*, 12 May 1847.

59. Treasury 64/363B, Gibbons to Jones, 19 Apr. 1847, enclosure in Jones to Trevelyan, 24 Apr. 1847.

60. J. S. Donnelly, Jr, 'The soup kitchens' in *New. hist. Ire.*, vii, p. 308.

61. 'Marshall's return', *C.C.* 5 Oct. 1847; *S.R.* 5 Oct. 1847.

62. The eastern side of Drinagh parish, in the Dunmanway Union, is not included here nor in the figures for mortality and emigration to follow.

63. T. P. O'Neill, 'The administration of relief' in R. D. Edwards and T. D. Williams (ed.), *The great famine: studies in Irish history 1845-52* (Dublin, 1956), p. 242.

64. Donnelly, 'Soup kitchens', p. 309.

65. P. Hickey, 'Cross is a reminder of famine times' in *C.E.*, 24 Mar. 1989.

66. *S.R.*, 17 July 1847.

67. 10 Vic. c. 31.

68. *The Nation*, 25 Sept. 1847; 2 Oct. 1847.

69. C. E. Trevelyan, *The Irish crisis* (London, 1848), pp 64-65.

70. *C.C.*, 5 Oct. 1847; *S.R.*, 5 Oct. 1847 (hereafter cited as 'Marshall's return').

71. J. Mokyr, *Why Ireland starved: a quantitative and analytical history of the Irish economy, 1800-1845* (London, 1985), pp. 262-66; P. P. Boyle and C. Ó Gráda, 'Fertility trends, excess mortality, and the great Irish famine' in *Demography*, xxiii (1986), p. 555.

72. *Census 1851*, pt v, i, 243.

73. *C.C.*, 22 Mar. 1847.

74. *The Nation*, 15 May, 3 Jun., 19 Jun., 1847.

75. Ibid., 29 Apr. 1847.

76. S. H. Cousens, 'The regional variation in mortality during the great Irish famine' in *R.I.A. Proc.*, 63 C, no. 3, 1963, p. 131.

77. Workhouse minute books, 1847.

78. *C.C.*, 7 Jan. 1847.

79. J. Lee, 'On the accuracy of pre-Famine Irish censuses' in J. M. Goldstrom and L. A. Clarkson (ed.), *Irish population economy and society: essays in honour of the late K. H. Connell* (Oxford, 1981), p. 54.

80. Cousens, 'Regional mortality', p. 130.

81. Pers. comm.

82. M. E. Daly, *The famine in Ireland* (Dublin, 1986), pp 100-01.

83. *Census 1851*, pt v, ii p. 35.

84. Boyle and Ó Gráda, 'Fertility trends', pp. 554-61.

85. These records are evidently complete.

86. *C.C.*, 7 Jan. 1847; *F.J.*, 23 Apr. 1847.

87. Newman to Grey, 4 Jan. 1847 in *Comm. corr.* ii, I.U.P., *Famine*, vol. 5, p. 460.

88. *Parl. gaz.*, p. 294.

89. *C.C.*, 13 Mar. 1847.

90. See note 104.

91. J. Popham, 'Report on the epidemic fevers ...' in *Dublin medical press*, viii (1849), p. 279.

92. One of these was Catherine Caverly, Cullanuller, whose godfather and grandfather was Eugene Hickey, a great-great-grandfather of the present author.

93. On starvation and fertility see J Bongaarts, 'Does malnutrition affect fecundity?' in *Science,* ccviii (1980), pp 564-69.

94. Boyle and Ó Gráda, 'Fertility trends', p. 554.

95. *C.C.*, 25 Feb. 1847.

96. *Fourteenth report of the commissioners of national education for the year 1847,*

pp 85-91, [981], H.C., 1847-48, xxix, pp. 219-225.

97. *Census 1851*, pt v, i, pp. 247, 253.
98. Ibid, pt v, ii. p. 240.
99. Cousens, 'Regional mortality', p. 129.
100. Lewis, *Topog. dict. Ire.*, i, pp. 497, 504.
101. *C.C.*, 29 May 1847.
102. Dunmanway workhouse minute book.
103. *Census 1851*, part V, i. p. 470.
104. D. Donovan, 'Observations on the peculiar disease to which the famine of last year gave origin and on the morbid effects of insufficient nourishment' in *Dublin medical press*, xix (1848), pp 67-68, 129-32, 257-58.
105. W. P. MacArthur, 'The medical history of the famine' in Edwards and Williams, *Famine*, pp 265-67.
106. P. Froggatt, 'The response of the medical profession to the great famine' in E. M. Crawford, *Famine: the Irish experience 900-1900: subsistence crises and famines in Ireland* (Edinburgh, 1989), p. 139.
107. On milk see E. M. Crawford, 'Dearth, diet and disease in Ireland, 1850: a case study of nutritional deficiency' in *Medical history*, xxviii (1984), pp. ??.
108. M. Crawford, 'Scurvy in Ireland during the Great Famine' in *Social history of medicine*, i, no. 3 (1988), p. 299.
109. 'Report on the epidemic fever in Ireland' in *Dublin journal of medical science*, vii (1849), pp. 103-04.
110. I. Murphy, 'Children in the Kilrush Union during the Great Famine' in *North Munster antiquarian journal*, xxiv (1982), p. 80.
111. *Census 1851*, part v, ii, 247-53.
112. S. H. Cousens, 'Regional death rates in Ireland during the great famine, from 1846 to 1851' in *Population Studies*, xiv, no. 1 (July 1960), p. 69.
113. K. A. Miller, *Emigrants and exiles* (New York and Oxford, 1985), p. 29.
114. Hickey, 'Four peninsular parishes', p. 212.
115. The youngest and only child of the Harrigans to be born in Canada was Dennis, who later married Catherine Ahearn and went to Minnesota, U.S.A. They were the maternal grandparents of the singer, Bing Crosby; see J. A. King, *The Irish lumberman-farmer* (Lafayette, 1982), p. 180; M. E. Fitzgerald, *The uncounted Irish in Canada and the United States* (Toronto, 1990), p. 292. W. D. Hamilton, *Old North Esk on the Miramichi* (Fredericton, 1979), p. 190.
116. A. R. M. Lower, *Great Britain's woodyard* (Montreal, 1973), pp 242-23.
117. Hickey, 'Four peninsular parishes', p. 270.
118. D. Corkery, *The hidden Ireland* (Dublin, 1975), p. 23.
119. Hickey, 'Four peninsular parishes', p. 441.
120. Donovan, 'Observations', p. 131.
121. *C.E.*, 30 July 1849.
122. *Illustrated London News*, 20 Feb. 1847.
123. T. Coleman, *Passage to America* (London, 1992), p. 134.
124. *Papers relative to emigration to British North American provinces, 1847-48*, pp 58-60, [50], H.C., 1849, xlvii, pp 254-56.
125. *S.R.*, 20 May 1847.
126. *F.J.*, 12 Mar. 1847.
127. *C.C.*, 3 Apr. 1847.
128. See note 59.
129. D. Fitzpatrick, 'Emigration, 1801-70' in *New hist. Ire.*, v, p. 577.
130. *The famine immigrants; lists of Irish immigrants arriving at the port of New York*

1846-1851 (Baltimore, 1983).

131. See note 124.

132. *C.C.*, 16 Sept. 1847.

133. J. Coombes, 'The cruise of the Margaret Hughes' in *Cork Holly Bough*, 1974, pp. ??.

134. *C.C.*, 21 Aug. 1847.

135. *C.C.*, 4 Sept. 1847.

136. *C.C.*, 21 Sept. 1847.

137. O. MacDonogh, 'Irish emigration to the United States of America and the British colonies during the famine' in Edwards and Williams, *Famine*, p. 366.

138. Coleman, *America*, p. 151.

139. M. O'Gallagher, *Grosse Isle: gateway to Canada 1833-1937* (Montreal, 1984), p. 135; Private correspondence from Grant Maxwell, a relation of the Fields as is also the present writer.

140. D. O'Donovan Rossa, *Rossa's recollections, 1838-1898* (Shannon, 1972), p. 142.

141. See note 91.

142. J. S. Donnelly, Jnr, 'Excess mortality and emigration' in *New hist. Ire.*, v, p. 355.

143. S. H. Cousens, 'The regional pattern of emigration during the great famine, 1846-1851' in *Transactions and papers of the Institute of British Geographers*, xxviii (1960), p. 121.

144. *S.R.*, 19 Jan. 1847.

145. Marshall to Commissioners, 20 Jan. 1848 in *Papers relating to the relief of distress and state of the unions in Ireland, 1848; Famine*, iii, p. 936.

146. I. Murphy, 'Kilkee and its neighbourhood during the second year of the great famine, 1846-1847' in *North Munster Antiquarian Journal*, xxiii (1981), p. 87.

147. *S.R.*, 6 Apr. 1847.

148. P. Froggatt, 'The response of the medical profession to ???', p. 148.

149. Daly, *Famine*, p. 68.

150. *C.C.*, 14 May 1850.

151. *Census 1851*, pt v, ii, pp. 14-15.

152. *Battersby's registry ... or Catholic directory of 1848* (Dublin, 1848), pp 341-42.

153. P. Hickey, 'Laurence O'Sullivan, P.P. Goleen (1828-48)'; E. Harris, 'Souper Sullivan' in *The Fold* (1986), pp 9-11.

154. Trench, *'Letters'*, p. 286.

155. *Second annual report of the commissioners for the administration of the laws for the relief of the poor in Ireland*, (Dublin, 1849), p. 14.

156. *C.E.*, 4 Sept. 1848.

157. *C.C.*, 27 Mar. 1847.

158. O'Donovan Rossa, *Recollections*, p. 148.

159. T. R. Malthus, *An essay on the principles of population* (London, 1973), pp. 44-45.

160. Quoted from *Das kapital*, in *Karl Marx and Frederick Engles; Ireland and the Irish question* (Moscow, 1971), p. 106.

161. *S.R.*, 13 Feb. 1847.

162. *C.E.*, 19 Aug. 1846.

163. A. M. Sullivan, *New Ireland*, i (Glasgow, 1877), p. 142.

164. E. M. Crawford, 'William Wilde's table of Irish famines, 900-1850' in Crawford, *Famine*, p. 7.

165. O'Rourke, *Famine*, p. 522.

166. Hickey, 'Four peninsular parishes', pp. 500-55.

167. L. M. Cullen, *An economic history of Ireland since 1660* (London, 1987), p. 132.

Plate 22.4   Boy and girl at Caheragh (*Illustrated London News*, 13 Feb. 1847).

Chapter 23

COUNTY CORK FOLKLORE AND ITS COLLECTION

GEARÓID Ó CRUALAOICH

The discipline of ethnology is under-represented in studies of the culture of Irish communities. This chapter is a contribution to the inclusion of an ethnological focus within the overall attempt to portray the life-style and world-view of the people of county Cork as these are reflected in history and oral tradition. The article seeks to draw attention to the considerable research resource that exists in the archive of primary ethnographic material deriving from the activities of the Irish Folklore Commission whose field-workers were active from the 1930s. The work of the Commission is nowadays the concern of the Department of Irish Folklore at University College, Dublin. It interests the folklore sections of Departments of Modern Irish and Irish History at other Irish universities, such as the *Béaloideas*/Irish Folklore division of the Department of Irish History at University College, Cork. The folklore sources also fall within the ambit of Departments of Anthropology and Sociology among others. With current moves towards interdisciplinary study and collaborative research, one envisages that the analysis of regional culture will henceforth address the materials of popular tradition – including folklore – as a fundamental part of the enterprise to describe and interpret the cultural heritage of all Irish communities.

The nature of folklore

The study of folklore deals with the collective representations and expressions of the popular world-view of communities or groups in a region's general population. At the heart of every such perspective is the creativity involved in acts of memory and imagination. Thus every world-view is being constantly renewed and recreated in the sayings and doings of individuals.[1] If we think of folklore as kinds of knowledge, then we think of individual members of a community or a group as carriers of that knowledge who participate in the process of remembering, performing and transmitting it to others in an ongoing way throughout both time and space. Like language or culture, viewed in their most general sense as human capacities acquired by socialisation and learning, folklore is globally unbounded. Just as the disciplines of linguistics and anthropology treat, for convenience sake, of the Dutch language or Nepalese culture, so too folklorists treat of areal, national, regional and local folklore under such labels as North-Western European, Irish, Munster, West Muskerry and so on. Folklore studies progress up and down the orders of discrimination and discreteness between the individual performer/informant and humankind as a species.

In this way we can understand the somewhat notional status of the concept 'county Cork folklore'. The representations and expressions of the popular world-view of communities and groups within Cork county both share features of these world-views with those of other communities and groups 'outside' and vary very significantly 'inside', among themselves, from time to time and from place to place. Nevertheless, we may usefully focus on something called 'the folklore of county Cork' if we bear in mind the essentially creative and process-based nature of folklore, as of all culture.

Folk knowledge, that popular world-view represented and expressed in the sayings and doings of communities or groups, is not always in verbal form only. Certainly what we call the major and minor genres of oral literature (tales, legends, folksongs, proverbs, riddles, nicknames etc.) are a conspicuous element of folklore but there are other features of comparable prominence. What we call material culture, for instance, the artefactual products of vernacular traditions of housing, clothing, food production, cooking, music-making and so on, is another significant domain of folklore. A third important aspect is that of popular religion. This involves the rituals and beliefs associated both with cults of popular Christianity and with partly-Christianised practices. The latter mostly derive from the ancestral or 'pagan' cosmology associated with pre-Christian religious systems in Ireland, for example, holy well cults.

All folk knowledge, all folklore, whether verbal or material or ritual/symbolic, is partly defined and identified by virtue of its being the subject and the product of the folklore process. As has been suggested, this means that folk tradition derives from a popular creative response to the experience of living in the world. It is the popular remembrance and expression of the collective representation of that experience by individual carriers. Such carriers of folklore act as performers and informants in respect of it, continually reshaping and renewing folk tradition out of their own creative adaptation of it by means of memory and imagination. Genuine folk tradition is a dynamic and developing popular channel of culture that flows largely outside of the formal – or official – channels of élite cultural communication. Such formal and official channels as schooling, print and broadcast media, industrial design, commercial training, church ceremonial and religious education, transmit official and élite versions of world-view. They disseminate standardised texts, orthodox beliefs and manufactured goods which in essence lack the personalised, spontaneous creativity that is the hallmark of folklore, verbal or otherwise.

Most people in Ireland today live in cultural worlds that seem filled up almost entirely with the products of formal, official, élite cultural communication. Folklore is thought of as something from the past, from a more innocent, pre-modern world. But the folklore process is an integral part of the cultural life of every group or community since all groups, of whatever size, consist of individuals who are, every single one, continually engaged in individual acts of memory and imagination and in behaviours that are informed by these acts, no matter how comprehensively some official values or standards predominate. Thus there is the folklore of the factory, the school, the television studio, the stock-market, the cattle-mart, the Dáil, the supermarket, Sunday mass or religious service, the bank, golf club, business lunch, theatre and so on.

In today's world, however, such folklore as is created out of the popular experience of our social life does not accrete over time into any extensive repertoire. This contrasts with the situation a century ago when the impact of formal channels of cultural communication on popular consciousness was much less. It is also the case that many traditional situations which served as occasions for the performance and transmission of representations and expressions of popular world-view (the 'rambling house' or 'scoraíocht-ing house', the turf-cutting *meitheal,* the knitting or quilting assembly, the wake, the pattern day) are practically extinct because of changing patterns of social organisation. People who remember these former facets of community life, or who know about them, are liable to imagine that with their passing folklore itself has passed away also. However other communal situations have come into being in contemporary experience that serve equally well as centres of transmission of portions of the admittedly less abundant repertoire of contemporary folklore: the bingo-hall, prayer meeting, lounge bar, launderette, bowling-alley, the trip to Knock/Medjugorje, the package holiday and so forth. The study of the folklore transmitted by means of these activities must, of course, go beyond ethnographic description of them and must bring together, classify and analyse the stock of recurrent verbal and behavioural motifs involved.

So like language (*qua* speech), folklore is 'going on' all the time, in such a way that the field of folklore is co-extensive with social life itself. It follows that the study of folklore – the folklore of Ireland, of

Munster, of Cork, of a single townland, street, estate or institution – can never be exhaustive. It can only aim to identify, analyse and interpret a reasonably representative sample of the ever-changing production of the folklore process.

County Cork oral tradition

Our knowledge of the folklore process and its products within the culture of county Cork is at its greatest for the era during which the Irish Folklore Commission was most active in the field-collection of folklore material through the agency of a variety of collection schemes. Since the days of Thomas Crofton Croker (1798-1854) in the early nineteenth century antiquarians and amateur folklorists had gathered the folk traditions of the Cork region. Under the aegis of the Gaelic League and the inspiration of the Anglo-Irish literary 'Revival', a more organised effort was made at the end of the nineteenth and the beginning of the twentieth centuries to identify active and talented carriers of rural Irish folklore, especially in the Irish-speaking areas. The founding in 1927 of The Folklore of Ireland Society and its journal *Béaloideas,* together with the establishment in 1930 of the state-sponsored Irish Folklore Institute, saw the collection and study of folklore in Ireland being put on a professional scholarly basis. In 1935 a full-time state-funded Irish Folklore Commission was established. Its honorary director was Antrim-born James Hamilton Delargy (*ob.* 1980), better known under the Irish form of his name, Séamus Ó Duilearga. He also held a chair of Irish Folklore at University College, Dublin. Housed on St Stephen's Green and in receipt of international scholarly financing for a specialist library and technical recording equipment, the Irish Folklore Commission quickly settled into the amassing, cataloguing and archiving of very extensive quantities of folklore matter flowing in from all over the country. The chief portion of these materials known as the Main Collection consists of transcriptions of field-collections and replies to questionnaires.

Professor Ó Duilearga recruited a team of a dozen or so full-time collectors to work under his direction. An extensive network of part-time collectors and correspondents was set up through which much collection was also effected. Material was gathered partly by special questionnaire and generally through the use of a *Handbook of Irish folklore* (for which see below, note 3), developed on the lines of a Scandinavian model by the archivist of the Commission, Dr Seán Ó Súilleabháin, a native of south Kerry. This *Handbook* is also the basis on which the Main Collection material from full-time and part-time adult collectors was catalogued. It is thus a vade-mecum for all those wishing to consult the folklore archive. A sound archive and an archive

C. Ó Síocháin

IMLEABHAR A 1607

Téarmaí, nathanna etc. ó Chléire	1-15
Breith leanbhaí, baisteadh etc.	1-15
Cleamhnais, pósadh	16-
Filí, filíocht	27, 93
An fharraige, éisc, báid etc.	passim
An aimsir	passim
Paidreacha	165,
Dúile neamh-shaolta	132-, 195, 199-240, 251-, 266-96, 299, 305-, 329-36, 357, 361-, 375
An Ghuí Ghann	107-12
Mallacht	110
Cláiríní búithre (bréagáin)	114-6
Large cake and curse, small cake and blessing (motif)	193-4
Fairies take a cow	195-6
Fairies take dead boy	197
Haunted house	198, 322
Pan is dead	206
Cruach Mháirtín tré thine!	212
cf. A.T. 301	214-5
Milking hare	230-1
A.T. 510	241-3
A.T. 910B	244-6
Seanfhocail	247
A.T. 1775	248-50
Silenced Irish priest and English king	256-60
Cailín a phós an diabhal!	261-2
Knife thrown at wave	263-4
Mermaid story	265
Sprid	289-90, 311
A.T. 168*	301-2
Weasels' funeral	303-
Robbers etc.	316-7
The Devil has no Irish!	319
Devil as a black dog	320
Station refused - priest's curse	323-4
Enchanted stag (Scottish lore)	325
Poteen-making (Scottish lore)	327
Churning	337-8
Festivals etc.	339-40, 356, 367-8, 380, 424-36, 465
Irishman in Chicago	341-3
Mails	343-4
Tobacco and flax	344
Ulster people settle in Connacht	344-7
Martins as landlords and judges	345
Bible readers	347

Plate 23.1 Sample page from Interim Clár ix of volume 1607 (Department of Irish Folklore, U.C.D.).

of visual material were also initiated and have grown over the years. Dr Caoimhín Ó Danachair from Limerick devoted sustained effort to these audio-visual holdings and also to the recording and mapping of material folk culture.

During the school-year 1937-38 a further extensive collecting effort took place with the cooperation of the state's Department of Education. In this scheme, known as The Schools Collection, primary school pupils throughout the state collected from their relatives and neighbours folklore and other information relating to a list of topics within the fields covered by the *Handbook*. It is frequently the case that this Schools Collection yields evidence of folklore and the folklore process for points of the country not covered by the efforts of many, or even any, adult collectors. This is obviously true as regards large areas like county Cork.

When the Irish Folklore Commission was disbanded in 1971, its archives and some of its staff moved to the Department of Irish Folklore at University Collge, Dublin. During the past twenty years the latter department has continued the work of the Commission while fulfilling its own teaching duties. Together with the Irish Folklore Council it has also engaged in the publication of folklore materials and scholarship, including items from or related to county Cork.

For county Cork folklore then, we have as main sources,[2] nineteenth-century publications by antiquarians like Crofton Croker, material collected and published by members of the Gaelic League and the largely unpublished corpus of matter gathered (mainly in the 1930s, 1940s and 1950s) by the Irish Folklore Commission. It is to a description of aspects of the county Cork material in the Main Collection of the Commission's manuscript archives that the remainder of this chapter is devoted.

In this connection, it may be useful, initially, to indicate the major headings under which the collecting – and the subsequent cataloguing and indexing – of the Cork folklore, as well as traditions from other counties, was carried out, on lines set down in the *Handbook of Irish folklore*.[3]

I. Settlement and Dwelling. II. Livelihood and Household Support. III. Communications and Trade. IV. The Community. V. Human Life. VI. Nature. VII. Folk Medicine. VIII. Time. IX. Principles and Rules of Popular Belief and Practice. X. Mythological Traditions. XI. Historical Tradition. XII. Religious Tradition. XIII. Popular Oral Literature. XIV. Sports and Pastimes.

Every one of the above rubrics had in turn more elaborate subheadings which set out the types of data to be sought under each particular section. Some examples may indicate the level of detail elicited:

I. *Settlement and Dwelling:* The District and its Townlands; the Dwelling House; Temporary Dwellings; Relics of the Past.

II. *Livelihood and Household Support:* The Care and Management of Livestock; Folklore of Domestic Animals and Birds; Agriculture; Trades and Occupations; Artificial Light in the House; the Fire; Food and Drink; Meals; Luxuries; Household Vessels and Utensils; Personal and Domestic Hygiene ....

V. *Human Life:* The Soul; the Sexes; Youth and Age; Individual Characteristics; the Human Body; Bodily Functions and Activities; Challenges; Contests and Feats; Marriage; Conception, Pregnancy and Childbirth; the Young Folk; Sickness; Death; the Wake; the Funeral; the Graveyard; the Grave; the Return of the Dead ....

VIII. *Time:* Measurement of Time; important Dates and Periods; Patterns and Local Festivals; Pilgrimages; Festivals of the Year; The Days of the Week; the Months of the Year.

IX. *Principles and Rules of Popular Belief and Practice:* Time and Space; Boundaries; Direction; Participation; Fate; Divination; Individuals Credited with Supernatural Powers; Talismans; Sorcery and Witchcraft; Emblems, Numbers and Colours; Speech and Silence; Traditional Code of Right and Wrong; Fictions ....

XIII. *Popular Oral Literature:* Storytellers and their Art; International Folktales told in Ireland; Irish Hero-tales; Male and Female Characters in Folktales; Animals and Birds in Folktales; Tales of Magic; Religious Tales; Tales of Origin; Prayers and Charms; Songs; Proverbs; Riddles ....

XIV. *Sports and Pastimes:* Occasional Pastimes and Celebrations; Wake-games and Amusements; Festivals, Amusements and Games; Classification of Games; Standard Games; Game-rhymes; Card-playing; The Playing of Music; Dancing; Singing; Dramatic Entertainments; Ball-games; Active Pastimes and Tests; Pastimes with Animals or Birds; Toys.

It may be noted here that the topics covered in the Schools Collection are themselves a reflection of the foregoing classification system, which is, in effect, the master-key to all the major archival sources. Among the topics of the Schools Collection[4] are the following:

Hidden Treasure; Riddles; Weather Lore; Local Heroes; Local Happenings; Severe Weather; Old Schools; Old Crafts; Marriage

Customs; The Penal Times; Place-Names; Bird Lore; Local Cures; Home-made Toys; Lore of Certain Days; Travelling Folk; 'Fairy Forts'; Local Poets; Famine Times; Games; Roads; Holy Wells; Herbs; The Potato Crop; Proverbs; Festival Customs; Care of Farm Animals; Churning; Care of the Feet; The Forge; Clothes; The Holy Family; Patron Saint; Fairs; Landlords; Food; Sport; Old Stories; Songs; Monuments; Bread; Houses; Buying and Selling; The Leipreachán; The Mermaid; Graveyards; Prayers; Strange Animals.

We know of just about three hundred people who, at various times and in varying degrees, collected folklore in Cork county which became part of the Main Collection. Just under fifty of these were women – an indication in itself of the male orientation of the collection enterprise and the archive of material resulting from it. There are no women, for instance, among the nine major county Cork collectors who, between them, collected more than two-thirds of the Cork material. Since folklore is an expression of the popular world-view of both women and men, girls and boys, and since much folklore is gender-specific for both genders, it follows that the female side of county Cork, as indeed of all Irish, folklore is severely underrepresented in the archive. This is not due to any lack of female performers/informants. It reflects rather the predominance of male collectors who are always, perforce, at a considerable disadvantage when it comes to collecting certain types of tradition. Obviously this is a situation not confined to Irish folklore or to folklore only as a discipline. There is wide appreciation today of how much of a male bias has pervaded all aspects of social and cultural studies heretofore, and of how necessary it is to take this factor into account when analysing and interpreting evidence produced under such conditions.

There is nonetheless a great deal of evidence in the Cork folklore material of the popular world-view of women – in so far as this is different from that of men – and more recent folklore-collecting technique has been appreciative of the need to overcome the gender deficiencies of former times. Used with sensitivity and caution, the archival material can be relied upon to yield evidence of the best quality possible for its time of the oral literature, the material culture and the ritual/religious domain of Irish and county Cork popular world-view in all its variety.

In all, the approximately three hundred collectors working in county Cork produced more than sixty-three thousand manuscript pages of folklore material between them. In terms of quantity gathered there are three main categories of collector, as follows:

Table 23.1

Categories of collector

Category:	Sex:	Status:	Number:	MS pages:
Major (more than 1,000 MS pages each)	All Male	Full-time	4	36,732
		Part-time	5	9,479
			9	46,211
Substantial (between 100-1,000 MS pages each)	7 Female	Part-time	7	1,799
	31 Male	Part-time	31	10,279
			38	12,078
Occasional (less than 100 MS pages)	41 Female	Part-time	41	
	c. 215 Male	Part-time	215	
			256	*c.* 5,000
Totals	48 Female 255 Male		303	*c.* 63,289

Included in the numbers of manuscript pages given in Table 23.1 for full-time collectors is a total of 2,263 pages from the Collection Diaries, which such full-time collectors were required to compile.

The list of the major-category collectors is shown in Table 23.2. It should be borne in mind that apart from Seán Ó Cróinín, the other full-time collectors shown gathered only tangentially in county Cork, their main fields of operation being elsewhere.

Table 23.2

Major-category collectors

Name:	Status:	Chief districts worked:	MS pages (approx.):
Seán Ó Cróinín	Full-time	Mid-Cork, South Cork, East Cork	30,868
Diarmuid Ó Cruadhlaoich	Part-time	Kinealmeakey	3,100
Seosamh Ó Dálaigh	Full-time	Bantry, Glengarriffe	2,100
Ciarán Ó Síothcháin	Part-time	Cape Clear	2,100
Eoghan Ó Súilleabháin	Full-time	Ardgroom	1,890
Tadhg Ó Murchadha	Full-time	Beara	1,874
Proinsias Ó Ceallaigh	Part-time	West Muskerry	1,843
Pádraig Ó Conaill	Part-time	Myross	1,379
Conchubhar Ó Ruairc	Part-time	Kealkill, Ballingeary	1,057

Of the thirty-eight substantial-category collectors, six, all males, produced in excess of five hundred pages. They may be listed (together with pages given in approximate numbers) as follows:

Table 23.3

Main substantial – category collectors

Name:	District:	Pages:
Ned Buckley	Knocknagree/Ballydesmond	565
Domhnall Ó Ceocháin	Cúil Ao/Ballyvourney	500
Mícheál Ó Cuileanáin	Skibbereen	970+
Liam Ó hIcidhe	Mitchelstown	800
Gearóid Ó Murchadha (Professor)	Cúil Ao	700

One female collector, Eibhlín Uí Bhuachalla, almost makes it onto this listing with 420 manuscript pages to her credit from the Ballyvourney district. Also in the 400-page range are Donnchadh Ó Céilleachair and Risteard Ó Suibhne whose collections are of West Muskerry provenance as well.

It will be apparent that one full-time collector, Seán Ó Cróinín, a native of Baile Mhic Íre, is responsible for almost one half of the entire county Cork corpus of folklore material in the Main Collection of the Irish Folklore Archive, with c. 31,000 manuscript pages out of c. 63,000. His contribution is ten times greater than that of the next highest collector, Diarmuid Ó Cruadhlaoich who worked on a part-time basis in the Ballineen-Enniskeane, Castletownkinneigh-Ahiohill district. Seán Ó Cróinín collected on all sides of the county. His *Cín Lae* or Collector's Diary is a valuable and highly instructive account of his own development as a collector. His formation took place under the tutelage of Séamus Ó Duilearga and Seán Ó Súilleabháin in Dublin and under the equal (if not *more* exacting) direction of the women and men from whom he gathered county Cork folklore so diligently and so copiously between 1938 and 1944, and again for a period from 1959 on. He died in 1965, aged only fifty years.

Seán Ó Cróinín became a full-time collector at the age of twenty-three and had not yet reached thirty years of age in 1944 when he stopped his first period of collecting. During that first phase his diligent and sensitive field-work, coupled with his accurate transcriptions, yielded several remarkable achievements. There are for instance the 1,500 manuscript pages from Seán Ó hAo (*Hamit*), one of the very last native Irish speakers from near Glandore in Carbery. One edited volume of this material has already appeared from the hand of Professor Donnchadh Ó Cróinín, Seán's brother, now alas also deceased. A second volume on which Donnchadh was working is being finished *post mortem* on his behalf and will, happily, also be in print. There is furthermore the material Seán Ó Cróinín transcribed in only seventeen days from Tadhg Ó Buachalla (*An Táilliúir*) of Gougane Barra. This has been edited and published by Aindrias Ó Muimhneacháin and constitutes a substantial textual supplement to Eric Cross's anecdotal work of reminiscence, *The Tailor and Ansty* (1942). The extensive material on the folk poets of West Muskerry which Seán transcribed from Pádraig Ó Cruadhlaoich (*Gaodhal na nGaodhal*) has been edited and published by Donnchadh Ó Cróinín, as have two substantial volumes from the 1,600 manuscript pages of folklore Seán transcribed in a three-month period from Amhlaoibh Ó Luínse (*Frúí Chonny*) of Cúil Aodha.

These six volumes[5] represent only a small fraction of the total amount of county Cork material collected by Seán Ó Cróinín. We must also remember that there is at least the same total amount again of Cork folklore in the archive from the hands of other collectors. Overall, the county Cork folklore in the Main Collection, when taken together with the material deriving from the Schools Collection of 1937-8, constitutes a huge and immensely valuable resource for those working on almost any aspect of the history and culture of the county. Its availability on microfilm as part of the manuscript holdings of the Boole Library at University College, Cork, together with the presence in the same library of microfilm indexes to the material, make the archive properly accessible on a local basis.[6] It is hoped that additional Cork folklore evidence will accrue from both county and city populations as the discipline of folklore continues firmly to establish itself in the ranks of those many domains of study concerned with the different facets of Irish civilisation.

County Cork mortuary ritual

By way of illustration, I wish to present an overview of county Cork folklore evidence regarding a single topic from the ritual/religious field of the region's tradition. This is the topic of mortuary ritual, the practices and beliefs associated with death and burial as reflected in the manuscripts of the Main Collection of the Irish Folklore archive. Permission to consult, copy and extract from these former Irish Folklore Commission documents now in the Department of Irish Folklore, University College, Dublin, is hereby acknowledged. The county Cork data used in this chapter derive in the main from field-work carried out in the 1930s. The performers/informants were generally elderly. The material, reporting what parents and grandparents said of their own young days, can be taken to reach back to the mid-nineteenth century. It comes from at least seven Cork communities ranging from Beara and

Bantry in the west to Araglen and Kilworth in the east, from Glandore on the south coast to Charleville on the northern border. It includes communities from the mid-county baronies of Kinealmeakey and West Muskerry. The data are arranged under six headings and written up here in the 'ethnographic present tense'. The style used reflects native Hiberno-English usage as normally found in the primary manuscript material from which the account is drawn. I believe that the sources illustrate the composite nature of county Cork popular world-view, especially the ambivalent admixture of items of Christian and native ancestral cosmology.

Overall this account of funerary ritual in the popular culture of county Cork tradition is cast in terms of an understanding of the structure of the 'wake' as a social assembly having both sacred and profane functions.[7] At the sacred level of significance, the 'wake' is presented as the occasion of the transition of the spirit of the deceased individual into the otherworlds of *both* Christian and native ancestral provenance. There is an emphasis on the performative agency of the *bean chaointe* or 'keening woman' in effecting transition/incorporation of the deceased into the otherworld of the ancestral kin-groups of which the departed one is henceforth to be a member. At the profane or sociological level, the 'wake' likewise articulates the process whereby the community of the deceased regenerates itself in the face of the mortal wound which the death of an individual member occasions. This reading of the funerary ritual of county Cork popular culture is compatible with ethno-logical analysis of funerary ritual in a wide range of traditional cultures. It attests to the richness of the folklore evidence that is available to students of Irish popular culture in this as in other fields of ethnology.

The occurrence of death

Certain features are a sure sign that a death is imminent in the community[8]. Among these may be listed the crowing of a cock by night or throughout the day,[9] the hearing by night of the death-tick in a wall or in an old timber bed,[10] the absence of a shadow thrown on the wall by a person lighting a lamp indoors at Hallowe'en,[11] the presence of grey crows about the house,[12] the hearing of the 'banshee', the super-natural female death messenger, in the vicinity of the household,[13] the meeting with a fairy or ghostly funeral on the road by night.[14]

Death itself is looked on as a punishment for sin.[15] Violent or sudden death is held in great awe since it is a sign of 'bad living' leading to a 'bad end'.[16] The death of a young person or child is taken as a sign that they were 'too good' for this sinful world.[17] The will of God is in operation behind all death[18] and an easy death after a long life is seen as a reward for good living.[19]

'Unnatural' deaths result in the dead person being 'in the fairies' and certain 'forbidden' acts bring danger of this type of death. Such acts are, for instance, interfering with 'the good people's property (forts, *sceach*-bushes, thorns) or removing or altering old passages or laneways and so causing annoyance and disturbance to 'the good people'. Such acts lead to ill-health and, ultimately, death.[20]

Before a person dies the 'habit' must be in the house and the dying individual is to be allowed touch it. It is said that as the point of death approaches there is a 'half-a-claim' from the world of the living (from this side) and a 'half-a-claim' from the other side on the dying person, and that when the dying individual lays his or her hand on the 'habit' they are 'more reconciled to go'.[21] Near the moment of death those in the house light the blessed candle and read and recite the litany of the dead.[22] Once death has taken place, the corpse should be left undisturbed for a certain period in order to allow the deceased to get safely to heaven and communicate with God regarding the state of his or her soul.[23]

It is believed that the souls of relatives dying far away come back to visit the old place one last time before taking flight to God. Such visitation is signalled by a loud knocking in the middle of the night.[24] It is held that people – and especially the elderly – come back to the place they frequented in this life. Consequently, the old man's walking stick is, after his death, left beside his bed every night for a half-year. His pipe, filled with tobacco, is left on the shelf above the bed. The deceased old woman's tea-caddy is for a similar reason left in the clevy (*poll an fhalla*) for a long time.[25]

Word spreads quickly of a death in a townland. Work stops in the fields and implements are abandoned 'as a mark of respect'. Work remains halted until after the burial.[26] Within the deceased's house the clock is stopped as soon as death occurs and mirrors are covered.[27] A sanction of prolonged critical gossip ensures that this is done. No dance or festive gathering takes place for half a year in a townland where a death occurs.[28]

Immediately after a death is announced, neighbours, especially the elderly and the female, start to congregate at the corpse-house; the younger men will mostly come there at nightfall. Two neighbours go with a family member to procure a coffin and wake-provisions: food, drink, tobacco, snuff. Nobody would dare to go on this errand alone, even in broad daylight.[29]

It is wrong and dangerous to go to or come from a wake alone since the souls of the deceased and of other ancestors are likely to be encountered in the vicinity of the corpse-house, and there is safety in numbers. Between midnight and day-break especially, the spirits of the dead and the fairies are likely to be very active about the corpse-house. At day-break some of the people at the wake start to go home. However, a certain number must stay until other neighbours arrive, because a corpse-house must never be left without company. The custom of bringing the body to 'the chapel' for the second night of the wake is opposed by many people on the grounds that this involves two 'funerals' and that it is displeasing to the deceased to be brought in and out of 'the chapel' in quick succession.[30]

Fairy 'keening' or lamentation is frequently heard in the vicinity of the corpse-house and such a phenomenon follows families. This fairy crying is not regarded as terrifying since it is proper that respect be shown to the dead from 'the other side' also. Sometimes a dead relative of the deceased will come back to the wake – a dead sister, perhaps. There are stories of fairy women coming into the wake to tell the household where they should bury a 'stranger', for instance an itinerant farm labourer or a traveller, who is being waked among them.[31]

Laying out the deceased
After a certain period has elapsed during which the corpse has been left undisturbed, it is washed and dressed and laid out by some local female who specialises in this work. On no account must any member of the family of the deceased handle the corpse or touch it while it is being thus readied for the wake. A male neighbour is got to shave a male corpse if this is considered necessary. When washed, the corpse is dressed and laid out on the kitchen table or perhaps on a bed where the corpse-house is large enough to have sizeable bedrooms. The face of the corpse should always look to the east.

The corpse is dressed in either the deceased's best clothes (the last worn to Mass) or else in a black or brown 'habit', a dress-like garment often associated with lay membership of a religious order. Some corpses are not dressed in a habit because of the belief that the person whose corpse wears a habit will not, for this reason, meet with his or her 'own' relatives or ancestors in the next life. A rosary bead is twined around the deceased's hands which are folded and joined on his or her breast. A prayer-book may be placed on the breast or under the deceased's chin.

While the feet of a corpse are usually fastened together during the wake either with a cord or a sock-pin (where socks are put on the feet), there is a great fear of confining the corpse with such foot-fastening still in place. If left undone this will prove to be a severe impediment to the deceased's activities in the next life of the otherworld. Also for this reason, no pin or clip is left in the 'habit' or other corpse-garment even though a number of these have been used in the dressing and laying-out procedure. The woman who lays out the corpse must undo the arrangement of the wake-room when the body is taken away. The tented linen sheets that stand or hang about the corpse during the wake must be taken down before the body is coffined. These, together with every scrap stripped off the table or bed on which the corpse was waked, must be bundled up into a heap in the centre of the room while the corpse is being coffined. The person who brings the loan of clothes or sheets to the wake-house has to be the person who takes these back again to where they came from. In the case of loaned sheets, the woman who washed the corpse must wet the four corners of the bundled sheets afterwards, before they can be sent away again.

The 'waking sheets' are five in number. They are kept at one house in every ploughland and may never be used for any other purpose. One of them goes under the corpse on the wake bed or on the kitchen table; one goes overhead, fastened to the ceiling; one goes to one side of the corpse and one each goes to its head and feet, these also fastened to the ceiling so that the corpse lies within a sort of linen tent.

Brass candlesticks for wakes are also kept at the same house as the sheets. Five candles are lit in them and kept lighting for a corpse dressed in a shroud or 'habit'. Three candles are lit and kept lighting in the case of a corpse not wearing this but dressed in its own clothes.

The pillows and bolster on which the corpse rested, the mattress of the bed and even the kitchen table on which the corpse was waked, will be turned over after the corpse is coffined. The two sides of the deceased's family will compete with each other to be the first to do these 'turnings' in an attempt to deflect from themselves the next succeeding death that is to occur. The length of time to such next succeeding death will have been gauged by the relative stiffness or limpness of the deceased's corpse during the wake. A limber corpse is regarded as a sure sign of impending further death in the family.

The little stumps of the first candles lit during the wake are kept in the house for a very long time, as they are used as a *leigheas* ('cure') for both people and animals. The water in which the corpse was washed is also regarded as having a 'cure' in it and is kept, for this purpose, by some people who will subsequently rub it on sores, saying at the same time 'In the name of the Father and of the Son and of the Holy Ghost'. Where it is not kept like this it is at least carefully retained until the end of the wake. Then, when the funeral leaves the house, it is 'thrown after the corpse' in the direction in which the coffin has moved off. To throw out the corpse-water before the corpse is regarded as a very dangerous thing to do. Instances where this was done were followed by a lot of trouble and misfortune for a long time after.

Crying over the corpse

It is not right for any member of the family to touch the corpse or go near it to express grief until it is laid out properly. Then the whole family assembles round the corpse and cries over it, talking to it and calling back the deceased. Later, when the corpse is coffined and just before the lid is put on, every member of the family must again come and cry over the corpse and kiss it. The final family crying is done outside the house just before the coffin moves off. When the family has finished their initial crying over the corpse, the neighbours cry over it in turn as they think fit, while they arrive at the wake-house during the course of the night. Also the special 'keeners' cry over the corpse from time to time during the wake. These are old women who are particularly good at crying and making extempore verses in praise of the deceased for which they are rewarded with drink and money. They are 'like poets' in the wake-house and their performance makes people very 'lonesome'. It also elates the whole assembly when they 'open up' in the middle of the night after the Rosary has been said. Such 'keeners' were sent for from miles away to come and perform at wakes and it was disrespectful to the deceased not to arrange to have keening at the wake and funeral. The keening women walk with the coffin during the funeral or ride with it in the horse-cart, often sitting on the coffin itself, if the journey to the graveyard is a long one.

Festive provisions of food, drink and tobacco

No one leaves the wake-house without receiving and eating some kind of a meal. Local girls help to provide this, just as local men are the ones who provide and tend to the fire which is kept blazing throughout the time of the wake. The company at the wake is fed several times during the night. There can be no shortage of food or drink since special supplies will have been acquired immediately following the time of death. Tea, it is said, is a great thing to dispel loneliness and sadness. Tea is made throughout the day for those coming in and out, and again throughout the night for those assembled inside. It is expected that there will be large quantities of food and drink available to the assembly for consumption during the wake.

There must also be plenty of snuff, tobacco and chalk pipes supplied for everyone to smoke. These chalk pipes will be given out to the men, either already filled with tobacco or together with a saucerful of cut tobacco from which each fills up his pipe. Similarly, saucerfuls of snuff are sent around among the women. Everyone at the wake, male and female, young and old, is expected to take tobacco or snuff in this fashion, and, on starting to either smoke or sniff it, to say *Beannacht Dé le hanamann na marbh* ('the Lord have mercy on the souls of the dead'). The consumption of tobacco and snuff continues throughout all the time of the wake and involves people who may otherwise be non-smokers and non-consumers of snuff. Readying the chalk pipes, the cut tobacco and the plates of snuff is an important part of preparations for a wake. Together with the tending of the fire it forms part of the deceased's male neighbours' responsibility.

This smoking goes on not only during the wake but also as part of the funeral. Baskets or boxes of filled pipes will have been placed on walls or bushes in the vicinity of the corpse-house for use by those coming to attend the funeral. A little before the funeral leaves the house a man goes on ahead with a basket of chalk pipes on his arm. As he meets people who are still on their way to the wake-house, or either coming to the funeral or waiting to meet it on the way, he gives each of them a filled pipe. Pipes that are left over after the wake and funeral are left in a basket on the grave. Anyone at all is welcome to take one.

Whiskey or *poitín* is also supplied to those attending a wake. A small amount is usually distributed to all, men and women alike, towards the middle of the night. The keening women will get drinks of whiskey according as they perform. On the day of the funeral, while the corpse is being coffined, the men in attendance are given a drink. There is a custom that the man giving out this drink spills a little of it into the coffin. It is believed that because of too much drink at wakes the priests made a rule that the corpse should be brought to 'the chapel' for the second night of the wake.

Festive behaviours

When people are waked on the kitchen table there is great sport at the wakes, with flutes and music and dancing. Sometimes mummers will be present during the night with everyone dressed up in different clothes. A wake can be like a wedding with all the fun and laughter. If there is no one to keep the 'fine boys' in check – say at the wake of an old woman who has few relatives and who is 'no loss' – then they get up to a great deal of 'devilment' as the night passes, tying people who doze off to sleep to the chairs, or the hen-coop on which they are stretched, or shaving, in their sleep, bearded old men who have dozed off near the fire.

Once the Rosary has been said after nightfall at a wake, then horse-play and rough tricks can be expected. 'Croosting' occurs with no objection or interference from the family of an elderly deceased. This involves the pelting of various individuals at the wake with little pieces of turf brought along specially in their pockets by the 'fine boys' to create mischief. Those 'prime lads' have great fun annoying some cranky man – knocking the clay pipe out of his mouth, for instance, by firing a *cadhrán* ('piece of hard turf') at him unawares. This type of general horse-play can amount to 'the devil's own kip-of-the-reel' – all sport and blackguarding and every fellow trying to be better (that is more outrageous) than the next.

It is known for the corpse to be secretly roped by tricksters during the wake so that it can be hoisted into an upright position in the middle of the night, striking terror and panic into the assembly – especially the women – who attempt to flee the house. Sometimes the people of the house are extremely angry at this and there is very nearly 'a real fight'. Other times a family will not mind, as such behaviour is half-expected. Given a chance they themselves would play the same tricks. There is generally some old man in each district who is well-known for organising and directing such 'devilment' at wakes. The 'prime boys' will send up to five miles for such a person to come to a local wake so as to indulge in sport and tricks.

Some of these gaming activities are organised set pieces. The young men will start to erect a pyramid of themselves and ask some innocent or inexperienced fellow to top it off for them, telling him to catch the cross-beam of the roof for a moment and then all running away so as to leave him suspended. Sometimes a not-so-innocent will allow himself to be duped like this but will extract revenge by suddenly flinging down ashes or soot into the eyes of those gazing up.

Occasionally an unsuspecting individual will be pounced on and made crouch in the centre of the floor as an anvil. Two or three others will start sledging him with their fists. The cry will be taken up: *Buail é, buail é, buail é trína chéile, buail é, buail é, buail é go léir* ('Beat him, beat him, beat him all over, beat him, beat him, beat him entire'), and maybe ten or twelve fellows in all will be pounding him. Someone will suddenly shout *Tá sé ag dóigheadh* ('he is burning'), whereupon the 'anvil' will be picked up and rushed either to a bucket of water or outside to a mud-patch to be doused. Another version of this game involves treating the victim as a spinning-wheel. Yet another involves having a patient, lying on the floor, visited and examined by all the 'doctors' at the wake and thus subjected to rough handling. In this game too, the victim sometimes turns the tables by suddenly throwing a concealed fistful of ashes or soot in the face of his 'visitor'.

On one occasion a group of five or six 'lads' going to a wake could not decide which of them should lead their party into the wake-house to go and stand over the corpse and cry a little, as it was customary for everyone attending a wake to do. They drew lots for the honour and it fell to a 'hardy boyo'. As they went in the door of the house some other one of them struck their leader a terrible blow on the ear-hole with his fist so that his crying over the corpse was remarkably authentic. The others had to back out of the door again with the need to burst out laughing.

'Brogue About' is regarded as the best and most popular game of all. For this, all the men sit around on the kitchen floor in a circle with their legs pulled up to them. An old shoe is passed round the circle under the raised knees and someone is prevailed upon to stand in the middle of the circle and try to intercept the shoe in its passage. As he turns to scan the circle of knees, he may be struck a crack of the shoe on the poll while his back is to whoever happens to have it. If it is a 'slow fellow' who is in the middle he may be a very long time looking for the shoe and will have to endure a great deal of punishment. In general this is regarded as a 'great' game.

Interment
When coffined, the deceased is brought out of the house feet-first. The coffin is put resting for a little while on two or four chairs in the open air. The family engage in their last crying over the deceased before the funeral moves off. When it does so, the chairs on which the coffin last rested will be knocked over together with other chairs and seating brought out of the house after the coffin itself. All these, together with the table inside the house on which the corpse is laid out (and which will have been knocked over at the time of coffining the corpse), will be allowed to remain in the fallen position until after the burial has taken place.

Four male relatives of the deceased, with the same surname, if possible, should be the ones who 'go under' the coffin when it is coming out of the house, when it is going into 'the chapel', again when leaving 'the chapel' (that is where the corpse is brought to 'the chapel' at all) and finally when entering the graveyard. There are memories of bodies being buried uncoffined, either carried to the graveyard on a stretcher or else in a coffin that is merely borrowed for the occasion and later returned to its owner. This was the 'hinge' coffin, so-called from the hinged end-board that swung to allow the body slide out into the grave. The coffin is preferably shouldered the whole way to the graveyard, especially if the deceased is well liked. Relays of men 'go under' the coffin as required. If the journey to the graveyard is a very long one, then after a mile or so the coffin can be placed in a horse-cart and drawn the rest of the way to the gate of the graveyard where close relatives again shoulder it.

The funeral procession goes by the longest traditional route to the graveyard, taking no short cut whatsoever, in accordance with the customary injunction *an timpeall chun an teampaill* ('the long way round to the churchyard'). Once brought into the graveyard on the shoulders of four close relatives, the coffin is carried all around the perimeter path in a sunwise (*deiseal*) direction before being brought to the grave. At the graveside, before the earth is piled in on top of the coffin, the screws on the lid are either loosened or withdrawn altogether to lie on the lid in the form of a cross. This is done to ensure that deceased persons have *cead a gcos* ('foot-room, liberty') in the otherworld.

It is reported as 'usual enough' not to have any priest in the funeral procession or at the grave, though in some places it has become the custom for two priests to attend every funeral. Where there is no priest present, the funeral, when it comes to a cross-roads, will halt, the coffin will be let down and the people all gather around it. Someone will then recite the *De profundis* and other prayers for the soul of the deceased.

A 'bog sod' should be carried in the end of every funeral. This is a 'blanket' of turf or top-sod about eight feet by four which is cut in a local bog or field and rolled in one piece onto a stick and tied with rope. This 'blanket' is unrolled after the burial and laid carefully in one piece over the filled grave.

The grave itself should always be aligned on an east-west axis. It should be opened or dug not by any relative of the deceased's but by a 'grave-digger' or else by a neighbour not having the same surname as the deceased. The grave is usually 'reddened' (that is opened by removing the top-sod and turning some earth) on the day after the death occurs. However, on no account can a grave be 'reddened' on a Monday, so that the grave of someone dying on Sunday is either opened that same day or else on the following Tuesday. A grave is usually opened by two men working together. When it is made, the two who made it cross their shovels over it. These are left in position until the burial time as a protection against interference with the grave by spirits or fairies. It is wrong both for people making a grave and those at a burial to clean boots or shoes afterwards on graveyard grass, and equally wrong to spit while in the graveyard.

Some people will open a grave but will on no account close it again themselves, even if it has been opened in error. Having been opened, a grave must receive something before being closed again, even if it is only half-opened. If nothing is put into a grave (even a partly-opened one) before closing it again, then it is sure to claim one of the family whose grave it is in a very short time.

Just as all those meeting a funeral – even a fairy funeral – on the road should turn and travel *trí choischéim na trócaire* ('the three merciful steps') with it, so those closest to the deceased (and to the grave at burial) should throw in three shovelfuls or three fistfuls of earth onto the coffin before the business of closing the grave begins in earnest. The noise of these first few shovelfuls of earth thudding onto the coffin causes the bereaved family to cry again in unison, a cry taken up once more and for the final time by any keening women present.

When a person has died and is buried, his or her clothes are given away to another to wear, as something that will benefit the soul of the deceased. The deceased's best suit of clothes, for instance, will be given 'in the name of God' to his best friend to wear to mass on the next three Sundays. These clothes may not be altered in size to suit the recipient. After the three Sundays on which they are worn to mass, they are often kept hanging up in the recipient's house until they melt away in moth-holes, just as it is believed the body of the deceased melts and withers away in a similar fashion in the grave.

Using folklore information

The above may help demonstrate the richness of oral traditional material in relation to funerary ritual in the popular culture of county Cork communities. The data illustrate the value to researchers on Irish culture of the folklore evidence that resides in the archive of the Irish Folklore Commission. Similarly rich testimony awaits those investigating other aspects of county Cork popular culture in such fields as story-telling, historical legends, belief systems, unofficial healing, traditional cosmology, goddess mythology, popular religion, calendar custom and so on. In light of the diversity and richness of this material, it is to be hoped that all students of the history and traditions of Irish communities will henceforth include the field of folklore within their focus.

References

1. Further discussion of the nature of folklore within the field of Irish studies will be found in G. Ó Crualaoich and D. Ó Giolláin, 'Folklore in Irish studies' in *The Irish Review*, v (1988), pp 68-74.

2. A comprehensive bibliography of published Irish folklore and folklore scholarship can be found in C. Ó Danachair, *A bibliography of Irish ethnology and folk tradition* (Cork, 1978) with a supplement in *Béaloideas*, xlviii-x (1980/81), pp 206-227.

3. S. Ó Súilleabháin, *A handbook of Irish folklore* (Dublin, 1942), reprinted in 1967 (Hatboro, Pennsylvania) and 1970 (Detroit).

4. [S. Ó Súilleabháin], *Irish folklore and tradition.* (Dublin, 1937).

5. D. Ó Cróinín, *Scéalaíocht Amhlaoibh Í Luínse* (Baile Átha Cliath, 1971); idem, *Seanachas Amhlaoibh Í Luínse* (Baile Átha Cliath, 1980); idem, *Seanachas Phádraig Í Chrualaoi* (Baile Átha Cliath, 1982); idem, *Seanchas ó Chairbre*, i (Baile Átha Cliath, 1985), ii in preparation; A. Ó Muimhneacháin, *Seanchas an Táilliúra* (Corcaigh, 1978).

6.   Anyone in the Cork area wishing to examine material in either the Main or the Schools Collection of the Folklore Archives should contact the Special Collections Desk on Floor Q-1 of the Boole Library, U.C.C.

7.   For a fuller treatment of this view of Irish funerary ritual see G. Ó Crualaoich, 'Contest in the cosmology and ritual of the Irish "Merry Wake"' in *Cosmos*, vi (1990), pp 145-160.

8.   Sample references are given in this section to the locations in the manuscripts of the folklore archive of the evidence presented. The abbreviation I.F.C. (for Irish Folklore Commission) is followed, in each instance, by the number of the manuscript volume and the pages therein on which the evidence cited is to be found. The place and year in which the information was collected are also indicated.

9.   I.F.C., MS 408, p. 308, Leap, 1937.

10.   Ibid.

11.   I.F.C., MS 42, p. 187, Charleville, 1929.

12.   I.F.C., MS 408, p. 308, Leap, 1937.

13.   Ibid.

14.   I.F.C., MS 550, p. 6, Enniskeane, 1938.

15   I.F.C., MS 550, p. 3, Enniskeane, 1938.

16.   I.F.C., MS 550, p. 4, Enniskeane, 1938.

17.   I.F.C., MS 550, p. 3, Enniskeane, 1938.

18.   I.F.C., MS 550, p. 4, Enniskeane, 1938.

19.   I.F.C., MS 550, p. 3, Enniskeane, 1938.

20.   I.F.C., MS 550, pp 4-5, Enniskeane, 1938.

21.   I.F.C., MS 107, pp 496-7, Kilworth, 1935.

22.   I.F.C., MS 107, p. 486, Kilworth, 1935.

23   I.F.C., MS 42, p. 185, Charleville, 1929.

24.   I.F.C., MS 550, pp 9-11, Enniskeane, 1938.

25.   I.F.C., MS 203, p. 99, Kealkill, 1935.

26.   I.F.C., MS 408, p. 75, Kilcaskin, 1937.

27.   I.F.C., MS 107, p. 487, Kilworth, 1935.

28.   I.F.C., MS 408, p. 309, Leap, 1937.

29.   I.F.C., MS 203, p. 96, Kealkill, 1935.

30.   I.F.C., MS 408, p. 74, Kilcaskin, 1937.

31.   I.F.C., MS 44, pp 122-23, Coomhola, 1933. The material discussed in the following five sub-sections is drawn from a similar range of evidence. It is however presented here without the inclusion of precise references.

Chapter 24

THE EVOLUTION AND INFLUENCE OF TOWN PLANNING IN CORK

KEVIN HOURIHAN

Introduction

This chapter is concerned with the development of urban planning in Cork city prior to the mid-twentieth century. Planning is a very wide-ranging process, involving the identification of a set of goals or objectives and the formulation of a set of measures to achieve them. Modern urban planning involves all aspects of the physical environment of towns and cities, including their centres and suburbs shopping, industrial and residential areas, open spaces and amenities, and the transport modes and links that bind them together. It also has a strong social and economic content since the built environment cannot be isolated from its residents and their employment.

To many people planning is a quintessentially modern phenomenon, a bureaucratic imposition that is at best frustrating and in its worst forms, corrupt and obstructive. Both perceptions are quite inaccurate. Urban planning has a long history. It seems probable that the early inhabitants of the Harappan cities in the Indus valley of modern-day Pakistan planned their settlements on a comprehensive and efficient basis in the third millennium B.C.[1] The first recorded use of planning in Europe was in the reconstruction of Greek cities after the defeat of the Persians in 479 B.C.[2] The author of these plans, Hippodamus of Miletus, is regarded as the father of modern town planning. Ever since, planning has been practised in European cities. Both the Greeks and Romans planned some of their cities in classical times and, even after the Dark Ages, planning re-emerged in medieval cities. The Renaissance, in particular, brought many innovations in city planning and design, and some of the most beautiful townscapes in Europe date from that period. The terrible problems that afflicted the industrial cities of the nineteenth century finally confirmed the need for comprehensive planning, and in the early twentieth century planning became statutorily recognised in most counties, and evolved into its present form. As a small and isolated city, Cork was never an innovator in planning or design, but its links with Britain and the Continent ensured that new developments were recognised in the city. This chapter attempts to trace the way in which

Cork's development was influenced by what was happening abroad. Most of the evidence is still visible in the physical fabric of the city, but there were also some proposals which never came to fruition.

The late medieval city

Late medieval Cork had much in common with other European cities. The medieval period had been of great importance in terms of the revival and expansion of cities after the Dark Ages, and through the development of new centres. Town planning had also become re-established, particularly through its use in the thirteenth century of planned colonial centres known as *bastides*.[3] A distinction is usually drawn between these and the planted towns which were more widespread. The latter include the Zahringer towns of Switzerland, the *terre murata* of the Florentine republic, and especially, the new towns established by the Germans in their expansion to the east. All of these differ from the *bastides* in that they generally had no predetermined plan, while the *bastides* were laid out in a regular pattern with streets, public buildings and often walls.

In terms of its form and design, medieval Cork had many of the characteristics of planted cities. The well-known bird's-eye view of the city in 1595[4] may be impressionistic but the details of the streets, churches and gates within the city are accurate, as are the landmarks outside the walls, so in the absence of large-scale archaeological investigation it provides the best available view of Cork at the end of the sixteenth century (Fig. 24.1).

The size of the walled city may have been determined by its site between the channels of the Lee, but it was very similar to typical *bastide* and planted towns. Cork's wall enclosed an area of some 700 by 260 yards. The *bastide* of Aigues-Mortes on the Mediterranean coast to the south of Arles measured about 690 by 320 yards, while the hill city of Carcassone was some 550 by 250 yards. The rectangular city walls were not as efficient as circular ones, both in terms of resisting an attack and also in enclosing space.[5] The city wall in Cork seems to have been a typical medieval single line with circular towers. By the seventeenth century the structure was obsolete and was being replaced in continental cities by the far more elaborate system devised by Sebastian de Vauban, Louis XIV's military engineer (Fig. 24.2)[6]

The internal form of Cork was also typically medieval. The wide, straight two main streets are similar to the commercial street *(Verkehrstrasse)* of German cities, which carried most wheeled traffic.[7] These streets were generally about 25 feet wide. The other streets were for residential use *(Wohnungsstrasserl),* often only seven or eight feet in width. A town square is shown opposite St Peter's

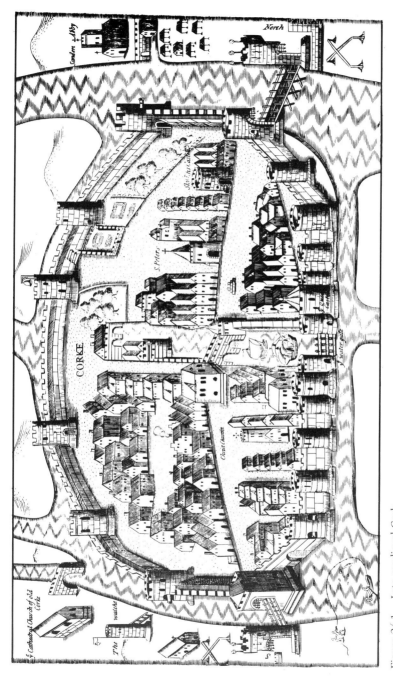

Figure 24.1 Late medieval Cork.
Source: *Pacata Hibernia.*

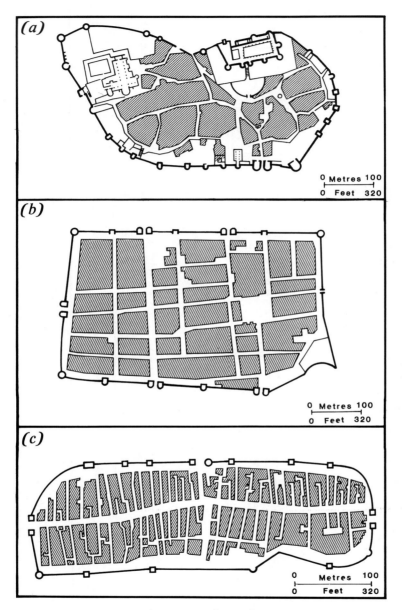

Figure 24.2 a Plan of Carcassone [France].
Source: Reference 3 (Morris, *Urban form*).
b Plan of Aigues-Mortes [France].
Source: Reference 3 (Morris, *Urban form*).
c Street-plan of late medieval Cork.
Source: *Pacata Hibernia*.

church in the present North Main Street. This probably served as the main market place in the city. The main streets in medieval cities often carried markets but Cork's streets were considerably narrower than the purpose-built market streets of, for example, the Zahringer new towns of the upper Rhine, which were 75 to 100 feet wide and running the full length of the towns between their gates.[8]

The buildings on the *Pacata Hibernia* map are gable-fronted, narrow and deep. Standard house plots in medieval planned cities were 24 feet wide and 72 feet deep, as street frontage was valuable and expensive.[9] A considerable amount of open space inside the walls is shown in the Cork map. Even allowing for artistic license, this may not be inaccurate. Contrary to popular belief, medieval cities were not too densely developed. Overbuilding was more common from the seventeenth century onwards as the towns grew more rapidly and any available space was built over.[10] The maps of eighteenth-century Cork show very dense development within the medieval site, but this may have occurred after 1595.

Overall, therefore, the appearance of Cork in late medieval times was fairly typical of cities elsewhere in Europe. There is no evidence of deliberate planning or design at that time. But there was a considerable amount of organised, collective effort as exemplified by the many urban ordinances and the then recorded-activities of the corporation.

The grand design

The influence of the Renaissance on urban design was profound. It began modestly with the building of a straight street, lined with palaces, in Genoa in 1470, but Renaissance theories of art, architecture and perspective were to dominate in European cities for the next four hundred years.[11] The finest results are found in the largest and most important cities like Rome, Berlin, Paris and London, although even in these cases the Renaissance designs never took the form of city-wide, comprehensive plans. Instead, they resulted in a series of monumental effects, designed to benefit the élite of society. Renaissance planning in Rome was instigated by the papacy, in Paris by the monarchy and in Amsterdam by the wealthy merchants.

Some of the preconditions of Renaissance planning were present in eighteenth-century Cork. The prosperity from the provision trade, the emerging merchant élite and the expansion outside the medieval city walls would all have favoured these new designs. However, the site of the city militated against them. Reclaiming new land was an expensive and time-consuming process; using it for parks or baroque squares would have been wasteful. Despite this, the elements of Renaissance design did penetrate to Cork.

A primary street was probably the most important aspect of Renaissance planning.[12] In Rome this took the form of an integrated system of streets linking the main pilgrimage churches in the city, but the idea is epitomised by single monumental avenues like the Champs Elysées in Paris and Unter den Linden in Berlin. In Ireland, there were no housing acts in the eighteenth century, and primary street planning was due to the 'Commissioners for Making Wide and Convenient Streets'.[13] The Wide Street Commissioners began as an *ad hoc* body appointed by parliament in Dublin in 1757. They were later given statutory powers of compulsory purchase of houses and sites, and achieved, in Craig's words, 'a very high degree of enlightened planning well in advance of their time'.[14]

Sixteen commissioners were appointed in Cork in 1765.[15] Despite having no funds until 1817, they were responsible for the layout of the South Terrace and Dunbar Street and the widening of Shandon Street. Their finest achievement was in the construction of Great George's Street (presently Washington Street). This street, with its regular building lines, heights and windows, epitomised the sense of symmetry and proportion which was central to Renaissance art. It was complemented by the building of the Courthouse in 1836. It has been suggested that the deflection of Great George's Street along the Grand Parade from its natural line linking up with St Patrick's Street was a conscious copying of John Nash's design for the Regent Street – Portland Place axis in London.[16] Nash's street makes enforced changes of direction at Picadilly Circus and Langtham Place, and he closed the vistas at these points with the Circus and All Souls Church. The architects of Great George's Street in Cork were James and George Pain, who had studied in London under Nash, and they may well have copied the Regent Street axis with its interesting employment of visual enclosure.

A second element of Renaissance design was the use of the gridiron for laying out residential areas.[17] One of its attractions was its use in classical city planning (such as that at Miletus), but it was also the urban equivalent of the ideal forms, the square and cube, which were fundamental to Renaissance architecture. The influence of the gridiron is evident in Rocque's map of 1759 (Fig. 24.3). The thirty acres of Dunscombe's Marsh were leased in 1710. Carty's map of 1726 shows some buildings on it, but by 1759 it had been fully developed along the axis of George's Street (modern Oliver Plunkett Street). These uniform streets and blocks contrast markedly with the medieval city nearby.

The greatest aesthetic achievements of Renaissance planning were in the form of enclosed squares.[18] Many were designed by the foremost

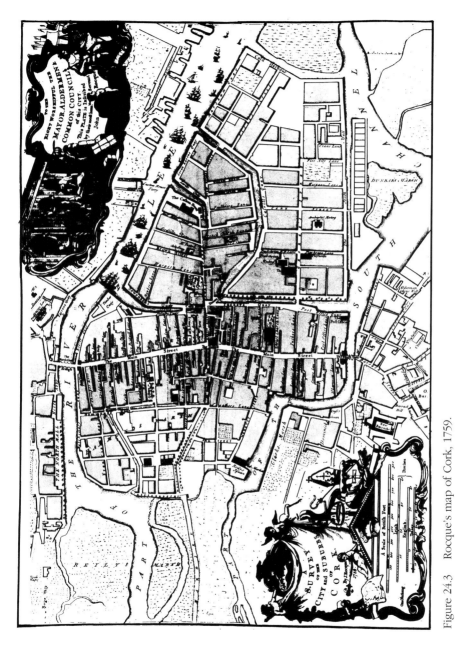

Figure 24.3   Rocque's map of Cork, 1759.
Source: J. Rocque, 'A survey of the city and suburbs of Cork' [London, 1759].

artists of their time, for example, Michelangelo's Piazza Campidoglio in Rome or Bernini's colonnade and Piazza for St Peter's Basilica. The reclaimed marshes in Cork were too valuable to be used for open space but there were some proposals for the development of squares. The new Corn Market was built in 1740 on Cornmarket Street and by 1750 Smith was arguing that a square should be opened in front of the building to 'form a handsome area, round which shops etc. might be erected'.[19] In the 1840s there were proposals for a new square, with a public monument in its centre, in front of the new courthouse on Great George's Street.[20] Neither square was constructed, and the city centre had no formal open space until Bishop Lucey Park was opened in 1985.

Another Renaissance element which almost came to Cork was a new town. New towns are planned developments which are consciously created for a specified objective. Their use is almost as old as urban planning itself, as for example, at Miletus and Priene in Asia Minor, and Alexandria in Egypt. During the twentieth century new towns have been widely developed in Great Britain, for example, Milton Keynes. New administrative capitals have been built for Australia (Canberra) and Brazil (Brasilia). During the Renaissance, they were generally initiated by princes or electors as expressions of their power and authority. Their design was strongly influenced by new theories of art and perspective, with generous landscaping, and even today the best of these remain very impressive and attractive. There had been several in France, such as Richelieu in the Loire Valley (founded by the Cardinal in 1620) and Versailles, and German examples include Karlsruhe and Mannheim.[21] In Britain, James Craig's design for a New Town in Edinburgh exemplified the concept.[22]

The Cork corporation decided in 1780 to reclaim the 230 acres of marshland south of the Navigation Wall. A central avenue, 90 feet in width, would form the east-west spine of the development, with north-south streets, 40 feet wide, intersecting with it every 100 yards (Fig. 24.4).[23] Building lots of 150 feet would be laid out along the streets. The plan is clearly similar to Edinburgh. If it had been implemented with suitable building controls, it might have provided Cork with a Georgian development as attractive as Newtown-Perry in Limerick.

The nineteenth century

Industrial urbanisation brought both unprecedented growth and pressures on European cities. Many were growing at rates of 2.1 per cent per annum at the fastest, doubling their populations every 34 years.[24] London had less than one million people in 1800, but some 6.5 millions at the end of the century.[25] Cities like Birmingham, Glasgow

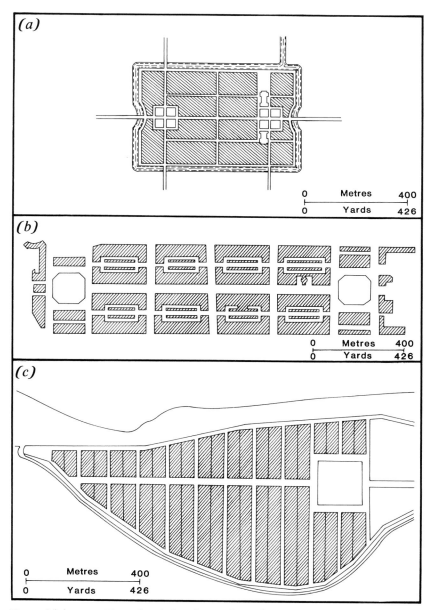

Figure 24.4   a   Plan of Richelieu [France], *c.* 1631.
                     Source: Reference 3 (Morris, *Urban form*).
             b   Edinburgh New Town, 1767.
                     Source: Reference 3 (Morris, *Urban form*).
             c   Proposed New Town, Cork, 1780.
                     Source: *Pacata Hibernia*.

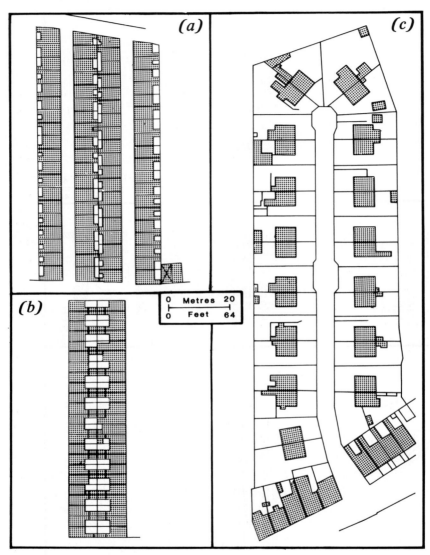

Figure 24.5 a Madden's Buildings, 1868.
b Sutton's Buildings, 1868.
c French's Villas, 1923.
Source: O.S., 1974, Scale, 1:1000.

and Manchester, which had been smaller and far less important than Cork in the eighteenth century, were growing even more quickly. This growth, combined with *laissez faire* capitalism, generated enormous pressures on housing, utilities and services of all kinds and led to severe ill-health in the urban populations. During the course of the century the scale of the problem was established through a series of select inquiries and parliamentary commissions. An understanding of the causes gradually emerged, and local authorities became actively involved in physical planning. Nineteenth-century planning in continental Europe was far more advanced with the Germans in particular adopting a system of 'town extensions'.[26] There were also the outstanding examples of Haussmann's reconstruction of Paris in the period 1853-70 and the development of the Ring in Vienna after 1858.[27]

In most respects Cork's experience in the nineteenth century was far closer to Britain than the Continent. There was one important difference, however: British cities were growing at unprecedented rates while Cork stagnated during the century. From a population of probably 100,000 in 1800, the city declined to some 80,000 in 1820 and varied little thereafter.[28] Economically also it was a time of stagnation. The provision and butter trades, the basis of eighteenth-century prosperity, were declining by the early nineteenth century and there was no large-scale manufacturing to replace them. Despite these differences, there are close parallels between the emergence of modern urban planning in Britain and the process in Cork. It was not a sudden development but rather the result of several decades of problems, inquiry and gradual understanding. Here three distinct phases can be recognised.

Phase I, 1840-1878: identifying the problems

In Britain the Municipal Corporations Act of 1835 was the beginning of the public response to the problems in the cities.[29] The corresponding Irish act of 1840 was far weaker and less democratic than the British one, as the franchise was confined to properly owners of £10 valuation or more. The powers amounted to passing by-laws for local government and nuisance abatement. Cork lost its liberties and was reduced to some three and a half square miles, subdivided into eight wards.

The characteristic of this phase was an increasing awareness of the social and physical problems of the city and a sense that something had to be done about them. Many of the problems in British cities peaked about mid-century. Back-to-back housing had become the normal type for workers, leading to poor ventilation and intense overcrowding.[30] In Cork this new style had not been used, but housing conditions were poor. In 1851, the census classified 78.6 percent of inhabited houses as first or second class but many of these had deteriorated into tenements, occupied by many families.[31] In Murphy's estimates, almost 70 per cent of the population lived in slums in that year, and that figure did not fall below 63 percent until 1891.[32] Gross population density was extremely high in the older area of the city (Table 24.1). This peaked in 1851 in St Peter's Ward at 238 persons per acre (over 152,000 per square mile).

The conditions of the streets and public utilities were equally wanting.[33] Street lighting had been introduced to Cork by a corporation act of 1718 and had been gradually upgraded. A piped water supply had started in 1768, but because of its cost (2 guineas per annum) it was confined to the wealthy. There was only one public fountain until the nineteenth century. All contemporary accounts stress the appaling physical conditions of the city centre: the dirt, smoke, open sewers, flooding, congested streets and overcrowded slums.[34] These problems must have been exacerbated by the topography of the city and by the slaughtering and provision trade. Health conditions were as bad as those of most British cities, with outbreaks of smallpox and cholera and an ongoing problem of typhus.[35] A paper read by Henry Biggs to the British Association meeting in Cork in 1843 examined living and health conditions in three contrasting streets in the city and quantified the problems involved.[36]

There seemed a clear relationship between over-crowding, poor housing and ill-health. In Pikes Lane (one of the many old lanes and small streets of the city centre which have long since disappeared), which was only four feet wide and had up to seven people sleeping in a single room with, on average, over 18 persons per house, 38 of the 145 inhabitants (26.2 per cent) had been sick in the previous twelve

Table 24.1
Gross population densities 1841-1926
(Persons per acre)

Year	Urban area	City centre	Highest density	Parish/Ward
1841	35.6	149.0	219	St Peter's
1851	37.8	171.3	237.9	,,
1861	35.4	147.5	215.3	,,
1871	34.7	110.6	138.0	No. 1 Centre
1881	35.4	92.8	109.6	,,
1891	33.3	79.2	128.6	,,
1901	30.3	70.3	92.5	,,
1911	30.5	60.8	78.9	,,
1926	31.3	54.8	79.7	No. 7 West

Source: Census, 1841-1926.

months. In contrast, Castle Street averaged fewer than six inhabitants per house with less than that total of people sleeping in one room and only nine of its 176 residents (5.1 per cent) had been ill in the previous year.

The response by public bodies to these problems was generally inadequate and disorganised, and considerably poorer than the British reaction to similar ones. The Towns Improvement Clauses Act was passed in 1817 and should have led to enhanced conditions. It provided for the paving of streets, better drainage and lighting, the removal of obstructions and the provision of recreational spaces – many of the elements which would have led to considerable improvement. Unfortunately, these proposals were optional and their implementation was left to the discretion of individual authorities. In Cork local acts were passed in 1852 and 1853. Under these the corporation did clear some congested streets and build some new houses, but this did little to benefit the poorer people and was opposed by them.[37] There were some other developments during this period.[38] Water supply and sewage disposal were improved. The Cork, Blackrock and Passage Railway Station was opened on Victoria Quay in 1850 and the station on the lower Glanmire Road followed in 1855. There were also transport improvements within the city, for instance, the introduction of a horse-drawn tram system in 1872. This proved to be uneconomic, however, and it was closed four years later. The South Slob, the site of the proposed new town of 1780, was reclaimed and Victoria Park was opened there in 1854. In 1869 it was converted into a racecourse, a function it retained until 1917. There was little improvement for the bulk of the population, however. Almost 11,000 families were still living in slums in 1871, and there were serious outbreaks of smallpox in 1872 and enteric fever in 1877.[39]

Phase II, 1878-1897: a more active response

This period began with several important acts related to physical planning. Under the 1874 Public Health (Ireland) Act, Cork corporation became an urban sanitary authority. This function applied to all borough corporations and towns of 6,000 people, but it added no new powers. Another Public Health Act of 1878 introduced comprehensive and updated sanitary laws which are still largely in effect today. A further important development came with the Artisans' and Labourers' Dwellings Improvement Acts of 1875 and 1879. Together these acts changed the role of the local authorities from one of control and standard-setting to one of an active involvement in physical development.

There was also a greater awareness of the need for planning and the potential benefits arising from it. In 1883 Robert Walker, the architect of the Cork Exhibition of that year, lectured to the Cork Literary and Scientific Society on the need for planning in the city.[40] His lecture stressed the importance of proper sanitation. He suggested some civic improvements, such as a town hall, a mansion house and a science and art building for the Literary and Scientific Society (he was 'quite tired of the delay' in providing the latter). His proposals for transport were more practical: they included a swivel bridge and a floating dock to protect the quays and flush the sewers as well as improving the berthing of ships. He also wanted more reclamation and a cattle market on the new ground. In many respects Walker's lecture now seems very dated, but its importance lies in the fact that it was the first comprehensive plan for the city.

In practice, planning largely consisted of slum clearance and the building of by-law housing. This new style of housing had developed in Britain in response to the prevailing miasmatic theory of disease transmission.[43] This held that most diseases were spread by vapours given off by rotting waste, so proper ventilation was essential. Back-to-back workers' housing was regarded as very unhealthy. The new model by-laws of the 1870s stipulated that every house should face onto an open street of at least twenty feet (thirty feet if used for traffic) and have an open space behind it to ensure the dwelling could be properly ventilated. In Britain the minimum by-law standards became the effective maximum for both local authorities and private developers, and the result was vast areas of 'Coronation Street' type buildings. Densities in these areas were very high (averaging 50 houses per net acre); their appearance was monotonous; they had no gardens or indoor toilets but they were a great advance on the slums and back-to-back terraces which preceded them.

The corporation built its first development in the new style in 1885-86. This was the 76 houses of Madden's Buildings on a 1.1 acre site in Blackpool. Each house had three rooms and cost £85 10s. 0d.[42] Between 1888 and 1892, three other corporation schemes were completed, providing another 270 houses (Table 24.2). All of these schemes are well preserved and are still in use today.

The Improved Dwellings Company was also active at this time. This group also followed the British precedent of philanthropic industrialists who had built workers' housing – in some cases, entire towns, like Saltaire near Bradford – during the nineteenth century.[43] These individuals' motivations ranged from self-interest (a happy worker being a productive one) to sincere concern for the poor and disadvantaged with, usually, a measure of missionary zeal (prohibitions on alcohol were common in such developments). The Cork company built over

Table 24.2
Public housing in Cork, 1886-1923

Development	Year	No.
Phase I		
Madden's Buildings	1886	76
Ryan's Buildings	1888	16
Horgan's Buildings	1891	126
Roche's Buildings	1892	128
TOTAL		346
Phase II		
Sutton's Buildings	1905	46
Barrett's Buildings	1906	73
Kelleher's Buildings	1906	50
TOTAL		169
Phase III		
McCurtain's Villas	1922	76
French's Villas	1923	30
McSweeney's Villas	1923	40
TOTAL		146

400 houses between 1870 and 1900, letting them only to workers who took a pledge of temperance, and as Murphy has noted, expressing its ethos in the names of the developments: Prosperity Square, Prosperous Place and Industry Street.[44]

These housing schemes were welcome developments, but they did nothing to alleviate the lot of the poorest section of society. The buildings had to be financed at commercial rates, and high rents (3s. 0d. to 3s. 6d. per week) were charged. This was much higher than the slum rents and limited the tenants to better-paid workers and artisans. The public health officers of the time were calling for houses at rents of 1s. 0d. to 1s. 6d.[45]

By the late 1890s the housing problem was being tackled. The percentage of families in slums fell to 44.1 in 1891 and to 12.6 in 1901. By British standards, Cork's problem was not excessive. Black spots in British cities were far larger; for example Liverpool, Manchester and Newcastle all had single areas with 30,000-50,000 people in them, while in Cork, the medical officer was estimating that 5,000 to 6,000 people lived in tenements unfit for human habitation.[47] The population density figures for the time also indicate the reducing scale of Cork's problem (Table 24.1). Medical belief at the end of the nineteenth century held that a town could not be healthy when its gross population density exceeded 25 persons per acre.[48] This was a rough guide: Cork's figure (30.3 p.p.a.) was far better than Liverpool (52 p.p.a.), Manchester or Birmingham (42 p.p.a.) but worse than Cardiff or Northampton (25 p.p.a.). On this scale, Cork was amongst the twenty worst cities in Britain or Ireland.

Phase III, 1898-1926: planning becomes a reality

The year 1898 was a turning point in the development of planning both in Cork and at an international level. The passing of the Local Government Act in that year extended voting to males of all ages. It also established Cork County Borough, giving the corporation most of its present-day responsibilities. A modern transport system was established in the city by the Cork Electric Tramway Service.[49] Six routes of narrow gauge track radiated from the Statue in St Patrick's Street. Electric trams had been developed in Germany by Siemens and first used for public transport in Berlin in 1881. Most British cities did not adopt the new trams until their transport systems came under municipal control in the late 1890s. Electric trams were fast and efficient and their arrival facilitated city-wide movement. This was the end, both symbolically and functionally, of the old cellular city.

The third important development in 1898 was the publication in Britain of a book titled: *Tomorrow: a peaceful path to real reform* by a parliamentary stenographer named Ebenezer Howard.[50] This book, which is still in print (under the title *Garden cities of tomorrow),* argued for decentralisation from the large industrial cities to purpose-built towns of about 30,000 population. This generated enormous interest, especially among wealthy industrialists like George Cadbury and W. H. Lever who had already built model towns for their own workers (Bourneville in Birmingham and Port Sunlight on Merseyside). It also coincided with the outbreak of the Boer War and the rejection by the army of huge numbers of recruits from the cities on the grounds of bad health.[51] This convinced even conservative elements of the need for physical planning in British cities.

The ideas of Howard and his co-workers were widely disseminated and led in 1913 to the First International Congress of Cities, Town Planning and Housing which met at Ghent in Belgium.[52] Cork corporation was represented by Alderman Beamish. In 1911, the Royal Institute of Public Health held its Annual Congress in Dublin.[53] Six of its eight sections were concerned with medical matters but the others were devoted to engineering, housing and planning. The eminent planner Patrick Geddes came to Dublin for this and presented an exhibition and a series of lectures on planning. This congress led directly to the establishment of the Housing and Town Planning Association of Ireland in Dublin in 1911.[54] A Cork branch was founded in 1913.[55] As part of a series of meetings outside Dublin, D. A. Chart lectured in Cork City Hall in 1913 on planning.[56] He stressed the benefits of planning – health, beauty and convenience.

The most important public lecture came in 1917 by D. J. Coakley, Principal of the School of Commerce, to the Technical Instruction Committee of Cork corporation.[57] His talk was impressive in its grasp of the current literature. He reviewed the situation in continental countries and cited studies in London, Liverpool and Dundee. Poor housing was still the major problem in Cork and Coakley made several proposals: new housing schemes in the suburbs; co-partnership housing; state subsidies for workers' housing; and encouraging land owners to develop their own estates. He also argued for a town planning competition similar to that in Dublin in 1914, and a civic survey, with legal planning powers for the corporation and the development of a plan. All of these suggestions were eminently practical and very similar to developments in Dublin and elsewhere.

In the meantime, corporation house building had continued intermittently. In 1905 and 1906 three new estates totalling 169 houses had been constructed. These retained the same straight-line plan as the earlier schemes, but they were larger two-storey buildings. They had no gardens and their back yards were not much larger than the first phase of public housing. The design of these buildings was not up to the standards of the more advanced municipalities in Britain. These had been inspired by a speculative middle-class development called Bedford Park on the west side of London.[58] In effect, this estate of semi-detached houses, in the emerging Queen Anne style, with very generous landscaping, became the model for middle-class housing of the twentieth century. It also inspired the municipal authorities of the late nineteenth century. London County Council was the most advanced of these, and it used the powers of the 1890 Housing Act to develop 'cottage-estates' of attractive houses with generous gardens and landscaping. The Old Oak Estate near Wormwood Scrubs in Acton is regarded as the most successful of these.[59] These influences are evident in the third phase of corporation building in Cork (Table 24.2). Even the title 'Villa' replaced the more proletarian 'Building' which had been previously used, and the new estates had far more attractive houses in short terraces with gardens to the front and rear.

The first comprehensive plans

The pressure for more comprehensive planning was maintained in the 1920s. The Cork Town Planning Association was founded in 1922 under the chairmanship of A. F. Sharman Crawford and in 1923 the Cork Progressives Association was launched.[60] One of their demands was for an enquiry into the activities of Cork corporation. The reform of municipal government was one of the main demands of Progressives in the United States also at this time.[61] In Cork, the corporation was dissolved in 1924 and Philip Monahan was appointed Commissioner.[62] The Town Planning Association then proceeded with its Civic Survey which was published in 1926.[63] According to the planning philosophy espoused by Patrick Geddes, a survey was an essential preliminary to producing a plan and there had been many calls for such a survey in Dublin.

The Cork Civic Survey was an exhaustive, impressive document which is still very modern in many ways. The most important problems in the city at that time have dominated planning ever since. Poor housing was a major consideration, with over one-fifth of the population still living in unhealthy conditions. There were three large concentrations of slums: the largest was west of Shandon Street and north of Blarney Street, with smaller areas off Barrack Street and in the west side of the Marsh. The Civic Survey recognised that a long-term housing programme would be necessary, and the corporation began building at Capwell in 1928. This was followed in 1930 and 1932 by over 300 houses at Turner's Cross and by the Gurranebraher development from 1934 onwards. The other pre-war schemes at Commons Road, Spangle Hill, Greenmount and Assumption Road were also a direct response to the slum housing identified in the Civic Survey, and even the post-war housing estates all followed the same philosophy of large-scale developments on green-field sites. It is only over the past fifteen years that the corporation has encouraged inner-city renewal and infill rather than development on the periphery.

Transport was the second major problem identified in the Civic Survey, including, in this context, a map of cattle movements into and out of the city. Aside from this, the diagnosis of the problem remains relevant today: the island site and the lack of bridges, together with the convergence of roads in the city centre were producing congestion. Transport has remained a serious problem in Cork despite later plans which focussed particularly on the problem.[64]

The third deficiency identified in the 1926 survey was the lack of public open space. Cork had only 0.54 acres per 1,000 residents compared with 5.7 acres in Dublin. (Modern requirements are for 2 hectares or almost 5 acres per 1,000 persons). The expansion of the city on reclaimed land during the eighteenth century discouraged the development of public squares or gardens. In many respects therefore the Civic Survey of 1926 established an agenda for planning and development which lasted for some sixty years.

Planning was still not established on a statutory basis. A Town Planning Bill was introduced in 1929, but was then postponed and replaced by a Town and Regional Planning Act in 1934.[65] An advisory plan for Cork was prepared under this act by Manning Robertson in 1941.[66] Although only fifteen years later than the Civic Survey Robertson's proposals were of a totally different nature. He argued for decentralisation from the old city to suburban-type developments with very generous provision of public open space. He envisaged the city growing to a population of 254,000 on 11,000 acres surrounded by a green belt where development would be prohibited. New roads would be built in and around the city centre to ease traffic movement. Altogether the scale of these developments was inappropriate to a city of Cork's size; they were influenced by the prevailing British planning philosophy of that time, as exemplified by Patrick Abercombie's plan for Greater London in 1944.[67]

Comprehensive urban planning was fully established in 1963 by the Local Government (Planning and Development) Act and the first legally-binding city plan was adopted by Cork corporation in 1969. Since then planning has had a dominant influence on shaping the city environment. This essay has attempted to show that, contrary to popular perceptions, the process of planning in Cork has been quite long and influential. Almost all aspects of city building, design and planning over several hundred years are still evident in the city today. Many of them deserve more attention than they presently receive from both the public and local authorities. They represent part of the city's heritage as much as any historic building or work of architecture.

References

1. D. Hamblin, *The first cities* (Amsterdam, 1973), pp 122-153.
2. R. Wycherley, *How the Greeks built cities,* 2nd ed. (London, 1962), pp 15-35.
3. A. Morris, *History of urban form* (London, 1972), p. 63.
4. *Pacata hibernia.*
5. Morris, *Urban form,* pp 69-70.
6. R. Dickinson, *The west European city,* 2nd ed. (London, 1961), p. 29.
7. Dickinson, *West European city,* p. 29.
8. Morris, *Urban form,* p. 95.
9. Ibid., p. 86.
10. Ibid., p. 71
11. Ibid., p. 103.
12. Ibid., pp 107-108.
13. M. Craig, *Dublin 1660-1860* (Dublin, 1969), p. 172.
14. Craig, *Dublin,* p. 174.
15. Caulfield, *Cork.*
16. M. Gough, 'A history of the physical development of Cork city', unpublished M.A. thesis, U.C.C. (1974), iii, p. 359.

17. Morris, *Urban form,* pp 108-9.
18. P. Zucker, *Town and square* (New York, 1959).
19. Smith, *Cork,* pp 403-04.
20. Windele, *Cork.*
21. Morris, *Urban form,* pp 153-58, 171-72, 176
22. C. and R. Bell, *City fathers: the early history of town planning in Britain* (Middlesex, 1972), pp 93-107.
23. The map is reprinted in *Cork. Hist. Soc. Jn.,* xxxiv, no. 140 (1929), p. 116.
24. K. Davis, *Cities* (New York, 1972), p. 17.
25. G. Cherry, *The evolution of British town planning* (Bedfordshire, 1974).
26. A. Sutcliffe, *Towards the planned city* (Oxford, 1981), pp 9-46.
27. S. Rasmussen, *Towns and buildings* (Liverpool, 1951), pp 160-171 and 145-49.
28. M. Murphy, 'The working classes of nineteenth-century Cork' in *Cork Hist. Soc. Jn.,* lxxxv (1980), p. 27.
29. Cherry, *British town planning.*
30. Sutcliffe, *Planned city,* pp 51-2.
31. *Census of Ireland 1851* (Dublin, 1856), vi, p. 230.
32. Murphy, 'Working classes', p. 29.
3. Gough, 'Physical development', p. 205.
34. Gough, 'Physical development'.
35. Murphy, 'Working classes', p. 29.
36. H. Biggs, *Annals of the county and city of Cork* (Cork, 1843).
37. Murphy, 'Working classes", p. 30.
38. Gough, 'Physical development', pp 222-24.
39. Murphy, 'Working classes', p. 29.
40. R. Walker, *The city of Cork: how it may be improved* (Cork, 1883).
41. Sutcliffe, *Planned city,* p. 51.
42. M. Gough, 'Socio-economic conditions and the genesis of planning Cork' in M. Bannon (ed.), *The emergence of Irish planning 1880-1920* (Dublin, 1985), p. 311.
43. Ball, *City fathers,* pp 215-286.
44. Murphy, 'Working classes', p. 30.
45. Gough, 'Socio-economic conditions', p. 311.
46. Murphy, 'Working Classes', p. 29.
47. Gough, 'Socio-economic conditions', p. 311.
48. Cherry, *British town planning,* pp 12-13.
49. Gough, 'Physical development', pp 240-1.
50. E. Howard, *Tomorrow: a peaceful path to real reform* (London, 1898).
51. G. Cherry, *Cities and plans* (London, 1988), pp 53-56.
52. Sutcliffe, *Planned city,* p. 173.
53. M. Bannon, 'The genesis of modern Irish planning' in Bannon, *Irish planning,* p. 196.
54. Bannon, 'The genesis of Irish planning', p. 201.
55. Ibid., p. 203.
56. Ibid., p. 204.
57. D. Coakley, *The general principles of housing and town planning* (Cork, 1917).
58. A. Edwards, *The design of suburbia* (London, 1981), p. 61.
59. Ibid., p. 91.
60. Gough, 'Socio-economic conditions', p. 319.
61. J. Friedmann and C. Weaver, *Territory and function* (London, 1979), p. 55.
62. Gough, 'Socio-economic conditions', p. 320.
63. Cork Town Planning Association, *Cork: a civic survey* (Liverpool, 1926).

64. B.K.S. Consulative Technical Services Ltd., *Cork traffic study report and recommendations* (Cork, 1968); Skidmore, Owings and Merrill, *Cork land use/ transporation plan* (Cork, 1978).

65. For a history of twentieth-century Irish planning see M. Bannon (ed.), *Planning: the Irish experience, 1920-1988* (Dublin, 1989).

66. M. Robertson, *County borough of Cork and neighbournood town planning report* (Cork, 1941).

67. Cherry, *Cities and plans,* pp 125-28.

Plate 24.1   The Firkin Crane Centre (Cork Archaeological Survey).

Chapter 25

CLASS, COMMUNITY AND THE IRISH REPUBLICAN ARMY IN CORK, 1917–1923

PETER HART

This was a war between the British Army and the Irish people.

Tom Barry[1]

Surely, what we chiefly do when we speak of the People is to make an historic reference to certain more or less defined loyalties, and to those who fought for them whether under Collins, Redmond, Davitt, O'Connell, or Wolfe Tone. It is a term, that is, which frankly excludes and frankly sets a boundary.

Seán Ó Faoláin[2]

Of all the revolutionary regimes which emerged in Europe in the wake of the Great War, the Irish republic in Cork[3] in 1922 was perhaps the least substantial and most curious. Republicans who opposed the treaty with England claimed that the whole island was an indivisible sovereign state, but in practice it was only in Cork and adjoining areas that they held effective power. Only in Cork were there republican censors, tax collectors and even postage stamps, all administered by the Irish Republican Army (I.R.A.)[4] which constituted the sole real authority in the county for the first eight months of 1922. This sketchy government was quickly dubbed, half-jokingly, the 'Republic of Cork'.[5]

It would be impossible to say exactly when and where this transient republic began and ended. People had given their allegiance to, and acted in the name of, 'the Republic' as an ideal or (il)legal fiction since 1917, and continued to do so after the end of the Civil War in 1923. In 1920 and 1921, many local communities began to call themselves 'the republic' after the police had withdrawn and the I.R.A. had taken control.[6] These village and parish republics reappeared after the Free State established itself, and the I.R.A. was still demanding allegiance – and taxes – in the same areas well into 1924. One National Army report described a portion of west Cork as being 'like the border of an independent state with our troops sallying occasionally into the enemy but never able to reach the most important centres'.[7]

More significant than any physical boundaries, however, were the

Plate 25.1   General Tom Barry (Cork Public Museum).

imagined ones which defined 'the Republic' in the minds of its adherents. The profusion of republics of all shapes and sizes in Cork between 1917 and 1923 suggests the complexity of this identity, and the variety of meanings that the term 'the Republic' held for different people. We can trace the boundaries of the imagined republic in the origins, attitudes and behaviour of the I.R.A., which embodied the revolution. Who did Tom Barry and his comrades have in mind when they acted in the name of 'the people' or 'the republic'? How did they define themselves and their loyalties? Who were they excluding?

The composition of the I.R.A.

First impressions

An enormous amount has been written about the I.R.A. and the name conjures up powerful images and symbols, but we still know very little about what sort of people joined and why. This question goes to the heart of political myths both new and old. Were the Volunteers a nation in arms or a 'murder gang' composed of thugs and loafers?

Most official commentators, whether British or Free State, echoed one English officer's caustic appraisal of the Cork I.R.A. as being made up of 'farmers' sons and corner boys who had no stake in the country'.[8] Opinions in the Royal Irish Constabulary ranged from the Inspector General's lofty declaration that the Volunteers were 'half educated shop assistants and excitable young rustics'[9] to the local sergeants, who knew them as 'insignificant' but generally 'respectable' young men.[10] This contemptuous tone was widely adopted. In Timoleague they were called 'ignorant country boys' and in Castletownbere 'raw country bogcutters'.[11] The Skibbereen *Eagle* referred to participants in one Volunteer parade as 'young rustics, bored by the vacuity of country life, and Skibbereen "sparks" wishful of a change from billiards'.[12] Such were the opinions of the Cork establishment.

The general consensus among soldiers, policemen and those with a stake in the country was that most rebels were unskilled youths with little social status and too much time on their hands. So pervasive were these stereotypes that 'the usual I.R.A. type' became a common description of suspects in military and police reports; British intelligence officers had to point out to their colleagues that 'it is a mistake to imagine that rebels can be recognised through their uncouth state, or by peculiarities of their dress'.[13]

Not surprisingly, I.R.A. members vehemently rejected the charges of being shiftless, uneducated hoodlums but, labels aside, they usually placed themselves within much the same modest social categories. They were indeed 'plain people' but they represented the hard-working and respectable heart of the nation. Republican contempt was reserved for the gentry, 'shoneens' and 'gombeen men' above them and the tinkers, corner boys and 'gutties' below. They would certainly include in their company good farm labourers and tradesmen, but countrymen might well have disputed the idea that theirs was an army of shop assistants. Rural rebels generally viewed towns with the gravest suspicion and would have heartily endorsed the view of Con Leddy, an I.R.A. officer from Araglen, that 'the country always was ahead of the towns'.[14] Most towns in Cork were felt by the local militants to be lacking in national fibre. Skibbereen's inhabitants 'were a race apart from the sturdy people of West Cork. They were different and with a few exceptions were spineless.' Midleton was 'a shoneen town'; Fermoy was 'essentially a loyalist town', and so on.[15]

On the other hand, I.R.A. units in northern and eastern parts of the county often thought that farmers, and large farmers in particular, held aloof from the struggle or, at best, were only fair-weather republicans. Ned Murphy, for example, thought that farmers around Mallow only joined the movement to avoid conscription and 'save their skins', and that 'the farmers' sons there never joined up the Volunteers, but the labourers were Volunteers in this area'.[16] One I.R.A. captain was even more blunt: 'God bless yeer souls ye pack of farmers whatever we are you are not much anyway'.[17]

Wealth and property were felt to be inimical to true patriotism. Indeed, the propertied were frequently blamed for the 'betrayal' of the republic and subsequent civil war. One intelligence officer from north Cork summed up the local Free Staters as 'the Farmers' Union [largely composed of strong farmers] and the Businessmen, Middle-Men, Landlord and Capitalist class'.[18] These groups were also identified with the old leadership of the Irish Party, who were presumed to be plotting their return to power and were intent on 'preserving the old ranks and grades in society'.[19] The natural corollary of such views was that, as Ted O'Sullivan, a staff officer of the West (3rd) Cork Brigade, put it, 'all the mountain and the poor areas were good'; he also asserted that small farmers and labourers were the backbone of the rebellion.[20]

In Cork city the I.R.A.'s social centre of gravity was again assumed to lie among the middling classes, between the genteel suburbs and the slums, each in their own way beholden to the British administration and British money. Volunteer membership was concentrated in working and lower-middle-class neighbourhoods like Blackpool and Evergreen. There were a few ardent republicans among the middle classes, such as the Gallagher and Kennedy families and their circle, but there were not many others who held memberships in both the I.R.A. and tennis clubs.[21]

All of these aspects of the I.R.A.'s identity applied to the officers as well as the rank and file. As Ernie O'Malley wryly observed in 1919: 'Often a man – a non-Volunteer – will point with pride and awe to the local President of the Sinn Féin Club; he would not dream of doing so where the local Volunteer Captain is concerned'.[22] The British Army's 1921 guide to 'Sinn Féin and the Irish Volunteers' ascribed the I.R.A.'s lack of proper discipline to the fact that the class background of the officers was 'exactly the same as the rank and file'.[23]

This lower-class sense of identity produced very little in the way of organisational class-consciousness. The I.R.A.'s dominant public values were the respectable middle-class ones of temperance, self-improvement and discipline, and these were taken very seriously by most officers and activists.[24] Many Volunteers were union members (for example, Michael Fitzgerald, the Commandant of the Fermoy Battalion in 1920, was also Secretary of the local Irish Transport and General Workers Union (I.T.G.W.U.) branch), and many participated in land disputes and strikes as individuals, but if the I.R.A. intervened it was almost always to protect property. Members of the I.T.G.W.U. were assumed to be allies, but only insofar as they directed their efforts toward the struggle for independence. Union organisers were considered a nuisance by leaders such as Seán Moylan and Liam Lynch. Lynch, while commander of the First Southern Division, declared that 'my experience is that certain organisers try to put Labour above Freedom, this may go on for some time, but not even their own individual members may stick this'.[25]

These tensions came to a head in late 1921 and 1922 when strikes in Whitechurch, Doneraile, Midleton and other parts of north and east Cork triggered I.R.A. responses which were immediately labelled anti-union. Embittered farm labourers complained that 'many of the farmers' sons are in certain organisations for their own benefit, and to use such against the workers', but they never mutinied or tried to use the army themselves.[26]

Just as striking farm and creamery workers felt that their employers exerted undue influence on the I.R.A., so militants within the movement sometimes lamented that local officers were chosen because of their social standing rather than their efficiency. When it came to fighting, however, the gunmen grew impatient with traditional social hierarchies:

> The chap generally elected Company Commander or Brigade Commandant was the man who was the biggest farmer or biggest shopkeeper's son in the district. Great men to parade with a flag who lent their prestige and their money to the fight, but they

Plate 25.2   Jer Dennehy, C. Conroy, Seán Ó Tuama and Seán Moylan, Spike Island 1921 (Cork Public Museum).

didn't fight, and those who didn't vamoose had to be shifted out of the way when the fighting started.[27]

Hardened guerrillas saw their flying columns as classless societies, united by patriotism. Florence O'Donoghue wrote that 'it is a wonderful comradeship this, of men drawn from every walk of life, from the Professor to the simple labourer, all united and contented in a noble service'.[28] The egalitarianism of active service sometimes bred a certain primitive jacobinism (Tom Barry once claimed that 'we had in effect been the first practical socialists in the country'[29]), as when land and cattle belonging to 'enemies of the Republic' were seized and redistributed in north and west Cork in 1921 and 1922. In many cases, though, these seizures were little more than the usual family and factional gambits to gain more land or stock.[30]

Whatever the levelling inclinations of some, Cork republicans as a group were no *sans-culottes*. If the social boundaries of 'the people' skirted around big farms and affluent suburbs, they also generally stopped short of the back lanes and workhouses inhabited by the 'undeserving' poor. These marginal sections of the population were classed as drunkards, thieves and prostitutes. It was assumed that recruits for the British and Free State armies were almost entirely drawn from such vice-ridden quarters, and ex-soldiers returning from the Great War were tarred with the same brush. Thus corner-boys and loafers, tramps and tinkers, and 'separation women' (soldiers' wives) were looked down upon both socially and politically by republicans.

The most striking feature of the Volunteers was not their class composition but their youth, and it was this factor which was most commented upon. For many observers this politicisation and radicalisation of the young – 'mere boys' – represented the real revolution, with the lines of conflict drawn between generations rather than parties. A Skibbereen judge spoke for many in 1921 when he concluded that 'the farmers themselves are anxious to settle down and want peace, but their sons won't let them, and the sooner they get rid of the sons the better for themselves, because the country is going to ruin by the actions of irresponsible boys'.[31] For once, 'the boys' were in charge. Volunteers often revelled in this revolt against their fathers and political and clerical father-figures.[32] A Bantry I.R.A. man recalled that 'our fathers and mothers were more or less against us at the time, but we all joined up, all the neighbours, all the young fellas'.[33] Another put it more succinctly: 'we didn't consult them'.[34]

Despite their new-found authority, however, the Volunteers discovered that their youth still prevented many people from taking them seriously. The Cork Brigades shared the chagrin of other Munster units at 'the general opinion that we are schoolboys out for a holiday'.[35] The I.R.A. responded by threatening those who ridiculed them with fines or expulsion from the country. One Castletownbere resident who made rude remarks about the rebels in a letter that was intercepted by the I.R.A. was fined £100 and warned 'that if he again uses such remarks against our forces he will suffer the extreme penalty'.[36]

Finally, Cork I.R.A. members were universally male and Roman Catholic. These may seem to be obvious points, but both were of the utmost importance. In fact, women were early and enthusiastic participants in the Sinn Féin movement, and were prominent in crowd violence on the streets of Cork and smaller towns in 1917 and 1918. As the fighting escalated, female activists were relegated to supporting roles within Cumann na mBan, the Volunteers' auxiliary organisation. This marginalisation of women was due to the increase in danger, but it was probably also related to the stagnation of the Sinn Féin party as it was eclipsed by the I.R.A. The latter organisation drew much of its strength from local youth culture and its informal networks of friends, cliques and gangs. Effective guerrilla action depended on these sorts of tightly-knit groups, and this process of male bonding actively excluded women. The following anonymous verse suggests a not unambivalent acceptance of this role:

> Harra for the Sinn Féin, the Sinn Féin are men,
> and if I were a boy I would go Sinn Féin with them.
> But as I am a girl I must lead a girl's life.
> But I'll do all in my power to be a Sinn Féin wife.[37]

Almost all I.R.A. men were practising Catholics, even under the Catholic church ban imposed during the Civil War. It is not their religiousness that is at issue, however, but their attitudes towards Protestants, who were present in Cork in considerable numbers, particularly in the south-west of the county and in the city. This attitude was one of increasing suspicion and hostility. The dominant image of Protestants was one of landlords and the ascendancy, the hereditary enemies. It was widely believed that Masonic Lodges and the Young Men's Christian Association were the seats of anti-republican conspiracies, and that loyalists were spying on their neighbours.[38] The I.R.A. occasionally tried to conscript Protestant men but this was only to extract money or intimidate opponents.[39]

These opposing images of the I.R.A. – its own and its enemies – parallel one another in some intriguing respects. Policemen, soldiers and guerrillas all agreed that the Volunteers were mostly men with little or no stake in the country because they were too young or too poor, and that the propertied population lacked the 'moral courage' to either join or oppose them. Each side looked on the other as a mob of armed hoodlums, and themselves as the upholders of decency. Both saw the 'rabble' and corner-boys as being on the other side. British (and some Free State) soldiers and many local Protestants 'regarded all civilians as "Shinners"'.[40] Everyone appealed to more or less the same labels and categories to place the I.R.A. and mark its social boundaries.

Further analysis

A range of other data exists which may be used to test the veracity of the foregoing impressions.[41] An analysis of this information yields the following tables which offer a statistical yardstick for comparison to the perceptions examined above:

Table 25.1

I.R.A.: composition and membership
Cork county (excluding Cork city)

Occupations	Officers			Rank and file			Census	
	1917-19	'20-'21	'22-'23	1917-19	'20-'21	'22-'23	1911	1926
Sample	139	186	99	255	680	329		
Percentage								
Farmer or son	28	27	29	29	31	19	45	41
Farm labourer	04	06	08	12	10	20	25	18
Un/semi-skilled	06	09	07	15	18	27		14
Skilled	23	24	24	21	18	21		08
Clerk	20	13	18	09	11	05		06
Merchant or son	12	13	05	07	06	03		05
Professional	05	04	04	01	03	02		02
Student	01	01	—	02	01	01		4
Other	02	04	04	02	02	02		05
Ages								
Sample	199	271	122	525	1,176	374		
Percentage								
Under 20	21	11	03	28	25	19		
20-29	58	59	71	56	58	66		
30-39	15	24	20	13	15	14		
40-49	02	04	05	03	02	01		
50-59	04	01	02	01	—	—		

Source: Reference 41.

The rebels came from a broad range of backgrounds and from most sectors of the local economy. The organisation had particular success among the building trades, motor drivers and drapers' assistants. Shoe and boot makers, living up to their international reputation for radicalism, were also prominent. Other occupations such as fisherman were almost completely unrepresented.[42] Artisans and tradesmen provided a solid core of support for the movement in both the city and county, just as they had for the Fenians fifty years before. Farming families, although under-represented, also usually provided at least a quarter of the I.R.A.'s members outside the city.

Upper-middle or upper-class people almost never became involved. Most of the 'professionals' in the I.R.A. were teachers, and assistant or part-time teachers at that, and so were at the lower end of the middle class. Similarly, nearly all skilled workers in the movement were apprentices or young journeymen. Those with merchant backgrounds were generally small shopkeepers and publicans or their sons. These upper social limits were matched by lower ones. Few I.R.A. men appear to have been unemployed or indigent. Nor were many casual labourers to be found in their ranks; there were, for example, very few dock workers in the Volunteers.

Those Volunteers who came from farming backgrounds followed much the same pattern. Over 80 per cent were sons working on their

Table 25.2
I.R.A.: composition and membership
Cork city

| Occupations | Officers | | | Rank and file | | | Census |
	1917-19	'20-'21	'22-'23	1917-19	'20-'21	'22-'23	1926
Sample	34	45	35	43	138	20	
Percentage3							
Un/semi-skilled	—	03	14	21	30	43	39
Skilled	33	38	41	45	39	33	25
Clerk	32	36	28	20	21	14	13
Professional	20	16	14	—	01	01	3
Merchant	02	02	—	03	03	03	06
Student	—	—	—	12	05	01	02
Other	11	07	03	—	02	04	11
Ages							
Sample	26	35	31	46	122	130	
Percentage							
Under 20	15	09	03	41	29	23	
20-29	62	66	65	46	64	62	
30-39	23	26	29	11	06	12	
40-49	—	—	03	—	01	02	
50-59	—	—	—	02	01	01	

Source: Reference 41.

father's land, a respectable occupation but one with little status or money. These youths came from farms of all sizes. Table 25.3 below shows the distribution of holdings by valuation within a rural I.R.A. company in west Cork, as compared with the general population of the District Electoral Division (D.E.D.) in which it was located.[43]

The values of the officers' farms were: £19, £32, £34 and £74. Judging by this sample (from an area of average wealth for west Cork), I.R.A. members tended to be drawn from reasonably successful families, and rarely from below the rural poverty line.

The most striking result shown by these tables is the extent to which Volunteers had non-agricultural occupations and, it may be inferred, lived and worked in urban rather than rural settings.[44] It would be wrong, however, to draw too sharp a line between the town and the countryside, as kinship and commerce linked them closely; many shop assistants and general labourers were farmers' sons. It is also worth noting that the sample is biased toward activists and those who came to official attention and so may not be a completely accurate reflection of the full membership. However, even with these qualifications, it is clear that the urban population of Cork outside the city was considerably over-represented and that this was a consistent feature throughout the revolutionary period. And if the very active city units are included, the urban orientation of the organisation becomes even more pronounced.

These basic characteristics were shared by both officers and men, but there were also important differences. By and large, officers tended to be older and of higher social status: white-collar workers rather than manual labourers. The most significant distinction was between farmers and their sons on the one hand and their employees on the other. Agricultural workers rarely became officers (although the chances increased slightly as time went on), especially in east Cork which was the main arena of rural class conflict. The farmers had a decisive edge in this respect, but did not dominate the I.R.A. as a whole. This helps

Table 25.3

Behagh company: rank and file value of land holdings (percentage)

	Up to £10	£11-20	£21-30	£31-40	£41-50	£51-100	£100+
1917-19	05	33	38	15	03	03	03
1920-21	07	27	40	13	07	03	03
1922-23	—	13	50	25	—	13	—
Manch D.E.D	30	30	21	10	03	03	03

Source: Reference 41.

account for its general neutrality during agricultural strikes and for the fact that it usually moved against strikers only when food supplies to urban markets were threatened.[45]

The data do not reveal any dramatic changes in the social structure of the I.R.A. between 1917 and 1923. After 1922, manual labourers began to replace farmers and white-collar workers among the rank and file, while the number of officers who were professionals or merchants declined. The army was becoming more proletarian. The leadership matured over the years and lost its adolescent fringe. Their followers remained quite young, suggesting a fairly constant intake of new recruits.

An examination of the sources, therefore, shows the Volunteers to have been more or less correct in their self-assessment. They were neither very poor nor very well off, but came from the central stratum of 'plain people' in between. The egalitarian image was somewhat illusory, as few unskilled workers became officers, but the organisation as a whole was predominantly lower-class.

The countrymen may well have been correct in viewing the towns as the centres of resistance to the Republic, but they were wrong in thinking that urban areas did not also contribute to the guerrilla war. This apparent polarisation within towns may have helped mobilise and radicalise the Volunteers; the presence of hostile civilians, as well as police and military garrisons, may have forced them to go on the run earlier and in greater numbers than their rural comrades.[46] I.R.A. fighters were partly right in seeing the farming class as reluctant republicans, but agricultural labourers were even less prominent until the Civil War.

Motivation for membership

So far we have discussed the social dimensions and attitudes of the I.R.A. in Cork, but this does not tell us why particular individuals joined the organisation. The question of personal motivation is oddly absent from most memoirs and first-hand accounts of the period. The majority of rebels seem to have regarded their political choices as completely natural, and their motives as self-evident, requiring little reflection.

It would be wrong to deny these men their very real convictions and ideals, but it seems clear that for the majority of Volunteers the decision to join was a collective rather than an individual one, rooted more in the local community than in ideology or formal political loyalties. Of course, there were exceptions, especially among the leadership. Men such as Terence McSwiney, and Tomás MacCurtain were 'republicans' and 'Sinn Féiners' well before the Irish Volunteers were founded. Nevertheless, the general tendency was for men to enter the organisation together with members of their families and peer groups. Companies were usually formed on local initiative by self-nominated organisers, often brothers or cousins. These men recruited volunteers from among their trusted 'pals' – relatives, co-workers, schoolmates, neighbours, Gaelic Athletic Association team-mates and so on.[47] The organisers and local 'big fellas' would then be elected as officers.

Thus for most I.R.A. men, joining the movement in its early days required little deliberate choice or effort. If you had the right connections, or were part of a certain family or circle of friends, you became a Volunteer along with the rest of your 'crowd'. If not, you probably stayed outside or on the fringes. These informal networks and bonds gave the I.R.A. a cohesion that its formal structure and drills could never have produced.

Figure 25.1 shows the evolution of the Behagh Company (see Table 25.3, p. 973) from 1915 to the end of the Civil War in 1923.[48] This unit covered nine townlands within the D.E.D., an area of approximately eight square miles. The Volunteers were first organised locally in the nearby town of Dunmanway and the men of Behagh originally belonged to this unit. They established their own company in 1917 which then became part of the Dunmanway Battalion. Here, as elsewhere, the movement spread from town to countryside.

The figure also illustrates the importance of family and neighbour-hood in the organisation. At every stage in the company's develop-ment, the number of members with brothers in the unit was never less than half the total. It may be assumed that an even larger percentage belonged to the same extended families. The company was also spatially tightly knit. Most of the Volunteers were immediate neighbours, clustered around several crossroads in the heart of the district. Significantly, three of the four officers, Captain Tom Donovan, First Lieutenant Tim Crowley and Adjutant Tim Coakley, lived side by side, forming, with their brothers, an organisational nucleus. As numbers increased in 1917 and 1918 the unit expanded somewhat to more distant townlands, but in 1922-23 its boundaries shrank back to its core area. Consciously or unconsciously, the self-defined perimeter followed a natural frontier of rivers, marshes and woods and excluded the three nearby Big Houses. This line very likely marked the horizons of everyday life for the local community. The main link with the outside world, the market town of Dunmanway, was also the Behagh Company's link with their superiors and the rest of the organisation. The ties and boundaries that defined the community also determined the shape of the I.R.A.

The revolution may have transformed 'the boys' into soldiers of the Republic (one excited Corkman wrote of his local crowd: 'the free and

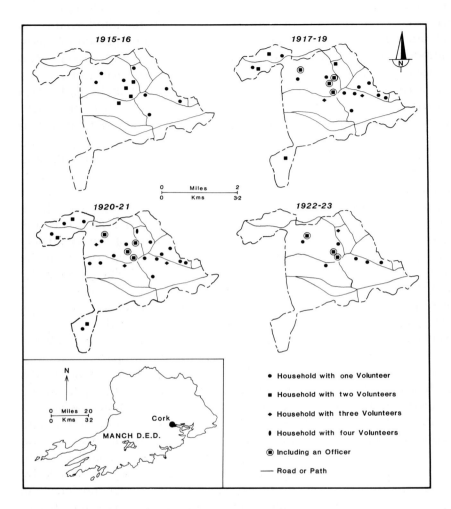

Figure 25.1   Origins of Volunteers, Manch D.E.D., 1915-23
Source: Reference 43.

easy going lads of Cahalanes Cross are quite the opposite now. They are "soldiers" ....'),[49] but they remained 'the boys' to those around them. The general use of this term to refer to the I.R.A. suggests that, as far as most people were concerned, the Volunteers' place in local society remained more or less the same.

However, while 'the boys' as a term of identity conveyed a sense of familiarity and either camaraderie or condescension, depending on the point of view, in other contexts it meant something quite different.

Traditional youth culture was one of subordination to parents, employers and priests, but it also contained an accepted element of ritualised rebellion which allowed for a temporary reversal of roles. On festival days such as St Stephen's Day, St Bridget's Day, All Hallows' Eve, Shrove Tuesday and wedding days, young men had a traditional right to wear disguises, march about in military fashion and demand money, food or entrance to houses, usually those of the better off. If these demands were not granted they would frequently exact a violent revenge, and so such events were often the occasion for rowdiness and confrontations with police. To symbolise this overturning of the normal code of deference clothes were often worn inside out, or else women's clothes were put on. These gangs, made up of a dozen or so members (drawn from family, friends and neighbours) and led by a Captain, were known as Wren Boys, Biddy Boys, Straw Boys, or just 'the Boys'.[50]

The role of such groups within the community was an ambiguous one. They mocked the established social order, to the annoyance of the police and respectable sections of society, yet the threat remained implicit. On the other hand, it was these same groups which acted to regulate the community according to popular standards of morality and justice. Unmarried mothers, adulterers, mixed (Protestant and Catholic) couples, land grabbers and offending landlords could all be pressurised by nocturnal visits or threatening letters to conform or leave. Of course, this role could be appropriated by a particular faction in a land, labour or political dispute, but even in these cases an appeal was usually made to local customs and rights.

'The boys', therefore, often represented the community, or at least thought they did, against local transgressors or outsiders. They patrolled the imagined boundaries and enforced conformity. This was a political sub-culture quite apart from the formal political arena which concerned itself with elections, parties and patronage. The two overlapped at election times when youthful enthusiasts were required as party followers and fighters, but young unpropertied men could not even vote until 1918. The players in one arena were almost never players in the other.

I.R.A. companies were a natural extension of this sub-culture and its unspoken assumptions and bonds. Most Volunteer 'operations' followed the Straw Boy/Wren Boy model very closely: the same disguises were worn and by far the most common activities were going to houses and demanding arms or money, robbing the mail-trains and intimidating recalcitrant neighbours, while dodging the police. The rebels' marching and drilling displays were equally derivative, as were the names they sometimes adopted, such as 'the Galty Boys' or 'the Hardy Boys'.[51] Nor did 'the boys' widen their political horizons when they joined the I.R.A. Although they canvassed, collected and provided protection for Sinn Féin at election time, Volunteers saw themselves as being apart from politics and parties altogether. One of the worst things that an I.R.A. member could say of another was that he was really only 'the Sinn Féin type'.[52]

The 'stake-in-the-country' men generally viewed the Volunteers with the same mixture of fear and contempt that they held for previous incarnations of 'the boys'. They were disorderly troublemakers who did not know their place, and they made the threat of youthful subversion real, at least for a few years:

> Then parent and priest may as well be dumb,
>   Their precepts were all ignored;
> And who can tell when the time will come
>   That their prestige will be restored;
> Then scant was the work of the plough or spade,
>   And employer kept silent beaks,
> For the boy was boss and the Mistress maid
>   In the time of the ten-foot pikes.[53]

Most Volunteers' experience of the revolution did not go far beyond the level of 'strawing' or following the 'wran'. One veteran told me that 'it was a very fluid business. If you were asked to do a thing, you went and did it'.[54] Frank O'Connor felt that 'if it was nothing else, it was a brief escape from tedium and frustration to go out the country roads on summer evenings, slouching along in knee-breeches and gaiters, hands in the pockets of one's trench-coat and hat pulled over one's right eye'.[55]

For others, like Liam Lynch, the I.R.A. was their whole life:

> Immediately he joined the Volunteers, Lynch ... associated only with comrades in the movement. From the very start when he joined the Sinn Féin Club and Volunteers in Fermoy he attended every meeting and parade and after business hours he invariably went to the Sinn Féin Club.[56]

Likewise, commitments and expectations could vary greatly over the years. Frank O'Connor, for example, moved from the fringes of the organisation in 1921 to full-time activity in 1922. When Volunteer companies were formed, or re-formed, in 1917 and 1918, very few of those who joined expected to fight a guerrilla war. At most, involvement might entail raiding houses for guns, rioting or a few months in jail. At this stage the organisation was not a revolutionary one. It was not even illegal.

By mid-1920 the dedicated revolutionaries within the I.R.A., often members of the clandestine Irish Republican Brotherhood such as Dan Corkery in Macroom, Sean O'Hegarty in Cork city or the Hales brothers of Ballinadee, had pushed the movement into open revolt. In the process an informal but recognisable division of labour grew up between this small hard core of committed activists, made up of both officers and men, and the membership at large, who became peripheral and occasional auxiliaries. The former went abroad in flying columns, monopolised the rifles and did most of the organising and fighting. The latter stayed at home, did scout duty, wrecked roads and bridges, robbed postmen and probably never fired a shot in anger.[57] Many nominal members who had joined in easier days were unwilling to do even this much, and had to be more or less forced into action.[58] In 1922 the bulk of these ordinary members withdrew altogether and their local companies melted away, leaving the guerrillas on their own.

Insiders and outsiders

Revolution meant the erosion of deference and social control within villages and parishes, and the rise to power of a county and nation-wide 'revolutionary élite' composed of previously unknown young men dedicated to the establishment of a republic.[59] However, although I.R.A. members in many respects rejected or moved outside the influence of traditional communal authorities and claimed (and believed them-selves) to be fighting for a national republic, their definition of the 'nation' followed the traditional boundaries of their local communities. 'The people' were those who fell inside these limits, and the enemies were those who fell outside. These marginal groups became the victim of the revolution.

Let us take, for example, those civilians shot by the I.R.A. as enemies. Between January 1920 and 11 July 1921 at least 146 so-called 'spies' and 'informers' were dealt with in this fashion, and 61 more were shot between 12 July 1921 and May 1923.[60] Thirty-six per cent of the victims were Protestants (who numbered approximately eight per cent of the Cork population) and eight per cent were 'tramps' or 'tinkers'. Seven were 'feeble-minded', five were identified by the I.R.A. as sexual deviants. Others belonged to the urban class of unemployed casual labourers and petty thieves. In addition, 29 per cent were ex-servicemen, many of whom also belonged to one or more of the above categories. All of these people were, in one way or another, outsiders, and were thus both suspect and vulnerable.

It might be suggested that Protestants and ex-soldiers were naturally hostile to the I.R.A. and more likely both to be working with the police or military, and to be shot. This was not so. The authorities obtained little information from either group and, in fact, by far the greatest damage was done by people within the organisation, or their relatives.[61] In any case, we can test this idea using the Cork Brigades' own 1921 lists of those identified as informers.[62] Only 17 per cent of these 157 suspects were Protestant and only 10 per cent were ex-soldiers. None were described as vagrants, mental incompetents or moral deviants. It is clear that members of certain marginal groups were much more likely to become victims and that they were often killed on the flimsiest of grounds, as reprisals or to set an example.

These murders were the culmination of a long process of exclusion and victimisation. Before Protestants and ex-soldiers were killed they were usually first ridiculed, denounced, raided, threatened, robbed and boycotted. Some were ordered to leave, having been found 'unworthy of a place in the citizenship of the Irish Republic'.[63] These people lived in a state of growing isolation and fear, and many fled the country, leaving their property to be divided up among the neighbours who had closed ranks against them.[64] The same process had earlier been directed against the local police.

Itinerants of all types, from unemployed drifters to 'tribes' of tinkers, were similarly harassed and eventually expelled from most towns and many country districts by the Volunteers, with the full approval of the local residents. As strangers without homes or families these victims were a natural focus for communal hostility and were acutely vulnerable. In the midst of terror and counter-terror they could vanish without a trace.[65]

This pattern of violence continued well after the British forces withdrew and throughout the Civil War. 44 per cent of those killed in 1922 and 1923 were Protestant, and 37 per cent were veterans of either the police or the army. These murders peaked in late April 1922 when, in three nights, fifteen Protestant men in south-west Cork were shot in their homes. This massacre may have been prompted by atrocities in Belfast and by the recent shootings of an I.R.A. officer while he was breaking into a house. One victim was called a 'Free Stater' by his attackers but the majority were elderly and apolitical. The gunmen wanted revenge, but they also wanted to exterminate or drive away all Protestants in the area. This idea of a final settlement of old grievances was a common one in 1921 and 1922.[66]

The dispossession and disempowerment of Protestants put into practice the youthful vision of 'the world upside down' inherent in the symbolism of the Wren/Straw/Biddy Boys. A Protestant businessman in Youghal reported that: 'one of my employees actually informed me that his day was coming and his name would yet be placed over the door of the business in place of my name'.[67] In a speech in April 1922, Seán

Moylan declared that 'they would give a call to the fine fat Unionists with fine fat cows. The domestic enemy was the most dangerous, and they would have to start fighting him now'.[68]

It is interesting to note that the April 1922 murders took place in and around Bandon, Dunmanway and Clonakilty, where the I.R.A. was most deeply divided between pro- and anti-treaty camps. It would appear that, rather than bring violence into the nationalist communities, the anti-treaty faction lashed out at the old external enemies. Despite the bloodiness of the Civil War which followed and the alienation of the I.R.A. from the general population, very few Free State supporters were killed. Neighbours, relatives and members of the same congregation did not turn on one another in this way.

Conclusion

Twenty years after he wrote the passage quoted at the beginning of this essay, Seán Ó Faoláin declared that the Cork I.R.A. 'could not, it must always be said, have done anything without the silence, patience, and loyal help of the whole people'.[69] This reversion to a language which he had earlier criticised suggests the power of the nationalist narrative of the revolution, which it portrayed as a straightforward struggle between 'the people' and their oppressors. The idea of 'the people', with its implications of unity and solidarity, was central to the I.R.A.'s corporate sense of identity and legitimacy, but it privileged a specific political and social group and excluded competing and marginal ones.

As Ó Faoláin himself suggested in 1943, 'the whole people', used as a political label, did not imply universality but rather the opposite. As traditional communal roles and networks were drawn on to create the I.R.A., local perceptions were polarised and a class of political and social outsiders was created. These included the police, ex-soldiers, travelling people and Protestants. Solidarity and alienation were two sides of the same coin. This radicalisation of community bonds and boundaries provided one of the main dynamics of the revolution in Cork.

Acknowledgement
I would like to acknowledge the support of the Social Sciences and Humanities Research Council of Canada in conducting this research.

References
1. T. Barry, *Guerilla days in Ireland* (Dublin, 1949), p. 207.
2. S. Ó Faoláin, 'The plain people of Ireland' in *The Bell* (October, 1943), p. 1.
3. Unless otherwise specified, 'Cork', in this essay, refers to both the city and county.

4. Another note on nomenclature: the organisation started as the Irish Volunteers in 1913 and this remained as the official name, but by 1921 the title 'Irish Republican Army' had been widely adopted. I have used the terms interchangeably, as they were used at the time.
5. It was also referred to as 'The Republic of Munster'. There were some people who took the idea seriously; see U.C.D., Ernie O'Malley papers, P17a/62, Father Dominic to Ernie O'Malley, n.d.
6. See, for example, C.A.I., Siobhán Lankford papers, U169c/17, Intelligence Officer, 4th Cork Bde to O/C Communications sub-area, 5 Feb. 1923.
7. Irish Military Archives (hereafter I.M.A.), A/0875, Chief of Staff's general situation report, 26 Sept. 1923.
8. Imperial War Museum (hereafter I.W.M.), Percival papers, Major A. C. Percival, 'Guerrilla warfare – Ireland 1920 – 21 [lecture no. 1].
9. P.R.O., CO/904/105, Monthly report of the Inspector General, Jan. 1918
10. P.R.O., CO/904/122, report on illegal drilling in Charleville, 18 Nov. 1917. See also the report from Rockchapel, 24 Nov. 1917, in the same file and *C.E.*, 26 May 1918.
11. U.C.D., Richard Mulcahy papers, P7/A/30, letter from E. O'Donovan, 28 Oct. 1921; I.M.A., A/0991/4, Officer Commanding [O/C] 1st Southern Division to O/C 5th Cork Brigade, 13 Sept. 1922
12. 20 July 1918.
13. I.W.M., Sir Peter Strickland papers, *Notes on the organisation and methods of Sinn Féin in the Sixth Divisional area*, 7 July 1921. An example of the use of the term 'the usual I.R.A. type' can be found in I.M.A., A/0413, [British] 6th Division circular, 28 Oct. 1920.
14. The quotation is taken from U.C.D., O'Malley papers, P17b/1230E, O'Malley's interview with C. Leddy.
15. The three remarks are from Barry, *Guerilla days*, p. 89, and U.C.D., O'Malley papers, P17b/112 and 132, interviews with E. Donegan and G. Power.
16. U.C.D., O'Malley papers, P17b/123, interview with N. Murphy. For other comment on farmers see ibid., P17b/112, interview with D. Browne, and U.C.D., Mulcahy papers, P7/A/27, Vice O/C 1st Cork Bde to O/C, 18 Nov. 1921.
17. P.R.O.I., Records of the Dáil Éireann Courts (Winding Up) Commission, D.É. 11/220, statement by J. O'Mahony, n.d. [1922].
18. C.A.I., Siobhán Lankford papers, U169b, 4th Cork Bde Intelligence memo, n.d. [1923].
19. C.A.I., Siobhán Lankford papers, U169b, letter from W. N., 13 May 1922.
20. U.C.D., O'Malley papers, P17b/108, interview with T. O'Sullivan.
21. See T.C.D., Records Office, Frank Gallagher papers, MS 10055, C. Saunders' diary for 1920.
22. I.M.A., A/0747, E. O'Malley to G. Plunkett, 5 Dec. 1919.
23. This pamphlet, printed in October 1920, can be found in the I.W.M., Strickland papers.
24. This puritanical side to the I.R.A. was often remarked upon by friends and foes alike. One of the former, Mrs W. (Sophie) O'Brien, reported that 'to offer a youth whiskey is almost to offend him', see her *In Mallow* (London, 1920), pp 7, 65-68.
25. U.C.D., Mulcahy papers, P7/A/34, O/C 1st Southern Division to the Chief of Staff [C/S], 13 Oct. 1921.
26. *Voice of labour*, 10 Dec. 1921. See also U.C.D., Mulcahy papers, P7/A/34, Adjutant 2nd Cork Bde to Adj. 1st Southern Div., 30 Sept. 1921; ibid., P7/A/34, O/C 5th Battalion to O/C 1st Cork Bde, 29 Oct. 1921, and the extraordinary article by

M. O'Regan, 'When the I.R.A. split on class issues' in *Labour news* (21 Aug. 1937), which deals with events in Bartlemy.

27. T. Barry interviewed by G. O'Mahony, 1968 (hereafter O'Mahony interview; tape in the possession of Mr O'Mahony, Cork city). See also N.L.I., F. O'Donoghue papers, MS 31,423, the comments of M. J. Costello in a letter to F. O'Donoghue, 11 Dec. 1951.

28. N.L.I., O'Donoghue papers, MS 31,176, O'Donoghue to 'Dhilis', n.d. [1921]. Every Cork I.R.A. veteran I interviewed stated quite definitely that there were no class tensions within the I.R.A.

29. O'Mahony interview.

30. I.M.A., DOD A/613 and A/8506.

31. *Cork County Eagle*, 5 Feb. 1921.

32. See U.C.D., O'Malley papers, P17b/112, interview with J. Minihan for one such episode.

33. R.T.É. Archives, A2790, interview with Mr O'Driscoll.

34. Interview with E. B., a Cobh I.R.A. veteran, 9 May 1989. As several of the veterans I interviewed asked not to be quoted by name, I will refer to all of them by their initials.

35. U.C.D., O'Malley papers, P17a/101, Adj., 2nd Southern Div. to Adjutant General [A/G], 17 Nov. 1921.

36. I.M.A., A/0991/4, O/C 1st Southern Div. to O/C Cork 5, 13 Sept. 1922. See also: C.A.I., Siobhán Lankford papers, U169b/21, letter from W. N., 27 Oct. 1921 and P.R.O., Irish Grants Committee, CO/762/97, O/C 7 Bn, 5th Cork Bde to Mrs Stratford, 27 June 1921.

37. N.L.I., O'Donoghue papers, MS 31,225.

38. See U.C.D., O'Malley papers, P17b/96, 111 and 112, interviews with F. O'Donoghue, N. Murphy and M. Murphy and C. Neenan.

39. For examples see P.R.O., CO/762/37 and 46, statements by J. Northridge and A. Stevens.

40. I.W.M., Percival papers, Major Montgomery to Percival, 14 Oct. 1923. Compare this to the following extract from the I.M.A., CW/OPS/14, Cork Command weekly survey, 24 Jan. 1923: 'it is evident that some members of the Army consider all inhabitants of Cork County as irregular'.

41. The ages and occupations of I.R.A. members were culled from a wide variety of sources, the most important of which are as follows. Newspapers: the *Cork Examiner, Irish Times, Cork County Eagle* and *Southern Star* for the years 1917-1923. Police reports: P.R.O., CO/904/102-116, monthly reports of the County Inspectors, 1917-21, and ibid., CO/904/122, reports on illegal drilling, 1917-18. Prison records: S.P.O., General Prisons Board records of DORA prisoners, 1917-20, and N.L.I., Art O'Brien Papers, MSS 8443-8445, lists of Irish prisoners in English jails, 1920-21. Also for the Civil War, I.M.A., P/1-P/6 and miscellaneous prisoners' location books and prison ledgers for Cork Command and elsewhere. I.R.A. records: C.A.I., Siobhán Lankford papers, unit and prison roll books and White Cross lists, together with I.M.A., A/series of documents, as well as documents in private hands.

The division of the occupational sample into the various categories follows G. Routh's methodology in his *Occupations and pay in Great Britain* (London, 1980). The category of 'clerk' includes shop assistants. The category of 'farm labourer' includes all those specified as such, along with two-thirds of those identified as 'general labourers' or just 'labourers'.

Both the 1911 and 1926 census figures are percentages of occupied males. 1911 figures are only partially given because the census categories do not match the ones given in this paper.

42. See S.P.O., DE 2/52, National Land Bank report on the West Carbery Co-op Fishing Society, 9 Oct. 1920.

43. N.L.I., O'Donoghue papers, MS 31,322, information about the members from T. O'Donovan's unpublished history of the company, also P.R.O.I., manuscript census returns for 1911, and Irish Valuation Office (hereafter I.V.O.) records.

44. It could be argued that these figures, which are biased towards those rebels who came to official attention, may reflect the better policing of towns in both the Black and Tan and Civil Wars. On the other hand, if this were the case, the number of countrymen in the sample should have gone down after 1919 when the Royal Irish Constabulary were withdrawn from most of their rural barracks and posts.

45. See, for example, U.C.D., Mulcahy papers, P7/A/30, Vice O/C to O/C 1st Cork Bde, 10 Nov. 1921.

46. See U.C.D., O'Malley papers, P17b/108, interview with T. O'Sullivan: 'Skibbereen was mostly Protestant and they [the Volunteers] stuck together better'.

47. One local pioneer who, along with his brother, organised a company in rural west Cork, told me that 'school pals came first' and that they only let in those whom they trusted. Interview with J. S., 2 Apr. 1988.

48. In addition to the sources listed in note 43, information for this figure maps was also drawn from N.L.I., O'Donoghue papers, MS 31,322, F. O'Donoghue's unpublished history of the Cork Volunteers up to 1916, and from interviews with E. Y., a veteran of the Dunmanway Company, on 3 Apr. and 3 June 1988. The figure is based on the O.S. maps located in the I.V.O.

49. P.R.O., CO/904/164, Censorship summaries precis, letter from Cork, 17 July 1918.

50. Systematic information on these practices can be found in the Schools Manuscripts in U.C.D., Department of Irish Folklore. 126 of these volumes deal with county Cork. See, especially, MSS S 283, p. 422; S 286, pp 120-121; S 291, p. 357; S 293, p. 162; S 339, pp 99-100 and S 343, p. 295. These customs existed throughout the county, but were beginning to die out in the 1920s and 1930s. See also the *Southern Star*, 13 Jan. 1917, and M. Ó Súilleabháin, *Where mountainy men have sown* (Tralee, 1965), p. 31. Finally, for some acute observations on youth culture in a small Munster town (Templemore) see N. Kevin, *I remember Karrigeen* (London, 1944), pp 30-36. For an extended discussion of this issue, see my article 'Youth culture and the Cork I.R.A.' in D. Fitzpatrick (ed.), *Revolution? Ireland 1917-1923* (Dublin, 1990).

51. See Buffs Regimental Museum, Canterbury, Mitchelstown Detachment war diary, 31 Jan. 1921 and M. J. Hoare, *The road to Glenanore* (London, 1975), p. 54.

52. See U.C.D., O'Malley papers, P17b/112, S. Daly interview. Most of the Cork I.R.A. veterans I interviewed had been active participants in several elections, but all were equally vehement that they had nothing to do with Sinn Féin or 'politics'.

53. N. Buckley, *The time of the ten foot pikes*, n.d. This poem can be found in the superb collection of B. Clifford and J. Lane (ed.), *Ned Buckley's poems* (Aubane Historical Society, 1987), pp 45-46. For further verses about the I.R.A. see *They also served* and *The battle of the bower*, ibid., pp 38-54. Buckley was a north-Cork poet and active Redmondite.

54. Interview with C. M., 28 Apr. 1989.

55. F. O'Connor, *An only child* (London, 1961), p. 202. See also S. Ó Faoláin, *Vive moi!* (London, 1965), p. 175.

56. N.L.I., O'Donoghue papers, MS 31,421, G. Power to F. O'Donoghue, 21 Dec. 1953.

57. See S. Ó Faoláin's comments in *Vive moi!*, pp 175, 180. Also U.C.D., Mulcahy papers, P7/A/19, H.Q. 1st Southern Division memo., 11 June 1921.
58. See, for example, the case of P. Casey in *I.T.*, 3 May 1921, and U.C.D., Mulcahy papers, P7/A/18, A. Stack to the Minister of Defence, 9 May 1921. There were many similar cases.
59. See D. Fitzpatrick, *Politics and Irish life* (Dublin, 1977), pp 222-24.
60. These figures were compiled from a wide variety of sources, mainly newspapers, I.R.A. documents and personal accounts. They probably underestimate the true figure by about 10 per cent as I only included those who were definitely killed by the I.R.A. and did not include hearsay reports. Also, many of these killings were secret, and some have undoubtedly remained so until this day.
61. See Percival, 'Guerrilla warfare – Ireland 1920-21' [lecture no. 1]; I.W.M., Sir H. Jeudwine papers, G.H.Q. Ireland, *Records of the rebellion in Ireland in 1920-21* [2 vols., May 1922], ii, pp 37-39, 55; and N.L.I., G. A. Cockerill papers, MS 10,606, Anon. [a battalion commander in Cork], 'Appreciation of the situation in Ireland', May 1921.
62. These can be found in I.M.A., A/0897.
63. P.R.O., CO/762/97, O/C 7th Bn, 3rd Cork Bde to Mrs Stratford, 27 June 1921.
64. For vivid personal accounts, see L. Fleming, *Head or harp* (London, 1965), O. P. Clark, *She came of decent people* (London, 1986) and L. Robinson, T. Robinson and N. Dorman, *Three homes* (London, 1938). There are hundreds of detailed accounts by victimised loyalists in Cork in P.R.O., CO/762, the files of the Irish Grants Committee, covering the whole revolutionary period.
65. For I.R.A. correspondence on the 'tramp nuisance' see I.M.A., A/0799, O/C 2nd Cork Bde to the Adjutant General, 24 June 1920, and ibid., A/0799, the A/G's reply of 25 June; also U.C.D., Mulcahy papers, P7/A/22, Director of Intelligence to C/S, 26 July 1921, and the Assistant C/S's comments thereon. See furthermore *C.E.*, 13 Aug. 1920. Local attitudes to travelling people throughout Cork are detailed in the Schools Manuscripts in U.C.D., Department of Irish Folklore. Of particular interest are MSS S 281, p. 45; S 283, p. 384; S 285, pp 92-93, 233; S 287, p. 350; S 294, p. 67; S 346, pp 58-59 and S 347, pp 441-443.
66. See U.C.D., O'Malley papers, P17b/111, interview with N. Murphy, and S. Moylan's speech in the Treaty debate: *Dáil Éireann official report: debate on the treaty between Great Britain and Ireland,* p. 146.
67. P.R.O., CO/762/50, John Brookes' statement.
68. *Cork Weekly Examiner*, 8 Apr. 1922. In fairness, it should be mentioned that Moylan, despite his rhetoric, had the best record of any Cork brigade commander in his treatment of Protestants.
69. Ó Faoláin, *Vive moi!*, p. 181.

Index of Places

ERRATA

p.272 line 13 for 'William' read Warham.

p.279 line 26 for '(ss p.281)' read (see p.281)

p.404 line 40 for 'Paccata' read Pacata

p.416 line 26 for 'Author' read Arthur

p.438 line 15 for '(Fig. 11)' read (Fig. 11.9)

p.535 line 27 for 'Annikissy' read Annakissy

p.564 line 21 for 'Berkely's' read Berkeley's